Dictionary
of the
Middle Ages

AMERICAN COUNCIL OF LEARNED SOCIETIES

The American Council of Learned Societies, organized in 1919 for the purpose of advancing the study of the humanities and of the humanistic aspects of the social sciences, is a nonprofit federation comprising forty-five national scholarly groups. The Council represents the humanities in the United States in the International Union of Academies, provides fellowships and grants-in-aid, supports research-and-planning conferences and symposia, and sponsors special projects and scholarly publications.

Carpet page from Lindisfarne Gospels. Hiberno-Saxon illuminated manuscript, *ca.* 700. BY PERMISSION OF THE BRITISH LIBRARY, COTTON NERO D. IV, fol. 210ᵛ

Editorial Board

Advisory Committee

Dictionary
of the
Middle Ages

JOSEPH R. STRAYER, *EDITOR IN CHIEF*

Volume 7

ITALIAN RENAISSANCE—MABINOGI

CHARLES SCRIBNER'S SONS • NEW YORK

Copyright © 1986 American Council of Learned Societies

Library of Congress Cataloging in Publication Data

Main entry under title:

Dictionary of the Middle Ages.

Includes bibliographies and index.
1. Middle Ages-—Dictionaries.   I. Strayer,
Joseph Reese, 1904–1987

| D114.D5 | 1982 | 909.07 | 82-5904 |

ISBN 0-684-16760-3 (v. 1)   ISBN 0-684-18169-X (v. 7)
ISBN 0-684-17022-1 (v. 2)   ISBN 0-684-18274-2 (v. 8)
ISBN 0-684-17023-X (v. 3)   ISBN 0-684-18275-0 (v. 9)
ISBN 0-684-17024-8 (v. 4)   ISBN 0-684-18276-9 (v. 10)
ISBN 0-684-18161-4 (v. 5)   ISBN 0-684-18277-7 (v. 11)
ISBN 0-684-18168-1 (v. 6)   ISBN 0-684-18278-5 (v. 12)

Published simultaneously in Canada
by Collier Macmillan Canada, Inc.
Copyright under the Berne convention.

1 3 5 7 9 11 13 15 17 19   Q/C   20 18 16 14 12 10 8 6 4 2

PRINTED IN THE UNITED STATES OF AMERICA.

The *Dictionary of the Middle Ages* has been produced with
support from the National Endowment for the Humanities.

The paper in this book meets the guidelines for
permanence and durability of the Committee on
Production Guidelines for Book Longevity of the
Council on Library Resources.

Maps prepared by Sylvia Lehrman.

Editorial Staff

Contributors to Volume 7

KLAUS AICHELE
Brooklyn College, City University of New York
LUDUS DE ANTICHRISTO

MANSOUR J. AJAMI
Princeton University
JARĪR; MAʿARRĪ, ABŪ 'L-ʿALĀʾ AHMAD AL-

GUSTAVE ALEF
University of Oregon
IVAN III OF MUSCOVY

ROBERT AMIET
Facultés Catholiques, Lyon
LYONESE RITE

JEFFREY C. ANDERSON
George Washington University
JAMES THE MONK

THEODORE M. ANDERSSON
Stanford University
LIED VOM HÜRNEN SEYFRID, DAS; LJÓSVETNINGA SAGA

MICHAEL ANGOLD
University of Edinburgh
JOHN III VATATZES; LASKARIDS

MARY-JO ARN
English Institute, Groningen
JEAN DE MEUN; KINGIS QUAIR, THE

ANI P. ATAMIAN
Columbia University
LAMBRON; LEO I/II OF ARMENIA; LEO V/VI OF ARMENIA; LUSIGNANS

BERNARD S. BACHRACH
University of Minnesota
JEWS IN EUROPE: BEFORE 900

GERSHON C. BACON
Bar-Ilan University, Ramat-Gan
JEWS IN RUSSIA

ANASTASIUS C. BANDY
LYDUS

JOHN W. BARKER
University of Wisconsin
JEAN BOUCICAUT

CARL F. BARNES, JR.
JEAN (JEHAN) D'ANDELI; JEAN DE BEAUCE; JEAN (JEHAN) DE CHELLES; JEAN DES CHAMPS; KRAK DES CHEVALIERS

ROBERT BARRINGER
St. Michael's College, University of Toronto
LEO III, POPE

CAROLINE M. BARRON
Royal Holloway College, University of London
LONDON

ÜLKÜ Ü. BATES
KIOSK

FRANZ H. BÄUML
University of California, Los Angeles
KUDRUN

ROBERT BEDROSIAN
KIRAKOS OF GANJAK; LIPARIT IV ORBĒLEAN

CAROLINE J. BEESON
KHWĀRIZMSHĀHS

HAIM BEINART
Hebrew University of Jerusalem
JEWS IN CHRISTIAN SPAIN

HANS BEKKER-NIELSEN
Odense Universitet
JÓN ÖGMUNDARSON, ST.; JÓNS SAGA HELGA; LAURENTIUS SAGA

ISAAC BENABU
Hebrew University of Jerusalem
JUDEO-SPANISH

ROBERT P. BERGMAN
The Walters Art Gallery
LEO OF OSTIA

IRENE A. BIERMAN
University of California, Los Angeles
IVORY CARVING, ISLAMIC; KHILʿA; KISWA

DALE L. BISHOP
KĀRNĀMAG-I ARDEŠĪR-I BĀBAGĀN

FOSTER W. BLAISDELL
Indiana University
ÍVENS SAGA

THOMAS W. BLOMQUIST
Northern Illinois University
LOMBARDS

PERE BOHIGAS
JORDI DE S. JORDI

C. E. BOSWORTH
University of Manchester
KURDS

LASKARINA BOURAS
LIGHTING DEVICES

CONTRIBUTORS TO VOLUME 7

BEVERLY BOYD
University of Kansas
KEMPE, MARGERY

CLEO LELAND BOYD
LINCOLN, RITE OF

CHARLES M. BRAND
Bryn Mawr College
JOHN II KOMNENOS; JOHN
KINNAMOS; KOMNENOI; LATIN
EMPIRE OF CONSTANTINOPLE

CYNTHIA J. BROWN
*University of California, Santa
Barbara*
JEAN, DUKE OF BERRY

ROBERT BROWNING
University of London
JOHN VIII XIPHILINOS, PATRIARCH;
JUSTINIAN I; LITERACY, BYZANTINE

LESLIE BRUBAKER
*Wheaton College, Norton,
Massachusetts*
KASTORIA; KATHOLIKON; KELLS,
BOOK OF; LACERTINE; LACTATIO;
LINDISFARNE GOSPELS;
LIPSANOTHECA; LOCULUS

LANCE W. BRUNNER
University of Kentucky
ITE CHANT

VINCENT BURANELLI
LYONS

DAVID BURR
*Virginia Polytechnic Institute and
State University*
JOACHIM OF FIORE

ROBERT G. CALKINS
Cornell University
JACQUEMART DE HESDIN; LIMBOURG
BROTHERS

AVERIL CAMERON
*King's College, University of
London*
JOHN OF EPHESUS

HENRY CHADWICK
Magdalene College, Cambridge
JOHN CHRYSOSTOM, ST.

FREDRIC L. CHEYETTE
Amherst College
LIVRES DE JOSTICE ET DE PLET, LI

STANLEY CHODOROW
University of California, La Jolla
LAW, CANON: AFTER GRATIAN

CAROL J. CLOVER
University of California, Berkeley
LAXDŒLA SAGA; LOKASENNA

MARK R. COHEN
Princeton University
JEWISH COMMUNAL SELF-
GOVERNMENT: ISLAMIC WORLD;
JEWS IN EGYPT

LAWRENCE I. CONRAD
*The Wellcome Institute for the
History of Medicine*
JĀḤIẒ, AL-; KUFA, AL-

JOHN J. CONTRENI
Purdue University
JOHN SCOTTUS ERIUGENA; LUPUS OF
FERRIÈRES

ELIO COSTA
York University, Ontario
LATINI, BRUNETTO

EDWARD J. COWAN
University of Guelph, Ontario
KENNETH I MAC ALPIN

H. E. J. COWDREY
St. Edmund Hall, Oxford
KING'S EVIL

JOSÉ LUIS COY
University of Connecticut
LÓPEZ DE AYALA

GLYNNIS M. CROPP
Massey University
JEU PARTI

SLOBODAN ĆURČIĆ
Princeton University
KONÀK

MICHAEL T. DAVIS
Mount Holyoke College
JEAN D'ORBAIS; JEAN DE RAVI;
KUENE, KONRAD; LABARUM;
LANGLOIS, JEAN; LANX;
LAPIDARIUM; LAST SUPPER;
LIBERGIER, HUGUES; LOCUS
SANCTUS; LOUP, JEAN

HELLE DEGNBOL
JÓMSVÍKINGA SAGA

PETER F. DEMBOWSKI
University of Chicago
LAISSE; LAI, LAY

GEORGE T. DENNIS
Catholic University of America
LATIN STATES IN GREECE

WALTER B. DENNY
*University of Massachusetts,
Amherst*
KILIM

LUCY DER MANUELIAN
KOŘIKOS

JAMES DICKIE
JINN

CHARLES DONAHUE, JR.
Harvard University
LAW, CIVIL—CORPUS JURIS,
REVIVAL AND SPREAD

E. TALBOT DONALDSON
Indiana University
LANGLAND, WILLIAM

FRED M. DONNER
University of Chicago
KHĀLID IBN AL-WALĪD

KATHERINE FISCHER DREW
Rice University
LAW, GERMAN: EARLY GERMANIC
CODES

DIANE L. DROSTE
*University of Toronto, Centre for
Medieval Studies*
LIGATURE

LAWRENCE M. EARP
Princeton University
LEONINUS

STEPHEN R. ELL
University of Iowa
LEPROSY

MENACHEM ELON
Supreme Court of Israel
LAW, JEWISH

MARCIA J. EPSTEIN
University of Calgary
JAUFRÉ RUDEL; LAI, LAY

STEVEN EPSTEIN
Duke University
ITALY, BYZANTINE AREAS OF

CONTRIBUTORS TO VOLUME 7

JOHN H. ERICKSON
St. Vladimir's Seminary
JOHN ITALOS

STEVEN C. FANNING
University of Illinois at Chicago Circle
LOMBARD LEAGUE; LOMBARDS, KINGDOM OF

SEYMOUR FELDMAN
Rutgers College
LEVI BEN GERSHOM

S. C. FERRUOLO
Stanford University
JACQUES DE VITRY

JOHN V. A. FINE, JR.
University of Michigan
JOHN ASEN II; KALOJAN; KRUM; KULIN; LAZAR HREBELJANOVIĆ

PETER G. FOOTE
University College, London
LAW, DANISH; LAW, SWEDISH

PATRICK K. FORD
Center for the Study of Comparative Folklore and Mythology, University of California, Los Angeles
MABINOGI

ROBERTA FRANK
University of Toronto, Centre for Medieval Studies
KENNING; KORMÁKS SAGA; KVIÐU-HÁTTR; LAUSAVÍSA

MARGIT FRENK
El Colegio de Mexico
KHARJA

EDWARD FRUEH
Columbia University
JOHANNES OF ST. VINCENT

RICHARD N. FRYE
Harvard University
KAᶜBA OF ZOROASTER

VICTORIA GABBITAS
Museum of Leathercraft, Northampton
LEATHER AND LEATHERWORKING

STEPHEN GARDNER
Columbia University
JOY, WILLIAM; LIERNE; LOCK, ADAM; LOTE, STEPHEN

NINA G. GARSOÏAN
Columbia University
JOHN OF ŌJUN, ST.; KAMSARAKAN; KARIN (KARNOY KᶜAŁAKᶜ)

ADELHEID M. GEALT
Indiana University
JACOPO DI CIONE; LIPPO MEMMI; LORENZETTI, AMBROGIO; LORENZETTI, PIETRO; LORENZO MONACO; LORENZO DI NICCOLÒ; LORENZO VENEZIANO; LUCCA DI TOMMÈ

DENO J. GEANAKOPLOS
Yale University
ITALIAN RENAISSANCE, BYZANTINE INFLUENCE ON

CHRISTIAN J. GELLINEK
University of Florida
KAISERCHRONIK; KARLMEINET; KÖNIG ROTHER

G. H. GERRITS
Acadia University
JORDAN OF QUEDLINBURG

JAMES L. GILLESPIE
Griswold Institute
JOHN OF GAUNT

HANS PETER GLÖCKNER
Johann Wolfgang Goethe Universität
JACOBUS (DE PORTA RAVENNATE); JOHANNES ANDREAE; JOHANNES MONACHUS

PETER B. GOLDEN
Rutgers University
KARAMANIA

OLEG GRABAR
Harvard University
JERUSALEM

JAMES A. GRAHAM-CAMPBELL
University College, London
JELLINGE STYLE

GORDON K. GREENE
Wilfred Laurier University
MA FIN EST MON COMMENCEMENT

JAMES GRIER
University of Waterloo, Ontario
LIBER USUALIS

JOHN L. GRIGSBY
Washington University
JEAN DE THUIM

MARY GRIZZARD
University of New Mexico
JOHN OF S. MARTÍN DE ALBARES; JORGE INGLÉS; JUAN AND SIMÓN DE COLONIA; JUAN DE BURGOS; JUAN DE FLANDES

ARTHUR GROOS
Cornell University
LAMPRECHT; LOHENGRIN

AVRAHAM GROSSMAN
Hebrew University of Jerusalem
KALONYMUS FAMILY

LAWRENCE GUSHEE
JEHAN DES MURS

BJARNI GUÐNASON
KNYTLINGA SAGA

JOSEPH GUTMANN
JEWISH ART

GREGORY GUZMAN
Bradley University
JOHN OF PLANO CARPINI

ABRAHAM S. HALKIN
JOSEPH BEN JUDAH BEN JACOB IBN ᶜAKNIN; JUDEO-ARABIC LITERATURE

NATHALIE HANLET
JOHANNES CANAPARIUS; JOHANNES OF ST. ARNULF; LANDOLFUS SAGAX; LANTBERT OF DEUTZ

EDWARD R. HAYMES
University of Houston
KÖNIG LAURIN

JOHN BELL HENNEMAN
Princeton University Library
JACQUERIE; LAW, FRENCH: IN SOUTH; LOUIS XI OF FRANCE

JOHN HENNIG
LITURGY, CELTIC

MICHAEL HERREN
York University, Ontario
ITINERARIUM EGERIAE

JUDITH HERRIN
Warburg Institute, University of London
LEO III, EMPEROR

xi

CONTRIBUTORS TO VOLUME 7

ROBERT H. HEWSEN
Glassboro State College
KABALA; KARS; KURA RIVER;
KUTᶜAISI

P. L. HEYWORTH
University of Toronto
KATHERINE GROUP

CONSTANCE B. HIEATT
University of Western Ontario
KARLAMAGNÚS SAGA

ROBERT HILLENBRAND
University of Edinburgh
KHAN

J. N. HILLGARTH
*Pontifical Institute of Mediaeval
Studies, Toronto*
LULL, RAMON

C. WARREN HOLLISTER
*University of California, Santa
Barbara*
KNIGHTS AND KNIGHT SERVICE

JOHN HOWE
Texas Tech University
LETALD OF MICY

DONALD GWYON HOWELLS
University of Glasgow
LAW, WELSH

ANNE HUDSON
Lady Margaret Hall, Oxford
LOLLARDS

JAY HUFF
JOHN OF AFFLIGHEM; JOHN OF
GARLAND

MAHMOOD IBRAHIM
*University of California, Los
Angeles*
JĪLĀNĪ, ᶜABD AL-QĀDIR AL-

ALFRED L. IVRY
Brandeis University
JUDAH HALEVI

RICHARD A. JACKSON
University of Houston
KINGSHIP, RITUALS OF:
CORONATION

WILLIAM E. JACKSON
University of Virginia
JOHANNES HADLAUB

PETER JEFFERY
University of Delaware
LITANY

GEORGE JOCHNOWITZ
*College of Staten Island, City
University of New York*
JUDEO-PROVENÇAL

JENNIFER E. JONES
LAZARUS, RAISING OF; LOGOS

WILLIAM CHESTER JORDAN
Princeton University
JOINVILLE, JEAN DE; LOUIS IX OF
FRANCE

WALTER EMIL KAEGI, JR.
University of Chicago
JULIAN THE APOSTATE; JUSTINIAN II

RICHARD W. KAEUPER
University of Rochester
JAIL DELIVERY; JUSTICES OF THE
PEACE

DANIEL H. KAISER
Grinnell College
LAW, RUSSIAN (MUSCOVITE)

IOLI KALAVREZOU-MAXEINER
*University of California, Los
Angeles*
JOSHUA ROLL

MARIANNE E. KALINKE
*University of Illinois at Urbana-
Champaign*
KLÁRI SAGA

DOUGLAS KELLY
University of Wisconsin
JOHN OF GARLAND

DALE KINNEY
Bryn Mawr College
JACOPO DI PIERO GUIDI; LANFRANC
OF MODENA; LATERAN

DAVID N. KLAUSNER
*University of Toronto, Centre for
Medieval Studies*
LLYWELYN AP GRUFFYDD

ALAN E. KNIGHT
Pennsylvania State University
JEU; JEU DE LA FEUILLÉE, LE; JEU DE
ROBIN ET MARION, LE

PAUL KNOLL
*University of Southern
California, Los Angeles*
JAGIEŁŁO DYNASTY

THOMAS KUEHN
Clemson University
LAW, SCHOOLS OF

VALERIE M. LAGORIO
University of Iowa
JULIAN OF NORWICH

ANGELIKI LAIOU
Harvard University
JOHN V PALAIOLOGOS; JOHN VI
KANTAKOUZENOS; JOHN VIII
PALAIOLOGOS; KANTAKOUZENOI;
LIUTPRAND OF CREMONA

IRA M. LAPIDUS
University of California, Berkeley
KHALDŪN, IBN

JACOB LASSNER
Wayne State University
KHAṬĪB AL-BAGHDĀDĪ, AL-

ARTHUR LEVINE
JACOBUS OF BOLOGNA; JUBILUS

KENNETH LEVY
Princeton University
KONTAKION

ARCHIBALD R. LEWIS
*University of Massachusetts,
Amherst*
LANGUEDOC

DAVID C. LINDBERG
University of Wisconsin
LENSES AND EYEGLASSES

AMNON LINDER
LAW, JEWRY

JOHN LINDOW
University of California, Berkeley
IÐUNN; LOKI

CHARLES T. LITTLE
Metropolitan Museum of Art
IVORY CARVING

DEREK W. LOMAX
University of Birmingham
LOPES, FERNÃO

CONTRIBUTORS TO VOLUME 7

MICHAEL P. LONG
Columbia University
LANDINI, FRANCESCO; LAUDA

LARS LÖNNROTH
KRISTNI SAGA

BRYCE LYON
Brown University
JOCELIN OF BRAKELOND; JOHN,
KING OF ENGLAND; JUSTICIAR;
LANFRANC OF BEC; LANGTON,
STEPHEN; LILLE

W. MADELUNG
The Oriental Institute, Oxford
JIHAD

GEORGE P. MAJESKA
University of Maryland
KAMENNAYA BABA; KIOT; KLEIMO;
KLIROS; KOKOSHNIK; KONTSOVKA

KRIKOR H. MAKSOUDIAN
JOHN I TZIMISKES; KATHOLIKOS;
KNIKᶜ HAWATOY; KORIWN; LAW,
ARMENIAN; LAW, CANON:
ARMENIAN; ŁEWOND; LOŘI

IVAN G. MARCUS
Jewish Theological Seminary
JEWISH COMMUNAL SELF-
GOVERNMENT, EUROPE; JUDAH BEN
SAMUEL HE-HASID; JUDEO-LATIN

T. L. MARKEY
University of Michigan
KARLSKRÖNIKAN

MICHAEL E. MARMURA
University of Toronto
KINDĪ, AL-

STEVEN P. MARRONE
Tufts University
KILWARDBY, ROBERT

JOHN HILLARY MARTIN, O.P.
JOHN OF PARIS

LAURO MARTINES
*University of California, Los
Angeles*
ITALY, FOURTEENTH AND FIFTEENTH
CENTURIES; ITALY, RISE OF TOWNS
IN

JOAQUÍN MARTÍNEZ-PIZARRO
Oberlin College
KETILS SAGA HÆNGS; KNUD
LAVARD; LEJRE CHRONICLE

RALPH WHITNEY MATHISEN
University of South Carolina
JORDANES

MICHAEL McCORMICK
*Dumbarton Oaks Research
Center*
KOLLEMA; KOLLESIS

LAWRENCE J. McCRANK
*Auburn University at
Montgomery*
LIBRARIES

DAVID R. McLINTOCK
University of London
LUDWIGSLIED

BRIAN MERRILEES
University of Toronto
JEU D'ADAM; JOHN OF HEWDEN;
JORDAN FANTOSME; LAI DEL DESIRÉ,
LE; LIVERE DE REIS DE BRITTANIE ET
LIVERE DE REIS DE ENGLETERRE

BARRY MESCH
University of Florida
JOSEPH IBN CASPI

JOHN MEYENDORFF
Fordham University
JOHN OF DAMASCUS, ST.; JOSEPH II,
PATRIARCH; LAW, CANON:
BYZANTINE; LITURGY, BYZANTINE
CHURCH

ROMUALD J. MISIUNAS
Yale University
LITHUANIA

MICHEL MOLLAT
*Institut de France, Academie des
Inscriptions et Belles Lettres*
JACQUES COEUR

ANNE M. MORGENSTERN
Ohio State University
JEAN MICHEL

JOHN H. MUNRO
University of Toronto
LINEN

HENRY A. MYERS
LAW, GERMAN: POST-CAROLINGIAN

LAWRENCE NEES
University of Delaware
LOMBARD ART

LEON NEMOY
Dropsie University
KARAITES

STEPHEN G. NICHOLS, JR.
University of Pennsylvania
LAI DU COR, LE

HELMUT NICKEL
Metropolitan Museum of Art
LANCE

THOMAS S. NOONAN
University of Minnesota
KIEVAN RUS

DONNCHADH Ó CORRÁIN
University College, Cork
LAW, IRISH; LEINSTER

BARBARA OEHLSCHLAEGER-
GARVEY
*University of Illinois at Urbana-
Champaign*
KOIMESIS

NICOLAS OIKONOMIDES
Université de Montreal
KATEPANO; LAW, BYZANTINE;
LOGOTHETE

ROBERT G. OUSTERHOUT
*University of Illinois at Urbana-
Champaign*
KARIYE DJAMI, CONSTANTINOPLE;
LAVRA

HERMANN PÁLSSON
University of Edinburgh
LANDNÁMABÓK

HERBERT H. PAPER
*Hebrew Union College, Jewish
Institute of Religion*
JUDEO-PERSIAN

DEREK PEARSALL
*Centre for Medieval Studies,
University of York, England*
LYDGATE, JOHN

FRANKLIN J. PEGUES
Ohio State University
JUSTICES OF COMMON PLEAS;
JUSTICES OF THE KING'S BENCH;
LAW, ENGLISH COMMON: TO 1272

CLAUDE J. PEIFER, O.S.B.
St. Bede Abbey
LEO I, POPE

xiii

CONTRIBUTORS TO VOLUME 7

DAVID A. E. PELTERET
New College, Toronto
KENTIGERN, ST.

KENNETH PENNINGTON
Syracuse University
JOHANNES TEUTONICUS;
LAURENTIUS HISPANUS; LAW CODES:
1000–1500; LAW, PROCEDURE OF

JAMES F. POAG
Washington University
JOHANN VON WÜRZBURG; KONRAD
VON STOFFELN

OMELJAN PRITSAK
*Ukrainian Research Institute,
Harvard University*
KHAZARS

ROSHDI RASHED
*Équipe de Recherche Associée,
Histoire des Sciences et de la
Philosophie Arabes, Centre
d'Histoire des Sciences et des
Doctrines, Paris*
KARAJI, AL-

THOMAS RENNA
Saginaw Valley State College
JEROME, ST.; JONAS OF ORLÉANS;
KINGSHIP, THEORIES OF; LEO IX,
POPE

NICHOLAS RESCHER
University of Pittsburgh
LOGIC, ISLAMIC

ROGER E. REYNOLDS
*Pontifical Institute of Mediaeval
Studies, Toronto*
KYRIALE; LAW, CANON: TO
GRATIAN; LITANIES, GREATER AND
LESSER; LITURGY, STATIONAL;
LITURGY, TREATISES ON

A. G. RIGG
*University of Toronto, Centre for
Medieval Studies*
LATIN LANGUAGE; LATIN
LITERATURE; LATIN METER

FRANÇOIS RIGOLOT
Princeton University
JEAN LEMAIRE DE BELGES

THEODORE JOHN RIVERS
LAW, GERMAN: EARLY GERMANIC
CODES

ELAINE GOLDEN ROBISON
JOHN OF CAPESTRANO, ST.

PAUL ROREM
LENT

LINDA C. ROSE
JEAN DE BRIENNE; JOHN KLIMAKOS,
ST.; JOHN IV THE FASTER,
PATRIARCH; JOHN OF NIKIU; JOSHUA
THE STYLITE; LATEEN SAIL; LEO I,
EMPEROR; LEO V THE ARMENIAN,
EMPEROR; LEO THE
MATHEMATICIAN; LIMITANEI;
LUKAS NOTARAS

MIRIAM ROSEN
Fordham University
KHĀNQĀH

C. ROUECHÉ
KEKAUMENOS

JAY ROVNER
LITURGY, JEWISH

TEOFILO F. RUIZ
*Brooklyn College, City University
of New York*
JULIANUS OF TOLEDO; LAW, SPANISH

JAMES R. RUSSELL
Columbia University
KARTĪR; LETTER OF TANSAR

J. JOSEPH RYAN
*St. John's Seminary, Brighton,
Massachusetts*
IVO OF CHARTRES, ST.

JOSEPH SADAN
Tel-Aviv University
KURST

PAUL SAENGER
Northwestern University Library
LITERACY, WESTERN EUROPEAN

KAMAL S. SALIBI
American University of Beirut
LEBANON

T. A. SANDQUIST
University of Toronto
JURY; JUSTICES, ITINERANT

PAUL SCHACH
University of Nebraska
KJALNESINGA SAGA

JACOB SCHIBY
JUDEO-GREEK

NICOLAS SCHIDLOVSKY
Smithsonian Institution
KANŌN

BERNHARD
SCHIMMELPFENNIG
Universität Augsburg
JUBILEE

JANICE L. SCHULTZ
Canisius College
JOHN OF SALISBURY

ALBERT SEAY
Colorado College
JACQUES DE LIÈGE; JOHANNES DE
GROCHEO

DAVID H. SELLAR
University of Edinburgh
LAW, SCOTS

IRFAN SHAHĪD
Georgetown University
LAKHMIDS

SERGEI A. SHUISKII
Princeton University
KHALLIKĀN, IBN

GIULIO SILANO
*Pontifical Institute of Mediaeval
Studies, Toronto*
JACOPONE DA TODI

LARRY SILVER
Northwestern University
KOERBECKE, JOHANN; KONRAD VON
SOEST; KRAFFT, ADAM; LIFE OF
MARY, MASTER OF THE; LOCHNER,
STEPHAN

BARRIE SINGLETON
*Courtauld Institute, University of
London*
JEAN DE LIÈGE; LAMBESPRINGE,
BARTHOLOMEW

DENNIS SLAVIN
Princeton University
JOGLAR/JONGLEUR

ROBERT J. SNOW
University of Texas
LAUDES, ACCLAMATIONS

JAMES SNYDER
Bryn Mawr College
JOOS VAN GHENT

xiv

CONTRIBUTORS TO VOLUME 7

PAUL SOLON
Macalester College
JOAN OF ARC, ST.

HAYM SOLOVEITCHIK
Yeshiva University, Bernard Revel Graduate School
JACOB BEN MEIR

PRISCILLA P. SOUCEK
New York University
JUNAYD; KAMKHĀ; KĀRGAH; KITĀBKHĀNA; KŪFĪ; LAQABI WARE

SVAT SOUCEK
JANISSARY; KHAN; KIRGHIZ

GABRIELLE M. SPIEGEL
University of Maryland
LOUIS VI OF FRANCE

RUTH STEINER
Catholic University of America
KYRIE

NORMAN A. STILLMAN
State University of New York at Binghamton
JEWS IN MUSLIM SPAIN; JEWS IN NORTH AFRICA; JUDAISM; JUDEO-ARABIC LANGUAGE

KENNETH R. STOW
University of Haifa
JEWS AND THE CATHOLIC CHURCH; JEWS IN EUROPE: AFTER 900; JEWS IN THE PAPAL STATES

SANDRA STOW
University of Haifa
JUDEO-FRENCH; JUDEO-ITALIAN

JOSEPH R. STRAYER
Princeton University
JAMES OF VITERBO; JORDAN OF OSNABRÜCK; LAMBERT OF HERSFELD; LAW, FRENCH: IN NORTH

SANDRA CANDEE SUSMAN
JACOPO DELLA QUERCIA

DONALD W. SUTHERLAND
University of Iowa
LAW, ENGLISH COMMON: AFTER 1272; LIBERTY AND LIBERTIES

R. N. SWANSON
University of Birmingham
LEGATES, PAPAL

EDWARD A. SYNAN
Pontifical Institute of Mediaeval Studies, Toronto
JOHN THE DEACON

ALICE-MARY M. TALBOT
KEDRENOS, GEORGIOS; KRITOVOULOS, MICHAEL

GEORGE S. TATE
Brigham Young University
LEIÐARVÍSAN; LÍKNARBRAUT

ROBERT TAYLOR
Victoria College, Toronto
LEYS D'AMORS

PAUL R. THIBAULT
Franklin and Marshall College
JOHN XXII, POPE

J. WESLEY THOMAS
University of Kentucky
KONRAD VON WÜRZBURG

R. W. THOMSON
Harvard University
K^CART^CLIS C^CXOVREBA

M. A. TOLMACHEVÁ
KHURDĀDHBIH, IBN

WARREN T. TREADGOLD
Hillsdale College
LEO VI THE WISE, EMPEROR

WILLIAM URBAN
Monmouth College
LÜBECK

GEORGES VAJDA
Centre Nationale de la Recherche Scientifique
JOSEPH BEN ABRAHAM AL-BAṢĪR; JOSEPH IBN SADDIQ

ANNE HAGOPIAN VAN BUREN
Tufts University
JEAN, DREUX; JEAN LE TAVERNIER; JEAN MIÉLOT; LATHEM, LIÉVIN VAN; LEFÈVRE, RAOUL; LIÉDET, LOYSET

AMY VANDERSALL
University of Colorado
LIUTHARD

JEANETTE A. WAKIN
Columbia University
LAW, ISLAMIC

ELLEN T. WEHNER
University of Toronto
LIVRE DE SEYNTZ MEDICINES, LE

ALFORD T. WELCH
Michigan State University
KORAN; LITURGY, ISLAMIC

WILLIAM K. WEST
LO CODI

ESTELLE WHELAN
KAABA

MARINA D. WHITMAN
KASHI; LAJVARD; LUSTERWARE

GREGORY WHITTINGTON
Institute of Fine Arts, New York University
JAMB; LANCET WINDOW; LOMBARD BANDS

BRUCIA WITTHOFT
Framingham State University
LEONARDO DI SER GIOVANNI

KLAUS WOLLENWEBER
Memorial University of Newfoundland
KOTZENMÄRE, DAS

KENNERLY M. WOODY
JOHN GUALBERTI, ST.

JAMES L. YARRISON
Princeton University
LĀDHIQIYA, AL-

RONALD EDWARD ZUPKO
Marquette University
JOURNAL; LAST; LEAGUE; LIVRE

Dictionary
of the
Middle Ages

Dictionary of the Middle Ages

ITALIAN RENAISSANCE—MABINOGI

ITALIAN RENAISSANCE, BYZANTINE IN-FLUENCE ON. The Byzantine influence on the Italian Renaissance cannot adequately be understood unless it is realized that during the same period Byzantium itself was experiencing the "Palaiologan" renaissance of letters; the Byzantine emigré scholars brought to Italy not only Greek texts but Palaiologan philosophical, philological, and literary interpretations as well as methods of teaching and study. The systematic teaching of Greek in Italy began in Florence in 1396 with Manuel Chrysoloras, whose pupils included many famous humanists (Leonardo Bruni, Pier Paolo Vergerio, Guarino da Verona, and others). His Greco-Latin grammar composed in the Palaiologan manner, and his method of translation (stressing contextual interpretation, not literal translation) and interest in certain Platonic writings as well as Plutarch, had an important impact in Italy.

During the Council of Ferrara-Florence (beginning in 1438), which brought many learned Greeks to Italy to discuss religious union with Rome, Greeks (especially Georgios Gemistos Plethon) introduced to—or better, interpreted for—Italian humanists previously unknown or unavailable Greek texts, especially the complete works of Plato. But Gemistos Plethon's sophisticated exegesis of Platonism was not truly understood until John Argyropoulos came in 1456 to teach in Florence, where he remained until 1471. Argyropoulos, formerly professor in Constantinople, acquired an acute knowledge of Latin and was therefore an ideal transmitter of Greek learning. Hired to teach Aristotelian works, his chief contribution lay in his systematic interpretation of Greek philosophy (especially Plato). He thus helped to reorient Florentine Humanism from its earlier rhetorical ("civic") emphasis to a metaphysical one.

The Florentine Platonic Academy, informally established by Cosimo de' Medici (1462) and inspired perhaps by Plethon, included Greeks and especially Latins such as its head, Marsilio Ficino (who, though not a student of Argyropoulos, was probably influenced by him), also Pico della Mirandola (1463–1494) and Angelo Poliziano (or Politian, 1454–1494), who had studied with Argyropoulos.

In mid-quattrocento Rome the Byzantine cardinal and scholar Bessarion directed an "academy" to produce more accurate Humanist (not Scholastic) translations of Greek works in philosophy and science and of the Greek church fathers. The chief translators were George of Trebizond (who first introduced to Italy the second-century Greek rhetorician Hermogenes) and Teodoro Gaza (Theodoros Gazes), a leading Aristotelian.

Venice assumed primacy in Greek studies from 1494 to about 1525. Ermolao Barbaro, the leading Venetian humanist, who studied in Rome with Gaza, promoted in Padua displacement of the dominant Averroist tradition of Aristotle in favor of the more authentic Greco-Byzantine tradition. Barbaro's efforts, along with Bessarion's earlier ones, led, later in 1497, to the appointment of the Greek Nicholas Leonicos Thomaeos to teach Aristotle at Padua "in the original (Greek) text." Meantime, in Venice, Aldus Manutius printed first editions of most of the important Greek classical authors. His chief collaborators were the Greek Markos Musouros, editor of Plato, and Demetrios Doukas, editor of the *Rhetores graeci.*

From Chrysoloras' appearance in Florence until 1535, the Italian humanists' mastery of Greek learning advanced from ignorance of the language (except in some works of Aristotle) to recovery and mastery of virtually the entire surviving corpus of Greek literature and philosophy in the original, a process in which the Byzantine exiles played the fundamental role as transmitters of texts, teachers, printers, and exegetes (among other things, of Greek drama, ora-

1

tory, history, and philosophy, including the ancient commentators on Aristotle).

BIBLIOGRAPHY

Deno J. Geanakoplos, "A Reevaluation of Influence of Byzantine Scholars on the Development of the *Studia humanitatis*, Metaphysics, Patristics, and Science in the Italian Renaissance (1361–*c.* 1521)," in *Proceedings of the PMR Conference*, **3** (1978), "Theodore Gaza, a Byzantine Scholar of the Palaeologan "Renaissance" in the Italian Renaissance," in *Medievalia et Humanistica*, **12** (1984), and "The Career of the Little-known Renaissance Greek Scholar Nicholas Leonicus Tomaeus and the Ascendancy of Greco-Byzantine Aristotelianism at Padua (1497)," in *Festschrift for J. Karayanopoulos* (1985). Also his *Greek Scholars in Venice* (1962), repr. as *Byzantium and the Renaissance* (1976), and *Interaction of the "Sibling" Byzantine and Western Cultures in the Middle Ages and Italian Renaissance* (1976); Paul Kirsteller, "Renaissance Thought and Byzantine Learning," in his *Renaissance Thought and Its Sources*.

DENO J. GEANAKOPLOS

[See also **Aristotle in the Middle Ages; Bessarion; Classical Literary Studies; Ferrara-Florence, Council of; Gemistos Plethon, Georgios; George of Trebizond; Manuel Chrysoloras; Plato in the Middle Ages; Translations and Translators, Byzantine.**]

ITALY, BYZANTINE AREAS OF. Byzantine areas of Italy in the south (the Mezzogiorno) roughly correspond with the modern regions of Abruzzi, Molise, Campania, Apulia, Basilicata, Calabria, and Sicilia, and cover roughly 38,200 square miles (99,000 square kilometers). Hills and mountains dominate the landscape; thus, while Italy's long coastline and central location in the Mediterranean basin attracted numerous invaders, they often found its rugged terrain difficult to conquer and hold.

In the early fifth century southern Italy first experienced the barbarian invasions; Alaric and his Visigoths continued their plundering march south after the sack of Rome in 410, and Vandals from North Africa raided the coastal areas. By the end of the century Theodoric had set up an Ostrogothic kingdom that included all of Italy; but in the south, except in Samnium, Ostrogothic settlement was slight. There the fifth century had been a period of general decline and economic stagnation. Theodoric's rule brought peace and a modest economic recovery.

Justinian attempted to restore Roman authority in the western parts of the empire lost during the previous century. In 535 his general, Belisarius, arrived in the south after a successful campaign in North Africa, and in this region the defeat of the Ostrogoths was rapid. Under Totila, however, the Ostrogoths rallied and ravaged much of southern Italy, only to be defeated by Belisarius' successor, Narses. The south was finally pacified by 555, and with the Pragmatic Sanction of 554 Justinian reorganized Italy and firmly incorporated it into what may now be called the Byzantine state. In the south there had been an economic collapse and a serious loss of population as a result of the Gothic Wars. The plague of 542 contributed to the decline. The Lombard invasion of Italy, beginning in 568, completed the cycle of catastrophe.

The Lombards were in the south by 570, and the conquest proceeded from the two principal Lombard strongholds at Spoleto and Benevento. Justin II (565–578) sent a relief expedition that was defeated in Campania; and Constantinople, pressed on many fronts, was in no position to offer further assistance to its Italian subjects. The Lombard conquest of the south was slow and methodical; by the mid seventh century Lombard dukes had organized virtually independent duchies at Spoleto and Benevento, and the Byzantines were confined to the extreme south at Taranto, Brindisi, southern Calabria, and another pocket of strength in the coastal cities around Naples.

Since the Byzantines still controlled Sicily and retained naval supremacy in the area, their footholds in the south were easily supplied and reinforced. Emperor Constans II, attempting to restore Byzantine rule in the west, landed at Taranto in 663 with a large army and pushed the Lombards back to Benevento, which he was unable to take. After the first visit by an emperor to Rome in almost three centuries, Constans established a capital at Syracuse and posed a serious challenge to both the Lombards and the Arabs in North Africa. His assassination in 668 marked the beginning of a long period of defeats for the Byzantines in the west. Under Romuald the Lombards took advantage of Byzantine disorder in the south, and by 680 the Greeks had lost Brindisi, Taranto, and most of Apulia, and held only the area around Otranto in Apulia and southern Calabria around Reggio. The western coastal cities of Gaeta, Amalfi, and Naples were drifting away from direct Byzantine rule. During this period the Arab raids on the south increased in intensity as well.

BYZANTINE AREAS OF ITALY

Key

Byzantine areas *ca.* 1000

0   100 Miles

0   100 Kilometers

TUSCANY

UMBRIA

Spoleto

DUCHY OF SPOLETO

ABRUZZI

Rome

CORSICA

ADRIATIC SEA

SAMNIUM

MOLISE

Garigliano R.

DUCHY OF BENEVENTO

Capua

Benevento

Bari

CAMPANIA

APULIA

Gaeta

Naples

THEME OF LONGOBARDIA

Brindisi

Salerno

Amalfi

BASILICATA

Taranto

TYRRHENIAN SEA

Otranto

SARDINIA

Rossano

Cosenza

CALABRIA

THEME OF CALABRIA

Reggio

Palermo

MEDITERRANEAN

SICILY

Syracuse

SEA

3

With some minor losses and gains, the Byzantine position in the south remained stable until the fall of Ravenna to Pepin I in 754 and the subsequent Frankish conquest of northern Italy. Constantinople faced immediate challenges in the Balkans and Asia Minor and internal divisions resulting from the iconoclastic controversy (726–843) and hence had no resources for the defense of southern Italy. Byzantine areas in Italy seemed destined to fall to the Lombards or Arabs. The Lombard duke Archis took the title of prince in 774 and ruled most of the south. The duke of Spoleto had become a vassal of the Frankish king. Arab raiding parties became a permanent fixture, and in Sicily the fall of Palermo (831) gave the Arabs the upper hand in their steady conquest of the island. Raiding on the mainland intensified; the Arabs took Bari and Taranto and were attacking at the gates of Rome in 846.

What remained of Byzantine Italy was Calabria and an increasingly smaller share of eastern Sicily. The duchy of Calabria, while in theory a dependency of the "theme" (Byzantine province) of Sicily, was left to defend itself. The transfer of church authority from Rome to Constantinople during the iconoclastic controversy helped to make Calabria in particular an important center of Greek religious practices, culture, and language. Refugees from Sicily (including many Greek monks opposing iconoclasm) and from other areas made Calabria the most Greek region of the west. In other districts of southern Italy that had been under Greek rule, the language remained a Latin vernacular and Greek practices were regarded as foreign. Some western cities, principally Naples, also retained a strong Greek heritage, but in those areas on the mainland recently lost, such as Cosenza and Taranto, Latin gradually dominated. The Roman church had lost considerable influence and property in Sicily and Calabria, but in Naples and Amalfi there was a vigorous local struggle between Roman and Greek ecclesiastic hierarchies and liturgies.

By the mid ninth century the Byzantine position had deteriorated in the south. With the Arabs threatening Rome, the papacy attempted to convince the Carolingian emperors to intervene in southern Italy. The Byzantines became allies of the Carolingian emperor Louis II (*ca.* 855–876) in his southern campaign, but the reconquest of Bari regained Constantinople nothing, and it was clear that the Franks had no intention of turning over to the Greeks any conquests they might make in the south. The Lombards took advantage of the disagreements between the two distant empires to enhance their own local influence. Under the Macedonian emperors Basil I (867–886) and Leo VI the Wise (886–912), the Byzantine position in Italy became more secure. Bari became Byzantine again in 876, and the Lombard prince of Benevento put himself under Byzantine authority. Around 885 the able general Nikephoros Phokas took command of the Greek forces in the south; he pushed the Arabs out of Calabria and reclaimed much territory from Salerno and Benevento.

Under Leo VI the government of the south was reorganized. Two themes were established: Longobardia on the east coast, ruled by a *strategos* (military governor) at Bari; and Calabria, under a *strategos* usually at Reggio. The Byzantines were more willing to rule directly, having become less trusting of their Lombard subjects. Leo also pursued a policy of colonization in Apulia and Calabria, and he fostered a reorganization of the church under Greek bishops. The Byzantines and their newly found Lombard subjects defeated the Arabs at Garigliano in 915 under the *strategos* Nicola Picingli and kept the mainland safe from the Arabs for a while. Naples and Gaeta returned to formal Byzantine protection.

The Byzantine revival in the south in the tenth century faced several serious challenges. Arab raiders several times forced the theme of Calabria to pay tribute. The Hungarian raids in Italy reached Campania in 922, and in the 940's threatened Longobardia as far south as Bari. The princes of Capua, who now controlled Benevento, were at first rebellious and succeeded in asserting their independence. The new Ottonian dynasty in Germany also challenged Byzantine rule in the south. When Otto I the Great (962–973) was at Benevento, the Lombard princes transferred their allegiance to him, and the Germans invaded Apulia and Calabria in 968 but with little result. A timely Byzantine marriage alliance with Otto's heir in 972 helped bring peace to the south, and Otto II obligingly crushed the Arabs in Calabria in 982.

This difficult political situation provided the background for a flowering of Greek culture in the south, principally centered in the Basilian monasteries of Calabria. The work of St. Nilus of Rossano (*ca.* 910–1005), hermit and monastic reformer, resulted in the great reputation of the Mecurion monastery and others he personally founded. Nilus helped to keep alive the eremitical tradition as well, and his own career witnessed many forced migrations caused by Arab raids. Nilus was widely venerated during his long life and was well known for his travels. His life demonstrates that Greek culture had set down strong roots in Calabria. Under Basil II (976–1025) the Byzantine position in the south was strengthened and consolidated. The emperor reorganized the government under a single *katepano* (chief) of Italy at Bari and supplied sufficient funds and troops. The successful general Basil Boiannes ended Arab raids, pacified the Lombards, and administered the initial defeats of the Normans. By about 1000 the Byzantine position in southern Italy was as strong as it had been at any time since the arrival of the Lombards.

BIBLIOGRAPHY

Jules Gay, *L'Italie méridionale et l'empire byzantin* (1904), trans. into Italian as *L'Italia meridionale e l'impero bizantino* (1930); André Guillou, "L'Italia byzantina dall'invasione longobarda alla caduta di Ravenna," in Giuseppe Galasso, ed., *Storia d'Italia*, I (1980); George Ostrogorsky, *History of the Byzantine State*, Joan M. Hussey, trans., 2nd ed. (1969); Giuseppe Pochettino, *I langobardi nell'Italia meridionale (570–1080)* (1930); Charles Wickham, *Early Medieval Italy: Central Power and Local Society 400–1000* (1981).

STEVEN EPSTEIN

[See also **Byzantine Empire: History; Lombards, Kingdom of; Ostrogoths.**]

ITALY, FOURTEENTH AND FIFTEENTH CENTURIES. The habit of seeing late medieval Italy as a study in political fragmentation, or of stressing the rise of large regional states such as Milan, depends tacitly upon the conceptual model of a centralized state. However, since no such state existed in Italy, there is something arbitrary about seeing Italian political affairs in the fourteenth century as moving toward the centralization of authority. Yet we cannot do without the model, for it enables us to make sense of a history that we would not otherwise know how to grasp. To take the opposite approach—to see the peninsula from the viewpoint of one of the small, independent communes or urban lordships, such as Siena or Ferrara—would give a picture of only one or two of its constituent parts, not of the larger—though by no means organic— whole. And although taking a route between the model and the fragmented reality seems to make logical sense, no historical narrative can sensibly accommodate it. Accordingly, we must draw on the

designated model, while also bearing its arbitrary aspects in mind.

Italy in 1300 was made up of more than forty different states, perhaps even as many as 300, depending upon how "state" is defined. The old kingdom of Italy—roughly the upper two-fifths of the peninsula, excluding Venice and the Papal States—was under the nominal rule of the Holy Roman Empire and still had an abstract juridical reality. But having been brutally beaten in its epochal clash with the papacy and Guelph cities, the imperial power in Italy had been reduced to a shifty, often venal, presence. Soon, too, with the transfer of the papacy to Avignon (1309), the Italian lands under papal rule verged on political disintegration, as towns and petty lords in the Romagna and Umbria did what they pleased, putting local autonomies foremost or willfully seizing neighboring territory.

In the north, along a line moving from east to west, the largest states de facto were the patriarchate of Aquileia; the republic of Venice; the urban lordships of Padua, Verona, Mantua, and Milan; the feudal seigniories of Piedmont, where the duchy of Savoy eventually predominated; and the republic of Genoa. Farther south, in Tuscany, lay the republican communes of Lucca, Pisa, Florence, and Siena. To the east of these, in the Papal States, were the Este lordship of Ferrara, the commune of Bologna, and a scattering of towns (each with a surrounding territory) to be ruled later on in the fourteenth century by petty despots such as the Malatesta (Rimini), Manfredi (Faenza), Ordelaffi (Forli), da Polenta (Ravenna), Montefeltro (Urbino), and Alidosi (Imola). Farther south were the commune of Perugia and the Patrimony of St. Peter, including Rome. Beyond them stretched the French Angevin realm of Naples, supposedly held under papal tutorship. Sicily and Sardinia had already been torn away from the Angevins by native revolt (the War of the Sicilian Vespers, 1282–1303) and Sardinia passed to the royal house of Aragon in 1324.

Within this broad spectrum of states, government varied enormously in its scope, efficiency, civility, social makeup, laws, and ideological presuppositions. The extremes lay in the differences between north and south, commune and kingdom; in the contrasts between feudalism and bustling commercial city, despotism and citizen consensus, fluid and more castelike nobilities. The great urban communes of the north stood at one extreme; at the other were the vast feudal holdings of the great barons of Angevin Naples and the Aragonese kingdom in Sicily (offi-

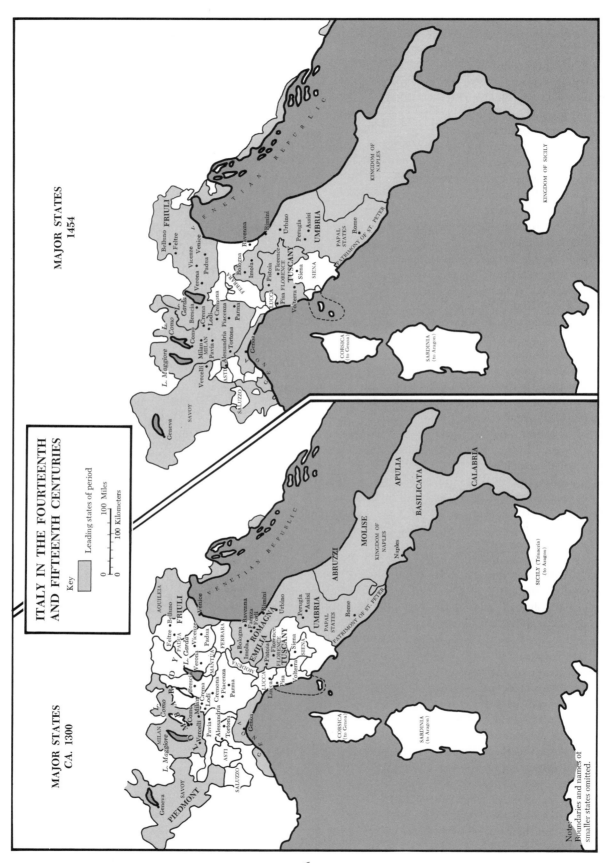

ITALY IN THE FOURTEENTH AND FIFTEENTH CENTURIES

Key

Leading states of period

0   100 Miles
0   100 Kilometers

MAJOR STATES
CA. 1300

PIEDMONT

Geneva

SAVOY

SALUZZO

ASTI

L. Maggiore

MILAN

Vercelli

Como

L. Como

Pavia

Lodi

Crema

Alessandria

Tortona

Brescia

L. Garda

Cremona

Piacenza

Parma

MODENA

Genoa

Vicenze

Padua

FRIULI

AQUILEIA

Belluno

Feltre

Verona

MANTUA

FERRARA

Bologna

Imola

Faenza

Forlì

Ravenna

Rimini

EMILIA ROMAGNA

Pistoia

Pisa

Lucca

LUCCA

Elsa

Volterra

FLORENCE

TUSCANY

Siena

SIENA

Urbino

Perugia

Assisi

UMBRIA

PAPAL STATES

Rome

PATRIMONY OF ST. PETER

ABRUZZI

MOLISE

KINGDOM OF NAPLES

Naples

APULIA

BASILICATA

CALABRIA

VENETIAN REPUBLIC

Venice

CORSICA
(to Genoa)

SARDINIA
(to Aragon)

SICILY (Trinacria)
(to Aragon)

Note: Boundaries and names of smaller states omitted.

MAJOR STATES
1454

SAVOY

SALUZZO

Geneva

L. Maggiore

Vercelli

ASTI

MILAN

Milan

Como

L. Como

Pavia

Lodi

Crema

Alessandria

Tortona

Brescia

L. Garda

Cremona

Piacenza

Parma

Genoa

Verona

Vicenze

Padua

Venice

Belluno

Feltre

FRIULI

VENETIAN REPUBLIC

FERRARA

Bologna

Imola

Ravenna

Rimini

Urbino

Pistoia

Pisa

Lucca

LUCCA

Volterra

FLORENCE

Florence

TUSCANY

Siena

SIENA

Perugia

Assisi

UMBRIA

PAPAL STATES

Rome

PATRIMONY OF ST. PETER

KINGDOM OF NAPLES

CORSICA
(to Genoa)

SARDINIA

KINGDOM OF SICILY

6

cially Trinacria). But there were also insuperable differences within Upper Italy, again in government by commune (associations of citizens), as in Genoa, and government by feudal fiat, as in Piedmont, large parts of Lombardy, the Friuli, the Romagna, and the Emilian–Tuscan Apennines.

Italy was becoming a complex patchwork of regional or local autonomies, which made allegiances difficult and frontiers unstable. There were civil wars and changing jurisdictions in the troubled realms of Naples and Sicily, popes determined to prevent the rise of a major power in Italy, the riot of urban political factions in the north, and the clash of republican communes with the spread of urban despotism (*signorie*). In this setting, once their desires or fears had been aroused, the larger political entities thrust out beyond their frontiers to conquer whatever they could. Thus Milan, the papacy, the Angevin and Aragonese kingdoms, Florence, Savoy, and Venice were involved in "a war of all against all." But even as these states expanded, acquiring more military muscle, they retained a high degree of intrastate variation, particularly the kingdom of Naples, the Papal States, and even the seigniory of Milan, all of which tolerated local legal custom, local courts, different ways of assigning and distributing local extraordinary taxes, and, in the north, occasional local assemblies of privileged citizens.

In the early fourteenth century there were three political storm centers, each of which helped to shape Italian destinies for generations to come. First, populous and industrious Milan, situated in the middle of the rich river plain of Lombardy, came fully under the rule of the Visconti, a feudal dynasty that swiftly spearheaded aggressive Milanese expansion. If the Visconti lords of Milan were to survive in such a fertile and politically fragmented region, they must extend and consolidate their gains again and again.

Second, when Pope Clement V (1305–1314) transferred the papacy to Avignon, he diminished the temporal power of the papacy in Italy, abandoned the Papal States to deepening turmoil and petty despots, and sowed the fears that would vindicate the divisive policies of the popes, who labored to keep all other Italian states relatively weak. Accordingly, the papal return to Rome (1377) intensified the anxieties of neighboring states, especially Florence. In the fifteenth century a line of Renaissance popes stubbornly followed a policy of nepotism, not only to find lordships for their families but also to protect and strengthen their pontificates. To be pope was to be locked into a struggle for power in the peninsula.

The eye of the third storm centered on Naples and Sicily. The establishment of a new dynasty by Charles of Anjou (1265–1278) had led to rebellion and civil war in Sicily, with the result that Sicily and its anti-Angevin nobility ended up under the rule of the house of Aragon.

The fourteenth-century storm centers had a major impact on only one of the two great seaports, Genoa, which became a prime target of Milanese expansion. Venice, preoccupied with its maritime empire and eastern emporia, was not a true contender on the Italian mainland until after 1400.

Matteo I Visconti, lord of Milan (1310–1322), was succeeded by a line of able direct descendants. Their ruling position in the city and its territories was accorded repeated legitimation by vote or acclamation in the large communal council of 900 and, when possible, by their confirmation as imperial vicars. Azzone Visconti (1328–1339) gathered Cremona, Piacenza, Crema, Lodi, Como, Vercelli, and Brescia into the Milanese fold, mainly by force of arms and by checking another ambitious signor, Mastino II della Scala of Verona. Under Lucchino Visconti (1339–1349), Asti, Parma, Tortona, Alessandria, and other towns were drawn into the Milanese state. Lucchino had the assistance of his brilliant brother, Giovanni, archbishop of Milan, who, as lord of Milan (1349–1354), seized Bologna from the papacy, acquired Genoa, struck deep into Tuscany, and, on his death, left a greatly enlarged political patrimony to his three nephews: Matteo, Galeazzo, and Bernabò. In 1385 the most important of these, Bernabò, was cunningly eliminated by his nephew (and son-in-law) Giangaleazzo, who became the first duke of Milan by buying the title from Emperor Wenceslaus in 1395. When Giangaleazzo died in 1402, his lands reached from Padua, across the Lombard plain, down to Assisi and Perugia, deep in papal territory. Florence alone had held out, though it stood on the brink of military collapse.

Despite its distance from Rome, the Avignon papacy did not lose interest in Italian politics or the Papal States, a prime source of income. But nearly every pope from John XXII (1316–1334) to Gregory XI (1370–1378) had to wage political and military campaigns against the Visconti and their chronic incursions into papal territory. Emperors and imperial claimants were also troublesome for the papacy. Henry VII, Louis of Bavaria, Frederick of Austria, and Charles IV flouted papal temporal claims and were usually able, on descending into Italy, to rally small armies of Ghibelline exiles or to incite Ghibelline leagues against the diplomacy and troops of papal legates. Consequently, in periods when papal recognition was denied to imperial claimants, popes themselves—such as Clement V and John XXII—temporarily claimed the imperial authority and appointed imperial vicars. For some years after 1314, Robert of Anjou (d. 1343), nominal king of Sicily (though in fact of Naples), went by the title of "vicar of all Italy." Always uneasy about Angevin machinations in central and northern Italy, popes never provided Robert with unstinting support—indeed, at times they entered into bitter conflict with him. The success of papal policy in Italy also depended in part upon the character of the cardinal legates. The most formidable of these, in his resolution to reconstitute the Papal States, was the Spaniard Gil Albornoz (1353–1367), a worthy rival to the astute archbishop and lord of Milan, Giovanni Visconti.

King Robert of Anjou failed on seven expeditions to wrest Sicily from Frederick III of Aragon (1295–1337). His anti-imperial policies were more successful, notably in Upper Italy, where he made alliances with Guelph centers such as Florence and used his forces to oppose both imperial claimants and the ever-busy Visconti of Milan. To hold the loyalty of his baronage he was forced to feudalize more of his lands, thus weakening the fiscal foundations of the crown. But the deepest wounds to the cohesion of the kingdom were inflicted later, in the reign of his granddaughter Joanna I, queen of Naples (1343–1382). A rivalry to the death between Joanna and her Hungarian cousins (Robert's father, Charles II of Anjou, had married a Hungarian princess) resulted in assassinations, civil wars, and two invasions of the kingdom (1347, 1350) by Louis I, king of Hungary. Charles III of Durazzo, descended from yet another branch of the family, had Joanna executed and was himself murdered in Hungary four years later (1386). It was owing to their preoccupation with Neapolitan and Hungarian affairs that these princes had been unable, in any realistic sense, to cast acquisitive eyes on central Italy.

In the last quarter of the fourteenth century, the Italian peninsula was dominated by three or four states. Having returned to Rome in 1377, the papacy was at once rent by the Great Schism (1378–1417), because of which popes Urban VI and Boniface IX had to employ urgent diplomacy to maintain the ecclesiastical obedience of the Italian states. On the high seas the keen and inveterate hostilities between Genoa and Venice climaxed in the Chioggia War (1378–1381), the outcome of which made Genoa eas-

ier prey for the Visconti, the Catalans, and the crown of France. Venice, in turn, experienced serious economic difficulties, being already much harassed by the Ottoman Turks in the Levant, the vital ground of Venetian trade. Meanwhile, along the southern frontiers of the ambitious Visconti state, Florence, in a time of political emergency, transformed its republican viewpoint into an ideological call for the "freedom of Italy" and the continuing independence of the existing city-states.

Italy's remarkable economic and demographic growth peaked in the decades around 1300. Not for centuries to come was the peninsula again to experience so much political novelty, zest, and movement, particularly as attested in the life of its urban communes. A forceful shaping vitality was evident in all spheres, including art and literature. The Italian banking houses of the Renaissance—Pazzi, Medici, Chigi, Strozzi—lacked the verve, numbers, ingenuity, and daring of their Sienese and Florentine counterparts of the early fourteenth century. The same is true of a comparison of differences between Venetian overseas merchants in 1300 and in 1500. Also, about 1320 Tuscany's woolen textile industry produced roughly double the amount of cloth that it produced after about 1350.

After 1350 the leading textile centers—Florence, Lucca, Siena, Perugia—were gravely troubled by unemployment, a rebellious proletariat, and deepening poverty. But the years 1315–1317 had already ushered in episodes of appalling famine, owing to crop failures and—it has been alleged—a crisis of overpopulation. Tax-farming records at Genoa reveal a disastrous decline in Genoese maritime commerce, possibly by 75 percent or more in the course of the century. And following the Black Death (1347–1349) much productive land all over Italy was to lie fallow for two or three generations.

Mention of the Black Death raises the question of population. Available figures profile catastrophic changes and reveal that Italy suffered the same decimated populations and shrunken productivities as the rest of fourteenth-century Europe. With the exception of luxury silks, overall economic output in fifteenth-century Italy was decidedly lower than it had been at the end of the thirteenth century.

In 1300, according to learned estimates, the population of the peninsula numbered about 11 million. Following bouts of famine after 1315 and after the epidemic spread of bubonic plague, this number had shrunk to 8 million by 1350 and was still the same half a century later, largely because of recurring outbreaks of mass infection. Florence in 1300 had a population of around 95,000 people; in the 1420's the total stood at about 40,000. The population of Genoa fell from 60,000–90,000 inhabitants in 1290 to about 36,000 in 1400. Innumerable villages and rural communes were wiped out. To take only one example, Pavia suffered epidemics in 1361, 1373, 1388, and 1399. Most other cities and rural clusters were subject to a similar pattern of recurrence.

The best historical thinking posits a concatenation of the forces that contributed to economic, demographic, and social decline, but the exact connections are elusive because the assumed guiding model is that of a "system" that can sustain only so much productivity and humanity. Some historians have argued that the limited capacities of any particular social system (and not a simple Malthusianism) account for economic and demographic fluctuation; when certain limits are reached, crises and breakdowns ensue until major readjustments have taken place.

Some of the terrible strains of the fourteenth century can be attributed to the impact of large, ravaging companies of professional soldiers, foreign and native, that sometimes numbered more than 5,000. They were captained by infamous commanders (condottieri) such as Werner von Ürslingen, Jean de Montreal, Conrad Wirtinger von Landau, and Sir John Hawkwood who hired themselves and their companies out on short-term contracts to republican communes and "tyrants" (signori). But when contracts were not renewed and stipends were cut off, they roamed savagely over the countryside, killing, pillaging, holding people for ransom, and generally disrupting agriculture or the entire flow of local trade and travel.

As a result of the fourteenth-century economic and demographic decline, Italian society suffered some loss of initiative and became more static. Henceforth, but more notably after 1400, there was less upward social movement; more people remained fixed in the stations to which they were born, or fell to a lower rung on the social ladder. In the countryside, down through the sixteenth century, more and more land was gathered into fewer hands, to the overwhelming advantage of princes, noblemen, urban oligarchies, and the rich metropolitan bourgeoisie. Sharecroppers (mezzadri) fell into chronic debt, many becoming as tightly bound to the soil as any tenth-century serf. Like rural Italy, cities recorded widening gaps between rich and poor, nobles and commoners, or political citizens and disenfranchised multitude. The early Italian Renaissance was an age not of deep vitality or expansion but of social cramping, visible chiefly in the political, economic, and demographic spheres.

It has been argued that the new, large scale of private building in fifteenth-century Florence, and perhaps in other cities, made for much prosperity in the construction and decorative arts industries. Many were thus able to improve their economic lot, despite difficult circumstances. But it remains to be seen how far the renewed vigor of the building trades, in a labor-intensive society, actually went to redistribute the wealth that tended, in most late medieval cities, to end up in relatively few purses.

A narrative of the principal events of fifteenth-century Italy must touch upon the six largest states: Venice, Milan, Savoy, Florence, the Papal States, and the Kingdom of Naples. A major share of the peninsula's economic and social resources went into the organization and maintenance of these states and their policies.

The death of Giangaleazzo Visconti (1402) issued in a brutal struggle for power at the Milanese court; subject lands and cities revolted; and the duchy was rent by civil war. The great menace to all of central and northern Italy had suddenly vanished. For the first time, the Venetian republic pushed deep into the Italian mainland, seizing Padua first, then Verona and Vicenza, and reaching next to take Belluno and Feltre (1401–1412). Venice would prey henceforth on the eastern boundaries of the Milanese duchy, driven by the claim that it had vital frontiers to secure there, but also moved to compensate for its losses to the Ottomans in the eastern Mediterranean. In the northwest the Milanese debacle permitted Amadeo VIII of Savoy to extend his domains both to the east and to the north, until he held most of Piedmont. These gains were accorded greater legitimacy when Amadeo received imperial recognition and the title of duke in 1416, an event that also helped convert the duchy of Savoy into a more ordered state.

Unlike Venice and Savoy, the republic of Florence was unable to take advantage of the short-lived Milanese collapse. Despite acquiring Pisa (1406) and some lesser towns, the Florentines failed to complete their dreamed-of takeover of Tuscany. Lucca and Siena, two tiny republics, remained an obstacle. Meanwhile, to the east and south the whole of papal territory was endangered by the brilliant young king of Naples, Ladislaus (d. 1414), who fought against the power of his great feudal barons, conquered Rome and Umbria (1413–1414), and was poised to strike at Tuscany and the Papal States when death struck him.

The Great Schism, centering on the drama of rival papal pretenders, was a blot on the pontifical dignity and retarded the consolidation of papal government. Not until Martin V's pontificate (1417–1431) did the papacy begin to recover its temporal losses. Soon, however, Rome had to confront yet another strong neighbor to the south: Alfonso V, king of Aragon, Sicily, and Sardinia, turned the ineptitude of Angevin policies to his advantage and seized Naples in 1442.

The Peace of Lodi and the Italian League (1454–1455) terminated the wars that had been triggered by the death of Filippo Maria, the last Visconti duke of Milan (1447). In these wars Venice, Alfonso V, and the great soldier Francesco Sforza fought for the spoils of the Milanese duchy while Florence, Savoy, and the papacy took sides or seized bits of territory. The armed struggle was won by Sforza, whose seigniorial claims to Milan were bolstered by his brilliant political and military skills and by his marriage to Bianca Maria, Filippo Maria Visconti's only child. Aside from confirming Sforza's seizure of Milan, the Italian League in effect recognized and endorsed the preeminence of the six leading states of the peninsula. But this *entente cordiale* was fleeting. The supposed balance of power was far from perfect; too many affairs of the first importance were still in flux.

After Francesco Sforza's death (1466) the old ambitions and fears reappeared and were stirred up into wars, most strikingly in the bullying war waged by Venice against Ferrara (1482–1484). The ambitions were chiefly those of an expansionist Venice, a revitalized papacy, and the Neapolitan-Aragonese kings. Florence and the Sforza rulers of Milan were moved more by fear: the former by nervousness over Venetian and papal designs, the latter by the knowledge that, as political upstarts, they required alliances against Venice.

These political fears and ambitions made up the background to the French invasion of the peninsula (1494), which ushered in the Italian Wars. Charles VIII of France, pressing the Angevin claim to Naples, led an army of 30,000 men and 40 pieces of artillery into Italy; Milan was thereby endangered, being also subject to a French dynastic claim. Venice and the great nepotist, Pope Alexander VI, quickly moved to profit from the invasion by grabbing territory or concluding advantageous agreements, while Florence and Savoy could do little more than yield to coercion. For the next sixty-five years the

overturning and reconstituting of Italian states was to be the business of armies of the crowns of France, Spain, and the Holy Roman Empire.

In 1500 Italy was a land of principalities, oligarchical republics, petty rural or urban despotisms, and feudal jurisdictions. Its frailties were less the result of political-territorial divisions than of crushing fiscal policies, resentful or passive subject populations, and unresponsive rulers and ruling elites. Venice could not count upon the allegiance of noblemen and rich burghers in its mainland dominions. The Milanese state was centralized at the top, in its tiers of leading officials, but was much fragmented in its subject communities and its numerous feudal enclaves. Savoy, the Papal States, and the Kingdom of Naples betrayed a similar pattern of decentralization. The papacy, moreover, given over to wholesale nepotism, was ready to trade its principles for grants of benefits to papal offspring and relatives. And Florence, riven by faction at home, was confronted abroad by rebellious subjects: Pisa, Pistoia, and Volterra. In short, the colossal burden of Italy's alienated populations and the widening cleavage between rulers and ruled exacerbated the peninsula's troubles in the face of foreign invasion.

It would be wrong, however, to suppose that a weakened Italy gave rise to a timid culture. Quite the opposite. There was no parallel elsewhere in Europe for the sum of Italian literary, artistic, and intellectual achievements in the fourteenth and fifteenth centuries.

Italian literature proper begins in the late thirteenth century, with an idealizing poetry of love and the verse of the "comic realists." Fresh, delicate, measured, and high-minded, the work of the love poets is better known because of Dante and Cavalcanti. But the realists—such as Rustico di Filippo and Cecco Angiolieri—also merit study. The sparkling vigor of their language and perception catches the dynamism of Italian burgher society, whereas the love poets speak for the more intellectual, aristocratic, and religious proclivities of the society. Petrarch, the greatest of the love lyricists, is the bridge to the Platonizing love poets of the early sixteenth century. But there persisted always a strong line of comic-realist verse. These two poetries offer the social historian essential evidence for tracking changes in mood, spirit, and consciousness.

Boccaccio is the leading name in prose fiction. The hundred stories of his *Decameron*—taken from legend, oral tradition, old stories, and contemporary anecdote—feature a colorful vernacular, as well as keenly drawn earthy characters and treatment of the themes of lust, avarice, vanity, folly, tenacity, and chicanery. Jocular stories *(facezie)* after Boccaccio were coarser and far less artful. The latinity of the fifteenth-century humanists delayed the development of Italian vernacular prose.

Italy's supreme artistic triumph occurred in the northern cities, in the stone, timber, and masonry of the urban churches and palazzi. Hundreds of those churches and more of the palazzi still stand as monuments to the energy and aesthetic eye of their builders. Virtually all the art of the period was intended for these edifices. Much of the ornamentation (and instruction by imagery) took the form of religious painting, a pursuit that raised numerous craftsmen from obscurity. From Giotto and Duccio in the early 1300's, to Masaccio, Piero della Francesca, and Giovanni Bellini in the fifteenth century, Upper Italy produced a procession of artists who seemed to revolutionize perception. They filled their frescoes and altarpieces with an ever more mundane humanity, one of their greatest accomplishments being their illusionistic turning of the picture space into a window that looked onto the everyday world.

The profound secularization of Italian culture— the cultural "processing" of experience along more worldly lines—took place in art and in political ideas no less than in upper-class life and letters. For the student who seeks to bypass the conventional boundaries and categories of the historical discipline, the art of the early Renaissance may be seen— its aesthetic appeal aside—as the record of a changing sensibility and an altering consciousness. Much fifteenth-century painting was keyed to the political and social needs, as well as to the life-style, of the princely courts and urban oligarchies. Both directly and indirectly such painting celebrated the groups and individuals who commissioned it.

In the intellectual sphere, the most fertile undertaking in the Italian peninsula at the end of the Middle Ages was Humanism. Defining it as the sustained study of classical literature and history, combined with a marked emphasis on rhetoric, experts take the origins of Humanism back to the literary activity of notaries and lawyers at Padua, Bologna, Florence, and other cities in the period around 1300. Petrarch is often considered the first full-fledged Humanist, owing to his love of antiquity and his mastery of classical rhetoric.

But if the search be for a broadly based movement, then we must look to the first decades of the fifteenth century, to groups of literati and intellec-

tuals at Florence, Padua, Venice, Bologna, Rome, and Milan. The pertinent names are those of Leonardo Bruni, Pier Paolo Vergerio, Francesco Barbaro, Guarino Guarini, Vittorino de Feltre, and Lorenzo Valla. They and their contemporaries turned Humanism into a course of education for the upper classes. They highlighted, for children as for adults, the study of grammar (Latin and Greek), rhetoric, history, poetry, and ethics. Their ideal was to fashion a complete personality, a whole man learned in languages, literature, philosophy, and history, although primary emphasis was given to rhetoric, the art of eloquence. This commitment to eloquence reveals that the product of humanistic education was intended to be an individual in close contact with other men, an advocate of public causes.

Despite the exuberance of its high culture, fifteenth-century Italy did not witness energetic forces of social innovation or social mobility. The apparent contradiction here is resolvable by noting that the upper classes achieved their highest measure of political security at home only in that century. Only then, too, when it was clear that the dominant political classes had turned into ruling castes, were the elite groups able to attain a decisive self-assurance; and only then could their artists and intellectual spokesmen transform this new awareness and self-confidence into corresponding cultural achievements. The result was a militant Humanism, a craze for the building and rebuilding of proud family palaces, a new architecture, and an art whose goals lay in the qualities of light, optimism, worldly affirmation, and a mimetic control over the visual environment.

BIBLIOGRAPHY

Hans Baron, *The Crisis of the Early Italian Renaissance,* 2 vols (1955, rev. 1-vol. ed. 1966); Sergio Bertelli, *Il potere oligarchico nella stato-città medievale* (1978); Gene A. Brucker, *Florentine Politics and Society, 1343–1378* (1962), and *The Civic World of Early Renaissance Florence* (1977); Romolo Caggese, *Roberto d'Angiò e i suoi tempi,* 2 vols. (1922–1930); Giovanni Cherubini, *Signori, contadini, borghesi* (1974); Giorgio Chittolini, ed., *La crisi degli ordinamenti comunali e le origini dello stato del Rinascimento* (1979); Benedetto Croce, *Storia del regno di Napoli* (1925), 5th ed. (1958); G. Falco, *La santa romana repubblica,* 2nd ed. (1954); Eugenio Garin, *Italian Humanism,* Peter Munz, trans. (1965); Frederick Hartt, *A History of Italian Renaissance Art,* 2nd ed. (1979); Denys Hay, *The Italian Renaissance in Its Historical Background* (1961), and *The Church in Italy in the Fifteenth Century* (1977); Jacques Heers, *Gênes au xv siècle* (1961).

Philip James Jones, *The Malatesta of Rimini and the Papal State* (1974), and *Economia e società nell' Italia medievale* (1980); Paul O. Kristeller, *Renaissance Thought* (1955, repr. 1961), and *Renaissance Thought and Its Sources*, Michael Mooney, ed. (1979); Frederic C. Lane, *Venice: A Maritime Republic* (1973); John Larner, *The Lords of Romagna* (1965), and *Italy in the Age of Dante and Petrarch* (1980); Emile G. Léonard, *Les Angevins de Naples* (1954); Gino Luzzatto, *An Economic History of Italy from the Fall of the Roman Empire to the Beginning of the Sixteenth Century*, Philip Jones, trans. (1961); Lauro Martines, *Lawyers and Statecraft in Renaissance Florence* (1968), and *Power and Imagination: City-States in Renaissance Italy* (1979); Guillaume Mollat, *Les papes d'Avignon*, 9th ed. (1949), trans. as *The Popes at Avignon* by Janet Love (1963).

Peter Partner, *The Lands of St. Peter* (1972); Ludwig Pastor, *The History of the Popes*, Frederick I. Antrobus and Ralph F. Kerr, eds., I–XII (1891–1912); Brian S. Pullan, *A History of Early Renaissance Italy* (1973); R. Romano and C. Vivanti, eds., *Storia d'Italia*, I–II, and supplements, especially *Annali*, I (1972–1978); Nicolai Rubinstein, *The Government of Florence Under the Medici (1434–1494)* (1966), and idem., ed., *Florentine Studies: Politics and Society in Renaissance Florence* (1968); V. Ruttenburg, *Popolo e movimenti popolari nell'Italia del '300 e '400*, G. Borghini, trans. (1971); Jerrold E. Seigel, *Rhetoric and Philosophy in Renaissance Humanism* (1968); L. Simeoni, *Le signorie*, 2 vols. (1950); F. Tateo, *I centri culturali dell'umanesimo* (1971); Alberto Tenenti, *Florence à l'époque des Médicis* (1968); Nino Valeri, *L'Italia nell'età dei principati, dal 1343 al 1516* (1949), and idem, ed., *Storia d'Italia*, 2nd ed., 5 vols. (1965–1967); John Humphreys Whitfield, *A Short History of Italian Literature* (1960).

LAURO MARTINES

[See also **Albornoz, Cardinal Gil; Angevins; Aragon, Crown of; Banking, European; Boccaccio; Bruni, Leonardo; Cavalcanti, Guido; Cecco Angiolieri; Clement V, Pope; Commune; Condottieri; Dante Alighieri; Duccio di Buoninsegna; Florence; Genoa; Giotto di Bondone; Guelphs and Ghibellines; Italy, Rise of Towns in; John XXII, Pope; Masaccio, Tommaso Cassai; Milan; Naples; Papal States; Petrarch; Pisa; Schism, Great; Sforza; Sicilian Vespers; Sicily, Kingdom of; Siena; Tuscany; Venice; Visconti.**]

ITALY, MUSLIMS IN. See **Sicily, Islamic.**

ITALY, NORMANS IN. See **Sicily, Kingdom of.**

ITALY, RISE OF TOWNS IN. The Lombard invasion of Italy in 568 was a Germanic migration that claimed unexpected victims. One of these was literacy. Within three generations—by the time of King Rothari's Edict of 643—Upper Italy had been turned into an illiterate expanse, in part at least because so many Romans of the educated sort had fled (and thus much of the detail of the invasion went unrecorded). Concentrated in the cities, the leading Roman families of the northern plain had escaped to Byzantine Ravenna and to Rome, accompanied by servitors and slaves. Imperial administration collapsed and the Germanic conquerors—perhaps some 200,000 in all—pushed aside what remained of the old ruling class. All the great landed estates and a large number of the lesser ones passed into Lombard hands, the biggest taker of booty being the king. In fear of their lives, many bishops, including the bishop of Milan, had deserted their dioceses; but others apparently remained to face the invaders.

Although war and disease had already diminished the population of late Roman cities, the Lombard invasion hastened the decline. By 750 nearly 100 episcopal towns had ceased to be diocesan centers, a trend not reversed by the conversion of the Lombards to Christianity. The invaders were warriors and tillers of the soil, not administrators, and they had no need of urban centers. They partitioned their Italian conquests into thirty-six duchies and imposed a yearly tax tribute amounting to one-third of the total agricultural product. Roman fiscal institutions broke down, seriously harming the cities, which had been centers of consumption and administration, not agglomerations founded on economic production and commercial exchange.

Writing of the seventh century, historians refer to "the ruralization and barbarization" of the central and north Italian cities. Pavia did not become a fixed capital because Lombard kings were often itinerant. In many cities the people tore up paved streets to satisfy individual building needs; they converted town squares and marketplaces to pasture land; and they turned more and more to agriculture, while the scope of the arts and crafts narrowed, by and large, to what could be produced in households. In Byzantine Italy, the cities also suffered Lombard attacks and destruction, but a few continued to prosper, notably Ravenna (until conquered by the Lombards in 751), Rome, and Naples. The "barbarization" of the surrounding areas reduced the flow of trade and traffic. Between the late sixth and ninth centuries, moreover, the princes of Naples, Amalfi, and Gaeta broke gradually away from subjection to Constantinople. Byzantine rule became a phantom presence and the three cities became the capitals, in effect, of independent states. The like was also true of Salerno and Capua, which broke away from the Lombard duchy of Benevento.

The explosive expansion of Islam had resulted, by the beginning of the eighth century, in Muslim control of North Africa and much of the Mediterranean. But historians have now seriously contested Henri Pirenne's thesis, according to which the Arab conquests severed commercial relations between East and West and all but expunged European cities outside Spain. Maurice Lombard and others have argued that the Arab victories released hoards of gold that stimulated commercial traffic with the Christian West. In any case, Italy remained a repository of towns; markets there survived, even when trade lapsed mainly into barter.

Historians detect strong signs of economic revival in the eighth century, but it may be well to see this period as transitional, so as to preserve a comparison with the ninth century, for which the evidence of movement and revival is conclusive. New urban sites, settled by refugees who had fled from the Lombards between the late sixth and the eighth centuries, now entered the historical scene: Venice, Comacchio, Ferrara, Viterbo, Troia, Fabriano, Corneto, Alessandria, and Aquila. After 750, with the Lombard conquest of Comacchio and Ravenna, Venice in particular benefited from quickening trade relations with the East. In the ninth century, if not earlier, the navigable tributaries of the Po River—the Lambro, the Ticino, and the Adda—took on a major importance in the revival of trade relations among ancient towns such as Pavia, Piacenza, Cremona, and Mantua, and in linking these, via the Alpine passes, to northern Europe.

In southern Italy, where the raids and conquests of the Saracens climaxed in the ninth century, the commercial lead was taken by Gaeta, Amalfi, Salerno, and Naples, whose merchants and sailors were in vital contact with North Africa, Egypt, and Constantinople, despite the militant pressure from Islam. Like Venice, Pavia, and Piacenza in the north, they received Eastern goods in transit or for regional consumption—chiefly pepper, nutmeg, cinnamon, cloves, ginger, and silk. In return, they exported lumber and iron, in addition to furs, metal goods, linen, hemp, sails, and slaves from Europe's Slavic frontiers.

The causes of the urban renaissance of the tenth and eleventh centuries were related to the economic and demographic "takeoff." A slowly improving agricultural technology, escalating rural productivity, possibly healthier populations (perhaps owing to more protein in the diet), a swelling flow of gold and silver, the booming of long-distance trade, and the pacification of the Magyars stimulated the rise and development of towns, particularly from the later tenth century on. Favored by Constantinople in commercial affairs, Venice and its shipping already excelled; but Pavia, Genoa, Pisa, Milan, Lucca, Florence, and Siena were also lively urban clusters. Their suburbs expanded, it seems, uninterruptedly. Milan had started building a new, wider circle of city walls as early as 850; Pavia, about 915, began to extend its walls; and so did little Cremona just over a century later (ca. 1030).

Commerce and changes in population deserve primary emphasis in accounting for the growth of Italian towns. Local marketing and long-distance trade made them what they were in the tenth century: social magnets that attracted more and more trade relations and rural immigrants. In the eleventh and twelfth centuries certain towns, set in populous countrysides, became major diocesan and administrative centers—capitals, really—as they began to exercise the power of petty states. The basis of their development into political capitals, however, lay in their vast new wealth and new trade relations, as well as in their fertile rural populations, which were ready and able to satisfy the expanding urban need for the consumption, labor, and transactions of immigrants.

Consequently, to the emphasis on trade and demography in the growth of cities must be added a nonurban but essential element, the productivity of the countryside. The Italian urban phenomenon would have been impossible without the continuous influx of people and foodstuffs from the agrarian hinterland. Even Venice—although it was not to have a noteworthy territorial share in the Italian mainland until the fifteenth century—relied heavily on immigrant sailors for its fleets and imported the bulk of its cereal grains from the rich lands of Apulia, Campania, and elsewhere.

Broad comparisons between the cities of southern and northern Italy in the eleventh and twelfth centuries touch at once on two or three major distinctions. In Upper Italy the quest for local urban autonomy became irresistible, and a large part of the nobility moved into the urban centers to reside and to pursue political ambitions, while retaining large estates in the countryside. In the south, on the contrary, in the succeeding Norman, Swabian, and Angevin kingdoms, cities remained under the rule of princes. Here the nobility did not seek to live in urban settings—often they disdained cities; and the middle class of urban craftsmen and merchants remained small, weak, or without any forceful political consciousness. This is not to say that the drive toward urban autonomy was absent in the south, for there were notable communal movements at Gaeta, Troia, Benevento, Bari, Salerno, and Amalfi, where associations of men sought to claim local municipal rights. But their successes were in no way comparable with the political victories of the northern communes. Local defense needs aside, southern cities did not dispose of their own armies and did not issue their own coinage. Furthermore, supreme authority over their city gates, walls, fortresses, ports, and markets failed to pass into local hands; these remained regalian rights of the southern crown. Although often intolerant of royal authority, Norman and later feudatories were more intolerant still of the ambitions of fledgling urban communes and in times of turmoil over the royal power were swift to block any urban attempts to seize local rights of the crown. In view of the claims of royal power and the might of the baronage, communes in the south were allowed to exist solely because localities and townships were more effectively ruled when royal government conducted its business there on the basis of formal dealings with local organizations and groupings.

In central and northern Italy most of the major urban sites—about forty in all—had Roman or even pre-Roman foundations, and cities that sprang up later, such as Venice and Ferrara, were unusual. Of the significant urban concentrations, some ten to twelve were to become true commercial centers: Venice, Genoa, and Pisa among seaports; Milan, Pavia, Florence, Lucca, Siena, Bologna, and Perugia among inland and river cities. But even lesser places—such as Piacenza, Parma, and Asti—produced merchants and moneylenders who crisscrossed western Europe and engaged in complex business transactions.

The cities of Upper Italy were, however, more than mere focuses of local traffic and international trade. Down to the late thirteenth century they were also bellicose societies caught up in the process of militant expansion. Bitter and drawn-out intercity wars became the order of the day, and urban ruling

groups boldly threw down challenges to the imperial-royal authority.

The Holy Roman emperors claimed the iron crown of the Italic kingdom: roughly north-central Italy, excluding Venice. They were challenged by the great urban communes, ranging from Milan and Genoa in the north down to Florence, Lucca, and Pisa in Tuscany. Along with numerous lesser communes, these had come into being between about 1080 and 1130. They appeared at first as sworn associations of important local residents: noblemen, substantial landowners, descendants of royal and episcopal officials, and a smattering of rich traders. Bound together by an oath, the associates (the commune) aimed—as at Piacenza, Milan, Genoa, Bologna, or Florence—to control the political life of the city, and this meant taking over the sum of public authority by negotiation, violence, or trickery. Almost immediately, therefore, the commune entered into conflict with one or more other claimants: the bishop, the resident or neighboring marquis or viscount (agents of the crown), or the crown itself—Henry IV, Frederick I, Henry VI, Frederick II.

From very early on, too, the commune sought to impose its will on the people and trade in the surrounding countryside or on the bordering sea. Larger cities conquered smaller ones; smaller ones seized lesser towns, villages, and rural communes. The result was an age of regional wars, lasting from the eleventh to the fourteenth century and even beyond. Venice, for example, claimed the "lordship of the Adriatic," and hence the right of control over all traffic that moved up the Adriatic to fan out into the Italian mainland. Genoa and Pisa made similar claims on the western coast, and so were continually at war until 1284, when a catastrophic naval defeat of Pisa at Meloria terminated the grand designs of that city-state. Another early victim of Genoa was the flourishing little port of Savona, lying just west of Genoa on the Italian Riviera.

The wars among Italian inland cities were no less ruthless. Planted in the heart of the northern plain, in a region of populous cities, the great commune of Milan was able, mainly by force of arms and diplomacy, to seize power over scores of cities and townships, including even the capital of the kingdom, Pavia, and to incorporate them all into a large regional state, later to be the duchy of Milan. Farther south, Florence battered its countryside until, by the end of the fourteenth century, it had taken Prato, Arezzo, Pistoia, and S. Gimignano. It also engaged in plots and wars that aimed ultimately at the seizure of the still independent city-states of Pisa, Lucca, and Siena.

Anxious about their Italian domains, the Hohenstaufen emperors fought to maintain their authority in Italy and to defeat the Lombard cities in league against them, but they were foiled by divisive German princes and especially by the popes, whose remarkable temporal claims climaxed in the thirteenth century. Nor were the great communes reluctant to stand up to the imperial armies. Under the terms of the Peace of Constance (1183), Frederick I was forced in effect to recognize the autonomy of the leading north Italian cities; for though the peace underlined the emperor's lordship and high claims, it also confirmed the right of local elections, local councils, communal control over surrounding lands, and rights of taxation, justice, and defense. The sovereign claims of the empire were quickly forgotten or spurned, and soon all major cities not included in the peace proceeded to exercise the same autonomies and privileges.

By 1150 urban Italians had turned themselves into the masters of maritime traffic between East and West. Earlier still, perhaps by 1100, Pisa, Lucca, and certain Lombard cities were probably exporting wool cloth to the Levant. In the course of the twelfth century, Italian merchants—including some from tiny northern towns—penetrated into most of the principal marketplaces of western Europe. Keeping with this ongoing flow of industry, Venetian and Genoese merchants pushed, in the thirteenth century, to the eastern shores of the Black Sea, to Astrakhan and Azerbaijan, and then to China, where in the early fourteenth century they established a colony at Zaytun (Zayton, Ts'üan-chou), on the Strait of Formosa. In the West, meanwhile, the Genoese sailed through the Pillars of Hercules, reached the Canaries, and then sought a direct link with India in the doomed voyage of the Vivaldi brothers, who attempted the circumnavigation of Africa in 1291. Some fourteen years earlier, if not before, Genoese merchant galleys had started making a yearly run north to England and Flanders, first calling at Cadiz and Seville. It was an achievement that surpassed the like of anything seen in the ancient world.

The demographic exuberance of the Italian cities kept pace with their expanding political, military, and mercantile frontiers. Since there are no reliable population figures for the eleventh and twelfth centuries, owing to an exiguous record, later figures and

conjecture must be relied upon for what came before. If the small port of Ancona on the Adriatic had 10,000 to 12,000 residents about 1200, as has been calculated, then it may be taken for granted that Venice, Milan, and Genoa had four to five times that number. Florence, it is estimated, had about 50,000 people; Bologna and Siena somewhat fewer; Pisa, Pavia, Lucca, Padua, Verona, and Perugia had even fewer, but still more than Ancona. The major cities at the end of the thirteenth century were (all figures are approximate): Milan (120,000–150,000), Venice (120,000), Florence (95,000), Genoa (60,000–90,000), Bologna (60,000), Siena (52,000), Pisa (38,000), Padua (38,000), Verona (38,000), Pavia (28,000), and Lucca (23,000). Farther south were Palermo (50,000), Rome (about 35,000), Naples (30,000), and Messina (25,000). Some twenty other cities, most of them in the upper part of the peninsula, had populations ranging from 10,000 to 20,000 or even more. No other part of Europe boasted so many populous cities. The persistent and dramatic increases in population had occurred between about 1080 and 1280, the period of urban Italy's greatest commercial and political exploits. Demographic and social vitalities coincided.

Despite the population figures for Palermo and Naples, the southern cities had not kept pace with their northern counterparts, as may be inferred from the absence in the above list of the once busy seaports of Gaeta, Amalfi, and Salerno. Explanations emphasize the retardant influences of the southern crown and nobility, the sacrifice of commercial to landed and grazing interests, and the differing values, mentalities, and ethnicities. It has also been persuasively argued, by P. J. Jones and others, that the trade and domineering attitudes of the north began to "colonize" the economy of the south in the eleventh century. Northern merchants, bankers, and middlemen seized the initiative and then, with the support of the local feudal baronage, made the southern economy dependent upon the goods, markets, and financial know-how of the north. Amalfi seems to have been almost the only southern city briefly to exhibit some of the colonizing and expansionist features of the great commercial communes of the north.

This thesis regarding an "imperialist" north squares with what is known about the ways in which Genoa, Milan, Venice, Florence, Pisa, and the other major urban centers conquered their neighboring seas or countrysides. No quarter was given. Lesser cities, townships, and rural communities were subjected by the great communes; henceforth the latter took the major decisions with regard to taxes, laws, military matters, and the administration of justice in the subject (often subjugated) lands. As "sovereign" cities they might entertain complaining petitions from their subjects, but the relationship was solely one of ruler to ruled; and such cities came in due course, through their courts and jurists, to claim the power of the prince in Roman law. Thus, the principal communes turned themselves, in the fourteenth century, into city-states.

The internal social and political constitutions of the leading cities comprise a vast field of study. Even in the eleventh century the larger urban clusters were far from having simple social structures. Their clerics and laymen included royal and episcopal officials, canons and penniless priests, feudal magnates, vassals, knights, free landholders, merchants, moneyers, tradesmen of both free and servile status, and local husbandmen and serfs. As city and population grew, local governing institutions became more complex. In the earliest period of the commune (1080–1130), most of its prominent and wealthy men quite likely affected noble rank, although the forebears of many of even the proudest had risen in rank only in recent times, beneficiaries of the dynamic character of tenth-century feudalism. After about 1140 an increasing number of "new men" gained membership in the commune; but the years from 1190 to 1225 circumscribe the period of revolutionary change, in the explosive rise of the *popolo,* a "popular" political movement. Among the great communes only Venice escaped the encounter with the *popolo,* for even Genoa was to experience popular agitations after 1250.

Well before 1200, on its way to becoming a petty state, the commune had developed a complex panoply of offices, councils, functions, and procedures. Chief among these were (1) the *parlamentum,* or general assembly of the whole commune; (2) the consulate, the chief executive body of the commune, often numbering from eight to twelve consuls; (3) a legislative council, which was to strip the *parlamentum* of most of its functions; (4) a formal body of advisers to the consuls; and (5) one or more communal courts that grew directly out of the consulate. These and other official groups were chosen exclusively from among the members of the commune by election, by co-optation, or by lot, depending upon the city.

About 1200, in the very years of the *popolo*'s emergence, the commune introduced a new official, the podesta *(potestas),* who was usually from another commune. He replaced the consuls as the executive head of the commune, but he was surrounded by a college of advisers and served for only six months or a year. Being an outside figure, the podesta was expected to exert more concentrated power and to stand above factions and rival family blocs. The importance of this is immediately evident: in the later twelfth century Genoa, Milan, Florence, Pisa, Bologna, Perugia, and most other major communes had experienced violent and prolonged civil strife among the nobility.

The *popolo,* meanwhile, had made a tempestuous appearance on the scene, with demands that complicated and intensified all public controversy within the cities. Most succinctly defined, the *popolo* was the organized body of the middle class (including its more affluent members), organized politically and militarily with a view to gaining a voice and a share of places in the political councils of the commune. Arrayed against the consular nobility (those who had monopolized the old communal consulate), the *popolo* was made up primarily of the sort of men who had long been denied a place in the commune.

The commercial revolution had elevated large numbers of men in wealth, hope, and ambition, especially in the bigger cities. Such men, looking for protective support and seeking to influence tax and trade policies, founded a diversity of guilds in the late twelfth century. But guilds were unable to stand up to the commune of noblemen, whereupon merchants, guildsmen, and other commoners banded together to form armed neighborhood societies. The collectivity of these, called the *popolo,* began to challenge the commune about 1200. By 1270 the *popolo* had triumphed in many cities, managing in some—Milan, Bologna, Florence, and Siena—to capture all the principal magistracies.

The height of power of the *popolo* (1250–1280), however, was also its turning point. Its momentum was spent, as was that of the leading guilds; and, like the guilds, the *popolo* began to turn more exclusive and oligarchical. Now in command of the city and commune, the richer and more eminent groups within the *popolo* backed away from reform policies or looked for compromises with the embattled nobility and "magnates" (rich men who put on the airs of noblemen and threw their weight around in the streets and marketplaces). A crossroads had been reached: from this time on, the central and north Italian cities inclined more and more toward despotic rule or stricter forms of oligarchy.

The vitality of the northern Italian cities had seemed endless during the twelfth and thirteenth centuries as they moved outward, conquered everything on their horizons, "colonized" the southern economy, and dispatched merchants to Africa, London, Russia, and even China. At the same time, far from keeping the peace at home, they gave rise to aspiring and aggressive social groups that entered into passionate conflicts. War, in the thirteenth century, became a costly commonplace, the more so as it was put increasingly into the hands of mercenaries.

By 1250 even the most pusillanimous of the larger communes had seized the sum of fiscal rights that had once belonged to the crown; such as an old hearth tax, the salt tax, tolls and excises, income from market rights, and profits from the administration of justice. But war, territorial ambitions and fears, and a hired soldiery put a relentless strain on communal expenses, with the result, after 1250, that cities were driven to find new sources of revenue. Chief among these were obligatory loans from citizens and taxes (gabelles) on most foodstuffs and goods brought into, or exported from, the city. In the fourteenth and fifteenth centuries these two sources, especially the first, came to account for the bulk of the public revenues of Venice, Milan, Florence, Siena, and most other capitals. Never short of ingenuity, the city-states revolutionized public finance in the course of the fourteenth century. They funded their public debts and introduced a system of deficit financing. For example, Venice and Florence took forced loans from citizens, paid interest on the monies borrowed, directed all major income into a central fund, and then—to complete the circle—used this fund to pay carrying charges on the debt, to pay the most pressing current obligations, and even to repay the principal. With its Casa di San Giorgio (the collectivity of bondholders), fifteenth-century Genoa employed an interesting and successful variation of this system.

Imagination and cleverness, however, did not guarantee a broader polity. City-states tilted toward despotism or narrowing oligarchy because of chronic warfare, social conflict, and virulent factional and fiscal strains; also, after 1348, because of plague, depopulation, and economic stagnation. The Italian urban economy did not recover from these setbacks for centuries. Nevertheless, by 1320 the cities of northern Italy had produced a culture, a range of values, and the institutions that went to make the early Italian Renaissance.

From Giotto around 1300 to Leonardo da Vinci in 1500, the art and architecture of the Renaissance depended upon the environment and patronage provided by cities such as Florence, Venice, Siena, Milan, and Ferrara. Not that the economy and labor power of the countryside were absent; but the initiative and innovations in culture, like the governing intellectual and moral influences, came from the cities—from their literacy, social structures, and political prepotency. It is sufficient in this connection to single out the process of secularization, perhaps the decisive characteristic of the Italian Renaissance. This process went back to the thirteenth-century cities, to the fervor of citizen commitment. The struggle for communal citizenship, for full membership in the worldly community, was converted into so intense an experience that the commitment passed over, as an attitude and then a point of view, into political theory, historical writing, and the local pride associated with major monuments of religious art.

From the late thirteenth century Italian prose and poetry carried the stamp of urban sights, burgher values, and mercantile pragmatism; or the stamp of a knowing idealism—as in the poets of the *dolce stil nuovo*—which was self-consciously erudite, polished, and given to a sophisticated playing with the oppositions between worldly and spiritual values. In painting, the saints came down from stylized Byzantine heavens to inhabit cities. City walls crowd the pictorial spaces of frescoes and panel painting; cultivated fields appear for the first time; and by the early fifteenth century, with Masaccio (*d.* ca. 1428), there are virtual snapshots of poverty and slums in a Renaissance city.

In order to highlight the viability of princely government, as at Milan and Mantua, or the cultural impact of republican political institutions, as at Florence and Venice, the historian must turn back again to the twelfth and thirteenth centuries, to the origins of the magistracies, electoral procedures, deliberative councils, fiscal and credit mechanisms, checks and balances, and administrative routines and expedients of the city-state.

But the worldly legacy of the city was to be borne above all by Humanism. From its origins in the late thirteenth century to its mature militancy in the fifteenth, Humanism catered preeminently to the civic and cultural needs of citizens. Supremely attracted by classical antiquity, the humanists turned its history and literature into a program of study for the ruling and wealthy classes of the cities. The high aims of this enterprise looked to eloquence: the art of the most persuasive speaking and writing—hence a social, public, even political, art.

BIBLIOGRAPHY

Gianluigi Barni and Gina Fasoli, *L'Italia nell'alto medioevo* (1971); Ottorino Bertolini, *Roma e i longobardi* (1972); Sarah Rubin Blanshei, *Perugia, 1260–1340* (1976); William M. Bowsky, *The Finance of the Commune of Siena* (1970); Robert Brentano, *Rome Before Avignon* (1974); Paolo Brezzi, *I comuni medioevali nella storia d'Italia* (1959, 2nd ed. rev. and enl. 1970), and *Il secolo di rinnovamento* (1973); Giorgio Cracco, *Società e stato nel medioevo veneziano* (1967); Emilio Cristiani, *Nobiltà e popolo nel comune di Pisa* (1962); Carlo Nicola de Angelis, *Le origini del comune meridionale* (1940); Teofilo Ossian de Negri, *Storia di Genova* (1968); Eugenio Dupré-Theseider, *La città medievale in Europa* (1958); Nunzio Federico Faraglia, *Il comune nell'Italia meridionale* (1883); Dino Gribaudi, ed., *Storia del Piemonte*, 2 vols. (1960); David Herlihy, *Pisa in the Early Renaissance* (1958), and *Medieval and Renaissance Pistoia* (1967); John Kenneth Hyde, *Padua in the Age of Dante* (1966), and *Society and Politics in Medieval Italy* (1973); Philip J. Jones, *Economia e società nell'Italia medievale* (1980); Frederic C. Lane, *Venice: A Maritime Republic* (1973); Archibald Ross Lewis, *Naval Power and Trade in the Mediterranean, A.D. 500 to 1100* (1951); Robert Sabatino Lopez, "The Trade of Medieval Europe: The South," in *The Cambridge Economic History of Europe*, II (1952), and *The Commercial Revolution of the Middle Ages, 950–1350* (1971); Lauro Martines, *Power and Imagination: City-States in Renaissance Italy* (1979); Charles William Previté-Orton, "The Italian Cities Till c. 1200," in *Cambridge Medieval History*, V (1926, repr. 1957); Yves Renouard, *Les villes d'Italie, de la fin du xe siècle au début du xive siècle*, 2 vols. (1969); Luigi Salvatorelli, *L'Italia comunale, dal secolo xi alla metà del secolo xiv* (1940); Attilio Simioni, *Storia di Padova* (1968); Antonio Viscardi and Gianluigi Barni, *L'Italia nell'età comunale* (1966); Daniel P. Waley, *Medieval Orvieto* (1952), *The Papal State in the Thirteenth Century* (1961), and *The Italian City-Republics* (1969).

LAURO MARTINES

[See also **Commune; Florence; Frederick II of the Holy Roman Empire; Genoa; Guelphs and Ghibellines; Italy, Fourteenth and Fifteenth Centuries; Lombard League; Lombards; Milan; Naples; Pisa; Ravenna; Siena; Trade; European; Tuscany; Urbanism: Western European; Venice.**]

ITE CHANT. *Ite missa est* ("Go, this is the dismissal") with the response *Deo gratias* ("Thanks be to God") is a dismissal formula concluding the Latin Mass. Vestiges of the formula can be traced as far back as the fourth century; during the early Middle Ages it was probably said after each Mass. By the eleventh century *Ite missa est* was replaced in a number of Masses (particularly those where the *Gloria in excelsis* was not said) by the formula *Benedicamus Domino.*

No systematic study of *Ite* chant has yet been made. The earliest music may have been simple recitation formulas, but by the eleventh century a number of more elaborate melodies were in use. Most of these melodies were adopted from other chants (particularly the *Kyrie eleison*), but a number seem to have been independently composed as well. Like the *Kyrie eleison,* the *Ite* chant is often supplied with *prosula*s, that is, syllabic texts added to the textless sections of the melody (see *Analecta hymnica* for editions of texts). Polyphonic settings of the *Ite* chant are not common and rarely form part of Mass cycles of the Ordinary from the later Middle Ages. The *Messe de Nostre Dame* by Guillaume de Machaut (*ca.* 1300–1377) is an important exception in this respect.

BIBLIOGRAPHY

Willi Apel, *Gregorian Chant* (1958, 3rd ed. 1966); Barbara M. Barclay, "The Medieval Repertory of Polyphonic Untroped *Benedicamus Domino* Settings," 2 vols. (diss., Univ. of California, Los Angeles, 1977); Clemens Blume and Guido M. Dreves, eds., *Analecta hymnica medii aevi*, XLVII (1905, repr. 1961), 409–416; Wilhelm Fischer, "Die Herkunft des 'Ite missa est' V. toni," in *Festschrift Alfred Orel zum 70. Geburtstag*, H. Federhofer, ed. (1960), 67–72; Frank Llewellyn Harrison, *Music in Medieval Britain* (1958); Joseph A. Jungmann, *The Mass of the Roman Rite*, Francis A. Brunner, trans., II (1955), 432–437.

LANCE W. BRUNNER

[See also **Gloria; Kyrie; Machaut, Guillaume de; Mass; Music, Western European.**]

IÐUNN is a goddess of Scandinavian mythology. Wife of Bragi (whose own status as a god is unclear), she does not appear in the list of fourteen *ásynjur* (goddess of the *æsir*) in *Snorra Edda* (*Gylfaginning*, chap. 22 [Finnur Jónsson's standard 1931 edition]), but her name figures among those of the gods invited to banquets with Ægir in *Lokasenna* and *Snorra Edda* (*Skáldskaparmál*, chap. 1). According to

Snorra Edda, Iðunn was the guardian of the gods' apples of youth (*Gylfaginning,* chap. 14), and her major moment in the mythology occurs when she and her remedy for old age are delivered to the giant Þjazi by Loki, thus causing the gods to age. Loki then assumes the form of a bird and rescues her, and the gods kill Þjazi. The ninth-century skald Þjóðólfr of Hvin (Norway) recounted the story at length in his *Haustlǫng* (strophes 1–13), a poem describing the decorative panels on a shield Þjóðólfr had received. Four centuries later, Snorri offered a consistent and more detailed version in *Skáldskaparmál* (chaps. 2–4, Finnur Jónsson's standard 1931 edition).

Much of the speculation on this myth has focused on the apples, for apples were not cultivated in Scandinavia in ancient times. Thus scholars have suggested that the myth was borrowed from some other source; one Irish analogue, the story of the sons of Tuirenn, seems particularly close. However, wild apples did grow in the north, and the Germanic and northern European languages share a cognate term for "apple" that could also refer to other fruits or to acorns.

Iðunn's role in the myth is typical: the giants covet such other goddesses as Sif and, particularly, Freyja. Indeed, Anne Holtsmark called Iðunn a local variant of Freyja. It is not difficult to regard Iðunn's apples as symbols of fertility. This is consistent with Iðunn's short exchange with Loki in *Lokasenna.* She tries to calm Bragi, and Loki calls her of all women the most eager for men, since she slept with her brother's slayer (strophes 16–18). If genuine, this otherwise unknown tale indicates Iðunn's further involvement in the mythology. There is, however, little evidence for cult activity.

BIBLIOGRAPHY

Sophus Bugge, "Iduns æbler," in *Arkiv för nordisk filologi,* 5 (1889); Anne Holtsmark, "Myten om *Idun og Tjatse* i Tjodolvs *Haustlǫng,*" ibid., 64 (1949), in which the author argues that Þjóðólfr's *Haustlǫng* is based on ritual drama; Edward O. G. Turville-Petre, *Myth and Religion of the North: The Religion of Ancient Scandinavia* (1964), 186–187.

JOHN LINDOW

[See also **Gylfaginning; Lokasenna; Skáldskaparmál.**]

ITINERARIUM EGERIAE. Also known as *Peregrinatio Aetheriae,* this treatise is one of the earliest examples of Christian pilgrimage literature. It is an account by a nun of her journey to Egypt, Palestine,

and Asia Minor. The work survives in fragmentary condition in an eleventh-century manuscript (Arezzo VI, 3), which was first published in 1887 under the title *S. Silviae Aquitanae peregrinatio ad loca sancta.* The opening pages are missing, and numerous attempts have been made to restore the names of both work and author. Editors and scholars have referred to the author variously as Silvia, Aetheria, Eucheria, and Egeria, the last now being generally accepted. Internal evidence and a reference in Valerius of Vierzo (a Spanish monk of the late seventh century) show that Egeria came from Spain or Aquitaine, the former being the more likely. Most authorities assign the data of the pilgrimage and the "diary" to about 400—recent research has endeavored to pinpoint the pilgrimage to 381–384. The content of some missing portions of the *Itinerarium* can be inferred from the *De locis sanctis* of Peter the Deacon (twelfth century).

The author's learning is not wide, and there are no quotations apart from the Scriptures. The latinity, which has been much studied, is a curious blend of contemporary Vulgar Latin and learned elements. The text gives valuable evidence for the meanings of liturgical and monastic terms in the late fourth or early fifth century.

Apart from the philological interest of the text, which is considerable, the *Itinerarium* is a very valuable document for students of Christian liturgy, piety, and archaeology in late antiquity. Egeria describes many churches in and around Jerusalem; she gives probably the earliest account of a regular Office in the Eastern monasteries and differentiates among various kinds of monks. There is also much of interest regarding the observation of the principal feasts, including the Nativity, Easter, and Pentecost.

BIBLIOGRAPHY

The most recent edition is in Aet. Franceschini and R. Weber, eds., *Itineraria et alia geographica,* 2 vols. (1965). The full text of *Itineraria Egeriae,* parallel passages from Peter Diaconus' *De locis sanctis,* plus a full text of that work are in vol. I; vol. II contains detailed *indices verborum* for the *Itinerarium* and the surrounding literature. Translation is in *Egeria's Travels, Newly Translated with Supporting Documents and Notes,* John Wilkinson, trans. (1971). See also P. Devos, "La date du voyage d'Egérie," in *Analecta Bollandiana,* 85 (1967); E. Löfstedt, *Philologischer Kommentar zur Peregrinatio Aetheriae* (1936).

MICHAEL HERREN

[See also **Peter the Deacon of Monte Cassino; Pilgrimage, Western European.**]

IUDICIA DEI. See **Ordeals.**

IVAN III OF MUSCOVY (1440–1505). Named co-grand prince when he was seven years old, during a critical period of the Muscovite civil war, Ivan became sole ruler in 1462, at the age of twenty-two. In his forty-three-year tenure, the longest yet for any member of his house, his realm trebled in size, stretching deep into former Lithuanian territory in the southwest and beyond the middle Volga in the northeast. The still independent principality of Ryazan and the independent city-state of Pskov acknowledged his suzerainty and respected his commands. This left the Tatar khanate of Kazan as the sometimes enemy of Muscovy in the north, but even this state came, at least temporarily, under Ivan's influence.

If historians have characterized Ivan as the "gatherer" of the Russian lands, he viewed himself as an emperor, the successor to the departed lords of Byzantium, as well as the inheritor of the title to the lands of the old Kievan realm, that is to say, of all the lands that once comprised Rus. The fall of Byzantium prompted Ivan III to seek foreign recognition for his imperial title. In 1472 he married Sophia, the niece of Constantine XI, the last Byzantine emperor, in the hope of advertising his connection and thereby strengthening his claim, but his cautious inquiries met with rejection by the rulers of the important Italian city-states, by the Habsburg rulers, and by the Ottoman sultan. Recognition came only from the politically weak, such as the Teutonic Order, some of the east Baltic towns, and the insignificant principality of Mazovia. With the determination that characterized the politics of the house of Muscovy, neither he nor his successors abandoned the quest.

At home Ivan became sovereign to his subjects and amassed greater authority over more Russians than had any ruler in the Russian north prior to the fifteenth century. What had passed for "liberties" in Muscovite society (the right of military servitors to transfer service at will and without penalty to other Orthodox princedoms, or to join the retinues of cadet princes of the Muscovite house) had crumbled during the period of the dynastic wars (1425–1452) and its aftermath. The consolidation of the northern principalities closed off the possibility of transferred allegiance and Ivan never permitted a return to the older system. The absence of institutional deterrents and the role of protector of the faith gave Ivan unlimited authority over his subjects, though he prudently sought to accommodate the interests of his aristocracy. If Ivan III may be viewed as the first autocrat of Muscovy, a variety of developments—beyond planning or desire—set the stage for the new form of governance.

BIBLIOGRAPHY

Gustave Alef, *Rulers and Nobles in Fifteenth-century Muscovy* (1983); Nikolai Andreyev, "Filofey and His Epistle to Ivan Vasil'yevich," in *Slavonic and East European Review,* 38 (1959); Ian Grey, *Ivan III and the Unification of Russia* (1964); Manfred Hellmann, "Moskau und Byzanz," in *Jahrbücher für Geschichte Osteuropas,* 17 (1969); Vasily O. Klyuchevsky, *A History of Russia,* C. J. Hogarth, trans., II (1912, repr. 1960), chaps. 1–4; Joel Raba, "The Fate of the Novgorodian Republic," in *Slavonic and East European Review,* 45 (1967).

GUSTAVE ALEF

[See also **Muscovy, Rise of.**]

IVANĒ MXARGRZELI. See **Zak^carids.**

ÍVENS SAGA is a prose adaptation of the medieval French *Yvain* of Chrétien de Troyes. At the end there is a statement that the Norse translation was made at the behest of King Hákon (that is, Hákon Hákonarson of Norway, 1217–1263). However, only later Icelandic copies now exist. The two oldest are fifteenth-century vellums, and the third primary manuscript is seventeenth-century paper. Thus, at least two centuries separate the original translation from the preserved texts, and it is difficult to say how much the latter have changed in the course of transmission. Furthermore, both vellums are defective, although for the most part the defects do not overlap. The third primary text presents a version characterized by shortening and considerable modification.

Íven, one of King Arthur's knights, sets out to avenge his kinsman Kalebrant after hearing the latter's tale of ignominious defeat by an unknown knight at a magic spring. Íven slays the knight in single combat but is trapped inside the knight's castle. He catches sight of the beautiful widow and falls in love with her. Through the good offices of Luneta, whom Íven once assisted at Arthur's court and who happens to be the confidante of the lady of the castle,

Íven and the lady are reconciled, and she is persuaded to accept him as her husband and the new defender of the spring. Arthur and his men now appear. Íven defeats Sir Kæi in defense of the spring, then invites everyone to a celebration.

After the festivities, Sir Valven (Gawain) persuades Íven that he must not risk losing his knightly reputation with a life of ease, but must come with them to seek further adventures. His lady grants him leave for one year and gives him a magic ring to protect him. However, Íven forgets his promise to return at the appointed time. A maid appears and demands the ring back—Íven is never to see his lady again. Overcome by remorse, Íven is struck by a fit of madness and wanders away from court. Later he is found and cured with a magic ointment by another lady, whose lands he then liberates from the attacks of an earl. Íven also rescues a lion from a dragon, and the lion becomes his devoted companion.

There follows a series of adventures. Íven, calling himself the Knight of the Lion, rescues various persons (Luneta, among others) from various perils. The culmination is a duel between Íven and Valven (each defending the cause of one of two sisters) in which neither recognizes the other—this ends in a draw, followed by recognition and general rejoicing. All that remains is for Íven to be reconciled to his lady. That is accomplished by Luneta through a ruse, and the saga ends happily.

The most obvious change in the saga compared with its French source is that of verse to prose, but there are others as well. The roles of the two sisters who are contending over their patrimony are reversed in the saga; it is the elder sister who is threatened with disinheritance and whose cause Íven defends, not the younger (as in Chrétien). In addition, two figures in Chrétien, the sister and a friend who helps her find Íven, are combined into one in the saga. A striking stylistic feature is the use of alliteration. This device is employed in Ívens saga with some effectiveness, especially in passages that require dramatic intensity.

Ívens saga does not show as much restructuring as Erex saga, but there is still some adaptation to native patterns.

BIBLIOGRAPHY

Ívens saga, Eugen Kölbing, ed. (1898); Ívens Saga, Foster W. Blaisdell, ed. (1979). A translation is Erex Saga and Ívens Saga: The Old Norse Versions of Chrétien de Troyes's Erec and Yvain, Foster W. Blaisdell and Marianne E. Kalinke, trans. (1977). See also Kalinke's "Characterization in Erex Saga and Ívens Saga," in Modern Language Studies, 5 (1975), and "Erex Saga and Ívens Saga: Medieval Approaches to Translation," in Arkiv för nordisk filologi, 92 (1977).

FOSTER W. BLAISDELL

[See also Arthurian Literature; Chrétien de Troyes; Erex Saga.]

IVO OF CHARTRES, ST. (Yvo, Yves) (ca. 1040–1115), French canonist, scholar, theologian. Born at Chartres, Ivo studied at Paris and at the Norman abbey of Bec under Lanfranc; a fellow pupil was Anselm, later archbishop of Canterbury. He served as priest at Nesle in Picardy, and from about 1078 was prior of the newly founded Canons Regular of St. Quentin, Beauvais. Elected bishop by the clergy and people of Chartres, and consecrated by Pope Urban at Capua in 1090, he governed his see ably until his death, 23 December, 1115.

A learned canonist and theologian, Ivo was involved in all the major issues of this age of turmoil and intellectual awakening. Although his opposition to the unlawful marriage of King Philip I caused his brief imprisonment in 1092, he firmly supported the legitimate rights of the monarchy despite a decade of strained church-state relations and stressed the necessity that both powers collaborate for social harmony. Ivo attended many assemblies for public affairs and church councils, including Clermont in 1095. Although he later expressed reservations about the First Crusade, he warmly supported the peace movement (Peace of God). He worked strenuously for the spiritual aims of the Gregorian reform, notably in his care for the monasteries and the canonical life of the clergy.

In the long investiture conflict Ivo based his stand on a more precise delineation of the bishop's dual role as spiritual ruler and temporal lord, and denied any sacramental meaning to the feudal ceremony, however conducted; he held that it could be tolerated to preserve peace, provided that free canonical election and consecration were observed. His conciliatory position drew papal disavowal, and charges of heresy by some, but aided settlement of the thorny problem in France and England, and ultimately with the German empire in the Concordat of Worms in 1122. The celebrity of the school of Chartres owed much to his enlightened leadership.

Ivo was often consulted for his expert opinions. His correspondence (some 300 letters) with lay and church leaders in France and abroad circulated widely and provides a primary source for understanding his life and times. Three collections of church law (*ca.* 1093–1096), undertaken at the instance of Urban II, influenced both canon law and theology. The chronological *Tripartita* (unedited) shows characteristic moderation. The topical *Decretum,* by including much regional law shunned by the Gregorian collectors, helped to reconcile the strict reform with Franco-German tradition. It was a mine of texts used by theologians and canonists, including Ivo himself for his more perfect *Panormia,* a handbook soon in widespread use. Its prologue is a milestone in the search for rules to harmonize discordant authorities and guide the application of church law with justice and mercy.

As leading canonist in the last phase of the ancient law before Gratian, Ivo served as bridge to the new age ahead. Twenty-five sermons include tracts on doctrinal and moral matters. His feast day is 20 May.

BIBLIOGRAPHY

Sources. Patrologia latina, CLXI (1855) (*Decretum* and *Panormia*), and CLXII (1854) (letters and sermons); *Yves de Chartres, Correspondance 1090–1098,* Jean Leclercq, ed. and trans. (1949).

Studies. Paul Fournier and Gabriel LeBras, "Yves de Chartres," in *Histoire des collections canoniques en occident,* II (1932), the best treatment of Ivo as canonist; Joseph de Ghellinck, *Le mouvement théologique du XIIᵉ siècle,* 2nd ed. (1948), 445–455; Hartmut Hoffmann, "Ivo von Chartres und die Lösung des Investiturproblems," in *Deutsches Archiv für Erforschung des Mittelalters,* **15** (1959); Stephan G. Kuttner, *Harmony from Dissonance: An Interpretation of Medieval Canon Law* (1960), and "Urban II and the Doctrine of Interpretation: A Turning Point?" in *Studia Gratiana,* **15** (1972); Rolf Sprandel, *Ivo von Chartres und seine Stellung in der Kirchengeschichte* (1962), a basic work.

J. JOSEPH RYAN

[See also **Investiture and Investiture Conflict.**]

IVORY CARVING

MATERIAL

The physical characteristics of ivory made it an especially desirable material for small-scale carvings during the Middle Ages. Its density of grain, rich tonality of surface, and responsiveness to precise carving made it an exotic substance in which many exquisite masterpieces were produced. The material itself was derived from several animals; elephant tusks were most frequently used because they were available in lengths that averaged six feet and weighed 70 to 100 pounds per pair. Walrus and narwhal tusks were used extensively throughout northern Europe and, significantly, from the tenth century were favorite materials for knife and sword handles in the Muslim world. According to various references, the ivory was transported via the fur trade routes from the Arctic Ocean. Another maritime ivory sometimes used was whalebone, which has a flecked surface and can be cut in rather large, flat pieces for decoration.

FUNCTION

Although ivory carving was practiced in Mediterranean countries from early times, the medieval period witnessed the introduction of new artistic forms for this material, for both secular and ecclesiastical purposes. Large ivory diptychs, decorated principally with images of consuls, commemorated administrations in the capitals of both the East and the West from about 400 to the mid sixth century. Such diptychs were elaborated into the larger format of double five-part wings for imperial use, focusing on a central image of the emperor. This organization of a diptych leaf became popular for the depiction of New Testament scenes in early Christian and Carolingian times. Containers in ivory, both cylindrical (pyxes) and box-shaped (*capsa*), had various functions.

Another, larger container was the bucket (situla). Four elaborately decorated holy water buckets survive from the Ottonian period. These situlae were carved from full sections of the elephant tusk. Larger curved sections of the tusk were used from the eleventh century on as oliphants, originally signal or hunting horns and also legal symbols of the transfer of land or property (so-called tenure horns), later ecclesiastical musical instruments and reliquary containers. As a result of this ecclesiastical use, most of the oliphants have survived. The covers of various kinds of liturgical manuscripts were decorated with ivory panels. In many instances precious ivories from earlier periods were adapted and thus preserved. Gold was often used in combination with these ivory covers, either inlaid or mounted behind ivory cut *à jour* (pierced through). Altar crosses in ivory or walrus tusk, sometimes with accompanying

Moses and the Brazen Serpent. Detail from cross attributed to Bury St. Edmunds, *ca.* 1150. NEW YORK, METROPOLITAN MUSEUM OF ART, THE CLOISTERS COLLECTION, 1963 (63.12)

free-standing statues of the Virgin and St. John, began to appear in the tenth and eleventh centuries. Some achieved extraordinary complexity in their minutely carved images, such as the walrus cross (sometimes attributed to Bury St. Edmunds) in New York, carved around 1150 (Metropolitan Museum of Art, The Cloisters; see frontispiece to vol. 10).

In Byzantium ivory was a preferred medium for small, portable icons, of which a number of examples survive from tenth- and eleventh-century ateliers in Constantinople.

Large ensembles of ivory panels decorated church furnishings, such as episcopal cathedras, as attested by early church inventories and the existence of the famous sixth-century chair (cathedra) of Maximian in Ravenna—probably assembled in Constantinople—which contains a rich iconographic program of Old and New Testament themes. Likewise, pulpits

and chancel doors adorned with ivory panels are documented, but none survives in the Latin West. Only in Coptic Egypt (Wadi Natrun) and in Byzantium (Mt. Athos) are there doors with inlaid ivories still in place. The golden pulpit (1002–1014) given by Henry II to Aachen is adorned with reused Coptic ivory panels and demonstrates the value given to the material itself.

During the Gothic period new categories of objects in ivory were introduced. Portable diptychs and triptychs, and especially tabernacles with a central statuette of the Virgin and Child enshrined within an architectural setting and protected by folding shutters, became essential pictorial accessories of private devotion. Ivories for secular purposes, decorated with subjects from mythology, history, or literature, form a large body of material. Production of ivory objects reached its peak in the fourteenth century; the medium never became popular during the Renaissance.

MEDIEVAL IVORY CARVERS

Little is known about specific ivory carvers during the Middle Ages. Only a few, whose works survive, are known by name. Among them is Tuotilo, recorded at St. Gall between 895 and 912, who made for Gospelbook covers several ivory panels that display a close dependence on the manuscript illuminations of the court school of Charles II the Bald.

Several mid-tenth-century ivory caskets (Madrid, Instituto de Valencia de Don Juan, and New York, Hispanic Society of America) are inscribed with the name of Khalaf, whose workshop at Madīnat al-Zahrāʾ near Córdoba produced a major group of Islamic ivories. One of the most revealing early medieval pieces is the reliquary arca shrine mounted with ivories (1053–1067) at San Millán de la Cogolla, Spain (dismantled and scattered in the early nineteenth century), a surviving fragment of which is signed by a Master Engelar and his son Redolfo. In addition to depicting the transportation of large elephant tusks for the project, this plaque shows the master carving a panel held by his son. Another professional artist, Master Hugo (illuminator, bronze caster, and probably ivory carver), was possibly responsible for the elaborate ivory cross sometimes attributed to Bury St. Edmunds. About the same time Savalo, working at St. Amand, signed a knife handle (Lille, Musée de Beaux-Arts), but no other works by him are known.

Sculptors better known for work in other materials were often responsible for works in ivory. The most familiar example is the magnificent large statuette of the Virgin and Child by Giovanni Pisano, which was made for the cathedral of Pisa in 1299.

Many ivories of the International Gothic period (*ca.* 1360–1430) have been attributed to the noted Embriachi family, which originated in Genoa and worked in Florence and Venice. Several large retables survive; the two most elaborate are those made for the Certosa of Pavia by Baldassare degli Embriachi and another, now in the Louvre, commissioned by Jean, duke of Berry, for the Abbey of Poissey.

CENTERS OF IVORY PRODUCTION:
EARLY CHRISTIAN AND EARLY BYZANTINE

Rome and Constantinople naturally became principal centers in the production of early medieval ivories, and the importance of the ateliers in these cities is almost incontestable. Around 400 the revival of

Justinian as Defender of the Faith. Diptych leaf from Constantinople, 2nd quarter of 6th century. PARIS, MUSÉE DU LOUVRE

Hellenistic excellence and taste generated by wealthy Roman families encouraged the production of ivories of superb quality. Pagan works, such as the diptych leaves of the Symmachi and Nicomachi (London, Victoria and Albert Museum, and Paris, Musée de Cluny), and Christian works, such as the panel depicting the Ascension and the Marys at the Tomb (Munich, Bayerisches Nationalmuseum), attest to the exceptional skill of the carvers. Many of these Roman carvings were treasured throughout the Middle Ages, becoming in part responsible for the revival of the late antique tradition in the court school of Charlemagne. Almost simultaneously with Rome, Constantinople became an important center for ivory. A diptych leaf with an archangel (sixth century; London, British Museum), with its refined aristocratic style, initiated a tradition in ivories for the Eastern capital. In the sixth century, under Justinian, the court workshop produced items of superb quality. The throne of Maximian in Ravenna and the diptych leaf with Justinian as defender of the faith (Paris, Louvre) are generally thought to have been produced at Constantinople in the second quarter of the sixth century. Provincial centers also flourished, and many ivories have been attributed to Ravenna, Milan, and Trier. In the eastern Mediterranean, ivories, especially pyxes, have been assigned to Palestine or Syria, but primarily on grounds of iconography.

CENTERS OF IVORY PRODUCTION: CAROLINGIAN

With the almost complete loss of sculpture in stone, stucco, and bronze, the ivories commissioned during the reign of Charlemagne offer a valuable key to the beauty and quality of the art produced for the court. Like the manuscript illuminations, the ivories

John the Evangelist. Plaque from court school of Charlemagne, early 9th century. NEW YORK, METROPOLITAN MUSEUM OF ART, THE CLOISTERS COLLECTION, 1977 (1977.421)

depended primarily on models from the early Christian period for their iconography and style. The covers of the Lorsch Gospels (London, Victoria and Albert Museum, and Vatican Library) clearly depended on such late antique models as the front panels of the throne of Maximian in Ravenna. The arrangement, iconography, and style of the book cover at Oxford (Bodleian Library, MS Douse 176) depend, in part, directly on two panels with scenes of the infancy and miracles of Christ produced in Rome about 400–410 (Berlin, Staatliche Museen, and Paris, Louvre). Parallels with manuscript illumination and the fact that several of the ivories formed the covers for these manuscripts indicate that the ivories must have been produced at the same scriptorium, probably at Aachen. The noble elegance of the figure style and the dynamism of composition characteristic of the court ivories are evident in the panel of the Virgin and the apostles from a larger representation of the Ascension (Darmstadt, Hessisches Landesmuseum).

In contrast to this plastic style of carving are the ivories of the "Liuthard group," named after the scribe of the Psalter of Charles the Bald who worked between 842 and 869. The covers of the Psalter (Paris, Bibliothèque Nationale, lat. 1152) illustrate psalms and display a striking correspondence to the spirited drawings of the Utrecht Psalter (Utrecht, University Library), the masterpiece of the Rheims scriptorium. Other ivories may be assigned to the court school of Charles the Bald, the location of which is uncertain in spite of the close affiliation of these ivories with the manuscripts produced at Rheims. The Drogo Sacramentary covers (ca. 850), which depict Gospel and liturgical scenes in ivory cut à jour, are associated with the first school of Metz, under Archbishop Drogo. A second "Metz" ivory group, produced in the third quarter of the ninth century, however, cannot be specifically linked with that city. The most important member of this group is the so-called throne of St. Peter (Vatican), constructed of wood and inlaid with à jour ivory strips carved with inhabited rinceaux. This chair, which is hidden from view within the ornate chair by Bernini, has a portrait of Charles II the Bald on the front, and eighteen panels, originally inlaid with gold, depicting the labors of Hercules. The throne may have been made for Charles's coronation in Metz as king of Lotharingia (869), and was certainly taken to Rome for his imperial coronation in 875. Although Carolingian ivory production diminished after 875, the style of this group, with volumetric figures and sharply defined acanthus borders, continued and even formed, in part, the basis for the first ivories of the Ottonian period.

CENTERS OF IVORY PRODUCTION: MIDDLE BYZANTINE

During the tenth and eleventh centuries, ivory carving flourished in Byzantium, where several ateliers, probably in Constantinople, can be distinguished. The ivories of the "painterly group" are undoubtedly based on painted models, as demonstrated by the close correspondence between the tenth-century illustrated Joshua Roll (Vatican, Biblioteca Apostolica) and several ivory panels based upon it with scenes of Joshua receiving ambassadors of Gibon, Joshua condemning to death the king of Jerusalem, and Joshua's army taking Ai (New York, Metropolitan Museum of Art).

Much of the chronology of the Middle Byzantine

Icon with Virgin and Child. Constantinople, mid 10th century.
RIJKSMUSEUM HET CATHARIJNE-CONVENT, UTRECHT

ivories is based on evidence now in Western collections. A Byzantine ivory depicting the Dormition of the Virgin is set into the cover of the Gospels of Otto III (r. 983–1002; Munich, Staatsbibliothek) and was certainly a contemporary gift to the West, possibly as part of the marriage dowry of the Byzantine princess Theophano who married Otto II in 972, thus providing a terminus ad quem. Other ivories are linked to emperors; the "Romanos group" is named after a plaque in Paris (Bibliothèque Nationale, Cabinet des Médailles) that probably depicts Christ crowning Emperor Romanos IV Diogenes and his wife Eudokia (1068–1071). The beginning of this type of coronation imagery is found in one of the few securely dated ivories, a representation of Constantine VII Porphyrogenitos (Moscow, State Museum of Fine Art), dated about 945. More characteristic of the court style is the plaque in Cortona of the reliquary of the True Cross made for Emperor Nikephoros II Phokas (963–969).

Generally the court style consists of figures carved in high relief, with angular and crisp draperies, and a formal elegance pervading the composition. Imagery was often drawn from the classic tradition, not only in style but also in content, achieving its highest artistic level in the Veroli casket (London, Victoria and Albert Museum), which depicts mythological subjects.

CENTERS OF IVORY PRODUCTION: ISLAMIC

In the medieval Islamic world, the major centers of ivory carving were Syria, Egypt, Spain, southern Italy, and Sicily. Cylindrical or rectangular caskets were the objects most commonly produced; the ivory was carved in relief, incised, stained, or painted and gilded. Most Islamic techniques and styles, such as incrustation, evolved from those practiced in Coptic Egypt. The most remarkable ivories—made under royal patronage—were carved in the Arab caliphate of Córdoba and Madīnat al-Ẓāhira. The finest caskets, those in London (Victoria and Albert Museum) and Madrid (Museo Arqueológico Nacional) dating from around 960, display panels of deeply cut vegetable arabesque and florid Kufic inscriptions.

CENTERS OF IVORY PRODUCTION: OTTONIAN AND ROMANESQUE

During the reigns of the Ottonian and Salian emperors, ivory carving became one of the primary media of artistic expression. The earliest series of carvings was commissioned by Otto I probably for an ambo or a chancel door and depicted New Tes-

Pyxis. Hispano-Mauresque from Córdoba, *ca.* 970. NEW YORK, METROPOLITAN MUSEUM OF ART, THE CLOISTERS COLLECTION, 1970 (1970.324.5)

which ivories may be assigned on either iconographic or stylistic grounds. Those of eleventh-century Liège are characterized by a vivacious "small-figure" style closely related to miniature painting. The ivory book cover of the Gospels of bishop Notger (Liège, Musée Curtius) is the most important piece of the group. In Cologne a number of walrus ivory carvings—game pieces and eleven square panels with New Testament subjects, each composed of numerous pieces of mounted ivory—are in the "pricked" style, so designated for the method of using small nicks to indicate drapery folds (London, Victoria and Albert Museum; New York, Metropolitan Museum of Art; Cologne, Schnütgen Museum). These remarkable deeply carved works of around 1150 indicate that Cologne was one of the most productive ivory centers during the Romanesque period.

In eleventh-century northern Spain, an atelier working for Ferdinand I of Castile (1033–1065) and Doña Sancha made a magnificent and intricately decorated ivory altar cross complete with a corpus (Madrid, Museo Arqueológico Nacional). Within the same Spanish artistic milieu of about 1100 should be placed the whalebone *Adoration of the Magi* (London, Victoria and Albert Museum), which has occasionally been linked to the English Romanesque art from the area of the English Channel.

tament scenes; it was originally destined for the cathedral of St. Mauritius, Magdeburg, before 962–973. The door or ambo was destroyed in a fire in the eleventh century and the carvings, preserved on caskets, were eventually dispersed. They are now in European museums (London, Paris, Berlin, Munich, and Darmstadt) and in the Metropolitan Museum of Art, New York, which owns the dedication panel. Iconographically the series depends upon a Byzantine narrative cycle, while the monumental quality of the style is strongly tied to the Carolingian tradition. The group may be the work of an itinerant atelier, yet it is connected to other ivories and stucco work produced in Milan for the successors of Otto I, for example, the situla ordered by Archbishop Gotfredus (975/975–980) for the entry of Otto II (Milan, cathedral treasury).

A number of ivories were made north of the Alps, but there is little agreement about their origin. A magnificent, softly plastic ivory Virgin and Child (Minz, Mittelrheinisches Landesmuseum) is traditionally attributed to Trier and the Master of the Registrum Gregorii (Gregory Master, active *ca.* 980–990). Cologne and Liège both were artistic centers to

Otto I offering Magdeburg Cathedral to Christ in Majesty. Ottonian altar panel, *ca.* 962–973. NEW YORK, METROPOLITAN MUSEUM OF ART, GIFT OF GEORGE BLUMENTHAL, 1941 (41.100.157)

Virgin and Child. Statuette with polychromy and gilding; French, before 1279. PARIS, MUSÉE DU LOUVRE

CENTERS OF IVORY PRODUCTION: GOTHIC

The diversity of Romanesque ivories contrasts with the stylistic homogeneity of thirteenth- and fourteenth-century ivories, which nevertheless introduced new iconographic forms. Increased availability of material and new demands for ivory carvings from the merchant classes encouraged increased pro-duction, and both secular and religious ivories survive in abundance from this period. By about 1250 Paris had become the preeminent center, with guilds authorized to carve such objects as mirrors, combs, and tablets. The earliest statuettes display strong similarities in style and composition to monumental sculpture. During his reign Louis IX (1226–1270) seems to have offered to the Ste. Chapelle an exquisite statuette of the Virgin and Child recorded in the earliest inventory datable before 1265 and not later than 1279 (Paris, Louvre). The statuette beautifully exemplifies this new monumental and aristocratic style, grand in conception but precious in execution. Diptychs, triptychs, and tabernacles in ivory appeared as objects for private devotion, in effect becoming the Latin equivalent of Byzantine icons. Particularly frequent are diptychs and triptychs with scenes from the life of Christ and of the Virgin, such as the early-fourteenth-century triptych of St. Sulpice du Tarn (Paris, Musée de Cluny). The Parisian origin of many of these works is accepted on stylistic and iconographic evidence; however, ateliers in eastern France, along the Rhine (especially Cologne), in England, and in Italy adapted the Parisian style, better known in most discussions of this period as the International Gothic style.

BIBLIOGRAPHY

Robert P. Bergman, *The Salerno Ivories: Ars Sacra from Medieval Amalfi* (1980); Danielle Gaborit-Chopin, *Ivoires du moyen âge* (1978); Adolph Goldschmidt, *Die Elfenbeinskulpturen aus der Zeit der karolingischen und sächsischen Kaiser und der romanischen Zeit, VIII.–XIII. Jahrhundert,* 4 vols. (1914–1926); Adolph Goldschmidt and Kurt Weitzmann, *Die byzantinischen Elfenbeinskulpturen des X.–XIII. Jahrhunderts,* 2 vols. (1930–1934); Raymond Koechlin, *Les ivoires gothiques français,* 3 vols. and portfolio (1924); Ernst Kühnel, *Die islamischen Elfenbeinskulpturen, VIII.–XIII. Jahrhundert* (1971); Joseph Natanson, *Gothic Ivories of the 13th and 14th Centuries* (1951), and *Early Christian Ivories* (1953); Wolfgang F. Volbach, *Elfenbeinarbeiten der Spätantike und des frühen Mittelalters,* 3rd ed. (1976); Kurt Weitzmann, *Catalogue of the Byzantine and Early Mediaeval Antiquities in the Dumbarton Oaks Collection,* III, *Ivories and Steatites* (1972); Paul Williamson, *An Introduction to Medieval Ivory Carving* (1982).

CHARLES T. LITTLE

[See also **Byzantine Minor Arts; Diptych; Gothic Art: Sculpture; Gothic, International Style; Giovanni Pisano; Hugo of Bury St. Edmunds; Oliphant; Pre-Romanesque Art; Situla; Tuotilo.**]

IVORY CARVING, ISLAMIC. In the Islamic Middle Ages ivory served as both a medium of artistic expression and an element of decoration for larger objects, usually fashioned of wood. The source of the ivory supply and the nature of ivory itself influenced the location of the workshops and the kinds of objects fashioned. Traditions within Islamic society affected the subject matter expressed in the decoration and the purpose and use of the objects.

In the Middle Ages ivory reached the Islamic lands via the overland trade routes from Africa. From the overland termini the ivory passed to the northern Mediterranean and the Arabian peninsula by sea. This routing probably explains the locations of ivory workshops: Egypt, Tunisia, Spain, Sicily, southern Italy, Syria, and Aden.

The nature of ivory, an animal tusk, restricted the range of its use for artistic expression, and tusk size and shape limited the proportions of a given piece. The carving of whole tusks (oliphants) is currently thought to be the work of Muslim craftsmen working in Norman Sicilian and southern Italian workshops. The oliphants themselves display patterns common in the Fatimid decorative repertoire: animal and human forms in a network of interlocked circles. Many caskets, vessels, and gaming pieces were fashioned from a full-diameter section of the tusk. Still more of the ivory work, however, was produced by carving, painting, and incising thin sheets or plaques that were fastened to a framework, usually wood. In addition, small carved or painted plaques were used as pieces of larger, elaborate works, either in incrustation or in intarsia. In the Mamluk period mosque furniture, including minbars, chairs, and platforms (*dikka*s), were decorated in this manner.

Always an import into Islamic lands, and thus a costly medium, ivory was used for luxury items. Within Islamic society, luxury of display was more often reserved for princely or private use than for religious purposes. Thus the types of items fashioned in ivory and the subject matter expressed on them reflect the taste of the wealthy, which had common referents over a broad geographic area: most of the carvings were on lidded containers intended to hold precious items. Caskets fashioned in the Islamic lands found their way into church treasuries as well as into the residences of the Muslim elite.

The decorative repertoire of the ivory pieces also reflected princely taste and changed over the course of the Middle Ages. While plant patterns with ani-

Casket. Córdoba (now in Pamplona), 1004. PHOTO: EDISTUDIO, BARCELONA

mal forms were a constant motif, the Fatimid Egyptian, and especially the Spanish, ivories depicted urban and courtly pastimes: dancers, musicians, falconers, and hunters. Some motifs represented signs of the zodiac and others seemed to serve as apotropaic devices. Decorative writing in Arabic became a prominent motif on the carved surface, especially in the Spanish ivories commissioned by Muslim royal patrons. The writing, which formed a prominent part of the design, not only expressed blessings to the owner but also gave information on patronage, workshop, and dating.

BIBLIOGRAPHY

John Beckwith, *Caskets from Cordoba* (1960); Perry Blythe Cott, *Siculo-Arabic Ivories* (1939); *Encyclopaedia of Islam*, new ed., I (1960), *s.v.* "ᶜĀdj"; Ernst Kühnel, *Die islamischen Elfenbeinskulpturen, VIII.–XIII. Jahrhundert* (1971).

IRENE A. BIERMAN

[See also **Fatimid Art; Islamic Art.**]

ĪWĀN. See Eyvān.

IWANĒ MXARGRZELI. See Zakᶜarids.

JACOB BEN MEIR, invariably known as Rabbenu Tam (*d.* 1171), possibly the most revolutionary Talmudist of the medieval period. Almost singlehandedly he revived talmudic dialectics, which had been dormant for well over half a millennium, and thus set in motion the unparalleled growth in Jewish law that took place over the next two centuries. His work underlies the great set of glosses to the Talmud known as the tosafot (additions). Their immediate impact was enormous—they were printed from the very outset alongside the text of the Talmud—and they have served to this day as the core of talmudic studies. Indeed, it would be no exaggeration to say, paraphrasing Whitehead, that much of the subsequent history of Jewish legal thought has been a series of glosses to the tosafot.

Intellectually Rabbenu Tam's achievement is inextricably bound up with that of his pupil and nephew, Rabbi Isaac ben Samud of Dampierre (d. ca. 1198). Rabbenu Tam himself wrote little, and what has survived (notably the *Sefer ha-Yashar*) is both textually corrupt and obscure; thus he was fortunate to have been followed by Rabbi Isaac, who systematically subjected almost the entire Talmud to dialectical analysis in his school. Rabbi Isaac's teachings, which incorporated both his own and his uncle's analyses, were set down by his pupils as tosafot and, spreading swiftly over Europe in either their original or edited forms, shaped the contours of all analytical (as opposed to codificatory) study of the Talmud.

A stormy, leonine personality, Rabbenu Tam was often embroiled in controversies, the exact cause and course of which are not always decipherable from the fragmentary evidence. Though he was not without occasional critics, his intellectual preeminence was unchallenged. Students flocked to his school from as far away as Kiev, and his fame was such that he is mentioned by the Spanish chronicler Ibn Daud, writing in Toledo around 1160/1161, to whom the entire northern French school, including Rashi, was unknown.

Given Rabbenu Tam's prestige and force of character, an active role in communal affairs would only have been natural. Sparseness of material again precludes any clear picture; but his repeated attempts to preserve the integrity of Jewish self-governance, as reflected in his ordinances against appeal in litigation to gentile authorities or use of gentile influence in communal affairs, is well documented, as is his famous ordinance requiring return of the dowry in the event that the wife died (childless) within the first year of marriage. To judge by these decrees, Rabbenu Tam's writ ran through the counties of Champagne, the royal lands, Greater Anjou and Poitou, and the duchies of Burgundy, Normandy, and Brittany. Given this impressive authority in fragmented northern France, it seems probable that Rabbenu Tam also coordinated the Jewish response to the Blois affair of 1171, when some thirty-one Jewish men and women were burned for the alleged murder of a Christian youth.

Little is known of his personal life. A grandson of Rashi and younger brother of Rabbi Samuel ben Meir, another famous Talmudist, Rabbenu Tam spent his early life in his father's town of Ramerupt. After narrowly escaping with his life during the Second Crusade, he moved to Troyes, Rashi's home town.

Although similarities between Rabbenu Tam and Abelard come quickly to mind, no links have been discovered so far between the parallel transitions from exegesis to dialectic that were occurring in northern French Jewish thought and in the works of Christian contemporaries.

BIBLIOGRAPHY

Israel Moses Ta-Shma and Nissan Netzer, "Tam, Jacob ben Meir," in *Encyclopaedia judaica*, XV (1972), offers a bibliography of studies in Hebrew. There is nothing in English.

HAYM SOLOVEITCHIK

[See also **Jews in Europe; Talmud.**]

JACOBITE CHURCH. See **Monophysitism.**

JACOB'S STAFF. See **Cross-staff.**

JACOBUS (de Porta Ravennate) (*ca.* 1120/1130–11 October 1178), glossator of Roman law. The documentary evidence about his activities covers roughly 1151 to 1169, and his death date appears in the necrology of S. Salvatore in Bologna. The attribute "de Porta Ravennate" suggests that he may have been a native of that quarter of Bologna. His father was Ildebrandus Alberti de Ugo de Boni; his wife's name was Julitta; and he had a daughter named Zugiana.

Among glossators of Roman law, Jacobus belongs to the generation after Irnerius. He was one of the *quattuor doctores*— the others being Hugo, Bulgarus, and Martinus—and was probably the youngest of them. These four gained eminence through their participation in the assembly at Roncaglia (1158), where they laid down the imperial privileges of the German emperor *(regalia)*. Jacobus also acted as a judge for the Bolognese podesta Guido de Sasso on 10 May 1151 and as an advocate for the abbey of Pomposa in a lawsuit against S. Maria de Reno in 1169. With Hugo, Bulgarus, and Martinus he is several times named among the legal experts surrounding the podesta—for instance, in 1154; in every case the *quattuor doctores* occupy a prominent rank. Alone among his colleagues Jacobus usually stressed his status as teacher and scholar.

Jacobus has left glosses on all parts of the *Corpus iuris civilis.* The leading manuscript in a group transmitting his glosses to the Codex Justinianus is MS Lat. fol. 275 in West Berlin, Staatsbibliothek Preussischer Kulturbesitz. One of the first treatises of penal law, the *Tractatus criminum,* which was edited in 1530 as a work by Placentinus, has for stylistic reasons been ascribed to Jacobus (by Hermann Kantorowicz). Jacobus' glosses are identified by his siglum "Ja." or "J."

BIBLIOGRAPHY

The *Tractatus criminum* was first attributed to Placentinus in the 1530 edition. It was reprinted in 1535 as *Placentinus, De varietate actionum libri VI.* The 1535 edition has been reproduced in facsimile with an intro. by Angelo Converso in Mario Viora, ed., *Corpus glossatorum juris civilis,* I (1973). *Summa de maiorum restitutione,* starting with the words "Subvenitus minoribus," is in Gustav Pescatore, ed., *Miscellen* (1889, repr. 1967); one distinction is in Emil Seckel, *Distinctiones glossatorum* (1911, repr. 1956), 352–353. References to other texts are in Helmut Coing, ed., *Handbuch der Quellen und Literatur der neueren europäischen Privatrechtsgeschichte,* I, *Mittelalter (1100–1500)* (1973). For references to manuscripts, see Gero Dolezalek, *Verzeichnis der Handschriften zum römischen Recht bis 1600,* 4 vols. (1972).

Studies. Still useful are Mauro Sarti, *De claris archigymnasii bononiensis professoribus a saeculo XI usque ad saeculum XIV,* 2 vols. (1769–1772, repr. 1962), I.1, and Friedrich Karl von Savigny, *Geschichte des römischen Rechts im Mittelalter,* IV (1850, repr. 1961). Most recent information is in Johannes Fried, *Die Entstehung des Juristenstandes im 12. Jahrhundert* (1974). See also Hermann Kantorowicz, "Il *Tractatus criminum,*" in his *Rechtshistorische Schriften,* Helmut Coing and Gerhard Immel, eds. (1970).

HANS PETER GLÖCKNER

[See also **Bologna, University of; Bulgarus; Corpus Iuris Civilis; Glossators; Hugo; Law, Schools of; Martinus Gosia.**]

JACOBUS DE VORAGINE. See **Golden Legend.**

JACOBUS OF BOLOGNA *(fl.* mid fourteenth century), Italian composer also called Jacopo da Bologna or Jacobus de Bononia. Apart from the period from about 1340 to 1360, there is virtually no extant biographical documentation. The main sources for the two decades in question are the texts set by Jacobus himself. That he was employed at the Visconti court in Milan until the death of Luchino in 1349 is suggested by the acrostic references to Luchino in the madrigal *Lo lume vostro* and in the motet *Lux purpurata.* The madrigal *O in Italia* refers to the birth of Luchino's twin sons in 1346. After 1349 Jacobus moved to the court of Mastino II della Scala *(d.* 1351) and of his brother and successor, Alberto *(d.* 1352), in Verona. The setting of Petrarch's *Non al suo amante* is the only known use of that poet's works by a contemporary composer, and likely stems from the Veronese years, when Petrarch maintained contacts with the Scala family. The madrigal *Nel bel giardino* refers to the Adige River in the vicinity of the ruling family's castle, and was probably written during this period as well. From Verona, Jacobus apparently returned to the service of the Visconti in Milan. The madrigals *Sotto l'imperio, Fenice fu',* and *Aquil'altera* relate to personages and events at the Visconti court up to 1360, and constitute the last evidence of his musical activities.

Until his departure from Verona, Jacobus participated in a musical competition with his best-known contemporaries, Magister Piero and Giovanni da Cascia. This involved the setting of similar or identical texts, and the use of disguised allusions to certain individuals, such as "Anna," through the literary device of wordplay known as *senhal.*

In addition to his short theoretical treatise, *L'arte del biscanto misurato* (The art of measured polyphony), thirty-four of Jacobus' works have been preserved intact, along with the single surviving voice of the motet *Laudibus dignis.* His music was widely disseminated and is known from nine manuscripts, the most important of these being the codices Squarcialupi (Florence, Biblioteca Medicea-Laurenziana, Palatino 87), Panciatichiano (Florence, Biblioteca Nazionale Centrale, Panciatichiano 26), and Reina (Paris, Bibliothèque Nationale, nouv. acq. frc. 6771).

Thirty-one madrigals make up the bulk of the music. Typically a madrigal by Jacobus consists of eight lines of text divided into two stanzas of three lines each and a concluding ritornello incorporating the final couplet. The most common rhyme scheme is *a b b, c d d, e e*. The two stanzas are set to identical music, while the ritornello is given its own setting, resulting in the musical form *a a b*. Some departures from this design occur through the use of three stanzas or two concluding couplets, or in the application of the poetic structure of the rispetto to the musical form of the madrigal. Jacobus' works also include the caccia *Per sparverare*, a *lauda* with incomplete text, and a motet. Two of the madrigals, *Giung'el bel tempo* and *Oselletto salvaço*, are sometimes referred to as "caccia-madrigals" because they combine the textual form of the madrigal with the canonic technique normally associated with the caccia.

Perhaps the most important composer of the early trecento, Jacobus occupies a critical position in a line of development leading through Landini to the composers of early-fifteenth-century Italy.

BIBLIOGRAPHY

W. Thomas Marrocco, *The Music of Jacopo da Bologna* (1954), contains texts and musical notation for all thirty-four compositions, plus the translation of Jacobus' theoretical treatise; an important review of this publication is John Ward, in *Journal of the American Musicological Society*, 8 (1955). See also Nino Pirrotta, ed., *The Music of Fourteenth-century Italy*, IV, *Jacobus de Bononia, Vincentius de Arimino* (1963), and "Jacopus de Bononia," in *Die Musik in Geschichte und Gegenwart*, VI (1957); *Polyphonic Music of the Fourteenth Century*, VI, W. Thomas Marrocco, ed., *Italian Secular Music by Magister Piero, Giovanni da Firenze, Jacopo da Bologna* (1967).

ARTHUR LEVINE

[See also **Caccia; Lauda; Madrigal.**]

JACOBUS OF LIÈGE. See **Jacques de Liège.**

JACOMART MASTER. See **Baçó, Jaime.**

JACOPO D'AVANZI. See **Avanzo, Jacopo.**

JACOPO DA VORAGINE. See **Golden Legend.**

JACOPO DELLA QUERCIA (*ca.* 1374–1438) was born in Quercia Grosso near Siena, son of a goldsmith and woodcarver, Piero di Angelo. He competed in the contest for the first bronze door of the Baptistery in Florence in 1401. In Lucca he carved a relief of St. Agnellus in the sacristy of the cathedral (1392), the tomb of Ilaria del Carretto in the cathedral (1406), and tomb slabs of the Trenta family and the Trenta altar in S. Frediano (begun after 1416); in Ferrara, a marble Madonna and Child executed for the cathedral (January to September 1406); in Siena, possibly a marble Madonna and Child above the Piccolomini Altar in the cathedral (1397–1398), the Fonte Gaia (1414–1419), the baptismal font in S. Giovanni (1417–1419), and decoration of the Casini Chapel in the cathedral (after 1436); in Bologna, the central doorway of S. Petronio (1424–1438, both de-

Acca Larentia (Roman goddess). Carving by Jacopo della Quercia from the Fonte Gaia, Siena, 1414–1419. ALINARI/ART RESOURCE, INC.

sign and execution) and the Vari-Bentivoglio monument in S. Giacomo Maggiore (after 1433); in S. Gimignano, a wooden Annunciatory Angel and Virgin Annunciate for the Collegiata (1421) now in the Municipal Museum. Jacopo had a major influence a generation later on the young Michelangelo.

BIBLIOGRAPHY

Giulia Brunetti, "Jacopo della Quercia and the Porta della Mandorla," in *Art Quarterly,* **15** (1952); C. Del Bravo, "Jacopo della Quercia at Siena," in *Burlington Magazine,* **117** (1975); Anne C. Hanson, *Jacopo della Quercia's Fonte Gaia* (1965); Ottavio Morisani, *Tutta la scultura di Jacopo della Quercia* (1962); N. Rondelli, "Jacopo della Quercia a Ferrara 1403–1408," in *Bullettino senese di storia patria,* **71** (1964); Charles Seymour, Jr., *Jacopo della Quercia* (1973), with full bibliography, and (with Hanns Swarzenski), "A Madonna of Humility and Quercia's Early Style," in *Gazette des Beaux-Arts,* **88** (1946).

SANDRA CANDEE SUSMAN

Prophet and music-making angels. Carvings from Florence Cathedral by Jacopo di Piero Guidi. PHOTO: BRUNO BALESTRINI

JACOPO DI CIONE (*fl.* 1365–1398), Florentine painter. He was an assistant of his older brothers Andrea Orcagna and Nardo di Cione, and he probably collaborated with Niccolò di Pietro Gerini and/or Niccolò di Tommaso. Jacopo's work shows a gradual shift away from pliable, relaxed forms in the 1360's to a rigid, stridently colored later style. His frequent collaborations make it difficult to isolate his hand, but chief among his accepted works are the *Coronation of the Virgin,* dated 1373, now in the Accademia, Florence, and the *Coronation of the Virgin,* in the National Gallery, London.

BIBLIOGRAPHY

Richard Offner and Klara Steinweg, *A Critical and Historical Corpus of Florentine Painting,* sec. IV, vol. III, *Jacopo di Cione* (1965).

ADELHEID M. GEALT

JACOPO DI PIERO GUIDI (*fl.* 1376–1412), architect and sculptor in Florence, a distinctive minor master. Surviving documented sculptures are five life-size Virtues on the Loggia dei Lanzi and three music-making angels for the cathedral facade. As an

architect, Jacopo is documented as consultant at the cathedral of Florence in 1384, and as foreman (*capudmagister*) in 1406. He also was commissioned to build a chapel at Figline Valdarno in 1390.

BIBLIOGRAPHY

Florence, Opera del Duomo, Museo, *Il Museo dell'Opera del Duomo a Firenze,* Luisa Becherucci and Giulia Brunetti, eds., I (*ca.* 1971); Manfred Wundram, "Jacopo di Piero Guidi," in *Kunsthistorisches Institut in Florenz, Mitteilungen,* **13** (1967–1968).

DALE KINNEY

JACOPO FRANCHI, ROSELLO DI. See **Rosello di Jacopo Franchi.**

JACOPONE DA TODI (Jacopo de' Benedetti) (*ca.* 1236–25 December 1306), poet and Franciscan friar. In Todi, the town of his birth, Jacopo de' Benedetti exercised the profession of notary and legal procurator. The hagiographic tradition surrounding him tells of the death of his wife, Vanna di Bernardino di Guidone, as the result of the collapse of a hall in which she was attending a party. Under her rich party robes Vanna was allegedly found to be wearing a penitential hair shirt; this discovery is said to have caused a profound crisis in her husband, who then (probably 1268) abandoned his profession and his comfortable life, and gave his goods to the poor.

For the next ten years Jacopone led a life of penance, possibly in connection with a confraternity of flagellants; he bound himself by vows but did not enter a convent until 1278. In that year he entered the Order of Friars Minor. Although Jacopone remained a lay brother all his life, he studied philosophy and theology, and established relations with some of the most notable personalities within the order. He took a conspicuous part in the disputes concerning the degree of strictness to be observed in the religious life of the order that divided his brethren. Jacopone was an ardent member of the Spiritual party and, in his poetry, expounded the radical views of his faction about absolute poverty and frequently excoriated what he saw as the laxity of the Conventuals.

At the beginning of Celestine V's pontificate, Jacopone addressed a poem to the pope in which he challenged Celestine to remain faithful to the ideals he had cultivated as a hermit and to guard the church from corrupt and simoniacal pastors. When Boniface VIII succeeded Celestine and abrogated some norms that his predecessor had published in favor of the Spirituals, Jacopone joined other opponents of the new pope and on 10 May 1297 signed a manifesto that, while appealing to a council, declared Boniface to have fallen from office. Boniface declared the rebels excommunicated and began the long siege of Palestrina, the castle in which Jacopone and other friars had joined the Colonna cardinals and other opponents of the pope. It was during this siege that Jacopone composed his most violent invective against Boniface, in which he accused the pope of perpetual intrigues and corruption. At the fall of Palestrina in September 1298, he was tried and jailed in the cellar of a convent, possibly in Todi.

At first Jacopone declared himself happy to be allowed to suffer imprisonment for the sake of the Lord and poverty. Eventually he addressed touching compositions to Boniface, begging at least to be absolved from excommunication if not released from his imprisonment. Boniface steadfastly refused to allow the release of the friar, who had to wait for the election of Benedict XI, in 1303, before being granted freedom and readmitted to communion. Jacopone, now aged and tired, lived out his last years in the convent of S. Lorenzo at Collazzone, between Perugia and Todi, where he died.

Jacopone's prodigious poetic activity, restricted to the genre of the *lauda,* was a faithful reflection of his personality and vicissitudes; this by no means limited the range of themes and tones adopted in his 102 compositions of this type.

The *lauda,* which had originated in rhythmic liturgical chant, became the basic devotional form of the multitude of confraternities that arose after the initial implementation of Lateran IV reforms. The *laude,* at first rudimentary litanic prayers, reached both artistic and doctrinal maturity in Jacopone's lifetime because of their adoption by the confraternities of the flagellants and by the Franciscan movement.

Jacopone may have been first drawn to the genre by his familiarity with the flagellants; his work expounds both the extremely ascetic devotion of the flagellants and the themes of primitive Franciscanism, but also retains the nature of a personal diary. Jacopone's *laude* are sparked by violent hates and loves that incarnate themselves in doctrinal forms intelligible even to the unlettered. Principal themes of his more explicitly autobiographical compositions are the tension in his condition of believing sinner and the contrasting states of enthusiasm and discouragement. Although Jacopone had the figure and example of St. Francis ever before his eyes, he was never able to share in the meekness and calm joy of his exemplar. Despite the many invectives against reliance on intellectual knowledge, Jacopone's poetry continues to reveal his juridical and theological training. Education in mysticism, which is the principal aim of Jacopone's poetry, is founded on books; if the poet enjoyed mystical graces, they do not surface in his work in the sort of spontaneous outbursts that characterize the works of St. Francis.

The central theme of Jacopone's mystical teaching is the insignificance of human life and experience, and the wisdom of giving up all for the sake of divine love. The horribly vivid and sarcastic descriptions of the futility of human ambition and activity, and Jacopone's merciless emphasis on the suddenness and awesomeness of death, have led critics to speak of his hate for himself and for all that is human. While there can be no denial of his identification of earthly life with sin and of existence with nothingness, it must be remembered that the poet's caustic analysis of reality is not an end in itself but what he proposes as the starting point of the ascent of the soul toward God. Nor is Jacopone's range of vivid expression used sparingly in the overwhelming, if rare, descriptions of rapturous joy that flows from the awareness of the divine presence and love granted to those who have understood their own misery and have denied themselves all that does not lead to God. Jacopone's *laude* remain among the greatest and most moving achievements of religious literature.

Uncertain traditions have attributed to Jacopone a collection of moral observations for use in meditation and a treatise on the mystical union. It is more probable that he composed the famous liturgical sequence *Stabat mater,* which bears much resemblance to his best-known *lauda,* "Donna del paradiso," which also deals with the sorrow of Mary at the sight of Christ's Passion.

BIBLIOGRAPHY

Franco Mancini, ed., *Le laude* (1974), offers the most authoritative edition of the poems. Other works attributed to Jacopone and a useful edition of the poems are in Franca Ageno, ed., *Laudi, trattato e detti* (1953, repr. 1971). The hagiographic materials about Jacopone are collected in Enrico Menestò, ed., *Le vite antiche di Jacopone da Todi* (1977). George T. Peck, *The Fool of God: Jacopone da Todi* (1980), although it suffers from weaknesses in the historical and theological analyses, provides translations of many *laude* and an extensive bibliography of works about Jacopone. See also Jacopone da Todi, *The Lauds,* Serge Hughes and Elizabeth Hughes, trans. (1982).

GIULIO SILANO

[See also **Franciscans; Italian Literature: Lyric Poetry; Italian Literature: Religious Poetry; Lauda.**]

JACQUEMART DE HESDIN (*fl. ca.* 1384–1409), a painter and manuscript illuminator in the service of Jean, duke of Berry. He was one of a number of artists who worked on the *Grandes heures du duc de Berry* (Paris, Bibliothèque Nationale, MS lat. 919). His only surviving work may be the *Way to Calvary,* a large miniature removed from the *Grandes heures* and now in the Louvre. He also illuminated the *Très belles heures,* known as the *Brussels Hours,* before 1402 (probably identical with the MS 11060–61, Brussels, Bibliothèque Royale).

BIBLIOGRAPHY

Robert Calkins, "The Brussels Hours Reevaluated," in *Scriptorium,* **24** (1970); Millard Meiss, *French Painting in the Time of Jean de Berry: The Late Fourteenth Century and the Patronage of the Duke* (1967), 194–228, 256–286.

ROBERT G. CALKINS

[See also **Gothic Art: Painting; Jean, Duke of Berry; Manuscript Illumination.**]

JACQUERIE. The word *Jacquerie* has often been used as a generic term for "a peasant rising, destructive but with no aim and no morrow," to quote Édouard Perroy. It is derived from the name Jacques Bonhomme, a colloquialism for humble folk, such as peasants or artisans. The actual rebellion that gave birth to the word took place in northern France in 1358, beginning on 28 May and lasting barely three weeks. In fact, contemporary sources do not offer much evidence that the Jacquerie of 1358 was an uprising of peasants. Inhabitants of rural communities certainly were involved, but the many royal letters of pardon describe the movement simply as a conflict of non-nobles against nobles, and identify most of the participants as artisans, stonecutters, petty functionaries, and even clergy, but rarely as cultivators of the soil.

The Jacquerie seems to have been triggered by an ordinance issued on 14 May 1358 by the regent of France, the dauphin Charles, following an assembly of the Estates at Compiègne which had been dominated by nobles hostile to Étienne Marcel, who was leading the Parisians in rebellion. As a means of curbing the growing brigandage by undisciplined men-at-arms, this ordinance called for defensible castles and fortifications to be put in good repair and stocked with provisions; those that could not be defended were to be destroyed.

The actual work of strengthening these fortresses fell upon stonecutters, laborers, and peasant subjects of the lords who controlled them. The very fact that they were to be strengthened enraged these rural inhabitants, who considered themselves poorly protected by their lords and saw little difference between the nobles and the brigands. Most of the latter were nobles or wished to be considered nobles. Although generally brutal to the villagers they encountered, they maintained courteous relations with most lords, and the nobles as a class were suspected of complicity with them. Defeats in battle had discredited the nobles as defenders of the realm without diminishing the pressure they exerted on their subjects. In a time of economic depression, rising taxes, and declining public order, the castles they were now to help repair seemed to the peasants to be instruments of tyranny rather than of protection. Scarcely a fortnight after the ordinance of Compiègne, the revolt began in the districts northeast of Paris.

The reinforcement of the castles was not, however, exclusively a measure against brigandage. Its other, and perhaps more immediate, purpose was to make it possible for the dauphin to prevent supplies from reaching rebellious Paris. Étienne Marcel was fully aware of this intention, and some chroniclers thought he initiated the Jacquerie. Whether he did so or not, his Parisians took advantage of the occasion to assault the castles of nobles in the vicinity of Paris. His men ventured as far as the château of Ermenonville, south of Senlis, which belonged to Robert de Lorris, a royal officer against whom Marcel had a particular grudge.

Modern accounts of the Jacquerie report the attacks on castles and the lurid details of atrocities committed against nobles and their families. Only recently, however, has it been recognized that these attacks followed a pattern. Not only the fortresses around Paris were assaulted, but also those near Amiens, Montdidier, Senlis, and Meaux. Contingents from the towns were involved in these operations, which, far from being aimless, suggest some sort of common effort to check the preparations of the dauphin and the nobles. The movement was strongest in regions that were relatively prosperous, and it had little backing in the more impoverished areas. The participants were clearly anti-noble: the Jacquerie was certainly a class conflict. Yet it was not a simple rising of peasants against their lords, and certainly not an undirected outburst by hopelessly destitute men. It bore every sign of being an effort, however desperate, to prevent the nobles from achieving a position of commanding power from which to intimidate the towns, whose representatives in recent assemblies had tried to shift the burden of taxation to the nobility.

Marcel's association with the Jacquerie has been called a great error, whereby he compromised the principles for which he stood by abetting irresponsible violence. Nothing could be further from the truth. Aside from the fact that his principles have been overrated and his selfish motives underrated, Marcel had already broken irrevocably with the nobility in February 1358, when his men murdered two prominent nobles in the dauphin's presence. One of these was the marshal of Champagne, who had been

a member of the reforming party opposed to the abuses in royal government that Marcel himself had criticized. His death outraged the nobles of Champagne, who played a prominent role in the assembly at Compiègne in May. Marcel and his allies in other northern towns were already committed to violence and to an anti-noble policy. Only in the Beauvaisis, where the worst atrocities occurred, does the Jacquerie seem to have pursued an independent course.

When the Jacques in Picardy treacherously murdered a member of the Picquigny family, they made a fatal blunder, for the Picquigny were friends of Charles of Navarre, who was usually allied with Marcel and whose resources at this time were superior to those of the dauphin. Charles assembled troops; and at Mello, Guillaume Cale, leader of the rebels, died under similarly treacherous circumstances. After their defeat at Mello on 10 June, the Jacques were hunted down and massacred. Just a day earlier, two relatives of Charles of Navarre had helped rout those who were besieging the dauphin's family at Meaux. Thus, the destruction of the Jacquerie was brought about by the one faction of the nobility that had been associated with Marcel in opposition to the dauphin. The latter, who had been unable to act effectively, was now in a position to devote his attention to the siege of Paris.

BIBLIOGRAPHY
Raymond Cazelles, "La Jacquerie, fut-elle un mouvement paysan?" in *Comptes rendus de l'Académie des Inscriptions et belles-lettres* (1978), is now the authoritative work. Siméon Luce, *Histoire de la Jacquerie*, 2nd rev. ed. (1984), is still the classic treatment. See also Michel Mollat and Philippe Wolff, *The Popular Revolutions of the Late Middle Ages*, A. L. Lytton-Sells, trans. (1973), 115–131 (part of a chapter entitled "Revolts Against Poverty"). Édouard Perroy, *The Hundred Years War*, Warren B. Wells, trans. (1951), can no longer be considered an acceptable source for the Jacquerie. On Marcel, see Jacques d'Avout, *Le meurtre d'Étienne Marcel* (1960). No treatment of this subject can neglect the scores of letters of pardon in Paris, Archives Nationales, Register JJ 86, some of which have been published in excerpts by Luce.

JOHN BELL HENNEMAN

[See also **Class Structure, Western; France.**]

JACQUES COENE. See **Coene, Jacques.**

JACQUES COEUR (*ca.* 1395–25 November 1456), merchant and royal treasurer, was born in Bourges, the son of a furrier. About 1422 he married Macée de Léodépart, daughter of the provost of the city. His first business ventures involved currency speculation and allegations of minting inferior coinage; there followed a commercial trip to the Near East in 1432 from which he returned penniless, having been robbed by pirates. In 1438 he was appointed royal treasurer *(argentier),* with the responsibility for supplying clothing, furs, jewels, arms, spices, and art objects to the court. He became creditor and, as a banker, moneylender to King Charles VII and to the royal household. In order to stock the warehouses of the Argenterie at Tours with luxuries, he fitted out at least six ships that sailed from Aigues-Mortes, and later from Marseilles, to Alexandria.

Wishing to manufacture luxury textiles (especially silks), Jacques had himself, his son Ravand, and his chief legal representative, Guillaume de Varye, enrolled in the silk guild of Florence. There, with some Italians, he organized a company to produce these goods. His commercial operations were not confined to providing goods for the royal court. They spread in all directions, over the sea and over a network of land routes, reaching Bruges and even Scotland. His agents and associates traded in the commercial centers of France—Rouen, La Rochelle, Limoges, Lyons, Avignon—and in the chief foreign markets—Bruges, Geneva, Genoa, Naples, Palermo, Barcelona, Valencia.

Jacques Coeur's political and financial enterprises were based principally on the confidence of Charles VII and on the numerous commissions that he was awarded. A member of the King's Council, he made himself indispensable by lending the money needed to reconquer Normandy from the English (1450), by reforming and stabilizing the currency (one much-used coin was called "le gros de Jacques Coeur") in 1447, and by assuring the credit of the kingdom's fiscal system. Thus, he placed the king in his debt and was able to use the revenues of the realm to carry on his business while he was royal commissioner in the assembly of the Estates of Languedoc and inspector general of the gabelle (salt tax). By exploiting the mines of the Lyons region, Jacques Coeur hoped to acquire silver for his oriental commerce, since in that part of the world silver was preferred to gold.

Diplomacy aided his business interests. Instead of resorting to armed reprisals, Jacques Coeur felt that it was more profitable to negotiate letters of marque with Genoa and with Alfonso V of Aragon, since friendly relations with those areas were essential for security in trading on the Mediterranean. His papal dispensation permitting trade with the infidels was renewed several times: when Jacques Coeur was a member of a mission to Rome in 1448, when he helped arrange the abdication of the antipope Felix V in 1449, and when, as a fugitive, he found asylum with Pope Nicholas V in 1455.

In Rome, as well as in Florence, Avignon, and Geneva, Jacques Coeur profited from the assistance of Italian bankers, whose loans made up for his lack of liquid capital. In fact, although his business affairs—by their scope, diversity, influence, and profitability—seemed to be brilliantly successful, they had a shaky foundation. Many of his debtors, short of cash, could meet their obligations only by ceding him their lands. Not content with having been ennobled in 1441, Jacques Coeur, like most men of his time, felt that to have high social position he had to be lord of many estates: St. Fargeau, Menetou-Salon, St. Gérand de Vaux, St. Haon, Ainag, and many others. He also built at Bourges the most beautiful French palace of the fifteenth century.

Jacques's success offended many and aroused jealousy. Charles VII was persuaded to act against him by the complaints and false accusations of envious rivals and dishonest debtors. The king may have felt that his agent was becoming too powerful. Jacques Coeur was arrested on 31 July 1451. The investigation and testimony took almost two years. Sentence was pronounced by a special commission on 29 May 1453. The former *argentier,* convicted of high treason, was condemned to perpetual banishment (as a commutation of a death sentence) and was forced to pay an enormous fine of 400,000 écus, equivalent to the value of all his possessions. It took Jean Dauvet, the prosecutor, almost four years to discover and to sell all of Jacques's assets. Dauvet had to travel throughout France, and his report gives a remarkably full record of the wealth and possessions of the condemned financier.

By the time this report was made, Jacques Coeur was dead. His friends, notably Jean de Village, had helped him to escape from the convent at Beaucaire. He went to Rome, where the pope took him under the protection of the church. While Jacques Coeur's agents carried on their activities from Barcelona and Marseilles to Palermo and the Levant, he himself joined a fleet sent by Calixtus III against the Turks. He died in Chios, perhaps in battle.

BIBLIOGRAPHY

Pierre Clément, *Jacques Coeur et Charles VII*, 2nd ed., 2 vols. (1866); L. Guiraud, "Recherches et conclusions nouvelles sur le prétendu rôle de Jacques Coeur," in *Mémoires de la Société archéologique de Montpellier*, 2nd ser., **2** (1900); Albert B. Kerr, *Jacques Coeur* (1927); Michel Mollat, ed., *Les affaires de Jacques Coeur: Journal du Procureur Dauvet*, 2 vols. (1952), and *Jacques Coeur, un "manager" du XVᵉ siècle* (in press).

MICHEL MOLLAT

[See also **Charles VII of France; Hundred Years War.**]

JACQUES DE BAERZE. See **Baerze, Jacques de.**

JACQUES DE LIÈGE (Jacobi Leodiensis, Jacobus of Liège) (*ca.* 1260–after 1330), music theorist and author of *Speculum musicae,* one of the great encyclopedias of musical knowledge. There is evidence that he studied at the University of Paris in his youth and, like most music students of the thirteenth century, concentrated his study on Boethius' *De institutione musica.* Jacques probably completed Books I–V of the *Speculum* in Paris between 1330 and 1340, composing Books VI and VII on his return to Liège. He may also have written what is now known as Anonymous I, the first of such treatises in Volume I of Edmond de Coussemaker's *Scriptorum de musica medii aevi nova series* (1864–1876, repr. 1963), as well as a work on psalm tones, now lost. Other than these facts and conjectures, nothing is known of Jacques's life.

Coussemaker was the first to discover and publish the manuscript of the *Speculum;* he published a list of chapter headings of Books I–V and a transcription of Books VI–VII in Volume II of the *Scriptorum* (pp. 193–433). Not knowing the authorship, however, Coussemaker attributed the treatise to Johannes de Muris (Jehan des Murs). Only in 1924 was the correct attribution made, this through the solving of a somewhat obscure acrostic. In recent years, Roger Bragard has prepared a new and complete edition that completely supersedes the partial and error-laden one by Coussemaker.

By all standards, the *Speculum* is an enormous work. It is divided into seven books, with some 521 chapters. The author tried to put into one treatise all

that he had learned in a lifetime of study and reading; the result is a true encyclopedia. It is, as its title states, a speculum, a "mirror," in which the art of music has been reflected and collected. Jacques was the speculative musician whose attention had been fixed on the human reflection of God's perfection; he was not unlike the medieval philosopher and theologian, who use human thought and reason to understand God and his creations. Music as a part of the quadrivium and a stage in the progression to metaphysics is the central core of the *Speculum.* Practical music, however, is a subject useful only as a support for theoretical ideas, which are of so much more value for the philosopher.

Book I works from the secure bases of Boethius and Macrobius and discusses the divisions of music and the importance of number as the moving force behind musical sound. As Jacques says, "Music is not to be taken as sound alone, but must be thought of as numbered sound." His authorities are mostly men of the past—Plato, Aristotle, Isidore, Pope Gregory the Great—but include one contemporary, Robert Kilwardby. Jacques also names Guido of Arezzo, the only practical musician so honored.

Book II extends the study of number to the proportions of musical intervals. In the 126 chapters of this book, all are explored in detail, with many diagrams and mathematical operations. Other writers do much the same, but not with such a complexity of details. Book III offers a set of corollaries to the propositions advanced in Book II, exploring the theses laid down by Boethius on such questions as the division of the tone into semitones, but with the detail possible only from a student at the University of Paris.

Jacques recapitulates the first three books in Book IV, but adds new meanings and classifications. Plainchant notation appears for the first time, as a means of showing intervals other than by ratios. Book V is the most abstract and the least practical of the first five books, bearing almost no relationship to the actual performance of music. In it, Jacques again turns to Boethius, with commentary on the last books of the *De institutione musica* in the scholastic manner.

The 113 chapters of Book VI return to performance practice, itemizing all the materials needed by the church musician, and discussing the principles and practice of plainchant. Again, while the fundamentals are the same as in other writers, Jacques is meticulous about giving details not found elsewhere. The climax of the book is an extensive *tonarius,* a classification of chants by musical characteristics, rather than by liturgical function. Jacques gives short poetic phrases as mnemonics to help in remembering the rules.

Book VII, only 48 chapters, concerns contemporary practice. It considers polyphony, from the simplest type to the complex counterpoint developed by the Notre Dame school in the twelfth and thirteenth centuries. Jacques also considers the changes that came in the fourteenth century as the result of the *ars nova.* He is a defender of the past and contrasts the techniques of the *ars antiqua* with those of the *ars modernorum.* He favors the style of composition, notation, and performance of his predecessors and heaps scorn and criticism on musicians of his own day, characterizing their work as being without authority, without tradition, arbitrary, and thus condemnable as contrary to reason.

For most readers of the treatise, Jacques seems little more than a peevish conservative who, unable to understand the innovations arising around him, vents his spleen at "modern" music and its proponents. Such a view of Jacques de Liège goes too far, however, for he is the supreme musical representative of the kind of intellectuality typical of the University of Paris, which also produced Thomas Aquinas. With his training in the method of rational and logical progression from one set of postulates to another, Jacques produced in his *Speculum* the same kind of masterpiece of musical speculation as did Aquinas in his philosophical and theological writings; the *Speculum* is a musical summa.

Of all the medieval music theorists, Jacques de Liège is certainly the one who most perfectly shows the heights to which scholasticism could rise when applied to music as a subject within the quadrivium. Nevertheless, his treatise received little or no attention in his own day, and he was never mentioned by later writers. In a sense he was born too late, for his masterwork came at a time (in music at least) when scholasticism was no longer able to withstand the new currents already seen in writers such as Philippe de Vitry and Marchettus of Padua.

BIBLIOGRAPHY

Roger Bragard, ed., *Jacobi Leodiensis: Speculum musicae,* 7 vols.; *Corpus scriptorum de musica,* 3 (1955–1973); John Caldwell, *Medieval Music* (1978); Albert Seay, "Musical Conservatism in the Fourteenth Century," in *Something of Great Constancy: Essays in Honor of the Memory of J. Glenn Gray* (1979), 144–157; F. Joseph Smith, "Ars Nova—A Re-definition?" in *Musica disciplina,* **18** (1964), 19–35, and **19** (1965), 83–97; Joseph Smits van Waesberghe, "Some Music Treatises and Their Interrelation," in *Musica disciplina,* **3** (1949), 25–31, 95–118; Oliver Strunk, ed., *Source Readings in Music History* (1950).

ALBERT SEAY

[See also **Ars Antiqua; Ars Nova; Boethius; Counterpoint; Kilwardby, Robert; Musical Treatises; Notre Dame School; Philippe de Vitry.**]

JACQUES DE VITRY (*ca.* 1160/1170–1 May 1240), preacher, historian, and churchman, was born into a wealthy bourgeois family in Vitry-en-Perthois, near Rheims, and educated in Paris, probably under Peter the Chanter. Little is known of his life until 1211, when he became an Augustinian canon regular and entered the monastery of St. Nicholas in Oignies, near Cambrai. It is likely that he previously had been a master in Paris and had served briefly as a parish priest in Argenteuil. While in Oignies (1211–1216) he became connected with the lay religious group centered around Mary of Oignies, an early leader of the Beguine movement. In 1213 he was commissioned to preach against the Albigensians and, in the following year, also began to preach a new crusade to the Holy Land. His renown as a preacher won Jacques election as bishop of Acre. He was consecrated in Perugia in July 1216 and arrived in Acre in November of the same year. Jacques was with the army of the Fifth Crusade at Damietta (1218–1221). Weary of the worsening situation in the East, he left Acre permanently to return to Europe in 1225. For the next three years he served the papacy in various capacities in Italy and the Low Countries. Then, in 1228, Gregory IX accepted Jacques's resignation as bishop of Acre and appointed him cardinal bishop of Tusculum in 1228. He remained in Rome until his death and was buried at Oignies.

Nearly 450 of Jacques's sermons survive, in four separate collections planned to serve as models for preachers: *Sermones dominicales (de tempore),* three sermons for each Sunday; *Sermones de sanctis,* 115 sermons for saints' days and feasts; *Sermones communes et feriales,* a small collection of 27 sermons for daily use; and 74 *Sermones vulgares* or *Sermones ad status,* which constitute one of the earliest and greatest collections of sermons addressed to specific social classes and religious groups. The last two collections are embellished with many illustrative anecdotes or moral exempla, derived both from literary sources and from personal experience, which were used to capture and hold the attention of the audience as well as to make the lessons of the sermons more intelligible. Both the *sermo ad status* and the use of exempla were innovative preaching techniques that Jacques helped to develop and popularize.

Jacques's other works include a life of Mary of Oignies (1213), an important source for the formative period of the Beguines; a collection of seven letters, dating from 1216–1221, and reporting events of his early years in the East and of the Fifth Crusade; and the *Historia Hierosolimitana abbreviata.* Although it was originally planned as a tripartite history of the crusades, only the first two books were completed. The first, the *Historia orientalis,* consists of a topography of the East and an account of events to 1179, based largely on William of Tyre. The more original second book, the *Historia occidentalis,* is a religious and moral history of the West that emphasizes the importance of new movements such as the Humiliati, Franciscans, and Beguines to the spiritual renewal of the church and to the success of the crusades. The projected third book would have carried the narrative through the Fifth Crusade. As a historian, no less than as a preacher, Jacques was a keen observer and frequently a harsh critic of the actions of the people of his time.

BIBLIOGRAPHY

The standard biography is Philipp Funk, *Jakob von Vitry: Leben und Werke* (1909). Of Jacques's works, there are critical editions only of part of his history and of the letters: John Frederick Hinnebusch, ed., *The Historia occidentalis of Jacques de Vitry* (1972); R. B. C. Huygens, ed., *Lettres de Jacques de Vitry* (1960). The *Vita Mariae Oigniacensis* is in *Acta sanctorum,* June 5 (1867), 547–572.

The *Sermones vulgares* were partially edited by J. B. Pitra in *Analecta novissima spicilegii Solesmensis, Altera continuatio,* II (1888). The exempla from this collection were printed by Thomas F. Crane as *The Exempla or Illustrative Stories from the Sermones Vulgares of Jacques de Vitry* (1890, repr. 1967). The *Sermones dominicales* were published by T. Lyngam (1575). The other collections have never been printed. There were, however, two simultaneous publications of the *exempla* from the *Sermones communes:* Goswin Frenken, ed., *Die Exempla des Jacob von Vitry* (1914); and Joseph Greven, ed., *Die Exempla aus den Sermones feriales et communes des Jakob von Vitry* (1914).

S. C. FERRUOLO

[See also **Beguines and Beghards; Crusades and Crusader States; Historiography, Western European; Preaching and Sermons, Western European.**]

JAGIEŁŁO DYNASTY. The Polish royal dynasty from 1386 to 1572 derived its title from the polonized name of the Lithuanian grand duke Jogaila (*ca.* 1351–1434). In an agreement with the nobles of Poland at Krewo on 14 August 1385, Jogaila/Jagiełło promised permanently to attach *(applicare)* his realm to the Kingdom of Poland *(Corona Regni Poloniae).* On 2 February 1386 he was accepted as king by the Polish nobility at Lublin. He entered Cracow on 12 February and converted to Christianity on 15 February, taking the baptismal name Władisław (Ladislas). Three days later he married the ruler of Poland, Jadwiga of Anjou, the second daughter of Louis of Hungary, who had succeeded the last Piast king of Poland in 1370. After confirming and enhancing the rights of the Polish nobility, Jagiełło was crowned king on 4 March. This personal union between Poland and Lithuania lasted for nearly two centuries before being transformed by the Union of Lublin (1569) into a constitutional bond. Jadwiga and Jagiełło's marriage was without issue, and she died in 1399. By the terms of agreements in 1401 at Radom and Wilno and in 1413 at Horodło, Jagiełło confirmed his own title as king of Poland and obtained the succession for his heirs by his fourth wife. His son Władisław III, who succeeded him, was killed while on crusade at Varna (1444). A second son, Casimir IV, grand duke of Lithuania from 1440, became king of Poland in 1447 and ruled for forty-five years. He was succeeded by his sons John Albert (1492–1501), Alexander (1501–1506), and Sigismund I the Old (1506–1548). The eldest son of Casimir IV, Władysław, ruled as king of Bohemia (1471–1516) and king of Hungary (1490–1516), being succeeded in both kingdoms by his son Louis (1516–1526).

During the reign of Jagiełło, royal authority was weakened by the continued rise of the great nobles of Little Poland, led by Bishop Zbigniew Oleśnicki of Cracow (d. 1455). It was they who taught the former pagan prince how to govern as a Western, Christian monarch. Noble ascendancy continued under Władysław III, who was only nine at his accession and who, after 1440, ruled Hungary as well. The monarchy temporarily recovered some of its authority under Casimir IV, for the king had a separate power base in Lithuania. Dynastic interests and foreign policy, however, undercut these gains. Agreements to ensure the family's succession and wars waged against the Teutonic Knights (1409–1411 and 1454–1466) required fundamental concessions to the nobility. By the end of the Middle Ages, the Jagiellonian monarchy had traveled very far along the road to the nobleman's paradise of the early modern period.

Although originally a Lithuanian dynasty, the Jagiellonians became thoroughly polonized. They were patrons of learning, refounding the University of Cracow in 1400 and providing substantial endowments. Jagiełło's victory over the Teutonic Knights at Tannenberg (Grunwald) in 1410 captured the imagination of the nation, and the dynasty provided a saint (Casimir) and a cardinal (Frederick) to the church from the generation of Casimir IV's sons. By virtue of Jagiełło's baptism and the subsequent conversion of Lithuania, the Jagiellonians assumed the missionary leadership in the East previously exercised by the Teutonic Knights. The dynasty was generally successful in reconciling the competing and often conflicting social, political, and religious interests of its multiethnic state. Under its rule Poland-Lithuania was a stable community.

BIBLIOGRAPHY

The standard genealogical guide to the Jagiełło dynasty is Zygmunt Wdowiszewski, *Genealogia Jagiellonów* (1968). The important, and still useful, study of the Jagiellonian period by Oskar Halecki, *Dzieje unii jagiellońskiej*, 2 vols. (1919–1920), should be supplemented by Henryk Samsonowicz, *Złota jesień polskiego średniowiecza* (1971). Biographical studies of each member of the dynasty, with bibliography, are in *Polski słownik biograficzny* (1935–). In English see, in addition to general histories of the period, Norman Davies, *God's Playground: A History of Poland,* I (1982), 115–155; Pawel Jasienica, *Jagiellonian Poland* (1978).

PAUL W. KNOLL

[See also **Lithuania; Poland.**]

JĀḤIẒ, ABŪ ᶜUTHMĀN ᶜAMR IBN BAḤR AL- (*ca.* 776–December 868/January 869), a prose writer of the ninth century whose works rank among the greatest classics of Arabic literature, as well as among the most important sources for the history of

medieval Islamic culture. He was notorious for his ugliness, and the sobriquet al-Jāḥiẓ (the bug-eyed) refers to a deformity that caused his eyes to protrude abnormally.

LIFE

Little is known about his early life. He was born in Basra, then one of the greatest cultural centers of the Islamic world. His family was of slave (possibly Abyssinian) ancestry, and he likely spent his childhood in poverty. Such conditions were hardly conducive to academic study, and only al-Jāḥiẓ's determination and insatiably inquisitive spirit could have led him to dedicate his life to scholarship. As a boy he had some training in a Koran school, but his real education came from attending lectures and discussions at the mosque, and in particular from frequenting the Mirbad, the vast economic and social center of Basra that teemed with throngs of traders, shopkeepers, sailors, peddlers, and vagabonds of every description. Bedouin poets, transmitters, and storytellers often came in from the arid steppe; and genealogists, philologists, and historians eagerly sought them out to record their verses and tribal traditions, and to study their dialects and vocabulary.

In Basra, then, al-Jāḥiẓ was exposed to all kinds of people and ideas, including the cultures of Persia and India. It was also here that he met and studied under some of the greatest scholars of early Islam, among them the philologists Abū ᶜUbayda, al-Aṣmaᶜī, and Abū Zayd al-Anṣārī. He eventually emerged as a master of the Arabic language; and his vivid style, sharp wit, and keen sense of human nature probably owe much to these early days.

At this stage of his career, al-Jāḥiẓ probably supported himself through teaching rather than writing, and the few allusions he makes to his early career indicate that these were difficult days. It is thus a tribute to the assimilative capacity of Islamic culture that al-Jāḥiẓ, who was not an Arab and had little contact with the Arab aristocracy in Basra, became such an energetic defender of the Arab community and Arab traditions. His first writings, treatises upholding the legitimacy of the ruling Abbasid dynasty, in 815/816 were brought to the attention of the caliph al-Maᵓmūn by a visiting Basran grammarian. The ruler was so impressed by them that he summoned al-Jāḥiẓ to Baghdad.

This was an opportunity of the greatest importance, since it enabled him to establish himself in the Abbasid capital. The move considerably broadened his intellectual horizons, for it was in Baghdad that he became familiar with translations from the classical Greek heritage (particularly Aristotle) and gained greater exposure to the rationalist speculative theology of Muᶜtazilism. His former colleague and fellow Basran al-Naẓẓām had become one of the prominent Muᶜtazilite thinkers of the day, and al-Jāḥiẓ soon became one of his leading advocates and a deeply committed follower of the doctrine.

His literary skills and religiopolitical views led the caliphs of the Muᶜtazilite era to regard al-Jāḥiẓ's work highly, but his direct contacts and sources of support were the powerful figures who surrounded the rulers. He was associated for a time with the chancery secretary Ibrāhīm ibn al-ᶜAbbās al-Ṣūlī, then with the vizier Muḥammad ibn ᶜAbd al-Malik al-Zayyāt, a personal enemy of the chief judge Aḥmad ibn Abī Duʾād. When the conflict between the two led to the fall of Ibn al-Zayyāt in 847, al-Jāḥiẓ fled to Basra. Aḥmad ibn Abī Duʾād had him brought back to Baghdad in chains and rags, but needed his services and eventually restored him to favor. Al-Jāḥiẓ enjoyed his patronage, and also the firm friendship of his son Muḥammad, for the next three years and wrote a number of important essays for them. But both patrons fell from favor in 851/852 and died shortly thereafter. Al-Jāḥiẓ then gravitated to the entourage of al-Mutawakkil's vizier al-Fatḥ ibn Khāqān.

Though Basra always remained a primary influence on his thought and works, al-Jāḥiẓ spent most of his career at Baghdad, and later the Abbasid palace city of Samarra. He was also familiar with Al-Kufa and Al-Ahwāz, traveled in the Arabian peninsula, and visited Damascus and Antioch in Syria. He makes no reference to any pilgrimage to Mecca. Al-Jāḥiẓ probably made his final return to Basra before the assassination of al-Mutawakkil and al-Fatḥ ibn Khāqān in 861. This was in effect his retirement, for by this time he was an old man and partially paralyzed. His date of death is well established as December 868/January 869.

WORKS

Despite the fluctuations in his fortunes, al-Jāḥiẓ seems to have been able to live very comfortably and to concentrate on his writing. The resulting literary output was massive—more than 200 works, about a third of which survive either wholly or in part. This vast bulk of material is of utmost importance to the historian of early Islamic culture and society, for al-Jāḥiẓ was an *adīb*, a man of letters proficient in a broad range of subjects covering all that an educated person was expected to know in order to articulate, criticize, and debate issues in the cultivated social circles of medieval Islam. He dealt with topics extending from philosophy and speculative theology to parody and satire, from history and literary criticism to geography, the natural sciences, and human nature.

It is, however, extremely difficult to characterize his works, since enormous diversity is a prominent feature of his style. Incapable of restricting himself to one side of an issue, al-Jāḥiẓ writes with deliberate disregard for order and peppers his discussions with ancillary statements, illustrative examples, and extravagant digressions. Drawing on almost the entire range of medieval Islamic learning, al-Jāḥiẓ provides readers with a vast variety of information and leads them through a virtual literary kaleidoscope in which the main themes and objectives are by no means readily apparent.

His own personality is very prominent. Reminiscences of personal experiences abound, and his discussions are often deeply personal statements of his own views. Al-Jāḥiẓ criticizes the dull, sober presentations of many of his contemporaries and insists that important issues can be dealt with in an entertaining way. In even his most serious works he introduces lighthearted anecdotes and witty observations, many of them sexually oriented (and, by rigid puritanical standards, obscene).

Typical of al-Jāḥiẓ's method is his main work, the *Kitāb al-ḥayawān* (Book of animals), which he began late in life and did not finish. A bestiary in that the author exhibits a profoundly Aristotelian interest in the nature and behavior of different animals, this work is in fact built on the Koranic theme that the world and everything in it is proof of God's existence, wisdom, justice, and mercy. In this magnificent work al-Jāḥiẓ uses his technique of disarray and digression to work in innumerable topics: history, theology, metaphysics, intellectual life, human nature, and sociology, to name a few. He has some particularly important points to make on aggression, the influence of the environment, and the evolution of animal species.

Al-Jāḥiẓ's other important works are *Al-Bayān wa'l-tabyīn* (Eloquence and elucidation), a humanistic compendium with particular reference to poetry and rhetoric; *Al-ᶜUthmānīya*, a political work on the earliest caliphs and the problem of the succession; *Al-Bukhalāʾ* (Misers), a lighthearted classic on avarice and avaricious men, including a plethora of priceless character sketches unrivaled in Arabic literature; and *Al-Tarbīᶜ waʾl-tadwīr* (The square and the circle), a collection of cultural and intellectual questions set to demonstrate, in an ironical manner, the pitfalls involved in servile adherence to traditional ideas, and the need to reexamine problems and to resort to independent rational judgment to solve them. In addition to these longer works, al-Jāḥiẓ wrote essays on points of Muᶜtazilite doctrine and aspects of the inquisition *(miḥna)* carried out to enforce it, tracts in defense of the Abbasids, works on Christians and Jews, non-Arabs, the Turks, the blacks, secretaries, tradesmen, thieves, and vagrants, and numerous epistles dealing with gratitude, envy, anger, jealousy, pride, indiscretion, friendship, humor, love and physical passion, sex, and obscenity.

The career of al-Jāḥiẓ had an impact of the highest importance on the development of Arabic literature and, indeed, on medieval Islamic literary culture. He lived at a time when Islamic culture had not yet established a clear pattern of direction. In this era of self-definition, the old established Arab traditions of philology and poetry, though now broadening to include such religiously oriented topics as Koranic exegesis, history, and law, proved in style and content too restricted to become either the vehicle for meaningful expression of the wide-ranging interests of a vast polyglot society, or, in consequence, the basis for an Islamic literary culture. Hence, they were insufficient for confronting the challenge of the Shuᶜūbīya, a movement, much supported by the Abbasid secretarial class, that sought to orient emergent Islamic society primarily on the foundations of the Sasanian courtly tradition and ancient Aramaean culture. That this challenge failed was in large part due to al-Jāḥiẓ. His early writing followed the lead of the secretarial works, and throughout his career he remained willing to accept much of value from the Persian tradition. But his roots lay in the Arabic humanities, and the rationalist arguments of the Muᶜtazila gave him the intellectual tools to uphold them. Probably feeling compelled to choose between the two camps, he became a sharp critic of the secretarial proponents of the Shuᶜūbīya and what he deemed their cynical pompous ways. But far more important, he demonstrated through his own work that bold initiative and experimentation could broaden and elaborate the old Arabic foundations into an exuberant and varied literary tradition that possessed, at the same time, a definite spiritual dimension.

Al-Jāḥiẓ was recognized as the preeminent litterateur of his day, and his work inspired and influenced most authors in the generations to follow. The tradition he played so vital a role in establishing gained both popular and official support, and the Arabic humanities, traditions, and lore were henceforth to remain the heart of medieval Islamic culture. The many surviving works of al-Jāḥiẓ are therefore not only important literary pieces but also a corpus of tremendous importance to our knowledge of this critical period in the historical formation of Islamic culture.

BIBLIOGRAPHY

By way of introduction, see Charles Pellat, ed., *The Life and Works of Jāḥiẓ*, D. M. Hawke, trans. (1969). Of the many works on al-Jāḥiẓ, the best are Charles Pellat, *Le milieu baṣrien et la formation de Ǧāḥiẓ* (1953), and "Ǧāḥiẓ à Baġdād et à Sāmarrā," in *Rivista degli studi orientali,* **27** (1952). On the judgment of posterity, see Charles Pellat, "Al-Ǧāḥiẓ jugé par la postérité," in *Arabica,* **27** (1980). For inventories of works, see Ḥasan al-Sandūbī, *Adab al-Jāḥiẓ* (1931), superseded by Pellat, "Gahiziana III. Essai d'inventaire de l'oeuvre ǧāḥiẓienne," in *Arabica,* **3** (1956), which is now dated.

Translations. Amr ibn Bahr al-Jahiz, *The Epistle on Singing Girls of Jāḥiẓ*, A. F. L. Beeston, ed. and trans. (1980); Joshua Finkel, "A Risālah of al-Jāḥiẓ," in *Journal of the American Oriental Society,* **47** (1927); Hartwig Hirschfeld, "A Volume of Essays by al-Jāḥiẓ," in Thomas Walker Arnold and Reynold A. Nicholson, eds., *A Volume of Oriental Studies Presented to Edward G. Browne on His 60th Birthday* (1922); Tarif Khalidi, trans., "The Boasts of the Blacks Over the Whites," in *Islamic Quarterly,* **25** (1981); Bernard Lewis, ed. and trans., *Islam from the Prophet Muhammad to the Capture of Constantinople* (1974), I, 23–24, 214–17; II, 55–57, 199–201, 210–16, 261; C. T. H. Walker, "Jāḥiẓ . . . on the 'Exploits of the Turks,'" in *Journal of the Royal Asiatic Society* (1915).

Studies. Miguel Asin Palacios, "El 'Libro de los Animales' de Jāḥiẓ," in *Isis,* **14** (1930); Marc Bergé, "Al-Tawḥīdī et al-Ǧāḥiẓ," in *Arabica,* **12** (1965); Marie Bernand, "Le savoir entre la volonté et la spontanéité selon an-Naẓẓām et al-Ǧāḥiẓ," in *Studia islamica,* **39** (1974); Susanne Enderwitz, *Gesellschaftlicher Rang und ethnische Legitimation: Der arabische Schriftsteller Abū ᶜUṯmān al-Ǧāḥiẓ (gest. 868) über die Afrikaner, Perser und Araber in der islamischen Gesellschaft* (1979); Josef van Ess, *Das Kitāb an-Nakṯ des Naẓẓām und seine Rezeption im Kitāb al-Futyā des Ǧāḥiẓ* (1972); Ibrahim Geries, "Quelques aspects de la pensée muᶜtazilite d'al-Ǧāḥiẓ selon *K. al-Ḥayawān*," in *Studia islamica,* **52** (1980); Tarif Khalidi, "A Mosquito's Wing: Al-Jāḥiẓ on the Progress of Knowledge," in *Arabic and Islamic Garland* (1977); L. Kopf, "The 'Book of Animals' (Kitab al-hayawan) of al-Jahiz," in F. S. Bodenheimer, ed., *Actes du VIIᵉ Congrès International d'Histoire des*

Sciences (1953); Jacob Lassner, *The Shaping of ᶜAbbāsid Rule* (1980), 116–136; David R. Marshall, "An Arab Humorist—al-Jāḥiẓ and 'The Book of Misers,'" in *Journal of the Faculty of Arts, Royal University of Malta,* **4** (1970); Charles Pellat, "Djāḥiz et la 'littérature comparée,'" in *Cahiers algériens de littérature comparée,* **1** (1966); Krystyna Sharżyńska-Bochénska, "Les ornements du style selon la conception d'al-Ǧāḥiẓ," in *Rocznik Orientalistyczny,* **36** (1973); Joseph de Somogyi, "Al-Jāḥiẓ and ad-Damīrī," in *Annual of Leeds University Oriental Society,* **1** (1958–1959), John MacDonald, ed., 55–60; Lakhdar Souami, "Introduction à la théorie du habar chez Ǧāḥiẓ: Définition et constitution," in *Studia islamica,* **53** (1981); Georges Vajda, "La connaissance naturelle de Dieu selon al-Ǧāḥiẓ critiquée par les Muᶜtazilites," in *Studia islamica,* **24** (1966); A. H. Mathias Zahniser, "Insights from the ᶜUthmāniyya of al-Jāḥiẓ into the Religious Policy of al-Maᵓmūn," in *Muslim World,* **69** (1979), and "Source Criticism in the ᶜUthmāniyya of al-Jāḥiẓ," in *Muslim World,* **70** (1980).

LAWRENCE I. CONRAD

[See also **Arabic Literature, Prose.**]

JAIL DELIVERY. The delivery of a jail refers to the trying of the accused felons within it. Before 1150, jail delivery may have been carried out by sheriffs or local justices, although there were always some prisoners who were sent to Westminster for trial before the king's justices, a practice that was both dangerous and expensive.

But the innovative work of Henry II (1154–1189) marks the true beginning of jail delivery. In the wake of the tough law-and-order measures instituted in the Assize of Clarendon (1166) and made tougher still in the Assize of Northampton (1176), the number of jails in England and the number of prisoners held in them greatly increased. With the establishment of the general eyre in the 1170's, jail delivery was one of the tasks given to its justices. Local officials—the sheriff, coroners, and bailiffs—would have everything in readiness when the justices arrived. The prisoners, or the accused who had been released on bail, were produced to be tried before the justices and a jury of people living in the neighborhood where the crime was committed. (The use of juries in criminal cases began in the thirteenth century.) If found guilty, the felon could expect swift execution. But as the business of the eyre increased, the overburdened justices moved more slowly and came less frequently. By the thirteenth century, new

measures were thus needed to clear the jails of their populations.

The system that obtained for most of the thirteenth century emerged in the 1230's. The crown provided for regular delivery of jails by commissions usually consisting of four county knights along with two royal justices. They might be charged with the delivery of a limited group of jails or even of all jails in the county. Sometimes the crown added to this charge the authority to adjudge land disputes, which were heard according to procedures known as assizes. Thus civil jurisdiction was linked with the criminal jurisdiction of jail delivery, though the powers were conferred by separate commissions. Sometimes one of the four commissioners was a professional justice with local connections; often a justice was appointed with power to add local associates. But despite all the variations, the outstanding features of the thirteenth-century system of jail delivery were a separate commission issued for each jail and a decidedly nonprofessional element in the use of local knights as judges.

Over the next four decades, from about 1292 to 1330, a new system of jail delivery took shape. In 1292/1293, Edward I replaced the ad hoc panels of local knights with pairs of permanent jail delivery commissioners who might be royal servants or locals. In 1299 he linked their work with the hearing of assizes by sending them to the jails according to a circuit pattern based on that established for assize justices in 1293. After taking the assizes, the justices remained together to deliver all the jails on their circuit. The new system had been in effect for only a short time when Edward II (1307–1327) reversed it and returned in large measure to delivery by local knights, thereby linking jail delivery to the peace commissions usually held by the gentry. He thus placed routine administration of criminal justice entirely in the hands of local knights. Edward III (1327–1377) returned to the system of his grandfather, Edward I. By 1330 jail delivery circuits had been reestablished and combined with assize circuits. Again, one set of justices held the assize and delivered the jails along their circuit. The judges who rode these circuits were usually not local knights but men from the central courts, justices and serjeants-at-law. Three times a year in theory—twice annually in practice—some of the best-qualified personnel from the central courts came out to the counties to do this work.

A broad account of the main stages in the history

of jail delivery, however, omits the numerous exceptions and additions to the basic structure. Many major towns were county seats where jail delivery could take place; urban concern over town rights thus would not be an issue, since townsmen would not have to be delivered outside their walls. Londoners usually were delivered at the Tower or at Newgate Prison. In the reign of Edward I, separate London commissioners, often mayors, former mayors, or former sheriffs, were appointed. Palatinates were allowed to make their own arrangements. During the thirteenth and fourteenth centuries some prisoners managed to have special commissions issued for justices to hear their charges against them alone; these commissions were very similar to special commissions of oyer and terminer. For the first half of the fourteenth century, periodic general commissions of oyer and terminer, known as trailbastons, gave justices powers to deliver jails, among much other work. From 1318 and for most of the rest of the fourteenth century, King's Bench was often itinerant and did some jail delivery on its tours. By the end of the fourteenth century, when assize and jail delivery powers were combined, the same justices often sat on commissions of the peace as well. Justices of the peace, moreover, had commissions of oyer and terminer. Thus the powers of a late-medieval justice arriving at a local jail might include jail delivery, assize, peace commissions, or even oyer and terminer.

BIBLIOGRAPHY

Marguerite Gollancz, "The System of Gaol Delivery as Illustrated in the Extant Gaol Delivery Rolls of the Fifteenth Century" (M.A. thesis, Univ. of London, 1936); Barbara A. Hanawalt, ed., *Crime in East Anglia in the Fourteenth Century: Norfolk Gaol Delivery Rolls, 1307–1316* (1976); Alan Harding, *The Law Courts of Medieval England* (1973); Roy F. Hunnisett, *The Medieval Coroner* (1961); Cecil A. F. Meekings, "List to Gaol Delivery Rolls and Files" (in Public Record Office, London); Ralph B. Pugh, *Itinerant Justices in English History* (1967), and *Imprisonment in Medieval England* (1968).

RICHARD W. KAEUPER

[See also **England; Jury; Justices, Itinerant; Justices of the King's Bench; Justices of the Peace; Law, English Common; Oyer and Terminer, Trailbaston.**]

JAIME BAÇÓ. See **Baçó, Jaime.**

JAIME FERRER THE ELDER. See **Ferrer the Elder, Jaime.**

JAIME SERRA. See **Serra, Pedro and Jaime.**

JALĀL AL-DĪN. See **Rūmī.**

JAMB, the vertical side of an opening in a wall, usually an archway, a doorway, or a window. The reveal is the side of an opening between a frame and the outer surface of a wall. In the Middle Ages, the jamb was often enriched with columns or colonnettes and, in the Gothic period, with statues. Jambs that support an arch are sometimes called *pieds-droits.*

GREGORY WHITTINGTON

JAMES OF VITERBO (*ca.* 1255–1308), the son of a prominent local family, the Capocci, in Viterbo, he became a member of the Order of Augustinian Hermits and studied at Paris in the 1270's and early 1280's. He had clearly shown ability as a young scholar and was sent back to Paris for theological studies. He succeeded the famous Egidius Colonna (also known as Aegidius Romanus), head of the Augustinians, as the master who was to represent that order in the teaching of theology at Paris. After seven years at the University of Paris (1293–1300), James returned to Naples to take charge of the rather inchoate theological faculty there. He enjoyed the favor of both the king of Naples and Pope Boniface VIII, and he defended the latter in his quarrel with Philip IV the Fair. He became archbishop of Benevento in September 1302, and several months later was appointed archbishop of Naples. James was beatified in 1914.

James of Viterbo wrote his famous treatise, *De regimine christiano,* late in 1301 or early 1302 before he became archbishop of Benevento. It was not, perhaps, the first treatise on the church as a political institution (as Arquillière suggested), but it was certainly one of the first to deal with a problem raised by many other thirteenth-century scholars, including Thomas Aquinas: if kingship, government, and law are natural forms of human behavior, and thus the result of God's will, and if even among the heathen there can be legitimate political authority, then how can the church claim superior authority? How can popes and bishops judge lay rulers? Or, to put the question another way, if legitimate authority was based on the consent, actual or implied, of the people (and this idea was also widely accepted by James' contemporaries), then how can the clergy interfere with what is manifestly God's will? James would answer that papal (and other ecclesiastical) power came directly from Christ as king, while secular powers came only from human nature and thus only indirectly from God. In the end, however, he admitted that while the church possessed temporal jurisdiction it would not exercise it "regularly and frequently," but should act only in case of necessity. Remembering that these words were written just as the great quarrel between Boniface VIII and Philip IV the Fair was beginning, this was good advice.

BIBLIOGRAPHY

Henri Xavier Arquillière, ed., *Le plus ancien traité de l'église: Jacques de Viterbe, De regimine christiano* (1926); Robert W. Carlyle and Alexander J. Carlyle, *A History of Medieval Political Theory in the West*, V (1926), 409–417; Michael Wilks, *The Problem of Sovereignty in the Later Middle Ages* (1963).

JOSEPH R. STRAYER

[See also **Boniface VIII, Pope; Philip IV the Fair; Political Theory, Western European.**]

JAMES THE CONQUEROR. See **Aragon, Crown of (1137–1479).**

JAMES THE MONK (*fl.* twelfth century?), called Kokkinobaphos after a Byzantine monastery of unknown location, is the author of six homilies on the Virgin and a set of unpublished letters (Paris, Bibliothèque Nationale, fonds grec, MS 3039) addressed to Irene Komnena, wife of Manuel I's brother Andronikos. Probably a member of the literary circle of the Komnenian court, which included Theodore

Prodromos, James is principally remembered because his writings were produced in deluxe illustrated editions.

BIBLIOGRAPHY

Aleksandr Ivanovich Kirpichnikov, "Perepiska monaxa Iakova s imperatricei," in *Letopis Istoriko-filologicheskago obshchestva pri imperatorskom novorossiiskom universitet,* 2 (1892); Karl Krumbacher, *Geschichte der byzantinischen Literatur,* 2 vols. (1897, and ed. 1970), 172; Henri Auguste Omont, *Miniatures des homélies sur la Vierge du moine Jacques* (1927); Cosimo Stornajolo, *Miniature delle omilie di Giacomo monaco e dell'Evangeliario greco urbinate* (1910).

JEFFREY C. ANDERSON

JANISSARY (Turkish: *yeni čeri,* literally, new troops), the salaried standing infantry of the Ottoman Empire. The first Janissary troops are believed to have been formed early in the reign of Sultan Murad I (1360–1389); the force was dissolved by Sultan Mahmud II in 1826.

Technically the sultan's slaves, they were initially recruited from his legal share (one-fifth) of war booty. Soon, however, a special recruitment called *devshirme* became the main source: forcible induction of the sultan's Christian subjects, mainly in the Balkans, where the greater part of the non-Muslim (*dhimmī*) population lived. The earliest known reference to this system of recruitment dates from 1395. The *devshirme* recruitment followed a fixed pattern and was supervised by a Janissary officer. Those chosen were boys and youths usually between the ages of eight and twenty; upon arrival at their destination—after 1453, usually İstanbul—they were reexamined and most were sent on to Anatolia to work among Turks in order to learn Turkish and Turkish ways; at the end of this period—some seven years—they returned to İstanbul and entered the ranks of *ajemi oghlans* (novice youths). After several years of training and instruction (which included the tenets of Islam), they entered the ranks of the Janissaries proper.

The chief reason for the creation and maintenance of the Janissary corps was the sultan's desire to possess a privileged, totally loyal military force, separated both from his Muslim subjects because of their non-Muslim birth, and from the Christian ones because of their conversion to Islam. The fact that they were not allowed to marry while in service and were in a permanent slave-master relationship to him further reinforced their isolation from society and their dependence on him. As converts to Islam, the Janissaries were among the foremost among the Ottoman *gazīs*, or warriors for the faith. In this respect they may have been affected by the legacy of such pre- and early-Ottoman Anatolian Muslim brotherhoods as the *ahīs* (*akhīs*), a legacy that may also have led to their eventual link with the Bektashi order of dervishes.

During the centuries of Ottoman expansion, the Janissaries were the elite troops; their effectiveness as the earliest well-trained, well-disciplined standing infantry of the Middle Ages contributed to the success of the Ottoman conquests in Europe and the Near East. Guarding the sultan in battle and at home was their concomitant duty; policing Istanbul was also within their purview. In the final centuries of its existence, however, the Janissary corps degenerated and became a social and financial burden on the Ottoman state.

BIBLIOGRAPHY

Hamilton A. R. Gibb and Harold Bowen, *Islamic Society and the West*, I.1 (1950), 56–66, 314–326; Halil Inalcik, *The Ottoman Empire: The Classical Age 1300–1600* (1973); Mehmet Zeki Pakalin, *Osmanli tarih deyimleri ve terimleri sözlüğü*, III (1972), 617–631; Stanford J. Shaw, *History of the Ottoman Empire and Modern Turkey*, I (1976), 122–125; Ismail Haki Uzuncarsili, *Kapikulu Ocaklari*, 2 vols. (1943–1944).

SVAT SOUCEK

[See also **Ottomans; Slavery, Islamic World; Warfare, Islamic**.]

JÁNOS HUNYADI. See Hunyadi, János.

JARCHA. See **Kharja**.

JARĪR (*d.* 728/729 or a little later), son of ʿAṭiyya ibn al-Khaṭafā ibn Badr, was one of the most illustrious medieval Arab satirists. He and two other great Umayyad poets, al-Farazdaq (*d.* 732) and al-Akhṭal (*d.* 708), constituted a distinguished trio who wrote in all poetic genres, especially satire, and excelled in each. Jarīr belonged to the Banū Kulayb clan, a branch of the Tamīm tribe that flourished in

the eastern part of central and northern Arabia. Of delicate constitution, short, and ugly, he married several women and had eight sons and two daughters, among whom were three minor poets. Perhaps because of his small physique, Jarīr had an indomitable passion for vituperation, a contentious temperament, and a sharp, cruel tongue. He initially tested his satirical mettle on poets of lesser magnitude but in 683/684 began his famous forty-year verbal dispute with al-Farazdaq, himself a great satirist. A minor intertribal quarrel prompted Jarīr to satirize al-Farazdaq, and they carried on a match for seven years before Jarīr traveled to Iraq to meet him. The subsequent hostile contact, which lasted until al-Farazdaq's death, dominated Jarīr's poetic career, and his satirical poetry assumed an even more venomous edge. Meanwhile, al-Akhṭal, who resided in northern Arabia, heard of this literary battle and the controversy over it, and dispatched his son Mālik to witness it and report to him. Mālik informed his father that he had found Jarīr "scooping [poetry] out of the sea while al-Farazdaq hewed [it] out of rock," meaning that Jarīr was a "natural" poet, whereas al-Farazdaq was "artificial," straining words and meanings. Al-Akhṭal then declared the one who "scoops out of the sea" to be the better poet. Ultimately he rescinded his judgment and sided, like most poets of the time, with al-Farazdaq. This brought al-Akhṭal into a scolding match with Jarīr, a dispute that lasted some nineteen years, during which al-Akhṭal satirized Jarīr with eleven poems and Jarīr responded with sixteen. However, the satires exchanged by Jarīr and al-Farazdaq, known as *al-naqāʾiḍ* (interchange of satires, polemic poems, flytings), became the most famous of their kind in Arabic poetry and were compiled in a separate collection of poetry (*dīwān*).

Lampoons, however, were not Jarīr's sole stock in trade; he was also a professional encomiast, an occasional poet who was ready to extol or revile whoever enjoyed or lost his favor. He was the court poet of al-Ḥajjāj (*d.* 714), the fearsome governor of Iraq, who eventually forwarded Jarīr to ʿAbd al-Malik (*r.* 685–705). ʿAbd al-Malik, who favored his great court poet al-Akhṭal—also Jarīr's rival—at first repulsed Jarīr but later received him graciously. Jarīr praised ʿAbd al-Malik with a magnificent poem that included one of the greatest panegyric lines ever composed:

Are not ye the best of those who on camel ride,
　　More open-handed than all in the world beside?

Of all the later caliphs whom he praised Jarīr was on good terms only with ᶜUmar II (717–720), with whom he shared piety, modesty, and religious fervor. In his old age Jarīr retired to his birthplace, Uthayfīya, where he died only a few months after the death of al-Farazdaq (whom he elegized in a fine poem).

The full thrust of Jarīr's poetry is perhaps best understood in the *naqāᵓiḍ* between him and al-Farazdaq. The themes that were prevalent in these masterful poems (113 in all) were fundamentally bedouin in character, and can be broadly classified in two major categories: boasting and taunting. Each poet would boast about the victories in battle of his own tribe and ridicule the other's losses. Exposing the faults and vices of each other and derisive abuse of the women of each other's tribe were abundant and virulent.

Jarīr was quite unlike al-Farazdaq, who was "dissolute, reckless and thoroughly undisciplined" (R. A. Nicholson). An eminent example of his chastity was the following line, for which he was castigated by Sukayna bint al-Ḥusayn (the great-granddaughter of the prophet Muḥammad):

> The heart-huntress came to visit you at night:
> This is no time for visiting;
> Please, depart in peace!

Sukayna exclaimed: "Shame on you! you called her a heart-huntress, but when she came to visit you, you rejected her. Couldn't you have said:

> "The heart-huntress came to visit you at night:
> You're welcome! could I but sacrifice myself for you!
> Please enter in peace."

Jarīr also excelled in love poetry, and he often started his *naqāᵓiḍ* with the conventional amatory prelude. His love poetry was set to music and sung by famous singers of the time. Some of Jarīr's lines in the genres of panegyric (line quoted above), *ghazal* (love poetry), and satire became proverbial and are considered as among the greatest of their kind. The two following lines are an example of his brilliant *ghazal*:

> Eyes that are fair and black have slain us
> And nay! have not revived the dead among us.
> They fell a man in love and leave him motionless,
> While they truly are the weakest of God's creatures.

His two most famous satirical lines, in which he lampooned both al-Farazdaq and al-Rāᶜī (another of more than forty poets that he summarily dealt with) are the following:

> Cast down thine eyes for shame! for thou art of Numayr—no peer of Kaᶜb nor yet Kilāb.
>
> . . . .
>
> Indeed, if Banū Tamīm became angry at you,
> You should consider all mankind angry too.

Jarīr was very prolific, and his poetry displayed a vast and impressive knowledge of various disciplines. Al-Farazdaq once said of Jarīr and himself: "How wanting is he, with all his chastity, of the firmness of my poetry; and how much I lack, with all my libertinage, the delicacy of his." As a "natural" poet Jarīr demonstrates a style characterized by limpidity, musicality, and a kind of raw elegance, especially in his love poetry and elegies. Despite occasional uncouthness and obscurity in his satires and panegyrics, his meanings were facile, his diction fluent, and his imagery concrete and accessible.

BIBLIOGRAPHY

Sources. There are two modern editions of the *dīwān:* one by Dār Ṣadir-Dar Bayrūt (1964); and a more scholarly one by Nuᶜmān M. Amīn Ṭaha, 2 vols. (1969–1971). The *naqāᵓid* were edited by Anthony Ashley Bevan as *The Nakāᵓid of Jarīr and al-Farazdak*, 3 vols. (1905–1912, repr. 1964).

Studies. Régis Blachère, *Histoire de la littérature arabe* (1952, repr. 1980); *Encyclopaedia of Islam*, both editions; Hamilton A. R. Gibb, *Arabic Literature*, 2nd ed. (1963), 42–43; Ibn al-Nadīm, *al-Fihrist*, Bayard Dodge, ed. and trans. (1970), 348–349; Reynold A. Nicholson, *A Literary History of the Arabs* (1907, repr. 1969), 238, 239, 240, 242, 244–246.

MANSOUR J. AJAMI

[See also **Akhṭal, al-; Arabic Poetry; Farazdaq, al-; Umayyads.**]

JARLMANNS SAGA OK HERMANNS. Also referred to as *Hermanns saga ok Jarlmanns*, this chivalric tale is extant in two main redactions, one found in two vellum manuscripts from the last quarter of the fifteenth century and the first part of the sixteenth century (edited by Agnete Loth) and the other preserved in one sixteenth-century vellum manuscript (edited by Hugo Rydberg and Bjarni Vilhjálmsson). Some forty-nine paper manuscripts of both redactions are known. The original version is probably not older than the first part of the fifteenth century.

The author attributes the work to Master Virgilius, who allegedly found it on the stone wall in the town of Licibon in France and included it in his book called *Saxafræði*. The story concerns the quest of an earl's son, Jarlmann, for the hand of Ríkilát on behalf of his sworn brother, King Hermann. By placing a magic ring on her finger and holding the ring until it becomes warm, Jarlmann causes the proud Ríkilát, skilled in the art of medicine, to fall in love with Hermann. While Jarlmann defends her against the army of an unwanted suitor, Ermanus, Hermann similarly repulses the attack of Romanus, an unwelcome suitor for the hand of Hermann's sister, Herborg. After Jarlmann returns to Hermann's court with Ríkilát, the king becomes so jealous of Jarlmann that the latter leaves. Shortly thereafter twelve cowled masons steal Ríkilát. Hermann sends for Jarlmann, asking him for help, and Jarlmann goes to the court of King Rudent, where he observes an incredible dance of supernatural creatures while airborne ships and poison-spewing dragons engage in battle amid earthquakes and landslides. Ríkilát, confined to a glass hall until her marriage to Rudent, is finally rescued by Jarlmann, who has feigned infatuation with Rudent's hideous sister, and by Hermann, who has been called to the rescue.

Analogues to *Konráðs saga, Karlamagnús saga, Mágus saga jarls, Klári saga,* and *Mírmanns saga* have been pointed out. Only one *rímur* version of the material is extant, composed in twelve stanzaic divisions and dating from before 1600.

BIBLIOGRAPHY

Finnur Jónsson, *Den oldnorske og oldislandske litteraturs historie,* 2nd ed., III (1924), 105–106; Agnete Loth, ed., *Late Medieval Icelandic Romances,* III (1963); Jón Þorkelsson, *Om digtningen på Island i det 15. og 16. århundrede* (1888), 167–168; Björn K. Þórólfsson, *Rímur fyrir 1600* (1934), 452–453; Bjarni Vilhjálmsson, ed., *Riddarasögur,* 6 vols. (1961), VI, 171–235.

PETER JORGENSEN

[See also **Karlamagnús Saga; Klári Saga; Konráðs Saga Keisarasonar; Mágus Saga Jarls; Mírmanns Saga; Riddarasögur.**]

JAUFRÉ RUDEL (*fl.* mid twelfth century), a Provençal troubadour, poet, and composer. Little is known about his life. A *vida* of doubtful accuracy calls him "prince of Blaja" (in southern France) and may connect him with a family of that name holding land on the Gironde near Bordeaux. A reference to him in a poem by his colleague Marcabru indicates that Rudel participated in the Second Crusade in 1147 and died abroad.

Seven surviving poems are ascribed to him, four of which have extant music. The best known of these is "Lanquan li jorn son lonc en mai." Jaufré Rudel is associated particularly with the concept of *amor de lonh,* the idealized distant love of a troubadour for a lady he never sees.

BIBLIOGRAPHY

Alfred Jeanroy, ed., *Les chansons de Jaufré Rudel,* 2nd ed. (1924); Rupert T. Pickens, ed., *The Songs of Jaufré Rudel* (1978).

MARCIA J. EPSTEIN

[See also **Marcabru; Troubadour, Trouvère, Trovador.**]

JEAN, DUKE OF BERRY (1340–1416), a vain and unscrupulous maneuverer during the political strife of early-fifteenth-century France. He is best remembered for his patronage of the arts, reflected in his magnificently decorated châteaus and his acquisition of the century's most beautiful manuscripts, of which the most celebrated is *Les très riches heures du duc de Berry* (Chantilly, Musée Condé), illuminated by the Limbourg brothers. Like other works produced under the duke's auspices, this model of elegance reflected many of the artistic tendencies of the time in its fusion of Flemish realism, of the refined Parisian style, and of Italian panel-painting techniques.

BIBLIOGRAPHY

Françoise Lehoux, *Jean de France, duc de Berri,* 4 vols. in 3 (1966–1968); Millard Meiss, *French Painting in the Time of Jean de Berry: The Late Fourteenth Century and the Patronage of the Duke* (1967); Jean Porcher, *Les très riches heures du duc de Berry* (ca. 1950).

CYNTHIA J. BROWN

[See also **Gothic Art: Painting; Jacquemart de Hesdin; Limbourg Brothers.**]

JEAN BOUCICAUT (*ca.* 1365–1421). Jean II le Meingre, called Boucicaut, swashbuckling *maréchal de France* (1391), fought in the Crusade of Nicopolis

(1396) and was captured by the Turks. Ransomed, he brought some military aid to the Byzantine emperor Manuel II (1399). He served an energetic term as French governor of Genoa (1401–1409). Later a provincial governor in France, he fought at Agincourt (1415) and died in English custody. He was also a poet, and as patron he commissioned the famous illuminated book of hours that bears his name (Paris, Musée Jacquemart-André, MS 27).

BIBLIOGRAPHY

Joseph M. A. Delaville le Roux, *La France en Orient au quatorzième siècle: Expédition du maréchal Boucicaut* (1885).

JOHN W. BARKER

[See also **Book of Hours; Crusades of the Later Middle Ages; France.**]

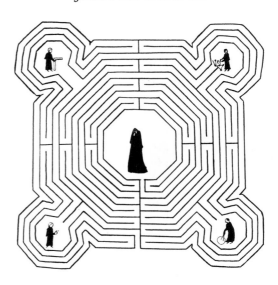

Jean d'Orbais (lower right). Rheims Cathedral, sketch of the nave-floor labyrinth by Jacques Cellier, late 16th century. FROM HANS REINHARDT, LA CATHEDRALE DE RHEIMS

JEAN (JEHAN) D'ANDELI (*fl.* 1200), first architect of the nave of the Gothic cathedral of Rouen after a fire destroyed much of the Romanesque cathedral on Easter Sunday, 1200. D'Andeli planned a four-story elevation with galleries, but he seems to have been quickly replaced by a certain Master Enguerrand, who modified the scheme and eliminated the galleries. Nothing else is known of Jean d'Andeli's career.

BIBLIOGRAPHY

Charles de Beaurepaire, "Notes sur les architectes de Rouen," in *Bulletin de la société des amis des monuments rouennais,* (1901); Armand Loisel, *La cathédrale de Rouen* (*ca.* 1910), 14–15; Henri Stein, *Les architectes des cathédrales gothiques* (1909), 61.

CARL F. BARNES, JR.

[See also **Gothic Architecture.**]

JEAN D'ORBAIS (*fl.* 1210–1220), depicted as one of the architects of Rheims cathedral in its (now-destroyed) nave-floor labyrinth. He may have been the designer of the choir. According to one seventeenth-century reading of the inscription of the maze, Jean "began the choir of the church" ("encommencea la coiffe de l'église"); and in a sixteenth-century sketch of the labyrinth by Jacques Cellier, Jean is shown drawing an apparent hemicycle plan. If Jean was the first architect of the cathedral, his stylistic vocabulary was formed by a sophisticated combination of elements drawn from Chartres, Sens, and earlier

Gothic buildings in Rheims. Despite his surname, Jean probably was not involved in the construction of the Abbey of Orbais.

BIBLIOGRAPHY

Robert Branner "Jean d'Orbais and the Cathedral of Reims," in *Art Bulletin,* **43** (1961), and "The Labyrinth of Reims Cathedral," in *Journal of the Society of Architectural Historians,* **21** (1962); Jean-Pierre Ravaux, "Les campagnes de construction de Reims," in *Bulletin monumental,* **135** (1977).

MICHAEL T. DAVIS

[See also **Rheims Cathedral.**]

JEAN DE BEAUCE (*d.* 28 December 1529), also known as Je(h)an Texier, was an architect of a number of works in the Flamboyant style at the Cathedral of Chartres. These include the steeple of the north tower of the west facade, 1507–1513; the choir screen, begun 1514; the organ loft, begun 1516 but abandoned in 1519; and the Pavillon de l'Horloge, 1520. He maintained a large workshop of glass masters and artisans.

BIBLIOGRAPHY

Marcel Aubert, *La cathédrale de Chartres* (1952), 11–12; Henri Stein, *Les architectes des cathédrales gothiques* (1909), 60.

CARL F. BARNES, JR.

[See also **Chartres Cathedral; Gothic, Flamboyant.**]

Choir screen by Jean de Beauce for Chartres Cathedral. Begun 1514. PHOTO: BERT BAKKER BV, AMSTERDAM

JEAN DE BRIENNE (*ca.* 1150–March 1237). Born to a family of the minor nobility in France, Jean de Brienne was a noted warrior and the husband of the heiress to the Kingdom of Jerusalem. He led the Fifth Crusade until he was ousted from command by his son-in-law Frederick II, the titular heir to Jerusalem, who crowned himself king in 1228. He then made an alliance with Pope Gregory IX against Frederick. In 1229 he was elected regent of the Latin Kingdom of Constantinople, even though he was at that time eighty years old, and two years later became coemperor with Baldwin II, who was still a child. In 1235 Jean defended Constantinople against the Laskarids of Nicaea and their Bulgarian allies, who were attempting to restore Byzantine rule. By the time Jean died, the Latin Kingdom consisted largely of the city of Constantinople and was in an extremely precarious state.

BIBLIOGRAPHY

D. M. Nicol, "The Fourth Crusade and the Greek and Latin Empires, 1204–61," in *Cambridge Medieval History,* IV, pt. 1 (1966); George Ostrogorsky, *History of the Byzantine State,* Joan Hussey, trans. (1956, rev. ed. 1969).

LINDA C. ROSE

[See also **Crusades and Crusader States: 1212 to 1272; Latin Empire of Constantinople.**]

JEAN (JEHAN) DE CHELLES, architect of the transept terminals (based mainly on those of St. Denis) and of seven choir chapels at Notre Dame in Paris, from about 1245 to about 1265. He died before the terminal of the south arm was completed and was honored by his successor, Pierre of Montreuil, in an inscription on its exterior dado stating that work was begun on 12 February 1258. No other works can be assigned to him.

BIBLIOGRAPHY

Marcel Aubert, *Notre-Dame de Paris* (1928), esp. 138, 149–154; Robert Branner, *St. Louis and the Court Style in Gothic Architecture* (1965), esp. 76–80.

CARL F. BARNES, JR.

[See also **Notre Dame de Paris, Cathedral of; Pierre of Montreuil.**]

JEAN DE LA LOUPE. See Loup, Jean.

Marie de France. Marble bust for St. Denis by Jean de Liège, *ca.* 1380. NEW YORK, METROPOLITAN MUSEUM OF ART, GIFT OF GEORGE BLUMENTHAL, 1941 (41.100.132)

JEAN DE LIÈGE (*d.* 1381/1382), of south Netherlandish origin, was an important sculptor of the French court from 1357 until his death. A student of and assistant to the Netherlandish sculptor Jean Pépin de Huy (active first half of the fourteenth century in Burgundy and Paris), he did his mature work for Charles V (*r.* 1356–1380). Jean's most important surviving works include effigies of Charles IV le Bel (*d.* 1328) and Jeanne d'Evreux (*d.* 1371) for Maubuisson Abbey (1372, now in the Louvre); a bust of Marie de France for St. Denis (*ca.* 1380, now in the Metropolitan Museum, New York); and the tomb of Philippa of Hainault in Westminster Abbey (1367).

While eschewing idealism, Jean's style has greater charm than that of the more rigorously realistic André Beauneveu (1360–1403), court sculptor for Jean, duke of Berry.

BIBLIOGRAPHY

Marcel Aubert, *La sculpture française au moyen âge* (1946); Lawrence Stone, *Sculpture in Britain: The Middle Ages* (1972).

BARRIE SINGLETON

[See also **Beauneveu, André; Charles V of France; Gothic Art: Sculpture; Gothic, International Style.**]

JEAN DE MEUN (Meung), surnamed Chopinel or Clopinel (1240/1260–1305), was born in the village of Meung-sur-Loire, southwest of Orléans. He attended the University of Paris and in contemporary documents is accorded the title "master." Few details of his life are known, but in the last years before his death he lived in the Faubourg St. Jacques, near the university.

It is clear from his writing that Jean was a well-read intellectual and a scholastic poet. He translated the *Military Art* of Vegetius, a fourth-century Latin writer, for Jean de Brienne, count of Eu (1284); Boethius' *Consolation of Philosophy* in verse and prose, dedicated to Philip IV the Fair; the *Life and Letters of Peter Abelard and Heloise;* the *Spiritual Friendship* of Ailred of Rievaulx (now lost); and Gerald of Wales's *Wonders of Ireland* (now lost). His own writings include his *Testament* (*ca.* 1296), his *Codicil,* and the bulk (nearly 18,000 lines) of the famous and influential *Romance of the Rose* (1270–1280).

In his works, Jean is violently antimendicant; in the *Romance* he mentions with great sympathy William of St. Amour, a secular master who wrote an attack on the mendicants. His antifeminism, so evident to some readers, is explained by others as a counter-balance to the unrealistic glorification of women in the works of such "courtly love" poets as Guillaume de Lorris, who wrote the opening of the *Romance.* Jean's language is never courtly but rather satirical, intellectual, scholastic, rational, and deeply Christian. At the same time Jean is revealed as a man imbued with a genuine sense of humor and a broad humanity.

BIBLIOGRAPHY

Sources. "Li testament de maistre Jehan de Meung" and "Le codicile de maistre Jehan de Meung," in *Le roman de la rose,* M. Méon, ed., IV (1814); *L'art de chevalerie, traduction du De re militari de Végèce,* Ulysse Robert, ed. (1897); *Traduction de la première épître de Pierre Abélard,* Charlotte Charrier, ed. (1934)—analysis of the remainder is in a University of Washington dissertation by Elizabeth Schultz summarized in *Dissertation Abstracts International,* **31** (1970), 767-A; "Boethius' 'De consolatione,' " Venceslas L. Dedeck-Héry, ed., in *Mediaeval Studies,* **14** (1952); *Le roman de la rose,* Félix Lecoy, ed., 3 vols. (1965–1970), also in English, Charles Dahlberg, trans. (1971).

Studies. Norman Cohn, *The World-view of a Thirteenth-century Parisian Intellectual: Jean de Meung and the Romance of the Rose* (1961); Lionel J. Friedman, " 'Jean de Meung,' Antifeminism, and 'Bourgeois Realism,' " in *Modern Philology,* **57** (1959); Ernest Langlois, "La tra-

duction de Boèce par Jean de Meun," in *Romania,* **42** (1913); Lucie Polak, "Plato, Nature, and Jean de Meun," in *Reading Medieval Studies,* **3** (1977).

MARY-JO ARN

[See also **Antifeminism; French Literature; Guillaume de Lorris; Romance of the Rose.**]

JEAN DE PARIS. See John of Paris.

JEAN DE RAVI (Ravy) served as master mason and sculptor at Notre Dame, Paris, between about 1318 and 1344. Continuing the work of his predecessor, Pierre de Chelles, Jean finished construction of the chapels and the enlargement of the tribune windows of the choir, as well as the rebuilding of the flying buttresses of the apse, in a taut, linear style that was a refined version of the Rayonnant vocabulary of the transept facades. During his tenure in office, the south side of the choir *clôture* sculpture was completed (*ca.* 1325–1335) and, possibly, its eastern extension was begun.

BIBLIOGRAPHY

Marcel Aubert, "Les architectes de Notre-Dame de Paris," in *Bulletin monumental,* **72** (1908), and *Notre-Dame de Paris: Sa place dans l'histoire de l'architecture du XIIe au XIVe siècle* (1920, 2nd ed. 1929), 148; Dorothy Gillerman, *The Clôture of Notre-Dame and Its Role in the Fourteenth-century Choir Program* (1977), 104–152.

MICHAEL T. DAVIS

[**Notre Dame de Paris, Cathedral of.**]

JEAN DE THUIM. Translator of the verse *Roumanz de Julius Cesar* and the prose *Hystore de Julius Cesar,* Jean bragged that in a mere four months he had adapted Lucan's *Pharsalia* and Caesar's *Commentaries* into Old French. Though most scholars, following Settegast, have attributed the verse translation to Jacot de Forest, Paul Hess argues convincingly that Jean wrote both texts. Closer adherence to the Latin sources hints, further, that the verse preceded the prose. Jean embroidered on his sources, added details to descriptions, and inserted a treatise on love reminiscent of Arthurian prose romances. He ended his story at Caesar's triumphant return to

Rome, with no glimpse of imminent treachery. Marilyn Bendena's dissertation may satisfy Gaston Paris's wish for a thorough study of Jean's translating techniques.

BIBLIOGRAPHY

Marilyn Bendena, *The Translations of Lucan and Their Influence on French Medieval Literature, Together with an Edition of the "Roumans de Jules Cesar" by Jacos de Forest* (diss., Wayne State Univ., 1976); Paul Hess, *Li Romaunz de Julius Cesar: Ein Beitrag zur Cäsargeschichte im Mittelalter* (1956), contains a useful bibliography; Franz Settegast, ed., *Li Hystore de Julius Cesar: Eine altfranzösische Erzählung in Prosa von Jehan de Tuim* (1881). See the review by Gaston Paris in *Romania*, 12 (1883).

JOHN L. GRIGSBY

[Translation and Translators, Western European.]

JEAN DES CHAMPS (*fl.* thirteenth century), French master mason who was master of the choir of Clermont-Ferrand Cathedral, begun in 1248 or, some say, even as late as 1262. He is associated with Clermont-Ferrand through two late transcriptions of the inscription on his tomb (destroyed about 1400), which had been in that cathedral. A Jean des Champs associated with Narbonne Cathedral in a document of 28 November 1286 may or may not be the Jean des Champs from Clermont. The many attributions traditionally made to Jean des Champs (cathedrals of Limoges, Rodez, and Toulouse, and other churches) are undocumented and untenable. Jean des Champs was alive in 1287 and may have died shortly thereafter.

BIBLIOGRAPHY

Carl F. Barnes, Jr., "Jean des Champs," in *Macmillan Encyclopedia of Architects*, II (1982); Michael T. Davis, "The Choir of the Cathedral of Clermont-Ferrand: The Beginning of Construction and the Work of Jean Deschamps," in *Journal of the Society of Architectural Historians*, 40 (1981).

CARL F. BARNES, JR.

[See also **Gothic Architecture**.]

JEAN HAY. See **Moulins, Master of.**

JEAN LEMAIRE DE BELGES (*ca.* 1473–*ca.* 1525). Considered the most important member of the *rhétoriqueur* tradition in France, Jean Lemaire de Belges was a humanist and a poet of great renown in the reign of Louis XII. Born in the town of Belges (Bavai) in northern France, he was brought up in Valenciennes by his uncle or godfather, Jean Molinet, the famous chronicler of the house of Burgundy, who initiated him into the literary games of the *grande rhétorique*. After receiving the lower ecclesiastical orders, Jean moved to Paris and registered at the Faculty of Arts. In 1498, at the age of twenty-five, he was employed as *clerc de finances* by the Bourbon court at Villefranche-sur-Saône. Soon Guillaume Cretin, a poet of some distinction, encouraged him to start a literary career and defend the merits of the French language. When Duke Pierre II died in October 1503, Jean wrote an allegorical poem, *Le temple d'honneur et de vertus,* which he dedicated to his new patron, Louis of Luxemburg, count of Ligny. This was followed by another dirge (*déploration*), *La plainte du désiré,* composed after Louis's death in December 1503, in which Paincture and Rhétoricque join in expressing Nature's grief in a very elaborate high style.

Hoping to attract her attention, Lemaire dedicated his new work to Queen Anne of Brittany; when he failed, he turned to Anne's rival, Margaret of Austria (1480–1530), daughter of Emperor Maximilian I and Mary of Burgundy. Margaret loved to be entertained by poets, painters, and musicians, and her favorite dwelling was in Pont d'Ain, near Lyons, the intellectual capital of France. Jean became her poet in residence and soon had the opportunity to eulogize his patroness when Margaret's second husband, Philibert, duke of Savoy, died in 1504, at the age of twenty-five. *La couronne Margaritique,* a vast allegorical composition in *prosimetrum,* was meant to praise Margaret's fortitude in the face of adversity (her famous motto, "Fortune infortune fort une," Fate greatly torments one lady, dates from that time). In a much lighter style Jean wrote two delightful rhymed letters, the *Épîtres de l'amant vert* (1505, published in 1510 or 1511), a masterpiece of wit and imagination. The first *épître* is a parody of the Ovidian farewell love letter, and the second plays on the mock-epic rendition of the *Aeneid* and the *Divine Comedy.*

Jean was twice sent to Italy by his patroness and visited Rome, Florence, and Venice. He seems to have been well acquainted with the Italian writers of his time, and used a number of historical and political documents of Italian origin in his later works, especially his monumental prose narrative, *Les illustrations de Gaule et singularités de Troie.* Meanwhile he continued to serve as Margaret's faithful court poet, writing official pieces when needed (*Les regrets de la dame infortunée*) and moving to Malines as her secretary when she was named regent of the Low Countries (spring 1507). After Jean Molinet died on 23 August 1507, Jean became the official chronicler (*indiciaire*) of the Burgundian states. He recorded much diplomatic activity in *La chronique annale* and celebrated the Treaty of Cambrai in *La concorde du genre humain*. His *Chansons de Namur* (1507), a poem of 39 stanzas greatly influenced by Molinet, exalts a Burgundian victory over the French and defends the humble virtues of the *petit peuple* against a decadent nobility ("armigère noblesse" with "mains polues," vv. 185–186).

Jean had many contacts with the great humanists of his time. In Lyons he met Symphorien Champier, "a very elegant philosopher, orator, historian and physician." In Dôle, Franche-Comté, he made friends with Heinrich Cornelius Agrippa von Nettesheim, the famous cabalist, who was then a lecturer at the university. He also was friendly with Jean Perréal, an influential painter, and other French artists, with whom he consulted frequently as he supervised the building of the Flamboyant Gothic church at Brou, near Bourg-en-Bresse. In 1509 he joined other poets in the propaganda against Venice (*La légende des Vénitiens*); translated an Italian lampoon against the Turks (*Les gestes de Sophy*); and wrote a polemic treatise against Pope Julius II, *Le traité de la différence des schismes et des conciles de l'église* (1511).

Finally, Jean resigned his position at Margaret's court and accepted Anne of Brittany's invitation to become her *indiciaire*. Immediately, in his *Épître du roi à Hector de Troie*, he gave an eloquent sample of his neo-Heroidian poetic talents at the court of Blois. Next, the three books of his monumental prose work *Les illustrations* were published (1511–1513). Based on John Annius (Nenni) of Viterbo's inaccurate work, this pseudohistorical reconstruction had a self-declared political purpose. Jean's last work, *La concorde des deux langages* (published in 1513), is an allegorical piece that reopens the debate about the primacy of the Italian culture over the French, with an obvious preference for the latter. The queen died on 9 January 1514, and there is no further mention of Jean after that date. He is referred to as the "late Jean Lemaire" in the 1526 edition of his works. Three charming *Contes de Cupido et Atropos*, the first two being generally attributed to Jean, were published in 1525.

Contrary to a common prejudice against the *grands rhétoriqueurs*, Jean was much more than a skillful, witty rhymer. He was a "universal man," with an immense curiosity in the most various domains. Philipp-August Becker called him, perhaps with too much enthusiasm, "der erste humanistische Dichter Frankreichs" (the first French humanist poet). Today, Renaissance scholars tend to play down his debt to Italian culture (although he introduced the terza rima into French poetics). Above all, he was the most vibrant apologist of the French language before Joachim du Bellay.

BIBLIOGRAPHY

Sources. François Rigolot, "Jean Lemaire de Belges," in Raymond C. La Charité, ed., *A Critical Bibliography of French Literature: The Sixteenth Century*, rev. ed. (1985); Jean Stecher, ed., *Oeuvres de Jean Lemaire de Belges*, 4 vols. (1882–1891, repr. 1969).

Studies. Philipp-August Becker, *Jean Lemaire, der erste humanistische Dichter Frankreichs* (1893, repr. 1970); Georges Doutrepont, *Jean Lemaire de Belges et la Renaissance* (1934); Jean Frappier, "L'Humanisme de Jean Lemaire de Belges," in *Bibliothèque d'Humanisme et Renaissance, 25* (1963); Henry Guy, "Jean Lemaire de Belges," in his *Histoire de la poésie française au XVIᵉ siècle*, I (1910, repr. 1968); Michael Frederich Owen Jenkins, *Artful Eloquence: Lemaire and Rhetorical Tradition* (1980); Pierre Jodogne, *Jean Lemaire de Belges, écrivain franco-bourguignon* (1972).

FRANÇOIS RIGOLOT

[See also **Rhétoriqueurs**.]

JEAN LE TAVERNIER (*fl.* 1434–*ca.* 1467), illuminator in Audenarde, near Ghent; he is also recorded in Tournai and Bruges, and as having worked on the decorations for the "Banquet of the Pheasant" (1454). His documented manuscripts, the *Hours of Philip the Good* (1454), in the Hague, and the *Chroniques et conquestes de Charlemagne* (1458–1460; Bibliothèque Royal, Brussels), have grisaille miniatures populated by many active figures in genre scenes. Both were made for Philip the Good, as were the two attributed volumes of the *Miracles de Notre Dame* (now in Paris and Oxford). Jean's full-color style, harder to identify, may be in certain manuscripts produced by the enterprise of Jean Miélot.

BIBLIOGRAPHY

L. M. J. Delaissé, ed., *La miniature flamande* (1959), also published as *Le siècle d'or de la miniature flamande* in *Handelingen van de Geschied- en Oudheidkundinge*

Kring van Oudenaarde, **12** (1960); Friedrich Winkler, *Die flämische Buchmalerei des XV. und XVI. Jahrhunderts* (1925).

ANNE HAGOPIAN VAN BUREN

[See also **Flemish Painting; Jean Miélot; Manuscript Illumination**.]

JEAN MICHEL, French sculptor responsible, with Georges de la Sonnette, for the earliest existing monumental *Entombment of Christ,* still preserved in the chapel of the hospital at Tonnerre, for which it was made. He is mentioned at Tonnerre from 1452 to 1454, when the monument was completed.

BIBLIOGRAPHY

William H. Forsyth, *The Entombment of Christ: French Sculptures of the Fifteenth and Sixteenth Centuries* (1970), 65–69, 188, 200–201; Theodor Müller, *Sculpture in the Netherlands, Germany, France and Spain 1400 to 1500* (1966), 57; Bernard Prost, "Le Saint Sépulcre de l'hôpital de Tonnerre," in *Gazette des beaux-arts,* 3rd ser., **9** (1893).

ANNE M. MORGANSTERN

[See also **Georges de la Sonnette**.]

JEAN MIÉLOT (*fl.* 1448–1472), writer and calligrapher, was born in Gueschard (or Gueschart) near Hesdin. He was secretary to Philip the Good of Burgundy from 1449 to 1467 and canon of St. Pierre in Lille, where he directed the production of books, from 1453 to 1472. His 1448 translation of the *Speculum humanae salvationis* was followed by thirty-three other translations of devotional or didactic texts. At least two layout mock-ups and several final copies in his hand are known, some of them possibly illustrated by Jean le Tavernier.

BIBLIOGRAPHY

L. M. J. Delaissé, ed., *La miniature flamande* (1959); Wolfgang Lutz and Paul Perdrizet, *Speculum humanae salvationis,* 2 vols. (1907–1909); Gianni Mombello, "Per la fortuna dell Boccaccio in Francia," Vittore Branca, ed., *Studi sul Boccaccio,* I (1963); Paul Perdrizet, des traducteurs de Phillippe le Bon," in *Revue d'histoire littéraire de la France,* **14** (1907), 472–482.

ANNE HAGOPIAN VAN BUREN

[See also **Jean le Tavernier; Manuscript and Book Production; Manuscript Illumination**.]

JEAN QUIDORT. See John of Paris.

JEAN, DREUX (*fl.* 1448–*ca.* 1466), calligrapher and illuminator born in Paris. He was official illuminator to Philip the Good of Burgundy, for whom he made books between 1448 and 1455, and, from 1464, to Charles of Charolais, the future duke. Living in Brussels, a member of the same confraternity as Rogier van der Weyden, Dreux Jean is probably the Master of the *Girart de Roussillon,* a Wauquelin manuscript now in Vienna (Vienna MS Cod. 2549) that was finished around the time of his appointment as official illuminator and presents a combined French and Rogierian style. The style was continued by the Master's assistants until the mid 1460's.

BIBLIOGRAPHY

L. M. J. Delaissé, ed., *La miniature flamande: Le mécénat de Philippe le Bon,* exhibition catalogue, Brussels/Amsterdam (1959); Antoine de Schryver, "Pour une meilleure orientation à propos de Maitre de Girart de Rousillon," in *Rogier van der Weyden en zijn Tijd: International Colloquium 1964* (1974); A. H. van Buren, "Jean Wauquelin de Mons et la production du livre aux Pays-Bas," in *Publication du centre européen d'études burgundo-médianes,* **23** (1983); Friedrich Winkler, *Die Flämische Buchmalerei* (1925).

ANNE HAGOPIAN VAN BUREN

[See also **Flemish Painting; Manuscript Illumination: Western European**.]

JEHAN. See also Jean.

JEHAN DES MURS (Johannes de Muris, John of Murs, Jean des Murs) (*fl. ca.* 1317–*ca.* 1345), French mathematician, astronomer, and theorist of music active in Évreux, Paris, Fontevrault, Mézières-en-Brenne, and Avignon. His books on music (about six, according to recent studies) were the most widely distributed and influential of his works, and were standard in university curricula for about 150 years. In their untraditional mode of exposition and their stress on temporal proportions, these works go hand in hand with the progressive French musical composition of the fourteenth century (the *ars nova*).

BIBLIOGRAPHY
Lawrence Gushee, "New Sources for the Biography of Johannes de Muris," in *Journal of the American Musicological Society,* **22** (1969); Emmanuel Poulle, "John of Murs," in *Dictionary of Scientific Biography,* VII (1973).

LAWRENCE GUSHEE

[See also **Ars Nova; Musical Treatises.**]

JELLINGE STYLE. The Jellinge style of Viking art is named for the decorative motif on a silver cup found in the Danish royal burial mound at Jelling, Jutland. It is characterized by a ribbon-shaped animal in profile with ornamental extensions to its body. It was in fashion from the end of the ninth to the late tenth century.

BIBLIOGRAPHY
Signe H. Fuglesang, "Early Viking Art," in *Acta ad archaeologiam et artium historiam pertinentia,* series altera, 2 (1982), 125–173, esp. 158–168; James A. Graham-Campbell, *Viking Artifacts: A Select Catalogue* (1980), chap. 9; D. M. Wilson and Ole Klindt-Jensen, *Viking Art,* 2nd ed. (1980), chap. 4.

JAMES A. GRAHAM-CAMPBELL

[See also **Viking Art.**]

Jellinge cup. Silver, tenth century. FIRST DEPARTMENT, NATIONAL-MUSEET, COPENHAGEN

JEROME, ST. (*ca.* 331–419/420), was, after Augustine, the greatest Latin father of the later Roman Empire. Born in Stridon (northeast Italy or Dalmatia) of wealthy Christian parents, he was educated in the liberal arts, and learned grammar from Donatus in Rome. During his stay at Trier, Jerome adopted an ascetic way of life, then popular in Western cities. In 372 he set out for Jerusalem in search of God. His odyssey led to Antioch, where he renounced classical learning in favor of the Bible. Taking his library with him, he entered the hermit life in Syria and never ceased thereafter to defend asceticism. In 379 Paulinus of Antioch, the leader of the Nicene-Trinitarian party, ordained Jerome a priest without pastoral obligations at Antioch. The next year Jerome met with Gregory of Nyssa and Gregory of Nazianzus in Constantinople.

Back in Rome in 382, Jerome acquired the patronage of Pope Damasus I, who asked him to revise the Old Latin version of the Bible and produce a standard version. He eventually translated the entire Hebrew Bible and some of the New Testament. While in Rome he gave spiritual advice to Christian women, particularly Paula and her daughter Eustochium. Jerome sharply attacked anyone who took issue with his translations, exegeses, relations with women, defense of asceticism and chastity, or association with Origen. He assailed Jovinian, Helvidius, Vigilantius, and his old friend Rufinus. In disgrace, partly because of his attacks on Roman clerics, he fled to the East, traveling much of the way with Paula, Eustochium, and other women. After they had toured Egypt and the Holy Land, Jerome and Paula established a double monastery in Bethlehem, where he spent most of the rest of his life. He continued to compose translations, biblical commentaries, and letters.

The life of Jerome reflects the tensions and fluidity within the later Roman Empire. He functioned within Christian intellectual circles, oblivious to his secular surroundings. His erratic career illustrates the penetration of asceticism in the West, the looseness of church organization, and the growing split between the Latin West and the Greek East. Jerome was a displaced loner whose ties with the ecclesiastical hierarchy were irregular and often turbulent. He was a major transitional figure between classical antiquity and medieval Christian civilization.

A protomedieval author, Jerome is primarily a doctor of the church. His enormous prestige was used to bolster points of dogma, ecclesiastical structure, and practices (sacraments, liturgy, relics, pilgrimages). For the Middle Ages, Jerome was the translator par excellence, the author of the Latin Vulgate, which became the textual basis of exegesis, theology, church decisions and discipline, and even changes in the secular sphere. Ironically, the Vulgate was later attacked by those wanting new translations from the Greek and Hebrew.

Jerome became the model of the Christian scholar, adept in translation, language, polemics, and learning both classical and Christian. With the spread of the idea of the *ecclesia primitiva* and classical humanism, he epitomized the union of scholarship and morality, of classicism and theology. He was himself one of the Christian writers he praised in his *De viris illustribus* (393–395). Abelard made him into a dialectician. Other medieval authors used Jerome to justify the rejection of pagan letters. His ambiguity about the city of Rome—as both Babylon and human glory—survived in medieval literature.

Jerome's scholarship was associated with the ascetic life. His actual conduct, as well as his polemic works, were summoned to support the hermit life and the propriety of monks' advising women. Jerome's lives of Hilarion and Malchus were used to champion both eremitism and cenobitism. His fervent defense of virginity and chastity served to transmit Greek Neoplatonic concepts of contemplation. Jerome unwittingly preserved some of Origen's opinions and methods. Paradoxically, medieval authors employed Jerome to endorse misogynist as well as feminist views of women.

Jerome's commentaries—such as those on Isaiah, Jeremiah, Ezekiel, Hosea, Jonah, and the Psalms—were influential both for content and for methodology. Although his allegorical and anagogical interpretations appealed to medieval exegetes, he later became known as the proponent of the literal/historical school. In the later Middle Ages Jerome's commentaries on Daniel and Matthew contributed to the prophecies of chiliasts concerning the era after the coming of Antichrist.

As a patristic writer Jerome defies classification. His uniqueness and unconventionality partially explain his enduring fame. He was an eccentric individualist whom the official church sometimes had difficulty absorbing. The Jerome myth rests on a combination of his irascible personality and his prestige as a biblical critic. With his translations, exegesis, methods of interpretation, and choice of canonical books, Jerome helped to shape the evolution of the Bible in Western culture. His feast day is 30 September.

BIBLIOGRAPHY

Sources. Patrologia latina, XXII–XXX (1863–1865); *Corpus scriptorum ecclesiasticorum latinorum, LIV–LVI, LIX (1910–1918); Corpus christianorum, series latina,* LXXII–LXXVIII (1958–1982).

Studies. Paul Antin, *Essai sur saint Jérôme* (1951); Yvon Bodin, *Saint Jérôme et l'église* (1966); Jean Gribomont, "Jérôme," in *Dictionnaire du spiritualité* (1974); Harald Hagendahl, *Latin Fathers and the Classics* (1958); John N. D. Kelly, *Jerome* (1975); Francis X. Murphy, ed., *A Monument to Saint Jerome* (1952); Angelo Penna, *S. Gerolamo* (1949); H. Sparks, "Jerome as a Biblical Scholar," in *Cambridge History of the Bible,* I (1970); Jean Steinmann, *Saint Jérôme* (1958), trans. by Ronald Matthews as *Saint Jerome and His Times* (1959); David S. Wiesen, *St. Jerome as a Satirist* (1964).

THOMAS RENNA

[See also **Bible; Church Fathers; Doctors of the Church; Gregory of Nazianzus, St.; Gregory of Nyssa, St.; Translation and Translators; Vulgate.**]

JERUSALEM. The main city of Palestine. Topographically the medieval city (roughly corresponding to what is known today as the Old City) lies over three hills with religiously charged names (Zion, Golgotha, Moriah) separated by the Tyropean valley. To the south is the Hinnom valley, and behind it another series of hills leading to Bethlehem, while to the east the Kidron valley separates Jerusalem from the higher range known by its most venerated spot, the Mount of Olives. Just a few miles to the east begins the Judean wilderness. There are no sources for water in Old Jerusalem; hence the city was provided with many cisterns and several artificial reservoirs (called pools) dug out of the rock around the city. Throughout the centuries the supplying of water through new cisterns, fountains, and later even aqueducts was one of the most meritorious acts of piety. Aside from services associated with the holiness of the city, Jerusalem has never had any significant economic base either in trade or in agriculture.

Jerusalem is a holy city having unique religious associations with Judaism, Christianity, and Islam. In the Middle Ages the visible forms of these associations were nearly exclusively Christian and Muslim, but Jewish associations continued to be deeply embedded in Jewish history and Jewish culture. The medieval history of Jerusalem, from Constantine the Great to Suleiman the Magnificent, consists in the interplay between fixed spatial features like hills and valleys, on the one hand, and high religious history or folk culture and memories, on the other.

Four periods can be outlined in this history: Byzantine Christian, Early Islamic, Crusades, and Mamluk and early Ottoman.

BYZANTINE CHRISTIAN

When Constantine transformed the Roman Empire into a Christian empire (324), Jerusalem was a minor provincial Roman city called Aelia Capitolina. It more or less coincided with the present Old City (an irregular square about one kilometer on each side), was probably walled, and included the standard monumental components of a Roman town: several temples, straight streets connecting main gates, statues of emperors, a military fortress, a tetrapylon, and possibly theaters. It was also a place of intensely, if unofficially, felt memories. Jewish pilgrims and travelers came to see the awesome ruins of the Second Temple in the southeastern corner of the city, occupying nearly one sixth of the area of Jerusalem. Christians maintained the memory of the life of Jesus, especially his Passion, throughout the city. It is important to stress that these activities and associations reflected far less high and literate religious attitudes than the humble, popular piety of frequently persecuted minorities.

The creation of a Christian empire, coupled with the move of the capital to Constantinople, transformed Jerusalem into the holiest city of the Byzantine world. This evolution was made visible in two ways: the construction of major monuments and change in use. The discovery of the True Cross by Empress Helena, however charged with legend it may have become, and the subsequent building of the Holy Sepulcher (335) were merely the beginnings of two and a half centuries of intense building all over the city and in its surrounding areas. Every moment of Christ's life was commemorated by large or small martyrium-type, central-plan sanctuaries, while congregational churches, usually on a basilican plan, served as places for the celebration of the Mass for local inhabitants and especially for pilgrims. None of these buildings have survived. The present Holy Sepulcher is but a shadow of what it must have been, but enough archaeological and written sources have remained to allow for reasonable reconstructions. On the other hand, the Church of the Ascension on the Mount of Olives, the Church of Zion, the great New Church built by Justinian, and sanctuaries dedicated to St. Anne, St. John the Baptist, St. Peter, St. Stephen, and St. James are

mostly known through literary sources alone. The extraordinary Madaba map (*ca.* 560–565), a large mosaic map of Palestine found in the small Transjordanian town of Madaba and containing a complete representation of Jerusalem, shows more than twenty churches or related holy buildings. An essential point is that the huge Temple area was left in ruins (except for a possible chapel to St. James in its southeastern corner), in order to fulfill the Gospel prophecy that "there shall not be left here one stone upon another that shall not be thrown down" (Matthew 24:2).

The second revolutionary change in Jerusalem was its new use. The population undoubtedly increased, but it was mostly its character that changed as it became a city for pilgrims. Hence it required the creation of a whole apparatus of hostels, monasteries, hospices, and other buildings for travelers. Little is known about the specifics of this organization, but one major change in the shape of the city can be attributed to it: the spread toward the south through the building of the so-called Wall of Eudokia (middle of the fifth century), which enclosed a few churches but mostly hostels. Furthermore, the function of Jerusalem as a place of pilgrimage led to the creation of an industry of holy objects reflecting its monuments (for instance, the celebrated pilgrim bottles known as the Monza vials from the Italian city where so many have been preserved) and to its impact on art and architecture elsewhere; even the remote Carolingian world, as well as much closer Syrian manuscript illustrators, saw direct or indirect inspiration in the monuments of Jerusalem.

EARLY ISLAM (638–1099)

Jerusalem surrendered to the caliph ᶜUmar in March or April 638 through a formal treaty that, among other things, forbade Muslims to take over Christian sanctuaries and allowed Jews to settle again in Jerusalem.

What happened to the city over the following four centuries is of fascinating complexity; much in the following summary is hypothetical or based on very recently uncovered archaeological data (the excavations south and southwest of the Temple area begun after 1967), on inscriptions, and on partial literary evidence. The most obvious change is the resacralization of the Temple area as a Muslim sanctuary. Under the impact of the Koranic revelation of Jerusalem as the first *qibla* (prayer direction) for Muslims, of the eventual localization of the Prophet's mystical night journey in Jerusalem, and of many early converts from Judaism to Islam, the ruined Temple of Herod was cleaned and refurbished; its gates, such as the Golden and Double Gates, were rebuilt; its platform (or platforms) were redone. The first major new monument to be built was the Dome of the Rock, completed in 691/692. The exact original purpose of this spectacular work of architecture is still a matter of controversy. Whether meant from the beginning as a monument commemorating the Prophet's journey (as it became later), whether formally an architectural proclamation of the new revelation in the city of its predecessors (as is indicated by its inscriptions), or whether a bizarre attempt at replacing Mecca (as is suggested by one medieval historiographic tradition), the Dome of the Rock truly modified the structure of the city of Jerusalem by creating a new Muslim pole in the eastern part of the city as a counterpart of the Holy Sepulcher in its western part. After the Dome of the Rock, a series of buildings gradually covered the old Herodian Temple and transformed it into the third holiest place of Islam, the Noble Sanctuary (Ḥaram al-Sharīf); the buildings included the Aqṣā Mosque (early eighth century with many later additions and repairs), fancy gates (mostly known from texts only), and small sanctuaries recalling various aspects of the Prophet's journey or memories of biblical prophets and patriarchs, such as Joseph, Jacob, and Abraham.

Unfortunately, subsequent modifications and especially the crusades make it difficult to establish a more precise chronology, except perhaps for the likelihood that key moments in the development of the Ḥaram were the reigns of the Umayyads (especially between 690 and 724), the Abbasids (early ninth century), and the Fatimids (early eleventh century). These are the periods when Jerusalem acquired its Arabic name, Bayt al-Maqdis or al-Quds, the Holy House or the Holy One.

It is even more difficult to reconstruct the human changes that must have taken place in Jerusalem. The new Muslim population was probably not very great and, as recent excavations have shown, newly arrived Arabs settled first to the south of the Ḥaram and slowly established themselves around the new holy place, principally to the north after the abandonment by the Fatimids, early in the eleventh century, of Eudokia's addition to the city. Jews returned to Jerusalem, settling probably in the general area of the present Jewish quarter south of the city. Even though dominated politically (as exemplified by the destruction of the Holy Sepulcher in 966, soon repaired), the Christians still formed the major portion of the population in Jerusalem. But they changed in character from a hellenized Christian group to an arabized one.

THE CRUSADES (1099–1244)

Short-lived though it was, the century and a half (actually barely a century, as little was done in the city after Saladin's victory of 1187) of Frankish rule was a turning point in the history of Jerusalem. First, it is a superbly documented period. Second, for the first time since Herod, Jerusalem was a royal capital. Third, the brutal assumptions of the conquering crusaders led to a total transformation of the features of the city and its influence.

In attempting to transform Jerusalem into a Western city, the crusaders destroyed a great deal of what had been there before and erected a great number of new buildings. Some were churches, such as that of the Holy Sepulcher, largely rebuilt with a new facade, and the restored Church of St. Anne; others were institutions, such as the centers of the money changers. But mostly they reinterpreted the monuments of Jerusalem without a knowledge of their actual history. The most interesting example is the Ḥaram area, which was taken to be the actual Temple of Solomon and thus was represented as an exemplar of Solomonic times throughout the Renaissance in paintings, one of many instances of misunderstandings developed in crusader times.

The building boom of the first half of the twelfth century must have been spectacular, since crusader remains still appear at many a street corner or have been reused in later buildings. One controversy about this activity, involving both construction and decoration, is the degree to which artisans were natives of Palestine or immigrants from the West. The mass building led to the slow filling of the Tyropean valley, thus removing the most visible natural landmark in the city up to that time. Finally, by paying little attention to the older physical and human structures of the city and by massacring or evicting many of its inhabitants, the crusaders unhinged the continuity of the development of Jerusalem without creating a new urban order that would have taken root in the city. In fact, only the Armenian (earlier also Georgian) quarter in the southwestern corner of the city is a direct urban result of the century of crusader occupation. At another level, however, the impact was more significant. In the West it created a mythology about Jerusalem, as maps and paintings for centuries represented a Jerusalem in Western garb, often with mystical overtones (for instance, it was shown as a round city with the four rivers of Paradise), and as orders created in and for Jerusalem—the Templars and the Knights of St. John—continued to play a role in Western history and society.

MAMLUK AND EARLY OTTOMAN (1260–1566)

The task of re-creating a Muslim Jerusalem fell to the lot of the Mamluk dynasty of Egypt. In a sense, Jerusalem became once again a provincial capital ruled from Cairo, but since it was more easily accessible than the holy places of Arabia, it became the focus of an enormous program of construction; more than 100 buildings, new or restored and repaired, are recorded in the 300 years that followed the final defeat of the crusaders. This program culminated in the rebuilding of the walls of Jerusalem and the redecoration in polychrome tiles of the Dome of the Rock by the Ottoman sultan Suleiman (1520–1566). It is not entirely by accident that this namesake of the second king of Israel made a point of symbolizing his huge empire by completing the rebuilding of Jerusalem. Until the late nineteenth century his Jerusalem remained one of the most perfectly preserved examples of a late medieval Islamic city of the Mediterranean area.

Suleiman only completed a process that had begun after 1260 and that consisted of three parts. In human terms, Muslims became the majority in the city and settled in its northern quarter as well as west of the Ḥaram. A diminished eastern sector was Christian, but the erection of two minarets near small sanctuaries flanking the Holy Sepulcher served to emphasize the superior place of Islam. Although Latin Christians were, for obvious reasons, particularly vulnerable to Muslim control and arbitrariness, all Christian groups became treated like minorities. Jews were resettled in the south-central part of the city. They had their own institutions, but their numbers were small during these centuries.

A second process was the rehabilitation of the Ḥaram. This included the building of large numbers of small commemorative monuments to prophets or to Muḥammad's journey, usually in an effort to recall pre-crusader ways. Probably following popular practices that had existed earlier, the Mamluks encouraged Muslim pilgrimage to Jerusalem and sponsored the special genre of pious books (faḍāʾil) describing the religious merits of Jerusalem and Palestine.

The most spectacular Mamluk process was the transformation of the northern and western edges of the Ḥaram and of the streets leading to it into a museum of hospices, madrasas, convents, libraries, fountains, and occasionally private tombs built by the ruling aristocracy. New streets and new shopping areas were created between these buildings, such as the beautiful Suq of the Cotton Merchants (Suq el-Qattanin). Altogether, the access to the Ḥaram became one of the best-preserved examples of the uniquely Mediterranean Islamic symbiosis between socially productive institutions and social or religious services.

The phenomenon can also be observed in Cairo and Aleppo, but it is particularly striking in Jerusalem because it is economically and socially less necessary in a small city, and therefore more important as a demonstration of an attempt to emphasize the holiness of the Ḥaram by surrounding it with the most eloquent examples of socially conscious Islamic purposes. It was possible because Jerusalem, often a place of exile for rebellious princes from Cairo, became a showplace of their piety.

BIBLIOGRAPHY

There is no acceptable book on medieval Jerusalem. Best introductions to sources are L. Hugues Vincent and F. M. Abel, Jérusalem, II, Jérusalem nouvelle (1926); Jan J. Simons, Jerusalem in the Old Testament (1952). Among recent works the most reliable, though incomplete, are Benjamin Mazar, The Mountain of the Lord (1975); Yigael Yadin, Jerusalem Revealed (1976). Medieval texts are in Palestine Pilgrims' Text Society, 13 vols. (1890–1897); John Wilkinson, ed., Jerusalem Pilgrims Before the Crusades (1977). See also Guy LeStrange, Palestine Under the Moslems (1890, repr. 1975), and History of Jerusalem Under the Moslems (197?), a reprint of the relevant chapters from the 1890 ed. The journal Levant (published by the British School of Archaeology in Jerusalem) contains reports of an ongoing survey of Islamic monuments in Jerusalem. For specific items see Michael Avi-Yonah, The Madaba Mosaic Map (1954); André Grabar, Ampoules de terre sainte (1958); Oleg Grabar, "The Umayyad Dome of the Rock," in Ars orientalis, 3 (1959), and, with Solomon D. Goitein, "Kuds, al-," in Encyclopaedia of Islam (new ed.).

OLEG GRABAR

[See also Crusader Art and Architecture; Crusades and Crusader States; Dome of the Rock.]

JERUSALEM, KINGDOM OF. See Crusades and Crusader States.

JEU, a French term designating various types of play, such as games, jests, and pastimes. From the late thirteenth century the term was also applied to dramatic works. It was used both as part of a title, as in Jean Bodel's *Jeu de saint Nicolas,* to which it was applied retroactively, and as a generic designation—for example, in the phrase *jeu de personnages* (play involving characters; dramatic play).

BIBLIOGRAPHY
Albert Henry, *Le Jeu de saint Nicolas de Jean Bodel,* 2nd ed. (1965), 185.

ALAN E. KNIGHT

JEU D'ADAM (also known as *Mystère d'Adam;* the Latin title is *Ordo representacionis Ade*). The earliest extant French drama, *Jeu d'Adam* was probably written by an Anglo-Norman author about the middle of the twelfth century. The play, which is unfinished, is in three parts: the story of Adam and Eve (590 lines), the slaying of Abel by Cain (154 lines), and a procession of prophets who predict the coming of Christ (198 lines to 561 lines, the length varying in different versions). The discourse is inoctosyllabic rhyming couplets and decasyllabic monorhyme quatrains. There has been considerable debate over the origins, whether insular or continental, of the work.

BIBLIOGRAPHY
Sources. The sole MS is *Ordo representacionis Ade,* Tours, Bibliothèque Municipale, MS 927. Editions are *Le Mystère d'Adam, an Anglo-Norman Drama of the Twelfth Century,* Paul Studer, ed. (1918); *Le Mystère d'Adam,* Paul Aebischer, ed. (1963); *Le Mystère d'Adam,* Leif Sletsjöe, ed. (1967), diplomatic edition; *Le Jeu d'Adam,* Willem Noomen, ed. (1971).
Studies. Erich Auerbach, *Mimesis,* Willard R. Trask, trans. (1953), chap. 7; Grace Frank, *The Medieval French Drama* (1954), 74–84; Lynette R. Muir, *Liturgy and Drama in the Anglo-Norman Adam* (1973).

BRIAN MERRILEES

[See also **Anglo-Norman Literature; Drama, French.**]

JEU DE LA FEUILLÉE, LE, a comic play from Arras written around 1276 by Adam de la Halle (also known as Adam le Bossu). This enigmatic work appears at first to be a satirical revue in which the author and some of his friends ridicule certain of their fellow citizens. Yet there is also a fairy scene, lending an air of unreality to the action. It is likely that Adam, by giving himself a central role in the play, has created a kind of psychodrama in which he acts out both his aspirations to become a great poet and his fears of failure. The play, with its mixture of fantasy, folly, and folklore, is sometimes seen as a medieval *Midsummer Night's Dream.*

BIBLIOGRAPHY
Adam le Bossu: Le Jeu de la feuillée, Ernest Langlois, ed., 2nd rev. ed. (1923, repr. 1965). See also Richard Axton and John Stevens, eds. and trans., *Medieval French Plays* (1971), 207–255; Jean Dufournet, *Adam de la Halle à la recherche de lui-même; ou, le jeu dramatique de la feuillée* (1974).

ALAN E. KNIGHT

[See also **Adam de la Halle; Drama, French; French Literature: After 1200.**]

JEU DE ROBIN ET MARION, LE, a pastoral play by Adam de la Halle of Arras (also known as Adam le Bossu). Written in the Picard dialect, probably between 1282 and 1287, it is thought to have been presented at the court of Robert II, count of Artois, which had moved to southern Italy following the Sicilian Vespers massacre of 1282. The first half of the play is a dramatized pastourelle, a type of narrative poem in which a knight declares his love for a shepherdess. Here the shepherdess (Marion) rejects the knight because she loves a shepherd (Robin). The second half of the play is a dramatized *bergerie* (pastoral poem), in which the couple join their shepherd friends for a picnic and games. The text is interspersed with rustic songs and dances that were familiar to the original audience.

BIBLIOGRAPHY
An edition is Ernest Langlois, ed., *Adam le Bossu: Le Jeu de Robin et Marion* (1923, repr. 1965). See also Richard Axton, *European Drama of the Early Middle Ages* (1975), 140–144; Richard Axton and John Stevens, eds. and trans., *Medieval French Plays* (1971), 257–302; Grace Frank, *Medieval French Drama* (1954, 2nd ed. 1960), 231–236.

ALAN E. KNIGHT

[See also **Adam de la Halle; Drama, French; French Literature: After 1200; Pastourelle.**]

JEU PARTI. The Old French *jeu parti* is a lyrical poetic form, usually made up of six strophes and two envois, that corresponds in structure and content to the Old French partimen. In this genre, which was used particularly by Thibaut de Champagne and the Arras trouvères, the poet-lover's monologue becomes a debate between two rival poets who, exchanging personal abuse, test contrary viewpoints on love and then leave the decision to the judges named in the envois.

BIBLIOGRAPHY

A collection of *jeux partis* is Artur Isak Edvard Långfors, ed., *Recueil général des jeux-partis français* (1926).

See also Jean Frappier, *La poésie lyrique en France aux XIIe et XIIIe siècles* (1960); Paul Remy, "De l'expression 'partir un jeu' dans les textes épiques aux origines du jeu parti," in *Cahiers de civilisation médiévale*, **17** (1974), 327–333.

GLYNNIS M. CROPP

[See also **French Literature: To 1200; French Literature: Lyric; Partimen; Thibaut de Champagne; Troubadour, Trouvère, Trovador.**]

JEWISH ART. Any discussion of medieval Jewish art must take into consideration the amazing cycle of paintings depicting biblical scenes found on the walls of the Dura Europos synagogue in Syria dating from the mid third century. The figural images arranged in three tiers on all four walls of the synagogue challenge the accepted historiography of the period and demand revision of the notion of a so-called normative Rabbinic Judaism that scholars have hypothesized. In addition, the firm conviction held in scholarly circles until very recently that a rigid iconoclasm prevailed throughout Jewish history is seriously questioned by this discovery. When the oft-quoted second commandment of the decalogue—"you shall not make for yourself a sculptured image" (Exod. 20:4 and Deut. 5:8), usually taken literally—is seen against the backdrop of complex social, political, and economic forces, it is clear that it is not a monolithic, unchanging concept that transcends particular historical contexts. It would be more accurate to speak of second commandments, in the plural, that mirror the multiple Jewish historical experiences.

Each Jewish society had to assimilate the biblical view of art to its own particular needs, necessitating new interpretations of the second commandment. Thus, the biblical injunction has meant something different in each historical context and must be evaluated accordingly. The very book that contains the second commandment elevates Bezalel, the desert artist, to unparalleled heights: "I have endowed him with a divine spirit of skill, ability, and knowledge in every kind of craft" (Exod. 31:1ff.). In any case, the dogmatic assertions of religious leaders in any specific social context are frequently not in harmony with the practices prevalent among large segments of their followers.

The Dura paintings also reopen the debate on the Jewish origins of Christian art. Josef Strzygowski first suggested in his *Orient oder Rom* (1901) that the ultimate source of many Christian Old Testament depictions may be in preexistent Hellenistic Jewish illustrated manuscripts, but the theory lacked substantive evidence. The Dura paintings, according to some scholars, supply the missing link between the lost Hellenistic Jewish art and the later Christian art. Scholars employ three arguments to support the hypothesis of illustrated Jewish manuscripts in antiquity: (1) that the Dura paintings were inspired by now lost illuminated Jewish manuscripts; (2) that iconographic motifs in the Dura synagogue, derived from lost Jewish manuscripts, survive in later Christian and Jewish art; and (3) that Jewish legendary motifs appearing in medieval Christian manuscripts reflect lost Jewish illustrated manuscripts.

The first argument is questionable because it is largely an argumentum ex silentio. No classical or early Christian illuminated manuscripts can be securely dated prior to the fifth century. Furthermore, no extant Hebrew illuminated manuscripts antedate the ninth century. Recent scholarship has suggested cartoons or pattern books as more probable sources for the Dura artists.

Supporters of the second argument might use such iconographic motifs in the Dura synagogue—for example, the hand of God, as symbolizing divine intervention to stop Abraham from slaying Isaac, and the ram tied or standing next to a tree—as proof because they also appear in early Christian, Byzantine, and later Jewish depictions of the Sacrifice of Isaac. These iconographic details vary from the biblical narrative, where an angel intercedes and the ram is caught in a thicket. Despite these similarities, there are also differences; only in the Dura synagogue is Isaac shown lying prone on the altar. Hence, these iconographic details may not have been

Water miracle; Aaron and the tabernacle; Abraham/Joshua (?); Elijah reviving the widow's son; Mordecai and Esther story. Frescoes from west wall of Dura Europos synagogue, mid 3rd century. YALE UNIVERSITY ART GALLERY

64

copied from the Dura synagogue or its hypothetical model but may simply have been inspired by extant literary traditions.

Similarly, there is a depiction of the daughter of Pharaoh, bathing nude in the Nile and discovering the child Moses while her three clothed maidens wait on shore. Again, as at Dura, the nude princess appears in the late-twelfth-to-thirteenth-century Christian illustrations of the Pamplona Bibles and in fourteenth-century Spanish Haggadah illuminations. However, though all these depictions share the motif of the nude princess, the later examples depart from the Dura painting by placing two nude maidens in the Nile with her. All that can be said with some certainty is that these illustrations are based on legendary elaborations of the biblical narrative, wherein the princess walks along the riverbank and dispatches a slave girl to fetch the basket from the water.

Referring to the third argument, supporters might point out that many Christian manuscripts contain legendary motifs which first appear in *aggadot* and midrashim (Rabbinic legends and homiletic writings). These extracanonical Jewish elements found in Christian art are frequently cited to substantiate the existence of lost Jewish illustrated manuscript cycles. A case in point are miniatures illustrating a Jewish tradition on the life of Abraham, according to which his search for the one God finally led him to reject the idol worship of his father, Terah. After Abraham had smashed his father's idols, King Nimrod ordered the iconoclast cast into the fire of the Chaldeans, from which he was miraculously rescued. This story appears in thirteenth- and fourteenth-century *Bible moralisée* and *Speculum humanae salvationis,* in Hebrew manuscripts from the fourteenth century on, and even in such fourteenth-century Persian manuscripts as Rashīd al-Dīn's *Jāmiᶜ al-Tawārīkh* (Collection of chronicles).

The images of this basic Jewish legendary motif in the three religions show such diversity in iconography and style as to refute the claim of a common, linear descent from lost Jewish manuscript models. After all, Jewish exegetical and homiletical methodology, as well as Jewish legends, such as Abraham in the fire, were freely adapted by both Christian and later Muslim writers for their own distinctive religious traditions.

Neither large cycles of paintings nor Hebrew manuscripts have survived from the Byzantine period. Evidence of the Jewish artistic tradition comes primarily from architectural sources, specifically Pal-

estinian synagogues, and it is only in the sixth century that there are dated examples. No clear picture of synagogue architecture has yet emerged from this period, and the rigid classification into three distinct groups—an early (second to fourth centuries), a transitional (late third to fifth), and a later type (fifth to eighth centuries)—has gradually been abandoned by scholars. Synagogues in Palestine may simply show regional variations.

Some of the synagogues, such as Bet-Alfa, dating from either the first or second half of the sixth century, follow the basilical plan, and their orientation for prayer is toward Jerusalem. These usages, however, are not universal and deserve more study.

Most interesting are the floor mosaics in Byzantine synagogues like Bet Alfa and Naarah, both dating from the sixth century. These mosaics continue a practice, traceable back to the fourth century, of three-panel mosaic floors. In the upper panel the Torah ark is usually flanked by a menorah and such symbols of the Jewish holidays as the shofar and the lulav and etrog (palm branch and citron, symbols of the Feast of the Tabernacles); the central panel usually has two concentric circles within a square. In the center, the frontal sun god Helios is depicted in his chariot. The second circle is divided into twelve radial units, one for each zodiacal sign. The corners of the square are decorated with busts of the four seasons. The bottom panel usually has a theme of salvation, perhaps the Sacrifice of Isaac, as at Bet Alfa. Only in the case of Bet Alfa and the neighboring synagogue of Bet-Shean are the names of the gifted Jewish folk artists known—Marianos and his son Hanina. The repertory of decorations used at Bet Alfa displays no unique Jewish characteristics. The popular inhabited vine scroll pavements, as well as the depiction of the suspended Isaac, are also found in Christian art. In the Gaza region, for instance, craftsmen in the fifth and early sixth centuries are known to have worked for Christian and Jewish patrons alike and to have produced similar types of mosaic floors. The inhabited scroll pavements of the synagogue of Gaza, dated 508/509, are closely related to the synagogue mosaic of Ma'on-Nirim and that in the Christian church at Shellal. There is no doubt that the Gaza structure is a synagogue because of the fortunate find of another mosaic belonging to it that depicts an Orpheus-like figure labeled David in Hebrew.

Aside from the Dura Europos synagogue frescoes and the mosaic floors of Palestinian synagogues, the major source of medieval Jewish art is to be found in the illuminated manuscripts from Islamic countries such as Egypt, Palestine, Yemen, and Persia and dating from the ninth and later centuries. They are also found in abundance in western Europe, where the finest examples date from the thirteenth to fifteenth centuries.

The earliest dated illuminated Hebrew manuscript from the Islamic East is the Moshe ben Asher codex (Cairo, the Karaite Synagogue), containing the books of the prophets. Dated 894/895, it is from Tiberias in Palestine. The codex, it should be noted, is a uniquely Christian form and was not adopted by Jews until post-talmudic times. (The most important Hebrew book for synagogal worship was the Torah scroll, or Pentateuch, which was never illuminated.) The Moshe ben Asher codex prefaces the biblical text with carpet pages similar to those in Koran manuscripts. Many of these Bibles may have been written by and for the Karaites, a schismatic Jewish movement that began in the eighth-century Abbasid East. The Karaites stressed asceticism and messianism and elevated the authority of the Bible. (They rejected the rabbinitic tradition, which looked to the Talmud as its authority.) The decorative motifs in the manuscripts—the abstract geometric patterns, the vegetal and floral ornaments with the palmette ansa attached to the outer design of the carpet page—are similar to decorative conventions found in Koran manuscripts. Even the gold and blue colors and the size of the manuscripts follow Islamic models. A few decorated pages contain schematic renderings of buildings, as does the Leningrad Bible, dated 929 and originating in Palestine or Egypt. On one page a square seven-branched lampstand appears in the center, above it the Ark of the Covenant flanked by two stylized leaves, perhaps symbolic of cherubim. To the side are such implements as the jar of manna, an altar, and Aaron's flowering rod. These schematic renderings may represent the wilderness tabernacle, since it was a metaphor for Scripture to the Karaites that may be illustrated here as in a related fragmentary page. It must be stressed that these tabernacle renderings bear little relation to early synagogue mosaics, nor do they link up with later Spanish Hebrew manuscripts that show the sanctuary vessels—an analogy frequently made by scholars. The synagogue mosaics depict the Torah ark flanked by the symbols of the Jewish holidays, while the Spanish Hebrew manuscripts show implements symbolizing the hope of the Spanish Jew that he would see the rebuilt messianic temple.

Most of the early decorated Hebrew manuscripts from Muslim Egypt and Palestine are Bibles, although some adornments are found in children's textbooks, liturgical books, and ketubbot (marriage contracts). They all employ artistic conventions used in contemporary Islamic art. An unusual feature in these manuscripts is the use of micrography (the outlining of human and animal figures by means of minutely written script) for the Masorah (critical notes on the text of the Hebrew Bible). In Islamic Hebrew manuscripts the shapes used are primarily geometrical and floral; in Christian Europe, shapes of animals and human figures are used. Apparently unknown in manuscripts of the Koran, these decorative games are recorded in Hellenistic and Christian writings and are found in Christian art. In surviving Christian examples, the figures have parallel rows of

Pentateuch carpet page. MS from Sanᶜa, Yemen, 1469. © GEORGE BRAZILLER, 1978

66

writing in order to fill a specific shape; the practice of having the letters themselves form the shape appears to be a unique Jewish invention.

Some surviving Bible manuscripts from fifteenth-century Yemen, probably the work of Jewish artist-scribes, contain decorations and colors inspired perhaps by Islamic enameled glass objects and designs on metal objects. The employment of biblical micrography for animal shapes marks a departure from the strictly geometrical and floral decorations in earlier Islamic Hebrew manuscripts.

Judeo-Persian illuminated manuscripts of the biblical epics written by Persian Jewish poets, such as Maulānā Šāhīn of the fourteenth century, have survived only in seventeenth-century renditions. These figural depictions of biblical and nonbiblical heroes are related in style and iconography to Safawid provincial manuscripts.

The earliest illuminated Hebrew manuscripts in western Europe come from the Franco-German region (Ashkenaz), where Jews had functioned as merchants since the tenth century. A two-volume Rashi commentary to the Bible, made in the region of Würzburg, Germany, in 1233 is the oldest illuminated Hebrew manuscript extant. Its seventeen miniatures reflect the late Romanesque style current in southern Germany. Again it should be emphasized that such depictions as the Sacrifice of Isaac in this manuscript bear little relation to earlier Jewish renderings of the theme. In style and iconography, the Würzburg Sacrifice of Isaac finds close parallels in such sculptured examples of the motif as the pulpit relief of the Schlosskirche at Wechselburg, of *ca.* 1235.

Unquestionably the richest Hebrew biblical illuminations from the Ashkenazic region are found in a Miscellany (London, British Library, MS Add. 11639), painted in the High Gothic style emanating from Paris. Dated to the last quarter of the thirteenth century and the early fourteenth century, its many miniatures include biblical, liturgical, and eschatological scenes. The most significant manuscript illuminated in Ashkenazic communities is the mahzor (literally, cycle)—a codex containing the obligatory prayers and piyyutim (additional liturgical poetry) for seven special Sabbaths and holidays. The huge format of these books suggests that they were intended for the synagogue and not for home use. As the Hebrew script uses no capital letters, initial letters so characteristic of Latin Christian manuscripts are rarely found. Instead, bold initial word panels predominate in these manuscripts. In some ways the

David and Goliath. MS painting, late 13th century. BRITISH LIBRARY, LONDON, MS. ADD 11639

mahzor was to Jewish tradition what the breviary was to Christian devotions. In fact, an inscription in one mahzor reads *Breviarium iudaicum*. Some of the most representative mahzorim date from the second half of the thirteenth and the early fourteenth century and come from southern Germany and the Rhineland. A special iconography evolved in the mahzor. A scale for weighing shekels was painted next to the liturgy for *Shabbat Shekalim* (pericope Scales); and signs of the zodiac and the labors of the months appeared next to the piyyut (liturgical poem) for dew, recited on the first day of Passover. Unique in some of these mahzorim and other Hebrew manuscripts from this region are human figures with animal and bird heads. No adequate explanation has yet been offered for them.

The most frequently illuminated Hebrew manuscript in fifteenth-century Germany is the Passover Haggadah. Stressing folklore and humor, the marginal illustrations deal with aspects of the seder liturgy. The style of the linear depictions reveals the impact of the new graphic techniques.

No illuminated Hebrew manuscripts survive from the Islamic phase of Spanish Jewish history. The earliest decorated manuscripts come from such flourishing Jewish centers as Toledo and Burgos in thirteenth-century Christian Spain. These manuscripts usually have arabesque carpet pages preceding the text. The most important illuminated Hebrew book of Christian Spain is the Passover Haggadah. Rabbinic in origin, the Haggadah was an integral part of prayer codices; it became a private, separate book only in thirteenth-century western Europe. Just as the private Latin psalter has pictorial Old Testament prefaces, so the fourteenth-century Spanish Haggadah manuscripts feature full-page nontextual miniatures, drawn primarily from the book of Exodus.

The Hebrew Bible, called *mikdashyah* (sanctuary of God) in Christian Spain, developed its own iconography during and after the late thirteenth century. On the preliminary folios preceding the biblical text it became customary to depict the gold and silver vessels which, according to rabbinic tradition, stood in Solomon's Temple and which, as noted earlier, gave visual expression to the messianic hope of beholding the rebuilt temple of Solomon.

In Italy, illuminated Hebrew manuscripts began to appear in the Rome region at the end of the thirteenth century. From the fourteenth century on, Christian illuminated legal texts from Bologna may have exerted an influence on the appearance of illuminated Hebrew legal codices, such as Maimonides' *Mishneh Torah* and Jacob ben Asher's *Arba^ca Turim*. Secular illuminated manuscripts like Avicenna's *Canon of Medicine* in Hebrew translation also become popular among Italian Jews. These manuscripts reveal the hands or influence of such Italian artists as Zenobi Strozzi, Leonardo da Besozzo, and Matteo di Ser Cambio.

Although literary sources mention ceremonial objects used in the observance of the Jewish holidays, the Jewish life cycle, and the liturgy of the synagogue, only two ceremonial objects have survived that can be securely dated to the fifteenth-century—a pair of *rimmonim* ("pomegranates," Torah headpieces) from Camarata, Sicily, and now in the Cathedral Treasury of Palma de Mallorca. These silver *rimmonim* are in the now familiar tower-shaped form and display decorative motifs familiar from Islamic art.

Few links can be established between the ancient synagogue architecture and what emerged in medieval Christian Europe. The oldest surviving synagogue is in Worms, Germany. Dating from 1175, it was razed by the Nazis in 1938 and recently restored. A woman's annex dates from 1213. Its twin-nave plan was adapted from monastic refectories and chapter houses of convents. The synagogal ark stood at the eastern end, but its most prominent feature was the pulpit (called *almemor*) situated in the center of the nave between columns. The double-nave plan used at Worms traveled eastward to Bavarian Regensburg, Bohemian Prague, and Polish Kazimierz, attesting perhaps to a basic cultural unity among Ashkenazic Jews.

Two beautiful surviving medieval examples of the many Spanish synagogues are to be seen in Toledo. The oldest extant is the thirteenth-century synagogue, now the church of S. Maria la Blanca, a basilica with four rows of octagonal piers supporting horseshoe arcades with stucco friezes. The other, now the church of El Transito, was built as a private synagogue in 1355–1357 for Samuel ha-Levi Abulafia, treasurer to King Pedro I the Cruel of Castile. A single nave hall, its walls are covered with arabesque panels and dedicatory inscriptions. The plans of the Spanish synagogues follow those of neighboring churches; the decorations frequently betray Mudejar influence.

BIBLIOGRAPHY

Joseph Gutmann, ed., *Beauty in Holiness: Studies in Jewish Customs and Ceremonial Art* (1970), *The Dura-Europos Synagogue: A Re-evaluation* (1973), *The Image and the Word: Confrontations in Judaism, Christianity, and Islam* (1977), *No Graven Images: Studies in Art and the Hebrew Bible* (1971), and *The Synagogue: Studies in Origins, Archaeology, and Architecture* (1975); Joseph Gutmann, *Hebrew Manuscript Painting* (1978); Rachel Wischnitzer, *The Architecture of the European Synagogue* (1964).

JOSEPH GUTMANN

[See also **Dura Europos; Manuscript Illumination: Hebrew; Mudejar Art; Palestine; Synagogue.**]

JEWISH COMMUNAL SELF-GOVERNMENT: EUROPE. The Jewish communities in medieval Europe enjoyed a large degree of religious and political autonomy or self-government. Except in the smallest villages and towns, disputes over issues of Jewish religious law were settled internally by local religious courts presided over by one or more rabbinical judges. Their jurisdiction encompassed areas of self-government covered by Jewish law, such as contracts, torts, marriage and divorce, dietary requirements, ritual purity, and Sabbath and holiday observance.

In addition to the religious court system managed by local rabbinical authorities, there also was a community board (kahal) of elders led by a parnas who administered questions of the Jewish community's public safety and social welfare. Unlike the religious judges, who were qualified by virtue of their competence in Jewish law, the elders derived their authority primarily from their age, wealth, family lineage, or influence with the Christian rulers. Although the community board might also include rabbinical judges, the board and not the religious courts was responsible to the Christian ruler to see that tax assessments were paid and that law and order were maintained. The elders were also responsible to the members of the Jewish community to intercede with the authorities if a threat to its security arose, and they also maintained a network of social welfare agencies.

Community funds were used to support the synagogue building and the ritual bathhouse (mikvah), to procure and repair the Torah scrolls used in the public liturgy, to provide schooling for the sons of indigent families or dowries for the daughters of the poor, and to meet the general needs of the ill, the aged, and other vulnerable members of the Jewish community such as orphans and widows. In addition to overseeing paid individuals who provided social services, the community board also supervised voluntary societies (ḥevrot) that specialized in religious duties such as visiting the sick, ritually preparing a body for burial, providing free loans, redeeming captives, and studying classical religious texts such as the Talmud.

Local Jewish communal authority rested on both Christian and Jewish theoretical foundations. From ancient times, the Achaemenid Persians, the Seleucids, and the pre-Christian Roman rulers had recognized the legitimacy of Jewish communities as religious polities. Imperial law required that qualified Jewish leaders regulate the community in accordance with Jewish "ancestral customs," which the Jews called Torah. But in the Theodosian Code (438), Christian Roman law modified pagan imperial policies of Jewish corporate toleration to comply with a theory of Christian subordinate toleration. Jewish self-government was now tolerated only in return for the Jewish minority's political, economic, and social subordination to the Christian majority.

In the Carolingian period, Charlemagne's son,

Louis the Pious, issued charters (privilegia) of royal support to individual Jewish merchants around 825. From the late eleventh century, the German emperors and various kings of England and Spain issued charters to Jewish communities supporting Jewish juridical autonomy and local self-government.

Apart from the Christian political theory of subordinate toleration that promoted Jewish collective legitimacy, Jewish tradition and unforeseen conditions of social isolation fostered local Jewish communal self-government in early Christian Europe. A third-century rabbinic source stipulated that the "townsmen could compel one another" to conduct local community business such as "to build a synagogue, purchase a Torah scroll," or "to make agreements" such as to regulate the community workers' wages (Tosefta, Bava Mezia 11:23). Such self-government had remained theoretical in Muslim lands, where Jewish communities were organized under central Jewish authorities (gaons, exilarchs); on the other hand, the Jews of the Rhineland and central Europe, northern France and England, Christian Spain, and Provence had to work out many of their own solutions to the new problems presented by a Christian society still economically underdeveloped and barely urbanized. Far from the control and guidance of the Babylonian or Palestinian Jewish leaders, most tiny local Jewish communities in early medieval Europe were on a Jewish frontier and improvised accordingly. In time the legal scholars legitimated spontaneous developments by applying to their communities the Talmudic precedent about local "townsmen." In this way, they made that text into a mandate for local Jewish self-rule that was to characterize hundreds of emergent Jewish communities in the new towns and settlements in Latin Christendom.

As worked out by legal scholars, a theory of association by voluntary consent underlay a Jewish community board's authority "to make agreements." It had the legal force of an oath or vow to follow the community's decisions. This oath, in turn, was theoretically derived from the one the Israelites had taken at Mt. Sinai when a covenantal bond was established with "those that are standing with us this day before the Lord our God and with those who are not here with us this day" (Deut. 29:14).

Implicit in this theory of a covenant by oath is the proviso that the violation of communal enactments entitles the community elders to punish the offender by using the ban of excommunication (herem), the ancient Jewish penalty for breaking an oath. The elders adapted this widespread and effective disciplinary measure from the religious judicial system and applied it not to violations of religious law enforced by rabbinical judges but to infringements of public ordinances executed by the community board. The ban resulted in the temporary or permanent social and religious ostracism of an individual. After being placed under the ban, a Jew could not eat, drink, study, pray, or do business with other Jews. Nor could his sons be circumcised or his dead be buried in the Jewish cemetery.

Aside from imposing the ban, community elders could exact fines; this practice was also taken over from the jurisdiction of Jewish religious courts and was derived from the verse, "And that whosoever came not within three days according to the counsel of the princes and the elders, all his substance shall be forfeited and himself separated from the congregation of the captivity" (Ezra 10:8). In addition to the ban and fines, the board could impose additional penalties such as flogging, imprisonment, or expulsion. Although Jewish courts generally did not have the right to impose capital punishment, Spanish rabbis passed death sentences on informers in the thirteenth and fourteenth centuries, and the secular authorities carried out the executions. Capital punishment also fell under Jewish jurisdiction for limited times later on in Poland.

Among the more innovative disciplinary measures adopted in northern Europe was the limitation of new residents in a community (*herem ha-yishuv*) to protect the economic welfare of current residents. At first, community membership included all resident families, but economic competition among the merchant settlers led boards to restrict new settlement. Since the late tenth century, the institution of trade monopoly (*maᶜarufya*) was widespread in the Rhineland. According to this practice, a Jewish merchant developed an exclusive business relationship with a Christian customer, and other Jews were prohibited from doing business with another Jew's client. As the Jewish population increased and economic opportunities contracted, decisions were made to redefine membership and the benefits accruing to it. By the eleventh century, communities in the Rhineland and in the growing area of the county of Champagne developed the residence restriction that defined who could become a new resident.

In the twelfth century, conflicts arose within the growing Jewish population, and additional provisions were made to promote social harmony. A person with a grievance could interrupt the public religious service and accuse the party he thought had wronged him (*ᶜikkuv ha-tefillah*). Another innovation was designed to reduce the risks to merchants who traveled and had to leave their property in another person's temporary custody. The ban on confiscation (*herem ha-ᶜikkul*) was widely practiced in northern and central European communities, and it forbade a person to confiscate an object entrusted to him for safekeeping, even though he subsequently acquired a claim against the owner.

As newer communities emerged with their own sense of local autonomy, issues of potential intercommunal jurisdiction arose. Already in the middle of the eleventh century, the elders of Troyes, in the county of Champagne, asked Rabbi Judah ha-Kohen, the head of the court and academy of Mainz, to define the limits of local rule. Rabbi Judah decided that in the area of general public welfare and security, each local community is completely autonomous, but if a community violated Torah law, another community or outside religious authority could interfere and hold it accountable. By the early thirteenth century, communities in Germany declared that each local Jewish court was autonomous, and on penalty of a "ban of the court" (*herem bet din*) any local court could summon a defendant to appear before it even if the party came from another locality.

The process of selecting local leaders in a Jewish community took various forms. In the less socially stratified smaller communities of northern Europe, the assembled male members of the community simply elected their heads, preferably by unanimous consent. In the larger communities of Spain, electors (*borerim*) were chosen in accordance with various rules designed to provide representation to all strata of society and prevent the undue influence of powerful family elites.

The process of tax collection also could be more or less controlled by the social elite. After the Christian authorities determined the amount of a tax, it was up to the Jewish community to decide how to assess the members and collect it. In Germany, taxes were determined by self-assessment accompanied by an oath. In Spain, on the other hand, disputes arose because the poor preferred self-declaration and the wealthy advocated a committee of assessors to assign each family its share.

In the early medieval Jewish communities, leadership roles were undifferentiated, and the same individual could serve as a rabbinic judge and also as a member of the community board. In pioneering communities in northern Europe, like Mainz, rabbinic authorities were not a professional class. Like most other Jewish men there, a rabbi made his living as a merchant but was expert in Jewish law. Like other merchants, religious judges paid their share of communal taxes. As communities grew, a paid rabbinate gradually developed, and in Germany it emerged only in the thirteenth century. Thus the ordinances of the intercommunal Rhenish synods of the 1220's provide that the elders cannot carry out a ban of excommunication without the knowledge of either the parnas or the "rabbi in his rabbinical capacity" *(rav be-rabanuto),* a term that suggests a formal institution. By the late thirteenth century, Rabbi Meir ben Baruch of Rothenburg *(d.* 1293) was asked about a Jew who contributed an endowment fund on condition that the accrued earnings from the fund would be used to pay the salary of the community rabbi, a clear indication of his professional status.

With the professionalization of the local rabbi, other individuals assumed particular responsibilities as cantor (hazan), a term sometimes used to refer to an assistant in the synagogue, or as experts in performing circumcisions (mohelim), or scribes (soferim), or ritual slaughterers of animals and poultry (shohetim). In the thirteenth and fourteenth centuries, a series of handbooks recording the laws and customs of the particular religious office was written for the specialized community functionaries.

Whereas in the northern communities a rabbi's jurisdiction was local until the late medieval period, in the thirteenth century the kings of Castile created a central rabbinic authority, the court rabbi *(rab de la corte),* to represent the Jewish subjects before the king. When such an appointee was also an outstanding Torah scholar, the Jewish community recognized him as "head of the Spanish exile." Such a position was occupied by Rabbi Todros ben Joseph Halevi Abulafia *(ca.* 1220–1298), who was a member of an aristocratic Jewish family of Toledo, during the reign of Alfonso X. In Aragon, on the other hand, several distinguished families and dominant scholars served the Jewish community but the office of chief rabbi was not created.

Complementing local communal governance in England, royally appointed officials supervised the records of loans made by increasingly influential Jewish moneylenders. By 1200 this office was filled by Christians, called justices of the Jews; they presided over the Exchequer of the Jews, a department of the Exchequer. The *presbyter Judaeorum,* who was appointed over English Jewry by the late twelfth century, was not a chief rabbi, but a wealthy Jewish royal appointee who served as the liaison between the court and the Jewish community.

At times, particularly strong personalities or the pressure of unusual circumstances led to intercommunal synods that enacted cooperative ordinances backed by the ban. One early effort in this direction was made by Rabbi Jacob ben Meir, known as Rabbenu Tam *(d.* 1171), the dominant Jewish authority of northern France. He tried to enlist the support of Jewish elders in southern France and in the Rhineland against Jewish informing to the Christian authorities and to reduce their influence on the selection of Jewish leaders.

Whereas Rabbenu Tam apparently circulated letters to different communities, the leaders of the three Rhenish towns of Speyer, Worms, and Mainz gathered in synods in 1220 and 1223 to legislate communal disciplinary measures. A synod was held in 1418 in Forli, in northern Italy, to pass sumptuary regulations and to discuss taking collective measures in dealing with the pope and to deal with problems facing the new Jewish communities in the region. In older communities like Spain, one regional synod met in Aragon in 1354, following the riots that accompanied the Black Death. The elders of Castile met in Valladolid in 1432 to deal with the disruptions caused by the riots of 1391 and the more proximate crisis posed to the community by the abolition in 1412 by John (Juan) II of Castile of Jewish jurisdiction over civil and criminal cases. The abolition in 1380 of Jewish jurisdiction over criminal cases was rescinded in 1432.

The tendency to organize on a regional basis achieved its most elaborate and effective expression in eastern Europe, where the rulers wanted the Jewish communities of Poland and Lithuania to form associations to facilitate tax collecting. Jewish representatives from the communities of Poland and Lithuania met at fairs in regional councils of rabbinical and community leaders from the middle of the sixteenth century until the Polish government abolished them in 1764, effectively marking the end of the most ambitious experiment in medieval communal government in Europe.

BIBLIOGRAPHY

Yitzhak F. Baer, "The Origins of the Organization of the Jewish Community of the Middle Ages" (in Hebrew), in *Zion,* 15 (1950), and *A History of the Jews in Christian Spain,* Louis Schoffman et al., trans., 2 vols. (1961–1966); Salo W. Baron, *The Jewish Community,* 3 vols. (1942–

1948); Haim Hillel Ben-Sasson, ed., *A History of the Jewish People* (1976); Louis Finkelstein, ed., *Jewish Self-Government in the Middle Ages* (1924); Louis I. Rabinowitz, *The Social Life of the Jews of Northern France in the XII–XIV Centuries,* 2nd ed. (1972); Cecil Roth, *A History of the Jews in England,* 3rd ed. (1964); Simon Schwarzfuchs, *Études sur l'origine et le développement du rabbinat au moyen âge* (1957); David M. Shohet, *The Jewish Court in the Middle Ages* (1931).

IVAN G. MARCUS

[See also **Commune; Exchequer of the Jews; Jacob ben Meir; Jews** (various articles); **Law, Jewish; Law, Jewry; Rabbinate.**]

JEWISH COMMUNAL SELF-GOVERNMENT: ISLAMIC WORLD. Islam granted the Jews, as it did other protected non-Muslim "people of the book," a substantial amount of autonomy to regulate their internal religious affairs. This dispensation, like so many other borrowed features of early Islamic administration, had its roots in the legal recognition accorded Judaism by the pre-Islamic regimes of Byzantium and Persia. Toleration of Judaism necessarily meant recognition of internal Jewish self-jurisdiction because Judaism, embodied in the Talmud, comprises a vast domain of civil law in addition to purely ritual observance and also because law at that time was personal, rather than territorial as it is today. The Islamic state was perfectly willing to accept this reality, since it had neither the desire nor the means to supervise Jewish daily affairs. So long as the Jews maintained discipline, paid taxes, and adhered to Islamic precepts requiring respect for the superiority of Islam, Muslim rulers were content to let them rule themselves.

Given this situation, it followed that the definition of Jewish self-government flowed from the Jews and that the Muslim government for the most part simply confirmed what the Jews devised. Rarely, if ever, is there evidence of unilateral Muslim initiation of new organs of Jewish self-rule. In fact, Muslim authorities meddled in internal Jewish affairs far less often than they did in those of the Christians, whose numbers were much greater and who, because they professed the same religion as foreign Christian powers, were seen as posing somewhat more of a threat.

HISTORICAL DEVELOPMENT

The privilege of self-government was canonized in the so-called Pact of ʿUmar, a document associated with the second caliph, ʿUmar ibn al-Khaṭṭab (r. 634–644), but probably not put into its well known literary form until the ninth century. In addition to the plethora of humiliating disabilities that this document imposes on all non-Muslims, in the version incorporated into the law code of the great Muslim jurist al-Shāfiʿī, who died in 820, it confirms the vital right to juridical autonomy:

> We shall not supervise transactions between you and your coreligionists or any other unbelievers nor inquire into them as long as you are content.... If one of you or any other unbeliever applies to us for judgment, we shall adjudicate according to the law of Islam. But if he does not come to us, we shall not intervene among you.

The procedure by which Islamic government followed through on its promise of autonomy is well illustrated by documents concerning the appointment of Jewish communal officials. A decree of an Abbasid caliph confirming the installation of a new head of the Jewish academy *(yeshivah)* of Baghdad in 1209 shows by its language both that the candidate's qualifications and prerogatives were defined by the Jews themselves and that the Muslim potentate merely gave the stamp of approval:

> Whereas Daniel ben Eleazar ben Hibat Allāh has petitioned us to be appointed head of the academy of the Jews in place of the deceased Eleazar ben Hillel ben Fahd, in the same manner and custom as applied to the latter; and whereas we have been informed how his coreligionists judge his endowments, qualities, and worthiness ... we hereby decree ... that he be appointed head of the academy of the Jews, after the fashion of the above-mentioned deceased and insofar as Ibn al-Dastūr also served as head of the academy. (Ibn al-Sāʿī, vol. IX, pp. 266–269)

Behind these phrases lies a process delineating the administrative relationship between the Islamic state and the Jewish minority. The community selected its own leader, presented a petition to the ruler vouching for his qualifications, and received in return a decree ratifying the appointment. This process was repeated with each change of administration, as is indicated by the references to Daniel's immediate predecessor and to an illustrious earlier incumbent, Samuel ben Eli ibn al-Dastūr (in office 1164–1193). The caliph's decree also specified the prerogatives to be enjoyed by the official. Probably the petition listed the leader's duties, since the Jews knew better than the Muslims how their political institutions operated. A remnant of such a petition, soliciting a Fatimid caliph's confirmation of the appointment of a candidate for the headship of the academy of Palestine and outlining his responsibilities, has been found in the Cairo Genizah.

EMPIRE-WIDE INSTITUTIONS

Jewish self-government, fully supported by the Islamic state, functioned on three intersecting levels: imperial, regional, and local. Two institutions of Jewish autonomy enjoyed political power on an empirewide basis during the first five centuries of Islamic rule. One was the office of head of the diaspora (Hebrew: *rosh ha-golah;* Aramaic: *resh galuta;* Arabic: *ra's al-jālūt*), known in modern scholarly literature as the exilarch. His seat was in Baghdad. The exilarchs claimed to be descended from King David, and this royal lineage formed the source of their authority among the Jews. The exilarchate originated in Parthian Persia and continued under the Sasanians, but appears to have been suppressed toward the end of Sasanian rule. Shortly after the Arab conquest of Iraq, the office was revived when the Muslims acceded to a Jewish request to install a surviving scion of the Davidic line named Bustanai in his hereditary position.

The exilarch's most important governmental prerogative consisted in the right to appoint judges *(dayyanim)* for provincial Jewish communities. He was also the principal representative of the Jewish minority before the Abbasid caliph and a respected member of the royal court. Eyewitness Jewish accounts of the comings and goings of the exilarch portray him as a miniature oriental potentate, honored in the synagogue like the caliph in his mosque, surrounded by doting servants and retainers, and provided with royal garb and transport upon his regular visits to the caliph's palace.

The other, and more significant, imperial governing authority among the Jews was the head of the academy (Hebrew: *rosh ha-yeshivah;* Aramaic: *resh metivta;* Arabic: *ra's al-mathība*). There were two academies in Iraq, called Sura and Pumbedita, and one in Palestine. Like the exilarchate, the academies had been founded in pre-Islamic times. However, their scope of authority became much enlarged as a result of the Islamic unification of southwest Asia and the Mediterranean lands. Called by the honorific "gaon" (plural, geonim), after a biblical phrase (Psalm 47:5), the academy heads in the Islamic period exercised undifferentiable spiritual and temporal authority over the Jews of the empire.

The source of their authority was rabbinic learning. For various reasons the Iraqi academies came to

enjoy intellectual and political supremacy early in the Islamic period, though the Palestinian gaon retained a certain measure of sovereignty over the Jews of adjacent Egypt when both countries belonged to the same empire, particularly under the Fatimids.

The geonim dispatched to distant communities judges trained in or at least accredited by their academies and also assigned other communal functionaries. Strong central control over Arabic-speaking Jewry was further cemented by the dissemination of authoritative answers (responsa) to questions about Jewish law, by the collection of revenue from locales, and by the dispensing of titles to distant supporters. In the Islamic world the bestowal of an honorific symbolized the political dependency of the recipient upon the granter. The Iraqi academies were more energetic in this matter than the Palestinian one—at once a cause and an effect of their early ascendancy.

As is to be expected in any system of government, the Jewish autonomous institutions having imperial pretensions periodically fell victim to political conflict and intrigue. Instances are recorded in which exilarchs deposed heads of academies and installed substitutes or in which academy heads ousted exilarchs. The two Iraqi academies vied for influence over imperial Jewry and for shares in the revenues sent from the provinces. Rivalry between exilarchal or gaonic candidates often led to political strife, even to temporary schism within one or the other of these institutions. Finally, the Palestinian academy, pushed into the background by the Iraqi geonim, occasionally strove to recoup some of its lost prestige by asserting claim to its ancient prerogative of regulating the Jewish calendar.

REGIONAL AND LOCAL INSTITUTIONS

The second plane on which Jewish self-government operated was the regional one. Regional Jewish leadership emerged, first in Spain in the tenth century, then in North Africa and Egypt in the eleventh. Usually these leaders bore the royal biblical title of "nagid" and exercised the type of authority formerly monopolized by the geonim and exilarchs. Most scholars believe that with the political breakup of the Abbasid empire in the tenth century, the rulers of the successor states in Spain, North Africa, and Egypt appointed regional Jewish authorities in order to sever Jewish contact with Baghdad. Detailed examination of an individual community, such as that of Fatimid Egypt, where the nagid's official title was *ra'īs al-yahūd* ("head of the Jews"), however, suggests that the process of detachment was more complex and may have owed more to internal than to external causes. According to this view, the regional Jewries gradually emancipated themselves from the strong control of the academies as they achieved demographic strength, economic self-sufficiency, and a level of indigenous religious scholarship rendering them less dependent upon the responsa and other types of spiritual instruction handed down by the geonim.

The third level, and fundamental cell, of Jewish self-government in the Islamic world was that of the local community. Local Jewish association had existed since Greco-Roman times, when it was focused on the synagogue. Councils of elders and various delegated officials performed religious and social functions binding each congregation into a self-sufficient community. Scholars are in disagreement over the extent to which local Jewish autonomy asserted itself during the heyday of Jewish imperial authority in the early Islamic centuries. Some believe that the authoritarian centralization of the geonim and exilarchs muted the independent spirit of local association. This is partly an argument from silence, since the extant sources for those centuries, largely legal writings of the geonim, reveal very little about life at the local level. Beginning with the early eleventh century, documentation from the Cairo Genizah provides rich detail about local communities in the Mediterranean lands. Here the local polity enjoyed considerable independence while maintaining a certain degree of deference toward imperial and regional Jewish leaders.

A chief characteristic of the local community—one vexing to those wishing to give a rational description of its structure—was a fluidity in the roles played by its officialdom. Fluidity of titles further clouds the picture. Nonetheless, certain features seem clear. First, the rank and file participated extensively in decisions affecting communal life. The "elders," not necessarily the oldest chronologically but certainly the most venerable in terms of prestige, represented the interests of the community at large and assisted the appointed local executive. When the rank and file felt wronged by their leaders, they often gave vent to their grievances by boycotting the synagogue, which was as much the focal point of Jewish public affairs as it was the place of prayer and study.

Where only one synagogue existed in a locality, its congregation was coterminous with the community. Where there were more than one (usually at most two, one each for Jews adhering to the Iraqi

and to the Palestinian liturgical rites), they functioned as a single community in matters of common concern. At the head of the community was the *muqaddam,* the appointed executive. This flexible Arabic title, meaning "one placed at the head," adopted the specific connotation of local community executive from the end of the eleventh century, when the regional nagid (in Egypt) inherited the prerogatives of the gaon. Prior to that, heads of congregations were appointees of the academies. The functions performed by the *muqaddam* depended upon his qualifications and upon local needs. For instance, he might serve as cantor, judge, teacher, scribe, fund raiser, or any combination thereof. In deference to the spirit of autonomy cherished by the locales, nagids showed responsiveness to local complaints about *muqaddam*s.

Unless it was a large community, a locality usually supported only one professionally trained judge *(dayyan),* who was appointed by the imperial or regional Jewish sovereign. Laymen joined with the expert judges to form the required quorum of three making up a rabbinical court *(beth din).* Adjudication of disputes between Jews was the most important self-governing function of the community. Another vital office was that of supervisor of social services, *parnas,* a word derived from the Hebrew verb meaning "to provide support." Several *parnasim* functioned in each community. They had charge of communal property, from which rental income was collected for the community chest, and of fundraising from individuals. Revenues from private and communal sources were expended on relief for the poor; on emoluments for Jewish public officials, scholars, and teachers of children of the poor; and on upkeep of synagogues. Charity proper appears to have been dispensed out of private contributions, whereas a disproportionate amount of the income from communal properties established as pious trusts went toward maintenance of the buildings and communal salaries.

Strife of the type that periodically surfaced in the imperial and regional institutions of Jewish autonomy often erupted at the local level as well. These disputes, frequently revolving around such matters as the appointment or the conduct of a local Jewish official, constituted another sign of the political vitality attending Jewish communal self-government.

BIBLIOGRAPHY
Simha Assaf, *Tequfat ha-geonim ve-sifrutah* (The gaonic period and its literature), Mordechai Margoliot, ed.

(1955), pt. 1; Yitzhak Baer, "The Origins of the Organization of the Jewish Community of the Middle Ages" (in Hebrew), in *Zion*, 15 (1950); Salo W. Baron, *The Jewish Community: Its History and Structure to the American Revolution*, 3 vols. (1948, repr. 1972), esp. I, 157–207; Eliezer Bashan, ed., *Mivḥar bibliographi ᶜal rashut ha-golah ha-nesiut ve-ha-negidut ba-mizraḥ* (Selected bibliography of the exilarchs, nesiim, and negidim in the Middle East), Haim Zeev Hirschberg, ed. (1974); Mark R. Cohen, "The Jews Under Islam: From the Rise of Islam to Sabbatai Zevi," in *Bibliographical Essays in Medieval Jewish Studies*, II (1976), and *Jewish Self-government in Medieval Egypt: The Origins of the Office of Head of the Jews ca. 1065–1126* (1980); Walter J. Fischel, *Jews in the Economic and Political Life of Medieval Islam* (1937, repr. 1969); Solomon D. Goitein, *A Mediterranean Society*, II, *The Community* (1971); Haim Zeev Hirschberg, *A History of the Jews in North Africa*, I, 2nd rev. ed., M. Eichelberg, trans. (1974), 205–256; Ibn al-Sāᶜī, *Al-jāmiᶜ al-mukhtaṣar*, IX (1934); Jacob R. Marcus, *The Jew in the Medieval World* (1938, repr. 1983), 287–292 (Nathan the Babylonian's account of Saadiah Gaon); Arthur S. Tritton, *The Caliphs and Their Non-Muslim Subjects: A Critical Study of the Covenant of ᶜUmar* (1930, repr. 1970), 78–88.

MARK R. COHEN

[See also **Exilarch; Gaonic Period; Jews in Christian Spain; Jews in the Middle East; Jews in Muslim Spain; Jews in North Africa; Nagid; Schools, Jewish.**]

JEWISH KHAZARS. See **Khazars.**

JEWISH OATH. See **Oath, More Judaico.**

JEWISH SCIENCE. See **Science, Jewish.**

JEWS AND THE CATHOLIC CHURCH. The relations between the Jews and the medieval church, as it was embodied in the popes and the hierarchy in particular, were governed consistently by a fully articulated theory. This theory originated in St. Paul's view, expounded in the Epistle to the Romans, that the true Israel is a spiritual body, composed of believers in Christ, and not the Israel of the flesh, the Jews, who erred by seeking salvation through following the laws of the Torah. Nevertheless, according to medieval theory, the Jews will not be rejected by God, and, indeed, will come to accept Christ at the end of days. The implication of this stricture that the Jews have a necessary role in Christian soteriology was later articulated in Augustine's theories. According to Augustine, the Jews are witness to Christian truth and the personification of Cain, despised murderers whose presence must be suffered. Augustine's ideas correspond to the principles of Roman law in the christianized empire, which sought to place the Jews in a state of subservience, as Christian theology indicated was proper. But Roman law also affirmed the fundamental rights of Roman citizenship and justice that Jews had always enjoyed. Theology and law were then combined in the letters and administrative decisions of Gregory the Great. One phrase he adopted from the Theodosian Code eventually came to typify all papal dealing with Jews: as much as the rights owed the Jews must not be denied them, so must the Jews themselves not overstep the limits which have been set, that is, those of Christian superiority and their own inferiority.

However, in Galatians and 1 Corinthians, Paul expressed a view of the Jews far different from that in Romans. They were Ishmael, the child of the slave woman, who must be driven out, and the leaven that sours the dough. Expanding on this theme, John Chrysostom called the Jews "degenerate, inebriate dogs," their synagogues houses of prostitution. In his *Eight Orations*, delivered at Antioch in 387, he warned Christians against polluting their faith and the Christian flock through contacts with the Jews in their homes and their synagogues. Those who stood idly by doing nothing to stop other Christians from judaizing through table fellowship and participation in Jewish rites became themselves "enemies of God."

This overwhelmingly negative view eventually became the popular one; it came to serve as a prime motivating ideology behind the late medieval Jewish expulsions, when men sought "opportunities" (as one sixteenth-century text describing the expulsion from Udine in Italy has it) to get rid of the Jews. The path to this end in Christian Europe began with the teachings of zealous purists, typified by the ninth-century bishop Agobard of Lyons, who dreamed of remolding European society according to the classic precepts of Christian reform. Like other contemporaries, who wished to have the whole of society operate exclusively on the basis of Christian principles, with kings dutifully following episcopal commands and interpretations, for Agobard, the very existence of the Jews in his world was a thorn. The church fathers had seen the Jew as the distorted reflection of Christianity and the enemy of the scattered Christian congregations. Not unexpectedly, the general christianizing of Europe had brought with it an escalation in the perceived scope of the imputed Jewish danger, and the Jew began to emerge as the enemy of society as a whole.

Enrolled in the forces of Antichrist, Agobard charged, the Jews had corrupted the emperor Louis the Pious himself. Contrary to Agobard's instructions, the emperor had endangered the church by allowing the Jews to flout the canons regarding the purchase and ownership of slaves and the free social intermingling of Jews and Christians.

Agobard's railings, however, had their limits. Though he might insinuate that the Jews were sexual monsters, unlike Chrysostom, he explicitly eschewed violence. He admitted, in the repressively severe code of laws he had drawn up, that the Jews should be controlled by legal means alone, and that they ought not to be subjected to arbitrary physical assault.

Others, who were clearly influenced by Agobard's teachings or other similar ones, went further and abandoned the Pauline-Augustinian tradition altogether. According to the writings of the early-twelfth-century abbot Guibert of Nogent, the Jews worked black magic in league with Satan to bring monks to the vilest pornographic acts, such as making "a libation of [their] seed" (Benton, p. 115) on the host. Other monastic chroniclers pictured the Jews as conspirators. It was the Jews who plotted the 1009 Muslim desecration of the Holy Sepulcher, wrote Raoul Glaber about forty years later. Thus, it was with justice that the "common will" of the faithful decreed the mass execution of the Jews by mob violence. The image of the Jews had become so negative that numerous texts routinely characterized all deviations from Christian orthodoxy as judaizing. If something is wrong and should be blotted out, the idea went, then it must be Jewish, at least in origin. The popes of this period too, such as Stephen IV (768–772), were not immune from calling Jews the "sons of darkness" and "Beliel," who threatened to corrupt the sons of light. In about 938, Leo VII consented to a request from the archbishop of Mainz to expel those Jews who would not become Christians. This situation was undoubtedly a product of early medieval turmoil and church weakness. Had it persisted, the teachings of Chrysostom, with their advocacy of violence, would surely have triumphed among churchmen and laymen alike, and all traces of the Pauline equilibrium would have disappeared.

There always would be certain churchmen whose concern for what they believed to be social purity would lead them to express these extremist, albeit uncanonical, positions. The preaching Franciscans of the fifteenth century, most notably Bernardino da Feltre, argued ceaselessly that only expulsion would end the plague of Jewish usury, or, more precisely, the plague of a Jewish presence itself. More extreme figures, such as the archdeacon of Écija, Ferrante Martinez, incited mobs all over Spain to initiate the devastating slaughters of 1391. Luther too, fearful of the so-called judaizing excesses of the sabbatarian sect of radical reformers, wrote, in *Concerning the Jews and Their Lies,* that if the Jews continue to threaten Christian integrity, their homes should be burned down. On the other hand, when the monk Rudolph (Radulf) urged mob violence against Rhenish Jews in 1146 during the Second Crusade, his mentor, Bernard of Clairvaux, successfully intervened to prevent a repetition of the massacres that had befallen the same Jewish communities in 1096 during the First Crusade. No friend of the Jews—he considered them possessed of a bovine mentality—Bernard emphasized that the canons and Christian charity made his actions obligatory.

Bernard signals a return among churchmen to the earlier equilibrium, a return undoubtedly related to an increasing level of stability in military, political, and church affairs. Bernard's position that Jews must be protected and their rights preserved, regardless of personal feelings, was already evident among churchmen during the First Crusade. The Hebrew chronicles recount that the Rhineland bishops took their obligations to protect the Jews with utmost seriousness. Nevertheless, these same bishops had also made known their conviction that the Jews would best save themselves, physically as well as spiritually, if they converted to Christianity. As was Bernard after them, therefore, the bishops were not motivated by personal whim, but by the dictates of law and theology. This fact has frequently gone unobserved by those historians who have followed the understandable reasoning of the medieval Jewish chronicles, which discriminated between friends and foes among the clergy rather than between upholders and violators of the canons.

From the late eleventh century, most churchmen array themselves along a spectrum in which the moderate Gregory the Great lies at one extreme and the harsh Agobard of Lyons at the other. It is therefore inappropriate to speak, as is invariably done, of a monolithic corpus embracing monks, canons, bishops, and popes, and label it the "church." With the possible exception of the papacy and the canon law, this "church" did not exist.

The Jews' difficulties arose with churchmen like Agobard who had eschewed violence yet still pursued the dream of a pure and perfected Christian society. This is a particularly apt characterization of the members of the two mendicant reforming orders, the Dominicans and the Franciscans. In thirteenth-century Spain, the Dominicans launched a three-pronged offensive in quest of Jewish converts: forced sermons, disputations, and the censorship of rabbinic literature were their prime missionary tools. (This campaign was something of an aberration, for it had long been accepted teaching that there was no sense in seeking Jewish converts before the time of the millennium, a teaching implied by Paul and confirmed by Augustine.)

The thirteenth-century Dominican conversion program aimed at Jews was an outgrowth of a wider mission to the East. To prepare missionaries, schools were established to teach Eastern languages, and a number of Dominicans thus became experts in Hebrew and rabbinic literature. The movement of Christian Hebraism, its roots already struck in earlier centuries, had now begun in earnest. By the sixteenth century, these Christian Hebraists went so far as to appropriate Jewish mysticism for their own purposes, seeing in the symbolism of the cabala the quintessential proof of the Trinity.

In the thirteenth century the great product of this movement was the *Pugio fidei* (*ca.* 1278) of Ramón Martí. The work typifies the Dominican confrontation with the Jews and Judaism. For the most part a point by point refutation of Judaism based on rabbinic midrashim, the *Pugio fidei* also describes post-Christian Judaism, in more vivid detail than had ever been used previously, as the faith of Satan. Yet, reflecting the position taken by one of those responsible for its compilation, the canonist and chief editor of Gregory IX's Decretals collection, Raymond of Peñafort, the *Pugio fidei* does not preach the expulsion of the Jews or the outlawry of Judaism; it only demands total stringency in the observance of the canons.

This hesitation about expulsion did not prevent the Dominicans from becoming deeply involved in the thirteenth-century papal Inquisition, and it is here that the potential danger of their program may be observed. Rabble-rousing, like that of the monk

Rudolph in the twelfth century or the Sevillian canon Ferrante Martinez in the late fourteenth century, presented so strong a threat to overall social stability that all leaders were eventually compelled to halt their provocative activities. Those on the border of this extremism, however, including not only the mendicants but also such prominent seculars as the thirteenth-century papal legates in France, the cardinals Robert of Courson and Odo of Châteauroux, managed to persuade secular leaders (kings among them) that it was their sacred duty to control the Jews with severe measures, including the use of the Inquisition. The Dominican inquisitors thus received royal support for their goal of overseeing the content of Jewish literature, the faithfulness to Christianity of new converts, and the conduct of those Jews known to have encouraged heresy by aiding former Jews to return to Judaism.

Apart from inquisitorial excesses, the danger of this institution lay in its effect on royal zeal. Louis IX of France became so aroused that he began to exceed the demands of the canons and to violate their safeguards as well, going so far as to assume a tutelary role over his clergy when it came to the Jews. He took the lead in destroying his Jewish chamber serfs. The perceived need to establish religiously pure political bodies eventually proved a cogent argument in favor of expulsion for him as well as for Edward I of England and Ferdinand and Isabella in Spain. In their zeal, the kings were surpassed only by the mobs stirred up by the ferment of popular piety. Their members were drawn from all ranks of society, and for them the Jews had become the source of all evil.

Nowhere is it possible to see more clearly the various nuances of the problems created for the Jews by churchmen and Christian theology than in the Talmud affair of the 1240's in Paris, initiated by a convert, Nicholas Donin. Parisian churchmen were the most instrumental in pursuing it, and the pope, Gregory IX, went along at first, for it appeared the Jews had correctly been charged with blasphemy and with observing a *Nova lex*, a fabrication and not the true law of the Torah. However, Innocent IV later honored a Jewish appeal to reexamine the talmudic texts, since the Jews were, at the least, guaranteed the right to profess authentic Judaism. Finally, a counterappeal by the legate Odo and forty-four Parisian masters went unheeded because Innocent IV had probably decided, apart from the justice of the Jews' complaint, that the course proposed by the Spanish Dominicans (to censor and exploit the Talmud for missionary purposes) was preferable to burning indiscriminately. In Paris, Louis IX decided the affair in 1254 by outlawing the possession and study of the Talmud in perpetuity.

The actions of Innocent IV typify the behavior of the popes toward the Jews. With rare exceptions, they accepted the dictates of tradition and the canons, above all, those codified in the great legal and theological collections of the twelfth and thirteenth centuries. Receiving strong episcopal support, even actions such as condoning a reasonable interest rate for Jewish lenders (rather than enforcing the absolute prohibition of interest that the canons seem to demand) were really quite defensible. They were grounded in the legal-theological principles that accepted the Jews and allowed them their good customs; they were not flagrant abuses of the canons, nor were they dearly bought exemptions. It is doubtful that bribes could regularly purchase papal protection. The sums cited on occasion by Jewish texts in connection with the popes were either stiff document fees of the kind demanded by the papal camera from Jews and Christians alike, or taxes paid by the Jews of the Papal States.

Obviously, not all the policies of the popes were unwaveringly consistent with one another; the law was, after all, always open to interpretation. Still, it would be ill-advised to judge the popes on the basis of individual pieces of legislation or actions. The actions of Innocent III at the Fourth Lateran Council in 1215, especially his introduction of a distinguishing mark on clothing, were consistent with the goal church theology and law had always advocated of maintaining a sharp social distance between Christians and Jews. The issues of whether to burn the Talmud, what powers to grant the papal Inquisition, and whether interest-taking should be prohibited or only regulated may also be assessed by similar standards. These were not innovations or fundamental changes in policy; they were the logical extrapolations from past ideals.

This overall adhesion to established principles is common to the Jewry policy of all popes. Their demands for punctilious observance or their sweeping exemptions were always justified, if sometimes tenuously, as consonant with the best interests of the Christian faith. Their deliberateness in observing the fundamentals is at times remarkable. Thus, if Innocent III threatened severe reprisals for Jewish violations of the canons and, in turn, waxed livid when they occurred, he also made it clear in his version of the bull (and canon) *Sicut judaeis non,* which he

named the *Constitutio pro Iudaeis,* that the church felt itself fully bound to protect Jewish rights. The snag, of course, was that Jewish rights were far from equal rights. The Jews were to be accepted and Judaism tolerated, said Innocent III, but they would have to acquiesce in Christian lordship with the bowed neck of the slave, for they had been consigned to perpetual servitude.

This theological concept, based on Galatians, sums up the essential thrust of the canons that concern Jews. From the sixth through the thirteenth centuries, canons had been enacted to govern such areas as the right of the Jews to live within Christian lands and to receive just (not equal) treatment; the degree of permissible social and commercial contact between Jews and Christians; the prohibition of Jewish mastery over Christians; the problems of conversion; and the right of the church to assert direct jurisdiction over Jews in certain areas. Under these broad headings, additional canons had accrued to regulate in detail the issues of interfaith table fellowship, the possession of slaves, the wearing of distinctive clothing, and the taking of usury (meaning any interest whatsoever). The most important of these (as well as of all other canons) were collected by Gregory IX in the Title, *De Iudaeis,* of his 1234 Decretals. It reflects faithfully the mature Jewry policy espoused and applied by the popes.

The theological mirror of the canons may, in turn, be found in the *Summa theologiae* of Thomas Aquinas. It contains the most concise statement of Jewish rights and disabilities that exists, and it shows beyond question the link between medieval and Pauline traditions concerning the Jews. At the same time, even Thomas did not represent a unanimously accepted position. Duns Scotus, for one, fiercely disagreed with him on the right of Jewish children not to be snatched from their parents for the purpose of baptism.

Contemporary Jews were aware of all this. Their expertise in church law and thought, which appears in various Hebrew polemics, was considerable; they were especially knowledgeable in papal theory, and with good reason. In the 1140's one Solomon ben Sampson had called the pope a devil. He erroneously believed the pope was responsible for the First Crusade massacres. By the end of the century, however, Ephraim of Bonn was praising Bernard of Clairvaux for preventing new massacres. By the 1250's Meir ben Simeon called on the king of France to follow the example of the pope in his dealings with Jews. Similarly, an anonymous thirteenth-century text that describes an alleged pogrom initiated in 1007 by the French king Robert the Pious studiedly advised Jews to pay lip service and more to papal claims to judge them in matters of religion. To be sure, the pope was no friend, but he was at least prepared to guarantee the Jews due legal process—the very thing that kings and other enemies, within and outside of the church, had striven so hard to deny them. The history of direct Jewish appeals to the popes and their positive responses is, consequently, long indeed. At a 1354 conclave in Barcelona, the Jews even petitioned the pope against allowing the Inquisition to violate the rules governing its jurisdiction over Jews.

With the accession of Paul IV in 1555, the medieval equilibrium was broken. Convinced that the end of days was near, he placed the Jews under his rule in a ghetto (the first true ghetto had already been established at Venice in 1516) and, by the use of heavy pressures, sought to achieve their immediate mass conversion. A similar policy had been pursued briefly in Spain, between 1412 and 1418, by the antipope Benedict XIII, under the influence of the Dominican Vincent Ferrer, and it resulted in many conversions. Paul IV was not so successful. Still, in theory and often in fact, his policies were maintained by each of his successors. With Paul IV, therefore, an epoch in church-Jewish relations had come to a close.

BIBLIOGRAPHY

Translations of medieval texts are in Thomas Aquinas, *Summa theologica*, Dominican Fathers of New York, trans., 3 vols. (1947–1948); St. Augustine, "Faith and Works, the Creed, in Answer to the Jews," Marie Liguori Ewald, trans., in his *Treatises on Marriage and Other Subjects* (1955); John F. Benton, ed., *Self and Society in Medieval France* (1970), esp. 134–137 and 209–211; Bernhard Blumenkranz, *Les auteurs chrétiens latins du moyen âge sur les juifs et le judaisme* (1963), mostly synopses; Wayne Meeks and R. L. Wilken, *Jews and Christians in Antioch in the First Four Centuries of the Common Era* (1978), with new translations of two of Chrysostom's orations; Martin Luther, "Against the Sabbatarians" and "On the Jews and Their Lies," Martin H. Bertram, trans., in *Luther's Works*, XLVII (1971).

Studies. David Berger, "The Attitude of St. Bernard of Clairvaux Toward the Jews," in *American Academy for Jewish Research, Proceedings,* **40** (1972); Bernhard Blumenkranz, "Deux compilations canoniques de Florus de Lyon et l'action antijuif d'Agobard," in *Revue historique de droit français et étranger,* 33 (1955); Peter Browe, *Die Judenmission in Mittelalter und die Päpste* (1942); Jeremy Cohen, *The Friars and the Jews* (1981); Solomon Grayzel, *The Church and the Jews in the Thirteenth Century* (1933); Manfred Kneiwasser, "Bischof Agobard von Lyon und der Platz der Juden in einer sakral verfassten Einheitsgesellschaft," in *Kairos,* **19** (1977); Ḥen-melekh Merḥavyak (Ch. M. Merchavia), *The Church Versus Talmudic Literature* (in Hebrew) (1970); Rosemary R. Ruether, *Faith and Fratricide: The Theological Roots of Anti-Semitism* (1974); Kenneth R. Stow, "The Church and the Jews: From St. Paul to Paul IV," in *Bibliographical Essays in Medieval Jewish Studies* (1976), *Catholic Thought and Papal Jewry Policy, 1555–1593* (1977), *The "1007 Anonymous" and Papal Sovereignty: Jewish Perceptions of the Papacy and Papal Policy in the High Middle Ages* (1984), and "The Jew as Alien and the Diffusion of Restriction: An Expulsion Text from Udine, 1556," in *Sefer Cassuto* (1985); Edward A. Synan, *The Popes and the Jews in the Middle Ages* (1965).

KENNETH R. STOW

[See also **Agobard; Anti-Semitism; Expulsion of Jews; Guibert of Nogent; Jews in Christian Spain; John Chrysostom, St.; Raoul Glaber; Raymond of Peñafort, St.; Talmud, Exegesis and Study of.**]

JEWS IN CHRISTIAN SPAIN. The Visigothic invaders of Spain (415) found a small Jewish settlement there. In general, it enjoyed a quiet life until Reccared converted from Arianism to Catholicism in 586. The Visigoths promulgated the first anti-Jewish laws in 589 at the Third Synod in Toledo. From then on persecutions, forced conversions, and expulsions became the basis of an anti-Jewish policy. The converted were forbidden to hold public offices that entailed any jurisdiction over old (that is, non-Jewish) Christians; nor were they allowed to enjoy any benefices. The Fourth Synod, held in Toledo in 633 under King Sisenand, produced the severest anti-Jewish legislation.

The Muslim invasion in 711 came at a time when the peninsula was most probably without many professing Jews, although some scholars maintain that there were small colonies of Jews scattered in isolated locations. But all agree that Jews arrived with the invaders and settled in various towns. When the Carolingian monarchy set out to push back the Muslim invaders and reconquer Barcelona (801), Jews also took part in resettling the Marca Hispánica (Catalonia). A limited number of Jews settled in various Christian nuclei in northern Spain. Jews found that they had access to and favorable treatment from the court of Sancho III the Great (1004–1035), king of Navarre. (During the last decade of his reign, Sancho could truthfully designate himself as king of Christian Spain; he ruled as Sancho I of Castile after 1027 and had virtual control of Aragon when it was incorporated into the kingdom of Navarre for part of his reign.)

A series of Jewish settlements came into being, basing their rights on *fueros,* privileges granted by the Christian rulers of northern Spain. Jews held land in full ownership (alodium) and as leaseholders. Many documents, some of them bearing Hebrew signatures, deal with transfers of land owned by Jews to church dignitaries and monasteries, and vice versa. It was then, in the early eleventh century, that the Jewish quarter of Barcelona came into existence; it endured until it was destroyed by the riots of 1391.

During the eleventh century the Jewish community was granted privileges in addition to those in the old code of common laws, the *Usatges* (compiled between 1053 and 1071). Every Jewish community, starting with the thirteenth century, was ruled by a varying number of elders, who formed a council. The influence of the town on the Jewish communal organization was greatest in Aragon. Barcelona, for example, had later a representation that based itself on three classes: the great one *(mayor),* the middle *(mitjana),* and the small, or lesser *(minor),* the criterion being the amount of taxes paid by the members of each class. Later, by the beginning of the fourteenth century, it had a council of thirty members (ten from each class), which patterned itself on the Christian municipal Council of One Hundred. Seven chosen *fieles,* or *secretarii* formed the executive body of the community, whereas the *adelantados* or *mukademin* (often identified with the *fieles*) had judicial duties to perform. (Another body, called *berurei averot,* composed of judicial officers recognized by the crown, supervised public morality. From its inception it was a typically Catalan institution, even after being transferred to other communities as well as to the Sephardic communities in sixteenth-century Turkey.) The king usually confirmed the rulings and constitution of the council. The same structure on a lesser scale was common also in a number of smaller communities. One of the main issues before the council was the yearly tax assessment, a major communal responsibility vis-à-vis the crown. Members of the council negotiated annually with the crown about the amount of taxes to be levied. It was an issue that caused tension and strife within the community. Nevertheless, the poor, those who dedicated their lives to the study of the Torah, and religious ministrants (rabbis, beadles) were exempt from taxes.

Legally, the Jews seem to have belonged to the ruler, a status consistent with the developing legal relationships that were prevalent elsewhere in Europe at that time. Indeed, Christians and Jews were recognized in Christian Spain as equals before the law. In Catalonia, a well-defined policy regulated the interrelationships among state, church, and Jews and offered protection to life and property. This was the situation in both Castile and Aragon. The Jews were a trustworthy element in the colonization of the borderland, such that a new type of settlement emerged in Castile on the king's land, known as *villa nova de iudaeis.*

The Jewish communities in Christian Spain developed in tandem with the various waves of the *Reconquista* drives. The reconquest of Toledo in 1085 should be seen as a turning point in the history of that community, which had already existed during the Muslim period. Cidellus (Joseph Ferruziel or Ferrizuel, *d. ca.* 1145) was appointed head of the Jews of the kingdom and acted as a special adviser and physician to Alfonso VI of Castile (1065–1109). Cidellus, himself a native of Cabra (near Córdoba and Granada), created new settlements by urging Jewish settlers to move from Muslim Spain to the Christian parts of Castile.

The main body responsible for the Jewish communal organization in Castile was the *concejo cerrado,* in which only members of the upper class of the local Jewish population were represented. The *veedores,* probably the administrative body within the council, played here an important role. The *mukademin* (adelantados) dealt with all daily matters of the community. The *bedin* (also known as *bedinus, vedi, albedin*), the supervisor and chief executive officer in the community, was a crown appointee. Furthermore, there were officers for works and voluntary communal organizations that took care of the sick and needy. Among such organizations were the burial societies (ḥevra kaddisha), which operated in almost every community.

The crown of Castile nominated a special person as *rab de la corte,* who was the chief Jewish official responsible for the distribution of taxes among the communities and who acted as appellate judge between Jewish litigants. The *rab de la corte* represented the Jewish community before the crown and acted as an intermediary between both sides. This typical Jewish courtier often served in the crown's administration and was considered a trusted servant of the monarch. The last *rab de la corte* of Castile was Abraham Seneor, who converted on 15 June

1492, and thus escaped the fate of his expelled brethren.

During the twelfth century Toledo, capital of Castile, became a center for Jewish translators and remained so well into the thirteenth century. Beginnings were made during the time of Alfonso VI of Castile, and the peak of activity was reached in the days of Alfonso VII (1126–1157). A collegium of translators of great reknown translated Arabic and Hebrew texts into Latin. Works on medicine, philosophy, astronomy, and other fields were brought to the knowledge of the West. Barcelona was another center of cultural creativity. Rabbi Abraham bar Hiyya wrote his works on mathematics and astronomy in that city.

The consolidation of Jewish life in thirteenth-century Spain was connected with the attitude toward the Jews of such rulers as James I of Aragon (1213–1276), and Ferdinand III (1217–1252) and Alfonso X (1252–1284) of Castile. This was the century of the great *Reconquista* drive toward the south; the frontiers established between Granada and the kingdom of Castile-León were to last until 1492. James I invited Jews from North Africa to settle in the newly conquered lands. Many answered his call and settled in the Balearic Islands (1224–1235) and the newly created kingdom of Valencia (1238/1239). The settlers were granted land and for some years enjoyed tax exemptions. They were active in local administration and in the central government, as mentioned earlier. Some also served as king's bailiffs. Others were diplomats in the service of their king, suppliers to the court, and tax farmers, who represented their brethren before the court.

The thirteenth century saw as well a great upsurge in Jewish learning. Great rabbis and scholars, such as Moses Nahmanides, Solomon ben Abraham Adret, Aaron ben Joseph ha-Levi (*ca.* 1235–1300), and their disciples, such as Rabbi Yom Tov ben Abraham Ishbili (Asbili, "of Seville," *ca.* 1250–1330), served their communities and Spanish Jewry. They wrote an abundance of works and studies. This was also the century of the cabala and the Maimonidean controversy, which arose in Spain and Provence and was not resolved until about 1300.

A decline in the Jewish status in Aragon became noticeable in the 1260's, an outcome of the fourth Lateran Council's (1215) decisions on the Jewish status. As early as 1228 James I had ordered, in accordance with these decisions, that no more than 20 percent interest be permitted on loans given by Jews. In the same decree Jews were also forbidden to hold

government posts, their oaths were declared invalid in litigations between Jews and Christians, and they were ordered to wear a special sign. The papal Inquisition was introduced into Aragon as well. Also, in 1263, the so-called Barcelona disputation between the convert Pablo Christiani and Nahmanides took place in the presence of the king. James's policy toward Jews should be considered in its twofold manifestation: on the one hand he made extensive use of their abilities and trustworthiness; on the other hand he implemented the church policies toward them and acted according to the advice given by Dominican and Franciscan friars. Although his son and heir Pedro III (1276–1285) followed a more rigorous anti-Jewish line, he nevertheless had to resort to the help of Jewish advisers and administrators. At this time Raimond Martini published his anti-Jewish work *Pugio fidei,* which later served as a manual for anti-Jewish propaganda.

In the *Reconquista* drive under the leadership of Ferdinand III and Alfonso X of Castile we find Jews as settlers in frontier areas and as mounted bowmen (*ballesteros*) in battle. Pope Gregory IX tried to induce Ferdinand to follow the anti-Jewish line of the church, but it seems that a realpolitik of reconquest restrained him from taking heed of the pope's exhortations. Only after the *Reconquista* had come to a halt did an anti-Jewish policy emerge, as expressed in the seventh part of the so-called *Siete partidas* legislation. Jews were still to be found in the king's service, for example, Todros ben Joseph ha-Levi Abulafia and Solomon ibn Zadok (Don Çulema), who acted as the king's envoy on various missions and served as chief tax farmer of Castile. The fate of Ibn Zadok's son Isaac (Çag de la Maleha), who was also in the king's service, was the gallows. He paid with his life for having taken the side of Sancho, the king's heir, in 1279.

The fourteenth century in Spain was a period of contraction and loss of Jewish services and influence. In Aragon James II (1291–1327) laid down the basis for an anti-Jewish line that held sway throughout the century: the rights of the Jews were to be preserved as long as they did not contradict the rulings of the church. A conversionist policy based on persuasion and conviction should be carried out. In 1306, however, James opened the frontiers of his kingdom to the Jews expelled from France and in 1320 acted with great vigor against the *Pastoureaux* (French crusaders against Jews and Muslims), who crossed the border into Aragon and Navarre. This policy was continued by Alfonso IV of Aragon (1327–1336) and his successor, Pedro IV the Ceremonious (1336–1387). The Black Death took its toll in this kingdom as well as in Castile, and the anti-Jewish riots that followed the plague struck a heavy blow to the Jewish communities. An attempt in 1354 to reorganize Aragonese Jewry along centralistic lines by forming a special central committee to lead all the communities failed.

Castile was then the scene of a clerical anti-Jewish attack. A conspicuous supporter of this attack was the convert Abner of Burgos (after conversion, Alfonso de Valladolid), who openly advocated a policy of persecution and forcible conversions. Nevertheless, Jewish influence was still prevalent at the court of Alfonso XI (1312–1350), in the person of the king's chief tax farmer, Don Yuçaf de Écija, who was also a member of the inner Council of the Kingdom. Ashkenazic traditions were brought to Spain by Rabbi Asher ben Jehiel, a pupil of Rabbi Meir of Rothenburg, who was appointed rabbi of Toledo. His descendants, especially his sons Rabbi Judah ben Asher and Rabbi Jacob ben Asher (author of a codification of Jewish law), played an important role in Jewish life, although many members of this family died during the 1348 riots. The first open demand for the expulsion of Castilian Jewry was made when a Moroccan army invaded southern Spain. Although the invader was expelled (1339), this anti-Jewish propaganda left its mark by stigmatizing the Jews as an unreliable element that at any time might join with the enemies of Spain. Alfonso tried to resettle Jews from southern Castile in the northern parts around the river Duero; a series of anti-Jewish restrictions were passed by the Cortes of Alcalá in 1348. An exceptional contribution to Spanish national culture in Castile was made by Rabbi Shem Tov ben Isaac Ardutiel, known as Santob de Carrión; his Hebrew and Spanish works (Proverbios morales) contained Jewish ethics. In Mallorca Jewish cartographers excelled: worthy of mention are Abraham Cresques (d. 1387) and his son Judah Cresques.

Pedro I the Cruel of Castile (1350–1369) did not succeed in restoring the Jewish communities, despite the help of his treasurer Samuel ben Meir ha-Levi Abulafia (whose synagogue and house stand today in Toledo as a monument to his greatness). Indeed, in 1360 or 1361 he was arrested and died in prison. The war waged against Pedro by his half-brother Enrique Trastámara brought to light a new element in the anti-Jewish propaganda. Enrique claimed that his aim was to free Castile from the "Jewish yoke" and from its enslavement in Jewish hands. Extortionate demands and heavy fines were imposed on Jewish communities in such cities as Burgos, Toledo, and Cuenca (each had to pay a million maravedi) for Enrique's war effort; those that failed to pay were to be sold into slavery. Many Jews perished during the invasions of the French and English mercenaries brought in by the contesting parties. Another blow fell on Jewish communities in Andalusia when Ferrant Martinez, the archdeacon of Écija, confiscated the synagogues in Seville and turned them into churches. Although Enrique had to reverse his anti-Jewish policy after having killed his brother and having been crowned, nevertheless the series of blows previously sustained by the Jews had already shattered the communities. It was then, as a consequence of the anti-Jewish drive initiated by Vicente Ferrer, that some Jewish dignitaries converted: Rabbi Solomon Halevi, rabbi of Burgos, became Pablo de Santa María and later went to Paris to study theology and was made bishop of Burgos; Samuel Abrabanel, one of the most important Jewish courtiers of his day, became Juan Sánchez de Sevilla and was appointed treasurer to the king.

On 4 June 1391 anti-Jewish riots started in Seville and spread throughout Spain. These riots cannot be seen as a social uprising. Rather, they were a joining together of all sectors of society—nobles and clergy, honorable citizens and town riffraff, soldiers and sailors. They were directed against the Jewish minority; and the only communities that survived were those that found ways to defend themselves, through either the king's presence there or some nobleman's intervention, or by means of the shelter given at a local castle. Approximately a third of the Jewish population was martyred; another third, including entire communities, accepted baptism; and many fled to North Africa or Granada. The old community of Barcelona ceased to exist. In all, of the Jewish population in Spain, estimated at about 600,000 before the riots, only about a third survived without converting.

Fifteenth-century Spain underwent a great socioreligious and political change. The state embarked on a clear anti-Jewish policy. Persecutions were followed by restrictions, prohibitions, and anti-Jewish legislation. Mention should be made of the 1412 Valladolid anti-Jewish laws. Also in that year, Gerónimo de Santa Fé, a convert to Christianity, initiated a disputation with a group of Aragon rabbis on Christian dogma and the messiahship of Christ. Known as the Tortosa disputation, it continued through the years 1413 and 1414, creating such havoc among the Jews that many of them converted out of despair.

The remainder of the fifteenth century, although witnessing some efforts at recovery on the part of the Jewish community, saw the development of the movement which advocated the total expulsion of Jews from Spain. When in 1474 Isabella and Ferdinand ascended the united throne of the kingdoms of Aragon-Castile, the demise of the Jewish community in Spain became inevitable. On 31 March 1492 the order of expulsion was signed; it was promulgated on May 1. On 31 July 1492 the last Jews left Spain, after more than a millennium of continuous settlement there.

BIBLIOGRAPHY

Yitzhak F. Baer, *A History of the Jews in Christian Spain,* Louis Schoffman and H. Halkin, trans., 2 vols. (1961–1966); Salo W. Baron, *The Jewish Community,* 3 vols. (1942, 1948); Haim Beinart, ¿*Cuando Ilegaron los judíos a España?* (1962), "Hispano-Jewish Society," in *Journal of World History,* **11** (1968), and *Trujillo: A Jewish Community in Extremadura on the Eve of the Expulsion* (1980); James W. Parkes, *The Conflict of the Church and the Synagogue* (1934, repr. 1961); Jaime Vicens Vives, *An Economic History of Spain,* Frances M. López-Morillas, trans. (1960).

HAIM BEINART

[See also **Expulsion of the Jews; Fuero; Inquisition; Jewish Communal Self-Government; Jews in Muslim Spain; Judeo-Spanish; Maimonidean Controversy; Martyrdom, Jewish; Nahmanides, Moses; New Christians; Pastoureaux; Polemics, Christian-Jewish; Sephardim; Toledo.**]

JEWS IN EGYPT. There is little information about the Jews in medieval Egypt prior to the tenth century. Ibn ʿAbd al-Ḥakam in his *Futūḥ Miṣr* (The history of the conquest of Egypt, North Africa, and Spain) states that 40,000 Jews remained in Alexandria after that city surrendered to the Arabs in 642. Though an evident exaggeration, this detail probably reflects Arab marvel at the large number of Jews in that bastion of Hellenistic Judaism during the Greco-Roman period. Egyptian Jews were on the same legal footing as the majority Christian population: a protected people (dhimmis), tolerated in return for payment of a poll tax and acknowledgment of Islamic precepts requiring respect for the superiority of Islam. Since the Byzantine revenue system had included a tax on persons—and, moreover, the

status of the Jews under Byzantine law had grown increasingly unfavorable—the advent of Islam can hardly have meant additional legal hardships for Egyptian Jewry.

During the first three centuries of Muslim rule, Jews migrated to Egypt from Iraq and Persia, where the majority of world Jewry lived at the time of the Arab conquests. Others came from adjacent Palestine and Syria. The fact that the great Jewish rabbinic scholar and philosopher Saadiah ben Joseph (from the Al-Faiyūm district in Upper Egypt) received his basic education in late-ninth-century Egypt attests to the presence of a viable community. On the other hand, the fact that Saadiah had to leave Egypt for Palestine and, ultimately, Iraq to complete his education and achieve scholarly and communal renown shows that Egyptian Jewry was still dependent upon those two pre-Islamic centers of Jewish learning.

Egyptian Jewry came into its own during the Fatimid period (969–1171), when Egypt became a major center of economic prosperity and Islamic political power, attracting Jewish merchants and scholars from the Abbasid domain. The Fatimids treated the Jews rather well, and several illustrious Jewish government officials helped to establish and administer the Fatimid bureaucracy. Instances of persecution, such as the pogroms against Christians and Jews under the deranged caliph al-Ḥakim (r. 996–1021), were exceptions proving the rule.

Some ninety communities are mentioned in documents from the Cairo genizah, dating from the eleventh century. Most of them were located in the Nile Delta region, but a number of settlements were distributed over Upper Egypt, both in fertile Al-Faiyūm and in commercially significant towns along the Nile. The twelfth-century Spanish Jewish traveler Benjamin of Tudela reported scattered population figures: 7,000 for Cairo-Fusṭāṭ, 3,000 for Alexandria, a total of 2,800 for ten small communities in Lower Egypt, and 800 for three settlements in Upper Egypt. These figures are of limited value for calculating the entire Jewish population; aside from the fact that Benjamin bypassed many more communities than he visited, it is not certain whether his numbers represent individuals or households. On the other hand, his data seem to reflect accurately the geographical distribution of Jewish settlement attested by Cairo genizah evidence on place-names.

The immigrant origins of most of Egyptian Jewry, at its peak population under the Fatimids, are indicated by the presence in many locales of Iraqi and/or Palestinian synagogues (congregations adhering either to the Babylonian or to the Palestinian liturgy). A considerable number of Karaite Jews, often wealthy and closely connected with the Muslim government, lived congenially alongside their Rabbinite Jewish neighbors. The Karaites, too, originated in Iraq and Persia. A third component of the mature Egyptian community consisted of North African Jews, mainly merchants, whose ancestry could usually be traced back to Mediterranean-bound emigrants from the Islamic East.

Until the middle of the eleventh century, Egyptian Jewry was administratively dependent upon the head of the academy (yeshiva) of Jerusalem, who was recognized by the Fatimid caliph as sovereign authority over the Jews in the empire. By 1100, however, and for the next four centuries, Egyptian Jewry had its own communal leader, called *raʾīs al-Yahūd* (head of the Jews) in Arabic and nagid (prince) in Hebrew. The nagid appointed judges and communal executives, and regulated all the other aspects of Jewish self-government formerly supervised by the Palestinian academy.

The Ayyubid period (1171–1250) was one of transition for the Jews, as for Egyptians generally. The Sunni Ayyubids, in their initial orthodox fervor and hostility toward the infidel crusaders, attempted to cancel some of the liberties enjoyed by non-Muslims under the Shiite Fatimids. Soon, however, the holy-war mentality gave way to peaceful relations with the European Christians, and Christians and Jews in Egypt were given relief from oppression. Other factors, principally economic, sowed the seeds of decline for the Jews of Egypt. Inflation, the rise of restrictive Muslim merchant guilds, the introduction of Islamic feudalism, and a devastating famine in 1201–1202 combined to reverse Egyptian Jewish fortunes. Sporadic internal signs of stress included a trend toward voluntary apostasy, an interest in Islamic Sufism, and Rabbinite imitations of Karaite rituals considered lax by Talmudic law. In this period Moses Maimonides (*d.* 1204) and his son Abraham (*d.* 1237), the intellectual and political leaders of Ayyubid Jewry, attempted to stem the tide of despair with various reforms, but to no avail.

The Mamluk period (1250–1517) witnessed a steady waning of Jewish status, economic well-being, and cultural achievement. Crusader and Mongol threats made the Mamluks especially jittery about possible non-Muslim disloyalty at home. At the same time, pious Muslim religious scholars campaigned to have non-Muslims relegated to their proper inferior position. Several severe decrees imposing the full weight of the humiliating disabilities of the Pact of ᶜUmar upon Christians and Jews are recorded during the first century of Mamluk rule. Jurists proposed even harsher measures, such as confining non-Muslims to ghettos or their outright expulsion—measures not enacted but nonetheless indicative of the worsening situation of the Jews and Christians.

Jews suffered also from the deleterious economic consequences of the conversion of Egypt to feudalism and statism under the Mamluks, as well as from the lower population of late medieval Egypt. Moreover, with the steady conversion to Islam of large numbers of Christians, social and religious disdain, economic resentment, and political suspicions came to be focused increasingly on the Jews.

Some descriptions of Mamluk Jewry in decline have been provided by late-fifteenth-century Jewish travelers. For instance, Rabbi Obadiah of Bertinoro, Italy, counted about 700 Jewish householders in Cairo in 1488, including 150 Karaite and 50 Samaritan families, while in the once bustling Jewish community of Alexandria he found a paltry remnant of 25. Obadiah's letters and the travel diary of his countryman, Meshullam of Volterra, who visited Egypt in 1481, confirm that the Mamluk decrees enforcing the Pact of ᶜUmar had achieved their purpose. The iron-handed rule of the Egyptian nagid, which both travelers described, was symptomatic of the community's debilitated condition. Weakened economically and demographically, and threatened by oppression, the Jews of Egypt needed autocratic leadership to prevent further disintegration.

BIBLIOGRAPHY

Eliahu Ashtor [Eli Strauss], *Toldot ha-Yehudim be Mitsrayim ve-Suryah* (The history of the Jews in Egypt and Syria under Mamluk rule), 3 vols. (1944–1970), and "The Number of Jews in Mediaeval Egypt," in *Journal of Jewish Studies,* 18 (1967) and 19 (1968); Benjamin of Tudela, *The Itinerary of Benjamin of Tudela,* Marcus N. Adler, ed. and trans. (1907, repr. 1967); Mark R. Cohen, *Jewish Self-government in Medieval Egypt: The Origins of the Office of Head of the Jews, ca. 1065–1126* (1980); Walter J. Fischel, *Jews in the Economic and Political Life of Medieval Islam* (1937, repr. 1969), 45–85; Solomon D. Goitein, *A Mediterranean Society: The Jewish Communities of the Arab World as Portrayed in the Documents of the Cairo Geniza* (1967); Norman Golb, "The Topography of the Jews of Medieval Egypt: Inductive Studies Based Primarily upon Documents from the Cairo Genizah," in *Journal of Near*

Eastern Studies, **24** (1965) and **33** (1974); Jacob Mann, *The Jews in Egypt and in Palestine under the Fātimid Caliphs,* 2 vols. (1920–1922, repr. 1970).

MARK R. COHEN

[See also Ayyubids; Benjamin of Tudela; Cairo Genizah; Egypt, Islamic; Fatimids; Ḥākim bi-Amr Allāh, al-; Mamluks; Nagid.]

JEWS IN EUROPE: BEFORE 900. The history of the Jews in Christian Europe from the fifth century to about 900 may be divided into two distinct periods. The first is confined to Jewish life in the barbarian kingdoms that flourished in Spain, Italy, and Gaul (there was no Jewish settlement in England). All of these polities came to an end in the wake of the Muslim conquests and before the end of the eighth century. The second period encompasses Jewish life in the Carolingian empire and in Byzantine Italy and northern Spain, environs that were generally under Carolingian influence. Two themes characterize the history of the Jews in the West during the five centuries under consideration here: the gradual elimination of the discriminatory Jewry law that had been codified by the Roman emperor Theodosius II (438) and the clear recognition by no later than the early Carolingian era that the Jews were a valuable part of society. In effect, they came to be treated in a manner not substantially different from that of the other loyal peoples of the empire and like the others were permitted to live according to their own laws. In this climate of equality, indeed occasionally of privilege, the Jews flourished and their communities grew.

Jewish communities were firmly established on the Iberian peninsula well before Christianity was introduced there, and apparently the Hispano-Jewish population was much larger and more important than were the Jewish communities in the other parts of western Europe. Throughout the Visigothic era the Jews remained a powerful and well-placed minority among other minorities in a highly fragmented and unstable political and social situation. The Jews controlled large estates, served in government, and were in positions of influence throughout the kingdom. Jewish armed forces could be a decisive factor in the defense of a city such as Arles (508). They even helped to take control of Narbonne (673). The Judeo-Goth Judila tried to usurp the Visigothic kingship (*ca.* 632). Thus in the period following the conversion of the Visigoths to orthodox Christianity during the last decade of the sixth century perhaps as many as six of the twenty-eight Visigothic monarchs who ruled during this era inaugurated ridiculously unsuccessful anti-Jewish policies that aimed at one time or another to deprive Jewish landholders of their estates, merchants of their markets, officials of their offices, and finally Jews, in general, of their religion and freedom. By about 711, however, the Jews joined with disaffected Goths, some Byzantines, and Hispano-Romans in support of a Muslim force led by Ṭāriḳ that overthrew King Roderick and the Visigothic kingdom. The success of this venture would seem to have aided the Jewish community, which flourished in both Muslim and Christian Spain for the next five centuries.

Under the Ostrogoths in Italy, the Jews were well treated and were in evidence at all levels of society—from senators to serfs and slaves, as well as in the government and the military. (Indeed, Jewish fighting forces were among the most effective elements in the garrison at Naples, when the city was besieged by the imperial army in 536.) Theodoric the Great (ruled 493–526) in his *Edictum Theodorici* (edict 143) guaranteed the privileges promised to the Jews in the Roman law but did not affirm the discriminatory limitations of the *Codex Theodosianus.* Although the Jews in Italy seem to have been neither as numerous nor as politically important as in the Visigothic kingdom, communities in dozens of Italian cities and towns have been identified. In some Sicilian and southern Italian towns the Jews appear to have been capable of making the difference with their taxes between bankruptcy and solvency.

In the highly fragmented political situation that followed the Byzantine reconquest of Italy and the Lombard invasions in the sixth century the Jews continued to flourish. In the north, Jews and Christians are known to have debated the relative merits of their respective faiths in public at the Lombard capital of Pavia (mid eighth century), while in the south Jewish communities grew and Hebrew culture was substantially revived. The importance of the Jews throughout Italy is also reflected in the letters of Pope Gregory I (590–604), who prohibited his bishops from depriving them of any of their rights. Indeed, he found himself in the unenviable position of having to cooperate with Jewish slave traders who were supported by Byzantine officials in the selling of Christian slaves.

The Jews of Merovingian Gaul like those in Spain and Italy were involved in all aspects of society. In government Jews served as judices and operated mints. However, it was probably in commerce and especially in the slave trade that members of the Jewish community were most prominent. In these activities they received royal support despite occasional clerical and even papal opposition. Apparently, the Jewish faction in a city such as Clermont was in a position to influence the choice of who would be bishop.

The Carolingians pursued a vigorous pro-Jewish policy that recognized the Jews as a people with their own law in much the same manner that Bavarians or Saxons were given recognition. In addition to basic legal parity, the Jews were the only non-Christians permitted to practice their religion. They served in government as judices, *tellonarii* (agents of the royal fisc), mint masters, and diplomatic envoys. The Carolingians actively encouraged Jewish merchant activity and settlement within the empire and on the frontiers as landowners and traders. Jews were recruited to help settle and garrison areas on the Spanish frontier from which Christians had been expelled by the Muslims.

Under Louis the Pious (r. 814–840) these policies were systematized and Jews were protected in their ownership, purchase, and sale of Christian slaves, in the employment of Christian laborers, the possession of their landed estates, and the building of new synagogues to meet the needs of an increasing population. Select Jewish merchants were also given special privileges and protection.

Jewish intellectual and religious life also flourished. The basis was established for the great rabbinical schools of the Rhineland, particularly at Mainz. In southern Italy (Venosa and Oria) and also in the Spanish March (Barcelona) academies thrived. Jewish scholars were welcomed at the imperial court; they discussed theological matters and even made converts, contrary to various legal prohibitions. Jews aided Christians in biblical study. Occasional efforts to oppose these policies by clerics such as that attempted by Archbishop Agobard of Lyons were crushed by the emperor.

BIBLIOGRAPHY

Bernard S. Bachrach, "Judacot and Judila: À *mise au point*," in *Classical Folia*, **31** (1974), and *Early Medieval Jewish Policy in Western Europe* (1977); Salo W. Baron, *A Social and Religious History of the Jews,* 2nd ed., III, IV (1957); Bernhard Blumenkranz, *Juifs et chrétiens dans le monde occidental, 430–1040* (1960), and *Les auteurs chrétiens latins du moyen âge sur les juifs et le judaïsme* (1963); Solomon Katz, *The Jews in the Visigothic and Frankish Kingdoms of Spain and Gaul* (1937); James W. Parkes, *The Conflict of the Church and the Synagogue: A Study in the Origins of Anti-Semitism* (1934); Andrew Sharf, *Byzantine Jewry from Justinian to the Fourth Crusade* (1971); Edward A. Synan, *The Popes and the Jews in the Middle Ages* (1965); Charles Verlinden, "À propos de la place des Juifs dans l'économie de l'Europe occidentale aux IXe et Xe siècles," in *Storiografia et storie: Studi in onore di Eugenio Duprè Theseider*, I (1974); *The World History of the Jewish People*, 2nd ser., *Medieval Period*, II, Cecil Roth, ed., *The Dark Ages* (1966).

BERNARD S. BACHRACH

[See also **Agobard; Anti-Semitism; Barbarians, Invasions of; Carolingians; Ecclesia and Synagoga; Merovingians; Ostrogoths; Polemics, Christian-Jewish; Slavery, Slave Trade; Theodoric the Ostrogoth; Visigoths.**]

JEWS IN EUROPE: AFTER 900. The Jews of medieval Europe were a source of no little concern for the general population; their very presence in society provoked conflict and violence. The number of Jews, however, was distinctly limited, as is clear from the accompanying table, compiled by Salo Baron (reflecting what he calls a "guesstimate"). Even in Spain, the country with the greatest Jewish population, Jews comprised less than 5 percent of the total. In no single city, moreover, were there more than 1,500 Jewish families.

Jews were constantly migrating. Rome, for example, was one of the few sites of continuous Jewish residence since the ancient period. In large sweeps, Jews moved from southern Italy to the Rhineland in the ninth to eleventh centuries, only to return to northern Italy 300 to 500 years later. Movement also occurred in the seventh century from Spain and the southern French littoral into the heart of France. The Muslim military and cultural advance two centuries later brought Jews once again into Spain. England had no Jews prior to the Norman Conquest of 1066; those who settled there afterward were expelled in 1290, not to be readmitted until the mid seventeenth century. The Jews of France were expelled in 1306, only to be readmitted twice before their final expulsion of the Middle Ages in 1394/1395. (Jews did not again live legally in the kingdom of France until the seventeenth century.) German Jewry, discounting the Rhineland slaughters of 1096,

Jews in the European Population

| | 1300 | | 1490 | |
Country	Jews	Gen. Population	Jews	Gen. Population
France	100,000	14,000,000	20,000	20,000,000
Holy Roman Empire	100,000	12,000,000	80,000	12,000,000
Italy	50,000	11,000,000	120,000	12,000,000
Spain	150,000	5,500,000	250,000	7,000,000
Portugal	40,000	600,000	80,000	1,000,000
Poland-Lithuania	5,000	500,000	30,000	1,000,000
Hungary	5,000	400,000	20,000	800,000
Total	450,000	44,000,000	600,000	53,800,000

SOURCE: Adapted from *Encyclopaedia judaica.*

grew steadily, until it too suffered local and regional expulsions in the fifteenth century. The Jews were expelled from Spain in 1492. This demographic pattern leads to the question of why the small and migrant Jewish population proved to be such a persistent thorn in the collective consciousness of the medieval Christian world.

CONSTITUTIONAL STATUS

The first answer to this question comes from an examination of Jewish constitutional status. Although it has often been characterized monolithically by terms like *servi camerae regis* (servants of the royal chamber or chamber serfs), in fact there was no uniform Jewish status except that of being *Judaei* (Jews), who were totally dependent on kings and other secular lords for any and all of their rights.

Such dependence did not necessarily remove Jews from normal legal processes. In England, for example, litigation to which a Jew was a party was tried before a local court. Still, kings interfered constantly and sometimes arbitrarily in such litigation, on the grounds that Jews were quasi chattels of the crown. Kings, furthermore, arrested Jews at will, made treaties with magnates preventing their movement from one region to another, restricted their right to own land or do business, and, ultimately, expelled them.

Barons at times opposed the royal monopoly over the Jews, especially when it worked to their disadvantage—as is apparent from the restrictions on Jewish lending found in the Magna Carta. The princes and cities of imperial Germany in the fourteenth and fifteenth centuries also demanded that the emperor transfer the rights over his chamber serfs to them. No one, however, challenged the existence of a special constitutional status removing Jews from other existing legal nexuses, whether feudal or local, and tying them directly to their rulers.

This situation grew out of the legal confusion of the tenth and eleventh centuries. The void created by the disappearance of Roman law left the Jews without any formal constitutional status. This was so even in the then regnant system of "personal law," for in that system the status of the Jews should have been that of "Roman citizens" living under Roman law.

The legal void did not affect Jews alone. Both Jews and certain non-Jews were forced to rely more and more on special privileges for many of their rights, sometimes including—for the Jews—the right of residence itself. Nevertheless, for non-Jews the growth of territorially based legal systems in the twelfth and thirteenth centuries marked the beginning of the end of the reliance on special privileges. In contrast, the Jews were not absorbed into this framework. Anxious to retain the powers and leverage acquired through grants of privileges, rulers—chiefly the emperor—claimed that the Jews were part of the fisc, that is, the crown. Later, in 1234/1236, Frederick II expanded this claim by asserting that the Jews were his chamber serfs, and thus special dependents of the crown.

Without the specific term "chamber serfdom," and with much regional variation, this pattern recurred nearly everywhere. It had but one exception. Jews did not become personal dependents but were integrated into territorial legal systems, as well as into the body politic, in the communes and duchies of northern Italy, where *ius commune* (medieval Romal law) was observed. This inclusion was mostly theoretical, however, for until the fourteenth and fifteenth centuries, few Jews lived in the region. Throughout medieval Europe, therefore, the Jews were constitutional outcasts, a status formalizing and concretizing the submissiveness that Christianity had prescribed as their proper behavior. Beyond that, the manipulations of "their Jews" by kings often occurred at the expense of magnates or members of other social classes. The status of the Jews, therefore, was frequently a source of friction and antagonism among Christians themselves or between Christians and Jews.

JEWS AND THE CHURCH

Medieval antagonism to Jews had many roots, beginning with the question of the right of Jews to exist. In principle, this question had been resolved by Paul, who declared in the Epistle to the Romans that Jews had a fixed place in the Christian order. From the first, however, church canons, councils, and fathers insisted that the Jewish status must be that of an inferior. In particular, Jews were to be excluded from all public office and rule over Christians, in accordance with biblical prophecy. Genesis 25:23 prescribed that the elder (Esau, identified with the Jews in Christian typology) was to serve the younger (Jacob, identified with the Christians); and Genesis 49:10, according to Christian exegesis, asserted that upon Jesus' appearance, the Jews were to surrender all political power.

In 1063 Pope Alexander II implicitly predicated the right of Jews to live within Christendom on their willingness to accept this stipulation, decreeing that in distinction to Muslims, Jews lived in peace among Christians, since "they are always prepared to serve." More explicit was Innocent III's insistence that Jews live in "perpetual servitude" (a purely theological term, not to be confused with the civil chamber serfdom or its variations), observing all the limitations of segregation and inferiority imposed upon them by the canons, and through their punishment bearing witness to Christian truth.

The failure to observe these limitations always provoked ire. So convincing are the railings of the ninth-century bishop of Lyons, Agobard, about Jewish political power that certain scholars have assumed this power was real. What in fact disturbed Agobard and many of his contemporaries, as his specific proposals make clear, was the absence of precise legal definitions of the parameters of Jewish existence. Such categories, established by the popes only beginning in the mid eleventh century, were usually based on preexisting canons. Jews were to have the full protection of the law and "due process," wrote Calixtus II (ca. 1120) in *Sicut Iudaeis,* the first formal exposition of the principal tenets of papal policy regarding the Jews, but they were also to yield at all times to the demands of the church. Thus, a fine balance between rights and restrictions was to characterize, as well as sustain, Jewish existence. This point

is elaborated in about 150 canons and reflected in the *Summa theologiae* of Thomas Aquinas.

But could this fine balance, reiterated time and again in specific papal decrees, operate in practice? There were those, like the Franciscans and Dominicans of the thirteenth century, who believed not, and expressed their doubts through their involvement in the burning or censorship of the Talmud and, later, through their overzealous exploitation of the papal Inquisition to punish converts reverting to Judaism as well their Jewish abettors. Yet, even the mendicants accepted the right of Jews to live within Christian society, as verbalized explicitly in 1274 by the former Dominican master general, Humbert of Romans. However, their fifteenth-century counterparts, primarily the Franciscans, charged the Jews with unforgivable violations of the canons ordering their submissiveness. Only expulsion, they insisted, could halt the Jewish crimes of blasphemy and unbridled usury.

These claims, exacerbated by accusations of Host and cross desecration and by blood libels—most notably that made by Bernardino da Feltre at Trent in 1475—brought even the popes to waver temporarily in their usual adherence to the principles set forth by Calixtus II. Nevertheless, no pope broke fully with the past until 1555, when Paul IV implemented a program aimed at achieving the complete integration of all Jews into Christian society through conversion. (Popes had always talked of conversion but had done little about it.) Thus the usually peaceful, if unequal, coexistence of the Jews and medieval papacy was brought to an end.

CONFLICT WITH THE LAITY

Scholars have typically portrayed anything but a peaceful coexistence, writing instead of ever increasing church pressure leading to attacks and expulsions. This picture, nevertheless, derives from a view of the church as an indivisible unity. Antagonism and physical threats, as distinct from canonical severity, emanated from extremists, both individuals and groups, acting in violation of the policies of the popes and the canons. What is more, Jewish existence was not threatened on a grand scale until extremist ideas were adopted and recast by lay society.

Most devastating was the medieval development of the idea that even minimal contact with things Jewish was corrupting and a threat to the whole of Christian society; with its roots in Galatians, it was most clearly expressed by the tenth-century bishop of Verona, Ratherius. High medieval lay society eventually adopted this point of view, which is not surprising, for it viewed itself in spiritual and pietistic terms. The French even spoke of themselves as a Chosen People dwelling in its Holy Land. Consequently, lay authorities were often more rigid and demanding than ecclesiastical ones; when, for example, the papacy allowed Jews to collect 20 percent interest, Louis IX of France forced the Jews to restore interest already collected. And Edward I purportedly justified his expulsion of Jews in 1290 by asserting the need to protect the "welfare of the kingdom from the heinous offence of usury." The Jews, in other words, were not to sully what contemporaries had begun to call the sacred patria.

PRESSURES AND VIOLENCE AGAINST THE JEWS

Expulsion, however, was a royal prerogative. Others, even magnates, were dependent on royal modifications of laws and practices when the Jews or their actions proved "offensive." Such "offenses" occurred in particular when rulers manipulated Jews, at times capriciously, for their own gain and to the disadvantage of the magnates. Thus, in 1269 magnates pressured the Lord Edward into prohibiting English Jews from taking feudal lands as surety for loans, thereby preventing the eventual reversion of those lands to royal hands or those of powerful royal favorites in the case of default.

The lower ranks of society did not enjoy the leverage of the nobility and understood little of legal niceties. It was they who were most deeply affected by the obvious isolation of the Jews in combination with the theological doctrine of Jewish perversity and consequent, necessary punishment. Why wait to attack the far-off Muslim enemy, asked popular crusading bands in the Rhineland (1096), when the Jewish enemy remained safe in their own lands?

Despite their ferocity, however, the crusade massacres were limited in scope. The main crusading army, massed in France and headed by higher clergy and nobility, did not attack Jews. Only in the first half of the fourteenth century is it possible to speak of violence occurring throughout western Europe within a unified period of time.

This violence was doubtless stimulated by many causes, among them natural phenomena like the outbreak of the Black Death in 1348. Nevertheless, a more fundamental explanation for the attacks—beginning with those instigated by the knight Rindfleisch in Franconia in 1298—must be sought in the overall breakdown then occurring in medieval society and in the insecurity generated by events like the arrest of Pope Boniface III in 1303 and the famine and economic downturn of the early fourteenth century. As in modern anti-Semitism, there occurred a striking example of a mass transference of rage from one source to another, and large numbers of people came to believe that by eliminating the Jews, otherwise incomprehensible problems would somehow miraculously disappear. Such reasoning was not the exclusive province of the lower classes, as the rioting throughout Spain in 1391, in which all of society participated, suggests.

In this way, the commonly held image of the Jew had become identical to that drawn by Agobard of Lyons in the ninth century: the minion of Antichrist, ever poised to threaten social integrity. It is no wonder, then, that modern historiography has spoken of a deterioration in the Jewish position. That deterioration, however, was not from good to bad, as is often said, but from bad to unacceptable—even the late-sixth-century Gregory of Tours reports incidents of crowd violence against Jews.

ECONOMIC FACTORS

Economic factors, too, shaped the Jewish image. The granting of consumption loans (pawnbroking)—the principal Jewish occupation in the High Middle Ages—has never been popular. Some, like Cardinal Robert of Courson in the thirteenth century, were even convinced that interest-taking and usury stood in the way of restoring a pristine society. Moreover, children who witnessed their mothers borrowing small sums from Jewish women lenders, of whom there were many, may have come to view the Jews as a threat to their security.

Most Jewish lending, in addition, took the form of "notorious usury," that is, openly granted loans with openly charged interest. Forbidden by "divine law," no authority could properly license it. The popes tried to circumvent the problem by objecting only to "immoderate interest." The kings of thirteenth-century France, England, and sometimes Spain, however, dissociated themselves from this ploy and closed down Jewish lending entirely. In the manner of the fifteenth-century Italian Franciscans—who, it should be noted, were skilled and at times innovative economists—these kings may have thereby been assuaging their consciences for condoning other, more subtle forms of investment and return.

Jewish lending activity was carried on by individuals like Aaron of Lincoln and Benedict of Norwich, reputedly among the wealthiest men in England, as well as by Spanish Jewish grandees who also served as tax farmers. There were women, too, who as a rule lent but a few shillings at a time. The most complex form of Jewish lending was the Italian loan bank regulated by a *condotta* (contract) between Jewish moneylenders and their rulers, in which a principal banker might operate branches with managers and employees in a number of towns.

Early medieval Jews were known for their activity in international commerce. Bishop Rüdiger Housemann of Speyer in the Rhineland invited Jews to settle in his city specifically for this purpose as late as 1084, and commerce was still a factor in the Jewish settlement of Poland in the thirteenth century. Although the Jews did not monopolize commerce, their involvement in it did not endear them to non-Jews. The ancient world's distrust of the merchant carried over directly into the Middle Ages.

There were Jewish artisans, most prominently in Sicily, and occasional farmers and viticulturists. (It is an error to think Jews could never own land.) There was even a guild of Jewish armorers in Rome. Still, lending was the principal occupation; no other large-scale option existed, despite the talk on the part of Aquinas and Edward I, among others, of rehabilitating Jews and directing them into crafts and agriculture.

But did Jewish lending and its profits have a general economic impact? Jewish taxes, in fifteenth-century Spain, for example, may have amounted to only 1 to 3 percent of royal revenues, not as high as 22 percent, as once thought. There was also the moral theological dilemma, as put to Thomas Aquinas by the duchess of Brabant: was it licit for Christian rulers to benefit from Jewish payments, since nearly all were the product of notorious usury? Still, Jewish monies did provide liquidity. The uncontested control of rulers over Jews permitted levying fines and extraordinary taxes at will, which could generate revenues capable of saving a kingdom from bankruptcy, as medieval men, who did have some grasp of the problems involved in currency outflows and the balance of payments, must have understood. Thus, the opposition of thirteenth-century royalty to Jewish lending created solvency problems for both the kingdoms and the Jews. It indicates a preference for spiritual over material motives, quite the opposite of what has traditionally been said of kings in regard to their dealings with Jews.

A related issue is that of the Jews and the economic cycle. Jewish loans often kept farmers, artisans, and merchants solvent. Hence, the economic recession and failures of the fourteenth and fifteenth centuries could easily be ascribed to Jewish manipulation, a view increasing the motivation for expulsions and attacks.

JEWISH SELF-GOVERNMENT AND LEADERSHIP

The organization of the Jewish community has been compared with that of the guilds, a comparison that ignores the fact that Jewish communities were highly structured long before guilds became formal entities. This view also incorrectly pictures the communities as closed, corporate entities with well-defined legal rights protected by the lay powers. Far from it, for by the late twelfth and thirteenth centuries, the Jewish communities had come to depend on arbitrarily drawn charters of only temporary validity for their privileges and rights.

Internal Jewish government, consequently, had two faces. Within the community it operated, in theory, according to halakhic definition and precision; the outside world, and secular authority in particular, was confronted with no little improvisation. Accordingly, a basic principle of Jewish political action and theory was to anticipate changes in lay governmental programs and prevent all but a select few representatives from dealing with the authorities. In response the authorities appointed official Jewish intermediaries: the Spanish *rab de la corte* (chief rabbi of the kingdom), the English *presbyter Iudaeorum,* and, although the office became hereditary, the Narbonese *rex Iudaeorum.* Normally defensive, Jewish leaders were sometimes daring, for example, suggesting, as they did at Barcelona in 1354, an appeal to the pope if royal support proved insufficient.

All Jewish communities exercised some measure of self-rule. In Spain, the community executed informers (with royal consent), and in early medieval Italy (if the 1054 Chronicle of Ahimaaz is not exaggerating) Jews also executed adulterers. The *rex Iudaeorum* held land alodially. In general, communal power varied inversely with the strength of lay government. In England, where the king was strongest, little, if anything, is known about Jewish internal government, perhaps suggesting it functioned on a low level. But there were exceptions. In mid-twelfth-century Champagne, ruled by a vigorous count, Jacob ben Meir (Rabbenu Tam) possessed quasi-comital powers over the Jews.

Assessing the extent of communal power is made difficult by the problem of determining the degree to which Jews were permitted, or obligated, to use their own law in deciding disputes. In the Carolingian period, charters allowing the Jews to use their "own law" most probably meant Jews *could* use Jewish law in addition to the barbarian Roman law normally considered their appropriate "personal law." Later medieval legal traditions corroborate this assumption, declaring that Jews may resort to their own law unless it clashes with local, canon, or common law (medieval Italian Roman law). Jewish legal *consilia* (responsa) also indicate that Jews could prefer Jewish over local law. This arrangement allowed the maintenance of a highly developed system of courts, at least those of arbitration. It is illusory, however, to think that governments did not interfere constantly in their operations. The execution of Jewish informers in Spain, for example, required explicit royal consent.

Originally, rabbinical leaders, commonly accepted as the source of teaching, interpretive, and, hence, legal authority, presided over Jewish courts and governmental institutions. Ahimaaz ben Paltiel, for one, punctiliously describes the generations of leadership exercised by his rabbinical ancestors in southern Italy. Lay forces, however, eventually replaced the rabbis. In thirteenth-century Narbonne, the council of *boni homines* superseded the *rex Iudaeorum,* who from then on functioned solely as the head of the local yeshiva. And the Hasidei Ashkenaz (pious of Germany) movement (twelfth and thirteenth centuries) may in part have been founded, and its precepts developed, in reaction to the loss of judicial and executive power suffered by its leaders, descendants of the foremost rabbinic and communal figures in the Rhineland, with roots going back to ninth-century Italy.

In a slight variation, probably related to the division of power in the Muslim East between the exilarch and the heads of the academies, rabbis and scholars in Muslim Spain complemented the lay leaders, into whose families they made a point of marrying. Andalusian Jewry's greatest luminary, Samuel ibn Nagrela (*d.* 1055/1056), famed as a halakhic scholar and poet, also exercised extraordinary powers as the nagid of the Jewish community and the vizier and military commander of the Taifa principate of Granada. In Christian Spain, on the other hand, lay leaders gained the upper hand.

A blatant effect of this increasing lay control was the "professionalization" and eventual subservience of the rabbinate to the laity, at times leading to the compromise of religious considerations in favor of practical ones. In fifteenth-century Germany, for example, rabbis competing for contracts and communal appointments were known sometimes to grant divorces for the sexual convenience of the parties involved. There was also concern that rabbis not make legal pronouncements affecting the constituents of colleagues in other communities. A further complication came from yeshiva heads. They saw themselves as superior in learning and religious probity to their "professionalized" counterparts, and therefore claimed a say in communal affairs. Finally, the appearance of legal codes in the later Middle Ages permitted laymen to challenge (not necessarily correctly) the decisions of rabbinical courts.

Important and independent rabbinic figures existed in all periods. As a class, however, the professionalized rabbinate of the fourteenth and fifteenth centuries stood at a far remove from the rabbinate of 200 and 300 years earlier. In terms of numbers, scholarship, and power, the rabbis of the earlier period were preeminent.

Perhaps the most significant factor in the shift of power from rabbinic to lay hands was the absence of formal criteria and governmental mechanisms for determining leadership. Rabbinic ordination (*semikhah*) had lost the official status it had had in the talmudic period. Hence, all power and offices within the community came through either consent or usurpation, invariably making it necessary to bolster ordinances and decisions by decreeing that a herem had been declared—meaning an agreement or common oath whose violation would provoke censure and possible excommunication. Similarly, local courts and jurisdictional limits were established by demonstrating that a scholar had once lived in a given district. There were also power struggles. Those between factions of Spanish courtiers, reflecting class or, more probably, family conflict, are well known.

Under these circumstances, questions arose concerning the need for a majority or unanimity in reaching decisions. In the German cities, where lay town councils developed, majorities prevailed; in nobility-ruled France, "the leading scholar or rabbi of the generation," and more than anyone else the aristocratic Rabbenu Tam, was sometimes able to impose the rule of unanimity. The specifics of Jewish internal administration thus reflected variations in regional non-Jewish government. At the same time, the Jewish champions of unanimity may have been anticipating the issue with which European representative institutions were to grapple in the thirteenth century: the challenge posed by the affirmation of Roman law that "what applies to all must be approved [ratified] by all."

Dependent on fickle and interfering rulers who had powers with only temporary validity and no true jurisdiction, and unsure of its own leaders and their official functions, Jewish self-government was, as Gibbon said, a collection of "partial institutions." Yet, that government did function to separate Jews from gentiles and, thus to reinforce the physical segregation and the sense of otherness characterizing medieval Jewish existence.

THE FAMILY

Perhaps nowhere were Jews more distinct from Christians than in their family life. A stable pattern characterized by a small nuclear family was the rule throughout the Middle Ages. There were, of course, quasi-aristocratic families tracing kinship and lineage over many generations; but, even here, each nuclear grouping described itself and appears in literary records as a distinct unit.

Three factors account for this phenomenon. The first two are the formal contractual mechanisms and the well-marked sexual parameters laid down in the Talmud, creating and defining family structure, with subsequent halakhic opinion nearly uniform on these subjects throughout the Middle Ages. Third, the Jews urbanized early, and legal elaborations fixing the number of permitted wives at one and the disposition of wealth through dowries and inheritance strengthened the forces inherent in the urban setting. The resulting Jewish family was small, affective (in an almost modern sense), and "proto-bourgeois." Records from the First Crusade suggest that the average "existing family" was two-generational and contained no more than two children at any given time. David Herlihy's description of fifteenth-century Italian city dwellers, stressing individualism and competition, seems applicable to Jews, especially those of the Rhineland, in the late eleventh century.

The difference between Jewish and Christian marital ideals was enormous, even if the Jewish marriage ceremony itself may have been influenced by Christian practices. Divorce, for instance, was both permitted and not rare; marriage was possible between first cousins; sexuality was considered a virtue. Thus, in discussing the Talmudic ruling permitting various coital positions, the twelfth-century Abraham ben David of Posquières declares that what a man and his wife agree upon in sex is both licit and good. And Isaiah of Trani (thirteenth century) sees marital lust as perfectly legitimate. In contrast, Raymond of Peñafort expresses the normative Christian teaching that sex, even for the purpose of procreation, has a sinful aspect.

This openness of the twelfth and thirteenth centuries was later curbed by mystical tracts insisting on a proper sequence of ritualized action during intercourse, in imitation of forces operating in the heavenly spheres. Yet, even here, the propriety—indeed, the obligation—to engage in sexual activity, especially within the framework of the law entitling the wife to sexual intercourse at fixed intervals, is never questioned.

The gulf between Jewish and Christian views on sexuality may explain the pornographic rantings of Guibert of Nogent (1053–1124) against the degeneracy of the Jews and their alleged role in the sexual perversion of monks; it doubtless contributed to expanding the religiously inspired picture of Jewish otherness.

SELF-CONSCIOUSNESS
AND INTELLECTUAL EXPRESSION

Jews showed great literary creativity. Even a brief listing of authors and their subjects makes this point: biblical exegesis—Rashi and Abraham ben Meir ibn Ezra; talmudic-legal study—Jacob ben Meir (Rabbenu Tam) and Jacob ben Asher; philosophy, theology, and its criticism—Judah Halevi and Joseph Albo; pietism—Moses ben Jacob of Coucy and Judah the Pietist; mysticism—Moses ben Shem Tov de León and Moses Nahmanides; belles lettres and poetry—Solomon ben Judah ibn Gabirol and Immanuel ben Solomon of Rome; history and chronicles—Abraham ibn Daud and Ahimaaz ben Paltiel. To this list may be added polemics, memoirs, religious odes, sermons, midrash, travelogues, and political theory.

Cultural creativity had political ramifications. Newly arisen courtier families in Christian Spain allied themselves at times with proponents of naturalistic Aristotelianism, while older Andalusian courtiers, trained in the Neoplatonic school, often opposed the new philosophic trends, their spokesmen, and their defenders. And, in Provence, antiphilosophic rabbis were instrumental in the burning of the books of Maimonides by the papal Inquisition in France in 1232. The political motives possibly informing the pietism of Hasidei Ashkenaz, fighting their loss of power to a new rabbinic leadership in the Rhineland, has already been noted.

Culture had its periodization and its geography. Southern Italy blossomed in the ninth and tenth centuries, and Rome was noteworthy in the late thirteenth and early fourteenth centuries. The tenth-to-twelfth-century golden age of Spain in poetry and philosophy was followed by great mystical creativity in the thirteenth and fourteenth centuries. The Rhineland produced legal and political ideas in the tenth and eleventh centuries and was then succeeded by the tosaphist legal commentators of Champagne and Paris in the twelfth century. The Rhineland reemerged into the limelight, first with Hasidei Ashkenaz in the early thirteenth century and, a number of decades later, with major codifications of rabbinic learning.

PERCEPTIONS OF THE GENTILE WORLD AND REACTIONS TO IT

Jews knew well the threats to their physical existence. This may be seen in the large number of chronicles and dirges expounding the ideology of kiddush ha-shem (martyrdom by self-inflicted wounds rather than conversion). But did they also understand the theoretical underpinnings of the Christian world and the possibilities for manipulating them? The anonymous chronicle recounting the "terrible events of 1007" and the *Milḥemet mitzvah* of Meir ben Simeon of Narbonne, both products of the mid-to-later thirteenth century, together with the record of the 1354 Jewish conference at Barcelona, leave no doubts about an intimate Jewish acquaintance with medieval papal and political theory and law. The pope is told that he alone has certain rights over the Jews in distinction to the king; an archbishop is warned that papal rather than royal teachings on usury should be his guide; and a complaint is lodged that papal edicts curbing the Inquisition in its dealings with Jews are not being properly observed. At the same time, Jews are admonished by their leadership to be fully submissive to papal demands, otherwise their rights will be endangered. Humiliating, without question, this was the only way to ensure papal protection of the Jews against arbitrary and unreliable kings. In defense of their self-esteem, Jews poked fun at Christian symbols and jested about the papal power of binding and loosing.

Jews considered Christianity to be idolatry; contact with it and with Christians was to be avoided. Only through a legal fiction, for instance, were business dealings with Christians allowed at all. Christians and Christianity, in fact, were seen as the

nemesis of Jewish well-being in much the way that Jews and Judaism supposedly were the nemesis of the Christians.

However, from the Jewish perspective, contact with Christianity was truly dangerous. The constant trickle of voluntary conversions occasionally became a torrent, as happened in Spain between 1412–1415. Therefore the suggestion of Menahem ben Solomon Meiri of Perpignan that Christianity was not idolatry was doomed to remain an isolated one. In distinction, Jews frequently spoke of Islam as monotheism, but this perhaps was because, unlike Christianity, Islam did not have a doctrine of the necessary conversion of the Jews. Contacts could be made and recognition given without the constant fear of subversion.

CONVERTS AND CONVERSION

The Christian world was highly ambivalent about converts. There was no simple merging by baptism into the Christian *patria communis,* as is evident in the case of the antipope Anacletus II, chosen along with Innocent II in the disputed election of 1130. Anacletus (Peter Pierleone) was the great-grandson of a Jew who had converted to Christianity and married a Christian noblewoman. Nevertheless, Jewish ancestry was still cited as a disqualification for his holding the papal office.

The most telling evidence of the ambivalence regarding converts are the name "new Christian," used to designate Spanish Jews who converted after the riots of 1391, and the *limpieza de sangre* (purity of blood) laws that discriminated against the new Christians in subsequent centuries. No single item, however, is more evocative of the dilemma of the convert than the "Letter of Maestro Andreas." Probably a fictional creation of the later-thirteenth-century Jacob ben Elie of Venice, the letter emotionally describes Andreas' rejection by a Christian society ever doubtful of his motives for converting. Tens of papal edicts commanding monasteries to provide food and other necessities to needy converts confirm Andreas' plaint.

THE MEDIEVAL JEWISH PREDICAMENT

Jews, thus, were a minority in an alien world. Theoretically, medieval society was monistic, resting harmoniously on complete spiritual homogeneity and unity. In practice, heretics, Muslims, and Jews, all permanent fixtures, disrupted this harmony. But society could, and did, mitigate the disruption by channeling irregular and deviant religious behavior in cases where it failed to root it out entirely. Co-existence was, therefore, made possible within a regulated framework. And where such regulation did in fact exist, as in the case of the Jews within the papally and canonically governed church, it was possible to achieve a status that was at least theoretically secure, however humiliating it was.

Nevertheless, the forces of regulation themselves could not always be kept under control. Their more radical exponents sometimes behaved like pilgrims, with a pent up pious zeal ever on the verge of exploding. Indeed, mendicants and kings, originally intended by the church to perform adjutant or executive regulatory functions, in the long run seized the initiative. Unable to make peace with the dissonance and the willful rejection of unity embodied by dissidents, and by Jews above all, they eschewed canonical restraints and espoused instead excess and violence. Opposition to the Jews, furthermore, was not all based on spiritual differences. The distinctive Jewish family life and constitutional status pointed squarely to inconsistencies, as well as to failings of structure and authority, in the medieval body politic. The very existence and presence of the Jew in Christian society, in other words, both attested to and symbolized its insufficiencies, in particular, the inability of the medieval world to achieve balance and proportion between its discordant forces. If, then, the Jewish physical presence in society was small, the Jewish psychological presence was enormous. No wonder it created traumas, and no wonder those traumas were dealt with by means ranging from legal repression, to expulsion, to physical attack. To have reacted to the Jewish presence with any lesser means would, for medieval society, have been a denial of its quest, however illusive and self-destructive, for harmony and unity, two of its most fundamental and, sometimes, utopian aspirations.

BIBLIOGRAPHY

Yitzhak F. Baer, *A History of the Jews in Christian Spain,* Louis Schoffman, trans., 2 vols. (1961–1966); Salo W. Baron, *A Social and Religious History of the Jews,* 2nd rev. ed. (1957–), esp. vol. XII; Haim Beinart, *Atlas Karta le-toldot 'am Yisra' el bi-yeme ha-benayim* (1981); Lawrence V. Berman *et al., Bibliographical Essays in Medieval Jewish Studies* (1976), esp. 15–105; Bernhard Blumenkranz, *Juifs et chrétiens dans le monde occidental, 430–1096* (1960); Robert Bonfil, *Rabbanut be-Italyah be-tekufat ha-Renesans* (1979); Peter Browe, *Die Judenmission im Mittelalter und die Päpste* (1942); Robert Chazan, *Medieval*

Jewry in Northern France: A Political and Social History (1973); Vittore Colorni, *Legge ebraica e leggi locale* (1945); Ze'ev W. Falk, *Jewish Matrimonial Law in the Middle Ages* (1966); David M. Feldman, *Birth Control in Jewish Law* (1968, repr. 1971); Louis Finkelstein, *Jewish Self-government in the Middle Ages* (1924, repr. 1972); Aryeh Grabois, "Mi-nesiut la-hanagat ha-parnasim: Ha-temurot ba-mishtar shel kehillat Narbonna ba-meah ha-yod-gimmel," in *Ummah ve-toldotehah,* pt.1 (1983); Solomon Grayzel, *The Church and the Jews in the Thirteenth Century* (1933); Avraham Grossman, *Hakhme' Ashkenaz ha-rishonim* (1981); William C. Jordan, "Jews on Top: Women and the Availability of Consumption Loans in Northern France in the Mid-Thirteenth Century," in *Journal of Jewish Studies,* **29** (1978).

Jacob Katz, *Exclusiveness and Tolerance: Studies in Jewish-Gentile Relations in Medieval and Modern Times* (1961); Guido Kisch, *The Jews in Medieval Germany: A Study of Their Legal and Social Status* (1949, 2nd ed. 1970); Maurice Kriegel, *Les juifs à la fin du moyen âge dans l'Europe méditerranéen* (1979); Gavin Langmuir, "*Tanquam servi*: The Change in Jewish Status in French Law About 1200," in Myriam Yardeni, ed., *Les juifs dans l'histoire de France* (1980); Cecil Roth, *A History of the Jews in England,* 3rd ed. (1964); Kenneth R. Stow, *Catholic Thought and Papal Jewry Policy, 1555–1593* (1977), "Papal and Royal Attitudes Toward Jewish Lending in the Thirteenth Century," in *AJS Review,* **6** (1981), and *The "1007 Anonymous" and Papal Sovereignty: Jewish Perceptions of the Papacy and Papal Policy in the High Middle Ages* (1984); Edward A. Synan, *The Popes and the Jews in the Middle Ages* (1965); Yosef Hayim Yerushalmi, *From Spanish Court to Italian Ghetto: Isaac Cardoso* (1971); Yisrael Y. Yuval, "An Appeal Against the Proliferation of Divorce in Fifteenth-century Germany" in *Zion,* **48** (1983); Israel Zinberg, *A History of Jewish Literature,* Bernard Martin, ed. and trans. (1972–).

KENNETH R. STOW

[See also **Abraham ben David of Posquières; Abraham ben Meïr ibn Ezra; Abraham ibn Daud; Agobard; Anti-Semitism; Ashkenaz; Banking, Jewish, in Europe; Black Death; Blood Libel; Clement VI, Pope; Converso; Ecclesia and Synagoga; Exchequer of the Jews; Expulsion of Jews; Family and Family Law, Jewish; Flagellants; Hasidei Ashkenaz; Historiography, Jewish; Host Desecration Libel; Jacob ben Meir (Rabbenu Tam); Jewish Communal Self-government: Europe; Jews and the Catholic Church; Jews in Christian Spain; Jews in the Papal States; Judah ben Samuel he-Hasid; Judah Halevi; Judaism: Kalonymus Family; Martyrdom, Jewish; Moses ben Shem Tov de Leon; Nahmanides, Moses; New Christians; Polemics, Christian-Jewish; Rabbinate; Rashi (Rabbi Solomon ben Isaac); Servi Camerae Nostrae; Solomon ben Judah ibn Gabirol; Usury; Usury, Jewish Law.]**

JEWS IN MUSLIM SPAIN. During the tenth through twelfth centuries, Jews in Muslim Spain enjoyed a brilliant period of material, cultural, and political achievement that gave rise to the notion, popularized by nineteenth- and twentieth-century historiography, of "the golden age of Spain." Although the unique Jewish civilization in Islamic Spain (called *Sepharād* in Hebrew and Al-Andalus in Arabic) came to an abrupt end with the Almohad conquest in the mid twelfth century, it continued in certain respects in Christian Spain, Provence, and North Africa, and eventually throughout the lands of the Sephardic Diaspora.

FROM MUSLIM CONQUEST TO SPANISH CALIPHATE

On the eve of the Muslim invasion in 711, the Jewish community was a bitterly disaffected element in Visigothic Spain because of the intermittent persecutions it had endured in the preceding decades. Thus, it welcomed Ṭāriq ibn Ziyād's invading forces and openly collaborated with them. In city after city, Ṭāriq and his lieutenant Mughīth organized local Jews into military garrisons to stand guard in their absence. This sort of cooperation was unique in the history of Islamic conquests and was due to unprecedented circumstances: The first Muslim invasion force was Berber, not Arab; their number was relatively small; and they were far more overextended than had been the case in earlier conquests. The cooperative spirit was modified the following year with the arrival of a large Arab army under Mūsā ibn Nuṣair.

During the first two hundred years of Muslim rule, the Jews seem to have maintained a low profile, and almost no mention is made of them in the Arabic sources. They simply became part of the larger subject population, with the usual rights and disabilities of non-Muslims, when the province was organized under caliphal authority and integrated into the Islamic social system. Furthermore, they had no role to play in the sanguinary internal Muslim dissensions that plagued Spain at this time.

The Jewish population of Spain grew considerably during the first two centuries of Muslim rule. Refugees from Visigothic persecution came back from North Africa, and there was immigration from the Muslim East. From a letter by Pope Adrian I, sent in 785 to the bishops of Spain, it may be inferred that Jews moved about freely and were unimpeded in their intercourse with the rest of the populace. Some Jews may even have felt confident enough to engage in proselyting activities among the demoralized Christian population at this time (to do so among Muslims would have been unthinkable). The end of the eighth century witnessed an outbreak of "Judaizing" heretical groups among the Christians of northern Spain.

In 838 Bodo, formerly a deacon at the court of Louis the Pious, arrived in Saragossa, where he converted to Judaism, adopting the name Eleazar. He then embarked upon an open campaign against Christianity and engaged in a literary polemic with the Spanish zealot Paulus Alvaro. According to Prudence of Troyes, Bodo-Eleazar served in the Muslim military and somehow convinced the Andalusian authorities to give Christians the unlikely choice of converting to Islam or Judaism. This apocryphal story may contain a garbled reference to the Judaizing heretical groups, who may have been the object of conversionary activities. It does indicate that the Jews in Spain were a force to be reckoned with.

Little is known of the nature of Spanish Judaism until the late eighth century. According to Spanish tradition, the teaching of the Babylonian Talmud was introduced into Iberia by the deposed exilarch from Baghdad, Natronai ben Ḥavivai, in 772. The first standardized prayer book for use by Spanish Jews was the seder (order of prayers) edited by Rabbi Amram Gaon around 850 as part of a responsum to a query from the Jews of Barcelona to the gaon in Iraq. This Jewish dependence upon Eastern scholarship had its parallel in the Muslim community of Spain as well.

THE RISE OF ANDALUSIAN JEWISH CULTURE

The development of a creative and highly independent Spanish Jewry coincides precisely with the period of general Andalusian self-assertion and self-realization that began with the declaration of an independent caliphate by ʿAbd al-Raḥmān III in 929 and then flowered under his successors. The sudden efflorescence of Andalusian Jewry was intimately linked to the rise of Ḥisdai ibn Shaprut (*ca.* 915–*ca.* 970), the remarkable Jewish physician, diplomat, and statesman who served at the court of ʿAbd al-Raḥmān III and al-Ḥakam II in Córdoba.

As the leading Jewish courtier in the realm, Ḥisdai acted as secular head of Spanish Jewry and bore the princely title of nasi. Like other great courtiers, he was a patron of the arts and sciences. As the leading Jew in Spain, he felt a special duty to be Maecenas to his brethren. His secretary, Menahem ben

Saruq, a poet and philologist, wrote the first Hebrew-Hebrew biblical dictionary: *Sēfer Pitrōnīm* (popularly known as *Maḥberet*), which later became popular in France and Germany. Another of Ḥisdai's protégés, Dunash ben Labrat, who was Menaḥem's bitter rival, pioneered in the adaptation of Arabic metrics to Hebrew poetry, setting the trend that became standard for Hebrew prosody in medieval Spain, and Provence. Not only the techniques but also the themes (including wine drinking, gardens, homosexual and heterosexual love) and aesthetic sensibilities of Andalusian Arabic poetry were adapted to what became the greatest revival of Hebrew language and literature since biblical times.

Ḥisdai singlehandedly embarked upon a program to make Spain a leading seat of world Jewry. He imported Hebrew books in such quantity that even Muslim writers, such as Ṣāᶜid al-Andalusī, made note of it. He carried on extensive correspondence with foreign Jewish leaders, including, it is alleged, the Khazar king Joseph. He loosened Spanish Jewry's dependence upon the Babylonian academies by appointing a brilliant Italian rabbi, Moses ben Ḥanokh, as the country's chief scholar *(rav)* and head *(rōsh)* of an independent yeshiva in Córdoba during the 950's or 960's. The spiritual autonomy of Spanish Jewry continued under Rabbi Ḥanokh ben Moses *(d.* 1014), Moses ben Ḥanokh's son and successor.

THE PARTY KINGS

The period of the "Party Kings" (1009–1090) that followed the collapse of the Córdoban caliphate witnessed the zenith of Andalusian Jewry. The political, ethnic, and social fragmentation of Muslim Spain offered talented and ambitious Jews extraordinary opportunities for government service. There arose a significant Jewish courtier class that held positions beyond the usual ones of physicians, purveyors, and petty bureaucrats found in other Islamic countries. Among them were high-ranking administrators such as Jekuthiel ibn Ḥasan (assassinated 1039) in Saragossa and Abraham ben Muhajir *(d. ca.* 1100) in Seville. The Jewish courtiers possessed a distinctive group ethos whose principal characteristics included a strong sense of elitism vis-à-vis other Jews, a harmonious synthesis of Arabic secular culture and Judaism, and a desire to attain social rank and political power.

The quintessential Jewish courtier was Samuel ha-Nagid, who served the Zirid kingdom of Granada as vizier from 1030 to 1056. He also commanded the royal army in the field, an unheard-of thing for a Jew in medieval Islam or Christendom. In addition to his political and military duties, he was head of the Jewish community, an outstanding talmudic scholar, a patron of the arts, and one of the four greatest masters of medieval Hebrew poetry. He groomed his son Jehoseph ha-Nagid to succeed him; the latter held the vizierate for ten years, until his murder in a popular uprising in 1066, during which the Jewish community of Granada was also destroyed. Jehoseph's death marks the end of the high point of Jewish political power and the beginning of a slow decline of the courtier class.

During the era of the Party Kings, Jewish literature was in full bloom. The poet Solomon ibn Gabirol (1021/1022–*ca.* 1058, known as Avicebron in Latin) composed moving Hebrew elegies for his murdered patron Jekuthiel ibn Ḥasan. At the court of Samuel ha-Nagid, where he found refuge, he produced Neoplatonic philosophical works, including the poetic *Keter Malkhut* (Kingly crown) and *Mekor Ḥayyim* (The source of life), which in its Latin translation *(Fons vitae)* had considerable influence on European Scholasticism. The philologist and grammarian Jonah ibn Janāḥ (990–1050) in Saragossa wrote the most scientific grammar *(Sefer ha-Dikduk)* of the Hebrew language prior to modern times, the second part of which contains the best medieval dictionary of Hebrew, *Kitāb al-Uṣūl* (Book of roots). The pietist Baḥya ibn Paquda (writing *ca.* 1080) composed one of the most enduring works of Jewish devotional literature, *al-Hidāya ᵓila farāᵓiḍ al-qulūb* (Guide to the duties of the heart).

UNDER THE ALMORAVIDS

With the Almoravid conquest about 1090, the twilight of Andalusian Jewry began. The pressure of the *Reconquista* and Almoravid religious zeal made interfaith relations less amicable. There was a steady decline in the number of Jews in the civil service. Already, Jews like the poet and literary critic Moses ibn Ezra *(d.* after 1135) were moving to the Christian north. One sign of the anxiety of the times was the outbreak of Jewish messianism, first in Córdoba sometime between 1110 and 1115, and later throughout Spain and Morocco in 1130.

But even while the Jews' political and social position had deteriorated, their culture flourished. Lucena had become a center of talmudic scholarship under Isaac Alfasi *(d.* 1103) and his pupil Joseph ibn Migash *(d.* 1141). Medieval Hebrew poetry reached its zenith in the verses of Judah Halevi (1075–1141). His "Songs of Zion" as well as other sections of his philosophical dialogue, the *Kuzari,* made him a major precursor of modern Zionism. His work was the culmination of Andalusian Jewish culture. Yet, at the same time, it embodied the rejection of that culture, since for Halevi there could be no substitute for the land of Israel. Setting out to realize the dream expressed by his poetry, Halevi left Spain in 1140 for Egypt and went from there to Palestine, where he died.

UNDER THE ALMOHADS

Between 1146 and 1172, the sectarian Almohads conquered what was left of Muslim Spain. They tolerated no non-Muslims. There were forced conversions en masse, creating a new class of crypto-Jews, many of whom eventually fled to the Christian north. Others, like the Maimonides family, fled to the Levant.

After the Almohad terror some Andalusian Jews resettled in the tiny Nasrid kingdom of Granada, where a small Jewish community remained until this last Muslim foothold in Iberia fell to Ferdinand and Isabella in 1492.

BIBLIOGRAPHY

Eliyahu Ashtor, *The Jews of Moslem Spain,* 2 vols., Aaron Klein and Jenny Machlowitz Klein, trans. (1973); Ibn Daud, *Sefer ha-Qabbalah,* Gerson D. Cohen, ed. and trans. (1967); Évariste Lévi-Provençal, *Histoire de l'Espagne musulmane,* 3 vols. (1950–1953); Norman A. Stillman, "Aspects of Jewish Life in Islamic Spain," in *Aspects of Jewish Culture in the Middle Ages,* Paul E. Szarmach, ed. (1979), and *The Jews of Arab Lands: A History and Source Book* (1979).

NORMAN A. STILLMAN

[See also **Baḥya ben Joseph ibn Paquda; Córdoba; Hebrew Poetry; Judah Halevi; Judeo-Arabic Language; Judeo-Arabic Literature; Maimonides, Moses; Polemics, Islamic-Jewish; Spain, Muslim Kingdoms of.**]

JEWS IN NORTH AFRICA. Throughout the Middle Ages, North Africa was the home of large and, at various times and places, culturally and economically significant Jewish communities. Jewish settlement in the Maghrib may go back to Punic times, although there is no concrete historical evidence to confirm this. There is, however, ample epigraphic and other evidence of an unbroken Jewish presence in the countries west of Egypt from Roman times to the Muslim invasions.

THE EARLY ISLAMIC PERIOD (CA. 650–850)

The century preceding and the century and a half following the Islamic conquest of North Africa is a rather shadowy period in the general history of the region and a veritable "dark age" in Jewish history. The Arab chronicles, most of which date from considerably later, make occasional mention of Berber tribes professing Judaism among the tribes that offered resistance to the conquerors. The most famous of the allegedly Judaized Berbers were the Jarawa of the Aurès Mountains in the central Maghrib (modern Algeria). Led by their queen, dubbed al-Kāhina (the sorceress) in the Arab sources, the Jarawa, in confederation with other Berber tribes, successfully repelled the Muslim invaders from the entire region as far as Barka for some five years until they were finally defeated and their queen killed in 693 or 698. The earliest versions of the episode with Kāhina fail to mention her being Jewish, which, in addition to the highly legendary nature of the accounts, makes the matter extremely doubtful. Native Jews are also mentioned in connection with the campaigns of Idrīs I (r. 788–791) to carve out the first independent Muslim kingdom in Morocco. References to urban Jewish comunities in North Africa during this early period are very few and oblique.

THE FIRST FLOWERING OF NORTH AFRICAN JEWRY (CA. 850–1140)

The blackout in North African Jewish history ends during the second half of the ninth century, at which time Jews are found in the major towns of the Maghrib: Fēs, Sijilmassa, Tlemcen, Tāhert (now Tiaret), and Qayrawān. The most important of these cities was Qayrawān, the capital of the province of Ifrīqiya and the principal metropolis in the Maghrib. Under the semi-autonomous Aghlabid emirs (800–909), and especially under the Fatimid caliphs (909–972) and their Zirid viceroys (972–1060's), Ifrīqiya became a crossroads of Mediterranean caravan routes and sea-lanes and a major stop on the greater Spain-to-India trade route, in which Qayrawānese and other North African Jewish merchants played a prominent role. The far-flung activities of these merchants are documented in detail in the papers of the Cairo genizah. Jewish economic prosperity reached its height under the heterodox Fatimids, who showed relatively more tolerance to their non-Muslim subjects than most Muslim rulers and did not impose the discriminatory tariffs prescribed by orthodox Islamic law for dhimmi merchants. The combination of general prosperity and a higher than usual degree of official tolerance fostered the growth and development of Jewish communities throughout the province, attracting many newcomers from the Islamic East as well.

During the second half of the tenth and the first half of the eleventh century, Qayrawān was the major spiritual and intellectual center of Jewry outside of Iraq. The "sages of Qayrawān" were noted in Hebrew literature for their religious and secular scholarship. The most famous of the sages was the physician and Neoplatonic philosopher Isaac ben Solomon Israeli (ca. 850–ca. 950), whose medical treatises, which included works on fever and ophthalmology, were standard texts in Europe well into the Renaissance and won him the title eximius monarcha medicinae. His pupil Dunash ibn Tamim (ca. 900–ca. 960), in addition to being a physician and philosopher, was active in the field of Hebrew grammar and philology, which had been developing in North Africa for some time, as is shown by the pioneer work of Judah ibn Quraysh of Tahert, written a generation or two earlier.

No other Jewish community outside of Iraq rivaled Qayrawān as a center of religious learning at this time. Two academies of higher learning (yeshivas) flourished there. One of these was founded in the late tenth century by Jacob ben Nissim ibn Shahin (d. 1006/1007), a scholar of Persian extraction and a correspondent of the Babylonian geonim. It was to him that Sherira Gaon addressed his famous Epistle, which is one of the major sources for the history of the gaonate. Jacob's son and successor, Nissim ben Jacob ben Nissim ibn Shahin, was a great rabbinical scholar and the author of many important works, including a talmudic commentary in Arabic, Miftāḥ Maghāliq al-Talmūdh (translated into Hebrew as ha-Talmud Mafte'aḥ Manulei, or Key to the locks of the Talmud), and a book of didactic and entertaining tales, Kitāb al-faraj baᶜd al-shidda (Book of relief after adversity), which became a model of its genre and enjoyed immense popularity throughout the centuries, appearing in various Hebrew translations and numerous printed editions from the early sixteenth century on.

Qayrawān's other prestigious yeshiva was the school of Ḥushi'el ben Elhanan (d. early eleventh century), an immigrant from Italy who introduced new approaches to the study of Jewish law. His son and successor, Ḥananel ben Ḥushi'el (d. 1057), who is known in Jewish tradition by the acronym RaḤ (for "our master Ḥananel"), achieved wide renown

throughout the medieval Jewish world for his commentary to the entire Babylonian Talmud, only part of which is extant.

The Jewish community of Qayrawān possessed a strong hierarchical organization that may have looked to Baghdad, with which it maintained close ties, as its model. The head of Qayrawānese Jewry was also the leading figure of the North African Jewish comunity. He was, as a rule, a prominent individual with ties to the Muslim ruler's court. Until the early eleventh century this official was known as the head of the congregations (rōsh ha-kehillōt). Beginning in 1015, however, and throughout most of the remainder of the century, he bore the illustrious title of prince of the diaspora (Negid ha-Golah), or nagid. The first nagid was Abraham ben Nathan, who was court physician to the Zirid emirs and a pillar of the Jewish community. The primacy of court Jews in communal affairs remained an outstanding feature of North African Jewish social organization throughout the Middle Ages and into modern times.

The second half of the eleventh century was a period of decline for much of North African Jewry. The province of Ifrīqiya, and Qayrawān in particular, suffered greatly from the looting and destruction that came in the wake of the invasions of the Banū Hilāl and Banū Sulaym bedouin in the late 1050's. The central Maghrib fell victim to the bedouin depredation in the decades that followed as the migration proceeded westward.

The Jewish community in Morocco remained immune to the decline in the rest of the Maghrib for several generations more. In the late eleventh and early twelfth centuries, Morocco, western Algeria, and Muslim Spain were joined under the rule of the Berber Almoravids, who despite their religious zeal and general bigotry showed no special intolerance toward Jews, as scholars of an earlier generation mistakenly believed. The great talmudist Isaac Alfasi (d. 1103), known in Jewish tradition by the acronym RIF, was active first in Morocco and later in Spain during the Almoravid period. His Sēfer ha-halākhōt (Book of laws) was the most important work on halakah prior to Maimonides' code. Although there was an overall decline of Jews in government service at this time, there were still a few with government ties, such as Abū'l-Hasan Meir ibn Kamniel (d. ca. 1142) and Solomon ibn al-Muᶜallim, his contemporary, who served as physicians at the Almoravid court in Marrakech.

During the later years of Almoravid rule, a wave of apocalyptic messianism swept through the Muslim West. Many Jews in Spain and Morocco, including the poet Judah Halevi, believed that the dominion of Islam would pass away in 1130. In Fēs, the visionary rabbi Moses Al-Da'ri brought many people to the brink of ruin with hysterical preparations for the coming of the Messiah, who Al-Da'ri declared would appear on Passover eve of that year.

THE ALMOHAD PERSECUTION (CA. 1140–1230)

The Almohad conquest of the entire Maghrib from Cyrenaica to Morocco (and including Muslim Spain) in the mid twelfth century was a cataclysmic event for North African Jewry. The conquests were accompanied by widespread massacres and destruction. The Almohads, who were sectarian Berbers, apparently did not extend the traditional protégé status to non-Muslims. Most of the urban Jewish population throughout their vast empire was forced to accept Islam, at least outwardly. Those communities that resisted were put to the sword. Their memory was immortalized in Abraham ibn Ezra's celebrated lament *Ahā yārad* (Oh, there descended), which contains a long litany of martyred congregations.

The Almohads did not demand much of the new Muslims at first except for the heavy taxes imposed upon all their subjects. However, since the religious fidelity of the forced converts who had accepted Islam under extreme duress was highly suspect, the Almohad authorities instituted a series of harsh discriminatory measures forcing the new Muslims to wear distinguishing clothing and severely limiting their civil rights and their freedom of economic endeavor. The persecution is described with great pathos by the philosopher Joseph ben Judah ibn Aknin, a contemporary of Maimonides and, like the great thinker, a refugee from the Almohad terror. In epistles of consolation addressed to their persecuted brethren, Maimonides and his father, Maimon ben Joseph, attempted to assuage the deep guilt of forced converts who could practice their Judaism only in secret.

North African Jewry emerged from the century of Almohad rule spiritually and numerically impoverished. Most of the Jewish intellectual leadership had fled to the more tolerant Muslim East or had accepted martyrdom. The Jews became the dhimmis par excellence in North African society, as no native Christian community survived the Almohad persecution.

THE POST-ALMOHAD SUCCESSOR STATES (CA. 1230–1550)

Jews lived in relative tranquillity in the Berber kingdoms of Hafsid Tunisia and Ziyanid Algeria throughout the late Middle Ages. Jewish cultural life was greatly enriched by the Sephardic refugees who fled to Algeria and Tunisia from the anti-Jewish disturbances in Spain and the Balearics in 1391. Under the leadership of men like Isaac ben Sheshet Perfet and Simeon ben Zemah Duran, Algeria became the spiritual center of North African Jewry.

Jewish life in late medieval Morocco was marked by greater ups and downs than in Tunisia or Algeria. The Merinid dynasty was not at all ill-disposed toward Jews, nor was it averse to employing them occasionally in high positions at court. All of the Jewish courtiers mentioned in the Arabic sources, however, met violent ends—for example, the members of the Waqqāṣa family (late thirteenth–early fourteenth century) and the ben Batashes (mid fifteenth century). There was palpable growth of hostility toward Jews among the Muslim populace during the Merinid period, and in 1438 the sultan ʿAbd al-Ḥaqq found it necessary to relocate the Jews of Fēs in a special quarter near the royal citadel for their protection. This quarter, the mellah, gave its name to the Jewish ghettoes that were established in Moroccan towns in the following centuries. The establishment of the Fēs mellah was indicative of the trend toward the increased social isolation of the Jews in late medieval Morocco. Throughout the later Middle Ages and into early modern times, the discriminatory laws governing Jews there were among the most strictly applied in the Muslim world. Jews were compelled to wear special black garments and to walk barefoot through the streets of the imperial cities in addition to the usual sumptuary laws and restrictions.

Despite the increasingly harsh social conditions, Moroccan Jewry was numerically and spiritually enriched by the arrival of large waves of refugees from the Iberian Peninsula after 1492.

BIBLIOGRAPHY

André N. Chouraqui, *Between East and West: A History of the Jews in North Africa*, Michal M. Bernet, trans. (1968); Solomon D. Goitein, *A Mediterranean Society: The Jewish Communities of the Arab World as Portrayed in the Documents of the Cairo Geniza* (1967–); Haim Z. (J. W.) Hirschberg, *A History of the Jews in North Africa*, trans. from the Hebrew by M. Eichelberg, 2nd rev. ed., I

(1974); Norman A. Stillman, *The Jews of Arab Lands: A History and Source Book* (1979); Jacob M. Toledano, *Ner ha-maᶜarav (La lumière du Maghreb)* (1911).

NORMAN A. STILLMAN

[See also **Aghlabids; Almohads; Almoravids; Ifriqiya; Maghrib, Al-; Marrakech; Qayrawān, Al-; Zirids.**]

JEWS IN RUSSIA. According to the earliest reliable evidence, Greek-speaking Jewish communities existed along the southern shores of the Black Sea from the beginnings of the Christian era. Ancient communities also existed in Armenia, Georgia, and the Caucasus, the latter area being the home of those Jews of Iranian origin later commonly known as Mountain Jews. Distant from the major Jewish centers, these communities left behind some physical remains in the form of synagogue ruins and tombstones, but no literary remains. Fragmentary information about Russian Jewry in the ancient and early medieval period stems from chance mentions in chronicles and travelers' accounts, hence it is impossible to estimate the size and extent of Jewish settlement in the region. The continuity of these settlements in the face of wars and migrations remains in dispute. Likewise for over a century a controversy has continued over the reliability of tombstone inscriptions transcribed by the Karaite scholar Abraham Firkovitch in the Crimea.

Jews fleeing Byzantine persecution or wars in Babylonia and Persia moved into outlying areas of Russian territory. The settlers included heterodox elements, such as Karaites and Samaritans. Notable church figures in the East, for instance Cyril in the ninth century, testify to their contacts with Jews, for both study and religious disputation. In this as yet "neutral" region on the periphery of Islam and Christendom, and with a lack of communal restraints, individual Jews ignored taboos against proselytizing activities, their most notable success being the conversion, in the mid eighth century, of the royal family and much of the aristocracy of the Khazar kingdom.

With the decline of Khazaria (from the mid tenth century onward), the center of gravity shifted to Kievan Russia, which became superficially christianized in the late tenth century. The intensity of anti-Jewish polemics tends to indicate continued Jewish missionary activity in the region, although the po-

lemics may also reflect stereotyped arguments from earlier Byzantine literature.

Kievan Jewry, though generally inarticulate, contained at least some affluent and learned elements. A Rabbi Moses of Kiev became a student of the noted Rabbi Jacob ben Meir (Rabbenu Tam) of France. During the twelfth century, Jews figure among the participants in political intrigues. An attack on Jewish supporters of the deceased duke Sviatopolk II in 1113 most likely stemmed from political rather than specifically anti-Jewish motivations. Kievan sources place Jews in at least two quarters of the city, and a "Jewish gate" is mentioned in chronicles in connection with a major fire in 1124 and local disturbances in 1146. The exact fate of these Jewish settlements in the wake of the Mongol invasion in the first half of the thirteenth century is unclear. A significant community of both Rabbinite and Karaite Jews did develop in the Crimea (particularly in Kaffa-Feodosia) under Genoese rule (*ca.* 1260–1475) and subsequently under the Tatar khans.

Religious intolerance and antiforeign sentiment for the most part kept Jews out of Moscow and Novgorod, though some came to Novgorod on business and evidently stayed on. The appearance of the "Judaizing heresy" in the 1470's cut short any further development of a Jewish presence. The sect, attributed to the missionizing of one Zechariah (Skharia), a Kievan Jew in Novgorod, spread among the clergy and nobility in both Novgorod and Moscow. Because our information on the sect comes mostly from hostile polemical sources, its doctrines cannot be precisely determined. Such elements as denial of the divinity of Jesus, denial that the Messiah had already come, use of Jewish prayers, observance of the Jewish Sabbath, and possible observance of Passover and circumcision figure prominently in the sources. Even taking into account the use of stereotyped images from earlier polemical literature, the doctrines of the sect and the arguments used against these Judaizers bear out the claim of Jewish instigation, though the movement was also connected to political struggles within the ruling circles of Muscovy. By the turn of the sixteenth century the heresy was stamped out, and an extremely intolerant view of Jews became the established state policy. From that time on, invasions, wars, and border changes occasionally brought Jews into Russian territory. Repeated orders expelling Jews from Russia attest to their presence, but no ongoing Jewish community would be established in Russia proper until the partitions of Poland in the late eighteenth century.

BIBLIOGRAPHY

Salo W. Baron, *A Social and Religious History of the Jews*, 2nd ed., III (1957), 213–220, XVII (1980), 116–128, and *The Russian Jew Under Tsars and Soviets*, 2nd ed. (1976), 1–9; Samuel Ettinger, "The Muscovite State and Its Attitude Towards the Jews," in *Zion*, **18** (1953) (Hebrew with English summary), and "Jewish Influence on the Religious Ferment in Eastern Europe at the End of the Fifteenth Century," in *idem et al.*, eds., *Yitzhak Baer Jubilee Volume* (1960) (Hebrew with English summary); Charles J. Halperin, "Judaizers and the Image of the Jew in Medieval Russia: A Polemic Revisited and a Question Posed," in *Canadian-American Slavic Studies*, **9** (1975).

GERSHON C. BACON

[See also **Khazars; Kievan Rus.**]

JEWS IN THE MIDDLE EAST. Jewish history in the Middle Ages is closely connected with that of Islam. At the time of the Islamic conquests, starting in 634, the great majority (perhaps 90 percent) of the Jews in the world lived in lands that were to become Muslim. From the very beginning of Islam, starting in the lifetime of the Prophet, there was a strong reciprocal influence between Islam and the Jews. Therefore, in order to better follow and understand the fate of the Jews in those countries, one has to start with Arabia, the cradle of the new religion.

JEWS IN ARABIA

The Koran mentions "the children of Israel," the Jews, several times. However, the sources from which historical knowledge about Jews in Arabia is drawn are found outside it. These are (1) talmudic literature, (2) inscriptions, (3) Christian literature, (4) pre-Islamic Arab poetry, (5) Islamic traditions about the Jahiliya (the pre-Islamic period) and the biography of the Prophet.

As indicated in the Bible, there had been close ties between Palestine and the Arabian peninsula since the dawn of history. Talmudic sources reveal that the southern and southeastern parts of Palestine (inclusive of Transjordania), which bordered Arabia, contained a dense Jewish population, and that there were close relations between Jews and the bedouin. There are many mentions of the bedouin in talmudic literature, mainly in those parts that were written in Palestine. As proven by inscriptions and by Arab traditions, Jews had penetrated deeply into the Arabian peninsula as well. The two big centers of Jewish settlement were the Hejaz in the north and center, and

Ḥimyar in the south. Starting from Elat (also Eilat; Arabic: Ayla; called Ezion-geber in the Bible, from which Greek Asia, used also in the Talmud, derives) south, the desert oases were inhabited and cultivated by Jews. Jews are described by Muslim traditionists as farmers par excellence, while the bedouin always avoided engaging in agriculture. Jews are also described as the founders of the city of Yathrib (later known as Medina). Some of those traditions fix Jewish settlement as early as the time of Moses, but more trustworthy ones date it at the time of the Jewish revolt against Rome (either the revolt of 66–70 or that of Bar Kokhba, 132–135). This is also confirmed by talmudic tradition.

Besides Medina, there are several other Jewish localities in Arabia mentioned in Muslim traditions, such as al-Ḥijr, Fadak, the Khaybar area, Wadi al-Qurā (the wadi of the villages), and Maqnā.

The other important area of Jewish settlement, in the southern part of Arabia (modern Yemen), was then called Ḥimyar. This is known from inscriptions (including a funerary one, from Bet She'arim in Palestine, mentioning people from Ḥimyar, the Homeritai). The settlements in that sector are also known from Byzantine sources, as early as Philostorgios, who wrote close to 425, referring to about 350. The kingdom of Ḥimyar became Jewish probably sometime in the fifth century. In 525 the Jewish king of Ḥimyar, Yūsuf 'As'ar (nicknamed Dhu Nuwās in Arab sources), was defeated by an Ethiopian army sent at the instigation of the Byzantines. The king apparently committed suicide, thereby ending that Jewish kingdom. Underlying this war was, on the one hand, a sharp animosity between Christians (Monophysites, centered mainly around the city of Najran) and Jews—the latter allegedly persecuted the former—and, on the other hand, the ambitions of the two world powers of that period, Persia and Byzantium. There were thus two hostile camps: Persia and the local Jews against Byzantium, Ethiopia, and the local Christians.

The Jewish presence in Ḥimyar and Hejaz certainly had something to do with the genesis of Islam; the Prophet was strongly influenced by Judaism, as can be seen from the many biblical themes and terms found in the Koran. However, it is still undecided whether this was due to a direct influence, or whether it happened through other channels, namely Christian or Manichaean sects that gained ground among the bedouin.

The main contact between the Prophet and the Jews was of a rather bellicose nature. Upon his ar-

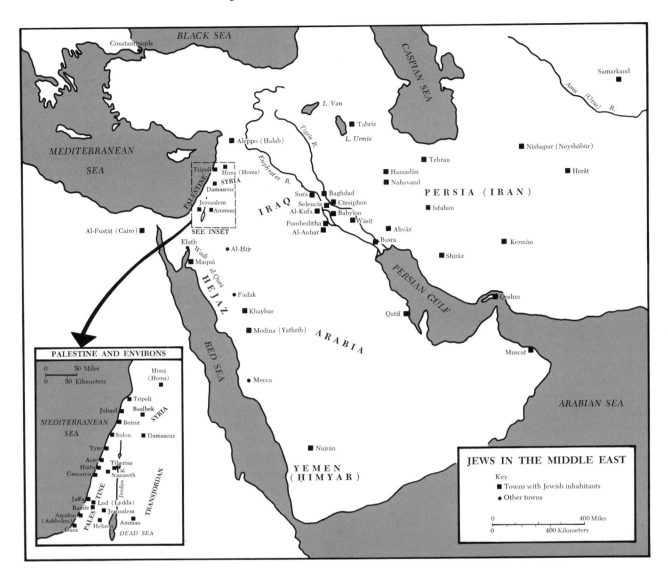

rival in Medina (the Hegira, 622), Muḥammad put an end to the alliances between the local bedouin, ever vying with each other, and the Medinese Jews. He then directed the newly established Muslim community (umma) to turn against the Jews.

According to Muslim tradition there were three major Jewish tribes at that time in Medina: the Banu Qaynuqāᶜ, described as jewelers; the Banu Naḍīr, the richest among them; and the Banu Qurayẓa. Several other Medinese Jewish clans were mentioned in the sources. There is a possibility that Medinese Jews were not in fact organized in tribes and that their designations stem from the names of ancient Arab tribes whose clients they had been in the past, and who had disappeared in the meantime. Medinan Jews were finally annihilated (after some of

them were expelled from the city); their fields and plantations, as well as their houses (or strongholds), were handed over to those companions of the Prophet who had fled with him from Mecca and now lacked any means of subsistence.

The men of the Banu Qurayẓa were all slaughtered as the Prophet looked on. Jewish properties in other parts of Hejaz were also gradually seized by the Prophet and the Jewish farmers reduced to the status of tenants. These confiscations enabled the Prophet to amass the means necessary for the formation and equipment of the Muslim army. However, Jewish localities which came under Muslim domination toward the end of Muḥammad's life were spared. Their inhabitants were subjected to a series of conditions specified in treaties of capitulation. These are

102

preserved in Muslim sources, and became a precedent for Muslim legislation concerning non-Muslims (dhimmis) from among "the people of the Book" *(ahl al-kitāb)*, namely Jews and Christians. By the treaties the local people were granted their personal safety, as well as that of their families, households, and belongings; they were permitted to keep their own religion and laws, with certain restrictions, such as that prohibiting the erection of new prayer houses. On the other hand, they had to hand over any weapons and riding beasts, and show submissiveness; they had to differ from the bedouin (the Muslims) in outer appearance (whence the origin of the yellow patch), and they had to pay various taxes, including poll tax and land tax.

Under the second caliph, ᶜUmar (634–644), Jews were completely and finally expelled from Hejaz, but not from the southern part of the peninsula. There they stayed on until modern times, but by the mid twentieth century all Yemenite Jews had emigrated to Israel.

JEWS IN PALESTINE AND SYRIA

After Bar Kokhba's revolt was crushed in 135, Emperor Hadrian forbade the Jews to enter the city of Jerusalem, which was then transformed into a pagan city called Aelia Capitolina, after the emperor (Aelius) and the Capitol, the Temple of Jupiter, in Rome. Jews, however, continued to live throughout Palestine and, together with the Samaritans, formed the majority of its population. In the third century Tiberias became the center for Palestinian Jews and the seat of the Sanhedrin, the council of sages and elders that presided over Jewish communities all over the world. Other important centers of communal leadership and learning were Caesarea and Ludd (Lydda).

The situation of the Jews worsened considerably after the empire was Christianized. Talmudic literature has retained echoes of severe persecutions during the early Byzantine period. The attitude of the gentile population also became excessively anti-Jewish, mainly under the influence of Christian preaching and writings. This internal tension led to several anti-Christian revolts, mainly by the Samaritans, in some of which the Jews seem to have taken part. Three major revolts are mentioned: in 484, around 500, and in 529 (under Justinian). The tension between the Jews of Palestine and the Byzantine authorities is also shown in early Byzantine codes; several acts of legislation are directed against the patriarch of the Jews (the nasi, head of the Sanhed-

rin) and his associate leaders, the *arkhipherekitai* (Hebrew: *rōsh ha-pereq*). No wonder, then, that the Jews of Palestine supported the Persians against the Byzantines. This support seems to have been particularly enthusiastic during the Persian conquest of Palestine in 614. There are conflicting reports of the Byzantine emperor Heraklios' attitude toward the Palestinian Jews after his victory over the Persians and the reconquest of Palestine in 628. Some sources say he decreed that all Jews must accept Christianity. Be that as it may, only six years later, the Muslim invasion of Palestine began.

All sources—patristic, Muslim, Jewish (both Karaite and Rabbinite)—are unanimous that there was a radical change in the status of Jerusalem after the Muslims conquered the city in 638: whereas for more than 500 years of Roman-Byzantine rule Jews had not been permitted to live in the city, they were now invited to settle there again. On this matter there is a certain amount of contradiction in the sources. The text of the treaty between the caliph ᶜUmar, who was presented with the city's capitulation, and the Christian population of Jerusalem, as preserved in Ṭabarī's chronicle, states explicity that the prohibition on Jewish residence in Jerusalem remains valid. On the other hand, there are other Muslim sources, as well as the Jewish ones, and even the Byzantine writer Theophanes, that bear witness to the renewal of the Jewish community of Jerusalem in ᶜUmar's day. The most probable explanation evidently is that, having yielded to Christian demands, ᶜUmar changed his mind a few years after the conquest. The Jews were then allowed to settle in the southern part of the city, which was in ruins. According to a fragment of a Jewish chronicle, they built a new quarter for themselves, using the debris of ruined houses. This quarter started at about what is known today as the Wailing Wall and in those days as the Priest's Gate; it stretched south to Mount Zion and then east to the eastern wall of the city. This is where the Jewish quarter evidently remained up to the crusader conquest. The northern part of the city remained Christian, whereas Muslims, mainly military, but also officials and scholars, stayed in the area of the Temple Mount, where the Dome of the Rock and the Aqṣā mosque were erected.

Another Jewish center that developed after the Muslim conquest was Ramle, the newly founded (*ca.* 715) capital of Palestine. The name *Filasṭīn* was given by the Muslims only to what was Palaestina Prima under Roman-Byzantine rule—that is, roughly the southern half of the country—whereas the rest was called Urdunn (Jordan) and its capital was Tiberias. There were also important Jewish communities in Hebron, Ascalon, Gaza, Haifa, Acre, Tiberias, and a group of smaller towns, mainly in Galilee. There is ample evidence about them in the Cairo genizah documents. These Jews probably were mainly the direct descendants of the Jewish population living there since the days of Joshua, but additional communities of Jews had arrived from Persia, Iraq, the Maghrib, Spain, and other countries.

The position of the Jews in Palestine improved considerably under Fatimid rule (from 969 on), but there was also much suffering and destruction during protracted wars waged by the Fatimids. Between 969 and 1029, Palestine was almost constantly a battlefield. Considerable influence at the Fatimid court was gained by such Jews as Ya'qub ibn Yūsuf ibn Killis, who became vizier under the caliph al-'Azīz in 977, after adopting Islam; Manasse ibn Ibrahim al-Qazzāz, the main representative of Fatimid authority in Damascus in the 980's; and, toward the middle of the eleventh century, the Tustari brothers, very influential merchants, one of whom was a top figure in Fatimid politics. These high-ranking Jews were generally strong supporters of the Palestinian Jewish population.

It was a widely accepted custom to launch appeals for Jerusalem, and donations for its Jewish population flowed in from all over the world. There also were special foundations in many Jewish centers, consisting of buildings and apartments for rent, whose revenue was for reasons of piety assigned to the Jews of Jerusalem. In addition, there was a continuous stream of Jewish pilgrims coming to the city from all over the world.

Palestine was the seat of a yeshiva of its own. This was the institution that had been known as Sanhedrin in antiquity. In contrast with later generations, when "yeshiva" meant an institution of learning (and many yeshivas were founded), in the period under discussion the yeshiva was a council of sages and elders. In fact the word "Sanhedrin" is a Greek loanword (synedrion) synonymous with Hebrew yeshiva (and Aramaic methīvā). The members of the yeshiva often still called themselves Sanhedrin, even in the eleventh century. The Cairo genizah has preserved more than 600 documents written by people of the Palestinian yeshiva or connected with it. Without these documents knowledge of the continued existence of this ancient institution would have been virtually nil.

The yeshiva of Palestine had its seat in Tiberias. Syriac (Christian Aramaic) sources telling the story of the war in Ḥimyar say that the main instigators of anti-Christian steps taken by the Jewish king were the "priests of Tiberias." There is no doubt that the reference is to the Sanhedrin of Palestine.

Tiberias was still an important center of learning during the early Middle Ages. Apparently some of the most popular Hebrew poets (payyetanim) lived there on the eve of Muslim conquest. It was also the main seat of the Palestinian Masoretes, who fixed the written vocalization of the Bible. The best-known of the Tiberias Masoretes was Aaron ben Moses ben Asher, who flourished during the first half of the tenth century. Exactly when the yeshiva was moved to Jerusalem is unknown, but it may have been around the middle of the tenth century. The first sources mentioning this yeshiva are connected with a sharp struggle that broke out between the Palestinian and the Babylonian Jewish leadership about the fixing of the calendar for the year 4682 of the Creation (A.D. 921/922). Saadiah Gaon, the main spokesman for the Babylonian camp, strongly criticized the Palestinian party, headed by Meir Gaon and his son Aaron. Fragments of pamphlets and epistles on this matter, written by both parties, were preserved in the Cairo genizah. The victory finally went to the Babylonians; the calendar of that year, as proposed by them, fits exactly with the calculations accepted since antiquity. It is hard to say precisely what prompted the Palestinians to diverge from these calculations; perhaps it was an attempt to achieve some compromise with the Karaites on matters of the calendar.

During the early Middle Ages there were many divergences between Palestinian rules and those of Babylonia; they are preserved, as listed in those days, in a special tractate. These differences consisted of rather trifling matters, such as whether the main holidays should be celebrated for one day (Palestinian custom) or two days (Babylonian), and no real religious schism developed.

The head of the yeshiva was called gaon, which seems to be an abbreviation of yeshivat ge'on Ya'aqov (the yeshiva "excellency of Jacob," a designation probably based on Ps. 47:5[4]). His chief assistant was the head of the court (av bet din), who dealt with legal disputes brought before the yeshiva by local communities. In addition, there were five other prominent leaders, called, according to their importance, "the third," "the fourth," and so on, composing a leadership of seven people in all. Much mation on the Palestinian yeshiva and its leaders is extant from the eleventh century. The list of the Palestinian yeshiva heads (geonim) can be reconstructed as follows:

Ẓemaḥ, 862–893
Aaron ben Moses, 893–910
Isaac, 910–912
Meir and his son Aaron, 912–926
Abraham ben Aaron, 926–933
Aaron ha-Kohen, 933–?
Joseph ha-Kohen ben ʿEzrūn, two years
ʿEzrūn (?) ben Joseph (?), thirty years
Samuel (ha-Kohen?)

. . .

Shemaʿyā
Josiah (?), spring of 1025
Solomon ha-Kohen ben Joseph, spring of 1025–21 August 1025
Solomon ben Judah, August 1025–April 1051
Daniel ben Azariah, 18 September 1052–August 1062
Elijah ben Solomon ha-Kohen, August 1062–November 1083
Evyatar ha-Kohen ben Elijah, November 1083–ca. 1110

Although the functioning of this central institution was based on the authority of learning and on the charismatic character of the leaders rather than on democratic principles, tranquillity was not its main feature. Thanks to Cairo genizah documents, several internal disputes of the eleventh century, which encompassed communities all over the world, are known. During 1038–1042 there even were two rival heads of the yeshiva (Solomon ben Judah and Nathan ben Abraham) struggling against each other, until the usurper was persuaded to give up.

Sometime around the Seljuk conquest of Jerusalem (which occurred in 1073, not 1071, as generally thought), the yeshiva had to leave Jerusalem and moved to Tyre. This harbor city, which played an important role in the economic life of that period, remained the seat of the Palestinian yeshiva for some forty years, after which it yielded to Damascus (nicknamed Ḥadrach in the documents of the period), and finally, probably in 1127, to Al-Fusṭāṭ (Old Cairo), then the main city of Egypt. During the 1080's and 1090's the Palestinian yeshiva was engaged in a sharp struggle with a scion of the exilarchic house, David ben Daniel. He had been proclaimed exilarch by his Egyptian followers, who probably wanted to see him become an overall leader of world Jewry. They were disappointed, however, and the Palestinian yeshiva kept its supremacy for an additional period, though

it was no longer in Palestine, now under crusaders' rule.

There is evidence of Karaite communities in several cities of Palestine and Syria: Jerusalem, Ramle, Ashkelon (Ascalon), Tyre, Damascus. The Karaites were far fewer in number than the Rabbinites; they all were relative newcomers, who arrived mainly from Persia and Iraq, beginning at the end of the ninth century. Their immigration was a result of intense propaganda to leave the Diaspora and settle in Palestine. In Jerusalem they founded their own quarter, situated outside the city wall, in the Samareitikē, opposite the southeastern corner of the Temple Mount, on the slopes of the Kidron valley. Some of their best-known writers and spiritual leaders of the tenth and eleventh centuries lived in Palestine.

The crusader conquest meant the destruction of all Jewish communities throughout Palestine, except Ashkelon, conquered by the crusaders only in 1153. Many refugees escaped to Egypt and Syria. Communities in those countries made great efforts to ransom Jews as well as Torah scrolls and other books that the crusaders held. However, small communities are mentioned by Benjamin of Tudela, who visited Palestine around 1170.

Not much is known about Jewish communities in Palestine in the later period, except that there still were several of them, including that of Jerusalem (where Jews settled again after Saladin retook Palestine from the crusaders). Communities in Palestine and Transjordania are mentioned by Ishtōrī ha-Parḥī, a writer of the first half of the fourteenth century. Toward the end of the fifteenth century the numbers of Jews in these communities increased considerably through the immigration of Jews from Spain, who suffered severe persecutions and were finally expelled from that country.

In Syria, where Jews had lived since antiquity, there were several important Jewish communities in the early Middle Ages: Damascus, whose ancient synagogue is mentioned in Muslim sources, and Ḥalab (Aleppo), which Jewish documents call by the biblical name of Aram-Zoba. The northern gate of Aleppo was known as *bāb al-yahūd* (the Jews' gate). Toward the end of the eleventh century Baruch ben Isaac, a famous scholar and leader of the community, lived in Aleppo. The city of Tyre had a large Jewish community, which was increased through the influx of Jewish merchants from the Maghrib. Jews in Tyre were engaged in the maritime trade, the city being at that time the main harbor of Syria-Palestine. They were also involved in the glass production for which

Tyre was then famous. There were communities in Tripoli, Jubayl, Beirut, Ḥimṣ (Homs), Baalbek, and other Syrian cities as well.

JEWS IN IRAQ AND PERSIA

Jews in these two countries constituted what is generally called Babylonian Jewry. In fact the lands of modern Iraq and Persia were politically united under Sasanian rule and remained united under the Muslims as well. There were Jews in Babylonia from the time of the destruction of the First Temple, when they were deported there by Nebuchadnezzar; many of them did not return to Palestine during Cyrus' reign. According to talmudic sources the Jews lived there in great numbers, some regions being completely Jewish. Jews were engaged in all branches of economic life, including agriculture. It appears that they also had the lion's share of the trade of the Persian kingdom, mainly the foreign trade of silk and of spices. Thus, until the Muslim conquest Babylonian Jewry was second in importance after that of Palestine, and famous for its scholars and institutions of learning. Talmudic sources bear witness to a competition between the two centers, with Babylonians seeking to become independent of Palestine in such a significant matter as fixing the calendar and the dates of the main feasts.

There is a common view among modern scholars that the situation of the Jews under Persian rule was better by far than that of their coreligionists under Roman, and later Byzantine Christian, rule. However, some information on the early Middle Ages is available about three waves of persecutions. The first occurred under Pērōz (Fīrūz reshīᶜa [the wicked one] in talmudic sources), beginning around 460, when the Jews of Isfahan were accused of having murdered two magi. Half of the city's Jewish population was then slaughtered and Jewish children forcibly converted to Zoroastrianism. There is also information on the killing, during the same period, of the exilarch and two leading Jewish sages.

The second period of persecutions was connected with Mazdak's revolution, around 500. There are some rather nebulous reports of how Jews had to suffer during that period, of general civil war throughout a whole generation. There is one passage, in a medieval Jewish chronicle (Seder Olam Zuta [The small order of the world]), which was interpreted to mean that Babylonian-Persian Jews under the exilarch Mar Zutra proclaimed their independence, lasting for seven years; but given the very unclear nature of the text, this must be taken with a grain of salt. It is also not clear who reportedly caused the Jews to suffer and brought about the killing of the exilarch and the head of the yeshiva: the revolutionaries under Mazdak or the Persian king and nobles.

The third period of persecutions occurred after the revolt of Bahrām Chubīn, the commander of the Persian army, and the murder of King Hormizd IV, in 589. After the Byzantine intervention and the taking of Maḥoza (Ctesiphon-Seleucia, the Persian capital), many Jews in this city were slaughtered by order of the new king, Xusrō II Abarwēz.

The attitude of the Jews in the Persian kingdom toward the Muslim invasion, which began in 633, is a somewhat puzzling matter. The only known Jewish sources relating to this period are the different versions of the Bustanai story. The core of this story consists of a meeting between the exilarch Bustanai and the caliph ᶜUmar, soon after the Muslim conquest. As a token of friendship, Bustanai was presented with a daughter of the defeated Persian king. Since its earliest known version, this tale has had a slanderous purpose; to show that the exilarchs of the Islamic period, the offspring of Bustanai, descended from a non-Jewish mother.

Syriac and Arab sources do not contain many explicit details concerning the ethnic nature of the indigenous population of Babylonia that submitted to Arab rule. However, a careful examination of the names and titles of these leaders, mentioned in early Muslim sources, reveals their Jewish identity. This may be shown by the nickname of one of them in Ṭabarī and other Muslim sources: Ibn Ṣalūbā. This nickname is obviously of Aramaic vintage and its only possible meaning is "son of the crucifier," a very common designation for Jews in Syriac sources. In light of this and other evidence, it appears that the leader of the local resistance against the Muslim invasion was none other than Bustanai the exilarch; his real name was Ḥananya or Ḥānān (in Muslim sources Ḥābān or Jābān, due to a confusion of the diacritical marks).

However unfriendly this first encounter between Babylonian Jews and the Muslim conquerors, the bedouin, may have been, Jews adapted to the new circumstances. They gradually acquired Arabic as a spoken language in addition to their own Aramaic. During the internal war between ᶜAli and the Umayyads, Jews sided with the former, as other elements of the indigenous population are known to have done. Due to the conditions created by Islamic rule, Jews migrated from villages and small towns to urban centers, among them newly created cities like Basra, Al-Kufa, and Baghdad.

During the Abbasid period Jews are known to have held a central position in the international trade of the caliphate, and in the control of its finances as well. The ninth-century Muslim geographer Ibn Khurdādhbih has given a description of the routes used by Jewish merchants, whom he calls Radhanites, and of the merchandise they traded. The routes stretched from Baghdad, then the center of world trade, to remote lands, from the Atlantic coast of Africa to China, and from the Slavonic lands and the lands of central Asia to the Arabian Peninsula and India, as well as the Christian countries of western Europe and Byzantium. Thought by many scholars to have been from southern France (Rhodanus [Rhône] > Rādhān), these merchants were in fact inhabitants of Iraq, coming from the region east of the Tigris, called Rādhān in early Syriac and Arab sources.

Jewish bankers, the so-called *jahābidha* (sing., *jahbadh*), played an important role in supplying funds for the always empty treasury of the Abbasid caliphs. Muslim sources dealing with the end of the ninth and the first half of the tenth centuries often mention them by name. There are also Jewish sources, preserved in the Cairo genizah, that have details about them. These were the families and offspring of Joseph ben Phinehas, of his son-in-law Netira, and of Aaron ben Amram. Besides their intense economic activities they were involved in Jewish community life, and there were family ties between them and the leaders of the yeshivas. The Radhanite merchants and these bankers and merchants of the later period can be considered a single social group or class that persisted for many generations, beginning with the Sasanian period. This continuum can perhaps be deemed to include the great families of Jewish international traders who, according to many genizah letters, were active in the Mediterranean trade of the eleventh century. Their Iraqi-Persian extraction is evident from the Persian terms they use in their letters. A characteristic feature of the activity of these traders and bankers is the frequent use of checks (Arabic: *suftaja;* Aramaic: *diyōqnē*). Through their financial connections they were able to transfer considerable sums of money donated by Jews of different lands to the yeshivas of Iraq (and also to that of Jerusalem).

However, the Jewish population of Iraq and Persia in general was by no means totally engaged in commerce and finance. The responsa of the geonim contain information on many other professions. As late as the eleventh century there is information on Jewish landowners and farmers, mainly of vineyards, and of Jewish artisans of all kinds. Jews also engaged in medicine and in a profession very popular in those days, astrology.

The main Jewish center was in Baghdad. It appears that the exilarch and the yeshivas left their former residences and settled in Baghdad sometime in the ninth century. (The yeshivas were formerly in Sura and Pumbedita; the exilarch first resided in Maḥoza, the Persian capital, later known as Madā'in, and then in a locality in southern Iraq, Qaṣr ibn Hubayrah.) Jews lived mainly in Karkh, the southwestern part of Baghdad and the main business section. Other important communities were in Basra, Al-Kufa, Wasit, Al-Anbār (near Pumbedita), Sura, and Isfahan.

The leadership of Babylonian Jewry remained in the hands of the exilarchs and the yeshivas, as it had been in Persian times. The exilarchs claimed descent from King David and enjoyed the respect of the Jewish masses as living reminders of their glorious past. The exilarchs are described in Muslim sources also as scions of "the prophet Dā'ūd." Apparently in earlier times the exilarch was recognized by the caliphs as supreme leader of the Jews in the whole world. As a result of internal conflicts, the exilarchate declined in the ninth century and the yeshivas gained control of Jewish communities throughout the Abbasid realm and even outside it. Still, the influence of the exilarchs was strong in the eastern, Persian regions. Jews of southern Iraq were under the leadership of the Sura yeshiva, and those of the north under that of Pumbedita, situated on the Euphrates.

An event of far-reaching importance was the conflict over the exilarchate that occured around 760, shortly after the Abbasid revolution. For some unknown reason, the exilarch's heir, Anan, was refused the position of his father; he then dissented and became the founder of a new sect, the Ananites, described as forerunners of the Karaites. A more critical view would doubt this version of Karaite beginnings and consider the Karaites the outcome of dissident sects that existed prior to Karaism. In the ninth century the central figure among Karaites was Benjamin al-Nah'āwendī. The center of Karaite activity was transferred to Palestine around 900, mainly through the preachings of the Karaite spiritual leader Daniel ben Moses al-Qūmisī.

The main matter of dissent on the Karaite side

was their refusal to accept any of the talmudic teachings (which they called *taqlīd*, tradition). Instead they relied exclusively on the interpretation of the Bible, made to totally depend upon *ijtihād*, the personal effort and common sense of the Karaites themselves. As in other matters, this attitude of the Karaites is strongly reminiscent of Muslim polemics, and even the terms they used were taken from the Islamic milieu.

Around the middle of the tenth century, due to the precarious situation in the Abbasid caliphate, which was ravaged by internal wars, many Jews left Iraq and settled in the Maghrib, then under Fatimid rule, as well as in Syria and Palestine. There was, however, a period of renaissance toward the end of the tenth and beginning of the eleventh centuries, when the Pumbedita yeshiva was ruled by Sherira Gaon and then by his son, Hai Gaon.

Throughout this earlier Muslim period Iraq was the main world center of Jewish learning. The literary production was mainly legalistic writings but there was also the beginning of Jewish philosophy, greatly influenced—or, rather, stimulated—by Muslim philosophers. In this respect, mention should be made of Saadiah Gaon, who was gaon of Sura, and his *Kitāb al-amānāt wa-al-Iᶜtiqādāt* (The book of beliefs and opinions).

Very little is known about later events and developments inside the Jewish population of Iraq. A central figure around the middle of the twelfth century was the gaon Samuel ben Eli, from whom there is a collection of letters preserved in the Cairo genizah. He was engaged in a polemic with his contemporary, Moses Maimonides. In addition, the names of several personalities from the exilarchic family are preserved, and also of some later heads of the Baghdad yeshiva. Benjamin of Tudela and Peraḥya of Regensburg, who visited Iraq in the second half of the twelfth century, have left rather enthusiastic descriptions of Jewish life in Baghdad and other localities. When the Mongols conquered Iraq (1258) their treatment of the Jews seems to have been better than that of other parts of the population. A Jew, Saᶜd al-Dawla, even attained the position of financial administrator under one of the Mongol rulers toward the end of the thirteenth century.

BIBLIOGRAPHY

Eliyahu Ashtor (Strauss), *History of the Jews in Egypt and Syria Under the Rule of the Mamlūks* (in Hebrew), 3 vols. (1944–1970); Michael Avi-Yonah, *The Jews of Palestine: A Political History from the Bar-Kokhba War to the Arab Conquest* (1976), 232–278; Salo W. Baron, "Saadia's Communal Activities," in *Saadia Anniversary Volume* (1943), and *A Social and Religious History of the Jews* (1965), III, 3–172; IV, 106–116; V, 209–288; Mark R. Cohen, "The Jews Under Islam: From the Rise of Islam to Sabbatai Zevi," in *Bibliographical Essays in Medieval Jewish Studies* (1976); Walter J. Fischel, *Jews in the Economic and Political Life of Mediaeval Islam* (1937), 1–44, 90–136; Moshe Gil, "The Constitution of Medina: A Reconsideration," in *Israel Oriental Studies,* 4 (1974), "The Rādhānite Merchants and the Land of Radhan," in *Journal of Economic and Social History of the Orient,* 17 (1974), "The Jewish Quarters of Jerusalem During Early Muslim Rule" (in Hebrew), in *Shalem,* 2 (1976), "The Babylonian Encounter" (in Hebrew), in *Tarbiz,* 48 (1978/1979), "The Scroll of Evyatar as a Source for the History of the Struggles of the Yeshiva of Jerusalem During the Second Half of the Eleventh Century" (in Hebrew), in *Jerusalem in the Middle Ages* (1979), and *Palestine During the First Muslim Period (634–1099)* (1983); Solomon D. Goitein, "Muhammad's Inspiration by Judaism," *Journal of Jewish Studies,* 9 (1958), and *Palestinian Jewry in Early Islamic and Crusader Times* (in Hebrew) (1980); Alexander D. Goode, "The Exilarchate in the Eastern Caliphate," in *Jewish Quarterly Review,* n.s., **31** (1940/1941); Haim S. Hirschberg, *Jews in Arabia* (in Hebrew) (1946); Jacob Mann, "The Responsa of the Babylonian Geonim as a Source of Jewish History," in *Jewish Quarterly Review,* n.s., 7 (1916/1917), 8 (1917/1918), *Texts and Studies in Jewish History and Literature* (1931–1935, repr. 1972), I, 63–356, 477–549; II, 3–66, and *Jews in Egypt and in Palestine Under the Fāṭimid Caliphs,* 2 vols. (1970); Joshua Prawer, *The Latin Kingdom of Jerusalem* (1972), 233–251; Norman A. Stillman, *The Jews of Arab Lands: A History and Source Book* (1979).

MOSHE GIL

[See also **Arabia; Cairo Genizah; Exilarch; Fatimids; Gaonic Period; Hejaz; Iran: History; Iraq; Islam, Conquests of; Islam, Religion; Jerusalem; Judaism; Karaites; Medina; Muḥammad; Nasi; Pilgrimage, Jewish; Saadiah Gaon; Syria; Xusrō II Abarwēz.**]

JEWS IN THE PAPAL STATES. Jews lived in Rome from before the first century B. C. By the early Middle Ages, as the letters of Gregory the Great (590–604) attest, Jewish centers had spread throughout the papal estates of central Italy. But in the following centuries, with the exception of isolated individuals in Lanciano, Gaeta, and Ancona, these centers disappeared. Conversely, by the twelfth century Rome had become, along with Salerno, the largest Jewish community in Italy (although the vast majority of Italian Jews resided in the south and in Sicily until their expulsion in the late fifteenth and the sixteenth centuries).

Extra-Roman communities are mentioned at the beginning of the fifteenth century with the diffusion of Jewish bankers throughout the peninsula. By 1500 there were well-established and economically stable communities in all parts of the Papal States. To pursue their policies of restriction and conversion more effectively, however, popes Pius V and Clement VIII dismantled these centers in 1569 and 1593, respectively, limiting Jewish residence to Rome and Ancona. This situation endured until the mid nineteenth century and the end of the Papal States.

The legal status of the Jews in the Papal States was governed by *ius commune* (Italian common law) in combination with church canons. These laws promised justice, but also made the Jews into legal and social inferiors. However, enforcement of the canons, especially the regulation calling for the wearing of a distinctive sign, was not consistent. Apart from variant interpretations of the canons given by different popes, this inconsistency probably resulted from lack of careful definition and division of governmental powers in Rome, and not from papal laxity or venality, as has been claimed. Moreover, regardless of the desires or the true strength of individual popes, Roman Jews looked unfailingly to the pope, with whom relations were usually pacific, as their protector. He was, in theory, their sovereign; and like all European Jews with respect to their rulers, they were the equivalent of his chamber serfs, if probably in a much modified form. The Jews acknowledged this sovereignty by offering a Torah scroll to each new pope, only to have it thrown to the ground. From the eleventh century (and perhaps as a direct result of a client relationship with the powerful Pierleoni family, which interceded with its other client, Calixtus II [*ca.* 1126]), the popes regularly issued a charter of protection to the Jews that was similar to charters given to monasteries. It was also based on the theological principle of Jewish witness to Christian truth. Known as *Sicut Iudaeis* and eventually incorporated into the canons, its protection was not ironclad, and it threatened to punish Jews who violated the canons circumscribing their actions. Under the terms of this clause (although the case was also clearly linked to Roman family frictions and politics), Elijah de Pomis was burned at the stake by order of the papal Inquisition in 1298.

Despite the numerous limitations placed on them, Jews were permitted the use of Jewish law in adjudicating internal disputes as long as it did not clash with *ius commune* or the canons. Prompted by a growing sophistication in the organization of the Papal States, but even more the result of an influx of non-Italian Jews from Spain and elsewhere that swelled the population and led to intergroup tensions that required calming, the 1524 *Capitoli* of Daniel da Pisa proposed regulating communal life by establishing a governing structure of concentric councils similar to that found in Jewish communities elsewhere, as well as in many Italian city-states. The only clear references to communal organization prior to that time are the extant decisions of the synods held at Bologna in 1416 and at Forlì in 1418, which authorized an intercommunal fund to acquire special papal letters of protection against the incendiary sermons of the Franciscan preachers. The names of Roman Jewish leaders from earlier centuries have survived, but the nature of their functions and, at times, even their existence are in doubt.

More is known of economic and cultural life. There were always Jewish international merchants and, in early times, estate owners. By the thirteenth century, however, most Roman Jews were concentrated in the production and marketing of textiles; in 1255 Alexander IV gave special customs exemptions to a guild of Jewish textile merchants. Jews also worked in the preparation of precious stones and dealt in incense and perfumes. In addition there were the lenders. Never comprising the majority of Papal States Jews, it was once thought that, beginning in the thirteenth century, Jewish lenders moved out from Rome and established Jewish centers of population throughout northern Italy. In fact, the northern lenders more likely originated in Naples and Sicily, if not Spain, France, and sometimes Germany. The lending services of the Jews (they rarely could be called bankers or financiers) proved so essential that even the Counter-Reformation popes maintained past traditions by severely regulating the Jewish rate of interest rather than forbidding loan banking altogether.

Jewish intellectual life flourished at roughly the same time that Rome and the papacy reached the peak of their European influence. In the late twelfth century the community of Paris wrote to Rome as a source of teaching authority. Poets, talmudists, and philosophers had been active since the late eleventh century; the most important of them were Nathan ben Jehiel of Rome, the author of a still useful talmudic dictionary, the *Arukh;* Judah Romano, a philosopher; and Immanuel of Rome, known for his sometimes ribald *Maḥbarot* (Notebooks) and sonnets.

Jewish culture declined in the fourteenth century but revived a century later with the appearance of papal physicians such as Bonet de Lattes, poets such as Moses da Rieti, and Renaissance-style philosophers such as Elijah Levita, Jacob Mantino, and Johanan Allemanno, many of whom were teachers of Christian humanists. The shock of the burning of the Talmud in 1553, followed by the establishment of the ghetto in 1555, signaled the start of the gradual impoverishment and cultural debilitation of Papal State Jewry.

BIBLIOGRAPHY

Vittore Colorni, *Gli Ebrei nel sistema del diritto commune* (1956); Solomon Katz, "Pope Gregory the Great and the Jews," in *Jewish Quarterly Review,* 24 (1933–1934); Attilio Milano, "I Capitoli di Daniel da Pisa e la communità di Roma," in *Rassegna mensile di Israel,* 10 (1935–1936), *Bibliotheca historica italo-judaica* (1954; supplemented 1954–1964; supplemented 1966 in *Rassegna mensile di Israel*), and *Storia degli Ebrei in Italia* (1963); Léon Poliakov, *Jewish Bankers and the Holy See from the Thirteenth to the Seventeenth Century,* Miriam Kochan, trans. (1977); Moses A. Shulvass, *The Jews in the World of the Renaissance,* Elvin I. Kose, trans. (1973); Kenneth R. Stow, *Taxation, Community, and State: The Jews and the Fiscal Foundations of the Early Modern Papal State* (1982); Hermann Vogelstein, *Rome,* Moses Hadas, trans. (1940).

KENNETH R. STOW

[See also **Jewish Communal Self-Government: Europe; Jews and the Catholic Church; Jews in Europe: After 900; Law, Canon: After Gratian; Law, Jewry; Papal States.**]

JIHAD signifies the armed struggle of Muslims against non-Muslims. In its general sense the Arabic term means exertion for a definite purpose. It appears in the Koran in the specific sense of fighting Arab idolaters, and it is imposed on Muslims as an important, meritorious duty. The theory of jihad in Islamic law reflects the situation of the early Muslim conquests. The earth is divided into the "abode of Islam" *(dar al-Islām)* and the "abode of war" *(dar al-ḥarb),* which must be brought under the rule of Islam by ceaseless jihad. Peace can never exist between the two territories; the permanent state of war may be interrupted only by the conclusion of an armistice, lasting for ten years at most. Ideally, at least one campaign into the "abode of war" should be carried out every year.

The aim of the jihad is not general conversion to Islam by force but the universal domination of Islam. Adherents of religions having scriptures could, on payment of a special tax, acquire the status of protected peoples that guaranteed safety of person and property as well as of religion. Initially, this status applied to Christians and Jews in particular, but in practice it was extended to Zoroastrians and members of most other religions. The actual offensive of jihad must be preceded by a formal invitation to the unbelievers to submit to Islam. Although in later times most enemies could be presumed to know the universal claim of Islam, a specific invitation was still in most cases considered preferable.

Jihad is generally considered in the religious law as a communal rather than an individual duty. Thus, if a sufficient number of Muslims carry out the duty, others are excused from it, in particular those lacking the material means. A son must have the permission of his parents to participate, a debtor, that of his creditor. Non-Muslims may be called upon to assist in the jihad. But in a case where the unbelievers take the offensive and threaten Muslim territory, jihad then becomes the duty of every able-bodied Muslim. Going even further, the Kharijites, who defined jihad as one of the "pillars of Islam," viewed it as a regular duty of every capable Muslim. Muslims killed in jihad were considered to be martyrs *(shahīd)* who entered paradise immediately.

The leadership of the jihad belongs to the imam, that is, the caliph for the Sunnites, or his representatives. A Sunnite law, however, generally recognizes the legitimacy of individual jihad unauthorized by the imam. This aspect became important historically as the caliphs and other rulers progressively neglected their responsibility for the jihad. Muslims desirous of fulfilling their religious duty gathered to live in *ribāṭs* (frontier fortresses) and engaged chiefly, though not exclusively, in defensive jihad. Acts of piracy against unbelievers could be considered as meritorious jihad. Groups of *ghāzīs* (raiders) carried out offensive jihad in the "abode of war." Much of Anatolia was thus conquered by Turkoman *ghāzīs* acting outside the control of caliph and sultan. The Shiites, on the other hand, considered jihad to be in abeyance and unlawful in the absence of their imam, except for defense against invaders.

The law distinguishes between the regular army and the volunteers, including nomadic tribes and individual town dwellers, who joined in the jihad after being called to arms by the imam. While the former are supported by regular pay, the volunteers must provide their own arms and mounts but are entitled to some support from the alms tax. Of the movable booty seized in jihad, one-fifth belongs to the imam. The rest is to be divided into shares among those present at the battle, each horseman receiving two or three times the share of a foot warrior. Land is commonly considered to become communal property of all Muslims, to be administered by the imam for their benefit. Captured enemies, including women and children, become slaves and are divided with the movable booty. The imam may, however, decide to exchange the male prisoners for Muslim prisoners of war, free them for ransom, or execute them. Those converting to Islam before capture go free and retain their property.

The lawbooks provide detailed rules for the conduct of the jihad, employment of ruses and siege equipment, ambushes, challenge to duel before battle, devastation of enemy land, destruction of fruit trees and flocks, the duties of the leader to the warriors and those of the warriors toward their leader, the discipline in the army, the conditions under which a Muslim is allowed to flee from the enemy, and the conclusion of an armistice. Although there was considerable variation in the views of the law scholars, these rules generally favored a humane conduct of war. They were derived from reports about the jihad under Muḥammad and the early caliphs and bear little relation to the actual practices of jihad under different conditions.

Wars between Muslims, although also often treated in the chapter on jihad in the lawbooks, were generally not considered to be jihad. Such lawful wars were those against apostates from Islam, rebels against the legitimate imam, and highway robbers. Only among the Kharijites was it common to view wars against other Muslims, whom they considered to be apostates, as jihad and often as more meritorious than the jihad against non-Muslims.

BIBLIOGRAPHY

M. Canard, "La guerre sainte dans le monde islamique et dans le monde chrétien," *Revue africaine*, 79 (1936); Daniel Bonifacius von Haneberg, *Das muslimische Kriegsrecht* (1871); Majid Khadduri, *War and Peace in the Law of Islam* (1955), 51–137; Mawerdi, *Les statuts gouvernementaux*, Edmond Fagnan, trans. (1915), 71–108; Albrecht Noth, *Heiliger Krieg und heiliger Kampf in Islam und Christentum* (1966).

W. MADELUNG

[See also **Law, Islamic; Warfare, Islamic.**]

JĪLĀNĪ, ᶜABD AL-QĀDIR AL- (1077/1078–1166), the most widely recognized Sufi saint, was born in the province of Jīlān, in northwest Iran, south of the Caspian Sea, where Hanbalism was strong. He went to Baghdad at age seventeen to pursue his studies in Hanbali circles but, rather than enrolling in the Niẓāmīya madrasa of Baghdad made famous by al-Ghazālī, he chose to study Hanbali law under the former Muᶜtazili Abu 'l-Wafāʾ ibn ᶜAqīl and the Hanbali *faqih* (someone versed in the science of Islamic law) Abu Saᶜd ᶜAli al-Mukharrimī. Al-Jīlānī received his Sufi training from Abu 'l-Khayr Ḥammād al-Dabbās. It was Abu Saᶜd ᶜAli al-Mukharrimī who placed the cloak (*khirqa*) on al-Jīlānī that signified the completion of his Sufi training. Thereafter, he spent twenty-five years wandering in the hinterland of Iraq, where he acquired a reputation as a Hanbali preacher rather than as a Sufi mystic. He returned to Baghdad in 1127 and six years later took over the headship of the madrasa of al-Mukharrimī. The school was enlarged and richly endowed after al-Jīlānī took over, and he resided in a *ribāṭ* (a Sufi center) attached to it. His family and a growing circle of disciples (*murīds*) lived in the *ribāṭ* as well. In addition to being a jurisconsult and a preacher, al-Jīlānī taught Koranic exegesis (*tafsīr*) and jurisprudence.

The Hanbali-Sufi connection that is evident in al-Jīlānī and later in the Qadirīya order might appear contradictory, since the Hanbalis have always been known to be anti-Sufi. But after the reconciliation between Sufism and Sunni Islam, many Hanbalis, the most celebrated of whom was Ibn Taimīya, were members of Qadirīya orders, especially the more moderate ones that continued to adhere strictly to the Koran and the Sunna of the Prophet.

As a teacher, a preacher, and a *faqih*, al-Jīlānī is not considered to have founded a Sufi order with a specific system or discipline. Nor is he considered to have been an ascetic, for he was married and left behind a considerable number of progeny, including at least fifty sons. Al-Jīlānī left few works, among them collections of sermons including *al-Fath al-Rabbani* and *Futuh al-Ghayb*. His more important work, *al-Ghunya li Ṭālibī Tarīq al-Haqq,* also appears to have originated in the form of oral sermons in which he set out his vision of the perfect man. The Qadirīya "way" (*tarīqa*) that is ascribed to him and to which many other orders trace their chain of authority (*silsila*) was largely the work of his sons, ᶜAbd al-Wahhāb (who took over the madrasa headship after his father died), ᶜAbd al-Aziz, and ᶜAbd al-Razzāq. They established the Qadirīya first as a localized group in Baghdad, with family branches in Hama and Damascus. When Baghdad was sacked by the Mongols in 1258, many of al-Jīlānī's descendants were massacred and his tomb was destroyed. Some of those who survived fled to Granada, where they established an order. When Granada itself fell, the descendants went to Fez, where another order was established. Al-Jīlānī himself is believed to have bestowed the *khirqa* on some of his *murīd*s, who propagated his name in Syria and Yemen.

Beginning in the fourteenth century, Sufi orders associated with al-Jīlānī proliferated, apparently because it was believed that by doing so they were promised paradise. He increasingly acquired the reputation of a saint who possessed holiness *(baraka)* and the ability to perform miracles. His biographies became filled with legends and miracles, to such an extent that he performed all the activities of the living while dead or was lord of the creation after God. The greatest spread of the Qadirīya order took place during the fifteenth century, eventually claiming adherents from India to west Africa. The order was recognized and patronized by the Ottomans, especially after their capture of Baghdad from the Safawids; Sultan Suleiman I the Magnificent rebuilt the tomb of al-Jīlānī in 1535, and it again became a popular refuge and an object of visitation.

BIBLIOGRAPHY

Arthur John Arberry, *Sufism* (1950, repr. 1970), 85; George Makdisi, "Ibn Taimīya: A Sūfi of the Qādiriya Order," in *American Journal of Arabic Studies*, 1 (1973); Annemarie Schimmel, *Mystical Dimensions of Islam* (1975); Margaret Smith, *Readings from the Mystics of Islam* (1950, repr. 1972), 77–78; John Subhan, *Sufism* (1970); John Spencer Trimingham, *The Sufi Orders in Islam* (1971); J. Van Ess, "Kadiriyya," in *Encyclopedia of Islam*, 2nd ed., IV (1978).

MAHMOOD IBRAHIM

[See also **Mysticism, Islamic; Sufism.**]

JINN (sing., *jinnī*, from *ijtinān*, "to be hidden"), a demonic, pre-Adamic order of creation. Islam accepts the idea of parallel universes; the jinn constitute an order halfway between man and angel that is normally invisible to mortals as part of the Unseen *(al-ghaib)*. Angels are created from light and, according to the Koran (55:15;15:27), jinn from smokeless fire; hence the nature of jinn is subtle and fugacious. Man, by contrast, is made of clay ("black mud altered"; Koran 15:26), which accounts for the failure of humans to perceive jinn. The moral structure of jinn is more complicated than that of angels; and, unlike them but like men, there are among them both believers and unbelievers (in Islam), whose retribution will be similar to that of man. Both are "dependent categories" (Koran 55:33) and equally the recipients of revelation, with the Prophet as apostle *(rasūl)* to both. Muslim jinn are avid readers of the Koran, and as Mecca there is the Mosque of the Jinn.

The social organization of jinn closely parallels that of man; according to the Koran they are divided into sects *(ṭarāʾif)*. They include many species inimical to man; particularly dangerous are the rebellious jinn *(mārid*s). These are devils who constitute an ever-present threat to mankind; a jinni described as *mārid* is clearly a devil *(shaiṭān)*. There are jinn and satanified jinn *(jinn mutashaittana)*; the universe is hemmed in and constantly menaced by demonic forces kept at bay only by the vigilance of the angels (Koran 37:6–10; 72:8–10).

Of the various species of jinn, the Koran singles out the afreet (Arabic: *ʿifrīt*) for special mention. The term is derived from *ʿafara* (to roll someone in the dust) and hence expresses insubordination; other concepts contained in the root are power and cunning, both of which the afreet possesses to an extraordinary degree.

The most dangerous of the satanified jinn is the *ghūl* (ghoul). The word does not occur in the Koran except as the abstract noun *ghaul*, signifying insidious destruction. The root connotes the ability to assume various forms: a ghoul can change into a bird or a woman, and an afreet can even change into smoke. This ductility is explicable in terms of its origin—it is created of essential fire. Ghouls are addicted to the consumption of human corpses.

Among afreets the female is more powerful than the male and can even marry humans. Though female ghouls can exist in their own right, their ability to change shape raises the question of incubation and succubation.

There are classes of jinn that are exclusively male or female; a *siʿla* is always female, and a *quṭrub* is always male; *siʿla*s are capable not only of succubation but also of fruitful sexual relations with humans. *Ghudār* are ogres in general, and the *ʿaqānqa* is a particularly unpleasant species. Possession is the chief danger posed by the jinn, and the Arabic word for "mad" *(majnūn)* means "possessed by a jinnī." Illustrations of jinn appear in the *Fetih Album,* preserved at İstanbul, and the feats of afreets figure throughout the *Arabian Nights.*

BIBLIOGRAPHY

Al-Bunī, *Shams al-ma ʿārif wa al-laṭāʾif al-kubrā* (n.d.), a grimoire (magician's book) listing of jinn and their corresponding conjurations; al-Damirī, *Hay-āt at-ḥayawān* (a zoological lexicon), A. S. G. Jayarkar, trans. (1906), I, 448ff.; Duncan B. Macdonald, *The Religious Attitude and Life in Islam* (1909, repr. 1965), lectures 5 and 10; Qazwīnī, *Aja ib al-makhluqāt* (1848), 368ff.

JAMES DICKIE

[See also **Angel/Angelology; Islam, Religion; Koran.**]

JOACHIM OF FIORE *(ca.* 1135–March 1202). Little can be said with certainty about Joachim of Fiore's life. The early biographical material is of doubtful accuracy. By 1184, when he appeared before Pope Lucius III seeking permission to write, he was living in the Cistercian monastery at Casamari in southern Italy, but for some time had been abbot of the monastery at Corazzo. During the succeeding years Joachim wrote extensively, first at Casamari and Corazzo and then in a hermit's cell at Petralata. The search for solitude finally led him to S. Giovanni in Fiore, where he founded the first house of the Florensian order (the rule of which was approved in 1196).

Joachim was soon famous. In the winter of 1190–1191 Richard the Lionhearted arranged an interview with him at Messina. Later in 1191 he again appeared before royalty, this time to denounce Emperor Henry VI. In general Joachim seems to have been on relatively good terms with the empire, however, and his monastery was the recipient of imperial privileges.

Joachim's major importance lies not in his actions but in his thought, particularly in his view of history. He was primarily an exegete who read Scripture according to two patterns, called by him *diffinitio alpha* and *diffinitio omega.* The former emphasizes the Trinitarian dimension of history, which Joachim saw as divided into three states or conditions *(status)* corresponding to the Father, Son, and Holy Spirit. The latter emphasizes the two dispensations, although the middle stroke of the omega suggests a third reality stemming from the other two. Both *diffinitiones* assume that there are only two

covenants and two testaments. The church and its corresponding document, the New Testament, will be valid until the second coming of Christ. Nevertheless, Joachim sees something important happening in his own age. The second *status* is dying away and the third is moving center stage. Because of the procession of the Holy Spirit from both Father and Son, the third *status* can be traced from the time of Elijah and from that of St. Benedict; yet in Joachim's time it is proceeding toward definitive separation from the second *status* and will characterize Christian life until the end of the world. Whereas the first *status* is characterized by an order of married persons and the second by an order of clerics, the third is characterized by an order of monks. It will feature a spiritual church, a spiritual understanding of both the New and Old Testaments, and joyful contemplation of heavenly things in a reign of peace that will endure until the last great persecution under Gog leads to final judgment and the end of the world.

Behind these general historical patterns lies a tapestry of subpatterns stemming from Joachim's search for *concordiae.* For example, the new and old dispensations, as well as history as a whole, are all divided into seven periods, each of which bears a family resemblance to corresponding periods. Thus the first period of Old Testament history is somehow analogous to the first period of New Testament history and to the first period of history in general, the second to the second, and so on. Again the threefold pattern provides the possibility of a triple concordance of events in the three *status.* Thus, if the first *status* is typified by the twelve patriarchs and the second by the twelve apostles, the third must contain twelve great abbots.

Joachim's reputation as a seer is closely related to his belief in these *concordiae.* Both Dante (*Paradiso* XIII, 141) and the liturgy of the Florensian order refer to him as "endowed with the prophetic spirit." Although Joachim denied that he possessed the gift of prophecy in the sense that the future was supernaturally revealed to him, he did claim a degree of spiritual understanding that enabled him to see the concordances underlying Scripture and, by manipulating them, to discover a historical pattern that could be projected both backward and forward in time.

The question of Joachim's orthodoxy was raised shortly after his death and is still debated. In 1215 the Fourth Lateran Council condemned his criticism of Peter Lombard's Trinitarian doctrine but left the rest of his thought untouched. Both the council and a papal decree of 1220 emphasized his essential orthodoxy. As the thirteenth century wore on, however, Joachim's apocalyptic views were put to various uses, some of them quite heterodox. In 1254 the Franciscan scholar Gerard of Borgo San Donnino caused a scandal by providing three of Joachim's works with an introduction and gloss that identified them as the Eternal Gospel scheduled to supersede the Bible in the dawning third *status*. A papal commission condemned Gerard's introduction without directly touching Joachim; yet the event raised doubts about him, and his notion of three *status* was condemned by a provincial council at Arles in 1263. Later in the century heretical groups such as the Apostolic Brethren and Guglielmites employed Joachim's thought in their own fashion; and Peter John Olivi, leader of the Franciscan Spirituals, drew on him to produce an apocalyptic view that, if not heretical in itself, inspired others to rebellion against the papacy.

Nonetheless, Joachim's views have continued to fascinate great men in every age. Dante was influenced by him in the Middle Ages and Savonarola in the Renaissance. In the twentieth century such diverse figures as William Butler Yeats and Carl Jung have appropriated Joachite thought in garbled fashion, and Wassily Kandinsky has described the course of modern art in terms that echo Joachim's theory of the three *status*.

BIBLIOGRAPHY

Sources. Expositio in apocalypsim (1527, repr. 1964); *Liber concordie novi et veteris testamenti* (1519, repr. 1964; first four books edited by E. Randolph Daniel, 1983); *Liber figurarum*, Leone Tondelli, Marjorie Reeves, and Beatrice Hirsch-Reich, eds., 2 vols. (1953), authorship disputed; *Psalterium decem chordarum* (1527, repr. 1965); *Tractatus super quatuor evangelia*, Ernesto Buonaiuti, ed. (1930).

Studies. Henry Mottu, *La manifestation de l'esprit selon Joachim de Fiore* (1977); Marjorie Reeves, *The Influence of Prophecy in the Later Middle Ages* (1969), and *Joachim of Fiore and the Prophetic Future* (1976); Marjorie Reeves and Beatrice Hirsch-Reich, *The Figurae of Joachim of Fiore* (1972); Delno West and Sandra Zimdars-Swartz, *Joachim of Fiore* (1983).

DAVID BURR

[See also **Franciscans; Historiography, Western European; Trinitarian Doctrine.**]

JOAN OF ARC, ST. (*ca.* 1412–30 May 1431). Born at Domrémy, one of five children in a farming family of comfortable means, the young Jeanne (or Jehanne) was later remembered as having been an energetic and devout child. She grew up during the Hundred Years War, a time of civil strife and foreign occupation when many areas of France, such as her native Barrois, were dominated by princes whose loyalty to either the English or the Valois claimants to the French throne was doubtful.

At thirteen Joan began hearing the "voices" (of Sts. Michael, Catherine, and Margaret) that guided her for the rest of her life. In 1429 she persuaded Robert de Baudricourt, captain of the nearest Valois garrison, to provide her with a small military escort for the dangerous journey to the yet-uncrowned dauphin's court. She left Vaucouleurs about 13 February and arrived at Chinon eleven days later. A fearful Charles VII delayed two days before yielding to public opinion and receiving her. Although the king was disguised, Joan immediately identified him. During a private interview she convinced Charles of her divine mission to help drive the English from France and to assist at his overdue coronation. According to legend she also confirmed his disputed legitimacy. After a three-week inquiry regarding her orthodoxy and chastity Joan was armed and given a commanding role in a sizable force to lift the English siege of Orléans.

In a series of letters Joan warned the English to withdraw. She then led reinforcements and supplies into the besieged city on 29 April. The revived French defenders launched a series of counterattacks and captured many of the encircling fortifications. By 8 May the dispirited English abandoned the siege. Characteristically, the pious Joan, who constantly urged confession on her troops, would not allow pursuit of the retreating forces as it was a Sunday. A month later Joan and the Valois army won a decisive victory in the field at Patay.

Expansion of the English occupation beyond Paris and Normandy would have dealt a serious blow to the Valois cause. Joan's victories at Orléans and Patay prevented such expansion by driving the English from the Loire Valley and destroying the myth of their invincibility. Her later campaign, which brought the king to Rheims for his coronation on 17 July, was the high point of her career. Since Joan's courageous example and inspirational leadership had helped restore the king's prestige and preserve his military position, she was briefly thrust

Joan of Arc. The earliest known rendering, sketched in the margin of the Paris Parlement's report of the relief of Orléans. PARIS, ARCHIVES NATIONALES

into the role of a political force at court. She came to be recognized as the leader in a faction favoring active war over intensified negotiations just as her own good fortune in war came to an end. She was wounded in an ill-supported assault on Paris in early September. Charles arranged a truce with Burgundy and disbanded the army. Although the king ennobled her family in December, her personal influence waned. When Burgundian forces besieged Compiègne in the spring, she left the court to travel there. On 24 May 1430 she was taken prisoner while leading a courageous rearguard action. Charles, to his eternal discredit, failed to ransom Joan, who he presumably felt had outlasted her usefulness.

Joan's male dress, claims to divine guidance, unorthodox behavior, and incredible success had all contributed to suspicions of heresy and sorcery, but her subsequent trial was essentially a political show intended to discredit the Valois cause. On 26 May representatives of the University in English-held Paris demanded that Joan be tried by the Inquisition. Under Burgundian pressure her captor surrendered his prisoner to the English in return for a sizable sum. Bishop Pierre Cauchon of Beauvais, aided by

the vice-inquisitor of France, Jean Le Maitre, assembled a court that met in the English stronghold of Rouen in early 1431. Though improperly held in a secular prison, guarded by male jailers, and denied counsel, Joan conducted a heroic, albeit hopeless, self-defense. She was eloquent under examination and steadfast when threatened with torture. Only when weakened by illness and her cruel confinement and faced with death did she submit. She was sentenced to a lifetime of imprisonment. Her later resumption of male dress under circumstances that remain unclear was taken as a sign of relapse, and she was condemned to be burned alive. Forceful and courageous even at her execution, she insisted on her innocence and asked the executioner to hold the cross high so that she could see it through the flames. Her last word was the cry "Jesus!"

Joan remained a controversial figure in the years immediately after her death. The inquiry into her trial, ordered by Charles VII in 1450, after his liberation of Rouen, was as political as the original trial since many of Joan's persecutors were by then in Valois service. In 1452 the papal legate to France, Cardinal Guillaume d'Estouteville, conducted a thorough but discreet investigation that invalidated the earlier trial and thus cleared Charles of any association with sorcery. Pope Calixtus III annulled the sentence of Joan in 1456. It was not until the nineteenth century that the "Maid of Orleans" became a popular national heroine. She was canonized in 1920.

Clouded by controversy in her day and shrouded in legend in our own, Joan of Arc still eludes modern scholarship. She embodied many of the great forces of her age, including the endemic violence that was the hallmark of late medieval civilization. Molded by the popular religious passion that would soon produce a church revolution, she helped to inaugurate modern French nationalism. Her deeds and her legend have been celebrated in notable literary and cinematic treatments by Friedrich Schiller, Mark Twain, George Bernard Shaw, Jean Anouilh, and Carl Th. Dreyer. Even after the myths are discarded, Joan endures as an astonishing figure. Her trip to Chinon, her acceptance by the suspicious Charles, the victories at Orléans and Patay, the coronation at Rheims, and her martyrdom in Rouen leave her greatness evident even to the most skeptical. By sheer force of personality she inspired people no less during her lifetime than centuries after her death. It is this emotional impact rather than her military service that provided her greatest contribution to the revitalization of the Valois cause and that continues to make her, as a heroine and saint, a spiritual force in modern French history.

BIBLIOGRAPHY

The key sources are Paul Doncoeur and Yvonne Lanhers, eds., *La réhabilitation de Jeanne la Pucelle*, 3 vols. (1956–1961); Jules Quicherat, ed., *Procès de condamnation et de réhabilitation de Jeanne d'Arc, dite la Pucelle*, 5 vols. (1841–1849); Pierre Tisset and Yvonne Lanhers, eds., *Procès de condamnation de Jeanne d'Arc*, 3 vols. (1960–1971). The most recent full biography is Frances Gies, *Joan of Arc: The Legend and the Reality* (1981), which should be supplemented by Malcolm G. A. Vale, *Charles VII* (1974), chap. 3. The most valuable study is Marina Warner, *Joan of Arc: The Image of Female Heroism* (1981).

PAUL SOLON

[See also **Charles VII of France; France; Hundred Years War; Inquisition; Valois Dynasty**.]

JOCELIN OF BRAKELOND (d. after April 1215). Little is known about the life of Jocelin of Brakelond, author of the chronicle of the Benedictine monastery of Bury St. Edmunds in Suffolk. Having entered the monastery in 1173, he came to hold a number of offices, including those of prior's (until 1182) and abbot's chaplain (1182–1188), guestmaster (1198–1200?), and almoner (1212). Though well educated, Jocelin was not a remarkable scholar. He is chiefly remembered for his vivid account of a great monastery and of the management and organization of its vast feudal lands. Written early in the thirteenth century, this account covers the years 1173–1202, with special attention to the life of Samson, the beloved abbot from 1182 to 1211. What makes this account so valuable is its collection of shrewd, wise, and humorous observations about the monks and their abbots. Jocelin was also the author of the martyrdom, now lost, of little St. Robert, a boy allegedly murdered by the Jews of Bury in 1181.

BIBLIOGRAPHY

See principally the edition and translation by Harold E. Butler, *The Chronicle of Jocelin of Brakelond Concerning the Acts of Samson, Abbot of the Monastery of St. Edmund* (1949). References to other studies are in Edgar B. Graves, ed., *A Bibliography of English History to 1485* (1975), 836–838.

BRYCE LYON

JOGLAR/JONGLEUR. *Joglar* is the Old Provençal term for "juggler" (Old French: *jogleor*). It is derived from the Latin *joculator* and may be found as early as the ninth century. *Jongleur*, which did not become common until the sixteenth century, seems to represent a conflation of *jogleor* and *jangleor* (liar, flatterer, or idle talker).

The origin of the *joglar* is uncertain. Some scholars (with Gaston Paris) believe that these men and women were direct heirs of the Roman *mimus*, the mime of the early Middle Ages. Others (including Edmond Faral) have sought to establish a case for the influence of non-Roman cultures as well.

Joglars were public entertainers who performed in towns, at fairs, and in courts. It was not unusual for more than 100 of them to attend and to entertain at the larger gatherings of the nobility. Although most traveled from town to town, some were fortunate enough to win permanent positions in the employ of nobles.

The literal translation of *joglar* does not convey a true sense of the *joglars'* versatility because the name implied a wide range of skills: juggling, singing, storytelling, mimicry, acrobatic feats, and playing musical instruments. The most common instrument was the vielle, giving rise to *vieleor* as a term often associated with *jogleor*.

Although many *joglars* performed music, they were not usually composers. It is likely that they played and sang songs from a popular repertory that included works of the troubadours and trouvères, and that they accompanied those poet-musicians instrumentally. The *joglars* performed the epic poems called chansons de geste, reciting them to repetitive musical formulas and perhaps accompanying themselves on vielles or harps. Since the tradition for the transmission of these works was oral, *joglars* (as well as the other performers of the Middle Ages) had to have well-developed memories.

The terms associated with *joglar* (such as *jangleor*) often carried strongly pejorative connotations. Joglars were vagabonds whose entertainments often included obscene or scatological references. Moreover, they were of a very low social class and were frequently denied legal protection and the sacraments of the church. Their lives were marked by poverty and hunger; they were forced to assume an attitude of servility toward noblemen. In the fabliau "Saint Pierre et le jongleur," the devil takes pity on the wretched state of a lowly *jouglere*, assigning him to stoke the fires of hell rather than to be thrown into its caldron.

Confréries (or *puys*) of *joglars* served a number of professional functions from as early as the twelfth century, such as providing a means for the dissemination of new music and poetry. A general effect of such societies (or guilds) was the gradual acceptance and elevation of the social status of professional musicians. The golden age of the *joglar* was the thirteenth century. Their subsequent decline was most likely related to the growth of secular theater.

BIBLIOGRAPHY

Edmond Faral, *Les jongleurs en France au moyen âge* (1910, 2nd ed. 1964); Raleigh Morgan, Jr., "A Lexical and Semantic Study of the Old French Jogleor and Kindred Terms" (diss., Univ. of Michigan, 1951), with extensive bibliography and citations, and "Old French *Jogleor* and Kindred Terms: Studies in Medieval Romance Lexicology," in *Romance Philology*, 7 (1953–1954); Gaston Paris, *La littérature française au moyen âge (xie–xive siècle)*, 2nd ed., rev. and enl. (1890), para. 20, pp. 36–37.

DENNIS SLAVIN

[See also **Chansons de Geste; Puy; Troubadour, Trouvère, Trovador.**]

JOHANITSA. See **John Asen II.**

JOHANN VON WÜRZBURG. All that is known of the activities of the German poet Johann von Würzburg must be inferred from his rhymed narrative work of nearly 20,000 lines, *Wilhelm von Österreich* (completed in 1314). He was apparently a learned bourgeois. The sources for his poem were given to him by a certain Dieprecht (who may have been his patron for a time and whose literary taste he praises), but the work is actually dedicated to dukes Frederick the Fair and Leopold I of Austria, to whom the poet must also have looked for support. Much of the action is set in the Near East, and some of the incidental material recalls the crusading activities of the Babenberg dukes Leopold V (1177–1194) and Leopold VI (1194–1230). The hero's title (von Österreich) would seem to indicate that the poem was intended as a glorification of the Austrian house; and the hostility toward Bavarians, which is repeatedly expressed, must certainly be seen in the context of the rivalry between Louis the Bavarian and Johann's putative patron, Frederick the Fair.

The vague historicity of the narrative is overlaid with a luxuriantly developed love interest and a series of fabulous and fictive adventures. Wilhelm, the son of Duke Leopold of Austria, is obsessed by his dream-vision of Aglye, the daughter of a heathen king, Agrant of Zyzya. He journeys to that distant realm and successfully woos the princess. Parental opposition leads to the lovers' separation. Aglye is betrothed to King Walwan of Frigia, who contrives to send Wilhelm on a deadly mission. Wilhelm escapes the fate intended for him and slays his rival. He then overcomes all obstacles, monsters, and magicians, until one decisive battle remains to be fought, against King Agrant. The battle takes place at Damietta (Leopold of Austria, Frederick of Swabia, Philip of France, and Richard of England are participants), and hostilities end with Wilhelm's complete vindication. When he is treacherously murdered at the poem's conclusion, Aglye, now his wife, dies of grief. Vassals swear the lovers' son eternal loyalty.

If the ordeals by combat, both fictive and quasi-historical, might be seen as a testimony to the vindicated prowess of "Austria," and thus its legitimation, the sentimental love relationship should be viewed as a tribute to the gentility of the house. Johann von Würzburg considered himself a modest follower of the earlier great authors of German chivalric romance, Wolfram von Eschenbach and Gottfried von Strassburg. Although Johann's complex allegorizing, his allusiveness, his emotional outpourings, and his multiplication of courtly splendors cannot disguise a certain lack of imaginative power and artistic control, the work is not without stylistic sensitivity and is altogether worthy of the poet's other professed model, Rudolf von Ems.

BIBLIOGRAPHY

An edition is *Johanns von Würzburg, Wilhelm von Österreich*, Ernst Regel, ed. (1906). Studies include Bernhard Beckmann, *Sprachliche und textkritische Untersuchungen zu Johann von Würzburg* (1937); Eckart Frenzel, *Studien zu Persönlichkeit Johanns von Würzburg* (1930); Friedrich Göhrke, *Die Überlieferung von Johanns von Würzburg "Wilhelm von Österreich" nebst einer Reimgrammatik* (1912); Eugen Mayser, *Studien zur Dichtung Johanns von Würzburg* (1931).

JAMES F. POAG

[See also **Austria; Babenberg Family; German Literature: Romance.**]

JOHANNES ANDREAE, also known as Giovanni d'Andrea or Jean d'André or Andréa (*ca.* 1270–7 July 1348), canonist, was probably born at Bologna, and not Rifredo, as has mistakenly been believed.

He was educated in Bologna, where he studied civil law with Martinus Syllimanus and canon law with Guido de Baysio, among others. Johannes also mentions that he was taught theology by John of Parma, referring probably to his preuniversity days. He took the doctorate in canon law between 1296 and 1300 and taught for most of his life. In 1301 he was professor of the *Decretals,* and in 1303 of the *Decretum.* He taught at Padua in 1307–1309 and 1319. Many details of his life are revealed in his works.

The jurist Baldus (*d.* 1400) addressed Johannes as *iuris canonici fons et tuba* (source and transmitter of canon law), for he had in fact raised the science of canon law to a new level. In addition to his legal activities he also rendered services to the city of Bologna and to the popes, especially John XXII, as legate.

Among his works the most important are his *apparatus glossarum* to the *Liber sextus* and to the *Constitutiones Clementinae,* which were soon to become *glossa ordinaria.* Almost as widely known and cited are his commentaries to the Decretals of Gregory IX and to the *Liber sextus;* they bear the title *Novella,* in honor of his daughter, Novella, who is said to have helped him prepare his lectures and even to have lectured herself, concealed behind a curtain so as not to disturb the students with her beauty. The trustworthiness of this information is subject to doubt, however. Johannes' lengthy additions to the *Speculum iudiciale* of Guillaume Durand must be noted, especially because he gives facts about the earlier canonists' lives and works that cannot be found elsewhere.

Johannes' influence was substantial and can be traced as far as statutory legislation in Friuli (1366) and Bohemia (*Ius regale montariorum* and the *Eisenacher Rechtsbuch*).

BIBLIOGRAPHY

Helmut Coing, ed., *Handbuch der Quellen und Literatur der neueren europäischen Privatrechtsgeschichte,* I, *Mittelalter: Die gelehrten Rechte und die Gesetzgebung* (1973); Gero Dolezalek, *Verzeichnis der Handschriften zum römischen Recht bis 1600,* 4 vols. (1972); Stephan G. Kuttner, *Reportorium der Kanonistik (1140–1234)* (1937), and his intro. to Johannes' *In quinque decretalium libros Novella commentaria* (1963), the best survey of life and works; S. Stelling-Michaud, "Jean d'André," in *Dictionnaire de droit canonique,* VI (1957); Friedrich Karl von Savigny, *Geschichte des römischen Rechts im Mittlealter,* VI (1850, repr. 1961), 98–125; Johann Friedrich von Schulte, *Die Geschichte der Quellen und Literatur des canonischen Rechts von Gratian bis auf die Gegenwart,* II (1887, repr. 1956), 205–229.

HANS PETER GLÖCKNER

[See also **Decretals; Decretum; Durand, Guillaume; Glossators; Law, Canon.**]

JOHANNES ANGLICUS. See Langlois, Jean.

JOHANNES CANAPARIUS was a monk, perhaps from Bohemia, who lived in Rome during the late tenth century. He wrote a life of Adalbert, bishop of Prague, martyred in 997, whom he had met in Rome. Johannes composed the vita at the request of Adalbert's companions and after a vision of his death. Later he added a *Translatio* and *Miracula Adalberti* to the life.

BIBLIOGRAPHY

Johannes' works are in *Monumenta Germaniae historica: Scriptores,* IV (1841), 581–595; *Monumenta Poloniae,* I (1864), 157–183. German translation is *Das Leben des Bischofs Adalbert von Prag,* Hermann Hüffer, trans., 2nd ed. (1891).

NATHALIE HANLET

JOHANNES DE GROCHEO (Grocheio) (*fl. ca.* 1300) is known only as the author of the musical treatise *Ars musice* (or *De musica*). Since he bases his discussion on musical practice as it was known in Paris, he may have been a student at the university there around the close of the thirteenth century.

Johannes' treatise is unusual for its time in that it is one of the few to discuss (albeit in the broadest terms) practical music and its manifestations in both the secular and the sacred spheres. The *Ars musice,* like most other treatises of its time, opens with an exposition of the materials of music, the derivation of its name, a discussion of its founder (Pythagoras), definitions of the four proportions used in music, consonances and dissonances, and intervals. In this it affirms a traditional position, using Isidore and

Boethius. Johannes makes it clear, however, that aside from these bows to the past, his interest does not lie in music as part of the quadrivium, with its importance for the philosopher or theologian. Rather, he emphasizes the practical and rejects Boethius' hallowed three-part division into *musica mundana, humana,* and *instrumentalis,* with its emphasis on the metaphysical and its use of music to represent God's creations. As a performer, Johannes bases his classification on "how the men in Paris use" music, and lists three categories: "vulgar" (secular monophony), "measured" (secular and sacred polyphony), and "ecclesiastical" (sacred monophony). Having identified these areas as his concern and taking up the elements common to all three, he presents the essence of letter notation, solmization with Guidonian syllables, staffed notation, and remarks on *musica ficta.* All of this is explored in a somewhat cursory manner, without detail or examples. Then he plunges into the main body of the work.

Vulgar (popular) music, according to Johannes, is monophonic and secular, either vocal or instrumental. It may range from serious *coronate* songs that are performed before kings and princes to dance songs for the young written on themes that will turn their thoughts away from improper things. Among the various types defined are the *stantipes,* the *ductia,* and the *rotundellus.* They are differentiated from one another by the subject matter of the poetry, the audience, and the musical form. Examples of each are given by the poetic opening line, some of which have been identified in various musical sources. These works may be performed by instruments, the variety and character of which are noted; some forms, when performed instrumentally, are different from their vocal counterparts. The section closes with a short discussion of how the works are composed. The need for close ties between text and music is emphasized, although how this is to be achieved is not covered. Dance pieces must be composed with clearly defined sections; some should have added percussion for accents.

Three areas of measured music are treated: the motet, the organum, and the hocket, each normally composed for two or three voices, the three-voice medium being the most popular in Paris. Johannes begins the section with a short explanation of the principles of temporal mensuration in order to explain what is implied by "measured." The normal unit of time called, appropriately, a tempus, may be divided into many parts: two, three, six, or, in the-

ory, an infinite number. Three tempora may be added together to make a perfection of three, the standard unit of polyphonic music. Mensural units are taken in metric patterns, known as the six rhythmic modes. They are notated by combinations of notes into groups of ligatures and single notes, so as to indicate the desired mode. Each of the three categories of measured music is then explored, with emphasis on their musical, poetic, and functional differences. The three forms are all composed consecutively, with a tenor written first or organized upon a preexisting melody, and the other voices then added above, line by line. Polyphonic conductus is considered a variety of organum in which, unlike in organum, the tenor is free-composed; organum tenors and those of motets are taken from "old songs."

Ecclesiastic song is the most important of the three categories, for its purpose is the highest, the worship of God. It is embodied in plainchant, music that is "ordained for the praise of the Creator and the service of God." In order to understand its nature, one must study its characteristic arrangement of series of notes in scalelike patterns known as ecclesiastical modes. Johannes repeats here in shortened form the rules that are part of the basic education of every choir singer. The various psalm tones are explained and hints are given about their correct performance. In the second part each service of the day is noted, with remarks on the various chants used in the particular liturgical act. There is no mention in this section of the place of polyphony in the services, although in the preceding section Johannes has noted that certain kinds of polyphony, especially organum, may be used within the church. In terms of function, plainchant is most appropriate and fitting. Some suggestions are made, for instance, on how to compose additional music for the liturgy, but these are few and of a most general nature.

The *Ars musice* is not a long work and, for the most part, is but a summary of material that is treated more comprehensively in other sources. The importance of Johannes' treatise, therefore, lies in his discussion of secular monophony, its forms, its audience, its poetry, its aesthetic and social functions. No other writer devotes so much attention to this subject, so that, although Johannes' remarks are often confusing, they are almost the only ones that provide any information.

BIBLIOGRAPHY

The Latin text in critical edition is in Ernst Rohloff, *Die Quellenhandschriften zum Musiktraktat des Johannes de*

Grocheio (1972). Translation is Johannes de Grocheo, *Concerning Music (De musica)*, Albert Seay, trans. (1967, 2nd ed. 1974). See also Patricia A. M. DeWitt, "A New Perspective on Johannes de Grocheio's Ars Musicae" (diss., Univ. of Michigan, 1973); Gustave Reese, *Fourscore Classics of Music Literature* (1957), 23–24; Hugo Riemann, *History of Music Theory, Books I and II*, Raymond H. Haggh, trans. (1962, repr. 1974), 123, 173–177, 179, 382.

ALBERT SEAY

[See also **Dance; Gregorian Chant; Hocket; Monophony; Motet; Musical Treatises; Organum.**]

JOHANNES DE MURIS. See **Jehan des Murs.**

JOHANNES DIACONUS. See **John the Deacon.**

JOHANNES HADLAUB (Hadloub, Hadloube) appears in a historical record from 1302 as the purchaser of a house in Zurich. Otherwise, information about him must be gleaned mainly from his poems.

Particularly important for questions about Hadlaub are songs 2 and 5, in which he mentions several prominent people from the Zurich area. Also significant is song 8, with a reference to a "diu liederbuoch" of a certain "Maness"—which is surely not, as has been supposed, the famous *Grosse Heidelberger (Manessische) Liederhandschrift* but certainly stands in an important relationship to it. Neither this relationship nor that between Hadlaub and the historical dignitaries he mentions has been established with absolute certainty.

The fifty-four poems preserved under Hadlaub's name, which appear in Karl Bartsch's anthology of Swiss poets, include mainly metrically loose treatments of thematic material that Hadlaub obviously inherited from earlier poets but made peculiarly his own. Most are songs about unrequited love *(hohe minne)*, influenced particularly by Heinrich von Morungen (*e.g.*, 3, 9, 17, 32, 49). Plaints of unrequited love also dominate the summer and winter songs (*e.g.*, 19, 21, 25, 28–30, 36, 40); Hadlaub has taken over from their creator, Neidhart von Reuental, little more than the basic idea. Interestingly, Hadlaub's answer to Neidhart's village bullies *(dörper)* appears in a poem (15) that is not expressly a winter song.

Similarly, Hadlaub's 35 and 41 make use of Walther von der Vogelweide's "Unter der Linden" (L 39, 11) but alter the bucolic mood by having the lover contemplate the use of force on his resisting beloved.

By contrast, Hadlaub's dawn songs (14, 33, 34, 50) feature admonitions to the furtive lovers to be sensible and part in time. Similarly, his autumn songs (18, 20, 44), an obvious heritage from Steinmar, tone down the frivolity, particularly the eroticism, to which Steinmar gave fairly free rein. On the other hand, Hadlaub's "Serena" (51), using the dawn song situation but depicting the meeting rather than the parting of secret lovers, has the aspiring lover vividly imagine just such eroticism. His "Romanzen" (1, 2, 4, 6) employ traditional motifs of Minnesang in the narration of vivid scenes in which lovers speak and act in ways that are not familiar to the traditional Minnesang or are, at most, only implicit in that tradition.

BIBLIOGRAPHY

An edition is Karl F. Bartsch, ed., *Die schweizer Minnesänger* (1886, repr. 1964), 283–361. Studies include Wolfgang Adam, *Die "Wandelunge." Studien zum Jahreszeitentopos in der mittelhochdeutschen Literatur* (1979); Hedwig Lang, *Johannes Hadlaub* (1959); Dietz-Rüdiger Moser, "Johannes Hadlaubs 'Nachtlied,'" in *Schweizerisches Archiv für Volkskunde*, 66 (1970); Herta-Elisabeth Renk, *Der Manessekreis, seine Dichter und die Manessische Handschrift* (1974).

WILLIAM E. JACKSON

[See also **Heinrich von Morungen; Middle High German Literature; Neidhart von Reuental; Steinmar; Walter von der Vogelweide.**]

JOHANNES MONACHUS (*ca.* 1250–22 August 1313), also known as Jean le Moine or Jean Lemoyne, canonist and bishop of Meaux, was born at Crécy (Picardie) and died at Avignon. After studying in Paris, where he was promoted *Doctor utriusque iuris*, he went to the papal curia in Rome, where he was an auditor for the Rota. In 1294 Johannes was made cardinal by Pope Celestine V. Boniface VIII made him vice-chancellor, and Johannes also served him as legate to Philip IV the Fair of France.

His works comprise an *apparatus glossarum* to the *Liber Sextus*, finished before 16 February 1301, which is probably the earliest commentary on this part of the *Corpus iuris canonici*, and glosses to the *Extravagantes* of Boniface VIII, especially to the bull *Unam sanctam* (two versions are in Paris, Bibliothèque Nationale, MSS/lat. 4701 and 4116), and of Benedict XI.

BIBLIOGRAPHY

Sources. See Johann Friedrich von Schulte, *Die Geschichte der Quellen und Literatur des canonischen Rechts von Gratian bis auf die Gegenwart,* II (1875–1880, repr. 1956), 192, n. 4. Early editions of his *apparatus glossarum* appeared at Venice (1585, 1602) and at Paris, as *Glossa aurea* (1535, repr. 1968).

Studies. The most comprehensive biographical works are F. Lajard, "Jean Le Moine, cardinal, canoniste," in *Histoire littéraire de la France,* 27 (1877); and Schulte, II, 191–193. More recent works are Helmut Coing, ed., *Handbuch der Quellen und Literatur der neueren europäischen Privatrechtsgeschichte,* I, *Mittelalter (1100–1500)* (1973), 377; Raoul Naz, "Jean le Moine ou Joannes Monachus," in *Dictionnaire de droit canonique,* VI, 112–113; A. M. Stickler, "Johannes Monachus," in *Lexikon für Theologie und Kirche,* V, 1062; A. van Hove, *Prolegomena ad codicem iuris canonici,* 2nd ed. (1945), 474.

HANS PETER GLÖCKNER

[See also **Law, Canon.**]

JOHANNES OF ST. ARNULF (*fl.* mid tenth century), monk and hagiographer. Entered the monastery at Gorze, then joined the abbey of St. Arnulf about 965. He wrote a life of his friend Abbot John of Gorze (*d.* 974) but did not complete it past 956. He also wrote lives of St. Glodesind and St. Gorgonius.

BIBLIOGRAPHY

Johannes' works are in *Monumenta Germaniae historica: Scriptores,* IV, 335–377; and *Patrologia latina,* CXXXVII (1853), 211–310. See also Max Manitius, *Geschichte der lateinischen Literatur des Mittelalters,* II (1923), 189–195.

NATHALIE HANLET

JOHANNES OF ST. PAUL IN ROME (*b. ca.* 910), prior of the monastery of St. Paul in Rome, wrote a Latin prose life of St. Odo of Cluny in three books (*ca.* 943). In a prologue he claims that it is based entirely on conversations he had with Odo around the year 938, but clearly other material is included. He

later produced a shorter, more strictly biographical version.

BIBLIOGRAPHY

Vita sancti Odonis is in *Patrologia latina,* CXXXIII (1853), 43–104. See also Max Manitius, *Geschichte der lateinischen Literatur des Mittelalters,* II (1923), 130–136.

W. T. H. JACKSON

[See also **Odo of Cluny, St.**]

JOHANNES OF ST. VINCENT, a monk of the eleventh and twelfth centuries, wrote *Chronicon S. Vincentii Vulturnensis* in four books. The chronicle begins, in the manner of Isidore, with the creation of the world and proceeds to a catalog of popes. It then proceeds to the founding of St. Vincent in 703. The fourth book brings the chronicle up to 1101.

BIBLIOGRAPHY

See Max Manitius, *Geschichte der lateinischen Literatur des Mittelalters,* III (1931), 552–555.

EDWARD FRUEH

JOHANNES SCOTUS ERIGENA. See **John Scottus Eriugena.**

JOHANNES TAULER. See **Tauler, Johannes.**

JOHANNES TEUTONICUS (Semeca, Zemeke) (*d.* 1245), professor of canon law at Bologna, was an influential canonist of the early thirteenth century. He studied at Bologna and heard Azo's lectures on Roman law. Although he never mentioned his teachers, he cited the glosses of Huguccio, Laurentius Hispanus, and Vincentius Hispanus frequently in his commentaries. He wrote his most important works in a remarkably short time, between about 1210 and 1218. Johannes left Bologna about 1218 and returned to Germany, where he held a number of positions in the churches of Halberstadt: scholasticus (1220), dean (1235), and provost (1241) of the cathedral chapter, and provost of St. Maria (1223).

Johannes' *Glossa ordinaria* to Gratian's *Decretum* was his most significant contribution to canon law. He completed this massive commentary in 1216, shortly after the Fourth Lateran Council. Although lacking great originality, his gloss comprehensively summed up a half-century of canonistic jurisprudence. Johannes' influence on later thought was mainly through this work, which contained a wide range of ideas about the proper structure of the church, the authority of the pope, the relationship of the church to the state, the role of the cardinals, and the rights of bishops. In general, Johannes supported the claims of Pope Innocent III to exercise temporal authority, but opposed many of his initiatives to centralize ecclesiastical authority and jurisdictional prerogatives.

Bartholomaeus Brixiensis revised Johannes' commentary in the mid thirteenth century by adding references to Pope Gregory IX's *Decretals* (1234) and appending his comments to some glosses. In Bartholomaeus' recension, Johannes' gloss was studied by every law student and copied into almost every manuscript of the *Decretum*. Fifteenth-, sixteenth-, and seventeenth-century glossed editions of the *Decretum* invariably print his apparatus. It is not an exaggeration to say that almost every lawyer, theologian, or polemicist of the later Middle Ages cited Johannes' *Glossa ordinaria*, which had become an "authoritative text."

In addition Johannes wrote a commentary on Pope Innocent III's official collection of canon law, *Compilatio tertia*, and on another collection of Innocent's decretals, the *Compilatio quarta*, that he himself compiled but that, for reasons not altogether clear, Innocent refused to authenticate. He completed a commentary on the constitutions of the Fourth Lateran Council shortly after its last session. Among his minor works are glosses to the *Arbor consanguinitatis et affinitatis* (Tree of consanguinity and affinity) and a set of thirty-six *Quaestiones disputatae* (Disputed questions [of law]). He also wrote a short *consilium* (ca. 1223–1232) while he was in Halberstadt.

BIBLIOGRAPHY

Sources. There are modern editions of books 1 and 2 of Johannes' apparatus to the *Compilatio tertia* and to the Fourth Lateran constitutions: *Johannis Teutonici Apparatus glossarum in Compilationem tertiam,* Kenneth Pennington, ed. (1981); *Constitutiones Concilii quarti Lateranensis una cum Comentariis glossatorum,* Antonio García y García, ed. (1981). See also G. Fransen, "À propos des Questions de Jean le Teutonique," in *Bulletin of Medieval Canon Law,* 13 (1983); Antonio García y García, "Glosas de Juan Teutónico, Vicente Hispano, y Dámaso Húngaro a los Arbores consanguinitatis et affinitatis," in *Zeitschrift der Savigny-Stiftung für Rechtsgeschichte,* Kan. Abt., 68 (1982); Kenneth Pennington, "A 'Consilium' of Johannes Teutonicus," in *Traditio,* 26 (1970).

Studies. Stephan Kuttner, "Johannes Teutonicus," in *Neue deutsche Biographie,* X (1974); Kenneth Pennington, "The Epitaph of Johannes Teutonicus," in *Bulletin of Medieval Canon Law,* 13 (1983), and "Johannes Teutonicus and Papal Legates," in *Archivum historiae pontificiae,* 21 (1983); W. Stelzer, "Johannes Teutonicus," in *Die deutsche Literatur des Mittelalters: Verfasserlexikon,* IV (1982).

KENNETH PENNINGTON

[See also **Law, Canon.**]

JOHN CHRYSOSTOM, ST. (348–407). John Chrysostom (golden-mouthed), archbishop of Constantinople from 398 to 404, was born at Antioch. The son of an army official, he studied rhetoric with Libanius but at the age of eighteen he was baptized a Christian and adopted an ascetic, eremitic life. Mortifications injured his health, so he returned to Antioch, where he became deacon in 381 and presbyter in 386. While deacon he wrote *De sacerdotio* (On the priesthood) to describe his ideals for the clergy. John's sermons attracted admiration; some he polished for publication, while the transmission of others was accomplished by private stenographers.

Chosen by Emperor Arcadius and his wife Eudoxia, John was consecrated on 26 February 398 to the see of Constantinople by Archbishop Theophilus of Alexandria. But his reforming zeal and centralizing of the finances of the city's churches won him enemies. Beginning in 400 tension rose between John and Eudoxia, who was offended by John's stern calls for renunciation of secular comfort and glory. The deposing at the Council of Ephesos in 401 of six simoniacal bishops alarmed metropolitans in Asia Minor, jealous of their independence. Four Egyptian monks whose ascetic theology derived from the controversial Origen appealed to John after being expelled by Theophilus of Alexandria. Invited to answer their charges, Theophilus enlisted support from the anti-Origenist Epiphanius of Constantia and decided to use John's many enemies to overthrow him. At a synod of thirty-six malcontent bishops at the Palace of the Oak, near Chalcedon, he condemned John in August 403 on trivial, bitter complaints that show how the clergy resented his reforms.

John retained a strong following. His exile was immediately revoked by the emperor. But two months later, when a silver statue of Eudoxia was erected facing his cathedral, John's complaints that the noise of the celebration disturbed the divine liturgy offended her. After he had compared her to Herodias and Jezebel, John was exiled to Cucusus, Armenia; then, to restrict his continued influence, he was roughly moved farther away. He died at Comana, Pontus. At Constantinople his disciples, refusing communion with John's successors, had Rome's support. But they were reconciled after a feast was established in John's honor.

John's posthumous influence was great; from the ninth century on, his name was attached to the Constantinopolitan liturgy. His sermons were widely read, copied, and imitated. First translated into Latin about 420 by a Pelagian, Anianus of Celeda, some were known to Augustine. They are a rich source for social history as well as for liturgy and church customs. Though they seldom break new ground in theology, their moral concerns are considerable and achieve original expression, especially in handling the concept of conscience. His preaching seeks to bring seriousness to the Christian profession and stresses the awe of the eucharistic mystery.

BIBLIOGRAPHY

Sources. An early edition of John's works is by Bernard de Montfaucon, 13 vols. (1718–1738), repr. with additions in *Patrologia graeca,* XLVII–LXIV.

Studies. The main (partisan) source for his life is Palladius' *Dialogus,* P. R. Coleman-Norton, ed. (1928). The best modern biography is Chrysostomus Baur, *Der heilige Johannes Chrysostomus und seine Zeit,* 2 vols. (1929–1930), translated by Sister M. Gonzaga as *John Chrysostom and His Time,* 2 vols. (1960–1961). The classic biography in Louis Sebastien Le Nain de Tillemont, *Mémoires pour servir à l'histoire ecclésiastique des six premiers siècles,* IX (1706), has not been superseded.

HENRY CHADWICK

[See also **Councils, Ecumenical; Reform, Idea of; Theophilus.**]

JOHN GUALBERTI, ST. (Giovanni Gualberto) (*ca.* 995–1073), founder of the Vallombrosan order. Although influenced by the eremitic circles associated with St. Romuald of Ravenna, John moderated their practices to conform more closely to traditional Benedictine monasticism. From his original monastery, which he established (1038) at Vallombrosa, he extended his influence over a number of other Tuscan monasteries, all of which formed the nucleus of one of the first true monastic orders. Like St. Romuald, he encouraged clerics to renounce private property and attacked simony, adopting the radical position that sacraments performed by simoniacs were invalid, a view that was opposed by St. Peter Damian, and defended by Humbert of Silva Candida.

BIBLIOGRAPHY

The main sources for the life of John Gualberti are Andrew of Strumi, *Vita Iohannis Gualberto,* in *Acta sanctorum,* 28, 12 Iuglo, c. IX, also in *Monumenta Germaniae historica: Scriptores,* XXX. 2, 1080–1104.

For modern discussions see Sofia Boesch-Gajano, "Storia e tradizione Vallombrosane," in *Bulletino dell'istituto storico italiano per il medio evo,* 76 (1964); Brunetto Quilici, *Giovanni Gualberto e la sua riforma monastica* (1943), also in *Archivio storico italiano,* 99–100 (1941–1942).

KENNERLY M. WOODY

[See also **Humbert of Silva Candida; Peter Damian, St.; Romuald of Ravenna, St.**]

JOHN KLIMAKOS, ST. (*ca.* 570–*ca.* 649). After reportedly spending forty years as a hermit in the Sinai Desert, Klimakos became the abbot of the monastery on Mt. Sinai and wrote the *Climax* or *Ladder of Paradise* (hence his name), a work that was very influential in Byzantine monasticism. The *Climax* consists of thirty chapters or steps (symbolizing the thirty unknown years in the life of Christ) that lead to spiritual perfection. The book is divided into two parts: the first twenty-six chapters are an analysis of the main vices that must be overcome in order to progress spiritually; the last four deal with the positive virtues: solitude, prayer, dispassion, and (in the final chapter) faith, hope, and charity. This work was translated into a number of languages, including Syriac, Arabic, Latin, and Church Slavonic, and was an especially important influence on the Slavs.

BIBLIOGRAPHY

The *Opera omnia,* in *Patrologia graeca,* LXXXVIII (1860), 631–1210, include Greek and Latin versions of the *Ladder of Paradise.* See also *The Ladder of Divine Ascent,* Lazarus Moore, trans. (1959).

LINDA C. ROSE

JOHN OF CAPESTRANO, ST.

JOHN OF CAPESTRANO, ST. (**John Capistran**) (24 June 1386–23 October 1456). After a religious crisis in 1415, John abandoned his legal and judicial career to become a Franciscan. He chose the rigorous but still small Observant branch, to whose subsequent expansion Capistran and his friend St. Bernardino of Siena greatly contributed. In 1418 John began his second public life, preaching and writing, combating the Fraticelli, defending the Observants against the Conventuals, and serving as papal legate and observant administrator. In the aftermath of the fall of Constantinople (29 May 1453) and the subsequent threat of Turkish advances into eastern Europe, John was commissioned to preach a crusade and to recruit crusaders to aid Hungarian resistance to the Ottomans. He played a dramatic role during the siege of Belgrade in July 1456, sending his crusaders into the citadel after the generals had called retreat, and thus received much credit for the victory that followed.

BIBLIOGRAPHY

There are no modern critical editions of John's works. See Aniceto Chiappini, *La produzione letteraria di S. Giovanni da Capestrano* (1927), and *Reliquie letterarie capestranesi* (1927), both registers of the saint's works; Johannes Hofer, *St. John Capistran, Reformer,* Patrick Cummins, trans. (1943). A more recent version of this work is *Johannes Kapistran: Ein Leben im Kampf um die Reform der Kirche,* 2nd ed. rev. by Ottokar Bonmann, 2 vols. (1964–1965).

ELAINE GOLDEN ROBISON

[See also **Franciscans; Hungary; Hunyadi, János.**]

JOHN OF DAMASCUS, ST.

JOHN OF DAMASCUS, ST. (**John Damascene**) (*ca.* 675–*ca.* 750), Greek theologian, hymnographer, and father of the church. He synthesized the Greek patristic thought that preceded him and gained the reputation of a classical exponent of orthodoxy throughout the Byzantine Middle Ages.

John was born in Damascus of the wealthy Manṣūr family; his father occupied a position there in the financial administration of the Christian community under the authority of the Muslim caliphs. After succeeding his father, John retired to the monastery of St. Sabbas (Mar Saba), near Jerusalem, about 700; there he acquired fame as theologian, polemicist, poet, musician, homilist, and ascetic writer. He died at St. Sabbas.

John's major work, used for years after his death as a standard textbook of philosophy and theology, is *Font of Wisdom (Pege gnoseos).* It is divided into three parts: (1) the "Philosophical Chapters," also known as the "Dialectics," an introduction to Greek philosophy emphasizing Aristotelian logic; (2) a history of heresies, which contains brief refutations of various false teachings listed in an approximately chronological order and including Islam; and (3) "Exact Exposition of the Orthodox Faith" *(Ekthesis),* in which the Trinitarian dogma, as formulated by the Cappadocian fathers (St. Basil the Great, St. Gregory of Nyssa, and St. Gregory Nazianzus), and the christological doctrine of the hypostatic union of the two natures of Christ occupy the most prominent place.

As a polemicist John published a number of small tracts against those unorthodox Christian groups that were in contact with his community in Damascus, among them the Nestorians, Monophysites, and Monothelites. He is most famous for having been the first to publish a systematic refutation of iconoclasm (his three "discourses" against those who rejected the holy images, written 726–730). For this he was formally anathematized (under his Arabic family name Manṣūr) by the iconoclastic council of Hieria (754), and glorified as a confessor by the Second Council of Nicaea (787).

As a hymnographer John had a lasting influence upon the liturgical tradition of the Byzantine church. Although some of the numerous attributions to "John the monk" found in the liturgical books are doubtful, he is certainly the author of the major hymns for Easter, Christmas, Epiphany, and other feasts. He also wrote many hymns of the weekly cycle, included in the book known as *Oktoechos* (Book of eight tones [modes]). The invention of the musical pattern of eight tones, applied throughout the hymnographical system of the Byzantine liturgy, is attributed to him, although no musical manuscript of his period has been deciphered.

John's sermons on feast days, such as the Dormition (August 15) and the Transfiguration of Christ (August 6), acquired great popularity and exercised theological influence. His *Sacra parallela* are anthologies of scriptural and patristic texts on the moral and ascetic dimensions of Christian life.

BIBLIOGRAPHY

Texts. Patrologia graeca, XCIV (1860); Bonifaz Kotter, ed., *Die Schriften des Johannes von Damaskus* (1969), and in an English translation as *On the Holy Images* (1978).

124

Studies. Hans Georg Beck, *Kirch und theologische Literatur im Byzantinischen Reich* (1959); Jaroslav Pelikan, *The Christian Tradition*, II, *The Spirit of Eastern Christendom (600–1700)* (1974); Keetje Rozemond, *La christologie de saint Jean Damascène* (1959).

JOHN MEYENDORFF

[See also **Byzantine Church; Christology; Church Fathers; Councils (Ecumenical, 325–787); Hymns, Byzantine; Icons, Theology of; Iconoclasm, Christian.**]

JOHN OF ŌJUN, ST. (Yovhannēs Ōjnecⁱi) katᶜolikos of Armenia from 717 to 728. One of the dominant figures of the medieval Armenian church, John (Yovhannēs [III]) is traditionally known as *Imastasēr* (the Philosopher) for his learning, which is said to have charmed even the Umayyad caliph al-Walīd.

John of Ōjun is particularly famous for his activity against the heretical tendencies in Armenia and for his regularization of the doctrine and customs of the Armenian church. Two of his polemical works have survived: *Against the Paulicians,* one of the main sources on this sect, which he identifies with the iconoclasts and accuses of consorting with sun worshipers, and *Against the Phantasiasts,* which condemns the extreme Monophysite followers of Severus of Antioch, who denied the reality of the Incarnation. John pursued his antiheretical activities by summoning two major councils. The Council of Dwin (719/720) specifically condemned the Paulicians in its thirty-second Canon and John's *Oratio synodalis* also contained allusions to these heretics, although the portion specifically directed against them has been lost. Still more important, the Council of Manazkert (725/726) marked the reunion of the Armenian and moderate Syrian Jacobite churches, rejecting the extremist positions of Julian of Halicarnassus and Severus of Antioch. In addition to his antiheretical works, John compiled a list of Armenian councils. His canons were subsequently included in the official Book of Canons of the Armenian church.

BIBLIOGRAPHY

John's writings are in *Teaṙn Yovhannu imastasiri awinecᶜwoy matenagrutᶜiwnkᶜ Domini Johannis philosophi Ozniensis ... Opera,* Awgerean/J. B. Aucher, ed. and trans. (1834). See also Nina G. Garsoïan, *The Paulician Heresy* (1967), 94–95, 135, 139–140, 161, 165, 177, 203, 209–210, 226; *Kanonagirkᶜ Hayocᶜ,* V. Hakobyan, ed., I (1964), 514–537, 646–647; Malachia Ormanean, *Azgapatum,* I (1912), 817–850, and *The Church of Armenia,* G.

Marcar Gregory, trans., 2nd ed. (1955); "Yovhannu imastasiri Hayocᶜ katᶜulikosi saks žolovocᶜ or elen i Haykᶜ," in *Girkᶜ Tʰtᶜocᶜ* (1901).

NINA G. GARSOÏAN

[See also **Armenian Church; Manazkert, Council of; Paulicians.**]

JOHN XXI, POPE. See **Peter of Spain.**

JOHN XXII, POPE (1244–4 December 1334), one of the popes of the so-called Babylonian captivity in Avignon. Born Jacques Duèse (Jacme Duesa in Provençal), he became a canon lawyer after schooling at Paris and Orléans. In 1308 he was named chancellor to King Charles II of Naples, in 1310 bishop of Avignon, and in 1312 a cardinal.

John's election to the papacy on 7 August 1316 ended a two-year vacancy of the papal throne. Already established in Avignon, he began an effective process of reform and reorganization in the spiritual, administrative, financial, and legal spheres of the church.

The Franciscan order had long been divided over the question of apostolic poverty, with the Spirituals professing the doctrine of absolute poverty and the Conventuals contesting it. John supported the Conventuals. In the bulls *Ad conditorem canonum* (8 December 1322) and *Cum inter nonnullos* (12 November 1323), he declared that Christ and the apostles had owned the goods they possessed, and that to deny this was heretical. Franciscans, therefore, could own property. Many of the Spirituals rebelled, and even elected one of their own as antipope (Nicholas V) in 1328, but John vigorously pursued them and their supporters, notably Emperor Louis IV of Bavaria, whom he had excommunicated.

In the administrative and financial spheres, John extended the process of centralization as he exercised his power of appointment to more and more church offices, and developed a more systematic taxation of these benefices. The cost, however, was a growing opposition to papal control.

In canon law the pope promulgated the *Liber septimus* (or *Constitutiones Clementinae*) (1317), a collection of decretals of Clement V, along with his own judicial decisions, known as the *Extravagantes communes.*

Beginning in 1331, John outlined his interpretation of the beatific vision, according to which the souls in heaven cannot contemplate the divine essence, and souls in hell cannot suffer true perdition, until Judgment Day. John spoke as a private theologian and met with a chorus of opposition. In the midst of the debates he fell sick and, on his deathbed, recanted.

BIBLIOGRAPHY

Jean XXII (1316–1334) Lettres communes analysées d'après les registres dits d'Avignon et du Vatican, Guillaume Mollat and G. de Lesquen, eds., 17 vols. (1904–1946); *Lettres secrètes et curiales du pape Jean XXII (1316–1334) relatives à la France,* August L. Coulon and Suzanne Clemencet, eds. (1906–1972). See also Guillaume Mollat, *The Popes at Avignon, 1305–1378,* Janet Love, trans. (1963).

PAUL R. THIBAULT

[See also **Avignon; Babylonian Captivity; Franciscans.**]

JOHN IV THE FASTER, PATRIARCH of Constantinople from 582 to 595, took the title "ecumenical [universal] patriarch," with its implicit challenge to the papacy of Rome. Pope Gregory I the Great (590–604) was, predictably, furious, even though there is evidence that the title had been used by the patriarchs since the beginning of the sixth century. Its precise meaning is debatable; it may have meant nothing more than patriarch of the ecumenical city. The title appears in the *Novellae* (new laws, of the *Corpus iuris civilis*) of Justinian referring to the patriarchs of Constantinople, but it does not appear to have been at that time a challenge to the power of the pope; rather, it seems to have been an assertion of primacy among the Eastern patriarchs. The controversy caused by John's assumption of the title resulted in the attempts by Emperor Maurice to redefine the status of the sees of Constantinople and Rome in the early seventh century.

BIBLIOGRAPHY

Alexander Vasiliev, *History of the Byzantine Empire* (1952), 173.

LINDA C. ROSE

[See also **Maurice, Emperor; Patriarch.**]

JOHN VIII XIPHILINOS, PATRIARCH (*ca.* 1010–1075), Byzantine jurist and patriarch and pupil

of John Mauropos. He taught law to Michael Psellos and subsequently criticized the latter's Platonist humanism. After being appointed head of the newly founded school of law (nomophylax) at Constantinople in 1045, he became a monk in Asia Minor in 1054 and from 1064 to 1075 served as patriarch of Constantinople. He probably wrote three studies in Roman law, but the corpus of homilies attributed to him is a later compilation, probably by his nephew of the same name.

BIBLIOGRAPHY

Joan M. Hussey, *Church and Learning in the Byzantine Empire* (1937, repr. 1963); Paul Lemerle, *Cinq études sur le XIᵉ siècle byzantin* (1977), 203–212; Wanda Wolska-Conus, "L'école de droit et l'enseignement du droit è Byzance au XIᵉ siècle: Xiphilin et Psellos," in Centre de Recherches d'Histoire et Civilisation Byzantines, *Travaux et mémoires,* 7 (1979).

ROBERT BROWNING

[See also **Law, Byzantine; Psellos, Michael.**]

JOHN THE KAT^COŁIKOS. See **John of Òjun, St.**

JOHN I TZIMISKES (*r.* 969–976), a Byzantine emperor of Armenian origin, related on his father's side to the Byzantine general John Kurkuas and on his mother's side to the Phokas family. Tzimiskes was a professional soldier; as general he participated in the campaigns against the Hamdanids of Syria and occupied the city of Samosata in 958. Under Nikephoros Phokas (963–969), John was elevated to the rank of domestic of the schools in the East and worked toward the reconquest of Cilicia. A court plot that ended the life of Nikephoros was responsible for his elevation to the imperial throne.

The short reign of John I Tzimiskes was marked by a major victory over the Russians in 971 and the restoration of the old Roman frontier on the Danube. In 972 Tzimiskes established close relations with the Western Empire by agreeing to a marriage between an Ottonian prince and a Byzantine princess; he then resumed the task of restoring the eastern frontier of the Byzantine Empire. According to the twelfth-century Armenian historian Matthew of Edessa, Tzimiskes marched to the very borders of Armenia before coming to terms with the Armenian

JOHN II KOMNENOS

Bagratid king Ašot III Oľormac (the Merciful) in 974. Tzimiskes then marched south to conquer Syria and Palestine. A year later he was probably poisoned.

BIBLIOGRAPHY

Leo the Deacon, *History*, C. B. Hase, ed. (1828); H. Grégoire, "The Amorians and the Macedonians 842–1025," in *Cambridge Medieval History*, IV.1 (1966), 105–192.

KRIKOR H. MAKSOUDIAN

[See also **Armenia: History of; Byzantine History; Domestic.**]

JOHN II KOMNENOS (1088–8 April 1143), Byzantine emperor. John II's succession to the throne upon the death of his father, Alexios I (16 August 1118), was contested by his sister, Anna Komnena, and her mother, Irene, on behalf of Anna's husband, Nikephoros Bryennios, but the plot was easily overcome. John was devout and puritanical; by preference he spent the bulk of his reign on campaign.

In southern Italy and Sicily, the Normans posed little threat during John's reign, since Roger II was still establishing his position. John's alliance with the German rulers Lothar II and Conrad III helped to keep the German and Norman fronts quiet. Hungary, however, increased its power in this period, and in 1128–1130 a series of border clashes occurred, without decisive result. When, in 1122, John attempted to expel the Venetians from their favored position in the empire, they launched raids on the Aegean islands, which forced the emperor to renew their privileges (1126).

The bulk of John's campaigns were in the East. He fought repeatedly with the Danishmendid emirs of east-central Anatolia, but in 1139–1140 failure to capture Niksar (Neocaesarea) frustrated his plans. He campaigned in 1137–1138 against the Armenian Rubenid rulers of Cilicia and the princes of Antioch; in 1137 Raymond of Antioch was compelled to accept Byzantine overlordship, and John entered Antioch in triumph. Raymond's Norman vassals, however, never really accepted Byzantine lordship; and a fresh "rebellion" of Antioch caused a new campaign in 1142–1143, during which John died in his camp in the Taurus Mountains, the victim either of assassination or of a hunting accident. His two eldest sons being dead, and the third in Constantinople, the succession passed (allegedly with John's approbation) to the youngest, who became Manuel I.

JOHN III VATATZES

BIBLIOGRAPHY

Joan M. Hussey, "The Later Macedonians, the Comneni, and the Angeli, 1025–1204," in *Cambridge Medieval History*, 2nd ed., IV. 1 (1966), 219–226, with bibliography, 858–867; Ioannes (John) Kinnamos, *Deeds of John and Manuel Comnenus*, Charles M. Brand, trans. (1976), 13–31, 209–210.

CHARLES M. BRAND

[See also **Anna Komnena; Antioch; Byzantine Empire; Danishmendids; Komnenoi.**]

JOHN III VATATZES (**John Doukas Vatatzes**) (*ca.* 1192–4 Nov. 1254), the greatest of the emperors of Nicaea. He belonged to a Thracian family prominent at the Byzantine court in the late twelfth century. Success in a tournament brought him to the notice of the Nicaean emperor, Theodore I Laskaris, who married him to his eldest daughter, Eirene (*ca.* 1216). John Vatatzes succeeded to the Nicaean throne on the death of Theodore in November 1221. At that time the Nicaean Empire was limited to scattered territories in western Asia Minor. By the time of his death, his dominions included not only the whole of western Asia Minor, but also Thrace, the southern Balkans, and the city of Thessaloniki. John Vatatzes had made the Nicaean Empire the most powerful state in the Levant.

He was a shrewd man, whose conquests were the result of a combination of opportunism and perseverance. In the words of a contemporary, George Akropolites, "He relied on his patience and would spend the spring in enemy territory and stay there during the harvest and even the autumn. If need be, he was willing to winter there." Such tactics were feasible only because of the underlying soundness of the Nicaean Empire. The emperor insisted upon stringent financial administration and upon efficient and profitable management of the imperial estates. It was said that he was able to present his empress with a crown paid for out of the profits of the imperial poultry farms. He also took steps to protect the Nicaean cloth industry against Italian and Muslim competition.

Empress Eirene died in 1239, and in 1244 John Vatatzes married Constance Lancia (Constance-Anna), the bastard daughter of his ally Emperor Frederick II Hohenstaufen. After his death, at Nymphaeum, he was venerated as a saint by the people of western Asia Minor. He was succeeded by Theodore II Laskaris, the only son of his first marriage.

BIBLIOGRAPHY

Silvano Borsari, "Federico II e l'Oriente bizantino," in *Rivista storica italiana*, 63 (1951); A. Heisenberg, "Kaiser Johannes Batatzes der Barmherzige," in *Byzantinische Zeitschrift*, 14 (1905); Demetrios I. Polemis, *The Doukai* (1968), 106–109.

MICHAEL ANGOLD

[See also **Frederick II of the Holy Roman Empire; Nicaea, Empire of; Theodore I Laskaris; Theodore II Laskaris.**]

JOHN V PALAIOLOGOS (1331/1332–1391), Byzantine emperor, reigned from 1341 to 1376 (when he was deposed by his son Adronikos IV) and from 1379 to 1391. Crowned on 19 November 1341, John V reigned initially under the regency of his mother, Anne of Savoy. The powerful John Kantakouzenos had had himself proclaimed emperor the month before, a situation that led to six years of civil strife. From February 1347 to November 1354 John V ruled jointly with John VI Kantakouzenos, then in his own right except for the deposition by his son (1376–1379) and a brief usurpation of the throne by his grandson John VII in 1390. During his reign the empire disintegrated under the pressure of the Serbs and the Turks, forces that John tried to combat by appeals to Rome and by his personal conversion to Catholicism in 1369.

BIBLIOGRAPHY

John W. Barker, *Manuel II Palaeologus (1391–1425)* (1969); Oskar Halecki, *Un empereur de Byzance à Rome* (1930); Jean Meyendorff, "Projets de concile oecuménique en 1367," in *Dumbarton Oaks Papers*, 14 (1960).

ANGELIKI LAIOU

[See also **Byzantine Church; Byzantine History; John VI Kantakouzenos; Schisms, Eastern-Western Church.**]

JOHN VI KANTAKOUZENOS (*ca.* 1295–15 June 1383), Byzantine emperor from 1347 to 1354. A member of one of the richest and most powerful aristocratic families, he held the offices of *megas papias* (keeper of the palace, an honorary office) and grand domestic under Andronikos III. He participated in all of Andronikos' major campaigns in Asia Minor, Bulgaria, and Epiros. After Andronikos' death, he disputed the regency named for young John V and proclaimed himself emperor (26 October

1341), while preserving the appearances of legitimacy by mentioning the names of John V and his mother, Anne of Savoy, before his own.

His coronation provoked a civil war in which the political issue was a struggle for the throne between members of the ruling class; the war, however, was also a social conflict, since Kantakouzenos' allies were mostly members of the landed aristocracy and his opponents of the merchant element, the sailors, and the poor of various cities. The civil war was especially violent in Thessaloniki but nonexistent in aristocratic strongholds such as Thessaly. Kantakouzenos was forced to rely on the aid of the Serbs (under Stefan Dušan) and the Turks, especially Umur of Aydin (Umur I Aydïnoghlu), with whom he had a lasting friendship. In 1345–1346 he called in the Ottomans. By the end of the civil war, almost all of Macedonia, Epiros, and Thessaly was in the hands of the Serbs, and the Turks were established in Thrace. Despite his alliance with the Turks, John made efforts to achieve church union with the West.

In December 1354 John VI abdicated and became a monk, taking the name Joasaph, but remained active in state affairs until his death. He was also involved in the hesychast controversy, which he helped to resolve in favor of the hesychasts (1351). He was an able soldier and a good diplomat, but his activities were destructive for the Byzantine state. A highly literate man, he left his memoirs (one of the principal sources for the period) and a number of theological works.

BIBLIOGRAPHY

Franz Dölger, "Johannes VI. Kantakuzenos als dynastischer Legitimist," in *Annales de l'Institut Kondakov*, 10 (1938); Paul Lemerle, *L'émirat d'Aydin, Byzance, et l'Occident* (1957); Donald M. Nicol, *The Byzantine Family of Kantakouzenos* (1968); Valentin Parisot, *Cantacuzène, homme d'état et historien* (1845); Günter Weiss, *Joannes Kantakouzenos—Aristokrat, Staatsmann, Kaiser und Mönch—in der Gesellschaftsentwicklung von Byzanz im 14. Jahrhundert* (1969); E. Werner, "Johannes Kantakuzenos, Umur Paša und Orhan," in *Byzantinoslavica*, 26 (1965).

ANGELIKI LAIOU

[See also **Byzantine History; Hesychasm; John V Palaiologos; Kantakouzenoi.**]

JOHN VIII PALAIOLOGOS (December 1392–October 1448), Byzantine emperor (from 1425) who sought to oppose the Ottoman advance by seeking help in Western Europe. Internally, he fought against Westerners, primarily in the Peloponnese, where the major possessions of the Byzantine Empire were then concentrated (1416–1418). He also assumed a warlike stance against the Ottomans when, in 1421, he backed a pretender against Murad II, thereby bringing Constantinople under Ottoman attack in 1422. In 1423–1424 John made an unsuccessful trip to Italy and Hungary in quest of Western aid. A decade and a half later, in 1437–1438, he led a deputation to the Council of Ferrara-Florence, which proclaimed the union of the Greek and Latin churches; but the union was never truly implemented, nor did Western help for the Byzantine state result from it.

BIBLIOGRAPHY

John W. Barker, *Manuel II Palaeologus (1391–1425)* (1969); Joseph Gill, *Byzantium and the Papacy, 1198–1400* (1979); Kenneth M. Setton, *The Papacy and the Levant, 1204–1571*, I (1976).

Angeliki Laiou

[See also **Byzantine History; Ferrara-Florence, Council of; Schisms, Eastern-Western Church.**]

JOHN, KING OF ENGLAND (1167–1216). Born on 24 December 1167, John, known as Lackland, was the fifth and youngest son of Henry II and Eleanor of Aquitaine. When his heirless brother Richard I the Lionhearted died in France from an infected wound on 6 April 1199, John succeeded to his French possessions and to the English throne. He was invested as duke of Normandy on 25 April in Rouen, and crowned king of England on 27 May. If the custom of primogeniture had been followed, the throne would have gone to John's nephew, twelve-year-old Arthur of Brittany, the posthumous son of John's elder brother Geoffrey, count of Brittany, who had died in 1186. But Arthur was considered too young and a foreigner (because he had always lived in Brittany), while John had the support of his mother and the majority of the English and Norman barons. By the Treaty of Le Goulet, concluded with Philip II Augustus of France on 22 May 1200, John obtained recognition of all his French fiefs in return for surrendering the city and county of Évreux and paying a relief of 20,000 marks.

Although John's first year augured well and although he was intelligent and able, he was a pampered youngest son, had a coarse humor, and was dishonest, suspicious, opportunistic, disloyal, lazy, and highly unstable. These defects of character caused a series of reverses throughout his reign that gave him the reputation of medieval England's worst king, reduced the royal power to its lowest point since the time of King Stephen (1135–1154), and altered the course of English history.

After the annulment of his barren marriage to Isabella of Gloucester, on 24 August 1200, John married Isabella, heiress to Angoulême (*d*. 1246), a move that increased his influence in southwestern France and infuriated Hugh le Brun, count of Lusignan, to whom Isabella had been betrothed. Failing to secure justice or compensation from John, Hugh appealed to Philip II, who summoned John to appear before his feudal court at Paris in 1202 to answer Hugh's charges that his behavior as feudal lord was improper. When John ignored the summons, Philip II declared him a feudal felon and pronounced forfeiture of all his French fiefs. War followed.

That summer, when Arthur of Brittany was besieging Eleanor of Aquitaine in the castle of Mirabeau, John, in a rare burst of energy, surprised the besieging force and captured Arthur and many of the leading Poitevin barons. His cruel treatment of the captives alienated any potential supporters he might have had in France; and when Arthur disappeared in the spring of 1203, it was widely believed that John had dispatched him with his own hands. In 1203 he lost Maine and Anjou. In March of 1204 the Château Gaillard fell to the French, and by May 1204 Normandy passed to Philip II, followed in the summer by Poitou and in 1206 by Brittany. All that remained to John was Aquitaine. In four years, mostly because of his military incapacity and incredible lethargy, he had lost the Angevin lands in France. Henceforth, England was to follow a quite different course that largely explains the uniqueness of English institutions.

Along with his French military fiascoes John was involved in an ecclesiastical dispute that was to divide and embitter his realm for eight years. When Hubert Walter, archbishop of Canterbury, died on 13 July 1205, there was dissension over the succession. Determined to choose their own man, the monks of Christ Church, Canterbury, secretly elected their subprior, Reginald. Learning of this act, John was furious and forced the election of his candidate, John de Grey, bishop of Norwich. Confronted with two archbishops-elect, Pope Innocent III proposed as candidate the eminently qualified Englishman Stephen Langton (d. 1228) and, over the objections of John's emissaries, consecrated Stephen archbishop in 1207. This highly impolitic action, unprecedented in England, triggered a break with John, who was widely supported by the barons. When John refused to accept Stephen, Innocent III placed England under interdict in March 1208. John retaliated in 1208 by confiscating all the possessions of clergy who observed the interdict, an act that drove most of them into exile and gave John their rich landed possessions. In 1209 John was excommunicated but received general support from the barons because the income from church lands obviated much lay taxation. Innocent III did not get the upper hand until 1213, when he gave his blessing to the projected invasion of England by Philip II. Faced with this challenge and the threat of deposition, John had to negotiate a settlement. In promising to accept Stephen Langton, to reinstate the exiled clergy, to compensate the church for its losses, to take England and Ireland in fief from Innocent III, and to pay an annual tribute to the Holy See, he suffered another humiliating defeat but gained Innocent III's support and deliverance from a French invasion.

This defeat was not his last. Since 1200 John's only success had been the Irish expedition of 1210 that enabled him to impose his control over the whole island and to introduce the English administrative system. Buoyed by this success and hoping to recover the lost French possessions, he patiently constructed a military and political alliance composed of Low Country and German princes, the German emperor (and John's nephew) Otto IV (1198–1215; d. 1218), and some French barons. By 1214 military preparations were complete. John advanced from La Rochelle in southwest France while the allied force struck through the county of Flanders. Soon John had to retreat, and in July 1214 the French overwhelmed the allied force at Bouvines, a victory that gave France political hegemony in western Europe for the next century.

In the autumn of 1214 John returned to a hostile kingdom. His frequent reverses had finally unleashed the pent-up hostility directed toward this king, whose unsavory character and insatiable greed bred hatred and fear. His manipulation of royal justice to destroy those he disliked led many barons to feel that only force could preserve them and their possessions.

Rebuffed time and again by John, a formidable group of barons revolted in the spring of 1215. Amid preparations for war by both sides, Stephen Langton and the respected baron William Marshal (d. 1219) worked to negotiate a settlement. An acceptable agreement was finally hammered out. On 15 June the barons and John met at Runnymede meadow, beside the Thames River near Windsor, where John put his seal to a rough draft of provisions. The final document, Magna Carta, was issued under the great seal on 19 June 1215.

Although Magna Carta was a victory for the barons and for constitutional principles of government, the most important being the enunciation that the king is, and shall be, below the law, John had no intention of keeping the agreement. Civil war soon erupted. John held his own against the barons, who had secured the aid of Louis, son of Philip II and later Louis VIII, until the autumn of 1216. Then, suffering from dysentery, the effects of tremendous exertion, and much drinking, he died on 18/19 October. The throne passed to his nine-year-old son, Henry III, with the papal legate Gualo and William Marshal as guardians. With John's death baronial resistance waned, and by the spring of 1217 the civil war ended. Unfortunately, the intelligence and extraordinary administrative ability that John had inherited from his father could never transcend the serious defects of his character.

BIBLIOGRAPHY

Partially outdated but still valuable because of interesting information garnered from the pertinent chroniclers is Kate Norgate, *John Lackland* (1902). A more modern and reliable study is Sidney Painter, *The Reign of King John* (1949). For John's loss of the French possessions see Frederick M. Powicke, *The Loss of Normandy, 1189–1204*, 2nd ed. (1961). John's policies and behavior as a ruler are delineated in John E. A. Jolliffe, *Angevin Kingship*, 2nd ed. (1963). For John's struggle with the church, see Christopher R. Cheney, *Pope Innocent III and England* (1976); Frederick M. Powicke, *Stephen Langton* (1928, repr. 1965). On the baronial revolt and Magna Carta, see James C. Holt, *The Northerners: A Study in the Reign of King John* (1961), and *Magna Carta* (1965); William S. McKechnie, *Magna Carta*, 2nd ed. (1914). The most concise account of John's reign is in Austin Lane Poole, *From Domesday Book to Magna Carta, 1087–1216*, 2nd ed. (1955).

BRYCE LYON

[See also **Angevins; England; Innocent III, Pope; Langton, Stephen; Magna Carta; Philip II Augustus; Walter, Hubert.**]

JOHN ASEN I. See **Peter and Asen.**

JOHN ASEN II (*ca.* 1196–1241), tsar of Bulgaria. John Asen II, son of Asen I, was heir to the Bulgarian throne when his uncle Kalojan died in 1207. Only about eleven years old, he fell victim to intrigues and had to be smuggled out of Bulgaria. He settled in Russian Galich. After the usurper Boril had acquired many enemies, John Asen's supporters summoned him back. They marched on Trnovo, the gates of which were opened to him. Thus in 1218 Asen became tsar of Bulgaria.

He inherited a weak state. Epiros, controlling Macedonia, was then the power in the Balkans. Asen took nearly a decade to subdue the boyars and rebuild his army. He recovered Beograd, Braničevo, and Vidin from Hungary. In the late 1220's Theodore of Epiros was planning to attack the Latins in Constantinople, where Baldwin II, a child, ruled. Needing a defender, the Latins offered John Asen an alliance by which his daughter would marry Baldwin and he would become regent in Constantinople. Theodore, with whom Asen had a treaty, suddenly attacked Bulgaria. Possibly he had learned of Asen's Latin negotiations. The Bulgarians were victorious at Klokotnica (1230). Theodore was captured, blinded, and imprisoned in Bulgaria. John Asen, who already held much of Thrace, then conquered all Macedonia and much of Albania.

His success ended the Latins' need for him, and they broke off negotiations. Angry, Asen allied with Nicaea against Constantinople. His daughter Helena married the Nicene heir. At the wedding (in 1235) the Bulgarians recognized the patriarch in Nicaea as ecumenical patriarch, in exchange for which the patriarch recognized the Bulgarian prelate in Trnovo as an autocephalos patriarch. The Nicenes and Bulgarians then besieged Constantinople. Soon seeing that a victory would give the Nicenes the city and replace the weak Latins with a strong Greek empire, Asen broke with Nicaea. The plague then struck Bulgaria, killing Asen's new patriarch, his son and heir, and his wife. Interpreting this as a sign of God's anger for breaking his alliance, he made peace with Nicaea in 1237. However, Constantinople did not yet fall. After John Asen's death his minor son, Koloman, succeeded and Bulgaria rapidly declined.

JOHN V. A. FINE, JR.

[See also **Autocephalos; Bulgaria; Byzantine Empire; Epiros, Despotate of; Kalojan; Latin Empire of Constantinople; Nicaea, Empire of.**]

JOHN DUNS SCOTUS. See **Duns Scotus, John.**

JOHN GERSON. See **Gerson, John.**

JOHN HUNYADI. See **Hunyadi, János.**

JOHN ITALOS (*ca.* 1025–after 1082), Byzantine philosopher. Born in southern Italy, John Italos studied under Michael Psellos at the University of Constantinople and in 1055 succeeded him as "chief of the philosophers." He commented on Plato, Aristotle's logic, Proclus, and Iamblichus, and attracted an enthusiastic following. He also acquired enemies in conservative ecclesiastical circles. In 1076–1077 nine propositions supposedly drawn from his teachings were condemned by a synod in Constantinople, though John himself, shielded by his patron, Emperor Michael VII Doukas, was not mentioned by name. In 1082, however, in the reign of Alexios I Komnenos, the case was reopened. John was banished to a monastery, and anathemas against him and his teachings were incorporated into the *Synodikon of Orthodoxy*, read annually on the first Sunday of Lent.

Modern scholars have questioned the nature and scope of John Italos' heresy. Not all the doctrines condemned in 1076–1077 are in his works, and many (preexistence and transmigration of souls, eternity of matter, self-subsistent world of ideas, apocatastasis) seem to be simply tenets of the Platonic tradition classified as heretical at the time of the condemnation of Origen in the sixth century rather than John's own thought. His opponents appear to have been alarmed above all by his apparent commitment to a metaphysics independent of Christian revelation, as seen, for example, in his Neoplatonic theory of "illumination," which assumes the connaturality of the purified intellect with the divine. They also opposed his application of philosophy to Christology, the Resurrection, and other dogmatic subjects, particularly since his dialectical virtuosity, expressed in an exaggerated pro-and-contra method of argumentation, could easily be construed as a cloak for skepticism.

John Italos' condemnation effectively curtailed development of an autonomous philosophy in Byzantium. Henceforth "Hellenic studies" could be pursued "for instruction," but adherence to the ancients' "foolish opinions" was to be rejected.

BIBLIOGRAPHY

Sources. Gregorius Cereteli, ed., *Joannes Itali opuscula selecta,* 2 fasc. (1924–1926); Perikles Joannou, ed., *Ioannes Italos, Quaestiones quodlibetales* (1956).

Studies. Jean Gouillard, "Le synodikon de l'Orthodoxie: Édition et commentaire," in Centre de Recherches d'Histoire et Civilisation Byzantines, *Travaux et mémoires,* 2 (1967); Perikles Joannou, *Christliche Metaphysik im Byzanz,* I, *Die Illuminationslehre des Michael Psellos und Joannes Italos* (1956); Pelopidas E. Stephanou, *Jean Italos, philosophe et humaniste* (1949).

JOHN H. ERICKSON

[See also **Heresies, Byzantine; Neoplatonism; Philosophy and Theology, Byzantine; Plato in the Middle Ages.**]

JOHN KINNAMOS (Cinnamus) (*ca.* 1143–after 1185), Byzantine historian. As an imperial secretary he frequented the court and accompanied Manuel I Komnenos on campaigns in the Balkans and Asia Minor. His history, composed in 1180–1182, was designed to cover the reigns of John II (1118–1143) and Manuel I (1143–1180), but the existing version breaks off in 1176. Kinnamos concentrated on the military history of the reigns, but also included accounts of theological controversies. Unlike his contemporary, Niketas Choniates, he eulogizes the emperors to excess. His style is clear, and much of his information is reliable.

BIBLIOGRAPHY

Epitome rerum ab Ioanne et Alexio [sic] Comnenis gestarum, Augustus Meineke, ed. (1836); *Deeds of John and Manuel Comnenus,* Charles M. Brand, trans. (1976).

CHARLES M. BRAND

[See also **Byzantine Literature; Historiography, Byzantine.**]

JOHN LYDUS. See Lydus.

JOHN OF AFFLIGHEM (*fl. ca.* 1100), also known as John Cotton, music theorist and author of a com-

prehensive treatise on music, *De musica cum tonario.* The author's discussion of organum as practiced in the early twelfth century (free organum) constitutes one of the two main theoretical sources on the subject from this period.

BIBLIOGRAPHY

Joseph L. James, "The *De musica cum tonario* by John of Affligem" (M.A. thesis, Ohio State University, 1955), is an English translation. See also Claude V. Palisca, ed., *Hucbald, Guido, and John on Music: Three Medieval Treatises* (1978), 87–190, for English translation by Warren Babb.

JAY HUFF

[See also **Musical Treatises; Organum.**]

JOHN OF BRIENNE. See Jean de Brienne.

JOHN OF EPHESUS (*ca.* 507–after 588), Monophysite bishop and church historian. In 542 John was sent by Justinian to convert pagans in Asia and was said to have inspired some 70,000 conversions. He was consecrated titular bishop of Ephesus about 558 but subsequently spent much of his time in Constantinople, where he knew the court intimately but nevertheless suffered intermittent persecution for his Monophysite beliefs.

John's *Church History,* written in Syriac, covers the years from Julius Caesar to 588, but only the third part (571–588) survives intact. Based on personal experience and containing a wealth of detail, it is an important source for the reigns of Justin II, Tiberius, and Maurice. However, its tone is strongly apologetic for the Monophysite cause (in contrast with Evagrius Scholasticus, the other main source for the period). Much of it was written while John was imprisoned in circumstances that required individual sheets to be smuggled out by friends. The arrangement of the surviving work shows many signs of this disjointed composition, being discursive and repetitive, and lacking the order and discipline of Evagrius' *Church History.* Like Evagrius, however, John admitted much secular material into his work, including military narratives. Despite its Syriac language, the work belongs to Constantinopolitan literature of the late sixth century; it shows the same fusion of secular and religious material that was emerging in other works of that era. Probably the most striking feature of the *Church History,* besides the attractive personal detail, is the black-and-white depiction of Orthodox and Monophysite personalities: thus Anastasius, quaestor under Justin II, and John Scholasticus, the patriarch, are shown as total villains for their instigation of persecution, while Justin II is depicted as a pathetic figure and Tiberius II as a romantic hero. John's *History* is an unusually personal document, written with the burning fervor of a member of a persecuted minority.

In addition, John wrote *Lives of the Eastern Saints,* also in Syriac, a collection of short lives of Monophysite holy men and women that is a rich source for material on everyday life in the Eastern provinces, the details of Monophysite-Orthodox relations, and asceticism in general.

BIBLIOGRAPHY

Sources. Part III of the *Ecclesiastical History,* Ernest W. Brooks, ed., is in *Corpus scriptorum Christianorum orientalium,* 3rd ser., III (1935). Extracts and French trans. of part II by F. Nau are in *Revue de l'Orient chrétien,* **2** (1897, repr. 1966), 41–68, 455–493. *The Lives of the Eastern Saints,* Ernest W. Brooks, ed. and trans. (into Latin), is in *Patrologia orientalis,* XVII (1923), iii–306, XVIII (1924), 511–698, XIX (1926), 151–285.

Studies. Pauline Allen, "A New Date for the Last Recorded Events in John of Ephesus' *Historia ecclesiastica,*" in *Orientalia Lovaniensia periodica,* **10** (1979); Susan Ashbrook [Harvey], "Asceticism in Adversity: An Early Byzantine Experience," in *Byzantine and Modern Greek Studies,* **6** (1980), and "The Politicisation of the Byzantine Saint," in Sergei Hackel, ed., *The Byzantine Saint* (1981); E. Honigmann, "L'Histoire ecclésiastique de Jean d'Éphèse," in *Byzantion,* **14** (1939), and *Évéques et évéchés monophysites d'Asie antérieure au VIe siècle* (1951).

AVERIL CAMERON

[See also **Historiography, Byzantine; Monophysitism.**]

JOHN OF GARLAND (Johannes de Garlandia) (*ca.* 1195–*ca.* 1272) was born in England. He studied at Oxford after the turn of the century, notably under John of London, went to Paris about 1217 or 1218 to continue his studies, and taught there for most of the rest of his life. He resided there in the Clos de Garlande, whence his name. It has been argued that he was a pupil of Alan of Lille, but this is unlikely. From 1229 to 1231 or 1232, John taught grammar at Toulouse, where he supported the suppression of heresy through his instruction and polemical writings. It is possible that he went to England, where he may have served as tutor to English princes, probably in the decade after his departure from Toulouse, but he was back in Paris by 1241.

John of Garland wrote treatises on grammar, rhetoric, logic, and poetics, including student wordbooks and dictionaries, as well as literary, moral, or religious works, including interpretative glosses and a mythography. In addition, he wrote on medicine, arithmetic, and music. However, the attribution to him of a number of these treatises is still uncertain.

The *Morale scolarium* (1241) is a fervent admonition to students to cling to the virtues and manners ideally associated with the life of the scholar: learning, urbanity, religion, and exemplary conduct. It is in elegiac stanzas.

The *Stella maris* (1249 or before), composed in rhythmic stanzas, is a lengthy recitation of the Virgin Mary's virtues and miracles, the whole intended to foster the moral awareness and zeal of the reader, especially of the Parisian students for whom John wrote. It thus contributed to the expanding cult of the Virgin in thirteenth-century France and England.

The more epic and polemical *De triumphis ecclesiae* (*ca.* 1252), in eight books of elegiac stanzas, is a diatribe against pagans and southern French heretics; it exhorts Christians, notably the church and the crown, to strive for the total extirpation of disbelief and error.

These works are often deliberately recondite and ornate. To understand them, even the medieval reader had to resort to glosses, or possess broad, detailed knowledge and an intelligence constantly alert to the often strained or radically abbreviated references and allusions, examples, and disquisitions that make up their intricate but coherent patchwork composition. The same is true for John's other literary productions: *De mysteriis ecclesiae* (1245), *Epithalamium beatae Mariae Virginis* (1220–1223, perhaps revised 1229–1232), *Integumenta Ovidii* (before 1241), and some minor works.

John practiced the technique of the gloss in the mythographic *Integumenta* to Ovid's *Metamorphoses.* Composed in elegiac stanzas, it is only 520 lines long. It is in fact an *abbreviatio,* like many accounts of the Virgin's miracles in the *Stella maris,* intended to guide students' reading of Ovid by providing some historical, scientific, and moral readings for the fables. The reader would need to have Ovid's poem at hand, for some glosses are terse to the point of being virtual one-word allegories that drastically reduce the original fables. Nevertheless, John's glosses survived into the Renaissance, either in whole or in part, in subsequent mythographies.

The *Parisiana poetria* (*ca.* 1220, revised *ca.* 1231–1235), perhaps John's best-known treatise today, derives from the tradition of the "arts of poetry," principally those by Matthew of Vendôme and Geoffrey of Vinsauf. His treatment preserves their emphasis on the place of verse and prose composition in the arts curriculum. And like them he draws extensively for his instruction on such authors as Bernard Silvester, Alan of Lille, and John of Hanville, as well as on his own works and inventions. The *Poetria* embraces metric and rhythmic versification, letter writing, prose composition (including the cursus), and some aspects of oration. Although John emphasizes basic ornamentation and versification, he also takes up the elements of invention (especially topical invention), arrangement, and selection in composition.

John adapted the commonplace comparison of the three orders of society illustrated for the Middle Ages by Vergil's three masterpieces: the aristocracy (*Aeneid*), the peasantry (*Georgics*), and the shepherds (*Bucolica*). He extended it to the representation of persons, places, and actions (*stylus materialis*), no doubt under the influence of rhetorical instruction on memory, glosses to Horace's *Art of Poetry*, and the emphasis in "arts of letter writing" on language appropriate to the writer's order, class, and station in society. He relates topical invention to the art of memory taught by Cicero, just as he borrowed the division into *personae* and *negotia* in topical description from Matthew of Vendôme, Geoffrey of Vinsauf, and, ultimately, Cicero in *De inventione*.

In the *Poetria* John's instruction on etymology served the purposes of his more specialized writings in lexicography and grammar, especially his topical dictionaries (he may have been the first to use the term "dictionary" for wordbooks in his *Dictionarius* [*ca.* 1220]), and various works on grammar that opposed the innovations of Alexandre de Villedieu and Evrard de Béthune.

All of John of Garland's writings evince broad, often ostentatious learning. His frequent historical, biblical, scientific, and literary references and comparisons are often couched in the obscure language admired by many of his contemporaries. Nevertheless, he was a prominent teacher. And by insistence on the quality of Latin style, he anticipated the late

medieval and early Renaissance humanists. He fought a vigorous, though largely unsuccessful, rearguard defense of the traditional arts of grammar and rhetoric against the encroachment into the curriculum of logic, Aristotelian studies, and new grammars.

Despite his prominence in the thirteenth century, modern scholarship has tended to neglect John of Garland, partly because he defended a sterile—or at least moribund—tradition in grammar and rhetoric after its eleventh- and twelfth-century brilliance, and partly because he assumed no important place among the new currents that emerged in thirteenth-century philosophy and the arts.

BIBLIOGRAPHY

John of Garland, *The Parisiana poetria*, Traugott Lawler, ed. and trans. (1974), contains the original text and an English translation, and an extensive bibliography. For early studies, see the excellent critical review in Louis John Paetow, *Morale scolarium of John of Garland* (1927), which also includes the annotated Latin text and an English prose paraphrase.

DOUGLAS KELLY

[See also **Geoffrey of Vinsauf; Grammar; Latin Literature; Matthew of Vendôme; Ovid in the Middle Ages; Rhetoric, Western European; Vergil in the Middle Ages.**]

JOHN OF GARLAND (**Johannes de Garlandia** or **Johannes Gallicus**) (*fl. ca.* 1240). The music theorist known by this name is the author of two treatises: *De plana musica* on plainchant, and *De mensurabili musica* on mensural (measured) music. The first is important primarily for its determination of the intervals usable in music; the second, for such topics as the rhythmic modes, consonance-dissonance classification of intervals, and types of organum (part music).

BIBLIOGRAPHY

Concerning Measured Music: De mensurabili musica, Stanley H. Birnbaum, trans. (1978). See also Rebecca A. Baltzer, "Johannes de Garlandia," in *New Grove Dictionary of Music and Musicians*, IX (1980), with bibliography.

JAY HUFF

[See also **Ars Antiqua; Musical Treatises.**]

JOHN OF GAUNT (March 1340–3 February 1399) was the fourth son of Edward III. He was born at

Ghent, and it is from his birthplace that Shakespeare popularized the designation "of Gaunt" in *Richard II*. John married Blanche, the heiress of Henry of Lancaster, and was created duke of Lancaster in 1362. His retinue made him England's leading magnate.

In the 1370's John played a major role in the affairs of England. Edward III was growing senile, and the prince of Wales (Edward the Black Prince, John's eldest brother) was in failing health. In 1373 John led a great expedition from Calais to Bordeaux, but he was unable to duplicate the spectacular military triumphs of his father and eldest brother. Although John was in part a victim of the new French policy of refusing battle, historians have blamed him for his failure. At home, he assumed increased direction of affairs. Challenged by a powerful group of clerics, he supported John Wyclif's protests against clerical dominion. Wyclif preached his doctrines before parliament, and John protected Wyclif from papal prosecution. In the Good Parliament of 1376, there was a reaction against John's supporters that led to the development of the impeachment process. He was, however, back in control by the time of his father's death in 1377.

John, suspected of sinister ambitions in the early years of Richard II's reign, was widely unpopular. His London residence, the Savoy, was a chief target during the Peasants' Revolt of 1381; only his absence on a diplomatic mission in Scotland saved his life. After 1381 John attempted to play the role of elder statesman between the king and a volatile faction of the baronage. His own ambitions had shifted to the Iberian peninsula.

In 1371 John had married Constance, heiress of Pedro I of Castile and León. Since Pedro had been murdered by his half brother Henry II, John claimed to be the legitimate king, a claim that was bound up with the complex diplomacy of the Hundred Years War and the Great Schism. He was able to mount an expedition against Castile (1386–1388), but it was a failure. He renounced his claim and married his daughter Catherine to King John I's son, the future Henry III.

John of Gaunt returned to England in 1389, to a tense political situation. Henry Bolingbroke, his son and heir, had joined in a successful attack upon Richard II's favorites. The role of elder statesman was now more precarious. In 1396 John married his mistress of some twenty years, Katherine Swynford, already the mother of four of his children, who were known as Beauforts. It was through the Beauforts

that Henry Tudor gained his claim to the throne. The marriage also made John the brother-in-law of Geoffrey Chaucer, whom he had long patronized. Richard II banished Henry Bolingbroke in September 1398, but he returned from exile late the following June or early July, four months after his father's death, to reclaim the Lancastrian inheritance and to seize the crown from his cousin.

BIBLIOGRAPHY

Ralph T. Bodey, *"Time-honour'd Lancaster"* (1926); Henry G. Richardson, *John of Gaunt and the Parliamentary Representation of Lancashire* (1938); Peter E. Russell, *The English Intervention in Spain and Portugal in the Time of Edward III and Richard II* (1955); Sydney Armitage Smith, *John of Gaunt* (1904); Robert Somerville, *History of the Duchy of Lancaster,* I (1953).

JAMES L. GILLESPIE

[See also **Castile; Chaucer, Geoffrey; Edward III of England; Edward the Black Prince; England; Henry IV of England; Hundred Years War; Impeachment and Attainder; Richard II; Wyclif, John.**]

JOHN OF HOWDEN (Hoveden) (*d. ca.* 1275), English writer and ecclesiastic, sometime clerk in the service of Queen Eleanor (wife of Henry III) and of Edward I. Most of his poetry is in Latin, but he wrote one French work, *Rossignol* (Nightingale), which is similar to his best-known Latin work, *Philomena,* an extended lyrical meditation on the life of Christ and the power of love in more than 1,000 stanzas.

BIBLIOGRAPHY

Frederick J. E. Raby, ed., *Poems of John of Hoveden* (1939); L. W. Stone, "Jean de Howden, poète anglo-normand du XIII⁰ siècle," in *Romania,* 69 (1946–1947).

BRIAN MERRILEES

[See also **Latin Literature.**]

JOHN OF MURS. See **Jehan des Murs.**

JOHN OF NIKIU (*fl. ca.* 700). John (Joannes), bishop of Nikiu in Egypt, was the author of a world chronicle, probably written in Coptic, that contains especially important material for the early reign of Emperor Heraklios, at the beginning of the seventh century. The manuscript is known in a Syriac version and an Ethiopic one. John was a Copt, which is to say a Monophysite, and was consequently opposed to both Justinian and Heraklios, whom he saw as persecutors of Monophysites. His account of the Arab conquests sees those events as a divine punishment of Heraklios for his heresy. Although it is clear that John was well informed about Egyptian affairs, his chronicle does not particularly focus on them but takes an imperial point of view.

BIBLIOGRAPHY

Robert H. Charles, trans., *The Chronicle of John, Bishop of Nikiu* (1916).

LINDA C. ROSE

[See also **Historiography, Byzantine; Monophysitism.**]

JOHN OF PARIS (*d.* 22 September 1306). Jean Quidort, also known as Jean Le Sourd (Surdus) and Praedicator Monoculus (if we follow Kaeppeli), was a Dominican priest and author who made important contributions in philosophy, theology, and especially in political theory. Recent scholarship attributes about twenty-five works to him; all are listed, with information on manuscripts and editions, in the 1975 bibliography by Thomas Kaeppeli.

John was born in Paris, but the date of his birth is uncertain. On the strength of his remark that he had heard the teaching of Peter of Tarentaise (later Pope Innocent V, who was in Paris 1259–1269), and of the supposed dates of his lectures on Peter Lombard's *Sentences* between 1284 and 1286, his birth is sometimes placed in the 1250's or even as early as 1240. Since we know that he received his master's degree in theology in 1304, this would mean that John was over fifty when he was granted his degree. While this is not impossible, it runs contrary to all we know of university practice, and has given rise to the opinion that his university career was extraordinary and that he was somehow an object of suspicion. John's remark may simply mean, however, that he had heard *about* the teaching of Peter of Tarentaise. If we accept Jean-Pierre Muller's closely reasoned arguments dating the lectures on the *Sentences* to 1292–1296, all the known dates for John's life fit into the normal pattern for a medieval uni-

versity professor and do not suggest that he had any special difficulties.

In his philosophical writings John appears as an ardent defender of the basic tenets of Thomas Aquinas, possessing a good grasp of his views on the nature of essence and existence, the unicity of substantial form, and the role of matter as the principle of individuation in corporeal things. His *Correctorium corruptorii "Circa"* (*ca.* 1282–1284) is an elaborate defense of the *Prima Secundae* of Thomas' *Summa theologiae* against the attacks of the Franciscan William de la Mare. After John—by then a member of his order—lectured as a bachelor on the *Sentences,* sixteen propositions based on his lectures were drawn up and these were denounced as erroneous to his superiors. John defended himself in an *Apology* (*Istos articulos non dixi, ut mihi imponuntur*) and conducted a disputation, about this time, on the nature of essence and existence, a work which is sometimes called the seventeenth question of his *Apology.* There is no evidence that he was condemned at this point and it is impossible to be sure if the attack upon him affected his subsequent university career. As a bachelor of theology John was obligated to preach sermons at the university. The several that have survived from 1293–1294 and 1301–1302 reflect the political and social unrest of the period and his own concern for justice.

In 1302 or early 1303, during the dispute between Pope Boniface VIII and King Philip the Fair, John wrote his best-known work, *De potestate regia et papali.* In it he tries to chart a middle course between those who say that the pope has power in the temporal as well as the spiritual realm since he stands in the place of Christ, and those who say that the pope and other prelates have no dominion over temporal matters. John argues that kingship, which is the rule of one person over a community for the common good, stems from the natural law and provides the basis for a civil authority independent of ecclesiastical control. The human race, however, is also directed to a supernatural goal, and proper guidance demands a ruler who is both divine and human, namely Christ. Christ has ceded his powers to the ministers of his church, who thus have power to direct mankind to this spiritual goal. This is the basis for a spiritual power that is independent of civil control. State and church can check each other if either fails in its purpose. Although John departs from medieval political theory and severely limits papal power in the secular realm, he nevertheless does not entirely support the views of Philip the Fair. In June 1303, along with his confreres at St. Jacques, John signed an appeal to a general council, requesting the examination of the legitimacy of Boniface VIII's papal election. There is no evidence, however, that he intended to act in Philip's behalf any more vigorously than his fellow Dominicans, much less support the extreme antipapist views of Pierre Flotte or Guillaume de Nogaret.

In 1304, as master, John conducted a disputation on the sensitive issue of the papal right to commission mendicant friars to hear the confessions of layfolk who were not their parishioners. John sharply defended the position of the pope as universal pastor, and rejected all arguments that parish priests, or even local bishops, had any rights to restrict the power of the pope in spiritual affairs. A year later John found himself in controversy again when he proposed an alternative to the theory of transubstantiation to explain the real presence of Christ in the Eucharist. John's theory was basically an "impanation" theory, an explanation already discussed in the eleventh century and later taken up again by Luther. Despite his plea (no doubt stemming from a pastoral concern) that it was better to have two explanations to defend the doctrine of the Real Presence than one, and his stated willingness to retract his somewhat controversial opinion, he was suspended from teaching and preaching and perpetually silenced by an episcopal board. John appealed his case to the papal curia, then at Bordeaux, but he died there awaiting an answer.

John wrote on controversial topics, but never in a polemical spirit. One can read his *De potestate regia et papali* without being made aware of the political battle that was then raging between the pope and the French king. His views on sensitive topics, such as the relations of church and state, the limits of the power of the pope and bishops, and the understanding of the Eucharist, are still of current interest. According to him, if the "regulations of the church seem to be disrupted by the needs of the people, it is the regulations that must give way," and he also believed that "prelates were not established to preside over the faithful, but to serve them." Along with his confrere Harvey Nedellec, John appears to have been the leading Dominican theologian in Paris at the end of the thirteenth century.

BIBLIOGRAPHY

Thomas Kaeppeli, *Scriptores ordinis praedicatorum medii aevi*, II (1975), 517–524, contains a complete listing of the manuscripts of John's works and their various editions and translations to 1975. An English translation of John's *De potestate regia et papali* is *On Royal and Papal Power*, Arthur P. Monahan, trans. (1974). For John's lectures on Peter Lombard's *Sentences* see Jean-Pierre Muller, *Jean de Paris (Quidort) O.P.: Commentaire sur les Sentences*, 2 vols. (1961–1964). See also Edward A. Goerner, *Peter and Caesar* (1965), 94–126; Jean Leclercq, *Jean de Paris et l'ecclésiologie du XIIᵉ siècle* (1942); John Hillary Martin, "The Eucharistic Treatise of John Quidort of Paris," in *Viator*, 6 (1975); Jean-Pierre Muller, "La date de la lecture sur les Sentences de Jean Quidort," in *Angelicum*, 36 (1959).

JOHN HILLARY MARTIN, O.P.

[See also **Aquinas, St. Thomas; Boniface VIII, Pope; Dominicans; Mass; Nogaret, Guillaume de; Peter Lombard; Philip IV the Fair; Philosophy and Theology, Western European; Political Theory, Western European.**]

JOHN OF PLANO CARPINI (*ca.* 1180–1252), a Franciscan friar, was the first papal envoy to travel to Mongolia, and thus to provide the Christian West with its earliest eyewitness account of the Mongols and their rapidly expanding empire. Upon his return in 1247, he wrote *Historia Mongalorum*, one of the better sources on the Mongols of the thirteenth century.

Considering the important positions he held in the church hierarchy—Franciscan Order official, papal envoy, papal legate, and archbishop—very little is known of John's personal life and activities. The meager documentation available reveals that John of Plano Carpini was most likely born in the Tuscan village of Pian di Carpini (Planus Carpinis in Latin; now Plano della Maggiore), near Perugia. He died on 1 August 1252, probably in his native Italy. Nothing is known of his family, infancy, and youth—not even when and where he was educated.

Since Pian di Carpini was close to Assisi, it is not surprising that John soon became a disciple and follower of St. Francis. He undoubtedly joined the Franciscans before the founder's death in 1226, and he quickly acquired a good reputation and important administrative offices in the order. John was sent to Germany in the early 1220's; he held the office of warden in Saxony in 1222 and became the provincial of Germany in 1228. There are several indications that he was provincial in Spain for three years, but no specific dates are given for this term of office. Except for this brief Spanish interlude, John spent most of his adult life as an administrator in Germany, where he was active in founding monasteries and sending his friars into Dacia, Hungary, Bohemia, Poland, Denmark, and Norway. The sources indicate that he watched over his friars and readily defended them before both bishops and princes. He was probably in Germany at the time of the Mongol invasion of eastern Europe, although some scholars argue that he was an official at the papal court between 1239 and 1245.

The Mongol threat to western Europe was still very real when Pope Innocent IV sent the first papal envoys to the Mongols in 1245; one of these papal missions was entrusted to John of Plano Carpini, an experienced and widely traveled cleric with energy, intelligence, and an exceptional knowledge of eastern Europe. Thus he was an ideal choice to lead an embassy to the Mongols, a two-and-one-half-year mission that proved to be physically hard on him, a very heavy man already more than sixty years old. Shortly after John's return in November 1247, Innocent IV sent him as a legate to King Louis IX, who was about to depart for the Middle East on his first crusade. Probably to reward him for his dangerous mission to the Mongols, Innocent appointed John archbishop of Antivari (now Bar) in Dalmatia in 1248. His episcopal reign was not without problems, for John soon found himself embroiled in a jurisdictional conflict with the archbishop of Ragusa (now Dubrovnik). The dispute was submitted to the Roman curia but John died before the issue was resolved.

Despite his many ecclesiastical offices and administrative positions, John's contribution to history rests primarily on his embassy to the Mongols and his subsequent account of the trip. Carrying papal letters, the friar left Lyons on 16 April 1245 and traveled through northeastern Europe and the Russian steppes. John was joined by Benedict the Pole in Breslau; this fellow Franciscan accompanied John to Mongolia as interpreter, and also wrote a brief account of their journey. The friars traveled through Poland and Russia, both of which had been devastated by the Mongols a few years earlier. Polish and Russian leaders provided them with advice and gifts for the Mongol leaders to ease their passage. Leaving Kiev on 3 February 1246, they arrived at Batu's capital of Sarai on the Volga on 4 April 1246. Batu, ruler of the western Mongol Empire and conqueror of eastern Europe, received the friars and had the pope's letters translated into Mongol; without com-

ment he ordered the friars to continue to the court of the great khan in Mongolia.

On 8 April 1246 John and Benedict began the most formidable part of their journey. With their bodies tightly wrapped against wind and fatigue, they traveled north of the Caspian and Aral seas, then through the Dzungarian Gap. On 22 July they arrived at the imperial camp of Sira Ordu, near Karakorum, the Mongol capital. The two intrepid friars had traveled about 3,000 miles in 106 days. Shortly after the arrival of the Franciscans, Güyük had been elected great khan. Along with several thousand envoys and representatives from all parts of the vast Mongol Empire, the friars witnessed Güyük's formal enthronement on 24 August 1246. The papal envoys were not granted a private audience with Güyük until November; they were then dismissed with a letter for the pope. They suffered greatly on the winter portion of the return trip via Sarai, Kiev, Poland, Bohemia, and Germany, and reached the pope at Lyons in November 1247.

Upon his return, and in response to frequent requests for information on Asia and the Mongols, John wrote down his observations and experiences in a work entitled *Historia Mongalorum*. This report consists of eight chapters on the Mongol lands, customs, religion, character, history, military organization and tactics, the peoples already conquered by the Mongols, and how best to oppose them on the battlefield. Military elements are stressed because John's mission had political-military overtones as well as the overt religious-diplomatic ones; Innocent IV had asked him to observe and evaluate the Mongol military machine and determine how best to resist it. In the ninth and final chapter, John gives a detailed account of his journey: places visited, his reception by various Mongol rulers, and people met en route. In regard to the last category, Christians he found living among the Mongols proved to be one of his main sources of information. Judging from the selection, and especially the spelling, of words and names in his report, most of John's information came from Russian and Turkish Nestorian Christians.

The *Historia Mongalorum* is John's only extant writing, and his historical significance thus rests on this single document. In terms of literary quality, his style is that of an efficient administrator experienced in pragmatic affairs; he writes in a simple, straightforward manner. Although not a literary masterpiece, the *Historia Mongalorum* is a model of concise and objective reporting. John's description of the Mongol customs, character, and history is one of the best treatments by any Western author; it is inferior to William of Rubruck's *Itinerarium* (he returned from the Mongols in 1255) only in personal and geographical detail. Although the friars failed to convert the Mongols and to persuade them to stop pillaging, John's history is especially important because it represents the first reliable account of the Mongols to appear in medieval Europe; particularly significant in this regard is John's exact listing of names: of the peoples conquered by the Mongols, of those still resisting in 1247, of the Mongol princes and rulers, and of witnesses to the truth of his report (individual merchants and Christians whom he met among the Mongols). These tallies are unrivaled in Western medieval literature and are thus of great historical value. It is unfortunate that John, the first European traveler to penetrate the heart of Asia, is usually overshadowed by Marco Polo.

BIBLIOGRAPHY

Sources. For years only the part of the *Historia Mongalorum* abstracted in Vincent of Beauvais's *Speculum historiale* was readily available; although there were many manuscript copies of the *Speculum* in existence after the 1250's, it was not printed until 1473. In his coverage of the Mongols, Vincent blended John's *Historia Mongalorum* with Simon of St. Quentin's *Historia Tartarorum,* written probably in 1248, after Simon returned from the Mongols in the Middle East. Two versions of John's *Historia* are extant: the first is an abbreviated account (extant in ten manuscripts) and the second is a fuller and more complete copy (four manuscripts). The texts were located, edited, translated, and studied after 1500.

The complete text of the *Historia Mongalorum* was first critically edited by Armand (M. A. P.) d'Avezac as *Relations des Mongols ou Tartares* (1838); the most recent and best critical edition is in Anastasius van den Wyngaert, *Sinica Franciscana,* I (1929), 3–130. The only English translation based on Wyngaert's text is in Christopher Dawson, ed., *The Mongol Mission: Narratives and Letters of the Franciscan Missionaries in Mongolia,* a nun of Stanbrook Abbey, trans. (1955).

Studies. J. J. Saunders, "John of Plan Carpini: The Papal Envoy to the Mongol Conquerors Who Travelled Through Russia to Eastern Asia in 1245–7," in *History Today,* 22 (1972); Denis Sinor, "John of Plano Carpini's Return from the Mongols: New Light from a Luxembourg Manuscript," in *Journal of the Royal Asiatic Society* (1957).

GREGORY G. GUZMAN

[See also **Batu; Mongol Empire: Europe and Western Asia; Mongol Empire: Foundations; Travel and Transport: Western European; Vincent of Beauvais.**]

JOHN OF SALISBURY (*ca.* 1115–25 October 1180), English humanist and philosopher whose career was marked by achievements in academic affairs, in diplomacy, and in ecclesiastical administration. Born near Salisbury, he began his studies in 1136 at Paris with Peter Abelard, Robert of Melun, and possibly Gilbert of Poitiers. William of Conches was also his teacher, at Chartres, or possibly at Paris. Peter Helias, Adam of the Little Bridge, and Robert Pullen were at least his acquaintances, and possibly his teachers. John was a papal functionary between 1148, when he attended the Synod of Rheims, and about 1154, when he became secretary and counselor to Theobald, archbishop of Canterbury. During the tenure of Theobald and his successor, Thomas Becket, John was also a representative of the archiepiscopal see at the court of Henry II and on the Continent. His support of Becket in the latter's quarrel with the king may have occasioned John's departure from England in 1164 and his subsequent stay at the abbey of St. Remi in Rheims. In 1170, however, John returned to England and was with his friend Thomas Becket at the time of his murder. In 1176 John was elected bishop of Chartres, where he remained until his death.

Between autumn 1156 and Easter 1157, when John was in disfavor with Henry II (possibly owing to his defense of ecclesiastical liberties), John worked on two major books, the *Metalogicon* and the *Policraticus,* which were completed in 1159 and dedicated to Becket, then the king's chancellor. The *Metalogicon* is a defense of the trivium and is generally conceded to be one of the first Western commentaries on Aristotle's lately recovered *Organon.* In this work John attacks those who deny the value of studying the trivium, especially logic, calling them Cornificians. John's accounts of personalities and their philosophical positions (in *Metalogicon* II, 17) constitute one of the major sources on the preeminent masters in the twelfth-century schools at Paris.

While many historians of philosophy agree that John's summary of various philosophical views on universals (*Metalogicon* II, 17) is accurate and helpful, few hold that his own reflections on this issue (especially *Metalogicon* II, 20) are of philosophical importance. This position has been challenged by Brian Hendley. Although John purports to be interpreting Aristotle, Hendley claims that he differs significantly from Aristotle and, in fact, propounds a view similar to that of John Locke. John of Salisbury agrees with Aristotle that genera and species have only mental existence and that they represent similarities of particular things; nevertheless, genera and species are "fictions" *(figmenta)*. That is, they do not correspond to the formal aspects of particular sensible things, as Aristotle holds; rather, they name or refer to natures or essences that have been inferred from sensible qualities. According to Hendley, then, John rejects the possibility of attaining, through abstraction or natural intuition, knowledge about sensible reality.

Penetration into the true natures of things through sensation and imagination is limited, but is advanced considerably by written and oral exchange of opinion and experience in which genera and species are employed. Eloquence, the effective use of language, is developed, and reading *(lectio)* and learning *(doctrina)* are facilitated, through the arts of the trivium. But God desires that man attain wisdom, or scientific knowledge, and hence he provides grace to assure this. Indeed, "the law of God has made faith the primary and fundamental prerequisite for understanding of the truth" *(Metalogicon* IV, 41), for through such understanding divine attributes are revealed, since natures disclose their cause.

Hendley allows that Locke may have abandoned his conviction that there are real essences; John of Salisbury did not. Still, the two Johns agree that if there are such natures, they can only be inferred from their sensible effects; that genera and species represent the ideas of the similarities of particular sensible things; and that communication and experience make possible progress in scientific insight.

In his *Policraticus* John discusses political legitimacy and the notion of the corporate state. Much research concerning the former has focused upon John's justification of tyrannicide, which contains many reservations and inconsistencies. Richard and Mary Rouse attempt to clarify John's teaching and provide a context to resolve the verbal contradictions. According to John, a tyrant is one who uses his power to violate the law, that is, "a certain [natural] fitness of things." The commonwealth is like an organism with the prince as its head, the church as its soul, and various other functionaries as other organs; hence, it can operate correctly only when the head (the prince) is sane. A tyrant is a corrupting influence on the rest of the body; no internal check can discipline him, and so he must be eliminated from without, by God himself, who may choose to act through a human agent.

Thus John's doctrine appears to be a moderate one, certainly not intended to be radical; indeed, it was offered to encourage the protection of the rights of the church by Henry II, who was not of such a character to be intimidated by spiritual threats. Still, the *Policraticus* seems to have been an influential work throughout the fourteenth and fifteenth centuries in the areas of political action and speculation.

John's other writings include *Entheticus, De dogmate philosophorum,* the *Life of St. Anselm,* the *Life of St. Thomas Becket,* and *Historia pontificalis* (Memoirs of the papal court). This last records his eyewitness perspectives on the papacy, especially from 1148 to 1151. John's letters, of a Latinity worthy of the quattrocento, reveal significant details of the controversy between Henry II and Becket.

BIBLIOGRAPHY
Sources. Joannis Saresberiensis postea eposcopi carnotensis, *Opera omnia,* J. A. Giles, ed., 5 vols. (1848, repr. 1969), also in J. P. Migne, ed., *Patrologia latina,* CXCIX (1855), 1–1040; *John of Salisbury's Memoirs of the Papal Court (Joannis Saresberiensis Historia pontificalis),* facing-page English trans. by Majorie Chibnall (1956); John of Salisbury, *Policraticus: The Statesman's Book,* Murray F. Markland, ed. (1979); *John of Salisbury, The Metalogicon,* Daniel D. McGarry, trans. (1955, repr. 1971).
Studies. Brian P. Hendley, "John of Salisbury's Defense of the *Trivium,*" in *Arts libéraux et philosophie au moyen âge* (1969), and "John of Salisbury and the Problem of Universals," in *Journal of the History of Philosophy,* 8 (1970); Hans Liebeschütz, *Mediaeval Humanism in the Life and Writings of John of Salisbury* (1950); Amnon Lindner, "The Knowledge of John of Salisbury in the Later Middle Ages," in *Studi medievali,* 18 (1977); Richard H. Rouse and Mary A. Rouse, "John of Salisbury and the Doctrine of Tyrannicide," in *Speculum,* 42 (1967); E. K. Tolan, "John of Salisbury and the Problem of Medieval Humanism," in *Études d'histoire littéraire et doctrinale* (1968).

JANICE L. SCHULTZ

[See also **Aristotle in the Middle Ages; Becket, Thomas, Saint; England: Norman-Angevin; Philosophy and Theology, Western European, Political Theory, Western European.**]

JOHN OF S. MARTÍN DE ALBARES, illuminator and deacon who signed the tenth-century Bible of León (now in León Cathedral). The Bible was written in 920, during the reign of King Ordoño II, for Abbot Mauro of the monastery dedicated to SS. María and Martín de Albares in León. The artist included animal, human, and geometric motifs that are derived from Byzantine and Moorish art.

MARY GRIZZARD

St. Luke. From Bible of León, illuminated by John of S. Martín de Albares, *ca.* 920. LEÓN, CATEDRAL DE LEÓN

JOHN PECKHAM. See **Peckham, John.**

JOHN QUIDORT. See **John of Paris.**

JOHN SCOTTUS ERIUGENA (*d. ca.* 877–879). The word *scottus* was used before the twelfth century to refer to anyone who came from Ireland. John Scottus, along with Sedulius Scottus, Josephus Scottus, and other compatriots, was one of many *scotti* who came to live, teach, and write on the Continent during the eighth and ninth centuries. Most of them were good scholars and teachers who received support and encouragement from Carolingian monarchs, bishops, and abbots. In some cases, however, their Irish customs and intellectual practices antagonized their continental counterparts.

John Scottus, who in one of his works referred to himself as Eriugena, "the one originating from Erin," first appears in the historical record in 850 or 851, when a bishop invited him to participate in a theological debate. At that time John resided and taught in the palace of Charles the Bald. He must have come to the Continent at least five to ten years before mid century in order to have acquired such a position and reputation. Biographical details are skimpy. Many of his works can be dated to the 860's. Most of John's teaching and writing appear to have been done in the ecclesiastical province of Rheims in northern France, especially near the cathedral towns of Soissons, Rheims, and Laon, and the royal palace at Compiègne.

John was a prodigious worker blessed with a keen mind and skills that were relatively rare in the ninth century. He commented on the arts, wrote poetry, engaged in theological controversy, translated important works of Greek theological speculation into Latin, wrote biblical commentaries and commentaries on some of the works he translated, and in his brilliant *Periphyseon* produced one of the most important and original works of the early Middle Ages. His thoughts and writings were developed in the company of his students and colleagues, who helped to spread his teaching. The fortunes of John's works are quite unequal. Some were well known in the Middle Ages and copied frequently, although not always under his name. Others did not circulate very widely and lay in relative obscurity until discovered by modern scholars. John Scottus is often classified as a philosopher and placed in the ranks of the great philosophers of the Western European tradition.

When John first came to the Continent, he probably began his teaching career by introducing students to the arts and to the Scriptures. A collection of glosses on difficult biblical vocabulary that he used may come from this period. He commented on one of the most important arts handbooks of the Middle Ages, *The Marriage of Philology and Mercury* by Martianus Capella, a late antique author. John's first venture into theology appears to have been the treatise *De praedestinatione,* written in approximately 851, which Archbishop Hincmar of Rheims and Bishop Pardulus of Laon asked him to write against the monk Gottschalk (Godescalc) of Orbais. Gottschalk was at the center of a bitter debate on the issue of double predestination, the notion that the good are predestined to eternal life and the evil are predestined to hellfire. John's contribution to the controversy revealed his debt to Augustine of Hippo, the liberal arts, and dialectical reasoning.

At this early stage in his career, John showed

some familiarity with the Greek language, or at least with Greek words. It used to be thought that all Irishmen came to the Continent as accomplished Hellenists. In John's case, his command of Greek clearly progressed while in the Carolingian realm. Carolingian rulers and some court scholars were very interested in things Greek from both a political and an intellectual perspective. John's first major translation was of the works of Pseudo-Dionysius the Areopagite, supposedly St. Paul's Athenian convert to Christianity but actually an unknown Greek author of about A.D. 500. A Greek manuscript of Dionysius' works had been given to Emperor Louis the Pious in 827 by the Byzantine emperor Michael Balbus. Abbot Hilduin of St. Denis near Paris translated the work soon after its arrival in Francia, but his translation was far from satisfactory. John's Latin version, undertaken sometime in the early 860's, represented a noticeable improvement over Hilduin's text. The translation of Dionysius was followed by translations of the *Ambigua* and the *Quaestiones ad Thalassium* of Maximus the Confessor, the *De imagine* of Gregory of Nyssa, and perhaps the *Ancoratus* (or *Sermo de fide*) of Epiphanius of Salamis.

John's translations, particularly those of the Dionysian corpus, added important new texts to the Western intellectual tradition. Since John was a scholar as well as a translator, exposure to the thought of the Greek fathers and to the general Neoplatonic tradition embedded in it opened up new intellectual horizons for him. His poetry, much of it written in honor of Charles the Bald, the Irishman's patron, or to be read before him on important occasions, is filled with Greek philosophical and theological phrases. More significantly, John's own work began to take a new turn. At home with the Scriptures, the Latin fathers, and the arts, he was inspired by his new acquaintance with Greek theological speculation to create his own intellectual synthesis.

The *Periphyseon* (also known as the *De divisione naturae*) is John's major work. He reworked portions of it during his life, leaving his handwritten notes in the margins of some of the extant manuscripts. In the *Periphyseon,* which is arranged as a dialogue between a master and his student, John addressed several themes central to Christian thought and often digressed to consider others. Creation, the divisions of nature, and the return of all being to its source provided the framework for the discussion. In addition to the *Periphyseon,* John wrote at least three other works.

In his commentary on the *Celestial Hierarchy* of Pseudo-Dionysius, he returned to a work he had earlier translated. He also wrote an enormously influential homily on the prologue to the gospel of John. Thirty of the fifty-four extant manuscripts attribute this work to Origen, and John Chrysostom and Gregory of Nazianzus are named seven times and one time, respectively. These false attributions no doubt contributed to the renown of the homily. They also demonstrate how profoundly influenced John was by the work of the Greek fathers. His last work, never finished, was a commentary on the Gospel of John. It exists in only one manuscript and bears many notes and additions in his own handwriting. John Scottus probably died while working on it.

BIBLIOGRAPHY

Walter Berschin, *Griechisch-lateinisches Mittelalter* (1980); Mary Brennan, "A Bibliography of Publications in the Field of Eriugenian Studies, 1880–1975," in *Studi medievali,* **18** (1977); Franz Brunhölzl, *Geschichte der lateinischen Literatur des Mittelalters,* I (1975), 467–475, 568–570; Édouard Jeauneau, *Quatre thèmes érigéniens* (1978), and "Jean Scot Erigène et le Grec," in *Archivum latinitatis medii aevi,* **41** (1979); Paolo Lucentini, *Platonismo medievale: Contributi per la storia dell'eriugenismo* (1979).

JOHN J. CONTRENI

[See also **Exegesis, Latin; Gottschalk of Orbais; Philosophy and Theology, Western European; Pseudo-Dionysius the Areopagite; Translation and Translators, Western European.**]

JOHN THE DEACON. This designation was applied to at least five medieval personages, of whom the earliest is the most important.

Pope John I. Prior to his accession, he was addressed by Boethius as "John the Deacon" in the dedications of three of his theological tractates: *Utrum pater et filius . . . , Quomodo substantiae . . . ,* and *Contra Eutychen et Nestorium.* John was one of the intellectual, orthodox Christians (including Symmachus, father-in-law of Boethius) whose requests impelled Boethius to write the *Quomodo substantiae.* This was to fulfill the Augustinian ambition that the understanding of faith be deepened through the application of Greek philosophical resources.

In 523 John, a native of Tuscany whose father's name was Constantius, was elected pope. At the time the Arian Ostrogoth Theodoric ruled as king at Ravenna; the orthodox emperor Justin I ruled from Constantinople. Theodoric sent John and others to Justin to attempt to persuade the emperor to mitigate his anti-Arian legislation; the legates succeeded on all points except the return of converted Arians to their original allegiance, for the pope had refused to plead this detail.

After crowning the emperor, the pope returned to Italy, where Boethius and Symmachus had been arraigned on a charge of *lèse majesté*, compounded in the case of Boethius by a charge of witchcraft and the use of forged documents. Both Boethius and Symmachus were executed; fear of Justin apparently prevented the execution of Pope John I. He died in prison, an exile at Ravenna, 18 May 526, accounted a martyr.

John the Deacon of Rome (ca. 824–before 882). Probably a monk of Monte Cassino, John was author of the best biography of Pope Gregory I the Great. He was a member of the court of Charles the Bald and, later, of the entourage of Pope John VIII.

John the Deacon of Naples (b. ca. 880). A hagiographer born at Naples, he was deacon of S. Gennaro by 906. He wrote a chronicle of the bishops of Naples covering the period 762–872 as well as notices on Sts. Severinus, Januarius, Sosius, the Forty Martyrs of Sebaste, and Procopius.

John the Deacon of Venice (d. after 1008) was the author of the earliest chronicle of Venice, including an eyewitness account of the rule of Peter II Orseolo (991–1009). He was named envoy of the doge to Otto III in connection with that emperor's visit to Venice in 1001.

John the Deacon of Rome (fl. mid twelfth century) was canon of the Lateran Basilica. At the request of Pope Alexander III (1159–1181) and the prior of the Lateran, he produced a third edition of his *Descriptio Lateranensis ecclesiae,* which he titled *Liber de Sanctis sanctorum.*

BIBLIOGRAPHY

Pope John I: Louis Duchesne, ed., *Le Liber pontificalis,* I (1886), 275–278; Roberto Cessi, ed., *Anonymus Valesianus,* in Rerum Italicarum Scriptores, XXIV, pt. 4, new ed. (1930), 20. *John of Rome (ninth century)*: Patrologia latina, LXXIV, 59–242. *John of Naples*: Monumenta Germaniae historica: Scriptores rerum Langobardicarum (1878), 424–435; Acta sanctorum—St. Severinus, Jan. I, 497–499; St. Januarius, Sept. VI, 874–878; St. Sosius, Sept. VI, 879–884; Forty Martyrs, Mar. II, 22–25. *John of Venice*: Monumenta Germaniae historica: Scriptores, VII (1846), 1–38; Patrologia latina, CXXXIX (1853), 871–940. *John of Rome (twelfth century)*: Roberto Valentini and Giuseppe Zucchetti, eds., *Codice topografico della città di Roma,* III (1946), 319–373.

EDWARD A. SYNAN

JOINVILLE, JEAN DE (*ca.* 1224/1225–1317), seneschal of Champagne and biographer of Louis IX. The Joinvilles were a family of Champagne (lords of Joinville) in whose house the seneschalsy of that county was hereditary at least from the late twelfth century, if not long before. The most famous member of the family was Jean, the confidant of Louis IX (St. Louis). Of his early life little is known, except that by 1240 he was already married. At Saumur in 1241 he met King Louis for the first time. The royal court had assembled there in order to celebrate the knighting of the king's brother, Alphonse, and his investiture with Poitou, a territory conquered from the English in the early thirteenth century.

Jean de Joinville's real fame was to come somewhat later, when he accompanied the king on the Second Crusade (1248–1254). Like the king he made careful preparations for the adventure, even joining with his cousin Jean, Lord of Apremont, to rent a ship. But disaster befell him on the crusade. He was captured with the king in Egypt in 1250; he was seriously ill at the time and was saved only by the efforts of an Arab physician. Released with the king after the negotiation of a treaty and the payment of ransom, Jean stayed with Louis four additional years in the Levant. He received money from the king to sustain his contingent of troops and, indeed, became the king's vassal. More than that, he became his close friend and the close friend of Louis's wife, Margaret.

After returning from the crusade in 1254, Jean had to correct the maladministration of his lands in Champagne, the legacy of his absence for six years. Another legacy of his crusading days was a recurrent fever that could occasionally incapacitate him. Nonetheless, from time to time Jean visited and advised his old friend the king, and stayed at court. There he had the famous squabbles over etiquette in Louis's presence with another of the king's friends, Master Robert of Sorbon, one of the royal chaplains.

In 1261 Jean remarried, his first wife having died probably the year before. His second wife brought considerable property to the marriage, and much of the remainder of his life was spent administering and protecting his estates. (His acerbic relations with local ecclesiastical authorities are notorious.)

Even though he was sick at the time, Jean, at the king's urging, obeyed a summons to the royal court in March 1267. In a dream he anticipated the reason for the summons: the king intended to go on crusade once again. Jean, remembering what had happened to his estates when he went away before, refused to accompany his overlord and opposed the whole plan. He regarded as mortal sinners everyone who encouraged the plans of the already physically weak king.

After the death of Louis on crusade in 1270, Jean frequently came to the court of his son and successor, Philip III. He continued his friendship with Louis's widow (who died in 1295) and maintained a keen interest in the process of Louis's canonization, at which he testified.

The reign of Philip III ended abruptly in 1285 with his death in the Aragonese crusade. His son, Philip IV the Fair, does not seem to have been a close friend of Jean; the seneschal made some very critical remarks about the quality of his rulership in the *Histoire de saint Louis,* which is Jean's lasting claim to fame. That book, written at the request of the royal family and dedicated ultimately to the future Louis X, occupied many of the remaining years of the old seneschal's life. It is regarded by Romance scholars as a monument of French prose and is certainly—with its refreshing anecdotes and critical spirit—the finest biography of the saint king.

Jean de Joinville seemed almost a monument to his contemporaries as he lived on and on, the grand old man. He outlived Philip IV (*d.* 1314) and spent some time in the entourage of his son, Louis X (*d.* 1316), whom he also outlived. His long familiarity with royal ritual made him a widely recognized expert on court ceremonial in the last decades of his life. He died 24 December 1317.

BIBLIOGRAPHY

Joinville's *Credo* and *Histoire de Saint Louis* are available in many usable editions; the best critical edition is that of M. Natalis de Wailly (1872, repr. 1972). A new critical edition with improvements but also with flaws is that of Noel Corbett (1977). Two convenient—though in style very different—English translations are those of René Hague, *The Life of St. Louis* (1955), containing both works; and Margaret R. B. Shaw, *Chronicles of the Crusades* (1963, repr. 1977), containing the *Histoire* only. A

full-length literary study of the *Histoire* is Maureen Slattery, *Myth, Man, and Sovereign Saint: King Louis IX in Jean de Joinville's Sources* (1985). The artistic history of the MSS of Joinville's *Credo* is treated in Lionel J. Friedman, *Text and Iconography for Joinville's "Credo"* (1958). An exhaustive consideration of Joinville's life, with an edition of his charters and those of other members of his family, is in Henri François Delaborde, *Jean de Joinville et les seigneurs de Joinville* (1894).

WILLIAM CHESTER JORDAN

[See also **Biography, French; Biography, Secular; Champagne, County; Crusades: 1212 to 1272; Louis IX of France; Seneschal.**]

JÓMSVÍKINGA SAGA was written by an Icelander about 1200, certainly no later than 1230. The introductory part relates the history of the Danish kings from the legendary Gorm the Childless to Harald Blacktooth. The main story concerns the Danish raiders called the Jomsvikings, who, according to the saga, in the tenth century formed a special warrior community at the stronghold Jómsborg on the Pomeranian coast.

The saga focuses on the Jomsviking chieftains, Pálnatóki and Sigvaldi, and on their manipulations of Danish royalty. Having helped Sveinn Forkbeard, the son of King Harald Blacktooth, to the throne by killing his father—in the most degrading manner imaginable—Pálnatóki enters the service of a Wendish king and founds Jómsborg. Sigvaldi, who assumes leadership after Pálnatóki's death, kidnaps and keeps fooling King Sveinn until the king turns the tables and in a drinking bout provokes the Jomsvikings into making a vow to invade Norway. This leads to their defeat in the great sea battle of Hjörungavágr, where the Norwegian Earl Hákon employs magic against them. Most of the Jomsvikings flee, but a few brave ones are captured. In the ensuing execution scene—the highlight of the narrative—they go, one by one, to their beheading with eloquent fearlessness. Most notable is Vagn, who puts a stop to the proceedings by slaying his would-be executioner, and is then pardoned by Earl Hákon's son.

Jómsvíkinga saga, which tells of the Jomsvikings in relation to the kings of Denmark and the earl of Norway, is classed among the kings' sagas; but it is the unpolished Jomsvikings who determine the course of the narrative, and the earl and the kings are ridiculed more than respected. The saga is marked by striking characters who make pithy remarks; its style is vivid but uneven. In this connection it is worth noting that *Jómsvíkinga saga* was written before the genre of *Íslendingasögur* was fully developed. The saga has been characterized as a historical novel with legendary traits in the manner of the *fornaldarsögur* and historians have regarded it with utter skepticism. But even though the saga is clearly a literary construction, it is now known from archaeological evidence and from writings of medieval historians that places and persons such as Jómsborg and Pálnatóki are not entirely fictional.

The construction of the saga presents some problems. The introductory part has been regarded by some scholars as a later addition, but it is more likely that the author drew on a written source, probably the *Óláfs saga Tryggvasonar* of Gunnlaugr Leifsson, and remolded the material so as to link it with the *Jómsvíkinga saga* proper. At the time the saga was written, the Jomsvikings had become famous in Iceland—there are allusions to them in poetry. It is believed that some of the rich tradition behind this saga also underlies contemporary historic writing in Denmark (Saxo, Sven Aggesøn). According to the saga, tales of the Jomsvikings were brought to Iceland by Icelandic skalds who had been present at the battle of Hjörungavágr; a few of their stanzas are quoted. The best-known poem about the Jomsvikings, *Jómsvíkinga drápa*, is based on the saga.

The manuscript tradition of *Jómsvíkinga saga* is rich: four independent medieval redactions are preserved, all descending from the same version of the saga yet quite at variance with one another. The oldest manuscript, AM 291 4°, from the end of the thirteenth century, is thought to contain the most original text; closely related to it is the text incorporated in *Óláfs saga Tryggvasonar hin mesta*, in the manuscript *Flateyjarbók*. The Stockholm Royal Library vellum manuscript 7 4°, from the beginning of the fourteenth century, contains a revised, abridged redaction, the style of which is terser, possibly the result of an attempt to approach the so-called classical saga style. Two more redactions are in AM 510 4°, from the sixteenth century, and in a Latin translation from around 1600 of a now lost medieval manuscript. Another and older version of the saga has been used in the historical works *Fagrskinna* and *Heimskringla*.

BIBLIOGRAPHY

The most recent edition is *Jómsvíkinga saga*, Ólafur Halldórsson, ed. (1969). For complete bibliography before 1937, see *Islandica*, 3 (1910), 34–39, and 26 (1937), 21–23. English translations (of the shorter redaction of the saga only) are Norman F. Blake, ed. and trans., *The Saga of the Jomsvikings* (1962); Lee M. Hollander, trans., *The Saga of the Jómsvíkings* (1955, 1971); Danish translation is Helle Degnbol and Helle Jensen, trans., *Jomsvikingernes Saga* (1978).

HELLE DEGNBOL

[See also **Óláfs Saga Tryggvasonar.**]

JÓN ÖGMUNDARSON, ST. (1052–1121), Icelandic churchman. Jón's life is best known from the saga about him (*Jóns saga helga*), despite some reservations about the historical accuracy of that work, which is in the tradition of hagiography rather than that of history. Information from the saga, combined with other sources, yields a fairly complete portrait of an important Icelandic churchman in the period not long after the conversion of his country to Christianity (*ca.* 1000).

Jón was born in southern Iceland and educated by Bishop Ísleifr Gizurarson (*d.* 1080) at Skálholt. It is reported that he traveled abroad as a deacon or subdeacon, visiting Rome and other places. The saga tells some entertaining stories from this period, but they are not easily verifiable. After his return to Iceland, Jón settled as priest and farmer at Breiðabólstaðr in Fljótshlíð, where he had been born; he married twice.

Since Ísleifr's consecration as the first bishop of Iceland in 1056, there had been only one bishop in the country, and around 1100 it was felt that a second diocese ought to be established in northern Iceland. As bishop-elect, Jón went abroad for consecration: first to Lund, from which Asser, who had become archbishop of the North (Scandinavia and Iceland) in 1104, sent him to Rome for dispensation because of his two marriages. He then returned to Lund, where he was consecrated 29 April 1106.

Jón was a successful administrator of the new diocese. He built a cathedral at Hólar, started a school with the help of teachers from abroad, and made arrangements for a Benedictine monastery to be established at Þingeyrar. Jón introduced the European learning and spirituality he had acquired during his travels, either directly from the Continent or through Lund, and he seems also to have organized a modest chapter at Hólar modeled on that of Lund. He is reported to have done away with those names of the days of the week that contained names of pagan gods—in the case of Thursday, for instance, replacing *þórsdagr* with *fimtudagr*. To this day, Icelandic is the only Scandinavian language with this lexical peculiarity, though credit for the achievement may well be ascribed to wishful hagiographic thinking by Jón's biographer rather than to reality.

In 1198 Þorlákr Þórhallsson (d. 1193), bishop of Skálholt, was declared a saint; at the same time or shortly after, reports of Jón's sanctity became known. In 1200 the day of his death, 23 April, was made his feast day, and in 1315 the day of his translation, 3 March, was added to the church calendar. Jón was venerated in Iceland but practically unknown elsewhere.

BIBLIOGRAPHY

Hans Bekker-Nielsen, "A Note on Two Icelandic Saints," in *Germanic Review,* 36 (1961); Magnús Már Lárusson, "Jón helgi Ögmundarson," in *Kulturhistorisk leksikon for nordisk middelalder,* VII (1962).

HANS BEKKER-NIELSEN

[See also **Jóns Saga Helga.**]

JONAS FRAGMENT. See Picard Literature.

JONAS OF ORLÉANS (before 780–842/843), born in Aquitaine, was bishop of Orléans from 818, succeeding Theodulf, until his death. He was involved in several reform synods, and in political events associated with Louis the Pious and the future Charles the Bald. He challenged the opinions of Agobard of Lyons and Ebo of Rheims. His *De institutione regia* (*ca.* 831) is a major text of Carolingian ecclesiology. In this tract, written for King Pepin of Aquitaine, Jonas asserts the prerogatives of the Frankish episcopacy in maintaining peace and justice throughout the empire. He emphasizes the pastoral functions of the bishops, who ultimately are responsible for upholding temporal order. As a mirror of princes the work exalts the majesty of the king—largely in conventional terms drawn from the Old Testament—whose task is conceived as a ministry of the church. The Christian prince is a model of virtue and a de-

fender of the oppressed. For Matfrid, count of Orléans, Jonas wrote *De institutione laicali,* a companion treatise, on the duties of married laymen. His *De cultu imaginum* was directed against Claudius, bishop of Turin; Jonas attempted to retain the veneration of images in churches without falling into image worship.

The career of Jonas typifies the growing influence of the Frankish episcopacy in politics, ecclesiastical discipline, and the liturgy. He attempted to define the respective duties of king and bishop in the face of imperial troubles, monastic withdrawal, and the power of lay magnates.

BIBLIOGRAPHY

Jonas' writings are in *Patrologia latina,* CVI (1864), 117–387. Studies include Étienne Delaruelle, "Jonas d'Orléans et le moralisme carolingien," in *Bulletin de littérature ecclésiastique,* 54 (1954); A. García Martínez, "El primer tratado político-religioso . . . Jonas de Orléans," in *Crisis* (Madrid), 4 (1957); Jean Reviron, ed., *Les idées politico-religieuses d'un évêque due IXe siècle . . . Jonas d'Orléans et son "De institutione regia"* (1930), with annotated text in Latin. See also R. W. Dyson, trans., *A Ninth-century Political Tract: The "De institutione regia" of Jonas of Orléans* (1983).

THOMAS RENNA

[See also **Carolingians and the Carolingian Empire; Theodulf of Orléans.**]

JONGLEUR. See Joglar/Jongleur.

JÓNS SAGA HELGA, one of the bishops' sagas, is an Icelandic Life of St. Jón Ögmundarson. It exists in three versions, all based on a translation or adaptation of a now lost Latin Life, composed shortly after 1200 by Gunnlaugr Leifsson (d. 1218/1219), a Benedictine monk of Þingeyrar.

Jón was declared a saint in 1200; and at the instigation of Guðmundr Arason, Gunnlaugr, who was highly esteemed for his learning and his skill as writer, was commissioned to produce a full Life of the first bishop of Hólar. To judge from the Icelandic translation, the Latin Life must have been a fine piece of hagiographic writing.

Version A represents the original translation or

adaptation best. It was written in the first half of the thirteenth century, and the chief manuscripts are from the beginning of the fourteenth century. Version B is somewhat augmented and is embellished in the florid style fashionable at the date of its composition, early in the fourteenth century. Lexicostatistical investigations suggest that this version might be attributed to Bergr Sokkason (d. 1350); the chief manuscript is from the mid fourteenth century. Version C, a conflation of A and B, is based on a fuller text of B than the extant one. It is known in two seventeenth-century manuscripts but has not yet been adequately edited.

In delightful contrast to some other bishops' sagas, such as *Árna saga biskups, Jóns saga* is not a historical record; rather, it is first and foremost a saint's Life, following the conventions of hagiographic composition. Whatever factual information Gunnlaugr had about St. Jón, who had died eighty years or so before the Latin Life was written, it had to be subordinated to the overall idea of describing how, with the grace of God, an Icelandic churchman, within the first century or so of the conversion of the country, was elevated to the highest office in the church and thence to sainthood. The description of St. Jón and his life is an exemplary portrait of an Icelandic churchman of the eleventh and early twelfth centuries, revealing much about the intellectual and spiritual climate of the age and vividly recounting the travels that were so much a part of the education of the Icelandic clergy.

BIBLIOGRAPHY

Editions are Jón Sigurðsson and Guðbrandur Vigfússon, eds., *Biskupa sögur*, I (1858), 149–260; Guðni Jónsson, ed., *Byskupa sögur*, II (1948), 1–175. Studies include Peter G. Foote, "Aachen, Lund, Hólar," in *Les relations littéraires franco-scandinaves au moyen âge* (1975), and "Bischofssaga (Byskupa sǫgur)," in *Reallexikon der germanischen Altertumskunde*, III (1978); Peter Hallberg, "Jóns saga helga," in Jakob Benediktsson *et al.*, eds., *Afmælisrit Jóns Helgasonar 30. júní 1969* (1969); Peter Koppenberg, *Hagiographische Studien zu den Biskupa sögur* (1980); Magnús Már Lárusson, "Jóns saga helga," in *Kulturhistorisk leksikon for nordisk middelalder*, VII (1962); Ole Widding, Hans Bekker-Nielsen, and L. K. Shook, C.S.B., "The Lives of the Saints in Old Norse Prose: A Handlist," in *Mediaeval Studies*, 25 (1963), esp. 317–318.

HANS BEKKER-NIELSEN

[See also **Bishops' Sagas; Guðmundr Arason; Jón Ögmundarson, St.**]

JOOS VAN GHENT (van Wassenhove) (active 1460–1475), Flemish painter working in Antwerp (1460–1464) and Ghent (1464–1468/1469), where he executed a large Crucifixion triptych (now in the Church of St. Bavo), about 1467. In 1469 he left Flanders for Italy, where he spent the rest of his life. In 1472 Joos was commissioned to paint the *Communion of the Apostles* altarpiece for the Confraternity of Corpus Christi in Urbino (now in the Church of S. Agatha, Urbino). After 1474 he worked for Duke Federigo da Montefeltro, assisting in the decoration of the Studiolo in the ducal palace of Urbino with twenty-eight bust portraits of illustrious men of antiquity and the Middle Ages (now divided equally between the Ducal Palace at Urbino and the Louvre) and personifications of the Seven Liberal Arts (several now in the National Gallery, London).

BIBLIOGRAPHY

Max J. Friedländer, *Die Altniederländische Malerei*, 14 vols. (1924–1937), III, 74–129; Jacques Lavalleye, *Juste de Gand, Peintre de Frédéric de Montefeltre* (1936); Erwin Panofsky, *Early Netherlandish Painting*, I (1953), 340–342.

JAMES SNYDER

[See also **Flemish Painting**; and picture overleaf.]

JORDAN FANTOSME, a clerk of Winchester and author of an Anglo-Norman chronicle of 2,065 lines (*ca.* 1174–1175) that recounts the border campaign of Henry II against his eldest son, known as the "Young Henry," and William the Lion of Scotland in 1173–1174. Although there is no evidence that Jordan participated in the campaign, his work gives the impression of being an eyewitness account.

BIBLIOGRAPHY

An edition is R. C. Johnston, ed., *Jordan Fantosme's Chronicle* (1981). See also Mary Dominica Legge, *Anglo-Norman Literature and Its Background* (1963), 75–81.

BRIAN MERRILEES

[See also **Anglo-Norman Literature; England: Norman Angevin.**]

JORDAN OF OSNABRÜCK (*d.* after 1283) was connected with the cathedral chapter of Osnabrück

Communion of the Apostles. Altarpiece panel by Joos van Ghent, 1472. © ACL BRUXELLES 1953

from about 1251 to 1283, probably as a canon. He wrote the work for which he is remembered, the *De prerogative romani imperii,* during or soon after the great interregnum, the period between the death of Conrad IV (1254) and the designation of Rudolf, Count of Habsburg, as emperor (1273). His work was completed by Alexander of Roes, probably about 1281.

Jordan believed, as did many other German schol-ars of this period, that the empire was absolutely necessary for the salvation of the Christian world. In his view the authority of the emperor is above that of all other rulers, whatever their titles. Since a Roman emperor could judge St. Peter, his successor can certainly judge and depose the pope. And if the emperor is superior to all other rulers, then no one can depose him.

The most interesting and probably the most influential part of Jordan's treatise is his justification of the electoral basis of the imperial office. Although in practice many emperors had been succeeded by their sons, the assent of the great princes of the empire had always been necessary; this right had hardened into a right of election during the twelfth and thirteenth centuries. Jordan argued that Charlemagne had instituted the election of the emperor by the princes because the rule of Christendom ("regnum ecclesie") was too important to be determined by accidents of heredity. It was all right for a mere kingdom such as France (which once had elected its king) to take its chances with hereditary succession but terribly dangerous for the empire, which had responsibility for all the Christian world. The elective principle would certainly have prevailed in any case; Jordan helped to give it intellectual respectability.

Jordan, and even more Alexander of Roes, his continuator, were suspicious of French claims to independent, if not superior, authority. The French (Franks) were indeed of German descent, but they were not unmixed Germans, as were the real Germans east of the Rhine. The French had the *studium* (primacy in scholarship) but the Germans had the empire. With the renewal of the empire under Rudolf, French claims to full independence, or even superiority, were vain.

BIBLIOGRAPHY

For a text of *De prerogativa* see H. Grundmann and H. Heimpel, eds., *Die Schriften des Alexander von Roes...*, in *Monumenta Germaniae historica: Staatsschriften des späteren Mittelalters*, I.1 (1958), 94–100. See also W. Schraub, *Jordan von Osnabrück und Alexander von Roes* (1910). Carl N. S. Woolf, *Bartolus of Sassoferrato* (1913), gives the fullest exposition of Jordan's views, but is most interested in the last section of the *De prerogativa*, which was not written by Jordan.

JOSEPH R. STRAYER

[See also **Alexander of Roes; Elections, Royal; Germany; Holy Roman Empire; Political Theory, Western European.**]

JORDAN OF QUEDLINBURG (*ca.* 1300–1370/ 1380), not to be confused with Jordan of Saxony, was born at Quedlinburg, Saxony. He was a prominent figure within the order of Augustinian Hermits, a teacher, a renowned preacher, and a widely read author of spiritual and homiletic literature. After studying in Bologna (1317–1319) and Paris (*ca.* 1319–1322), Jordan returned to Germany and taught

in a number of Augustinian monasteries. From at least 1346 to 1351 he was the provincial of the Augustinian Hermits in Thuringia-Saxony, following which he devoted most of his time to his literary endeavors until his death in Vienna (or Vienne, France). Perhaps his most important, and his most mature, work is the *Vitasfratrum*, a historical-ascetical treatise, completed in 1357. Also important are three large collections of sermons: *Opus postillarum, Opus "Jor" sermonum de tempore*, and *Opus "Dan"* or *Sermones de sanctis*, all written after 1357. Fourteen other works are commonly attributed to Jordan, two of which are no longer extant. Especially through the four writings named, he influenced late medieval spirituality to a considerable degree.

BIBLIOGRAPHY

For complete bibliographies of Jordan's writings, see Rudolf Arbesmann and Winfridus Hümpfner, eds., *Jordani de Saxonia Liber vitasfratrum* (1943); Robrecht Lievens, *Jordanus van Quedlinburg in de Nederlanden* (1958), 5–25. See also F. Mathes, "The Poverty Movement and the Augustinian Hermits," in *Analecta Augustiniana*, **31** (1968) and **32** (1969).

G. H. GERRITS

[See also **Augustinian Friars; Preaching and Sermon Literature.**]

JORDANES (Jornandes) was a Goth who served initially as a notarius in the Italian kingdom of Theodoric in the early sixth century. He later converted from Arianism to Catholicism and seems to have become a cleric; some scholars identify him as the contemporary bishop of Jordanes of Croton. About 550 he composed *On the Origin and History of the Goths,* usually called the *Getica,* which summarized the now lost *Gothic History* of Cassiodorus. Shortly thereafter Jordanes wrote *Survey of the Times; or, On The Origin and History of the Roman Race,* usually called the *Romana,* based upon the lost history of the Roman senator Aurelius Memmius Symmachus. Some scholars believe both works were written at Constantinople. Jordanes is the earliest surviving Gothic historian; his works, which include much material available nowhere else, were intended to justify the Gothic dominion over the Romans.

BIBLIOGRAPHY

Texts of the *De origine actibusque Getarum* and the *De summa temporum vel origine actibusque Romanorum* are in *Monumenta Germaniae historica: Auctores antiquissimi,* V, pt. 1 (1882). There is a translation of the *Getica* by Charles C. Mierow: *Jordanes, The Origins and Deeds of the Goths* (1915). Bibliography and commentary are in *Clavis patrum latinorum,* 2nd. ed. (1962), nos. 912–913; Martin von Schanz, Carl Hosius, and Gustav Krüger, *Geschichte der römischen Literatur* ... IV, pt. 2 (1920, repr. 1959), 115–120.

RALPH WHITNEY MATHISEN

[See also **Cassiodorus; Ostrogoths.**]

JORDI DE S. JORDI (*ca.* 1395–*ca.* 1425), Valencian poet who wrote in the Catalan-Provençal language. He served under Alfonso V of Aragon in the latter's campaigns in Sardinia and Corsica (1420); captured in 1423, he was for a short time held prisoner in Naples. A member of Alfonso's court, Jordi himself belonged to an aristocratic family. These biographical facts play an important part in the courtly love poetry that he wrote before his untimely death.

Eighteen of Jordi's poems survive, most of them on the theme of love, and some employed elements from the earlier troubadour tradition, which he improved upon. His work is also reminiscent of Petrarch's. Among his surviving works are the *Stramps* (unrhymed verses, once set to music) and *Presoner,* in which he tells of his imprisonment in Naples.

BIBLIOGRAPHY

An edition of Jordi's poetry is Martí de Riquer, *Jordi de Sant Jordi: Estudio y edición* (1955). Studies include Paul Russell-Gebbet, "Medieval Catalan Literature," in Peter E. Russell, *Spain: A Companion to Spanish Studies* (1976); Arthur Terry, *Catalan Literature* (1972), 38–39.

PERE BOHIGAS

[See also **Catalan Literature; Spanish Literature: Lyric Poetry.**]

JORGE INGLÉS, painter in Castile, mid fifteenth century. His retablo for the chapel of Buitrago, Madrid (1455), is the first painting of certain authorship in Castile to be executed in the Hispano-Flemish style. His name indicates he may have come from England, but there is no documentation for his origin. His paintings show the influence of Rogier van der Weyden, from whom he seems to have derived

his slender, angular figures and light-suffused landscapes.

BIBLIOGRAPHY

José Gudiol Ricart, *Pintura Gotica,* in *Ars Hispaniae,* IX (1952).

MARY GRIZZARD

JOSEPH II, PATRIARCH (*d.* 1439), was patriarch of Constantinople from 1416 to 1439. With a large Byzantine delegation, including Emperor John VIII Palaiologos, he traveled to Ferrara and then Florence to accomplish the reunion of the Eastern and Western churches. At the time of the council he was an octogenarian, and he died (10 June 1439) before the end of the sessions. Of Bulgarian ancestry, but speaking fluent Greek, he was reticent during the initial stages of the debates but seems to' have been convinced by the Latin arguments and ready to sign the document of union. His tomb is in the Church of S. Maria Novella in Florence.

BIBLIOGRAPHY

Joseph Gill, *Personalities of the Council of Florence* (1964), and *The Council of Florence* (1959).

JOHN MEYENDORFF

[See also **Councils, Western; Ferrara-Florence, Council of; John VIII Palaiologos.**]

JOSEPH BEN ABRAHAM AL-BAṢĪR (Yūsuf al-Baṣir) (*d. ca.* 1040), theologian and doctor of Karaite law. His works, composed in Judeo-Arabic and preserved in fragmentary condition, concern the ritual law and theology of the Karaite sect. In both of his theological works—a summary (*Kitāb al-Muḥtawī*) and a later, more developed treatise (*Kitāb al-Manṣūrī*)—he followed closely, but adapted to the needs of his community, the Kalām Muᶜtazilite of the Basra school, discussing such subjects as atomism, God's attributes, and a defense of God's goodness in a world of manifest evil. Al-Baṣīr was inspired particularly by the writings of the qadi ᶜAbd al-Jabbar, his contemporary. In a very literal Hebrew version of his works made shortly after their composition by his student, the Byzantine Karaite Tobias ben Moses of Constantinople, al-Baṣīr's two treatises were to nourish Karaite doctrinal teaching until the end of the sect's creative period at the close of the fifteenth century.

BIBLIOGRAPHY

Zvi Ankori, "Ibn al-Hiti and the Chronology of Joseph al-Basir the Karaite," in *Journal of Jewish Studies,* 8 (1957), and *Karaites in Byzantium* (1959); Georges Vajda, "Les études de philosophie juive du moyen âge depuis la synthèse de Julius Guttmann," in *Hebrew Union College Annual,* 43 (1972), and "Les problèmes des sanctions divines, du repentir et questions connexes selon Yūsuf al-Baṣīr," in *Revue des études juives,* 137 (1978).

GEORGES VAJDA

[See also **Karaites; Judeo-Arabic Literature; Muᶜtazila, al-; Philosophy and Theology, Jewish: In Islam.**]

JOSEPH BEN JUDAH BEN JACOB IBN ᶜAKNIN

JOSEPH BEN JUDAH BEN JACOB IBN ᶜAKNIN (*ca.* 1150–1220), also known as Ibn ᶜAknin, was a Jewish philosopher and poet born in Barcelona of Spanish-Jewish stock. He lived in Fēs, Morocco, much of his life, a forced convert to Islam who hoped eventually to return to Judaism. A friend of Maimonides, he wrote (in Hebrew) a commentary on the mishnaic tractate *Pirkei Avot* (Ethics of the Fathers) and (in Arabic) a philosophic commentary on the *Song of Songs,* an ethical treatise on *The Hygiene of the Soul,* and a large, unpublished compilation of Jewish law.

BIBLIOGRAPHY

Julius Guttmann, *The Philosophy of Judaism,* David W. Silverman, trans. (1964); Abraham S. Halkin, "Classic and Arabic Lore in Ibn Aknin's *Hygiene of the Soul,*" in *Proceedings of the American Academy of Jewish Research,* 14 (1944), "Ibn Aknin's Commentary on the Song of Songs," in *Alexander Marx Jubilee Volume* (1950), "Ibn Aknin— His Intellectual World" (in Hebrew), in *Harry A. Wolfson Jubilee Volume* (1965), and *idem.,* ed., *Ibn Aknin's Commentary on the Song of Songs,* with Hebrew trans. (1964).

ABRAHAM S. HALKIN

[See also **Jews in North Africa; Maimonides, Moses; Philosophy and Theology, Jewish: In Islam.**]

JOSEPH IBN CASPI

JOSEPH IBN CASPI (Joseph ben Abba Mari ibn Kaspi) (1279/1280–1340) was a Jewish philosopher and exegete who was born in Argentière (hence the name, from *Kesef,* "silver"), and lived in southern France and northern Spain, even visiting Egypt. His writings are all in Hebrew and deal with philosophy, theology, biblical exegesis, morals, and anti-Christian polemics. Caspi considered himself a disciple of Moses Maimonides (1135–1204) and wrote commentaries on Maimonides' *Guide of the Perplexed.*

The major influences on Caspi, besides the Jewish theologians Abraham ibn Ezra and Maimonides, were the Islamic philosophers al-Fārābī, Ibn Sīnā (Avicenna), Ibn Rushd (Averroës), and the Neoplatonist al-Baṭalyawsī (1052–1127). His approach to religion was considered radical, and he suffered from the hostility of his more conservative Jewish coreligionists. He died in Valencia.

BIBLIOGRAPHY

Caspi's literary activity has been examined in Barry Mesch, *Studies in Joseph ibn Caspi* (1975). For a general appreciation of Caspi's contributions, see Israel Zinberg, *A History of Jewish Literature,* Bernard Martin, ed. and trans., III (1973), 115–124.

BARRY MESCH

[See also **Fārābī, Al-; Maimonides, Moses; Philosophy and Theology, Jewish: in Islam; Rushd, Ibn; Sīnā, Ibn.**]

JOSEPH IBN SADDIQ

JOSEPH IBN SADDIQ (Joseph Ben Jacob ibn Ẓaddik) (*d.* 1149), Jewish poet and theologian active in Córdoba, where he died. His treatise in Judeo-Arabic—only a Hebrew version has been preserved— owes its title, *Sefer ha-Olam ha-Qatan* (Book of the microcosm), to the amount of space in the text devoted to the theme of the parallelism between the "little world" or microcosm (man) and the vast universe as described in Greek philosophy. This parallelism leads man to an introspection given final form by the quest for spiritual perfection culminating in bliss.

In its detail the doctrine as stated by Saddiq reveals the combined influences of Aristotelian psychology; the Neoplatonic metaphysics of Isaac Israel and Solomon ben Judah ibn Gabirol; the rational organization of the dogma of divine unity formulated by Baḥya ibn Paqūdā, inspired by Saadiah Gaon (Saᶜadya ben Joseph) and Dāwūd al-Muqammiṣ; and, with certain reservations, the defense of God's goodness found in kalam theodicy. The whole of Saddiq's thought is crowned by a spiritualized eschatology.

BIBLIOGRAPHY
Alexander Altmann, "Ẓaddik, Joseph ben Jacob ibn," in *Encyclopaedia judaica*, XVI (1971); Georges Vajda, "Les études de philosophie juive du moyen âge depuis la synthèse de Julius Guttmann," in *Hebrew Union College Annual*, 43 (1972); Harry A. Wolfson, "Joseph ibn Ṣaddiḳ on Divine Attributes," in *Jewish Quarterly Review*, 55 (1965).

GEORGES VAJDA

[See also **Gaonic Period; Muqammiṣ, Dāwūd al-; Philosophy and Theology, Jewish: In Islam; Saadiah Gaon; Schools, Jewish.**]

JOSHUA ROLL. The Joshua Roll is a unique Byzantine example of a horizontal *rotulus* (now 10.5 meters long and about 0.3 meter high) illustrating scenes from the Old Testament story of Joshua in a continuous sequence of drawings. Below the drawings an excerpted Septuagint text summarizes the events. Although the roll is a tenth-century creation, the drawings go back to earlier depictions of this story. The *rotulus* may have celebrated the exploits of an emperor in the guise of an Old Testament hero. Candidates are Nikephoros II Phokas and especially John I Tzimiskes, whose campaigns were directed toward the reconquest of the Holy Land, as were those of Joshua.

BIBLIOGRAPHY
Theodor Birt, *Die Buchrolle in der Kunst* (1907); *Josua-Rolle: Vollständige Faksimile-Ausgabe im Originalformat der Codex Vat. Pal. Graeco 431 der Biblioteca Apst. Vaticana* (1983); Hans Lietzmann, "Zur datierung der Josuarolle," in *Mittelalterliche Handschriften. . . . Festgabe zum

60. Geburtstag von Hermann Degering . . . (1926); *Rotulo (ill.) di Giosuè*, in Codice Vaticano Palatino greco 431, 2 vols. (1905), with 15 color plates; Meyer Schapiro, "The Place of the Joshua Roll in Byzantine History," in *Gazette des beaux-arts*, 6th ser., 35 (1949); Kurt Weitzmann, *The Joshua Roll, a Work of the Macedonian Renaissance* (1948).

IOLI KALAVREZOU-MAXEINER

[See also **Manuscript Illumination: Byzantine and Islamic.**]

JOSHUA THE STYLITE (*fl.* late fifth–early sixth centuries) was one of the earliest and best of the Syrian historians. He seems to have been a Monophysite. Knowledge of his chronicle, which is lost, is possible only because an abridged version of it was incorporated later in the work of Dionysius of Tel-Mahré. Joshua's chronicle, written in Syriac and probably composed in Edessa at the beginning of the sixth century, begins in 395–396 and ends in 506. It details the war between the Persian and Byzantine empires and is dedicated to an abbot named Sergios. There are excellent descriptions of the siege warfare of the time and of weapons. Joshua tells of the Goths, who formed part of the Byzantine armies, and of the Huns; he also includes material on daily life: harvests, taxation, and prices of food.

BIBLIOGRAPHY
Bernard Lewis and Peter M. Holt, eds., *Historians of the Middle East* (1962); Charles C. Torrey, "Notes on the

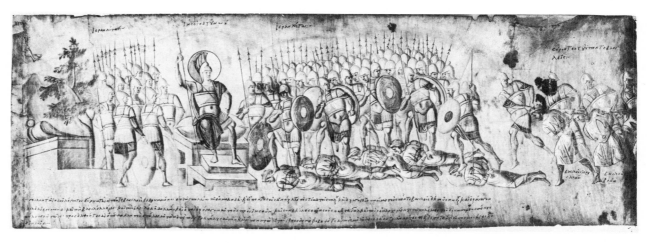

Triumph of Joshua. From the Joshua Roll, 10th century. VATICAN LIBRARY, MS PALAT GR. 431

JOSTICE ET PLET, LIVRE DE

'Chronicle of Joshua the Stylite,'" in *Hebrew Union College Annual*, **23**, pt. 1 (1950–1951).

LINDA C. ROSE

[See also **Dionysius of Tel-Mahré; Historiography, Byzantine.**]

JOSTICE ET PLET, LIVRE DE. See **Livres de Jostice et de Plet.**

JOURNAL, a measure of area in France that originally referred to the amount of land a man with a team of oxen could work in one day. It varied in size depending on the terrain, the nature of the cultivation, the quality of the soil, and the like. Since the *journal* was used almost everywhere in France (only the *arpent* was more prevalent), each region tended to adopt its own local standard during the sixteenth and seventeenth centuries.

Most of these *journals* were in the range of twenty to thirty ares, but some were as small as one to two ares and some as large as fifty-five to sixty ares. There never was a Parisian standard promulgated for this unit. In medieval French manuscripts such variant spellings as *jorna, jornaul, jorneil, jornel, jornel, journau, journelle, journiau,* and *jornault* were common. Such Middle French forms as *journel* and *jornaul* were derived from the Latin *diurnalem* of the day.

RONALD EDWARD ZUPKO

[See also **Arpent; Weights and Measures, Western European.**]

JOUSTING. See **Games and Pastimes.**

JOY, WILLIAM (*fl.* mid fourteenth century). As master mason at Wells Cathedral from 1329 until the mid 1340's Joy designed and constructed the new choir and the remarkable scissorlike strainer arches of the crossing. Perhaps trained near Bristol, he was also master mason at Exeter Cathedral (*ca.* 1342–1352), where he probably oversaw construction of the facade, and built other churches, such as that at Ottery St. Mary, Devon.

JUAN AND SIMÓN DE COLONIA

BIBLIOGRAPHY

Jean Bony, *The English Decorated Style* (1979), 51, 86–87 (notes 22, 26); John H. Harvey, *English Medieval Architects* (1954), 151; Robert Mark, "The Inverted Arches of Wells Cathedral: A Technical Interpretation," in *The Friends of Wells Report for 1974*, 12–17; Geoffrey Webb, *Architecture in Britain: The Middle Ages*, 2nd ed. (1965).

STEPHEN GARDNER

JUAN AND SIMÓN DE COLONIA. Juan de Colonia (Hans of Cologne, *fl. ca.* 1442–1481), was an architect and sculptor of German origin who introduced the Flemish style into the architecture of Burgos. After producing exotic, pointed steeples for the cathedral of Burgos, he became its master of works in 1454. Before his death in 1481, he completed the plans for the Carthusian monastery of Miraflores in Burgos and may also have designed the Chapel of the Visitation in the cathedral.

Simón de Colonia (*fl. ca.* 1482–1511), the eldest son of Juan, was the most important Burgos architect of the second half of the fifteenth century. He practiced the Isabelline style, employing aspects of the Flemish style practiced by his father. His masterpiece (1482–1498) in Burgos Cathedral is the burial chapel of the constable of Castile, Pedro Fernández de Velasco. Directly inspired by the Flamboyant Gothic burial chapel (1430 [monument, 1489]) of Álvaro de Luna in Toledo Cathedral, the Burgos chapel is crowned by an unusual vault. The dome, bearing an eight-pointed star with open tracery, helped launch the Burgos school of architecture, which continued into the sixteenth century.

Between 1486 and 1499, Simón de Colonia also completed the lower part of the rich Isabelline facade of the church of the monastery of S. Pablo in Valladolid. As master of works of Seville Cathedral between 1497 and 1502, he modeled its lantern on the steeples designed by his father at Burgos Cathedral.

BIBLIOGRAPHY

José Camón Aznar, *La arquitectura plateresca* (1945); Fernando Chueca Goitia, "Arquitectura del siglo XVI," in *Ars Hispaniae*, XI (1953); Theodor Müller, *Sculpture in the Netherlands, Germany, France, and Spain: 1400–1500* (1966); Agostín D. Sanpere and Juan A. de Lasarte, "La escultura hispano-flamanca. Burgos: Los Colonia," in *Ars Hispaniae*, VIII, 355–365; Leopoldo Torres Balbas, "Arquitectura gótica," in *Ars Hispaniae*, VII (1952).

MARY GRIZZARD

Arms of Doña Mencia de Mendoza, supported by wild women. Carving by Simón de Colonia from chapel of the constable, Burgos Cathedral, 1482–1498. PHOTO: WIM SWAAN

154

The Annunciation. Tempera panels by Juan de Burgos, *ca.* 1350. COURTESY OF THE FOGG ART MUSEUM, HAR-VARD UNIVERSITY. GIFT OF META AND PAUL J. SACHS

JUAN DE BURGOS (*fl.* mid fifteenth century), an International Gothic artist active in Burgos, where the International Gothic movement lasted through the third quarter of the fifteenth century—longer than elsewhere in Spain. Judging from his only known work, the signed *Annunciation* panels (*ca.* 1450, now in the Fogg Museum, Cambridge, Mass.), his style is closely related to that of Nicolás Francés of León (*fl. ca.* 1424–1468), which has similar facial types and massive forms.

BIBLIOGRAPHY
"Juan de Burgos," in Fogg Art Museum, Harvard University, *Collection of Medieval and Renaissance Paintings,* II (1919), 246–248.

MARY GRIZZARD

JUAN DE FLANDES (*fl. ca.* 1496–1519) was an artist whose activity centered in Palencia, in northern Spain. He may have come from Flanders or been trained there, for he shows the influence of Hans Memling and Gerard David. In Spain he had several ecclesiastical employers as well as the patronage of Queen Isabella I. Among his works are a portrait of the queen (*ca.* 1500), of which there are many copies, and the *Reina católica* altarpiece (*ca.* 1495), composed of small panels (between twenty-seven and forty-six of them) portraying the life of Mary. These panels are scattered in many public and private collections.

BIBLIOGRAPHY
E. Bermejo, *Juan de Flandes* (1962), in Spanish; C. Eisler, "Juan de Flandes's St. Michael and St. Francis," in *Bul-*

Christ's descent into Limbo. Panel painting from the *Reina católica altarpiece* by Juan de Flandes, *ca.* 1495. COURTESY OF PALACIO REAL, MADRID

letin of the Metropolitan Museum of Art, n.s. **18** (1959–1960); F. J. Sánchez Cantón, "El retablo de la reina católica," in *Archivo español de arte y arqueologia*, **6** (1930) and **7** (1931).

MARY GRIZZARD

JUAN MANUEL. See **Manuel, Don Juan.**

JUAN REXACH. See **Rexach, Juan.**

JUBE. See **Screen.**

JUBILEE. Derived from the Hebrew word *yōbēl*, which means "ram" or "ram's horn," the Old Testament jubilee was a year of atonement proclaimed after every forty-nine years for restitution of social injustices and announced "on the tenth day of the seventh month . . . throughout the land" by the blowing of a ram's horn (Leviticus 25:8–9). St. Jerome Latinized the Hebrew word to *iubilaeus* in allusion to the Latin verb *iubilare* (to shout). True to its Old Testament derivation, the term meant a fifty-year cycle, especially since the twelfth century. From that time on, it stood for regularly recurring feasts in honor of a saint: perhaps by 1126 at Santiago de Compostela (fifty years after the beginning of the cathedral and shrine of St. James) and certainly in 1220 at Canterbury (fifty years after St. Thomas Becket's death). From 1300 it also served to designate the Holy Year, first in Rome and then in other pilgrim centers.

BIBLIOGRAPHY

Raymonde Foreville, *Le jubilé de St. Thomas Becket du XIII⁰ au XV⁰ siècle (1220–1470)* (1958), and "L'idée du jubilé chez les théologiens et les canonistes (XII⁰–XIII⁰ siècles) avant l'institution du jubilé romain (1300)," in *Revue d'histoire ecclésiastique*, **56** (1961); Herbert Grundmann, "Jubel," in *Festschrift für Jost Trier* (1954); G. Lambert, "Jubilé hébreu et jubilé chrétien," in *Nouvelle revue théologique*, **72** (1950); Nicolaus Paulus, *Geschichte des Ablasses im Mittelalter*, II and III (1922–1923); Bernhard Schimmelpfennig, "Die Anfänge des Heiligen Jahres von Santiago de Compostela im Mittelalter," in *Journal of Medieval History*, **4** (1978).

BERNHARD SCHIMMELPFENNIG

[See also **Holy Year; Pilgrimage, Western European; Santiago de Compostela.**]

JUBILUS. In the Gregorian Alleluia chants, the jubilus is the melisma to which the final syllable of the word "allelluia" is set. The construction of the jubilus sections ranges from the somewhat improvisatory style of melodies directed toward specific high points and cadences, to more tightly controlled manipulations of material involving various patterns of repetition and producing formal plans such as *a b a* and *a a b*. The music of the jubilus is often reused in the alleluia verse section, most notably at the end (but also internally). By the ninth century the widespread practice of adding text to the jubilus had become an important factor in the development of the sequence.

BIBLIOGRAPHY

Willi Apel, *Gregorian Chant* (1958); Richard L. Crocker, *The Early Medieval Sequence* (1977); Karlheinz Schlager, "Jubilus," in *The New Grove Dictionary of Music and Musicians,* IX (1980).

ARTHUR LEVINE

[See also **Gregorian Chant.**]

JUDAH BEN SAMUEL HE-HASID (The Pietist)

(*ca.* 1149–1217) was a descendant of the Qalonimide (Kalonymus) family from Italy and of Rabbi Abun of Le Mans. His life is not well documented, being mediated mainly through legends first written down in fifteenth- and sixteenth-century Hebrew and Yiddish hagiographic cycles derived from earlier oral traditions. He was born in Speyer and studied with his father and other authorities there. About 1195 he moved to Regensburg, where he established a synagogue later associated with his name.

Of Rabbi Judah's theological writings, the most significant survives only in quotations. *Sefer ha-Kavod* (Book of divine glory) deals with the problem of anthropomorphism. Other works, extant in manuscript, are a commentary to the liturgy in which the number of letters of the prayers is numerologically associated with esoteric meanings; a truncated manuscript of over 300 pages, which deals with angels, the influence of the stars, and the permutations of the letters of God's names; and mystical poems on the divine unity. His son Moses Saltman compiled Judah's Bible commentary in the form of *reportationes.*

Judah ben Samuel's major achievement in pietism is *Sefer Ḥasidim* (Book of the pietists), which is a speculum of late-twelfth- and early-thirteenth-century Germany and Jewish society there, and is filled with exempla. The first sixteen paragraphs of this work were written by Judah's father, Samuel the Pietist. Judah's special innovation is his description of a sectarian circle of pietists who follow charismatic "sages" (hakamim) and confess their sins to them. In his program for an ideal Jewish society, the pietists are to serve God's complete will by avoiding unnecessary contact with nonpietist Jews. Many of the ideas that Judah advocated were preserved by his relative and disciple, Rabbi Eleazar ben Judah of Worms, who eliminated Judah's sectarianism and proposed instead a personalist form of pietism di-

rected at ameliorating the spiritual life of individual Jews, not at designing a sectarian ideal community.

BIBLIOGRAPHY

The English translation is Judah ben Samuel, *Medieval Jewish Mysticism: Book of the Pious,* Sholom Alchanan Singer, trans. (1971).

Studies include Avigdor (Victor) Aptowitzer, *Mavo le-Sefer Rabiyah* (Introductio ad Sefer Rabiah) (1938), 343–350; Joseph Dan, *Torat ha-sod shel ḥasidut Ashkenaz* (The esoteric theology of Ashkenazi Hasidism) (1968); Jacob Freimann, "Mavo" (Introduction) to Judah ben Samuel, *Sefer Ḥasidim,* Jehuda Wistinetzki, ed., 2nd ed. (1924), 1–9; *Germania judaica,* I (1963), 293–294; *The Ma'aseh Book,* Moses Gaster, trans. (1934), II, 336–395; Ivan G. Marcus, *Piety and Society: The Jewish Pietists of Medieval Germany* (1981).

IVAN G. MARCUS

[See also **Eleazar ben Judah of Worms; Hasidei Ashkenaz; Jews in Europe; Philosophy and Theology, Jewish.**]

JUDAH HALEVI

(*ca.* 1075–1141), Hebrew poet and philosopher, was born into comfortable and cultivated surroundings at either Toledo or Tudela, in Muslim Spain. He showed an early talent for poetry that brought him into contact with Moses ibn Ezra and other leading Hebrew poets of Andalusia. Following the Almoravid conquest of 1090–1094, Judah traveled widely through the northern, Christian part of the peninsula, becoming familiar with many poets, men of affairs, and statesmen. In Toledo he practiced medicine at the court, but the murder of his Jewish patron in 1108 caused him to resume his travels, which took him through Andalusia and the Maghrib. Although personally successful in all his endeavors, Judah was disappointed with the political regimes of his day and finally decided to emigrate to Palestine. He died en route to the Holy Land, in Alexandria (though legend has him killed upon arriving at his destination).

About 800 of Judah's Hebrew poems are extant, and they cover the entire range of medieval Hebrew poetry, both secular and religious. The influence of Arabic poetry is found in the structure and style of many of his poems, as well as in their content. Typical of the period are his lyrical love and drinking poems, as well as his eulogies and laments. Judah's poetic gifts often burst through the clichés of genre, attesting to a passion for love and friendship that infused his entire life. It is in his national poetry, however, that Judah found his own voice, thereby earning lasting esteem and eminence. His 350 religious poems (piyyutim) composed for the Jewish festivals blend past with present, and national destiny with the personal fortunes of the poet. Particularly noteworthy are his "Songs of Zion," some thirty-five original poems that express deep attachment to the land of Israel, symbol for Judah of his people's promise and fulfillment.

Judah's literary skill served him well in his philosophical magnum opus, *The Book of Argument and Proof in Defense of the Despised Faith,* commonly known as *Sefer ha-Kuzari.* Kuzari is the name given to the king of the Khazars, a Turkic people living mostly along the Caspian Sea, some of whom converted to Judaism in the eighth century. Judah's book, written between 1120 and 1140 in Judeo-Arabic, is a fictional and often artfully contrived account, in dialogue form, of the reason for this conversion, an act that is viewed as recognition of the superiority of Rabbinic Judaism to Islam, Christianity, and Karaite Judaism.

Essentially, the work is a sustained critique, partially on philosophical grounds, of philosophy itself, in the amalgam of Neoplatonist Aristotelianism represented, for Judah, by Ibn Sīnā. Influenced strongly by the Muslim theologian al-Ghazālī, Judah finds the philosophers vulnerable in their basic physical and metaphysical arguments for an independent yet ever-present set of four elements, and for individually immortal souls (V, 14). Consciously contrary to philosophical convention, he insists that history and commonly held beliefs offer demonstrative proof for the assertions of traditional Judaism. This argument is buttressed by theories of the natural superiority of the people and land of Israel, a status that, for Judah, ensures their survival but does not render them immune from a severe proto-Zionist critique. Zionist too is the conclusion of the book, in which Judah's spokesman sets off for the Holy Land.

BIBLIOGRAPHY

The Judeo-Arabic original and a twelfth-century Hebrew translation are in *Das Buch al-Chazarī des Abū-l-Ḥasan Jehuda Hallewi, in arabischen Urtext sowie in der hebräischen Übersetzung des Jehuda Ibn Tibbon,* Hartwig Hirschfeld, ed. (1887). The Judeo-Arabic has been reedited as *Kitāb al-radd wa-'l-dalīl fī 'l-din al-dhalīl* (The book of refutation and proof on the despised faith), David H. Baneth and Haggdi Ben-Shammai, eds. (1977). There is also a new Hebrew translation, *The Kosari of Yehuda Halevi,* Judah Kaufman, trans. (1972). Hartwig Hirschfeld's 1906

translation, *Judah Hallevi's Kitāb al Khazari,* remains the only complete translation of this work in English, but there is an abridged translation by Isaac Heinemann, *Kuzari: The Book of Proof and Argument* (1947), repr. in *Three Jewish Philosophers* (1960, 1974). For English translations of Halevi's poetry see *Selected Poems of Jehudah Halevi,* Nina Ruth Salaman, trans., Heinrich Brody, ed. (1973).

See also, in Hebrew, Yoḥanan Silman, "God and Matter in the Light of the Hierarchic Relationships in the Kuzari" (Ph.D. diss., Hebrew University, Jerusalem, 1973), and, in English, Herbert Davidson, "The Active Intellect in the *Cuzari* and Hallevi's Theory of Causality," in *Revue des études juives,* 131 (1972).

ALFRED L. IVRY

[See also **Hebrew Poetry; Jews in Christian Spain; Jews in Muslim Spain; Judeo-Arabic Literature; Khazars, Jewish; Philosophy and Theology, Jewish.**]

JUDAISM is the religion, thought, and way of life of the Jews. The term developed in Hellenistic Jewish circles (Greek: *ioudaismos;* see 2 Macc. 2:21). It was adopted by Christians to refer to the Jewish faith (Gal. 1:13ff) as a parallel and in contradistinction to Christianity (Greek: *christianismos*). There is no precise term for Judaism in medieval Jewish usage. The Hebrew word *torah* (teaching), which has other significant meanings, is the word that is most often used to express the notion of the entire corpus of Jewish teaching, while the word *Israel* (Hebrew: *Yisrā'ēl*) is the principal term for the Jewish people.

EARLY RABBINIC JUDAISM

Already in later antiquity the process that would transform ancient Israelite religion into Judaism was well under way. The synagogue (Hebrew: *bēt keneset;* Greek: *synagōgē,* place of assembly) had come into being sometime in the sixth century B.C. during the Babylonian exile. The central importance of the Torah, or Pentateuch, as the core of Jewish Scripture was firmly established under Ezra and Nehemiah in the fifth century B.C. The Pharisaic approach to living as an unceasing series of consecrated acts, which fused religion and daily life into an integrated whole, had won the day in Palestine and in the neighboring centers of Jewish population after the destruction of the Second Temple in A.D. 70. Worship through prayer totally replaced the defunct sacrificial cult. Indeed, the very word for the sacrificial service (*avodah*) was now applied to prayer service. The Hebrew Bible was canonized by the rabbinical council at Jabneh (Jamnia) at the end of the first century and its consonantal text was established. The interpretation of sacred writ by midrash, or homiletic exegesis, became common as a rich midrashic literature began to develop. It was believed (on the basis of such passages as Exod. 34:27) that the great mass of oral tradition had been given to Moses along with the written Torah at Sinai and passed down orally from generation to generation. It was refined, systematized, and set down in the Mishnah (Instruction) by the Palestinian patriarch Rabbi Judah ha-Nasi around the year 200. This corpus was further elaborated and discussed in the Gemara (Completion) of the Palestinian and Babylonian Talmuds (Learning), the former redacted in the middle of the fourth century, the later in the early part of the fifth and completed in the sixth century.

It was during the Middle Ages, however, that Judaism—its practice, institutions, and thought—crystalized and developed its distinctive form. Any survey of this process must be preceded by a summary of some of the basic beliefs and practices of Rabbinic Judaism, that is, the talmudic and midrashic foundation upon which medieval Judaism was built.

The faith of Rabbinic Judaism. The religious faith that is expounded by the rabbis in the Talmud and in the ancillary midrashic literature is firmly rooted in the Hebrew Bible. This faith rests upon two fundamental doctrines: the belief in the One God of the universe, and the divine selection of the Jewish people (Israel) as the bearers of this belief and its witness before all mankind. These concepts are implicit in the scriptural profession of faith known as the *Shema,* which is recited in the morning and evening prayer services and upon lying down to sleep: "Hear O Israel, the Lord is our God, the Lord is One" (Deut. 6:4). According to one view expressed in the Babylonian Talmud (BT Tractate *Makkot* 23b–24a), the 613 commandments of Judaism can be reduced to the single essential principle of faith in God as enunciated by the prophet Habakkuk: "The righteous shall live by his faith" (Hab. 2:4).

God in Rabbinic Judaism is the almighty creator of the world, and one of his common epithets is *Ribbono shel Olam* (Master of the universe). Even as he is the world's master, he provides and sustains it. Like the God of the Bible, he is conceived of as a king, and his divine rule is referred to as the Kingdom of Heaven. Though a king, God is not a tyrant (ᶜ*Avoda Zara* 3a), and righteousness (Hebrew: *ẓedakah*) is one of his two primary attributes. He is also conceived of in Jewish piety as a father, and his

other primary attribute is loving-kindness (Hebrew: *ḥesed*). The combined aspects of God as ruler and parent are expressed in the important prayer that begins "Our Father, Our King," a dictum from the so-called Ethics of the Fathers.

Although there is divine providence, man is given free will in accordance with the statement of the Palestinian tanna Rabbi Akiva (*ca.* 50–135) "All is foreseen, but freedom of choice is given; and the world is judged with goodness, and all is in accordance with the works" (Mishnah Tractate *Avot* 3:15). Another Talmudic dictum says: "Everying is in the hands of Heaven, except the fear of Heaven" (BT Tractate *Berakhot* 33b).

The God of Rabbinic Judaism is both transcendent and intimate, at one and the same time above the world and yet pervading it. Thus he is referred to by metonomy as *Shamayim* (Heaven) and also as *Shekhinah* (Omnipresence or Divine presence). He is also *Ha-kadosh barukh Hu* (The Holy One, blessed be He) and *Ha-Makom* (The place, again in the sense of omnipresence). The tetragrammaton (YHWH), now read as Adonai (The Lord), and the word God (Hebrew: Elohim) are now reserved primarily for liturgy.

The raison d'être of Judaism rests upon the belief that God not only revealed himself to humanity, but has made known his will for the conduct of life. For all people he has revealed the basic Noachian code with its seven commandments, and for his chosen people he has revealed the Torah, both written and oral. Although the Torah exists for all mankind, it is Israel's acceptance of it that has made them God's "special treasure" (Exod. 19:5) and "a light unto the nations" (Isa. 42:6). Indeed, had they not accepted it, they would not differ from the pagan nations (Num. Rabbah 14:10 and Exod. Rabbah 47:3). In carrying out God's will, the rabbis taught, Jews were working as partners with the Deity in fulfilling the divine plan and helping to usher in the rule of righteousness on earth.

Despite the disappointments encountered by Jewish messianism in Christianity and other sectarian movements of lesser consequence, and despite the disaster brought on by the messianic expectations of the Bar Kokhba rebellion (132–135), Rabbinic Judaism never abandoned its faith that the kingdom of righteousness would eventually be ushered in by the Messiah, a great leader and teacher of the House of David. However, it was incumbent upon Jews to wait for that time. Until then, they must pray for the welfare of their secular rulers (Mishnah Tractate

Avot 3:2). Rabbinic Judaism never lost faith that the dispersed people of Israel would be restored to their land, their subjection would be ended, and the Temple would be reestablished.

Alongside the messianic ideal based upon the biblical prophets, Rabbinic Judaism held eschatological beliefs unlike those of the ancient Israelites. These beliefs were influenced in part by Zoroastrianism, with which the Jews had first come into contact during the Babylonian exile.

According to rabbinic belief, the righteous will be rewarded in paradise (Hebrew: *Gan Eden*), while the wicked will be punished in hell (Hebrew: *Gehinnom*). The function of the latter, however, is considered mainly purgatorial. Most sinners will be punished for only twelve months in the flames (*Eduyyot* 10).

The practice of Rabbinic Judaism. As noted above, prayer replaced sacrifice in Rabbinic Judaism. Prayer was considered by the rabbis to be the sacrificial service of the heart (BT Tractate *Ta^canit* 2a, commenting on Deut. 11:13). Where the Temple had had two daily services (morning and afternoon) for weekdays, the synagogue had three with the addition of an evening service. Following the Temple custom, an additional service was performed after the morning service on Sabbaths and festivals. The holiday cycle was that of the Bible with the addition of the festivals of the Second Temple period, Purim and Hanukkah.

The core of each service was the so-called Eighteen Benedictions (Hebrew: *Shemoneh Esreh,* also known as Amidah) redacted by the Palestinian patriarch Rabban Gamaliel at the end of the first century. However, the texts of prayers were not set down in writing for approximately six hundred years because of the disapproval of the rabbis of the talmudic period. In addition to the obligatory prayers, the service was adorned with liturgical compositions known as piyyutim (sing., piyyut, from Greek: *poiētēs*). The authors of the piyyutim remained anonymous until the sixth century. However, beginning with the Palestinian payyetan Yose ben Yose, many of these poets became known by name, and a very rich liturgical and devotional poetic literature developed throughout the Middle Ages.

Although formal prayers could be recited by individuals in private, the rabbis emphasized the superiority of communal prayer (BT Tractate *Berakhot* 8a). The quorum for a congregation was established as ten adult males (thirteen being the age of religious majority). The stress placed upon public prayer was an important element in preserving the strong communal character of medieval Jewish life.

In addition to the formal prayer services, Rabbinic Judaism developed a detailed system of ritual blessings to be recited throughout the day when awakening, washing, eating, drinking, and going to sleep. Special benedictions were prescribed for beholding natural phenomena such as a rainbow, for hearing good tidings, for receiving bad news, or for completing a lesson of study. There were appropriate blessings for occasions throughout the life cycle (circumcision, marriage, and others) and for such occasions as coming into the presence of a temporal monarch or a sage. An entire tractate of the Talmud is devoted to the subject of blessings (*Berakhot*). The rationale behind the elaborate system was to make the Jew continually aware of the divine presence.

Despite the tremendous value placed upon prayer in Rabbinic Judaism (even God prays, according to the Talmud; namely that his mercy should overrule his judgment), even greater value was placed upon the study of Torah, both written and oral. The rabbinic ideal was the study of Torah for its own sake (Hebrew: *Torah li-Shemah,* Mishnah Tractate *Avot* 6:1). Study was also deemed important because it led to the practice of religion (BT Tractate *Kiddushin* 40b). In fact, some rabbis maintained that a boor could not truly be pious (Mishnah Tractate *Avot* 2:5).

Because of the primacy accorded to study in Jewish life, education was an essential part of Jewish observance in the Rabbinic period and throughout the Middle Ages. The custom of regular Torah readings on Mondays, Thursdays, Sabbaths, and holidays was already part of the synagogue ritual by the late second century. Preaching in the synagogue had been a common practice since Second Temple times, and from the Rabbinic period on sermons were delivered whenever possible on Sabbaths, festivals, and fasts. People came in droves to hear accomplished preachers (PT Tractate *Horayot* 3:7, 48b).

THE SPREAD OF RABBINICAL JUDAISM

At the dawn of the Middle Ages the largest community by far of world Jewry lived in the Mesopotamian province of the Sasanian Persian Empire, which was called by the Jews Babylonia. Babylonia was the creative center of Judaism from the third to the eleventh century. Here the Babylonian Talmud, which in later generations would spread throughout the Jewish world as the constitutional framework for normative Judaism, was taught and interpreted in the great academies known as yeshivas. In late antiquity there had been several of these schools in Babylonia. However, by the beginning of the Middle Ages two had survived, one at Sura on the southern end of the Euphrates and the other at Pumbedita further north along the same river. There was also a third academy outside of Mesopotamia, the venerable Tiberian yeshiva in Palestine. The Babylonian academies were centers of religious authority for Jews in the Sasanian Empire. The Palestinian academy was the most authoritative institution for Jews in the Byzantine Empire.

At the end of the sixth century the heads of the Babylonian academies took on the title of *Rosh yeshivat ge'on Ya^c akov* (The head of the academy of the pride of Jacob), which later generations contracted to gaon (pl., geonim). It is not known when the heads of the Palestinian academy took on the gaonic title, for little is known about the school in Palestine prior to the tenth century.

The Muslim conquests of the seventh and eighth centuries united the majority of world Jewry within a single state that extended from Spain and North Africa in the west to central Asia and the borders of India in the east. In the second half of the eighth century, the geonim of Babylon—which was now the Arab province of Iraq and the political, cultural, and economic center of the caliphate—began to emerge as the leading religious authorities of world Jewry. The geonim were the great propagators and expounders of the Babylonian Talmud, which they sought to make into the constitutional framework for the entire Jewish community. They based their claims to legitimacy and preeminent leadership on the contention that they were the sole possessors of the living and authoritative rabbinic tradition that went back ultimately to Moses at Sinai. They exerted a great educational influence over the masses in Babylonia through public teaching sessions, known as *kallot,* which were held twice a year during the months of Adar (February–March) and Elul (August–September). Those who could studied at the academies during the rest of the year as well. As freedom of movement within the Islamic world increased in the second half of the eighth century, merchants who were alumni of the academies helped to spread the prestige and influence of those institutions abroad. They sometimes acted as local representatives of the gaonic academies in the far-flung cities of the caliphate where they settled.

The Jewish communities of the Diaspora sent queries (Hebrew: *she'elot*) on law, ritual, and textual exegesis to the academies. These were accompanied by contributions that, the geonim emphasized, had a merit comparable to the annual shekel paid to the Temple. The geonim answered the queries with responsa (Hebrew: *teshuvot*), authoritative legal opinions. Their decisions frequently bore the admonition "This is the halakhah (religious law) and there is no moving from it." For most Jews the authority of geonim was supreme because it was the interpretation of divine law and there could be no appeal. For future reference, gaonic responsa were frequently copied and collected in the Jewish communities through which they passed.

The Palestinian academy differed from the Babylonian on various points of law and ritual (for example, in the Palestinian rite the Torah was read in the synagogue in a triennial cycle, whereas in the Babylonian rite the reading took only one year). Nevertheless, the different academies recognized each other's orthodoxy. The Palestinian academy was increasingly overshadowed by its sister institutions in Babylonia, and by the twelfth century the Babylonian form of Rabbinic Judaism had become the dominant rite—with local variations—worldwide. The earliest prayerbooks, which led to greater standardization of the liturgy, were issued by the Babylonian academies. The first such prayerbook was the *Seder* (Order) of Rabbi Amram Gaon, which was sent to the Jews of Spain at their request around 860. The *Seder Rav Amram* included all of the regular prayers in accordance with the annual cycle for weekdays, Sabbaths and festivals, new moons, fasts, and the post-biblical holidays of Hanukkah and Purim. Each section was preceded by the pertinent laws (halakhot). At the end of the prayer book were the special blessings and prayers for use in daily life (such as grace after meals) and events in the life cycle (circumcision, marriage, burial, and others). Later prayerbooks, such as the Ashkenazic *Maḥzor Vitry* of the late-eleventh-century French rabbi Simḥah ben Samuel, made considerable use of the *Seder Rav Amram.*

Babylonian Rabbinic Judaism prevailed even though the gaonic academies themselves declined in the eleventh century and were gradually supplanted by independent centers of Jewish creativity in North Africa, Spain, Italy, Provence, northern France, and the Rhineland as the Jewish world became increasingly decentralized.

The growth of new centers was an organic process that evolved with the spread of the Babylonian Talmud and talmudic scholarship and was in complete harmony with the rabbinic ideal of study as a supreme virtue. New schools of higher learning, which were also called yeshivas, were established to meet local needs and not as rivals to the gaonic academies. The special status of the latter was marked by the prayer for their welfare and the welfare of their scholars, which remained in the liturgy even after they had disappeared.

One of the earliest centers outside of Babylonia was the city of Al-Qayrawān in Ifrīqiya (Tunisia). Here a yeshiva was founded in the late tenth century by a Persian scholar, Rabbi Jacob ben Nissim Ibn Shahin (d. 1006/1007). His son and successor Rabbi Nissim ben Jacob (d. 1062) wrote an important commentary on the Talmud in Arabic, entitled *Miftāḥ Maghāliq al-Talmūd* (The key to the locks of the Talmud). A second yeshiva was opened in Al-Qayrawān in the eleventh century by the Italian rabbi Ḥushiʾel ben Elhanan. Italy had been within the orbit of the Tiberian academy, and Ḥushiʾel introduced the use of the Palestinian Talmud as an ancillary tool for the study of halakah alongside the more complete Babylonian Talmud. Ḥushiʾel's son and successor, Rabbi Hananel (d. 1057), became one of the most renowned Jewish scholars of the Middle Ages and was often referred to by the acronym RaḤ. He wrote one of the first complete commentaries to the entire Babylonian Talmud, a work that enjoyed wide circulation throughout Europe during the Middle Ages, but has survived only in part down to the present.

Despite their own high level of scholarship, the Jews of Al-Qayrawān maintained close ties with the Babylonian academies well into the eleventh century. Other communities, however, made the break more sharply. The Jewish community of Muslim Spain, for example, gave up all dependence upon the gaonic authorities after 972, when the Italian scholar Rabbi Moses ben Ḥanokh established his own school in Córdoba under the patronage of the Jewish courtier Ḥisday ibn Shaprut. As *rav rosh* (chief scholar) of Spanish Jewry, Moses ben Ḥanokh issued his own responsa and never sought the opinions of the scholars in Babylonia. His yeshiva produced an independent generation of Spanish rabbis, including his son and successor, Rabbi Ḥanokh ben Moses, and the great courtier, warrior, and poet Samuel ha-Nagid (Ismail ibn Nagrelᶜa), who also produced a talmudic commentary that has survived only in part.

The Babylonian tradition of Rabbinic Judaism had come into Christian Europe at least as early as

802, when the Babylonian scholar Machir arrived in Narbonne. Around the same time the Kalonymus family of Lucca, which apparently had ties with both the Palestinian and Babylonian academies, came to Mainz at the invitation of Charlemagne or perhaps Charles the Bald. By the late tenth century a complete commentary to the Babylonian Talmud was available in Christian Europe. This early commentary was the work of Rabbi Gershom ben Judah of Mainz, who was known as *Meʾor ha-Golah* (Light of the Exile). He had studied in Provence and later returned to northern Europe, where he established his own yeshiva. Under his leadership a new independent Jewish center began to evolve. For reasons of distance and difficulties of communication, this area had never had the same sort of intimate ties that Mediterranean Jewry had maintained with the gaonic academies. Rabbi Gershom issued far-reaching legal reforms (Hebrew: *takkanot*), which helped lay the foundations of Ashkenazic Judaism. Among these was his ban against polygamy, which has remained binding upon Ashkenazic Jews. Rabbi Gershom's talmudic commentary, however, was superseded by the great work of Rashi of Troyes (1040–1105), who also wrote the standard Hebrew commentary on the Bible. Rashi's lucid commentary finally made the Babylonian Talmud accessible to Jews everywhere. His work was followed by the additional commentaries of Rashi's disciples, who were known as the tosaphists and who combined their master's techniques with the methodologies of Rabbi Isaac ben Jacob Alfasi (d. 1103) of Spain and others whose works were now becoming available in northern Europe. The tosaphists firmly established France and Germany as preeminent centers of talmudic study.

THE SECTARIAN CHALLENGE TO RABBINIC JUDAISM

One of the most serious challenges to the Babylonian rabbinic tradition was posed by the fundamentalist Karaite sect, founded in the second half of the eighth century by Anan ben David, a disappointed candidate for the exilarchate (the secular leadership of Babylonian Jewry occupied by putative descendants of the Davidic royal house). This sectarian movement denied the authenticity of the oral Torah, and hence of gaonic authority. Anan and his followers accepted only the Bible (Hebrew: *mikra*, whence their later name of *karaʾim*—karaites, or Bible readers) as the source of Jewish law. Anan himself seems to have had a strong ascetic tendency, and his general approach to scriptural exegesis for the extrapolation of Jewish law is almost invariably harsher than that of Rabbinic Judaism. For example, the prohibition against kindling fires on the Sabbath in the Mosaic code (Exod. 35:3) is interpreted by Anan and most of the early Karaite scholars as constituting a total ban against all fire on the Sabbath, even if the flame were kindled before Friday evening. Thus, the Sabbath eve was spent in total darkness. Anan also forbade sexual intercourse between husband and wife on the Sabbath by means of a very forced interpretation of the ban on agricultural labor. (In Rabbinic Judaism, on the contrary, connubial relations are considered among the joys of the Sabbath.) Anan tended to be considerably stricter with regard to the laws of purity, dietary regulations (for example, he totally rejected the talmudic notion of *shi^c urim*, or the "minimal quantities" that were necessary to make something ritually unfit), and consanguineous marriage. Anan put forth his new interpretations in a work entitled *Sefer ha-Mitzvot* (Book of commandments), which he composed in Aramaic.

Karaism absorbed a number of smaller sectarian groups that had been founded in Persia during the late seventh century; they were influenced by Iranian religion and were themselves strongly ascetic in orientation. These groups included the Isawites (followers of the messianic pretender Abu ^c Īsā al-Iṣfahānī) and the Yudghanites. Karaism may also have absorbed some small remnants of Jewish sects that had their origins in pre-Rabbinic times.

Because of its appeal to individualism, Karaism eventually failed to create a well-organized, unified movement. Anan's dictum "Search thoroughly in the Torah, and do not rely upon my opinion" left the movement open to continual divisions from within. Nevertheless, Karaism was a force to be reckoned with in Judaism during the ninth and tenth centuries, when it had some of its best intellectual leadership in such men as Benjamin ben Moses al-Nah^ᵓāwendī and Daniel ben Moses al-Qūmisī. In rejecting the oral Torah and returning to the scriptural text, the Karaite scholars were forced of necessity to develop the sciences of Hebrew grammar and lexicography as well as biblical exegesis. They also seem to have been the first Jewish theologians to employ the tools of Greek philosophy, which had shortly before come into vogue in Muslim circles. Like the Mu^c tazilites in Islam, they were vigorously opposed to any but allegorical interpretations of anthropomorphisms in scripture. Rabbinic literature, by contrast, abounded with anthropomorphic descriptions of God, and as

such was the object of Karaite attacks. The questions of anthropomorphism, rational knowledge of God, and many other philosophical points were taken up by the Karaites at the very time that these issues were being raised in other quarters, both Jewish and non-Jewish. Hence the Karaite threat to mainstream Judaism was all the more serious. In order to combat the Karaites, Rabbinite Jews were forced to take up the same weapons.and, of course, to address some of the same burning issues. Thus, the challenge of Karaism proved to be an important stimulus to Rabbinic Judaism, especially in the areas of biblical exegesis, Hebrew language studies, and philosophy.

The fight against Karaism was taken up most effectively by one of the outstanding figures of medieval Judaism, Saadiah Gaon (882–942). Even before becoming gaon of Sura and while still in his early twenties, Saadiah wrote a devastating critique of the founder of Karaism, entitled *Kitāb al-Radd ^c alā ^c Anan* (The book of response against Anan). He again responded to many of the intellectual issues raised by Karaism in his philosophical masterpiece *The Book of Beliefs and Opinions* (Arabic: *Kitāb al-ᵓAmānāt wa-al-I^c tiqādāt;* Hebrew: *Emunot ve-ha-De^ᵓot*), written six years before his death. Saadiah also provided some of the basic tools for Rabbinite scholars to counter Karaite interpretations of the Bible. He composed the first Hebrew dictionary, the *Agron,* and prepared pioneering studies in Hebrew grammar. He also wrote a rational, philologically sound commentary to accompany his Arabic translation of the Bible. Because of the all-encompassing scope of his endeavors on behalf of Judaism, Saadiah was often referred to by later scholars as "the Gaon" and was dubbed by Abraham ben Meir ibn Ezra, the great twelfth-century Spanish exegete, "the chief spokesman in every area." Saadiah also played a vital role in meeting the challenge posed to Judaism by the Hellenistic renaissance of the medieval Muslim world.

THE DEVELOPMENT OF JEWISH PHILOSOPHY
Between 850 and 1200, the Islamic world experienced a revival of Greek science and philosophy. Hellenic learning in Arabic translation exerted a profound cultural influence upon both Muslims and Jews that was felt in religious and secular thought.

Early Rabbinic Judaism and Greek philosophy. Judaism had already encountered Hellenism centuries earlier in Greco-Roman times, and there were at the beginning of the Common Era a number of Jewish communities that had assimilated many of the ideals of Hellenic culture. The most important of these communities was Alexandria, which produced the standard Greek translation of the Bible, the Septuagint, and the well-known Jewish philosopher Philo.

However, the irreconcilable conflict between Jewish monotheism and Hellenic paganism was later continued between Judaism and Christianity. The latter was the political and cultural heir to the Hellenistic world, inheriting many of its anti-Semitic prejudices, and Rabbinic Judaism turned its back upon Greek philosophy, even as the church fathers were making it into "the handmaiden of the Christian religion." The only significant philosopher mentioned by name in the Talmud is Epicurus, and in fact, *apikoros*, which literally means "Epicurean," became a standard term in rabbinic usage for a heretic. Although there are many Greek loanwords in the Hebrew and Aramaic of the Talmud and Midrash, Greek philosophical terms are notably absent. Even the dialectics of talmudic argumentation with its associative logic stands dramatically apart from Greek syllogistic reasoning. For the rabbis of the talmudic period, wisdom was Torah learning, and Torah learning only, while secular learning was considered to be of ephemeral value.

The rationalist challenge to Rabbinic Judaism. The intellectual and spiritual ferment within the Muslim world that accompanied the introduction of the Greek corpus in the ninth century posed many of the same challenges for Judaism that it did for Islam. Many Jews, particularly in the new middle class, were troubled by the apparent contradictions between religion on the one hand and science and philosophy on the other. For example, Judaism held that the world was created ex nihilo, whereas in the Aristotelian system it was formed from eternal matter. Judaism held that the highest truths were those revealed by God, whereas a fundamental tenet of Greek philosophy was that all truths could be reached by the powers of reason. The competing claims to truth made by the numerous schools of thought that flourished during this period only increased many people's spiritual uncertainty.

Jewish freethinkers, like their Muslim counterparts, appear at this time. One such Jewish dissident was the Persian heretic Ḥiwi al-Balkhī, who was active in Khorāsān during the mid ninth century. He denied the very foundation of Judaism as a revealed religion. Ḥiwi composed a book, no longer extant, which apparently enjoyed wide circulation, and in which he raised two hundred questions attacking the

Bible on rational grounds. He criticized the injustice of the biblical God, denied miracles on the basis of experiential knowledge, and scoffed at the crude anthropomorphisms. As has been noted above, the issues of God's justice and of anthropomorphisms were major concerns of the Muslim Muᶜtazilite theologians and had been taken up in Judaism by the Karaites. Benjamin al-Nahᵓāwendī, for example, separated God from the anthropomorphisms of the Bible by advancing the theory of a demiurge angel created by God to carry out the actual work of creation (like the Logos of Philo) and to act as God's intermediary with the world. According to Benjamin, the anthropomorphic passages in the Bible were actually referring to this demiurge and not to God himself.

These were by no means new questions in Judaism. The question of theodicy is raised in the Bible itself—most notably in the book of Job, but also elsewhere (for example, Gen. 18:20–33). Already in the Bible, too, there is a marked internal tension between the sublime transcendence of God, his total otherness, and the human terms with which he is frequently described. In early Second Temple times certain emendations of the Hebrew text were made by scribes in order to eliminate some of the most offensive anthropomorphisms. The Jewish translations of the Bible went still further by interpreting certain passages in which God is described with human attributes either allegorically or with circumlocutions. Even in rabbinic literature, particularly in the legendary material (Haggadah), where anthropomorphisms abound, there is often the qualifying phrase "as if such things were possible" (Hebrew: *kivyakhol*). The rabbis of the Talmud did note on occasion that "the Torah speaks in the language of mortals," and they warn that the attributes employed in praising God are totally insufficient. (See, for example, BT Tractate *Berakhot* 33b, where Rabbi Ḥanina tells the parable of a king who possessed millions of gold coins, but was praised for owning millions of silver ones. "Was this not in fact an insult to him?" the rabbi asks.) Despite these sporadic rabbinical caveats, anthropomorphisms were numerous in the Bible and Jewish literature and were taken literally in popular belief. They also loomed large in esoteric circles. For Jewish mystics, God enthroned appeared in his glory as the supernal man (see Ezekiel's vision, Ezek. 1:26). There was even a cabalistic work on "the measurement of the divine body" (Hebrew: *Shiᶜur Komah*).

The philosophic defense of Rabbinic Judaism. The

challenges raised by freethinkers, like Ḥiwi, and sectarians, like the Karaites, seemed all the more threatening because they touched upon genuine Jewish theological concerns that were also current in the general intellectual climate of the day. Furthermore, many of these critiques were seized upon by Muslim polemicists against Judaism. Rabbinite Jews met the challenge by offering a rational exposition of Judaism through philosophy. As noted above, the first leader to champion Rabbinic Judaism in this way was Saadiah Gaon.

Saadiah's philosophic chef d'oeuvre, *The Book of Beliefs and Opinions,* was written—as the author acknowledges in his introduction—with the aim of clearing up the spiritual doubt (Arabic: *shubha*) of his contemporaries. The book is written in Arabic, rather than Hebrew, so that it might be easily understood by the educated layman, who was most likely to be perplexed by the conflicting views of the different religions, sects, and philosophical schools. In his introduction, Saadiah explains that people fall into doubt because of fuzzy thinking, and he shows how they can dispel doubt and distinguish between true and false beliefs on the basis of the four fundamental types of knowledge: (1) knowledge from sensory perception, (2) knowledge from self-evident first principles, (3) knowledge from syllogistic reasoning, and (4) knowledge passed down by reliable tradition. According to Saadiah there is also knowledge from revelation. There can be no contradiction between scientific knowledge and knowledge from revelation because both proceed from the same divine source. Anything in the biblical revelation that appears to be in conflict with reason needs to be interpreted allegorically.

For Saadiah the beliefs of Judaism are rationally demonstrable, even the belief in God. In chapter 1, he deduces the existence of an eternal Creator who made the world ex nihilo. He employs three proofs based upon the nature of the world (which is finite, composite, and subject to accidents) and a fourth proof based upon the nature of time (if time were infinite, the present would not exist). He also examines twelve non-Jewish theories of cosmogony and refutes each one of them. Having proved *creatio ex nihilo* and the existence of God, Saadiah turns in chapter 2 to the unity of God and addresses the problem of divine attributes. He explains that these qualities are metaphorical, are not comparable to their mundane equivalents, and do not imply any multiplicity that would contradict the perfect unity of God's nature. Rather, they are due to the poverty of

human language in expressing such an exalted concept. This strongly anti-anthropomorphic stance of Saadiah remained henceforth the normative view of Rabbinic Judaism.

After dealing with the essential questions of God and creation, Saadiah turns to the relationship between the Creator and his creatures, specifically with regard to the revelation of divine law and the nature of that law (chap. 3). The divine laws are of two types: rational laws, which can be deduced by reason; and traditional laws, such as ritual commandments and the dietary laws, which cannot be arrived at by reason alone and which can be known only through revelation. For example, reason dictates that society ban murder, because if left unchecked, people would annihilate one another. On the other hand, ritual laws are inherently neutral in character from the point of view of reason, but they have nevertheless a positive value which can be explained rationally. For example, the laws of defilement and purity teach men humility and reverence and heighten their consciousness of the holy. Revelation, according to Saadiah, is necessary for both rational and traditional laws because the mind takes time to arrive at the truth and also because it only apprehends the general principles, but not necessarily the details and ramifications. Hence the need for prophecy, scripture, and tradition. In answer to Christian and Muslim claims to the contrary, Saadiah—in complete accord with rabbinic tradition—argues that the laws revealed to the prophets, set down in the Bible, and passed from generation to generation are eternally valid and cannot be abrogated.

Saadiah's treatment of the divine law leads logically into a discussion of obedience and disobedience, compulsion and justice (chap. 4). God in his mercy and justice has given man the power and the ability to do what he has commanded. Man's ability to act or to abstain from acting implies both freedom of choice and responsibility. But how can man have true freedom of will if God has foreknowledge of all things? Here, for the first time in Jewish thought, Saadiah formulates one of the essential philosophical questions that has occupied the minds of Jewish thinkers ever since. God's knowledge is not the cause of the existence of things, for they would have then existed from eternity even as God's knowledge is eternal. God knows what choice a man will ultimately make, but the choice is indeed the person's. Although other leading Jewish thinkers, for instance Judah Halevi in his *Kuzari,* adopted Saadiah's explanation, not all found it satisfying. The late medieval Spanish Jewish philosopher Joseph Albo (*d. ca.* 1440) argued in his *Sefer ha-Ikkarim* (Book of principles) that Saadiah's explanation in no way solved the problem since if God's knowledge depends upon reality, rather than reality upon God's knowledge, then God's foreknowledge cannot be maintained.

Saadiah next turns to the nature of good and evil deeds and how they leave their impress upon the human soul (chap. 5). At the same time, he tries to solve the difficult theological problem of why the righteous and the innocent suffer. Saadiah sets forth in clear fashion the rabbinic doctrine that there is, in addition to the suffering of punishment and of testing, a "suffering of love" for which God in his wisdom has prepared a special reward. He likens this latter form of suffering to punishment inflicted by a loving father to protect his child or bitter medicine administered to reduce an illness.

Saadiah's description of the nature of the human soul (chap. 6) became the standard view among medieval Jewish philosophers. The three words for soul in the Hebrew Bible (*nefesh, ruaḥ,* and *neshamah*) are interpreted as being indicative of the soul's three faculties. For Saadiah, *nefesh* in the Bible refers to the faculty of appetite, *ruaḥ* indicates the faculty of passion and courage, and *neshamah* the faculty of knowledge. Although these faculties follow Plato's famous tripartite division, Saadiah and those who came after him, as for example Maimonides, insist upon the essential unity of the soul. Saadiah provides a strong rational defense of the Jewish belief in the resurrection of the dead (chap. 7), which, though generally held, had never been set forth in such a manner.

Again following Rabbinic tradition, Saadiah harmonizes two conflicting views regarding the time of Israel's ultimate redemption. That redemption will take place either at the preappointed time or, alternatively, at the time when Israel through genuine repentance proves itself worthy of being redeemed (chap. 8).

Saadiah further uses rational arguments to uphold the existence of reward and punishment in the world to come. He explains that the Torah, nevertheless, speaks mainly of reward in this world (chap. 9) because prophecy usually treats in greatest detail urgent events near at hand and is more circumspect about events in the distant future. He also expands upon certain Rabbinic doctrines that heaven and hell are not actual places, but subtle essences, a form of

light in the world to come that will have opposite effects upon the righteous and the wicked.

Finally, in keeping with the Hellenistic tone of thought that was in vogue during his time, Saadiah concludes his theological magnum opus with an appended treatise (chap. 10) in which he recommends the golden mean as the ideal manner of conduct in this world.

Saadiah successfully defended Rabbinic Judaism from the onslaught of rationalist freethinking and Karaism, and he laid the foundations upon which medieval Jewish scholastic theology and philosophy were built. Even Maimonides, who disagreed with Saadiah on many basic philosophical issues, concedes that "were it not for Saadiah, the Torah might well have disappeared from the midst of Israel" (*Epistle to the Jews of Yemen*).

Saadiah's approach to Jewish theology was very much along the methodological lines of the kalam theologians in Islam, particularly the Muᶜtazilite school, and kalamic influence remained strong in mainstream Judaism for the next two and a half centuries. Succeeding geonim at Sura, such as Samuel ben Hophni (*d.* 1013) and Saadiah's son Dosa (*d.* 1017), followed in the rationalist tradition of Saadiah. Throughout the major Jewish intellectual circles in the Muslim world the study of philosophy came to be viewed as an integral part of the study of Torah. Indeed, in some quarters primacy was given to the former.

PHILOSOPHICAL TRENDS AND SYNTHESES

In the populous Jewish centers of North Africa and Spain, Neoplatonism came into vogue during Saadiah's lifetime. Jewish philosophers such as Isaac ben Solomon Israeli and his pupil Dunash ibn Tamim (*d.* after 955/956) in Al-Qayrawān, and Solomon ben Judah ibn Gabirol, Baḥya ben Joseph ibn Paquda, and Joseph ben Jacob ibn Ẓaddik (*d.* 1149) in Spain, viewed God as the Neoplatonic first cause from which emanates a hierarchical universe of hypostases. These philosophers sought to achieve the ascent of the soul through ethical and intellectual discipline to an ultimate union with the Divine. Unlike Saadiah, the Neoplatonists were not primarily concerned with proving the existence of God or justifying the tenets of Judaism per se, but rather with understanding the relation of God to this world. Isaac Israeli (*d. ca.* 955), the father of Jewish Neoplatonism, tries to link his philosophical ideas with Jewish beliefs. For example, he connects the traditional concept of bliss in paradise with the ultimate felicity of divine union. On the other hand, Solomon ibn Gabirol (*d. ca.* 1057), the greatest of the Jewish Neoplatonists, in his major work, the *Fons vitae* (Hebrew: *Mekor Ḥayyim*), sets forth a system that is devoid of any specifically Jewish content. It is probably for this reason that the greatest influence of the book was in medieval Christian circles (via the Latin translation of Johannes Hispalensus and Dominicus Gundissalinus). Ibn Gabirol's metaphysical poem "The Kingly Crown" (Hebrew: *Keter Malkhut*), which expresses many of the same ideas as his *Fons vitae,* had a more lasting place in Jewish religious literature due to its devotional quality, which made it appropriate for liturgical use. Because of the confession of sins at the end of the poem, it was adopted by many Sephardic Jews for reading on Yom Kippur.

One Neoplatonist who did have a very considerable impact on subsequent Judaism was Baḥya ben Joseph ibn Paquda of Saragossa (*fl. ca.* 1080). His devotional handbook *The Guide to the Duties of the Heart* (Arabic: *al-Hidāya ilā farāʾiḍ al-Qulūb;* Hebrew: *Ḥovot ha-Levavot*) combines Saadiah's rationalist theology with a pietism that has mystical overtones. Baḥya's manual—as its title implies—deals with the inner man and the soul's quest for spiritual perfection and union with the Divine Light. Just as Saadiah's *Beliefs and Opinions* marked the first attempt at a systematic presentation of Jewish theology, so Baḥya's *Duties of the Heart* represents the first systematic presentation of Jewish ethics. Through the Hebrew translation made by Ibn Tibbon in 1161, *The Duties of the Heart* came to enjoy great popularity among European Jewry, not only among mystics and pietists, but among the masses as well because of its homely warmth and sincerity.

During the middle of the twelfth century, Jewish philosophy came to be dominated by Aristotelianism. Although there were some Jewish Aristotelians in tenth-century Iraq, the first milestone in the turn toward this philosophical trend came in Spain with the appearance of Abraham ben David Halevi ibn Daud's (*d. ca.* 1180) *The Exalted Faith* (Arabic: *al-ʿAqīda al-Rafīʿa;* Hebrew: *Ha-Emunah ha-Ramah*). The new trend exhibited a strict rationalism in contradistinction to the Neoplatonic mysticism. It also showed a greater awareness of the boundaries separating religious faith and philosophical reason than did the kalamic theologians like Saadiah.

The chief exponent of Jewish Aristotelianism,

and indeed the greatest Jewish thinker of the entire Middle Ages, was Moses Maimonides (*d.* 1204). Maimonides, also a consummate legal authority, was acutely aware of the dilemma of the believing Jewish intellectual. Such a person had studied philosophy and was troubled by the contradictions between faith and reason, but was not satisfied with Saadiah's kalam arguments; it was for this sort of Jewish intellectual that Maimonides composed his *Guide of the Perplexed* (Arabic: *Dalālat al-Ḥā'rīn;* Hebrew: *Moreh Nevukhim*). It had a profound impact upon almost all subsequent medieval Jewish philosophers, and even those who disagreed with its views—and they were not inconsiderable—could not ignore them.

Maimonides' *Guide* is essentially a work of philosophic exegesis. In it he undertakes to explain in a thorough and systematic fashion the anthropomorphic and anthropopathic terms in Scripture, as well as unclear biblical parables. The book is aimed exclusively at an intellectual elite and is written in an obscure and often contradictory style in order to keep its esoteric message from the uninitiated. In his other writings, however, Maimonides conveyed many of his philosophical and theological ideas in a popular form, as, for example, in the first and last books of his great law code, *Mishneh Torah.*

Maimonides' uncompromising rationalism rekindled the fires of controversy between Hellenistic and anti-Hellenistic forces within Judaism in a manner not seen since talmudic times. Many rabbis in Christian Europe who had been unaffected by the revival of Greek philosophy and science in the Islamic world considered Maimonides' rejection of literal biblical images and of many elements of haggadic legend as nothing less than heresy. The controversy continued throughout the thirteenth and fourteenth centuries, with occasional bans against the work in certain communities. Although the conflict between rationalists and antirationalists was never entirely resolved, the healing powers of time and Maimonides' tremendous personal prestige removed the *Guide* from the center of the conflict and accorded it a place within the literature of mainstream Judaism.

ANTIPHILOSOPHICAL AND
NONPHILOSOPHICAL TRENDS

The rejection of philosophy in traditionalist circles. Maimonides' extreme rationalism was the lightning rod for a storm of controversy between the forces of rationalism and antirationalism within the Jewish community. However, although the rationalists had dominated since the time of Saadiah, there had been opposition to Greek philosophy and rationalist interpretations of Judaism long before the Maimonidean controversy completely polarized the two camps.

Hai Gaon (d. 1038), the head of the Pumbedita academy and a leading interpreter of halakah, was opposed to the teaching of philosophy to children in Jewish schools. He criticized other geonim, including his own father-in-law, Samuel ben Ḥofni, for "frequently reading the works of Gentiles."

The ultimate rejection of rationalist philosophy as the key to understanding Judaism came from one trained in the Hellenistic tradition—Judah Halevi (ca. 1075–1141). Halevi was recognized in his own lifetime as the laureate of Hebrew poetry in Spain. As a physician, he had been educated in accordance with the Greek curriculum, in which philosophy had a major part. In his later life, he came to reject philosophical rationalism in his masterful dialogue *The Book of Argument and Proof in Defense of the Despised Faith* (Arabic: *Kitāb al-Ḥujja waal-Dalīl fī Naṣr al-Dīn al-Dhalīl*; Hebrew: *Sefer ha-Hokhakha veha-Re'aya le-Haganat ha-Dat ha-Bezuya*). It was popularly known as *The Kuzari* after one of its two principal characters, the king of the Khazars, whose conversion to Judaism provides the dramatic setting for the dialogue.

Speaking through the rabbi who answers the questions of the Khazar king, Halevi argues that philosophy fails in the metaphysical sphere. Religious certainty is obtainable only through the experience of divine revelation, and history shows that only the Jewish people have had an undisputed collective religious experience of the theophany. Christianity and Islam not only attest to that essential fact, but take it as their own point of departure. For Halevi, prophecy is an inherent faculty of the Jewish people, a mark of their divine election, which enables them to approach the *Shekhinah* (Divine presence). Just as the Jewish people are "the pick" of mankind (see *Kuzari* I, 95), so the land of Israel is preeminent among all the countries of the earth (*Kuzari* II, 9–24). The perfect religious life is possible only there.

Judah Halevi's glorification of Rabbinic Judaism, his unabashed nationalism, and his philosophical rationalism won his book a lasting place in traditionalist circles. It was also popular among the cabalists of the thirteenth century and later mystics such as the hasidim. Along with his stirring cycle of poems known as the "Songs of Zion," it remained a classic expression of the traditional Jewish longing to return to Israel and a precursor of modern Zionism.

It should be noted that unlike the vehement opponents of philosophy who were so vocal during the Maimonidean controversy of the thirteenth and fourteenth centuries (men like Solomon ben Abraham of Montpellier, Abba Mari, known as Astruc of Lunel, and Asher ben Jehiel), Judah Halevi was not against philosophy per se. Indeed, he considered it the supreme intellectual achievement. However, according to Halevi, its validity was limited to the physical realm, and it could never provide a path to religious certainty. As noted above, the dynamic tension between the proponents and opponents of philosophy was never completely resolved within Judaism. One attempted compromise was the ban issued by Rabbi Solomon ben Abraham Adret in Barcelona in 1305, which prohibited the study of physics and metaphysics before the age of twenty-five.

Mystic and pietistic trends. Since at least Second Temple times subterranean mystic currents had flowed beneath the mainstream of Judaism. Some scholars believe that early Jewish mysticism developed under the influence of Greek and/or Persian religious trends, while others believe that it was an indigenous product of the inner dynamism of Palestinian Jewry in the late Second Temple period. During the Rabbinic period esoteric and theosophic speculation was rampant among the heretical sects, but it was also cultivated by some leading rabbis. No less venerated halakic sages than Rabbi Johanan ben Zakkai and Rabbi Akiva were engaged in the Mysteries of the Divine Chariot (Hebrew: *maᶜaseh merkavah*; see Ezek. 1:4–28) and the Mysteries of Creation (Hebrew: *ma aseh bereshit*). By the gaonic period, a considerable mystic literature had built up that included the *Heikhalot* books (the *heikhalot* being the celestial palaces), the *Shiᶜur Komah* (the measurement of the divine body), and the *Sefer Yezirah* (Book of creation). The latter was highly regarded throughout the Middle Ages and merited commentaries by Saadiah, Isaac Israeli, Dunash ben Tamim, the Italian physician Shabbetai Donnolo (d. ca. 982), and the Spanish scholar Judah ben Barzillai (d. early twelfth century).

Mystical movements of many different shadings developed all over the Jewish world during the High Middle Ages. Their common denominator was the urge for a more intimate relation with God, the ultimate stage of which was a *unio mystica* known as the embrace (Hebrew: *devekut*). This intimate relationship was to be achieved through an especially pious way of life. The practitioners of this piety were known as hasidim, a term that in rabbinic literature designated those who maintained the highest standards of religious and ethical practice.

One of the earliest and most important of these mystic-pietist movements was that of Hasidei Ashkenaz, which began in the eleventh and flowered during the twelfth and thirteenth centuries. The movement started and was centered in Germany, but spread into northern France and even England. While insisting upon the unity and incorporeality of God, the Hasidei Ashkenaz also emphasized the immanence of the Godhead, which pervades all things. The fervent love of God was another basic tenet of the movement. The ultimate demonstration of love for God was "the sanctification of the Divine Name" (kiddush ha-shem), or martyrdom. This love was manifested by the Jews' holy combat against Christian idolatry and, as such, was fervently desired. The Hasidei Ashkenaz were in the forefront of the martyrs during the massacres that accompanied the crusades. Their piety, their ethics, and many of their religious practices (including aspects of liturgy) left a lasting imprint on European Jewry.

Another hasidic movement was that founded in Egypt by Abraham Maimonides (d. 1237), the son of Moses Maimonides. His movement, which also had adherents in Palestine, exhibited the strong influence of Muslim Sufism. Abraham Maimonides tried to revive such ancient Jewish practices in prayer as prostration and raising the hands in supplication. He also produced a manual for pietists entitled Kifāyat al-ᶜĀbidin (Complete guide for the servants of God). Both his innovations and the excessive, almost heretical-sounding expressions of mystical ecstasy by some of his followers aroused considerable opposition among other Jews, and the movement had neither the longevity nor the lasting influence of Hasidei Ashkenaz.

The most esoteric of the medieval Jewish mystic movements was that of the cabalists, which began in Provence in the twelfth century and spread to Spain at the beginning of the thirteenth. Deriving its name from the Hebrew word kabbālāh ("tradition," particularly of an esoteric kind), the movement comprised two main trends—one theosophic and Gnostic, the other Neoplatonic and philosophic. The ultimate goal for the cabalist was "cleaving unto God" (Hebrew: devekout), and great store was set upon mystical "intention" (Hebrew: kavvanah) in prayer. The cabalists produced an enormous esoteric literature, of which the most important work is the Sefer ha-Zohar (Book of splendor), written mainly in Spain between 1280 and 1286. Gershom Scholem, the leading historian of Jewish mysticism, has called the book "the most important evidence for the stirring of a mythical spirit in medieval Judaism." The book later became a classic Jewish text in both Ashkenazic and Sephardic Jewry, and parts of it were even incorporated into the liturgy.

The cabalist movement did not terminate in the Middle Ages, but continued to develop and to spread into modern times. It had a profound influence on later Judaism in prayer, custom, and ethics.

THE TREND TOWARD LEGAL CODIFICATION

As noted at the very outset of this article, it was during the Middle Ages that Judaism crystallized and developed its distinctive form. One of the most important single processes that brought this about was the progressive trend, spanning the entire medieval period, toward the codification of the Jewish law (halakah). The Talmud was recognized as the extrabiblical source of law, but it was not a code. It was an encyclopedic discussion that provided the foundation and framework for a comprehensive and systematic legal system.

The first real codex that had a marked influence on later codes was the Halakhot Pesukot (Judicially determined laws) of Yehuday Gaon (second half of the eighth century). Composed in Aramaic, its material was arranged topically as well as by talmudic tractates. The Halakhot Pesukot omitted laws that had fallen into desuetude (such as laws concerning the sacrificial cult) and laws with relevance only to the Holy Land and therefore not observed in the Diaspora. The Halakhot Pesukot spread quickly throughout the entire Jewish world. There were numerous adaptations and abridgments and a Hebrew translation, all of which attest to the important need that it filled.

About a century later, a more complete code was put together, in the opinion of most scholars both medieval and modern, by Simeon Kayyara in Babylonia. This work, entitled Halakhot Gedolot (Great corpus of laws), also included laws no longer in practice and gave new names to certain groups of laws.

The next milestone in the evolution of codification came in the late eleventh century with the appearance of the Sefer ha-Halakhot (Book of laws) by the North African-born Spanish scholar Isaac ben Jacob Alfasi (d. 1103). Alfasi's work was essentially an abridgment of the Talmud, and hence was often called *Talmud Katan* (Little Talmud). This code enjoyed tremendous prestige throughout the entire Jewish world up to modern times and was the subject of numerous commentaries.

Not long after Alfasi's death, there began to appear books of legal decisions in which laws (halakhot) had been extrapolated from talmudic discussions. The process culminated in the systematic, comprehensive, and indeed revolutionary code of Maimonides, the *Mishneh Torah* (Repetition of the Torah), also known as the *Yad ha-Ḥazakah* (The strong hand). Maimonides' code classified Jewish law by subject matter and was based upon all of the talmudic and post-talmudic legal literature then in use; it omitted all of the discussions and controversies. The book itself became the object of controversy because of its great boldness in determining the halakhah in each instance without offering any citation of the sources themselves and without presenting any alternative opinions. Nevertheless, Maimonides' method eventually won the day, and his beautifully clear, concise Hebrew style influenced the language of later codes. Maimonides divided his monumental work into 14 books which were subdivided into 83 parts totaling 1,000 chapters and 15,000 paragraphs. He states explicitly in his introduction that his compendium was written "in plain language and unadorned style so that the entire Oral Torah might become systematically known to all" and that "all the rules should be accessible to young and old." Unlike his predecessors, Maimonides included laws no longer in force with the view that his *Mishneh Torah* might someday constitute the legal code of the reestablished Jewish commonwealth.

Many codes of varying scope appeared in Europe during the twelfth and thirteenth centuries. They were arranged along pre-Maimonidean lines and were not as convenient as the *Mishneh Torah*. During the first half of the fourteenth century, however, a new code appeared in Spain. It combined the convenience of Maimonides' compendium, new halakhic material generated during the previous two hundred years, and elements of the older codes that had wider acceptance among many sectors of European Jewry. This was the *Sefer ha-Turim* (Book of columns) by Jacob ben Asher (*d.* 1340). Ben Asher's code arranged Jewish law under four very convenient general headings. This new and more practical arrangement was later adopted by Joseph Karo (*d.* 1575) for his *Shulḥan Arukh*, which came to be recognized as the single most authoritative code throughout the Jewish world. Karo considered Alfasi, Maimonides, and Ben Asher the three pillars of Jewish legal teaching.

CONCLUSION

Judaism has never in its long history been static and unchanging, nor has it been monolithic and entirely homogeneous. Nevertheless, it may be said that most of its devotional, intellectual, and legal framework, as developed in the Middle Ages and described here, has been preserved in great measure by traditional Jewry and has had a not inconsiderable influence even among reformist and secularist Jewish movements in modern times.

BIBLIOGRAPHY

English translations of medieval texts are Judah Halevi, *Kitab al Khazari*, Hartwig Hirschfeld, trans. (1905 and later eds.); Moses Maimonides, *Guide of the Perplexed*, Shlomo Pines, trans. (1963); Saadya Gaon, *The Book of Doctrines and Opinions*, Samuel Rosenblatt, trans. (1948).

Studies. Jacob B. Agus, *The Evolution of Jewish Thought from Biblical Times to the Opening of the Modern Era* (1959); Salo W. Baron, *A Social and Religious History of the Jews*, 17 vols. (1952–); Isidore Epstein, *Judaism: A Historical Presentation* (1959); Louis Finkelstein, ed., *The Jews, Their History, Religion, and Culture*, 4th ed. (1970–1971); Louis Ginzberg, *Geonica*, I, *The Geonim and Their Halakic Writings* (1909, 2nd ed. 1968), and *On Jewish Law and Lore* (1955, repr. 1970); Solomon D. Goitein, *A Mediterranean Society*, II, *The Community* (1971), and *idem*, ed., *Religion in a Religious Age* (1974); Julius Guttmann, *Philosophies of Judaism*, David W. Silverman, trans. (1964); Abraham Z. Idelsohn, *Jewish Liturgy and Its Development* (1932, 1960, 1967); Max Kadushin, *The Rabbinic Mind* (1952, 3rd ed. 1972); George Foot Moore, *Judaism in the First Centuries of the Christian Era*, 3 vols. (1930–1932), and *History of Religions*, II, *Judaism, Christianity, and Mohammedanism* (1929); Henry Malter, *Saadia Gaon: His Life and Works* (1921, repr. 1969); Solomon Schechter, *Studies in Judaism* (1st–3rd ser.), 3 vols. (1896–1924, repr. 1945); Gershom G. Scholem, *Major Trends in Jewish Mysticism*, 3rd ed. (1954); Norman A. Stillman, *The Jews of Arab Lands: A History and Source Book* (1979); Georges Vajda, *Introduction à la pensée juive du moyen âge* (1947); Hirsch J. Zimmels, *Ashkenazim and Sephardim* (1958, 1969).

NORMAN A. STILLMAN

[See also Baḥya ben Joseph ibn Paquda; Cabala; Exegesis, Jewish; Gaonic Period; Gershom ben Judah; Hasidei Ashkenaz; Israeli, Isaac; Judah Halevi; Karaites; Maimonidean Controversy; Maimonides, Abraham ben Moses; Maimonides, Moses; Martyrdom, Jewish; Rabbinate; Rashi; Saadiah Gaon; Schools, Jewish; Solomon ben Judah ibn Gabirol; Talmud, Exegesis and Study of.]

JUDEO-ARABIC LANGUAGE. "Judeo-Arabic" is a general designation for various forms of Arabic spoken and written by Jews. Three stages may be distinguished in the history of the language: Proto-Judeo-Arabic, Classical Judeo-Arabic, and Modern Judeo-Arabic.

PROTO-JUDEO-ARABIC

Prior to the rise of Islam, the only Jews speaking Arabic were the Jewish tribes of the Arabian Peninsula. Their everyday language was similar to that of their Arab neighbors save for the admixture of Aramaic and Hebrew words expressing specifically Jewish religious and ethnocultural ideas. The Arabs referred to this early Judeo-Arabic dialect as *al-ya-hūdiyya* (Jewish speech). Some of the Hebrew and Aramaic terminology of this early Judeo-Arabic, as well as a number of religious concepts, passed into the speech of the Arabs.

The art of writing was extremely limited in sixth- and seventh-century Arabia. Jews certainly wrote documents in Arabic, using Hebrew characters, but they produced no Judeo-Arabic literature. The only Arabic literary form at the time was poetry composed and transmitted orally, according to strict conventions in the supratribal idiom of classical Arabic. The poems of the sixth-century Jew Samuel ben ᶜĀdiyā (al-Samaw'al), for example, cannot be considered Judeo-Arabic because they are entirely devoid of Jewish linguistic or conceptual content.

There is no organic link between Proto-Judeo-Arabic and classical Judeo-Arabic.

CLASSICAL JUDEO-ARABIC

With the Islamic conquests of the seventh and eighth centuries, the majority of world Jewry came under Arab rule. Arabic became the language of the new ecumene, as Aramaic and Greek had been before, only over an ever larger area. Along with other peoples in this vast empire, the Jews adopted the language of the conquerors. As Arabic spread among the urban masses of the caliphate, however, it underwent a variety of transformations and developed into Middle Arabic (actually Middle Arabic dialects), which was distinguished from the old Arabian (proto-Arabic) dialects by the loss of the case endings, an analytical rather than synthetic structure, and an enriched vocabulary.

By the tenth century, Arabic had become the daily language of the Jews, and they were using it for nearly all forms of written expression, including religious queries and responsa, documents, textual commentaries, and everyday correspondence. Only poetry was written exclusively in Hebrew, as a Jewish nationalistic response to the ideal of the Arabic of the Koran. For Islamic civilization Arabic poetry was the ultimate national art; for the Jews, biblical Hebrew was the divine language, superior to all others, and thus a formidable challenge to Arabic.

Jews normally wrote Arabic in Hebrew characters, which were already familiar to them because the reading of Hebrew was taught from early childhood for religious purposes. In addition, although the Jewish intelligentsia could read Arabic script with at least some degree of facility, books by Muslim writers were frequently transcribed into Hebrew letters for more convenient reading.

Since Hebrew lacks several consonants found in Arabic, a system of diacritical points was adopted—albeit somewhat haphazardly—to augment the Hebrew alphabet (for example, the Arabic *ẓā'* was indicated by a dotted *ṭēt*, in close imitation of the Arabic writing system). There are minor deviations in the transcription of Arabic sounds into Hebrew characters among different writers (for example, both the Hebrew *gīmel* and ᶜ*ayin* with a diacritical were used for the Arabic *ghayn*).

Although Jews sought to write in classical Arabic (which was the only acceptable form of written expression in the Islamic world), few had the rigorous training necessary for writing the literary language flawlessly. Furthermore, not having been nurtured on the Koran and ancient Arabic poetry, nor imbued with the ideal of *al-ᶜarabiyya* (Arabic as the language of revelation and divine perfection), Jewish writers were less careful to maintain the strict dichotomy between the classical written language and the living spoken language. The styles of Jewish writers varied from what may be considered classical Arabic with some Middle Arabic elements (as in Saadiah Gaon's translation of the Bible and his *Book of Doctrines and Beliefs* or in Maimonides' *Guide of the Perplexed*) to a slightly classicized Middle Arabic bristling with colloquialisms. The latter style predominates in the family and business correspondence of members of the middle and working classes preserved in the Cairo genizah. One of the most common dialect features in these documents, which date mainly from the late tenth to the mid thirteenth centuries, is the use of the forms *nfᶜl/nfᶜlū* for the first-person singular and plural of the imperfect verb (instead of standard *'fᶜl/nfᶜl*), which is a hallmark of Maghrebi dialects.

In addition to the script, the most common unifying features of all forms of medieval Judeo-Arabic are the use of quotations from the Bible and the Talmud in the original Hebrew and Aramaic, and the easy assimilation of Hebrew loanwords into Arabic.

MODERN JUDEO-ARABIC

Modern Judeo-Arabic arose in the late fifteenth century and has continued down to modern times. Its main characteristic is its colloquial nature. This shift from classical and Middle Arabic to modern communal vernaculars resulted mainly from the increased social isolation of the Jews of the Arab world in the later Middle Ages.

BIBLIOGRAPHY

Yehoshua Blau, *A Grammar of Mediaeval Judaeo-Arabic* (1961), in Hebrew, and *The Emergence and Linguistic Background of Judaeo-Arabic* (1965); Solomon D. Goitein, *A Mediterranean Society,* I (1967), and *Jews and Arabs* (1974); G. D. Newby, "Observations About an Early Judaeo-Arabic," in *Jewish Quarterly Review,* n.s. **61** (1970); Moritz Steinschneider, *Die arabische Literatur der Juden* (1902); Norman A. Stillman, "Response to Professor Joshua Blau," in Herbert H. Paper, ed., *Jewish Languages: Theme and Variations* (1978), *The Jews of Arab Lands* (1979), and "Some Notes on the Judaeo-Arabic Dialect of Sefrou (Morocco)," in Shelomo Morag *et al.,* eds., *Studies in Judaism and Islam* (1981).

NORMAN A. STILLMAN

[See also **Arabic Language; Cairo Genizah.**]

JUDEO-ARABIC LITERATURE. The rapid expansion of the Muslim empire over vast areas in Asia and Africa during the seventh century brought myriad non-Muslims under its sway. Among their subject peoples, large numbers of Christians, Zoroastrians, and pagans, as well as some Jews, adopted the faith of the dominant group. Generally much more cultured than their conquerors, they introduced into Islam a thirst for learning. Muslim Arab intellectuals became interested in the achievements of the ancient Greeks, Persians, and Hindus in medicine, mathematics, science, theology, and philosophy. An active translation program was initiated to make those works available in Arabic. By the tenth century the islamized, Arabic-speaking world possessed the treasures of other civilizations, and Muslim intellectuals were themselves producing original Arabic studies in the various disciplines.

The Jews within the Muslim world gradually

learned to speak and even to compose in Arabic, which had displaced the Aramaic vernacular. Some of them were deeply affected by the intellectual pursuits of their countrymen. In addition to the traditional lore that they learned as children, such Jews were stimulated by much of the secular culture that had come into their world through translations: medicine, mathematics, astronomy and astrology, science, theology, and philosophy. Traditional Jewish learning was not left untouched by this contact with secular scholarship. In particular, standards of rationalist thinking were applied to the study of Jewish texts.

Under the impact of the cultured environment and in response to the challenge of the Karaites (sectarians who rejected the traditional subservience to rabbinic interpretations of Scripture and who insisted on their right to learn how to serve God by studying the Bible), some rationally inclined students turned to exegesis. Saadiah Gaon (882–942), Samuel ben Hophni (*d.* 1013), Judah ibn Bal^{c}am (*ca.* 1050–1100), Tanḥum of Jerusalem (*d.* 1291), and others wrote commentaries of varying lengths on the Pentateuch and on other parts of Scripture. They sought to get at what the text really meant, to smooth apparent contradictions, to suggest rational interpretations of the marvels and miracles recorded in the Bible, to explain away the numerous anthropomorphisms, and to shed light on obscure and difficult passages. These commentators were followed by others who wrote in Hebrew and utilized many of the contributions of the earlier exegetes. Knowledge of Hebrew grammar, a prerequisite for obtaining the correct meaning of the Bible, was treated in a number of studies, two of which deserve mention. Judah ben David Ḥayyūj (*ca.* 945–*ca.* 1000) was the first to recognize that a triliteral root is the basis of the language and that all verb forms, and almost all nouns, are traceable to basic three-letter stems. His disciple Jonah ibn Janāḥ (first half of the eleventh century) compiled a grammar in which his conclusions and those of his master and other predecessors are offered to serve as a full-sized portrait of Hebrew; his dictionary completes this offering. The realization that the comparative study of Hebrew, Aramaic, and Arabic can aid considerably in understanding the Bible motivated the monograph of Judah ibn Quraysh (second half of the ninth century) of North Africa.

Rabbinic literature was also treated in Arabic. Saadiah Samuel ben Hophni and Ḥefez ben Yazliʾah (tenth century) in Iraq, Nissim ben Jacob (*ca.* 990–

1062) in Qayrawān, and others prepared full commentaries or scattered explanations of parts of the Talmud, sent responsa to inquirers, and sought to rationalize its contents. They compiled laws and decisions on particular themes, such as inheritance, contracts, dietary prohibitions, and phylacteries. Maimonides (1135–1204), the greatest of them, produced a magnificent commentary on the Mishnah and a comprehensive code of doctrines, practices, ritual, and future hopes.

Despite the dominance of Arabic in Jewish prose works written in the Islamic world, poetry was composed in Hebrew. The Jewish poets wanted to display the excellence of the language of their Bible, just as their Muslim peers aimed to emulate the inimitable Koran. But the influence of Arabic poetry on Hebrew verse is telling, particularly in Spain. The creation of secular poetry on nature, friendship, love, reflections, and special occasions is clearly the result of contact with Arabic verse. So too are the innovations of rhyme, meter, and stanza; rich imagery; and the individualism of the poets, an offshoot of the rationalism that was the hallmark of the time. A unique book in Arabic, by the well-known Hebrew poet Moses ibn Ezra (*ca.* 1055–after 1135), is devoted to the rhetoric of the Bible and later Hebrew poetry.

It was in philosophy that the most novel departure from traditional patterns of thought and doctrine occurred. Christian and Muslim writers took over the concerns of the ancient Greeks regarding the origin of the universe, the essence of matter, the nature of life, ethics, and psychology. The sacred writings and traditions of their religions played a major role in their quest to resolve the almost unavoidable clash between the philosophic views on these problems and the positions of their revealed religions. (Philo Judaeus, in the first century, had offered a solution that, through various channels, was adopted by the later thinkers, who also assumed that both sources of their information were valid.)

Jewish intellectuals, too, learned classical philosophy from Arabic translations and from the contributions of later Christians and Muslims; and they, likewise, sought to reconcile revealed religion with philosophy as they grappled with similar religious doctrines of creation, God's attributes, revelation, and reward and punishment. Thus, Jewish philosophic writings can be arranged in three groups, all quite similar to their Arabic counterparts. One, represented by Saadiah Gaon, first established that the universe was created, a doctrine that necessarily implied the existence of God. This reasoning is similar to the conclusions of the followers of Kalam. Although Saadiah did not subscribe to their physical theories or to God's attributes, his views on the soul, free will, the good life, and other issues resemble their doctrines.

Maimonides was definitely one of the *falasifa,* philosophers who were criticized by most Muslims and Jews for giving their primary loyalty to Aristotle rather than to tradition. Even though he differed with the Greek master on some fundamental issues, such as creation and providence, he was undoubtedly a philosopher-Jew. Very learned in world and Jewish literature, he subscribed to transmitted traditional teachings, the elements that guided his thought clearly visible in the truths he reached philosophically. His opponents challenged him for arriving at religious beliefs rationally and for his unorthodox doctrines. Nevertheless, he had many disciples, and for centuries afterward his philosophy served as the point of departure for Jewish thinkers.

Neoplatonism infused with the theology of Judaism found its fullest medieval expression in the work of the poet Solomon ben Judah ibn Gabirol (1020–1058). The original Arabic version is lost; the text is preserved in a medieval Latin translation, *Fons vitae.*

Since the work lacks biblical and rabbinic references, it did not gain popularity among Jewish philosophers, save among mystical writers; and, until modern times, it seems not to have been translated into Hebrew in its entirety.

BIBLIOGRAPHY

Julius Guttmann, *Philosophies of Judaism,* David W. Silverman, trans. (1964), 47–241; Abraham S. Halkin, "Judeo-Arabic Literature," in Louis Finkelstein, ed., *The Jews,* II (1949, 4th ed. 1971); Moritz Steinschneider, *Jewish Literature from the Eighth to the Eighteenth Century,* William Spottiswoode, trans, (1857, repr. 1970), 59–203.

ABRAHAM S. HALKIN

[See also **Arabic Poetry; Maimonides, Moses; Philosophy and Theology, Jewish: In Islam; Solomon ben Judah ibn Gabirol.**]

JUDEO-FRENCH does not designate any particular speech, language, dialect, or jargon, but qualifies medieval French texts written by Jews, whose mother tongue was in no way different from that spoken by the other inhabitants of the region. Rather, the written word had a specific appearance: the Jews preferred Hebrew characters. This script, evolving from the transliteration of Latin speech, had its own orthographic rules: the Latin [k], when later pronounced [tʃ] in Old French, was still rendered by p, but with a diacritic mark indicating its new value (p̌); the Latin [j], becoming [dʒ], was rendered ' , as in French, until the thirteenth century, when ɉ, corresponding to the French g, was introduced. This interference, due to the knowledge of French writing in Latin characters, perscribes a circumspect treatment of these texts. Yet, the Hebrew script, with its diacritical marks and vowel points, offers a more reliable picture of the phonetic system of the author's dialect.

The best-known Old French words in Jewish texts are in the glosses of Rashi's (1030 or 1040–1105) commentaries on the Bible and the Talmud. Throughout the twelfth and thirteenth centuries, rabbis in France, as well as in England and Germany, interspersed their writings with French words. Indeed, Jews in these countries studied and even prayed in their respective Old French dialect, as some full-length prayers and songs attest.

Far more important are the biblical glossaries and dictionaries, which contain tens of thousands of Old French words in various *oïl* dialects, testifying to a complete vernacular version in use by French Jewry since the tenth century.

The study of this material has yielded some precisions on the phonetics of old French (for example, [y], [s], [j] > [ʒ]; closing of nasal vowels), as well as on the use of verbal forms (for example, present participle, imperfect tense), and in the field of lexicology, where the Hebrew counterpart admits of a more accurate definition of the Old French term. Its greatest contribution is the light it sheds on the hermeneutics of the Jews in medieval France and the role of French in Jewish exegesis.

BIBLIOGRAPHY
Menahem Banitt, "Une langue fantôme: Le judéo-fran-çais," in *Revue de linguistique romane*, 27 (1963), *Le glossaire de Bâle* (1972), and *Rashi, Interpreter of the Biblical Letter* (1985); David S. Blondheim, *Les parlers judéo-romans et la Vetus Latina* (1925); Arsène Darmesteter, *Reliques scientifiques*, I (1890), 103–307; Raphael Levy, *Trésor de la langue des juifs français au moyen âge* (1964).

MENAHEM BANITT

[See also **Rashi (Rabbi Solomon ben Isaac).**]

JUDEO-GERMAN. See **Yiddish.**

JUDEO-GREEK. The Judeo-Greek language was commonly spoken among Greek Jews (Romaniots) until the arrival of the Spanish exiles at the end of the fifteenth century. Generally, in places where large numbers of the newcomers settled, their culture displaced the Greek culture and language of the local Jews. This occurred, for example, in Thessaloniki, but not in small and distant places like Janina, Arta, or Corfu, where Judeo-Greek survived.

The Judeo-Greek language is almost identical with standard Greek, although it is written in Hebrew letters. In addition, the vocabulary and especially the religious terminology, phonetics, and morphology contain Hebrew and Aramaic elements. Judeo-Greek texts may be divided into three categories: glossaries of the Bible, translations of the Bible from the original Hebrew text, and original verse (including folk songs and liturgical poetry).

The oldest known Judeo-Greek codex is a 124-word glossary containing a translation into Greek (in Greek letters) of the names of plants mentioned in the Mishnah (from the tractates of *Kilayim* and *Shviᶜit*). However, experts are divided on when that glossary was composed. Paleographic indications seem to rule out the possibility that it was written before the ninth century.

Another glossary contains a list of 300 terms for God's names in Hebrew, as well as their translation into Aramaic and Judeo-Greek. The glossary was probably written in the fourteenth or fifteenth century, judging by paleographic evidence. Phonetic phenomena indicate that it was composed in Crete. The author was a well-educated Jew versed in the Septuagint and other Jewish-Hellenistic literature. Another glossary of that period is now in the archives of the National Library in Jerusalem. It contains a translation in Judeo Greek of words from Psalms, Lamentations, and Ecclesiastes, as well as a brief commentary in Hebrew, and was probably written in Candia (Crete). At the head of the hand-written manuscript is "written in 1578." Many other glossaries of the Bible and of individual biblical books were compiled in later periods, especially since the nineteenth century.

The most important translation into Judeo-Greek appeared in the Constantinople Polyglot Bible of 1546. Some researchers believe it was actually written much earlier, since the text contains several archaic terms and lacks Turkish words. But this phenomenon is common to all Judeo-Greek texts. There are also two known translations of the book of Jonah. One, dated 1263, is in the Bodleian Library at Oxford. The second is included in the Yom Kippur prayer book used by Romaniots and dates from the fifteenth century.

Among the old Greek congregations the Judeo-Greek folk poetry was most widespread in Janina and Corfu. These texts are poems (called *pizmonim*, *piyyutim*) from the local Judeo-Greek liturgy that were not included in the prayer books sent from other European congregations. They were composed by local rabbis, and the acrostics sometimes reveal the poets' names. The first to discover the Romaniots' poetry was a Greek linguist in Corfu, Spyridon Papageorgios, who published his findings in 1881. In 1889 and 1890 Moisis Caimis, the editor of a Jewish periodical in Corfu, *Israilitis Khronografos*, published several poems. Other researchers, such as Papadopoulos-Kerameos and Schwab, subsequently published their findings.

The Judeo-Greek compositions were written in dialects generally similar to those spoken in the area where the author lived. However, there were special characteristics common to all Judeo-Greek translations and original works that distinguished them from standard Greek dialects in several respects. First, Hebrew and Aramaic words are used, especially words relating to prayers, Jewish tradition, and blessings and curses. Turkish elements entered the Judeo-Greek language after the fifteenth century, when the area was occupied by Turkey (such elements entered common Greek at the same time). Second, Judeo-Greek contains archaisms from ancient Greek. Third, special intonations made the Jews' speech different from that of others. In order to write Greek in Hebrew letters, the writers used similar-sounding consonants and the Hebrew punctuation signs to account for the vowels. In morphological terms the Hebrew syntax influenced translators and writers, resulting in several characteristics that are held in common with other languages spoken by the Jews in the Diaspora.

BIBLIOGRAPHY

Moshe Altbauer and Jacob Schiby, "A Judeo-Greek Glossary of the *Hamesh Megillot*" (in Hebrew), in *Sefunot*, 15 (1971–1981); Daniel Goldschmidt, "Judaeo-Greek Bible Translations of the Sixteenth Century" (in Hebrew), in *Kirjath Sepher*, 33 (1957–1958); Dirk Christiaan Hesseling, *Le cinq livres de la loi (le Pentateuque): Traduction en*

Néo-Grec publiée en caractères hébraïques à Constantinople en 1547, transcrite et accompagnée d'une introduction, d'un glossaire et d'un fac-simile (1897); Joseph Matsa, *Yanniotika Evraika Traghoudhia* (1953), and "Jewish Poetry in Greek" (in Hebrew), in *Sefunot*, 15 (1979–1981); Moïse Schwab, "Sept épitaphes hébraïques de Grèce," in *Revue des études juives*, 58 (1909); Joshua Starr, "A Fragment of a Greek Mishnaic Glossary," in *Proceedings of the American Academy for Jewish Research*, 6 (1934–1935).

JACOB SCHIBY

JUDEO-ITALIAN. The term "Judeo-Italian" is used in connection with a number of manuscripts produced in Italy between the late eleventh and the sixteenth centuries and written in Hebrew characters. Their main linguistic elements are those of the southern-central Italian dialects. Nevertheless, the language of these manuscripts displays conspicuous differences from those dialects, such as a unique lexical patrimony (Hebrew roots with Italian endings; Hebrew words, especially of a liturgical nature, that did not lend themselves to translation), special linguistic structures (Semitic syntactic construction in many phrases), and the persistence of many lexical forms already obsolete in the surrounding linguistic norm.

Textual evidence led Umberto Cassuto to hypothesize the existence of a true dialect that served as a common means of expression for the Jews of Italy. On the other hand, Menahem Banitt saw these texts as mere literary exercises. Having examined the varied contents of the Judeo-Italian texts, ranging from paraphrases of the Bible to glossaries containing practical terms, Giuseppe Sermoneta has proposed that there must have been a common means of communication that linked the Jews of Italy linguistically. Still, he claims that Judeo-Italian was not a specific and well-defined dialect but, rather, a "linguistic mode" that arose as a result of the interaction between the dialects spoken by the various copyists and the cultural heritage embodied in traditions of Jewish exegesis and textual interpretation. Therefore, according to Sermoneta, the special characteristics of Judeo-Italian were established not by specific phonetic, morphological, or lexical data but by the historical, sociological, and cultural conditions of the various Jewish communities.

The oldest examples of Judeo-Italian are in tenth-century Hebrew texts, such as *Megillat Aḥimaʿaz* and *Sefer Josippon,* in which isolated glosses made their way into the body of the Hebrew text. Works of the eleventh through the thirteenth centuries, most notably the *Arukh* of Nathan ben Jehiel, the *Responsa* of Samuel ben ha-Yatom, and the *Midrash Sekhel Tov* of Menahem ben Solomon, contain articulated lists of glosses.

In the thirteenth and fourteenth centuries full-length translations, especially of the Bible and the siddur (a prayer book), as well as glossaries and original literary works, appeared. Best-known are the translation of Moses ben Joseph Kimhi's grammar, *Mahalakh Shevilei ha-Da^c at,* Judah Romano's glossary to Maimonides' *Mishneh Torah,* and an anonymous elegy on the Ninth of Av.

BIBLIOGRAPHY
Max Berenblut, *A Comparative Study of Judaeo-Italian Translations of Isaiah* (1949); Umberto Cassuto, "Un'antichissima elegia in dialetto giudeo-italiano," in *Archivio glottologico italiano,* 22–23 (1929); Giuseppe Sermoneta, *Un glossario filosofico ebraico-italiano del XIII secolo* (1969), "Considerazioni frammentarie sul giudeo-italiano," in *Italia,* 1 (1976), and "Considerazioni frammentarie sul giudeo-italiano II," in *Italia,* 1 (1978).

SANDRA STOW

JUDEO-LATIN. There is a small but significant corpus of Latin texts that Jews wrote in Hebrew characters and that Cecil Roth called "Judeo-Latin." In addition to an Anglo-Jewish charter, there are Latin quotations in Hebrew polemical writings directed against Christians as well as Hebrew incantations and prayers.

Some Christian converts to Judaism made use of their knowledge of the Vulgate in the defense of Judaism and the attack on Christianity. Several examples are found in the *Nizzahon vetus,* a thirteenth-century German-Jewish religious polemic. Its many quotations from the Vulgate, rendered in Hebrew characters, derive in large measure from the Christian education of Jewish proselytes, such as Isaac the Proselyte and Abraham the Proselyte, mentioned in the book. Another instance of Judeo-Latin in polemics is Joseph ben Nathan Official's *Sefer Yosef ha-Mekanne* (The book of Joseph the zealot), from thirteenth-century northern France (Sens).

Most learned Jews in northern Europe knew some Latin words or phrases through oral transmission, not from the study of texts. Occasionally a technical term in vogue appears in a Hebrew work. Thus in *Sefer Hasidim* (The book of the pietists), a thirteenth-century pietistic work from the Rhineland, the author stipulates that Jews should study Torah, "not other kinds of learning such as [Christian] dial[ec]tica" (J. Wistinetzki, ed., par. 752).

And it is from oral, rather than written, sources that the second type of Judeo-Latin evidence, prayers and incantations, derives. For example, part of an Italian- or German-Jewish formula for searching for buried treasure by means of a divining rod includes a passage that Moritz Güdemann transcribed thus:

> *Deus cuius providentia in sua dispositione non fallitur te suppliciter exoramus ut noxia cuncta submoveas et omnia nobis prospera concedas in nomine Dei vivi creatoris omnium creaturarum etc. in nomine Dei sancti El Eloa Sabaot Agla Adonai Tetragrammaton etc. qui vivis et regnas in secula seculorum.*

God whose providential care does not err, we humbly entreat You to remove all harmful things and grant to us all favorable things, in the name of the living God of all creatures, etc., in the name of the Holy God, El Eloa Sabaot Agla Adonai Tetragrammaton, etc., who lives and reigns for ever.

Another example, from a thirteenth-century German-Jewish manuscript in Paris (Bibliothèque Nationale, MS Heb. 326), refers to an ordeal by Psalter (*judicium cum psalterio*) in which the following non-christological version of a Christian formula is used: "omnipotens sempiterne deus qui cunctas tu ex nihilo creasti [et qui] hominem de limo terrae formasti ..." (Omnipotent sempiternal God who created everything out of nothing [and who] formed man from the mud of the earth ...).

In certain incantations Jews even used such christological expressions as "Maria" and "Parakletos." One additional instance is even more striking. In the Rhenish ceremony in which a Jewish boy first learns the Hebrew alphabet, the teacher and then the child recite the entire alphabet forward and backward. Then the child twice recites the last four letters of the Hebrew alphabet in the form of a word. Those four letters spell KRS(h)T, apparently a garbled transformation of *Christ(e).*

BIBLIOGRAPHY
Yitzhak Baer, "The Religious-Social Tendency of *Sepher Hassidim* (in Hebrew), in *Zion,* n.s. 3 (1937); David Berger, ed. and trans., *The Jewish-Christian Debate in the*

High Middle Ages: A Critical Edition of the Niẓẓaḥon vetus (1979), English pp. 31–32; Moritz Güdemann, *Geschichte des Erziehungswesens und der Cultur der abendländischen Juden*, 3 vols. (1880–1888, repr. 1966), II, 333–337; Joseph ben Nathan Official, *Sefer Yosef ha-Mekane*, Judah Rosenthal, ed. (1970); Judah ben Samuel he-Hasid, *Sefer Ḥasidim*, Jehuda Wistinetzki, ed. (1924); Colette Sirat, "Une formule divinatoire latine dans deux manuscrits hébreux," in *Revue des études juives*, **125** (1966); Joshua Trachtenberg, *Jewish Magic and Superstition* (1939).

IVAN G. MARCUS

[See also **Polemics, Christian-Jewish.**]

JUDEO-PERSIAN. The term "Judeo-Persian" is applied to the form of Modern Persian written by Jews in the Hebrew alphabet. There are also varieties of spoken Persian used in various Jewish communities in Iran, but these are not written. Judeo-Persian is very close to Standard Classical Persian. Nevertheless, the Jewish texts have special orthographic, morphological, syntactic, and lexical usages that differ considerably from the corresponding Islamic variety of Persian, which is written in a modified Arabic script. In addition to the Hebrew and Aramaic loanwords that have become integrated into Judeo-Persian, there are also native Persian words that were lost in Islamic Persian. The Jewish writer was generally not constrained by the canons of Classical Persian orthography, and thus wrote a kind of Persian that more accurately reflects what was actually pronounced. Judeo-Persian is therefore an extremely important independent textual source that sheds light on the history of the Persian language. Forms abound in its texts that accord well with what is otherwise known only from Modern Colloquial Persian—a variety that is not normally represented in written form today except in restricted literary instances.

Judeo-Persian texts are primarily of four types: translations of Hebrew originals (such as books of the Bible), original compositions on Judaic themes (the poetry of Shahin, Imrānī, and others), personal letters and documents, and numerous transcriptions into Hebrew script of a large number of works of Islamic Persian literature (Ḥāfiẓ, Saᶜdi, Neẓāmi, and others).

The earliest known Modern Persian texts are eighth-century inscriptions written in the Hebrew alphabet, a practice that continued well into the twentieth century. Thus Judeo-Persian has extended contemporaneously over the entire 1,200 years of the history of Modern Persian.

Judeo-Persian translations of the Bible (chiefly of the Pentateuch) form an important and varied textual source. The oldest text is that of the Pentateuch known from a unique manuscript in the British Library. It bears a colophon with a date equivalent to 1319, although the translation is much older. Others are known from later periods, notably a text in the Vatican Library acquired in the late sixteenth century. The Tavus text of the Constantinople Polyglot Bible (1546) was once thought to be the oldest of this genre, and much attention was paid to it because it was reprinted (in Perso-Arabic script) in the Walton Polyglot Bible in England in the mid seventeenth century. It thus formed the basis for the study of Modern Persian in the West. These and other translated versions follow the pattern of word-by-word rendition of the Hebrew original, in much the same manner as is known from Persian translations of the Koran or from translations in other holy book traditions.

The greatest Judeo-Persian writer, Shahin of Shiraz (*fl.* fourteenth century), composed a number of poetic works, notably a lengthy poem in rhyming couplets in which he tells the stories of the Pentateuch. His language is almost totally devoid of Hebrew loanwords, and he uses Islamic nomenclature from Arabic for many of the names of the biblical personages, a practice that is widespread in the work of other Judeo-Persian authors. In this extensive poem Shahin draws on a wide variety of post-biblical—midrashic and haggadic—sources, as well as on Islamic legendary tradition. The poet Imrānī (*fl.* sixteenth century), in a continuation of Shahin's work entitled *Fatḥ-nāma* (Book of victory), elaborates in poetic form all the material from the Book of Joshua up to the coronation of King David. He also composed a number of other works, including the lengthy philosophico-didactic poem *Ganj-nāma* (The book of the treasure), which renders the popular mishnaic text *Pirkei Avot*.

Judeo-Persian language and literature are of considerable importance for several reasons: as textual testimony for the history of the Jews of the Persian-speaking world; as a well-documented example of the languages that can be labeled "Jewish languages" for which a special "interlinguistics" may be formulated; as evidence for the history of the Persian language from a tradition independent of the Islamic mainstream linguistic sphere; as an important source for the sociolinguistic aspects of religious styles and registers in a language; and as an instance of how a Semitic language structure has been fused with an Indo-European one (in the case of Judeo-Persian there is the further example of Hebrew-Aramaic elements added to an already fused Arabic-Persian case).

Much remains to be done in the study and analysis of Judeo-Persian language and literature, since so little has been published. The major collections of manuscripts are in the following libraries: British Library (London), Bibliothèque Nationale (Paris), Royal Danish Library (Copenhagen), Hebrew University and National Library (Jerusalem), Ben-Zvi Institute (Jerusalem), Jewish Theological Seminary Library (New York), Hebrew Union College–Jewish Institute of Religion Library (Cincinnati).

BIBLIOGRAPHY

Jes Peter Asmussen, *Studies in Judeo-Persian Literature* (1973); Walter J. Fischel, "Israel in Iran: A Survey of Judeo-Persian Literature," in Louis Finkelstein, ed., *The Jews: Their History, Culture, and Religion*, 2 vols. (1949, 4th ed. 1970–1971), II; Gilbert Lazard, *La langue des plus anciens monuments de la prose persane* (1963), 128–134, and "La dialectologie du judéo-persan," in *Studies in Bibliography and Booklore*, 8 (1968); Amnon Netzer, *Muntakhab-e ash'āre Fārsī az asār-e yahudiyāh-e Irān* (1973); Herbert H. Paper, "Research in Judeo-Persian: Needs, Deeds, and Prospects," in *World Congress of Jewish Studies, Fifth, Jerusalem, 1969: Proceedings*, IV (1972), *Biblia Judaeo-Persica: Editio variorum* (microfilm) (1973), and "Judeo-Persian," in Herbert H. Paper, ed., *Jewish Languages: Theme and Variations* (1978); Abraham Yaari, *Sifrei Yehudei Bukhara* (1942).

HERBERT H. PAPER

JUDEO-PROVENÇAL. The term "Judeo-Provençal" has two different meanings. It may refer to a language—written in Hebrew characters but otherwise very close to Provençal—that was used for Jewish religious texts in the Middle Ages. Or it may refer to a spoken language (used also in popular writings) that showed marked divergences in grammar, lexicon, and phonology from other dialects of Provençal.

Religious texts include a fragment of a poem about Queen Esther by Crescas du Caylar (*ca.* 1327); a group of liturgical poems, called piyyutim in He-

brew and *obros* in Judeo-Provençal, written in both languages in alternating verses; and a complete prayer book for women, which is noteworthy because it includes a unique blessing: "Blessed art Thou, O Lord our God, king of the universe, who made me a woman." This prayer book, typical of Jewish translations of the period made in other countries, is basically a word-for-word translation from the Hebrew original. Its syntax, therefore, does not reflect the speech of a Romance language.

The spoken language may have been called Shuadit. Its age is a matter of dispute, but its existence is first attested in comic works written by non-Jews. One such work may date from the early sixteenth century and is called "Lou sermoun di Jusiou" (The sermon of the Jews). Another is a Christmas carol called "Reviho-te Nanan," composed in the seventeenth century. It is a dialogue between a convert to Christianity and a Jew named Nanan (a nickname for Abraham). At the end of the carol, Nanan too decides to become a Christian. These comic texts show that Jews were recognized as having a different way of speaking. On the other hand, such parodies may not be good samples of Judeo-Provençal, since the writers were not native speakers. Moreover, they may have distorted certain phonetic or grammatical features for comic effect. A more recent work is a play called *Harcanot et Barcanot*, composed around the year 1820. Szajkowski believes the author to be a Jewish lawyer from Montpellier named Bédarride.

Among the phonetic traits found in these varied sources is the merger of [ž] and [š]. Thus, *jour* (day) is spelled *chour* in the "Sermon of the Jews." In words of Hebrew origin, the letters *samekh, sin,* and *thaw* are all pronounced [f]. Thus *fuf* (horse), from Hebrew *sus*.

Jews were expelled from Provence in 1498, and the only place in southern France where they could legally reside was the Papal States. After the French Revolution, when Jews were free to live anywhere in France, Judeo-Provençal began to disappear. The writer Armand Lunel (1892–1977) was the last speaker of the language, and he had learned it from his grandparents, not from his parents. The only remnant of spoken Judeo-Provençal is a version of the song "Had Gadya," still occasionally sung at Passover seders.

BIBLIOGRAPHY

George Jochnowitz, "Shuadit: La langue juive de Provence," in *Archives juives*, 14 (1978), and " . . . Who Made Me a Woman," in *Commentary*, 71 (1981); Armand Lunel,

Juifs du Languedoc, de la Provence, et des États français du Pape (1975); Pierre Pansier, "Une comédie en argot hébraïco-provençal de la fin du XVIIIᵉ siècle," in *Revue des études juives,* 81 (1925); Susan Milner Silberstein, *The Provençal Esther Poem Written in Hebrew Characters c. 1327 by Crescas de Caylar* (diss., Univ. of Pennsylvania, 1973); Zosa Szajkowski, *Dos loshn fun di Yidn* (The language of the Jews in the four communities of the Comtat Venaissin) (in Yiddish) (1948).

GEORGE JOCHNOWITZ

JUDEO-SPANISH is a Jewish language of Hispanic stock spoken and written by Jews of Spanish origin. Phonetically and morphologically it reflects pre-sixteenth-century Spanish, and the influence of Hebrew is notable particularly in lexical areas associated with religious practices. Through contact with the languages of those Mediterranean countries in which Jews settled after their expulsion from Spain in 1492, Judeo-Spanish has admitted elements from Turkish, French, Italian, and Moroccan Arabic, and within the eastern Mediterranean dialects there are phonetic variations that reflect the transformation undergone by Spanish at the close of the fifteenth century. The language is also referred to as Ladino or Spanyol and, in Morocco, as *Hakitía.* Ladino, which originally referred only to the language used in translations of sacred Hebrew texts, has been gaining wider currency.

Up to the beginning of the twentieth century, the language was generally written in Hebrew characters, using the standard Hebrew alphabet with diacritics, to accommodate Hispanic phonemes. Early texts appeared in "square" characters, either with or without vowels, but the bulk of printed material is in the cursive rabbinic script (Rashi script). In 1928 the Turkish authorities banned publication in Hebrew characters, which resulted in the adoption of the Roman alphabet.

After their expulsion from the Iberian peninsula and at the invitation of Sultan Bajazet II, Jews settled in the Ottoman Empire and important Judeo-Spanish-speaking communities grew in present-day Bulgaria, Greece, Israel, Rhodes, Romania, Turkey, and Yugoslavia. From the end of the fourteenth century, persecuted Spanish Jews were also given shelter in North Africa, and Judeo-Spanish-speaking communities are still found along the northern coast of Morocco. The twentieth century saw the annihilation of many of the Balkan communities by the Nazis as well as a general movement away from the tradi-

tional centers and toward Israel, Europe, and the Americas, resulting in the gradual disappearance of the language.

Although the first editions of the Judeo-Spanish Bible translations appeared in the sixteenth century, they are believed to reflect an earlier tradition elaborated by the Jews long before their expulsion. Other liturgical works were translated at an early date, and there are still Jewish communities (in İstanbul, Salonika, Jerusalem, Tehran, Tangier, Gibraltar, and in the Spanish and Portuguese congregations of Amsterdam) where prayers are recited in Judeo-Spanish on certain occasions.

Up to the eighteenth century, most of the literature is rabbinic, the chief exponent being the *Me'am Lo'ez,* which was begun in Constantinople in 1730 by Jacob Culi. An encyclopedic work, it is structured mainly on the Pentateuch and spans the sources of Jewish thought. The nineteenth century witnessed the growth of a popular literature in Judeo-Spanish, including novels, plays, popular histories, translations of major European novels, as well as the birth of the Judeo-Spanish press.

Among the earliest examples of Judeo-Spanish verse are some *kharjas* by Judah Halevi written in Hebrew characters, and there exists a fragment of an early Judeo-Spanish poem on the biblical story of Joseph. However, it is in the realm of oral literature, and particularly in the *romances* (ballads), that speakers have preserved their ancient Spanish heritage.

BIBLIOGRAPHY

Texts are in Samuel G. Armistead and Joseph H. Silverman, *The Judeo-Spanish Ballad Chapbooks of Yacob Abraham Yoná* (1971); Ignacio González Llubera, ed., *Coplas de Yoçef* (1935); Vidal Sephiha, *Le ladino, judéo-espagnol calque: Deutéronome* (1973). Marius Sala, *Le judéo-espagnol* (1976), is a bibliographical study. See also José Benoliel, "Dialecto judeo-hispano-marroquí o Hakitía," in *Boletín de la real academia española,* **13** (1926), **14** (1927), **15** (1928), **32** (1952); Cynthia M. Crews, *Recherches sur le judéo-espagnol dans les pays balkaniques* (1935); Raymond R. Renard, *Sépharad: Le monde et la langue judéo-espagnole des Sephardim* (1966).

ISAAC BENABU

[See also **Spanish Language.**]

JULIAN OF NORWICH (1342–1416/1423), an English anchoress and mystic, author of the *Reve-*

lations of Divine Love, which has been acclaimed as one of the major spiritual works of the Middle Ages.

As a girl Julian wished for three gifts from God: recollection of Christ's passion; an illness at thirty; and the three wounds of true contrition, loving compassion, and affective longing for God. Her wishes were fulfilled in the *Revelations*. On 8 May 1373, when she was thirty, she lay dying from a serious illness, attended by her mother and friends. As the local priest held a crucifix before her eyes, she began to experience a series of sixteen visions or "showings" and was miraculously cured. These visions, which focused on the crucified Christ, occurred over a five-hour period, with the sixteenth taking place on the following evening. Her account of this experience appeared in a short version of the *Revelations* recorded shortly after the event, and a long version set down after almost twenty years of insightful meditation.

Manuscript evidence indicates that the *Revelations* did not enjoy a large audience, there being only one fifteenth-century copy of the short version, three postmedieval manuscripts and two extracts of the long version, and the Serenus Cressy edition of the long text, published in 1670, which attests to the continuing interest in Julian among the exiled English Benedictine communities on the Continent. The renascence of interest in the *Revelations* in the late nineteenth century has continued throughout the twentieth.

Although both texts were dictated to an amanuensis—a practice also followed by Birgitta of Sweden (1303–1373) and Catherine of Siena (*ca.* 1347–1380)—Julian's claim that she was "unlettered" is belied by her profound grasp of church teachings and Scriptures, her familiarity with earlier and contemporary mystical authorities, and her literary gifts. A comparison of the two texts reveals that the long version is more concerned with the significance of the visions, shows a greater assurance on Julian's part, and has two important additions: the central allegory of the lord and the servant (chaps. 51–57) and the excursus on the motherhood of God (chaps. 58–61). Like its precursor, the long version proclaims Julian's message of joy in Christ, sorrow for sin, and God's love, not to a restricted audience of contemplatives but to her fellow Christians "who desire to be Christ's lovers."

Julian's language is simple and moving; Christ's love is homely and courteous; all creation resides in a hazelnut held in the palm of a hand; and God is seen in a point (an instant of time). Yet she explores and elucidates the deepest mysteries and theological concerns of Christianity: creation, redemption, Divine Providence; sin; the pardox of evil (sin) and God's all-embracing love; the indwelling of the Trinity at the apex of the soul; the Mystical Body of Christ; the motherhood of God invested in Christ as Wisdom; and man's spiritual childhood.

Julian's "showings" and certain aspects of her theology have been questioned by some scholars, but the consensus finds her visions valid and her theology sound.

BIBLIOGRAPHY

The best edition of the *Revelations* (both versions) is *Showings,* Edmund Colledge and James Walsh, eds. (1978). Also see Ritamary Bradley, "The Motherhood Theme in Julian of Norwich," in *14th-Century English Mystics Newsletter,* 2, no. 4 (1976); André Cabussut, "Une dévotion médiévale peu connue: La dévotion à Jésus nôtre mère," in *Revue d'ascétique et mystique,* 25 (1949); Paul Molinari, *Julian of Norwich: The Teachings of a Fourteenth-Century English Mystic* (1958); Brant Pelphrey, *Love Was His Meaning: The Theology and Mysticism of Julian of Norwich* (1982).

VALERIE M. LAGORIO

[See also **Middle English Literature; Mysticism.**]

JULIAN THE APOSTATE (Flavius Claudius Julianus) (*ca.* 331/332–26 June 363), Roman and Byzantine emperor, was born to Basilina and Julius Constantius; his father was murdered after the death of his half brother Constantine I. Although raised as a Christian, Julian bitterly directed his resentment for the murder of his father against the persons and policies of Constantine and his sons, and thus against Christianity. His interest in pagan rites and lore was aroused by pagan teachers and his studies in Nicomedia, Ephesus, and Athens. His cousin, Emperor Constantius II, raised him to the rank of caesar in 355 and sent him to Gaul to lead resistance against Germanic invasions. His victories over the Germans won him fame among his soldiers and aroused among certain pagan literary circles hopes for a pagan revival.

A complex conspiracy induced Julian's soldiers to proclaim him Augustus—that is, emperor—at Paris late in the winter of 360. Negotiations failed to secure a settlement with Constantius, but his unexpected death permitted Julian to occupy Constantinople unopposed in December 361. He had already openly revealed his commitment to a revival of pagan rites. After appointing officials who were loyal to him, he began restoring pagan temples and encouraging his subjects, by means of treatises, public letters, and astute patronage and persuasion, to resume worshiping the gods. He also forbade Christians to teach literature. Pagan rhetoricians and philosophers contributed their literary efforts to his program. The most important work of Julian was his polemical treatise *Against the Galilaeans* (Christians), which survives in fragmentary form.

Preparatory to his campaign against Persia, Julian left Constantinople for Antioch in Syria, where he encountered much Christian opposition and ridicule. He departed from Antioch on 5 March 363 to invade Persia, probably planning to consolidate his power and confirm the correctness of his religious policies by conquering Persia. After initial successes he died from a wound suffered during a skirmish. His intellectual paganism had won only limited support, and the pagan revival collapsed with his death. Yet his reign had been the center of some of the most important intellectual ferment of the fourth century.

BIBLIOGRAPHY

Julian's writings are in *The Works of the Emperor Julian*, Wilmer Cave Wright, trans., 3 vols. (1913–1923, repr. 1930). See also Joseph Bidez, *La vie de l'empereur Julien* (1930); Glen W. Bowersock, *Julian the Apostate* (1978); Walter Emil Kaegi, Jr., "Constantine's and Julian's Strategies of Strategic Surprise Against the Persians," in *Athenaeum*, **69** (1981), "Domestic Military Problems of Julian the Apostate," in *Byzantinische Forschungen*, **2** (1967), "The Emperor Julian at Naïssus," in *L'antiquité classique*, **44** (1975), and "The Emperor Julian's Assessment of the Significance and Function of History," in *Proceedings of the American Philosophical Society*, **108** (1964).

WALTER EMIL KAEGI, JR.

[See also **Byzantine Empire: History; Roman Empire, Late.**]

JULIANUS OF TOLEDO (*ca.* 642–690), theologian and church official, was born into a family of converted Jews. He studied with Eugenius II, archbishop of Toledo (647–657). Julianus probably became involved in a conspiracy to overthrow King Wamba and crown his rival, Erwig, as ruler of Visigothic

Spain in 680. As archbishop of Toledo (680–690), he presided over the twelfth (680–681), thirteenth (683), fourteenth (684), and fifteenth (688) councils of the Visigothic church in Toledo. As head of the twelfth council he was commissioned to answer, in his *Apologeticum fidei*, the pronouncements of the Sixth Ecumenical Council of Constantinople (also known as the Third Council of Constantinople, 680–681). Pope Benedict II (684–685) found some of his ideas theologically unsound. Julianus wrote other theological treatises, hymns, a history of Wamba's reign, and a biography of St. Ildefonsus *(Elogium Ildefonsi)*. All of these works are listed in Julianus' biography by Felix, bishop of Toledo (693–700).

BIBLIOGRAPHY

J. N. Hillgarth, "Julian of Toledo in the *Liber Floridus*," in *Journal of the Warburg and Courtauld Institutes*, **26** (1963), and "St. Julian of Toledo in the Middle Ages," in *Journal of the Warburg and Courtauld Institutes*, **21** (1958); A. K. Ziegler, *Church and State in Visigothic Spain* (1930).

TEOFILO F. RUIZ

[See also **Eugenius II of Toledo; Councils (Ecumenical, 325–787); Spanish Literature: Latin; Visigoths.**]

JUNAYD (**Junayd Naqqāsh al-Sultānī; Junayd of Baghdad**) (active late fourteenth century) was a painter whose known works illustrate a manuscript (dated 1396) containing the poetry *(khamseh)* of the Persian poet Khwājū Kirmānī (1280–1351) now in the British Library, London (Add. 18113). The artist's signature, "Junayd Naqqāsh al-Sultānī," is incorporated in the architectural decoration of an illustration depicting the wedding night of the Persian prince Humāy and the Chinese princess Humāyūn (fol. 45b). Junayd's use of the epithet "al-Sultānī" probably indicates that he was linked to the court of the contemporary ruler of Baghdad, Sultan Aḥmad ibn Uwais (1382–1410) of the Jalayirid dynasty. A link between Junayd and the Jalayirid court is also suggested by a reference to him contained in a sixteenth-century essay by Dūst Muḥammad, who also describes Junayd as the student of an earlier Jalayirid court painter, Shams al-Dīn.

Junayd's paintings are notable for their courtly settings and a finesse of detail in the rendering of costumes, buildings, and landscapes. They prefigure, in this regard, the style and mood favored during the fifteenth century, particularly at the Timurid court in Herāt.

BIBLIOGRAPHY

Ivan Stchoukine (Shchukin), *Les peintures des manuscrits tîmûrides* (1954), 33–35; Norah M. Titley, *Persian Miniature Painting and Its Influence on the Art of Turkey and India* (1983), 27–34.

PRISCILLA P. SOUCEK

[See also **Islamic Art and Architecture; Timurids.**]

JURY, a body of neighbors summoned by a public officer to give under oath a true answer to some question. Juries were widely used during the medieval period for a variety of purposes. English juries, the subject of this essay, were used in two distinct phases of criminal trials. The jury was first utilized in the indicting stage, as a device to produce accusations. At a later date the jury was adopted to determine whether an accused person was innocent or guilty.

The history of the indicting or grand jury in England begins with a textual passage in the late-tenth-century laws of King Ethelred II the Unready (978–1016), which ordered twelve sworn men of the neighborhood to accuse all guilty persons. The ordinance clearly foreshadowed the indictment process set forth in the Assize of Clarendon some 190 years later in 1166 by Henry II. Thus far, however, no evidence has been discovered that links the two in any way. It is probably correct to assume that Henry II devised the accusing jury independently.

The Assize of Clarendon dealt with a multitude of matters, most of which relate to the administration of criminal justice. One of Henry's prime concerns was to reinforce the accusation procedure of the time. Before 1166 there were two ways to indict criminals. The most popular was accusation by the victim or his survivors. A second process was accusation by a fellow criminal who hoped to escape the rigor of the law by indicting his accomplices. Article I of the Assize of Clarendon states:

> King Henry, on the advice of all his barons, for the preservation of peace, and for the maintenance of justice, has decreed that inquiry shall be made throughout the several counties and throughout the several hundreds through twelve of the more lawful men of the hundred and through four of the more lawful men of each vill upon oath that they will speak the truth,

whether there be in their hundred or vill any man accused or notoriously suspect of being a robber or murderer or thief, or any who is a receiver of robbers or murderers or thieves, since the lord king has been king.

The procedure outlined at Clarendon was reaffirmed a decade later (1176) in the Assize of Northampton, which specified that, if possible, knights should make up the hundred jury, and added arson and forgery to the list of indictable offenses. These early experiments with the grand jury proved relatively successful. Later legislation and modifications were concerned mainly with keeping the jurors free from coercion. The grand jury remained a fixture of criminal procedure long after the end of the Middle Ages.

During the early medieval period the guilt or innocence of persons accused of crimes was determined by means of ordeals. The essence of the trial was the ordeal, which took a variety of forms, all purporting to reveal the judgment of God. The ordeal of cold water, for example, tried the accused by lowering him into a pool. If he was accepted by the water—that is, if he sank—he was innocent. If rejected—that is, if he floated—the accused was guilty and subjected to the appropriate punishment. Other popular ordeals used heated iron and boiling water. All required the blessing of the instrument by a priest and a suitable ritual.

The assizes of Clarendon and Northampton specify ordeal of cold water as the regular mode of trial for those indicted under their provisions. They also reveal that Henry II had less than total faith in the verdict of the ordeal. Both contain provisions for the exile of persons of "bad renown and publicly and evilly reputed," even if they were found innocent by the judgment of God. Nor were laymen the only skeptics; from a very early period some churchmen decried the church's participation in the ordeal.

In the thirteenth century matters came to a head. The Fourth Lateran Council (1215) forbade all clergy to take part in ordeals. This robbed the ordeal of all religious sanction and meant it could no longer be used as a means of trial. In England the decree was obeyed almost immediately and created a very large problem for the courts. The only official reaction to this dilemma occurred in 1219. The justices, about to depart on eyre (circuit), were told to keep those accused of greater crimes in prison, if they suspected them of being guilty. Those accused of medium crimes should be allowed to abjure the realm. Persons accused of lesser crimes should be allowed to go free if they found pledges for good behavior.

Clearly, these provisions were intended as temporary expedients, but King Henry III never gave any further direction in this matter. The justices were left to work out a solution on their own. Their solution, developed during the half century after 1219, was the petty or trial jury.

Even before the Fourth Lateran Council's decree, certain disputes in criminal proceedings had been referred to a jury. When a defendant alleged the accusation against him was brought out of hate and envy, the justices put this allegation to a jury because the jurors would know the motives of the accusor. If a jury could determine the motive of an accusor, then why could it not also determine the guilt or innocence of the accused? Moreover, for a generation the courts had employed juries in civil litigation touching matters of the gravest importance. The solution must have seemed almost painfully obvious.

The petty jury was not without problems of its own, however. Its members were selected from among those who served on the grand juries. Nothing prevented a juror from serving on both a defendant's grand and petty juries, and complaints were registered against this. Finally, in 1352, a statute permitted defendants to challenge jurors on this ground. Moreover, since the petty jury was a substitute for the judgment of God, it was not at first obvious that defendants could be forced to accept the verdict of mere humans. By 1275 Edward I was confident enough to impose the petty jury by statute:

> ... notorious felons who are openly of evil fame and who refuse to put themselves upon inquest of felony at the suit of the King before his justices, shall be remanded to a hard and strong prison as befits those who refuse to abide by the common law of the land.

The *prison forte et dure* of the statute was somehow transformed into *peine forte et dure,* torture by pressing with heavy weights. The accused had to either accept the jury or suffer a slow and painful death. Obviously guilty felons sometimes chose the latter in order to avoid forfeiture of their goods and chattels.

At the end of the Middle Ages, Sir John Fortescue described the petty jury in *De laudibus legum Angliae.* His was a jury whose members were judges of fact, not of law, impartial men with open minds who found their verdict from presentations in the court and not from their own knowledge. They were very like the modern petty jury. Nonetheless, the petty jury retained something of the inscrutability of its predecessor, the ordeal. Its deliberations were secret and privileged; its answers unanimous, simple, and unqualified.

BIBLIOGRAPHY

Sources. Sir John Fortescue, *De laudibus legum Angliae,* S. B. Chrimes, ed. and trans. (1942); *The Laws of the Kings of England from Edmund to Henry I,* A. J. Robertson, ed. and trans. (1925).

Studies. S. F. C. Milsom, *Historical Foundations of the Common Law* (1969); Theodore F. T. Plucknett, *A Concise History of the Common Law,* 5th ed. (1956), and *Edward I and Criminal Law* (1960); Sir Francis Pollock and Frederic W. Maitland, *The History of English Law Before the Time of Edward I,* 2nd ed., 2 vols. (1952).

T. A. SANDQUIST

[See also **Clarendon, Assize of; Councils, Western (1215–1274); Fortescue, Sir John; Henry II; Law Codes: 1000 to 1500; Law, English Common: To 1272; Ordeals.**]

JUSTICES, ITINERANT (in eyre). The use of traveling royal justices in England has a long and complex history. As early as the reign of William the Conqueror, they were sent to sessions of the shire courts. Under Henry I the scope of their activity was expanded considerably, but the collapse of central government that marked King Stephen's reign (1135–1154) ended these early experiments. This article is concerned with the use of itinerant justices by Henry II, under whom the eyre became a permanent institution, the *iter ad omnia placita* (general eyre). During the fourteenth century the general eyre was superseded, though itinerant justices continued to be employed in other ways well past the end of the medieval period.

Henry II came to the throne in 1154. During the first decade of the reign, he struggled to reestablish the political and financial stability of royal government. Henry was then prepared to begin the formidable task of reasserting royal judicial supremacy throughout his realm. He did so in 1166 by dispatching two powerful magnates on an eyre. Their task was to enforce the provisions of the Assize of Clarendon, promulgated earlier that year. Henry intended that the two justices should cover the whole of the kingdom with their eyre, but in fact the north and west of England escaped their attentions. The assize focused on the problems of crime and violence. Though it may not have established radical new procedures for the presentment of criminals, as was once believed, the stern uniformity with which the two royal justices enforced the assize was without precedent. The hurried building of county jails and the digging and blessing of ordeal pits were evidence of their activities.

In 1176 Henry embarked on a still more inventive and ambitious attempt to punish the perpetrators of crimes. Richard fitz Nigel (or Fitzneale) in the *Course of the Exchequer* describes the process:

> ... the King once more essayed to renew the "golden days" of his grandfather; and, making choice of prudent men, he divided the kingdom into six parts, so that the justices chosen, whom we call "Justices in Eyre," might go on circuit through them and restore the rights which had lapsed. They, giving audience in each county, and doing full justice to those who considered themselves wronged, saved the poor both money and labor. (Charles Johnson, ed. and trans., p. 77)

For two years the king's justices worked at enforcing the Assize of Northampton (1176). It and the earlier Assize of Clarendon were concerned primarily with criminal activity. In 1176, however, the justices broadened the scope of their eyre by dealing with a number of feudal matters. They received oaths of fealty on behalf of the king, collected information about the custody of castles, and made inquiries "concerning escheats, churches, lands and women, who are in the gift of the king."

In 1179 Henry introduced the Grand Assize, a new procedure for use in disputes over the ownership of land. More royal justices were dispatched to administer this and other, less solemn, procedures used to determine right to possess land, the true heir, and right to present church benefices. In the last decade of Henry's reign the Assize of Arms (1181) and the Assize of the Forests (1184) were added to the justices' burdens. In effect the king, by means of itinerant justices, brought within the ambit of royal jurisdiction a great body of litigation previously dealt with by feudal and local courts.

By 1194 royal justices on eyre were being issued a set of articles (chapters) of inquiry. The appearance of these articles of the eyre clearly marks the emergence of the general eyre. Subsequently, individual chapters were modified or dropped, and new chapters were added in response to royal command, popular demand, and legislation. The 1194 articles of the eyre, however, remained the prototype as long as the general eyre was a feature of English judicial practice.

The evolution of the eyre from the Assize of Clar-

endon to the end of the twelfth century involved important changes in the arrangement of the king's courts. The court of common pleas, for example, had its origins in a measure of 1178 providing that five judges were perpetually to follow the person of the king and dispense justice. This was done in response to the demand for ready access to royal justice. As the quantity of the litigation increased, the king found it necessary to create a body of professional judges. Many came from the church and the universities, but throughout the reigns of Henry and his sons Richard I and John, the lay element remained strong in the royal judiciary.

There are many indications that the general eyres were a considerable burden to the populace. A chronicler tells how, in 1233, the men of Cornwall fled to the woods when the justices approached. By 1250 an attempt was made to limit the holding of the general eyre in any county to a maximum of once in seven years. The reason behind the fear and resentment is easy to understand. From the beginning the eyres had been the result of mixed motives. Law and order were socially desirable ends for all law-abiding persons, but in the Middle Ages the exercise of justice was also a source of profit. The eyre had always been a great financial gain for the king and a correspondingly great oppression for his subjects. Richard I collected huge sums, first for his crusade and later to pay his ransom. John exploited the fiscal possibilities of the general eyre to help support his unsuccessful ventures on the Continent. Later kings used the general eyre, or merely the threat of one, to relieve their subjects of money needed by the royal Exchequer. The money came from fines levied against litigants and from procedural fees. Amercements were rendered against counties, townships, and individuals for dereliction of duty or negligence in pursuit of the king's interests.

The power of the general eyre is manifested by the fact that its sessions comprehended all other royal courts. Pleas normally heard by the county and hundred courts were automatically transferred to the justices on eyre. Even pleas currently before any of the justices at Westminster from the county where a general eyre was in session were adjourned to the general eyre.

Yet the eyre was even more than a court *ad omnia placita*. The justices undertook a searching examination of all administrative and judicial business that had transpired in the county since the last general eyre. The king intended not only that his justices should provide an impressive display of royal power in action but also that they would do their best to ensure that the king's commands were fulfilled between visitations. To these ends the sessions of the general eyre in the thirteenth century were solemn affairs.

Bracton, writing about 1250, describes the arrival of the justices and their staff thus:

> First let the writs be read which authorize and empower them to proceed on eyre, that their authority may be known. When these have been heard, and if the justices so wish, let one of the senior and more distinguished among them publicly declare in the presence of all the reason for their coming, the purpose of the eyre and the advantage to be derived from keeping the peace: . . . And [let him declare] that the king orders all his lieges, in the faith whereby they are bound to him and as they wish to save their possessions, to lend effective and diligent counsel and aid for the preservation of his peace and justice and the suppression and extirpation of wrongdoing. (Samuel E. Thorne, trans.)

Early in the proceedings the justices had juries empaneled from each hundred, borough, and liberty within the county. Each jury was given a copy of the chapters (*capitula*) of the eyre. By Bracton's day the chapters numbered more than fifty. Among them the following provide a good indication of the wide scope of the justices' inquiries:

> Of young men and maidens who are and ought to be in the king's wardships: who they are, who have them and through whom, and how much their lands are worth.
>
> Of churches in the king's gift: which churches they are, who hold them and by whom they were presented.
>
> Of purprestures made against the king: whether on land or in the sea or in fresh water, whether within a liberty or without or elsewhere, no matter where.
>
> Of measures established and sworn throughout the realm: whether they have been adhered to as ordained, and whether the keepers of measures have taken a bribe from anyone that he may buy by one set of measures and sell by another.
>
> Of deceased Christian usurers: who they were, and what chattels they had, and who has them. Of the chattels of slain Jews and their pledges, debts and charters, and who has them.
>
> Of forgers and clippers of coins.
>
> Of burglars and malefactors and their harbourers in time of peace.
>
> Of fugitives: if any have returned after flight without the permission of the lord king.
>
> Of outlaws and their chattels: who has them, and whether outlaws have returned without warrant.

> Of those who have not pursued as they ought outlaws and burglars who crossed their lands.
>
> Of defaults, that is, of those who have been summoned to be here before the justices and are not present, and of those who did not come on the first day.
>
> Of the escape of thieves.
>
> Of poachers in parks and fishponds, who they are.
>
> Of the excesses of sheriffs and other bailiffs: whether they have fomented litigation for the purpose of acquiring lands or wardships or of obtaining money or other profits by which justice and truth are stifled or suffer delay.
>
> Of sheriffs and other ambidextrous bailiffs who take bribes from both sides. (Samuel E. Thorne, trans.)

After receiving a copy of the *capitula*, the jurors retired to prepare their written answers (*veredicta*) to the above inquiries. These were submitted to the court at a time appointed by the justices. The justices then settled down to the task of examining the jurors and hearing litigants. The inevitable result of their activity was a fine or amercement, duly entered upon the rolls that recorded the fiscal results of the eyre. In due course the sheriff of the county would receive orders to collect these monies and transmit them to the Exchequer at Westminster.

The middle of the thirteenth century was the high point of the general eyre. From the king's point of view it was a great financial success. Income from this source rose steadily throughout the first half of the century. The royal servants in the law were so adept at exploiting this aspect of justice that Matthew Paris thought the eyre of 1240–1241 nothing more than a plundering expedition to fill the royal coffers. Probably most of the jurors who prepared *veredicta* for the justices would have agreed with him.

Yet by the end of the thirteenth century a great transformation had taken place. The general eyre had become only an occasional thing, useful to the crown as a threat but no longer indispensable for the provision of royal justice. The eyre had suffered from two basic difficulties almost from its origins. First, it was intended to be general in its coverage of the realm as well as in the nature of its jurisdiction. But never, in the more than one hundred years of its existence, did the eyre travel in regular and ordered circuits. Groups of counties were visited by the justices, but the groups varied from eyre to eyre and, hence, the frequency of visitation varied from county to county. Some counties escaped visitation for ten, fifteen, or even twenty years. A few parts of England lay entirely outside the eyre system. Those areas outside the eyre or infrequently served by it were handled in various other ways, but the fact that the crown never established any system to provide uniform coverage of the whole realm is suggestive. To some extent the eyre responded to those areas where the need was greatest or where the possibility of financial gain was greatest.

Second, the eyre was by nature intermittent. It had to be, since in the early part of the thirteenth century the eyre utilized the bulk of the judicial talent in the kingdom. Until 1249 the court of common pleas was disbanded during a general eyre. Those who suffered from the exactions of the justices demanded less frequent visits and petitioned Parliament to this effect. On the other hand, litigants generally desired more frequent provision of at least certain aspects of royal justice. Nearly everyone wanted cases in which they were personally involved to be tried cheaply, expeditiously, and locally. Even in its heyday it was necessary to supplement the general eyre with itinerant justices with limited commissions. By the end of the thirteenth century, the functions of the general eyre were being taken over to an increasing extent by a wide variety of judicial commissions, many staffed with nonprofessionals. These looked after such matters as jail delivery, trying particular assizes, and sometimes even individual cases. By then, improved access to the court of common pleas at Westminster also provided an outlet for litigation that had previously been handled by the general eyre.

Thus, the manifold functions of the general eyre were dispersed among various institutional arrangements that had grown up alongside the eyre, which was not so much succeeded as superseded. During the fourteenth century, eyres were held sporadically and covered only a few counties. They became an occasional means of extortion and punishment rather than an important arm of royal government. New sources of income for the crown, such as the tax on wool and woolfells, and parliamentary grants, more adequately met the needs of the late thirteenth and the fourteenth centuries. Of course the mechanisms that superseded the eyre were not free to their clients; they too provided income for the crown.

The legacy left by the general eyre was the notion that a strong bond existed between justice and the regulation of local government. Many of the chapters of the eyre show how searching were the justices' inquiries about the conduct of local officials and communities. The amercement rolls are filled with the evidence of the justices' relentless punishment of neglect or malfeasance in the conduct of public duties. Without the eyre the abuses of local government would have remained hidden. Self-government was an economic necessity in the Middle Ages. No central authority could finance the complex bureaucracy needed for any alternative. In England for more than a century the general eyre provided the crown with the means for strict supervision of local authorities and created self-government at the king's command. This aspect of the work of the general eyre was not replaced when it ended. Local government lapsed into the hands of the gentry, with predictable results.

BIBLIOGRAPHY

Medieval works treating the eyre include Henry de Bracton, *De legibus et consuetudinibus Angliae*, Samuel E. Thorne, trans., II (1968); Richard fitz Nigel, *The Course of the Exchequer*, Charles Johnson, ed. and trans. (1950); Ranulf de Glanville, *The Treatise on the Laws and Customs of the Realm of England Commonly Called Glanville*, George D. G. Hall, ed. and trans. (1965).

Among records of eyres are *Crown Pleas of the Wiltshire Eyre, 1249*, C. A. F. Meekings, ed. (1961); *The Roll of the Shropshire Eyre of 1256*, A. Harding, ed. (1981).

See also William Craddock Bolland, *The General Eyre* (1922); Helen Maud Cam, *Studies in the Hundred Rolls* (1921); Doris Mary Stenton, *English Justice Between the Norman Conquest and the Great Charter* (1964); Ralph V. Turner, *The King and His Courts* (1968).

T. A. SANDQUIST

[See also **Assize, English; Exchequer, Court of; Jury; Justices of Common Pleas.**]

JUSTICES OF COMMON PLEAS. "Court of common pleas" is a modern term used to refer to the central English law court that was known to contemporaries in the medieval period as the "common bench." In the last part of Henry II's reign (1154–1189), three judicial tribunals administered justice on behalf of the king. One of these was the circuit court of traveling judges that went out from Westminster periodically to hear pleas in a certain group of assigned counties. These circuits were called "eyres," and the judges were "itinerant" because they traveled. This system of English circuit justice first appeared in the reign of Henry I (1100–1135). Another group of judges comprised a second tribunal that heard pleas in the presence of the king. This, too, was a traveling court, for the medieval king was an itinerant king who constantly moved about his kingdom.

Also from the last years of Henry II, a third court sat within the precincts of the royal palace at Westminister on the Thames, a few miles upstream from London. Westminster was already the chief royal residence; and the officers of the royal treasury and the Exchequer performed their duties in Westminster Hall. There was a natural connection between the fiscal and the judicial, for justice involved royal financial rights and the collection of fines and amercements, and the officers of the Exchequer often helped the judges (and sometimes served as judges) in this third court. Most of all, the Westminster court heard the pleas of persons who, because of distance and difficulty of travel, were unable to bring their suits before the king's court or the eyre courts as those two tribunals moved about the countryside. This third court also treated the unfinished business that was sent back from the two traveling courts.

All three courts dealt with the same kinds of cases, which may for the most part be called "common pleas"; no one of them specialized in a particular kind of litigation. In fact, it may be better to think of them in the last years of the twelfth century not as three courts but as three different sets of judges. And in the early years of John's reign (1199–1216), they were still far from being clearly three separate courts, and even farther from handling different kinds of law cases. As the struggle between King John and Pope Innocent III grew sharper after John's excommunication in 1209, the king closed the sedentary court at Westminster, probably because of a shortage of judges. His excommunication meant that those judges who were clerics would no longer serve him in any one of the three courts.

During much of the period after 1209, John used only one set of judges—those who accompanied him about the country—to do the work of the eyre judges and the "bench" judges who were accustomed to sit at Westminster. With this single group of judges he usually opened each of the four judicial terms of the year—Michaelmas, Hilary, Easter, and Trinity—by sitting for perhaps a week at Westminster and then moving out into the counties on a prearranged itinerary. Not until the struggle over Magna Carta had completely subsided and his young son, Henry III, had attained his majority and taken over the rule of the kingdom did these three sets of judges reappear on a regularized basis.

Because of the uncertainty and irregularity of court sessions in the last years of John's reign, the barons who forced Magna Carta upon him in 1215 provided for more certain justice in article 17, which stated that "common pleas (communia placita) shall not follow our court but shall be held in some definite place." This article did not stipulate that Westminster was to be that "definite place"; but since judges had sat there for years before Magna Carta, it was natural that a group of them should be reestablished at Westminster during Henry III's minority. When the other two courts resumed their activity, the court at Westminster became the permanent sedentary court, hearing cases throughout the four judicial terms of the year.

In the course of the thirteenth century, the term "common bench" (communis bancus) came increasingly to be applied to this court to set it apart from the court that sat "in the presence of the king" (the coram rege). The common bench was most often referred to in terms of the justices who sat on it (justiciarii de banco), and the pleas that were heard there (placita de banco). By the end of the thirteenth century, the term "common bench" was recognized by all, and throughout the medieval period identified the court that, with few exceptions, held its sessions regularly at Westminster, and that in modern times has acquired the popular name "court of common pleas."

The justices who sat on the bench in the late twelfth and thirteenth centuries came from various backgrounds. The English kings often chose clerks in minor orders to be judges. These men rarely advanced to holy orders, although some did become archdeacons and a very few left their judicial careers to become bishops. These clerks were valuable judicial officers because they were literate, were fairly well educated, and sometimes had formal training in canon and civil law. In addition to salaries, the king could reward them by presenting them, or favoring their presentation, to church livings in the form of prebends, canonries, and benefices. Laymen also held judgeships, and although in the early days of the bench Henry II had some of the great barons serve very occasionally, and perhaps for special purposes, such powerful men did not comprise the regular personnel of the bench. The lay judges who became professional and permanent figures in this court came from obscure knightly families scattered across England. These laymen had acquired their knowledge of the law by working as undersheriffs or stewards of more powerful families, or engaging in many ways in the daily judicial and fiscal business of the county and of other local units. Geoffrey fitz Peter, who became one of the most important judges during the reign of King John, was the son of a forester.

During the long reign of Henry III (1216–1272), a pattern is discernible wherein several clerks in minor orders served bench judges as their personal clerks and, through the experience gained in such employment, rose to become notable judges. Such a clerk might work for years on the bench and on eyre, managing various kinds of legal processes, and acting as writer and custodian of writs, court rolls, and other legal records. Martin Pattishall of Northamptonshire was the clerk of a well-known lay judge, Simon Pattishall, for many years in the early thirteenth century before becoming a bench judge about 1220. He trained his clerk, William Raleigh, who became a prominent judge in the 1230's; and Raleigh certainly employed Roger Thurkelby for some time before the latter rose to a seat on the bench in 1240. Thurkelby's judicial career spanned twenty years, but other bench clerks did not have long apprenticeships followed by equally long judgeships. Robert Nottingham, an obscure judge who served Robert Lexington, also a clerical judge, from 1230 to 1245, succeeded to the bench upon his master's retirement in the latter year. Lexington's career as a judge covered twenty-five years; Nottingham served for only two years before retiring.

In the thirteenth century bench judges were also drawn from the ranks of more specialized clerks who were called "keepers of the rolls and writs of the bench." Such a person was originally the chancellor's deputy on the bench, the first formal appointment of such an officer being made in 1246, when the king named Roger Whitchester, of a Northumberland family, to this position and provided for his salary. Whitchester had probably been associated with the bench since 1230 as William York's clerk, and he served as "keeper" from 1246 until 1254, when he was promoted to the bench. Before he became a bench judge, the king had assigned him to numerous commissions as a judge of assizes. Of the eight keepers of rolls and writs between 1246 and 1314, seven eventually moved to judgeships on the bench. One of the better-known of these was Elias Beckingham, who was probably in judicial service as early as 1258, when he was Hugh Bygod's clerk in the Essex assizes. Twenty years later he was appointed keeper of the rolls and writs of the bench. In 1285 he was moved from this office to a seat on the bench and was the only member of the common bench to survive the wholesale dismissal of judges in

1290; Beckingham then served for another seventeen years, until his death. His entire legal career covered fifty years.

Justices of the common bench had much more to do than merely attend to the litigation before them. The longest of the judicial terms, Michaelmas, usually lasted eight weeks. Each of the other three terms lasted four weeks or less. This left considerable time between terms, and the judges then went into the counties to execute assize commissions, jail delivery commissions, and oyer and terminer commissions, and to perform other judicial duties. In the late twelfth century and for most of the thirteenth, the common bench judges also had to staff the frequent eyres that took royal justice into the counties. There were not enough bench judges to manage the eyres, and additional nonprofessional judges had to be added to accomplish the circuits. Furthermore, in the attempt to keep the bench functioning while the eyres were under way, not all of the bench judges went out on eyre. But enough did go out to deplete the personnel of the bench; and on certain occasions, during heavy eyre work, the bench sessions were suspended.

Edward I (1272–1307) brought this state of affairs to an end in the early years of his reign; he stopped assigning bench judges to eyres, and the court at Westminster sat regularly during all four terms, year after year. The eyre judges of Edward I's reign can be thought of as career judges with repeated eyre commissions, and were never given appointments to the common bench. A notable exception to this custom occurred in 1290, when the king appointed John Mettingham to be chief justice of the common bench after he had removed all of the bench judges, except Elias Beckingham, on charges of corruption. Mettingham's chief judicial work before that time had been confined to twenty years of eyre commissions, a field in which he had acquired a notable reputation and had won the respect and confidence of the king. The tradition of relieving the common bench judges of eyre work did not continue under the two succeeding kings, for Edward II and Edward III assigned certain judges from both benches to the eyres that they commissioned. But it really mattered little, for the eyres were coming to an end: Edward II commissioned only two—for Kent in 1313 and for London in 1321—and Edward III, after four crowded eyres in the first years of his reign, abandoned the institution altogether.

The most important change in the personnel of the common bench throughout the entire medieval period occurred in the last years of the thirteenth century, when Edward I began to choose judges from among men who were professional pleaders (in modern terms, "barristers"). Historians have sometimes described this change as a shift from clerical judges to lay judges, but analysis of the change shows that the lay judge involved in this shift was a particular kind of layman. He had acquired a specialized training that caused him to be increasingly identified with the professional pleader, a person who had spent many years practicing as a lawyer before the common bench and in other courts. This professional class of pleader is not clearly in evidence until the early years of Edward I's reign. When the pleader first appeared in the 1270's, he carried the Latin title *narrator,* one who specialized in delivering, in place of the litigant, the "narration" or opening complaint in a lawsuit. This specialist stood in sharp contrast with another agent in the early legal profession, the attorney, who was a more generalized lawyer. The attorney managed the details of legal process and represented a litigant in various ways but did not plead in court. Almost any literate person having a practical acquaintance with the legal system could serve as an attorney: a relative, a friend, or a neighbor. The rise of the attorney to professional status is a more obscure process, although it was contemporaneous with the rise of the pleader.

In contrast to the attorney, the pleader was an expert in oral legal argument. Not only did he deliver the opening complaints in a lawsuit; his major task, whether he served plaintiff or defendant, was to combat and defeat his opponent's arguments and to clarify and specify the major points in a suit that could win the case for his client. In effect, he was a trial or courtroom lawyer. Nothing is known of the institution or process through which the earliest pleaders received their highly technical training. Later, in the fourteenth and fifteenth centuries, the Inns of Court provided this professional preparation and the narrators were eventually called "serjeants-at-law." In the late thirteenth century, when they first appeared, their most important attribute was their extensive and thorough knowledge of the common law, of legal process, and of the new statutes, a knowledge exceeded only by that of the judges.

In 1290, when Edward I reconstituted the common bench after the judicial scandals, he named William Gisleham, a professional pleader from Suffolk, to one of the five judgeships. Gisleham not only had engaged for several years in private practice; he also had served as the king's pleader in the quo warranto

suits of the 1280's, initiated by the king to clarify the conditions of franchises. Within the next seven years Edward appointed two other professional pleaders, William Bereford and William Howard, to the common bench. Both of these men had been prominent legal practitioners, and Bereford was to enjoy one of the longest judicial careers in English history.

Still, at the end of Edward's reign in 1307, of six judges on the common bench, three were clerical; and of the three laymen, only two, Bereford and Howard, were former pleaders. The change was completed under Edward II (1307–1327) and Edward III (1327–1377). At the end of the former's reign, all five common bench judges were laymen and four were former pleaders. By 1337, when the number of judgeships had been increased to eight, all came from the ranks of the professional pleaders. And, with only one or two exceptions, all of the later judges of the medieval common bench came from the same group. It could be said that the legal profession had captured the judiciary. A possible disadvantage of this development lay in the absence of diversity in the judges' professional backgrounds, diversity that might have had a beneficial influence on the development and application of English law. On the other hand, the major advantage of this new situation was obvious. From that time on, the judicial administration of England would lie in the hands of judges whose understanding of the law arose from the common, extensive, and rigorous experience of the practicing lawyer.

The careers of most medieval judges never crossed the political watersheds of factional struggle, violent political change, and royal displeasure. But when such events did occur, the results were often puzzling and difficult, if not impossible, to explain. John Stonor, the son of an Oxfordshire freeholder, studied law at London in the first years of the fourteenth century, was admitted to the bar about 1313, and assumed a seat on the common bench in 1320, when the struggle between Edward II and Thomas of Lancaster was moving to its violent conclusion. Stonor was one of those who had to give judgment against the Mortimers in 1322, thereby storing up for himself the resentment of the baronial opposition. Yet in 1327, when that opposition achieved its victory in the deposition of the king, Stonor was permitted to remain on the bench. Two years later he was appointed chief baron of the Exchequer for a few months, and then returned to the common bench as its chief justice. In 1331, shortly after the young Edward III had assumed complete control of his government, he removed Stonor from the chief justiceship for unspecified reasons but appointed him a puisne justice of the same bench a month later, an equally mystifying move. He served on the bench until Trinity term 1335, and then in July 1335 Edward III reappointed him chief justice of the common bench, the second time that he had held that office. It is difficult to find acceptable explanations for any of these changes. The important point is that whatever the vagaries of fortune, Stonor persisted and endured in his professional career.

The next change was more comprehensible, for in the violent reaction of Edward III against his ministers in 1340, he removed Stonor once more and imprisoned him in the Tower of London. But no charges have ever been discovered against him, and in the Easter term of 1342, he sat again as a puisne justice of the common bench. In the following judicial term the king again made him chief justice, for the third time, and he served in that post until 1354, when, decrepit and ill, he retired from the bench and died a few months later.

John Stonor's career illustrates both the vulnerability of judges to political change and royal caprice, and the ability of these men to recover from misfortune and prosper professionally. Stonor also represents the durability of literate activity and tradition among certain of the medieval English gentry: he was the first important member of a moderately influential Oxfordshire landed family, and more than a century later his direct descendants had retained that influence and left to future generations a treasury of correspondence that brilliantly illuminates the social customs and outlook of their class in the late fifteenth century.

Most of the judges of the common bench were as fortunate as Stonor in recovering from momentary setbacks; and the bench was remarkably stable during the last two centuries of the medieval period, despite notable crises in the fourteenth century and the prolonged political turbulence in the fifteenth century. A total of seventy-four men served as judges of the common bench in the fourteenth century. The bench had usually carried a complement of five justices in the preceding century, and in the fourteenth century this average rose to six, reaching eight on occasion and falling as low as three. If ten judges who served less than three years are deducted from the total, each of the remaining sixty-four served an average of ten years, clear proof of stability.

The distinction of the longest judicial career on the medieval common bench belongs to William

Bereford, who served from 1294 until his death in 1326, a span of thirty-two years. He was practicing as a lawyer in the 1270's, so his entire legal career covered some fifty years. From 1309 until his death he was chief justice. John Stonor's judicial career was not quite as long as Bereford's, considering his several absences from the bench. The third-longest career was probably that of William Thirning, who came to the common bench after the violent judicial upheaval of 1388. During the political revolution of 1399, when Richard II was deposed, Thirning, as chief justice, was the most conspicuous judicial figure in the deposition proceedings and in the settling of the crown upon Henry IV. He continued to serve until 1413, when his career of twenty-seven years came to an end.

In summary, therefore, the common bench was one of three royal courts that arose in England in the late twelfth century. The king drew its judges at first from the nonprofessional ranks of the clergy and the laity, but by the early fourteenth century those judges became exclusively laymen drawn from the ranks of professional lawyers. Although adverse political conditions affected the court from time to time, it maintained a remarkable stability of personnel throughout the medieval period and played the most important role in the daily development and application of the English common law.

BIBLIOGRAPHY

Lists of judges of the common bench from 1272 to 1422 are in George Osborne Sayles, ed., *Select Cases in the Court of King's Bench,* I (1936), cxxix–cxxxv; IV (1957), xci–xcv; and VI (1965), lxvi–lxxxi. Studies include Alan Harding, *The Law Courts of Medieval England* (1973); Margaret Hastings, *The Court of Common Pleas in Fifteenth-Century England* (1947); Franklin J. Pegues, "The Clericus in the Legal Administration of Thirteenth-Century England," in *English Historical Review,* 71 (1956); Doris Mary Stenton, *English Justice Between the Norman Conquest and the Great Charter, 1066–1215* (1964).

Franklin J. Pegues

[See also **Edward I of England; Exchequer, Court of; Justices, Itinerant; Justices of the King's Bench; Law, English Common.**]

JUSTICES OF THE KING'S BENCH. The English court that was later known as the "King's Bench" first appeared in the late twelfth century, during the reign of Henry II (1154–1189), who is called the father of the English common law because he made it possible for every English freeman to find legal remedy in his royal courts in cases that earlier had been tried in baronial courts or other private franchisal courts. He accomplished this in part through the renovation and expansion of the system of itinerant or eyre judges, who made periodic circuits through English counties, bringing the king's justice to the local countryside. Henry also began the practice of having judges hear pleas on a regular basis within the royal palace at Westminster, on the Thames near London. In addition to these two groups of justices, he took a third and smaller group with him as he traveled about his kingdom, and these judges heard cases in his presence. This was the "King's Bench." Extremely little is known about it during the last part of Henry's reign and during that of his son, Richard I the Lionhearted (1189–1199), because both kings were rarely in England.

The King's Bench became prominent during John's reign (1199–1216) as the court that held pleas in the presence of the king *(coram rege)*. At John's death his son Henry III (1216–1272) was nine years of age and too young for many years to have such a court. In a reorganization of governmental offices in 1234, the King's Bench reappeared fully constituted, and its history can be studied thereafter in a continuous fashion.

Through most of the medieval period, the most certain, and often the only, way to identify the King's Bench in the records is through the occurrence of the term *coram rege*. But the phrase *bancus regis* (king's bench) appeared frequently as time went on, and usually with phrases such as *justiciarii de banco regis* (justices of the king's bench) and *placita de banco regis* (pleas of the king's bench). For some time into the thirteenth century, pleas must have been heard literally in the presence of the king. But as the volume of business grew, this became impractical as a strict rule. The judges needed most of all to have the king's opinion and consultation easily available at short notice. Even this was impossible for long periods in the reigns of Henry III and Edward I when they were out of the kingdom. Such a period was the long absence of Edward I in 1286–1289, during which the King's Bench sat regularly, although the king was not in England. Nevertheless the king maintained the tradition of occasionally presiding over sessions of his own bench, and not until the fifteenth century did he absent himself permanently from this court.

For a long time the jurisdiction of the King's

Bench differed little from that of the other two courts, the common bench and the justices on eyre. All three heard common pleas, but the eyre justices had the additional duty of dealing with criminal justice in the counties. A person could sue a common plea in an eyre, or in the common bench, or in the King's Bench, and sometimes one of the three was chosen for geographical convenience. In addition to common pleas, the King's Bench had a special jurisdiction: it could correct error in either of the other two courts, and it had authority to hear, or summon before it, any case that touched the king. The ability of the eyres to deal effectively with crime decreased, and by the beginning of the fourteenth century, the king recognized that special efforts were needed to control crime. He gradually placed this burden on the King's Bench, so that by 1330 this court had assumed the entirely new task of administering criminal justice by hearing and processing criminal indictments. Criminal justice was to constitute a large part of its work thereafter.

Until the late thirteenth century, the king chose the judges of the King's Bench, as he did the eyre judges and those of the common bench, from lay persons who may have acquired legal experience as stewards of great lords, and who were invariably landholders, and from clerks in minor orders who had similar experience, as well as education and perhaps some training in canon and civil law.

More is known of the clerical than of the lay judges in the early period. William Raleigh, who headed the reconstituted King's Bench in 1234, was a clerical judge. He had learned much law by serving as a clerk to another judge, Martin Pattishall, for some fifteen years. After Pattishall's death in 1228, Raleigh received a judgeship on the common bench and in 1234 became senior justice on the King's Bench. He left this court in 1239 when his prominence in the king's service assisted him in being elected bishop of Norwich and, later, bishop of Winchester. During his years on the two benches, he may have trained another clerk, Henry Bracton, who became a judge of the King's Bench and the best-known name in the medieval judiciary for his monumental treatise on English law.

Ralph Hengham (*ca.* 1240–1311) is one of the best-known medieval English judges, and perhaps the most complete model of the clerical judge. Nothing is known of his education, but all young clerks who followed his career pattern had received some education, probably in a cathedral school. Hengham began his judicial career in the 1260's as a clerk to

Giles Erdington, one of Henry III's judges. From the experience gained in this employment he was appointed to the King's Bench in 1270, the common bench in 1272, and again to the King's Bench in 1273. He probably became chief justice of this court immediately (1274) and retained the post until his removal from office in 1290.

The judges of both common pleas and King's Bench played a role in the legal business of the king's council when it met; the chief justice of the King's Bench, because of his special position, played the most important role in that council when it discussed and made legislation. Edward I issued a large amount of legislation that sought to expand legal remedy and jusice, and Hengham had a large, perhaps the largest, share in drafting the provisions of such famous laws as the Statute of Gloucester (1278) and especially the Second Statute of Westminster (1285), the largest single piece of legislation made by an English king up to that time.

Like all clerical judges, Hengham pursued a major career, that of a royal judge, and a minor career, that of a churchman. Because of the demands of his judicial career, he was necessarily nonresident and usually nonfunctioning in the various church offices he held. These ecclesiastical livings added appreciably to his income. In 1294 Hengham possessed fourteen ecclesiastical livings, scattered through at least five dioceses; these made him a notable, if not a notorious, pluralist. In addition to holding rectories, prebends, and canonries, he was chancellor of Exeter in the 1270's and archdeacon of Worcester from 1287 to 1288. Hengham received these church livings through the patronage of the king, bishops, and great nobles. As a clerical judge with extensive extrajudicial involvement, he was bound to be suspected of conflicts of interest and of favoritism in his judicial conduct. This ill will contributed to the charges brought against him in 1290, when he was convicted of judicial maladministration, removed from office, and sentenced to pay a heavy fine.

At this moment in his life Hengham had perhaps the best-informed legal mind in England, and he continued to serve as legal consultant to various persons and institutions. Within ten years the king's rancor against him subsided, and Edward I appointed him chief justice of the common bench in 1301, a position he held until he retired from public office in 1309. During his earlier career as chief justice of the King's Bench, he had written two law tracts on procedure, the *Summa magna* and the

Summa parva, and thereby had become one of only five medieval English judges whose authorship of legal treatises is definitely known.

Hengham was one of the last clerical judges, for the King's Bench, like the common bench, underwent a change in the late thirteenth century, when the king began to name practicing lawyers (pleaders) to judgeships, and these lawyers were invariably laymen. The first such judge was Gilbert Thornton, who became chief justice of the King's Bench in 1290, after the disgrace of Hengham. This happened at the same time that William Gisleham became the first pleader to sit on the common bench. Like Gisleham, Thornton had spent the preceding decade in private practice and also as a king's serjeant suing the king's cases in the quo warranto campaign of the 1280's. Thornton was the only such person on the King's Bench until his death in 1295; then William Ormsby assumed a judgeship that he held for about seven years. While two other professional pleaders advanced to judgeships in the early years of Edward II's reign (1307–1327), not until 1320 were all three seats of the King's Bench occupied for a while by professional lawyers: Henry Scrope, Robert Mablethorp, and Henry Spigurnel. And not until some thirty years later, at mid century, did the professional lawyers acquire permanent control of seats in this court. In this respect the development of the King's Bench paralleled closely that of the common bench.

From their earliest appearance in the twelfth century until the late thirteenth century, the judges of the two central courts as well as the eyre judges were free from serious charges of corruption or malfeasance. But this situation changed in 1289, when Edward I returned to England after three years in France and heard reports of serious professional misconduct among his judges. The charges stung the king, probably because the alleged offenses had occurred during his absence. In deep anger he removed most of the eyre judges, all of the King's Bench justices, and all but one member of the common bench. The most notable of the accused were the two chief justices, Thomas Wayland and Hengham. In the case of the former, the king confiscated his lands and Wayland, after fleeing to a church for sanctuary, was permitted to abjure the realm and go into exile. Most of the other judges, including Hengham, were tried and fined, and none but Hengham ever appeared again in the courts.

As the fourteenth century progressed, charges of corruption were more frequently leveled at judges of both benches, and they sometimes fell victim to social and political strife that had not enveloped them in the earlier period. Although Edward II's reign was full of political tension, the judges seem not to have suffered for that reason. The only recorded instance of judicial misconduct involved William Inge, who had served for three years on the common bench and had become chief justice of the King's Bench in 1316, succeeding Roger Brabazon. After less than two years he was accused and convicted of tampering with writs, and of purchasing land from a litigant while a plea concerning that land was in progress.

The purge of 1340–1341 was the most serious royal attack on the judges since 1289. It was probably directed at members of the council for maladministration, however, and the judges fell under the royal displeasure for that reason more than for judicial misconduct. At least half the judges were removed and some were even imprisoned, but the charges were never clear, and most judges returned to the king's service within a short time. The case of Richard Willoughby in particular deserves comment.

Willoughby, whose father had been a lawyer, had become a justice of the King's Bench in 1331, when he was kidnapped and held for ransom by the Folville gang of Leicestershire, a group of lawless men, with knights, clerks, a constable, and priests among them, who terrorized several counties for more than twenty years. He became chief justice of the King's Bench in 1338 but fell under grave accusations in 1340. By "clamor of the people" he was charged with selling the laws as if they were cows and oxen. The lengthy process gives no details of the charges because Willoughby attacked the procedure that was used against him. He was finally sentenced to a heavy fine, but the king soon pardoned him and he was restored to office at Michaelmas 1341 and served until 1357.

The frequency of incidents of judicial malfeasance and the equal frequency with which the king pardoned and restored discredited judges to their posts were persistent features of Edward III's reign (1327–1377). Recognizing the temptation to corruption, the king instituted a new oath for judges in 1346 and warned William Thorp, the new chief justice of the King's Bench, that if he violated the oath, he would be drawn and hanged, and his property confiscated. In 1350 Thorp was convicted of bribery by a special judicial commission. He confessed, and at the king's special order was sentenced to the promised punishment. A few months later the king pardoned him, and a year later he was serving as a baron of the Exchequer, with judicial commissions of assize and of oyer and terminer.

The increased level of everyday violence in fourteenth-century England and a corresponding deterioration of popular respect for judges and the law produced a greater incidence of verbal abuse, assault and battery, and even homicide, of the judges. Separate from this was the mass violence on a large scale that occurred during the Peasants' Revolt of 1381. Confined mainly to Kent, London, and East Anglia, the depredations of the mobs and gangs were extremely severe on local and royal officials. One notable victim was John Cavendish, chief justice of the King's Bench, a native of Suffolk and especially hated for his severity in recent judicial commissions. While he was trying to escape to sanctuary, a gang caught him in the open countryside, beheaded him, and paraded his head on a pike through the county to Bury.

The greatest suffering of the judges came in the political crisis of 1386–1388, when they were caught in the crossfire between lords and king. In their efforts to remove the undue influence of the young king's favorites, the lords in 1386 imposed a commission of control and inquiry over the king's household and impeached his major adviser. To resist this restriction on royal power, Richard II (r. 1377–1399) put a series of questions to the judges of both benches in 1387. Robert Tresilian, chief justice of the King's Bench, may have suggested these tactics to the king. In fact, Tresilian was the sole judge sitting on the King's Bench at that time. The answers given by him and the common-bench judges could have been argued from the premises of the common law. They told the king that the powers of the commission constituted "accroachment" of royal power, and that those responsible for the commission could be considered traitors.

In violent recrimination the lords who opposed King Richard accused Tresilian and others of treason. Tresilian went into hiding but was discovered, brought before Parliament, and sentenced to execution. The common-bench judges who had answered the king's questions were also sentenced to death, but their sentences were commuted to exile in Ireland.

The political troubles of the fourteenth century pale in comparison with the military and political conflict of the fifteenth century that is called the

Wars of the Roses. The career of John Fortescue (*ca.* 1390–1479) serves as a model for the young lawyer's rise to judicial office in the fifteenth century while also illustrating the vagaries of fortune endured by a judge during great political strife. The son of a Devonshire knight, Fortescue studied law at Lincoln's Inn. He became a serjeant-at-law, a fully qualified practitioner, in 1430 and was appointed a king's serjeant eleven years later. During this early professional period he served as a justice of the peace thirty-five times in various counties, carried out judicial commissions, and on a few occasions sat in parliament.

Fortescue's advancement to chief justice of the King's Bench was remarkable because it came only one year after his appointment as king's serjeant. For the next nineteen years he managed that particular court until the Yorkist claimant, Edward IV, won the crown from Henry VI in 1461. Fortescue was replaced on the bench and his estates forfeited because he remained loyal to the Lancastrian side; he lived for the next ten years in Scotland and France, writing tracts on law and government.

When Henry VI made his last bid for power in 1471, Fortescue returned to England; the Yorkists proclaimed him traitor and captured him in the Battle of Tewkesbury. Within months Edward IV gave him a general pardon, and Fortescue served on the king's council for two years after that. He never returned to the King's Bench, but it is highly likely that if he had been a younger man at that time, the Yorkist king might well have restored this Lancastrian judge to his former judicial post.

Before the onset of war, Fortescue's career as King's Bench justice, however unusual his talent as a jurist, typified the activities that judges of both benches had performed for two centuries. In addition to ordinary service on the bench, they served in numerous other capacities. Between the four annual court terms they went into the counties with commissions of assize, oyer and terminer, and jail delivery. They also performed special investigations and tasks, and were expected to attend meetings of council and Parliament. Sometimes the king assigned them, as Edward III did Geoffrey Scrope, to embassies overseas. In these respects Ralph Hengham's career in the thirteenth century was little different from Fortescue's, except that Hengham was a churchman and reached the bench by a different path. Once the judges were selected exclusively from professional pleaders, their training and advancement to the bench had common features.

Despite the incidents of corruption and violence that sometimes claimed them as victims, the justices of the King's Bench were in general jurists of great ability and gave an indispensable continuity to judicial administration. During the fourteenth century, thirty-eight men served in this court. Sixteen had temporary appointments, were substitutes, or otherwise had careers of four years or less. Each of the others served an average of twelve years, a clear indication of institutional stability. And when kings were displaced—Edward II in 1327, Richard II in 1399, Henry VI in 1461, and Richard III in 1485—the orderly administration of justice continued almost without interruption.

In sum, the King's Bench was an English royal court that, from its inception, dealt with the same types of cases as did the common bench. In this respect, as one of two courts sharing the same jurisdiction, it gave the English judicial system a feature not possessed by that of any other European state. At the same time it was a superior court, able to correct the errors of the common bench, and it dealt particularly with cases of personal concern to the king. In the fourteenth century it gradually developed an additional area of work by assuming the administration of criminal justice. Its judges, in legal training and technical abilities, were not different from those of the common bench. Judges were often moved from one bench to the other without difficulty. The volume of business treated by the King's Bench, however, was usually not more than half, and often less than half, of that handled by the common bench. Perhaps because of this, the complement of the King's Bench was ordinarily three judges rather than the six to eight of the other court. For almost half of the fourteenth century, only two justices sat on the King's Bench, and for three brief periods, only one. It had its particular importance in its closeness to the king and in its frequent need to consult him.

BIBLIOGRAPHY

The largest amount of information on the origins, development, operations, and personnel of the medieval King's Bench is found in the introduction to each volume of George Osborne Sayles, ed., *Select Cases in the Court of King's Bench*, 7 vols. (1936–1971); lists of judges of the King's Bench for the period 1269–1422 are in the appendixes of vols. I (1936), IV (1957), VI (1965). Studies of the lives and careers of individual judges of the King's Bench include the introduction to Sir John Fortescue, *De laudibus legum Angliae*, Stanley Bertram Chrimes, ed. and trans. (1942); Bertha H. Putnam, *The Place in Legal History of Sir William Shareshull* (1950); the introduction to

Radulphi de Hengham Summae, William Huse Dunham, ed. (1932); E. L. G. Stones, "Sir Geoffrey le Scrope (c. 1285–1340), Chief Justice of the King's Bench," in *English Historical Review,* 69 (1954).

FRANKLIN J. PEGUES

[See also **Justices, Itinerant; Justices of Common Pleas; Law, English Common; Westminster, Statutes of.**]

JUSTICES OF THE PEACE. The seals that medieval English kings used to authenticate their acts represented the king on one foil armed and armored, mounted as a knight charging his enemies; the other foil showed him seated, holding an orb and the sword of justice, ready to uphold the good laws he swore to defend in his coronation oath. Both aspects of this responsibility for the peace were important in the long process that transformed the keepers of the peace, who at first acted primarily as military captains, into the justices of the peace, who lost the military function but acquired broad judicial and administrative power in the countryside.

The period in which the justices of the peace arose—what might be termed the prehistory of the office—has been traced to the late twelfth and early thirteenth centuries. The need to provide for the defense of coasts and border areas promoted the appointment of special commissioners to keep the peace in particular areas, such as the Welsh border and the southeastern coast, and officers named primarily for border defense could easily be given responsibilities for keeping the peace in inland counties as well. Although the sheriffs, who were considered the normal keepers *(custodes)* of their shires, might be given this added responsibility, commissions went to others as well. At first these commissions named the king's familiars rather than local men, but the Barons' War in the mid thirteenth century brought a significant change.

In order to offset the power of sheriffs and to secure control of royal castles, the king's baronial opponents in 1263 placed a keeper of the peace *(custos pacis)* in every county. Formerly, a commission for keeping the peace *(ad pacem conservandam)* created an ad hoc official or temporarily gave added authority to sheriffs; such commissions operated, however, only in counties where some special need existed. The new keepers of 1263 became distinct from the sheriffs and were established throughout the realm. This baronial system of keepers with mixed military and police functions survived the royal victory in 1265 and was useful in restoring order to troubled districts. Often called "captains" as well as "keepers," these men saw to the selection of troops and assessed their pay upon the community. The king's keepers, however, were appointed only intermittently and were not part of the uniform scheme of local administration by local men instituted by the king's baronial opponents. The sheriffs and their subordinates were still the essential peace officers; *custodes pacis* were not found throughout the realm. Keepers were appointed for many counties as a precautionary measure in 1277, when Edward I and the great lords went campaigning in Wales; and by the time another general appointment was made in 1287, the functions of the keeper were changing.

In 1287 peace and military roles began to diverge. The keepers, reflecting their military origins, were to inspect the readiness of local men for war according to the provisions of the Statute of Westminster (1285), but after 1287 they were no longer military leaders. In time their military role was taken by the wardens of the Welsh and Scottish marches, the late medieval military lieutenants, and the Tudor lords lieutenant of the counties. The keepers themselves were moving in a different direction and would eventually become judicial officers. Two indicators of future development are evident in 1287: these first primarily judicial *custodes* were men of lesser status than the essentially military keepers, and their number had increased to two in each county (perhaps paralleling practice in judicial commissions).

Some of the basic movements in late-thirteenth- and early-fourteenth-century English law and administration were involved in the change in the keepers' role. As the king's government expanded its capabilities and learned (partly from the baronial opposition of 1258–1267) the need to police its agents, a vast new jurisdiction emerged. The legal category of trespass, brought into the royal courts by the relatively simple, inexpensive, and informal complaint (querela) rather than by formal and expensive writs, encompassed both the disputes of the countryside and the rising volume of complaints directed against the king's ministers, who seemed, in popular imagination, to be always increasing in number and in wickedness. This new trespass litigation, formerly left to uncertain local remedy, came into royal courts by means of a simple device. A litigant could charge that his opponent had broken the king's peace, that he had come by force and arms against the king's peace (*vi et armis et contra pacem domini regis*), whether the offense was brutal assault or illegal fruit picking. By its very vigorous attempt, in some degree successful, to maintain a tolerable level of internal peace and to provide remedies for wrongs, the crown had generated a demand for justice beyond the capacity of existing royal institutions. Whether or not crime and disorder were increasing on some absolute scale (as the complaints of contemporaries would indicate) cannot be determined; but the evidence does show that Englishmen wanted their complaints heard by royal judges and that the crown tried one experiment after another in the attempt to meet this need by means of suitable judicial officers and institutions. The justices of the peace emerged from this experimentation through a process that was slow, marked by significant reverses, and far from inevitable.

The Statute of Winchester provided the core around which the judicial powers and responsibilities of the keepers could grow; it was entrusted to their enforcement from 1287. The keepers were to see to routine police matters: every town and village must maintain watchmen; town gates must be closed at night; underbrush must be cut back from the roads to deprive robbers of cover. They were also to inspect the arms of the local citizenry, so that an effective force would be available when the hue and cry was raised against evildoers. But apparently a decade earlier the keepers were recording breaches of the peace for later trial before the king's justices; the instructions of 1287 to set down all infringements of the Statute of Winchester may simply have extended the practice. In 1300 keepers became justices, but only with regard to offenses committed by the king's officials against the Magna Carta or the Forest Charter. Yet the scope of their jurisdiction was quite restricted, and the critically important determining or judging power did not last.

During the first half of the fourteenth century the results of a struggle going on largely out of view can be seen: the crown now gave peace officers determining power (as in 1316, 1329, 1332, 1338, 1350, 1361, 1368), now withdrew it (as in 1327–1328, 1330, 1332, 1344, 1364). At issue were not only the power contained in the commissions but also the men who would be appointed as keepers or justices to exercise them. In other words, the question of personnel may have been as important as the question of judicial power; certainly the issues were closely linked.

From one point of view, the constant changes in peace commissions took on the coloration of a great

constitutional contest. The parliamentary commons backed the creation of true justices of the peace, urging the crown to commission local gentlemen with full power to pass sentence on the accused. Gradually the commons triumphed over the resistance of a central government that preferred not to accept local notables in such positions and chose to rely on professional lawyers or magnates. Even when pressure from the commons secured commissions appointing justices of the peace, the crown might, as on several occasions in the reign of Edward III (1327–1377), nullify their effect by appointing great lords to act as overseers or supervisors of the justices. Writing in 1929, Bertha Putnam, the pioneering investigator of the justices of the peace, saw the commons campaign on their behalf as farsighted, a "definite policy for local government" in which "it was the commons, rather than the central government, who first recognized the value of the 'pivot' of the English constitution."

A somewhat different perspective results if this policy for local government is read, as the work of Alan Harding forcefully suggests, as a bid for gentry control of countryside justice. In clamoring for local men as justices, the commons were of course urging the appointment of themselves or men like them (the gentry and leading burgesses) to positions that could place the royal stamp of approval on an authority in the counties and boroughs that they saw as their natural right. In time every country gentleman who counted was placed on the commission of the peace almost automatically. The central government may not have been merely obstinate and authoritarian in its resistance to local justices of the sort the commons wanted; principle as well as the professional jealousy of the king's justices may have been at work. If it can be assumed that the crown was motivated by a general concern for order in the countryside, it had ample reason to resist the movement in favor of justices of the peace; evidence well known in Westminster clearly indicated that the appointment of local men as powerful justices was hardly conducive to order.

The experiment with special commissions of oyer and terminer showed from the 1270's on how readily judicial powers that had been passed out to local men provided them with powerful weapons for their feuding; it also showed what a troublesome stream of complaint might come to the crown as a result. Moreover, the conduct of the early keepers and justices scarcely inspired confidence. In 1316 (to take one example from the scores of unpublished complaints preserved in the Public Record Office, London), John of Massingham charged that a band of men who coveted some of his land broke into the house where John and his mother were dining and savagely beat them both; the intruders were led by "Robert de Ingaldesthorp, knight, constable, and keeper of the peace ... and other unknown evildoers." In such cases the pivot of the constitution appears as a significant part of the problem of disorder.

Whatever the motives of officials in Westminster and whatever the effects on law and order in the countryside, the keepers did become justices. Edward III seems to have overcome the traditional royal reservations about justices of the peace through a prudent assessment of the support he needed to fight the war in France. The king could scarcely call upon the countryside leaders to pay war taxes and lead warrior contingents while denying their ideal of local justice and administration. As a 1348 petition from the commons pointed out, "Residents are best fitted to deal with local needs." Certainly the statute of 1361 (34 Edward III c. I), once thought to be the virtual creator of the justices, simply sanctioned a transformation that had long been coming. After a last gasp of serious opposition to the justices of the peace in 1364–1386, a second statute (42 Edward III) restored their full powers.

The exact content of the judicial and administrative powers of the justices cannot be thought of as an unvarying constant either wholly present or wholly absent at any particular time. The scope of the determining power varied according to the terms of the commission given the justices and the statutes enacted in Parliament. From 1332 the justices were prohibited from hearing suits of felony or trespass brought by suit of party, that is, they could no longer give damages to plaintiffs. The lesser crimes justifiable before justices of the peace were known as indictable trespasses until sixteenth-century lawyers created a special legal meaning for the term "misdemeanor"; the actions for which a litigant could collect damages then became simply trespasses. By the mid fourteenth century the number of justices had increased considerably and included both unlearned local gentlemen and men of law. An act of 1344 set a minimum number of justices (a quorum), primarily those learned in law, who must be present when felony charges were determined. The requirement was sporadically extended after 1389, when two quorums were established, one for determining felonies and one for all other offenses. By 1430 a single quorum

for all offenses was reestablished and gradually increased in size. Although the justices had only two major peace statutes to enforce, Winchester (1285) and Northampton (1328), the total number of statutes regulating their power was vast. Before 1485 as many as 133 statutes concerning justices of the peace had been passed; the Tudors would add 176 more.

Until 1359 the justices of the peace kept a vestige of the military role so important in their origins. Although they had not personally commanded local troops after 1287, the power of array, first added to their commission in 1338, was included sporadically until 1346 and then appeared regularly until 1359. The commission of array empowered the justices to select suitable men to serve in the local levies of troops. The system gave great discretion and much opportunity for graft to arrayers, and the previous commissions had generated heated complaints about the oppressions and extortions committed by arrayers; these difficulties may have prompted the crown to experiment with array power entrusted to peace officers whose early functions had included taking the view of arms. But when the justices of the peace lost array power in 1359, finally and permanently snapping their link with military levies (whether for war or police work), their powers had not been reduced. Eliminating military duties may have simply cleared the way for more substantial administrative responsibilities, especially in the implementation of a growing body of economic legislation.

The crown gave justices of the peace economic powers for brief periods in the reign of Edward II and again in 1350–1352, in the wake of the plague. But for seven years thereafter the important regulations enacted by the Statute of Laborers and intended to hold down wages in a labor shortage were entrusted to separate justices of laborers. Thus the justices of the peace made their real entry into the field of economic regulation only in 1368, when they were given responsibility not only for the new labor laws but also for control of such offenses as forestalling and regrating (buying up goods before they came to the usual markets in order to take "excessive gayne"); they were likewise given supervision over weights and measures. Some of their formal responsibilities may have proved in practice impossible, such as enforcement of the reactionary Statute of Cambridge (1388), which forbade workers to move about without sealed letters from the justices, attempted to conscript laborers' children for agricultural work, and ordered that statutory maximum wages be maintained. Moreover, given the sheer volume of their economic duties, one wonders how the justices were able to keep track of them all, let alone vigorously prosecute all offenders; the range of their charge extended from the size of hogsheads and the preservation of salmon to the most general and controversial labor legislation of the day.

If in some duties the justices were occupying regulatory ground that had been formerly the preserve of the guilds, in other ways their work entered the hazy territory of moral supervision (an entry possibly made easier by the obvious moral component in economic matters). During the fourteenth and fifteenth centuries the justices of the peace were instructed to do justice on such village figures as the frequent nightwalker and the frequenter of taverns beyond the proper time. Even some matters that might seem properly justiciable in ecclesiastical courts went to the justices of the peace. Statutes against Lollards added duties to their growing list in the fifteenth century.

As the competence of the justices was extending into new areas of jurisdiction, they were being superseded in actual practice, in the final stages of criminal cases, by justices who had formal legal training; the justices of the peace were instructed to leave difficult cases to the judges of the King's Bench or to justices of assize and jail delivery. But if they thus lost ground as criminal-law judges, the justices of the peace continually increased their administrative powers, especially in the field of economic regulation. By the close of the Middle Ages, they had gone far toward the domination of local government for which they are famous.

Across the entire range of cases, from felonies to sumptuary legislation, the justices relied on the presenting jury for evidence of wrongdoing. The charge (or list of articles of inquiry) given to the jurors varied as the powers of the justices fluctuated. In its earliest known form the charge was based on the commission given the justices and on the peace measures of the Statute of Winchester; this list was supplemented during the fourteenth and fifteenth centuries by clauses drawn from the older articles of the general eyre and from the general commissions of oyer and terminer known as trailbaston. The charge also reflected the wide authority of the justices over both common-law and statutory offenses, and included articles for which no specific warrant existed either in commissions or in statutes.

In fact, the charge to the jurors, far from being stereotyped, was likely written up by local peace officials and their clerks rather than by Westminster justices; it may have varied from one county to the next. In answering the questions put to them by the justices, the jurors at first spoke from their own knowledge; like most medieval jurors, those sworn in before justices of the peace were expected to be knowledgeable, not impartial. Accusations presented by persons not serving as jurors began to appear only after the mid fourteenth century. The origins of such third-party accusations seems to have been the informal plaints or bills, the querelae, which were so important in the general evolution of the office of justice of the peace. The justices might act on a bill themselves, or they might give it to jurors; if the jurors declared it a "true bill," it became an indictment presented at a session of the peace. Some bills apparently were handed directly to jurors and, if in correct form, became legal presentments.

Like most medieval courts, sessions of the peace could be large and formal meetings with nearly all justices present and cases from the entire county brought under judgment, or they might be more informal and restricted sessions supervised by some of the justices and concerned with only a few cases. General sessions were ordered to be held four times a year by statutes of 1351, 1362, and 1414; though actual practice varied, they were known as quarter sessions. These sessions, usually held in a royal castle, guildhall, or shire hall, might bring together several hundred people—twenty-four law-abiding men from each hundred (from which the nine to sixteen jurors for the hundred were selected), the sheriff of the county, coroners, constables, seneschals, bailiffs of liberties and their subordinates, representatives of vills, and the accused. In trespass cases many of the accused admitted their guilt and were fined without further process. Those denying guilt were given a jury trial in the usual common-law form. Conviction for trespass was punishable by fine; for felony, by hanging.

Hangings of convicted felons were not the only dramatic scenes at the sessions of the peace. Despite their reassuring name, the court sessions were sometimes anything but peaceful; existing records show assaults on jurors and justices, and sometimes the complete disruption of the court. On occasion justices opposed to one another appeared with their fully armed followings ready to do battle. Such scenes serve as reminders that justices of the peace evolved in a very turbulent society in which they participated quite fully. Alan Harding has suggested that the king found it difficult to distinguish between the justices and the outlaws, since both maintained armed gangs. The justices can hardly be thought of as primarily the king's men, carefully chosen by him to meet the problem of order in a troubled countryside. With more truth it could be claimed that the justices chose themselves and that they regulated and defined the many statutes and commissions concerning this office. Without a sizable body of paid civil servants and judges, the crown could scarcely satisfy the expectations of public order and redress of grievances that royal policy had created, nor settle the vast amount of litigation it had encouraged, by any other means than by turning to the existing local powers.

In short, the overextension by the crown—or, from another point of view, the escalation of public expectation—forced kings to turn to the gentry as justices for breaches of the peace and administrators of a growing body of economic regulation now seen as a proper concern of the state. The triumph of the justices of the peace thus marks the ebbing of a tide of centralization in law and administration that had long flowed in the direction of Westminster with its small corps of royal bureaucrats and professional lawyers. But judicial power vested in the "natural" countryside leaders cannot be easily thought to be more just or more conducive to public tranquility than a system based on Westminster officials. By capturing the broad base of royal justice, the peace officers became the representatives and exemplars of the common law to most Englishmen; by using their office so often and so blatantly for their own quarrels and local advantage, the justices of the peace may have helped to create the lack of respect for law notorious in late medieval England.

BIBLIOGRAPHY

Marguerite Gollancz, ed., *Rolls of Northamptonshire Sessions of the Peace* (1940); Alan Harding, "The Origins and Early History of the Keeper of the Peace," in *Transactions of the Royal Historical Society,* 5th ser., **10** (1960), and *The Law Courts of Medieval England* (1973); Elisabeth C. Kimball, ed., *Records of Some Sessions of the Peace in Lincolnshire, 1381–1396,* 2 vols. (1955–1962), and *Records of Some Sessions of the Peace in the City of Lincoln, 1351–1354, and the Borough of Stamford, 1351* (1971); J. B. Post, "The Peace Commissions of 1382," in *English Historical Review,* **91** (1976); Bertha H. Putnam, "The Transformation of the Keepers of the Peace into the Justices of the Peace," in *Transactions of the Royal Historical Society,* 4th ser., **12** (1929), *Kent Keepers of the Peace, 1316–1317* (1933), *Proceedings Before the Justices of the Peace in the Fourteenth and Fifteenth Centuries* (1938), and "Shire Officials: Keepers and Justices of the Peace," in

James F. Willard, William A. Morris, and William H. Dunham, Jr., eds., *English Government at Work,* III (1950); Rosamond Sillem, *Records of Some Sessions of the Peace in Lincolnshire, 1360–1375* (1937).

RICHARD W. KAEUPER

[See also **Law, English Common; Trespass.**]

JUSTICIAR. After his conquest of England in 1066, William I, duke of Normandy and king of England, and his successors had to divide their time between the two possessions. Until the thirteenth century most of them spent the greater part of their time on the Continent, fighting the French kings and administering Normandy and other French acquisitions. They had therefore to delegate regalian authority in England to trusted persons. These officials, described variously as regent, custodian, or prefect, were given wide authority. They supervised much of the administration while the king was present, and during his absence they governed as vice-regents. Under William I the best-known was perhaps Lanfranc of Bec, archbishop of Canterbury (1070–1089). William II Rufus (1087–1100), with talent only for fighting, left most of the governing to capable administrators. One such administrator, Ranulf Flambard, bishop of Durham, who never had more than the rank of chaplain, converted the temporary vice-regency into a more permanent and well-defined office. He was undoubtedly the first justiciar *(justiciarius),* as these vice-regents came to be styled.

Of singular administrative ability, Flambard was unscrupulous, a weakness that led to his fall from power under Henry I (1100–1135) and his eventual replacement in 1107 or 1108 by Roger, bishop of Salisbury (d. 1139), who had already served the king well as chancellor. The first to be called justiciar (as were all royal justices), Roger became known as second after the king. Surrounding himself with a dedicated group of officers who implemented his financial, legal, and political policies, he developed the functions of the office of justiciar and then set out to remodel much of Norman administration. His financial innovations led to the development of the Exchequer, over which he presided at its accounting sessions. As chief justice he directed the procedure of the royal court as well as the missions of the itinerant justices begun under Henry I. He was the royal mediator between spiritual and lay powers and did whatever was required for the government to be effective. Although associated with every aspect of royal government, he belonged to no department; he was above them all, a kind of medieval prime minister. Roger held this powerful office until 1139, when King Stephen removed him.

There was no justiciar during the period of civil war between Stephen and Henry I's daughter Matilda. With the return of peace and the accession of Henry II in 1154, the justiciar again became preeminent. During Henry II's reign and the early years of Henry III's reign (1216–1272), a succession of great justiciars, all associated with the rapid progress in law and administration, and empowered with executive discretion, raised the office to the apogee of its power. This period has been justly called the "age of the justiciars."

From 1155 to 1168 Henry II split the authority of the justiciar between two prominent barons, Robert de Beaumont, earl of Leicester, and Richard de Lucy. Robert de Beaumont, however, consistently served as vice-regent during Henry's absence. He helped to prepare the Constitutions of Clarendon and was a key negotiator with Thomas Becket. Upon Robert's death in 1168, Richard de Lucy became and remained sole justiciar until his retirement in 1178. For a year the office remained vacant. Then Ranulf de Glanville (d. 1190), an impressive and able person and author of the first text on the common law, *Treatise on the Laws and Customs of England,* became justiciar. He had worked his way up in the royal service and called attention to himself by his accomplishments as a warrior, sheriff, justice in eyre (circuit justice), and justice of the King's Bench. Although many of Henry II's legal and administrative innovations had been introduced before 1180, Glanville ensured their success by his shrewd and efficient supervision.

Upon his accession in 1189, Richard I the Lionhearted dismissed Glanville and reverted to the practice of divided authority by appointing Hugh de Puiset, bishop of Durham (d. 1195), and the chancellor William Longchamp (d. 1197). William quickly reduced Hugh to impotence and assumed so much authority in such an arbitrary manner that in 1191 Richard I appointed Walter of Coutances (d. 1207) as justiciar. Walter fulfilled his functions with skill and loyalty for the next two years.

His successor, Hubert Walter, was a gifted administrator and the greatest of the justiciars. Trained by Glanville, whom he had served as a clerk, Walter had achieved by 1189 a place as baron of the Exchequer and justice of the small council. Under Richard he had also become bishop of Salisbury, had partic-

ipated in the Third Crusade, and had returned in 1193 to help collect the ransom money to free Richard from captivity in Germany. He was justiciar until his resignation in 1198, thereafter serving as chancellor until his death in 1205. Since Richard I went to France almost immediately after his release from captivity, Walter actually governed England for five years. To finance Richard's French wars, he introduced a new land tax called the carucage (a tax assessed on the number of plowlands held by an individual), the first land tax since the abolition of the danegeld in 1162. In 1195 Walter issued instructions to the itinerant justices that expanded the scope of their judicial and administrative powers and may possibly have created a new local peace officer called the coroner.

Hubert was succeeded by Geoffrey Fitzpeter, earl of Essex, an efficient justiciar until his death in 1213, whereupon John appointed one of his Poitevin favorites, Peter des Roches (d. 1238), then bishop of Winchester. Efficient and clever, Peter was extremely unscrupulous, a trait that did not endear him to John's baronial enemies. Peter lost the justiciarship upon John's death (1216) amid civil war and was succeeded by Hubert de Burgh (d. 1243). Until his dismissal in 1232, Hubert, the last of the great justiciars, wielded extraordinary power during the long minority of Henry III. He managed, however, to alienate many of the barons. A friend of Peter des Roches, Stephen de Segrave, replaced Hubert as justiciar until 1234, when he was dismissed. The office then lapsed despite attempts by the baronial enemies of Henry III to revive it in 1258–1261. With the fall of Hubert de Burgh the office of justiciar became in reality only a monument to the strong government of the Norman-Angevin kings.

BIBLIOGRAPHY

For a detailed study of the justiciar, see Francis James West, *The Justiciarship in England, 1066–1232* (1966). The following works deal extensively with some of the principal justiciars: Christopher Cheney, *Hubert Walter* (1967); Clarence Ellis, *Hubert de Burgh: A Study in Constancy* (1952); Edward J. Kealey, *Roger of Salisbury, Viceroy of England* (1972); Geoffrey V. Scammell, *Hugh de Puiset, Bishop of Durham* (1956); R. W. Southern, "Ranulf Flambard and Early Anglo-Norman Administration," in *Transactions of the Royal Historical Society,* 4th ser., **16** (1933); Charles R. Young, *Hubert Walter, Lord of Canterbury and Lord of England* (1968). See also John E. A. Jolliffe, *Angevin Kingship,* 2nd ed. (1963).

BRYCE LYON

[See also **England: Norman-Angevin; Exchequer; Exchequer, Court of; Glanville, Ranulf de; Lanfranc of Bec; Law, English Common; Roger of Salisbury; Walter, Hubert.**]

JUSTINIAN I (**Flavius Petrus Sabbatius Justinianus**) (*ca.* 482–11 November 565), Roman emperor 527–565, was born at Tauresium (Illyricum, probably near Niš) about 482 of Latin-speaking peasant stock. Brought to Constantinople about 490 by his maternal uncle Justin (later Justin I), who had migrated to the capital and made a career in the imperial guard (the Excubitors), the young Justinian received a thorough education and served for some time as an officer in the imperial guard. The details of his early career, however, are unkown. On the death of Emperor Anastasius (518), Justinian played a leading part in the negotiations and intrigues that led to his uncle's proclamation as emperor. During Justin's reign (518–527) Justinian was his right-hand man and, as Justin drifted into senility, he became the power behind the throne. During these years he formed a liaison with Theodora, a former actress, but was at first prevented from marrying her by his aunt, Empress Euphemia, and by the Roman law that prohibited marriage between senators and theatrical performers. In 525, after Euphemia's death and a change in the law, Justinian and Theodora were married. On 4 April 527 Justinian was crowned coemperor. On the death of Justin, he became sole emperor (1 August 527). Justinian saw himself both as the heir to Roman traditions of imperial power and as invested by God with an authority that was in principle limitless. From the outset he aspired to restore Roman rule in the West, where Germanic kingdoms had been set up in Italy, Gaul, Spain, and Africa. Disengagement from the inconclusive war against Persia that he had inherited was a precondition for operations in the West. After a victory at Dara in 530, more apparent than real, peace was concluded in the East in 532. In 533 a seaborne expedition to Africa under the command of Belisarios destroyed the Vandal army in two battles and restored Roman rule in Africa. Justinian rewarded Belisarios with a triumph of unexampled magnificence on his return to Constantinople in 534.

After several years of diplomatic negotiations with the Ostrogothic rulers of Italy and secret correspondence with Amalasuntha, daughter of King Theodoric, Justinian launched his Italian expedition, again under the command of Belisarios, in 535. The imperial forces took Rome in December 536, defended the city against a siege by superior Gothic forces in 537–538, and occupied Ravenna, the Gothic capital, in 540. But a renewed outbreak of war with Persia and Hun raids on the Danube frontier prevented the war in Italy from being pressed to a successful conclusion. The Goths showed unexpected resilience, especially under King Totila (541–552), who for a time recovered almost all of Italy. Two further campaigns under Belisarios (544–548) and Narses (552–554) were needed to defeat the Ostrogoths, and a few pockets of Gothic resistance held out until 562. The long years of war left Italy devastated and demoralized. In 551 a brief campaign reestablished Roman rule in southern Spain without ending Visigothic control of most of the Iberian Peninsula.

The Persian war that erupted with the capture of Antioch in 531 by King Xusrō I Anōšarwān (*r.* 531–579) dragged on inconclusively, with a few brief truces, until 561. The main theater was in the western Caucasus, where the Persians were anxious to dominate Armenia and gain an outlet to the Black Sea that would enable them to threaten Constantinople. The Romans frustrated these aims, but only at the cost of large payments to Persia. In the Balkans increasing pressure from Slavonic tribes, from Hun groups, and in the 560's from the Avars led to successive invasions of imperial territory, some of which penetrated to within a short distance of Constantinople.

This threat from a mobile foe could not be countered by victory in a pitched battle. Justinian followed a policy of fortification in depth and the sowing of discord among the invaders by diplomacy and bribery. The failure of his successors to retain control of the northern Balkans does not imply that Justinian's policy was not the best possible at the time. Dazzled by the prospect of reconquest in the West and by the traditional conflict with Persia, he and his contemporaries did not realize the scale and seriousness of the movement of peoples in central and eastern Europe.

Justinian's codification of Roman law began in 528 under the inspiration—and from 529 under the direction—of the lawyer Tribonian. It comprised the *Code* (*Codex,* a collection of all imperial enactments still valid), completed in 529, the *Digest* (a compilation of authoritative opinions of Roman jurists) and the *Institutes* (a textbook for students), both completed in 533, and a series of new laws or

Novels (Novellae post codicem constitutiones), mostly published before the death of Tribonian in 542. Conservative in intent, Justinian's legislation in fact cleared away many antiquarian survivals and adapted the law to the needs of his age. Its effect upon the subsequent development of European law is beyond measure. Justinian's administrative reforms aimed at ending abuses rather than at radical change. Yet his measures against tax evasion and illegal exercise of power by great landowners won him the bitter hostility of the aristocracy, who in any case despised him as an upstart.

Justinian's public works included, besides fortifications, underground cisterns for the water supply of Constantinople, a bridge over the river Sangarius on the main road east, the restoration of cities damaged by earthquake or war, a new city near his birthplace (called Justiniana Prima), and above all churches: S. Vitale in Ravenna, begun under the Ostrogoths about 525 and completed by Justinian in 547; St. John the Evangelist at Ephesus; and Hagia Sophia at Constantinople, a building without parallel in boldness of conception and magnificence of execution (begun in 532 under the supervision of Isidoros of Miletos and Anthemios of Tralles and completed in 537).

Justinian was convinced that it was his duty to maintain unity of belief and organization in the church. The Latin church of the West, with its Augustinian theology and its long experience of separation of religious and secular authority, was unsympathetic to what it saw as imperial interference in religious affairs. Doctrinal disputes on the relation between the divine and human natures of Christ divided the Chalcedonians of East and West from the Monophysites of the East. Justinian strove throughout his reign to bring the dissident groups together by persuasion or by force. His policy toward the Monophysites oscillated between toleration and persecution, partially mitigated by the favor that Theodora showed toward the Monophysites. From 543 on he sought to find common ground with the Monophysites in the condemnation of allegedly Nestorian doctrines professed by three earlier theologians: Theodore of Mopsuestia, Theodoret of Cyrrhus, and Ibas of Edessa, the so-called Three Chapters. This policy antagonized the Latin West without satisfying the Monophysites. The final condemnation of the Three Chapters by the Fifth Ecumenical Council in 553 solved nothing. The Western church remained sullenly hostile, while persecution turned the Monophysites from a dissident group within the church

into a parallel church that became dominant in Syria and Egypt.

The economic difficulties of the long years of war, aggravated by the pandemic of bubonic plague in 542–543, led to much opposition, not only from the landowning classes but often from the people of Constantinople as well. The Nika riot of 532 nearly cost Justinian his throne and was ended only by means of a savage massacre. Lesser outbreaks occurred throughout his reign. Justinian appointed no coemperor who could automatically succeed him, and as he grew older there was a series of conspiracies by would-be successors. When Justinian died, a virtual coup d'état placed his sister's son, Justin II, on the throne.

BIBLIOGRAPHY

Gian Gualberto Archi, ed., *L'imperatore Giustiniano* (1978); John W. Barker, *Justinian and the Later Roman Empire* (1966); Robert Browning, *Justinian and Theodora* (1971); Aikaterine A. Christophilopoulou, *Byzantinē historia*, I (1975); Charles Diehl, *Justinien et la civilisation byzantine au VIe siècle*, 2 vols. (1901); Isrun Engelhardt, *Mission und Politik in Byzanz: Ein Beitrag zur Strukturanalyse byzantinischer Mission zur Zeit Justins und Justinians* (1974); Berthold Rubin, *Das Zeitalter Iustinians*, I (1960); Ernst Stein, *Histoire du Bas-Empire*, II (1949); Percy Neville Ure, *Justinian and His Age* (1951); Alexander Vasiliev, *Justin the First: An Introduction to the Epoch of Justinian the Great* (1950).

ROBERT BROWNING

[See also **Belisarios; Byzantine Church; Byzantine Empire: History (330–1025); Constantinople; Corpus Iuris Civilis; Early Christian Architecture; Early Christian Art; Hagia Sophia; Isidoros of Miletos; Italy, Byzantine Areas of; Law: Byzantine; Law, Canon: Byzantine; Monophysitism; Theodora I, Empress; Urbanism, Byzantine; Warfare, Byzantine.**]

JUSTINIAN II (668/669–711), Byzantine emperor, son of Constantine IV, and the last emperor of the Heraklid dynasty. Justinian's first reign lasted from 10 July 685 to late 695, and his second extended from the summer of 705 to 4 November 711.

During his first reign, Justinian II confronted the rising threat of the Bulgars to the north and the Arabs to the southeast under the very powerful Umayyad caliphs. The instability of his reign partly resulted from those grave dangers. Lack of adequate manpower required him to transfer the population of Cyprus to the mainlaind, as well as to attempt the conscription of Slavic prisoners. The attribution of the so-called *Farmer's Law* to his first reign is unproven, but important canonical decisions were taken by an ecclesiastical council that he approved, the Council in Trullo, which is also known as the Quinisextum Council (691–692). It is incorrect to assert, as some historians have done, that Justinian II instigated widespread purges of aristocratic families during his first reign.

Beginning in 692, Justinian authorized the striking of gold solidi that displayed the head of Christ Pantokrator, a precedent in numismatic history and in the official use of religious images, one that escalated the religious polemic with the caliphate.

After ruling for ten years, Justinian lost his throne as the result of a palace conspiracy, and suffered the splitting of his nose (hence his epithet Rhinotmetus) and exile to the Crimea. Leontius, a former strategos of the Anatolic theme, imprisoned in the praetorium and inexplicably freed after three years, replaced him as emperor (695–698). Justinian escaped from the Crimea after marrying the sister of the Khazar khan. Renamed Theodora, she bore Justinian a son, Tiberius. Justinian recaptured Constantinople with the aid of the Bulgar khan Tervel, executed Leontius and his successor, Tiberius III (698–705), and purged his opponents (although he did not slay all aristocrats). His efforts to punish the Crimean port of Cherson in 710 led to his overthrow and execution on the orders of Philippicus Bardanes, who succeeded him as emperor (711–713).

BIBLIOGRAPHY

James D. Breckenridge, *The Numismatic Iconography of Justinian II* (American Numismatic Society Notes, no. 144) (1959); Constance Head, *Justininian II of Byzantium* (1972); Andreas N. Stratos, *Byzantium in the Seventh Century,* Marc Ogilvie-Grant, trans., V (1980).

WALTER EMIL KAEGI, JR.

[See also **Byzantine Empire: History; Councils (Ecumenical); Farmer's Law; Iconoclasm, Christian; Mints and Money, Byzantine.**]

JUSTINIANIC CODE. See Corpus Iuris Civilis.

KAABA (Arabic: *Kaᶜba,* cube), a prismatic structure in Mecca that serves as the focal point of prayer and

pilgrimage for Muslims throughout the world. It has existed in some form since pagan times, when it was the leading shrine in Arabia.

While the Prophet Muḥammad was still a young man, the Kaaba was destroyed by fire. With the assistance of a foreign craftsman, it was rebuilt, on a larger scale, in alternating courses of stone and wood, a technique native to Abyssinia.

The hegira of Muḥammad and his followers from Mecca to Medina took place in 622; this event marks the beginning of the Islamic calendar. During their first months at Medina, the Muslims followed the practice of Jewish tribesmen there and faced in the direction of Jerusalem while praying. Only after about a year and a half did the Prophet reverse their orientation *(qibla);* since then Muslims everywhere have prayed facing in the direction of the Kaaba at Mecca.

After the Muslim conquest of Mecca in 630, Muḥammad retained the Kaaba as the focal point for prayer; in addition, he adapted the established pagan

The Kaaba. PHOTO: HALUK DOGANBEY. © PAUL ELEK PRODUCTIONS LTD. 1963

pilgrimage to Mecca, with its ritual circumambulation of the Kaaba, to Islamic purposes.

The adoption of this venerated Arabian shrine as the literal center of Islam had a profound impact on the course of Islamic civilization. Most immediately apparent is the fact that every mosque had to be oriented in the direction of the Kaaba, in order to provide the correct *qibla* for communal prayers. Several methods of determining the *qibla* were used, with varying degrees of accuracy. This requirement was taken seriously, and when, from time to time, the *qibla* of a new mosque was found to have been calculated incorrectly, the building would be torn down and rebuilt—as happened, for example, at Wāsiṭ in Iraq in the early eighth century.

Even more important culturally was the requirement that every adult Muslim (with a few exceptions) make the pilgrimage (*ḥajj*) to Mecca at least once in his or her lifetime. The holy city was thus, from the beginning, a center of contact among believers from all corners of the world, providing opportunities for travel and the exchange of goods and ideas; as a consequence, a cosmopolitanism cutting across all social levels was built into the very fabric of Islam and no doubt contributed materially to the remarkable cultural unity that characterized the Islamic Middle Ages.

The Kaaba as it stands today has been rebuilt several times since the death of the Prophet. At the first such rebuilding, in 683, the Abyssinian technique of alternating courses was given up in favor of local stone; to the extent possible, these stones have been reused in subsequent reworkings of the building. The Kaaba is kept covered with a black cloth (*kiswa*), decorated with bands of Koranic verses embroidered in gold.

BIBLIOGRAPHY

K. A. C. Creswell, *Early Muslim Architecture*, I, 2nd ed., pt. 1 (1969), 1–6, 11–13, 62–64; B. Lewis, "Ḥadjdj," in *Encyclopaedia of Islam*, new ed., III (1971); A. J. Wensinck, "Ka^Cba," in *ibid.*, IV (1978).

ESTELLE WHELAN

[See also **Arabia; Islam, Religion; Islamic Art and Architecture; Kiswa; Mecca; Muḥammad; Qibla.**]

KA^CBA OF ZOROASTER (Persian: *Ka^Cba-yi Zardušt*), the local name for an Achaemenid stone structure at Naqsh-e Rustam, 5 kilometers (3.1 miles) north of Persepolis in Fārs province, Iran. The cubical structure faces the cliff where the corpses of Darius and other Achaemenid rulers were placed in chambers hewn from the rock and where there are rock reliefs depicting early Sasanian kings.

The original purpose of the building, which has one chamber and blind windows, is disputed, although the suggestion that it was a tomb or a fire temple has yielded to the theory that it was either a place where the royal corpse was prepared for interment or a vault for royal insignia in Achaemenid times. The use of a tooth chisel on the stone suggest that the Ka^Cba dates from the time of Darius (*ca.* 500 B.C.).

After the fall of the Achaemenids nothing is known about the Ka^Cba, unless it is the structure that appears on the obverses of coins struck by the Frataraka dynasty of Persis (modern Fārs province). It is only in Sasanian times that the Ka^Cba reappears in history.

Šābuhr I (*r.* 240–262) had a trilingual inscription (Parthian, Middle Persian, and Greek) engraved on the sides of the structure. This inscription, comparable to the *Res gestae divi Augustus,* gives a list of the lands ruled by Šābuhr and details of his wars against the Romans. In the first campaign he claims to have defeated Gordian III (in 244) and to have forced Philip the Arab to pay an indemnity. In the second campaign (*ca.* 256) Šābuhr says he annihilated a Roman army and then conquered and plundered many cities in Syria and Anatolia, including Antioch, capital of the Roman province of Syria. In the third campaign (*ca.* 259) he captured Valerian and many Roman notables, and again ravaged many cities. The rest of the inscription tells of fire temples and religious rites that Šābuhr established, followed by a list of dignitaries in the courts of his predecessors as well as in his own court. This inscription is a valuable source for knowledge of the Sasanian court, offices, and titles.

Another inscription, in Middle Persian only, is on one side of the Ka^Cba. It tells of the rise to power of a Zoroastrian priest named Kerdīr (Kartir) who began his career under Šābuhr and was elevated to the nobility and chief priesthood of the empire under Bahrām II, grandson of Šābuhr (*r.* 276–293).

In Šābuhr's inscription the Ka^Cba is called a *bun-xānag* (literally "foundation house"), which may mean that it was a shrine or repository for the Avesta, sacred book of the Zoroastrians, or other documents. Since there are so many Achaemenid and Sasanian rock reliefs on the cliffs of Naqsh-e Rustam facing the Ka^cba, and since the city of Istakhr was nearby, the site, which was enclosed by a wall, may have had special significance for the Sasanians. The Ka^cba is mentioned by authors in the Islamic period, but it had lost its original significance even though local people regarded it with some awe.

BIBLIOGRAPHY

See Erich F. Schmidt, *Persepolis*, III (1970), 34–49; and for the inscriptions, André Maricq, "Res gestae divi Saporis," in *Syria*, 35 (1958); M. Sprengling, *Third Century Iran* (1953).

RICHARD N. FRYE

[See also **Avesta; Naqsh-i Rustam; Šābuhr (Shahpuhr) I; Sasanians; Zoroastrianism.**]

KABALA (Greek: Khabala; Latin: Cabalaca; Armenian: Kapalak; Arabic: Qabala), the earliest known capital of Albania, an ancient and medieval kingdom of southeastern Caucasia. Located near the site of the present village of Kabala, some fifty miles (about eighty kilometers) southeast of Nukha, Kabala lay north of the Kura River between the streams called Seboj (Durian-*chai*) and Kesios (Geok-*chai*). After the partition of Caucasia between Rome and Sasanian Iran in 387, Kabala became the first residence of the *marzpan* (viceroy), the Persian governor-general of Albania; its district, comprising some 598 square miles (about 1,550 square kilometers), became known as Ostan-i-Marzpan (court or seat of the *marzpan*). After the transfer of the Albanian capital to Bardha^ca (Armenian: Partaw), south of the Kur, about 460, Kabala continued to exist and was an Albanian bishopric from at least the fifth century until as late as the tenth. Taken by the Arabs in the seventh century, Kabala became a part of the kingdom of Shirvan. Laid out in the form of an irregular rectangle and surrounded by a wall with eleven bastions, Kabala was a center for the production of corn and silk. It was destroyed by Tamerlane in 1386–1387.

BIBLIOGRAPHY

Sowren T. Eremyan, *Hayastanĕ ĕst "Ašxarhac^coyc^c"i* (1963), 58, 75, 105; Omar S. Ismizade, "Kabala stolitsa drevnei kavkazskoi Albanii," in Igrar Aliev, ed., *Voprosy*

istorii Kavkazskoi Albanii (1962); Guy Le Strange, *The Lands of the Eastern Caliphate* (1905, repr. 1966), 181; Kamilla V. Trever, *Ocherki po istorii i kulture Kavkazskoy Albanii* (1959), *passim*.

ROBERT H. HEWSEN

[See also **Albania (Caucasian); Shirvan.**]

KABBALAH. See Cabala.

ĶĀḌĪ. See Qadi.

KAFTAN. See Caftan.

KAIROUAN. See Qayrawān, Al-.

KAISERCHRONIK. The *Kaiserchronik* (Chronicle of the emperors) was written by an unknown clerk (or clerks) connected with Ratisbon (Regensburg), Bavaria, around 1150. In 17,283 lines with end rhyme, it narrates in epic form the history of thirty-two Roman and eighteen German emperors, and also presents the stories of four fictional rulers. Therefore, it cannot be regarded as a genuine world history *(chronica mundi)*. The imperial biographies are painted in black and white; the subjects are either wicked (Nero) or virtuous (Constantine the Great), depending on whether they hindered or furthered the advancement of Christianity.

The narrator takes the founding of Rome as his starting point and shows the spread of Roman power and Christian virtues into Germany until 1147, when he stops in the middle of a crusade sermon delivered by St. Bernard of Clairvaux. The style, which is even (and contains splendid dialogues) in the Roman part (lines 43–14,281), seems inferior in the German part (lines 14,282–17,283).

The infusion of legendary matter is rather extensive; the fullest examples are the legend of St. Silvester, connected with Constantine (2,827 lines), and that of Faustinianus (2,871 lines), placed between the apocryphal emperor "Jovinus" and Nero. It is in these "historiae" (embellishments) that the poem excels and starts to repay the reader's efforts in otherwise heavy reading. The *Kaiserchronik* also undertakes to relate the salvation history *(Heilsgeschichte)* of mankind.

The popularity of the *Kaiserchronik* from the second half of the twelfth century until the sixteenth century must have been widespread, for fifteen manuscripts and eighteen fragments have been located. The oldest text, from the middle of the twelfth century, is part of the Vorau Codex. The copying, enlarging, shortening, excerpting, and rerhyming continued, particularly in Bavaria, until the end of the sixteenth century. By 1300 the *Kaiserchronik* had become the first major German poem to be recast into a prose version. The latter was often attached to the well-known Swabian law code, the *Schwabenspiegel*. The *Kaiserchronik* was the first epic account of the Roman Empire in the vernacular. Many subsequent German chroniclers incorporated narrative material from it.

BIBLIOGRAPHY

A critical edition is *Deutsche Kaiserchronik,* Edward Schröder, ed., in *Monumenta Germaniae historica: Deutsche Chroniken,* I (1892, repr. 1964). Studies include Helge Eilers, *Untersuchungen zum frühmittelhochdeutschen Sprachstil am Beispiel der Kaiserchronik* (1972); Christian J. Gellinek, *Die deutsche Kaiserchronik* (1971); K. H. Hennen, "Strukturanalysen und Interpretationen zur Kaiserchronik" (diss., Cologne, 1977); Ernst Friedrich Ohly, *Sage und Legende in der Kaiserchronik* (1940, repr. 1968).

CHRISTIAN J. GELLINEK

[See also **Chronicles; Germany; Historiography, Western European; Holy Roman Empire; Kingship, Theories of: Western Europe.**]

ḴĀLĪ. See **Rugs and Carpets.**

KALLIKAN, IBN. See **Khallikān, Ibn.**

KALOJAN (also called Joanica, *d.* 1207) was a younger brother of Peter and Asen, the founders of the Second Bulgarian Empire. He was sent to Con-

stantinople as a hostage after the 1188 treaty between Byzantium and Bulgaria. Within three years he escaped home and began leading raids against Byzantium. After Peter's death in 1197, he became ruler of Bulgaria. The raids against the Byzantine Empire increased until Kalojan agreed in late 1201 or early 1202 to a treaty which restored to the Byzantines the parts of Thrace he had occupied. Kalojan was soon again on the offensive, occupying Niš. He also fought with the Hungarians, taking Braničevo from them in 1203.

In 1204 papal legates crowned Kalojan king and granted his bishop in Trnovo the title of primate. Kalojan felt this justified calling himself "tsar" and his bishop, "patriarch." These relations with Rome had no lasting impact. In 1204 Constantinople fell to the Fourth Crusade. Kalojan quickly began expanding into Thrace, regularly replacing Greek bishops with Bulgarians. He offered the crusaders an alliance against the Greeks, but the crusaders, bent on obtaining Thrace for themselves, rejected it. Thus in 1205, when Greek magnates in Thrace revolted against the Latins, the rebuffed Kalojan willingly aided them. Baldwin I, the Latin emperor, marched against him. At Adrianople, Kalojan's Bulgarians were victorious. Baldwin was taken prisoner and died in Bulgarian captivity. This greatly weakened the newly established Latin empire and also guaranteed the survival of the Greek state of Nicaea, since the defeat at Adrianople forced the recall of a Latin army which was then attacking the Greeks in Anatolia. After Adrianople, still in 1205, Kalojan conquered more of Thrace and most of Macedonia. Sources hostile to him stress his brutality to the subjugated Greek population. He died (some sources suggest he was murdered) during a siege of Thessaloniki in 1207, shortly after his Bulgarians had killed Boniface of Montferrat, the crusader king of Thessaloniki. Bulgaria then rapidly declined until it was revived by Kalojan's nephew John Asen II in the 1220's.

JOHN V. A. FINE, JR.

[See also **Bulgaria; Peter and Asen.**]

KALONYMUS FAMILY, a distinguished Jewish family whose descendants in the tenth through thirteenth centuries were among the most prominent authors of rabbinical literature and works of mysticism in northern Italy and Germany, and served as community leaders. The Greek name of the family testifies to its apparent southern Italian origin. According to a thirteenth-century tradition, passed down by the Ashkenazi Hasidim, the forefathers of the family were brought to Germany from Lucca in the year "849 after the destruction of the Temple" (that is, in 917) by King Karl. Since Conrad I, and not a king by the name of Karl, reigned in Germany in 917, most scholars believe that the reference is to Charles the Bald or Charles the Fat, whose reigns included the 870's and 880's, respectively. Others placed the event in 982, during the reign of Otto II.

However, a thorough study of the annals of these kings, as well as of the descendants of the family, rules out any possibility of accepting these propositions. The period of its activity proves that the family did indeed migrate around 917. The event was attributed to Charlemagne ("Karl" in the tradition) in order to heighten its importance—a common practice in thirteenth-century Europe among many peoples.

The most famous family member was Meshullam ben Kalonymus (930–1005), who spent most of his life in Lucca. Numerous questions on Jewish law, sent to him from all centers of Jewish settlement in Christian Europe and the Byzantine Empire, constitute a valuable historical source for the study of the period. Meshullam ben Kalonymus and his father helped to lay the foundations for the development of magnificent centers of Jewish scholarship in Christian Europe. For centuries the members of the family were renowned in Jewish society and produced many of the leaders of the various communities. They are also recorded as having received privileges from the rulers and as having been courtiers and familiars of royalty.

The family exercised a considerable influence on the culture and outlook of medieval German Jewry in three principal spheres: (1) the preservation and development of mysticism—a number of the leaders of the Ashkenazi Hasidism movement, which flourished at the end of the twelfth century and during the thirteenth century, were descended from the family; (2) the development of liturgy, which occupied an important place in synagogue prayer and exerted a significant impact on the congregants in the Middle Ages; (3) formation of the spiritual image and outlook of many Ashkenazi Jews—kiddush hashem (martyrdom) was one of the ideals in whose formation members of the family played an important role.

Scholars and leaders by the name of Kalonymus

were active at the same time in the communities of Provence. It is possible that they were connected with the Italian-German branch of the family, but no clear evidence exists for this supposition.

BIBLIOGRAPHY

See Joseph Dan, *The Esoteric Theology of Ashkenazi Hasidim* (1968), 9–45; Avraham Grossman, "The Migration of the Kalonymus Family from Italy to Germany," in *Zion,* **40** (1975), and *The Early Sages of Ashkenaz* (1980), chap. 1 (all in Hebrew).

AVRAHAM GROSSMAN

[See also **Hasidei Ashkenaz; Jewish Communal Self-Government: Europe; Jews in Europe; Liturgy, Jewish.**]

KAMENNAYA BABA (plural, *kamennye baby*), a small, primitive, stone or clay female figure such as those unearthed in the steppe areas of Russia, Siberia, and Anatolia. These statuettes, dating from the fifth century B.C. to the thirteenth century A.D., normally show a very full and rotund female body. They are connected with various Turkic peoples who inhabited these regions. Although occasionally interpreted as remnants of matriarchy, these figures are more likely connected with primitive fertility cults.

BIBLIOGRAPHY

Lexikon der Kunst, II (1971), 519; Alexander L. Mongait, *Archaeology in the USSR,* M. W. Thompson, trans. (1961), 94–96.

GEORGE P. MAJESKA

KAMKHĀ (kimkhwā) is the Persian term for a type of silk cloth. Both the term and the fabric appear to be of Chinese origin. In China *chinhua* designated a silk cloth brocaded in gold with floral designs, but the Near Eastern usage may be less precise. For Ibn Khurdādhbih (*d. ca.* 911) and al-Thaᶜālibī (*d.* 1038), *kamkhā* is a Chinese fabric the manufacture of which appears to have spread to Iran only after the Mongol invasion. Ibn Baṭṭūṭa mentions that in 1355 *kamkhā* was being produced in Nishapur, Baghdad, and Tabriz, locations where the Mongols had established workshops (*kārgah*s) for the manufacture of silk textiles. Gradually the fabric became known in eastern, central, and western Europe, where it was designated by terms deriving from *kamkhā: kamuka* in the Balkans, *camorcán* in Spanish, *camocca* in Italian, and "kimcob" in English.

BIBLIOGRAPHY
ᶜAlī Akbar Dehkhodā, *Loghat-nāma* (1972); Gerhard Doerfer, *Türkische und mongolische Elemente im Neupersischen,* III (1975), 602–606; Robert B. Serjeant, *Islamic Textiles* (1972), 31, 69, 113, 150, 218.

PRISCILLA P. SOUCEK

[See also **Silk; Textiles, Islamic.**]

KAMMERKNECHTSCHAFT. See **Servi Camerae Nostrae.**

KAMSARAKAN, one of the great noble houses of early medieval Armenia, descended from the Iranian clan of the Kāren and allied by marriage with the royal Armenian Arsacids. The Kamsarakan were lords of Širak and Aršarunikᶜ in west-central Armenia, and their lands stretched south and west into the district of Basean. The lords *(tanutēr)* of the house were honored on occasion with the imperial titles duke, *curopalate,* and *anthypatos.*

The Kamsarakan usually supported the pro-Byzantine policy of the Mamikonean. Their opposition to the Sasanians apparently led to their temporary disgrace early in the fifth century, but they seem to have regained their power rapidly and it continued to grow during the marzpanate. The *curopalate* Nersēh Kamsarakan became prince of Byzantine Armenia (*ca.* 689/690–691). Like that of their allies the Mamikonean, the position of the Kamsarakan declined in the eighth century. They were totally ruined after the disastrous rebellion of 771/772 against the caliphate and were compelled to sell their domains of Širak and Aršarunikᶜ to the Bagratid heir, Ašot Msaker. Thereafter the name of the Kamsarakan disappears from Armenian historical sources, but the later house of Pahlawuni, which was to play an important role in the eleventh through thirteenth centuries, seems to have been descended from them.

BIBLIOGRAPHY
Nikolai Adontz, *Armenia in the Period of Justinian,* Nina G. Garsoïan, ed. and trans. (1970), 210–212, 237–238, 414 (n. 66), 447–448 (n. 42), 498 (n. 76), 511–512 (n. 36), 516 (n. 53), 524 (n. 81); Gérard Garitte, *La Narratio de rebus Armeniae* (1952), 440, no. 59; K. Kogean, *Kamsarakannere tearkᶜ Širakay ew Aršaruneacᶜ* (1926); Cyril Toumanoff, *Studies in Christian Caucasian History* (1963), 171 (n. 90), 206–207 and n. 236, and *Manuel de généalogie et de chronologie pour l'histoire de la Caucasie chrétienne* (1976), 266–270, 530.

NINA G. GARSOÏAN

[See also **Armenia: History of; Bagratids; Marzpanate; Pahlawuni; Sasanians.**]

KANŌN (canon), poetic form in medieval Byzantine hymnography based on an established series of nine biblical canticles. The nine odes in a *kanōn* paraphrase the canticles; each begins with a model strophe *(heirmos)* establishing a metrical pattern for a series of strophes *(troparia)* that follow. Throughout the year numerous *kanōnes* for feasts and saints are sung at the morning service *(orthos)* as part of the daily liturgy. St. Andrew of Crete *(d. ca.* 740), composer of a lengthy penitential *kanōn* for Lent, is among the first known authors of this form.

BIBLIOGRAPHY
Miloš Velimirović, "The Byzantine Heirmos and Heirmologion," in *Gattungen der Musik in Einzeldarstellungen,* I (1973), 192–244; Egon Wellesz, *A History of Byzantine Music and Hymnography,* 2nd ed. (1961, repr. 1963).

NICOLAS SCHIDLOVSKY

[See also **Byzantine Church; Heirmos; Hymns, Byzantine; Liturgy, Byzantine Church; Troparion.**]

KANTAKOUZENOI, Byzantine aristocratic family. The first known member is a soldier active during the reign of Alexios I Komnenos (1081–1118). The name appears to derive from a toponymic (Kata-Kouzenan), in which case the family originated in the area of Smyrna, in Asia Minor. In the course of the twelfth century, the Kantakouzenoi acquired extensive landed possessions in the Peloponnesus, and during the fourteenth century in Thrace and Macedonia. They emerged as one of the most important families of the Byzantine Empire in the thirteenth century, and continued to hold this position until the fall of the empire. Their connection with the Peloponnesus persisted; a Kantakouzenos served as its governor from about 1286 to about 1294, and the first despot of the Morea was Manuel Kantakou-zenos, appointed in 1349. Members of the family in the Byzantine or Serbian lands are traceable through the fifteenth century.

BIBLIOGRAPHY

Aleksandr P. Kazhdan, *Sotsyalny sostav gospod-stvuioshevo klassa Vizantii xi/xiii vv* (1974); Donald M. Nicol, *The Byzantine Family of Kantakouzenos ca. 1100–1460* (1968); Dionysios A. Zakythēnos, *Le despotat grec de Morée,* 2 vols. (1932–1953, repr. 1975).

ANGELIKI LAIOU

[See also **Alexios I Komnenos; Byzantine Empire.**]

KARĀ MUHAMMAD. See **Qara Muhammad.**

KARĀ QOYUNLU. See **Qara Qoyunlu.**

KARĀ YUSUF. See **Qara Yusuf.**

KARAGÖZ FIGURES. See **Qaragöz Figures.**

KARAITES, a Jewish sect that does not acknowl-edge the authority of the postbiblical Jewish tradi-tion (so-called oral law) incorporated in the Talmud. It is the only Jewish sect (not counting the Samari-tans) that has survived for more than 1,200 years and is still in existence. Its name is variously explained as "scripturalists" and as "callers [to the original bib-lical faith]."

HISTORY

The sect originated within the confines of the me-dieval Muslim empire, principally as a result of the intellectual and social ferment within the Jewish community in Iraq, which enjoyed substantial auton-omy in its internal affairs and was administered by a bureaucracy headed by the exilarch (who represented it before the caliph's court) and by the presidents of the rabbinic academies. The sect represents a link in the ancient chain of resistance on the part of some

elements of Jewry to the oral law and its official tra-dents and administrators. Earlier links were the Sad-ducees, the Essenes, and the Dead Sea sectarians, al-though there is no clear evidence of direct influence by them upon Karaism.

The consolidation of the vast Muslim empire in the seventh and eighth centuries enabled discon-tented elements (mostly poorer tenant farmers and artisans) in Iraqi Jewry to migrate to the largely mountainous eastern and northern provinces of the former Persian empire, where they came into close contact with the awakening Persian resistance, under the banner of Shiism, to the hegemony of the Arab conquerors. The earliest known sectarian leader, Abū ᶜĪsā (also known as Obadiah) of Isfahan, tried to follow the example of his Persian compa-triots by rising in armed revolt against the Arab au-thorities, but he was quickly defeated and slain. None of his local successors chose to follow his war-like example.

By the middle of the eighth century his followers, called Isunians or Isfahanians, had returned to met-ropolitan Iraq, where they attracted a member of the top-rank rabbinic aristocracy named Anan ben David. According to the traditional rabbinic account (known only from a quotation by a twelfth-century Karaite writer), Anan was next in line for election as exilarch but was rejected in favor of his brother be-cause of his unorthodox views. He forthwith seceded from the synagogue and founded the Karaite sect. The historicity of this account is open to some serious doubt, but it seems clear that Anan's social position and superior learning brought considerable support to the budding sect, particularly as he pro-ceeded to compose a code of sectarian law (*Sefer ha-mitzvot* [Book of precepts]), the earliest known Karaite literary document. His authority, however, was recognized only by his immediate followers, the Ananites. Subsequent sectarian teachers (Ishmael of ᶜUkbara and Meshwi al-ᶜUkbarī, Benjamin ben Moses al-Nah'āwendī, Malik al-Ramlī, Mūsā [Moses] al-Zafārānī [also known as Abū ᶜImran al-Tiflīsī], Daniel ben Moses al-Qūmisī) disagreed with Anan on many points of law. Benjamin al-Nah'āwendī (second quarter of the ninth century) is, so far as is known, the first to use the collective term "Karaites" for the several schismatic groups.

By the start of the tenth century, the schism had spread from its original Iranian-Iraqi birthplace into Palestine (Jerusalem, where Daniel al-Qūmisī was the first eminent Karaite scholar to settle), Syria (Da-mascus), and Egypt (Cairo). Karaite missionaries traveled far and wide, preaching to Rabbinic audiences (Islamic law forbids heterodox missionary activity among Muslims), apparently with little success, at least among the educated classes (with the exception of Anan, no Karaite scholar is known to have been originally a rabbinic Jew). At first some sort of modus vivendi seems to have prevailed between Karaism and Rabbinic Judaism, but in the first half of the tenth century the situation changed radically. Saadiah Gaon (882–942), a native of Egypt and president of the Rabbinic academy at Sura in Iraq, a brilliant and influential scholar, published a series of polemical works in which he condemned Karaism as outright heresy. The effect of this sudden blow was immense: it deprived Karaism of the only missionary field open to it and extinguished its hope of eventually converting all of Jewry. On the other hand, the challenge of Saadiah's scholarly criticism gave rise to the golden age of Karaite literature (tenth and eleventh centuries), compelled the squabbling sectarian groups to coalesce into a more or less unified sect, and fostered some modest but vital modification of the excessive rigor of its teaching.

The First Crusade (1099) put an end to all Jewish activity in Palestine and much of Syria, and caused the Karaite academy in Jerusalem, which had trained scholars from many lands, to go out of existence. New Karaite settlements were established in the Byzantine Balkans, Cyprus, Spain, the Crimea, Lithuania, and Poland. The Constantinopolitan community, under both Byzantine and (after 1453) Ottoman Turkish rule, developed a fruitful scholarly production. The decline of Turkey in the eighteenth and nineteenth centuries shifted the leading role to the Crimean and Lithuanian communities, which subsequently came under Russian rule. Soon thereafter the leadership of the Russian communities succeeded in obtaining from the czarist government full civil rights for Karaites by disclaiming any historic and national kinship with their persecuted Rabbinic brethren—the only such instance in Karaite history.

LITERATURE

Anan's code of law, of which only fragments have been discovered, was written in Aramaic, the language of the greater part of the Talmud; Benjamin al-Nah'āwendī and Daniel al-Qūmisī used Hebrew for their own legal and exegetical works. The overwhelming bulk of later Karaite literature composed by writers in Muslim countries, down to the fifteenth century, was written in Arabic. The Balkan, and later Russian, authors used Hebrew, at first very

clumsy and overloaded with Greek and Arabic loanwords but later more fluent, and in recent times occasionally also the spoken Karaite-Tatar dialect (written in Hebrew characters), which originated in the Crimean communities under the Tatar khanate.

The golden age of Karaite literature opened with Yūsuf Ya‘qūb (Jacob) al-Kirkisānī (second quarter of the tenth century), a prolific writer and independent thinker, whose code of law (Kitāb al-anwār [Book of lights]) is a veritable treasure trove of early Karaite history and thought. He was followed by Salmon ben Jeroham, a bitter polemicist against Saadiah; Japheth ben Ali, the premier early Karaite Bible commentator; and David Ben Abraham Alfasi, a learned philologist and author of a Hebrew-Arabic lexicon of the Bible. In the eleventh century the Karaite academy in Jerusalem was staffed by several eminent scholars: Joseph ben Noah (its president), Aaron ben Jeshua, Joseph ben Abraham ha-Kohen ha-Ro'eh al-Baṣīr (an eminent philosopher), and Jeshua ben Judah.

In the Balkans a group of translators rendered several classical Karaite works from Arabic into Hebrew, thus making them accessible to European Karaites who knew no Arabic. In 1148 Judah ben Elijah Hadassi began to compile a Hebrew encyclopedia of contemporary Karaite knowledge (Eshkol ha-kofer [Cluster of henna]). Other authors were Jacob ben Reuben, Moses ben Abraham Dar‘ī (a prolific poet), Samuel ben Moses al-Maghribī (whose code of law, compiled in 1434, is the last such work written in Arabic), David ben Se'adel ibn al-Hītī (author of a concise but valuable chronicle of Karaite scholars), and Moses ben Samuel of Damascus (a Syrian poet and civil servant who was forcibly converted to Islam in 1354 by his princely master, was compelled to make the pilgrimage to Mecca, and finally escaped to Cairo, where he described his experiences in Hebrew verse).

The thirteenth to fifteenth centuries in the Balkans produced Aaron ben Joseph the Elder (late thirteenth century), the compiler of the official Karaite liturgy; Aaron ben Elijah the Younger (d. 1369), author of a tripartite summa of Karaite learning treating philosophy, law, and biblical exegesis; and Elijah ben Moses Bashyazi (d. 1490), author of the now most authoritative code of law (Adderet Eliyahu [Mantle of Elijah]).

DOGMA AND PRACTICE

Except for the rejection of the Talmud, there is no basic difference between Karaite and Rabbinic belief.

Indeed, the Karaites found themselves compelled to construct something like a Talmud of their own, in the form of numerous precepts and rules derived from the Bible by way of analogic deduction or based only on the consensus of their scholars—it was impossible in the medieval world to go on living entirely under the biblical legislation composed a thousand or more years earlier.

It is in practical theology that Karaism parts company with Rabbinism, mostly on the side of greater rigor. Thus it rejects the Rabbinic mathematical calendar (hence Karaite holy days do not always coincide with Rabbinic ones), the Rabbinic dietary rules, and the Rabbinic use of fire (kindled before Sabbath eve) during the Sabbath for light or cooking. The Karaite law of incest, even after the mild reform effected by Jeshua ben Judah, is far more restrictive than the Rabbinic one. Polygamy was never explicitly outlawed in Karaism (as it was in Rabbinism), but in practice appears to have been, even in Muslim countries, extremely rare, and certainly impossible in the Christian West. The Karaite liturgy is also different from the Rabbinic one.

Except for Russia, where the Karaite leadership deliberately renounced all kinship with Rabbinic Jewry, Karaism has always asserted its fraternal solidarity with the adherents of Rabbinic Judaism, however serious and long-standing their disagreements may be. There is no historical evidence of any Karaite attempt to merge with Islam or Christianity. Karaism has thus always remained a genuine, albeit dissident, product of Jewish thought, tradition, and history.

BIBLIOGRAPHY

Simḥah Pinsker, *Liqqūṭē qadmōniyyōt (Zur Geschichte des Karaismus und der karäischen Literatur)*, 2 vols. (1860–1903, repr. 1967 [or 1968]–1969), continues to be valuable for the original documents published there for the first time. Jacob Mann, *Texts and Studies in Jewish History and Literature*, II, *Karaitica* (1935, repr. 1972), is a massive collection of documents and studies, the major part of which deals with the period after 1500. Raphael Mahler, *Karaimer (Karaites, a medieval Jewish movement for deliverance)* (in Yiddish) (1947), trans. into Hebrew as *Ha-Kara'im* (1949), regards Karaism as a movement toward political and socioeconomic liberation, rather than toward theological dissidence. The Karaite anti-Saadian polemics are discussed by Samuel A. Poznanski, *The Karaite Literary Opponents of Saadiah Gaon* (1908). Leon Nemoy, ed. and trans., *Karaite Anthology* (1952), is a selection of extracts in English translation from the most important documents before 1500. The leading Karaite philosophers are discussed in Isaac Husik, *A History of Medieval Jewish Philosophy* (1916). P. Selvin Goldberg, *Karaite Liturgy and Its Relation to Synagogue Worship* (1957), is to be supplemented by Leon Nemoy, "Studies in the History of the Early Karaite Liturgy: The Liturgy of al-Qirqisānī," in *Studies in Jewish Bibliography, History, and Literature in Honor of I. Edward Kiev* (1971).

See also Zvi Ankori, *Karaites in Byzantium* (1959); Salo W. Baron, *A Social and Religious History of the Jews*, V (1957), 209–285, 388–416; André Paul, *Écrits de Qumran et sectes juives aux premiers siècles de l'Islam: Recherches sur l'origine du qaraïsme* (1969); Naphtali Wieder, *The Judean Scrolls and Karaism* (1962).

LEON NEMOY

[See also **Jews in the Middle East; Judaism; Saadiah Gaon.**]

KARAJĪ, AL- (al-Karkhi), Abū Bakr ibn Muḥammad ibn al-Ḥusayn (al-Ḥasan) (*fl. ca.* 1000), a mathematician active in Baghdad. Virtually nothing is known of his origins, teachers, or education, except what he himself wrote: "When I arrived in Iraq and saw how both small and great people loved and venerated science, I began to write works on arithmetic and geometry, one quickly after another, until I went back to the mountain countries [cities located between Azerbaijan, Iraq, Kordestan, Persia, and the lands bordering on the Caspian Sea] where I came to stay." It is confirmed by others that al-Karajī wrote all his mathematical and almost all his scientific works in Baghdad.

Al-Karajī's contribution is most important in algebra and arithmetic. His three extant treatises on mathematics have often been referred to by subsequent mathematicians and bibliographers: *al-Fakhrī* and *al-Badīᶜ*, both on algebra, and *al-Kāfī*, on arithmetic. There are two other extant texts, a short elementary treatise on algebra, ᶜ*īlal-ḥisāb al-jabr* (Oxford, Bodleian, I, 986, 3), and a fragment on the arithmetic triangle, cited by al-Karajī's thirteenth-century successor, the mathematician al-Samawᵓal. In addition to his books on mathematics, al-Karajī wrote an engineering work on "extraction of underground waters" (*Inbaṭ al-miyāh al-khafiyyat*). Other works attributed to him seem to be lost.

In order to understand al-Karajī's importance and the meaning of his contribution, it is necessary to review briefly the conception of algebra since it had been established as an autonomous discipline by al-Khwārizmī at the beginning of the ninth century. In his *Algebra* al-Khwārizmī conceives albegra mainly as a theory of equations of the first and second degrees. He examines associated binomials and trinomials and then discusses the solution of arithmetic and geometric problems, which, according to his view, can all be reduced to one of six basic equations.

The successors of al-Khwārizmī, expecially Abū Kāmil, developed the algebraic calculus and the rational Diophantine analysis. The elaboration of the tools of abstract algebraic calculus made it possible for al-Karajī to conceive a new mathematical project: the arithmetization of algebra. In the words of one commentator, he enabled the algebraist "to work with unknowns with all the arithmetic instruments, just as the arithmetician works with the knowns." This involves a transposition and extension of elementary arithmetic operations—the algorithms as well as Euclidean division or the extraction of roots—to algebraic terms and expressions, and particularly to polynomials. Thanks to the arithmetization of algebra, al-Karajī arrived at the construction of the algebra of polynomials and also gained a better understanding of the algebraic structure of real numbers. One of the consequences of this new project was the algebraic interpretation of Book X of Euclid's *Elements*. Previously considered a geometry book by most mathematicians, it was reinterpreted by al-Karajī as a book on algebra. According to this new view, its concepts refer not only to geometric magnitudes but also to magnitudes in general, numerical as well as geometric.

In *al-Badīᶜ*, al-Karajī also studied the radicals through operations of elementary arithmetic, and in the text cited by al-Samawᵓal he developed the tools of calculus, such as the table of binomial coefficients and its formation law, and the expansion

$$(a + b)^n = \sum_{m=0}^{n} \binom{n}{m} a^{n-m} b^m$$

for integer n, demonstrated with an old-fashioned form of mathematical induction.

It was as an algebraist that al-Karajī undertook an important inquiry into the Diophantine analysis. We know that seven books of Diophantus' *Aritmetica* were translated into Arabic by Qusṭā ben Lūqā at the end of the ninth century. They correspond to the first seven books out of thirteen promised by Diophantus, according to a newly established sequence. We also know that Abū Kāmil contributed to the development of Diophantine analysis in his treatise on algebra. In *al-Fakhrī*, al-Karajī reproduces one part of the first book of Diophantus and most of the text of the following three books. This summary, in which al-Karajī interprets the *Aritmetica* algebraically, has guided the present author in the authentication of the presumably lost Greek books by Diophantus. In *al-Badīᶜ*, al-Karajī resumes his inquiry into Diophantine rational analysis (known as *fī al-ᵓIstiqrāᵓ*), which constitutes a separate subject of algebra. It deals with Diophantine equations or systems of equations that the author tries to solve within the corpus of rational numbers.

Thus, with al-Karajī, algebra is no longer confined to the study of algebraic equations. In this respect, however, the contribution of al-Karajī remains modest: he takes up again, like his predecessors, the six canonical equations of the first and second degrees in order to solve equations of higher degree: $ax^{2n} + c = bx^n$, $bx^n + c = ax^{2n}$, $ax^{2n+m} = bx^{n+m} + cx^m$. It is in this tradition inaugurated by al-Karajī that mathematicians would attempt to resolve the cubic equation with radicals.

Al-Karajī's work marked forever arithmetic algebra. He stands at the beginning of a whole tradition, which brings together the most important algebraist-arithmeticians from the twelfth until the fifteenth century, such as al-Samawᵓal, al-Fārisī, al-Kāshī, and also the most notable Western mathematicians, such as Leonardo of Pisa (Leonardo Fibonacci).

BIBLIOGRAPHY

Editions and translations are *Inbaṭ al-miyāh al-khafiyyat* (1945); *L'algèbre: Al-Badīᶜ d'al-Karagī*, Adel Anbouba, ed. (1964), with a useful introduction; *Extrait du Fakhrī*, Franz Woepke, ed. and trans. (1853, repr. 1982); *Kāfī fīl Hisāb*, Adolf Hochheim, ed. and trans., 3 vols. (1878–1880), in German; al-Samawᵓal ibn Yaḥyā al-Maghribī, *al-Bahir en algebre d'as Samawᵓal*, Salah Ahmad and Roshdi Rashed, eds. (1972), in Arabic, with al-Karajī's text on the arithmetic triangle.

See also Diophantus, *Les Arithmetiques* (1984), especially the trans. of al-Karajī's text in the notes; Roshdi Rashed, "Al-Karaji," in *Dictionary of Scientific Biography*, VII (1973), "Les travaux perdues de Diophante (I)," in *Revue d'histoire des sciences*, **26** (1974), and *Entre arithmétique et algèbre: Recherches sur l'histoire des mathématiques arabes* (1984).

ROSHDI RASHED

[See also **Mathematics.**]

ḲARAKHANIDS. See **Qarakhanids.**

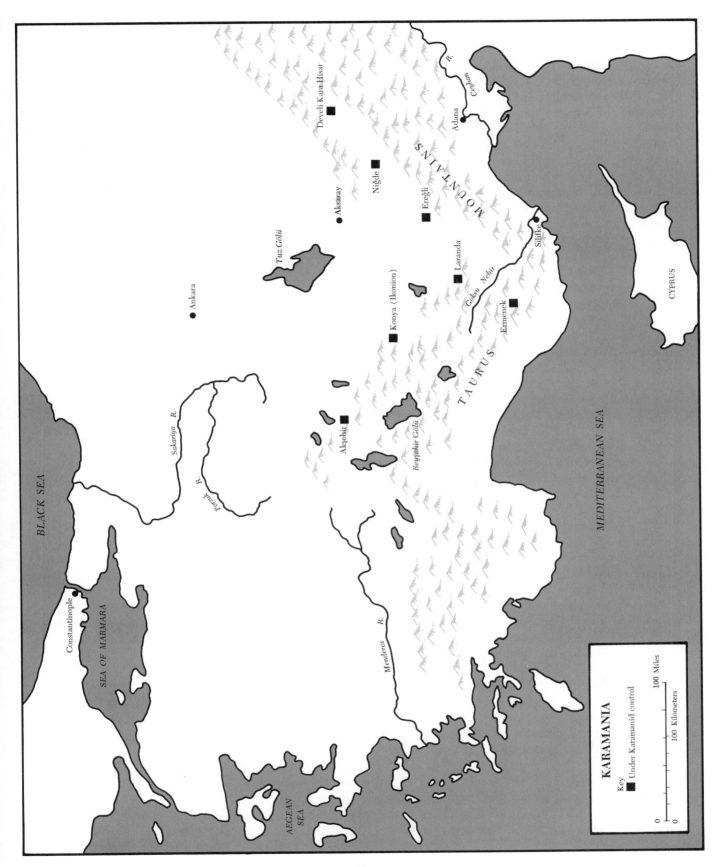

BLACK SEA

SEA OF MARMARA

Constantinople

AEGEAN SEA

Sakariya R.

Porsuk R.

Menderes R.

Ankara

Tuz Gölü

Aksaray

Develi Kara Hisar

Niğde

Ereğli

Adana

Ceyhan R.

Silifke

Göksu Nehir

Laranda

Ermenek

Konya (Ikonion)

Akşehir

Beyşehir Gölü

TAURUS

MOUNTAINS

MEDITERRANEAN SEA

CYPRUS

KARAMANIA
Key
■ Under Karamanid control

100 Miles

100 Kilometers

0
0

213

KARAMANIA, a Turkoman beylic in the western Taurus region. It was an important Anatolian power (*ca.* 1250–1475); Laranda was its capital. The Karamanids also controlled Konya (Ikonion), Niğde, Silifke, Ermenek, Ereğli, Develi Kara Hisar, Aksaray, Akşehīr, and other important centers at various times. Being restless Turkomans, the Karamanids sought to reduce Seljuk and Mongol interference in their affairs. Such a policy often produced cooperation with the Mamluks of Egypt and unleashed disruptive forces among the Seljuks. The Mongols viewed the Karamanids as a major obstacle to their control of Anatolia.

The origins of the dynasty are obscure. The Karamanids and their tribal followers appear to derive from the Avshar grouping of the Oghuz. Although they may be placed in Ermenek as early as about 1225, they did not fully emerge until the second half of the thirteenth century. Karaman Beg, involved in Seljuk-Mongol-Mamluk struggles and in warfare against Cilician Armenia, perished while campaigning against the latter about 1263. His son Mehmed Beg (*d.* 1278) attempted to place his own "Seljukid" candidate, Siyāvush (Jimri), in Konya. This and his pro-Mamluk activities cost him his life at the hands of the Mongols. The Karamanids, continuing a desultory struggle against the Mongols, survived the collapse of the latter and even benefited from it.

Thus ᶜAlāᵓ al-Dīn Beg (*ca.* 1361–1398) became a major Anatolian power. His expansionism and support of Tamerlane would not be forgotten by the Ottomans. Following the death of Murad I, his father-in-law, in 1389, ᶜAlāᵓ al-Dīn Beg encouraged the western Anatolian begs to revolt against Ottoman domination. This led to the first of several clashes with Bāyazīd I, son and successor to Murād I, who subsequently captured and executed him in 1396 and annexed his lands. Tamerlane's triumph in 1402 restored Mehmed Beg (*d.* 1423); and Ibrahim Beg (*d.* 1464) continued to make attempts on Ottoman possessions. In 1475 Mehmed II decided to end the problem and incorporated Karamania into the Ottoman state.

This territory also contained a Turkish-speaking Greek Orthodox population (the *Karamānli*) whose origins are still much debated.

BIBLIOGRAPHY

Sources. Ibn Bībī, *Al-Avāmir al-ᶜAlāᵓiya fī-l-Umūr al-ᶜAlāᵓ-īya* (1956), also in *Receuil de textes relatifs à l'histoire des Seljoucides,* IV, Martin T. Houtsma, ed. (1902);

Ahmed Şikārī, *Karaman oğulları tarihi* (1946); Feridun N. Uzluk, ed. and trans., *Selçuknāme* (1952).

Studies. Claude Cahen, *Pre-Ottoman Turkey,* J. Jones Williams, trans. (1968). A detailed bibliography is in F. Sümer, "Ķarāmān-Oghullarī," in *Encyclopaedia of Islam,* IV (1978). On the Turkish language written in Greek script by the Christians of Karamania, see J. Eckmann, "Anadolu Karamanlı ağızlarıha ait araştırmalar," in *Ankara Üniversitesi Dil ve Tarih-Coğrafya Fakültesi Dergisi,* 8 (1950). See also Ismail Hakki Uzunçarşili, *Anadolu Beglikleri* (1969).

PETER B. GOLDEN

[See also **Anatolia; Bayazid I Yildirim; Mamluk Dynasty; Mongol Empire; Murad I; Ottomans; Seljuks; Tamerlane; Turkomans;** and map overleaf.]

KĀRGAH, a Persian term, synonymous with *Kār-Khāneh,* for a place of manufacture of various goods but especially of brocaded or embroidered silks. As such the *kārgah* was associated with China and connected also with some of the cities along the silk route such as Samarkand or Bukhara. During the Mongol period *kārgah*s were also established in Nishapur, Baghdad, and Tabriz. These *kārgah*s were under state control and served a function parallel to that of the *ṭirāz* factories of earlier centuries. The workers in these factories were sometimes slaves and the goods they produced were often given to officials as part of their compensation in lieu of salary. It has not been possible to identify the goods produced at these *kārgah*s among the few surviving textiles of the Mongol period.

BIBLIOGRAPHY

ᶜAlī Akbar Dihkhudā, *Lughat'nāmah* (1971); Muhammad Pādshāh, *Farhang-i Ānandrāj* (1956–1963?), V, 3328; Rashīd al-Dīn Ṭabīb, *Jamiᶜ al-tawārīkh,* Abdul-Kerim Alizade, ed., III (1957), 30, 179, 342, 414, 539.

PRISCILLA P. SOUCEK

[See also **Textiles, Islamic; Ṭirāz.**]

KARIN (KARNOY KᶜAŁAKᶜ) (Greek: Theodosiopolis; Arabic: Qālīqāla/Ḳālīḳāla; Turkish: Erzurum), major strategic and commercial center in northeast Anatolia between the upper valleys of the Euphrates (Kara-su) and the Araks (Araxes) on the main east-west highway from Asia Minor to Iran and the East. The Armenian name of the city, Karin, or more correctly Karnoy K^{c}ałak^c (the city of Karin), was derived from the name of its district, known to classical authors as Karenitis/Carenitis. The Arab name of the city, Qālīqāla, was derived from Karnoy K^{c}ał-ak^c, despite the fanciful etymology given by the historian al-Balādhurī.

In the fourth century, Karin seems to have formed part of the domain of the Armenian Arsacid kings, and it was the residence of the last ruler of the western portion of Greater Armenia after its partition in 387. The city was renamed Theodosiopolis by the Byzantines, who fortified it in 415. It was further fortified under Justinian I in the sixth century, according to the contemporary historian Procopius (*On Buildings*, III. v. 3–12). At first the residence of the *comes Armeniae*, the city became the seat of the *magister militum per Armeniam* under the Justinianic reform, as well as the anchor point of the Byzantine defense in the East.

The strategic importance of Karin continued through much of the Middle Ages. It was first taken by Ḥabīb ibn Maslama in 653, settled with an Arab garrison, and included in the Muslim fortified border zone (*Iqlīm al-thughūr*) facing Byzantium. A century later (751–752) the city was briefly retaken by Emperor Constantine V, who razed its walls and deported the neighboring population to the Balkans, but it was rebuilt almost at once by the Arabs and remained a Muslim emirate, occasionally recognizing Bagratid overlordship, for nearly two centuries. Recaptured in 949 by the Byzantines, who replaced its Muslim population with Greeks and Armenians, the city and its district were ceded to the *curopalate* David of Tayk^c (or Tao) in 979. Upon his death the city reverted to the empire and was refortified by Basil II in 1018. It once more became an administrative center as the residence of the strategos of Basil's newly created theme of Iberia until the capital of the theme was shifted to Ani in 1045. At the same time, the nearby commercial city of Arcn, whose population was drawn largely from Karin/Theodosiopolis, profited from the active transit trade of the area.

The final return of Theodosiopolis to Muslim domination came in the second half of the eleventh century. When Arcn was sacked and destroyed by the Seljuk Ibrāhīm Ināl in 1048/1049, its population fled to the protective fortifications of Karin/Theodosiopolis, which they began to call Arcn-Rum/Arzān ar-Rūm. Ruled by the local dynasty of the Sal-

tukids, the city was taken in 1201 by the Seljuks, who were, in turn, forced to recognize the overlordship of the Mongols after 1243. Little is known of the internal history of the city in the twelfth and thirteenth centuries, but the numerous mosques and other elegant monuments dating from this period testify to a considerable prosperity. A new period of crisis began with the decline of the Mongol Ilkhanid dynasty in the fourteenth century. The city passed successively to rival Mongol and Turkoman groups for nearly two centuries until its final incorporation into the Ottoman Empire after the Battle of Caldiran in 1514, when it resumed its former administrative position.

BIBLIOGRAPHY

Nikolai Adontz, *Armenia in the Period of Justinian*, Nina G. Garsoïan, trans. (1970), 43–44, 98–100, 115–116, 119–124, 219, 284, 332; al-Balādhurī, *The Origins of the Islamic State*, I, Philip K. Hitti, trans. (1916, repr. 1968), 305, 309–310, 312–313, 320; Claude Cahen, *Pre-Ottoman Turkey*, J. Jones-Williams, trans. (1968), 106–108, 115, 118, 125–133, 154, 163–165, 242, 322; Ernst Honigmann, *Die Ostgrenze des byzantinischen Reiches* (1935), 10, 16, 18–19, 21–22, 42–43, 79–80, 151, 157–158, 162, 180–181, 183, 211–219; Heinrich Hübschmann, *Die altarmenischen Ortsnamen* (1904, repr. 1969), 415–416; Guy Le Strange, *The Lands of the Eastern Caliphate* (1905, repr. 1976), 115–118; Hakob A. Manandyan, *The Trade and Cities of Armenia in Relation to Ancient World Trade*, Nina G. Garsoïan, trans. (1965), 87–90, 133, 145–146, 148–149, 179, 182, 186–187; Aram Ter-Ghewondyan, *The Arab Emirates in Bagratid Armenia*, Nina G. Garsoïan, trans. (1976), 21–24, 32–33, 88–91, 109, 115, 127–129, 131–133, 139–142.

NINA G. GARSOÏAN

[See also **Armenia, Geography; Armenia: History of.**]

KARIYE DJAMI (Camii), Constantinople. One of the best surviving Byzantine monuments of the capital, the former church of Christ in the Chora monastery gives a good impression of Palaiologan art at the highest level of patronage, preserving significant remains of mosaic, fresco, and sculptural decoration, as well as marble revetments. Foundations date to the sixth century and the naos to the twelfth, but the present form of the building is primarily the result of the enlargement undertaken about 1316–1321 by the statesman and scholar Theodore Metochites, whose dedicatory portrait survives above the naos

Dormition of the Virgin. Mosaic from the Kariye Djami, Constantinople, early 14th century. © THE BOLLINGEN FOUNDATION, 1966

portal. An irregular but picturesque assemblage of ancillary chambers was added, including two narthexes and a funeral chapel (*parekklesion*). The decoration, on which the fame of the church rests, includes narrative mosaic cycles in the narthexes of the life of the Virgin and the infancy and miracles of Christ. The naos mosaics have almost entirely disappeared; of the festival cycle, only the Dormition of the Virgin survives. The *parekklesion* is decorated with frescoes of an eschatological nature, including the Last Judgment and Anastasis. The manneristic style, termed "overripe" by Otto Demus, is pivotal to the understanding of Palaiologan art. The building was converted to a mosque in 1511 and to a museum in 1945.

BIBLIOGRAPHY

Paul A. Underwood, *The Kariye Djami*, 4 vols. (1966–1975), see esp. Otto Demus, "The Style of the Kariye Djami and Its Place in the Development of Palaeologan Art," IV, 107–161.

ROBERT C. OUSTERHOUT

[See also **Byzantine Art; Theodore Metochites.**]

KARLAMAGNÚS SAGA is an Old Norse translation of the Charlemagne cycle of the chansons de geste and Carolingian romances that originated in France in the eleventh and twelfth centuries. The compilation was made in Norway around the middle of the thirteenth century, during the reign of Hakon IV (1217–1263), in large part drawing on earlier Norwegian and Icelandic translations of individual works. There is no single complete manuscript of the saga. However, the various extant manuscripts, taken together, provide a full text. Carl R. Unger classified these manuscripts into two groups, called *A* and *B*, a convention followed in subsequent scholarship on the saga. The original *A* compilation survives in two imperfect later manuscripts and two earlier fragments. A later *B* redaction was written in Iceland in the fourteenth century (although it survives only in later copies). Variants from two manuscripts and two fragments of this version were printed by Unger, and another manuscript has since been discovered.

The date of the saga compilation indicates that some of its translations may preserve versions of certain texts that are earlier than extant versions in the original languages. Thus, especially where the original has been lost, the various saga versions are of great value to students of a number of early poems.

The "complete" saga consists of ten parts. Part I, untitled in the manuscripts that contain it, describes the rise to power and early, pre-Roncesvalles career of Karlamagnús (Charlemagne) and appears to be based on a lost French compilation which itself included brief versions of a number of works. The now lost *Chanson de Basin* and versions of *Girart de Vienne*, the Saxon wars (against "King Vitakind"), and the *Voyage* (or *Pèlerinage*) *de Charlemagne* are among the more important segments of the *A* compilation. Part II, "Olif and Landres," concerns the trials of an unfairly accused queen, here said to be the sister of Karlamagnús; it appears only in the later *B* version. A prologue says that the tale of Olif was translated from a version "found" in Scotland, which was clearly one of the earliest Middle English romances. The saga probably preserves features of a French version antecedent to such analogues as *Doon de la Roche*.

Parts III through VI concern wars waged by Karlamagnús before Roncesvalles (Runzival). Part III, "Oddgeir the Dane," is based on an early version of *La chevalerie Ogier de Danemarche*. In it the young Oddgier (Ogier) proves himself during the course of a campaign in Italy. In Part IV, "King Agulandus,"

Rollant (Roland), some of whose exploits were reported in Part I, is the most prominent hero. Its setting, Spain, is taken from the Latin Pseudo-Turpin chronicle, which it follows for about a quarter of the section. The rest is based on a version of the *Chanson d'Aspremont* which was very close to extant texts of that poem. Part V gives a second account of the Saxon wars, "Guitalin the Saxon," in a version likely to have been taken from the source of Jean Bodel's *Chanson des Saxons*, unlike that in the first part of the *A* version (omitted in the *B* redaction). Part VI, "Otuel," an abbreviated version of the French *Chanson d'Otinel*, takes Karlamagnús back to Italy. However, the campaign there is the least important part of this tale of the conversion of a heathen champion to Christianity and his subsequent defeat of a potentially equally worthy heathen who chooses to fight as champion of the heathen creed.

Part VII, "Journey to Jerusalem," gives a significantly different version of material in the first part of the *A* version, this time a very close rendition of the comic *Voyage de Charlemagne en Orient* based on a text that was probably, in some respects, slightly better than the surviving Anglo-Norman text of the poem. Part VIII, "The Battle of Runzival," is, of course, a version of the *Chanson de Roland*. It is often very close to the Oxford text, especially in the beginning, but derives from a variant version with features which have been preserved in the other *Roland* manuscripts.

Part IX, "Vilhjálm Korneis" (William Shortnose), is a brief but diverting account of the later years of its hero, known in French sources as Guillaume d'Orange, who must emerge from religious retirement to come once more to the aid of Karlamagnús. It is in several ways a better-told version than the French *Moniage Guillaume* analogues. Part X, entitled "Miracles and Signs," gives a third, very pious, account of the emperor's apocryphal journey to Jerusalem and Constantinople, and other edifying details of his services to Christianity, ending with his death and funeral. This section, along with Part IX, is preserved only in the later *B* version, but at least part of it (and no doubt all of "Vilhjálm Korneis") must have been in the original compilation. Much of it derives from Pseudo-Turpin, but the most important source is the *Speculum historiale* of Vincent of Beauvais.

Aside from its interest as a repository of early textual traditions, *Karlamagnús saga* is important in that it is the more extensive of only two extant compilations of the "Matter of France." Like the Arthurian cycle, Carolingian romances were compiled in historical and chronicle compendia such as the Pseudo-Turpin, but aside from the saga there is only one similar compilation adhering largely to poetic sources, the Welsh *Ystoria de Carolo Magno*, which contains, in the same order, five of the ten narratives of the saga, from similar, mostly Anglo-Norman, sources. While the Welsh and Norse versions may both have been modeled on a lost compilation made in the British Isles, the saga is the more important surviving account. As a work of literature, it may suffer by comparison with the Arthurian compilations, but such comparisons should be made with caution in view of the long and complex history of the stages through which the "Matter of Britain" passed.

In fact, we should note that if *Karlamagnús saga* is uneven in its achievement, sometimes repetitive, and sometimes contradictory, so is the greatest of Arthurian compilations, Malory's *Morte Darthur* (1469–1470), which represents the culmination of a tradition, not a pioneering effort to amalgamate previously separate narratives into a coherent sequence. The saga, on the other hand, is certainly such an effort, whatever its relation to a putative British model may be. *Karlamagnús saga*, however pallid it may seem in comparison with such Icelandic masterpieces as *Njáls saga*, is also written with a narrative skill well above the average of medieval romance narrative.

The original translators and compilers added transitions and explanations and, even more important, cut and reorganized the material so as to draw attention away from the often repetitive action and focus more sharply on the issues involved in its human confrontations. The *B* redactor further improved the consistency, coherence, and dramatic impact of the work, eliminating material he must have found confusing, confused, or distracting. He also effectively expanded underdeveloped sections, especially that concerning the war against Agulandus.

As a result of this process of selection and revision, every part of the saga advances the central theme, which is embodied in the figure of Karlamagnús as the ideal Christian ruler and surrogate of God. There is almost no trace here of the often capricious and tyrannical monarch of the "rebellious barons" cycle of French Carolingian romance, nor do lesser heroes usurp the king's preeminence. Rollant, for example, frequently engages in rash actions which endanger his side, but Karlamagnús, or others acting for him and/or for God, intervene to save the situation. Thus Rollant, for all his heroic qualities, remains subordinate to Karlamagnús, the recipient of God's fuller revelation and directives. Neither Karlamagnús nor any other Christian hero (with the possible exception of Turpin, toward whom the *B* redactor in particular shows notable reverence) is ever to be confused with God; for all Christians are human, including Karlamagnús, and therefore fallible; hence such comedy as that of the Part VII version of the "Journey to Jerusalem." But Christians characteristically recognize and repent their sins, doing their best to make reparations to God and their fellow men—or even, as in the case of Vilhjálm Korneis, to dumb beasts. This awareness distinguishes the true Christian from the heathen or the traitor to the Christian cause.

Heathenism, in turn, is seen as self-defeating. Its adherents' refusal to believe the truth is reflected in their wrongheaded behavior, especially in the mutual distrust rife among them and their irrational belief in the efficacy of material objects and brute force. They are inevitably overcome by the patience, courage, and courtesy born of respect for one's fellow creatures, as well as by the clarity of vision, which characterize the Christians. This basic contrast is interestingly exemplified in the saga's handling of that stock chanson de geste character the heathen warrior who would have been superb "if only he had been a Christian." No two examples are quite alike. Part IV's Jamund is doomed by his poor judgment, although he is as valiant as any Christian, while his subordinate, Balam, makes a thoughtful conversion to Christianity and lives to reap suitable rewards. Part III's Karvel is apparently to be forgiven for his refusal to convert. He at least acknowledges the superiority of the Christian cause and helps it to triumph, even though he considers it disloyal to defect permanently.

On the other hand, the stubborn heathen Klares of Part VI is differentiated from his counterpart Otuel only by the latter's providential conversion. Klares is doomed to defeat because he rashly offers to defend the truth of the pagan faith in solemn judicial combat. Invariably, the behavior of the unenlightened (even if shortly to be converted) heathen is almost comically stupid. Such consistency in treating heathen versus Christian characteristics is one of the virtues of the saga compilation, which manifests values which are hardly naïve or out-of-date, even for those who may find the sectarian aspect repugnant.

The saga lacks the powerful ambiguities and mythic suggestiveness through which Arthurian romance captivates the imagination of succeeding generations. The difference between the two "matters" is implicit in their subjects. Unlike Arthur, Charlemagne was a relatively recent, well-documented historical figure who was already regarded as a saint when the legends attached to his name took their literary form. Whereas Arthur could be envisioned as "passing" in a mysterious fashion, defeated in an archetypal battle with his next of kin, Charlemagne was known to have died in his bed, a prosaic circumstance which could be enlivened only by adding details adducing evidence of his sanctity. The relative flatness of the ending of the Charlemagne cycle apparently did not bother medieval Scandinavians, who preserved more Carolingian romances in various forms than they did those of the Arthurian variety.

The hagiographic aura of the end of *Karlamagnús saga* can be seen to be a suitable conclusion. One of the points made in the final version of that ending is that later Christian kings could not be expected to live up to the values symbolized by Karlamagnús. The saga reveals Christian society's limitations and imperfections, but it aims to keep its ideal in sight. Karlamagnús, aside from the few missteps which keep him human, is that ideal incarnate, and it is appropriate to conclude with an account of his apotheosis.

The saga's popularity in Scandinavia over several centuries is witnessed by a number of works which are generally agreed to derive from one version or another. The most important of these is the Danish *Karl Magnus Krønike*, an abridgment of the *A* version which preserves sections of the older compilation now missing in the extant saga manuscripts. The Swedish *Karl Magnus* contains only Parts VII and VIII. There are also a number of later Icelandic *rímur* cycles as well as ballads from Norway, Denmark, and the Faroes which attest to the long survival of the material, at least in oral tradition.

BIBLIOGRAPHY

The only complete edition of the saga in the original language is *Karlmagnús saga ok kappa hans*, Carl R. Unger, ed., 2 vols. (1860). An edition in modern Icelandic orthography without textual variants is *Karlmagnús saga og kappa hans*, Bjarni Vilhjálmsson, ed., 3 vols. (1950). The only complete translation is that of Constance B. Hieatt, *Karlmagnús Saga: The Saga of Charlemagne and His Heroes*, 3 vols. (1975–1980), in English. Four of the ten sections of the saga have been reedited and published with a French translation in *Karlmagnús saga, Branches I, III, VII, et IX, edition bilingue par Knud Togeby et Pierre Hal-*

leux, Agnete Loth, ed., and Annette Patron-Godefroit, trans. (1980), with afterword by Povl Skårup.

On Part I, see Paul Aebischer, *Textes norrois et littér-ature française du moyen âge,* I (1954), and *Textes norrois et littérature française du moyen âge,* II (1972), which contains a translation of this part.

On Part II, see Hamilton M. Smyser and Francis P. Ma-goun, Jr., *Survivals in Old Norwegian of Medieval English, French, and German Literature* (1941), which contains a translation, and Hamilton M. Smyser, "The Middle English and Old Norse Story of Olive," in *PMLA,* 56 (1941). On Part III, see Knud Togeby, *Ogier le Danois dans les littératures européennes* (1969). On Part IV, see Peter G. Foote, *The Pseudo-Turpin Chronicle in Iceland: A Contribution to the Study of the Karlamagnús Saga* (1959), which also comments on other parts and the saga as a whole. On Part VI, see Paul Aebischer, *Études sur Oti-nel: De la chanson de geste à la saga norroise et aux ori-gines de la légende* (1960). On Part VII, see Paul Aebischer, *Les versions norroises du "Voyage de Charlemagne en Orient"* (1956). On Part VIII, see Paul Aebischer, *Rolan-diana Borealia: La saga af Runzivals bardaga et ses dé-rivés scandinaves comparés à la Chanson de Roland* (1954); and Eyvind Fjeld Halvorsen, *The Norse Version of the Chanson de Roland* (1959), which is also a valuable commentary on other sections and the saga as a whole. On Part IX, see Smyser and Magoun, cited above for Part II; it contains a translation.

A valuable contribution to the critical analysis of the saga is Carol J. Clover, "Scene in Saga Composition," in *Arkiv för nordisk filologi,* 89 (1974).

The more recent edition of *Karl Magnus Krønike* (1960) is edited by Poul L. Hjorth.

CONSTANCE B. HIEATT

[See also **Arthurian Literature; Chansons de Geste; Faroese Ballads; Matter of Britain, Matter of France, Matter of Rome; Pseudo-Turpin; Rímur; Roland, Song of; Scandi-navian Literature: Rhymed Chronicles.**]

KARLMEINET, a title derived from the Latin form of the name Carolus Magnitus (Karl der Grosse or Charlemagne), is a book about the Frankish em-peror. An early-fourteenth-century compilation by an unknown Rhenish poet, it contains the legendary life story of Karl from youth to death in about 35,000 lines with end rhymes. It is arranged in six books.

1. *Karl und Galie:* Karl spends his youth as a ser-vant in a kitchen of a village near Paris and flees to Spain, where he grows up as a pagan. With the help of his foster father he regains France. Traveling in-cognito in Spain he wins princess Galie (his former foster sister) as his wife, after she has been baptized (*ca.* 14,000 verses).

2. *Morant und Galie:* Karl's wife Galie is falsely accused of adultery with his vassal Morant of Rivere. Both are jailed, but set free, once their innocence has been proven in a duel (*ca.* 5,300 verses).

3. *Karls Kriegsfahrten* (Karl's campaigns): a hap-hazard compilation of Karl's frequent campaigns and his three subsequent marriages and liaisons, re-sulting in many illegitimate children. Karl voyages to the Holy Land and to Santiago de Compostela. His octagonal dome at Aachen (Aix-la-Chapelle) is constructed (*ca.* 5,300 verses).

4. *Karl und Elegast:* Under the assumed name of Albrecht, Karl (at the behest of an angel who appears in his dream), and the Black Knight Elegast, whom he had formerly banished undeservedly, go on a rob-bery spree in the Carolingian palace. After several adventures Elegast becomes Karl's brother-in-law (*ca.* 1,300 verses).

5. *Karl und Rolant:* follows the outline of Pfaffe Konrad's *Rolandslied* (*ca.* 8,300 verses).

6. *Ospinel (Oliver) und Magdalie:* Inserted into the preceding book, this is the story of Ospinel, king of Babylonia, who tries to woo Magdalie, daughter of the king of Marselis. In order to win her hand, he promises the defeat of Karl's Twelve Peers. Although Ospinel manages to defeat one of them, Turpin, he is killed in a duel by Oliver with Durendart (Rolant's sword). Finally Magdalie becomes a Christian and is married to the victor, Oliver (*ca.* 1,100 verses).

Epilogue. *Karls Tod* (Karl's death): occurs in his seventy-second year (*ca.* 500 verses).

The books that comprise *Karlmeinet* derive from various sources. The source for book 1 is ultimately a French chanson de geste, although East Middle Netherlandish transmission is likely. For book 2 a French or Latin source is likely. Book 3 is indirectly dependent on Vincent de Beauvais' *Speculum histo-riale* as well as Jacob van Maerlant's *Spieghel histo-riael.* Book 4 is translated from the East Middle Netherlandish romance *Karel ende Elegast.* For book 6 French and Latin derivations have been as-sumed as likely also, and the epilogue depends again mainly on Vincent de Beauvais.

The only manuscript which contains all seven sto-ries is *A* (fifteenth century) in the *Landes-und Hoch-schulbibliothek Darmstadt,* folio 2290, 540 leaves, which has been edited by Adelbert von Keller, *Karl Meinet* (1858, repr. 1971). The other ten manuscripts are fragmentary.

The *Karlmeinet* is important testimony to Charlemagne's literary afterlife in fourteenth-century Germany, despite the fact that the center of the cult lay in France.

BIBLIOGRAPHY

A chronological, annotated bibliography has been prepared by Cola Minis, *Bibliographie zum Karlmeinet* (1971). Minis provides a codicological description of the extant manuscripts. A history of the Dutch *Karel ende Elegast* has been edited by J. Bergsma, in *Klassiek Letterkundig Pantheon,* CXXXII (1960).

Studies. Udo von der Berg, "Konrads Rolandslied und das Rolandslied des Karlmeinet," in *Rheinische Vierteljahrsblätter,* **39** (1975); Theodor Frings and Elisabeth Linke, "Rätselraten um den Karlmeinet," in *Mediaeval German Studies Presented to Frederick Norman* (1965); Karl-Ernst Geith, "Rolands Tod: Zum Verhältnis von 'Chanson de Roland' und deutschem 'Rolandslied,'" in *Amsterdamer Beiträge zur älteren Germanistik,* **10** (1976); Márta A. Holmberg, *Karlmeinet-Studien* (1954); Heinrich Tiefenbach, "Zur Sprache von 'Karl und Galie,'" in *Amsterdamer Beiträge zur älteren Germanistik,* **8** (1975).

CHRISTIAN J. GELLINEK

[See also **Chansons de Geste; Charlemagne; Matter of Britain, France, Rome; Rolandslied; Vincent of Beauvais.**]

KARLSKRÖNIKAN (KK) is the longest (9,628 lines) of the Scandinavian rhymed chronicles. It was completed in its earliest version in 1452 by an unknown redactor and is usually interpreted as being the work of two different anonymous Swedish authors: lines 1–2,765 comprising the so-called *Engelbrektskrönikan* (The Engelbrekt chronicle); and lines 2,766–9,628, the *Karlskrönikan* proper. The first of these describes the rebellion of the Dalecarlian folk hero Engelbrekt Engelbrektsson against Erik of Pomerania from about 1432 until he was murdered on 4 May 1436. The second portion describes the rise of Karl Knutsson (later to become Charles VIII of Sweden), Engelbrekt's ruthless former co-commander, as he seeks to consolidate the kingdom under his rule. Terminating at a politically inconclusive point, the chronicle was then extended by the three *Sturekrönikor,* which cover the periods 1452–1470, 1470–1487, and 1488–1496.

The combination of *Erikskrönikan* (the earliest of the Scandinavian rhymed chronicles), *KK,* and the three Sture chronicles has been termed *Stora rimkrönikan* (The great rhymed chronicle), which cov-

ers nearly two and a half centuries of Sweden's history (from 1249 to 1496). While of slight value as a literary work, *KK* is the most credible contemporary source that has survived to inform us of this turbulent period in Sweden's history. In contrast to *Erikskrönikan,* by far the more imposing as a literary work, *KK* is also know as *Nya krönikan* (The new chronicle), while the former is known as *Gamla krönikan* (The elder chronicle).

The manuscripts containing *KK* reveal many hands, emendations, and false readings. Only one manuscript, Cod. Holm. D 6 (Stockholm, Royal Library), consisting of 126 leaves scripted in 1452, contains it as an independent work; this is also the earliest text that has survived. The Engelbrekt chronicle is thought to derive in part from German chancery writer Johan Fredebern and in part from other contemporaneous sources (although it is still a contested matter precisely how much of *KK* derives from each source). A convincing case has been made that Fredebern composed lines 1,262–2,765 sometime between 1436 and 1438. Only so much is certain, however: the first portion of *KK* attests several Low German hapax legomena and is thus of distinct linguistic and cultural value. It is a direct witness of Low German influence on the Swedish of the time.

BIBLIOGRAPHY

Karlskrönikan has been edited by Gustaf E. Klemming, *Svenska medeltidens Rim-Krönikor,* 3 vols. (1865–1868). For a discussion of the extent of Fredebern's contribution in comparison with that of others see Erik Noreen, "Författarfrågor i 'Nya eller Karlskrönikan' (RK2)," in *Arkiv för nordisk filologi,* 55 (1939).

T. L. MARKEY

[See also **Chronicles; Erikskrönikan; Scandinavian Literature: Rhymed Chronicles.**]

KĀRNĀMAG-I ARDEŠĪR-I BĀBAGĀN (or Pāpakān) (The book of the deeds of Ardešīr, son of Papak) is a Middle Persian work of the late Sasanian period that deals with the foundation of that dynasty. It is one of the few extant examples of historical writing in Middle Persian, although it is clear from Arabic and Classical Persian sources that a substantial Middle Persian collection of Iranian historical traditions, the *Xwadāy nāmag* (Book of kings), had been compiled by Zoroastrian priest-scribes.

The *Kārnāmag* was apparently the basis for the rendering of the Ardešīr legend found in Firdawsī's great Persian epic, the *Shāhnāma* (Book of kings).

Although the *Kārnāmag* has little value as a historical record, it does reflect the persistence of the romantic tradition surrounding Cyrus, the founder of the Achaemenid dynasty, a tradition preserved in Herodotus' account in the first book of the *Persian Wars*. This account bears comparison with other "dynasty-founder" stories common in the ancient Near East: the prophecy of a future ruler (often in a dream), the efforts by the ruling dynasty to kill the future ruler, the nurture of the future ruler by shepherds, the precocious display of leadership abilities, the period of tutelage in a rival court, the triumphant return. This is an interesting feature in view of the Sasanians' general ignorance of the Achaemenids, their knowledge seemingly being limited to an awareness of the first and last "Dārās" (Dariuses), and this probably by way of the Alexander romance.

The *Kārnāmag* is also notable for its anti-Arsacid (Parthian) bias, a common feature of Sasanian Zoroastrian writing. The Arsacids (who were Iranian but not Persian) are depicted as petty dynasts, responsible for the fragmentation of the Iranian empire and for the decline of religion.

BIBLIOGRAPHY

Mary Boyce, "Middle Persian Literature," in *Handbuch der Orientalistik*, I: *Iranistik*, IV (1968), 57–60; Arthur E. Christensen, *Les gestes des rois dans les traditions de l'Iran antique* (1936).

DALE L. BISHOP

[See also **Ardešīr (Ardashir, Artaxeres) I; Pahlavi Literature; Sasanians; Shāhnāma; Xwadāy Nāmag.**]

KARS (Armenian: Karuc^c Berd; Persian/Arabic: Ḳarṣ, Ḳārṣ, or Ghars), an Armenian town and fortress on the Axurean River (Kars-çay) in the district of Vanand. Founded by the Urartians (ninth through sixth centuries B.C.) and probably identical with Ptolemy's Khasira/Khorsa, Kars first became important as one of the capitals of Bagratid Armenia (928–961). In 962 Ašot III ceded Vanand to his brother Mušeł (Mushegh), who founded the kingdom of Kars (Vanand) but whose grandson, Gagik-Abas II, ceded it to the Byzantines in 1064 (it was taken by the Seljuks later that year). During the Bagratid period, Kars

grew rich on the transit trade between Ani and Erzurum, and it was during this time that the present cathedral was built. Kars was subsequently taken by the Seljuks (1064), the Georgians (1074), the Seljuks again (1080), the Kipchaks (destroyed 1153), the Georgians (1204), the Mongols (1239), Tamerlane (destroyed 1387), the Black Sheep (1412), the White Sheep (1467), and the Ottomans (1534), becoming Ottoman again in 1578.

BIBLIOGRAPHY

Aram Ter-Ghewondyan, *The Arab Emirates in Bagratid Armenia*, Nina G. Garsoïan, trans. (1976), 64, 69, 95, 104, 143; Jean Michel Thierry, "À propos de quelques monuments chrétiens du vilayet de Kars (Turquie)," in *Revue des études arméniennes*, n.s. 3 (1966) and 8, and *La cathédrale des Saints-Apôtres de Kars: 930–943* (1978); Cyril Toumanoff, *Studies in Christian Caucasian History* (1963), 202, 486, and "Armenia and Georgia," in *Cambridge Medieval History*, IV, pt. 1 (1966).

ROBERT H. HEWSEN

[See also **Armenia, Geography; Armenia: History of.**]

KARTĪR or Kirdēr (third century), Zoroastrian high priest under the first seven Sasanian monarchs, from Ardešīr I (224–241) to Narseh (293–303). He is mentioned together with other low-ranking officials as a *hērbad* (a priest of the second rank) in the inscription of Šābuhr I on the Ka^c aba-yi Zardušt from about 262. In a Manichaean Middle Persian text on the last journey of Mani (the founder of Manichaeism), the hostile king Bahrām I (273–276), in the company of Kirdēr, son of Ardawān, accuses the prophet; however, Kirdēr may not be Kartīr the priest. The Zoroastrian Pahlavi books do not mention Kartīr at all, although he has left four inscriptions in Middle Persian (more than any single Sasanian king), according to which he seems to have gained enormous power in the course of his long career. Since other high priests (such as Tansar) are mentioned often and favorably in various texts, Kartīr seems to have been deliberately consigned to oblivion. Perhaps his successful ambitious career was seen as a dangerous precedent and a potential threat to the balance of classes and powers in the Sasanian state.

All four inscriptions, recorded in the reign of

Bahrām II (276–293), are in Fārs. The longest and best-preserved is below that of Šābuhr I on the Kaᶜba of Zoroaster (KKZ). Another, on the cliff face of Naqsh-i Rustam (KNRu) opposite the Kaᶜba of Zoroaster, is near the bas-relief depicting Šābuhr's triumph over Valerian (KNRm). The shortest is at Naqsh-i Rajab (KNRj), with Kartīr himself apparently in bas-relief with raised finger. It is near the investiture scene in bas-relief of Ardešīr I and the supreme God, Ohrmazd (KNRb). The fourth, at Sar Mašhad (KSM), is near a bas-relief interpreted as depicting Bahrām II slaying lions that are attacking him, his family, and Kartīr.

With the exception of an eschatological narrative in KSM, the contents of the four inscriptions are nearly identical. Kartīr enumerates his services to the crown and the *yazata*s (spiritual beings worthy of worship): the enthronement of sacred fires, bringing joy to men of the Magian estate and satisfaction to the holy creations of water, fire, and animals. He boasts of having suppressed Jews, Orthodox Christians, Brahmins, Mandaeans, Nestorian Christians, Manichaeans, and Buddhists both in Ērānšahr and in foreign lands conquered by the king of kings. He claims to have converted people of the "cult of demons" and "unbelievers" to belief in Ohrmazd, and to have punished heterodox Magi, destroyed images, and financed the restoration of the orthodox cult with the issue of many charters and rescripts. Kartīr was *mōbad* (Zoroastrian priest) and *hērbad* under Šābuhr I; under Hormizd I (273) he received the additional title of "*mōbad* of Ohrmazd," which he retained under Hormizd's brother, Bahrām I; Bahrām II added the title *Boxt ruwān ī Warahrān* (Soul savior of Bahrām). The duties and powers of the last two titles are not known, and they do not seem to have been continued under the later Sasanians.

In KSM, Kartīr describes a voyage to observe the delights of heaven and the punishments of hell in the company of a woman of light from the East, probably his *dēn* (the spiritual embodiment of one's deeds), and a man of his own form, probably his *frawahr* (the incorruptible essence of one's spirit). The particulars of his vision accord with the spirit journey described in the Pahlavi *Ardāy Wīrāz Nāmag* and with the image of the next world in other texts. Such journeys in Zoroastrian tradition come at times of social discord as supernatural affirmation of the truth of the Mazdean way. Although Kartīr's ambition may have been perceived after him as a threat to that order, he nonetheless deserves credit for establishing

the Zoroastrian church as the stable foundation for the pillar of Sasanian kingship.

BIBLIOGRAPHY

Michael Back, *Die sassanidischen Staatsinschriften* (1978); Richard N. Frye, "The Middle Persian Inscription of Kartīr at Naqš-i Rajab," in *Indo-Iranian Journal,* 8 (1965); Philippe Gignoux, "L'inscription de Kartir à Sar Mašhad," in *Journal asiatique,* 256 (1968); Walter B. Henning, "Mani's Last Journey," in *Bulletin of the School of Oriental and African Studies,* 10 (1942); Vladimar G. Lukonin, "Kartir i Mani," in *Vestnik Drevnei istorii,* 3 (1966); Martin Sprengling, *Third Century Iran: Sapor and Kartir* (1953).

JAMES R. RUSSELL

[See also **Ardešir (Ardashir, Artaxeres) I; Kaᶜba of Zoroaster; Naqsh-i Rustam; Šābuhr (Shahpuhr) I; Sasanians; Zoroastrianism.**]

KᶜARTᶜLI. See Georgia: Geography.

KᶜARTᶜLIS CᶜXOVREBA (Life of Georgia) is a corpus of Georgian historical writings also known as the Georgian Annals. (There are also other Georgian historical works not included in the *Kᶜartᶜlis Cᶜxovreba.*) The collection was begun in the eleventh century; more material was added through the fourteenth century. Finally, at the beginning of the eighteenth century, King Wakhtang VI (who was also responsible for the compilation of a code of Georgian law) appointed a commission of scholars to revise, correct, and amplify the collection. This resulted in the edition translated by Marie-Félicité Brosset. Since then earlier recensions have come to light.

The official collection contains seven works:

1. The *History of the Kings of Kᶜartᶜli* (Georgia) covers the history of Georgia from the earliest times down to the fifth century A.D. This work includes the folklore of Georgian origins (which it attempts to correlate with the biblical genealogies of Noah's offspring), the legendary story of Alexander the Great's invasion of the Caucasus, and an account of the conversion of the Georgians to Christianity by St. Nino. This last is printed as a separate section in the Georgian edition of Qaukhchishvili.

2. The *History of King Wakhtang Gorgasali* is at-

tributed to a certain Juansher (eighth century), husband of the niece of Archil II. It gives an account of the deeds of King Wakhtang I (d. 510) and brings the history of Georgia down to the eighth century.

3. The *Martyrdom of King Archil II* concerns that event, which took place in 786.

These three works were edited by Leontius Mroveli; the date of his redaction has been variously ascribed to the eighth or the eleventh century. An Armenian adaptation was made in the twelfth century, the collection being ascribed as a whole to Juansher.

The rest of the collection contains four additional works:

4. The *Chronicle of K^cart^cli*. This is an anonymous work covering the period from the death of Archil II to late in the eleventh century, composed in 1072–1073.

5. The *History of the King of Kings* is an anonymous work concerning David II Aghmashenebeli (the Restorer or the Builder), who reigned from 1089 to 1125.

6. The *Histories and Eulogies of the Sovereigns* is an anonymous thirteenth-century work dealing primarily with the reign of Queen Tamara (1184–1212).

7. The *History of the Mongol Invasions,* the final work, is also anonymous and deals with the period from Tamara's death to the mid fourteenth century.

BIBLIOGRAPHY

The most recent edition of the Georgian text is by Simon G. Qaukhchishvili, *K^cart^clis C^cχovreba,* 2 vols. (1955–1959). The only full translation remains that of Marie-Félicité Brosset, *Histoire de la Géorgie, première partie,* 2 vols. (1849–1850). For further bibliography see Cyril Toumanoff, "Medieval Georgian Historical Literature: VIIth–XVth Centuries," in *Traditio,* 1 (1943), "The Oldest Manuscript of the Georgian Annals: The Queen Anne Codex (QA), 1479–1495," in *Traditio,* 5 (1947), and the introduction in his *Studies in Christian Caucasian History* (1963), 11–29.

R. W. THOMSON

[See also **David II (IV) the Builder; Georgia: Political History; Georgian Literature; Georgians (Iberians); Tamara; Wakhtang Gurgaslani.**]

KASHI, a Persian word that can refer to all glazed pottery but usually is defined more narrowly as glazed tilework for wall surfaces. *Kashi* is an abbreviation of *Kashani,* meaning "from the [Iranian] city of Kashan," a name that might derive from *kas,* the Semitic word for glass. Kashan has been identified as an important medieval center of ceramic production because tiles survive with inscriptions saying they were made in Kashan. Kashani tileworks are noted for their designs painted in gold luster and range in date from *ca.* 1200 to *ca.* 1340. They maintain a remarkable conservatism in style, explainable partially because a single family of Kashan potters dominated the industry for more than three generations. From its widespread usage during the thirteenth century in Iran, the tradition of covering a wall with glazed tile became an indelible hallmark of Islamic decoration.

The decorative tilework tradition did not originate in Kashan but goes back as far as the thirteenth century B.C. in Khuzistan, where tiles were employed on walls, perhaps to reduce humidity. The natural flowering of tilework may be the result of the affinity of the basic Near Eastern building material, baked or sun-dried bricks, for glazed bricks. But tilework fell into disuse with Hellenistic domination of the region, when mosaic surface ornament tended to prevail, and when Sasanian builders preferred carved and molded stucco work. Since painted tiles tended to be made in the same factories, by the same techniques, and in the same style as painted pottery, glazed tilework regained favor in the Islamic world when the Abbasids began to support the development of ceramics as an art form. The evidence for a ninth-century polychrome luster tile tradition stems from excavations at Samarra and from tiles still embedded in the walls of the great mosque in Qayrawān in Tunisia (dated 862). Luster tiles continued to be made in Iran until the fourteenth century, but were superseded by underglaze painted tiles, often in blue and white. A technical brilliance in underglaze polychrome tiles was reached in the fifteenth- and sixteenth-century Ottoman mosque tiles.

"Kashi" used as a generic term may also include mosaic faience that developed not in the potter's workshops but as an extension of architectural brickwork introduced to render more legible the inscriptions on the facades of eleventh-century Iranian buildings. Pieces of monochrome glazed brick were cut into small pieces, then joined together by pouring clay mortar in from the back side to fill the spaces between the pieces. The earliest known complete mosaic faience wall is the Ala-ed-Din mosque in Konya, dated 1220. Fine Iranian examples such as the mausoleum of Uljaytū in Sultaniya (1304–1316)

Kashi decoration from Prayer Hall of Blue Mosque, Tabriz, *ca.* 1465. PHOTO: HENRY DE SÉGOGNE. © MAZENOD, PARIS, 1976

Hagii Anargyri. Small basilican church at Kastoria, *ca.* 1000. FOTO MARBURG/ART RESOURCE

and the Blue Mosque of Tabriz (1465) survive. Cuerda seca, another tilework technique, exemplified by the interior walls of the Alhambra, achieved a rich array of colors and avoided the problem of the mingling of unstable runs in the kiln by tracing the design with an incised outline and filling it in with a greasy manganese pigment. The outline formed a container wall that, when burned, looked like a roughened, black "dry cord." The laboriousness of these alternative processes favored the long-standing dominance of underglazed painted tiles for Near Eastern wall coverings.

BIBLIOGRAPHY

Oliver Watson, "Persian Lustre-painted Pottery: The Rayy and Kashan Styles," in *Transactions of the Oriental Ceramic Society*, **40** (1973–1975), plates 1–16.

MARINA D. WHITMAN

[See also **Ceramics, Islamic.**]

KASTORIA, a town in southern Macedonia supporting numerous Byzantine churches dating from the late ninth to the end of the twelfth century. With the exception of the Koubelidiki, the churches are small basilicas, and all seem to have been commissioned by local families. The masonry technique employed is consistent: the exterior walls are composed of mortared rubble, faced with brick and stone arranged in distinctive decorative patterns. Interiors are often covered with frescoes.

BIBLIOGRAPHY

Ann Wharton Epstein, "Middle Byzantine Churches of Kastoria: Dates and Implications," in *Art Bulletin,* **62** (1980).

LESLIE BRUBAKER

[See also **Basilica.**]

KATEPANO, a Byzantine official whose title *(kata + epano)* means chief. Until the tenth century the *katepano* was usually the head of a small coastal region or ethnic minority in the empire (such as the Mardaïtai of Attaleia). From around 970 on, the term designated a high-ranking officer, such as commander of heavy cavalry stationed in a frontier region (for example, Byzantine Italy) or governor of such a region, with authority over several local strategoi; in this respect the term seems to have been the Greek equivalent of *dux* and is the origin of the

English word "captain." By the twelfth century the *katepano* had increased fiscal responsibilities. The title itself disappeared in that century but was the origin of the term *katepanikion*, a small fiscal district that was common during the thirteenth and fourteenth centuries.

BIBLIOGRAPHY

Hélène Glykatzi-Ahrweiler, "Recherches sur l'administration de l'empire byzantin aux IXe–XIe siècles," in *Bulletin de correspondance hellénique*, **84** (1960), 64ff, also published separately the same year; Ljubomir Maksimović, *Vizantijska provintsijska uprava u doba Paleologa* (1972), 43ff, with detailed English summary; Nicolas Oikonomidès, *Les listes de préséance byzantines des IXe et Xe siècles* (1972), 344; Georgios Theocharides, *Katepanikia tes Makedonias* (1954).

NICOLAS OIKONOMIDES

[See also **Byzantine Empire: Bureaucracy.**]

KATHERINE GROUP. The texts commonly referred to by this name are Middle English religious pieces—saints' lives, pious and homiletic treatises, meditations—found chiefly in two manuscripts: Oxford, Bodleian Library, MS Bodley 34, and British Library, MS Royal 17.A.XXVII. MS Bodley 34 contains (in the order cited) the lives of the virgin martyrs St. Katherine (hence the title), St. Margaret, and St. Juliana; *Hali Meiðhad,* a tract in praise of female chastity; and *Sawles Warde,* an allegorical and homiletic treatise, which is a free adaptation of chapters 13–14 of Book IV of *De anima,* ascribed to Hugh of St. Victor (*d.* 1141). The same texts are found in the same order in MS Royal 17.A.XXVII, except that *Hali Meiðhad* is omitted and *On Lofsong of ure Lefdi,* a paraphrase of a Latin verse prayer of Marbod of Rennes, appears after *Sawles Warde.*

These texts have greater claims to the attention as a group than as single works. Their interest is that in the form they have survived, in MS Bodley 34 in particular, the different texts display linguistic characteristics of a consistency seldom found in a Middle English manuscript. What is more remarkable is that these characteristics are also found in other manuscripts—recognizably in Royal 17.A.XXVII, the sister manuscript of Bodley 34; in Cotton Titus D.XVIII and Cotton Cleopatra C.VI, both of the latter being texts of a rule for anchorites preserved

without title but generally known as *Ancrene Riwle*—and in Cotton Nero A.XIV, which contains the *Ancrene Riwle* and other religious texts, and strikingly in Corpus Christi College, Cambridge, MS 402, one of the earliest versions of the *Ancrene Riwle,* there named in the rubric to the manuscript itself, *Ancrene Wisse.*

Even though they are the work of different scribes, the similarity between the language of Bodley 34 and Corpus 402 is so close in phonology and accidence, in vocabulary and idiom, and in the nature and stability of their spelling systems, that analysis can scarcely distinguish them in the smallest details.

J. R. R. Tolkien demonstrated the linguistic consistency of the group, proposed a localization in Herefordshire, and suggested a date (on linguistic grounds) of not much before 1225, if that early. Tolkien's dating is supported by paleographical evidence: N. R. Ker, in the introduction to Tolkien's edition of *Ancrene Riwle,* assigns MS Bodley 34 to the first quarter of the thirteenth century, while a date later than 1224 is fixed for the Corpus MS of *Ancrene Wisse* by the reference to "ure freres meonurs" (fol. 16^v), since the Franciscans arrived in England in that year.

The date and localization proposed by Tolkien have gained wide acceptance, and are supported by circumstantial evidence, such as the thirteenth-century inscription in the Corpus MS recording its presentation to the Augustinian abbey of St. James the Apostle at Wigmore in northwestern Herefordshire, near the Welsh border. The existence in the mid thirteenth century of a chapel dedicated to "Saincte Juliane," not far from Wigmore, and a reference by the author of *Ancrene Riwle* to "ower englische boc of seinte margarete" may be evidence of local interest in those saints, which could explain the presence of their lives in MS Bodley 34.

There is no agreement on the identity of the author of the texts and not much on the question of whether they are the work of one or many. But it seems likely that S. T. R. O. d'Ardenne is right in her claim that they are the products of an especially active and influential center or school rather than the work of a single busy author and universal provider of devotional literature.

They belong to a tradition that reaches beyond the Conquest to Aelfric. The connection between the alliterative prose of the Katherine Group and that of Aelfric's saints' lives and homilies has often been made—though John C. Pope, Aelfric's editor, properly refuses to accept the Katherine Group texts as metrical even in the loose Aelfrician sense. But apart from their historical and archaeological importance (which has been much exaggerated), they represent a considerable achievement in their own right: a cultivated and expressive language for literate people— a serviceable, self-confident, occasionally exuberant prose, rhetorically sophisticated (though sometimes merely rhetorically elaborate) with a relaxed and cordial fit between itself and the ideas it expresses and the ends for which it was employed.

BIBLIOGRAPHY

Bibliographies are in *New Cambridge Bibliography of English Literature,* I (1974), and *A Manual of the Writings in Middle English, 1050–1500,* II (1970). For a useful list of the chief editions and translations of the Katherine Group and associated texts, see the edition of parts VI and VII of *Ancrene Wisse* by Geoffrey Shepherd (1959). New editions, with bibliographies, are Robert W. Ackerman and Roger Dahood, eds. and trans., *Ancrene Riwle, Introduction and Part I* (1984); Simonne R. T. O d'Ardenne and E. J. Dobson, eds., *Seinte Katerine* (1981); Bella Millett, ed., *Hali Meiðhad* (1982).

Karl D. Bülbring recognized the affiliations of the language of the Katherine Group with the ninth-century Mercian glosses in the Vespasian Psalter as early as 1901 in his "*E* and *Æ* in the Vespasian Psalter," in *An English Miscellany Presented to Dr. Furnivall in Honour of His Seventy-fifth Birthday* (1901, repr. 1969). J. R. R. Tolkien's discussion of the dialect he named the "AB language" is in "*Ancrene Wisse* and *Hali Meiðhad,*" in *Essays and Studies,* **14** (1929). The fullest account of the AB language is in *Þe Liflade ant te Passiun of Seinte Iuliene,* S. T. R. O. d'Ardenne, ed. (1936, rev. ed. 1961). See also H. M. Logan, *The Dialect of the Life of Saint Katherine* (1973). Also see Eric J. Dobson, *The Origins of Ancrene Wisse* (1976), which attributes the work to an Augustinian canon writing at Wigmore Abbey, Herefordshire, *ca.* 1215–1222.

P. L. HEYWORTH

[See also **Ancrene Riwle; Middle English Literature.**]

KATHOLIKON (Catholicon), the principal church of a Greek monastery (for instance, Hosios Lukas in Phocis). The term is derived from the Greek *katholikos,* the head of a number of monasteries located within the same area.

LESLIE BRUBAKER

[See also **Monastery.**]

KATHOLIKOS (katᶜolikos), a word of Greek origin, meaning "general" or "universal," and originally applied to the secular superintendent of finance in each diocese at the time of Constantine the Great. In certain sixth-century Greek sources it appears as the official title of archbishops, *katholikos episkopos,* and of superiors of several monasteries in the same city. The use of the word as the title of a metropolitan bishop seems to be of an earlier date in Syriac and Armenian. In the acts of the Council of Seleucia-Ctesiphon, which took place in February 410, Isaac, the bishop of Seleucia-Ctesiphon, is referred to as the *katholikos* of the East. The title also appears in his signature. In the Armenian version of the canons of the councils of Nicaea and Antioch, which were translated in the 430's, the Greek *metropolitos* (metropolitan) is frequently translated as *katholikos.*

The earliest application of the title to the chief bishop of Greater Armenia—if it is not an interpolation—is to be found in Koriwn's *Life of Maštocᶜ,* written in the 440's, in which the patriarch St. Sahak, bishop of Arsacid Armenia, is referred to as *katᶜolikos* (the Armenian form) on two occasions. The Armenian writers of the fifth century and thereafter occasionally use the title for the bishops of Rome, Constantinople, Caesarea, and frequently for those of Georgia and Caucasian Albania. The Armenian form of the word, *katᶜolikos,* indicates that it was borrowed from Greek, but the alternate form *katᶜulikos,* which is probably just as old as the first, suggests Syriac influence. The Armenian *katᶜolikos* was originally the bishop of Arsacid Armenia. The Armenian sources from as early as the seventh century indicate that the *katᶜolikoi* received ordination. The present-day tradition of anointing the crown of his head is also old and attested from the ninth century.

In the early twelfth century, the bishops of Ałtᶜamar challenged the authority of the *katᶜolikos* and began to use the title, thus creating a schism in the Armenian church. Even after the schism had ended in the fourteenth century, they retained their title. In a similar manner, the bishops of the city of Sis, the capital of Cilician Armenia where the *katᶜolikoi* resided in the fourteenth century and the first half of the fifteenth century, continued to use the title even after the transfer of the patriarchal throne of Vałaršapat in 1441.

During the Middle Ages and in modern times the title *katholikos* has also been used by the heads of the Nestorian, Georgian, and Caucasian Albanian churches. Ever since the seventeenth century, the head of the Armenian Uniates in Lebanon has also borne the title *katᶜ olikos*-patriarch of Cilicia

BIBLIOGRAPHY

Vardan Hacᶜuni (Hats'owni), *Katᶜolikosan ĕntrutᶜ-iwn ew jeřnadrutᶜiwn patmutᶜean mēj* (The Election and Ordination of Katholikoi in History) (1930); Koriwn, *Patmutᶜiwn varucᶜ S. Maštocᶜ vardapeti* (A History of the Life of Holy Maštocᶜ Vardapet), P. Nersēs Akinean, ed., in *Mechithar-Festschrift* (1949), 171–320, esp. note 13 of Akinean's commentary (in Armenian), 283–287; Geoffrey William H. Lampe, *A Patristic Greek Lexicon* (1962, repr. 1976); *Syndicon orientale; ou, recueil de synodes nestoriens,* Jean Baptiste Chabot, ed. and trans. from Syriac (1902).

KRIKOR H. MAKSOUDIAN

[See also **Armenian Church; Byzantine Church.**]

KAXETI. See **Georgia: Geography.**

KAYKHOSRAW I. See **Qaykhosraw I.**

KEDRENOS, GEORGIOS (Georgius Cedrenus) (*fl. ca.* 1100), is known only for his compilation of a world chronicle, the *Synopsis historiōn,* which covers the period from the creation of the world through the Old Testament kingdoms and the Roman Empire, up to the reign of the Byzantine emperor Isaac Komnenos (1057). His work is unoriginal and of little value as an independent historical source, since much of the section dealing with the period up to 800 is based on such authors as Pseudo-Symeon, Theophanes Confessor, and George the Monk; from 811 on, the chronicle is virtually a verbatim copy of John Skylitzes.

BIBLIOGRAPHY

The *Synopsis* is in *Corpus scriptorum historiae Byzantinae,* Immanuel Bekker, ed., 2 vols. (1838–1839); *Patrologia graeca,* CXXI (1864), 24–1165, and CXXII (1864), 9–368. See also Herbert Hunger, *Die hochsprachliche profane Literatur der Byzantiner,* I (1978), 393–394, with full bibliography; K. Schweinburg, "Die ursprüngliche Form der Kedrenchronik," in *Byzantinische Zeitschrift,* 30 (1929–1930).

ALICE-MARY M. TALBOT

[See also **George the Monk; Historiography, Byzantine; Skylitzes, John; Theophanes Confessor.**]

KEEP. See **Dungeon.**

KEKAUMENOS, the family name of the author of an eleventh-century Greek text, *Strategikon,* found in a single fourteenth-century manuscript now in Moscow (Synod. 435). An initial section of unknown length is lost, and there are lacunae and apparent dislocations in the surviving text. The composition is principally addressed to the author's sons, as advice on general conduct in civil and military affairs, illustrated by vivid anecdotes drawn mainly from contemporary events; there is also a section of advice for an emperor. The style is straightforward and appealing. This is a text of major importance for the political and social history of eleventh-century Byzantium.

BIBLIOGRAPHY

The complete text, with a brief introduction, was published as *Cecaumeni Strategicon,* B. Wassiliewsky and V. Jernstedt, eds. (1896, repr. 1965 under Kekaumenos). See also Kekaumenos, *Vademecum des byzantinischen Aristokraten,* Hans Georg Beck, ed. and trans. (1956), a German trans. of the *Strategikon,* with brief notes. Gennadi Grigorevich Litvarin has published a new text, with Russian trans., a very full commentary, and a bibliography, as *Sovety i rasskazy Kekavmena* (1972). A new edition, with English trans. and commentary, is being prepared by C. Roueché.

The first major study of the work is Paul E. Lemerle, *Prolégomènes à une édition critique et commentée des "Conseils et récits" de Kékauménos* (1960).

C. ROUECHÉ

[See also **Byzantine Empire.**]

KELIM. See **Kilim.**

KELLS, BOOK OF, a richly illustrated Insular Gospelbook, usually dated to about 775–800, housed in the monastery of Kells from at least 1006 until 1653, when it was sent to Dublin; since 1661/1682, it has been at Trinity College, Dublin (MS 58). The Book of Kells is the most elaborately decorated of the Hiberno-Saxon manuscripts; the density of the decoration and the high quality of its minute, precise detail may have occasioned Gerald of Wales's reference in the twelfth century to a manuscript that appeared to be the work of angels rather than of men.

Although the organization, most of the formal motifs, and many of the iconographic motifs of the manuscript have parallels in other Insular works, the

Temptation of Christ. From the Book of Kells, *ca.* 775–800, Trinity College Dublin, MS 58, fol. 202v. COURTESY THE BOARD OF TRINITY COLLEGE, DUBLIN

precise date and place of origin of the Book of Kells remain controversial. It has been attributed to scriptoria in Northumbria, Ireland, and Scotland, and dated from the beginning to the end of the eighth century. In content and arrangement the decoration of the Book of Kells builds on earlier Insular practice (for instance, the Book of Durrow: Dublin, Trinity College Library, MS 57), including a cross carpet page, four symbols pages, canon tables, evangelist portraits, initial pages and illuminated initials within the text. The four additional full-page miniatures—

the Virgin and Child, the arrest of Christ, the temptation of Christ, a figure (Christ or one of the evangelists) and angels—are unusual but are associated with text passages singled out in other Insular Gospelbooks, particularly Durham, Cathedral Library, MS A.II.17 (*ca.* 700), a manuscript that has been connected with Lindisfarne. As in the Book of Kells and the St. Gall Gospels (Stiftsbibliothek, codex 51), the Durham Gospels contains full-page miniatures of events from Christ's life. The miniature of the Virgin and Child in the Book of Kells (fol. 7v) is iconographically related to another Lindisfarne product, the Cuthbert reliquary (*ca.* 698).

The meticulous accuracy of the ornament of the Book of Kells presupposes familiarity with the style of the Lindisfarne Gospels (London, British Library, MS Cotton Nero D.IV), a manuscript produced at Lindisfarne, probably between 695 and 700. Among preserved Insular examples, the Lindisfarne Gospels seems directly to anticipate the Book of Kells also in the use of arcaded canon tables, the abandonment of the diminuendo headpiece—common in Insular manuscripts since the Cathach of St. Columba (600–625)—in which each letter is progressively smaller, and the panel-like arrangement of much of its decoration.

Other motifs in the Book of Kells cannot be traced in works connected with Lindisfarne: the foliate ornament, rare in Insular decoration, has been connected with a manuscript of Bede, now in Leningrad, apparently produced in one of the twin monasteries of Wearmouth and Jarrow about 746, as well as with continental Carolingian ornament; Pictish influence may have inspired the interlaced human figures and fantastic animals that occur throughout the manuscript. The peculiar format of the canon tables, which seem faithfully to imitate a defective model, was once thought to reflect Carolingian practice but is now considered to rely on a Northumbrian exemplar of the early eighth century; the inclusion of symbols of the evangelists in the canon table arcades (beast canon tables) has parallels both from northern England (for instance, fols. 1–5 of the Maeseyck Gospels, early eighth century, possibly from York) and from Carolinigian France (for instance, London, British Library, MS Harley 2788, of *ca.* 795).

The prefatory texts of the Kells Gospels are closely allied with those of the Book of Durrow, a Gospelbook (*ca.* 675–680) assigned to either Northumbria or Ireland; the quality of the parchment and the quire structures of the two manuscripts are similar and have been compared with the Durham Gospels. The script of the latter book has also been associated with the Book of Kells.

BIBLIOGRAPHY

E. H. Alton, Paul Meyer, and G. O. Simms, *Evangeliorum quattuor Codex Cennanensis,* 3 vols. (1950–1951), facsimile and commentary. See also Jonathan J. G. Alexander, *Insular Manuscripts, 6th to the 9th Century* (1978); Carl A. Nordenfalk, *Celtic and Anglo-Saxon Painting: Book Illumination in the British Isles 600–800* (1977).

LESLIE BRUBAKER

[See also **Canon Table; Carpet Page; Celtic Art (with illustration); Durrow, Book of; Evangelist Symbols; Gospelbook; Lindisfarne Gospels; Manuscript Illumination; Migration and Hiberno-Saxon Art.**]

KEMPE, MARGERY (Burnham) (ca. 1373–after 1438), a controversial mystic of Lynn, Norfolk, whose dictated memoirs, discovered in 1934, are considered to be the first autobiography in English. Known for incessant lamentation over the sufferings of Christ, which she considered to be divinely inspired and beyond her control, she was ridiculed, imprisoned, and examined for heresy (she was found innocent). Few believed in her, a notable exception being her husband, to whom she had borne fourteen children. After she began to live as a mystic her husband agreed to live with her in sexual abstinence.

Kempe's autobiography was long considered merely a bizarre account of her pilgrimages to Jerusalem, Rome, and Santiago. It has found some sympathy in recent times as the life of a woman misunderstood and harassed in a time that saw the burning of Lollards and of Joan of Arc (1431). Kempe's life as a mystic followed a pattern not uncommon in the Middle Ages: a materialistic existence was interrupted by illness with delirium, followed by conversion and the search for a spiritual way. She is often compared to Julian of Norwich, whom she had met, and to St. Birgitta of Sweden, whose disciples she had known.

BIBLIOGRAPHY

The Book of Margery Kempe, Sanford B. Meech and Hope Emily Allen, eds. (1940), was modernized as *The Book of Margery Kempe,* William E. Butler-Bowdon, ed. (1944, repr. 1957). See also Clarissa W. Atkinson, *Mystic and Pilgrim* (1983); Louise Collis, *Memoirs of a Medieval Woman* (1964); Sheila Delaney, "Sexual Economics, Chau-

cer's Wife of Bath, and *The Book of Margery Kempe,*" in *The Minnesota Review,* n.s. 5 (1975); David Knowles, *The English Mystical Tradition* (1961), 138–150.

BEVERLY BOYD

[See also **Birgitta of Sweden, St.; Julian of Norwich; Mysticism.**]

KENNETH I MAC ALPIN (Cináed mac Ailpín) (*fl.* 840/841–858), the first ruler of the united kingdoms of the Dalriadic Scots and the Picts. He flourished in a period obscured by the paucity of reliable primary sources, and his reign was further obfuscated through the ill-considered speculations of later antiquarians and historians.

It is certain that Kenneth was a member of the Cenél Gabráin, a kindred or clan named for the Dalriadic king who was a contemporary of St. Columba. Kenneth's somewhat shadowy father, Alpin, is said to have reigned briefly in both Dál Riata and Pictland, though possibly at different times.

Kenneth's career was strongly affected by the ferocity of the Viking attacks on Dál Riata and Pictland. In 836, as king of Dál Riata, he received the assistance of Godfrey mac Fergus, lord of Oriel in Ireland and subsequently ruler of the Hebrides, against the Norsemen. Three years later "many of the noblest of the Picts fell" in a battle against the Vikings. Kenneth exploited the consequent Pictish weakness by marching east to crush all resistance and thus made himself ruler of the two kingdoms, traditionally in 843.

Kenneth had thus fulfilled the tantalizingly obscure "Berchán's Prophecy," which alleged that he would "by force of his strength . . . feed ravens . . . would reign in the east after using the strength of spears and of swords, after violent deaths, after violent slaughter." Berchán also recorded a tradition, echoed in a lost Irish saga and repeated in several medieval sources, that the demise of the Picts resulted from Scottish treachery; the Scots somehow betrayed their enemies at a banquet and cast them into a prepared pit. The most authoritative source, the *Scottish Chronicle,* relates that Kenneth invaded England six times, confidently pushing his frontier south and seizing Dunbar and Melrose in the process. He was recalled to Pictland when the Vikings, probably Danes, raided east along Strathmore to attack the ancient stronghold at Cluny and the new ecclesiastical *caput* of Dunkeld. In 849 the relics of

St. Columba were divided because of the Viking threat to Iona, part going to Kells in Ireland and part, under Kenneth's supervision, to the new church that he had built at Dunkeld.

There is no evidence to support the twelfth-century antiquarian tradition that Kenneth introduced the "Laws of Mac Alpin." He died at the royal hall (*palacium*) of Forteviot in present-day Perthshire in 858. The oft-repeated tradition that he and many of his successors were buried at Iona is false.

BIBLIOGRAPHY

Alan Orr Anderson, *Early Sources of Scottish History, A.D. 500–1286*, 2 vols. (1922), I, cxlvii, cxlviii, cliii–clv, clvii, 267–275, 279–280, 287–292, 354, and notes; Marjorie O. Anderson, *Kings and Kingship in Early Scotland* (1973), 43–48, 196–200, 249–250, 288–291; Edward J. Cowan, "The Scottish Chronicle in the Poppleton Manuscript," in *Innes Review*, 32 (1981); Archibald A. M. Duncan, *Scotland: The Making of the Kingdom* (1975), 56–59.

EDWARD J. COWAN

[See also **Dál Riata; Scotland, History.**]

KENNING. The kenning, a distinctive feature of skaldic poetry and of *dróttkvætt* verse in particular, is rare in Eddic poetry and rarer still in West Germanic verse. It is a periphrasis, consisting of two or more substantive members, that takes the place of a noun. The term is probably derived from the expression *kenna við* (to express or describe one thing by means of another). For instance, the kenning "ship of the desert" (camel) consists of a base word (ship) and a definer or determinant, a noun to which this base word is made to relate (desert). The definer is most typically a noun in the genitive case (the desert's ship), but the kenning can also be a substantive compound, the first element of which limits the range of the second (the desert-ship). Taken together, the two nouns have a significance that neither has separately.

The kenning proper is to be distinguished from the *kend heiti* (qualified name), although thirteenth-century Icelandic theoreticians did not draw clear-cut boundaries between the two. The *kend heiti* is any circumlocution in which the base word literally refers to the concept designated by the whole. One kind of *kend heiti* is the designation of someone or something through a statement of family relationship: Baldr is Odin's son, earth is Thor's mother. In another kind of *kend heiti,* men are denoted by their

deeds: Sigurd is the slayer of Fáfnir, a king is a distributor of rings. Old English and Old Saxon poetry make extensive use of the *kend heiti.*

Barely 100 items are expressed by kennings in skaldic verse; among these are warrior, woman, ship, blood, battle, shield, sword, hand, gold, and carrion beasts. The base words used to designate men are names of divinities and masculine tree names; for women, goddess names, tree names of feminine gender, and feminine words for earth. Gold and silver, battle, weapons, armor, and ships are used as definers in men-kennings, while women are generally defined by what they wear and what they serve. It has been said that early skaldic poetry uses kennings of general applicability (so that all men-kennings, for example, are interchangeable without any loss in meaning), and that only later in the tradition are nonce-kennings with specific senses favored; it is probably unwise, however, to assume that kennings were ever chosen arbitrarily, without regard to their poetic associations and implications.

Some kennings involve pagan recollections (a woman is "Freyja of the necklace"; blood is "wounds of the giant's neck") and legendary lore (gold is "sun of the Rhine" or "seed corn of Fýris-plains"). Others are more like riddles, metaphoric comparisons pointing to hidden correspondences in the universe (stones are "bones of the earth"; the sea, "plain of the lobster"). The definer of a kenning could be expanded by further kennings: a warrior is the "raven's feeder"; he is also, therefore, the "feeder of the swan of the resounding wave of wounds" (wave of wounds = blood, its swan = raven). A kenning consisting of more than three elements is called *rekit* (driven). An abbreviated kenning consisting only of a base word is called a half-kenning.

The kenning appears fully developed in Bragi's *Ragnarsdrápa* and is highly elaborated in the works of the tenth-century skalds Egill Skallagrímsson, Eyvindr skáldaspillir, and Einarr skálaglamm. Eleventh-century official poets such as Sighvatr generally avoided mythological kennings, but these reappeared in number in the following century.

BIBLIOGRAPHY

Hallvard Lie, "Skaldestil-studier," in *Maal og minne* (1952), and "*Natur*" og "*unatur*" i skaldekunsten (1957), 42–64; Edith Marold, *Kenningkunst: Ein Beitrag zu einer Poetik der Skaldendichtung* (1983); Rudolf Meissner, *Die Kenningar der Skalden* (1921); James B. Spamer, "The Kenning and the Kend Heiti: A Contrastive Study of Periphrasis in Two Germanic Poetic Traditions" (diss.,

Brown Univ., 1977); Einar Ól. Sveinsson, "Dróttkvæðaþáttur," in *Skírnir*, 121 (1947); Jan de Vries, *De skaldenkenningen met mythologischen inhoud* (1934).

ROBERTA FRANK

[See also **Anglo-Saxon Literature; Dróttkvætt; Skaldic Poetry.**]

KENTIGERN, ST. (*d.* 612), is the patron saint of Glasgow and the first recorded bishop of the British (Celtic) kingdom of Strathclyde. The ninth-century Welsh Annals report that he died in 612, one of the few statements about him accepted by most scholars. He is also known as Mungo, probably representing the Celtic word "my" (sometimes used of early saints) followed by a hypocoristic form of his name, though the sources seem to have interpreted "Mungo" as meaning "my dear." Glasgow Cathedral is dedicated to him under the latter name.

Kentigern is commemorated in several lives and church offices. The earliest life, extant only in fragmentary form, appears to date from the mid twelfth century. It was probably known to Jocelyn, a monk of Furness in Lancashire, who composed a life about 1180, at the request of Bishop Jocelyn of Glasgow. These may ultimately draw on an early written life, though the suggested date of the latter has ranged from the seventh to the eleventh century. Each extant early life is a farrago of tales drawn from folklore, the Bible, and hagiography. A folklore motif, current in Jocelyn's day though rejected by him, is that Kentigern was born of a virgin. Another version of his parentage, in the earliest life, claims that his father was Ewen (Owein, Yvain), which suggests an association with the Arthurian cycle of legends. The unusual account of his death, however, may have some historical basis. He died in a warm bath on the octave of the feast of Epiphany (13 January), the day he had customarily conducted a baptismal service. The story, recounted to explain the date of his feast day, appears to be a garbled allusion to a baptismal service, which in the early church was celebrated on Epiphany in some places and involved a descent into a stone-lined cistern.

BIBLIOGRAPHY

Primary sources include Nennius, *British History and The Welsh Annals*, John Morris, ed. and trans. (1980), 46, 86; Jocelyn, *Vita Kentegerni*, and the anonymous *Vita Kentegerni imperfecta*, in Alexander P. Forbes, ed., *Lives of S. Ninian and S. Kentigern* (1874), 27–133 (trans.), 159–252 (text); "Office of St. Kentigern in the *Sprouston* (or *Edinburgh*) Breviary," ibid., xciv–c.

Studies include John MacQueen, "Yvain, Ewen, and Owein ap urien" and "A Reply to Professor Jackson," in *Transactions of the Dumfriesshire and Galloway Natural History and Antiquarian Society*, 33 (1956, for 1954–1955) and 36 (1959, for 1957–1958), respectively; Kenneth H. Jackson, "The Sources for the Life of St Kentigern," in Nora K. Chadwick *et al., Studies in the Early British Church* (1958), 273–357; David McRoberts, "The Death of St. Kentigern of Glasgow," in *Innes Review*, 24 (1973).

DAVID A. E. PELTERET

[See also **Strathclyde, Kingdom of.**]

KETILS SAGA HÆNGS. The story of Ketil hæng (salmon) is one of the Old Norse sagas known as *fornaldarsögur* (stories of early times or legendary sagas). *Ketils saga* is brief. The hero is born and raised on the island of Hrafnista, which lies across from Ramsdal in northern Norway. As a child he shows no promise, spending his time lying by the fire. Very soon, however, he shows his anxious father what he can do by killing an aggressive neighbor and then a dragon that haunts the northern part of the island. Years of poor crops cause Ketil to go on fishing expeditions in various fjords, where he runs into man-eating giants and hideous troll women. He soon earns a reputation for exterminating these creatures. The high point of the saga is Ketil's expedition to Finnmark, where he befriends the sorcerer Brúni and makes love to his daughter, the giantess Hrafnhild. On his way home, Ketil encounters and kills Gusi, Brúni's brother and king of the Finns, and obtains thereby Gusi's three magic arrows, the Gusisnautar, which become an heirloom among the men of his family. Hrafnhild later bears him a son, Grímr loðinkinni (hairy cheek), but because of the opposition of his family, Ketil is unable to live with her. He marries another woman, by whom he has a daughter, and swears an oath that his daughter will never have to marry against her will. The second part of the saga covers various duels between Ketil and his daughter's rejected suitors, as well as armed encounters with troll women and with an outlaw. Ketil dies of old age at Hrafnista, leaving his property to Grímr loðinkinni.

The sagas of Ketil and Grímr as they have survived were probably written early in the fourteenth century, and may have been put together only to provide ancestors for Örvar-Oddr (Arrow-Odd), the far more famous protagonist of *Örvar-Odds saga*. It must be pointed out, however, that Ketil and Grímr are mentioned as men of Hrafnista and ancestors of early settlers of Iceland by the Icelandic *Book of Settlements (Landnámabók)* and by the genealogies in *Egils saga Skallagrímssonar*. Their stories must therefore have existed in oral tradition long before they were put down in writing.

Besides some loose stanzas, *Ketils saga* contains, four verse dialogues in Eddic meter and diction that may be described as *sennur* (exchanges of invective between the hero and his foes).

The *fornaldarsögur* of the men of Hrafnista (Ketil, Grímr, Örvar-Oddr) are linked by common use of certain folktale patterns and motifs, notably those of the "Bear's Son Tale," better known from *Beowulf* and *Grettis saga*. Other elements of continuity are the theme of giant- and troll-killing and the passing down of the Gusisnautar among the males of the family.

Ketils saga and *Gríms saga* are found together in three vellum manuscripts of the fifteenth century, both in the Arnamagnaean collection: AM 343a 4°, AM 471 4°, and AM 576 4°.

BIBLIOGRAPHY

Ketils saga hængs is in Guðni Jónsson and Bjarni Vilhjálmsson, eds., *Fornaldar sögur Norðurlanda*, I (1943), 243–266. See also Marlene Ciklamini, "Grettir and Ketill hængr, the Giant-Killers," in *Arv*, 22 (1966); Andreas Heusler and Wilhelm Ranisch, eds., *Eddica minora* (1903), lxix–lxxv; Joaquín Martínez-Pizarro, "Transformations of the Bear's Son Tale in the Sagas of the Hrafnistumenn," in *Arv*, 32–33 (1976–1977).

JOAQUÍN MARTÍNEZ-PIZARRO

[See also **Fornaldarsögur; Gríms Saga Loðinkinna; Örvar-Odds Saga**.]

KHALDŪN, IBN (1332–1406), Arabic historian. Walī al-Dīn ᶜAbd al-Raḥman ibn Muḥammad ibn Khaldūn was born in Tunis, the son of an Andalusian family of scholars and scribes who had migrated from Spain to North Africa before 1248. He was destined to follow in the family tradition. His education consisted of religious subjects, including Koran and *ḥadīth* (the sayings of the prophet Muḥammad), Islamic law, Arabic grammar, and secular and rational sciences, such as logic, mathematics, and philosophy.

It was intended to provide him, as a future scribe, with the combination of worldly knowledge and religious wisdom that would be essential to his position in court society.

Despite his background and education, Ibn Khaldūn's career did not progess in the usual way. He proved to be a temperamental man and had a stormy career, moving from court to court and master to master, seeking political influence and personal security. His first position was in the service of the Hafsids of Tunis, his family's patrons. In 1352 he was appointed scribe of the chancery (ᶜalāma), his duty the signing of official papers with the name and title of the sultan. Soon after his appointment he left, traveled for two years, and then moved to the Marinid court at Fēs, where he was involved in factional conspiracies that obliged him to move in 1362 to the court of Muḥammad V in Granada. In 1365 he went to Bougie, where he was appointed *hajib* (head of government), with part-time duties as preacher in the citadel mosque and teacher of law. During these years Ibn Khaldūn composed a commentary (written before 1364) on the *Burda*, a famous poem in praise of Muḥammad, a summary of Ibn Rushd (Averroës), a treatise on logic, a work on arithmetic, a commentary on jurisprudence, and an epitome of al-Razi's theological work. At Bougie his career reached its apogee as he combined the role of administrator with that of cultivated courtier, scholar, and philosopher.

This was a short-lived success. In 1366 the Hafsid emir of Constantine conquered Bougie and shattered Ibn Khaldūn's career. There followed some ten years of occasional clientage, diplomatic missions, and uncertain prospects. Ibn Khaldūn oscillated between pursuit of his disrupted political career and retirement from public life. For a time he undertook to represent Abū Hammu of Tlemcen as a diplomatic agent to the bedouin tribes of North Africa. In 1370 he retired to the ribat of Abū Madyan to devote himself to religious learning. Soon he was persuaded by the Marinid sultan, and later again by Abū Hammu, to resume his diplomatic missions to the Arab tribes. By 1375 he had exhausted his political credit, and was obliged to retire for four years to Qalᶜat Ibn Salāma. This retreat, a turning point in Ibn Khaldūn's career, was forced by the complicated and tumultuous political circumstances of the time, and by his own restlessness, ambition, and penchant for intrigue. Behind the circumstantial factors, however, lay a deeper conflict between public life and scholarly and religious interests, between the active and the contemplative life.

Between 1376 and 1379 Ibn Khaldūn composed the first draft of the *Muqaddima* (Introduction [to his history of Islam]) and his *History of the Berbers*. The *Muqaddima* is best known as a theory of history, but it is also an encyclopedic work that includes a résumé of the religious culture of his age.

History was a new topic for Ibn Khaldūn. The choice of subject implied an effort to understand the connection between worldly activity and religious concerns on several levels. History allowed Ibn Khaldūn to embrace knowledge without forgoing potential action and without committing himself to permanent withdrawal from politics. To retire into teaching or to study philosophy or law, or to become a Sufi, would be to surrender the active pole of his worldly political existence to the passive pole of the inner life. History allowed him to postpone action and to reflect upon the possibility of recombining learning and action.

More immediately, history was a subject of practical utility. It was part of the education of the scholar and scribe because it contained examples of proper etiquette and good advice on political matters, and imparted the wisdom implicit in the actions of great men of the past. In addition, history was religious instruction. Muslim history turned on the life of the Prophet and his companions, and the deeds of the early caliphs and the great teachers of Islam. It contained a record of rewards and punishments that could teach men God's will and intentions. Proponents of history held that it inculcated lessons of patience, resignation, humility, and piety. It exposed the fragility of power, wealth, and striving, the uncertainties of fate, and the insecurity of existence. History confronted man with his limits and encouraged patient resignation before God's providence.

History, then, as understood in Muslim culture, was not concerned with the flow of time, but with the qualities of persons who could serve as examples for later generations. Containing political lessons, religious implications, and an implicit morality of resignation, history held images of how religious values were worked out in the course of worldly involvements. It was the record of the this-worldly manifestation of Muslim religiosity. History was thus another form of God's revelation and guidance. It was a secular literature leading to religious fulfillment.

For Ibn Khaldūn, this view had an immediate personal significance. In the *Muqaddima* he gives examples of how misunderstanding of history leads workers, artisans, teachers, and other people of low status to aspire to political power and authority that they cannot really possess. These examples helped him come to terms with the true position of the scribe. In the early days of Islam, he points out, the scribe was a minister of state and a member of the ruling elite. In his own time the true political rulers were the sultans, the royal families, and the chiefs of the tribes that supported them. Now the scribe was only a servant. From history he could gauge his realistic prospects, temper his ambition, and reestablish his respect for the legitimacy of the established dynasties and the given social order.

History was important on yet another level, and on this new level Ibn Khaldūn rose above the traditional meaning to create within his culture a virtually unique philosophic concept of the totality of historical change. Taking as a basis the encyclopedic tradition in Muslim historical scholarship, Ibn Khaldūn made history a comprehensive study of human experience. Using the philosophic tradition, he raised history from the knowledge of the particulars to a comprehensive understanding of the whole of human civilization.

His theory of the rise and fall of empires and the development of civilization is widely acclaimed for its originality and penetration. Ibn Khaldūn's theory began with the premise that society is essential to humans; and to ensure the existence of the community, a leader is necessary. From leadership and collective life comes ^{c}aṣabīya (the devotion to the values and interests of the group, or group solidarity). It leads to conquest and the founding of dynasties and empires. The establishment of empires, according to the theory, is the basis of civilization. Larger populations sustain specialization of labor, generate a surplus product, and make possible the construction of cities and monumental buildings. Taxation concentrates wealth to permit the formation of an elite that patronizes the luxury crafts and stimulates prosperity. Rulers patronize scholarship, religion, and art, and inspire new cultural accomplishments by bringing the contributions of a new dynasty to peoples of different heritages. Civilization also embodies a moral or religious goal. Large-scale civilizations can exist only when natural virtue is supplemented by rational or religious principles. In the Muslim world the caliph represents the divine law and attempts to implement it in the society at large.

Yet Ibn Khaldūn understood that however important dynasties and empires are to civilizations, they of necessity subvert their own achievements. Though their power is based upon group loyalty, rulers inevitably seek to monopolize power and glory, enjoy luxury, and detach themselves from their obligations to their followers. They replace those followers with new clients, servants and slaves who are beholden to them alone. The original members of the ruling group drift away from their devotion to the regime because they are tempted by the luxuries of civilized life. As the state weakens, exploitation grows, taxes rise, the general economy is depressed, and there follows a decline in the arts, crafts, and culture, which lose their patronage and fall into decay. Civilization corrupts the dynasty and thus destroys itself. The cycle of decline is completed by the rise of a new group with ͨaṣabīya; it has the cohesiveness and moral virtue to overthrow the old, corrupted civilization, establish a new dynasty, and begin the historical cycle again.

Thus, for Ibn Khaldūn history is cyclical, and the rise and fall of dynasties represents the rise and fall of material prosperity and cycles of intellectual and artistic vitality. Historical cycles are also moral cycles, for new regimes inspire moral fervor, piety, and devotion to their rational or religious purposes, while decline entails corruption, demoralization, and the decline of the religiously oriented society. The end of each cycle, however, does not necessarily mean a return to barbarism, for each civilization leaves a lasting residue in the development of cities, the refinement of crafts, and the pursuit of intellectual and religious sciences.

This vision of the historical cycle became of personal importance to Ibn Khaldūn. From this larger perspective he was able to evaluate the conditions of North Africa in his time. He noted that it was a region of particular instability, since it experienced the constant rise and fall of dynasties. At the same time he noted that the eastern parts of the Muslim world, especially Egypt, were centers of lasting civilized accomplishment. Furthermore, Ibn Khaldūn may have come to understand that because of the ephemeral quality of regimes, the life of the politician was futile; religion was the lasting residue and bulwark of civilization. With these lessons in mind, he was able to form a resolve to return to public life, not in North Africa but in Egypt, and not as a scribe but as a religious scholar and judge. With the completion of his *Muqaddima* and his *History of the Berbers*, Ibn Khaldūn returned to the public world. After a short stay in Tunis, he renounced the life of the scribe and in 1382 began a new career as a historian and scholar, teacher of law, and judge and religious administrator in Egypt.

Until his death in 1406, Ibn Khaldūn served at times as chief judge of the Malikite school of law and as administrator of Sufi institutions with rich endowments. His new career in a new land echoed his old. In Egypt he devoted himself to historical scholarship, to teaching religious law, and to the application of the law to problems of everyday life, but the new career involved him in familiar political problems. High-ranking professors, judges, and administrators of religious institutions were appointed by the sultan, held influential positions at court, and profited from the administration of public funds. In his new position Ibn Khaldūn found himself involved in the same conflicts among scholarly vocation, religious principles, and secular actualities. As Walter Fischel put it, "He suffered . . . from an inner conflict between an urge for action and the wielding of power and influence on the one hand, and a devotion to learning, research, and scholarship on the other." Although his occupation and his land of residence were new to Ibn Khaldūn, he had re-created a situation that preserved the essential tensions between private ambitions and political actualities, scholarship and public life, learning and action, power and morality, and secular and religious concerns. A new theory of history had led Ibn Khaldūn to a new career that perpetuated the fundamental problems of the old. His life illustrates the still more profound tension in Islamic culture between the claims of this world and of the world to come.

BIBLIOGRAPHY

Sources. Histoire des berbères . . ., William MacGucken de Slane, trans., 4 vols. (1852–1858), rev. ed. by P. Casanova (1925–1956); *Muqaddima*, Arabic ed. by E. M. Quatremère, *Les Prolégomènes d'Ebn Khaldun*, 3 vols, (1858), trans. by Franz Rosenthal as *The Muqaddimah*, 3 vols. (1958, 2nd ed. 1967); *al-Taͨrīf bī ibn Khaldūn*, Muhammad ibn Tāwīt al-Ṭanjī, ed. (1951), his autobiography.

Studies. Walter J. Fischel, *Ibn Khaldūn in Egypt* (1967); Yves Lacoste, *Ibn Khaldoun—Naissance de l'histoire passé du Tiers-monde* (1966), trans. by David Macey as *Ibn Khaldun: The Birth of History and the Past of the Third World* (1984); Muhsin Mahdi, *Ibn Khaldūn's Philosophy of History* (1957); Erwin I. J. Rosenthal, *Political Thought in Medieval Islam* (1958); Franz Rosenthal, *A History of Muslim Historiography* (1952, 2nd ed. 1968).

IRA M. LAPIDUS

[See also **Historiography, Islamic**.]

KHĀLID IBN AL-WALĪD (*d. ca.* 642), Muslim general and companion of the prophet Muḥammad. A prominent member of the powerful clan of Makhzūm from the Meccan tribe of Quraysh, he was distantly related by marriage to the Prophet. Little is known of his early life. Like most of his clan, he opposed Muḥammad's teachings in Mecca and continued to do so for some years after the Prophet had fled to Medina in 622. In the military clashes between Muḥammad and the Meccans he played an important role because of his talents as a tactician and cavalry commander; at Uḥud, fighting against the Muslims, he was able to turn the tide of battle in the Meccans' favor by exploiting a brief lapse in discipline in the Muslims' ranks. It appears that he embraced Islam late, after it had become clear that the struggle between Muḥammad and the Quraysh was going in the Prophet's favor. The exact date of his conversion is disputed, but it seems unlikely that it occurred before the Prophet's siege of Khaybar in 628, since he had commanded the Meccan cavalry at Al-Ḥudaybiya a few months earlier.

After Khālid's conversion the Prophet lost no time in utilizing his military talents. In 629 Khālid participated in the large campaign that engaged the Byzantines at Muʾta in southern Syria, taking charge after the original commander was killed and leading the army safely back to Medina. At the conquest of Mecca (630) he was in command of the right wing of Muḥammad's large army. Shortly thereafter he was sent to pacify the tribe of Khuzayma, near Mecca, and he later participated with the Prophet in the Battle of Ḥunayn and the siege of Al-Ṭāʾif. In the year before Muḥammad's death, Khālid is said to have led campaigns against Dūmat al-Jandal (now Al-Jawf) in northern Arabia and against the town of Najrān in the Yemen. Clearly he was among those late converts from the Quraysh aristocracy who received favored treatment from Muḥammad in his last years as a means of ensuring their loyalty.

With Muḥammad's death and the outbreak of the *ridda*, the first caliph, Abū Bakr, put Khālid in command of an army charged with subduing rebellious tribes in northern and northeastern Arabia. In 632 he quickly restored the allegiance of the tribes of Asad, Ṭayyiʾ, and Tamīm in several skirmishes in the Najd, and then marched against the most serious opposition to Islam, that of the rival prophet Musailima among the Ḥanīfa tribe in Al-Yamāma (eastern Arabia). He quashed this threat in the bloody Battle of ʿAqrabāʾ (633). In the course of these campaigns, Khālid came under verbal attack from some of the early converts for his behavior, especially for ordering the execution of a tribal chief and immediately marrying his widow; but Abū Bakr left him in command and early in 634 ordered him to march with about 1,000 men against unsubdued Arab tribes living along the Euphrates in Iraq. Khālid's campaigning there saw the reduction of several Arab towns (Al-Ḥīra, ʿAyn al-Tamr, Al-Anbār, perhaps Al-Ubulla) and the conquest of Arabic-speaking tribal groups such as Shaybān and ʿIjl, often with the aid of sympathetic segments within the tribes. He also made forays farther up the Euphrates, to Dūmat al-Jandal, on the trade route from Iraq to Syria, and to the Hejaz, which he helped reconquer. Abū Bakr soon ordered Khālid to reinforce the Muslims engaged in fighting the Byzantines, however, and after a daring march across the desert to Syria (recounted with romantic embellishments in the Arabic chronicles), he joined his small force to the Muslim armies there.

The sources disagree on Khālid's exact role in the conquest of Syria. According to some, he was the supreme commander of operations in Syria, whereas others consider him to have been only a subordinate commander under Abū ʿUbayda ibn al-Jarrāḥ, but all agree that he was prominent in the sieges of Bostra, Damascus, and Ḥims, and in the battles of Ajnādayn, Faḥl, and the Yarmūk. It does appear, however, that his powers of command were sharply reduced by the second caliph, ʿUmar ibn al-Khaṭṭāb, after his accession in 634, for ʿUmar abruptly discontinued Abū Bakr's policy (continuing that of Muḥammad) of favoring Quraysh aristocrats for command positions, and gave the appointments instead to early converts. Although Khālid is still mentioned in connection with later episodes in the conquest of Syria, such as the occupation of Jerusalem, Qinnasrīn, and Aleppo, he is much less prominent than before. Except for leading some of the summer raids into Byzantine Anatolia, he seems to have faded from public view, settling down in Ḥims, where his descendants continued to be of local importance. He died there (or perhaps in Medina).

BIBLIOGRAPHY

Arabic sources include al-Balādhurī, *Futūḥ al-buldān*, trans. by Philip K. Hitti as *The Origins of the Islamic State* (1916, repr. 1966); Ibn Ḥajar al-ʿAsqalānī, *al-Iṣāba*, I, no. 2190; Ibn Hishām, *Sīra*, trans. by Alfred Guillaume as *The Life of Muhammad* (1955); al-Ṭabarī, *Tarīkh al-rusul wa-al-mulūk*, 15 vols. (1897–1901); al-Wāqidī, *al-Maghāzī*, Julius Wellhausen, ed. (1902), 77ff. See also Fred M. Donner,

The Early Islamic Conquests (1981); Elias S. Shoufani, *Al-Riddah and the Muslim Conquest of Arabia* (1973); William Montgomery Watt, *Muhammad at Medina* (1956).

FRED M. DONNER

[See also **Iraq; Islam, Conquests of; Syria.**]

KHALLIKĀN, IBN, Aḥmad ibn Muḥammad (22 September 1211–30 October 1282), an Arab judge, was born into a well-established family of Erbil, in Iraq. Although his father died soon after his birth, he studied with renowned scholars at Aleppo, Damascus, and Mosul. By 1239 he lived in Cairo, where in 1249 he was appointed deputy to the *qadi al-qudat* (judge of judges). In 1261 the Mamluk sultan Baybars appointed him "judge of judges" of Damascus; he held that office, providing justice and judicial administration, for six years. In 1271 Ibn Khallikān returned to Cairo, where he taught until Baybars' death in 1277, then was reappointed to his former post in Damascus in 1278. He fell victim to political intrigue in 1280, spent three weeks in prison, then resumed his duties. He was dismissed early in 1281, being out of favor with the new sultan, Qalawun.

Ibn Khallikān became famous as the author of the first comprehensive biographical dictionary, *Wafayāt al-aᶜyān wa-anbāᵓ abnāᵓ al-zamān* (Obituaries of celebrities and reports of the sons of their time), in which the entries were in alphabetical order. He decided to omit the usual entries on the Prophet and his companions, the Muslims of the second generation, and the first four caliphs. In his preface he states explicitly that he means to entertain and edify. The work, written between 1256 and 1274, consists of some 826 (or 855) biographies of persons from all respectable professions whose death dates were known to the author. They provide a vivid portrait gallery and a colorful mosaic of the intellectual life in the Islamic world during its first seven centuries. The numerical breakdown (in the 826 version, with some overlap) reveals 161 jurists, 147 poets, 145 rulers and generals, 95 philologists, 94 historians and prose writers, 87 traditionists, 42 preachers and ascetics, 41 viziers, 32 judges, 21 Koranic expositors, 19 philosophers and physicians, 17 theologians, and 3 musicians. The length of an individual entry varies according to the importance or interest of the person, but increases toward the end of the dictionary, perhaps indicating definitiveness. The usual entry has the following pattern: full name, a brief charac-

terization regarding merits in his profession, his place in the Muslim tradition (with whom he studied, whom he taught, what he wrote, examples of verses [for poets]), the date of death, and the vocalization of proper names mentioned in the entry.

Ibn Khallikān proved to be an acute observer of human behavior and eager to emphasize his subjects' social inclinations and sexual preferences. He was also a perceptive critic of versification and style. As a result, the *Wafayāt* provided its intended audience with historical information in the *adab* form. The literarization of history proved a success, for the book was widely circulated and laid ground for a new type of biographical writing. It was continued by Ibn al-Ṣuqāᶜī (*d.* 1325) and supplemented by Ibn Shākir al-Kutubī (*d.* 1363).

BIBLIOGRAPHY

The fullest and most up-to-date edition of the *Wafayāt* is that by Iḥsān ᶜAbbās (1968–1972), complemented by A. J. al-Tahir's *Mulāḥazāt ᶜala Wafayāt al-aᶜyān* (1977). The English translation by Baron Mac Guckin de Slane, *Ibn Khallikan's Biographical Dictionary*, 4 vols. (1843–1861, repr. 1970), is dependable if puritanical; extracts from it were used by Edward V. Lucas in his *A Boswell of Baghdad* (1917).

Although no study of Arabic historiography omits Ibn Khallikān, the only monographic studies seem to be Heinrich Ferdinand Wüstenfeld, *Ueber die Quellen des Werkes: Ibn Challikani Vitae illustrium virorum* (1827), and Hartmut Fahndrich, "Man and Men in Ibn Khallikan" (diss., UCLA, 1972). The latter branched into two articles: "The *Wafayāt al-aᶜyān* of Ibn Khallikān: A New Approach," in *Journal of the American Oriental Society,* 93 (1973), and "Compromising the Caliph," in *Journal of Arabic Literature,* 8 (1977). See also Ján Pauliny, "Die Anekdote im Werke Ibn Hallikāns," in *Asian and African Studies* (Bratislava), 3 (1967); Sergei A. Shuiskii, "Abu Nuvas v svode zhizneopisanii Ibn Khallikana," in *Voprosy vostochnogo literaturovedeniya i tekstologii* (1975).

SERGEI A. SHUISKII

[See also **Arabic Literature, Prose; Biography, Islamic.**]

KHAN *(khān),* a term meaning "ruler" and used chiefly in those medieval countries that were either Turkish or influenced by Turks, both pre-Islamic and Islamic. The term is believed to be of inner Asian origin, appearing among the Orkhon Turks (sixth to eighth centuries, in the territory of present-day Mongolia), but it is thought to have been borrowed from the Ruan-Ruan (possibly identical with the

Avars), who in turn would have taken it from the Sien-Pi (the earliest attested date, in Chinese sources, being *ca.* A.D. 240).

In Orkhon Turkish, the term, spelled as *qan,* appears alongside the longer form *qaghan;* these two terms, while at times used synonymously, more often implied a difference of degree: *qaghan* meaning a supreme, universal ruler, *qan* a lesser one, implicitly subordinate to the former. Both this interchangeability and difference accompanied the destinies of the two terms throughout their history even after their orthography had become modified by the Arabo-Persian script and phonetics to *khān* and *khāqān.* The choice of form, however, was affected, up to a point, by personal style and position in a sentence: thus *qaghan/khāqān* tended to be used independently or separately from the ruler's name, while *qan/khān* more often followed the name (as in the poem *Qutadghu bilig,* in reference to an eleventh-century Qarakhanid ruler: "This *khāqān*'s name has been recorded in a book"; " ... Ulugh Bughra *Khān* ..."). Both in early Islamic and in European records, the longer form, *qaghan,* appears to have been noticed and applied to Turkish rulers of various ranks. The tenth-century geographical compendium *Ḥudūd al-ʿĀlam* enumerates several *khāqān*s of inner Asia (such as the *khāqān* of the Kirghiz in southern Siberia), while Byzantine and Russian chronicles mention the *qaghan* of the Khazars. Some Russian sources even refer to a *qaghan* of the Rus, probably on account of a dynastic family tie between the houses of Rurik and the Turkic royal clan of Ashina.

The term passed in both its forms from Turkish into Mongolian, where the distinction of degree reasserted itself, possibly due to the hierarchical structure of the Mongol empire. Paradoxically, Genghis, the founder of the empire, is called *khān* in Mongol documents (probably in deference to the initially more modest extension of his realm, when he was at first the ruler of a restricted political formation), whereas his successors, rulers of what was claimed to be a universal empire, were invariably referred to as *qaghan*s.

In the medieval Islamic world, the terms *khān* and *khāqān* (and sometimes *qāʾān*) spread chiefly through the medium of Persian political terminology, and were in this manner adopted by Ottoman Turkish, where they survived with similar connotations until relatively recently, chiefly in official documents and on coins. Thus Süleyman the Magnificent (sixteenth century) is referred to in an

endowment document as "the victorious imperial *khāqān* ... Sultan Süleyman *Khān.*" Meanwhile in other parts of the Islamic world, chiefly in Iran and in the Indian subcontinent, the term *khān,* the only survivor, depreciated to the point of denoting a middle level of officialdom, and even became an epithet attached to any name.

BIBLIOGRAPHY

Gerard L. M. Clauson, *An Etymological Dictionary of Pre-Thirteenth-Century Turkish* (1972), 611, 630; Gerhard Doerfer, *Türkische und mongolische Elemente im Neupersischen,* III (1967), 141–179; Annemarie von Gaban, *Das Leben im uigurischen Königreich von Qočo (850–1250)* (1973), 67–71.

SVAT SOUCEK

[See also **Crimea, Khanate of; Genghis Khan; Mongol Empire.**]

KHAN, a building designed to house a caravan. As is so often the case in Islamic architecture, the range of synonyms for a building type illuminates its various overlapping functions. In eastern Islamic lands, the common term is caravanserai *(karvansarāī),* which connotes a place for the protection of trade; in the Near East, *funduq* (inn); and in the Maghrib, ribat, which implies a brief stopover. The word "khan," widely used throughout the Islamic world, can often mean "private house."

Khans served a wide variety of people. Strategically sited khans commanding important passes, fords, bridges, or crossroads would have a combined civil and military function, and thus might have a garrison. At the official level they might be part of the state intelligence network *(barīd)*: couriers bearing important messages and documents would speed along the major routes, halting at khans to change their mounts. Merchant caravans, itinerant craftsmen in search of commissions, wandering scholars, professional geographers or travelers, pilgrims, occasionally even the ruler and his retinue—all would derive benefit from the institution.

Most significant rural khans are to be found in Syria, Anatolia, and the Iranian world, which for this purpose includes India. The khans of Ayyubid and Mamluk Syria feature an open courtyard with a vaulted walkway surrounding it. They are often strongly fortified with guardrooms, crenellations, and machicolations, as well as bastions; but few have any private accommodations. In the axially ordered khans of Seljuk Anatolia, executed in well-dressed stone, a marked divison is maintained between the open courtyard bordered by arcades and the narrower three-aisled stables behind it on the same axis (Sulṭān Khān). Other khans in Anatolia have only a covered hall or an open courtyard with annexes for chambers and stables. The plain exteriors of these khans are relieved by infrequent animal sculpture and by a single, often very elaborate portal (Zazadin Han). Over a hundred such khans from the thirteenth century survive, bearing witness to state patronage aimed at encouraging east-west and north-south trade. The Ottoman period is best represented by huge khans for pilgrims, with mosques, baths, shops, and other facilities nearby.

It was in Iran and central Asia that the khan saw its fullest development. These khans have a fortified exterior, a cruciform courtyard with a central well and stables at the diagonals or in long corridors flush with the exterior wall, and an array of vaults and domes. Khans bordering the desert often have a lighthouse minaret, built to guide caravans forced by the heat to travel at night (Gaz). At the intersection of major routes, entire caravan cities sprang up, offering facilities for many hundreds of travelers.

Urban khans were far rarer than their rural counterparts. Most surviving examples are postmedieval and can be found in Turkey, Syria, and the Iranian world. They served trade rather than travel and hence shops and storage space normally took precedence over stables.

BIBLIOGRAPHY

Oktay Aslanapa, *Turkish Art and Architecture* (1971), 147–161; N. Elisséeff, "Khān," in *Encyclopaedia of Islam*, new ed., IV (1978); Godfrey Goodwin, *A History of Ottoman Architecture* (1971); John D. Hoag, *Islamic Architecture* (1977), 237–242; George Michell, ed., *Architecture of the Islamic World* (1978); Behçet Ünsal, *Turkish Islamic Architecture in Seljuk and Ottoman Times, 1071–1923* (1959).

ROBERT HILLENBRAND

[See also **Funduq; Hān; Islamic Art and Architecture; Ribat; Seljuk Art and Architecture; Trade, Islamic.**]

KHĀNQĀH, an Arabized form of the Persian *khān-agāh,* meaning "hall" or "house," denotes a communal residence commonly associated with the Sufis, or Muslim mystics. It first appears in late-tenth-century texts, both Arabic and Persian, describing particular establishments in eastern Iran and the adjoin-

ing region of Transoxiana. Elsewhere such an establishment is known as a ribat (Iraq), *tekke* (Turkey), *zāwiya* (Africa), or *dargāh* (India).

Significantly, the earliest *khānqāh*s (tenth century) were associated with a group of Manichaeans reported to be living in Samarkand and with a Muslim sect known as the Karrāmīya, who were found in Khorāsān, Transoxiana, Gorgan, and Tabaristan. But these diffuse origins were soon obscured by the proliferation of Sufi *khānqāh*s in the same area, and in fact a Sufi prototype was subsequently invented for the historical literature in the form of a fictitious eighth-century *khānqāh* said to have existed in Palestine.

The emergence of the Sufi *khānqāh* reflects the expansion of mysticism within Islam from informal groups of disciples meeting in the master's home or workplace to a fixed community institution. The earliest code of conduct for the *khānqāh* is attributed to the Khorāsānī master Abū Saᶜīd ibn Abi'l-Khayr (d. 1048), whose ten rules addressed various obligations of prayer, respectful relations among the residents, and assistance to the poor, the needy, and other outsiders. Not long after the time of Abū Saᶜīd, the Sufi *khānqāh*s, like the mosque colleges (*madrasa*s) of the religious establishment, came under the patronage and control of Seljuk rulers, first in Iran and then farther west in Syria. This practice was continued by the Ayyubids and Mamluks in Syria and Egypt from the twelfth to the sixteenth centuries. In the Muslim East, meanwhile, following the Mongol invasions of the thirteenth century, Sufi orders and their *khānqāh*s spread to India, where they soon attracted the patronage of the Delhi sultanate. The expansion of the Ottoman Turks in the sixteenth century similarly brought Sufi establishments (*tekke*s) to North Africa, where they remained an important social force into the twentieth century.

While the various functions of the institution required certain facilities—living quarters for the shaykh (master) and his family, cells for disciples, guest rooms, a large kitchen and dining room, and a mosque and ceremonial hall—there is no specific building type associated with the *khānqāh*. With increased government sponsorship, the Sufi establishments came to be incorporated into elaborate complexes, but the Sufis themselves ceased to use them as residences.

BIBLIOGRAPHY

Jacqueline Chabbi, "Khānḳāh," in *Encyclopaedia of Islam*, new ed., IV (1978); George Michell, ed., *Architec-*

ture of the Islamic World (1978); Annemarie Schimmel, Mystical Dimensions of Islam (1975); J. Spencer Trimingham, The Sufi Orders in Islam (1971).

MIRIAM ROSEN

[See also Dervish; Islamic Art and Architecture; Mysticism, Islamic; Ribat.]

KHANS OF CRIMEA. See Crimea, Khanate of.

KHARJA, also spelled jarcho, harǧa, jarŷa, khardja, is the last qufl (second part of a strophe) of the Hispanic-Arabic poetic form called muwashshaḥ, invented in the tenth century and adopted also by Hispano-Hebrew poets. Conceived as an independent unit and a pointe, the kharja gives the cue to the meter and rhymes of the poem. It is a quotation offering a strong contrast to the rest of the muwashshaḥ; its language is preferably colloquial Arabic and Romance, its style "close to the speech of the common people and the phraseology of thieves," according to Ibn Sanāᵓ al-Mulk (1155–1211).

The discovery in 1948, by Samuel M. Stern, of twenty Romance kharjas in Hebrew muwashshaḥs of the eleventh through thirteenth centuries was a major event in medieval literary scholarship. They turned out to be two-to-four-line poems written in Mozarabic dialect with some admixture of Arabic words and phrases. They are most often uttered by a lovelorn girl, frequently addressing her mother or her beloved (ḥabīb). For instance: "What shall I do or what / will become of me? / My love, / Do not go away from me!"; "I will not sleep, Mother, / At the break of day / Abū al-Qāsim comes, / The face of dawn"; "The holiday is approaching, alas, / and I'm still without him! / My heart is aching for him."

Some of these texts were written before the poems of the first troubadours, and thus constitute the earliest known vernacular European lyrics. Being feminine poetry and using a simple and emotional style (as opposed to the masculine and sophisticated poetry of the troubadours), they were identified by scholars with the primitive chansons de femme and Frauenlieder, which, since the Romantic period, have been assumed to be the oral antecedents of literary Western lyrics. The term kharja has often been used since then in the misleading sense of "Mozarabic feminine (folk) song," thus excluding the Arabic kharjas and avoiding the obviously contrived character of many of them. Others may have been in-

spired by oral songs but were not necessarily identical with them.

Since 1948 more Romance (or rather bilingual) kharjas have been discovered, mostly in Hispano-Arabic muwashshaḥs, increasing the total number to more than sixty. They present serious textual problems, having been written in Semitic characters by scribes unfamiliar with Mozarabic, a dialect about which little is known today. As a whole they offer a mixture of Romance and Arabic features in form, content, and poetic expression.

The same merging of traditions is also visible in the much more numerous Arabic kharjas, which have been neglected until recent years. In these there are striking similarities to the Mozarabic corpus as well as great differences. In both types the prosody is Romance, the rhymes either Romance or Semitic; medieval Hispanic or French motifs and devices alternate with Islamic ideas and metaphors.

BIBLIOGRAPHY

Margit Frenk Alatorre, Las jarchas mozárabes y los comienzos de la lírica románica (1975), and (as Margit Frenk) "La lírica pretrovadoresca," in Erich Köhler, ed., Les genres lyriques (1979); Linda Fish Compton, Andalusian Lyrical Poetry and Old Spanish Love Songs (1976); Richard Hitchcock, The Kharjas: A Critical Bibliography (1977); James T. Monroe, "The Muwashshaḥāt," in M. P. Hornik, ed., Collected Studies in Honour of Américo Castro's Eightieth Year (1965), and "Studies on the 'Harǧas': The Arabic and the Romance 'Harǧas,'" in Viator, 8 (1977).

MARGIT FRENK

[See also **Arabic Poetry; Chansons de Femme; Mozarabic Literature; Spanish Literature.**]

KHATCHKᶜAR. See Xačᶜkᶜar.

KHAṬĪB AL-BAGHDĀDĪ, AL- (Aḥmad ibn ᶜAlī ibn Thābit, 1002–1071), jurist, traditions scholar, and preacher (khaṭīb) at Baghdad. Born in Hanīqiyā, a small village near Baghdad, the son of a local preacher, he received a traditional religious education. Following early training, he traveled extensively, studying at various theological centers throughout the Islamic world. The Khaṭīb established himself at Baghdad in 1028. His great reputation for scholarship and preaching earned the enmity of rival scholars. In 1059 the successful rebellion of al-Basāsīrī forced the Khaṭīb to flee to Damascus for eight years.

The Khaṭīb's great reputation as a scholar in the religious sciences is acknowledged by his various biographers, who credit him with having written at least eighty-one works. A number of these works are preserved, including his greatest contribution to Islamic learning, *Taʾrīkh Baghdad* (History of Baghdad). According to the medieval biographer Ibn Khallikān, "Had he written nothing but this history, it would have been sufficient for his reputation." The printed edition of this work consists of fourteen volumes of more than 7,800 biographical entries arranged alphabetically, although this system was not consistently applied. The earliest collections of biographical information were according to chronological layers *(tabaqah)*. Each layer signified a generation, although there was no agreement as to the number of years in a generation. In the tenth century, theologically oriented local histories had a wide geographical distribution; besides increasing the number of biographical entries, some of these works abandoned the chronological division for an alphabetical arrangement. The obvious advantage to the new arrangement was that it made for an easier system of reference, requiring only the full name and not the details of the subject's life. Unlike secular local histories, these works were conceived of as handbooks for scholars of the religious sciences, in particular the students at the various local centers of theological learning.

The Khaṭīb's history is, however, more than a dictionary of scholars. The biographical sections are preceded by a detailed introduction that deals with the topography and toponymy of Baghdad. The juxtaposed accounts of topography and history form perhaps the most important source on the physical arrangement of the city and its pattern of growth. There were other attempts at describing the physical arrangement of Baghdad, but from what must have been a fairly substantial body of literature only a few texts and many scattered fragments remain. Because the Khaṭīb prefaced his accounts with a chain of authorities, it is possible to glimpse the works of authors whose accounts are otherwise known only by title.

Given its great reputation, the work of the Khaṭīb was never displaced by later research. It was, however, slavishly copied and brought up to date by a series of supplements *(dhayl)* also employing the alphabetical arrangement. Each succeeding generation thus added its list of representative scholars.

BIBLIOGRAPHY

Al-Khaṭīb's main work is *Taʾrikh Baghdad*, 14 vols. (1931, repr. 1968). Elements of the topographical introduction to the *Taʾrikh* have been translated and annotated by Georges Salmon as *L'introduction topographique à l'histoire de Baghdādh* (1904) and by Jacob Lassner as *The Topography of Baghdad in the Early Middle Ages: Text and Studies* (1970).

JACOB LASSNER

[See also **Biography, Islamic.**]

KHAWADA NAMEH. See **Xwaday Namag.**

KHAZARS. The name "Khazar" is attested in Chinese, Iranian, Armenian, and Syriac sources long before the establishment of the Khazar empire (the kaganate) in the 650's. The name, of Altaic origin, first occurs with the attribute *ak* (or *aq*) (white or western)—*Akkachir > Akatsir*—as a part of the fifth-century empire of Attila. The Khazar realm was one of the Eurasian nomadic steppe empires (*paces*, from *pax*, the Latin word for peace and dominion), in which a confederation of military charismatic clans (*Männerbünde*) and international merchants ruled over the nomadic tribes of the steppe and the sedentary populations in the oases and rural areas.

During the Byzantine-Sasanian struggle for hegemony in the first decades of the seventh century, the Western Turkic kagan T'ong Jabghu supported Heraklios I. In the middle of the century, when the Chinese destroyed the Western Turkic empire, the son of T'ong Jabghu established himself in what is now Daghestan (in the fifth century it was the territory of the Khachirs, called Khazars by the Turks), thereby founding the Khazar kaganate. The ruling Turkic clans in the Khazar realm were the Old Turkic imperial dynasty A-shin-na (< *achina*, white wolf), and the influential tribes of the dynasty of the Kagans/Kabars. The leading mercantile tribe was the Iranian *Varāz/Varač* (Khazar form: *Barč/Bolč*); the latter was also the dynasty of the "kings" or majordomos. A member of that dynasty was King Joseph, who corresponded with the Spanish Jewish leader Ḥisdai ibn Shaprut (*ca.* 960).

The 300-year history of the Khazar empire is presented here as divided into eight periods. During the first two periods (650–685, 685–720) its government, situated in Daghestan (with Semender and Belendjer as centers), was busy establishing control over the territory it had wrested from the Onogurs of Magna Bulgaria, as well as all of Transcaucasia. By 685 the two traditional sedentary powers—the Byzantine Greeks and the Arab Umayyads (successors to the Iranian Sasanids) had established their own condominium in Transcaucasia (Armenia, Georgia, Albania/Azerbaijan), omitting the Khazars as their partners. The ensuing Khazar sallies into Transcaucasia and their interference in the Byzantine civil war during the troubled years 695–711 brought no lasting results.

The next period, 721–750, was dominated by the second Arab-Khazar war (721–737) for hegemony over Transcaucasia, with varying success for both sides. The Khazars conquered Ardabīl, the capital of Azerbaijan, in 731, and Marwān ibn Muḥammad led a successful march into the interior of Khazaria (737). There were two permanent results of that confrontation. First, much of the population of the areas destroyed during the war (basically Alani and Bulgars) migrated to the north, mainly to the shores of the Azov Sea, the basins of the Donets and the Don, the lower Volga, and the area between the rivers Terek and Kuma. The capital of the realm was also transferred north, to the estuary of the Volga. This was Atīl, a twin city of the Iranian type: Sarigchin or al-Bayḍā (Arabic) and Khamlikh or Khvalisy (Old Rus). The second result was the first conscious encounter by the majordomo with the syncretistic Judaism in Ardabīl, which resulted in his private conversion (731).

During 750–800 there were only casual Khazar attacks on Transcaucasia, the last being in 799. The commercial Khazar clans, headed by the Barč/Bolč, entered into cooperation with the international Frankish (Jewish) merchant corporation, centered in the Rhône basin (Arabic: Al-Rādhānīya). Khazaria became a very important link in the transit trade between Western Europe and the Near East and Far East. The customs offices of Šārkel (on the Don River) and Atīl (on the Volga) were producing great revenues, especially from the slave trade. Now the majordomo officially accepted Judaism, and started imposing that religion on the steppe peoples, including (ca. 799) the kaganate. The seeds of the pax's self-destruction were thereby planted, since the majordomo and his amateur missionaries were not in a position to impose a sedentary political structure together with the sedentary religion of Judaism.

The next period, 800–840, brought new challenges. The Avar pax was destroyed by Charlemagne

(796), and it was necessary to fortify the western frontier, which had become a power vacuum. The Turkic Kabars revolted, seeking to defend the traditional steppe religion and the kaganate. They were defeated, however, and the fugitive kagan found refuge in the Middle Volga trading factory of the Franko-Frisian-Scandinavian (Varangian) international merchants' company called Rus. This was the birth of the Rus kaganate (ca. 839) and the Rurikid dynasty. The Rurikids immediately started to expand toward the Oka River, causing the future Hungarians to move toward the Don basin (Lebedia), where they joined the Khazar realm for some forty years. Now the majordomo imposed Judaism on another member of the Kagan dynasty, with the result that, beginning about 840, the kaganate lost its political and ideological base, retaining only a ceremonial character. All power was now vested in the majordomo, called in the sources *ikhshedh bäg, melekh* in Hebrew, and *malik* in Arabic, meaning "king." In the meantime, the Turkic Torki/Oghuzes defeated and expelled from central Asia the originally Tocharian Pechenegs, who became the eastern neighbors of Khazaria (ca. 830–840).

During the period 840–880, the joint forces of the Khazars and the Torki/Oghuzes failed to annihilate the Pechenegs; at the end of the period the latter defeated the future Hungarians and took over the Donets-Don basin. This constant change of political power resulted in the economic ruin of the territory. The defeated Hungarians left for Pannonia in 896; the inhabitants of the Donets-Don basin moved to the Volga-Kama basin and became known as Volga Bulgars. Being Muslims (all steppe empires practiced complete religious tolerance), they established trade relations with the new commercial Samanid state in central Asia; the Khazar government was still able to maintain its suzerainty over the Volga Bulgarians and obtain a portion of their revenue.

From the last two periods, 880–930 and 930–965, three local sources, all written in Hebrew, survive: the fragments of the chronicle of the last three majordomo kings: Benjamin (ca. 880–ca. 900), Aaron (ca. 900–ca. 920), and Joseph (ca. 920–ca. 960); the so-called Khazar correspondence (ca. 960); and the Kievan letter (ca. 930), discovered in 1962, which includes a Khazarian remark.

Around 930 the Rus kagan Igor conquered Kiev and initiated the Dnieper "route from the Varangians to the Greeks." Since Constantinople had replaced Baghdad as the center of commerce, the Khazarian Volga routes soon became obsolete. In 965

Igor's son and successor Sviatoslav delivered a finishing blow to Khazaria. The realm disintegrated into its component parts, which joined the new masters of the steppe and Eastern European cities: the Rus, the Pechenegs, and the Torki/Oghuzes.

BIBLIOGRAPHY

Mikhail Illarionovich Artamonov, *Istoria Khazar* (1962); Douglas M. Dunlop, *The History of the Jewish Khazars* (1954); Norman Golb and Omeljan Pritsak, *Khazarian Hebrew Documents of the Tenth Century* (1982); Peter B. Golden, *Khazar Studies,* 2 vols. (1980); Pavel K. Kokovtsov, *Evreysko-khazarskaya perepiska v X veke* (1932); Gyula Moravcsik, *Byzantinoturcica,* 2nd ed., 2 vols. (1958), esp. I, 81–86 (bibliography); Svetlana A. Pletneva, *Khazary* (1976), and Pletneva, ed., *Stepi Evrazii v epokhu srednevekovia* (1981); Omeljan Pritsak, "The Khazar Kingdom's Conversion to Judaism," in *Harvard Ukrainian Studies,* **2** (1978), and *The Origin of Rus',* I (1981); Bernard D. Weinryb, "The Khazars: An Annotated Bibliography," in *Studies in Bibliography and Booklore,* **6** (1963) and **11** (1976).

OMELJAN PRITSAK

[See also **Russian Nomads: Invasions of.**]

KHIL᷄A, an ensemble of fine cloth garments bestowed by Muslim rulers as a mark of honor. The robes, belts, and head coverings that comprised the *khil᷄a* varied locally and changed over time. Black robes distinguished the official Abbasid *khil᷄a;* inscribed bands, the Fatimid; ermine and brocade, the Mamluk.

BIBLIOGRAPHY

Irene A. Bierman, "Art and Politics: The Impact of Fatimid Uses of Tirāz Fabrics" (diss., Univ. of Chicago, 1980); Leo A. Mayer, *Mamluk Costume* (1952), 56–65; R. B. Serjeant, "Materials for the History of Islamic Textiles," in *Ars islamica,* **9–16** (1942–1951).

IRENE A. BIERMAN

[See also **Costume, Islamic.**]

KHURDĀDHBIH, IBN (Ibn Khurradādhbih), Abū'l-Qāsim ᷄Ubayd Allāh ibn ᷄Abd Allāh (820/ 825–912/913), the "father of Islamic geography," was born in Khorāsān and grew up in Baghdad. His

Maḥmūd of Ghazna donning a *khil᷄a.* Miniature in MS of Rashīd al-Dīn's *Jāmi᷄ al-Tawārīkh,* A.D. 1000.
© E. J. BRILL 1979

family, of Persian Zoroastrian extraction, had been in Abbasid civil service since their conversion to Islam. In his adult life Ibn Khurdādhbih served as the director of the post and intelligence service in Jibāl and later as postmaster general in Baghdad and Samarra. In Samarra he was close to the court and eventually achieved the court rank of boon companion to the caliph al-Muᶜtamid (870–892).

These two careers, as well as his origins, determined the scope and focus of Ibn Khurdādhbih's writing. An expert in *adab,* he composed a manual for courtiers *(Kitāb al-nudamāᵓ wa'l julasāᵓ)* and instructions on correct behavior at recitals *(Adab al-samāᶜ),* as well as two sociogastronomic treatises, *Kitāb al-sharāb* (On drinking) and *Kitāb al-ṭabīkh* (On culinary art). None of these survives. Music was more to him than entertainment. He was acquainted with the famous musician Isḥaq al-Mawaṣilī and wrote the partially preserved work *Kitāb al-lahw wa'l-malāhī* (On playing and the musical instruments). His family background probably inspired his *Kitāb jamharat ansāb al-Furs wa'l-nawāqīl* (Principal genealogies of the Persians and of the transplanted population). This, and his *Kitāb al-taᵓrīkh* (History), are preserved only in quotations.

Ibn Khurdādhbih's claim to fame is based on the geographic treatise *Kitāb al-masālik wa'l-mamālik* (Book of routes and kingdoms). The earliest extant work of Islamic geography, it is in an abridged, but more or less complete, state. The first work of the "Iraqi school," it probably follows an earlier Persian pattern while showing familiarity with Greek geography, specifically Ptolemy and the concept of continents. It deals primarily with the Islamic world, its boundaries, and the neighboring peoples and states. Iraq, as the heart of the Abbasid realm, occupies a central position in both the description and the geopolitical concept of the world. This system, of Iranian origin, divided the inhabited world into seven great kingdoms, six of which formed a circle around the seventh, Iran (replaced in the Islamic tradition by Iraq). Other areas described in great detail are Khorāsān and Mawerannahr.

A specifically Islamic feature is the chapter on *qibla.* The dry data of mathematical geography are followed by commercial and postal itineraries of varying degrees of detail and accuracy, partially based on official materials and archival sources available to the author. To these are added stories of curiosities and lively accounts of customs and traditions. It is apparent that the developing scholarship of the Islamic state created a methodological re-quirement for a new mold into which the mass of newly acquired information could be fitted. The book signaled the establishment of a new genre of administrative geography and was recognized as a pioneering work by contemporaries. Repeated imitations by later scholars, often under the identical or similar titles, led orientalists to attach the name "Routes and Kingdoms" to the genre.

BIBLIOGRAPHY

Casimir-Adrien Barbier de Meynard, "Le *Livre de routes et de provinces,* par Ibn-Khordadbeh, publié, traduit, et annoté par . . . ," in *Journal asiatique,* 6th ser., 5 (1865); Carl Brockelmann, *Geschichte der arabischen Litteratur,* I (1898), 225–226, and supp. I (1937), 404; Michael Jan de Goeje, ed., *Bibliotheca geographorum Arabicorum,* VI (1889); Father A. Khalifa, *Mukhtār min Kitāb al-lahw wa'l-malāhī li 'bn Khurradādhbih* (1961); Ignati Yulianovich Krachkovsky, *Izbrannie sochinenia,* IV (1957), 17, 23, 80, 147ff.; André Miquel, *La géographie humaine du monde musulman jusqu'au milieu du 11ᵉ siècle,* I (1967), 85–92.

M. A. TOLMACHEVA

[See also **Geography and Cartography, Islamic; Postal and Intelligence Services, Islamic.**]

KHWĀRIZMSHĀHS (or more properly Khwārazmshāhs), the rulers of Khwarizm (Khwārazam), a central Asian province lying along the lower course of the Oxus River (Amu Darya) and its delta on the Aral Sea in the modern Uzbek SSR. (It is the ancient Chorasmia, and modern Khiva.) This well-irrigated agricultural region (northward is the Jaxartes River [Syr Darya]) is surrounded by deserts that kept it relatively secure from attack and external cultural influences. For example, the indigenous Iranian language, Khwarazmian, flourished as the general language until its gradual turkification during the reign of the Seljuk Khwārizmshāhs (beginning eleventh century). The title "Khwārizmshāh" is traced back to semilegendary Iranian kings. Its historical use is standardly ascribed first to the dynastic house of the Afrīghs (305–995). Subsequently it became popular to the extent that it was used by local rulers regardless of the ethnic background of the dynast or any particular political ties. By the end of the twelfth century, however, the title Khwārizmshāh came to be associated with an independent Islamic Turkic empire; for about a half-century the Khwārizmshāhs led the greatest military power in the Islamic world.

Historically the Khwārizmshāhs were the most significant dynasty to evolve out of the decentralized appanage (*iqtāᶜ*) system of the great Seljuks. From 1055 the Seljuks, assuming the title sultan, became in effect protectors of the Abbasid caliph, the continuing symbol of Muslim unity and authority. The appanage system gave more autonomy to local governors, among whom were the Khwārizmshāhs. Out of this the Khwārizmshāhs arose to challenge the Seljuks and replace them as protectors of the caliph and the Islamic community.

The dynastic founder of the Khwārizmshāhs was a Seljuk slave who obtained the status of "keeper of the royal wash bowl" and was eventually appointed governor of the appanage Khwarizm. But his grandson Atsiz (1127–1156) is considered the true founder because he was able to consolidate his power and transform Khwarizm into a political center to rival that of the great Seljuks themselves. He accomplished this by subjugating the neighboring nomads based in the lower areas of the Syr Darya and substantially increasing his Turkish mercenary forces. This in turn provided the base for the success of his grandson, Tekish (Täkäsh) (1172–1200), who gave the Khwārizmshāhs their independence from the Seljuks.

At the same time the Abbasid caliph al-Nāṣir (1180–1225) began to cherish hopes of eliminating the Seljuks as well. Caliph and Khwārizmshāh found themselves allies against a common Seljuk foe. Tekish, acting in the name of the caliph, marched westward and destroyed the Seljuks (1194). Assuming the title "sultan," he now replaced them as protectors of the caliph. His son, Muḥammad, persisted in the same dynastic goal and expanded their empire to its greatest territorial limits from the frontiers of India to Iraq. This inevitably brought him into conflict with the caliph, who by now sought independence from Khwārizmshāhs and Seljuks alike. The climax came in 1217 when Muḥammad led a campaign against Baghdad itself.

Meanwhile, the political situation in east Asia changed dramatically. The Mongols, led by Genghis Khan, turned from their campaigns in China to attack the Khwarizmian empire. By 1221 they had taken the capital, Gurganj, and Muḥammad, fleeing for his life before the invading Mongols, died in obscurity. During the next ten years his son, Jalāluddin (1120–1231), pursued from India to Syria and harried to his death, attempted vainly to resist the Mongols and restore the Khwārizmshāh dynasty.

BIBLIOGRAPHY

W. Barthold (Vasilii Vladimirovich Bartold), *Turkestan Down to the Mongol Invasion* (1968); Clifford E. Bosworth, "Khwārazm" and "Khwārazm-Shāh," in *Encyclopaedia of Islam*, 2nd ed., IV (1978); René Grousset, *The Empire of the Steppes: A History of Central Asia*, Naomi Walford, trans. (1970); Marshall G. S. Hodgson, *The Venture of Islam*, II (1974).

CAROLINE J. BEESON

[See also **Mongol Empire: Foundations; Seljuks; Turkomans.**]

ḲIBLA. See **Qibla.**

KIDDUSH HA-SHEM. See **Martyrdom, Jewish.**

KIEVAN RUS. Kiev was the first state to arise among the East Slavs. Created during the second half of the ninth century, it was named for the city of Kiev on the right (or west) bank of the middle Dnieper River, where its grand princes resided from about 880 until the second quarter of the twelfth century. Although the Kievan state had fragmented into a series of virtually independent principalities by the mid twelfth century, these principalities, as a whole, are referred to as Kievan Rus until the time of the Mongol conquest (1236–1240).

TERMINOLOGY

There is some controversy about the proper name for the Kievan state and its inhabitants. The East Slavic tribes of the Kievan era formed the nucleus for the Great Russian, Ukrainian, and Belorussian (White Russian) peoples of later times. Those who wish to stress the Kievan ancestry of Muscovite Russia and the Russian empire prefer the term "Kievan Russia." On the other hand, the sources of the Kievan period employ the self-appellation "Rus" rather than "Russian." Consequently, those who wish to emphasize the fact that the Kievan state was not Great Russian prefer the term "Kievan Rus."

A similar dispute concerns the language of the Kievan period. Some scholars claim that a unified East Slavic language existed and call it Old Russian. Others believe that the various East Slavic tribal di-

alects never coalesced into a standard literary language that, in any case, should be known as Old Rus.

TERRITORY

Kievan Rus lay almost entirely within the forest-steppe and forest zones. The early Kievan state was confined primarily to the region between Novgorod in the north and Kiev in the south. In the course of time, colonization and conquest expanded its frontiers westward to the Polish and Hungarian borders, northward to the lower Northern Dvina River, eastward to the upper Volga and Oka rivers, and southward to the border with the steppe zone. From the late tenth to early twelfth centuries, Tmutarakan on the Taman Peninsula of the northeastern Black Sea coast also formed part of the Kievan state.

THE EARLY EAST SLAVS

Since the East Slavs became the dominant ethnic group in the Kievan state, much attention has been devoted to their history in the pre-Kievan era. In particular, scholars have sought to determine when, how, and why they first settled in the lands of present-day Russia. Unfortunately, no consensus has been reached and these fundamental questions are still unresolved. The specialists who claim that the supposed Slavic homeland was located within Rus (usually placed between the middle Dnieper and the lower Danube rivers) have failed to prove that Slavs actually inhabited this area since time immemorial. Scholars who maintain that the Slavs migrated into the Russian lands from some other area disagree about where these Slavs came from, when they first migrated into Rus, and how they came to inhabit the Kievan lands. Given the nature of the historical, archaeological, and linguistic evidence, it is most difficult, if not impossible, to trace East Slavic prehistory earlier than the middle of the first millennium of the Christian era with any certainty.

Of the various theories concerning the development of the East Slavs since the mid first millennium, the most convincing argues that some of the Slavs located along the lower Danube and adjacent regions began to migrate north and east into the forest-steppe on the right bank of the Dnieper starting in the sixth century. This migration was most likely an attempt to escape the harsh repression of the Avars, who had conquered the lower Danubian basin in the mid sixth century. In any event, the earliest undisputed Slavic sites within the Kievan lands are on the right bank of the Dnieper and date from the sixth/seventh centuries. These sites belong to the Korchak culture (named for the village of Korchak, west of Kiev), the eastern European variety of the Prague-type culture, and they indicate that the East Slavs of this time had a relatively simple agrarian society. By the eighth and ninth centuries, the East Slavs had settled the forest-steppe on the left (or east) bank of the Dnieper and had begun to colonize the forest zone of northern Russia.

The written sources of the Kievan era contain comparatively little information about early East Slavic history. The chroniclers, who all wrote several centuries later, noted some eleven major East Slavic tribes and their general locations. Unfortunately, their brief comments about the society and customs of these tribes usually take the form of a Christian commentary on the false practices of the East Slavic pagans. It appears, however, that the East Slavs had a political structure with tribal leaders or princes (*kniazi*) and elders, as well as various social customs. Archaeological data reveal that the East Slavs of the

forest-steppe still had a relatively simple agrarian society in the mid ninth century. As before, clusters of a few small settlements were located along riverbanks. The people in these villages apparently practiced some form of slash-and-burn agriculture and made most goods for themselves. Study of the grains found at sites from this era point to the growth of wheat, rye, barley, and millet. Society was uncomplicated, local, and self-sufficient.

The migration of the East Slavs into the forest zone brought them into contact with a variety of non-Slavic peoples. Balts, for example, occupied the upper Dnieper basin, Belorussia, and west-central Russia, while West Finns and Volga Finns inhabited east-central Russia and much of the forest zone north of the Volga. As the East Slavs moved north, they displaced, killed, or assimilated the native Balts and Finns, although some pockets of those groups survived for many centuries. The process of assimilation left an important Baltic substratum among the Belorussians and a significant Finnic substratum among the Great Russians. Thus, while the East Slavs constituted the largest single ethnic group in the Kievan state, its population was multinational from the very beginning. In addition to the various Balts and Finns, there were Turks, Poles, Scandinavians, Jews, central and western Europeans, Greeks, South Slavs, and assorted Near Eastern peoples in the Kievan state.

THE ORIGINS OF THE KIEVAN STATE

The earliest Russian chronicles, which date from about the mid eleventh century, record that around 860 the East Slavic and Finnic tribes of northern Russia invited from overseas a certain Rurik and his Varangian (Viking) Rus to come and rule over them. Rurik and his followers established themselves as rulers of Novgorod and other towns of northern Russia, and his successors went on to develop the Kievan state. The descendants of Rurik, the Riurikovichi, provided all the princes of the Kievan era; and all the Muscovite rulers down to the son of Ivan the Terrible (Fedor I Ivanovich, *d.* 1598) traced their ancestry back to the semilegendary Rurik. Those who believe that the chronicle account is substantially accurate are known as Normanists, since they believe that Normans or Vikings established the Kievan state. On the other hand, various Russian scholars have long denied that Vikings from Scandinavia founded the first Russian state. These anti-Normanists maintain that the East Slavs established their own state; that the Vikings played a minor role, at most, in the creation of this state; and that there is no real truth in the "invitation" to Rurik.

Neither the Normanist nor the anti-Normanist approach is completely satisfactory. While the evidence for the ninth century is not abundant and can be interpreted in different ways, there is no doubt that some Vikings were active in different parts of present-day European Russia by the mid ninth century. By the second half of the ninth century, if not earlier, some of these Vikings had begun to settle in Russia. The origins of the Kievan state cannot be understood by ignoring these Vikings and their activities as the anti-Normanists too often do. On the other hand, Normanists have traditionally ignored the East Slavs and their society in the ninth century. The early Vikings who came to Russia had to deal with an established and developing East Slavic society. Nevertheless, the heart of the Normanist controversy revolves around the authenticity of the "invitation" to Rurik, and this writer believes that while the chronicle account may well contain inaccuracies, it probably contains more than just a few grains of truth.

POLITICAL HISTORY

The political history of the Kievan state can be conveniently divided into several periods, which are based on the reigns of the Kievan grand princes listed below:

Rurik, *ca.* 860–879
Oleg, 879–912
Igor, 913–945
Olga (as regent), 945–964
Svyatoslav I, 964–972
Yaropolk I, 972–980
Vladimir I, 980–1015
Svyatopolk I, 1015–1019
Yaroslav the Wise, 1019–1054
Mstislav (coruler), 1024–1036
Izyaslav I, 1054–1078
Vsevolod, 1078–1093
Svyatopolk II, 1093–1113
Vladimir II Monomakh, 1113–1125
Mstislav, 1125–1132
Yaropolk II, 1132–1139

The first period encompasses the reign of Rurik in Novgorod. Perhaps the most notable event came when two of his followers, Askold and Dir, left Rurik, went south down the Dnieper, seized control of Kiev, and from there led the first Russian attack on Constantinople in 860. The Kievan state thus possessed two major centers from its very inception: Novgorod in the north and Kiev in the south.

The second period began soon after Rurik's death when his kinsman and successor, Oleg, moved south, invaded Kiev, killed Askold and Dir, and made Kiev the capital in 882. Having united Novgorod and Kiev under one ruler, Oleg initiated two major developments that were to characterize the period until Svyatoslav's death in 972. The first was the conquest of the East Slavic tribes and their conversion into tribute-paying subjects of the Kievan prince. This bloody struggle lasted until the late tenth century and saw the Kievan princes forcibly put down strong opposition and repeated revolts. By the time of Vladimir I, almost all East Slavs had been incorporated into the Kievan state.

As the Kievan state expanded, its early leaders sought to establish an active trade with Byzantium. Following the example of Askold and Dir, Oleg and Igor launched attacks upon Constantinople in 907 and 941–944 in order to force Byzantium to grant favorable trading conditions. It was Svyatoslav I, however, who had the most ambitious plans in this regard. Abandoning a highly successful campaign along the Volga in which he had destroyed the Khazar empire, Svyatoslav invaded Bulgaria at the request of Byzantium. Once established there, he announced his intentions to transfer his capital from Kiev to the Danube delta. But these plans had to be abandoned when the now alarmed Byzantines defeated Svyatoslav in 971. On his return journey to Kiev, Svyatoslav was killed (972) by the Pechenegs and his skull made into a drinking cup. With his death the days of the great Viking-like overseas expeditions came to an end.

The third period, an era of internal consolidation and development, is sometimes considered the high point of the entire Kievan era. Led by such famous grand princes as Vladimir, who introduced Christianity to the people of Kiev (988–989), and Yaroslav the Wise, the Kievan rulers concentrated on the establishment of those customs, practices, and institutions that came to characterize Kievan society. The basic problem faced by the grand princes of this period was how to unite and govern the vast lands and heterogeneous peoples that had been added to the Kievan state during the previous century.

While struggling to create a sound foundation for Kievan society, these grand princes also had to face a new and persistent threat from the Turkic nomads of the Russian-Ukrainian steppe: the collapse of the Khazar empire had left Kiev exposed to these Asian nomads. Seeking slaves and booty, the Pechenegs became a major danger during the tenth century. Despite the success of some of their raids, the grand princes of this period were able to contain the nomadic threat. Vladimir built a distant early warning system along the southern frontiers of Rus, and Yaroslav decisively defeated the Pechenegs in 1036. At the same time, relations with the Turkic nomads were not always hostile. These nomads acted as intermediaries in trade with the south and served as auxiliaries in the Rus armies; their leaders even intermarried with the Rus princely families. Nevertheless, the danger from the steppes became very real in the late tenth century.

After Svyatoslav's death, a protracted war of succession ensued among his sons, from which Vladimir I eventually emerged victorious around 980. During the first years of his reign, the chroniclers describe Vladimir as a staunch supporter of paganism as well as a lecherous prince who kept at least 800 concubines. Nevertheless, it was Vladimir who converted Rus to Orthodox Christianity. Christianity, however, had first appeared in Rus about a century earlier, and Vladimir's grandmother, Grand Princess Olga, was the most famous convert (ca. 955). Regrettably, the available sources do not explain why paganism proved unsatisfactory or why Orthodox Christianity was selected to become the new state religion. They simply tell of representatives of Islam, Judaism, Roman Catholicism, and Orthodoxy visiting Kiev and Rus representatives being sent abroad to obtain a firsthand look at these religions. Around 988 Vladimir I sent Rus mercenaries to help the Byzantine emperor Basil II (d. 1025), in exchange for his sister Anna's hand in marriage. When Basil failed to keep the bargain, Vladimir captured the Byzantine city of Tauric Chersonese (Chersonesus; modern Kherson) in the Crimea. He kept Chersonese until Basil's sister arrived, after which he converted, married Anna, returned Chersonese to the emperor, and went back to Kiev, where he began to convert his subjects by force. With the spread of Orthodox Christianity, Byzantine ideas and practices in music, art, architecture, literature, law, philosophy, political theory, and education took root in Rus.

Vladimir may well have decided that only one of the prophetic religions could provide the unifying force for his diverse realm. In such a case, the close trade ties with Byzantium, which went back almost a century, made Orthodoxy the natural choice. There was one problem, however. The subordina-

tion of the head of the Rus church, the metropolitan, to the head of the Byzantine church, the patriarch, provided the emperor with an opportunity to use religion to influence Kievan secular affairs. This difficulty was not readily resolved, and continued until the reign of Yaroslav (d. 1054).

Following Vladimir's death, his sons fought the second protracted war of succession. After the Battle of Listven in 1024, the two remaining contenders, Yaroslav and Mstislav, divided the Kievan state along the Dnieper, with Yaroslav ruling the right bank and northern Rus while Mstislav ruled the left bank and Tmutarakan. When Mstislav died in 1036 without an heir, Yaroslav became grand prince of a reunited Kievan Rus.

Yaroslav's reign as undisputed grand prince (1036–1054) was one of the most brilliant periods in the entire history of Kievan Rus. The Pechenegs were soundly beaten, the famous cathedrals of St. Sophia in Kiev and Novgorod were built, learning and education were strongly encouraged, and the codification of Rus's first written law code, the *Russkaya Pravda*, was begun. There is no doubt that Kiev under Yaroslav was one of the most advanced capitals of Europe.

While Yaroslav fostered the spread of Byzantine culture and art, he simultaneously fought to maintian the rights of Rus vis-à-vis Byzantium. In 1043, for example, commercial conflicts with Byzantium led him to launch the last Rus attack on Constantinople. Although a Byzantine-appointed metropolitan reached Kiev in 1039, the problem of religious subordination was not settled, and in 1051 Yaroslav temporarily appointed his own choice, the Rus Ilarion, as metropolitan. Although Yaroslav was not completely successful in dealing with Byzantium, he clearly ranks as one of the greatest grand princes of Kiev.

The death of Yaroslav inaugurated the fourth period, a time in which Rus was beset by two great problems. In the mid eleventh century the Polovtsy/ Cumans replaced the Pechenegs as rulers of the steppe. From this time until the early thirteenth century, the Polovtsy raided the Kievan lands periodically and, as often as not, defeated the Rus armies. The danger from the steppe was exacerbated by the increasing political disunity within Rus. In an attempt to avert the bloody civil wars that had followed the deaths of Svyatoslav and Vladimir, Yaroslav, on his deathbed, drew up a plan for dividing political power among his sons. Soon after his death, however, a new struggle for the succession erupted. In this struggle the power of the grand prince in Kiev was slowly eroded. Members of the princely family increasingly saw themselves as autonomous local rulers rather than as the grand prince's local representatives. Few princes respected the lands of their rivals, and Polovtsian auxiliaries were frequently used to destroy the lands of these rivals. Attempts by the Rus princes to restore stability at several peace conferences failed. Thus, the period after Yaroslav was characterized by the decline of the grand princely power, the growth of powerful but competing local interests, and incessant Polovtsian raids.

These centrifugal trends and the constant nomadic raids were temporarily halted by Vladimir II Monomakh (d. 1125) and his sons. Their reigns thus represent the fifth period in Kievan history. Monomakh, who was already famous for his victories over the Polovtsians, was selected in 1113 as grand prince in order to heal the violent social conflicts that erupted after his predecessor's death. His reforms eliminated the worst abuses and, despite the brevity of his reign, he was the last great grand prince of Kiev. While Mstislav (1125–1132) was able to preserve the stability and unity created by his father, the reign of Yaropolk II brought the resurgence of local interests and the renewed weakening of central authority. This time no Kievan prince was able to reverse the centrifugal trends.

The sixth and final period in Kievan history encompasses the century before the Mongol conquest and was distinguished by the breakdown of the Kievan state into several virtually independent principalities. The number of principalities varied because emerging cities within a principality constantly attempted to assert their independence and strong princes almost always sought to conquer weaker neighboring principalities.

Kiev, now the capital of one such principality, was constantly threatened by the neighboring rulers of the Chernigov, Galician-Volynian, and Suzdal principalities. As a result, the princes of Kiev tended to wield very limited power for short periods of time. The political decline of Kiev can be compared with the growing political power of Suzdal in the upper Volga region. Under such men as Yuri Dolgoruki (Long Arm, d. 1157), Andrei Bogoliubskii (1157–1174), and Vsevolod Bolshoe Gnezdo (Big Nest, 1177–1212), the Suzdal princes sought to assert their independence from both townsmen and boyars within their domain while extending their power eastward into the Volga Bulgar lands, northwestward into the Novgorod lands, and southwestward toward Kiev.

During the eleventh and twelfth centuries, Novgorod exploited the breakdown of Kiev's power to create its own form of self-rule. The prince here was not hereditary, as elsewhere, but a military commander who served at the pleasure of the city assembly (veche). At the same time, oligarchs and townspeople fought for control of the veche. Novgorod also emerged as the chief center for Rus's Baltic trade, for it was there that German and Rus merchants met to exchange their goods. Kiev, Suzdal, and Novgorod typify the diversity found within Kievan Rus during its last century.

The constant conflicts among the Russian principalities made them prey to foreign attacks. Enemies such as the Polovtsians, Hungarians, Poles, and Germans, however, were never able to conquer the Russian lands. Thus, the Russian princes were completely unprepared for the Mongol invasion of 1236–1240, even though the Mongol victory over a group of Russian princes at the Battle of the Kalka River in 1223 should have served as a warning. The Mongols conquered one by one the Russian principalities, which never seriously attempted a united resistance. The Kievan period now gave way to the era of Mongol rule.

KIEVAN SOCIETY AND ECONOMY

Numerous efforts have been made to categorize or label Kievan society. Many Soviet scholars, for example, have tried since the early 1930's to demonstrate that Kievan Rus was feudal. They argue that its predominantly agricultural economy was characterized by large estates worked by an enserfed peasantry, and they expressly reject the views of pre-Revolutionary scholars who emphasized the importance of foreign trade and slave labor. No label yet suggested for Kievan society is completely satisfactory. The Kievan period lasted for four centuries and the Kievan lands stretched from the steppe to the Arctic and from Poland to the western Urals. Furthermore, the population of the Kievan state included a variety of ethnic groups at different stages of development and with divergent social patterns. No one label can possibly describe such a diverse society accurately. Consequently, it would be better to abandon the effort to find some single, all-encompassing term and instead focus upon the diversity within the Kievan socioeconomic structure.

The overwhelming majority of the people were peasants. Because of the paucity of sources, the relative importance of slash-and-burn agriculture, as opposed to some form of crop rotation, is not clear. There is also a lack of precise information on the nature of the basic social unit; the commune, the extended family, and the nuclear family all have their advocates. Nevertheless, the life of the average peasant was probably governed more than anything else by the fact that primitive implements, traditional methods, and little fertilizer led to very low grain yields. The peasants lived most of the time at subsistence level, with barely enough to feed themselves and their few animals (domestic animals such as cattle and pigs were also raised). As a result, the peasantry was always very dependent upon the surrounding forest for its survival. The forest supplied wood for homes, implements, and warmth, as well as the animals needed for meat and pelts. Animal skins could also be exchanged for other goods. The abundant fish from forest streams and the many berries and mushrooms from the woods provided other sources of food that were often more reliable than subsistence farming. Given this situation, it is misleading to debate, as some have done, whether agriculture or forest products were more important in Kievan society. Both were essential for the peasant. In addition, this dual dependence on forest and farm meant that peasants settled in small numbers over large areas, creating a land-intensive, low-density way of life.

In the ninth century most East Slavs belonged to an unstratified agrarian society whose members dwelt in small, scattered villages. Within this society new groups began to emerge. The end of Khazar-Arab hostilities in the Caucasus led to the growth of Islamic trade with eastern Europe, a trade in which furs and slaves from eastern Europe were exchanged for Islamic silver coins (dirhams). It was this trade, centered in Khazaria and Volga Bulgaria along the Volga, that attracted the Vikings to Russia. Seeking the source of these dirhams, Viking merchant-marauders, along with East Slavic and other traders, soon established regular contact with Islamic merchants. To obtain the furs and slaves they needed, these merchant-raiders began to demand tribute in furs from the native population and to kidnap prospective slaves from nontributary peoples. Since these warrior-merchants were militarily superior, they gradually established their domination over the indigenous inhabitants. Thus, a multinational ruling group of merchant-warriors whose life was based on trade and whose centers were fortified towns slowly emerged within Rus.

Kievan Rus thus began with a dual socioeconomic structure: the vast majority of peasants living in scattered hamlets and the small, heterogeneous ruling group of the towns who monopolized foreign trade. During the next century or so, this pattern remained basically unchanged, although some alterations occurred. The establishment of the capital at Kiev led to an active trade with Byzantium, a trade that soon rivaled the older Eastern commerce along the Volga. As time went on, the conquered East Slavs and other subjects of the grand princes changed from tributaries into taxpayers, and a network of local governors collected taxes in local centers. Towns slowly began to develop as places of safety in wartime, as markets for international commerce and local trade, and as centers of political-administrative and ecclesiastical power. These emergent cities consisted of two main areas: the citadel or kremlin, usually located on a high, easily protected spot and serving as the residence of the prince and his retinue; and the commercial region, or *posad,* located outside the kremlin and containing the workshops and dwellings of merchants, artisans, and workers.

During the eleventh century, major changes began to take place in Kievan society. Rus trade with the Near East and Byzantium was temporarily disrupted because of the collapse of the Khazar state, the cessation of the influx of Islamic silver into eastern Europe, the Polovtsian conquest of the steppe, and the weakening of Byzantium. While Rus trade with the south continued, Novgorod's growing commerce with the Baltic gained in importance. By the early thirteenth century, Novgorod had concluded its first written agreement with the German merchants of the Baltic, and Smolensk had developed an active trade with the Baltic via the Western Dvina River and Riga.

Internally, the eleventh century marked the appearance of private property in land. The origins, extent, and significance of large private estates form one of the most controversial topics in Kievan history. This controversy will probably never be resolved, because the few sources of the time generally ignore this phenomenon and focus on political events. Furthermore, contemporaries never explained the meaning of various key terms used in the several documents that do deal with the problem. In any event, it appears that princely landholding dates from the eleventh century. Soon after, members of the princely retinues (boyars) and the church began to acquire estates. As already indicated, many Soviet scholars maintain that these estates were feudal in nature. This interpretation is not convincing, because recent scholarship, both Soviet and Western, has shown that many peasants preserved their freedom until the Muscovite era. The collection of taxes from these free peasants has apparently been confused with the extraction of manorial dues from serfs.

Recent research also suggests that private property was not as extensive as once thought, that it came from virgin forest rather than already occupied peasant land, and that these estates were worked not by serfs but by slaves and various semifree peoples who had special obligations to a landowner. Furthermore, large estates were primarily devoted to raising livestock rather than to producing food; princes, boyars, and the church obtained food primarily through taxes, legal fees, and subsistence payments to officials, all made in kind by free peasant taxpayers.

The picture of late Kievan society that emerges, while not clear in all details, contains great diversity in the lower stratum. Most people were still free peasants. Besides slaves, there were apparently an increasing number of semifree people who had become dependents. The slaves and dependents apparently provided the labor on the private estates.

The ruling groups were still very involved in trade, as can be seen in Novgorod, but the share of their total income derived from taxes and from their private estates was increasing. The merchant-marauders of the earlier period, who were all completely slavicized by now, had divided into professional merchants and members of the governing class. The retinue of the early princes was the nucleus for the boyar class, the medieval Russian parallel of the Western nobility. The boyars, however, did not possess fiefs, and thus had no service obligation to a prince or other lord. Boyars served princes for as long as was mutually convenient, and when they received land as a reward, it was in the form of an allod. Thus, the original trader-warrior group now contained a vast spectrum of merchants, princes, and boyars comparable with the many gradations of peasants.

This growing diversity of Kievan society was also manifested in the towns. In them a large number of artisans and workshops produced a growing variety and number of goods; potters and smiths supplied everyday needs, and highly specialized craftsmen such as jewelers catered to a more limited market. These artisans challenged the power of the princes and boyars within the towns, and more than once an unpopular prince was replaced by the town assembly (veche), and hated boyars had their houses looted and were forced to flee.

In conclusion, no single term can adequately comprehend all the heterogeneous elements in Kievan society or describe the diversity of the economy. "Serfdom" and "feudalism" are not appropriate terms for Kievan Rus. Unfortunately, no one has yet come up with a label or term that is acceptable.

BIBLIOGRAPHY

Bibliographies. Among basic reference and bibliographic works, the following should be noted: Stephan M. Horak, comp., *Russia, the USSR, and Eastern Europe: A Bibliographic Guide to English Language Publications 1964–1974* (1978); Paul L. Horecky, ed., *Basic Russian Publications: An Annotated Bibliography on Russia and the Soviet Union* (1962); Charles Morley, *Guide to Research in Russian History* (1951). Among the more specialized bibliographies is Peter A. Crowther, comp., *A Bibliography of Works in English on Early Russian History to 1800* (1969).

Current American publications can be found in *The American Bibliography of Slavic and East European Studies* (1956–). Current western European works are treated in the *European Bibliography of Soviet, East European, and Slavonic Studies,* the first volume of which covered 1975.

See also the *Bolshaia sovetskaya entsiklopedia,* 30 vols., 3rd ed. (1970–1976), for which an English translation has been published: *The Great Soviet Encyclopedia;* and *The Modern Encyclopedia of Russian and Soviet History,* 15 vols. to date.

Sources. The single most important source for the Kievan period is the *Povest vremennykh let,* or *Tale of Bygone Years,* often referred to in English as the *Russian Primary Chronicle* or the *Nestor Chronicle.* The *Povest* covers the time up to the early twelfth century and appears in two versions called the Hypathian and Laurentian. For a useful English version, see Samuel H. Cross and Olgerd P. Sherbowitz-Wetzer, eds. and trans., *The Russian Primary Chronicle: Laurentian Text* (1953). Another chronicle which covers the Kievan era is *The Nikonian Chronicle: From the Beginning to 1240,* 2 vols., Serge A. and Betty Jean Zenkovsky, eds. and trans. (1984).

The period from the early twelfth century to the Mongol conquest is covered in continuations of both versions of the *Povest.* The continuation of the Hypathian version for the years 1118–1200 has been translated by Lisa Lynn Heinrich as *The Kievan Chronicle* (1978). A further continuation covering the period from 1201 to 1292 has recently been translated by George A. Perfecky, *The Hypathian Codex, Part Two: The Galician-Volynian Chronicle*

(1973). One of the many chronicles of Novgorod and Pskov was translated by Robert Michell and Nevill Forbes as *The Chronicle of Novgorod, 1016–1471* (1914).

The law codes, trade treaties, donative charters, and other documents of the Kievan period, while not numerous, form an invaluable source of information. The most important of these materials have been collected together in the first two volumes of the series *Pamiatniki russkogo prava*, I, *Pamiatniki prava Kievskogo gosudarstva, X–XII vv.* (1952), and II, *Pamiatniki prava feodal'no razdroblennoi Rusi, XII–XV vv.* (1953). The *Russkaya Pravda* has been translated into English by George Vernadsky in *Medieval Russian Laws* (1947; repr. 1955, 1969), 26–56.

Various non-Russian sources contain information on Kievan Russia: the Byzantine Constantine Porphyrogenitos, *De administrando imperio*, Gyula Moravcsik, ed., R. J. H. Jenkins, trans., 2 vols. (1962–1967); the Islamic *Hudud al-ᶜAlam, The Regions of the World: A Persian Geography 372 A.H.–982 A.D.*, V. Minorsky, trans. (1937, 2nd ed. 1970), and *A History of Sharvan and Darband in the 10th–11th Centuries*, V. Minorsky, trans. (1958); and the western European Adam of Bremen, *History of the Archbishops of Hamburg-Bremen*, Francis J. Tscham, trans. (1959); Snorri Sturluson, *Heimskringla; or, The Lives of the Norse Kings* (various translations); *The Chronicle of Henry of Livonia*, James A. Brundage, trans. (1961); and *The Livonian Rhymed Chronicle*, Jerry C. Smith and William L. Urban, trans. (1977).

Various non-Russian sources describe the Mongol conquest of Russia and its immediate aftermath. For the Chinese sources see E. Brettschneider, *Mediaeval Researches from Eastern Asiatic Sources*, I (repr. 1967). The basic Islamic sources are Ata Malik Juvaini, *The History of the World Conqueror*, J. A. Boyle, trans., 2 vols. (1958); and Rashīd ad-Dīn, *The Successors of Genghis Khan*, J. A. Boyle, trans. (1971). The best-known western European sources are found in Christopher Dawson, ed., *The Mongol Mission* (1955), and R. A. Skelton, *et al.*, eds., *The Vinland Map and the Tartar Relation* (1965).

Literary and religious sources provide important information about many aspects of Kievan life often neglected by chronicles and charters: the twelfth-century epic poem *The Song of Igor's Campaign*, Vladimir Nabokov, trans. (1960), although its authenticity and dating have been questioned; "The Narrative, Passion, and Encomium of Boris and Gleb," trans. by Marvin Kantor in *Medieval Slavic Lives of Saints and Princes* (1983); and the *Life of St. Theodosius*, in G. P. Fedotov, ed., *A Treasury of Russian Spirituality* (1965), 11–49.

Many excellent collections of excerpts from sources of the Kievan period are available in different languages. For English works with excerpts from sources of the Kievan era, see Basil Dmytryshyn, ed., *Medieval Russia: A Source Book, 900–1700* (1967, 2nd ed. 1973), 3–113; George Vernadsky, Sr., ed., *A Source Book for Russian History from Early Times to 1917*, I, *Early Times to the Late Seventeenth Century* (1972), 3–46, 61–64, 69–71; Serge A. Zen-

kovsky, ed., *Medieval Russia's Epics, Chronicles, and Tales*, rev. ed. (1974), 41–211, 249–255.

Studies. A good exposition of the Ukrainian approach to the Kievan era can be found in Michael Hrushevsky, *A History of Ukraine* (1941), 20–122. Single-volume studies of the Kievan era include B. Grekov, *Kiev Rus*, Y. Sdobnikov, trans., Dennis Ogden, ed. (1959); B. A. Rybakov, *Early Centuries of Russian History*, John Weir, trans. (1965); George Vernadsky, *Kievan Russia* (1948). The origins of the East Slavs and their early history are treated in Marija Gimbutas, *The Slavs* (1971).

The number of works dealing with the origins and early history of the Kievan state is enormous. The spectrum of opinion regarding these controversial problems is reflected in T. J. Arne, *La Suède et l'Orient* (1914); Imre Boba, *Nomads, Northmen, and Slavs: Eastern Europe in the Ninth Century* (1967); Nora Chadwick, *The Beginnings of Russian History* (1946); H. R. Ellis Davidson, *The Viking Road to Byzantium* (1976); Gerhard Laehr, *Die Anfänge des russischen Reiches* (1930); Henryk Paszkiewicz, *The Origin of Russia* (1954), and *The Making of the Russian Nation* (1963); Omeljan Pritsak, *The Origin of Rus*, I (1981); Ad. Stender-Petersen, *Varangica* (1953); Vilhelm Thomsen, *The Relations Between Ancient Russia and Scandinavia and the Origins of the Russian State* (1877); Alexander A. Vasiliev, *The First Russian Attack on Constantinople in 860–61* (1946); George Vernadsky, *Ancient Russia* (1943), and *The Origins of Russia* (1959).

Specific aspects of Kievan history and society are examined in some detail in a variety of specialized studies: Martin Dimnik, *Mikhail, Prince of Chernigov and Grand Prince of Kiev* (1981), discusses the last years of the Kievan era and the early Mongol period; G. P. Fedotov, *The Russian Religious Mind: Kievan Christianity* (1946); John Fennell, *The Crisis of Medieval Russia, 1200–1304* (1983), treats the period *1200–1240*; Ellen S. Hurwitz, *Prince Andrej Bogoljubskij* (1980); M. W. Thompson, comp., *Novgorod the Great: Excavations at the Medieval City* (1967); M. N. Tikhomirov, *The Towns of Ancient Rus*, Y. Sdobnikov, trans., D. Svirsky, ed. (1959); Russell Zguta, *Russian Minstrels* (1978).

Thomas S. Noonan

[See also **Agriculture and Nutrition; Bogoliubskii, Andrei; Boyar; Muscovy, Rise of; Novgorod; Oleg; Olga/Helen; Rurik; Russian Nomads, Invasions of; Slavs; Tmutarakan, Khanate of; Trade, European; Vikings; Vladimir, St.; Vladimir Monomakh; Yaroslav the Wise.**]

KILIJ ARSLAN. See **Qïlïj Arslan II.**

KILIM (also *kelim, gilim*), a term used to describe both a technique of weaving and carpets woven in that technique. The technique itself is also known as tapestry weave or weft-faced plain weave. In it wefts of colored yarn, which form the fabric design, are packed down to cover the warps. The doubling-back of the wefts to form the design of the fabric necessitates either small slits along the warps or an interlocking of wefts through each other or around a shared warp. The term "kilim" for such carpets is used in the Middle East, although rugs and tapestries have long been woven in this technique in pre-Columbian America, northern Europe, and Egypt, independent of the more familiar Islamic kilims.

The weaving of slit-tapestry rugs in the Middle East is an ancient practice; kilim fragments were found in the fifth-century B.C. Pazyryk burial site in Siberia. Numerous fragments from medieval times have been excavated at Al-Fusṭāṭ in Egypt, their technique virtually identical to that of many of the "Coptic" textiles of the Middle Ages. Although the kilims woven in Islamic lands, judged on the basis of surviving examples, were long thought to be the products of village and nomadic weavers, recent discoveries of examples in curvilinear court designs leave open the possibility that kilims may have been a "high art" form since medieval times.

The kilim technique seems to have come to Europe through Egyptian, Byzantine, or Roman examples. The earliest European church tapestries woven in the technique, such as the eleventh-century Cloth of St. Gereon from Cologne and the Halberstadt tapestries of the late twelfth century, show no relation in iconography or design to surviving fragments of medieval Islamic kilims and probably represent an independent artistic evolution.

Kilim (slit-tapestry) weave, showing vertical and diagonal boundaries between color areas. FROM IRENE EMERY, THE PRIMARY STRUCTURE OF FABRICS: AN ILLUSTRATED CLASSIFICATION (WASHINGTON, D.C.: THE TEXTILE MUSEUM, 1966)

BIBLIOGRAPHY

Walter B. Denny, "Classical Roots of Anatolian Kilim Designs," in *Hali*, 2 (1979); Anthony N. Landreau and W. R. Pickering, *From the Bosporus to Samarkand: Flat-Woven Rugs* (1969); Alexander L. Mongait, *Archaeology in the USSR*, M. W. Thompson, trans. (1961), 94–96; Yanni Petsopoulos, *Kilims* (1979), 17–25.

WALTER B. DENNY

[See also **Rugs and Carpets; Tapestry Weaving.**]

KILWARDBY, ROBERT (*ca.* 1215—10 September 1279), English church official. He studied at Paris and then taught arts there from about 1237 to about 1245. He returned to England, entered the Dominican order, and studied theology at Oxford, where he was regent master in the late 1250's. In 1261 he was elected prior provincial of the English Dominicans, and in 1272 he was appointed archbishop of Canterbury. His most celebrated act as archbishop was the condemnation of thirty articles in logic, grammar, and natural philosophy issued at Oxford on 18 March 1277. Along with the nearly simultaneous condemnation at Paris, this was part of a conservative reaction against the teachings of certain university scholars, including Thomas Aquinas, who were seen by some as having taken purely philosophical principles too far. In 1278 Kilwardby was named cardinal bishop of Porto. He died at Viterbo.

BIBLIOGRAPHY

Kilwardby's *Quaestiones in librum tertium Sententiarum*, I, *Christologie*, Elisabeth Gössmann, ed. (1982), and *De ortu scientiarum*, Albert G. Judy, ed. (1976), present the most important of his works yet to be published in critical editions. The edition by Judy contains a fine summary of the evidence for the chronology of Kilwardby's life and a nearly complete bibliography. There is also Kilwardby's *De natura relationis*, Lorenz Schmücker, ed. (1980), with some bibliographical entries omitted by Judy. For a fuller biography, but one that must be corrected by more recent work on certain details of dating, see Ellen M. F. Sommer-Seckendorff, *Studies in the Life of Robert Kilwardby, O.P.* (1937). Among studies of his thought and his place in intellectual controversy, see Daniel A. Callus, *The Condemnation of St. Thomas at Oxford*, 2nd ed. (1955); Dorothea E. Sharp, "The 1277 Condemnation by Kilwardby," in *New Scholasticism*, 8 (1934).

STEVEN P. MARRONE

[See also **Thomism and Its Opponents.**]

KINDĪ, AL-, Abū Yūsuf Yaᶜ**qūb ibn Isḥāq** (ca. 800–ca. 870), the first Islamic philosopher. Born in Al-Kufa, Iraq, he belonged to the South Arabian tribe of Kinda—hence his name al-Kindī (the Kindite). He was educated in Al-Kufa, Basra, and Baghdad, but very little is known about his philosophical training. His close association with the translation of Greek philosophy into Arabic by Syriac-speaking Christian scholars suggests the possibility that he may have had some of these scholars as philosophy teachers. The Abbasid caliphs al-Maᵓmūn (d. 833), al-Muᶜtaṣim (d. 842), and al-Wāthiq (d. 847) were his patrons and he was a tutor to a son of al-Muᶜtaṣim. For reasons not fully known, he fell out of favor with the caliph al-Mutawakkil (d. 861) and his library was confiscated (it was returned to him later).

The first in a line of Islamic philosophers who were physicians and scientists as well, al-Kindī produced works that cover a wide range of subjects: philosophy, theology, logic, astronomy, astrology, alchemy, arithmetic, geometry, and music. An early medieval Arabic source mentions some 240 of his works, of which only a small number have survived. Judging from these, probably most of the lost works were short treatises. The medieval Latins knew some of his treatises in translation, such as *De somno et visione, De intellectu,* and *Liber de quinque essentiis.* Of his surviving Arabic treatises, the longest and philosophically most important is his *fī al-Falsafa al-Ūlā* (On first philosophy), dedicated to the caliph al-Muᶜtaṣim. Platonic, Aristotelian, and Neoplatonic concepts are recast in it to forge a philosophical perspective consistent with generally accepted Islamic views of the world's creation. Divided into four chapters, it is a remarkable piece of energetic, sustained argument.

After a short introductory chapter in which he defends and recommends the study of philosophy, al-Kindī devotes a lengthy second chapter to a detailed argument to prove the world's temporal creation ex nihilo. An infinite body is impossible, he tries to show, since its supposition must lead to the affirmation of unequal infinities, a contradiction. He argues that motion and time must be finite. A static body, he then maintains, is also impossible. Body, by definition, must be in motion. Hence the world's creation cannot be interpreted as merely the initiating of motion in an already existing, but static, body. The world's creation is ex nihilo.

The third and fourth chapters are devoted to proving the existence of the True One and to demonstrating his uniqueness and utter oneness. The pluralities in the various categories of the existents around us, al-Kindī argues, are composed of unities. But these unities, he tries to show in detail, belong to the existents accidentally, not essentially. Whatever belongs accidentally to one thing derives its existence from another thing wherein it exists essentially. Hence the accidental unities in the world must ultimately derive from an existent who is essentially one. This is the True One, God. Moreover, without unity, there can be no existence. The True One, the bestower of accidental unities to the world, is the bestower of its existence.

As a philosopher, al-Kindī was "Islamic" both in the cultural sense of this term and in the sense that his philosophy was in harmony with generally accepted Islamic religous beliefs. Thus he upheld not only the doctrine of the world's creation ex nihilo but also (in a shorter treatise) the doctrine of bodily resurrection. In this he differed from the other major medieval "Islamic" philosophers, who denied both these doctrines. Although, properly speaking, al-Kindī did not establish a philosophical school, he did have followers. He pioneered the philosophical venture in medieval Islam, setting the stage for the philosophical developments that were to follow.

BIBLIOGRAPHY

A translation is *Al-Kindī's Metaphysics*, Alfred L. Ivry, trans. (1974), with introduction and commentary. A listing of al-Kindī's works is Nicholas Rescher, *Al-Kindī: An Annotated Bibliography* (1964). See also George N. Atiyeh, *Al-Kindī: The Philosopher of the Arabs* (1966); William L. Craig, *The Kalām Cosmological Argument* (1979); G. Endress, *Proclus Arabus* (1973); J. Jolivet, *L'intellect selon Kindī* (1971).

MICHAEL E. MARMURA

[See also **Aristotle in the Middle Ages; Philosophy and Theology, Islamic.**]

KINGIS QUAIR, THE (The king's book), probably written in 1423/1424 by James I of Scotland, is a fine Chaucerian dream vision that draws from both Lydgate's *Temple of Glas* and Boethius' *Consolation of Philosophy.* It recounts in rhyme royal the encounters of the lovesick narrator with Venus, Minerva, and Fortune.

BIBLIOGRAPHY

The most recent edition is *The Kingis Quair*, John Norton-Smith, ed. (1981). See also Ian Brown, "The Mental

Traveller—A Study of the *Kingis Quair*," in *Studies in Scottish Literature,* 5 (1968); Andrew von Hendy, "The Free Thrall: A Study of *The Kingis Quair*," ibid., 3 (1965); John Preston, "Fortunys Exiltree: A Study of the *Kingis Quair*," in *Review of English Literature,* n.s. 7 (1956).

MARY-JO ARN

[See also **Middle English Literature.**]

KING'S EVIL. There is evidence that from the late thirteenth century, the kings of France and England regularly sought to heal by their touch sufferers from scrofula (struma, glands). A tubercular infection of the lymphatic glands leading to chronic enlargement and degeneration, the term scrofula was also applied to other disorders of the neck and face; it was known popularly as *le mal le roy* (the king's evil), and in Latin as *morbus regius* (or *regis*).

The Latin term had, however, a complex development. In classical authors, in the *Etymologiae* of Isidore of Seville (*ca.* 560–636), and in some medieval sources, it signified jaundice. Patristic writers, including St. Jerome, applied it to leprosy and like diseases, and it kept this meaning in the works of such late-eleventh- and early-twelfth-century writers as Goscelin of St. Bertin and William of Malmesbury. Only gradually did it come to mean scrofula. Soon after 1066 the *Vita Ædwardi regis* recorded the first healing miracle by King Edward the Confessor (1042–1066), that of a woman with infected throat glands whom the author—probably a monk of St. Bertin—clearly regarded as scrofulous, although some symptoms were of leprosy. However, William of Malmesbury, Osbert of Clare, and Ailred of Rievaulx, who told the story in the twelfth century, followed the *Vita* in avoiding the term *morbus regius.*

By the mid thirteenth century the symptoms of leprosy were increasingly confused with those of scrofula; since the former was becoming a less common disease, the term *morbus regius* was now applied to the latter. Thus, in a medical work written about 1250, probably at Montpellier, Gilbert the Englishman gave an account of scrofula in which he associated leprous with scrofulous symptoms, and also spoke of it as *morbus regius* "because kings cure this disease." Up to this time, however, there is little suggestion that kings did so regularly. Edward the Confessor's miracle was an isolated token of personal sanctity. Helgaud, the biographer of the second Capetian king of France, Robert II the Pious (996–1031), represented him as similarly curing the

sick, including lepers, by touching their diseased members and signing them with the cross.

Clear evidence of repeated touching begins just before 1124, when Abbot Guibert of Nogent claimed to have seen the fifth Capetian king, Louis VI (1108–1137), perform his "customary miracle": By his touch and by the sign of the cross he healed people who came "in crowds" with scrofula of the neck or other parts of the body. Guibert noted that Louis's father, Philip I (1060–1108), had eagerly done likewise until his sins deprived him of the power. Guibert seems to have had reservations about Louis's custom, for he sought to restrain him; he also noted—almost certainly correctly in the Norman period—that no English king had ventured to do the like.

A year or two later William of Malmesbury's opposition was more pronounced. Probably with Guibert's passage in mind, he stigmatized as false the view that royal healing miracles flowed from hereditary endowment rather than from personal sanctity. From this time until about 1250 there is a dearth of evidence save a general observation, in a letter of about 1185 from Peter of Blois to the court clerks of Henry II of England (1154–1189), that contradicted William of Malmesbury: The best proof of the holiness of a king's anointing was his capacity to clear up a groin disease and to cure scrofula. This evidence suggests that in France from Louis VI's time, if not from his father's, and perhaps also in early Angevin England, kings sometimes touched for scrofula, thereby exciting controversy among clerics about the powers of the king as *christus Domini.* But it is doubtful whether the healing of scrofula—not yet identified with the *morbus regius*—was a regularly exercised and generally recognized royal attribute.

There is a little evidence that in France King Louis IX (1226–1270) touched for scrofula, especially after his return in 1254 from the unsuccessful Seventh Crusade, whereupon he intensified all his religious observances. In the French royal household accounts that survive from the later Middle Ages there is certainly attested a regular custom of touching for the *morbus regius* (scrofula). In 1307/1308 many sufferers came to Philip IV (1285–1314) from as far as Lorraine, Spain, and Italy; such long-distance travelers received substantial sums in alms. The touching of people from many parts of France itself may be presumed. In England, where public records are plentiful, Exchequer accounts afford evidence of touching from 1276/1277, when the king's confessor disbursed a penny to each of 627 persons cured of the *morbus regius*. The practice is thus attested there from the reign of Edward I (1272–1307), but since it was firmly established so soon after his return from crusade in 1274, it is likely to have grown up in the latter years of his father, Henry III (1216–1272). Henry visited Louis IX in 1254 and 1259/1260, and he may well have imitated the Capetian example.

From this time, in face of some medical skepticism, touching for the king's evil became a settled usage of the French and English kings, in England until 1714 and in France until 1789; kings touched irrespective of their personal character or dynastic legitimacy. The custom is best regarded as a sign of the emergence in France and England of national monarchies concerned to underline the spiritual qualities and functions of the kingly office. There is no evidence that it was practiced elsewhere.

From the reign of Edward II (1307–1327), English kings had a custom on Good Friday of offering gold and silver from which finger rings having healing properties were made. Beginning in the fifteenth century, they instead rubbed between their hands ready-made rings that were held to be effective against cramps and epilepsy, and hence became known as "cramp rings." In England, forms of service for touching for the king's evil and blessing cramp rings have survived from about 1500; a form for touching for the king's evil was printed in some prayer books from the reign of Charles I (1625–1649) to 1719.

BIBLIOGRAPHY

Modern study of the king's evil begins with Marc Bloch, *Les rois thaumaturges* (1924, repr. 1961), trans. by J. E. Anderson as *The Royal Touch* (1973); but Bloch's account of the early development should be treated with reserve. A penetrating reassessment of the evidence is Frank Barlow, "The King Evil," in *English Historical Review*, 95 (1980), repr. in his *The Norman Conquest and Beyond* (1983). For liturgical texts, see *Monumenta ritualia ecclesiae anglicanae*, dissertations and notes by William Maskell, 2nd ed., III (1882, repr. 1970), 388–397.

H. E. J. COWDREY

[See also **Leprosy; Medicine, History of.**]

KINGSHIP, RITUALS OF: CORONATION. The word "coronation" is the shorthand form in English of a series of interwoven ceremonies that may be ex-

pressed by other words in English or in other languages: *consecratio, inauguratio,* or *coronatio* in Latin; *die Weihe* or *die Krönung* in German; and *consecration, couronnement,* or *sacre* in French. These may be used in combination (for example, "consecration and coronation" in English), or one may also speak simply of "the anointing." In every case, nevertheless, the intention of a given writer is not usually to restrict the sense of the term to any one aspect of the ceremonial, and all terms refer to the ritual that formally invested a monarch with his office. The ceremony was composed of four elements, some of which survived only vestigially, if at all, in some countries: the election, the acclamation, the anointing, and the crowning.

The ceremonial of crowning is older than that of anointing. Crowning was practiced in the Byzantine East, just as it had been in ancient Rome, and there were also biblical models for it. The first certain coronation in the medieval West is that of Charlemagne on Christmas Day, 800. Anointing, on the other hand, was practiced in Visigothic Spain as early as the seventh century. The pouring of oil upon a king's head was based upon the biblical model of the high priest's anointing of Hebrew kings, and the occidental act had obvious Davidic connotations. The Visigothic precedent appears to have been unknown in Frankish lands, however. For that reason, the early history of the rite must be regarded as an independent development among the Franks. Thus it is in the Frankish lands that the European precedent was set: When the papal legate anointed Pepin the Short in 751, he inaugurated a tradition that was to be repeated for the same king by the pope himself in 754; royal unction has ever since remained a part of European custom.

If, as Carlrichard Brühl has argued, anointing and crowning were joined into a single ceremony from the very moment of the former's introduction, then the rite developed unusually quickly for a liturgical act. It is more likely that the crowning was originally regarded as an act that created the secular ruler and that the anointing did the same for the spiritual ruler; the two were often administered in different times and places under the early Carolingians. From the coronation of Louis the Pious in 816, both were sometimes performed at the same time, and before the end of the ninth century Hincmar of Rheims had composed several texts that wove them into a unified ceremony. These texts became the foundations for the rite in all occidental countries, and some of the prayers and benedictions that the archbishop of

Rheims adopted, adapted, or composed are still to be found in the English ceremony.

The other two elements of the early ceremony require brief mention. In the Carolingian age Frankish kingship was theoretically elective. That certainly does not mean that there was anything like a democratic process involved, but only that certain barons could exercise enough power to select one or another member of the royal house as king. Although elections in the ninth and tenth centuries must always be interpreted within the context of contemporary political circumstances, permanent elective elements did enter coronation ceremonial, and they remained present in the liturgy and acts of various countries until the end of the Middle Ages. There was also almost always some sort of acclamation, which was a public expression, viva voce, of acceptance of the new monarch by those present at the ceremony. This was derived from the biblical shout, "God save the king" (1 Sam. 10:24).

The various elements were first brought together in the Frankish kingdom of the Carolingians and not in England as was formerly thought. Thence they spread throughout the several kingdoms of the Carolingian empire in the ninth century, to England at a very early date, and eventually to the rest of Europe. The liturgical character of the ceremony caused it to appear in numerous benedictionals and sacramentaries, and it is found in one form or another in a great many of the surviving medieval pontificals. English innovations were adopted in the West Frankish kingdom, as were East Frankish novelties, and all three kingdoms interacted upon each other to create a rite that was truly international, which has made it difficult to unravel its early history. Each country eventually displayed peculiarities that distinguished the history of its cermonial from that of its neighbors.

The ceremony of the Carolingian empire played a formative role in the creation of all other coronation rites in the West, as is demonstrated by the introduction of crowning in 800. The continuous elective nature of the imperial dignity, the requirement that the emperor be crowned by the pope, the complications of the journey to Rome, and eventually even the failure of many emperors to be crowned there— all these sharply distinguished the imperial ceremonial from its counterpart in the monarchies. Further oddities of the imperial ceremony included the kissing of the pope's feet twice during the ceremony, a coronation oath unlike that of any of the kings, and the holding of the pope's stirrup while the latter

mounted his horse after the ceremony. Furthermore, the liturgy was very different from that of the kings. The last emperor to be crowned at Rome by a pope was Frederick III in 1452. The ceremony was last performed for Emperor Charles V, who was crowned in 1530 at Bologna.

More important for the German rulers than their coronation as emperor was their coronation as king of the Romans (that is, of the Germans) at Aachen. This ceremony, normally performed by the archbishop of Cologne, gave them their practical political authority—to the extent that they possessed such—and the right to style themselves king and "emperor elect." Furthermore, as successors to Charlemagne, who had assumed the Lombard royal title, they had the right to a coronation at Milan with the iron crown of Lombardy. Finally, the emperors could have themselves crowned king of Burgundy at Arles. Very few German rulers were able to realize all four of the coronation rites to which they were entitled.

The primary liturgical singularity of the German ceremony was the scrutiny (*scrutinium*), a series of questions put to the king before his anointing. There was also a well-developed formal query to the people present inquiring if they wished that he who was about to be anointed be king. Nevertheless, it is difficult to associate either of these exclusively with Germany because numerous French texts borrowed the scrutiny from German ones, and there is a formal consent of the people in the French and English ceremonies as well.

The English kings were crowned at various places until William the Conqueror gave precedence to Westminster in 1066, after which they were normally crowned there by the archbishop of Canterbury. There is almost nothing to distinguish the English from the continental ceremonies during the Anglo-Saxon period except that the Anglo-Saxons were the first to formulate an oath that was not exclusively for the benefit of the bishops of the realm; this oath came to be copied and sworn on the Continent. With the Conquest, subtle differences crept into the English rite. The coronation oath came to be taken in the vernacular French (there also exists an Anglo-Saxon translation of one of the coronation oaths), whereas other monarchs swore their oaths in Latin down to the end of the Middle Ages. This marks a significant secularization of the ceremony, and the alliance of crown and church was never to be as close in England as it became, for example, in France. The most famous singularity of the English ceremony, the king's champion's challenge at the post-coronation banquet, may not have come into being before the thirteenth century. By far the most important English innovation after the Conquest is an addition to the coronation oath of 1308, by which the king swore to preserve "the laws and the customs" of the realm.

Coronations in France were performed at various places until 1129, when Philip, the eldest son of Louis VI, was crowned co-king (he died two years later and never reigned alone); after that, all medieval ceremonies took place in Rheims, the archbishop there usually officiating. It now appears that, until the early thirteenth century, the French ceremony followed essentially the German rite. Then it became necessary to revise the ceremony considerably on account of the adoption of the legend of the Holy Ampulla (which treats of the little vial of chrism sent from heaven at the moment of Clovis' baptism by Remigius of Rheims). The Holy Chrism that the ampulla contained is first mentioned in connection with a coronation ceremony in 1131 (coronation of Louis VII as co-king with his father, Louis VI). Three thirteenth-century texts—built upon tenth-century predecessors—incorporated the legend and created a ceremony that thereafter was essentially only elaborated upon. The Holy Chrism was thereby given a central role in the French ceremony and in French kingship, both of which, therefore, sharply distinguished France from other monarchies. Jean Golein wrote during the reign of Charles V that the king of France is anointed, "not with oil or balm fabricated by the hands of a bishop or apothecary, but with the celestial holy liquor that is in the Holy Ampulla" (*Traité du sacre*, 1372).

Like the English monarchs, the French touched for the king's evil (scrofula, a tuberculous skin disease) after their sacring, and the ability to touch successfully was considered a proof of the legitimacy of the king and the efficacy of royal unction. The French ceremony was peculiar also in that a major role was played in it by the twelve Peers of France after they came to be defined in the early thirteenth century.

Other countries had their traditions, too. The Norwegian kings were usually crowned at Niðoaros (Trondheim), the Swedes at Uppsala, the Neapolitans at Naples, and so on, and there were special insignia in most countries (like the holy crown of St. Stephen in Hungary or the Stone of Scone in England).

The variety of coronation ceremonials over so many centuries makes it impossible to give even the briefest outline of the course of a ceremony. In almost every case there was a lengthy liturgical act that included numerous prayers and benedictions, anointing, investiture with the symbols of office (crown, scepter or scepters, royal mantle, royal orb in some cases, ring, sword), and there may have been an investiture with symbols of knighthood (boots or sandals, and spurs). The ceremony usually closed with a mass, during which the monarch sometimes read the Evangel and made an expensive offering to the coronation church. Many countries terminated the ceremony with some sort of procession and post-coronation banquet. There are records of French ceremonies that began with the arrival of the assisting clerics at the church at 6:00 A.M. and that ended with the departure of the newly crowned sovereign only at 2:00 P.M. or later.

The constitutive aspect of the coronation ritual was extremely important in the earlier Middle Ages, and no one could claim to possess fully the royal title until he was anointed and crowned. This explains the haste with which William II Rufus (1087–1100) had himself crowned at Westminster—he wished to preempt any claims his brothers might have. The early Capetians solved the problem of succession by having the successor crowned co-king during the father's lifetime. Although it has been recently argued that the practice was largely the result of a series of accidents, it surely helped to establish the dynasty firmly upon the throne.

At the end of the Middle Ages the coronation was still looked upon as a necessity even though it was no longer juridically necessary: for example, before Charles VII's coronation at Rheims in 1429, Joan of Arc consistently referred to him as *gentil Dauphin*. In every country in which a coronation rite was essential, the mere fact that it had to be performed by a high official of the church inextricably bound the secular office of government to the Christian religion and flavored the character of medieval kingship.

BIBLIOGRAPHY

Marc Bloch, *The Royal Touch: Sacred Monarchy and Scrofula in England and France*, J. E. Anderson, trans. (1973); Alfred Boretius and Victor Krause, eds., *Capitularia regum Francorum*, in *Monumenta Germaniae historica: Legum*, sec. II, 2 (1897), containing the best edition of the texts of Hincmar of Rheims; Cornelius A. Bouman, *Sacring and Crowning: The Development of the Latin Ritual for the Anointing of Kings and the Coronation of an Emperor Before the Eleventh Century* (1957); Carlrichard

Brühl, "Fränkischer Krönungsbrauch und das Problem der 'Festbrönungen'," in *Historische Zeitschrift*, **195** (1962); Edward S. Dewick, ed., *The Coronation Book of Charles V of France (1338-1380)* (1899), the best edition of the lengthiest of the medieval French coronation *ordines*; Reinhard Elze, ed., *Die Ordines für die Weihe und Krönung des Kaisers und der Kaiserin* (1960), complete edition of the *ordines* for the coronation of the emperor; Robert Folz, *The Coronation of Charlemagne, 25 December 800*, J. E. Anderson, trans. (1974); Robert S. Hoyt, "The Coronation Oath of 1308: The Background of 'les leys et les custumes'," in *Traditio*, **11** (1955); Richard A. Jackson, "Les manuscrits des *ordines* de couronnement de la bibliothèque de Charles V, roi de France," in *Le moyen âge* (1976), and *Vive le Roi!: A History of the French Coronation from Charles V to Charles X* (1984); John Wickham Legg, *Three Coronation Orders* (1900); Leopold G. Wickham Legg, *English Coronation Records* (1901), the most complete collection of English texts, but badly in need of revision; Andrew W. Lewis, *Royal Succession in Capetian France* (1981); Janet L. Nelson, *Politics and Ritual in Early Medieval Europe* (1985); Henry G. Richardson, "The Coronation in Medieval England: The Evolution of the Office and the Oath," in *Traditio*, **16** (1960); Percy Ernst Schramm, *Festschrift Percy Ernst Schramm*, Peter Classen and Peter Scheibert, eds., 2 vols. (1964), *A History of the English Coronation*, Leopold G. Wickham Legg, trans. (1937), and *Der König von Frankreich: Das Wesen der Monarchie vom 9. zum 16. Jahrhundert*, 2nd ed., 2 vols. (1960); Claire Richter Sherman, "The Queen in Charles V's 'Coronation Book': Jeanne de Bourbon and the 'Ordo ad Reginam Benedicendam'," in *Viator*, **8** (1977).

RICHARD A. JACKSON

[See also **Anointing; Charlemagne; Hincmar of Rheims; King's Evil; Kingship, Theories of: Western Europe.**]

KINGSHIP, THEORIES OF. The period 800–1400 abounds in speculative analyses of political ideas in western Europe. The modern student, however, may be repelled by the apparent static quality of this mass of writing, which seems repetitive, abstract, and unrealistic. Far from claiming originality, medieval authors usually insist on their orthodoxy. They deal with problems that appear anachronistic, and their arguments appear overburdened with biblical, patristic, and classical references. Yet the Middle Ages transmitted to the modern world many of its concepts of government, law, sovereignty, legislative authority, judicial procedures, natural law, representation, and the state. Westerners have never com-

pletely lost the medieval passion for reducing political questions to basic universal principles.

Much of medieval political thought concerns monarchy because of the widespread existence of this type of regime—in England, Germany, Spain, Sicily, eastern Europe, and numerous principalities. The received corpus of patristic literature reflects the thought world of the later Roman Empire, with its imprint of Hellenistic forms of monarchy. For purposes of analysis, medieval theories of kingship can be isolated from their setting within church-state conflicts. Kingship will be considered here only as it appears in formal writings. Nothing will be said about the development of general attitudes toward monarchy as seen in other types of sources, such as juridical decisions and vernacular literature.

Although certain themes in monarchical thought do recur, the attempts of modern historians to synthesize all kingship theories in the Middle Ages are unsatisfactory. Scholars after World War I often exaggerated the constitutional elements in kingship. More recently others have emphasized the transition from liturgical to law-based kingship. While this distinction is useful—particularly as a tool in assessing the influence of ecclesiology—it requires qualifications (such as the role of public law in kingship theory). Since the 1960's the most popular theory of medieval kingship imposes a descending-ascending structure on all political thought. Descending here refers to power derived from God and his vice-regent on earth. The ascending thesis locates power in the people. But this contrived conceptual frame is misleading and simplistic, especially in its interpretations of "theocracy" and Aristotelian influence. Since the 1950's most scholars have focused on the specific political context in which works on kingship were composed. They have generally avoided the older "history of ideas" (*Ideengeschichte*) method, which tends to divorce ideas from their political environment.

CAROLINGIAN KINGSHIP

The idea of monarchy had few defenders in the Germanic West. Romano-Byzantine emperorship had little effect on theories of Germanic kingship. Frankish law codes and chronicles suggest an elective form of monarchy (although not incompatible with hereditary succession), and a king who was expected to wage war effectively, defend regional custom and privileges, protect the clergy and their property, and maintain the peace. Gregory of Tours (538/

539–594/595) praises rulers who settle disputes and safeguard churches and monasteries. The more optimistic Venerable Bede (672/673–735) places kings in the flow of providential history. God has selected certain kings to eradicate idolatry and heresy, to assist in spreading true doctrine and ecclesiastical discipline, and to provide examples of Christian conduct. But the total influence of these Germanic and Germano-Christian ideas of kingship upon Carolingian thought was slight.

Carolingian theories of kingship owed much to St. Augustine of Hippo (354–430) and Pope Gregory the Great (*ca.* 540–604), who together established the vocabulary and thought frame for political discourse in the Middle Ages. For them, kings have the important function of providing social peace, which lessens the occasions for sins of violence and allows the clergy to carry out their salvific duties. God uses rulers to punish sinners and provide a remedy for sin. But Augustine hestitates to go beyond this negative government function. The ruler is neither the embodiment of justice nor a moral leader. Gregory distinguishes clearly between the king's office and his person. As a kind of pastor who sets an example of ascetic virtue for his subjects, the ideal prince grudgingly abandons his prayerful solitude when God beckons him to love his neighbor. While the service of others is praiseworthy, in Gregory's view the political life remains a distraction from the spiritual life—hardly a promising intellectual environment for the creation of a philosophy of politics.

Charlemagne was the first Germanic king to infuse a clear sense of moral purpose into government. His adviser Alcuin (*ca.* 730–804) perceived a moral dimension in Charlemagne's actions and proclamations. The preservation of peace was a means that the emperor used to Christianize and civilize the Western empire. Governmental laws and coercion were to be supplemented by a network of schools. Less pessimistic than Augustine about the possibility of a reign of justice on earth, Alcuin envisioned an empire of mutual cooperation among Christians. His notion of *pax et concordia* implies some degree of earthly happiness. Charlemagne's empire was an approximation of the City of God, a replica of the Kingdom of Heaven on earth. Alcuin stressed the king's responsibilities to the church, which served to give political cohesion to his realm. Although the church enjoyed a quasi-independent status, it was closely associated with imperial administration. It never occured to Alcuin that the church could become a threat to royal authority.

Alcuin was no political thinker, but his exhortations to Charlemagne helped to establish a twofold legacy of kingly duties: protection of the church and leadership in promoting Christian behavior. Ninth-century churchmen would incorporate this twin function into their ecclesiologies. While Alcuin made God the source of all political authority, and emphasized the king's religious duties, he owed little to the sacral kingship expressed in Frankish and Anglo-Saxon traditions. Charlemagne's court scholars were fond of calling him a king-and-priest, but this fuzzy idea was never intended to supersede his public authority. When eulogists made Charlemagne another David, they were thinking more of his moral functions than of his priestly ones.

The idea of monarchy was closely scrutinized after the death of Charlemagne. External attacks on the empire, internal dissension, ineffective kings, assertive bishops and metropolitans, and beleaguered monks all served to encourage the affected groups to give more precision to the nature of royalty. The more far-reaching of these discussions were by clerics who usually treated kingship in the context of the unitary church. Jonas of Orléans (*d.* 843) in his *De institutione regia* makes the king a servant or minister of the church. Although the chief responsibility for peacekeeping belongs to the episcopacy, the latter must summon the king to assist in this undertaking. The prince in his turn aids the church in its salvific mission by living an exemplary life. The king should be just, merciful, kind, pious, and courageous. He aids orphans, widows, and the poor. Since God has ordained two separate jurisdictions within Christian society, the king should limit himself to temporal matters unless the bishops explicitly ask him to intervene in ecclesiastical affairs—for instance, to enforce an anathema.

In several treatises Hincmar of Rheims (*ca.* 806–882) elaborates on the king's dignity and duties, including specific suggestions on issues of public policy. His king is above all a promulgator of laws. He sustains church canons and clerical immunities. Even the bishops are subject to Roman imperial law; they are not to hamper the king in the performance of his secular duties. God set up princes in order to punish the wicked, and maintain the peace through the enactment and execution of the law.

Hincmar's definition of kingship comes close to that contained in the canonical collections of the period (mid ninth century), such as those of Pseudo-Isidore and Benedictus Levita. Pseudo-Isidore indicates that kings have enforced the church's conciliar decrees. Benedictus attempts to demonstrate the king's duty to use terror to uphold ecclesiastical privileges. Thus the higher clergy saw the king as a functionary of the church, an instrument that permits them to perform their task of saving souls. Of course the king operates in his own jurisdictional sphere, but this role is of secondary concern for the clerical authors. Although Hincmar was suspicious of all princes and wary of extensive royal power, he was on the whole more worried about kings becoming too weak than becoming too strong. He and other clerical writers of the time denied any right of resistance to royal *auctoritas*. Whatever the personal attributes of a particular prince, the office of the ruler is divinely sanctioned. Perhaps God does not literally command the prince to do a particular act, but he did create the institution of monarchy. No responsible churchman after the death of Louis the Pious in 840 would advocate rebellion in the tumultuous Western kingdoms.

In the writings of Hincmar, Jonas, and other episcopal authors there are extended treatments of the king's private virtues. It was believed that the prince's public qualities were manifestations of his personal life as a Christian. One of the contributions of ninth-century political thought was to make the "mirror for princes" (*speculum principis;* German: *Fürstenspiegel*)—an ancient literary genre that had been Christianized by Hellenistic and Byzantine apologists—a feature of Western monarchical thought throughout the Middle Ages.

Smaragdus of St. Mihiel (*d.* after 825) was the first Westerner to compose a Christian *Fürstenspiegel*. His *Via regia* is a guide to Christian ruling. The king should be unequaled in wisdom, justice, prudence, humility, mercy, detachment, patience, receptiveness to counsel, and the love of God and neighbor. Kingship is as much a matter of being someone as it is of doing something. Governments and policies are passing; virtue endures forever. The king in the *Via regia* and in subsequent speculum literature generally resembles the iconlike saint in medieval hagiography. Ninth-century thinkers sought the absolute and the eternal. They often idealized kings in universal terms isolated from time and place.

Smaragdus' archetype is also a description of a lay spirituality. In his mirror for monks (*Diadema monarchorum*) he carefully contrasts the two ways of life in the church. The monk is an ascetic in a monastery. The king is an ascetic in the world. His sense of duty moves him to assume the "burden" of governing. He would prefer, as Louis the Pious had done, to retreat into solitude. Pope Gregory had envisioned secular rulership as a kind of pastoral life; kings and bishops were both prelates. Smaragdus helped to launch a *speculum principis* tradition that made the king an activist ascetic.

Henceforth kingship was never able to free itself completely from this connection with the monarch's conduct as an ordinary Christian. The ascetic components in Smaragdus' royalist ideal are even more prominent in works by later monks. In the 850's Sedulius Scottus wrote his influential *De rectoribus christianis* in the same vein. But Sedulius makes more of the king's peacekeeping service than did Smaragdus. The king must crush rebellions and restrain pretentious bishops. It is not enough to establish temporal peace, since the absence of war can still be the occasion of a "bad" peace (*pax mala*). The Christian king should impose a "good" peace (*pax bona*) founded on true justice. He will guard monasteries from pagan marauders and local bishops. For Sedulius a genuine peace is essentially spiritual, the reign of Christ's justice. Yet his image of Christ's kingdom in this world has little to do with social justice or material prosperity. Sedulius' speculum vacillates between the search for a just order and an ideal of detachment.

The semiascetic king of Smaragdus and Sedulius appears in the royalist thought of other ninth-century monks, including Druthmar, Lupus of Ferrières, Notker of St. Gall, and Paschasias Radbertus. While the king's virtues in these writings are generally similar to those in the works of Jonas of Orléans and Hincmar of Rheims, the ecclesiological implications of the royal potestas are less discernible. Although the monastic authors are hesitant to trace the king's authority to God through the instrumentality of the hierarchical church, they helped to establish a literary tradition of the ascetic view of kingship that lasted until the early twelfth century. The influence of ascetic kingship roughly coincides with the period when the cultural influence of monasticism was at its greatest intensity. Given the presence of monks in royal courts, it is understandable that they should attempt to fashion an ideal of kingship in their own image. Monks, after all, looked to lay princes for protection.

As imperial authority disintegrated after Louis the Pious' death, monastic authors placed their trust in regional kings and lesser princes. Even in Anglo-Saxon England the popularity of ascetic kings can be seen in Asser's *Life of King Alfred* (*ca.* 893) and the anonymous vita of Edward the Confessor (written probably soon after his death in 1066). The close connection between secular rulership and lay spirituality appears in the account by Abbot Odo of Cluny (ca. 879–942) of Count Gerald of Aurillac, the lay lord who wages war for Christ, however reluctantly. Gerald's defense of the church against its enemies is spiritually meritorious. In Helgaud's life of Robert II the Pious (r. 996–1031) the king is a Christ figure who performs miracles, intercedes for his people before God, and instructs wayward bishops in theology. Abbot Odilo of Cluny (962–1049) makes Emperor Otto I and his wife Adelaide "philosophers" (that is, monks) who adapt the peace of the cloister to the needs of the entire empire. Similar expressions of saintly kingship can be seen in Ottonian imperial art.

In Anglo-Saxon England and early Capetian France the higher clergy also divinized the origin and function of monarchy, the best hope of stability. In Ottonian and Salian Germany the idea of regal pontificalism was especially pronounced because of the proximity of the German church to the monarchy. Through proprietary churches and lay investiture, the German king was the effective head of the church (caput ecclesiae). He performed all ecclesiastical functions except the sacramental. The boundary between lay and ecclesiastical rights was obscured by ceremony. By unction the king became the Lord's anointed. He was crowned "by the grace of God."

INVESTITURE CONTROVERSY

The investiture controversy between Pope Gregory VII and King (later Emperor) Henry IV, which started in 1075, gave medieval kingship its distinctive characteristics. Much of the ninth-century theorizing about secular authority had been done within speculations about the makeup of the church. Clerical thinkers displayed scant interest in defining the scope of the temporal power's legitimate authority, although the ruler's public powers were certainly recognized. But it was not until the late eleventh century that defenders of royalty accentuated the relative autonomy of the temporal order, thereby preparing the ideological way for the later emergence of the state and of state-church conflicts. Royalists (Henricians) were compelled to champion the temporal realm's independence against the papalists (Gregorians), who rendered the temporal subordinate to the spiritual.

This rush of kingship theories was a spontaneous reaction to the novel claims of the papalists. As a result, the responses of King Henry IV and his backers often have a hasty, confused quality about them. They are convinced that Gregory VII is usurping royal authority, but they seem less sure about the exact nature of that authority. They accuse the pope of interfering with the king's God-given rights. Since the king has cognizance over matters that the pope does not, the latter has no right to depose and excommunicate him. From this starting point the Henricians waver between two sets of arguments: regal-sacerdotal and dualist.

The traditional regal-sacerdotal arguments would seem better suited to justify the king's hold over German (and Italian) bishoprics and abbeys. Henry IV himself suggests such an approach in his assaults on Gregory VII. German kings had long encouraged a religious aura around their symbols of majesty. This quasi-priestly aspect of the monarchy harmonized with the king's various jurisdictional rights over ecclesiastical and lay lands. Since German princes and Italian cities often resisted Ottonian and Salian ambitions, the kings naturally emphasized their special position over all other types of authority. In their view, God entrusted his emperors with the power to suppress rebellions and preserve the peace.

Against the Gregorians the Henricians argued that the king had to restore peace and unity to all of Christian society. Even prelates should submit to imperial authority whenever the emperor was punishing evildoers, correcting sinners and heretics, administering justice, repelling foreigners on the borders, and assisting the helpless.

But another theme in Henrician literature is the dualist division between the temporal and the spiritual. The pope's improper attacks on the king disrupt the church's right order. The church's weapon is the Word; the state's, the sword. Popes too are subject to kings in temporal matters. Within the Gelasian and Isidorian traditions this dualist argument is simple and compelling. God established two jurisdictions within the church militant, and put one head over each. But the king can ask the pope in exceptional cases to help him. Similarly, the pope can ask the king to assist him in performing his sacramental duties and in prodding recalcitrant evildoers. The Henricians had to admit that many bishops possessed property in their own right, but this complication was at first not closely examined. The pope, then, cannot meddle in temporal matters on his own initiative, except perhaps in the patrimony of St. Peter.

The historian should not insist on too sharp a distinction between the regal-sacerdotal and the dualist viewpoints, for they are often combined in the same treatise or letter. A reasoned defense of secular authority was, after all, something fairly new. The Henricians had difficulty dealing with the obvious inferiority of temporal reality as compared with the spiritual, the prelatic anointing of kings and emperors, the basically nonsacramental character of royal unction, the Donation of Constantine (an eighth-century document, allegedly written by Constantine, in which the popes are given jurisdiction over the whole of western Europe), the clerical duty to care for the souls of laymen, the clerical prerogative to define temporal cases, the papal right to intervene in temporals when sin is involved, and the canon law with its ecclesiastical privileges. It would be anachronistic to expect a more cogent or precise analysis of kingship, for neither the papalists nor the royalists perceived all the ideological and practical implications of their propositions. The Henricians seem frantic in their attempts to muster a wide range of arguments from Roman law, rights of prescription and conquest, conciliar and papal decrees, canonical collections, the Bible, patristics, classical authors, Roman and Carolingian history, and customary law. By contrast, the papalist defense appears more self-consistent and self-confident.

The investiture controversy influenced subsequent discussions of kingship in the following ways:

1. Kingship henceforth was usually examined within the context of the two-power relationship.

2. The question of the origin of political authority was inseparable from considerations of kingship. In general, royalists made God the direct source of royal power. Papalists interposed the Roman church between God and ruler.

3. Political theory became more dualist. Both royalists and papalists recognized the king's right to administer the temporals of his realm. The differences between the two lay in the extent of the church's authority in temporals. The clerical writers gradually expanded the number of cases in which the church could legitimately intervene in those temporal affairs normally reserved for princes. Since the king derives his authority ultimately from the church, the latter should determine his competence, at least in select instances. The king is the church's assistant, commissioned to use the sword to defend ecclesiastical possessions, true doctrine, and the downtrodden. But while the royalists likewise recognized the church's corporate unity, they retorted that the king was re-

sponsible only to God when temporals were involved. The royalists made few claims to intervene in spiritual affairs; they were simply protecting themselves from ecclesiastical encroachments. By the fourteenth century, however, the situation was reversed; it was the church that sought to barricade itself against the royalist claim of emergency jurisdiction. Prior to 1300 churchmen had used Gelasian dualism to safeguard the church from lay intrusions against temporals; after 1300 the lay powers used the same doctrine to sanctify such intrusions.

4. As a corollary, royalists made less use of the traditional regal sacerdotal argument. Theologians refined their definitions of priesthood (sacerdotium) and its prerogatives. Canonical thought and procedure clarified the parameters of ecclesiastical jurisdiction. The Carolingian "king and priest" (rex et sacerdos) was falling into disuse. The royal unction was said to be a sacramental, not a sacrament. As kingship became desacralized, the pope assumed the title of vicar of Christ (vicarius Christi). Many imperial symbols were transferred to the Roman see, the hub of an increasingly centralized church. Certainly thaumaturgical kingship survived in popular beliefs and liturgical ceremonies, particularly in France and England. The Norman Anonymous (or Anonymous of York, ca. 1100) testifies to the strength of the notion of rex Christus, the earthly monarch who participates in the nature and rulership of Christ the King. Since Christ's royal power was superior to his sacerdotal power, the earthly king's power is superior to that of the bishop, whose jurisdictional competence stems directly from the king. Unlike his more Gelasian contemporaries, the Norman Anonymous combines sacramental and political authority in the Christian king, a figure of the Heavenly Melchizedek. As Christ was both human and divine, he possessed magistracy in both temporal and spiritual realms—and so, consequently, does his royal typus on earth. But this Christocentric approach to kingship was already out of date by 1100, as kings in Germany, France, England, and Spain had come to rely more on legalistic justifications.

5. As the role of monks changed, the ideal of ascetic kingship faded. Peter Damian's (1007–1072) nonascetic view of monarchy illustrates this transition to more law-based ideas of rulership. In his letters to King Henry IV, Peter makes the usual homages to the king as a type of Christ and God. But Peter forgoes lecturing the king on his private virtues. Instead, he concentrates on the royal office, which carries with it the charge to defend the

church, particularly by expelling simoniacs. In his speculum for King Henry I of England (written *ca.* 1102–1105), the monk Hugh of Fleury also dwells on the dignity of secular power. The king protects the people from evil, and rules both laity and clergy in justice and equity. Since the king is the *imago Dei* and the bishop the *imago Christi,* the former rules the latter just as the Father rules his Son. The monarch leads men to heaven through coercion and laws; the priest, through the word of doctrine. The king defends orphans, widows, and the poor. His most prominent virtues are sobriety, justice, prudence, and temperance. Hugh of Fleury's portrait of the perfect king seems closer to the cultured king of John of Salisbury's *Polycraticus* than to the ascetic *typus* of Smaragdus' *Via regis.*

The decline of ascetic kingship is more pronounced in the writings of other twelfth-century monks. Suger's vita of Louis VI, a speculum for the young Louis VII (written between 1137 and 1145), is superficially cast in a hagiographical mold. Before beginning his kingly career, Louis VI announces that he longs to become a monk at the monastery of St. Denis. He gets his wish at the close of his reign, when he is permitted to die at St. Denis, wearing the monastic habit. But virtually the entire vita is about Louis VI's exterior life—the suppression of rebellion in the domain and the defense of the church—not about his interior disposition. Odo of Deuil's crusade chronicle of Louis VII mentions the king's personal virtues only as an aside. The monastic reformer Bernard of Clairvaux (1090–1153), an ardent supporter of the dignity of the royal office, avoids any suggestion that kings act as models of ascetic virtue, a role reserved for monks and prelates. He praises his model prince, Count Theobald, as an upholder of the church's liberty and a righteous defender of the oppressed. Bernard's ecclesiology will not permit him to grant any other functions to lay lords. The spiritual duties of each order—monastic, clerical, and lay—are kept distinct.

6. The "problem of the empire" became a major theoretical issue following the breakup of the Carolingian empire into many kingdoms and principalities. Monarchs outside Germany tried to justify their independence of the emperor. The emperor in his turn had to justify his autonomy vis-à-vis the pope.

7. The papalist conception of secular authority was further developed. Since the spiritual realm was ontologically higher than the temporal, spiritual leaders were superior to temporal ones in the church. The pope thus held both swords, but he

could allow princes to wield the temporal sword on his behalf. The papacy's struggle with emperors indirectly undermined the emperor's theoretical claims over the national kingdoms and encouraged French and English kings to assert their temporal independence of imperial dominion. Adages such as "The king is emperor in his own realm" and "The king recognizes no superior in temporals" are expressions of this resistance to imperial claims. It might be noted that Pope Innocent III (1198–1216) saw in the French king's independence an implicit acceptance of the papacy's incidental jurisdiction in the temporals of France. The later, more extreme claims of papalists—such as Egidius Colonna, James of Viterbo, Augustinus Triumphus, from the late thirteenth and early fourteenth centuries—expanded the sphere of extraordinary competence, but their ideological beginnings lay in the investiture conflict.

8. To counter the papalist claims, royalists were obliged to search for bases of political power outside theology and ecclesiology. As royalists lost faith in the polemic worth of royal sacerdotalism, they were inclined to place the locus of political authority in Roman law, natural law, and the people.

JOHN OF SALISBURY AND THE LAW

The most important treatise on kingship in the twelfth century was the *Polycraticus* of John of Salisbury (*ca.* 1110–1180). This work reflects the current tendencies in monarchical thought and suggests some new directions. Although much of the book echoes the clichés of the *Fürstenspiegel,* it also focuses on the institutions of the body politic. John's king is above all a wise and pious Christian who sets the moral tone for his subjects. He is a self-disciplined paragon of virtue. He punishes evildoers, administers justice, leads his army against God's enemies, protects his people. The king is subject to the law of the land and the higher law of God, as revealed in the Scriptures. The influence of Gregorian clericalism is evident. The church summons kings to perform those temporal tasks—such as the punishment of criminals—that would demean the spiritual arm. Kings are lesser officials in the church who assist the clergy in their spiritual work.

But within this Gregorianized *speculum principum* John of Salisbury achieves a tour de force unequaled in previous medieval writings on politics. Especially noticeable is the lessening of the ascetic and sacral aspects of kingly virtue. John's ruler, guided by moderation, seems worldly compared with Smaragdus' prince. The king is literate and urbane, steeped in biblical/patristic and classical learning. He acquires wisdom from pagan authors, and tries to elevate his subjects to the level of Sophia. Special attention is given to the role of classically educated counselors who help to educate the monarch in justice.

John's frame of reference is not the church universal or the empire but, rather, the res publica, meaning England. The king is an intergral part of the realm. Even John's discussion of the two powers is placed within the individual kingdom. The commonwealth is an autonomous unit, analogous to the human person, that places obligations on all subjects, including clergy. All parts of the body are interdependent and relate to the proper functioning of the whole. The head is the king; the soul, the clergy; the heart, the senate; and so on. The importance of the clergy in the body politic, however, must not be overemphasized, for the head often acts in its own right. The point is that the king and the clergy cooperate within a corporate juridical entity. Such a notion of organic unity compelled theorists to conceive of kingship in terms of obligations to the community. It is a short step from the commonwealth to the "community of the realm."

The law defines the interrelationship of the parts of the res publica. The king may be a lawmaker, but he is under the law, just as is any other member of the realm. By "law" John appears to mean customary law, in addition to natural law and divine law. Whatever he meant by "positive law," John was in agreement with the twelfth-century tendency to define monarchy in juridical terms. Later jurists would look to the *Polycraticus* as a rationalization of limited monarchy. Despite the anachronisms in the book, it does hint at the constitutionalist side of English legal writings evident from Bracton in the thirteenth century to Fortescue in the fifteenth century.

John's unexpected interjection of tyrannicide into his tract is not necessarily a restriction of royal power. Rather, he intended to warn Henry II of England (or Roger II of Sicily) against abusing his God-given authority. God sometimes appoints human agents to correct or even kill unjust kings, although John certainly did not advocate such measure against Henry II. John's bold analysis of tyrannicide is consistent with his personal view of kingship. No king is indispensable or sacrosanct, since all men can be corrupted. Paradoxically, John's discussion of tyrannicide serves to demonstrate the importance God places on political rule in his economy of

salvation. He even resorts to violence to ensure that good kings assist him in governing the universe.

DUALISM ESTABLISHED: 1150–1296

Theories of kingship after John of Salisbury are markedly dualist. The king's sacral powers are largely passed over. He is the head of his realm in temporals and receives his authority directly from God. Kingship theories move toward further clarification without always being tied to ecclesiology or two-power controversies. No doubt the developments in canon law, papal centralization, and theology—which further elucidated ideas such as priesthood, power of the keys, investiture of prelates, unction, sacraments, sin—encouraged royalists to expand their notions of monarchy. But even more important was the growth of de facto royal power and monarchical institutions, particularly in Angevin England. The utilization of Roman law in the national kingdoms greatly strengthened the king's authority in his judicial and legislative functions.

Italian civilians circumvented many feudal constraints on imperial authority by making the emperor the source of the law. He is a public power who can abolish bad laws and create new ones whenever necessity or utility requires. The national kings outside Germany adopted the new science of jurisprudence to disentangle the crown's rights from the mass of other claims. The focus on public law enabled royalist thinkers to make the king responsible for maintaining the common good of the realm. Kingship from about 1150 to 1296 dealt less with the need to defend the realm from external attack than with the valuable service the monarch provides his people by administering justice, upholding customary law, and clarifying lines of judicial authority. Royalist writers told of the marvelous advantages that would result from a royal government less inhibited by regional interests and personal privileges.

The king's function as a lawmaker obliged thinkers to confront the classic problem of his relation to the law. The Germanic and feudal traditions had stressed the ruler's subservience to custom, and his duty to seek counsel and make decisions in council. It was of course assumed that the king was under God's law. In the twelfth and thirteenth centuries royalist writers often stress the necessity for kings to rule with justice, equity, and reason. But most assert that the king is not legally bound to obey the law. He cannot be coerced to follow the law because he is responsible only to God, who punishes despots.

Since he is morally obligated to obey human positive law, he is not absolute or arbitrary.

Aside from civilian and canonist thought, the most far-reaching analysis of the problem appears in the works of the lawyer Henry de Bracton (*d.* 1268). The king as *solutus legibus* (not bound by the laws) is under no man. He cannot be legally compelled to submit to positive law, even though in his coronation oath he swears to obey it. He is not subject to human justice and punishment. Bracton never read Carolingian treatises on kingship, but he does place the king under God and law (*sub deo et lege*), being obliged to follow God's commands and moral law. Bracton's kingship is impersonal, constitutional, and within the English, Germanic, and biblical traditions. Yet he uses the revived Roman law to bolster the king's authority in legislative and, especially, judicial matters.

The king's relation to the law was further clarified in thirteenth-century discussions of natural law. Civilians and Aristotelians used natural law to shield secular authority from ecclesiastical claims. With the idea of natural law, royalists attempted to bypass the two-swords theory that had placed ultimate jurisdiction in the hands of the clergy, particularly the pope. Natural law provided a convenient way of submitting the king to the law while simultaneously keeping him unfettered by custom.

In his *De regno* (also known as *De regimine principum*) Thomas Aquinas (*ca.* 1225–1274) demonstrated the feasibility of a reasoned defense of natural-law monarchy, without resorting to the moralizing and the analogies of the *Polycraticus*. The strong kingship in the *De regno* is, to be sure, not completely consistent with Aquinas' views on mixed monarchy (monarchy combined with aristocracy and democracy) and the law, expressed in his other works. Yet he presses hard for a naturalist explanation of the origin and makeup of the political community. His king is firmly established within the body politic and the natural law. The prince can override positive law when the common good requires such action. The state's primary function is to lead subjects to natural virtue by the use of right reason. From there, the clergy will provide the necessary grace and spiritual assistance to complete the requirements for salvation. Although ultimately the handmaiden of the church, the temporal power possesses a relative good. Aquinas wants to reduce the church's involvement in temporals and the state's involvement in spirituals. His kingship is basically ecclesiological and theological.

The Aristotelian Egidius Colonna (*ca.* 1247–1316) liberated Thomist kingship from its two-power framework. His ideal king is less constrained by the law, the community, and the clergy. In his *De regimine principum* Egidius places the king below natural law but above positive law. He uses Aristotle's idea of the best man to illustrate the advantages of flexible royal rule. He justifies even hereditary succession by means of a naturalist analysis of royal government *(regimen regale)*. To ensure that the prince possesses a commitment to the common good, he must be properly educated from his early years.

While Egidius' use of Aristotle buttressed similar ideas of public necessity in natural and positive laws, his exploitation of Aristotle permitted royalists to attribute a positive, yet extra-ecclesiastical, function to temporal power. In his attempt to construct a self-sustaining theory of monarchy based on Aristotle's *Politics,* Egidius chose not to complicate his theory by discussing royal prerogatives in spirituals. Like that of most contemporary Scholastics, Egidius' thought is academic, experimental, and provisional. His concept of the common good prepared the ideological way for casual or incidental jurisdiction. He came close to this principle when he gave implicit permission for the king to lead his people to natural virtue, to interfere in the church's temporals, to abrogate custom in the interest of the common good, to tax privileged lands and persons. His *De regimine principum* was enormously popular in the fourteenth century precisely because it did not press the argument from the common welfare into more controversial areas, thus giving the tract the appearance of objectivity and universality.

Egidius states flatly that it is better to be ruled by the best man than by the best laws. But at the time the more usual response to this *questio,* as found in the commentaries on Aristotle's *Politics* (such as that of Peter of Auvergne) and the quodlibets, is tilted toward the best laws. It is better to be ruled by the best laws per accidens because human princes will likely succumb to passion. But per se the best man is preferable, because he can apply abstract principles to concrete instances. Despite the authors' qualification that, alas, the great man probably cannot be found, they ennoble the principle of monarchy. It might be noted that Aristotelian writers scrutinize not the origin of kingship but the benefits to be had in a *regimen regale.* Their utilitarian argument is that the general welfare is best served when someone enforces existing laws efficiently and justly.

Egidius shows the advantages of both the best man and the best laws, without attempting to harmonize them. His preference for the best man is balanced, without comment, by a discussion of the need for the king to respect customary law and seek counsel. In keeping with the *Fürstenspiegel* tone of his educational program, Egidius describes the kind of advisers who should surround the king.

In the fourteenth century Aristotle's *Politics* and *Ethics* were often summoned to defend the rights of the community. But royalists found in the same texts support for royal forms of government. The English secular Scholastic Walter Burley (*ca.* 1275–after June 1344) in his commentary on the *Politics* suggests that monarchy—and hereditary succession—is best, although with the usual limitations imposed by law and custom. Royalists were attracted to Aristotle's treatments of the common good and the naturalist polity. It is not surprising that they professed to see in the *Politics* the Peripatetic's approval of the great man, for even the ancients drew the same conclusion.

NATIONAL KINGSHIP: 1296–1315

Kingship theories emerged from controversy. Ninth-century bishops struggled to free themselves from king and pope. The investiture dispute involved the king's right to grant authority to churchmen. Baronial resurgences obligated lawyers such as Bracton to explain how royal prerogatives worked within the English legal and judicial traditions. Using civilian jurisprudence and historical arguments, Hohenstaufen emperors assailed popes who blocked imperial incursions into Italy. At the end of the thirteenth century, French and English kings encountered papal resistance when they taxed their clergy without Rome's consent.

King Philip IV the Fair (1285–1314) and Pope Boniface VIII (1294–1303) exchanged diatribes over the degree of royal jurisdiction in the French church; the conflict started in early 1296 when Boniface issued a bull prohibiting secular taxation of the clergy without papal approval. In the course of this struggle both sides came to remake their respective perceptions of kingship. Philip's publicists contended that the king had the right to tax church lands in a national emergency. During the investiture controversy the Henricians had emphasized the origin of temporal authority in order to counter papal claims over temporals. In the clash between Philip IV and Boniface VIII, the royalists concentrated on the king's duty to protect his kingdom from external foes (usually unnamed, since the English and Flemish were presumably Christian). They found the source of secular authority in history, Roman law, theology, Scripture, and ecclesiastical decrees; according to their arguments, the king had casual jurisdiction over all temporals in the realm, including those of the clergy.

Modern historians refer to Henry IV's defenders as Henricians, but they never refer to Philip IV's supporters as Philipians. And for good reason. The new royalists do not personalize the tax issue. They focus not on King Philip IV, but on the realm of France. The king is but a member of the body politic. While his normal task is to protect custom and privilege, he occasionally suspends custom when the kingdom is threatened. The clergy cannot reply that their landed possessions are exempt, since former kings gave them to the church. The *Disputatio inter clericum et militem,* an anonymous tract written in France between 1296 and 1303, makes the cleric appear unpatriotic for his unwillingness to contribute to the nation's defense. Kings provide clerics with their physical needs so that the latter can better care for souls. Surely the king can repossess these lands if the priests are derelict in their holy duties. They should not complain if the king occasionally taxes their lands, since the revenues are used to protect the clergy and their property.

The publicists cleverly associate the defense of the realm with the popular grumbling about church wealth. They exploit the widespread demand for a more spiritual church and make Philip the Fair a zealous reformer. Although the major thrust of the royalist line is dualist—the king is the chief guardian of the realm's temporals—the religious element is not ignored. In the *Rex pacificus* (an anonymous tract published in 1301) the king defends a holy realm and a holy people. The kingdom is a kind of mystical body *(corpus mysticum),* an analogue of the church. For Guillaume de Nogaret (*ca.* 1260–1313) Philip's attack on Boniface is in fact a defense of the faith and the universal church. The royalist position is intermingled with crusade terminology and ecclesiological images. The commonplace defense of the realm somehow becomes the defense of the church. The king's custody of the realm's temporals legitimizes his control of the clergy.

The foremost defense of Philip IV is the *De potestate regia et papali* of John of Paris (written in 1302). In this Thomist work casual jurisdiction provides the link between church and state. To shore up his conciliar theory, John places the origin of monarchical authority in the people. But in fact he uses the people *(populus)* as a rhetorical device to consolidate the royal grip over the French church. Certainly John's two-power theory presumes a unified Christian society. But both powers actually function independently of each other, except for those rare instances when one head is deficient—and even then the king's acual and de jure powers surpass those of the pope. The inherent goodness of the res publica justifies the king's nearly absolute authority in time of danger. The clergy are in effect absorbed into the political order, without meaningful appeal to outside aid or special prerogatives.

The apologists for Boniface VIII generally deny the natural origin of regna. They often take the extreme view that all temporal authority derives from papal overlordship. In his *De ecclesiastica potestate* (*ca.* 1301) Egidius Colonna—the author of the royalist *De regimine principum* in 1285!—grants the papacy dominion over all temporals. The king holds his kingdom insofar as he is loyal to the church. Modeled after Augustine's City of God, the church determines the function of the lower orders in the hierarchy of peace. When antipapal writers propose a world monarchy, they tend to restrict the church to spirituals. In *De monarchia,* a philosophical argument for a universal empire (from shortly after 1300), Dante separates the spheres of operations for the two powers. The philosopher-king coordinates the particular regna in a peaceful world order, in which all human potential is realized. Engelbert of Admont (*ca.* 1250–1331) insists that the empire must be preserved because it provides a degree of justice, peace, and self-sufficiency not possible in the smaller kingdoms.

Following the decline of the empire after 1250, papalists, imperialists, and royalists debated the relation of the kingdoms to the empire. Canonists and theologians were divided over the issue. Some of them, such as Hostiensis (*ca.* 1200–1271), would have kings subject to the emperor. Others agreed with Innocent III that the king of France recognized no superior in temporals. But by 1300 most papalists preferred to place kings under the emperor, who himself was subordinate to the Roman see. Philip the Fair's propagandists used Romanist and Aristotelian arguments in favor of the king's independence in temporals. Pierre Dubois, an official at Philip's court, would have the French king become the new universalist head of a revived Christendom. With the launching of a crusade the king was to restore peace to Europe by means of international arbitration.

Imperialists in the fourteenth century continued to defend imperial authority. With a grasp of political reality Bartolo da Sassoferrato (1313/1314–1357) distinguishes between the de jure rights of the emperor over the regna and the de facto independence of the latter. Since the imperial office is elective, writes Lupold of Bebenburg (*d.* 1363), the church of Rome has no jurisdiction over the empire. The king of Germany is supreme in the empire before he ever receives the title of emperor. Lupold is more interested in defending the rights of the German ruler than in making unrealistic claims over the provinces of the Holy Roman Empire. He and other post-glossators developed a theory of the ruler's legal sovereignty. While the power of the prince is unlimited, he is obligated to will only what is for the common good of society. He is bound by the jus gentium (law of nations) to make useful laws.

The political realism of the civilians is absent in the more extreme of the papalist theories. Rejecting the traditional dualism of the two powers, Augustinus Triumphus (*ca.* 1275–1328) makes the pope the supreme regal power. The laws of merely secular kings can have validity only when they are approved by the pope. The Portuguese Franciscan Alvaro Pelayo (or Alvarus, *d. ca.* 1349) grants the natural origins of the temporal powers; but they are imperfect until the church sanctifies them by grace. The supreme pontiff, who holds the fullness of power in both spiritual and temporal matters, has the right to appoint, correct, and depose any monarch in Christendom.

Kingship theories in the fourteenth century retained many of the assumptions found in ninth-century tracts. The literary traditions within which these ideas were expressed help to account for this remarkable continuity. Remnants of Alcuin's synthesis survive. First, the king is seen as a moral guide who leads his people to Christian virtue and, at least indirectly, to heaven. Even William of Ockham (*ca.* 1285–1349), who sharply desacralized secular government, assigns an ethical purpose to rulership, although this end is achieved more by coercion than by moral example. Second, the ruler's chief function is to maintain peace and right order. Third, monarchical government protects the church. The clergy are secured in their persons and their property in order that they may carry out their spiritual duties.

But changed conditions had affected kingship. The empire was in disarray, while the national monarchies were strong. The papacy's prestige dwindled after Boniface VIII's death in 1303. The development of the two laws (natural and positive), scholastic methods, and Aristotelian categories gave substance to monarchical thought. Writers had learned how to defend monarchy without extensive reference to ecclesiological frameworks. The king was still, of course, the minister of God (minister Dei), but on terms defined by the throne, not the church. Ironically, the late medieval prince used the notion of minister Dei to defend royal interventions in church temporals. Casual jurisdiction was taken to be an expression of the king's conventional duty to safeguard ecclesiastical goods.

Carolingian ecclesiology was implicitly dualist. But late medieval dualists, such as William of Ockham, make the temporal order function almost in its own right, with scant reference to ecclesiastical direction. Carolingian writers had emphasized the interdependence and mutual necessity of both powers—an idea greatly expanded from the eleventh century on. Fourteenth-century royalists, however, reduced the points of contact between the two powers. They moved closer to the acceptance of church and state as distinct entities, each operating within its own sphere. They often restricted the clergy to evangelical concerns, and expanded the crown's rights over the temporals of both laity and clergy.

Seven themes are evident in late medieval theories of kingship. First, there is an emphasis on the realm as the pivot from which to define monarchy. This convergence on a specific kingdom gave royalists the advantage of attaching the king's person to an object of loyalty that was more abstract and permanent. The king was the embodiment of the kingdom and its inhabitants. He derived his power and duties from the realm, which largely existed apart from the empire and the Holy See. Any threats to the survival of the regnum obligated the crown to increase its demands for contributions from its subjects. The modern notion of the state is implied in the ratio status regni (reason of the state of the realm).

Second, as a corollary, the realm is seen as a nation with its own customs and traditions. The subject should be loyal not only to the monarch but also to his fatherland (patria) and to the national community. Rising national sentiment served to unite the people with their ruler.

Third, royal authority is closely identified with the common good of the realm. This idea of the general welfare is associated with the king's casual jurisdiction, which he and he alone evokes in times of national emergency. In normal times he is simply to protect the rights and privileges of his subjects.

Fourth, the king's peacekeeping role is almost an end in itself, only loosely related to the lofty ideal of natural or divine justice. Marsilius of Padua (d. ca. 1342) strips away the metaphysical basis of government by extolling the ruler's duty to use coercion in the cause of social order. If dissension is to be curbed, power must be localized in a single place.

Fifth, monarchy is a desirable form of government because it is utilitarian. Fourteenth-century kingship, to be sure, did not lose its religious aura. The Carmelite Jean Golein, a translator at Charles V's court, said that the French monarch put on the royal religion with his anointment robes. The king was a priestly ruler, the head of a mystical body. Legends of thaumaturgical power and the oriflamme were very much alive in France. So, too, were the commonplace arguments in favor of monarchy as inherently the best form of government. Aristotelian defenses of one-man rule abound, as do analogies of earthly kingdoms with their heavenly prototypes. The issue of hereditary versus elective monarchy was debated. But increasingly theorists point to the benefits that result from a well-administered monarchy of whatever kind. They give less attention to philosophical rationalizations and more to de facto advantages that subjects will obtain. William of Ockham has no illusions about the merits of monarchical rule. No godlike prince for him. He simply wants a leader who possesses the will and the means to punish criminals. His descriptions of the ideal regime are qualified with cold realism.

Sixth, the king is more explictly bound to the law and the community. This stress on the king's duty to obey the law runs parallel with the contemporary tendency to extend his legislative and judicial authority. The tensions between those two trends often can be found in the same treatise. The continuous appeal of limited monarchy was due largely to the presence of groups in the realm who opposed the spread of royal authority. Theory to this extent reflected institutional reality.

In Spain the Reconquest spurred royalist writers to exalt the king's God-given powers. Borrowing from the Roman law, the Siete partidas, a major legal code from the second half of the thirteenth century, makes the monarch responsible for administering justice to his people. Other writers warn of the evils of tyranny. Francesc Eiximenis (ca. 1326–1409) depicts the views of the cortes and the nobility. The king is bound by a contract with the community to uphold the latter's interests.

The drift to limited monarchy was especially

marked in England, where the pact between king and community was firmly established within English traditions and social structures. Magnates, knights, and burgesses could often cooperate against an authoritarian crown. When kings felt too constrained by barons and parliament, they asserted their prerogatives. Richard II (1377–1399) insisted that he could legislate by himself, and could tax his subjects as he saw fit. The struggles between crown and parliament in the fourteenth century produced a body of theory that would prove useful for later proponents of both limited and unlimited kingship. Constitutionalists such as Sir John Fortescue (1385/1395–after May 1479) drew upon these earlier defenses of parliament, popular consent, and the common law. But the theoretical foundations of Tudor absolutism were laid in the same period, with considerable help from the English clergy.

Calls for checks on royal power by European theoreticians were, however, generally moderate and cautious. They did not advance popular sovereignty, popular participation in royal decisions, political-institutional restraints on the king, or extensive individual rights of subjects. Their idea of limitation referred mainly to the prince's moral duty to rule in the interests of the common good (bonum commune), within the confines of the natural law.

Seventh, the royal grip on ecclesiastical possessions is tightened. The monarchies demanded contributions from the church for both the defense of the church and the defense of the kingdom. The dualist assumptions of the royalist writers are increasingly salient. The Somnium viridarii, a tract written about 1376, is a systematic defense of the French king's rights in church temporals. The author skillfully incorporates these rights into his treatments of the crown's sovereignty and inalienability. The radical Songe du vergier (ca. 1378), a vernacular popularization of the Somnium, links the clergy's obligations more explicitly to the crown as a public power and also to the nation as a fatherland (patrie). The king's right of casual jurisdiction permits him to intervene in the church's immunities.

John Wyclif (ca. 1328–1384) makes the king a virtual pastor of souls who diligently compels the clergy to perform their spiritual duties. Since the administration of property is a worldly activity, the clergy should be disendowed in the interest of the entire church. Presumably the secular ruler is one of the righteous elect. His interest in the salvation of his subjects obligates him to assume jurisdiction over church property when the clergy are lax, and directs

such property to pious ends. A proto-Erastian, Wyclif made the prince a powerful reformer. But the king's functions are largely negative, for his charge is to punish evildoers, not to inspire subjects to virtue. Wyclif's two-power theory is less dualist than that of most of his contemporaries. His reformist kingship represents a significant minority tradition that influenced later theories of state interference in church policy.

CONCLUSION

It is difficult to generalize about kingship theories in western Europe after 1400 because they conformed more closely to the national conditions of the particular countries. As two-power theories and elaborate ecclesiologies became increasingly unrealistic after the failure of the conciliar movement, each monarchy had to adapt its own ideological traditions to changed political circumstances. The speculum principis exhortations continued to remind kings of the need to be virtuous and to do justice. But they were adjusted to the writer's disposition concerning his monarch: whether he wanted to expand or restrict royal authority. Medieval theories of kingship did not move in a linear direction toward either the constitutional or the absolutist thought of the sixteenth and seventeenth centuries. These latter theories drastically reshaped their medieval antecedents. But one assumption in particular survived beyond medieval kingship: government should possess a high moral purpose. Kingship theory stubbornly kept its ties to an idea of government that was subordinate to natural and divine laws. Not until the nineteenth century did European political thought discard its medieval frame.

BIBLIOGRAPHY

Charles C. Bayley, "Pivotal Concepts in the Political Philosophy of William of Ockham," in *Journal of the History of Ideas,* **10** (1949); Marc Bloch, *The Royal Touch,* J. E. Anderson, trans. (1973); Lester K. Born, "The Perfect Prince: A Study in Thirteenth- and Fourteenth-century Ideals," in *Speculum,* **3** (1928), and "The *Specula principis* of the Carolingian Renaissance," in *Revue belge de philologie et d'histoire,* **12** (1933); Robert W. Carlyle and Alexander J. Carlyle, *A History of Mediaeval Political Theory in the West,* 6 vols. (1903–1936); William A. Chaney, *The Cult of Kingship in Anglo-Saxon England* (1970); Lowrie J. Daly, *The Political Theory of John Wyclif* (1962); Dante Alighieri, *On World Government; or, De monarchia,* Herbert W. Schneider, trans. (1957); Pierre Dubois, *The Recovery of the Holy Land,* Walter I. Brandt, ed. and trans. (1956); E. Ewig, "Zum christlichen Königsgedanken im

Frühmittelalter," in *Vorträge und Forschungen*, 3 (1954); John N. Figgis, *The Divine Right of Kings* (1896; 2nd ed. 1914, repr. 1965).

John E. A. Jolliffe, *Angevin Kingship* (1955, 2nd ed. 1963); John of Paris, *On Royal and Papal Power*, John A. Watt, trans. (1971); John of Salisbury, *The Statesman Book*, John Dickinson, trans. (1927, 1955, 1963); Ernst H. Kantorowicz, *The King's Two Bodies: A Study in Medieval Political Theology* (1957); Fritz Kern, *Kingship and Law in the Middle Ages*, Stanley B. Chrimes, trans. (1939, 1956); Ewart (Kellogg) Lewis, *Medieval Political Ideas*, 2 vols. (1954); Bryce D. Lyon, *A Constitutional and Legal History of Medieval England* (1960); Marsilius of Padua, *The Defender of the Peace*, Alan Gewirth, trans. (1967); Arthur S. McGrade, *The Political Thought of William of Ockham* (1974); Charles H. McIlwain, *The Growth of Political Thought in the West* (1932); Theodor E. Mommsen and Karl F. Morrison, trans., *Imperial Lives and Letters of the Eleventh Century* (1962); Karl F. Morrison, *The Two Kingdoms* (1964); John B. Morrall, *Political Thought in Medieval Times*, 2nd ed. (1962); Alessandro Passerin d'Entrèves, *Dante as a Political Thinker* (1952).

Ian S. Robinson, *Authority and Resistance in the Investiture Contest* (1978); Jean Pierre Royer, *L'église et le royaume de France au XIVe siècle d'après le "Songe du vergier" et la jurisprudence du Parlement* (1969); Percy E. Schramm, *A History of the English Coronation*, Leopold H. Wickham Legg, trans. (1937), and *Der König von Frankreich*, 2 vols. (1939–1960); Beryl Smalley, ed., *Trends in Medieval Political Thought* (1965); Joseph R. Strayer, *Medieval Statecraft and the Perspectives of History*, J. Benton and T. Bisson, eds. (1971); Gerd Tellenbach, *Church, State, and Christian Society at the Time of the Investiture Contest*, R. F. Bennett, trans., 2nd ed. (1959, repr. 1970); Thomas Aquinas, *On Kingship*, Gerald B. Phelan, trans. (1949); Walter Ullmann, *A History of Political Thought: The Middle Ages* (1965); Michael Wilks, *The Problem of Sovereignty in the Later Middle Ages* (1963); George H. Williams, *The Norman Anonymous of 1100 A.D.* (1951).

THOMAS RENNA

[See also **Alcuin of York; Alfred the Great; Aquinas, St. Thomas; Asser; Augustine of Hippo, St.; Augustinus Triumphus; Bartolo da Sassoferrato; Bede; Benedictus Levita; Bernard of Clairvaux, St.; Bracton, Henry de; Carolingians and the Carolingian Empire; Charlemagne; Dante Alighieri; Decretals, False; Dictatus Papae; Disputatio inter Clericum et Militem; Donation of Constantine; Edward the Confessor, St.; Egidius Colonna; Eiximenis, Francesc; Engelbert of Admont; Fortescue, Sir John; Gelasius I, Pope; Gregory of Tours, St.; Gregory I the Great, Pope; Gregory VII, Pope; Helgaud; Henry I of England; Henry II of England; Henry IV of Germany; Hincmar of Rheims; Hostiensis; Hugh of Fleury; Investiture and Investiture Conflict; James of Viterbo; John of Paris; John of**

Salisbury; Jonas of Orléans; Louis VI of France; Lupold of Bebenburg; Lupus of Ferrières; Marsilius of Padua; Nogaret, Guillaume de; Notker Teutonicus; Ockham, William of; Otto the Great; Peter Damian, St.; Philip IV the Fair; Pierre Dubois; Roger I of Sicily; Sedulius Scottus; Siete Partidas; Smaragdus of St. Mihiel; Somnium Viridarii; Suger of St. Denis; Wyclif, John.]

KIOSK (Turkish: *köshk*), in Turkey, a small building intended for pleasure, retreat, or observation. A pleasure kiosk is situated at a locale where it commands a pleasant view of a natural or artificial landscape. A kiosk is usually a freestanding structure. It may consist of a single room, of several rooms, or even of more than one story, but it is not equipped to serve as a residence. A kiosk can be part of a larger structure, semidetached from it. A glassed-in pavilion or a penthouse is referred to as a kiosk. The furnishings traditionally consist of cushions and low tables decorated with lively patterns and rich colors. The interior beauty is to match that of the outside and please the senses of the occupant.

ÜLKÜ Ü. BATES

KIOT (or *kivot* [Russian], from the Greek *kibotos*, ark), a wooden icon case, usually highly decorated with carvings or painting, sometimes with doors. It ranges in height from a few inches to a few feet, and is found in Orthodox churches or in homes, usually holding a particularly revered icon. The word is also used to denote a large, freestanding frame or shrine for an icon, such as is found in Orthodox churches.

GEORGE P. MAJESKA

[See also **Icons, Manufacture of.**]

KIRAKOS OF GANJAK (1200/1210—1271/1272), one of the most important Armenian historians of the thirteenth century. The few biographical details known about him are drawn primarily from his *History of Armenia*. According to this, Kirakos received his early education in eastern Armenia, at the monastery of Getik. Subsequently he studied for a prolonged period with the historian Yovhannēs

Vanakan (d. 1251). His education was interrupted by the invasions of the Khwārizmshāh Jalāl al-Dīn Mangūbirdī, beginning in 1225, during which time Vanakan and his students fled several times to more secure places. In 1236 Vanakan and Kirakos were taken captive by the invading Mongols. They were kept for several months and employed by the Mongols as secretaries, until they were able to escape. Almost nothing is known about the remaining years of Kirakos' life. In 1251 he participated in a movement to crush a rebellion in the church. Around 1255 he interviewed the Cilician Armenian king Hetᶜum I (1224–1268) in eastern Armenia, after the latter's return from a visit to Batu Khan.

Kirakos' *History* is a lengthy work in sixty-five chapters, narrating the history of Armenia from the fourth century to 1266/1267, where it ends abruptly. The work is most valuable for twelfth- and thirteenth-century events because the author utilized now-lost Armenian works on the Seljuks. He was an eyewitness to the Mongol invasions, and during his captivity he learned Mongolian. Chapter 32 of the *History* contains a lexicon of fifty-five Mongolian terms with their Armenian equivalents, one of the earliest monuments of the Mongolian language. Furthermore, Kirakos had access to the most influential Armenian lords of the period, which also made him well qualified to write about the workings of his own society.

BIBLIOGRAPHY

Sources. The critical editon of Kirakos' *History of Armenia* is *Patmutᶜiwn Hayocᶜ*, Karapet A. Melikᶜ-Ōhanjanian, ed. (1961). *Istoria Armenii*, L. A. Khanlarian, trans. (1976), is a Russian version of this classical Armenian text. A full French translation of an earlier, noncritical text was made by Marie Félicité Brosset, *Deux historiens arméniens: Kiracos de Gantzac . . .* , I (1870–1871).

Studies. Robert G. Bedrosian, *The Turco-Mongol Invasions and the Lords of Armenia in the 13–14th Centuries* (diss., Columbia, 1979); John Andrew Boyle, "Kirakos of Ganjak on the Mongols," in *Central Asiatic Journal*, 8 (1963), and "The Journey of Hetᶜum I, King of Little Armenia, to the Court of the Great Khan Möngke," in *Central Asiatic Journal*, 9 (1964); P. H. Oskean, "Der Geschichtsschreiber Kyrakos von Ganzak" (in Armenian), in *Handes Amsorya*, 36 (1922).

ROBERT BEDROSIAN

[See also **Armenia: History of; Armenian Literature; Hetᶜum I; Historiography, Armenian.**]

KIRGHIZ, a Turkic, Muslim people of central Asia, purported to be the principal nationality of the Kirghiz SSR within the USSR. Kirghiz medieval history consists of two distinct periods: that of the Yenisei Kirghiz, who lived in the southern part of central Siberia and developed a composite semisedentary civilization between the sixth and thirteenth centuries, and that of the Tien Shan Kirghiz, who were partly formed from Yenisei Kirghiz tribes that had migrated to the westernmost reaches of the Tien Shan Mountains, primarily between the thirteenth and fifteenth centuries, in the wake of Mongol invasions.

Chinese and Islamic sources, as well as archaeological evidence, show the Yenisei Kirghiz as a Turkic-speaking ethnic group that had superimposed itself, and eventually turkicized, the older Paleosiberian populations of the upper Yenisei. Some of these autochthonous populations were called Khakas, so that the ethnonyms Kirghiz and Khakas were at times used interchangeably in Chinese sources. The Kirghiz became the ruling group in the kingdom, whose sovereign was called *khan* or *qaghan* in Kirghiz and *azho* in Khakas. The headquarters of this ruler was in the only Kirghiz town mentioned by name, Kemijkat. The political structure of the kingdom reached relative sophistication, to the point where, in addition to the ruler, there was a government with ministers and other officials. Stockbreeding, agriculture, hunting, fishing, mining, and handicrafts, as well as trade, were practiced by various segments of the population.

In 840 the Kirghiz destroyed the Uighur khanate centered in Mongolia and until about 926 were the dominant power in inner Asia. They continued to have peaceful relations with China but extended their rule southwestward into Chinese Turkistan. After the collapse of their empire in Mongolia and Turkistan, the Kirghiz continued to enjoy an independent existence on the Yenisei until they became in 1207 and, more lastingly, in 1218 the first foreign nation to be conquered by Genghis Khan's Mongols.

The Yenisei Kirghiz shared the written cultural tradition of inner Asian Turks, using a script partly derived from a Syriac alphabet, partly from native Turkic symbols. The runelike angularity of this script resulted from the fact that it was used mainly for inscriptions cut into tombstones. A great number of such tombstones have been found on the territory of the Yenisei Kirghiz; they reveal considerable wealth in herds and land owned by certain individuals, suggesting the privileged position of Kirghiz aristocracy. Some indicate the presence of Manichaeism among the otherwise heathen Yenisei Kirghiz.

In their new homeland in the western Tien Shan Mountains of central Asia, the Kirghiz absorbed the remnants of the older local populations as well as various Mongol components that had migrated there. They kept some features of their Yenisei civilization while abandoning others, becoming almost exclusively mountain nomads of the seasonal vertical transhumant type. Stockbreeding almost entirely replaced agriculture. There were no permanent settlements, and portable felt tents (yurts) became the only type of dwelling. Sheep, horses, camels, and, in the southern parts of the western Tien Shan and in the Pamirs, yaks were raised. The handicrafts and trade decreased, and the runelike writing system disappeared. An oral art was practiced, however, in which epic poetry reached perhaps the highest degree of perfection among the Turkic peoples. The Tien Shan Kirghiz, unlike the Yenisei ones, never formed a unified kingdom. Rather, it was their language, way of life, and complex tribal structure that provided the common denominator. Most of these transformations are believed to have been completed by the end of the fifteenth century. The islamization of the Kirghiz, however, did not begin until the following century.

BIBLIOGRAPHY

Vasili V. Barthold, *Kirgizy (Istoricheskii ocherk)* (1927), reprinted in his *Sochinenia,* II, pt. 1 (1963), 471–543, and "Kirgiz," in *Encyclopaedia of Islam,* new ed., IV (1980); René Grousset, *The Empire of the Steppes,* Naomi Walford, trans. (1970); Sergei V. Kiselev, *Drevniaia istoria Iuzhnoi Sibiri* (1951); Leonid R. Kyzlasov, *Istoria Tuvy v srednie veka* (1969).

SVAT SOUCEK

[See also **Mongol Empire, Foundations.**]

KIRMIZ. See **Qirmiz.**

KISWA, the textile covering of the Kaaba, the most sacred of the Muslim sanctuaries. Traditionally, the Muslim ruler controlling Mecca renewed the kiswa annually at the time of the hajj. Providing the kiswa made the mark of the sovereign visible to all Muslim pilgrims. Covering the Kaaba began as early as the time of the second caliph, ᶜUmar ibn al-Khaṭṭāb, in 634. The name of the caliph, his vizier, the weaving site, and the date were usually inscribed on the kiswa. Often several layers of fine cloths and many colors, even stripes, were used.

BIBLIOGRAPHY

Ibn Jubayr, *The Travels of Ibn Jubair,* V, William Wright, ed. (1852), and Michael J. de Goeje, ed. (2nd rev. ed. 1907), 83, 95, 127; Ferdinand Wüstenfeld, ed., *Die Chroniken der Stadt Mekka,* II (1859, repr. 1964), 54, for an extract from al-Fāsī; R. B. Serjeant, "Material for a History of Islamic Textiles," in *Ars islamica,* **15–16** (1951), which provides an English trans. of an extract from al-Fāsī.

IRENE A. BIERMAN

[See also **Kaaba; Textiles, Islamic.**]

KITĀBKHĀNA, a Persian term for a library or a place where books were copied and bound. The introduction of paper into the Islamic world in the mid eighth century stimulated both the production and the collection of books. By the early ninth century sizable collections were known, and some were formally organized as libraries. In Islamic libraries books were customarily grouped by subject and placed flat on shelves in cupboards. A register of the library's contents was often made. In some libraries readers were provided with writing materials so that they might prepare their own copies.

Library collections evolved in conjunction with the intellectual concerns of the Islamic community. Those of mosques naturally contained texts of religious importance. Private libraries had a wider range of materials. Some early collections, such as that of the Abbasid caliph al-Maʾmūn, included works in Greek or Syriac for study and translation into Arabic. Wide-ranging collections were also assembled by the Fatimid rulers in Cairo and the Spanish Umayyads in Córdoba. The Fatimid library is said to have been rich in historical texts, and the Umayyad one was noted for its literary works.

After the fall of these dynasties their libraries were dispersed. Some books were destroyed, but many were sold at auction and entered other collections. With the proliferation of madrasas during the eleventh and twelfth centuries, new libraries were created for them.

Many libraries used scribes and bookbinders to maintain or augment their collections. During the fourteenth century, private or court libraries began to produce luxury books with rich illuminations and even paintings. This trend is particularly evident in Iran, where the *kitābkhānas* of the Jalayirids, Timurids, and Turkomans became as much centers of producing books as repositories for them.

BIBLIOGRAPHY

Adam Mez, *The Renaissance of Islam,* S. Khuda Baksh and David S. Margoliouth, trans. (1937, repr. 1973), 172–177; Olga Pinto, "The Libraries of the Arabs During the Time of the Abbasides," F. Krenow, trans., in *Islamic Culture,* 3 (1929).

PRISCILLA P. SOUCEK

[See also **Córdoba; Libraries; Madrasa; Ma^ɔmūn, al-; Manuscripts and Books: Islamic.**]

KIVORII. See **Darokhranitelnitsa.**

KJALNESINGA SAGA, which was probably composed about 1320, is based on older sagas, on various other written and oral sources, and on place names. The only fully developed character is Búi Andríðsson, who seems to be modeled on the titular hero of *Qrvar-Odds saga,* and who dominates the action of the story from beginning to end. He is unique among saga heroes in that, as a young man, he carries no other weapon than a sling.

Because of his refusal to sacrifice to the pagan gods, Búi is outlawed. In retaliation he burns down the pagan temple—the detailed description is a borrowing from *Eyrbyggja saga* or *Heimskringla*—and slays the owner's son. After a series of skirmishes and the abduction of a young woman, Búi sails to Norway on the advice of his prescient foster mother. Here King Harald Fairhair punishes him for the desecration of the temple by sending him in search of a chessboard, which is in the possession of Harald's foster father, the giant king Dofri. Búi spends the winter with the giant's daughter, with whom he en-

genders a son, and returns in the spring with the chessboard. King Harald now demands that he wrestle a black giant, whom he kills by crushing his ribs on a pointed rock—a loan from *Finnboga saga.* Twelve years after his return to Iceland Búi meets his own end by having his ribs crushed on a rock in a wrestling match with his son. Búi's death was no doubt intended to be understood as poetic justice for his callous reluctance to avenge the death of his father, who was slain by the owner of the temple destroyed by Búi. Búi's treatment of Esja, his fostermother, and especially of the two women who bore his children was also callous.

Kjalnesinga saga is one of the better examples of late sagas of native heroes *(Íslendingasögur),* which were strongly influenced by the popular sagas of ancient times *(fornaldarsögur).* Its chief purpose seems to have been entertainment. It is preserved intact in one vellum from the second half of the fifteenth century and in several vellum fragments and numerous paper transcripts.

BIBLIOGRAPHY

Kjalnesinga saga, in *Íslendinga sögur,* XII, Guðni Jónsson, ed. (1947), and in *Íslenzk fornrit,* XIV, Jóhannes Halldórsson, ed. (1959). See also "The Saga of the Men of Keelness," in *Four Icelandic Sagas,* Gwyn Jones, trans. and intr. (1935).

PAUL SCHACH

[See also **Eyrbyggja Saga; Family Sagas, Icelandic; Finnboga Saga.**]

KLARA HÄTZLERIN. See **Hätzlerin, Klara.**

KLÁRI SAGA. The tale of Klárus is an Icelandic *riddarasaga* (tale of chivalry) presumably composed in the middle of the fourteenth century. The work holds a unique position among the Icelandic *riddarasögur,* which generally contain no factual information regarding the circumstances of their composition. *Klári saga,* however, commences by informing us that the story was recounted by Bishop Jón Halldórsson, who had found the original, a Latin metrical narrative, in France. No such work is known today. The Norwegian Jón Halldórsson was bishop of Skálholt from 1322 to 1339, but around

1300 he had studied, as a young Dominican monk, in Paris. It is not clear from the opening statement in *Klári saga* whether Jón Halldórsson himself had translated the story or whether he had told it, and someone else had later written down his account from memory.

The "King Thrushbeard" motif—the taming of a haughty, cruel princess—is at the heart of *Klári saga*. When Klárus, son of Emperor Tiburcius of Saxland, learns about the beautiful Princess Serena, daughter of the king of the Franks, he becomes infatuated with her and is determined to marry her. Although his teacher, the wise Master Perus of Arabia, tries to dissuade Klárus from the undertaking, the latter persists in his plan to woo Serena. For his apparent lack of table manners at a festive meal, Klárus is verbally abused by the princess and then driven away from court. By appealing to her cupidity, however, Klárus finally succeeds in marrying Serena, but only after repeated frustrations and humiliations. The lengthy denouement depicts the vengeance Klárus wreaks on his wife for her earlier cruelty to him. During her various trials and tribulations she proves to be a model of patience and fidelity. The saga concludes with some moralistic reflections.

Klári saga bears traces of a Latin original in the use of the double dative, and in certain un-Norse participial constructions. Loanwords regularly appear with proper Latin inflection. The title of the work, *Klári saga* (The tale of Klárus), shows use of Latin forms, and the saga is replete with rhetorical questions reminiscent of Latin usage. The saga's indebtedness to the courtly style of the translated *riddarasögur* is manifested primarily through a moderate use of synonymous collocations and alliteration.

The two oldest redactions of *Klári saga* are preserved in MS AM 657b, 4to (*ca.* 1350) in the Arnamagnæan Institute in Copenhagen, and in Codex Holm. 6, 4to (*ca.* 1400) in the Royal Library in Stockholm. In addition to these two repositories, manuscripts of *Klári saga* are also in the National Library of Iceland in Reykjavik, and in the British Museum. A metrical version of *Klári saga*, the *Rímur af Clares og Serena*, is known from eighteenth-century manuscripts (JS 58, 4to; Lbs 638, 4to) in the National Library in Reykjavik.

BIBLIOGRAPHY

Gustaf Cederschiöld, ed., *Clari saga*, in *Altnordische Saga-Bibliothek*, 12 (1907); Bjarni Vilhjálmsson, ed., "Clari saga," in *Riddarasögur*, V (1954); Alfred Jakobsen, *Studier i Clarus saga: Til spørsmålet om sagaens norske proveniens*, in *Áprbok for Universitetet i Bergen*, Humanistisk Serie, 1963, no. 2 (1964); Erik Wahlgren, *The Maiden King in Iceland* (1938).

MARIANNE E. KALINKE

[See also **Riddarasögur.**]

KLEIMO (or *kleima*), a seal or stamp, as in a hallmark. In icon painting the *kleimo* is the border of small narrative scenes surrounding the main picture. They are usually scenes from the life and miracles of the saint who is the major figure of the icon, but they may also depict other saints or scenes that are related to the major subject.

GEORGE P. MAJESKA

[See also **Icons, Russian.**]

St. George and the Dragon with *kleimo* showing scenes from the saint's life. Russian icon painting, 14th century. RUSSIAN MUSEUM, LENINGRAD

KLIROS (Greek: *kleros,* literally, "clergy") is the raised platform located outside the iconostasis on the left and right sides of the front of an Orthodox church. These areas, sometimes blocked from the view of the congregation by icons in tall frames, are the traditional areas for the cantors and choirs during divine services. The fact that the *kliros* has two parts is a relic of the earlier tradition of antiphonal singing.

GEORGE P. MAJESKA

[See also **Iconostasis**.]

KNEZ LAZAR. See **Lazar Hrebeljanović.**

KNIGHT IN THE PANTHER SKIN. See **Shot͑a Rustaveli.**

KNIGHTS AND KNIGHT SERVICE. Traditionally, the western European lay aristocracy of the tenth, eleventh, and twelfth centuries was viewed as an elite of landholding knights. Scholars were inclined to accept, though not without qualification, the contemporary formula dividing society into those who prayed, those who fought, and those who toiled—*oratores, bellatores, laboratores.* It was recognized that *bellatores* might vary enormously in wealth and power: some were landless household knights, while others occupied alods rather than fiefs and thus owed no feudal service. Nevertheless, the typical knight was seen as a fief holder who rendered homage and service to his lord in return for the fief. The lord might in turn be the fief-holding vassal of a higher lord, while the knight might be served by knightly vassals one step down on the feudal pyramid.

As a result of more recent scholarship, this hierarchical concept has been largely rejected, at least for most of western Europe in the period before about 1200. The warrior aristocracy is now commonly divided into at least two distinct groups, knights and *nobiles,* that coalesced only in the later twelfth or thirteenth century. Until then, knights occupied a distinct and intermediate level in European society: above the peasantry, below the aristocracy. The *nobiles* were wealthy hereditary landholders exercising broad jurisdictional powers. The knights were their military retainers, usually of humble means, defined by their military vocation rather than their lineage.

The distinction between the older and newer views arises in part from a difference in the definition of knight. Formerly the term was associated almost exclusively with a mastery of the techniques of mounted combat, certified by the dubbing ceremony. The knight, or chevalier, was the armored warrior mounted on his war-horse. Ultimately from *cheval,* the French for horse, comes the English word "chivalry," the code of knightly behavior. St. Anselm listed as the equipment necessary to the knight his war-horse—his "most trusty companion"—together with bridle, saddle, and spurs, and the knight's own arms, his hauberk, helmet, shield, lance, and sword. Since such equipment was possessed by *nobiles* and military retainers alike, and since the ceremony of investiture with arms (dubbing) was, in one form or another, common to all, earlier scholars grouped all mounted, fully armed warriors into a single knightly elite, differing in wealth and power but sharing a single vocation and ideology.

Recent scholarship, while continuing to accept these views up to a point, has tended to stress what Joseph R. Strayer calls "the two levels of feudalism." A series of detailed studies of social structures in various regions of France and the Low Countries has disclosed a gap between the great noble families and their knightly retainers.

Georges Duby, drawing on his meticulous examination of the Mâconnais, sees the nobles (*principes, proceres,* or *optimates*) and the knights (*milites*) emerging as a two-tiered aristocracy toward the end of the tenth century. The nobles were responsible for maintaining peace and public order because of their assumption of royal authority or, in some instances, the possession of a special charisma based on their descent from heroes or saints. The ordinary knights, the *milites,* were their auxiliaries and dependents, lacking a distinguished lineage and possessing little or no land. In the beginning, *nobiles* and *milites* did not normally intermarry, and contemporary records routinely distinguished between them. But as the eleventh century progressed, the gap narrowed, Duby argues, until by about 1100 "the French aristocracy formed a single whole," an *ordo militum.* Further regional studies have widened the gap between *nobiles* and *milites,* and postponed their assimilation to the late twelfth or thirteenth century.

This view, now generally accepted, denies an aristocratic status to ordinary knights until the time of their absorption into the old nobility. The absorption occurred at different times in different regions, but nowhere, not even in Duby's Mâconnais, can it be dated before the mid twelfth century. Until then the *nobiles* constituted a distinct socioeconomic group, descended for the most part from great Carolingian families, preserving its distinctiveness by avoiding nonaristocratic marriages, and never identified in contemporary sources simply as *milites*. The very term *miles* implied dependence: before the twelfth century, writers seldom identified someone as a *miles* without naming his lord. William of Poitiers reported that the future William the Conqueror, as duke of Normandy, scornfully denied that he was a mere *miles* of the king of France. For although princes and *nobiles* were dubbed to knighthood and shared with their ordinary knights the vocation of the *bellator,* they participated in warfare as commanders, not common warriors. They, not their *milites*, exercised political and jurisdictional authority, the power to coerce and to command.

Gradually, however, the *milites* began to blend into the old aristocracy. They acquired aristocratic privileges and jurisdictional rights, married into the old families, sometimes erected fortified dwellings on their lands, and ceased to be identified by a separate, nonaristocratic title. The sources began referring to holders of military tenures, great and small, as *domini* (lords) while the term *miles* came to acquire such prestige that it became a fitting appellation for even the greatest warrior-aristocrat. The growing dignity of the knightly title owed much to the emphasis placed by the church on the vocation of the Christian warrior. The dubbing ceremony became a "sacrament of knighthood." Some scholars have associated the elevation of knights with the crusading movement and the renown of military orders such as the Knights Templars and Teutonic Knights. Others have pointed to the celebration of knightly prowess in contemporary literary works such as the *Song of Roland, Tristan and Iseult,* and the Arthurian romances. Whatever the reasons for it, the fusion of *milites* and *nobiles* resulted in a new aristocracy of knight-landholders of varying degrees of wealth set against the nonaristocratic majority of the lay population.

Recent scholarship, in short, is largely agreed that knights—*milites*—emerged around the late tenth century as a separate class of military retainers in the entourages of great families, usually serving as garrisons in their castles. In time many *milites* acquired lands, but they remained a class apart until the later twelfth or thirteenth century. Such, roughly, was the pattern in Namur, Picardy, Flanders, Hainault, Troyes, Burgundy, Poitou, Normandy, and elsewhere. In Germany there emerged a class of unfree knights, *ministeriales,* who served in the military retinues of kings, bishops, and nobles, and during the thirteenth century blended into the free nobility.

This two-tiered model has necessarily been presented in an oversimplified form. For one thing, it ignores the castellans, a lesser aristocratic group whose appearance in the late tenth century coincided with the emergence of castles as instruments of defense and territorial control. More generally, the sources for various regions employ a considerable variety of terms for knights and nobles, some of which strongly suggest the existence of intermediate levels. Writers in the Mâconnais around 1100 distinguish between common knights (*milites gregarii*), knights of moderate nobility (*milites mediae nobilitatis*), and knights of the highest nobility (*milites primi nobilitatis*), and it seems unlikely that the boundaries between these groups were sharply etched. The Norman sources disclose a hierarchy of at least three tiers—*nobiles* (or *divites*), *magnates* (or *proceres*), and *milites* (or *equites*)—and here too some blurring at the edges can be detected. Again, adventurous young knights from noble families might serve in the military retinues of other lords. There is evidence from several French regions of noble cadet lines slipping downward into the status of *milites,* and in a number of instances, particularly in the strongly governed Anglo-Norman state, of *milites* ascending into the nobility through royal favor and marriages to noble heiresses. Sally Harvey has detected a class of common, smallholding knights in post-Conquest England, yet the pipe rolls and feudal surveys of Henry II's reign display a socioeconomic spectrum extending from the holders of fractions of knights' fees to the holders of scores and even hundreds of fees.

Surveys of knights' service were undertaken during the twelfth century in England, Normandy, Champagne, Norman Sicily, and elsewhere. They mark an important advance in the systematization of the feudal military obligation. Originally all *milites* in good health were expected to fight in their lords' battles, but in time, as kingdoms and principalities coalesced, great princes imposed exact quotas of knights on their tenants in chief. The earliest evidence for such quotas comes from England under William the Conqueror, who, as most scholars would now agree, imposed military quotas on virtually all his tenants in chief, churchmen and laymen alike, in numbers ranging up to sixty knights and possibly more. The abbot of Abingdon, for example, owed thirty knights to the king's host and the same number for garrison duty at Windsor Castle. When King Henry I summoned these knights to the royal army in 1101, one of Abingdon Abbey's military tenants declined to serve and the abbot was obliged to find a substitute. The king expected thirty knights, and it would not do to send him twenty-nine. The era of quantification had dawned, at least in Norman England, and it was now a relatively easy step for the monarchy to transmute the quota into a monetary payment in lieu of military service. Such payments, known as scutage (shield money), became commonplace in twelfth-century England. As knights gradually settled on their lands, and as their service was increasingly restricted by custom—to forty days a year within the boundaries of the realm—the monarchy often found it more convenient to take their money rather than their service and to hire obedient, battle-ready mercenary knights in their place.

By at least the early 1130's the Norman kings of England had imposed similar military quotas on their tenants in chief in the duchy of Normandy. During the twelfth and thirteenth centuries the practice of assigning quotas and commuting them for money payments spread from England and Normandy into various parts of France, and into distant lands that had fallen under French influence—southern Italy, Sicily, Greece, and the Crusader States. In the course of the thirteenth century, as knightly equipment became increasingly elaborate and costly, heirs of knightly families began to postpone the ceremony of knighthood and sometimes to remain unknighted throughout their lives. Having become assimilated into a hereditary nobility, they were now assured of their social and economic position through the inheritance of their patrimony and aristocratic status. No longer did their freedom and sustenance depend on their knightly vocation. An heir of knightly lineage might now spend his entire life as a squire or valet without jeopardizing his social position.

Ever since their first appearance, knights had owed their military importance to the dominant role of armored cavalry in warfare. The twelfth-century Byzantine princess and historian Anna Komnena declared that the impact of a charging body of French knights was such as "might rupture the walls of Babylon." Throughout the twelfth and thirteenth centuries, foot soldiers continued to participate in com-

bat, and on occasion a commander would order his knights to dismount "so that they might make a more determined stand." But after the beginning of the fourteenth century the military domination of the mounted knight was challenged decisively by major advances in infantry tactics. With the coming of the longbow, pike, halberd, and cannon, knights relinquished their role as a warrior elite. But as they did so, they placed all the more emphasis on their social prerogatives and chivalric ethos. Knightly pageantry became more ostentatious, heraldry more intricate. The new age witnessed a proliferation of elaborate tournaments and of new knightly orders, such as the Order of the Garter. The great museum collections of knightly arms and armor, banners, and emblems are apt to date from late medieval or early modern times, when the knightly style had become more colorful and ornate than ever before but when knights no longer dominated the battlefields of Europe.

BIBLIOGRAPHY

George T. Beech, *A Rural Society in Medieval France: The Gâtine of Poitou in the Eleventh and Twelfth Centuries* (1964); Marc Bloch, *Feudal Society*, L. A. Manyon, trans. (1961); Constance B. Bouchard, "The Structure of a Twelfth-century French Family: The Lords of Seignelay," in *Viator*, **10** (1979), esp. 45–46; Éric Bournazel, *Le gouvernement capétien au XIIᵉ siècle, 1108–1180* (1975); Jacques Boussard, "Les mercenaires au XIIᵉ siècle: Henri II Plantagenet et les origines de l'armée de métier," in *Bibliothèque de l'école des chartes*, **106** (1946), and "L'enquête de 1172 sur les services de chevalier en Normandie," in *Recueil de travaux offert à M. Clovis Brunel*, I (1955); Robert Boutruche, *Seigneurie et féodalite*, 2 vols. (1959–1970); Marjorie Chibnall, "Mercenaries and the *familia regis* under Henry I," in *History*, **62** (1977); Noël Didier, *Le droit des fiefs dans la coutume de Hainaut au moyen âge* (1945); Georges Duby, *La société aux XIᵉ and XIIᵉ siècles dans la région mâconnaise* (1953), and *The Chivalrous Society*, Cynthia Postan, trans. (1977), esp. 112–122, 158–170; Theodore Evergates, *Feudal Society in the Baillage of Troyes Under the Counts of Champagne, 1152–1284* (1975), esp. 144–153 and comprehensive bibliography of regional studies; Guy Fourquin, *Lordship and Feudalism in the Middle Ages*, Iris Lytton Sells and A. L. Lytton Sells, trans. (1976), esp. 78–87; François Louis Ganshof, *Feudalism*, Philip Grierson, trans. (1952); Léopold Genicot, *L'économie rurale namuroise au bas moyen âge (1199–1429)*, I, *La seigneurie foncière* (1943), and II, *Les hommes. La noblesse* (1960)—vol. II containing a fundamental contribution to the current conception of *milites* and their relations with the nobility—and "La noblesse au moyen âge dans l'ancienne 'Francie': Continuité, rupture, ou évolution?" in *Comparative Studies in Society and History,* 5 (1962); Olivier Guillot, *Le comte d'Anjou et son entourage au XIe siècle,* 2 vols. (1972); Sally Harvey, "The Knight and the Knights Fee in England," in *Past and Present,* no. 49 (1970).

Charles H. Haskins, *Norman Institutions* (1918); C. Warren Hollister, *The Military Organization of Norman England* (1965), esp. chap. III; Jean François Lemarignier, *Le gouvernement royal aux premiers temps capétiens, 987–1108* (1965); Archibald R. Lewis, *The Development of Southern French and Catalan Society, 718–1050* (1965), esp. 287–314; Ferdinand Lot and Robert Fawtier, gen. eds., *Histoire des institutions françaises au moyen âge,* I, Michel de Bollard, *Institutions seigneuriales* (1957); Jane Martindale, "The French Aristocracy in the Early Middle Ages," in *Past and Present,* no. 75 (1977); Lucien Musset, "L'aristocratie normande au XIe siècle," in Philippe Contamine, ed., *La noblesse au moyen âge, XIe–XVe siècles: Es sais à la mémoire de Robert Boutruche* (1976); Édouard Perroy, "Social Mobility Among the French *Noblesse* in the Later Middle Ages," in *Past and Present,* no. 21 (1962); Timothy Reuter, ed. and trans., *The Medieval Nobility: Studies on the Ruling Classes of France and Germany from the Sixth to the Twelfth Century* (1978); Sir Frank Stenton, *The First Century of English Feudalism, 1066–1166,* 2nd ed. (1961); Joseph R. Strayer, "The Two Levels of Feudalism," in Robert S. Hoyt, ed., *Life and Thought in the Early Middle Ages* (1967); Peter W. Topping, ed. and trans., *Liber consuetudinum Imperii Romaniae. Feudal Institutions as Revealed in the Assizes of Romania, the Law Code of Frankish Greece* (1949); Léo Verriest, *Noblesse, chevalerie, lignages* (1959); Ernest Warlop, *The Flemish Nobility Before 1300,* 2 vols. (1975), esp. I, 11–18, and bibliography; Karl Ferdinand Werner, "Untersuchungen zur Frühzeit des französischen Fürstentums (9. bis 10. Jahrhundert)," in *Die Welt als Geschichte,* **18** (1958), **19** (1959), **20** (1960).

C. WARREN HOLLISTER

[See also **Arms and Armor; Castellan; Cavalry, European; Chivalry; Class Structure, Western; England: Norman-Angevin; Feudalism; Fief; Ministerials; Nobles and Nobility; Scutage; Squire, Esquire.**]

KNIK^C HAWATOY (Seal of faith) is presumably a seventh-century Armenian *catena patrum* (literally, chain of the Fathers) containing theological excerpts from the works of early Christian and Armenian Fathers. According to the full title of the book, it first circulated during the pontificate of Kat^cołikos Komitas (617–622). This information has led certain scholars to think that Komitas himself had a hand in the compilation of the *Knik^c*. Other scholars, how-

ever, identify it with a work entitled *Hawatarmat* (Root of faith), which is attributed to the mid-seventh-century Armenian theologian Yovhannēs Mayragomec^ci.

The 1914 edition *(editio princeps)* of the *Knik^c Hawatoy* is based on a single codex copied between the fourteenth and sixteenth centuries. According to critics, however, the catena in its present state cannot be a seventh-century compilation for the following reasons: (1) there is no indication in the work itself that Kat^cołikos Komitas had any role in the task of gathering or editing the contents; (2) Yovhannēs Mayragomec^ci, from whose works there are excerpts in the *Knik^c*, is mentioned more than once as "blessed," an epithet that he could not have used before his own name; (3) the *Knik^c* contains excerpts from the writings of the eighth-century theologian Step^canos, bishop of Siwnik^c; (4) there are also excerpts from the *Yačhxapatum girk^c*, a work attributed to St. Gregory the Illuminator, but not known to Armenian writers until the eleventh century. These facts indicate that the present text is either a later compilation or a revised edition of a seventh-century catena.

Knik^c Hawatoy is divided into ten chapters, each of which is devoted to a different topic, such as the Trinity, the Incarnation, and the incorruptibility of the body of Christ. It contains both lengthy and short excerpts from the writings of more than fifty Fathers. The medieval editor who compiled the work generally followed the fifth-century Monophysite patriarch Timothy Aelurus' treatise against the Council of Chalcedon (451).

The purpose of the *Knik^c Hawatoy* was to provide the Armenian theologians with texts needed to defend the anti-Chalcedonian position of the Armenian church in discussions with the Byzantine theologians. The long excerpts from the Armenian translation of the treatise of Timothy Aelurus, dating from the mid sixth century, testify to this.

Besides the introduction to the first modern published edition, there is still no serious comprehensive study of *Knik^c Hawatoy,* which also contains excerpts from hitherto unknown works, for example, the letter of Eznik of Kołb to Maštoc^c.

BIBLIOGRAPHY

The edition is *Knik' Hawatoy ĕndhanur surb ekełec'woy yułłap'ař ew s. hogekir harc'n meroc' dawanut'eanc' yawurs Komitas kat'ułikosi hamahawak'eal,* hrataraku't'iwn Karapet episkoposi, ĕndarjak naxabanov (The seal of faith of the holy catholic church, excerpted from the declarations [of faith] of our orthodox and inspired fathers, compiled at the time of Katholikos Komitas, edited by Bishop Karapet, with a lengthy introduction) (1914).

For a general bibliography *see* Gérard Garitte, *Documents pour l'étude du livre d'Agathange* (1946). Studies include Ervand G. Tēr Minasean, "*Knik^C Hawatoy žołovacun ew Hayoc^C ekełec^Cu dawanabanakan dirk^Cē Z ew Ē darerum*" (*Knik^C Hawatoy* and the dogmatic position of the Armenian Church in the sixth and seventh centuries), in Ervand G. Tēr Minasean, *Patma-banasirakan hetazotut^Cyunner* (Historical and philological studies) (1971), 88–118.

KRIKOR H. MAKSOUDIAN

[See also **Armenian Church.**]

KNITTING. See Textiles; Wool.

KNUD LAVARD (also Cnut Lavard) (*ca.* 1096–1131). The son of Erik I the Good of Denmark (1095–1103) and his wife, Bodil, Knud Lavard ("Lord" or "Bread-giver") spent the period after his father's death and the rise to power of his uncle, Niels Estridsen, in the court of Lothair, duke of Saxony and later Holy Roman Emperor. Around 1115, after his return to Denmark, he bought the office of earl of Slesvig from King Niels. The area around Slesvig, on the southern border of Jutland, was exposed to constant invasions by the Slavic tribes of the Lübeck area, as well as to raids by Saxon and Frisian outlaws and Danish robber barons. Knud Lavard took radical measures against the depredators, and soon brought the troubled area back under the control of the Danish crown.

In the course of this campaign, he fought victoriously against Henrik, king of the Slavic tribes, who was related to the Danish royal family. Henrik and Knud Lavard reached a settlement, and when Henrik died, Knud bought the dignity of *knés* (ruler) of the Wends from Lothair. Shortly before this, he had married Ingeborg, the daughter of Prince Harald (Mstislav) of Novgorod.

Knud's great success and evident thirst for power brought him the mistrust of King Niels and his son Magnus. After much friction, mutual suspicion, and accusations, Magnus murdered Knud in the forest of Haraldsted on 7 January 1131. Knud was buried in the Church of Our Lady in the nearby town of Ringsted. His present grave at Sankt Bendt's Church in Ringsted dates back to the seventeenth century.

The murder unleashed four years of civil war led by Knud's brother Erik against Niels and Magnus. In 1134 Magnus died in battle at Hammerness (Skåne) and Niels was murdered in Slesvig, where he had taken refuge. The avenger became Erik II the Memorable (1134–1137).

Knud Lavard's popularity and the treacherous manner of his murder made it possible for his successors and descendants, from Erik II to Valdemar I, to strengthen their position by encouraging his cult as a saint and martyr. Already at the time of his death, springs were said to have welled up miraculously at the place where he died and also in Haraldsted, at the spots on which those carrying his body had allowed it to rest. Erik II founded a Benedictine monastery at Ringsted and endowed it generously. It was probably there that the English monk Robert of Ely wrote the first vita of Knud Lavard, from which short extracts survive. Knud was canonized by Pope Alexander III in 1169, and the translation of his remains took place on 25 June 1170. The earliest extant vita of Knud is in the form of readings *(lectiones)* for the liturgical offices on the feasts of his passion and his translation. These are preserved in a Kiel manuscript dated about 1200. The breviaries of Lund, Roskilde, Odense, and Slesvig celebrate Knud on both feasts with extracts from the vita of his office. The breviaries of Århus and Västerås each celebrate only one of his feast days: translation and passion, respectively. Knud was traditionally the patron of guilds in Ringsted and Slesvig; after his canonization he was claimed as patron by many more. He is represented in frescoes at the churches of Ringsted, Vigersted, and Hvidbjerg.

BIBLIOGRAPHY

Sources. Martin C. Gertz, ed., *Vitae sanctorum Danorum*, II (1910), 169–247, and *Chronicon Roskildensis*, in *Scriptores minores historiae danicae medii aevi*, I (1917), 3–33; Carl af Petersens and Emil Olson, eds., *Knytlinga saga*, in *Sogur Danakonunga*, II (1925). For Helmold of Bosau, see *Helmolds Slavenchronik*, Bernhard Schmeidler, ed. (1937), 96–102, and in English translation, *The Chronicle of the Slavs by Helmold, Priest of Bosau*, Francis J. Tschan, ed. and trans. (1935), 152–158. For Saxo Grammaticus, see *Saxonis gesta Danorum*, Carl Knabe and Paul Herrmann, eds., rev. by Jørgen Olrik and Hans Raeder, I (1931), 334–412.

Studies. Hans T. Olrik, *Knud Lavards liv og gærning* (1888); Niels Skyum-Nielsen, *Kvinde og Slave* (1971), 63–77, 81–83.

JOAQUÍN MARTÍNEZ-PIZARRO

[See also **Denmark; Roskilde Chronicle.**]

KNÝTLINGA SAGA, an Icelandic collection of lives of Danish kings, dating from the middle of the thirteenth century. "Knýtlingar" is the name of the royal family and means literally "descendants of Knút" (Cnut), but it is probably derived from the name of Cnut the Great (d. 1035), the most powerful member of the family although not its founder, since the title of the collection is a late one. The original name may possibly have been *Sǫgur Danakonunga,* similar to the original name of *Heimskringla,* the sagas of the kings of Norway.

Knýtlinga saga covers Danish history for two and a half centuries from King Harald Bluetooth to King Knud VI (*ca.* 936–1187). As preserved today it is a direct continuation of *Skjǫldunga saga,* which ended with Gorm the Old, Harald Bluetooth's father. Originally the work commenced with an account of prehistoric Danish kings adapted from one version of *Jómsvíkinga saga,* but this beginning was left out when *Knýtlinga saga* and *Skjǫldunga saga* were united. In other respects the saga is relatively well preserved and exists in many manuscripts, the oldest one dating from about 1300.

The question of the sources of *Knýtlinga saga* is a very intricate problem, as yet unresolved. It is clear, however, that the author used many and various sources, both Icelandic and Danish, to which he sometimes vaguely refers. He had older Icelandic historical works and skaldic poetry to draw upon, among others an *Eiríksdrápa,* an obituary poem about King Erik Ejegod ("the ever-good," *d.* 1103). Saxo later used this poem as an authority in his *Gesta Danorum. Heimskringla* provided an inspiration and a model as well as a source, but the author generally tried to avoid following any one source too extensively and preferred to turn to other available materials. The consequence is that the first twenty-five chapters are both heterogeneous and fragmentary. On the other hand, the life of St. Knud (*d.* 1086), which constitutes the bulk of the work, exhibits a more artful form of saga, with conflicts, climax, and the tragic death of a saint.

The belief that an independent Icelandic "Life of St. Knud," written about 1200, was inserted virtually unchanged into *Knýtlinga saga* and was later lost in its separate form is untenable. Some speeches in the "Life of St. Knud" are based on Snorri Sturluson's speeches, and Snorri's description of St. Óláf has greatly influenced that of St. Knud. The author also used Danish sources, presumably a legendary story of St. Knud by Ælnoth and Saxo's narratives in *Gesta Danorum,* but because of the method and narrative technique of *Knýtlinga saga* there are numerous deviations from these older texts.

The last part of *Knýtlinga saga* tells of St. Knud's successors, with the life of St. Knud Lavard (*d.* 1131) and the warfare of the Danes in Wendland (eastern Germany) as the dominant plot. Danish annals were among the author's sources. Today, however, it is a matter of heated dispute whether his accounts are based directly on Saxo's work or whether there was a common authority in a lost historical work. The former hypothesis seems to be preferable.

Knýtlinga saga is to a large degree molded in an artistic saga style. Its historical value is no less apparent, however, since it contains stories and contemporary poems that are found nowhere else.

There is some likelihood that the author was Óláfr Þórðarson (*d.* 1259), Snorri's nephew, for he was a learned man who stayed in Denmark at the court of King Valdemar the Victorious (*d.* 1241), from whom he received "lore and narratives." While at court he may have conceived the ambition of composing a history of the Danish kings, which would raise their position in Icelandic saga writing to one of equality with the kings of Norway.

BIBLIOGRAPHY

Gustav Albeck, *Knýtlinga: Sagaerne om Danmarks konger* (1946), and "Knýtlinga saga," in *Kulturhistorisk leksikon for nordisk middelalder,* VIII (1963); Svend Ellehøj, "Omkring Knýtlingas kilder," in *Middelalderstudier. Tilegnede Aksel E. Christensen,* Tage E. Christiansen, ed. (1966); Bjarni Guðnason, "Saxo och Eiríksdrápa," in *Nordiska studier i filologi och lingvistik: Festskrift tillägnad Gösta Holm,* Lars Svensson, Anne Marie Wieselgren, and Åke Hansson, eds. (1976), and *Danakonunga sǫgur* (1982); Finnur Jónsson, *Knýtlingasaga, dens kilder og historiske værd* (1900); Rikke Malmros, "Blodgildet i Roskilde historiografisk belyst," in *Scandia,* 45 (1979); *Sǫgur Danakonunga,* Carl af Petersens and Emil Olson, eds. (1919–1925); Curt Weibull, "Saxo: Kritiska undersökningar i Danmarks historia från Sven Estridssons död till Knut VI," in *Historisk tidskrift för Skåneland,* 6 (1915), and "Knytlingasagan och Saxo: En källkritisk undersökning," in *Scandia,* 42 (1976).

BJARNI GUÐNASON

[See also **Cnut the Great; Jómsvíkinga Saga; Knud Lavard; Norse Kings' Saga; Skjǫldunga Saga.**]

KOERBECKE, JOHANN (*fl.* 1432–1491), Westphalian painter, was active in Münster. He is best known for his *Marienfelde Altarpiece* (1457), the wings of the *Langenhorst Altarpiece* (*ca.* 1445), and

The Annunciation. From *Marienfelde Altarpiece* by Johann Koerbecke (1457). M. A. RYERSON COLLECTION (33.1064), © The Art Institute of Chicago, all rights reserved

his later work, the *Freckenhorst Altarpiece*. His work is linear and decorative, employing gold grounds for slender, angular figures.

BIBLIOGRAPHY

Johannes Sommer, "Johann Koerbecke," in *Westfalen Sanderheft*, 5 (1937); Alfred Stange, *Deutsche Malerei der Gotik*, VI (1954), 14–20.

LARRY SILVER

[See also **Gothic Art: Painting.**]

KOIMESIS, one of the twelve major feasts in the Orthodox Church, commemorates the death or dormition (sleep) of the Virgin and is known today in the West as the Assumption (which, however, stresses Mary's bodily resurrection rather than her death). The account of the dormition may have originated in Egypt and Syria. Its celebration began in

Jerusalem and reached the West by the sixth century, as Gregory of Tours (*d.* 594) attests. The Byzantine emperor Maurice (582–602) fixed the feast day at August 15, where it has remained.

A fourth-century apocryphal account of the Koimesis, falsely attributed to pseudo-Melito, bishop of Sardis (second century), provided many of the legendary details. St. Modestus of Jerusalem (*d.* 634) established its dogma in a famous encomium. Homilies of St. John of Thessaloniki (*d.* 649) and St. John of Damascus (*d. ca.* 749/750) provided sources for later liturgy and iconography.

In Byzantine art the Virgin is shown on her deathbed, surrounded by the apostles (usually St. Peter at her head and St. John at her feet), with Christ in the center carrying the soul of his mother, as depicted in an ivory panel possibly carved in Constantinople prior to 972 (book cover, MS Clm. 4453, Munich, Staatsbibliothek). In twelfth-century and later depictions, apostles arrive on clouds, orders of angels hover above, and three hierarchs appear, as seen in the wall painting of the Dormition, dated about 1295, at the church of St. Clement (church of the Peribleptos) in Ohrid (ancient Lychnidus) in present-day southern Yugoslavia. A common detail is the representation of Athanios (Jephonias), a fanatical

Dormition of the Virgin. Steatite carving, *ca.* 1000. VIENNA, KUNSTHISTORISCHES MUSEUM

Jew whose hands were cut off for touching the Virgin's funeral bier.

BIBLIOGRAPHY

Hans-Georg Beck, *Kirche und theologische Literatur im Byzantinischen Reich* (1952), 502; Martin Jugie, *La mort et l'assomption de la Sainte Vierge* (1944); Philippe Verdier, *Le couronnement de la Vierge* (1980), esp. chaps. 3 and 4; Antoine Wenger, *L'assomption de la Vierge dans la tradition byzantine du VIᵉ au XIIᵉ siècle* (1955).

BARBARA OEHLSCHLAEGER-GARVEY

[See also **Assumption of the Virgin; Byzantine Art; Marian Feasts; Serbian Art and Architecture; Twelve Great Feasts.**]

KOKOSHNIK (plural, *kokoshniki*), originally the exterior ends of the onion-shaped vaults *(bochki)* of sixteenth- and seventeenth-century Russian wooden architecture, named after their supposed resemblance to a type of medieval female headdress. Cop-

Church of the Transfiguration showing *kokoshniki*. Kizhi Island, Karelian SSR, 1714. PHOTO: KLAUS G. BEYER

ied in masonry first in Pskovian receding corbels, *kokoshniki* elsewhere tended to become decorative rather than structural elements and to be used in receding ranks to soften transitions between different architectural levels and elements.

GEORGE P. MAJESKA

[See also **Bochka; Russian Architecture.**]

KOLLEMA (Greek, "something that has been glued"), an ancient technical term used in the manufacture and sale of papyrus to designate a single sheet of writing material. Many such *kollemata* were glued end-to-end to form a roll *(volumen)* of papyrus.

BIBLIOGRAPHY

Naphtali Lewis, *Papyrus in Classical Antiquity* (1974), 79–83; Eric G. Turner, *The Typology of the Early Codex* (1977), 43–54.

MICHAEL MCCORMICK

KOLLESIS, (Greek, "a gluing"), a modern technical term designating the joints produced by gluing together many sheets *(kollemata)* of papyrus to form a roll, the ancient form of book.

MICHAEL MCCORMICK

[See also **Codex; Manuscript and Book Production; Papyrus.**]

KOMNENOI. The Komnenoi family ruled the Byzantine Empire during the years 1057–1059 and 1081–1185. They rose to prominence in the eleventh century as landholders near Kastamonu (Castamona, near the Black Sea) in north-central Asia Minor and as leaders of the rising military aristocracy. Isaac Komnenos led a military revolt against Michael VI Stratiotikos (1056–1057), which ended in his usurpation as Isaac I (1057–1059). When Isaac retired to a monastery, his brother John refused the throne.

John's widow, Anna Dalassena, had ambitions for her sons. Her third son, Alexios Komnenos, fought valiantly against the Turks and rebel generals but was drawn into revolt against Nikephoros III Botaneiates (1078–1081) by maternal pressure and the emperor's suspicion. Alexios had the support of his wife's family, the Doukai, and of most of the army.

Alexios I (1081–1118) and his son John II (1118–1143) surmounted numerous problems: the Turkish occupation of Asia Minor; Norman and Pecheneg attacks on the Balkans; and the passage of the First Crusade through Byzantine territory. From the firm military and territorial base they had created, Manuel I (1143–1180) attempted further expansion. He tried too much, on too many fronts, and left an exhausted empire.

The Komnenoi intended to reassert Byzantium's imperial greatness. In Western affairs, from 1081 to 1157 the Byzantines strove for an alliance with the German emperors against Norman ambitions. Under the Komnenoi the Byzantines repelled Norman attacks under Robert Guiscard in 1081–1085, under Guiscard's son Bohemond I in 1107–1109, and under Roger II of Sicily in 1147–1149; a Byzantine counterthrust against Norman Italy (1155–1157) failed, however. Thereafter, Manuel joined the Normans, the pope, and the Lombard cities against Frederick I Barbarossa of Germany. In the Balkans, to secure the Danube frontier, the Byzantine army crushed the Pechenegs, reduced the Serbs to vassalage, and ended the long wars against Hungary in 1172 with the imposition of Manuel's protégé, Béla III.

In the East, the Komnenoi were less successful. Even through Alexios restored Byzantine authority in western Asia Minor and John recovered territory on the north and south coasts, they were unable to stop the Turks from raiding in every direction from their capital at Ikonion. In 1176 Manuel was severely defeated by the Turks at the Battle of Myriokephalon. An independent Armenian state developed in Cilicia. Despite repeated efforts, the Komnenoi obtained only passing recognition of their authority over Antioch and nominal suzerainty over the Kingdom of Jerusalem.

Internally, the Komnenoi strove to restore organized government. They brought the aristocracy to heel by means of marriage alliances, firmly controlled the church, reinstituted sound money, and revived the army with the *pronoia* (grants) system.

Manuel I was unable to conciliate his cousin Andronikos; his youthful heir, Alexios II (1180–1183), was under the control of his mother, who as regent was unable to resist Andronikos' advance. The latter made himself regent in 1182, then emperor (Andronikos I, 1183–1185). His oppression and his failure to

stem a brutal Norman attack on Thessaloniki in 1185 led to his downfall and the end of the dynasty.

The Komnenoi gave Byzantium a century of stability, and their combined reigns witnessed remarkable achievements in art, literature, and scholarship.

BIBLIOGRAPHY

Charles M. Brand, *Byzantium Confronts the West, 1180–1204* (1968), 1–75, 160–175; Joan M. Hussey, "The Later Macedonians, the Comneni, and the Angeli, 1025–1204," in *Cambridge Medieval History,* 2nd ed., IV, pt. 1 (1966), with bibliography.

CHARLES M. BRAND

[See also **Alexios I Komnenos; Andronikos I Komnenos; Anna Komnena; Byzantine Empire; Doukas; John II Komnenos; Manuel I Komnenos.**]

KONÀK (or *konaq*), a Turkish word meaning a halting place or, later, an inn, a mansion, or a government house. It is used to identify a number of residential building types found in Islamic architecture and in the post-Byzantine architecture of the Balkan countries. In the latter context it frequently refers to monastic dormitories and to the urban residences of the wealthy.

SLOBODAN ĆURČIĆ

[See also **Islamic Art and Architecture; Khan.**]

KÖNIG LAURIN is a Middle High German narrative poem from the cycle of stories about Dietrich von Bern (Theodoric I the Great "of Verona"). The poem seems to have been very popular in the late Middle Ages, and it survives in a large number of manuscripts from the fourteenth and fifteenth centuries. The story and its earliest literary versions probably date from the mid thirteenth century.

The poem follows the model of the romance with fairy-tale elements rather than the heroic model found in such poems as *Alpharts Tod.* The form reflects this choice as well in its use of short rhymed couplets in place of the strophic form employed elsewhere. The story begins with a challenge to Dietrich's court in the form of a famous rose garden in the Tyrol surrounded by a silken thread. The owner of the garden, the dwarf king Laurin, demands the left hand and right foot of anyone who breaks the thread. Dietrich and Witege ride out to challenge Laurin and, after numerous fights and the introduction of a new plot element—Laurin has abducted Künhilt, the sister of Dietleip, one of Dietrich's retainers—the dwarf is defeated. He invites Dietrich and his men into his castle inside a hollow mountain. Künhilt tells her brother that she is being well treated but that she wishes to be rescued, because the dwarfs are heathen. Still wanting revenge for the destruction of his rose garden, Laurin drugs Dietrich and his men, and imprisons them. Künhilt brings her brother his armor and a ring that allows him to see the invisible dwarfs. She then covers the magic stone that gives light in the underground castle. In the darkness Dietrich and his men fight the dwarfs. Laurin is captured, Künhilt is rescued, and the poem concludes with Laurin accepting Dietrich's friendship and Christian baptism.

In one manuscript there is a continuation in which Laurin's uncle Walberan comes to Verona (Bern) to rescue Laurin from Dietrich. After a brief single combat with Dietrich, Walberan decides to make peace, and there is a general celebration.

The motifs of dwarf warriors and of magic rings and caps that give the wearer invisibility and great strength are familiar from the *Nibelungenlied* as well as from the more fantastic narrative of the period. *König Laurin* seems to be typical in its combination of characters from heroic legend with fairy-tale plots and motifs that produced many such narratives during the later Middle Ages. Scholarly attempts to link the story with Germanic heroic legend have been interesting but inconclusive. The poem is composed in a rough meter of four-stressed rhymed couplets.

BIBLIOGRAPHY

Ruth R. Hartzell Firestone, *Elements of Traditional Structure in the Couplet Epics of the Late Middle High German Dietrich Cycle* (1975), 153–217; Joachim Heinzle, *Mittelhochdeutsche Dietrichepik* (1978), 23–26 (plots of various versions), 192–204 (textual criticism), and 298–313 (complete list of known manuscripts); Georg Holz, ed., *Laurin und der kleine Rosengarten* (1897), a critical reconstruction of several versions; Oskar Jänicke, ed., *König Laurin*, in *Deutsches Heldenbuch*, I (1866), an attempt at a critical text; P. B. Wessels, "König Laurin, Quelle und Struktur," in *Beiträge zur Geschichte der deutschen Sprache und Literatur* (Tübingen), 84 (1962).

EDWARD R. HAYMES

[See also **Middle High German Literature; Theodoric the Ostrogoth, Emperor**.]

KÖNIG ROTHER is the oldest and most beautifully narrated Middle High German wooing story *(Brautwerbung)*. A Rhenish work of 5,197 lines with end rhymes, it was composed in the 1150's for a Bavarian (perhaps Ratisbon or Tengelingen) audience.

Rother, a legendary bachelor king, is depicted as the ideal Christian ruler, unsurpassed in power, stature, lineage, wealth, virtue, and magnanimity. He lacks only a wife and heir, and is counseled to seek his bride abroad, where he wins no less a princess than the daughter of Constantine, emperor of Byzantium. He loses her by trickery but, in disguise, wins her back just as she is about to fall into the hands of an unworthy heathen. Eventually he fathers Pippin, and thus is the grandfather of Charlemagne. After Rother discharges his dynastic responsibilities, he and his Greek wife retire to a monastery.

The structure of the work is tripartite, resting on an older narrative layer that must have contained the story in two versions. The high point of the narrative is the wooing scene (beginning with verse 2,235), in which Rother's disguise is penetrated; it belongs to the best narrative material in precourtly German literature. *König Rother* is intimately related to a number of other prominent wooing stories, above all the Anglo-Norman *Romance of Horn* (ca. 1170) and the thirteenth-century Old Norse *Vilcinasaga* (which forms part of the *Þiðreks saga*). But *König Rother* also continues older narrative traditions such as are found in Athenaeus' story of Zariadres and Odatis (230), Firdawsī's *Gushtâsp and Katayoun* (Persian, ca. 1000), and *Digenis Akritas* (tenth–twelfth centuries). These oriental stories were popular in twelfth-century Bavaria because of dynastic and commercial interests in Constantinople.

The most important issue in the tale of *König Rother* is not who may have sponsored the telling of this story but its main political thrust. It consists of a seemingly comic transfer of royal lineage to the Carolingian line through marriage *(translatio imperii per nuptias)* by which the superiority of the Carolingian house over that of the Byzantines was to be "proved." *König Rother* was read until about 1300 and became largely unknown by 1400. It influenced several later minstrel epics.

BIBLIOGRAPHY

Sources. Two older critical editions are Theodor Frings and Joachim Kuhnt, eds., *König Rother* (1922, 2nd ed. 1961), and Jan de Vries, ed., *Rother* (1922). A newer, masterful edition is Günter Kramer, ed. and trans., *König*

Rother: Geschichte einer Brautwerbung aus alter Zeit (1961). An English translation is Robert Lichtenstein, trans., *King Rother* (1962).

Studies. Michael Curschmann, "'Spielmannsepik': Wege und Ergebnisse der Forschung von 1907–1965" (two articles), in *Deutsche Vierteljahrsschrift für Literaturwissenschaft und Geistesgeschichte*, **40** (1966); Christian J. Gellinek, *König Rother: Studie zur literarischen Deutung* (1968); Uwe Meves, *Studien zum König Rother, Herzog Ernst und Grauer Rock (Orendel)* (1976); Walter J. Schröder, *Spielmannsepik*, 2nd ed. (1967), 87; Klaus Siegmund, *Zeitgeschichte und Dichtung im König Rother: Versuch einer Neudatierung* (1959); Ferdinand Urbanek, *Kaiser, Grafen und Mäzene im König Rother* (1976).

CHRISTIAN GELLINEK

[See also **Middle High German Literature; Romance of Horn.**]

KONINC ERMENRÎKES DÔT. See **Ermenrîkes Dôt.**

KONRAD FLECK. See **Fleck, Konrad.**

KONRAD, PFAFFE. See **Rolandslied.**

KONRAD VON SOEST (*fl. ca.* 1394–1422), German painter, active around Dortmund, is best known for the *Niederwildungen Altarpiece* (signed and dated 1403, now in the Evangelischer Kirche, Wildungen), containing scenes of Christ's infancy and passion, Pentecost, and the Last Judgment. There are certain stylistic affinities to Netherlandish painting, possibly the result of contacts with artists or with manuscript illuminations from France or Burgundy. He also painted an altarpiece (*ca.* 1420) for the Marienkirche in Dortmund and triptych wings of female saints (St. Ottilie and St. Dorothea) now in Münster.

Niederwildungen Altarpiece. Konrad von Soest, 1403. COURTESY WESTPHALIAN MUSEUM OF ART AND CULTURAL HISTORY

BIBLIOGRAPHY

Rolf Fritz, "Zur westfälischen Tafelmalerei um 1400," in *Westfalen*, 27 (1948), *Der Dortmunder Marienaltar* (1950), and *Conrad von Soest: Der Wildunger Altar* (1954); Paul Jonas Meier, *Werk und Wirkung des Meisters Konrad von Soest* (1921); Paul Pieper, "Die altwestfälische Malerei," in *Westfalen*, 27 (1948); Alfred Stang, *Deutsche Malerei der Gotik*, III (1938), 22–31, *German Painting* (1950), 11, 24, plates 67–69, and *Conrad von Soest* (1966); Kurt Steinbart, *Konrad von Soest* (1946).

LARRY SILVER

[See also **Flemish Painting; Gothic Art.**]

KONRAD VON STOFFELN (*fl.* second half of the thirteenth century). The name Konrad von Stoffeln is appended in a scribal notation to one of the two surviving manuscripts of the short German narrative poem *Gauriel von Muntabel.* The scribe of this manuscript identifies Konrad as the author of the poem he has copied. There is a Swabian noble family with the name von Stoffeln appearing in chronicle listings for the second half of the thirteenth century (the probable time of the work's composition), but there is no hard evidence that Konrad was a member of this clan of *Freiherren.* Although the author assures his readers that his narrative is based on a written source, this claim appears improbable. The poem seems to be the poet's own rather free combination from a number of sources.

Central to the poem is the popular medieval story of the love of a mortal man for a fairy goddess, a motif found, for example, in the tale of the Swan Knight, in Marie de France's *Lay of Lanval,* in the *Lay of Graelant,* and in many other works as well. Also visible is the influence of Ulrich von Zazikhoven's *Lanzelet,* Wirnt von Grafenberg's *Wigalois,* Der Pleier's *Meleranz,* and Der Stricker's *Daniel vom blühenden Tal.* Wolfram's and Hartmann's romances may have influenced Konrad's work as well.

Gauriel von Muntabel is the story of a knight's liaison with a fairy queen. This love must remain a secret, however, and is qualified by the hero's promise to his lady never to reveal her existence. When he boasts openly of his beloved's beauty, he loses her favor. He sickens and is rendered malformed. As Knight of the Goat (a goat accompanies him on his adventures) he must regain his lady's favor (and his former appearance) by the successful performance of a series of difficult tasks, which include combat with three of the most renowned knights of the Round Table and a journey to the Perilous Land.

The poet lists Hartmann von Aue, Wolfram von Eschenbach, and Gottfried von Strassburg as his models. Gottfried's *Tristan* (*ca.* 1210) was surely a particularly strong influence on the metrical form of *Gauriel,* and Hartmann's Arthurian romances (particularly *Iwein*) extremely important sources for *Gauriel's* plot. Gauriel, Knight of the Goat, completes the tasks assigned to him with the help of a goat companion, just as Iwein, the Knight of the Lion, reconquers the affection of his beloved, relying in critical moments on the aid of his comrade the lion. But the symbolic impact typical of Hartmann's treatment of the animal figure is lacking in Konrad's work.

Gauriel von Muntabel is an eclectic product of the late courtly period. Like so many works of its time, the poem is stylistically not without merit, but in its exploitation of established traditions it seems superficial, even confused. Some of the difficulty critics have had with the work, however, should probably be traced to faulty transmission and editing.

BIBLIOGRAPHY

Edition. Gauriel von Muntabel, eine höfische Erzählung aus dem 13. Jahrhunderte, Ferdinand Khull, ed. (1885, repr. 1969).

Studies. Karl Deck, *Untersuchungen über Gauriel von Muntabel* (1912); Emanuel von Roszko, *Untersuchungen über das epische Gedicht Gauriel von Muntabel* (1903); Vinzenz Seunig, "Der Gauriel-Dichter als Nachahmer Hartmanns von Aue," in *Festschrift der 50. Versammlung deutscher Philologen und Schulmänner dargebracht von Mittelschulen der Kronländer Steiermark* (1909).

JAMES F. POAG

[See also **Arthurian Literature; German Literature: Romance; Gottfried von Strassburg; Hartmann von Aue.**]

KONRAD VON WÜRZBURG (*ca.* 1220/1230– 1287) was one of the most versatile and prolific writers of Middle High German literature. Historical records tell only that he died in 1287 in Basel, leaving behind a house, a wife, and two daughters. Additional biographical information can be gleaned from his works, which indicate that he was born between 1220 and 1230 in Würzburg of a middle-class family, had a good education, may have lived for a while in the lower Rhineland area of Germany, and spent the last two decades of his life in Basel as an independent author. There he supported himself by writing on commission for the nobility, higher clergy, and wealthy patricians of the city and the surrounding area. Attempts to determine a relative chronology of his works on the basis of their language and style have been inconclusive.

Konrad's particular talent shows itself to best advantage in his verse tales, the most distinguishing characteristics of which are their historical settings, pronounced didactic tendencies, and exploitation of the grotesque and ugly. All are told in smooth couplets without the awkward inversions and obvious rhyme fillers that abound in most medieval verse tales.

The poet's best work is the humorous story *Heinrich von Kempten*. When the title hero is condemned to death by Emperor Otto at a banquet, he throws the emperor down on the table, draws his knife, and threatens to kill him unless amnesty is granted. Otto revokes the sentence, but orders the knight never to appear before him again. Years later, during the siege of an Italian city, Heinrich is taking a bath when he sees the emperor being attacked by the enemy. Leaping from the tub, the knight seizes sword and shield and rushes naked to Otto's aid. He thus rescues his sovereign and regains his favor. The amusing descriptions of incongruous situations—the great emperor lying among the dishes of the banquet table and the nude warrior fighting so boldly—together with Otto's comically ironic remarks make it one of the most popular of medieval tales. According to the epilogue, this parody of the courtly manners and deeds of Arthurian romance was based on a Latin source. It is somewhat different, however, from the two extant Latin versions of this story.

Das Herzmaere belongs to the many medieval stories that tell of death for love. Because of the jealousy of his ladylove's husband, a knight takes leave of her and travels to the Holy Land, where the pain of separation makes him mortally ill. On his deathbed he asks that his heart be brought back to the lady. His squire attempts to carry out this wish but is intercepted by the husband, who takes the heart and has it prepared for a meal. After the lady has unknowingly eaten it, she is told what was served, whereupon her own heart breaks and she too dies of love. Konrad employs a well-balanced structure of prologue, tale, and epilogue, of narrative alternating with dialogue. The influence of Gottfried von Strassburg's *Tristan und Isolt* (*ca.* 1210)—Gottfried is praised in Konrad's prologue—can be seen both in the polished verse and in the plot. The basic story is a very old one that came to Europe from India about the beginning of the twelfth century. Three versions that are approximately contemporaneous with Konrad's have a historical, medieval poet as the hero: the Provençal Guilhem de Cabestanh, the French Châtelain de Coucy, and the German Reinmar von Brennenberg (*d.* before 1276). Many other variants are extant.

In *Der Welt Lohn* the hero, Wirnt von Grafenberg (author of the Arthurian novel *Wigalois*), is introduced as a gallant nobleman who is devoted to the pursuit of honor in all knightly activities. While he is reading a love story, a woman of superlative beauty enters his room and tells him that she is the one whom he has always served. Wirnt is delighted to have such a charming ladylove but has to confess that he has never seen her before. When he asks her name, she says that she is Dame World (Frau Welt) and, turning to go, exposes a back that is infested with maggots, snakes, and toads, and covered with repulsive sores. The knight is so affected by the sight that he leaves on a crusade and spends the rest of his life atoning for his former worldliness. The story is a masterpiece of vivid description, suspense, and sharp contrasts: the earlier and the later disposition of the hero, and the front and the rear view of Dame World. Konrad's description of this creature was probably the source for the representations of her that appear on the portals of the cathedrals at Basel and Worms. The inspiration for the story may have come from several poems by Walther von der Vogelweide.

Except for the beginning, which has been lost, and several other lacunae, most of Konrad's *Der Schwanritter* (Knight of the swan) has been preserved. The extant portion starts with a scene at Charlemagne's court where the duchess of Brabant accuses the duke of Saxony of illegally seizing her land and the duke, a brother of her late husband, defends himself, demanding a trial by combat. An unknown knight, who has just arrived in a swan-drawn boat, offers to represent the duchess and is victorious. On the condition that she is never to ask his name, he marries her (or her daughter; a lacuna makes this obscure) and becomes ruler of the land. Eventually the fatal question is asked and the knight departs as he came. Although the separate episodes are well written and interesting, the story as a whole is disappointing. The poet's interest in legal proceedings and his desire to exploit the drama of combat caused him to expand these trial scenes at the expense of the personal relationship of the knight and his wife. Moreover, by abandoning the traditional fairy-tale elements with their aura of mystery and by presenting the hero's timely arrival as an instance of divine intervention, Konrad makes the hero's departure seem both arbitrary and heartless. The source of *Der Schwanritter* was apparently a version of *Le Chevalier au cygne.*

Das Turnier von Nantes (Nantheiz) is unusual among verse tales in that it has very little plot. Indeed, it is hardly more than a description of a large and colorful tournament in which 4,000 knights take part. The tournament takes place, appropriately enough, at the capital city of King Arthur. However, the participants are not of Arthur's world but are Konrad's contemporaries, and their armorial bearings are described accurately and at length. The hero of the tournament, called King Richard of England, was no doubt Richard, earl of Cornwall, who was chosen king of Germany in the disputed election of 1257. Since the work seems to be a panegyric for which the author hoped to be rewarded, it was probably composed between 1257 and 1259, the date when Richard returned to England. It is important primarily as an early example of heraldry verse.

Considering the widespread interest in religious legends during the late thirteenth century, it is not surprising that Konrad should receive commissions to put some Latin saints' lives into German verse. He composed three such works, each treating a different type of church hero: *Silvester* (an account of the pope who brought about the conversion of Constantine), *Alexius* (the story of an ascetic who renounced everything that did not further his personal salvation), and *Pantaleon* (a recital of the sufferings and death of a famous Roman martyr). The legends of Silvester and Alexius were especially popular in Konrad's time, as indicated by the many Latin and vernacular treatments, but he obviously did not find them attractive as literary material. His versions are little more than direct translations of his Latin sources, with no rearrangement of events for artistic effect, little imaginative language, frequent repetition of formulaic expressions, and generally careless versification. Pantaleon was a more congenial subject, perhaps because the various attempts to kill him—by fire, wild beasts, drowning, the wheel, and the sword—offered possibilities for dramatic description and suspense. Konrad's treatment of this saint, therefore, shows not only better craftsmanship, but also greater independence in the selection and disposition of the episodes. In none of the three legends is there any indication that the author was by nature especially pious.

Even a casual examination of Konrad's three longer verse narratives reveals that he, like so many otherwise gifted medieval writers, lacked the ability to arrange material on a large scale around an idea, a character, or a situation in such a way that each part fits into an integrated whole. Nevertheless, these works contain too many fine scenes and episodes to be labeled failures. The most successful, because it is the best coordinated, is *Engelhard* (6,504 verses), which was based on a Latin version of the story of Amicus and Amelius.

Engelhard, the son of a Burgundian nobleman, and Dietrich, the son of the duke of Brabant, are close friends who are serving at the court of the king of Denmark. Engelhard and the king's daughter Engeltrud fall in love, spend a night together in a garden, and are surprised there the next morning by a knight who reports them to the king. In order to save the honor of his sweetheart, the hero denies having been with her, and a trial by combat is arranged to determine the truth of the matter. Engelhard believes his guilt will cause him to lose and therefore asks Dietrich, who is his exact double, to take his place. His friend does so and defeats the accuser. Engelhard then marries the princess, eventually becomes king of Denmark, and has two sons. Meanwhile Dietrich, now duke of Brabant, contracts leprosy. He dreams that he can be cured only by bathing in the blood of Engelhard's children. When his friend learns of the dream, he kills the boys and gathers their blood for Dietrich's bath. The duke is healed, and God rewards Engelhard's great loyalty by restoring his sons to life. In his prologue Konrad declares that his narrative deals above all with loyalty. Because of the influence of *Tristan,* however, he develops the Engelhard-princess relationship to a self-contained story that takes up more than a third of the verses. This detracts from the thematic unity, but the many excellent lyrical passages in the love story are adequate compensation. Other verse novels that have left a significant mark on *Engelhard* are *Willehalm von Orlens* by Rudolf von Ems, and *Cligés* by Chrétien de Troyes.

The faults and virtues of *Engelhard* reappear in accentuated form in Konrad's *Partonopier und Meliur* (21,784 verses). This novel was based on the French *Partonopeus de Blois (ca.* 1150), which also inspired Dutch, English, and Norse versions. Partonopier, the nephew of the king of France, becomes lost during a hunt and is carried by a mysterious boat to an apparently empty castle, where he spends the night. In the darkness the princess Meliur, whose magic has brought him there, comes to his bed. He wins her love but must promise not to look at her in the light for two and one-half years, after which time she can marry him. When a year has passed, Partonopier journeys to France to visit his family. His mother is convinced that Meliur is in reality a devil and persuades the hero to take a small lantern back with him so that he can look at her while she is asleep. When he sees the princess, she loses her magic powers and renounces him. He returns to France and wanders about in the forest like a wild man. At last, with the help of Meliur's sister, he is able to take part in a tournament, the prize of which is the hand of the princess. He is declared the winner, he regains the lady's favor, and they are married.

Partonopier und Meliur contains some of Konrad's best writing. His descriptions of the wondrous castle, the idyllic landscape surrounding it, and the nightly meetings of hero and heroine are filled with poetry and charm. On the other hand, thousands of verses are devoted to battles that have little to do with the main story. Although the work records the experiences of a youth from the age of thirteen to maturity, it is not an education novel, whatever the author's intention might have been. The reader does not see him learning and developing as a result of his experiences. It is also not a psychological novel, as has been suggested. Konrad had neither the ability nor the inclination to portray the inner nature of his characters.

Konrad's last novel was his monumental *Trojanerkrieg,* a work of more than 40,000 lines that breaks off—perhaps because of the death of the author—at the point where Patroclus dies. The chief source was the *Roman de Troie* of Benoît de Sainte-Maure (*ca.* 1165), which was supplemented by material from Ovid, Statius, and possibly other Latin writers. Like Benoît, Konrad begins his story many years before the quarrel of Achilles and Agamemnon, starting with Hecuba's dream that her unborn child would cause the destruction of Troy. This is followed by extended accounts of the births of Paris and Achilles, the story of Jason and Medea, the conquest of Troy by Hercules, the quarrel of the goddesses over the golden apple, the abduction of Helen, and other events to which Homer alludes only briefly, if at all. Konrad was more than halfway

through his work before he described the Greeks preparing for their invasion.

Although the novel achieves a certain unity through its consistent emphasis on the immutability of fate, it remains basically an unintegrated series of loosely connected episodes in which the speech and actions of the characters, both gods and mortals, are highly stylized. Indeed, the effect is often that of a collection of allegories whose events appear as illustrations of universal truths. This metaphorical trait is made more pronounced by the broadening of the conflict to a world war, with the races of Europe and Africa taking part on the side of the Greeks and the Asian peoples supporting the Trojans. At the same time the work is pervaded by an air of rationalism that lends characteristics of the thirteenth-century bourgeoisie to gods and heroes alike. The demand of Konrad's public for love stories was supplied by lengthy accounts of the relationships between Jason and Medea, Paris and Helen, and Achilles and Deidamia. The popularity of the *Trojanerkrieg* is attested by the twenty manuscripts and fragments that have been recorded and the influence it exerted on later writings.

Konrad's lyric poetry, like his narrative verse, treats both secular and religious subjects and is compared in a variety of forms. There are twenty-one *Minnelieder* (love songs), six *Spruch* cycles, a *Spruch* being a secular song dealing with subjects other than love, three dawn songs (albas), two *Leiche* (lays), and two long poems composed for recitation rather than for singing. The love songs are traditional in theme and tone and have none of the ironic humor, parody, or vulgarity to be found in many of the courtly love songs of the second half of the thirteenth century. Konrad's love songs have several distinctive features. All but four of them dispense with the fiction of autobiography, with the result that they are eulogies of women in general or commentaries on love rather than revelations of emotional reactions to personal situations. Thus, they tend to resemble *Sprüche.* Another characteristic feature is the prevalence of scenes of nature. All but one of his songs begin with a description of a season, and in many cases these summer and winter scenes carry over into the second and third stanzas as part of the basic theme, instead of remaining merely a device to establish a mood or provide poetic similes. A third characteristic of Konrad's love songs is the incomparable virtuosity with which he plays with rhyme and meter. In some compositions the complex patterns are so smoothly integrated that they almost escape attention; in others the poet ostentatiously flaunts his technical skill. In one song, for example, each syllable in every line rhymes with the corresponding syllable in another line, with little or no distortion of sense or word order. Since these works were sung rather than simply read, this virtuosity must have greatly impressed and charmed Konrad's public. The prominence of nature, the prevailing happy mood (only two songs are lover's laments), the lively rhythms, and the fact that five of the love songs have refrains make it likely that these were dance songs.

The *Sprüche* and dawn songs exhibit the same technical proficiency that is found in the minnesongs but are otherwise less distinctive. The *Sprüche* present religious and moral teachings, complaints about the parsimonious rich (who apparently do not buy Konrad's verses), and two eulogies. The *Leiche* are more significant. One is devoted to the praise of Mary and Christ and contains some rather unusual similes and metaphors. The other is a *Minneleich* that has many references to medieval and classical literature and some direct criticism of the poet's own rude and lawless time (that of the imperial interregnum after the death of Frederick II in 1250). At the end the narrator admonishes Venus to awake and oppose war by spreading love. He calls the composition a dance song which he sings for the ladies.

The theme of some of the *Sprüche* is further developed in one of Konrad's two long lyric poems, "Die Klage der Kunst." In stanzaic form this work presents an allegorical trial in which Lady Art brings charges against False Generosity before the court of Queen Justice, because incompetent bunglers have received gifts while she herself is neglected. In her decision the queen denounces the rich who do not support Art and directs the narrator to inform them that fortune will not bless those who care nothing for Art. In the introduction to his other long poem, "Die goldene Schmiede," the poet declares that he wishes to forge in the smithy of his heart an ornament worthy of the queen of heaven, Mary. He goes on to praise her in a rhapsodic hymn of 2,000 lines with an uninterrupted series of colorful and imaginative similes, symbols, and metaphors. It is a magnificent tour de force of highly ornamental language that is unparalleled in German medieval literature.

In Konrad's narrative and lyric verse a talented craftsman adapts a wide variety of traditional romantic materials for a somewhat rationalistic audience. He does so by such means as playing down or omitting supernatural elements not connected with Christian doctrine or church history, by using his-

torical figures and precise geography, by exploiting the gruesome and macabre, and by developing extended court scenes with their legal argumentation. The author remains detached from his works to the extent that his narrator seldom interprets, his love songs become didactic commentaries, and his panegyric to Mary assumes a liturgical, rather than a personal, tone. Konrad was popular with his contemporaries and had a considerable influence on later writers up to the end of the medieval period.

BIBLIOGRAPHY

The editions of Konrad's work and much of the secondary literature are listed in Eduard Hartl, "Konrad von Würzburg," in *Die deutsche Literatur des Mittelalters: Verfasserlexikon,* II (1936); and Horst Brunner, "Konrad von Würzburg," in *Die deutsche Literatur des Mittelalters: Verfasserlexikon,* 2nd ed., V (1985).

Recent studies of Konrad's writings include: Helmut de Boor, "Die Chronologie der Werke Konrads von Würzburg, insbesondere die Stellung des Turniers von Nantes," in *Beiträge zur Geschichte der deutschen Literatur,* 89 (1968); Thomas Cramer, "Minnesang in der Stadt: Überlegungen zur Lyrik Konrads von Würzburg," in *Literatur, Publikum, historischer Kontext* (1977); Hans Joachim Gernentz, "Konrad von Würzburg: Charakter und Bedeutung seiner Dichtung," in *Weimarer Beiträge,* 7 (1961); Regina Renate Grenzmann, *Studien zur bildhaften Sprache in der "Goldenen Schmiede" Konrads von Würzburg* (1978); Timothy R. Jackson, *The Legends of Konrad von Würzburg: Form, Content, Function* (1983); Gerhard P. Knapp, *Hector und Achill: Die Rezeption des Trojastoffes im deutschen Mittelalter* (1974); Barbara Könneker, "Erzähltypus und epische Struktur des *Engelhard:* Ein Beitrag zur literarhistorischen Stellung Konrads von Würzburg," in *Euphorion,* 62 (1968); Inge Leipold, *Die Auftraggeber und Gönner Konrads von Würzburg: Versuch einer Theorie der "Literatur als soziales Handeln"* (1976); Wolfgang Monecke, *Studien zur epischen Technik Konrads von Würzburg: Das Erzählprinzip der "Wildekeit"* (1968); Ursula Schulze, "Konrads von Würzburg novellistische Gestaltungskunst im *Herzmaere,*" in *Mediaevalia litteraria: Festschrift für Helmut de Boor zum 80. Geburtstag* (1971); Gisela Werner, *Studien zu Konrads von Würzburg "Partonopier und Meliur"* (1977).

J. WESLEY THOMAS

[See also **German Literature: Romance; Middle High German Literature.**]

KONRÁÐS SAGA KEISARASONAR, an Icelandic saga of unknown authorship, is preserved in six vellum manuscripts from the mid fourteenth to the sixteenth century and in some thirty-five paper manuscripts. Probably written in its original form around 1300, the more recent of the extant versions has been edited once, in 1859, and the older on three occasions. Oriental motifs as well as connections to *Gǫngu-Hrólfs saga, Ívens saga,* and the German tale *Loher und Maller* have been seen in the saga.

The story, which is said at one point to have been written down by the emperor of Constantinople and sent to Germany and Denmark, and at another to have been found by a cleric on a street, deals with Konráð, son of the king of Saxland, who is raised at the court of an earl in the kingdom. The earl's son, Roðbert, returns with his foster brother to the king's court, where he seduces Konráð's sister (for which he is subsequently banished). Roðbert convinces Konráð to accompany him to Miklagarð (Constantinople), where he uses his skill in languages to pass himself off as the king's son and the monolingual Konráð as his retainer. After overcoming numerous dangers to which the emperor and Roðbert expose him, and after having taught himself Greek, Konráð announces his true identity to the entire Byzantine court. The emperor betroths his daughter, Matthildr, to him on the condition that he go to deserted, snake-infested Babylon to find the mate to a certain green stone. Matthildr offers the hero invaluable advice, including the effects of crowing cocks and squealing pigs on lions and elephants, respectively. After adventures that progress exactly as the princess has predicted, Konráð, accompanied by a grateful lion, returns with treasures, including the sought-after stone, wins a joust against the emperor, humiliates Roðbert and has him banished, and sails home with Matthildr to Germany.

One *ríma* of eight stanzaic divisions is extant from before 1600, while seven eighteenth- and nineteenth-century *rímur,* all unedited, are known to exist.

BIBLIOGRAPHY

Gustav Cederschiöld, ed., *Fornsögur Suðrlanda* (1884); Jennifer M. Hunt, ed., "The Major Text of *Konráðs saga keisarasonar* with a Thesaurus of Word Forms" (M. Phil. thesis, Univ. of London, 1972); Finnur Jónsson, *Den oldnorske og oldislandske litteraturs historie,* 2nd ed., III (1924), 104–105; Margaret Schlauch, *Romance in Iceland* (1934), 43, 75–77; Finnur Sigmundsson, *Rímnatal,* 2 vols. (1966); Gunnlaugur Thórðarson (Þórðarson), *Konráðs saga keisarasonar er fór til Ormalands* (1859); Jón Thorkelsson (Þorkelsson), *Om Digtningen på Island i det 15. og 16. Århundrede* (1888), 161, 162, 173, 178; Björn K. Thórólfsson (Þórólfsson), *Rímur fyrir 1600* (1934), 395–398; Bjarni Vilhjálmsson, ed., *Riddarasögur,* III (1954, repr. 1962), 269–344; Jan de Vries, *Altnordische Literaturgeschichte,* II (1967), 536; Theodor Wisén, *Riddara-rímur* (1881).

PETER JORGENSEN

[See also **Fornaldarsögur; Gǫngu-Hrólfs Saga; Ívens Saga.**]

KONTAKION, the first major genre of Byzantine liturgical hymnody, cultivated between the fifth or early sixth century and the ninth century. The foremost composer of kontakia was St. Romanos Melodos, a converted Syrian Jew who was active at Constantinople during the first half of the sixth century. Kontakia in effect are long metrical sermons—theological, narrative, and at times dramatic elaborations of biblical and hagiographic subjects. Two to three dozen long, metrically similar stanzas called *oikoi* are generally grouped together in a kontakion, sharing the same short concluding refrain *(ephymnion)* and often linked by their first letters in an acrostic spelling the name of the poet-composer *(melode)* and/or the liturgical occasion. The *oikoi* are introduced by a shorter strophe of differing metrical structure called the *koukoulion* or *prooimion,* which was perhaps composed later but nevertheless shares the common refrain. Some five dozen to seven dozen kontakia are attributed to Romanos, including works for most major feasts of the liturgical year. The most celebrated kontakion is the so-called *Akathistos,* a hymn of uncertain authorship, honoring the Virgin Mary. The kontakion's function as a long poetic commentary on the feast was gradually taken over by the genre of liturgical hymnody called the *kanōn,* which grew in popularity during the eighth century. Although the old kontakia were reduced to the *prooimion* and first *oikos,* they retained a place in the service and are still sung today. The earliest musical style for kontakia was probably simple and syllabic, but little if any trace of the original music remains. Since the ninth century, kontakia have been sung in a variety of florid styles in the Byzantine and Old Slavonic traditions.

BIBLIOGRAPHY

J. Grosdidier de Matons, *Romanos le mélode et les origines de la poésie religieuse à Byzance* (1975); Kenneth Levy, "An Early Chant for Romanus' *Contacium trium puerorum?*" in *Classica et mediaevalia,* **22** (1961), and "The Earliest Slavic Melismatic Chants," in Christian

Hennick, ed., *Fundamental Problems of Early Slavic Music and Poetry* (1978); P. Maas and C. A. Trypanis, *Sancti Romani melodi cantica: Cantica genuina* (1963), and *Sancti Romani melodi cantica: Cantica dubia* (1970); *Monumenta musicae byzantinae*: IV, *Contacarium Ashburnhamense*, C. Høeg, ed. (1956), and VI, *Contacarium palaeoslavicum mosquense*, A. Bugge, ed. (1960); J.-B. Pitra, *Analecta sacra spicilegio Solesmensi parata*, I (1876); Oliver Strunk, "Some Observations on the Music of the Kontakion," in his *Essays on Music in the Byzantine World* (1977).

KENNETH LEVY

[See also **Byzantine Church; Hymns, Byzantine; Kanòn; Liturgy, Byzantine Church.**]

KONTSOVKA (plural, *kontsovki;* Russian for tailpiece) is the decorative ornamental design, often drawn in two colors, used to mark divisions between texts in medieval Slavic manuscripts. Although usually geometric in form, *kontsovki* with stylized vegetation motifs are by no means unknown. Smaller ones are often used to fill out lines.

GEORGE P. MAJESKA

Kontsovka. 17th century. PLOVIDIV, NARODNA BIBLIOTEKA, MS 42, leaf 100

KONYA. See Ikonion.

KORAN, the sacred scripture of Islam, containing the revelations recited by the prophet Muḥammad to the people of Mecca and Medina over a period of about twenty years up to the time of his death in 632. The term comes from the Arabic *qurʾān* (recitation),

the earliest attested usage of which occurs in the Koran itself, where it seems to represent the Syriac *qeryānā* (scripture reading, lection), as used in Christian liturgy. At the same time, it is formed on a common verbal noun pattern from the Arabic verb *qaraʾa* (recite, read), which also occurs in the Koran, usually in reference to Muḥammad reciting the revelations. The name of the Islamic scripture reflects the fact that it first appeared in oral form. Moreover, it is in its recited form, memorized in part by all Muslims and essential to the daily prayers, that the Koran has had the most significance for Muslims through the centuries.

GENESIS

The origins and early development of the Koran are closely related to Muḥammad's prophetic experience and his various roles as founder of the Muslim community. In his native city of Mecca he was for about ten years a prophet-preacher, called in the Koran a "warner" *(nadhīr),* delivering messages from God in the form of cryptic prophetic oaths and oracles, and later more extended, sermonlike recitations. During this Meccan period Muḥammad seems to have received and memorized the revelations at night (see Suras 73:1–8, 75:16–19, 87:6f.; Koran references in this article follow the verse-numbering system of the 1923 Egyptian edition), and then recited them during a public ritual called a *ṣalāt,* performed each morning and evening (11:114, 17:78, 20:130–132). While he recited, his followers listened in silence (7:204); at various points in the service they prostrated with him (84:20f.) and probably recited praise formulas. Muḥammad's main prophetic role in Mecca was thus as the recipient and reciter of messages from God that were oral in form and liturgical in function. Fundamental changes in his roles and in the nature and functions of the Koran occurred in Medina after the Hegira in 622. There, as the religious and political leader of the Muslim community, he served as worship leader *(imām)* and public speaker *(khaṭīb)* in weekly services held at noon on Fridays. These services became the main setting for the public recitation of new revelations and revised and expanded versions of old ones.

The main turning point in the history of the Koran during Muḥammad's lifetime occurred, however, not at the time of the Hegira, as is generally assumed, but a year or so later, when he began to adapt the Meccan collection of liturgical material called the Recitation *(al-qurʾān)* to form a written scripture for the Muslims, called the Book *(al-kitāb).*

Islamic tradition records the names of several secretaries who wrote down revelations he dictated in Medina. For a while this task must have occupied a good part of Muḥammad's time, but the responsibilities of leading the rapidly growing Muslim community forced him to leave it unfinished. To what extent he was responsible for the final form and arrangement of the Koran is uncertain. It seems likely that he dictated most of the Koran to his corps of scribes, and that at the time of his death most of the individual suras had reached approximately their final form.

HISTORY

That Muḥammad left no official text of the entire corpus of the revelations is virtually certain. Some of his followers began to make collections during his lifetime, and soon after his death several more or less complete codices existed. Some of these codices acquired authoritative status in the more important intellectual centers of the rapidly expanding Islamic empire: Ibn Masᶜūd's in Al-Kufa, Abū Mūsā's in Basra, and Ubayy ibn Kaᶜb's in most parts of Syria. Thus, as with other scriptures, the development of semiofficial metropolitan texts preceded the establishment of a canonical text. A number of private collections are also mentioned in the sources, such as those of Muḥammad's cousins, ᶜAlī ibn Abī Ṭālib and ᶜAbd Allāh ibn al-ᶜAbbās.

The first official recension of the Koran was prepared under the authority of the third caliph, ᶜUthmān, about twenty years after Muḥammad's death. The orthodox view is that this "ᶜUthmānic text" was only a revision of a recension made under the first caliph, Abū Bakr, at the urging of ᶜUmar, who was to become the second caliph, and that the purpose of this revision was simply to remove dialectical irregularities that had crept in. But the various accounts of an earlier official recension contain many contradictions as to who authorized it and why, and they all seem to be attempts by later Islamic tradition to diminish the significance of the old codices and make the official text seem older than it actually is. In general, ᶜUthmān's recension seems to have been accepted immediately as the standard text. Serious opposition to it is recorded only in Al-Kufa, where Ibn Masᶜūd is said to have rejected it and where his followers continued to study and copy his text for many years.

At first the Koran was written only in a bare consonantal form that lacked not only the vowel signs but also the diacritical points that later distinguished certain consonants from others: s and sh, r and z, and, in some positions, b, t, th, n, and y. The readers had the freedom of choice (ikhtiyār) to read the basic text however they thought best, and they took advantage of this freedom, thus giving rise to an increasing number of variants. In 934 the freedom of ikhtiyār was severely curbed when the leading Koran scholar of the day, Abū Bakr ibn Mujāhid, selected seven systems of reading the entire text, called readings (qirāʾāt; sing., qirāʾa), and persuaded the viziers Ibn ᶜĪsā and Ibn Muqla to prohibit the use of all others, including the old codices. Some eminent scholars who at first refused to conform were publicly condemned and forced to renounce their earlier views. But demands for freedom continued, and two versions (riwāyāt; sing., riwāya) came to be accepted for each of the Seven, while some scholars tried to expand the number of canonical readings to ten or as many as fourteen.

Eventually the pressure of orthodoxy prevailed, and only one version, the Kufan one of Ḥafṣ (d. 805), based on the reading of ᶜĀṣim (d. 744), is now used nearly everywhere in the Islamic world except for parts of Africa where a Medinan reading is still used. The widely acclaimed Egyptian standard edition of 1923 adopted the version of Ḥafṣ, thus giving it a certain canonical supremacy in practice if not in theory. A modern critical text of the Koran has not yet appeared. A plan to produce such a text was announced in the 1930's by Arthur Jeffery and some German colleagues who collected a vast number of variants from the early sources. But World War II brought an abrupt halt to the project, and it has not been taken up again.

DESCRIPTION

The Koran is a book in the Arabic language about four-fifths the length of the New Testament. It consists of 114 units called suras (Arabic: sūra; pl., suwar), varying in length from two lines (ten words) to more than 700 (as many as sixty pages) in a modern printed edition. The suras are divided into loosely rhymed verses that also vary considerably in length and style. Some verses are short and rhythmic, with a consistent rhyme or assonance that is integral to the content (see, for example, Suras 91, 92, 97), while others are long and prosaic, often with short statements or formulas attached to the ends to provide the rhyme (for example, 2, 4, 5). Some suras are carefully composed literary pieces with central themes, consistent rhetorical form, or other unifying features (such as Sura 12, a long account of the story of Joseph; Sura 26, a series of seven prophet stories with the same two-verse refrain and other features of consistent schematic form; and Sura 55, a long, seventy-eight-verse litany with the same rhetorical question serving as almost every other verse, beginning with verse 13).

Most suras, however, are composite, consisting of segments or pericopes on different themes from different dates, often loosely joined with little apparent connection of thought. This disjointedness almost certainly goes back to Muḥammad and is to be explained by the fact that the Koran had no set form during its oral stage. The revelations were revised from time to time as they were repeated on different occasions, and older material was often expanded or inserted into new contexts, sometimes with a change in the rhyme.

The parts of the Koran that appear to be the oldest are similar in form and content to the veiled utterances of the soothsayers (kuhhān; sing., kāhin) of Muḥammad's day. In some of these there is no indication that the message is from a deity (as in Suras 101–103); in others Muḥammad seems to be the speaker (as in 81:15–21, 84:16–19, 92:14–21). In most parts of the Koran, however, God is the speaker, indicated usually by the plural of majesty, "we," but occasionally by first-person-singular grammatical forms. In Meccan parts of the Koran, Muḥammad is often the addressee of the message, indicated by second-person-singular forms (as in the beginnings of 73, 74, 87, 93, 94, and parts of longer suras, such as 17:45–111). Meccan parts of the Koran feature, besides the oaths and oracles mentioned above, accounts of the "signs of God" (āyāt; sing. āya) in nature (as in 6:95–105, 13:2–4, 16:3–16), stories of earlier peoples who were destroyed by God for rejecting his messengers (such as 7:59–93, 11:25–95, 21:48–77, 26:10–191), creation stories (such as 15:28–44, 17:61–65, 38:71–85), and descriptions of the Last Judgment, paradise, and the hellfire (such as 37:38–74, 43:70–77, 56:1–56).

In Medinan passages new themes are introduced, with increasing stress on political, legislative, and military matters, and there is also a change of emphasis in the dramatic form, with most passages being addressed not to Muḥammad but to specific groups of his contemporaries: the Jewish tribes of Medina (frequently in Sura 2), Muḥammad's followers (frequently in Sura 5), and occasionally his opponents and his wives. Muḥammad is more frequently referred to in the third person, as the Messenger of God (rasūl Allāh), the Prophet (al-

nabī), or sometimes by name (all three forms occur in 33:38–40).

In the early manuscripts the suras were separated only by the basmala, the formula "In the name of God, the Merciful, the Compassionate," which now stands at the beginning of each sura except Sura 9. This formula was not part of the earliest revelations, but came to be used by Muḥammad in the middle or late Meccan years to introduce each recitation of a portion of the Koran. When the suras were put into their final, written form, the basmala was placed at the beginning of each as a divider. Its absence at the beginning of Sura 9 thus suggests that at one time 8 and 9 were regarded as a single sura.

Just after the basmala in twenty-nine suras there is a letter or group of letters of the Arabic alphabet, usually called in European languages "the mysterious letters." Whether they were intended to have any actual or symbolic meaning is uncertain. Some early authorities offered a variety of abbreviation theories—for example, that alr and ḥm together stood for the divine name al-raḥmān—while others said they had mystical significance based on their numerical values, or were simply signs stressing the Arabic nature of the revelation, or sounds to arouse the hearers. Although the presence of these letters cannot now be fully explained, it is clear that they have an important role in the history of the text of the Koran.

The first sura and the last two serve as a kind of introduction and conclusion to the Koran. Sura 1, called "The Opening," is a short, seven-verse prayer, and 113 and 114, known as "the two [suras] of taking refuge," are charms for warding off evil powers. After Sura 1 the suras are arranged roughly in order of descending length, a principle that probably goes back to the Prophet and is well attested in other ancient and medieval writings. Other factors—such as dates, main themes, introductory formulas, and the presence of groups of mysterious letters—also affected the arrangement of the Koran, especially where certain groups of suras have been kept together despite varying length—for example, 10–15, dealing mainly with prophet stories and beginning with the letters alr (except that 13 has almr); 40–46, all beginning with ḥm; and 57–66, a group of short Medinan suras.

CHRONOLOGY

The Koran is a historical document that reflects Muḥammad's changing situation and responds constantly to the specific needs and problems of his contemporaries. It offered encouragement to the Prophet in times of persecution, rebuttal to accusations made against him by his opponents, and advice and instructions on political, military, and religious matters. Major doctrines and regulations for the emerging Muslim community were introduced in stages that are not always clear, with apparent contradictions and inconsistencies. For these and other reasons it is essential to know the approximate dates of many passages, and at least the chronological order of others, if they are to be understood fully. However, the Koran is not in any chronological order, and critical scholars have not been able to agree on a system for dating its various parts.

The traditional dating is based on the assumption that the present suras were the original units of revelation, that is, that except for a few verses in some suras each sura was revealed all at once, or during a short period of time before the next sura was begun. This view led to the practice of designating each sura as "Meccan" or "Medinan," and then to attempts to determine the exact chronological order of all the suras as wholes. For several very good reasons, however, the early Koran scholars were unable to agree even on whether some suras were Meccan or Medinan, much less on the exact chronological order of all of them.

One complicating factor was that a number of passages came to be connected with stories that arose in the attempts to reconstruct the life of the Prophet—for instance, associating 53:1–18, 74:1–7, and 96:1–5 with his call to prophethood, 17:1 with a miraculous Night Journey, and 19 and 20 with the time of the emigration of most of his followers to Abyssinia. From these and similar accounts there arose a genre of Islamic literature called "the occasions of the revelation" *(asbāb al-nuzūl)*, which popularized legendary accounts involving the dating of parts of certain suras.

Another complicating factor was the theory of abrogation *(naskh)*, which arose in order to resolve inconsistencies within the Koran and to enable the jurists to use it as a source for Islamic law. Acknowledging the inconsistencies, the jurists and others argued that the latest verse on any subject abrogated all earlier verses that contradicted it. Long lists of "abrogating and abrogated (verses)" *(al-nāsikh wa-l-mansūkh)* were then compiled by those seeking Koranic proof texts for their own particular views. Eventually an order of suras attributed to Ibn ᶜAbbās came to be widely accepted, and with a few changes

was adopted by the editors of the Egyptian standard edition of the Koran.

Since the middle of the nineteenth century, Western scholars have proposed a variety of Koran dating systems. The one that has gained the most acceptance is that of what might be called the "four-period" school of Gustav Weil, Theodor Nöldeke, Régis Blachère, and others. Weil divided the "Meccan suras" into three periods, distinguished largely on the basis of style and phraseology. He and his followers accepted the Muslim assumptions that the suras were the original units of revelation, that it was possible to arrange them in chronological order, and that Islamic tradition provided a sound basis for dating parts of the Koran.

These assumptions were cast into serious doubt by the research of Richard Bell, who concluded that the suras are far more complex than was previously assumed; that the revelations underwent considerable revision, including expansion and replacement of older passages with new ones; and that this revision involved written texts and was done during Muhammad's lifetime under his supervision. A survey of Bell's provisional dating shows that he regarded only one fourth of the 114 suras as being composed completely of Meccan material, one fourth as being completely Medinan, and half as having significant amounts of material from both before and after the Hegira. Much remains uncertain, but the evidence seems to support Bell's main conclusions.

INTERPRETATION

The Koran became the ultimate authority in all Islamic legal and religious matters, and its correct interpretation became an important branch of Islamic learning called *tafsīr* (exegesis, interpretation). The most highly respected type of Koran interpretation was *tafsīr bi-l-ma'thūr* (traditional exegesis), consisting of the collection and careful transmission of traditions *(ahādīth;* sing., *hadīth)* on the "occasions of the revelation" and on the meaning or interpretation of specific verses. This type of exegesis reached its zenith in the thirty-volume commentary by al-Tabarī (*d.* 923), which remains unparalleled in its field. The most eminent and original commentaries since the time of al-Tabarī are the *Kashshāf* (Unveiler) by al-Zamakhsharī (*d.* 1144), which exhibits an extraordinary perceptiveness and knowledge of Arabic language and grammar, and the "Great Commentary" by Fakhr al-Dīn al-Rāzī (*d.* 1210), which excels in painstaking theological and philosophical analysis. An increasing tendency toward the use of personal opinion and philosophical speculation during the first six Islamic centuries reached a certain conclusion with al-Rāzī's commentary, after which individual initiative and expression in Koran commentary were successfully discouraged until modern times. One later commentary must be mentioned, the still-popular *Lights of the Revelation* by al-Bayḍāwī (*d.* 1316), which is basically an abridgment of al-Zamakhsharī's work, assimilating it to Sunni orthodoxy and expanding it in places with details from other sources. These and several other classical commentaries have been reprinted frequently in Arabic in modern times, but none has been translated in full into any European language.

One reason for this is the strongly entrenched view that scholarly study of the Koran must be done in Arabic. The Koran, revealed expressly as an Arabic book for Arabs (see 12:2, 42:7, 43:3), must be recited in Arabic in the ritual prayers even by non-Arabs. Moreover, the prevailing attitude today is that a translation is not the Koran itself, but an "interpretation." Muslims have translated the Koran into other languages since the tenth century, but as interlinear or parallel column paraphrases. The first Latin translation, completed in 1143 by Robert of Ketton at the behest of Peter the Venerable, enjoyed wide circulation in manuscript and served as the basis for the first translations into Italian (1547), German (1616), Dutch (1641), French (1647), and English (1649–1688).

BIBLIOGRAPHY

Arabic editions and translations. Al-Qurʾān al-karīm (1923, often reprinted) is the Egyptian edition generally accepted by Muslims as the standard edition and is rapidly replacing Gustav L. Flügel's *Corani textus arabicus* (1834, often reprinted) in the West. For a chart converting Flügel's verse numbers to those of the Egyptian edition, see William Montgomery Watt, *Bell's Introduction to the Qurʾan* (1970, repr. 1977), 202–203. Paret's German translation and Blachère's French one give both numbering systems, Paret giving the Egyptian first, Blachère giving Flügel's first. Some Indo-Pakistani editions, notably the Ahmadīya ones today, use a different system; for a conversion chart, see Herbert U. Weitbrecht Stanton, *The Teaching of the Qurʾan* (1919, repr. 1969), 117–134.

Among the many English translations, the following are recommended: Abdullah Yusuf Ali, *The Holy Qurʾan: Text, Translation, and Commentary* (1934; 3rd ed. 1938, repr. 1968), probably the most reliable oriental translation, but with some later theological views read into the text and defended in the notes; Marmaduke M. Pickthall, *The Meaning of the Glorious Koran* (1930, rev. ed. 1976), a popular trans. stressing what the Koran means to Muslims, with Egyptian and English text and numbering only in the 1976 ed.; Richard Bell, *The Qurʾan Translated, with a Critical Re-arrangement of the Surahs,* 2 vols. (1937–1939), a valuable translation and critical study of the text, but difficult for the general reader to use; Arthur J. Arberry, *The Koran Interpreted* (1955), widely used, attempts to reproduce in English the literary qualities of the Arabic, but with undue consistency, literalness, and ambiguity in places. The standard French and German translations are Régis Blachère, *Le Coran,* 2nd ed. (1966), with valuable notes; Rudi Paret, *Der Koran: Übersetzung,* 2nd ed. (1966, repr. 1979).

Concordances and indexes. Hanna E. Kassis, *A Concordance of the Qurʾan* (1983), based on Arberry's translation but arranged by the Arabic roots, with indexes to the English terms. The following Arabic concordances are recommended: Muḥammad F. ʿAbd al-Bāqī, *Al-Muʿjam al-mufahras li-alfāz al-qurʾan al-karīm,* (1945, repr. 1968), to the Egyptian standard edition; Gustav L. Flügel, *Concordantiae Corani Arabicae* (1842, often reprinted), to Flügel's text. Useful select subject indexes are in Watt, *Bell's Introduction,* 215–240; Blachère, *Le Coran,* 681–743; Stanton, *Teaching,* 75–110, older but still useful; and in the translations by Yusuf Ali, Pickthall, and others.

Commentaries in English. David S. Margoliouth, *Chrestomathia Baidawiana: The Commentary of el-Baidāwī on Sura III* (1894); Alfred F. L. Beeston, *Baidāwī's Commentary on Surah 12 of the Qurʾan* (1963); Helmut Gätje, *The Qurʾan and Its Exegesis,* Alford T. Welch, trans. and ed. (1976), selections mainly from al-Zamakhsharī and al-Bayḍāwī but also from other classical Sunni, Shiʿa, Sufi, and modern commentaries. Some modern commentaries have been translated into English: Abul Kalam Azad, ed. and trans., *The Tarjumān al-Qurʾān,* 2 vols. (1962–1967), covering only Suras 1–8 and stressing modernist issues; (Syed) A. A. Maudoodi, *The Meaning of the Quran,* 4 vols. (1970–1973), covering only Suras 1–9, largely traditionalist and devotional. One modern Shiʿa commentary is S. V. Mir Ahmed Ali, *Commentary on the Holy Qurʾan* (1975). Rudi Paret, *Der Koran: Kommentar und Konkordanz,* 2nd ed. (1977), is valuable especially for references to the literature on key terms and individual passages and for cross references. William Montgomery Watt, *Companion to the Qurʾan* (1967), based on Arberry's translation, has brief comments elucidating passages that are difficult for the general Western reader.

Introductions and general studies. Watt, *Bell's Introduction,* based on Richard Bell's 1953 work, the standard introduction in English; Theodor Nöldeke and Friedrich Schwally, *Geschichte des Qorāns,* 2nd ed., 2 vols. (1909–1919), vol. III by Gotthelf Bergsträsser and Otto Pretzl

(1938), the most comprehensive introduction to the Koran in any European language, now needs updating; Régis Blachère, *Introduction au Coran*, 2nd ed. (1959, repr. with revisions 1977), less detailed and less critical, but valuable especially on problems involving the language of the Koran. Among the recent studies, Kenneth Cragg, *The Event of the Qurʾān* (1971) and *The Mind of the Qurʾān* (1973), are perceptive attempts to guide the general Western reader.

The classic European study of *tafsīr* is Ignaz Goldziher, *Die Richtungen der islamischen Koranauslegung* (1920, repr. 1952), which for the early period must now be supplemented with Nabia Abbott, *Studies in Arabic Literary Papyri*, II, *Qurʾānic Commentary and Tradition* (1967), especially 92–113, and John Wansbrough, *Quranic Studies* (1977), esp. 119–246, not, however, intended for the general reader. For modern Muslim studies and bibliography, see Johannes M. S. Baljon, *Modern Muslim Koran Interpretation* (1961); J. J. G. Jansen, *The Interpretation of the Koran in Modern Egypt* (1974).

Recent studies on Koranic themes. Youākim Moubarac, *Abraham dans le Coran* (1958); Salih H. al-Shamma, *The Ethical System Underlying the Qurʾān* (1959); Daud Rahbar, *God of Justice: A Study in the Ethical Doctrine of the Qurʾān* (1960); Toshihiko Izutsu, *God and Man in the Koran* (1964); Dirk Bakker, *Man in the Qurʾān* (1965); Toshihiko Izutsu, *Ethico-religious Concepts in the Qurʾān* (1966); K. Wagtendonk, *Fasting in the Koran* (1968); Thomas O'Shaughnessy, *Muhammad's Thoughts on Death: A Thematic Study of the Qurʾanic Data* (1969); S. el-Saleh, *La vie future selon le Coran* (1971); Johan Bouman, *Gott und Mensch im Koran* (1977).

Bibliographies. See Watt, *Bell's Introduction*, 173–181, and the bibliography in Alford T. Welch, "Ḳurʾān," in *Encyclopaedia of Islam*, new ed., V (1981). Rudi Paret, ed., *Der Koran* (1975), provides reprints of a selection of important articles on various Koranic themes and issues, mainly in English and German. For a complete list of articles on the Koran, see James D. Pearson, comp., *Index islamicus 1906–1955* (1958), 56–63, and the Koran sections in each five-year supplement.

ALFORD T. WELCH

[See also **Friday Prayer; Ḥadith; Islam, Religion; Law, Islamic; Muḥammad; Ṭabari, al-.**]

KOŘIKOS (Korykos; Corycus). The fortress of Kořikos on the coast of Cilicia comprised an island castle (Kis Kale) with towered walls and a land castle rebuilt by the Byzantine emperor Alexios Komnenos in the early twelfth century. Shortly before 1167, when Benjamin of Tudela visited Kořikos, it be-

longed to King Tᶜoros II of the Cilician Kingdom of Armenia and marked its western frontier.

There are Armenian inscriptions with the names of kings Leo I/II (1206) and Hetᶜum I (1251) on the island castle's main tower.

From 1359 to 1448 the fortress belonged to Cyprus, and by the mid fifteenth century was the property of the Karamanid Turks.

BIBLIOGRAPHY

Thomas S. R. Boase, ed., *The Cilician Kingdom of Armenia* (1978); George H. Forsyth, "Architectural Notes on a Trip Through Cilicia," in *Dumbarton Oaks Papers*, **11** (1957); Ernst Herzfeld and Samuel Guyer, *Meriamlik und Korykos* (1930); Victor Langlois, *Voyage dans la Cilicie, 1852–1853* (1861); Wolfgang Müller-Wiener, *Castles of the Crusaders*, John M. Brownjohn, trans. (1966).

LUCY DER MANUELIAN

[See also **Cilician Kingdom.**]

KORIWN (active early fifth century), Armenian writer, whose *Life of Maštocᶜ* (*d.* 439) is thought to be the earliest original work in Armenian. Our knowledge about him derives mostly from his work, in the introduction of which he refers to his "special status as a pupil" of the vardapet Maštocᶜ, the man who invented the Armenian alphabet. This is why he claims he was singled out by his schoolmates to write the *Life*. Koriwn was probably among the earliest pupils of Maštocᶜ to become literate in Armenian and to be sent out as a teacher to the different districts of Armenia.

Koriwn's place of origin has been a matter of controversy, since the interpretation of a certain passage in the *Life* (chap. 15) has led several scholars to consider him a man of Georgian extraction who later became bishop of Georgia. Modern scholars, however, have rejected this interpretation, and some have even emended the text.

From the *Life* we learn that Koriwn was the assistant and associate of Maštocᶜ (Mesrob). This indicates that he was greatly involved in the cultural movements of the period. In the mid 420's he and his classmate Łewond were sent to Constantinople to join their two associates, Eznik of Kołb and Joseph of Pałnatun, in order to translate the works of the Greek fathers into Armenian. They returned to Armenia soon after 431, bringing with them the canons of the councils of Nicaea and Ephesus, an authoritative copy of the Scriptures, and several works of the Greek fathers. Koriwn probably composed the *Life of Maštoc^C* in the mid 440's, since the last date-able event mentioned in it is from 443. Koriwn's name is not mentioned in connection with the anti-Persian uprising of 449–451, which was instigated by several of his classmates. He had probably died before the commencement of the rebellion.

The *Life of Maštoc^C*, which is a hagiographical work, is Koriwn's only known opus; there is also a shorter medieval epitome of this work. Stylistic similarities between the *Life* and the fifth-century histories of Agat^Cangełos and P^Cawstos Buzand, and the Armenian translations of the Books of the Maccabees and the Euthaliana (short summaries of New Testament books attributed to Euthalius) in the Armenian Bible, have led certain scholars to attribute these to Koriwn as well.

BIBLIOGRAPHY

Norayr Biwzandac^Ci, *Koriwn vardapet ew norin t^Cargmanut^Ciwnk^C* (Koriwn Vardapet and his translations) (1900); Koriwn, *Vark^C Maštoc^Ci* (Life of Maštoc^C), Manuk Abełean, ed. (1941, repr. 1962), Bedros Norhad, trans. into English (1965).

Krikor H. Maksoudian

[See also **Armenian Church, Doctrines and Councils; Armenian Literature; Armenian Saints; Bible, Armenian; Eznik of Kołb; Historiography, Armenian; Maštoc^C, St.**]

KORMÁKS SAGA, an Old Norse family saga, is preserved in *Mǫðruvallabók* (ca. 1340); fragments survive in a later manuscript, AM 162 fol. (ca. 1400). The saga, which probably dates from the early thirteenth century, is a biography of the Icelandic skald Kormákr Ǫgmundarson (ca. 930–970) and tells of his lifelong, unfulfilled love for a woman called Steingerðr.

Kormáks saga contains a higher proportion of poetry than any other family saga. In the standard Icelandic edition, *dróttkvætt* stanzas take up about a third of the entire number of lines. These occasional verses *(lausavísur)* are represented as spur-of-the-moment improvisations by the poet in response to a specific situation. Kormákr recites sixty-four stanzas, mostly about his unhappy love; Holmgǫngu-Bersi recites fourteen, mostly about war; and even Steingerðr is given a quatrain in which she states her determination to have Kormákr.

The narrative follows in general the conflict pattern of other skald biographies, such as *Bjarnar saga Hítdœlakappa, Gunnlaugs saga,* and *Hallfreðar saga*. Kormákr competes against each of Steingerðr's husbands, Bersi and Þorvaldr, even though it was his failure to attend his wedding to Steingerðr that led her to marry them. He manages to have Bersi so crippled in a duel that the squeamish Steingerðr divorces him. Kormákr provokes Þorvaldr with insulting verses, public misconduct with his wife, and a blow from a tiller; but only when Kormákr saves Steingerðr from pirates does Þorvaldr relinquish his wife. Kormákr is as willing as ever, but Steingerðr will have none of him. He ends his life as a Viking in the British Isles, dying of injuries received in a battle with a giant in Scotland.

The relationship between the poetry and prose of *Kormáks saga* is still unsettled. The traditional view is that the stanzas are genuine tenth-century compositions and that the romantic outlines of Kormákr's life were preserved in oral tradition until the saga was written down in the thirteenth century. Others accept the verse as authentic, but regard the prose biography as late and freely invented; the converse—authentic biography and spurious verse—is theoretically possible but unlikely. Some believe that the stanzas were composed no earlier than the twelfth century and were accepted as genuine or at least early by the saga author and his audience. Others conceive of both poetry and prose as the free creation of the saga author. The last possibility can probably be ruled out on the basis of the striking discrepancies in the saga between certain verses and their accompanying prose, occasions on which the saga author completely misunderstands a skaldic kenning or allusion. Finally, it has been argued that both verse and saga were influenced by the story of Tristan, whose Old Norse saga was written in Norway in 1226, and that Kormákr's poetry shows the direct impact of troubadour poetry.

According to *Skáldatal*, Kormákr worked for Earl Sigurðr of Lade (d. 962) and for Haraldr gráfeldr (king of Norway, ca. 960–970); fragments of his official verse are preserved in *Snorra Edda,* but this aspect of the poet's life is ignored in his saga. Like the other *skáldasǫgur* (sagas of poets), *Kormáks saga* tells little about the artistic and political strivings of its skald protagonist and quite a lot about his duels, litigation, and love life. Far from the courts at which he won fame, the tenth-century skald is depicted in these narratives as a cantankerous, even boorish and mean-spirited, man who rejects or is rejected by women and who converts his little domestic wrongs into strangely memorable verse.

BIBLIOGRAPHY

Sources. Kormáks saga, Einar Ól. Sveinsson, ed., in *Íslenzk fornrit,* VIII (1939); *The Sagas of Kormák and the Sworn Brothers,* Lee M. Hollander, trans. (1949).

Studies. Theodore M. Andersson, *The Icelandic Family Saga* (1967), and "Skalds and Troubadours," in *Mediaeval Scandinavia,* **2** (1969); Bjarni Einarsson, *Skáldasögur* (1961), 52–164, and "The Lovesick Skald," in *Mediaeval Scandinavia,* **4** (1971); Einar Ól. Sveinsson, "Kormakr the Poet and His Verses," in *Saga-Book of the Viking Society,* **17** (1966).

ROBERTA FRANK

[See also **Family Sagas, Icelandic; Skáldatal.**]

KOSOVO. See Serbia.

KOTZENMÄRE, DAS *(Die halbe Decke),* a late-fourteenth-century Middle High German verse tale *(Märe)* transmitted in six versions, ranging from 122 to 230 lines, with varying details and differing social milieux.

A wealthy old widower, after an honorable and charitable life, gives his house and possessions to his twenty-year-old son, who fails to show any sense of gratitude or respect. The feeble old man is first driven from the family table and then, when his daughter-in-law gives birth to a son, from his own room. He is obliged to subsist miserably in an unheated space under the staircase, where he is finally all but forgotten. During a particularly cold winter he begs his little grandson to ask his father for an old blanket *(Kotze).* But the ungrateful and greedy son cuts it in two, giving one half to the child and retaining the other. Moved by his grandfather's tearful gratitude, the child returns to his father to demand the other half. "This," he explains upon inquiry, "is for you when you are in need of it in your old age." Out of the mouth of the innocent child the shaken father hears the word of God; he repents and quickly restores the old man to his place of honor in the household. The moral of the tale is: Honor your father and mother, and teach your children likewise.

The subject of this didactic tale, expounding an ancient and vital social command, is attested in the early traditions of India *(Rigveda);* it was known widely in medieval Latin exempla (Jacques de Vitry; Vincent of Beauvais' *Speculum morale).* Similarities in the *Kotzenmäre* with two Old French versions ("La houce parti" and "C'est de la houce" in Anatole de Montaiglon's collection of fabliaux) suggest a Latin exemplum as the common source. The motif subsequently found its way into the *Meistersang,* Hans Sachs's *Spruchgedichte,* and Clemens Brentano's *Des Knaben Wunderhorn* (1805–1808).

BIBLIOGRAPHY

Hanns Fischer, *Studien zur deutschen Märendichtung* (1968), 304f., 327; Margaret D. Howie, *Studies in the Use of Exempla, with Special Reference to Middle High German Literature* (1923); Ulla Williams, "Das Märe von der halben Decke in der mhd. Literatur" (diss., Univ. of Kentucky, 1971), and "Die halbe Decke," in *Die deutsche Literatur des Mittelalters: Verfasserlexikon,* III (1980).

KLAUS WOLLENWEBER

[See also **Fabliau and Comic Tale; Jacques de Vitry; Mären; Middle High German Literature; Vincent of Beauvais.**]

KRAFFT, ADAM (also Kraft) *(ca.* 1455/1460–1508/1509), leading Nuremberg stone sculptor. Krafft is best known for reliefs in sandstone that are akin to paintings in that full attention is given to settings and there are layers of space. Emphasis is on vivid facial expressions and figure interactions. Krafft's works include the Schreyer-Landauer monument in St. Sebald's (1490–1492), the tabernacle in St. Lorenz's (1493–1496), the Pergenstörffer monument (1498–1499) (originally in St. John's Cemetery, now in the Frauenkirche), the *Stations of the Cross,* which formerly lined the road to St. John's Cemetery (now in the Germanisches Nationalmuseum), and the *Entombment* (1506–1508) (in St. John's Cemetery).

BIBLIOGRAPHY

Wilhelm Schwemmer, *Adam Kraft* (1958); Jeffrey Chipps Smith, *Nuremberg: A Renaissance City 1500–1618* (1983), 24–27, 61; Dorothea Stern, *Der nürnberger Bildhauer Adam Kraft* (1916); Gert von der Osten and Horst Vey, *Painting and Sculpture in Germany and the Netherlands 1500–1600* (1969), 18–20.

LARRY SILVER

Adam Krafft. Self-portrait from base of *Sakramentshaus*, St. Lorenz, Nuremberg, 1493–1496. PHOTO: WIM SWAAN

Krak des Chevaliers, 12th–13th centuries. PHOTO: A. F. KERSTING

KRAK DES CHEVALIERS, the most imposing and best-preserved example of crusader military architecture in the Levant. The name is a corruption of the Syriac *karka* (fortress). Set on an approximately 2,000-foot (650-meter) plateau in present-day northwestern Syria, the site guards roads leading from the interior of Syria to the coast of the Mediterranean. A Muslim castle, Hosn al-Akrad, stood on the site. The site was captured by Frankish knights in 1110 after the First Crusade had ended in 1099 and was fortified, after 1142, in a series of building campaigns by the Knights Hospitalers of St. John of Jerusalem over the next century and a half.

The Krak des Chevaliers fell on 8 April 1271 to the Muslims, who enlarged and refortified it thereafter. Military engineers who built the Krak des Chevaliers later employed a number of its features in French military architecture.

BIBLIOGRAPHY

Paul Deschamps, *Les châteaux des croisés en Terre sainte,* I, *Le crac des chevaliers* (1934), and "Le crac des chevaliers," in *Terre sainte romane* (1964).

CARL F. BARNES, JR.

[See also **Castles and Fortifications; Crusader Art and Architecture.**]

KREMLIN. See **Moscow Kremlin, Art and Architecture.**

KRISTNI SAGA, an account of the conversion of Iceland to Christianity in the year 1000 and the earliest history of the Icelandic church, probably written in the latter half of the thirteenth century. It is preserved in the manuscript *Hauksbók,* dating from the early fourteenth century. The sources for the account may be traced as far back as the early twelfth century, a little more than 100 years after the conversion is said to have taken place. In its main outlines the story is also found in Ari fróði's (Ari the Learned's) *Íslendingabók,* in the various versions of *Óláfs saga Tryggvasonar,* and in *Njáls saga. Kristni saga,* however, contains a much more detailed account than any of the other sources. It is attributed to Sturla Þórðarson (d. 1284), lawman of Iceland and nephew of Snorri Sturluson.

BIBLIOGRAPHY

An edition is *Kristnisaga, Þáttr Þorvalds ens víðfǫrla, Þáttr Ísleifs biskups Gizurarsonar, Hungrvaka,* Bernhard Kahle, ed. (1905), 1–57. See also Oskar Brenner, *Über die Kristni-Saga* (1878); Dag Strömbäck, *The Conversion of Iceland: A Survey* (1975).

LARS LÖNNROTH

[See also **Njáls Saga; Oláfs Saga Tryggvasonar.**]

KRITOVOULOS, MICHAEL (*ca.* 1400/1410–*ca.* 1470), Greek historian, also known as Kritoboulos or Kritopoulos. After the fall of Constantinople to the Turks in 1453, he entered the service of Sultan Mehmed II (Muḥammad II, 1430–1481) the Conqueror and was named governor of Imbros, his native island, in 1456. His *History,* which survives in a single manuscript in the Seraglio Library in İstanbul (İstanbul, Topkapi Sarayi, Codex G.İ.3), describes in five books the first seventeen years of the reign of Mehmed II (beginning in 1451) from the Turkish point of view and praises the sultan in glowing terms. His style is, however, strongly reminiscent of his ancient Greek forebears, especially Thucydides.

BIBLIOGRAPHY

The edition of Diether R. Reinsch, *Critobuli Imbriotae Historiae* (1983), supersedes all earlier editions. For translations see Philippe A. Dethier, *Vie de Mahomet II,* in *Monumenta Hungariae historica: Scriptores,* XXI, pt. 2 (*ca.* 1875), 7–368; Charles T. Riggs, *History of Mehmed the Conqueror by Kritovoulos* (1954), in English and based on Dethier. See also N. P. Andriotēs, "Kritoboulos ho Imbrios kai to historiko tou ergo," in *Hellenika,* 2 (1929); V. Grecu, "Kritoboulos aus Imbros," in *Byzantinoslavica,* 18 (1957); Herbert Hunger, *Die hochsprachliche profane Literatur der Byzantiner,* I (1978), 499–503, with good bibliography; A. Pertusi, *La caduta di Constantinopoli,* II (1976), 228–251.

ALICE-MARY M. TALBOT

[See also **Historiography, Byzantine; Mehmed (Muḥammad) II.**]

KRUM (*r. ca.* 803–814), one of Bulgaria's greatest warrior rulers, was originally a Bulgarian chieftain from Pannonia. Nothing is known about his activities in Pannonia nor about his acquisition of the Bulgarian throne. Shortly after his accession, in about 805, Krum fought a successful war with the Avars which enabled him to unite the Bulgars of the west, in Pannonia, with those of the east. How far his state then extended westward is unknown; some scholars propose to the Timok River, while others suggest it was to the Tisza River. With the collapse of the Avar khaganate, in this period, the Bulgars replaced the Avars as overlords over the Slavs and proto-Rumanians living in the territory north of the Danube up to the Carpathians and east to the Dnieper. In 807, for an unknown reason, the Byzantines launched a raid against Bulgaria. In retaliation, in 808, Krum's troops raided along the Struma River and in 809 took Sardika (modern Sofia). Then, in 811, the Emperor Nikephoros I himself led a large Byzantine force against Bulgaria which sacked Krum's capital of Pliska. Krum's Bulgars ambushed and destroyed the Byzantine army on its way home, however. During the battle Nikephoros was killed and his skull was made into a drinking cup. In 812 Krum followed this victory by taking the Byzantine Black Sea ports of Develtos and Mesembria. The next year he defeated a major Byzantine force sent against him, then took much of Thrace (including Adrianople) and ravaged the suburbs of Constantinople. In these conquests of 812–813 he transferred many Byzantine subjects to Bulgaria, where many were enrolled as soldiers. In 814 he again marched on Constantinople with a massive army but died of a stroke en route.

Krum's gains against Byzantium in Thrace were not to be lasting. A treaty between Byzantium and Krum's successor, Omurtag, restored the Balkan Mountains as the Byzantine-Bulgarian border. Krum also issued a law code, the first for the Bulgarian state, whose text (except for a fragment) has not survived. He tolerated all ethnic groups; Bulgars, Avars, Slavs, Greeks (including deserters to him), and even an Arab are mentioned as serving him. In occupied Byzantine territories he used Greeks in high administrative positions. Though a great warrior, he regularly tried diplomacy first. Throughout the 811 campaign he extended peace offers, which Nikephoros ignored. He also offered a treaty to the Byzantines throughout 812 and 813; only after Byzantine rebuffs of his offers did he launch his attacks.

BIBLIOGRAPHY

John V. A. Fine, Jr., *The Early Medieval Balkans* (1983), 94–105; Steven Runciman, *A History of the First Bulgarian Empire* (1930), 51–70.

JOHN V. A. FINE, JR.

[See also **Byzantine History; Bulgaria; Nikephoros I.**]

KUDRUN. The epic poem *Kudrun* is transmitted in only one manuscript, the *Ambraser Heldenbuch* (Codex Vindobonensis, s.n. 2663), which was written by Hans Ried at the request of Emperor Maximilian I between 1504 and 1516. The language of the manuscript is Early New High German. The *Kudrun,* however, is in its transmitted form originally a Middle High German epic of 1,705 four-line stanzas, varying between *Nibelungen* stanzas and *Kudrun* stanzas. The latter are distinguished from the *Nibelungen* stanzas by the fact that the sixth hemistich has four instead of three stresses, the eighth has six instead of five stresses, and both have feminine rhyme. The epic was written in Austria or Bavaria about the middle of the thirteenth century, in any case not before 1230/1240, but the manuscript from which Hans Ried copied probably dated from the fifteenth century.

The narrative is tripartite, consisting of the adventures of Hagen (first–fourth *aventiure*), the story of Hilde (fifth–eighth *aventiure*), and the story of Kudrun (ninth–thirty-first *aventiure*). Both stylistically, in its oral-formulaic content and density, and thematically, in its employment of traditional narrative themes, the poem reveals its ultimate provenience in the oral tradition.

The first part relates the abduction of young Hagen by a griffin, his finding three similarly abducted princesses in the wilderness, his eventual destruction of the brood of griffins, and his return to Ireland—with the princesses, one of whom he marries—on a passing ship. In the second part, King Hetel of Denmark sends out suitors on his behalf for the hand of Hilde, Hagen's daughter. This is a dangerous undertaking, since Hagen has all suitors for his daughter's hand killed. Hetel's men, pretending to be in flight from Hetel, however, are received as guests at Hagen's court, where Wate demonstrates his fighting skill and Horant impresses father and daughter with his singing. With the connivance of Hilde they manage to abduct her, hotly pursued by Hagen. Upon landing on their home shore, they join forces with Hetel and face Hagen. The ensuing battle ends in reconciliation, and Hetel marries Hilde with Hagen's blessing.

The third part is devoted to the suits of Kings Sivrit, Hartmut, and Herwig for the hand of Hetel's daughter, Kudrun. All are rejected, but after a battle Herwig is accepted. Before the marriage can take place, however, Sivrit attacks the lands of Herwig, whose future father-in-law, Hetel, goes to his aid. Meanwhile, Hetel's castle is conquered by Hartmut and his father, Ludwig, who abduct Kudrun. Hetel and Herwig catch up with them on the "Wülpensand," where a devastating battle takes place. Hetel is killed; Ludwig and Hartmut flee with the remnant of their army and with Kudrun. In the land of Ludwig and Hartmut, Kudrun resists all attempts to make her accept Hartmut. After fourteen years an army led by Herwig, Sivrit, and Kudrun's brother Ortwin appears and takes bloody revenge. The narrative ends in general conciliation and a quadruple marriage.

The history of the first part of *Kudrun,* the Hagen story, presumably does not go back beyond the strophic epic of the thirteenth century. It consists mainly of narrative matter native to the epic of the late twelfth and early thirteenth centuries. Aspects of the Hilde narrative, on the other hand, can be traced in the Germano-Judaic *Dukus Horant* of the fourteenth century, the *Rolandslied* and the *Alexanderlied* of approximately the middle of the twelfth century, the Old Norse *Skáldskaparmál* of the first half of the thirteenth century, the Old Norse *Sörla þáttr* in the *Flateyjarbók* of the latter part of the fourteenth century, the *Gesta Danorum* of Saxo Grammaticus from the beginning of the thirteenth century, the two Eddic Songs of Helgi—one from the eleventh century and one from the twelfth—a considerable number of *Folkeviser,* and the Old English *Deor* of the eighth century and *Widsith* from the late seventh century. The story of Kudrun, on the other hand, is seen either as having evolved from a Kudrun narrative that existed independently from that of Hilde, or as a creation of the poet of the transmitted

Kudrun, who used the narrative of Hilde and other bride-abduction stories as a basis. But not only the antecedents of *Kudrun* appear to be shrouded in considerable uncertainty; subject to debate as well is the relationship between *Kudrun* and the *Südeli* and *Meererin* ballads, which reflect motifs of the narrative of Kudrun's captivity.

Obviously the question of the function of *Kudrun* in its transmitted form at the time of its composition in the thirteenth century is particularly pressing. To maintain, in reaction to nineteenth-century evaluations of the poem, that its function is "little more" than "entertainment" is merely begging the question. More recent interpretations rest on the basis of the obvious relationships between *Kudrun* and the *Nibelungenlied.* Seen in this perspective, *Kudrun* is an antitype to the *Nibelungenlied,* just as Kudrun is antitypical to Kriemhild and the conflict between Kriemhild and Brünhild is countered by the conciliatory functions of the women in *Kudrun.* This "lateral" function of the narrative is accompanied by the "vertical" relationships among the generations. The Hilde narrative, for instance, may be seen as antitypical to the Kudrun story in that it is determined by the laws of revenge, whereas the latter is characterized by a spirit of conciliation: in the cases of Hagen, Hetel, and Hilde, youth acts for the sake of conciliation, while the older generation acts for the sake of revenge. A solely "vertical" analysis of *Kudrun,* however, cannot answer the question of its function in the mid thirteenth century. But whatever the perspective in which the relationship of *Kudrun* to the *Nibelungenlied* is seen, its dependence on the latter makes it clear that its function in the mid thirteenth century can perhaps best be understood as a commentary on the earlier poem, as well as on the entire epic tradition upon which it draws.

BIBLIOGRAPHY

A facsimile edition of the MS text of *Kudrun* is *Kudrun, Die Handschrift,* Franz H. Bäuml, ed. (1969). The best edition of a MHG text of the epic is that of Karl Bartsch, rev. with new introd. by Karl Stackmann, *Kudrun,* 5th ed. (1965).

For the older secondary literature, see the bibliography of Albert Fécamp, *Le poème de Gudrun* (1892), 237–260; Hermann Schneider, *Germanische Heldensage,* I.1, *Deutsche Heldensage* (1962), 534–541, bibliography for 1928–1960 by Roswitha Wisniewski. Problems of *Kudrun* research are treated in Werner Hoffmann, "Die Hauptprobleme der neuren 'Kudrun'-Forschung," in *Wirkendes Wort,* **14** (1964), and *Kudrun: Ein Beitrag zur Deutung der nachnibelungischen Heldendichtung* (1967); Roswitha

Wisniewski, *Kudrun* (1963). Problems of interpretation are extensively discussed in Ian Campbell, *Kudrun: A Critical Appreciation* (1978).

FRANZ H. BÄUML

[See also **Ambraser Heldenbuch; Brynhild; Dukus Horant; Middle High German Literature; Nibelungenlied; Rolandslied; Skáldskaparmál.**]

KUENE, KONRAD (*ca.* 1400/1410–1469), architect and sculptor. Kuene served as *Dombaumeister* at Cologne Cathedral from about 1445 until his death. Little is known about his architectural activity at the cathedral; he may have worked on a portion of the north aisle of the nave, the southern tower of the west facade, and the foundations of the northern tower of the west facade. His high professional standing is attested to by his 1459 appoint-

Archbishop Dietrich von Moers. Carving by Konrad Kuene from the tomb in Cologne Cathedral, 1460. FROM HANS PETER, DER DOM ZU KÖLN, 1248-1948 (1948)

ment as director for northern Germany by the Regensburg masons' lodge.

Kuene was equally adept as a sculptor. His attributed oeuvre, characterized by powerful, expressive figures, embraces such important monuments as the tabernacle in the parish church at Kempen, the four statuettes of masons' saints on the tomb of his predecessor, the architect Nikolaus von Bueren (d. 1445), and the tomb of Archbishop Dietrich von Moers (completed 1460), both in Cologne Cathedral.

BIBLIOGRAPHY

Heinrich Appel, "Die Bildwerke des Kölner Dombaumeisters Konrad Kuyn (d. 1469)," in *Wallraf-Richartz Jahrbuch,* 10 (1938); Paul Clemen, *Der Dom zu Köln* (1937); E. Kühnemann, "Zum plastische Werke des Dombaumeisters Konrad Kuene," in *Kölner Domblatt,* 6/7 (1952); Johann Jacob Merlo, "Zwei Denkmale Kölner Dombaumeister aus dem 15. Jahrhundert," in *Zeitschrift für christliche Kunst,* 1 (1880), and *Kölnische Künstler in alter und neuer Zeit* (1895), 507–513; Theodor Müller, *Sculpture in the Netherlands, Germany, France, and Spain: 1400–1500* (1966), 67–69, pl. 79.

MICHAEL T. DAVIS

[See also **Architect, Status of.**]

KÜRNBERGER, DER. See Der von Kürenberg.

KUFA, AL-, a city founded in central Iraq during the early Islamic conquests. After Saᶜd ibn Abī Waqqāṣ' decisive victory over the Sasanians at Al-Qādisīya in 637, all of Iraq quickly fell to the Arab forces. Saᶜd's army first established a base at Ctesiphon (Al-Madāʾin), the former Sasanian capital, but this site proved unsatisfactory, probably because the city was within striking distance of Sasanian forces in Persia. Saᶜd soon withdrew to a more secure position on the Euphrates River about 120 kilometers south of Ctesiphon, likely in order to command the routes around the north end of the great swamps of southern Iraq. Here, in 638 or 639, he founded Al-Kufa as a permanent garrison and a base for further military operations.

The earliest town was a simple military bivouac, with the tribal contingents all encamped on their own grounds (*khiṭaṭ*) around a central mosque and a headquarters for the governor. Roads roughly radiating from this central area separated the tribal plots, and there were numerous stretches of open ground (*jabbānāt*) that were used as pasture for animals, exercise fields, tribal cemeteries, and mobilization points. The population of the town was probably more than 100,000 by 656.

Like Basra, Al-Kufa was a base for the Arab conquest of areas farther east. Armies launched from it pushed into the Persian highlands, capturing Isfahan and Rayy. At the same time, Al-Kufa administered the agricultural lands of central and northern Iraq, and its military leaders managed the rich estates that had belonged to the Sasanian crown. All this made the garrison town a lively, prosperous center and hastened its transformation into a proper city. The economic and military prospects brought immigrants pouring into Al-Kufa from Arabia, and the tribal plots expanded in all directions and became more densely populated. Tents and huts gave way to mud-brick houses crowded along narrow, winding lanes, and during the governorship of Ziyād ibn Abī Sufyān (670–673) the congregational mosque and the governor's headquarters, by now a palace, were rebuilt. Further improvements were made by the governor Khālid al-Qasrī (723–737), who built Al-Kufa's famous covered markets.

The city's first burst of rapid growth diminished after about ten years, for the conquest of the heartlands of Persia had by then pushed the frontiers of Islam to far more distant lands. At this point, Basra began to surpass Al-Kufa, for while the former's armies were conquering the rich province of Khorāsān, Al-Kufa's had the difficult and less fruitful task of reducing Azerbaijan. At the same time, the population of Al-Kufa was coming under enormous social pressures. From the time of its founding, the town had contained contingents from numerous tribal groupings, all maneuvering for control of the province's resources. This comprised an element of serious instability, and was rendered all the more grave by the presence of a large Yemeni minority and by uncontrolled immigration of newcomers demanding more equitable distribution of grants and stipends. On a more general level, the provincial capitals were all evolving into the real centers of power in the nascent Islamic empire, and as such grew resentful of efforts by the caliphate to control them from Medina.

For such reasons Al-Kufa soon became a major center of ferment and dissent as early Islam sought its identity as a politico-religious entity. A number of prominent Kufans were involved in the murder of the caliph ᶜUthmān in 656, and thus, in the ensuing civil war, the city cast its lot with ᶜAlī ibn Abī Ṭalib. It served as his capital, and many Kufans fought for him at the battles of Al-Jamal (the Camel) (656) and Ṣiffīn (657). The instability of the situation in the city was already clear. Although many Kufans, particularly those from the Yemenite tribes, were fervent supporters of ᶜAlī, many of the tribal chieftains viewed him as a threat to their privileged position and so gave him only halfhearted support. It was also among the Kufans that there emerged the Kharijite movement, which arose from intransigent elements opposed to ᶜAlī's decision to accept arbitration to end the war with Muᶜāwiya.

This basic lack of cohesion persisted as the salient feature of the Kufan social and political scene in Umayyad times. The city remained a focus for the radical ideology of the Kharijites. Meanwhile, the faction (Shīᶜa) of ᶜAlī remained loyal to his memory. Agitation by Ḥujr ibn ᶜAdī al-Kindī (executed in 671) led to more serious unrest when the Shīᶜa prevailed upon ᶜAlī's son Ḥusayn to come to Kufa to lead them. This agitation was quelled by the suppression of the Kufan Shiᶜa late in 679, and by the massacre of Ḥusayn and most of his retinue at the Battle of Karbalāʾ at the beginning of 680. The Shīᶜa of Al-Kufa remained implacable, however, and its resistance to the Umayyads was soon manifested in several violent episodes: the fatal march of the Tawwābūn (Penitents) in 684, the rebellion of Mukhtār (685–686) and the rise of the Kaysānīya movement, and the revolts of Zayd ibn ᶜAlī (740) and ᶜAbd Alāh ibn Muᶜāwiya (744).

Against both the Kharijites and the Shīᶜa stood the established tribal leaders (ashrāf). These chieftains had no liking for rule from Syria, but supported the Umayyads as a regime dependent upon the same tribal principle that guaranteed their position in Iraq. As a rule, they cooperated with the Umayyads and almost always led their followers against the forces of insurrection. The only instance of general Kufan unity came in 700–701, when the city joined in the great Iraqi rebellion of Ibn al-Ashᶜath. When Ḥajjāj ibn Yūsuf crushed this revolt, both Basra and Al-Kufa were demilitarized; a new capital was founded at Wāsiṭ, and from there all Iraq was henceforth ruled by an occupation force of Syrian troops. Al-Kufa's role as the focus of Shiite Islam nevertheless continued. It was from there that Shiism eventually spread into Persia (particularly to Qom), and from there that clandestine agents were sent to organize anti-Umayyad propaganda in Khorāsān. When the ensuing rebellion succeeded, it was in Al-

Kufa, in 749, that Abū 'l-ᶜAbbās was invested as the first Abbasid caliph.

Al-Kufa served for a short time as the de facto capital of the Abbasids. Though neither Abū 'l-ᶜAbbās nor his successor, al-Manṣūr, lived there on a regular basis, the treasury and administration were based in al-Kufa until al-Manṣūr began construction of a new capital at Baghdad in 762. Meanwhile, the city's development continued apace. Walls and new buildings were erected, and new ideas and social elements were introduced with the influx of troops and supporters of the victorious Abbasids. Although Al-Kufa was again to be the scene of occasional violent unrest, its population was becoming too mixed for it to pose any serious threat to the regime.

Abbasid Al-Kufa was famous for dates, silk, and perfumes, but was primarily renowned as a center of scholarship. Arabic writing was perfected there, and Kūfī was for centuries the Arabic literary script par excellence. Jurisprudence as a field of study began in Al-Kufa, where there arose such great scholars as Abū Ḥanīfa (d. 767) and Abū Yūsuf (d. 798). The related sciences of prophetic tradition (ḥadīth) and Koranic exegesis (tafsīr) also appeared there at an early date. Whatever Al-Kufa lacked in comparison with Basra's achievements in verse and theology, it more than compensated through its contribution to historical writing. Without the works of such great Kufan historians as Abū Mikhnaf (d. 774), Sayf ibn ᶜUmar (d. 796), Naṣr ibn Muzāḥim, the first historian of the Shīᶜa (d. 827), and the genealogists Muḥammad ibn al-Sāʾib al-Kalbī (d. 763) and his son Hishām (d. 819), precious little would be known about early Islamic history beyond the confines of Arabia. Finally, Al-Kufa was the second major center, after Basra, for the study of Arabic grammar. Based on the work of its master, al-Kisāʾī (d. 795), it produced a long line of grammarians and philologists who did much to establish a firm basis for Arabic linguistic studies.

Al-Kufa began to decline in the twelfth century. This was an era of chronic instability and insecurity from which Iraq generally suffered; but even before this, the essential raison d'être for a town like Al-Kufa had disappeared. Long since demilitarized, it could not maintain itself in an empire in which the established Arab tribes no longer dominated political or economic affairs. Its role as an academic center was eclipsed as Baghdad assimilated the heritage of Al-Kufa and Basra and lured away their scholars. And even its role as a focus of Shiism suffered when the Buyids, in the mid tenth century, established a major shrine at nearby Najaf, where the tomb of ʿAlī was believed to be located.

From 996, when the Buyid emir Bahāʾ al-Dawla granted Al-Kufa as a fief *(iqṭāʿ)* to the bedouin Uqaylids, the declining city was subjected to increased spoliation by nomadic elements. When the traveler Ibn Jubayr visited it in the late twelfth century, it was ruined, sparsely populated, and subject to frequent raids by local bedouin. Ibn Baṭṭūṭa confirms that the city had declined even further by the fourteenth century, and in Ottoman times it was only a small borough of little consequence lying close by the ruins of the once-great city.

BIBLIOGRAPHY

Al-Kufa was declared an archaeological site in 1938, and excavations have proceeded irregularly since that time. Most of the reports are in Arabic in the journal *Sumer;* but see Muḥammad ʿAlī Muṣṭafā, "Preliminary Report on the Excavations in Kūfa During the Third Season," in *Sumer,* **19** (1963); Keppel A. C. Creswell, *Early Muslim Architecture,* 2nd ed. (1969), I, i, 22–26, 38–40, 43–44, 46–58, excellent on architecture and urban history. On the founding of Al-Kufa, see Else Reitemeyer, *Die Städtegründungen der Araber im Islam* (1912). There is an excellent summary of Kufan history, with detailed bibliography of primary and secondary sources, in the article by Hichem Djaït in *Encyclopaedia of Islam,* new ed., V (1980); for further details, see Julius Wellhausen, *Das arabische Reich und sein Sturz* (1902), translated by Margaret Graham Weir as *The Arab Kingdom and Its Fall* (1927); Louis Massignon, "Explication du plan de Kūfa (Irak)," in *Opera minora,* Y. Moubarac, ed. (1963), III; M. A. Shaban, *Islamic History: A New Interpretation* (1971–1976); Michael G. Morony, *Iraq After the Muslim Conquest* (1984). On the politico-religious movements of Al-Kufa, see Julius Wellhausen, *Die religiös-politischen Oppositionsparteien im alten Islam* (1901), ed. and trans. by R. C. Ostle and S. M. Walzer as *The Religio-political Factions in Early Islam* (1975); W. Montgomery Watt, "Shīʿism Under the Umayyads," in *Journal of the Royal Asiatic Society* (1960); Martin Hinds, "Kūfan Political Alignments and Their Background in the Mid-Seventh Century A.D.," in *International Journal of Middle East Studies,* **2** (1971); Hichem Djaït, "Les Yamanites à Kūfa au Ier siècle de l'Hégire," in *Journal of the Economic and Social History of the Orient,* **19** (1976); Redwan Sayed, *Die Revolte des Ibn al-Asʿat und die Koranleser* (1977); S. Husain M. Jafri, *The Origins and Early Development of Shīʿa Islam* (1979). For Kufan contributions to medieval Islamic culture, see Joseph Schacht, *An Introduction to Islamic Law* (1964), 23–68; Ramzi Baalbaki, "Arab Grammatical Controversies and the Extant Sources of the Second and Third Centuries A.H.," in Wadād al-Qāḍī, ed., *Studia arabica et islamica: Festschrift for Iḥsān ʿAbbās on*

His Sixtieth Birthday (1981); Abd al-ʿAziz Duri, *The Rise of Historical Writing Among the Arabs,* Lawrence I. Conrad, ed. and trans. (1982).

LAWRENCE I. CONRAD

[See also **Abbasids; ʿAli ibn Abi Ṭalib; Alids; Basra; Buyids; Iraq; Shiʿa.**]

KŪFĪ (Kufic), an Arabic adjective denoting something connected with the city of Al-Kufa in Iraq and often used specifically to describe an angular script employed in Koranic manuscripts and monumental epigraphy during the eighth to twelfth centuries. Muḥammad ibn Ishaq al-Nadīm (*d.* 990) mentions the *kūfī* script as one of several used for copying the Koran. Later, Islamic and Western authors used the term more generally to describe any script with angular letters. The prototype of these scripts probably originated in late-seventh-century Syria; their subsequent association with Al-Kufa was undoubtedly strengthened by the reputation of that city as a leading center of religious studies during the eighth and ninth centuries. When used on architectural structures, *kūfī* was often subject to decorative elaboration.

BIBLIOGRAPHY

Nabia Abbott, *The Rise of the North Arabic Script and Its Ḳurʾanic Development* (1939), 17–30; Adolf Groh-

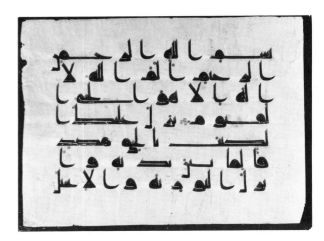

Kūfī script (Koran) on parchment. Mesopotamian, early 9th century. THE METROPOLITAN MUSEUM OF ART, ROGERS FUND, 1937 (37.99.2)

308

mann, *Arabische Paläographie*, pt. II (1971), 71–231, in *Österreichische Akademie der Wissenschaften*, XCIVa.

PRISCILLA P. SOUCEK

[See also **Alphabets; Calligraphy, Islamic; Kufa, Al-; Manuscripts and Books, Islamic.**]

KULIN, the first major ruler (ban) of medieval Bosnia (*ca.* 1180–*ca.* 1204), acquired his banate under obscure circumstances. He was able to assert Bosnia's de facto independence from Hungary while retaining loyalty to the pope. To try to regain their influence, the Hungarians in 1192 persuaded Pope Celestine III to transfer the Bosnian Catholic church from the jurisdiction of Dubrovnik to that of Split. Kulin successfully resisted this, maintaining close relations with the archbishop of Dubrovnik. He was accused by the Hungarians and the archbishop of Split of giving asylum to and sympathizing with heretics who fled to Bosnia from Dalmatia. Kulin cleared himself with Rome, and at Bilino polje in 1203 he participated in a local church assembly that promised to accept a series of reforms and reaffirmed Bosnia's loyalty to Rome. Kulin built at least two Catholic churches and granted Dubrovnik extensive commercial privileges in a charter of 1189. He is not mentioned in the sources after 1203.

BIBLIOGRAPHY

S. Ćirković, *Istorija srednjovekovne bosanske države* (1964); Vladimir Ćorović, "Ban Kulin," in *Godišnjica Nikole Čupića*, 34 (1921), 13–41.

JOHN V. A. FINE, JR.

[See also **Bosnia; Hungary.**]

KURA RIVER (Georgian: Mtkvari; Armenian: Kur; Greek: Kyros or Kyrnos; Latin: Cyrus). The principal river of south Caucasia (in present-day Turkey, Georgian SSR, and Azerbaijan SSR), the Kura has its sources in the springs of a circular swampy valley, the former district of Koļ or Kola, in north-central Armenia and descends rapidly to the north to water the plain of east Georgia (Iberia). Thereafter, it flows through the arid and steadily broadening steppes of Azerbaijan, and after joining the Araks flows another sixty miles to enter the Caspian Sea. The Kura flows past the cities of Axalkᶜalakᶜi (Akhalkalaki), Axalcᶜixe (Akhaltsikhe), and Tiflis (Tbilisi) and near Ganjak, Bardhaᶜa, and Šamxor (Shamkhor). Its tributaries include the Aragvi (Argava), Alazani (Alazan), and Iora from the north and the Xrami (Khram) and Terter from the south. Its entire length is 941 miles (1,515 km), draining a basin of some 72,500 square miles (188,000 sq km).

BIBLIOGRAPHY

David S. Margoliouth, "The Russian Seizure of Bardhᶜa in 943 A.D.," in *BSOS* (1918); Eduards Veidenbaums, *Putevoditel po Kavkazu* (1888), 41ff; Aleksandr Yakubovskii, "Ibn Miskaveikh o pokhode Rusov v Berdaa v 332 g.–943/4 g.," in *Vizantiiskii vremennik*, 24 (1923–1926), 63–92.

ROBERT H. HEWSEN

[See also **Araks River; Armenia: Geography; Bardhaᶜa; Caucasia; Ganjak; Georgia: Geography.**]

ḲURAYSH. See Quraysh.

KURDĀBIH, IBN. See Khurdādhbih, Ibn.

KURDS, an Indo-European people who at present inhabit much of the eastern and southern parts of Anatolia in Turkey, the northwest of Iran (the northern part of the Zagros chain, the northern and northeastern parts of Iraq, and the northeasternmost part of Syria). Soviet Transcaucasia also has significant Kurdish groups. Statistics of the total number of Kurds vary, since different countries apply varying ethnic and linguistic criteria of what constitutes "Kurdishness"; recent estimates have ranged between 5.5 million and 13.5 million. The western Iranian language of Kurdish is quite distinct from New Persian; there are three main groups of dialects, Northern, Central, and Southern, the first of these being the most conservative, retaining, for example, case and gender distinctions lost by the others. Traditionally, Kurdish has been written in various modifications of the Arabic script, as it is still written in Iraq and Iran, but the Armenian script has been used, and in recent years, Latin and Cyrillic scripts have also been devised, especially for northern Kurdish. There is a rich oral folk literature, and Kurdish poets are known to have flourished from the fifteenth century on, but literature, in the first place poetry, actually written down in Kurdish does not seem to date back beyond the seventeenth century. The extensive literary production that began then is flourishing today. Since early Islamic times the Kurds have produced notable scholars (for example, the literary biographer in Arabic, Ibn Khallikān of Erbil, *d.* 1282, and the Ottoman Turkish historian Idrīs Ḥakīm Bidlīsī, *d.* 1520), but these have usually written in one of the three great literary languages of the Islamic Middle East: Arabic, Persian, or Turkish.

The actual name "Kurdistan" for the land of the Kurds seems to date only from the Seljuk period, when Sultan Sanjar (*d.* 1157) created a province of that name based on a town north of Hamadān. Nevertheless, the historical origins of the Kurdish people have been sought as far back as Sumerian and Assyrian times (second millennium–early first millenium B.C.). It is true that Herodotus mentions no people readily identifiable with them, but Xenophon mentions the country of the Karduchoi in his *Anabasis* (401–400 B.C.), and from that time classical authors called a region on the left bank of the Tigris Corduene (Aramaic: [Beth] Qardū) and referred to various kings of the Karduchoi. Whether these Karduchoi were ancestors of the modern Kurds is unproven. Probably by the time of the expansion of the Muslim Arabs, the term "Kurd" was being applied to a congeries of Iranian or Iranized tribes that may well have contained also Semitic and Armenian elements.

Under Islam, the Kurds appear as a tribally organized people with both nomadic and sedentary elements; component tribes are enumerated in the Arabic sources from the tenth century onward. They early acquired a reputation as a bellicose and predatory people, so that in classical Islamic literature, *Kurd* and its plural, *Akrād*, are synonymous with "brigands." The caliphs had frequently to send punitive expeditions into the Kurdish mountain areas in order to put down rebellions and to curb Kurdish raids on the lowland regions of the Fertile Crescent (for example, on Mosul). The period of the "Iranian intermezzo" of the tenth and eleventh centuries, when hitherto submerged Iranian peoples came to the fore militarily and politically, involved primarily the Dailamites of the Elburz Mountains region, but various Kurdish groups also burst out at this time and formed principalities which were in practice autonomous of the Baghdad caliphate. Thus we have the Shaddadids in western Azerbaijan (*ca.* 951–1174), founded by the adventurer Muḥammad b. Shaddād, subsequently with branches at Dwin (now near Erevan in the Armenian SSR) and at Ganja (or Ganzha) in Arrān (in czarist times Elizavetpol, now Kirovabad in the Azerbaijan SSR); these emirs played a considerable part in jihad against the Christian Georgians, Armenians, and Byzantines. The Rawwadids of Tabriz (early tenth century–1071) were probably ultimately of Arab stock but became thoroughly Kurdicized. They and other Kurdish chiefs of the region tried to stem the westward migrations of the Turkomans in the eleventh century but ended up as vassals of the Seljuks. The Hasanuyids (Ḥasanwayh; *ca.* 960–1014) flourished in the central Zagros and supplied troops to the Buyid emirs of Persia and Iraq. The Marwanids of Diyarbakir (983–1085) held this strategically placed region on the southern and western fringes of Armenia and Kurdistan and thus achieved an importance beyond their actual power; they were on good terms with the Byzantine emperors, and Naṣr al-Dawla ibn Marwān (*d.* 1061) was used by Constantine X to secure the release of the Georgian prince Liparit IV Orbēlean, captured by the Seljuks.

In general, the inflow of Turkoman nomads from the east spelled the end of an independent role for these Kurdish powers, but the Kurds continued to figure prominently as contingents in the armies of various Turkish rulers and atabegs. Intermarriage between Kurds, Arabs, Persians, and Turks was frequent, but one of the most significant historical facts concerning the Kurds of the crusading period was the Kurdish origin of the Ayyubid dynasty, that of Saladin and his successors (1169–late fifteenth century). Ayyūb ibn Shadhi (*d.* 1173), founder of the line and father of Saladin, arose from the Hadhbānī tribe of Kurds, and settled at Dwin; and the Kurdish element in both the armies and the administration of the Ayyubids always remained notable.

The Mongol invasions and their domination of much of the Middle East eclipsed the political role of the Kurdish tribes, but throughout succeeding centuries the Kurds continued to be an intractable element, jealous of their autonomy, between such rival powers as the Mamluk, Ilkhanid, and Turkoman dynasties, and then, later, between the Ottoman Turks and the Persian Safawids.

BIBLIOGRAPHY

The primary source material on the Kurds has to be gleaned from a wide range of works in Arabic, Persian, Turkish, Armenian, and Georgian, but preeminent among all of these is the Persian history of the Kurds by Sharaf al-Dīn Bidlīsī, *Sharaf-nāma* (completed in 1596). This work, describing the history of the Kurds from ancient times, was later translated into French by François B. Charmoy as *Chèref-nâmeh* (1868–1875). The best general treatment of the Kurds and their history is "Kurds, Kurdistān," in *Encyclopaedia of Islam*, 2nd ed. (1981). For the Kurdish origins of the Ayyubids, see Vladimir F. Minorsky, *Studies in Caucasian History* (1953), 107–157.

C. E. BOSWORTH

[See also **Armenia; Ayyubids; Buyids; Dwin; Georgia; Ilkhanids; Indo-European Languages, Development of; Iran, History; Islam, Conquests of; Khallikān, Ibn; Mamluk Dynasty; Mosul; Ottomans; Saladin; Seljuks; Shaddadids.**]

KÜRNBERGER, DER. See **Der von Kürenberg.**

KURSĪ ("seat"; plural, *karāsī*; Syriac: *kurseyāʾ*; Hebrew: *kissé*). In the Middle Ages a *kursī* was a small tray table or stool used for ceremonial purposes and occasionally in the home (the Eastern table is usually so low that those using it have to sit on a carpet or pillow). In Islamic religious writings and glosses on the Koran (in which *kursī* is used in the context of God sitting on a throne), the term should mean "footstool," but—in order to avoid an anthropomorphic connotation—commentators and philosophers explained it allegorically or claimed that "throne" and *kursī* are the names of the two uppermost of the seven heavens surrounding the earth. *Kursī* can also be defined as "support," "slab," one of the characters on or under which a hamza is placed, or one of the parts of a flintlock rifle. In modern usage, *kursī* means "chair" (a seat with a back and, sometimes, armrests).

BIBLIOGRAPHY

Solomon D. Goitein, *A Mediterranean Society*, IV (1983); Joseph Sadan, *Le mobilier au Proche-Orient médiéval* (1976).

JOSEPH SADAN

[See also **Furniture, Islamic.**]

KUTᶜAISI (Kutaisi) (also Kutᶜatᶜisi; Armenian: Kota; Greek: Kytaia, Kotatission, or Oukhimerion [for the citadel]), the traditional capital of West Georgia. Located on the Rioni River, Kutᶜaisi remained the capital after the unification of Georgia in 1008, until the recapture of Tiflis (Tbilisi) in 1122. The northern part of Kutᶜaisi consisted of a citadel and a fortified upper town. To the south, across the river, lay the commercial center. Sacked by the Seljuks in 1074–1079 and by the Khwārizmshāh Jalāl al-Dīn in 1228, Kutᶜaisi was burned by the Ottoman Turks in 1512 and 1691. In 1462 the city became the capital of the new West Georgian kingdom of Imeretᶜi and maintained that position until the state was annexed by Russia in 1810. Kutᶜaisi is noted for its cathedral, one of the most remarkable cruciform churches in Georgia. Near the city stands the Gelatᶜi monastery (twelfth century), whose academy was the greatest cultural center of medieval Georgia.

BIBLIOGRAPHY

William E. Allen, *A History of the Georgian People* (1932, repr. 1971); Károly Gink and Erzsébet Csemegi-Tompos, *Georgia: Treasures, Towers, and Temples,* Inez Kemens, trans. (1975), 65–66; David Marshall Lang, *The Last Years of the Georgian Monarchy* (1957); Rusudan Mepisashvili and Vakhtang Tsintsadze, *The Arts of Ancient Georgia* (1979); Jules Mourier, *Guide au Caucase* (1894), 80–83.

ROBERT H. HEWSEN

[See also **Gelatᶜi; Georgia: Geography.**]

KVIÐUHÁTTR, the Old Norse name for one of the chief meters of skaldic poetry, is a syllable-counting refinement of the Eddic meter *fornyrðislag*. In *kviðuháttr*, even lines retain the two stressed and two unstressed syllables of *fornyrðislag*, but odd lines are shortened by one unstressed syllable. As a result, the odd lines of *kviðuháttr* usually have only one alliterating syllable. Resolution of two short syllables to create one long syllable occurs, as in *fornyrðislag*, but is rarer. The regular alternation of three- and four-syllable lines gives *kviðuháttr* a distinctive swaying rhythm, slow, balanced, and ceremonial.

Kviðuháttr couplets are found in the poetic inscription on the ninth-century Rök stone in Östergötland, although they may be accidental as the form is not sustained:

> *Réð Þjóðríkr*
> *hinn þurmóði ...*

Theodoric, the fierce-hearted, ruled ...

The first poem in *kviðuháttr* that has come down to us is Þjóðólfr (Thiódólf) of Hvín's *Ynglingatal*, a genealogical poem from about 900; the meter is regular, but stanza length varies:

... *ok allvald*
Yngva þjóðar
Loka mær
at leikum hefr.

... Loki's daughter [the goddess Hel]
has the king of Yngvi's race at her pleasure.

Kviðuháttr was the special meter of the Old Norse genealogical praise poem. In addition to *Ynglingatal*, it was used for Eyvindr Finnsson Skáldaspillir's *Háleygjatal* in the tenth century, the anonymous *Nóregs konungatal* in the late twelfth, and Sturla Þórðarson's *Hákonarkviða* in the thirteenth. The meter occurs infrequently in nongenealogical praise poems. An exception is Þórarinn Loftunga's *Glælognskviða* in the early eleventh century, a poem that may have been composed as a Christian response to *Ynglingatal*. Egill Skallagrímsson's (*ca.* 910–990) two long poems in *kviðuháttr*—*Sonatorrek* and *Arinbjarnarkviða*—form a class by themselves. Stylistically, *kviðuháttr* exhibits a fondness for wordplay on proper names and for congruent kennings *(nýgervingar)*.

BIBLIOGRAPHY
Lee M. Hollander, *The Skalds: A Selection of Their Poems* (1945), 4, 7, 76; Hallvard Lie, *"Natur" og "unatur" i skaldekunsten* (1957); Edward O. G. Turville-Petre, *Scaldic Poetry* (1976), xxxiii–xxxiv; Klaus von See, *Germanische Verskunst* (1967), 47–49.

ROBERTA FRANK

[See also **Eddic Meters; Eddic Poetry; Egill Skallagrímsson; Eyvindr Finnson Skáldaspillir; Kenning; Skaldic Poetry; Sturla Þórðarson.**]

KYRIALE is a relatively modern term assigned to parts of manuscripts, usually graduals or full missals, containing music for the ordinary of the Mass. The structures of kyriales vary greatly, and the parts of the ordinary may be troped or rhymed. Earlier examples of kyriales began with groups of Kyrie melodies (hence the term "kyriale") sometimes paired with a few Gloria melodies. Longer groups of Gloria melodies followed. At this point, in a few kyriales, sequences could be introduced. Then came groups of

Sanctus melodies, followed by those for the Agnus Dei. Credo melodies, usually limited in number and musical complexity, concluded the kyriale and did not fall between the Gloria and Sanctus, as might have been expected. Occasionally chants for the *Ite* or *Benedicamus* were added to kyriales, and these were generally very short unless troped. In later medieval manuscripts the groups of melodies for the Kyrie, Gloria, Sanctus, Agnus Dei, and Credo were broken up and used to form distinct "Masses."

BIBLIOGRAPHY
Dom D. Catta, "Aux origines du kyriale," in *Revue grégorienne*, 34 (1955); Virgil Fiala and Wolfgang Irtenkauf, "Versuch einer liturgischen Nomenklatur," in Clemens Köttelwesch, ed., *Zeitschrift für Bibliothekswesen und Bibliographie, Sonderheft* [1], *Zur katalogisierung mittelalterlicher und neuerer Handschriften* (1963), 105–137; Andrew Hughes, *Medieval Manuscripts for Mass and Office* (1982), 628, 735–737, 749–751.

ROGER E. REYNOLDS

[See also **Agnus Chant; Agnus Dei; Benedicamus Domino; Creeds, Liturgical Use of; Gloria; Gradual; Ite Chant; Kyrie; Missal; Sanctus.**]

KYRIE (Greek: "Lord"), the first of the chants of the Ordinary of the Mass. The complete text is "Kyrie eleison" (three times), "Christe eleison" (three times), "Kyrie eleison" (three times). In the early church, "Kyrie eleison" (Lord, have mercy) was said or chanted by the congregation as part of a litany in response to supplications voiced by the priest, deacon, or cantor, with the number of repetitions varying freely. The Ordo of St. Amand, dating perhaps from the early ninth century, clearly defines the form of the Kyrie as it is sung toward the beginning of the Mass, following the Introit.

Margaretha Landwehr-Melnicki has studied melodies for the Kyrie in nearly 500 manuscripts dating from the tenth to the eighteenth centuries. Of the 226 melodies thus collected, 26 form a group of widely known chants; these appear in sources from at least three different regions, over a period of several centuries. Of this group, 18 are included (along with others) in the Vatican Edition of chant, available in the *Liber usualis* and *Graduale romanum*. For thirteen of them, the earliest preserved source is of the tenth century (the Kyries of Masses I, II, III, IV, VI, VII, XIV, XV, XVI, XVIII, and Kyries *ad lib.* I, V, and VI); for four, the eleventh century (Kyries of Masses III and XI repeated in a different reading as Kyrie *ad lib.* X–XII and *ad lib.* V); for two, the twelfth century (Kyries of Masses VIII, and IX and X [fundamentally the same melody]); and for one, the thirteenth century (Kyrie of Mass XVIIb).

"Kyrie eleison" is often treated in medieval manuscripts as having five syllables (the two adjacent *e*'s are elided). In the musical settings, one finds typically a single note or a neume (representing two, three, or perhaps four notes) on each of the first two syllables, then a melisma (a longer chain of notes) on the central *e*, and a return to the simpler style for the ending. But there are many exceptions to this. The music may be the same for each acclamation until the last (*aaa, aaa, aab*), or follow the form of the text, varying the melody at the end (*aaa, bbb, aaa'*). Another possibility is *aba, cdc, efe'*; but the musical form most frequently found is *aaa, bbb, ccc'*. Sometimes all the acclamations end alike.

Of the tenth-century melodies surveyed by Melnicki, nearly half end on D, the others on E and G. Later G becomes the most popular final; nearly two-thirds of the eleventh-century melodies and half the twelfth-century melodies end on G. But in every century after the tenth, there are some new Kyries on each of the four finals possible for ecclesiastical chant. The character of the melodies is a little different from that of the Proper chants of the classic repertory, which are evidently earlier. Among features that set the Kyries apart stylistically is the tendency in certain melodies ending on D to stress the notes a fifth and an octave above the final (A and D respectively) in such a way that they assume structural importance. Melodies descend stepwise through the interval of a fifth (or even further) without pausing to double back; or, alternatively, they may skip certain notes, as would be done in the classic repertory.

In many early sources, Kyries appear in double versions: the melody is written out once to the Kyrie eleison text, and then again to another text, one that expresses the same thought in Latin in more detail, and fits the melody in such a way that there is one syllable for every note (or nearly so). Such texts are now called *Kyrie prosulae*; but in the older studies, as for example in Vol. 47 of *Analecta hymnica*, where many of them are edited, they are called tropes for the Kyrie eleison. It used to be thought that in every case the melismatic form of the melody existed first, before the text was fitted to it, but it now appears that in at least some cases melodies were composed only after the Latin text had been written. In addition to these Latin-texted versions of the Kyrie eleison, there are also a few true tropes for the chant. They consist of rather brief phrases intended to introduce the chant as a whole, or one of its sections, and are provided with musical settings of their own, in neumatic style.

Polyphonic arrangements of the Kyrie eleison were made as early as the eleventh century. Accompaniments for the chant melody were provided either in note-against-note style, or with many notes in the added voice for each note of the chant. In some later settings, the chant was abandoned entirely.

BIBLIOGRAPHY

David A. Bjork, "Early Repertories of the *Kyrie Eleison*," in *Kirchenmusikalisches Jahrbuch*, **63** (1979), and "The Kyrie Trope," in *Journal of the American Musicological Society*, **33** (1980); Joseph A. Jungmann, *The Mass of the Roman Rite*, Francis A. Brunner, trans. (1951), I, 333–346; "Kyrie eleison," in *The New Grove Dictionary of Music and Musicians*, X (1980); Margaretha Landwehr-Melnicki, *Das einstimmige Kyrie des lateinischen Mittelalters* (1955, repr. 1968); *Liber usualis* (1950), edited by the Benedictines of Solesmes with intro. and rubrics in English.

RUTH STEINER

[See also **Gradual; Gregorian Chant; Liber Usualis; Litany; Mass; Melody; Music; Tropes.**]

LABARUM. The labarum was the standard of later Roman emperors, particularly Constantine. According to Eusebius (*Vita Constantini* I.1. 30–31), the labarum was formed by a tall lance surmounted by a crown bearing the Chi-Rho monogram of Christ and a crosspiece from which a purple, gem-encrusted cloth was suspended. Eusebius describes imperial portraits as being part of the labarum, but it is unclear whether he is describing the original standard or one he had seen years after the labarum had come into use. The labarum appears frequently on sarcophagi in the fourth and fifth centuries and, without the monogram, as an attribute of Byzantine emperors.

BIBLIOGRAPHY

Henri Leclerq, "Labarum," in *Dictionnaire d'archéologie chrétienne et de liturgie*, VIII, 1 (1928); Angelo Lipinsky, "Labarum," in *Lexikon der christlichen Ikonogra-*

Sarcophagus from Lateran Palace, Rome, showing the labarum. 4th century. VATICAN, MUSEO PIO CRISTIANO

phie, III (1971); George H. L. F. Pitt-Rivers, *The Riddle of the Labarum and the Origin of Christian Symbolism* (1966).

MICHAEL T. DAVIS

[See also **Christogram.**]

LACERTINE, a pattern formed of intricately interlaced ribbons with zoomorphic terminals, which often clasp their own, or an adjoining, "body" in their mouths. It may have originated in Syria or Egypt, and may have been transmitted from the Middle East by Scytho-Sarmatian art, but its most common form appeared around 540 in the Germanic Animal Style II, in which the predominant animal is a snake. Lacertine ornament reached the British Isles by 624–625, as is shown by objects from the Sutton Hoo royal ship burial. It subsequently figured prominently in Hiberno-Saxon manuscripts—where the snake was supplemented by a wide variety of other animals and, in the Book of Kells, even by humans—and continued throughout the medieval period.

BIBLIOGRAPHY

Carl Nordenfalk, *Celtic and Anglo-Saxon Painting* (1977); Marvin C. Ross and Philippe Verdier, *Arts of the Migration Period in the Walters Art Gallery* (1961); Bernhard Salin, *Die altgermanische Tierornamentik* (1935).

LESLIE BRUBAKER

[See also **Anglo-Saxon Art; Animal Style; Celtic Art; Interlace; Kells, Book of; Migration and Hiberno-Saxon Art; Sutton Hoo.**]

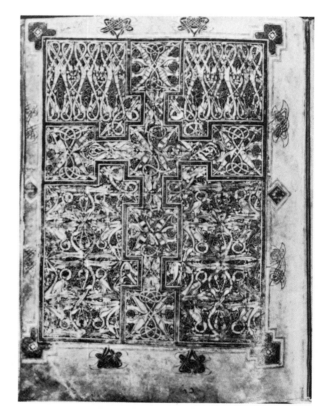

Cruciform page with lacertine ornament. From Lichfield Gospels, probably Welsh, early 8th century. COURTESY OF THE DEAN AND CHAPTER, LICHFIELD CATHEDRAL

LACTATIO, the Virgin nursing the Christ child; also known as the *Galaktotrophousa* or Virgo Lactans. Representations show the Virgin, usually seated but occasionally standing, holding the child on her lap or in her arms. The Christ child either holds his mother's exposed breast or nurses. Although the image is visually derived from Egyptian renderings of Isis nursing Horus, the ultimate textual source for the Lactatio may be Clement of Alexandria's remarks on the power of the Virgin's milk (*Paidagogos,* I.6). Though a second-century Roman catacomb painting showing a seated woman holding a child on her lap is sometimes cited as the earliest example, the true Lactatio probably originated in Eastern monastic circles in the fifth or sixth century, an early witness being the apse painting of cell 1,725 in the monastery of Jeremiah at Saqqara (late sixth or seventh century).

BIBLIOGRAPHY
Victor Lasareff, "Studies in the Iconography of the Virgin," in *Art Bulletin,* **20** (1938); Émile Mâle, *L'art religieux en France: Étude sur l'iconographie du moyen âge,* III (1949), 147–149.

LESLIE BRUBAKER

[See also **Coptic Art.**]

LĀDHIQIYA, AL- (ancient Laodicea, modern Latakia), seaport on the Mediterranean coast of modern Syria, is located on the Raᵓs Ziyāra headland between Alexandretta (now Iskanderun), to the north, and Tripoli, to the south. Seleukis I Nikator founded Laodikeia hē epi Thalassē, Laodicea on the Sea, one of five cities named for his mother, Laodike, on the ruins of Phoenician Ramitha in the 280's B.C.; it became one of the four most important Seleucid cities. The Romans acquired Laodicea in the mid first century B.C. when they subdued the Near East. It passed thence into the Eastern Roman Empire, at which time Justinian I made it a provincial capital.

The Arab armies under ᶜUbāda ibn al-Ṣāmit al-Ansārī conquered Laodicea (636) and made it part of the province of Ḥimṣ (transcribing its name as Al-Lādhiqiya). The Byzantines raided it about 718–719 and again in 910, but Al-Lādhiqiya continued under Muslim rule until 968, first under Umayyad governors and then under the Abbasids and their Tulunid, Ikhshidid, and Hamdanid vassals. In 968 the Byzantine emperor Nikephoros II Phokas (*r.* 963–969, known as "the White Death of the Saracens") succeeded in conquering much of northern Syria, in-

cluding Al-Lādhiqiya. The Byzantine-Muslim frontier stabilized south of Al-Lādhiqiya for about a century, but the area returned to Muslim control during Byzantium's domestic troubles of the mid eleventh century. It and other cities passed, in 1086, from the emir of Shaizar to Malikshāh, the Seljuk Turkish sultan.

Al-Lādhiqiya's importance as a seaport drew the first crusaders and caused it to change hands from Turks to crusaders to Byzantines to crusaders to Byzantines to the crusader count of Antioch and back, finally, to the Byzantines between 1097 and 1104. Tancred of Antioch retook Al-Lādhiqiya in 1108, making it part of the Principality of Antioch and his chief port. ᶜImād al-Dīn Zengī (Zangī; *r.* 1127–1146), the governor of Aleppo and Hama, raided in the vicinity of Al-Lādhiqiya in 1136 and took 7,000 captives and 100,000 head of livestock. Earthquakes struck the city in 1157 and 1170. The latter quake was sufficiently severe that it led to a truce between Muslims and crusaders, a truce that the Christians broke in 1171 by seizing two Egyptian ships at Al-Lādhiqiya. These seizures drew a retaliatory raid in that year from Nūr al-Dīn Maḥmūd (*r.* 1146–1174) of Aleppo.

Saladin took Al-Lādhiqiya from the crusaders in 1188, sent off the crusaders in the waiting Sicilian fleet, carried away marble from the city, and permitted the native Christians to remain upon payment of *jizya* (a poll tax). Al-Lādhiqiya remained in Muslim hands until 1260 despite Hospitaler raids in 1204–1205, though an army from Aleppo is said to have thrown down its walls in 1223 to prevent the crusaders' taking and fortifying it. This control served to isolate crusader Antioch from Tripoli and to limit its access to the sea to St. Simeon on the Orontes River.

Hulagu, the Mongol conqueror of Persia (and founder of the Ilkhanid dynasty), received Al-Lādhiqiya with his conquest of Aleppo and then granted it to Bohemond VI of Antioch in return for the latter's support in the Mongol capture of Damascus (1260). Baybars, the Mamluk victor over the Mongols at ᶜAyn Jālūt (3 September 1260), took revenge for this support by sacking Antioch in 1268, leaving Al-Lādhiqiya as the only remnant of the crusader Principality of Antioch. The king of Jerusalem ransomed it from Mamluk attack in 1275. But the Mamluk sultan Qalāᵓūn (1279–1290), taking advantage of a war among the Christians over Acre (1287) and earthquake damage to Al-Lādhiqiya's walls, seized it and put it into service as Aleppo's port. It remained of significance in Mediterranean trade into the fifteenth century and fell to the Ottomans in 1517. Al-Lādhiqiya's importance throughout the medieval period, as from its founding, was as a Mediterranean port providing an entrepôt for the larger, more important inland population centers: Antioch, Aleppo, Hama, and Ḥimṣ.

BIBLIOGRAPHY

Because of its generally subordinate role, the history of medieval Al-Lādhiqiya must be sought in the context of events affecting northern Syria as a whole or in the histories of that area's major inland population centers. See "al-Lādhiḳīya," in *Encyclopaedia of Islam,* new ed., V, with bibliography. In works such as Kenneth M. Setton, ed., *A History of the Crusades,* 2nd ed., I–III (1969–1975), or Ernst Honigmann, *Die Ostgrenze des byzantinischen Reiches von 363 bis 1071* (1935), only occasional mentions of Al-Lādhiqiya appear.

JAMES L. YARRISON

[See also **Aleppo; Baybars al-Bunduqdārī; Crusades and Crusader States: To 1192; Ḥimṣ; Hulagu; Malikshāh; Qalāʾūn; Saladin; Syria.**]

LADINO. See **Judeo-Spanish.**

LADY CHAPEL. See **Chapel.**

LAI, LAY. *Lai* is an Old French poetic and musical term derived probably from the Old Celtic (unattested) *laidh* (poem or song accompanied by [a] musical instrument[s], or a musical composition); it was first applied to octosyllabic poems of the Arthurian cycle written in Breton. Alternative derivations include *leudus,* which appears in sixth-century Vulgar Latin, referring to a vernacular song; the Old High German *Leich* (dance song); the Irish *loîd* (bird song); and the Classical Latin *laudes* (praise). The English "lay" appears to be a borrowing from the French. Like most medieval vernacular terms designating literary forms, *lai* had a variety of applications. Modern scholars distinguish principally between lyrical and narrative *lais.*

LYRICAL *LAIS*

Lyrical *lais* seem to have been cultivated by the Provençal troubadours. In northern France they were composed between the twelfth and fifteenth centuries. Like its counterpart the *descort,* the lyric *lai* is a strophic poem with a widely varying number of stanzas—as few as four, as many as twenty-four. The stanzas are seldom symmetrical, each being sung to a different melody, a structure possibly related to stanzaic liturgical compositions such as the sequence. The number of lines in each stanza varies, the average being twenty to twenty-five. The *lai* is characterized by a preference for short lines of two to eight syllables. The stanza is usually constructed on two rhymes.

Thematically the *lai* differs but little from other medieval French lyrics. Courtly love furnishes the usual subject, but the poet also may praise the Virgin or explore other religious or didactic themes. During the fifteenth century the *lai* became predominantly religious. Lyric *lais* are often inserted in long narrative works of prose or poetry and are clearly distinguishable from surrounding poetic material in the latter case. Shorter, freer *lais* are occasionally found within late Arthurian prose romances.

Early *lais* give the impression of a sprinkling of internal rhymes ornamenting an essentially narrative structure. They may represent a vernacular imitation of the inventive wordplay found in Latin ecclesiastical poetry of the time, in which serpentine rhymes and cross-rhymes produce the effect of parlando declamation when the text is recited, and enhance structural cohesion when it is sung. The absence of repetitive poetic and musical structures for the early *lais,* often written by poets whose works included the stanzaic forms of the trouvères, suggests that the *lai* was regarded by poets and composers as a tour de force for invention: avoidance of large-scale repetition may have been a mark of competence, although internal repetition of short melodic phrases is common. Among the trouvères who wrote *lais* were Thibaut de Champagne, Gautier de Dargies, Colin Muset, and Jaque de Cysoing.

In the fourteenth century there was some formalization of the *lai* into twelve stanzas, of which the first and last might be similar in rhyme scheme and music. This type accounts for two of the four *lais* inserted in the *Roman de Fauvel* (1310–1314) and for the majority of those written by Guillaume de Machaut. Guillaume treated the form as a vehicle for musical invention; his *lais* explore the boundaries of *ars nova* mensuration, and four of them contain stanzas that may be sung in canonic or combinative polyphony.

Lais appeared in the repertories of Jean Froissart,

Eustache Deschamps, Christine de Pizan, and Alain Chartier, the successors of Guillaume de Machaut. The form declined in the fifteenth century, possibly because it was associated primarily with monophonic music.

NARRATIVE *LAIS*

Narrative *lais,* short stories in verse, were composed between about 1170 and 1230. (After that time, short verse fiction continued in France under such names as fabliau, *essemple, conte,* and, above all, *dit.*) It is customary now to distinguish between "Breton" and "courtly" *lais.* The name "Breton" was given because of the presence of Celtic local color (place-names and personal names) and certain folkloric and supernatural elements, and because the poets themselves sometimes claimed to have utilized Breton sources. None of those supposed sources is extant.

"Breton" and "courtly" *lais* were both composed in octosyllabic rhymed couplets. Their average length was from 300 to 400 verses. Love and adventure are the unifying themes of their stories. The heroes and heroines, of noble birth and, usually, of noble heart, dwell mostly in a real world, but they also enter easily into the otherworld of faerie. The best-known, and artistically most accomplished, "Breton" *lais* are those of Marie de France. Other "Breton" *lais* are anonymous: *Graelant, Guingamor, Desiré, Tydorel, Tyolet, Espine, Melion, Doon, Trot.* Among the best-known "courtly" (non-"Breton") *lais* are *Cor, Mantel, Ignaure, Haveloc,* and *Ombre.* Some other narrative poems traditionally considered *lais*—such as *Aristote, Lecheor,* and *Vair palefroi*—should be considered fabliaux.

The Middle English "Breton" lays—such as *Sir Launfal* (in another version *Sir Landevale*), *Lay le Freine, Emaré,* and *Sir Gowther*—are derived either from Marie de France or from other French *lais.* The model for *Sir Orfeo (Kyng Orfew)* is now lost, as are, probably, many other Old French *lais.*

BIBLIOGRAPHY

Alfred Jeanroy, Louis Brandin, and Pierre Aubry, eds., *Lais et descorts français du XIIIᵉ siècle* (1901, repr. 1975); Jean Maillard, *Évolution et esthétique du lai lyrique* (1963), and *Problèmes musicaux et littéraires du lai* (1958); Gilbert Reaney, "The Lais of Guillaume de Machaut and Their Background," in *Proceedings of the Royal Music Association,* 82 (1955–1956), and "Concerning the Origins of the Medieval Lai," in *Music & Letters,* 39 (1958); Thomas C. Rumble, ed., *The Breton Lays in Middle English* (1965); Prudence M. O'Hara Tobin, ed., *Les lais anonymes des XIIᵉ et XIIIᵉ siècles* (1976); Ferdinand Wolf, *Über die Lais, Sequenzen und Leiche* (1841).

PETER F. DEMBOWSKI
MARCIA J. EPSTEIN

[See also **Anglo-Norman Literature; Ars Nova; Arthurian Literature; Descort; Fabliau and Comic Tale; Fauvel, Roman de; Machaut, Guillaume de; Marie de France; Troubadour, Trouvère, Trovador.**]

LAI DEL DESIRÉ, LE, a late-twelfth-century French lay, possibly written in England, that recounts how the hero, Desiré, falls in love with a fairy mistress by whom he has two children but whom he must leave to fulfill his obligations at the court of the king of Scotland. A brief visit from his son, now grown, brings him back to the magic land of his mistress, but he returns a second time to court. Finally the mistress brings her son and daughter to court— he to be knighted, she to be married—then leaves, taking Desiré back to her kingdom.

BIBLIOGRAPHY

E. Margaret Grimes, ed., *The Lays of Desiré, Graelent, and Melion* (1928, repr. 1976); Francisque Michel, ed., *Lais inédits des XIIᵉ et XIIIᵉ siècles* (1836).

BRIAN MERRILEES

[See also **Anglo-Norman Literature.**]

LAI DU COR, LE. Best-known for romances of courtly life and love, Arthurian literature also boasts a number of shorter poems called lays, a form adapted from Celtic sources and sung to musical accompaniment. One of the most intriguing, the 594-line *Lai du cor* (Lay of the horn), appears to have been composed in England at the end of the twelfth century by an otherwise unknown poet who names himself, in the last few lines, Robert Biket.

Writing in Anglo-Norman, the Old French dialect used in England, Biket takes as subject an old folk motif, the test of wives' chastity by a magical device (here a magical drinking horn). Generally made of elephant ivory with elaborate carving, drinking horns served as exotic signs of wealth used on ceremonial occasions.

Lays often take a central symbol of their tale as a title (for instance, "The Honeysuckle," "The Nightingale," "The Cloak"), thereby stressing the association of love and magic—romance as an escape to "the otherworld"—that Celtic poetry contributed to the European conception of love. By its title, the *Lai du cor* marks the horn's centrality to the story, and then goes on to associate the exotic and the magical with it.

At the feast of Pentecost, Arthur holds a festive court in Caerleon. Into the hall rides a messenger holding a carved ivory horn circled by four golden bands and covered with precious gems. A silver band around the top contains a hundred tiny golden bells. "In the time of Constantine," it is said, "a wise and valiant fairy had made the horn so that even the softest brushing of the bells would set them to tinkling a music more enchanting than any harp or lute, or siren of the sea, could make."

The messenger strikes the bells, and everything in Arthur's court abruptly halts: All the knights stop eating, the waiters drop cups and plates, the ladies cease flirting, the baker slices his hand instead of the bread, and Arthur and the other kings and nobles stop talking. In the dramatic silence the messenger gives the horn to Arthur as a gift from a King Mangoun3, then abruptly departs.

At this point the horn, like love itself when it turns from enchantment to jealousy, assumes a sinister cast. Closer examination reveals letters carved on the horn. Arthur calls his chaplain to read them; the chaplain looks at the writing, pales, and begs to remain silent. Arthur insists, and the priest reveals that the horn had been created by an angry and embittered fairy as a device for revealing the unchastity of women and the ridiculous romanticism of men, who believe themselves perfect lovers when, in fact, they are cuckolds, objects of derision.

Only the husband of a chaste wife could successfully drink from the vessel. Others would have the contents of the horn spilled over them upon raising it to their lips. Ever imprudent, Arthur insists on testing the horn's powers forthwith. As the ladies of the court look slyly at their lovers, who laughingly observe that "Today you'll see jealous husbands put to the test and cuckolds suffer," Arthur has the horn filled with spiced wine, then raises it to his lips, only to have the contents spill all over him.

Furious, he rushes at Guinevere with raised dagger; his knights barely prevent him from striking. They calm him by observing that one can be unchaste in thought as well as in deed, and that it's natural for married women to have occasional unchaste thoughts. All husbands present, they suggest, should try the horn; if no one else fails, then Arthur can

punish Guinevere. One by one the noble husbands test themselves, only to have the wine soak them.

By now the lay has made its point. To conclude, it introduces a beautiful young woman who "looks like a good fairy," the wife of Caradoc Strong-Arm. She urges Caradoc to make the test in her honor. "For," she says, "I would never take a lover, no matter how powerful or handsome, besides yourself; you are my lover." Naturally, Caradoc drinks from the horn without difficulty, even saluting the king with a hearty "Wassail" as he drinks. Arthur rewards him by confirming the possession of the land he holds in fief; everyone finishes the feast and all return home, apparently determined to be better husbands: "They bring their wives back, those who love them more than ever."

Scholars have long been puzzled by the lay, sensing its ambiguous status vis-à-vis the romance tradition. The uncertainty translates into generic instability as some critics see it as parody, more fabliau than lay, more epic than romance. Even the verse form, primarily hexasyllabic rather than the more usual octosyllables, has led to confusion of dating (first around 1150, now *ca.* 1200 or the third quarter of the twelfth century) and even of form. One critic argues that it has an epic alexandrine (twelve-syllable long lines), rather than the shorter, more unusual, six-syllable form.

No scholar has yet remarked on the lay's destabilizing effect on the concept of love poetry. It equates language and love as ambivalent sign systems continually revealing and concealing hidden meanings and inner emotions: the contradictory poles of desire and duty. The horn serves as a metaphor for language and for women, revealing the sense in which, like tests, they are vessels, containers of substance placed there by others—husbands, authors, stewards—all very sure of the meaning and value of these contents. But humans and their artifacts—whether language, texts, or even enchanted horns—have a disconcerting habit of revealing their difference by exposing the very illusions they might be called upon to confirm. So whatever its genre, the *Lai du cor* apparently seeks to question the assumptions of the reigning love ethic a good three quarters of a century before Jean de Meun's *Roman de la Rose.*

BIBLIOGRAPHY
Sources. Le lai du cor has been preserved in only one MS: Oxford, Bodleian Library, MS Digby 86. Editions include Philip E. Bennett, ed., *Mantel et Cor: Deux lais du*

XIIe siècle (1975); Heinrich Dörner, ed., *Robert Biquet's Lai du Cor mit einer Einleitung über Sprache und Abfassungszeit* (1970); C. T. Erickson, ed., *The Anglo-Norman Text of the Lai du Cor* (1973); Fredrik Wulff, ed., *Le lai du cor: Restitution critique* (1888).

Studies. Philip E. Bennett, "Some Reflections on the Style of Robert Biket's *Lai du cor*," in *Zeitschrift für romanische Philologie,* 94 (1978); Ernst Hoepffner, "The Breton Lais," in Roger Sherman Loomis, ed., *Arthurian Literature in the Middle Ages* (1959, repr. 1969); Stefan Hofer, "Bemerkungen zur Beurteilung des Horn- und Mantellais," *Romanische Forschungen,* 65 (1953–1954); Mary Dominica Legge, *Anglo-Norman Literature and Its Background* (1963), 132–133; Beate Schmolke-Hasselmann, "L'intégration de quelques récits brefs arthuriens (*Cor, Mantel, Espée*) dans les romans arthuriens du XIIIème siècle," in Danielle Buschinger, ed., *Le récit bref au moyen âge: Actes du colloque des 27, 28, et 29 avril 1979* (1981); Otto Warnatsch, ed., *Der Mantel, Bruchstück eines Lanzeletromans des Heinrich von dem Türlin, nebst einer Abhandlung über die Sage vom Trinkhorn und Mantel und die Quelle der Krone* (1883, repr. 1977), 58–84.

STEPHEN G. NICHOLS, JR.

[See also **Anglo-Norman Literature; Arthurian Literature; Courtly Love; Oliphant.**]

LAISSE (also called *tirade*), a unit of narration in Old French and Old Provençal epic poetry. This feminine noun, derived from the verb *laisser* (to allow, to let go), originally signified a bond that allows an animal only a certain amount of movement (that is, a leash). By figurative use it acquired the meanings "bond" in general, "group of lines in poetry," "song," and, finally, "epic strophe constructed with the same assonance or, sometimes, with the same rhyme." Laisses are highly irregular in length. They can have as few as four and as many as two hundred verses, the average number being about twenty. Since French epics are not only chronicles of deeds but also songs of deeds (chansons de geste), the laisse is not only a unit of narration but also one of melody. Not much is known about the musical aspects of the laisse. It is generally supposed that it was characterized by three melodies: an initial one (*timbre d'intonation*), a developmental one, and a concluding one. In certain chansons de geste the concluding melody corresponds to the "orphan verse" (*vers orphelin*), the short, six-syllable line placed at the end of the laisse.

The laisse is a link in the chain of the story, and while it constitutes a formal unit, based on asso-

nance and on melody, its most important function is to contribute to the unfolding of the narration. Much of the art of the Old French epic stems from various kinds of linkage between individual laisses. The following are the most important: The last line or lines of the laisse are repeated in the first line or lines of the next laisse with, of course, a different assonance. A second kind of linkage is the *laisse similaire,* a repetition of the narrative content in (usually three) consecutive laisses. Such repetition, found chiefly in older *chansons* (notably in *Roland*), enhances the lyric quality of the epic, deepens its psychological purport, and heightens its artistry.

BIBLIOGRAPHY

Jacques Chailley, "Études musicales sur la chanson de geste et ses origines," in *Revue de musicologie,* 27 (1948); Peter F. Dembowski, "Le vers orphelin dans les chansons de geste et son emploi dans la "Geste de Blaye," in *Kentucky Romance Quarterly,* 17 (1970); Mildred K. Pope, "Four *Chansons de geste:* A Study in Old French Epic Versification," in *Modern Language Review,* 8 (1913), 9 (1914), and 10 (1915), a pioneering study of the laisse in conjunction with the more general problems of versification in four epics; Jean Rychner, *La chanson de geste: Essai sur l'art épique des jongleurs* (1955), 68–125, an analysis of the laisse in nine representative songs, chiefly from the point of view of their oral diffusion.

PETER F. DEMBOWSKI

[See also **Assonance: Chansons de Geste; French Literature.**]

LAJVARD is the Persian name for the dark blue lapis lazuli stone. By using cobalt oxide, which produces a deep resonant blue when fired in the kiln, an appearance similar to lapis lazuli is produced on a ceramic glaze. The word lajvard therefore began to be applied to the metallic pigment and to a class of ceramic wares that resembled lapis lazuli. Lajvardina wares have a sapphire or occasionally turquoise blue ground decorated with a lotus, dragon, or phoenix amid delicate geometric and arabesque patterns in black, red, and white enamels.

To further embellish these somber, opulent luxury vessels, gold leaf was added, a process explicitly detailed by Abūl-Qāsim in a ceramic treatise of 1301. He explained that *mithqal* (about five grams) of gold is beaten between paper into twenty-four sheets, then cut with scissors into small angular pieces to be stuck with glue onto the glaze. The expense of

Lajvardina bowl in dark blue, with red, white, and gold decoration. Kāshān, Iran, 13th century. THE METROPOLITAN MUSEUM OF ART, FLETCHER FUND, 1934 (34.151)

lajvardina manufacture, necessitating the use of large amounts of gold, expensive cobalt, and extra work and firings for enamel and gilding, may partially explain its short life of a hundred years. Judging from the introduction of Far Eastern motifs, a fashion that became prevalent during the Mongol period in Persia (1256–1393), and chronological evidence provided by the stratigraphy of excavations at Takht-i Sulaymān in northern Iran, together with literary references (a letter received in 1308 by the vizier Rashīd al-Dīn describing lajvardina dishes as gifts from the sultan of Delhi) and two dated examples from 1315/1316 and 1374/1375, lajvardina production seems to have continued only until the end of the fourteenth century.

BIBLIOGRAPHY

Arthur Lane, *Later Islamic Pottery: Persia, Syria, Egypt, Turkey,* 2nd ed. (1971), 7–8.

MARINA D. WHITMAN

[See also **Ceramics, Islamic; Faience.**]

LAKHMIDS, an Arab dynasty that ruled Al-Ḥīra on the lower Euphrates for some three centuries before the rise of Islam and played a decisive role in the his-

tory of the Arabs in that period. Al-Ḥīra and the Lakhmids did not belong to the world of the Mediterranean but were drawn into its orbit because of their clientship to Persia and their consequent participation in the Sasanian war effort against Byzantium.

The founder of the dynasty, ʿAmr ibn ʿAdī (*fl.* last quarter of the third century), was also the founder of Al-Ḥīra. In addition to his record as a warrior, he appears as the protector of Manichaeism after it was outlawed in Persia. His son, Imruʾ al-Qays, also cut a large figure in the military annals of the Lakhmids but went over to the Romans; he died in 328 and was buried at Namāra in the *provincia* Arabia.

Lakhmid history in the fourth century is obscure, but in the fifth it is illuminated by three illustrious names: al-Nuʿmān, nicknamed Al-Aswar ("the One-Eyed"), and al-Sāʾiḥ ("the Wanderer"), who visited the Syrian St. Simeon between 413 and 420; his son Mundhir (*ca.* 418–452), who took part in the Byzantine-Persian war of 421–422; and, toward the end of the century, Nuʿmān II (498–502), who began a series of operations against Byzantium that may have been a prelude to the Persian war of Anastasius' reign (502/503–505).

The sixth century witnessed the peak of Lakhmid aggressiveness against Byzantium. The redoubtable Mundhir III (503–554) ravaged the frontier for almost fifty years. In addition to warring continually with the Ghassanids, the Arab clients of Byzantium throughout this period, he conceived the strategy that culminated in the defeat of the Byzantine army under Belisarios at Callinicum in 531. Finally, the Ghassanid Ḥārith turned the tide against him and he died in battle in 554. It was Mundhir's ubiquitous presence along the Roman frontier that induced Justinian I around 530 to reorganize the Ghassanid phylarchate and concentrate power in the hands of a supreme phylarch.

Lesser kings succeeded Mundhir—three of his sons—but in 580 Al-Ḥīra had a capable ruler in the person of his grandson, Nuʿmān III. After a reign of some twenty years (580–602), during which he reasserted the prestige of the Lakhmids with the Arabs and the Persians, Xusrō II Parvīz had him killed, and with his death Lakhmid rule over Al-Ḥīra came to an end. The fall of the Lakhmids was fraught with disaster for the Sasanians, since they were the latter's shield against the Arabs of the Arabian Peninsula. When those Arabs appeared in the 630's as Muslim conquerors, the Lakhmid shield was no more.

The significant role they played in the history of

the Arabs derives from their association with Al-Ḥīra, for three centuries the great center of cultural diffusion among the Arabs of pre-Islamic times. Although the Lakhmids officially adopted Christianity only in the reign of their last king, al-Nuᶜmān III, their city, Al-Ḥīra, had become a major center of Christianity in the Orient, whence that religion spread in Arabia and the Persian Gulf area. Even more important is the fact that the Arabic script developed in Al-Ḥīra; with the spread of Islam over a wide belt of the globe, it was destined to become one of the major scripts of the world.

BIBLIOGRAPHY

The main Arabic source is al-Ṭabarī, *Tārīkh,* trans. into German by Theodor Nöldeke, *Geschichte der Perser und Araber zur Zeit der Sasaniden* (1879, repr. 1973). The standard work on the Lakhmids is still Gustav Rothstein, *Die Dynastie der Lahmiden in al Ḥīra* (1898). References to the Lakhmids in the classical and Syriac sources are collected in these two works. Other Arabic sources are Masᶜūdi, *Murūj,* Charles Pellat, ed., II, 213–220; Ḥamza al-Iṣfahānī, *Taᵓrīkh,* ed. Beirut, 83–97; Yaqūt, *Muᶜjam al-Buldān* (Beirut) II, 495–543. For more recent studies on the Lakhmids, see Franz Altheim and Ruth Stiehl, *Die Araber in der alten Welt,* 5 vols. (1964–1969), II, 313–328, and V/1, 358–373; M. J. Kister, "Al-Ḥīra: Some Notes on Its Relations with Arabia," in *Arabica,* 15 (1968); Irfan Shahid (Kawar), "The Arabs in the Peace Treaty of A.D. 561," in *Arabica,* 3 (1956), "Ghassan and Byzantium: A New *Terminus a Quo,*" in *Der Islam,* 35 (1959), and "*Byzantino-arabica:* The Conference of Ramla, A.D. 524," in *Journal of Near Eastern Studies,* 23 (1964).

IRFAN SHAHĪD

[See also **Byzantine History (330–1025); Calligraphy, Islamic; Ghassanids; Hira, Al-; Sasanians.**]

LAMB OF GOD. See Agnus Dei.

LAMBERT OF HERSFELD (*ca.* 1025—1081/1085), historian. Educated at Bamberg, he became a Benedictine monk and a strong advocate of the Cluniac reform. He transferred to Hasungen in 1077 and was elected abbot soon after Hasungen had joined the group of Cluniac monasteries in 1081. He died soon afterward, perhaps as late as 1085.

Lambert's *Annals of Hersfeld* is the outstanding historical work of the period. As in all similar works, there is nothing original in the first part

(which goes back to 1040). The next section, covering 1040 to 1069, is based on more recent sources; and from 1069 to 1077 the work is all his own. Lambert wrote in a vivid, almost novelistic style, quoting or paraphrasing the demands and replies of the parties involved in the bitter contests that marked the investiture struggle. The most famous example is his account of Henry IV's submission to the pope at Canossa.

Unfortunately, Lambert was a better writer than he was a historian. As might be guessed from his support of Cluny, he was opposed to Henry IV and a strong supporter of Gregory VII and the nobles who rebelled against Henry. Thus his account of the events at Canossa cannot be trusted, and his reports of the discussions between Henry and the Saxon nobles are at best only partially accurate. On the other hand, it is clear that Lambert did understand the basic principles involved in the struggle: the demand of the church to be free from lay control, the duty of the king to consult with his nobles and maintain justice, and the right of rebellion against an unjust king. Lambert stated these principles eloquently, and thus his work aids in the understanding of the atmosphere in which the investiture struggle took place, even when his account is not reliable about the facts.

BIBLIOGRAPHY

The text of the *Annals* is in *Monumenta Germaniae historica,* V (1844), 134–263. See also Robert W. Carlyle and Alexander J. Carlyle, *A History of Medieval Political Theory in the West,* III (1928), 130–132, 155–157; James Westfall Thompson, *A History of Historical Writing* (1942, repr. 1967), 187–188.

JOSEPH R. STRAYER

[See also **Benedictines; Canossa; Cluny, Order of; Gregory VII, Pope; Henry IV of Germany; Historiography, Western European; Investiture and Investiture Conflict.**]

LAMBESPRINGE, BARTHOLOMEW (*fl. ca.* mid fifteenth century), Dutch-English goldsmith, was one of the leading London artists who collaborated on the tomb of Richard de Beauchamp at St. Mary's, Warwick, about 1450. The contracts survive imperfectly, but the side figures' dramatic character gives evidence of the influence of Flemish-Burgundian sculpture in England at this time. Lambespringe's main official role was gilding and finishing these figures and, presumably, the effigy as well.

BIBLIOGRAPHY

John G. Nichols, *Description of the Church of St. Mary, Warwick, and of the Beauchamp Chapel* (ca. 1838); Lawrence Stone, *Sculpture in Britain: The Middle Ages,* 2nd ed. (1972), 207–209.

BARRIE SINGLETON

[See also **Metalsmiths, Gold and Silver.**]

LAMBRON, also known as Lambro or Namrun, was the fortress-seat of the Hetᶜumid dynasty of Cilician Armenia. Along with the castle of Baberon, Lambron controlled one of the main routes through the Cilician Gates in the Taurus Mountains of western Cilicia. It was thus of great strategic importance for the control of Cilicia and the object of conflict between the Hetᶜumids and the Rubenids in their struggle for mastery over the area. It remained an impregnable fortress, having been unsuccessfully besieged by the Rubenid Mleh in 1171–1172 and by Ruben III in 1182. The Rubenids were able to capture Lambron only when Leo I/II, later the first king of Cilicia, invited the Hetᶜumids of Lambron to a banquet and promptly arrested them. Ruins of the castle of Lambron show it to have been a large fortress, consisting of five chambers the outlines of which followed those of the plateau on which it was located, as was the case with many Cilician castles.

BIBLIOGRAPHY

Ghevont M. Alishan, *Sissouan, ou l'Arméno-Cilicie* (1899); Thomas S. R. Boase, ed., *The Cilician Kingdom of Armenia* (1978); F. C. R. Robinson and P. C. Hughes, "Lampron, Castle of Armenian Cilicia," in *Anatolian Studies,* 19 (1969).

ANI P. ATAMIAN

[See also **Cilician Gates; Cilician Kingdom; Hetᶜumids; Leo I/II of Armenia; Rubenids.**]

LAMENTATION, in Christian iconography, the scene of expressing grief over the dead body of Christ after the Deposition and before the Entombment. The Gospels make no mention of the lamenting of the dead Christ, although this act is mentioned in the apocryphal Gospel of Nicodemus. The artistic convention of depicting this pause to lament is thought to reflect certain funerary rites in the

Christian East and West. It is often difficult to distinguish between images of the Entombment and the Lamentation. Typically, Mary, the mother of Christ, and Mary Magdalene, shown expressing immense grief while attending the body of Christ, are the emotional focus of such scenes.

BIBLIOGRAPHY

Gertrud Schiller, *Iconography of Christian Art,* Janet Seligman, trans., II (1972), 174–179.

JENNIFER E. JONES

[See also **Crucifixion; Early Christian Art; Iconology.**]

LAMPRECHT (*fl. ca.* 1150) was a cleric who identified himself as the author of two verse narratives, *Tobias* and *Alexander.* Since the dialect of his works is Moselle-Franconian and an excursus in *Tobias* mentions the founding of Trier, his literary activity has traditionally been associated with that city, although Cologne and even Regensburg have also been suggested as his place of residence.

Lamprecht's *Tobias* is transmitted only in two late-twelfth-century fragments from the flyleaves of a manuscript (Berlin, Ms. germ. quart. 1416), which contain the initial 274 verses of the work. The text follows the Old Testament book of Tobias to the death of Sennacherib in chapter 1, occasionally citing other biblical passages and adding moralizing comments.

The *Alexander* marks an important turning point in the history of Middle High German literature, both as the first treatment of a worldly theme and as the first adaptation of a French rather than a Latin work. Lamprecht identifies his source as Alberich von Bisinzo (probably Pisançon), who wrote in a Franco-Provençal dialect in the early twelfth century. Alberich's principal sources are Julius Valerius, the *Historia de preliis,* and the interpolated Quintus Curtius. The only surviving fragment of Alberich's work breaks off after 105 verses in the middle of a description of Alexander's education. Lamprecht translates the same passage in 180 verses, a result of his tendency to gloss and the difficulty of adapting French octosyllabic *laisses* into four-beat rhymed couplets. He also pauses to explain geographical names of biblical significance and to expand battle descriptions, which include important references to heroes of Germanic saga (Sigurd, Hilde, Wolfwin).

The *Alexander* survives in three versions of differing lengths and degrees of adaptation. The version closest to the original is in the composite Vorau manuscript (*V* = Stiftsbibliothek Cod. 276 in Bibliothek des Augustiner-Chorherrnstifts in Vorau/Steiermark), where the narrative is brought to a sudden conclusion with the death of Darius. The final verses, 1,497–1,533, appear to be the work of a continuator. A second continuator (**BS* or **X*), writing about 1160, completed the same version as that used by the Vorau manuscript, using further sources, especially the *Iter ad Paradisum* and its description of Alexander's adventures in the fabulous East.

This expansion provided the model for further redactions. *B*, the *Basler Alexander* (4,734 verses), apparently stems from an Alemannic intermediary of the thirteenth century and survives as part of a fifteenth-century chronicle (Basel University Library E VI 26). *S*, the *Strassburger Alexander* (7,302 verses), transmitted in a manuscript from 1187 and destroyed with the Strassburg University Library in a fire in 1870, is notable for the introduction of courtly elements and its comparative stylistic refinement. It appears, depending upon interpretations of relative chronology, to have exerted significant influence on the style and development of courtly romance, especially on the works of Eilhart von Oberge and Heinrich von Veldeke. Although Lamprecht's original conception remains a subject of controversy, the Strassburg redaction appears to treat Alexander as a figure who is ultimately consistent with the theme of the transience of earthly glory.

BIBLIOGRAPHY

Editions are *Lamprechts Alexander nach den drei Texten mit dem Fragment des Alberic von Besançon und den lateinischen Quellen*, Karl Kinzel, ed. (1884); Friedrich Maurer, ed., *Die religiösen Dichtungen des 11. und 12. Jahrhunderts*, II (1965), 517–566. See also Herwig Buntz, *Die deutsche Alexanderdichtung des Mittelalters* (1973); George Cary, *The Medieval Alexander*, D. J. A. Ross, ed. (1956); W. Schröder, "Der Pfaffe Lamprecht," in *Die deutsche Literatur des Mittelalters: Verfasserlexikon*, 2nd ed., V (1985).

ARTHUR GROOS

[See also **Alexander Romances; German Literature: Romance.**]

LAMPS. See **Lighting Devices.**

LANCE, a pole arm or staff weapon used for thrusting, the principal armament of a knight. Medieval pole arms consisted of two basic components: the usually wooden shaft and the steel head or point, the shape of which varied greatly with the purpose. Though late Roman and Byzantine cavalry had twelve-foot-long lances *(kontós)*, up to the eleventh century knights in western Europe carried much shorter lances, eight to ten feet in length. Their double-edged, leaf-shaped heads had a pair of lugs or "wings" at the sockets, serving as stops to prevent penetration too deep for easy withdrawal. This "winged" lance could be wielded freehand, and even thrown, as well as couched under the arm.

After the eleventh century—following closer contact with Byzantium by way of the crusades—the knightly lance was some twelve feet long, like the *kontós,* and the couched position was the only feasible one. This knightly lance had a short, narrow blade, without "wings" or stops; the tapering shaft increased in thickness toward the butt, with a thinner grip section. Tournament lances were tipped with blunt coronels; their handgrips were protected by steel vamplates.

The older "winged" lance was adapted as a hunting spear for dangerous game, such as boar or bear, which was best kept at a distance. For a slip-proof grip the shafts of these boar spears were wrapped with crisscrossed leather straps studded with big-headed nails or given a knobby surface by nicking selected saplings to produce scar tissue.

In the infantry, spears seven to eight feet long, often with "wings," were commonly carried up to the fourteenth century. In imitation of the phalanx of classical antiquity, the city militias of the Italian Renaissance developed long infantry lances, which were adopted by Swiss and German citizen soldiers and mercenary infantry. Their pikes were about twelve to fifteen feet long, the short tips fastened to the shafts by long strips of iron to prevent their being chopped off easily. The disciplined pikemen's square was practically invincible and dominated European battlefields up to the mid seventeenth century. The disadvantage of the overlong pike was that it proved effective only in close formation. Many foot soldiers preferred more versatile pole arms, which could be used not only for the thrust but also for hacking and hewing. The most popular pole arm in Switzerland, Germany, and Bohemia was the halberd, which had an elaborate head combining an ax blade, a stabbing spike, and a rear hook. Swiss hal-

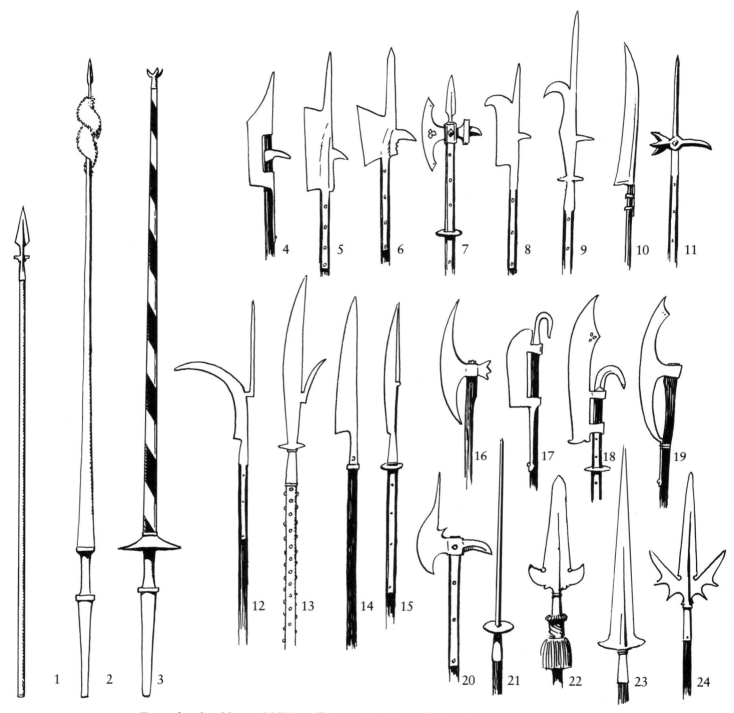

Types of medieval lances: (1) "Winged" lance, 10th–11th c.; *(2)* Knightly lance, late 15th c.; *(3)* Tournament lance, late 15th c.; *(4)* Swiss halberd (Sempach type), 15th c.; *(5)* Swiss halberd (Bernese type), 15th c.; *(6)* German halberd, late 15th c.; *(7)* Poleaxe, French or Burgundian, 15 c.; *(8)* Bill, English, 15th c.; *(9) Roncone,* Italian, 15th c.; *(10) Sturmsense,* 15th–16th c.; *(11)* Lucerne hammer, Swiss, 15th c.; *(12) Faucard,* French, 15th c.; *(13) Glaive,* Italian, 15th–16th c.; *(14) Couse,* south German or Austrian, 15th–16th c.; *(15) Vouge,* Burgundian, 15th c.; *(16) Guisarme,* English, 14th c.; *(17)* Lochaber axe, Scottish, 15th–17th c.; *(18) Gläfe,* Saxon, 16th c.; *(19)* Berdiche, Russian, 15th–17th c.; *(20) Mordaxt,* Swiss, 15th c.; *(21) Ahlspiess,* Bohemian, 15th c.; *(22)* Partisan, Italian, 16th c.; *(23)* Ox-tongue partisan, Italian, 15th–16th c.; *(24) Korseke (Chauve-souris),* Italian, 15th–16th c. ALL DRAWINGS BY AUTHOR berds developed into distinctive local types (Sempach, Bern, and Zurich).

The poleax was similarly constructed with ax blade, spike, and a rear hammerhead; together with the bill it took the place of the halberd in western Europe and England. The Italian *roncone* was a bill with a large forward cutting hook; both bill and *roncone* were originally peasant weapons developed from the pruning hook. Peasant levies—and rebels—made use of tools at hand, such as straightened scythes or threshing flails with added spikes. Hammers, sickles, or knives set on long shafts became the Lucerne hammer, *faucard* (fauchard), *glaive,* and *vouge* (voulge). Broad-bladed axes became *guisarmes* in France and England, Lochaber axes in Scotland, *Gläfen* in Germany, *Mordaxt* in Switzerland, and *berdiche* in Poland and Russia. By adding spikes for stabbing and smashing, armorers turned long-handled clubs into weapons which, with black humor, came to be called *goedendag* ("have a good day") in Flanders and *Morgenstern* ("morning star") in Switzerland.

Pole arms designed for stabbing only included the mail-piercing *Ahlspiess* with its three-foot-long spike and small guard plate, and, at the other extreme, the wide-bladed partisan with symmetrical parrying hooks at the base of the blade. During the fifteenth century several subtypes of partisan developed: the long-bladed ox tongue *(langue-de-boeuf),* the *korseke* with batwing-shaped parrying hooks *(chauve-souris),* the *runka,* and the *Friulian spetum.* The *Ahlspiess* was used in fifteenth-century Bohemia and Austria; the partisan was Italian in origin but spread during the sixteenth century, into northern countries, where it became fashionable as equipment for palace guards. A greatly reduced form of partisan, the spontoon, was carried by infantry officers of the seventeenth and eighteenth centuries as a badge of rank. Throwing spears (javelins) played only a very minor role in western Europe, although in Hungary and Transylvania a well-equipped horseman might carry two or three short (three-foot) darts *(djerids)* in a special quiver, following the Turkish model. The lances of nineteenth-century light cavalry regiments—lancers, lanciers, and uhlans—were not of the heavy type used by the medieval knight, but were light shafts adopted from Polish uhlans, Turkish *sipahi*s, and Russian Cossacks.

BIBLIOGRAPHY

Arturo Puricelli-Guerra, "The Glaive and the Bill: The Evolution of Farm Tools into the Most Basic of Pole-arms," in Robert Held, ed., *Art, Arms, and Armour,* I (1979–1980); William Reid, *Arms Through the Ages* (1976); Heribert Seitz, *Blankwaffen,* 2 vols. (1965–1968).

HELMUT NICKEL

[See also **Arms and Armor; Bow and Arrow/Crossbow; Cavalry; Warfare.**]

LANCELOT. See **Arthurian Literature.**

LANCET ARCH. See **Arch.**

LANCET WINDOW, a long, slender window topped by a steeply pointed or lancet arch. In a traceried window, the term applies to a section of the larger window that is shaped like a lancet window (also called a lancet light). It was widely used in the thirteenth century, particularly in northern France and England.

GREGORY WHITTINGTON

[See also **Arch; Tracery.**]

LAND TENURE. See **Tenure of Land, Islamic, Slavic, Western European.**

LANDINI, FRANCESCO (1325/1335–1397), Italian composer, poet, singer, and organist of the fourteenth century. He was the leading figure on the Florentine musical scene throughout most of the latter half of the trecento. Landini's father, Jacopo del Casentino (d. 1349), was a founding member of the Florentine guild of painters. Francesco was born in Fiesole or Casentino, both near Florence, and is buried in the church of S. Lorenzo in Florence.

Until recently, most of what was known about Landini's biography was based on information provided by Filippo Villani's late-fourteenth-century *Liber de civitatis Florentiae famosis civibus.* Francesco lost his sight in infancy or early childhood when he contracted smallpox. Despite his blindness, he had established himself as a premier singer, poet, and organist by the 1360's. Recent research has shown that Landini was employed as an organist at the Florentine monastery of Sta. Trinità in 1361 and at the church of S. Lorenzo beginning in 1365. According to Villani, his excellence in poetry and music earned Landini the *corona laurea*, bestowed upon him at Venice during the 1360's by Peter I of Cyprus. Villani reports that Petrarch was a member of the jury which awarded the crown to the composer. Landini is also supposed to have invented a type of string instrument that Villani calls a *Serena serenarum*. Whether this instrument was ever actually built remains unknown. Documentary evidence reveals that Landini was also involved in the building and tuning of organs, serving as an advisor in two major organ-building projects for the church of Santissima Annunziata in 1379 and the cathedral of Florence in 1387.

On the basis of contemporary accounts, it appears that Landini was most admired for his skill as a player of the organetto (a small, portable organ). Significantly, his name appears in musical sources not as Landini, but as Francesco delgli orghany or Franciscus Cecus Horghanista. His tombstone in S. Lorenzo depicts Landini with his organetto, as does the portrait of the composer appearing in the magnificent Squarcialupi Codex, a major source for Landini's musical works. A description of Landini's musical talents that illustrates the almost mythical stature he had attained in his lifetime is provided by Giovanni Gherardi da Prato in his retrospective account of Florentine culture and society of the 1380's, *Il Paradiso degli Alberti*. He describes an occasion on which Landini was asked to play his organetto while "a thousand birds were singing." The birds grew silent as they listened to the sweet strains of the composer's music. Then they joined in the song, singing louder than before, and while his audience watched in awe, a single nightingale lit upon the branch above Landini's head.

Literary references to the composer often portray him as a man of a strongly intellectual cast of mind. By all accounts, Francesco was well versed in the theoretical aspects of music and the other liberal arts. Da Prato praised his "divine intellect" and his understanding of "the most subtle proportions of musical number." He emphasized that Francesco "could discuss not only his music, but all the liberal arts, because he was so erudite in all these matters." The humanist Cino Rinuccini wrote of "Francesco, physically blind, but illuminated by his soul, who

knows the theory as well as the practice of music." Landini himself offered evidence of his academic musical leanings in his madrigal *Musica son,* in which the allegorical figure Musica laments that the new generation of composers is not interested in studying her theoretical background as part of the quadrivium, but only in writing popular songs.

The most important witness to the intellectual side of Landini's personality is his lengthy invective in Latin verse written against detractors of the English Franciscan philosopher William of Ockham (*d.* 1349). The poem was a response to the upsurge of humanist sentiment in Florence, which marked the 1370's and 1380's. The humanist intellectuals condemned the syllogistic "barbarisms" of British dialectic as part of their own propaganda campaign based on the imitation of classical authors. In his invective, Landini attacked one representative of the new movement who, "severe with his superciliousness and proud of his open mouth, seeks to resound through the uneducated masses of the rabble and philosophizes among the effeminate crowds." Although this "impudent layman" is never named, Landini's scorn was probably directed toward Luigi Marsili, prior of the Augustinian monastery of S. Spirito in Florence in the 1380's. Marsili, following the example of his friend and mentor Petrarch, was an outspoken champion of late-fourteenth-century humanism. Marsili's ideas, especially popular among the youth of the upper middle class, were rejected by the more conservative elements of Florentine society with which Landini aligned himself. Representatives of this well-to-do circle (for example, members of the Alberti and Corsini families) often had strong financial or political interests in Paris, Bruges, and the papal court at Avignon, one of the most important musical centers of the late fourteenth century. The tastes of this cosmopolitan segment of Landini's Florentine audience may have been partially responsible for the markedly French character of much of his music. Another source of French influence on Landini's music could have been the presence of the Augustinian composer Guglielmus de Francia in Florence in the 1360's.

The influence of the French polyphonic style is most evident in Landini's three-voice ballate. Landini composed forty-nine works of this type (the form of which corresponds to the French virelai). More than half of these exhibit style traits generally associated with the French chanson style of the fourteenth century, such as *verto* (open) and *chiuso* (closed) endings (corresponding to the *ouvert* and *clos* endings of the French *formes fixes*) and untexted lower voice parts (tenor and contratenor). These works most likely date from after 1370. The ninety-one two-voice ballate, although not all early works, are characterized by a more traditional Italian style. Landini's early ballata style is closely related to that of the northern Italian madrigal, a genre associated primarily with the courts of the Veneto and Milan in the first half of the trecento. The popularity of the madrigal in Florence was rapidly eclipsed by that of the ballata after about 1370, and Landini himself composed only twelve madrigals. The dramatic rise in the popularity of the ballata in this period must have been inspired largely by Landini's efforts in the genre. His use of graceful melodic contours and expressive dissonances and his sense of tonal coherence (as reflected in such works as the well-known *Gram piant' agl'ochi*) combined to create some of the most engaging music of the fourteenth century.

Landini's name is often associated with a particular cadential formula in which the resolution of the leading tone to the final is interrupted by a move downward to the sixth degree of the scale, the final then being approached by the skip of a third. Although this "under-third cadence" is more typical of the polyphony of the fifteenth century, Landini seems to have been the first composer to utilize the formula regularly. For this reason it is often referred to today as a "Landini cadence."

BIBLIOGRAPHY

For a more complete bibliography, and for further details relating to Landini's life and works, see Kurt von Fischer, "Landini, Francesco," in *The New Grove Dictionary of Music and Musicians,* X (1980). For the current state of documentary research on Landini, see F. Alberto Gallo, "Lorenzo Masini e Francesco degli Organi in San Lorenzo," in *Studi musicali,* 4 (1975). Material relating to Landini's part in the battle between the humanists and the logicians can be found in Michael P. Long, "Francesco Landini and the Florentine Cultural Elite," in *Early Music History,* 3 (1983). The musical works are edited by Leo Schrade in *Polyphonic Music of the Fourteenth Century,* IV(1958). Von Fischer's "Ein Versuch zur Chronologie von Landinis Werken," in *Musica disciplina,* 20 (1966), provides a guide to the dating of Landini's works on the basis of stylistic and textual criteria.

MICHAEL P. LONG

[See also **Ballata; Music, Western European; Ockham, William of.**]

LANDNÁMABÓK (The book of settlements) is a unique document in world literature, describing in remarkable detail the genesis of the Icelandic nation. After a brief mention of early references to the island, of Irish anchorites living there before the settlement, and of its discovery by the Norsemen, the book proceeds to list, in geographical order, the names of more than 400 settlers who made their home in this new world during the period 870–930, defining the land claims of each and every one of them, and embodying a good deal of information about the lives of many individuals down to the eleventh century. The book reveals a remarkably precise local knowledge of every part of the country, and the numerous genealogies included in the work appear to be equally reliable. The main section of *Landnámabók* is clearly cyclical in arrangement, taking the reader clockwise, settlement by settlement, round the whole island.

There are five extant versions of *Landnámabók,* one of them a fragment. The earliest, *Sturlubók,* compiled by Sturla Þórðarson (1214–1284), probably about 1275–1280, is preserved in a seventeenth-century manuscript. Next is *Hauksbók,* compiled by Haukr Erlendsson (d. 1334), parts of which, dating from about 1306–1308, survive in his own handwriting. The third medieval version, *Melabók,* which appears to have been compiled in the first decade of the fourteenth century, has been associated with Snorri Markusson of Melar (d. 1313), and survives only on two vellum leaves dating from the fifteenth century. However, it was in a much better state in the seventeenth century, when it was used for the compilation of *Þórðarbók,* which was written by Þórður Jónsson of Hítardalur (d. 1670). Slightly earlier than *Þórðarbók* is the *Skarðsárbók,* compiled by Björn Jónsson of Skarðsá (not later than 1636), who based his work on *Sturlubók* and *Hauksbók.*

These five versions, however, had their antecedents. The most explicit evidence for this is found in Haukr Erlendsson's epilogue to his redaction of *Landnámabók:*

> Now the account of the settlements of Iceland is completed, according to what wise men have written, first the priest Ari Þorgilsson the Wise, and Kolskeggr the Wise. But I, Haukr Erlendsson, wrote this book, following the book which was written by Sturla the Lawman, a most learned man, and also that other book, written by Styrmir the Wise. (Turville-Petre, p. 104)

According to this statement, there were two versions of *Landnámabók* earlier than Sturla's: one compiled by Ari Þorgilsson (1068–1148) and Kolskeggr Ásbjarnarson, probably about the beginning of the twelfth century; and the other by Prior Styrmir Kárason (d. 1245), about 1220. It has been shown by Jón Jóhannesson that *Styrmisbók* is best reflected in *Melabók,* since both Sturla and Haukr added a good deal of material from other sources, particularly the *Íslendingasögur;* however, since *Melabók* no longer exists apart from the two leaves, we must depend on *Þórðarbók* for detailed evidence of its nature. It has proved harder to reconstruct a hypothetical text of Ari and Kolskeggr, because Styrmir evidently added a good deal to this, his source.

BIBLIOGRAPHY

Editions. Ari Þorgilsson fróði, *Íslendingabók. Landnámabók,* Jakob Benediktsson, ed., 2 vols. (1968); Jakob Benediktsson, ed., *Skarðsárbók* (1958). The most recent translation is Hermann Pálsson and Paul Edwards, trans., *The Book of Settlements: Landnámabók* (1972).

Studies. Theodore M. Andersson, *The Problem of Icelandic Saga Origins* (1964); Jakob Benediktsson, "*Landnámabók:* Some Remarks on Its Value as a Historical Source," in *Saga-Book of the Viking Society,* **17** (1970); Barði Guðmundsson, *The Origin of the Icelanders,* Lee M. Hollander, trans. (1967); Jón Jóhannesson, *Gerðir Landnámabókar* (1941), and *A History of the Old Icelandic Commonwealth,* Haraldur Bessason, trans. (1974); Sveinbjörn Rafnsson, *Studier i Landnámabók: Kritiska bidrag till den isländska fristatstidens historia* (1974); E. O. G. Turville-Petre, *Origins of Icelandic Literature* (1953, repr. 1967).

HERMANN PÁLSSON

[See also **Iceland; Sturla Þórðarson.**]

LANDOLFUS SAGAX (*ca.* 977–*ca.* 1026), Italian historian. His *Historia romana* is a rewriting and continuation of Paul the Deacon's eighth-century *Historia romana,* as well as of the earlier histories of Eutropius (*Breviarium ab urbe condita*) and Jordanes (*De summa temporum*). Landolfus extends his chronicle to 813, using as a source the ninth-century work of Anastasius.

BIBLIOGRAPHY

Landolfus' work is in *Monumenta Germaniae historica: Auctorum antiquissimorum,* II, Hans Droysen, ed. (1877), 225–376. See also Max Manitius, *Geschichte der lateinischen Literatur des Mittelalters,* I (1911), 214, 681.

NATHALIE HANLET

[See also **Historiography, Western European; Jordanes; Paul the Deacon.**]

LANFRANC OF BEC, also known as Lanfranc of Canterbury (*d.* 24 May 1089), was born early in the eleventh century at Pavia. He studied Roman law at Bologna and then went to France, where he became master of the cathedral school at Avranches in 1039. Going to the monastery of Bec in Normandy in 1042, he founded a school there, became prior, and established himself as one of the foremost authorities in logic and dogmatic theology. Orthodox in his views, Lanfranc defended the doctrine of transubstantiation against the attacks of Berengar of Tours. In 1070 he went to England to become archbishop of Canterbury and a trusted councillor of William the Conqueror. Lanfranc supported moderate Hildebrandine reform in England, reorganized the dioceses, and toiled for workable relations between church and state. An astute and realistic churchman, he served both church and state well.

BIBLIOGRAPHY

The most comprehensive study of Lanfranc in English is A. J. Macdonald, *Lanfranc: A Study of His Life, Work, and Writing,* 2nd ed. (1944). Older but still useful is Heinrich Böhmer, *Kirche und Staat in England und in der Normandie* (1899); See also Frank Barlow, "A View of Archbishop Lanfranc," in *Journal of Ecclesiastical History,* **16** (1965); Richard W. Southern, "Lanfranc of Bec and Berengar of Tours," in Richard W. Hunt, William A. Pantin, and Richard W. Southern, eds., *Studies in Medieval History Presented to F. M. Powicke* (1948).

BRYCE LYON

[See also **Berengar of Tours; England: Norman-Angevin.**]

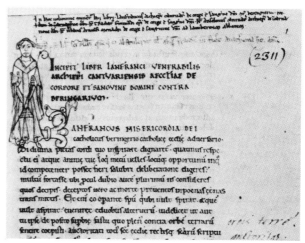

Lanfranc of Bec portrayed as monk-bishop in a manuscript (*ca.* 1100) of his treatise against Berengar. OXFORD, BODLEIAN 569 (2311), fol. I

LANFRANC OF MODENA (*fl. ca.* 1100), architect of Modena Cathedral, and praised in his time as "mirificus edificator." With the sculptor Wiligelmus, he worked on commissions associated with Countess Matilda of Tuscany. His cathedral at Modena (begun 1099, altar consecrated 1106) survives almost intact; its distinctive, modular design with timber roofing represents an erudite personal style that is traceable in other Po Valley churches.

BIBLIOGRAPHY

Pietro Galavotti, *Le più antiche fonti storiche del Duomo di Modena,* 2nd ed. (1974), 44–59; Arturo Carlo Quintavalle, "La cattedrale di Cremona, Cluny, la scuola di Lanfranco e di Wiligelmo," in *Storia dell'arte,* 18 (1973), and "Piacenza Cathedral, Lanfranco, and the School of Wiligelmo," in *Art Bulletin,* 55 (1973).

DALE KINNEY

[See also **Matilda of Tuscany; Wiligelmus of Modena.**]

LANGLAND, WILLIAM (*d.* after 1388), the reputed author of *The Vision of William Concerning Piers the Plowman,* a poem written in alliterative long lines during the last decade of the reign of Edward III and the first of Richard II. The work is of much historical interest because of its attacks on the corrupt practices both of the church and of the state, and because its titular hero Piers, a poor plowman of Christlike virtue, became a mythic figure of Christian integrity invoked by the rebels in the Peasants' Revolt of 1381 and often in the next centuries by supporters of the reformation of the English church. The poem's extraordinary sweep and intensity, which caused a basically conservative work to be adopted by rebels and protestants, also make it one of the greatest religious allegorical poems in English, rivaled only by Spenser's *Faerie Queene.* It is preserved in three distinct versions, which have the form of a series of dream visions purportedly experienced by a narrator also named Will; aside from what may be inferred from what the author allows his surrogate Will to tell us about himself—and little may be safely inferred—nothing is known of William Langland. Even his authorship of the poem, or of one or another version of it, has often been questioned; indeed, the matter of Langland's authorship was for many years almost the exclusive focus of *Piers Plowman* criticism, and is not yet a wholly dead issue.

The three versions, which are preserved in some fifty-three manuscripts, consist of a short form of about 2,400 lines, presumed to be the earliest form and referred to as the *A*-text; a form more than three times longer, the *B*-text, a revision of the *A*-text with many inserted additions plus a continuation of more than 4,000 lines for a total of about 7,300; and the *C*-text, a revision of the *B*-text up to a point some 850 lines from the end that despite many substantial additions and subtractions of material is virtually the same length as *B.* All three versions are divided—*B* and *C* rather haphazardly—into sections called passus (steps), and each begins with a prologue.

The *A*-text has the prologue plus eleven passus, and the action breaks off abruptly at the end. However, a Passus XII, or fragments of it, appears in three manuscripts: the longest version of this (117 lines) concludes with a declaration by one John But that he had made "this end" because Will had died after he had "wrought what here is written and other works both / Of Piers the Plowman and much people also." What "this end" refers to is not clear, and how much, if any, of *A* Passus XII (88 lines in the second manuscript, 20 in the third) is by Langland is impossible to determine. Since the two longer versions of XII hurriedly bring the narrator toward death in a way that is reminiscent—even echoic—of the ending of the *B*- and *C*-texts, it is possible that But wrote all of Passus XII in order to give the seemingly unfinished version an ending consonant with the one he knew it had in other manuscripts. Neither the *B*- nor the *C*-text shows any direct reflection of *A* Passus XII; both continue straight on from the action of *A* Passus XI. The *B*-text has a total of twenty-one passus, *C* of twenty-three, each including a prologue.

The presumed order of composition of the three versions is not capable of absolute proof, but comparison of the texts suggests strongly that *B* is the intermediate version and *A* the earliest; the order has rarely been questioned, and never persuasively. All versions circulated in manuscript during the later fourteenth, the fifteenth, and the sixteenth centuries, but Robert Crowley's three printings of a *B*-text version in 1550 tended to make the intermediate text the most available to readers. This is the most artistically satisfying of the versions, and even after the great edition of all three texts by W. W. Skeat in 1867–1884 it has remained the chief center for criticism of the poem. Literary references to *Piers Plowman* without more precise identification generally refer to the *B*-text.

AUTHORSHIP AND DATE

The most persuasive evidence for William Langland's authorship of the poem is its specific attribution to him in a Latin note written in an early-fifteenth-century hand on the last leaf of one of the oldest surviving C-text manuscripts, Trinity College, Dublin, D.4.1. This note reports that the father of William "de Langlond," Stacy de Rokayle, was of gentle birth (*generosus*) and lived in Shipton-under-Wychwood, a tenant of the Lord Spenser in the county of Oxford, and that William wrote the "book that is called Piers Plowman." The handwriting of this note is the same that recorded on the same leaf several notes showing familiarity with contemporary matters in the part of the country Langland is said to have come from. There seems no good reason to doubt the authority of this note, even though it fails to explain why Langland did not take his father's surname.

That the author's name was Langland receives further support from a note originating with the sixteenth-century antiquarian John Bale, who thought, however, that the author's first name was Robert: this mistake probably arose through the misreading of a phrase in the first line of the poem's second major part, "yrobed in russet" (*B* VIII 1), as "I Robert in russet." Because the poet calls his narrator Will, it is to the narrator rather than the author that the scribes are referring in incipits and explicits referring to Will. But that this was the author's own name seems to have been recognized by the scribe of a manuscript dated *ca.* 1425 whose explicit refers to the "Book of William" concerning Piers the Plowman, a formulation significantly different from the more common reference the "Vision of Will" concerning Piers. In one of the sixteenth-century manuscripts that has the Bale note about Robert Langland a second hand has added, "Robert, or William langland made pers ploughman."

Finally, that the poet's first name was William and his surname Langland is suggested most strikingly by an anagrammatic signature in a *B*-text line spoken by the narrator: "I haue lyued in londe ... my name is longe wille." Scribes and readers have registered in the margins their understanding that these words contain the elements of the name William Langland, none more clearly than the sixteenth-century reader who recorded the injunction, "nota the name of thauctour."

The principal inference that has been drawn concerning Langland—that he was a cleric in minor orders—emerges from a key passage in the C-text. Will awakes at the end of the Meed story (*C* VI), but before he goes back to sleep he has a waking encounter with the allegorical figures Reason and Conscience. This encounter occurred, he says, when he was living with his wife Kit in a cottage in Cornhill in London, and at a time when he still had his health and was able to work, and enjoyed a good, lazy life. To Reason's question why he is not supporting himself as a laborer, he answers ironically that he is too tall to stoop low, and too weak to work. To the charge that he is living by begging, he offers a most evasive excuse: when he was young, his father and his friends sent him to school, where he learned what Holy Writ meant, and ever since has found no life he liked except "in these long clothes." Hence he makes his living by praying for the souls of those who give him food, visiting their households once a month or so. Since he is a cleric with the tonsure, he considers himself exempted from menial occupations. When Conscience demurs at this excuse for begging, Will admits that he has wasted much time; but, like a merchant who hopes to make one supremely profitable bargain, Will hopes some time to get a "gobbet" of God's grace that will redeem all his misspent time. After Conscience and Reason exhort him to lead a more licit life, he goes to church and falls asleep and dreams more of his poem.

In this passage it is hard not to see in the fictional Long Will the poet himself, William Langland. Presumably Langland had a good deal of education and took the tonsure, but instead of continuing upward into holy orders he married (Will's wife is mentioned again, as well as a daughter), though he continued to dress as a cleric and, having no regular ecclesiastical position, supported himself in a clerical manner by praying for the souls of his benefactors, probably people interested in him as a poet. The anomaly that in his poem he pours scorn on those who live by begging and on clerics without positions in the church is one that he was well aware of: in the very first lines of the poem Will tells us that he was dressed "in the habit of a hermit unholy of works," and elsewhere he admits that his long clothes made him look like a "loller"—apparently a term used to describe (among others) peripatetic, unattached members of the clergy. Yet Langland seems to have been as ready as Will to sacrifice respectability in order to do what he thought he ought—Will to find the ideal of Do-Well, Langland to write of Will's search. When in the C-passage Will boasts that he knows in his conscience what Christ would like him to do, though Will does not say what that is, it can only be the writing of *Piers Plowman*.

There is little evidence by which to assign a precise date to either the *A*-text or the *C*-text. References that occur in *A* in the Lady Meed incident, and especially the resemblance of Meed to Alice Perrers, notorious for her corruption of the courts and her domination of Edward III in the last years of his life, suggest composition in the late 1360's or early 1370's. For the *C*-text there seems to be a terminus ad quem of 1388, the year in which Thomas Usk, whose *Testament of Love* contains clear echoes of *C*, was beheaded; a passage that may refer to the Second Statute of Laborers, passed in September 1388, after Usk's death, is possibly an addition made very late in the poet's career. As with *A*, topical references are too broad to yield a precise date of composition.

There is much firmer evidence for dating the *B*-text 1376–1379. Clear references appear to events that occurred in the last year of Edward's reign, including the Good Parliament of 1376, and to the situation in England when the boy King Richard was crowned, including, perhaps, a passage reflecting the coronation itself. An apparent allusion to the warfare between the rival popes in 1379 suggests that the composition was in process for several years. But what intervals passed between the abandonment of the *A*-text and the *B*-revision, or the completion of *B* and the *C*-revision, are unknown.

THE POEM

The headings in the manuscripts of all three versions distinguish between two major sections, the first of which (the *Visio*) is called by the same name some of the explicits use for the whole poem, "The Vision of William Concerning Piers the Plowman": this consists of two dreams, after each of which the narrator wakes. The second section (the *Vita*) is called "The Life of Do-Well, Do-Better, and Do-Best According to Wit and Reason": this consists of a single dream in *A*, but of seven in *B* and six in *C*. The concept of Do-Well is one that comes to Will suddenly at the very end of the *Visio* and becomes the object of his search for much of the rest of the poem. In the *Visio* the narrator's dreams come to him while he is merely wandering about the country in search of "wonders." As a result, Will is a more passive observer than he is when he is engaged actively in a search and participating more directly in the action.

In his dreams in the *Visio*, he is granted only one interview with an allegorical figure, Lady Holy Church, while in the *Vita* he meets and questions a host of allegorical figures and sometimes takes strong exception to their replies, though their loquacity is often such that he has a hard time getting a word in edgewise.

The *A*-text breaks off with Will's eloquent denial of the usefulness of learning in obtaining salvation, but in *B* and *C* he continues his often obstreperous search through dream and dream-within-dream until, as the poem nears its end, he gradually withdraws from his active role and becomes once more the passive observer he had been in the *Visio*. *Visio* and *Vita* are alike in their sharp satire, especially of friars and corrupt clergymen, in their mingling of digressive homily with poetry of great intensity, and in their constant discussion of the most basic tenets of Christianity. Will's questions imply that the poet believed that the answer to the question of why the well-taught Christian society of late-fourteenth-century England was so badly behaved lay in a general failure to apprehend first principles.

Society and its behavior are the subject of Will's first dream, which comes to him while he is lying by a brook in the Malvern Hills. He sees in a dream a fair field full of folk, situated between a lovely tower on a hill and a dreadful donjon in a dale. The folk are of all sorts, from the top to the bottom of society, behaving as people of the world do in all sorts of occupations. Langland's penchant for satire ensures that most seem to be doing their work badly or dishonestly. The dream of the fair field is expanded in the *B*-text to include a rather cryptic glimpse of the political situation in England under the young King Richard. While Will is still surveying the field, Lady Holy Church appears to him and speaks of the behavior of the folk and of the significance of the two towers. The fair one is occupied by Truth or God, the other by Wrong or the Devil. It is characteristic of the poem that while Truth's abode is visible from the field at the very beginning, the search for Truth is a constantly recurring theme throughout, as if what seems present and immediate is actually remote and elusive.

Will, who often shows the slow-wittedness shared by many medieval first-person narrators, does not recognize Lady Holy Church when she appears despite the fact that she speaks in terms of basic Christian doctrine. When he learns who she is, he at once asks her how he might save his soul. How one may attain salvation is a question often asked, and often answered, in the poem, so often that the search for salvation is sometimes said to be the chief theme. But as is customary with Langland, the very obviousness of the question conceals the extreme difficulty implicit in the seemingly simple answer it is apt to evoke. Thus when Holy Church explains that Will must practice charity, which she identifies with Truth, he objects that her answer is unsatisfactory for he has no "natural knowledge" of Truth; she must teach him better "by what power it originates in my body and where." Holy Church is angered by Will's obtuseness, but her reply, that knowledge of Truth is "a natural knowledge that teaches one in one's heart to love God," simply imputes to him the very thing he claims he lacks. Like other of Langland's seemingly august allegorical personifications such as Conscience and Reason, Holy Church is both human and fallible: she is like a Sunday school teacher impatient of her pupils' failure to grasp what seems to her self-evident.

The exchange between Will and Holy Church is paradigmatic of much that occurs in the poem. The questions he asks his interlocutors are usually simple, and the answers are generally (though not always) right, but the suggestions, like those offered by Lady Holy Church, are easier stated than acted upon. If things were as simple as she suggests, there would be no need for a poem based on the premise that Christianity has little reality except within the human heart, where it is to be apprehended not merely by the intellect but by the entire spirit. To gain such an apprehension, Will (and the human will) must live long, travel far, and dream much. The poem is a dramatization of an individual's attempt to learn the Truth in his heart.

Having been told, if unsatisfactorily, how to know the Truth, Will asks Holy Church to teach him how to know the False. Her answer is a protracted illustration of falseness: she points to a beautiful woman clad in rich scarlet (characters come and go in Will's dreams with truly dreamlike abruptness) who is her greatest enemy, Lady Meed. The following incident is Langland's most sustained piece of narrative and affords him a fine opportunity to exercise his powers as a satirist. It also affords him another opportunity to illustrate the complexity of the seemingly simple. Lady Meed (Reward) is about to be wedded to False with the assistance of unsavory allegorical figures such as Favel (Flattery), Liar, and Fickle-Tongue, as well as a number of officials of the church and of the civil service. But Theology, hear-ing of the wedding, objects that Meed must not be wedded to False since God has granted that Meed be given to Truth, despite Holy Church's contempt for her. To determine the true nature of Meed—to straighten out her ambiguity—is the object of much of the subsequent action. Theology recommends that Meed and her fiancé False go to London to find out in the law courts whether their marriage would be valid. The whole wedding party takes off in a marvelously grotesque procession: Meed rides on a sheriff "shod all new," Simony and Civil Law ride on summoners, and Liar becomes a "long cart" to carry some of the rabble. But when the King hears of what is going on and orders that False and his fellows be arrested, all run away, leaving Lady Meed alone to be taken into custody.

Treated as a privileged prisoner, Lady Meed at once begins to corrupt the secular and ecclesiastical authorities with bribes and promises of bribes. The King, who, like Theology, thinks she is of some potential benefit to society, offers her as wife to one of his knights, Conscience. But Conscience indignantly refuses her, and in a long speech he condemns her as a whore who gives illicit rewards to all comers, perverting justice with her largesse. Meed replies to these charges by arguing that meed in the sense "reward" is an absolutely necessary principle in society, which, since all work or serve for pay, could not function without it. She argues that even Conscience makes use of reward. In an extended topical reference, she accuses Conscience of causing the King (here Edward III) to settle the French wars by accepting only a "little silver"—a reference to the Treaty of Bretigny of 1360, by which Edward gave up his claim to the French throne in return for a huge sum. If Meed had been in charge, she says, the King would have defeated the French and rewarded his followers with parcels of the captured country.

The King is greatly impressed by Meed's defense, and Conscience is forced to offer a rebuttal. He tries to refute her claim that she represents payment for services rendered by making distinction between true meed, which is what God awards the just in the afterlife, and "meed measureless," which seems to denote any reward given on earth: Lady Meed is the latter. But so ideal a definition is too simplistic, leaving society with no word for legitimate compensation. The point bothered Langland, who in the C-text adds a passage in which Conscience, using an ingenious analogy from grammar, argues that the system of rewards by which society seems to function does not properly depend on the desire for gain but rather on the love and loyalty which exist between the servant and the served, of which reward is merely the tangible token. The idealism of *B*'s definition remains; but another aspect of Langland's idealism is seen in *C*'s determination not to let *B*'s oversimplification remain unmodified.

In her final appearance, Meed resolves any lingering doubts by her own bad behavior. She appears in the judgment hall and interferes with the King's justice by offering to settle criminal cases with cash payments to the victims. The King, influenced by Reason, now realizes that Meed is a perverter of justice. He vows to rule his realm henceforth with the aid of Conscience and Reason—a moment of the triumph of virtue which, like other such moments in the poem, seems short-lived.

In all three texts Will wakes after Meed's condemnation, but in *A* and *B* he goes to sleep almost immediately to continue his dreaming. He hears a sermon, preached by Conscience in *A* and by Reason in *B*, to all the folk on the field, exhorting them to live better. As a result they go to confess their sins to Repentance, confessions that Will hears as emanating from personified deadly sins. These confessions, six in *A* and all seven in *B*, are probably the best-known part of the poem. Though Pride and Lechery receive only a few lines, Envy, Avarice, Gluttony, Sloth, and Wrath (omitted in *A*) are developed with great art, as allegorical figures, to be sure, but speaking as people in conditions appropriate to the sins they represent. This extraordinary mingling of allegory and realism generates a vitality that rivals that of the pilgrims in Chaucer's General Prologue to the *Canterbury Tales*. Here follows, in the *C*-text, the quasi-autobiographical episode (described above) relating to Langland's clerical status.

After Will falls asleep following this incident, the *C*-text proceeds as had *A* and *B* (though *C* amplifies the confessions with material transferred from a later part of *B*). When the confessions are completed, in all three texts "a thousand of men" set off penitently in search of St. Truth. But no one knows where to find him—a palmer they meet has never heard of him—until a plowman suddenly "puts forth his head": this is the first appearance of Piers, the simple farmer whose name became the poem's. Piers knows the elusive Truth well, having served him, he says, for many years, and he instructs the pilgrims how to reach him. But the folk say they need a guide, since they find confusing Piers's directions, which lead the traveler through the Ten Commandments and other basic Christian precepts. Piers offers to

lead them himself if they will first help him plow his half acre.

All agree to this proposal and they work hard for a time; but then their enthusiasm wanes, and many sit about idly. Piers, whose natural leadership is made stronger by a good measure of righteous wrath, calls upon Hunger to get the idlers back to work, and Hunger's arrival makes everyone work strenuously. Piers, highly conscious of his obligation to feed society, asks Hunger how he should treat people who refuse to work, and receives good moral advice. But having proved to be a helpful moralist, Hunger, like other of Langland's allegorical personifications, then shows an unexpected though not unnatural aspect of himself— he refuses to depart until he has been well fed. Piers and the people have to labor frantically to satisfy him, whereupon he goes to sleep like an overfed glutton, and everyone stops work. Langland knew that hunger made men both overwork and, when they could, overeat—hunger's effect is not simple, but cyclical.

At the beginning of the final section of the *Visio*, Truth sends Piers a message telling him to stay home and plow his field, and sends a pardon for him and those who help him plow. Truth's message to stay at work confirms Piers's function as the economic basis of society, while his being the principal recipient of the pardon tends to make him the spiritual basis as well. Langland discusses the pardon at some length and the matter of who will or will not qualify for it: in general it will apply to all those who behave as they should. At the end of this discussion, a priest approaches Piers and asks to see his pardon so that he may interpret it for him. Will himself sees that the pardon consists of only two lines: "They that have done good shall go into life everlasting; and they that have done evil into everlasting fire." In these lines, actually from the Athanasian Creed, the priest says he can find no pardon, presumably because the reward of good and the punishment of evil do not involve pardon, which applies only to sin. Of course, the very fact that a virtuous man can achieve everlasting life is itself a pardon, effected by Christ's sacrifice, but the priest is technically correct within the limited context of his thought.

In the *A*- and *B*-texts, Piers reacts surprisingly by tearing the pardon apart "in pure anger," after which he vows to cease from manual labor and to devote himself henceforth to prayers and to penance. The poet gives us no hint for the motive of his anger, which is exacerbated when the priest scornfully asks him where he got the learning he shows when he quotes Scripture as a reason for his sudden vow. No wholly satisfactory explanation for the tearing of the pardon has been advanced, but the analogy with Moses' destruction of the tablets of the law after his descent from Sinai, while far from exact, is suggestive. Moses was also angered at the behavior of a priest, Aaron, who led the people to worship the golden calf. Furthermore, in the patristic tradition, Moses' angry action was considered a type of the replacement of the Old Law by the New, an action signifying a movement from something supremely good to something better. Piers himself is clearly moving from his position as simple farmer to that of a dedicated and authoritative exponent and teacher of Christian doctrine, which is what he is when we next meet or hear of him in the *B*- and *C*-texts (he does not reappear in *A*).

In Piers's imitation of Moses we get an illustration of the poet's belief that the individual Christian must relive Scripture historically as well as spiritually. But the *C*-poet, perhaps yielding to complaints that the scene made Piers seem impious by destroying a pardon sent from Truth, breaks off with the priest's announcement that he can find no pardon, omitting the tearing of the pardon and Piers's quarrel with the priest. Thereafter in all three texts Will awakens and broods upon the meaning of his dream. He comes to the conclusion (as so often, one a little aside from the point) that, while papal pardons are efficacious, at Judgment Day the surest pardon is Do-Well. It is here that Do-Well first appears, soon to be joined by his grammatical kinsmen Do-Better and Do-Best.

Here the *Visio* ends; and with the *Vita* begins Will's search for Do-Well. While still awake, he questions two Franciscan friars, who tell him Do-Well dwells with them. Will denies this stridently, sharing his author's scorn for the friars' self-satisfaction. Once more asleep, Will encounters "a much man, like to myself," who turns out to be Thought. Like many of the allegorical personifications Will meets, Thought is an aspect of his own psyche. In answer to Will's question, Thought gives a definition of the three Do's that fails to satisy him. Wit (Intelligence) suddenly appears and gives other definitions, which still do not satisfy Will. Wit's wife, Dame Study, rebukes Wit for wasting advice on one whose motives she suspects. She excoriates Will for wanting knowledge that she assumes he will misuse. Will's courtesy pacifies her, and she sends him on to Clergy (Learning). Will is warmly welcomed by

Clergy and his wife, Dame Scripture, and Clergy again defines the Do's.

All these definitions Will receives vary, but in general Do-Well appears to be a person in active, secular life who lives and makes a living in accord with Christian teaching; Do-Better seems more contemplative, withdrawn from secular activity, living in patience and charity, and helping and teaching others; Do-Best seems to be an ecclesiastical executive, one who punishes the wicked and cares for the good, a bishop or a pope. These definitions accord roughly with the several manifestations of Piers Plowman. We have already seen him making a transition from Do-Well to Do-Better in the Pardon scene, and his handling of the people who helped him plow his field foreshadows his final appearance as executive.

A misconstruction of some of Clergy's remarks starts Will thinking of predestination, fear of which brings him to the not entirely logical conclusion that learning is of little help in attaining salvation, and the *A*-text breaks off with Will's eloquent condemnation of learning: apparently Langland had introduced into his poem issues he was unable to solve in poetry. In *B* and *C* the action is resumed with a kind of allegory of the poet's abandonment of his quest in favor of more worldly though unspecified activity, which he pursued for a number of years. When Fortune, to whom he had submitted himself in this period, abandons him he returns to the quest. After a series of dialogues with Scripture, with Lewte (Justice), and, in *B*, with an unnamed interlocutor who becomes in *C* Recklessness, an aspect of Will, he has a marvelous inner dream in which Kind (Nature) takes him up on a mountain and shows him a vision of the natural world without humanity. But Will has reached his lowest point in understanding, and the reverence he feels for God's ways as they appear in the natural world is dispelled when he takes his vision to prove that all the animals save man are guided by reason: therefore he rebukes Reason for not guiding men. Reason tells him to mind his own business, and Will awakes back into the outer dream, ruefully aware that he has spoiled an opportunity to make progress in his search.

This conclusion is confirmed by a figure who appears to him and tells him that he should not have rebuked Reason. Will follows the newcomer, who introduces himself as Imaginative, actually Will's own constructive memory, the faculty that enables human beings to make proper sense of their experience. Imaginative answers a number of questions that have puzzled Will, and most especially explains to him the importance of clergy, learning, in the Christian scheme. With characteristic Langlandian irony, Imaginative chides Will for writing when there are already enough books to teach what Do-Well is—and enough pairs of friars.

But Imaginative suddenly vanishes, and Will awakes. When he sleeps again, it is Conscience who comes to comfort him. He is invited to take dinner with Clergy, and finds himself at a side table with Patience, eating sour food of penance while a fat doctor of divinity sits at the head table munching victuals of the best. The doctor is thought to be modeled on a contemporary Dominican, and Will's outrage at his smugness provides a fine bit of double-edged satire. Will asks his usual question about the Do's, and after the doctor gives his definition, Conscience calls upon Clergy for his. Clergy refuses to answer on the grounds that Piers Plowman has denied learning any value except for love, that is, except insofar as it teaches love. In *B*, Patience then defines the Do's as to learn, to teach, and to love God and one's enemies, placing stress on the last. In *C*, Piers suddenly appears and speaks the definition given to Patience in *B*, after which he disappears.

The treatment of Piers in this scene helps explain how he eventually took on a life almost independent of his creator. Will, the poet's surrogate, has just treated the guest of honor with ill-tempered satirical wit that we have come to associate with the poet himself, and has had to be hushed by Conscience and Patience. These same august allegorical figures recognize Piers as a superior authority. Thus at the same time that we are encouraged to identify the poet with the badly behaved Will, we see the poet's other creation, Piers, at his most exalted, and the difference in the moral order of the two makes it seem impossible that the person Will resembles could possibly have created Piers. It is hardly surprising that some critics have supposed that Piers Plowman must have had mythic existence before Langland wrote his poem. And at the end of the scene Conscience takes on his own independent life when he suddenly vows to leave Clergy and to become a pilgrim with Patience, despite Clergy's claim that he can teach him more than Patience can.

Will follows the pilgrims, who soon come upon a person identified as both a minstrel and a wafer-seller, the busiest of men, Hawkin the Active Man, whose coat is stained with many spots of dirt. These are his sins, which he confesses to Patience at length, a kind of repetition of the earlier confessions of sin that *C* avoids by transferring much of the confession to them. Patience preaches Hawkin a sermon on the life of patient poverty, through which one may avoid the deadly sins. Patience seems to suggest that Do-Well cannot be made actual in an active life. Paradoxically, in order to do well, one must really move toward Do-Better by living the life of patient poverty. After Patience's sermon Hawkin is left wailing for his sins. In *B*, Will wakes to wander the country like a lunatic, still in search of Do-Well, despite the discouraging example of Hawkin. Reason finally takes pity on Will and rocks him to sleep. There appears to him an extraordinary creature with many names, the chief of which is Anima (Soul or, in the theological sense, Life). In *C*, Will does not wake, and the creature, renamed Liberum Arbitrium (Free Will), appears to him in a continuation of his previous dream.

Anima–Liberum Arbitrium, a kind of model of the human psyche with all its functions such as thought, reason, and memory, takes Will a step further along the path Piers has already trod, from the active outer world into his own soul, where, conditioned by patient poverty, one learns to practice love. Anima–Liberum Arbitrium speaks most eloquently of Charity, whom Will says he has never known. In *B*, Anima tells Will that without Piers Plowman's help one will never know Charity, for Piers alone can look into men's wills. Anima then conflates two biblical texts (1 Cor. 10:4; Matt. 16:18) into a kind of identification of Piers with Christ: *Petrus id est Christus.* Apparently Piers is seen as an aspect of Christ, human nature at its best, historically that human nature which craved redemption and which Christ took upon himself when he became man. Piers the simple virtuous farmer has left his half acre to become the Christlike exponent of Christian charity, has gone all the way from Do-Well to Do-Better.

In *C*, Anima's association of Piers with Christ is weakened, and in the following scene, where in *B* Piers plays a major role, he is replaced in *C* by Liberum Arbitrium. In *B*, Anima, responding to Will's inevitable objection that despite Anima's discussion he still does not know what charity means, describes it as the fruit of a tree named Patience which grows in an orchard called man's heart. This tree is in the care of Piers Plowman and his associate Liberum Arbitrium. At the mention of Piers's name, Will faints, and in a dream-within-a-dream Piers shows him the tree. In *C*, Liberum Arbitrium takes Will directly to the tree, and there is no secondary dream.

The Tree is the most complex of all Langland's images. It symbolizes both Patience and Charity, and since it is propped by the three piles of the Trinity, it symbolizes also the Trinity, the interaction of whose three parts is the cause of charity. Since man is made in the image of God, the Tree grows within man's heart. Its fruits are marriage, widowhood, and virginity—analogues of the three parts of the Trinity. Piers (Liberum Arbitrium in *C*) describes how he defends the tree with the three piles, and Will asks if he might taste an apple; when the tree is shaken, the fruit that falls from it turns out to be the prophets and patriarchs. This fruit the Devil seizes as it falls and bears off to limbo. It appears that the tree has become also an image of that Tree of the Garden of Eden whose fruit tempted Eve to original sin. In *B*, Piers angrily seizes the second pile of the Trinity, the Son, and hits out after the Devil. This action is at once followed by—seemingly causes—Christ's Incarnation. Gabriel visits the Virgin and Christ is conceived. The poet then gives a summary narrative of Christ's life and death. In *C*, the final violent section is taken by Libera Voluntas Dei, the free will of God, into whom Liberum Arbitrium has suddenly metamorphosed.

The summary of Christ's life and death is a kind of reading of Scripture, but as always Will must not only read it but live it, and he now begins a journey that will take him to Jerusalem on the first Good Friday. On a mid-Lenten Sunday he meets successively with Abraham (Faith) and Moses (Hope), each of whom is seeking a knight named Christ, who alone can release the souls lying in Abraham's bosom and seal the commandment Moses received on Mt. Sinai. Will and his companions are overtaken by a Samaritan riding on a mule who is hastening to a joust in Jerusalem. He is not specifically identified as Charity or as Piers or as Christ, but his succor of a man who falls among thieves (whom neither Faith nor Hope could help) shows him to be in some sense all three. He explains the doctrine of the Trinity to Will at great length and with considerable ingenuity, though the relevance of the doctrine to Christ's sacrifice, which we are about to witness, is hard for the modern reader to understand.

When the Samaritan hurries away to Jerusalem, Will wakes and wanders wildly until he once more sleeps. He dreams he is in Jerusalem on Palm Sunday, where he sees one who is "like the Samaritan and somewhat like Piers Plowman" riding barefoot on an ass's back, like a knight who comes to be dubbed. Will witnesses the Crucifixion, which he describes simultaneously as a tournament in which the Christ-knight jousts with Death and as a literal crucifixion. When Christ dies, Will follows him to hell. Here he hears the Four Daughters of God disputing about the great light before hell's gates, with Mercy and Peace arguing that Mary's son has come to release the souls of the patriarchs and prophets, while Truth and Righteousness indignantly deny that those in hell can ever be let out. As Christ appears at hell's gates the devils argue with one another about whether he can despoil hell of their prey. In a marvelous passage, Christ explains that he has come to claim what was stolen from him in the Garden of Eden, and that he has become man in order to redeem man—a trick to cheat a trickster. Hell's gates break open, Christ frees those souls he wishes, the Daughters of God kiss one another, and Will wakes to summon his wife and daughter to Easter Mass.

With this triumphant scene a poet more sanguine might well have closed his poem. But, surprisingly, Christ's triumph is not man's Do-Best, nor does the universal hope it brings long survive. In the last two passus of the poem (unrevised in the *C*-text), Will witnesses the founding of the church and its ultimate subversion by the friars, and the poem ends like a true apocalypse. In Piers Plowman's final appearance, he has become St. Peter and the type of the good pope, and as such he is also Do-Best. Conscience tells Will that before ascending to heaven Christ gave Piers power to forgive all men their sins who pay what they owe to Piers's pardon. Will himself watches the descent of the Holy Spirit on the Apostles at Pentecost, and sees the Spirit in the form of Grace join with Piers. In a reversion to the agricultural imagery of Piers's first appearance, Grace distributes seeds—skills by which men may earn honest livings and the four cardinal virtues by which they may govern themselves. The half acre becomes the whole earth on which Piers and Grace cultivate Christiantity, and a barn called Unity or Holy Church is erected wherein Christians may store their grain and take refuge against the attacks of Antichrist.

The latter begins his attacks as soon as Grace and Piers go off to cultivate the earth. Conscience has the common people fortify Unity and withdraw into it for safety. But the cardinal virtues are perverted into tools of self-gratification, and Antichrist's attack on Unity becomes fiercer. Will awakes from his sleep not knowing where to find food to support himself.

While still awake, he meets Need, who advises him to pervert the cardinal virtue of temperance by making a virtue of necessity, that is, to be needy, as Christ was, but to make of neediness an excuse for begging his livelihood. Will goes to sleep and dreams how Antichrist ultimately overcomes Unity when, at Clergy's request, Conscience allows the begging friars to enter: their easy confessions poison Contrition, and Unity is wholly corrupted. The narrrator, now an old man ready for death, hears Conscience in despair vow to become a pilgrim and go to find Piers Plowman, who alone may remedy what has happened. Conscience cries after Grace until Will awakes for the last time. Like Truth so many times in the poem, Do-Best has been found and lost. Piers has become the elusive symbol of the leader of the true church whom many in the Reformation were to adopt as their own.

BIBLIOGRAPHY

Editions. All texts: W. W. Skeat, *The Vision of William Concerning Piers the Plowman Together with Vita de Dowel, Dobet, and Dobest, Secundum Wit et Resoun,* 4 pts., 5 vols. (1867–1884), reduced to 2 vols. with the three texts printed in parallel form (1886). A-text: George Kane, ed., *Piers Plowman* (1960), authoritative edition; Thomas A. Knott and David Fowler, *Piers the Plowman: A Critical Edition of the A-Version* (1952). B-text: George Kane and E. Talbot Donaldson, *Piers Plowman* (1975), authoritative edition; A. V. C. Schmidt, *The Vision of Piers Plowman: A Critical Edition of the B-Text* (1978), useful annotation. C-text: Derek Pearsall, *Piers Plowman by William Langland: An Edition of the C-Text* (1978).

Studies. A. J. Colaianne, *Piers Plowman: An Annotated Bibliography of Editions and Criticism, 1550–1977* (1978). The following studies are generally of the B-text unless titles specify otherwise: David Aers, *Piers Plowman and Christian Allegory* (1975); Ruth M. Ames, *The Fulfillment of the Scriptures: Abraham, Moses, and Piers* (1970); Judith H. Anderson, *The Growth of a Personal Voice: Piers Plowman and The Faerie Queene* (1976); Robert J. Blanch, ed., *Style and Symbolism in Piers Plowman* (1969); Morton W. Bloomfield, *Piers Plowman as a Fourteenth-century Apocalypse* (1962); Mary Carruthers, *The Search for St. Truth: A Study of Meaning in Piers Plowman* (1973); Nevill K. Coghill, *Langland: Piers Plowman* (1964); E. Talbot Donaldson, *Piers Plowman: The C-Text and Its Poet* (1949); T. P. Dunning, *Piers Plowman: An Interpretation of the A-Text,* rev. ed., T. P. Dolan, ed., (1980); Robert Worth Frank, Jr., *Piers Plowman and the Scheme of Salvation: An Interpretation of Dowel, Dobet, and Dobest* (1957); Greta Hort, *Piers Plowman and Contemporary Religious Thought* (1938); S. S. Hussey, ed., *Piers Plowman: Critical Approaches* (1969); George Kane, *Piers Plowman: The Evidence for Authorship* (1965); Elizabeth D. Kirk,

The Dream Thought of Piers Plowman (1972); Jeanne Krochalis and Edward Peters, eds. and trans., *The World of Piers Plowman* (1975); John Lawlor, *Piers Plowman: An Essay in Criticism* (1962); Daniel M. Murtaugh, *Piers Plowman and the Image of God* (1978); Dorothy L. Owen, *Piers Plowman: A Comparison with Some Earlier and Contemporary French Allegories* (1912); D. W. Robertson, Jr., and Bernard F. Huppé, *Piers Plowman and Scriptural Tradition* (1951); Elizabeth Salter, *Piers Plowman: An Introduction* (1962); Ben H. Smith, Jr., *Traditional Imagery of Charity in Piers Plowman* (1966); Edward Vasta, ed., *Interpretations of Piers Plowman* (1968).

E. TALBOT DONALDSON

[See also **Allegory; England; Middle English Literature; Seven Deadly Sins; Visions.**]

LANGLOIS, JEAN, "citizen of Troyes, crusader, former master of the fabric of St. Urbain," has been proposed as the designer of the church of St. Urbain, Troyes, a masterpiece of the Rayonnant Gothic style, and its first architect between about 1263 and 1266. Accused of embezzling 2,500 livres from the construction fund, he had left Troyes by 1267. However, the designation "master of the fabric" may refer to the financial or administrative official charged with the maintenance of an edifice. Jean Langlois's access to large sums of money would imply that his duties were of an accounting rather than an architectural nature.

BIBLIOGRAPHY

Studies. Robert Branner, "A Note on Pierre de Montreuil and Saint-Denis," in *Art Bulletin,* 45 (1963); Francis Salet, "Saint-Urbain de Troyes," in *Congrès archéologique de France,* 113 (1955).

MICHAEL T. DAVIS

[See also **Gothic, Rayonnant.**]

LANGTON, STEPHEN (*d.* 9 July 1228), archbishop of Canterbury during the turbulent reign of King John. The date of birth for Stephen Langton is not known, but his father was Henry, lord of the manor Langton-by-Wragby in Lincolnshire. As a youth Langton went to Paris for study, obtained a degree, and then became a respected theologian. During his twenty-five years at Paris he wrote his celebrated *Questiones,* which discuss current theological issues such as the limits of obedience to episcopal authority and the papal power of dispensation. At Paris, Langton came to know Lothario dei Segni, who was to become Pope Innocent III in 1198 and, as pope, invited Langton to Rome. In 1206 Langton was made cardinal-priest of St. Chrysogonus and at the same time became involved in the dispute between King John and Innocent III over the election of the archbishop of Canterbury.

At the death of Archbishop Hubert Walter in 1205 the younger monks of Christ Church, Canterbury, secretly elected as archbishop their subprior, Reginald, instead of acceding to John's will and electing Bishop John de Gray of Norwich. Furious, John then forced the monks to elect John de Gray. Innocent III, declaring both elections void, ordered the monks' representatives, who had come to Rome, to hold a new election in his presence. On his advice they elected Langton, whom Innocent III consecrated on 17 June 1207. This action so angered John that he banished the monks of Canterbury and declared that he would never accept Langton's election. In reply Innocent laid England under interdict in 1208 and excommunicated John in 1209. Until the dispute was settled in 1213, Langton lived at Pontigny in France, where Thomas Becket had also resided in exile. Though he protested against John's behavior, Langton adopted a conciliatory attitude and several times attempted to negotiate a settlement, which came only when King Philip Augustus of France accepted the invitation of Innocent III to invade England and depose John. John then had to recognize Langton, who went to England in July 1213 and absolved John.

Langton then associated himself with the developing baronial opposition to John, and assumed a leading role at meetings of the barons and in their negotiations with John. He was at St. Albans on 4 August 1213, where it was proclaimed at a great council that the laws of Henry I should be observed. Later, at a meeting of barons at St. Paul's in London he read the Coronation Charter of Henry I, and the barons declared that they would fight for its observance. Despite his intellectual leadership of the opposition, however, Langton did not want war and on several occasions forestalled conflict. But so frustrated were the barons by the spring of 1215 that they took up arms. During May and early June Langton and the respected baron William Marshal worked to produce an agreement that would be acceptable to the barons and John. This agreement ultimately became Magna Carta, ratified by both parties at Runnymede meadow on the Thames with Langton serving as a conciliatory force and spokesman for John. It is quite certain that Langton drafted most of the provisions guaranteeing the liberties of the church.

Soon after John's acceptance of Magna Carta Langton went to Rome to attend the Fourth Lateran Council. There Innocent III suspended him because of his failure to enforce papal censures against the barons fighting John, a suspension that continued for two years, until the deaths of Innocent and John. In 1218 Langton returned to England, and from then until his death in 1228 he was a loyal supporter of the young Henry III. He was responsible for the departure from England of the papal legate Pandulf and for the papal promise that no legate would reside in England while he was archbishop.

A theologian of note and an accomplished administrator, Langton was one of the most able archbishops of Canterbury. His greatest legacy was his creative and moderate statesmanship in the period between 1213 and 1216 and his considerable part in the formulation of Magna Carta.

BIBLIOGRAPHY

The principal study of Stephen Langton is Frederick M. Powicke, *Stephen Langton* (1928). See also Powicke, "A Bibliographical Note on Recent Work upon Stephen Langton," in *English Historical Review,* **48** (1933). For Langton as a theologian and churchman see George Lacombe and Arthur M. Landgraf, "The *Questiones* of Cardinal Stephen Langton," in *New Scholasticism,* **3** (1929), **4** (1930); George Lacombe and Beryl Smalley, "Studies on the Commentaries of Cardinal Stephen Langton," in *Archives d'histoire doctrinale et littéraire du moyen âge,* 5 (1930); Phyllis B. Roberts, *Studies in the Sermons of Stephen Langton* (1968). For sources in translation see *English Historical Documents, 1189–1327,* III (1975).

BRYCE LYON

[See also **England; Innocent III, Pope; John, King of England; Magna Carta.**]

LANGUEDOC. Though Languedoc is sometimes referred to as that entire area of France south of the Loire and Burgundy whose inhabitants spoke Occitanian dialects quite different from those of northern France, a more restricted use of the term is advisable. This definition considers Languedoc to be a province of southern France bounded by the Rhône, western Toulousan, the Massif Central, the Pyrenees, and the Mediterranean. It first assumed its general boundaries in the late eleventh century, when it was controlled by Count Raymond IV of St. Gilles, of the house of Toulouse. By 1271 it had passed to the control of the kings of France, who united Toulouse proper and the seneschalsies of Beaucaire and Carcassonne to form a royal provice that remained intact down to the time of the French Revolution.

The area now called Languedoc began its medieval existence as part of a Visigothic kingdom with its capital at Toulouse. After Clovis defeated the Visigoths at Voillé in 507, part of it became Frankish but most continued to be ruled by the Visigoths as the province of Septimania until its conquest by the Arabs in 718. For the next six decades Languedoc was a battleground between the Carolingians and the Muslims, during which time its Aquitainian and Gothic upper class suffered severely and the entire countryside was thoroughly devastated.

For about half a century after 778, Languedoc formed part of a Carolingian kingdom of Aquitaine; those years saw peace return, a revived church and monastic system, and resettlement of the countryside. After 829, however, effective Carolingian control gradually lessened until, by the end of the century, it had ended completely. Attempts were made by magnates like the counts of Toulouse-Rouergue to form viable principalities in the area, but they failed abysmally during the course of the tenth and early eleventh centuries—thwarted by the lesser nobility, who refused obedience, new castles and a castellan class that could not be controlled, and by the practice of dividing lands equally among all heirs in accordance with the legal system of the region.

In the late eleventh century, Raymond IV of St. Gilles, as count of Toulouse, duke of Narbonne, and marquis of Provence, laid the foundations of a united Languedoc. Before he had completed his work, however, he left on the First Crusade; his twelfth-century heirs, Alphonse Jourdain, Raymond V, and Raymond VI, were unable to build on what he had begun. Instead, they found themselves on the defensive against the pretensions of the rival house of Aragon and unable to control their great vassals, the Trencavels of Béziers-Carcassonne, the counts of Foix, and the Guillems of Montpellier, or even their own city of Toulouse, and all of them were practically independent by 1208.

Though Languedoc remained politically fragmented during this period, it made great economic and cultural progress. Cities arose, foreign trade grew, and a great fair appeared at St. Gilles—all of which helped to produce a new middle class quite

similar to that of northern Italy, as well as a vital Romanesque art and architecture and a troubadour poetry patronized by the nobility. The church failed to respond to the reform spirit of the age and was unable to stop the spread of new and dangerous heresies, those of the Waldensians and, especially, the Albigensians.

The inability of Count Raymond VI of Toulouse to suppress the Albigensian heresy in his domains caused Pope Innocent III to launch a northern French crusade against Languedoc, led by the able and ruthless Simon de Montfort. In 1213 Simon defeated a combined Aragonese-Toulousan army at Muret and killed King Pedro II of Aragon in the process, but neither he nor his sons were able to crush the Midi's political resistance to their rule or to extinguish heresy. As a result, in 1226 a second army, led by King Louis VIII, had to move south; it finally defeated the southern French once and for all. By 1229 most of Languedoc was under direct royal control, and by 1271, despite a few revolts following the deaths of Raymond VII and Alphonse of Poitiers (both of whom had controlled Toulouse), the entire province had become part of the royal domain, and remained so until the end of the Middle Ages.

Though the period of the Albigensian Crusade saw considerable fighting and damage in parts of western Languedoc near Toulouse and Béziers, the thirteenth century was, generally speaking, a time of steady economic progress. Languedoc's major cities, Toulouse, Narbonne, and Montpellier, grew rapidly in size, reaching a population of some 35,000 each by 1300. Smaller towns also were increasing in size, as was the population of the countryside. Merchants from the Midi began to compete with Italian traders in Mediterranean markets from Syria west to Tunisia and Valencia, and St. Louis built a new port at Aigues Mortes to rival Marseilles and Barcelona. A number of local fairs appeared and merchants of the region, led by those of Montpellier, began to go in large numbers to the fairs of Champagne. Though husbandry and grazing continued to flourish along marshy shores and mountain uplands as well as in the flat plains, it was industrial progress that proved most spectacular, especially in textile production, milling, and the making of arms. There was also considerable moneylending, which developed into banking as new techniques of capitalism were copied from the Italians. By the end of the century, Languedoc had become a region that economically and socially resembled Italy more than any other part of western Europe.

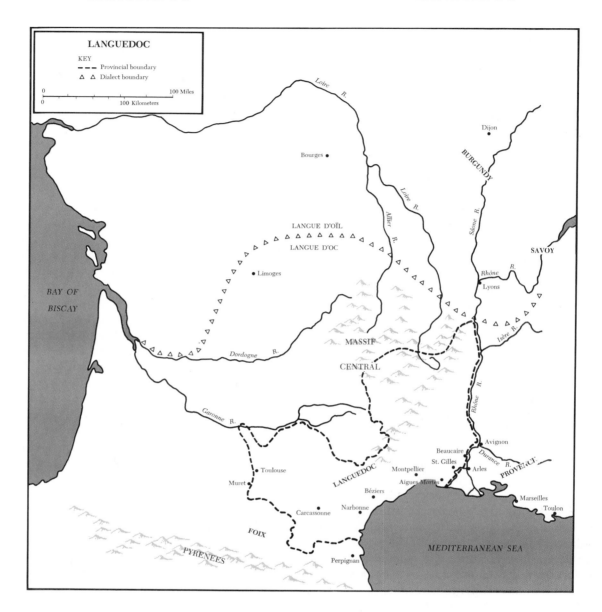

The control of Languedoc by the Capetians after 1229 had important political and social consequences, though in some ways it did not prove to be too burdensome. The local nobility was not dispossessed; towns with consulates (supreme governing bodies) continued an autonomous existence; and below the level of royal governor or seneschal, most royal officials were not northerners but recruits from the local region. Even the legal system, as it had evolved during the twelfth century, remained relatively unchanged. Nevertheless, slowly but surely royal authority began to erode elements of local particularism until, by the end of the century, it had attracted the talents of such able administrators as Pierre Flote to the Paris of Philip the Fair. An In-

quisition supported by the Capetians slowly but surely ended the Albigensian heresy in areas such as Toulouse and Béziers where it had had many adherents.

During the thirteenth century considerable cultural change took place as well. One of the more significant was the disappearance of the troubadours, in part because after 1229 neither the lower nobility nor magnates like the count of Toulouse were willing to serve as their patrons. They sought patronage at the more distant courts of Frederick II and Manfred of Sicily, Alfonso X the Wise of Castile, and James (Jaume) I the Conqueror of Aragon. As troubadour culture declined, however, learning grew in importance. Montpellier developed its twelfth-century schools into a university that was the most important center for medicine and Roman law outside of Italy, and the university in Toulouse, founded by the papacy as a center of orthodoxy, took firm root. A new Gothic style from the north influenced the building of churches such as St. Sernin in Toulouse, as a civilization still largely Occitanian became increasingly influenced by that which held sway north of the Loire.

At the beginning of the fourteenth century, royal government continued to expand its authority, and after 1337 a lieutenant of the king regularly served as governor of the entire province. Representatives of the clergy, the middle class, and the nobility regularly came together as an Estates-General of Languedoc to vote subsidies to the crown. Montpellier, the region's principal port, which had long been shared with the house of Aragon, became completely French in 1349. The economic growth of the entire area continued, with Toulouse and Montpellier reaching a population of some 40,000 each by the 1340's and Narbonne not far behind. Furthermore, although much traffic now reached northern Europe by way of Savoy and its Alpine passes or through the Straits of Gibraltar, and the fairs of Champagne had begun to decline, the move of the papacy to Avignon stimulated the economy of the region sufficiently to make up for most of this loss. It was hardly noticed at first that no more virgin lands existed for an expanding rural population to exploit, and that more and more foodstuffs had to be imported from areas such as Sicily.

Then a series of disasters struck. In 1337 the Hundred Years War began; and within a decade bands of mercenaries, used by both the English and the French, began to wander through Languedoc, devastating the countryside. In 1348 the Black Death arrived, and in certain areas carried off half of the urban and rural population. It returned in 1361 in outbreaks that proved equally devastating. The ruin of the Bardi and the Peruzzi in Florence affected capitalists in Languedoc who were closely tied to these banking houses. And by the 1360's and 1370's famines regularly struck the region. Social discontent disturbed the decaying towns, and jacqueries such as the Tuchins were rife in the countryside. By 1402 the city of Toulouse had lost two-thirds of its population, and Montpellier had only 15,000 inhabitants. Narbonne declined as its port silted up, and the papacy, which had to share its authority with a rival Rome, ceased to stimulate the local economy. The great magnate Gaston Phoebus of Foix could defy the central government, which was able to exercise authority only fitfully during the reign of Charles V. It was an impoverished province that faced the fifteenth century.

After 1400, changes affected Languedoc very slowly. Though most warfare between the English and the French took place north of the Loire and the province remained loyal to Charles VII when he resided at Bourges, social revolts and depredations by mercenary bands continued to be endemic. Languedoc also suffered when the Avignon papacy finally collapsed after 1417. Only gradually was the new royal government of Charles VII and Louis XI able to restore order. At the same time institutional changes of some importance began to appear. The Estates-General of Languedoc began to meet more regularly, especially before 1450, and a new Parlement was established to centralize the province's judicial system. The customary law, especially that dealing with family and matrimonial matters, began to change and show the direct influence of Roman law as it was applied elsewhere in the realm. Though Languedoc kept its special character and continued to use local officials in royal administration, it began to find itself more and more integrated into the France of the north.

Economically, the situation began to change by mid century as well. Jacques Coeur, who controlled royal finances for the king, began to revitalize the region's foreign commerce by organizing a merchant fleet at Aigues Mortes to trade with the Levant and by setting up his business headquarters in Montpellier. This provided Montpellier with its last brief period of commercial glory before it began to lose ground to Marseilles, which had just been annexed to the royal domain. By the last years of the century, the countryside had started to prosper again and a new international fair had been organized at Beaucaire as a rival to Lyons further north. Montpellier's university recovered its ancient vigor and Toulouse revived as a center of intellectual life. Even the troubadours returned to the region as their poetry was somewhat artificially stimulated by the patronage of King René of nearby Provence. After a century of disaster, Languedoc slowly revived, but less as a center of a special Occitanian civilization than as a vital part of a vigorous French nation.

BIBLIOGRAPHY

The primary source is Claude de Vic and Joseph Vaisette, *Histoire générale de Languedoc*, II–IX (1875–1885). Studies include André Armengaud and Robert Lafont, eds.,

Histoire d'Occitanie (1979), 54–281; Archibald R. Lewis, *The Development of Southern French and Catalan Society, 718–1050* (1965); Jonathan Sumption, *The Albigensian Crusade* (1978); Walter L. Wakefield, *Heresy, Crusade, and Inquisition in Southern France, 1100–1225* (1974); Philippe Wolff, *Histoire du Languedoc* (1967), 110–263.

ARCHIBALD R. LEWIS

[See also **Aquitaine; Black Death; Castellan; Cathars; Consuls, Consulate; Fairs; Famine in Western Europe; France; Hundred Years War; Inquisition; Jacques Coeur; Montpellier; Representative Assemblies; Toulouse; Trade, European; Troubadour, Trouvère, Trovador.**]

LANTBERT OF DEUTZ (*d.* 1170) wrote the *Vita Heriberti* (*ca.* 1050), a life of St. Heribert, archbishop of Cologne and founder of the monastery at Deutz. At the insistence of Archbishop Hermann of Cologne, who felt that the *Vita* did not include enough of Heribert's miracles, Lantbert later composed the *Miracula sancti Heriberti*. He was made abbot of St. Lorenz in Liège in 1060 and lived there until his death.

BIBLIOGRAPHY

Vita Heriberti, in *Monumenta Germaniae historica: Scriptorum*, IV (1841), 739–753; *Miracula sancti Heriberti, ibid.*, *Scriptorum*, XV, pars II (1887), 1245–1260; Max Manitius, *Geschichte der lateinischen Literatur des Mittelalters*, II (1923), 364.

NATHALIE HANLET

[See also **Hagiography.**]

LANX. The lanx was a large shallow circular or rectangular dish used in antiquity to carry fruits and victuals. The trays often reached weights of 100 pounds and, as seen in such outstanding examples as the Corbridge lanx, were decorated by elaborate figural compositions. The lanx probably served as one of the principal sources for the paten in early Christianity.

MICHAEL T. DAVIS

[See also **Paten.**]

LAODICEA. See Lādhiqiya, Al-.

LAPIDARIUM, a treatise on the properties and virtues of stones, was a frequent work of classical Greek and Roman authors, such as Ptolemy and Dioscorides (in his *De materia medica*), and was written and elaborated throughout the Middle Ages. In the early seventh century Isidore of Seville compiled descriptions of stones emphasizing their mineralogical variety and practical uses. A different tradition is represented by Marbod, bishop of Rennes from 1096 to 1123, whose *Liber lapidum seu de gemmis* (written between 1067 and 1081 while Marbod was schoolmaster at Rennes) gives an account of the legendary and magical virtues, as well as the real qualities, of sixty stones. Perhaps the outstanding medieval lapidarium was the *Lapidario* of Alfonso X, completed in 1250. This lavishly illustrated treatise coordinated nearly 500 stones with the signs of the zodiac, stars, temperatures, and letters of the alphabet.

BIBLIOGRAPHY

Alfonso X, *Lapidario*, Sagrario Rodríguez M. Montalvo, ed. (1981); *Dioscorides de materia medica*, Max Wellmann, ed. (1906–1907); Isidore of Seville, *Etymologiae*, in *Patrologia latina*, LXXXII (1850); Marbod of Rennes, *Liber lapidum seu de gemmis, ibid.*, CLXXI (1854); Lynn Thorndike, *A History of Magical and Experimental Science*, I (1929), 775–782.

MICHAEL T. DAVIS

[See also **Alfonso X; French Literature: Didactic; Gems and Jewelry; Marbod of Rennes.**]

LAQABI WARE, a type of medieval Islamic pottery. The use of the Arabic term *laqabi* (*lakabi*, "painted") to describe this ware is, however, of modern European origin. Examples of *laqabi* ware contain carved designs embellished by the addition of colored glazes. This decorative technique may have been used to simulate the appearance of cloisonné enameled vessels. Originally assumed to have been made in Iran, this ware is now thought to have come from Syria. It may have been influenced in its decorative themes and techniques by Byzantine ceramics and enamels.

BIBLIOGRAPHY

Arthur Lane, *Early Islamic Pottery* (1947), 36; David Talbot Rice, *Islamic Art* (1965), 68.

PRISCILLA P. SOUCEK

[See also **Ceramics, Islamic.**]

Persian *laqabi* plate of Seljuk period, mid 12th century. COURTESY OF THE FREER GALLERY OF ART, SMITHSONIAN INSTITUTION, WASHINGTON, D.C. (29.11)

LASKARIDS. An aristocratic Byzantine family that provided the empire of Nicaea with its ruling house. The name probably derived from the Arabic for soldier *(al-ᶜaskar)*, which suggests that they came from the eastern frontiers of the Byzantine Empire.

The Laskarids rose to prominence in the late twelfth century. In 1199 Theodore I Laskaris (1204–1221), the founder of the empire of Nicaea, married Anna, a daughter of Emperor Alexios III Angelos (1195–1203), and was designated his heir apparent. Theodore had at least six brothers, who gave him invaluable support when he was establishing the Nicene Empire. After his death in 1221, the Nicene throne passed to Theodore's son-in-law, John III Vatatzes, whose only son and heir, Theodore, took the surname Laskaris. Theodore II died in August 1258, leaving his seven-year-old son, John IV Laskaris, to succeed him.

John Laskaris' rights were progressively set aside by the usurper Michael VIII Palaiologos (1259–1282) until, on Christmas Day 1261, John was blinded and imprisoned. This act sparked an uprising by the Nicene borderers. Support for the deposed child emperor also came from the Arsenites, the followers of Patriarch Arsenios (1254–1259, 1261–1264), who had been deposed for protesting Michael Palaiologos' usurpation. Laskarid sentiment was so strong that in 1290 Emperor Andronikos II Palaiologos (1272–1328) visited John Laskaris in prison to seek his forgiveness. This act failed to dissipate legitimist feeling. The Laskarid cause went into decline only after the death of John Laskaris (*ca.* 1305). But until the fall of Constantinople in 1453, and even later, Laskaris remained a prestigious surname. It was claimed by such notable men as John Laskaris Kalopheros, prominent in the later fourteenth century in promoting the interests of Byzantium in the West, and by the scholars Janos and Constantine Laskaris, who carried on the Byzantine traditions of scholarship in Western Europe after 1453.

BIBLIOGRAPHY
Demetrios I. Polemis, *The Doukai* (1968), 106–111, 139–140.

MICHAEL ANGOLD

[See also **Arsenius Autorianus; Byzantine Empire: History; Latin Empire of Constantinople; Michael VIII Palaiologos; Nicaea, Empire of; Theodore I Laskaris; Theodore II Laskaris.**]

LAST, a measure of capacity (a unit of account) for dry and liquid products in England that etymologically was derived ultimately from the Old English *hlæst*, a load or cartload. The most common lasts, consisting of 12 barrels of varying capacities (*ca.* 17.76 to *ca.* 19.92 hectoliters), were used for ashes, barrel fish, beer, butter, iron, pitch, potash, and soap. Other lasts were used for bowstaves, 600; feathers, 1,700 pounds (771.103 kilograms); flax, 600 bonds; grain, 10 seams or 80 bushels (*ca.* 28.19 hectoliters); gunpowder, 24 barrels or 2,400 pounds (1,088.616 kilograms); herrings, 12,000; hides, 20 dickers or 200 in number; raisins, 24 barrels or 24 hundredweight (1,219.248 kilograms); salmon, 6 pipes or 504 gallons (*ca.* 19.08 hectoliters); salt, 10 weys or 420 bushels (*ca.* 148.00 hectoliters); and wool, 12 sacks or 4,368 pounds (1,981.290 kilograms).

RONALD EDWARD ZUPKO

[See also **Weights and Measures, Western European.**]

LAST SUPPER, THE, recounted in all four Gospels, encompasses the episodes of the meal shared by Christ and his disciples on the eve of his Crucifixion, and the announcement of Christ's betrayal by Judas. The earliest images of a communal repast of Christ and his followers, as in the crypt of Lucina in the catacombs of S. Callisto in Rome, likely concern the future meal in heaven promised by Christ to the faithful. Early Christian and Byzantine visualizations of the Last Supper, which began to appear in the sixth century in the Rossano Gospels and in S. Apollinare Nuovo, Ravenna, represent Christ and the disciples reclining around a sigma-shaped or circular table in the manner of a Roman banquet. The rectangular table appeared in the West, beginning in the late ninth or early tenth century, as the separation and identification of Judas assumed an increasing importance. From the beginning, depictions of the Last Supper often included the washing of the feet of the apostles. In Byzantine art the liturgical character of the Last Supper was stressed by the scene of the Communion of the apostles, in which Christ ritualistically distributes the bread and chalice to the twelve. In the West this sacramental theme gained ascendancy only in the later Middle Ages.

BIBLIOGRAPHY
Eduard Dobbert, "Das Abendmahl Christi in der bildenden Kunst bis gegen den Schluss des 14. Jahrhunderts," in *Repertorium für Kunstwissenchaft,* 13 (1890), 14 (1891), 18 (1895); Laura Hibbard Loomis, "The Table of the Last Supper in Religious and Secular Iconography," in *Art Studies,* 55 (1927); Elisabeth Palli Lucchesi, "Abendmahl," in *Lexikon der christlichen Ikonographie,* I (1968); Louis Réau, *Iconographie de l'art chrétien,* II, pt. 2 (1957); Gertrud Schiller, *Iconography of Christian Art,* Janet Seligman, trans., II (1972), 24–41.

MICHAEL T. DAVIS

[See also **Bouts, Dirk; Feet, Washing of; Ferrer I (The Elder), Jaime; Holy Week.**]

LATAKIA. See **Lādhiqiya, Al-.**

LATEEN SAIL (Latin sail), a triangular sail suspended by a long yard at an angle of about forty-five degrees to the mast. The lateen sail was a vast improvement over the older fixed sail and it made possible a great advance in medieval seafaring. Fastened to the gunwales, it could be moved according to the direction of the wind, and consequently allowed for more flexibility in navigation because it permitted sailing closer into the wind. It probably appeared in the eastern Mediterranean in the second century, and was used in both the feluccas of the Mediterranean and the dhows of the Arabian Sea.

BIBLIOGRAPHY
Encyclopaedia Britannica, 11th ed. (1910–1911).

LINDA C. ROSE

[See also **Navigation; Ships and Shipbuilding.**]

LATERAN, the site and buildings of the cathedral of Rome, comprising the early Christian cathedral itself, a detached octagonal baptistery, the papal palace *(patriarchum),* and miscellaneous dependencies including monasteries, a hospital, and schools. Today only the baptistery, rebuilt by Pope Sixtus III (432–440), and Vasallectus' thirteenth-century cloister adjoining the church survive in medieval state. The basilica has undergone multiple remodelings, and today it shows the work of Francesco Borromini in the nave (1646–1650), Alessandro Galilei on the facade (1730–1732), and Virginio Vespignani in the apse (1876–1886). The palace was mostly demolished by Pope Sixtus V, beginning in 1586; its only surviving parts are the oratory of St. Lawrence *(Sancta Sanctorum),* the *scala santa,* and the apse of the *aula magna* of Leo III, with its mosaic decoration remade under Benedict XIV (1740–1758).

"Lateran" comes from the name of the Roman family, Laterani, whose property near the Porta Asinaria was confiscated in A.D. 65. The church, officially named St. John by the seventh century, commonly was called Basilica Constantina after Constantine the Great, who donated the site to the Roman Church in 312–313, and sponsored the original church building. Possibly a thank offering for Constantine's victory over Maxentius, the basilica was the first Christian building officially sponsored by a Roman emperor. Its design, drawn primarily from civic and sacral-imperial antecedents, presumably was influential. A wooden-roofed basilica with planar, brick-faced walls, it had a nave, four aisles defined by four colonnades (eighty columns in all), and a single apse at the west. Most immediately impressive were its size (maximum length 333.3 Roman feet, width 180 Roman feet; or 98.53 meters by 53.46 meters) and its splendid decoration and outfittings in marbles, mosaic, and precious metals.

Medieval contributions included rebuilding and decoration commissioned by Pope Sergius III (904–911) following an earthquake in 896 that caused the nave to collapse; the twelfth-century addition of an east porch signed by Nicolaus Angeli (Niccolò d'Angelo); and construction of a transept and new apse, decorated by the mosaicist Jacopo Torriti, commissioned by Pope Nicholas IV, in 1291 (mosaic remade in the nineteenth century).

The palace grew from a core of Roman residential structures, donated with the basilica by Constantine, to a complex of lavish dining and reception halls, chapels, porticoes, and countless utilitarian rooms and buildings. Repeatedly pillaged, the *patriarchum* was often refurbished and continually enlarged by popes from the seventh through the thirteenth centuries. It had great prestige, evidenced by Charlemagne's emulation of it in his palace *(quod nominavit Lateranis)* at Aachen.

The Lateran was visited by churchmen and pilgrims from all over Europe. Ecumenical councils were held there, including the great affairs of 1123 and 1215, and among its relics the Lateran boasted the Ark of the Covenant and other Judaica. There was a unique collection of ancient statuary, including the bronze "Caballus Constantini" (equestrian Marcus Aurelius), on display in the square outside the transept. After the jubilee of 1300, the Lateran's medieval history ended abruptly, and sadly. The palace was abandoned in 1304; after Avignon the popes' primary residence was the Vatican. The basilica burned in 1308; just repaired, it burned again in 1361.

BIBLIOGRAPHY

Tilmann Buddensieg, "Le coffret en ivoire de Pola, Saint-Pierre et le Latran," in *Cahiers archéologiques,* **10** (1959); Johannes Diaconus, *Descriptio lateranensis ecclesiae,* in Roberto Valentini and Giuseppe Zucchetti, eds., *Codice topografico della città di Roma,* III (1946, repr. 2 vols. 1960); Louis Marie Olivier Duchesne, ed., *Le Liber pontificalis,* 2nd ed., 3 vols. (1955); Richard Krautheimer, Spencer Corbett, and Alfred K. Frazer, *Corpus basilicarum christianarum Romae,* V (1977); Philippe Lauer, *Le palais de Latran* (1911); Ursula Nilgen, "Das Fastigium in der Basilica Constantiniana und vier Bronzesäulen des Lateran," in *Römische Quartalschrift,* **72** (1977); John Bryan Ward-Perkins, "Constantine and the Origins of the Christian Basilica," in *Papers of the British School at Rome,* **22** (1954); Jens T. Wollesen, "Die Fresken in Sancta Sanctorum," in *Römisches Jahrbuch für Kunstgeschichte,* **19** (1981).

DALE KINNEY

[See also **Early Christian and Byzantine Architecture.**]

LATERAN COUNCILS. See **Councils, Western.**

LATERCULUS. See **Polemius Silvius.**

LATHEM, LIÉVIN VAN (Livinus van Laethem) *(fl.* 1454–1493), Flemish painter and manuscript illuminator. Having joined the guild of painters in Ghent in 1454, Liévin van Lathem was working for Duke Philip the Good by 1459, probably in the latter's residence in Ghent. He soon moved to Antwerp, where he joined the guild of painters in 1462 and where he remained for the rest of his life. Lathem was among the highest paid of the painters making decorations for the wedding of Duke Charles the Bold in 1468. In the 1480's he served as court painter to Maximilian of Austria (Emperor Maximilian I), who inherited the Netherlands from Charles's daughter Mary of Burgundy.

In 1469 Lathem collaborated with the scribe Nicolas Spierinc on a book of hours for Charles the

Madonna and Child, MS illumination by Liévin van Lathem from *Hours of Mary of Burgundy,* 15th century. VIENNA, OSTER-REICHISCHE NATIONALBIBLIOTHEK, COD. 1857, fol. 24

Bold. Antoine de Schrijver has identified a manuscript in the Durrieu collection (Larivière) as the one in question and has consequently assigned to Lathem the works formerly given to Philippe de Mazerolles (d. 1479). Among them are a *Roman de Gilles de Trazignies* (Chatsworth Bakerwell, Duke of Devonshire collection, MS 7535); copies of Raoul Lefèvre's *Histoire de la conquête de la toison d'or* and the anonymous pseudo-Aristotelian *Livre des secrets* (Paris, Bibliothèque Nationale, MSS fr. 331 and 562); and a large part of the *Hours of Mary of Burgundy* (Vienna, Osterreichische Nationalbibliothek, cod. 1857).

BIBLIOGRAPHY

Jozef Duverger, "Hofschilder Lieven van Lathem (ca. 1430–1493)," in *Jaarboek der koninklijk Museum voor Schone Kunsten Antwerpen* (1969), 97–104; Franz Unterkircher and Antoine de Schrijver, "Gebetbuch Karls des Kuhen vel potius Studendenbuch der Maria von Burgund," in *Kommentar* (1969), 42–45; Alphonse Wauters, "Liévin van Lathem," in *Biographie nationale de Belgique,* XI (1890–1891), cols. 421–424; Friedrich Winkler, "Studien zur Geschichte der niederländischen Miniaturmalerei des XV. und XVI. Jahrhunderts," in *Jahrbuch der kunsthistorischen Sammlungen des allerhöchsten Kaiserhauses,* 32 (1915).

ANNE HAGOPIAN VAN BUREN

[See also **Flemish Painting; Manuscript illumination, Western European; Mary of Burgundy, Master of; Spierinc, Nicolas.**]

LATIN CROSS. See **Cross, Forms of.**

LATIN EMPIRE OF CONSTANTINOPLE (1204–1261). The so-called Latin Empire of Constantinople was founded by Western Europeans when the Fourth Crusade conquered Constantinople on 12 April 1204. It came to an end on 25 July 1261, when the Byzantines retook the city. The empire claimed suzerainty over Thessalonica (Thessaloniki), Greece, and the Aegean islands, but in reality it seldom exercised authority outside of eastern Thrace, Bithynia, and Troas.

In a contested election the crusaders chose the count of Hainault and Flanders as Emperor Baldwin I (1204–1205). Baldwin proved too impetuous in battle; after his capture and death at the hands of the Vlach-Bulgarians, his brother Henry followed him as regent and then emperor (1206–1216). Henry was the most capable of the Latin rulers; his intelligence

and kindness won the support of his non-Latin subjects, and his military skill extended the empire's boundaries. He was succeeded by his sister Yolande and her husband, Peter of Courtenay; Peter was crowned by the pope in 1217 but never reached Constantinople. He was captured by the Greeks of Epiros and died in prison. His son Robert was crowned (1221) in Constantinople, but proved so unworthy that his own barons drove him away; he died in Greece in 1228. Peter's youngest son, Baldwin II (b. 1217), was underage, so Jean de Brienne was chosen emperor in 1229. Jean (or John, as he and his successors are known) did not reach Constantinople to be crowned until 1231; he ruled until his death in 1237. John's daughter Maria married young Baldwin. John was a capable general, but his miserliness alienated his followers. Baldwin II (1237–1261) had no talent for government and spent as much time as possible in Western Europe, residing in royal courts while in quest of funds. The feebleness and ineptitude of the rulers contributed to the early decay of the Latin Empire.

Personal incompetence was compounded by the terms of three documents that each new ruler had to swear to uphold. In March 1204, prior to the city's capture, an agreement among the crusaders provided for the divison of spoils, election of emperor and patriarch, distribution of fiefs by a commission on which the new emperor would have no voice, and limited rights for the new emperor. The second document, of October 1204, prescribed a division of territory; the emperor, the Venetians, and the non-Venetian crusaders each received land near the capital and additional shares in more remote regions. (The actual apportionment of Latin territories, however, owed more to accident of conquest than to the proposed division.) In October 1205 a treaty between the regent Henry and the Venetian podesta specified that the emperor could act only with the consent of a council made up of the podesta, his councillors, and the principal non-Venetian vassals of the empire. Terms of military service were specified; judges appointed by the council (not the emperor) would decide cases of failure to fulfill military obligations.

The Latin emperors claimed to be the continuators of Constantine the Great's empire. They retained Byzantine ceremonial for coronations, imperial insignia (purple boots, eagles), and court titles, but the reality of their power was that of a feudal monarch. Their control over such great vassals as the kings of Thessalonica, the princes of Achaea, and the dukes of Athens and of the Archipelago was tenuous;

the Venetians possessed the greatest concentration of power in the empire, and their views might conflict with the emperor's.

The empire was confronted almost at once by an array of problems. Three Byzantine successor states sprang up: at Trebizond, descendants of Andronikos I Komnenos founded the empire of the Grand Komnenoi; at Nicaea (Nikaia), Theodore Laskaris, a son-in-law of Alexios III Angelos, established himself and presently claimed an imperial title; in northwestern Greece, Michael I Doukas, an illegitimate relative of the Angeloi, created what became the despotate of Epiros. Nicaea and Epiros were to present serious dangers to the Latin emperors. In the northwest, Ioannitsa (or Kalojan), ruler of the Vlach-Bulgarian (or Second Bulgarian) Empire, initially tried to conciliate the crusaders. Only when they rejected his advances did he put himself at the head of a coalition of Slavs and discontented Byzantines to attack crusader garrisons in Thrace. To recover Adrianople and Demotika, Baldwin and Enrico Dandolo, the Venetian doge, hastened westward with a small force. In April 1205 they encountered Ioannitsa near Adrianople; the crusaders were put to flight, Count Louis of Blois was killed, and Emperor Baldwin was captured. Only the skill of the aged Dandolo rallied a part of the army; many Franks fled and allegedly took ship at once for the West. Baldwin perished in captivity. After Dandolo's death (ca. 1 June 1205), Baldwin's brother Henry regained the friendship of the Byzantines of Thrace and restored somewhat the empire's position.

For the first decades of the Latin Empire's existence, the Bulgarian-Thessalonian-Epirote front posed the chief dangers. Boniface of Montferrat, disappointed candidate for the imperial crown, had been compensated with the kingdom of Thessalonica, but his rivalry with Baldwin (and later Henry) was barely patched over. Ioannitsa devastated Thrace in 1205–1206. Only the almost simultaneous deaths of Boniface and Ioannitsa in 1207 rescued the empire from its difficulties. Three candidates sought the Bulgarian crown, and Henry was able to use their conflicts to his own advantage. In Thessalonica, a lengthy minority and tensions between the queen mother and the regents allowed Henry to assert his authority there in 1209. He advanced into Greece in the same year, took Thebes by force, and received the homage of Euboea (Negroponte) and Achaea. Even Michael of Epiros became a vassal, though a most unreliable one. Henry's final years represent the highest point of the Latin Empire.

Michael of Epiros was succeeded by his half brother Theodore (1214–1230), while Henry's death in 1216 left the empire without competent leadership. Theodore expanded his domains into Thessaly and Macedonia, until Thessalonica itself passed into his hands in 1224. Theodore's vaulting ambition knew no bounds; he called himself "emperor" and challenged Bulgaria for control of Thrace. But John Asen II (1218–1241), who had reunified the Bulgarian Empire, defeated and captured Theodore at Klokotnitsa (1230).

The Latin Empire, in the meantime, had been the passive spectator of these struggles; Emperor Robert of Courtenay owed his entrance into Constantinople to John Asen's kindness, and Latin rule scarcely extended eighty miles west of Constantinople. After 1228, Asen hoped to become regent and even father-in-law of the young Baldwin II, but was frustrated by the introduction of John of Brienne. John was able to hold off the Bulgarians and even to defeat a combined Bulgarian-Byzantine army outside Constantinople in 1235. A year later a similar attack was halted by the arrival of an army from the principality of Achaea. The Bulgarian Empire weakened following John Asen's death in 1241, but the feeble Baldwin II was in no position to utilize the opportunity.

The Nicene front now became the crucial one. Theodore Laskaris (who was crowned in 1208 as Theodore I and died in 1222) cooperated with Ioannitsa against the Latins, but was severely defeated by Emperor Henry in 1211. By the ensuing treaty the Latin Empire won much of Bithynia and Troas, from Nicomedia to Adramyttion (modern Edremid). After Henry's death Empress Yolande maintained tranquillity on the Nicene front by marrying a daughter to Theodore I. His successor, John III Vatatzes (1222–1254), was more vigorous. After a victory over Emperor Robert's troops in 1225, he left the Latin Empire only Nicomedia and the capital's Asian suburbs. Occupying the Gallipoli Peninsula, John obtained the first Nicene territory in Europe. Here his continuing rivalries with "Emperor" Theodore of Thessalonica and John Asen helped the Latin Empire survive. After the Battle of Klokonitsa, John III was content to cooperate with the Bulgarian ruler.

After John Asen's death, Vatatzes profited from many of his conquests. In 1246 the Bulgarian territories in southern Thrace and Macedonia passed to the Nicenes, and Thessalonica was yielded by inhabitants who disliked the current scion of the Epirote house. In the ensuing years, the Nicenes drew a tightening ring around Constantinople, but seldom fought directly with the Latins. Rather, John III negotiated with the papacy in the hope that the city would be peacefully surrendered to him in return for acceptance of Catholic doctrine and papal supremacy. John's son Theodore II (1254–1258) was preoccupied with wars against Serbia, Bulgaria, and Michael II of Epiros. The Latin Empire, strengthless, survived on borrowed time.

Religious affairs and negotiations with the papacy preoccupied both Latin and Nicene rulers. Control of the church in the Latin Empire had been promised to whichever party (Venetian or non-Venetian) failed to win the imperial throne in the first election. The Venetians, who lost the election, therefore proceeded to name clerics who elected a Venetian, Thomas Morosini, as patriarch. Pope Innocent III reluctantly accepted this choice and recognized Constantinople as a patriarchate. He and his successors, however, strove to break the Venetian stranglehold on the office, with slight success. Another cause for interminable disputes was the subject of church property; except for a small proportion, the crusaders had divided among themselves Byzantine ecclesiastical property along with other lands and portable wealth. This proved irrecoverable in most areas; the popes forced a new division, whereby the church was supposed to receive an eleventh of all properties. Nonetheless, the patriarchs of Constantinople were chronically impoverished, forced to borrow from Venetians and others.

Clerics who arrived from the West were interested only in the highest ecclesiastical posts: archbishoprics, bishoprics, cathedral prebends, or the principal urban churches in Constantinople. The parish clergy in the countryside and most towns remained Greek-speaking; only a few would acknowledge papal overlordship. Even in the capital, Greek clerics refused allegiance to the Latin patriarch and retained contact with the exiled Orthodox patriarch at Nicaea.

A few Latin monasteries had existed in Byzantine territory before 1204, notably in the Venetian quarter of Constantinople. These were now reinforced by a significant monastic establishment. The Cistercians and the military orders were active, and after 1220 they were joined by Franciscans and Dominicans.

Negotiations for reunion of the Orthodox and Catholic churches were repeatedly renewed during the Latin Empire. Discussions between Western and Byzantine ecclesiastics began as early as December 1204. Not least among the barriers to agreement were the memories of the crusaders' sack of Constantinople (especially their abuse of churches and church property), and the Latins' desire to impose tithes (hitherto unknown in the East) on the Orthodox laity. The principal issues under discussion were liturgical usages, the *Filioque* (procession of the Holy Spirit from the Son as well as from the Father), and papal supremacy. The personality of such negotiators as Cardinal Pelagius (1214) exacerbated the situation. Franciscan and Dominican envoys in 1234 were unable to reach agreement with the Nicene church. John III hoped that the pope would offer him Constantinople in return for acceptance of union with Rome. By 1254 Innocent IV recognized that a Byzantine reconquest was unavoidable. He would even accept the Orthodox patriarch at Nicaea as patriarch of Constantinople, if it would further the cause of reunion.

One of the major internal problems of the Latin emperors was to win the support of the native population. At first the crusaders were favorably received in many locales. The populace of Constantinople, deprived of its natural leaders, was prepared to accept a crusader as emperor. The peasants generally viewed a change of masters without complaint; at Thebes, Adramyttion, and other places the townspeople welcomed the victors of 1204, in hopes of protection from external foes and an end to excessive taxation. Yet after a few months Latin oppressors had alienated many of their new subjects. By early 1205, Ioannitsa had won the support of the peasantry and upper classes of Thrace, who for a time aided his campaign against the crusaders. Later the population of the countryside came to look to Epiros or Nicaea for rescue.

Only Emperor Henry showed any skill in winning the affections of the natives. A noble Byzantine, Theodore Branas, accepted crusader rule because he had long been enamored of the French princess Agnes-Anna, widow of Alexios II and Andronikos I; Henry made Theodore lord of Demotika and Adrianople. Henry was so favorably received by the native population that he was able to utilize Greek troops against the Byzantine successor states. His justice was celebrated; later courts refused appeals against judgments made during his reign. Above all, he respected Orthodox religious preferences and refused to allow the papal legate, Cardinal Pelagius, to close the Greek churches of the capital. Henry's successors, however, were less wise; they ignored or oppressed the Byzantine populace, and Baldwin II indignantly repudiated the allegation that he consulted Greek advisers. The populace of Constantinople and its vicinity awaited eventual Byzantine recovery of the capital.

The position of the Venetians was another persistent internal problem. Although they initially claimed large territories, they ultimately held only trading stations, commercial privileges, and a few limited landholdings. Their interests did not always accord with the emperor's, yet through the imperial council they had virtual veto power over his actions. After a brief experiment with local election in 1205, the podesta (head of the Venetian community in Constantinople) was chosen by the doge every few years. While the Venetians generally were loyal to the empire, they did not hesitate to make commercial treaties with its chief enemies, Nicaea and Epiros.

The complexities of imperial succession necessitated a series of regents, beginning with Henry, who served while his brother's fate was in doubt. Conon de Béthune, one of the principal personages of the Fourth Crusade, was regent in 1216–1217 and again in 1219; in the interval (1217 until her death in 1219) the Empress Yolande ruled in behalf of her husband, the captive Peter of Courtenay. Her daughter Mary was briefly regent when Emperor Robert fled the city (1228); subsequently the brothers Narjot and Philippe de Toucy (who could claim French royal blood through Theodore Branas and Princess Agnes-Anna) held the office at various time. The temporary nature of their positions hindered the regents from making decisions or setting policies. Baldwin II repeatedly absented himself from the empire: He was in Western Europe at Jean de Brienne's death in 1237 and did not return until 1239; he was away again from about 1244 to 1248, in 1249, and often during the Latin Empire's final decade.

A besetting problem of the empire was poverty. Even at its largest, there were too few enfeoffed knights to defend the realm, and mercenaries had to be sought. After the loss of the bulk of the empire's territories (1217–1225), only mercenaries and such volunteers as the pope could obtain were available. The Venetians monopolized trade, and paid few commercial tolls. Western mercenaries repeatedly abandoned the bankrupt Latin Empire to enroll in the service of the Nicenes, the Epirotes, or even the Bulgarians and Turks. Baldwin II was particularly needy; his trips to the West were to solicit funds and troops from the pope, the Venetians, Queen Blanche

of France and her son Louis IX, and even the king of Castile. To secure funds, he parted with the most precious relics that remained in Constantinople after the crusaders' sack. Such irregular transfusions could not replace missing revenue, and the empire's last years were penurious.

The cultural life of the Latin Empire was almost equally barren. Not all Orthodox-Catholic religious interaction was hostile; there were some conversions to Catholicism, and the Franciscan order attracted converts and bilingual offspring of mixed marriages. While few translations of classical or patristic Greek sources were carried out in Constantinople during the Latin Empire, the way was prepared for translations, by Franciscans and others, of Latin theologians (Augustine, Thomas Aquinas) into Greek. These works were to have great influence on Byzantine thought in the ensuing century. In Constantinople, at the church now called Kalenderhane Djami, an artist with seeming south-Italian affinities produced a small group of frescoes illustrating the miracles of St. Francis. These date from the last decade of the empire and are its sole surviving artistic creation.

The end of the Latin Empire, although long expected, came suddenly. In 1259 Michael VIII Palaiologos usurped the Nicene throne. In 1261 one of his armies, under Alexios Strategopoulos, passed near Constantinople on its way to campaign against the Bulgarians. At the same time the Venetian fleet and a large part of the garrison had sailed north to secure the island of Daphnusia in the Black Sea. On the night of 24/25 July 1261, with the assistance of Byzantines living in and near the city, Strategopoulos' troops were admitted to Constantinople. There was little resistance; Baldwin II fled, abandoning his imperial insignia. He was to spend the rest of his life (to 1273) in quest of assistance to recover his empire. On 15 August, Michael VIII entered Constantinople and was crowned anew at Hagia Sophia. The city was decayed, even half ruined, but the Byzantine Empire had regained its ancient capital.

BIBLIOGRAPHY

Basic works with recent bibliographies include Antonio Carile, *Per una storia dell'impero latino di Constantinopoli* (1972, 2nd ed. 1978); D. M. Nicol, "The Fourth Crusade and the Greek and Latin Empires, 1204–1261," in *Cambridge Medieval History*, IV, 1, 2nd ed. (1966); Robert Lee Wolff, "The Latin Empire of Constantinople," in *idem* and Harry W. Hazard, eds., *The Later Crusades, 1189–1311*, 2nd ed. (1969).

Recent works on internal history include Antonio Carile, "Alle origini dell'impero latino d'Oriente: Analisi quantitativa dell'esercito crociato e ripartizione dei feudi," in *Nuova rivista storica,* **56** (1972); Benjamin Hendrickx, "Les institutions de l'Empire latin de Constantinople (1204–1261): Le pouvoir impérial (l'empereur, les régents, l'impératrice)," in *Byzantina,* **6** (1974), "Les institutions de l'Empire latin de Constantinople (1204–1261): La cour et les dignitaires," in *Byzantina,* **9** (1977), and "The Main Problems of the History of the Latin Empire of Constantinople (1204–1261)," in *Revue belge de philologie et d'histoire,* **52** (1974); David Jacoby, "Les états latins en Romanie: Phenomènes sociaux et économiques (1204–1350 environ)," in XVᵉ Congrès internationale des études byzantines, *Rapports et co-rapports,* I, pt. 3 (1976); Robert Lee Wolff, *Studies in the Latin Empire of Constantinople* (1976).

For works on foreign affairs, see Michael Angold, *A Byzantine Government in Exile* (1975); Claude Cahen, *Pre-Ottoman Turkey,* J. Jones-Williams, trans. (1968); Speros Vryonis, Jr., *The Decline of Medieval Hellenism in Asia Minor and the Process of Islamization from the Eleventh Through the Fifteenth Century* (1971).

On relations with the papacy, see Joseph Gill, *Byzantium and the Papacy 1198–1400* (1979); Kenneth M. Setton, *The Papacy and the Levant, 1204–1571,* I (1976).

CHARLES M. BRAND

[See also **Baldwin I of the Latin Empire; Bulgaria; Byzantine Empire; Constantinople; Crusades and Crusader States; Epiros, Despotate of; Jean de Brienne; Latin States in Greece (with map); Nicaea, Empire of; Trebizond.**]

LATIN LANGUAGE. Medieval Latin, the learned lingua franca of Western Europe until the end of the Middle Ages, must be distinguished from Vulgar Latin, the ancestor of the Romance languages. It is the direct descendant of Classical Latin, and is the main subject of this article, which is divided as follows: (1) the difference between Vulgar Latin and Medieval Latin; (2) the nature of Latin in the Middle Ages—its fundamental conservatism and how it was learned; (3) the main differences between Classical Latin (abbreviated CL) and Medieval Latin (ML): (*a*) vocabulary, (*b*) accidence and syntax, (*c*) pronunciation and spelling.

VULGAR LATIN

Even in the first century B.C. there was in Rome a distinction between the spoken, popular language (the demotic language) and literary, learned Latin. The extent of this split is uncertain; it may at first

have been no more significant than the difference between colloquial and educated English in the present day. Eventually, however, the two became quite distinct: the literary, learned language was preserved from change, through education; the spoken language, like all spoken languages, continued to develop and change. As Latin-speaking colonists, farmers, and soldiers spread throughout Italy and then into the provinces of Spain and Gaul, their language developed into separate dialects with their own forms, structures, and pronunciations. This spoken language, known as Vulgar Latin, thus formed the basis for the Romance languages: Italian, Spanish, Portuguese, French, Catalan, Provençal, and Romanian.

Latin is a synthetic language, depending on its inflections to indicate the relationship among words, tenses, moods; thus the root *ambul-* is modified by its endings alone: *ambul-at* (he is walking), *ambul-abat* (he was walking), *ambul-avisset* (he would have walked). Similarly, *genu* (knee), *genu-s* (of the knee), *genu-um* (of the knees). Inflected languages depend less on word order than do analytic languages such as English. Vulgar Latin gradually developed from a highly inflected language into an analytic one: compare the Latin *stilus amitae meae* (the pen of my aunt, my aunt's pen) with the French *la plume de ma tante.*

The development of Vulgar Latin properly belongs to the study of Romance philology, but a few of its tendencies affect Medieval Latin. Some early texts show the influence of Vulgar Latin: The *Itinerarium Egeriae* (*ca.* 400) can be regarded as Vulgar Latin or as debased literary Latin. Much later, the Strasbourg Oaths (842) are still recognizably Latin in the form sworn by the followers of Charles the Bald, but are taught as part of the history of the French language. In pockets of Roman imperial influence charters in very debased Latin are found; inscriptions throughout the Roman world show a casual attitude to grammar and concord (agreement of gender, case, and number). After a certain date, however, one must distinguish between the Latin that is in direct descent from Vulgar Latin (and thus is a precursor of a vernacular) and the literary Latin that has been influenced by vernacular languages (or is simply ungrammatical). The certain point of distinction is reached only when enough vernacular texts appear to make it possible to be sure just what the spoken vernacular was like: by the twelfth century, to take an extreme example, there is no difficulty in distinguishing Latin from French.

LATIN IN THE MIDDLE AGES

The conservatism of the Latin language. The literary language, unlike Vulgar Latin, was preserved from most of the ordinary pressures that contribute to linguistic change, mainly because the basis of teaching was an established literary heritage of authors and authorities. Even in classical times Latin was taught in schools. Throughout its history as the language of education and of educated discourse—for more than a thousand years—Latin was always a *learned* language, a fact of considerable importance for its development. Although it was spoken in schools and universities, and although anyone with any pretensions to education and literacy throughout the Middle Ages was, almost by definition, nearly bilingual in Latin and his own vernacular, no one spoke Latin as a native tongue.

Consequently, Latin was preserved from changes resulting from the processes of analogy that have affected all vernacular languages, especially through the learning processes of children. Children, at the time of their greatest capacity for learning to speak—before the age of four—work mainly by analogy and generalization: if the plural of "egg" is "eggs," then the plural of "bag" is "bags"; if the past of "keep" is "kept," then the past tense of "sleep" is "slept"; and so on. This process, however, spills over to eradicate anomalies: unless a pattern is so common as to resist analogical reduction (such as "I am," "you are," "he is"), a child tends to reduce abnormal forms to fit the pattern. A child must be taught, either by the weight of contrary usage or by instruction, to reject analogical plurals such as "mouses," "gooses," and "childs," and past tenses such as "swimmed," "singed," and "drived." In the absence of such correction, the linguistic change may become permanent: this is how the Old English plural *scipu* became Modern English "ships"; and the past tense *weop* became the Modern English "wept."

Latin, however, was always learned by instruction; the rules were learned first. Consequently, Latin usage could always be referred back to the authority of grammar books, and was not subject to the influences of analogy. No such standards of correctness existed for English until after the Renaissance, and formal teaching in English grammar is a relatively recent development. This is why English changed considerably between 700 and 1400, whereas Latin stayed much the same throughout its history. The author of *Beowulf* would have found even Chaucer's English totally incomprehensible. Cicero, however, would have had no difficulty reading a fifteenth-cen-

tury Latin chronicle. (He would, however, have had to familiarize himself with some different spelling conventions, would no doubt have been puzzled by some features of the syntax, and would not have known all the words.)

How Latin was learned. Latin was taught from grammar books and from texts; the former changed little throughout the Middle Ages, but the selection of texts (and thus the influences on practice) did change from time to time. The standard primer of Latin grammar until the Renaissance was the *Ars minor* of Aelius Donatus (fourth century), whose *Ars maior* was used by more advanced students. Even more important was the *Institutiones grammaticae* of Priscian (sixth century). Donatus and Priscian together formed the core of grammatical teaching. The theory of language had been studied from early times, as in the *De lingua latina* of Varro (second century B.C.). The *Etymologiae* of Isidore of Seville (*ca.* 570–636) was one of the most useful encyclopedias available in the Middle Ages; its first few books are organized according to the seven liberal arts, the first of which is *grammatica*, the study of grammar. Isidore's account of the nature of the Latin language was well known. Advanced studies, such as that of Eutyches (Priscian's disciple), on the conjugation of the verbs, were also available. Later in the Middle Ages two versified grammars were written: the *Graecismus* of Evrard (Eberhard) of Béthune (*d.* 1212) and the *Doctrinale puerorum* of Alexandre de Villa Dei (Ville-Dieu) (*ca.* 1170–1250). Both of these are extant in many copies. Being in verse, they were easily memorable, and tags from them (such as lists of feminine nouns ending in *-us* and rules for the construction of impersonal verbs with accusative and genitive) occur throughout the margins of medieval manuscripts, perhaps as aides-mémoire to the scribes or simply as well-remembered verses.

How did the medieval student acquire his Latin vocabulary? Students nowadays have fairly rigid notions about the usage of Latin vocabulary, distinguishing prose words from poetic, and "classical Latin" from "late Latin." Such distinctions depend ultimately on dictionaries that record not only the meaning of words but also their usage. The development of the Latin dictionary, however, was slow; even what is today considered an elementary principle, alphabetical arrangement, did not develop until the later Middle Ages. At first, students seem to have learned their vocabulary from "class lists," in which words were grouped according to subject matter (for instance, terms of agriculture, plants, animals, warfare, justice). Encyclopedias such as the *Etymologiae* were similarly arranged. Many short word-lists were available from the late classical period on, and have been collected and edited by Georg Goetz. The first major Latin dictionary was the *Elementarium doctrinae rudimentum* of Papias (mid-eleventh century); it was followed by the *Panormia* of Osbern of Gloucester (mid-twelfth century) and the extremely popular *Liber derivationum (Magnae derivationes)* (1190–1192) by the canonist Huguccio. These dictionaries culminated in the great *Catholicon* (1286) of Giovanni Balbi of Genoa (Johannes Januensis), by far the most comprehensive dictionary before modern times. It was arranged strictly alphabetically and, like most medieval dictionaries, indicated the declension of a noun (by giving the genitive form) or the conjugation of a verb, and occasionally supported its definitions by a quotation. The *Catholicon* was, after the Bible, one of the first works to be printed, perhaps by Gutenberg, in 1460.

The absence of a historical dictionary meant that Latin was less intolerant of neologisms, Graecisms, and words taken from the vernacular languages; there was no standard authority against which to check the status of a word, and so there was no purism nor hostility to innovations in vocabulary. In addition, the class-list type of vocabulary (like *Roget's Thesaurus*) tended to be all-inclusive and would include as many words as possible, irrespective of origin. Thus, a poetic word like *ensis* came to be a usual word for "sword"; many words strange to us would be included in lists as apparent synonyms. This fact should make the reader cautious in labeling a medieval author's vocabulary exotic; strict standards of latinity are inappropriate to the Middle Ages. All the major dictionaries are from Latin to Latin; the first Latin-English dictionary is the very short fifteenth-century *Promptorium parvulorum* (The children's storehouse).

Since Latin dictionaries and Latin grammars were written in Latin, no one could teach himself Latin; the role of the teacher, at least in the early stages, was all-important. Aelfric's *Colloquy* (tenth century) gives a picture of a schoolmaster taking his class through basic vocabulary, asking each boy in turn how he makes his living, what animals he catches, and so on. Once basic grammar was learned, from Donatus and Priscian, the class would be taken slowly through a text, construing each word and commmenting on the grammar.

Many texts were prepared specifically for teaching purposes. An example is the eleventh-century "Canterbury Classbook" (now Cambridge University Library, MS Gg. 5.35, which also contains the "Cambridge Songs"). The texts in this book are laid out on the page with wide margins and ample space between the lines to incorporate interlinear glosses, equivalent words, and comments above each word in the line. These glosses, usually in Latin, provide synonyms and grammatical and syntactical information, clarifying the tense and mood of the verb, the cases of the adjectives and nouns, and the antecedents of pronouns. The fact that the synonyms are in Latin suggests that the glosses were used to extend the student's vocabulary. There are also some construe marks: as Latin word order (especially in verse) is alien to speakers of more analytic languages, such as English and French, words were marked by a series of dots or symbols or sequential letters (*a, b, c, d, e*) to show the order in which they were to be construed. Some of the glosses give basic information on history, geography, and mythology, and even allegorical interpretations. Many glossed texts are, in effect, annotated editions. Some classical and medieval texts were studied with well-established commentaries (in which grammatical and lexical information predominated), such as Servius' commentary on Vergil and Donatus' commentaries on the comedies of Terence, both from the fourth century.

The most important influence on medieval latinity was not so much the grammar books as the texts that were studied. Modern students look mainly to Golden Age Latin writers—Caesar, Cicero, Livy, Vergil, Horace, Ovid—as authorities for style and usage. In the Middle Ages, however, the best-known texts were, first, the Vulgate Bible of Jerome (fourth century) and the church's liturgical texts, and then the authors studied in the educational curriculum. A great part of the liturgy is biblical in origin, and the best-known parts of the Bible would be those that formed a regular part of the services. The Old Testament was translated into Latin from Hebrew, and the New Testament was translated from Greek; thus, both Hebrew and Greek idioms found their way into ecclesiastical Latin.

The educational curriculum certainly contained classical authors, but also included both ancient authors no longer generally taught and medieval texts. Fairly simple reading was provided by "libri Catoniani": these contained such easy texts as Cato's *Distichs*, a collection of proverbs in verse couplets (*ca.* third century), the fables of Avianus (often supplemented later by the fables of Walter of England or of Alexander Neckam), and the *Eclogue* of Theodulus (a ninth- or tenth-century debate between Truth and Falsehood, which relates pagan mythology and biblical history). The "Canterbury Classbook" provided a reading program of Christian Latin poetry—Juvencus, Arator, Prudentius, up to very difficult texts such as those of Aldhelm.

Thus, the fact that Latin was learned formally, from grammars and texts, preserved it from essential change; on the other hand, the texts used—particularly Christian ones—produced a different kind of orthodoxy from that which derives from a purely classical education. Also, the absence of an authoritative dictionary allowed considerable freedom in lexical innovation.

DIFFERENCES BETWEEN MEDIEVAL LATIN AND CLASSICAL LATIN

There is no such thing as Medieval Latin, if by it is meant a language with a fixed grammar and vocabulary; there are simply varieties of Latin written in the Middle Ages. The only common denominator for all these varieties is the fundamental grammar supplied by Donatus and Priscian. On the other hand, many of the divergences from Classical Latin are so widespread as to be described as medievalisms and may be found in most medieval authors.

Vocabulary. Even in the classical period Latin absorbed a number of Greek words. Some were words for ordinary things, such as *artopta* (Greek: *artoptēs,* baking pan). Most, however, were at the literary level, where Greek had a sophisticated philosophical terminology; words such as *philosophia* were easily absorbed into Latin. The early Christian church developed initially in Greek-speaking centers, and ecclesiastical vocabulary was heavily indebted to Greek: *diabolus* (Greek: *diabolos,* devil), *diaconus* (Greek: *diakonos,* deacon), *ecclesia* (Greek: *ekklesia,* church), *presbyter* (Greek: *presbyterōs,* priest), *episcopus* (Greek: *episkopos,* overseer [bishop]), *paroecia, parochia* (Greek: *paroikia,* district outside the community [parish]), *hebdomada* (Greek *hebdomas,* from *hepta,* seven [week]), *synagoga* (Greek: *synagōgē,* assembly, synagogue), *allegoria* (Greek: *allēgoria,* allegory). Similarly, some Hebrew words, adopted first into Greek and then transliterated into the Latin Bible, became part of ordinary religious vocabulary—for instance, *pharisaeus* (Greek: *pharisaios;* Hebrew: *pārash,* separate [Pharisee]). The influence of Greek waned after the early Christian period, but in the latter Middle Ages, as Greek philosophy and science were rediscovered, technical vocabulary was increased by words such as

usia (Greek: *ousia,* being), *noys* (Greek: *nous,* intelligence), and words for plants, celestial objects, and medicine, among others.

The spread of the Roman Empire across Europe caused the assimilation of many non-Latin words into ordinary Latin vocabulary. Isidore's *Etymologiae* (early seventh century) contains some words of Germanic origin (for example, soap from *sapa*). The pressure of vernacular languages was felt at all periods, especially in topics for which Latin had no terminology. In accounts and records scribes would often simply use a vernacular word, either because they did not know a Latin equivalent, or for greater precision. Sometimes the word should not be regarded as Latin at all (as in *una buketta* [a bucket]); the only criterion by which to assess the latinity of a word is the frequency of its occurrence and, particularly, its capacity to behave like a Latin word—to decline like a Latin noun or adjective, to conjugate like a verb, or to be modified by the addition of prefixes and suffixes.

The process can be illustrated by some words for land and landholding: the Germanic root *feu-* (Old English: *feoh,* property; Old Frisian: *fiu;* Modern English: *fee*) produced the Latin *feodum* (fief), *feodalis* (feudal). The Germanic *mark-* (boundary; Old English: *mearc*) produced the Latin *marca,* and thus many derivatives meaning "someone living by a boundary": *marcensis, marcianus, marcisius.* Latin roots were also used in word formation: *tenēre* (to hold) developed the technical sense "to hold (property) from someone else"; hence *tenens* (a tenant), and thus *tenementum* (tenement, house). The word "forest" has an interesting history. The Latin adverb *foris,* meaning literally "outside the gates," came to refer to land outside the cultivated demesne; hence, the word *for-estum* was formed, meaning "the uncultivated land, the bush"; this in turn generated such derivatives as *disafforesto* (deforest, clear for cultivation—*dis + ad + foris + -tum,* noun suffix + verbal ending), and a further noun, *disafforestatio* (deforestation).

Ordinary word formation proceeded unchecked by lexicographical purism. The infinitive form of the verb is often used as a substantive noun: *esse* (being, in a philosophical sense), *tuum velle* (your wish), *pro posse* (according to one's ability). A feature of both Vulgar Latin and Medieval Latin is the spread of diminutive forms: *dominicella, domicella* (from *domina,* mistress), whence the French *demoiselle* (girl) and the English "damsel." Similarly, *soliculum* (from *sol,* sun), whence the French *soleil* (sun). The roots *cantus* (song) and *cantor* (singer) produced *cantaria, cantuaria* (chantry), *cantoria* (office of cantor), and similar words for church offices. Another innovation adopted into philosophical Latin (and ultimately into common vernacular usage) was *realis, realiter* (real, really), from *res* (thing).

Metaphor was another source for new vocabulary. The Persian word for "king" (*shāh*) produced the medieval Latin *scaccum* (the game of chess); as a board marked with black and white squares was used for counting money, the *scaccarium* became the "exchequer." A *cancellum* (originally meaning "boundary, enclosed space") came to mean "chancel," and produced *cancellarius* (chancellor). A *placitum* first came to mean "decree," from the phrase *placitum est (regi)* (it has pleased [the king]); from meaning "decision of the court" it came to mean "request for a decision," and thus "plea"; from it were formed such nouns as *placitor* (one who hears pleas, judge).

Other technical phrases came to be used as nouns: *quo warranto* (by what warrant?) came to mean the writ itself; a *quodlibet*, literally "whatever," came to mean "disputation," because it was originally an examination on "whatever you like," that is, a general examination. It was declined as a neuter noun, with the plural *quodlibeta*. In some words the meaning may have changed first in the vernacular derivative and then been transferred back to the Latin word from which it was derived. Thus the Latin *causa* (cause, case, affair) produced the French *chose* (thing), and in turn the Latin *causa* came to be a synonym of *res* (thing).

A comprehensive account of Medieval Latin vocabulary would be misleading, as the lexicon varied according to place and time. Naturally, philosophical vocabulary is usually confined to philosophical contexts, and technical to technical, but in Medieval Latin there is also the geographical dimension. The vocabulary of an English document is likely to be peculiar to Anglo-Latin (or, during the French-speaking period of medieval England, Norman-Latin). This is one reason why modern dictionaries of Medieval Latin are organized on national lines, such as R. W. Latham's *Revised Medieval Latin Word-List from British Sources*. There are also dictionaries of French-, Hungarian-, and Polish-Latin. This local vocabulary must be distinguished from what might be called Common Medieval Latin, which would include ecclesiastical terminology and the vocabulary of science (though not technology, which tends to be derived from vernacular words for

tools), philosophy, astronomy, medicine, mathematics (with Arabic influence), and music.

In addition to these natural extensions of the vocabulary, arising from external pressures of other languages or from original deficiencies, there were a few deliberate stylistic movements that cultivated an exotic vocabulary. The most remarkable is the style known as Hisperic Latin (apparent in the *Hisperica famina* of the seventh century, the style of Aldhelm, and even as late as Abbo of St. Germain's *Bella Parisiaca* in the late tenth century); this style involved coinages from obscure roots (usually Greek). Hisperic words, however, did not outlive the poetic fashion for which they were created.

Developments in Medieval Latin vocabulary can be paralleled in the history of most languages; words change meaning and new words are added to the lexicon, from foreign sources or on the basis of existing roots. In one respect Medieval Latin differed from other languages: its words did not become archaic or unusable because of semantic change. It is no longer possible in Modern English to use the word "silly," for example, in its Middle English sense "innocent"; the connotations of the word have changed too much. In Latin, however, since the ancient authors were still used as the basis of education, their vocabulary remained available in its original senses.

Accidence and syntax. In all periods of the Middle Ages there are examples of "poor" Latin; the difficulty is to classify them according to their significance. They may result simply from an individual's inadequate grasp of Latin grammar, for not all medieval clerks were competent Latinists. There are, for instance, a record of the oral examination of one clerk who clearly had no understanding of Latin case endings, and a fifteenth-century English translation of *Alexander's Letter to Aristotle* showing that the author had no idea how to translate *ut* and the subjunctive. The use of abbreviation marks is often a sign, one suspects, that the scribe was unsure exactly what ending to use.

Some "bad grammar" may, however, be of more linguistic significance. First, in early periods (before the eighth century in Germany, for example) it may involve examples of Vulgar Latin, that is, Latin that might in time have become a full-fledged Romance language, if it had not been displaced by another language. Second, it may be a sign of local usage; this is especially important in spelling variations, where local pronunciations may be reflected in the spelling of Latin, but can also affect syntax. Finally, it may be a widespread medieval usage. In all places and periods examples of "good" Latin (that is, Classical Latin) must also be expected. Individual scholars could always go back to classical texts as their models and thus write impeccable Latin—but the existence of such fluent Latinists does not mean that writers who did not conform to classical practice were necessarily out of step.

Accidence—the inflections of nouns, adjectives, verbs—is generally that of Classical Latin. In some charters written before the Carolingian period, all grammatical rules (even the distinction between the nominative and accusative cases) appear to be totally unknown, but most writers (other than the merely incompetent) decline and conjugate Latin words according to classical practice. A few analogical forms occur—that is, the reduction of apparent anomalies to a more general pattern. Greek nouns ending in -ma (which should have the genitive singular ending in -matis, the plural in -mata) are sometimes declined as feminine first declension (like porta); similarly, neuter plural nouns ending in -ia are sometimes treated as feminine singulars. There is sometimes confusion between nouns of the second and fourth declensions (both of which end in -us in the nominative). The dative singular of totus (CL: toti) sometimes appears as toto (by analogy with bonus); in Classical Latin the dative singular of unus is uni in all genders, but in Medieval Latin the feminine singular dative is sometimes une (= CL unae). Fourth-conjugation verbs with the first-person singular ending in -io (infinitive, -ire) are sometimes confused with those of the first conjugation (-io, -iare), and vice versa. Classical Latin deponent verbs have sometimes been re-formed to an active pattern, especially in the passive voice. Similarly, the gerundive often has an active sense; for instance, nocenda venena is the equivalent of nocitura venena (harmful poisons).

Latin accidence was firmly entrenched in the grammar books, but syntax was given less attention. Consequently, Medieval Latin syntax was less restricted by authority and shows more variation from classical practice. Variations arise from two sources: the influence of the vernacular languages (for instance, of English on Anglo-Latin) and the difficulty or strangeness of some classical constructions.

Medieval Latin is generally much simpler than Classical Latin; relationships between parts of the sentence are more explicit—for example, clauses of purpose or reason (introduced by ut, cum, quod) are often introduced in the main clause by a clarifying adverbial phrase (ad id, ad hoc, ad eam causam).

Some authors use a more "natural" word order, with the object and indirect object after the verb. Analytic expression sometimes replaces Classical Latin synthesis, for example by the use of auxiliary verbs: thus, volo ire (CL: ibo, I will go), debeo ire (CL: mihi eundum est, I ought to go), habeo quidquam facere (I have to do something, from the sense "I have something to do"), habeo eum interfectum (I have killed him); compare French: je l'ai tué (CL: eum interfeci), tres erant ambulantes (CL: tres ambulabant, there were three men walking, three men were walking). Sometimes the gerund is used instead of the present participle: ambulando loquebantur (CL: ambulantes loquebantur, they spoke while walking). The ablative absolute construction is not always used correctly: sometimes it is replaced by the nominative absolute, and sometimes it is used where the subject or object of the main sentence is involved (that is, where Classical Latin would have used the nominative or accusative).

In subordinate clauses of time, dum and cum are used interchangeably for "when," with either the indicative or the subjunctive mood. Purpose clauses are introduced not only by ut and ne but also by quo (in CL used only with a comparative adjective or adverb), quatinus, and quominus (lest). Purpose is often expressed simply by the infinitive: veni eam videre (CL: veni ut eam videam, I have come to see her). Result clauses are often introduced by quod, for instance, in tantum quod (to the extent that), as well as by ut. In Classical Latin impero (order) is followed by ut + subjunctive; iubeo (order), by the infinitive. These distinctions are not maintained in Medieval Latin, in which impero + infinitive and iubeo + ut are common; Medieval Latin also uses volo ut + subjunctive (I wish that). The strict Classical Latin rules governing the sequence of tenses (and the distinction between historic and primary tenses) are often ignored, especially in conditional clauses. In fact, many Medieval Latin writers are careless about tenses in general; not only is the historical present often used side by side with the ordinary past tense, but aspect is often ignored, so that perfect, pluperfect, and imperfect tenses are often used together to refer to the same event. Negative commands are often formed by ne (or non) + subjunctive, a usage given great currency because of its frequency in Cato's Distichs.

Indirect discourse (accusative + infinitive construction in CL) is often introduced by quod, followed by a finite verb (usually indicative, occasionally subjunctive). This is parallel to English and

French *(he said that . . . , il a dit que . . .),* but also may have been reinforced by the Greek *hoti* + finite verb, a usage that came into Latin through the Vulgate Bible. As *quod* also meant "because," *quia* and *quoniam* (both originally meaning "since" or "because") were also commonly used to introduce indirect speech. Rules for indirect speech are carelessly observed. Sometimes *quod* appears to introduce direct speech: *dixit quod ibi fuissem* (he said "I was there," meaning "he said that he was there"); in this example the verb could equally well be in the indicative (*dixit quod ibi fui* or *fueram*). Indirect questions are often introduced by *si, utrum,* or *numquid;* in direct questions the Classical Latin distinctions between *-ne, nonne,* and *num* are not always observed.

Classical Latin does not use a definite or indefinite article: *vir ivit* can mean "a man came" or "the man came." Greek expressed the definite article by *ho, he,* or *to,* and occasionally used *tis* (a certain) for the indefinite article. In Medieval Latin the definite article is usually expressed by *ille, illa, illud* (the ancestor of the French *le, la*), *iste,* or, for greater emphasis, *idem* (in CL meaning "the same"), *prefatus, memoratus,* or *predictus,* all literally meaning "the aforementioned." The indefinite article is usually *quidam* (in CL meaning "a certain") or forms of *unus* (one). Pronouns are used less precisely than in Classical Latin: *se* and *sibi* are not always used reflexively, and often *eum* is used to refer back to the subject of the sentence (CL: *dixit se adesse,* ML: *dixit eum adesse,* he said he was there). The pronouns *quisquam* and *aliquis* are used almost interchangeably.

The instrumental case is often expressed by means of a preposition such as *cum, ab, de, per* (French: *par;* compare English "through"), or *ex*—for instance, *eum cum gladio interfecit* (he killed him with a sword). Prepositions are used in several nonclassical ways: *ad* often has the meanings of the French *à* or the English "at" (and is sometimes used where CL would use a dative, or before place-names—for instance, *ad Romam ire;* CL: *Romam ire,* to go to Rome). Perhaps as a result of this weakening of *ad,* the sense "up to" is often expressed by *usque ad* or simply *usque; apud* (CL: *cum* + ablative) often means no more than "with" (compare French *avec,* which is derived from *apud*), but sometimes means "in the writings of" (for instance, *apud Abelardum,* in Abelard's writings). *Pro* and *pre* (CL: *prae*) both came to mean "on account of" and are often confused; *iuxta* can mean "according to" (as in *iuxta Augustinum,* according to Augustine; CL: *se-*

cundum): *de* can have all the senses of the French *de,* or the English "of" (Matthew Paris writes *abbatia de Oseneie,* the abbey of Osney; *de clero pars magna,* a great part of the clergy).

Many of the departures from Classical Latin syntax occur at points that give the most difficulty to modern students—ablative absolute; sequence of tenses; rules for use of the subjunctive, accusative and infinitive, reflexive pronouns—but should not be regarded on that account as failures in latinity. They simply reflect the extent to which Classical Latin was an alien language even to educated medieval scholars. Many of the developments (such as the use of *ille* as a definite article, or the use of the ablative of the gerund) were inherent possibilities even in Classical Latin; others were reinforced by tendencies in the vernacular languages or by usages inherited, via the Latin Vulgate Bible, from Greek or Hebrew. Modern scholars should be very cautious before labeling a medievalism "ungrammatical" and before emending a text to conform to classical practice.

A few sentences from the thirteenth-century chronicle of Matthew Paris will give an idea of some of the usages found in ordinary Medieval Latin prose: (1) *credebant enim confidenter ut essent honorem pro honore recepturi* (for they confidently believed that they would receive respect in return for respect): *credo . . . ut* + subjunctive, for CL *credo* + accusative + infinitive; (2) *cuius querulis sermonibus cum rex attonitus nimis compateretur, misit properanter comitem Waranniae cum armata manu Oxoniam, eos qui latuerant Romanos eripere et scholares arripere* (since the king was astonished and very sympathetic to his words of complaint, he quickly sent the Earl of Warenne to Oxford with an armed band, to rescue the Romans who had gone into hiding and to arrest the scholars): *misit* + infinitive of purpose, for CL *ut* or *qui* + subjunctive; (3) *quo cum die praefixo pervenissent, tractatum est diligenter per episcopos ut salvaretur status clericalis universitatis* (when they arrived there on the assigned day, it was carefully arranged by the bishops that the position of the whole student body should be preserved): impersonal construction *tractatum est . . . per* for CL *episcopi egerunt, operam dederunt,* and *per* (by) for CL *ab* + ablative; (4) *tandem suggestum legato ab episcopis et universitate cleri quae ibidem in praesenti fuit, quod certaminis discrimen a familia sua sumpsit exordium* (finally, it was suggested to the legate by the bishops and the whole university body which was there that the crisis of the dispute had its origin in the legate's own household):

impersonal construction *suggestum (fuit)*, as in example (3), *in praesenti fuit* for CL *aderat, quod* + indicative for CL accusative and infinitive, the phrase *universitas cleri* (as *universitas clericalis* in example [3]) means "the whole of the clergy"—"the entire student [and faculty] body"—"the university").

Pronunciation and spelling. In the sixteenth century Erasmus complained that there was such diversity in the pronunciation of Latin throughout Europe that speakers from different countries could not understand each other, even though they were speaking the same language. Until the late nineteenth or early twentieth century (that is, until it had been reformed according to Classical Latin), Latin pronunciation in schools derived directly from medieval pronunciation. The old pronunciation can still be heard in legal phrases such as sine die (pronounced in English [sai-ni dai-i], to rhyme with *tiny* and *die* + *-ee*) or ultra vires (vai'rees). Evidence for medieval pronunciation consists in the testimony of Erasmus and seventeenth-century writers on pronunciation (which must be used cautiously), rhymes, and spellings. The following account applies principally to England and France in the later Middle Ages.

The Classical Latin diphthongs *ae* and *oe* fell together with *ē* at an early date; all three should be pronounced as long close *ē* (French *été*, English "take"), so that *cēdo* and *caedo* (and also *sēdo*) were homophones. Spellings and rhymes suggest that *au* was close to long close *ō* (English *hope*). Although Serlo de Wilton's *De differentiis* (twelfth century) shows a clear knowledge of the distinction between vowels that were naturally short or long (*Scorto nemo placet nisi dextram munere placet*, distinguishing *plăcēre* [please] from *plācāre* [soothe]), some writers of quantitative verse take great liberties with vowel length, perhaps indicating that there was some uncertainty in ordinary spoken Latin. The seventeenth-century English scholar Robert Robinson, an expert on pronunciation, shows that short vowels in open syllables were, for him, long (CL: *păter, lĕvis, mŏra*), and this is confirmed by loanwords such as *labor,* which must have been taken into English with a long *ā* (CL: *lăbor*). Compare also the legal Latin *nisi* (nai-sai).

Consonantal *u* was unquestionably pronounced [v] (not [w]), as is shown by borrowings (*verbal, derive*) and by occasional spelling confusion between *u/v* and *b* (which sometimes caused confusion between future and perfect in *-abit/-avit*). After *q,* however, *u* appears not to have been pronounced (it

was probably not pronounced fully even in Classical Latin), and rhymes between *decor* and *aequor* are common. Initial *i/j* before a vowel, and intervocalic *i,* may have had the English *j* sound (as in "edge"), as is shown by borrowings such as "justice" and "trajectory," and by the spelling *magestas* (majesty, also influenced by *magis,* more). Initial and medial aspirate *h* (*honor, traho*) seems to have been reduced to a rough breathing or lost altogether, as is shown by many spellings (*abet* = *habet, ac* = *hac,* and conversely *honus* = *onus, trahicio* = *traicio*). Serlo distinguishes *amo* (I love) from *hāmo* (hook) as though only the length of the vowel would indicate the distinction. Loss of *h* is seen in many vernacular languages at the same time.

Before a front vowel *c* was pronounced *s,* and *sc* was pronounced *ss;* this is indicated frequently by spellings and backspellings, and by words adopted into the vernacular (compare English *cede*). There is no evidence in England or France for the Italian *tch* pronunciation. As there appears to have been only a marginal distinction between double and single consonants, it seems likely that *c, s, sc,* and *ss* were pronounced identically before front vowels; thus, the following sets are homophones: *caedo/sedo/cedo; ecce/esse; dicit/discit.* Before a back vowel *c* remained hard, as is shown by occasional spellings with *ch* and *k* (*charus* [dear], *karissimus* [dearest]). Before a front vowel *g* was probably a fricative (as in the English "edge"), but the evidence is slight; compare such borrowings as "germane." Posttonic prevocalic *-ti-* is usually to be pronounced *-ci-* (*-si-*), with semivocalic *-i-,* as in *ratio, nuptiae* (ML: *racio, nupcie*), except after certain consonants, such as *c* and *x: mixtio, fictio.* From verse it is clear that words such as *racio* are often disyllabic.

Final *-d* seems to have been unvoiced to *t* (*haut* = *haud*); *ph* was identical with *f,* as in modern pronunciation (*spera* = CL: *sphaera,* sphere, is a special case). As in Classical Latin, *th* was pronounced *t*: the Modern English *th* in "theater" is the result of "learned" interpretation. Intervocalic *-gn-* in words such as *dignus* was, as in Classical Latin, a palatal, not a velar, sound; it should be pronounced *-nny-,* as in British "innumerable"; spellings using *ngn* are an attempt to represent the sound. Post vocalic *m* was a plosive, as is shown by intrusive *p* in words such as *dompnus* (= *domnus* < CL *dominus,* master), *dampnum* (= *damnum,* loss); compare the English "empty," from Old English *æmtig.*

Until recently editors of Medieval Latin texts frequently "classicized" the spellings (for instance, by substituting *ae* for *e*); this practice has obscured much of the evidence for Medieval Latin pronunciation, and has given the illusory appearance of a standard orthography. Consequently, subsequent editors have often been unable to recognize genuine Medieval Latin forms. Although Medieval Latin spelling is more regular than that of the vernacular languages (simply because it had a long-established traditional literature on which to base its spellings), there was still considerable fluidity and flexibility. After about 1000 *e* was almost invariable for the Classical Latin *oe* (*celum* = *coelum*, *obedire* = *oboedire*) and for the Classical Latin *ae* (*puelle* = *puellae*, *seuus* = *saeuus*). The distinction between *u* and *v* is purely orthographic: in early Medieval Latin *u* is found in all positions; later texts sometimes use *v* initially (*vnde* for *unde*). Similarly, *j* is simply an orthographic variant of *i* and appears both initially (*justicia*) and after *i* (*hijs* = *hiis* = CL: *his*, ablative plural of *hic*).

The following spellings, though not invariable, are very common:

CL *-ti-* > ML *-ci-* (*concepcio*; conversely, ML *conditio* for CL *condicio*)
CL *-gn-* > ML *ngn* (*dingnus*)
CL *c* > ML *s* before *e, i* (*seu* = CL *ceu*)
CL *s* > ML *c* before *e, i* (*cetus* = CL *saetus*)
CL *sc* > ML *ss* before *e, i* (*nessit* = CL *nescit*)
CL *sc* > ML *s* before *e, i* (*silicet, septrum*)
CL *c* > ML *sc* before *e, i* (*conscitus* = CL *concitus*)
CL *h* sometimes lost (*abere, trait* = *habere, trahit*); conversely, *h* is sometimes intrusive (*habundare, trahicio* = CL *abundare, traicio*)
CL *ph* > ML *f* (*filosofus*)
CL *f* > ML *ph* (*nephas, prophari* = CL *nefas, profari*, influenced by *propheta*)
CL *th* > ML *t* (*tronus*)
CL *ch* > ML *c* (*corda* = CL *chorda*)
CL *c* > ML *ch* (*charus*)
CL *i* > ML *y* (*yemps* = CL *hiems*)
CL *y* > ML *i* (*misterium*)
CL *quu* > ML *qu* (*equs*)
CL *qu* > ML *c* (*secor* = CL *sequor-secutus*)
CL *c* > ML *qu* (*loquutus* = CL *locutus-loquor*)
CL *mn* > ML *mpn* (*ympnus* = CL *hymnus*)
CL *x* > ML *xc* (*excerceo, excitium* = CL *exerceo, exitium*)
CL *x* > ML *xs* (*exsitium* = CL *exitium*)
CL *xs* > ML *x* (*extare* = CL *exstare*)
CL single consonant often doubled (*altissonus*)
CL double consonant often single (*opidum*)
CL *-d* > ML *-t* (*nequit* = CL *ne quid*; conversely, *nequid*, he cannot = CL *nequit*

Unstressed vowels are often confused (ML *discendo* = CL: *descendo*).

Some common Medieval Latin spellings include: *autor* (CL: *auctor*), *sepero* (CL: *separo*), *puplicus* (CL: *publicus*), *occianus* (CL: *oceanus*), *Jubiter* (CL: *Juppiter*), *Adriane* (CL: *Ariadne*), *albestus* (CL: *asbestus*), *optuli* (CL: *obtuli*). Medieval Latin, of course, spells biblical names according to their Vulgate form: Dalida (Delilah), Salamon (Solomon), Esdra (Ezra), Esaias or Ysaias (Isaiah); many biblical names are indeclinable (Ysaac/Isaac), but Adam often has the genitive Ade.

CONCLUSIONS

The humanists of the Renaissance finally succeeded in elevating Classical Latin as the norm of Latinity; they reformed the spelling of Latin to that of antiquity (taking editors wtih them into the classicization of texts that were in fact medieval and introducing spellings that the authors themselves would not have recognized). They established as norms the syntax, style, and vocabulary of Classical Latin, removing the vast number of intrusions that had entered the vocabulary since the fourth century. Pronunciation, however, was not reformed until relatively recent times. Only very recently have scholars come to see that Medieval Latin, although it never had a standard lexicon, grammar, or orthography, nevertheless had customary usages that should not be removed by ill-directed classicizing.

BIBLIOGRAPHY

Ancient grammatical works are in Heinrich Keil, ed., *Grammatici latini*, 7 vols. (1857–1880). For grammars written in the Middle Ages, see James J. Murphy, *Medieval Rhetoric: A Select Bibliography* (1971), 42–54. On Vulgar Latin, see Veikko Väänänen, *Introduction au latin vulgaire* (1963). There is no comprehensive modern grammar of Medieval Latin. For a bibliography on specific points, see Martin R. P. McGuire and Hermigild Dressler, *Introduction to Mediaeval Latin Studies*, 2nd ed. (1977), 277–284.

Useful general works include Karl Langosch, *Lateinisches Mittelalter* (1963); Dag L. Norberg, *Manuel pratique de latin médiéval* (1968); Karl Strecker, *Introduction to Medieval Latin*, Robert B. Palmer, trans. (1957). There are summaries in many modern anthologies: Charles H. Beeson, ed., *A Primer of Medieval Latin* (1925, repr. 1953); Richard A. Browne, *British Latin Selections A.D. 500–1400* (1954); Karl P. Harrington, ed., *Mediaeval Latin* (1925). Ancient (and some medieval) glossaries are in Georg Goetz, *Corpus glossariorum latinorum*, 7 vols. (1888–1923). Dictionaries of Medieval Latin are Charles du

Fresne du Cange, *Glossarium ad scriptores mediae et infimae latinitatis* [begun in 1687], Léopold Favre, ed., 10 vols. (1883–1887, repr. 1937–1938); Ronald E. Latham, *Revised Medieval Latin Word-List from British and Irish Sources* (1965), and *Dictionary of Medieval Latin from British Sources* (1975); Jan F. Niermeyer, *Mediae latinitatis lexicon minus*, 2 vols. (1976); Alexander Souter, *Glossary of Later Latin to 600 A.D.* (1949).

A. G. RIGG

[See also **Anthologies; Catalan Language; Cato's Distichs; Encyclopedias and Dictionaries, European; French Language; Grammar; Hiberno-Latin; Hisperic Latin; Huguccio; Indo-European Languages, Development of; Isidore of Seville, St.; Italian Language; Papias; Portuguese Language; Priscian; Provençal Language; Prudentius; Romanian Language and Literature; Spanish Language.**]

LATIN LITERATURE. In all countries of western and central Europe (except Iceland), from the time of the conversion to Christianity to the end of the Middle Ages, the language of education—and thus of "literature"—was Latin. As late as 1350 no one could have foreseen that Latin would ever cease to be the language of knowledge and culture. For roughly a thousand years, from 400 to 1400, Western literature means Latin literature. Literature in the vernacular languages may now be regarded as more significant (as the forerunner of future developments) and therefore more appropriate for modern students to learn. Medieval scholars, however, may well have regarded literature in the vernaculars as a sign of cultural backwardness and of a failure in education.

For convenience, the subject is here divided into the following periods: (1) beginnings until the early seventh century; (2) seventh to ninth centuries; (3) tenth and eleventh centuries; (4) twelfth century; (5) thirteenth century; (6) fourteenth and fifteenth centuries. Latin literacy grew more or less steadily (with some interruptions) throughout the Middle Ages until its greatest flowering in the twelfth and thirteenth centuries. After that time it was overtaken by its own success: the spread of general literacy among the laity produced a new reading public, which, however, was literate not in Latin but in the vernacular languages.

This article deals only with works that are considered literary in modern terms. Chronicles, natural science, theology, philosophy, laws, letters, sermons, and similar works are excluded unless they are (*a*)

incidentally literary (such as twelfth-century cosmological poetry), (*b*) indicative of literary accomplishments (for instance stylistically), (*c*) influential on later literature (Boethius), or (*d*) in a genre that corresponds to one now regarded as literary ("fictional" sermon exempla). Even with these limitations, the coverage, particularly in the later periods, is necessarily cursory and selective.

There are two opposed but complementary ways of looking at Medieval Latin literature. The first, characterized by the work of Ernst Curtius, sees Latin literature as part of a continuum from Roman rhetorical education; literature is simply the outgrowth of the educational curriculum, particularly of the second part of the trivium, rhetoric. All literary expression can be analyzed in terms of the teaching and exemplary texts that lie behind it; the writer learned his craft through grammars and handbooks of rhetoric, and so his writing can be viewed as a series of figures and tropes.

An epic, for example, can be analyzed in terms of its exordium (invocation to the muses and/or patron, modesty prologue, statement of subject matter) and its set pieces (such as descriptions of people, places, or battle scenes according to rhetorical precepts). Many short poems can be interpreted simply as rhetorical imitations within a genre, even as school exercises. Certain set themes—"Wealth does not bring happiness," "The inevitability of death," "The transitoriness of fame"—are regarded not so much as statements of universal truth but rather as rhetorical *topoi*. This approach tends to be skeptical about personal poetry—love poems, praise of great men, requests for money—where a literary analogue is available.

The opposed approach looks for originality in sentiment and expression. It stresses the emergence of new forms (such as rhyme and rhythm), new themes (often shared with vernacular literatures), and new sentiments (attitudes to love, Christian pathos, penitential humility). Both approaches are necessary, and the two must be applied simultaneously. Each work must be regarded as a product of its literary environment (whether ancient or contemporary) and as, possibly at least, an individual and unique statement. Recent approaches, however, have sought a more fundamental understanding of medieval attitudes to literature—first, by investigating medieval discussions of myth and fabulous narrative (and thus, ultimately, of fiction) and, second, by analyzing the terms of criticism and literary analysis in the medieval accounts (*accessus*) of earlier authors.

BEGINNINGS TO EARLY SEVENTH CENTURY

With the conversion of Rome to Christianity the church inherited not only a language that was the common tongue of the Roman Empire but also an ancient and pagan tradition. Many Christian thinkers, such as Tertullian, Jerome, and Augustine, were apprehensive about the effects of an educational system that was at best secular and often explicitly pagan. In theory Roman Stoicism had much to offer Christianity: the fictitious correspondence between St. Paul and Seneca testifies to the debt acknowledged by Christians to Roman philosophy. Both Christians and Stoics, for example, shared (at least in theory) the ideal of poverty. Roman education, however, was elitist and aristocratic, whereas the church professed humility and egalitarianism. Even training in Latin itself involved a separation from the ordinary spoken language of the people, the demotic language, and a concentration on style (such as Ciceronian prose) that was in contrast with the *sermo humilis* of the Gospels. As usual in such circumstances, the church adopted and adapted the devil's weapons and gradually developed a Christian Latin literature to stand beside, if not to replace, the ancient pagan authors—but in twelve hundred years Medieval Christian Latin never totally lost its classical pagan strains.

Although Medieval Latin literature might be said to begin with the first Christian poet—perhaps Commodian, though his dates (third, fourth, or fifth century) are disputed—several pagan authors and texts of the third and fourth centuries must be included in an account of Medieval Latin, partly because they seem generally to have been accepted into the Christian tradition and partly because they became important in Christian Latin education. The proverb collection known as the *Disticha Catonis* (late second century or third century) became part of the educational curriculum and was often quoted in the Middle Ages (for instance, by both Chaucer and William Langland). Servius' commentary on the *Aeneid* (late fourth century) was a basic handbook for the elucidation of classical poetry—mythology, meter, language, and ancient history; the commentaries of Donatus on the comedies of Terence (mid-fourth century) were also well known.

The educational system itself—the trivium and quadrivium—was celebrated in Martianus Capella's (*fl.* 410–429) *De nuptiis Mercurii et Philologiae,* which itself became an educational classic. Macrobius' commentary (fourth century) on Cicero's *Somnium Scipionis* provided a popular but detailed account of ancient physics and cosmology. The Latin versions of Dictys Cretensis and Dares Phrygius (who had both supposedly written eyewitness accounts of the Trojan War) provided the Middle Ages with their principal sources for the Trojan War; less well known was the epitomized *Ilias latina,* 1,000 lines long, attributed to a Pindarus (perhaps Baebius Italicus). The *Fables* of Avianus (*ca.* 400) brought the Aesopian tradition of beast fable into the Latin literary tradition and became a popular school text. Many of the texts now included in the *Appendix Vergiliana* may have been composed in this period, but others (such as the *Moretum*) may be as late as Carolingian. The North African *Anthologia latina* (sixth century), preserved in the Codex Salmasianus, formed the nucleus of (or model for) later poetic anthologies. Lactantius (*ca.* 300) was converted by Christianity, but his poem on the *Phoenix* was probably written early in his life, as it shows no sign of Christian allegory. Claudian (*ca.* 400) also wrote a poem on the *Phoenix;* he was not a Christian, but his poems, especially *De raptu Proserpinae,* were very popular in the Middle Ages.

We may now turn to Christian literature. The Latin Bible (not only Jerome's authoritative Vulgate [fourth century] but also earlier translations such as the *Vetus latina*) provided, together with the liturgy, the fundamental starting point for all Christian Latin poetry. Perhaps the first, and most obviously new, contribution of Christianity to Latin literature is seen in the hymns composed for the daily Office and for specific religious feast days, for both monastic and congregational use.

Although Augustine's *Psalm Against the Donatists* is effectively rhythmical, and although the hymns of Ambrose and later poets are often analyzed in search of rhyme and rhythm (in order to discover the origins of later rhythmical verse), we should first emphasize the classical nature of the hymns. Hymns could have been produced in popular rhythms (perhaps based on the Psalms), but the early hymnists chose to put classical quantitative verse to the service of religion. Some freedoms in meter, no doubt demanded or encouraged by the fact that the hymns were sung, do not alter the fact that the basic meters are the classical iambic dimeter, iambic dimeter catalectic, and trochaic septenarius.

Few of the hymns of Hilary of Poitiers (fourth century) survive. The first great name in hymn writing is Ambrose of Milan (*ca.* 350–397), and after him comes the Spanish poet Prudentius (348–405), whose *Cathemerinon* and *Peristephanon* provided hymns respectively "for the daily round" and on the early Christian martyrs. In the sixth century the basic hymnal was amplified by the great poet Venantius Fortunatus, whose *Pange lingua* and *Vexilla regis prodeunt* have retained their popularity into modern times. After this time we find specifically organized hymnals, such as the Spanish *Mozarabic Hymnary* (of uncertain date; MSS of the collection date from the end of the ninth century, but many of the hymns are much older) and the Irish *Antiphonary of Bangor* (end of the seventh century); national hymnals often celebrate locally popular saints and martyrs.

The greatest challenge to Christian poets was the Latin epic. Although no one ever succeeded in rivaling Vergil, biblical history provided plenty of worthy themes. Some attempts were made to christianize Vergil, partly through interpretations of the Fourth Eclogue and its apparent prophecy of the birth of Christ. One curious attempt was made by Proba, wife of a proconsul, whose "Cento" used lines and half-lines from Vergil's works in praise of Christ. The Spanish poet Juvencus (fourth century) wrote a very Vergilian epic in about 3,000 lines, narrating the story of the Gospel.

Prudentius' *Psychomachia* is also in epic style and was one of the most influential poems of the age. It describes, battle by battle, the victory of the Virtues over the Vices in the struggle for possession of the human soul. It influenced personification allegory and the description of the Sins throughout medieval literature. The *Heptateuchos* by the Gallic poet Cyprian (*ca.* 400) tells the story of the Old Testament up to the Book of Judges. Claudius Marius Victor (fifth century) took the first few chapters of Genesis as the theme of his *Alethia*. The most sensitive treatment of the fall of man, almost Miltonic in its subtlety, is by Avitus (*d. ca.* 519), bishop of Vienne. The African poet Dracontius (end of the fifth century) treated the fall of man in his epic *De laudibus Dei*. The Roman poet Caelius Sedulius (fifth century) wrote a more comprehensive two-book epic; his *Carmen Paschale* narrates the Gospel story of the Passion together with all the Old Testament material that foretells it. Arator (sixth century) followed the biblical narrative fairly closely in his *Acts of the Apostles*.

Not all poetry by Christians was epic, or even religious. One of the most interesting poems, by Ausonius (*ca.* 310–*ca.* 395), is a description of the river Moselle and its scenery. His younger contemporary Paulinus of Nola (*ca.* 353–431) wrote mainly religious verse. Other Gallic poets of the age include Sidonius Apollinaris, Auspicius of Toul, Paulinus of Perigueux (who wrote a life of St. Martin based on that by Sulpicius Severus), Paulinus of Pella, (Tiro) Prosper of Aquitaine, and the prolific Magnus Felix Ennodius (*ca.* 473–521).

In addition to Venantius Fortunatus, the sixth century produced several authors of great literary significance. Boethius (*ca.* 480–524/526) is mainly known for his translations of Greek philosophy into Latin, but his *Consolatio Philosophiae*, written while he was awaiting execution, had immense literary influence through both its *prosimetrum* form (combination of prose and verse, perhaps written in imitation of Martianus Capella's *De nuptiis*) and its descriptions of Fortune and her wheel and the vanity of human fame. Boethius' solution of the problem of free will and divine providence continued to influence writers up to Chaucer. The *Elegies* of Maximian (sixth century) contributed greatly to medieval portrayals of old age and the *senex amans*.

Isidore of Seville (*ca.* 570–636) is famous mainly for his *Etymologiae* (or *Origines*), a comprehensive encyclopedia of human knowledge. He begins with the Seven Liberal Arts and proceeds to medicine, agriculture, warfare, and other fields, illustrating each article with quotations from both biblical and pagan sources. The *Etymologiae* (used extensively by Hrabanus Maurus in his *De universo,* also known as *De rerum naturis*) was one of the most important compendia of general knowledge in the Middle Ages. Isidore's *Synonyma*, the consolation by Reason of a despairing man, had considerable influence on medieval consolation literature as late as Hoccleve's *Dialogue*.

SEVENTH TO NINTH CENTURIES

Spain continued to produce poets, such as Eugenius II of Toledo, King Sisebut, and Ildefonsus, but the centers of Latin culture now moved to the north. Rome had never conquered Ireland, but it was to Ireland that Latin culture passed in the sixth century, and Irish scholarship continued to be important into the ninth century. Solitude-seeking monks took to Ireland a script based on Common Roman and developed there a distinctive Insular script, which eventually spread to Britain. The exotic poetic style known as Hisperic (or "hermeneutic"), a strange mixture of Latin, Greek, and Hebrew, developed in Ireland; one of its early exponents was the grammarian Virgilius Maro of Toulouse, but it is seen most strikingly in the school texts known as *Hispe-*

rica famina. It is also seen in the *Altus prosator* of Columba (*ca.* 521–*ca.* 597), whose life was written by Adamnan. Ireland is especially noted for hymn writing—the *Liber hymnorum,* the *Bangor Antiphonary,* and the hymns by Sechnall (Secundinus) and Columbanus (*d.* 615).

Celtic mainland Britain produced little literature until (ironically) Gildas' (*ca.* 500–570) *De excidio,* a lament on the final conquest of Britain by the Saxons. In fact, it was only after the Anglo-Saxon conquest and the Christian missions of St. Augustine of Canterbury, Hadrian, and Theodore of Canterbury that the island produced any literature of note. The first major Anglo-Latin poet was Aldhelm (*ca.* 640–709), whose *De virginitate* was very popular; his prose and poems show Hisperic influence. Northumbria produced the most important literary figure of the age, Bede (672/673–735), who is famous not only for his *Historia ecclesiastica* but also for his works on meter and computus.

In the eighth century, the consolidation by Charles Martel of the Frankish kingdom in Gaul and Germany (where the Englishman Boniface, another poet, had been the leading missionary) made possible the flourishing of literature at the court of Charles Martel's grandson, Charles the Great—what is known as the Carolingian Renaissance. The leading figure in the Carolingian literary circle was another Englishman, Alcuin of York (*ca.* 730–804), himself a poet; his high regard for literature is seen in his description of the library at York. The court circle at Aachen was very cosmopolitan, including not only Gallic and German poets but also scholars from Ireland and Italy. The most outstanding poets of the court were Alcuin himself, Theodulf of Orléans (the best), Angilbert, and Modoin. Their affection for the classics is seen in the nicknames they used: Alcuin was Flaccus (Horace), Angilbert Homer, Theodulf Pindar, and Modoin Naso (Ovid). Other leading literary figures at the court included Einhard (the biographer of Charlemagne), the Italian Paul the Deacon, Peter of Pisa the grammarian, Paulinus of Aquileia, the Irishman Dungal, and the Irish grammarian and geographer Dicuil.

The historical importance of the Carolingian Renaissance, however, consisted not so much in the writing of poetry as in the copying of texts—many classical texts are preserved solely, or primarily, in copies made in this period—and the development of a script in which to do so. The Carolingian minuscule became almost a universal script for the next three centuries; it was the basis for the reform of handwriting in the fifteenth century and is thus the origin of the modern printed alphabet. The impetus of the Carolingian revival continued through the ninth century and ensured that, despite the ravages of the Vikings, Latin culture survived.

One great scholar was Hrabanus Maurus (*ca.* 780–856), a pupil of Alcuin, whose encyclopedic *De universo* was based on Isidore's *Etymologiae.* Hrabanus' pupil Walafrid Strabo (808–849) was once credited with the *Glossa ordinaria,* but is now known mainly for his poems. The age continued to produce poets: Ermoldus Nigellus, Gottschalk of Orbais (who was condemned for heresy), and Florus of Lyons. Irish scholars, such as St. Donatus of Fiesole, Colman, the philosopher John Scottus Eriugena, and the poet Sedulius Scottus, continued to be influential in continental monasteries. Poets of the second half of the ninth century include Hincmar of Reims, Heiric of Auxerre, Ermenrich of Ellwangen, Micon of St. Riquier, Agius of Corvey, Hucbald of St. Amand (who wrote an amusing poem on baldness), and Radbod of Utrecht. Probably from this century is the *Ecloga Theoduli* (the identity of Theodulus is unknown), a debate in a classical setting between Truth and Falsehood; its epitomes of biblical stories and pagan mythology made it an important school text throughout the Middle Ages, and many commentaries were written on it.

One fashion of the age was a fondness for elaborate "picture poems," which used acrostics (of initial letters) but also telestichs (of final letters)—and even diagonal arrangements—to spell out words; some poems even made pictures out of letters in the middle of the poem. Akin to this verbal craftsmanship, perhaps, is the riddle; the early collection by Symphosius (fourth/fifth century) was imitated by the Anglo-Saxon Tatwine and by Eusebius. In addition, the Hisperic style of difficult Latin had not entirely died out: in 896 Abbo of St. Germain wrote a three-book epic on the Viking siege of Paris, the *Bella Parisiacae urbis,* of which the third book contains deliberately arcane vocabulary, which is then explained by glosses.

TENTH AND ELEVENTH CENTURIES

From the tenth century onward, Latin literature thrived throughout the whole of western Europe. Only a few authors and works can be mentioned individually from this point on. Monasteries continued to be the main centers of literature and scholarship during this period. Irish influence declined; Germany under the three Ottos became more prominent and more distinct from French literary circles than in the Carolingian era; Italian authors continued to be influential in imperial circles; Anglo-Latin stayed relatively isolated, but even before the Norman Conquest there were many contacts between England and northern France.

During the tenth century the rhythmical sequence became an established literary form. It was particularly developed by Notker Balbulus and was soon used for secular as well as religious purposes. By the end of the eleventh century disyllabic rhyme was normal in rhyming verse, particularly in the leonine hexameter; monosyllabic rhymes, in hexameters and other kinds of verse, are found even earlier. Rhythmical verse became common but remained secondary to the quantitative hexameter and elegiac couplet.

In England the decline in learning that had been deplored by King Alfred (r. 871–899) was arrested by the monastic reforms (the Benedictine Reform) made by Dunstan and Ethelwold. Abbo of Fleury visited England in the late 980's as a teacher, and his *Life of St. Edmund* was translated into the vernacular by Aelfric. Prose literature, especially hagiography, thrived; Asser's biography of Alfred parallels the tributes made to Charlemagne by Einhard. Prose and poetry continued to be written in the Hisperic style. In the ninth century Aethelwulf celebrated the *Lives of the Abbots,* and in the tenth we have Frithegod's poem on St. Wilfrid and several poems by Wulfstan of Winchester, including a metrical version of Lantfred's *Life of St. Swithin.* Perhaps of English origin is the Pseudo-Ovidian *De mirabilibus mundi* (eleventh century?). Otherwise, Anglo-Latin poetry reemerges only after the Norman Conquest, with the epigrams of Godfrey of Winchester (formerly of Cambrai) and the poems (including the *Vita S. Malchi*) of Reginald of Canterbury, both born in France, and with the work of Lawrence of Durham, the first post-Conquest native poet.

In this period Germany produced many Latin poets, such as Fromund of Tegernsee (*ca.* 960–1008). From the monastery of St. Gall came Ratpert, Waldrammus, and perhaps Gerald, author of the epic *Waltharius.* The *Waltharius* is one of the few Latin epics that draw on Germanic legend; in Vergilian style it recounts the love of Walter and Hildegund, the treachery of Gunther, and the conflicting loyalties of Hagen. Hrotswitha, abbess of Gandersheim (*ca.* 935–1000), wrote many poems but is mainly famous for her "Terentian" comedies on religious themes, such as the farcical *Dulcitius* (which man-

ages to extract burlesque from martyrdom) and the *Abraham,* notable for its brothel scene. From the tenth century we also have the first example of liturgical drama, the *Quem quaeritis* trope. The anonymous *Ruodlieb* (*ca.* 1050) is unfortunately only fragmentary; it is full of lively scenes but seems very episodic. From the Rhine Valley came a verse anthology that must lie behind the extant *Cambridge Songs;* this collection contains both rhythmical verse and sequences, as well as classical extracts set to music, on all manner of topics—erotic, humorous, political, philosophical, and religious—and must have been compiled no earlier than 1039. One major poet of the eleventh century was Wipo, chaplain at the royal court of Conrad II. The satires of Sextus Amarcius attack sins in an uninspired way. More interesting is Embricho of Mainz's long epic on the life of the prophet Muḥammad, which was still being read three centuries later.

Tenth-century Italy produced the anonymous epic *Berengarii imperatoris gesta* and the accomplished poetry of Liutprand, bishop of Cremona, as well as many famous anonymous short poems such as the *O Roma nobilis.* The most famous Italian man of letters of the eleventh century was Peter Damian. Under Desiderius (later Pope Victor III) the abbey of Monte Cassino produced many scholars and poets, including Guaiferius (Waifarius) and Alphanus of Salerno; the latter wrote not only medical treatises and translations (in the already established medical tradition of Salerno) but also personal poetry. Theobald of Monte Cassino wrote a versification of the prose *Physiologus,* a popular bestiary. Alphanus' contemporary, Amatus, wrote a verse history of the Norman dynasty in Sicily. Most importantly, an otherwise unknown Italian scholar named Papias wrote an alphabetically organized dictionary, the *Elementarium doctrinae rudimentum,* the basis for many future dictionaries.

From tenth-century France came the anonymous beast epic *Ecbasis captivi* (with monosyllabic leonine rhyme), which tells the story of a lost calf that is caught by a wolf. In France we begin to see the rise of the cathedral schools that were to dominate the twelfth century and that became the nuclei of universities. One of the leading scholars at Rheims was Gerbert of Aurillac, later Pope Sylvester II, and one of its principal poets was Godfrey of Rheims. At the great abbey of Cluny the abbot Odo wrote religious poems, and at Chartres the poet Fulbert was outstanding.

In the second half of the eleventh century we

begin to see the emergence of major poets, anticipating the literary splendors of the next century. The three most important French Latin poets of the period are Baudri, Hildebert, and Marbod. Baudri (Balderich) of Bourgueil (1046–1130) wrote verse epistles (some in imitation of Ovid's *Heroides*), saints' lives, a versification of Fulgentius, a history of the crusades, and a long poem, in vision form, to Adela, countess of Blois. His contemporary, Hildebert of Lavardin (1056–1133), archdeacon of Le Mans and archbishop of Tours, was one of the most important Latin poets of the Middle Ages, and his works remained popular for centuries. His life of St. Mary of Egypt and his poem on the Mass, *De mysterio missae* (often found in combination with a similar one by Petrus Pictor), were especially popular; his short poems and epigrams occur frequently in the anthologies. Symptomatic of Hildebert's stature is the number of poems erroneously attributed to him in medieval manuscripts, such as Peter Riga's *Susanna* and *Agnes* and Bernard Silvester's *Mathematicus*. Often associated with Hildebert in manuscripts is Marbod (*ca.* 1035–1123), bishop of Rennes, famous for his *Liber lapidum* and *Liber decem capitulorum* and his life of St. Lawrence. Marbod's works also were absorbed into the anthologies; his pupil Geoffrey of Vendôme (*ca.* 1070–1132) was also a poet.

TWELFTH CENTURY

The term "twelfth-century renaissance" can be applied not only to the flourishing of philosophy and natural science but also to literature. The older verse forms, hexameters and elegiac couplets (now often rhymed), remained the most common meters, but rhythmical poetry gained considerably in popularity. In addition to the rhythmical sequence, new fixed rhythmical stanzas became very popular for all kinds of poetry, especially for satire—the "regular Victorine sequence" (the *Stabat mater* stanza) and the asclepiadic and goliardic quatrains. The verse *comoedia* was developed. Rhetorical theory made new advances both in letter writing and in poetic composition. Science and literature came together in cosmographic poetry. Prose became a common vehicle for the literature of entertainment.

There was no single cause for all this activity. Among the contributing factors were the greater stability of European Christianity (after the end of the Viking incursions) and the effective christianization of the whole population; the Cistercian movement and its mystical fervor; and, above all, the growth

(side by side with the traditional monasteries, which continued to flourish) of schools around the great cathedrals. Centers such as Paris, Bologna, and Orléans contained large numbers of students who were destined not for monasteries but for careers in ecclesiastical or secular administration. This audience of students in turn bred lecturers and scholars, and from the interaction between them came new ideas, new interests, and new areas of research. Several secular courts also promoted literary activity, notably those of Henry the Liberal of Champagne and especially Henry II of England. It was fashionable during this period to lament the decline of the arts beside the study of law or philosophy, but in fact the arts prospered quite well.

France and Norman England dominated the literary scene. Cultural contacts between England and France, which had always been strong, were reinforced by the Norman Conquest of 1066 and by the accession of Henry II, who united England with a large part of France. Scholars and poets crossed the channel frequently. Many great English men of letters were educated at Paris or Orléans or held posts in French monasteries; conversely, many French writers spent much time in England. The court of Henry II included, at some time or another, most of the important literary figures of the day.

The reign of Henry II produced another, unexpected, literary stimulus: the murder of Archbishop Thomas Becket in 1170 gave rise to a large literature of poems, hymns, satires, and lives of the sanctified martyr. The foremost literary figure of the century was John of Salisbury (*ca.* 1115–1180); from a literary point of view, his most important work was the *Polycraticus*, a "rule for princes," full of anecdotes and dedicated to Becket.

The *De nugis curialium* of Walter Map (*ca.* 1140–1209) contains witty anecdotes, ghost stories, and tales of the macabre, with much incidental satire on the court and on religious orders. Map also wrote some poems, though not those attributed to him by John Bale in the sixteenth century. The letters of Peter of Blois (*ca.* 1135–1212) were designed for public consumption as epistolary models and enjoyed enormous popularity for centuries; Peter also wrote some entertaining poems. Alexander Neckam (1157–1217), of St. Albans and Cirencester, has been described as "one of the most remarkable scholars of the second half of the twelfth century"; his immense learning and range of literary skills can be seen in his *De naturis rerum*, his *Corrogationes Promethei*, his poem *De laudibus divinae sapientiae*, and his earlier verse fables the *Novus Avianus* and *Novus Aesopus,* as well as in his many theological works.

Geoffrey of Monmouth's *Historia regum Britanniae* (written 1136–1138) was denounced even in the twelfth century as utter fabrication, but much of his account of pre-Saxon British history has been justified by modern scholarship and archaeology. His work may have been designed to provide the Norman kings of Britain with a legendary past (that is, a lineal descent from Troy) to rival and replace the Germanic ancestry of the now-defeated Anglo-Saxons. Whatever his motives and historical value, he was responsible for the diffusion of the Arthurian legend throughout Europe. He also wrote a verse *Vita Merlini.* Another writer associated with the court of Henry II was the prolific Gerald of Wales (*ca.* 1146–1223); his accounts of Ireland and Wales (based on personal experience), his autobiograpical writings, and his *Speculum ecclesiae* are full of amusing anecdotes and are very polished and literate.

Another "anecdotist" was Gervase of Tilbury (*ca.* 1140–1220); he spent most of his life as a provincial administrator in the service of the emperor Otto IV, to whom he dedicated his *Otia imperialia,* now famous especially for its "ghost stories." Collections of prose stories often had a moral purpose. The *Disciplina clericalis* of Petrus Alfonsi (1062–*ca.* 1140) takes the form of a dialogue between father and son. The *Historia septem sapientum* (or *Dolopathos*) by John of Alta Silva (Haute-Seille), written about 1184, was based on an Eastern legend. The English Odo of Ceriton made a collection of prose fables about 1200.

The history of Troy was a popular theme for poets, perhaps stimulated by Geoffrey of Monmouth's account of the Trojan diaspora. Very popular were Pierre de Saintes' *Viribus arte minis* and the anonymous *Pergama flere volo* (in rhyming elegiacs). Full-length epics on the same theme were written by Simon Chèvre d'Or or Aurea Capra (the *Ylias*) and by Joseph of Exeter in six books (*ca.* 1185).

The story of Alexander the Great produced epic poems by Walter of Châtillon and Quilichinus of Spoleto; the story was told in prose in the *Historia de preliis.* The fictitious letters (of a much earlier date) between Alexander and Aristotle were widely popular throughout the Middle Ages; Alexander's contained material on the "Wonders of the East," and Aristotle's was a "Mirror for Princes."

Crusade literature was naturally common, and the theme of Jerusalem, old and new, was central to the epic on *Solomon's Temple* by Acardus of Arroasia (*d.*

ca. 1136), prior of Jerusalem; it was concluded by his successor Gaufridus. Contemporary or local themes were chosen by several Italian poets: Donizo of Canossa (*d. fl.* 1115) wrote an epic on the Countess Matilda and Italian history; William of Apulia wrote the *Gesta Roberti Wiscardi;* Godfrey of Viterbo (*ca.* 1125–1192) wrote the *Speculum regum* and the *Pantheon,* a world history in goliardic meter. Peter of Eboli (*d.* 1219 or 1220) wrote poems on Sicilian history and the baths at Puteoli. Moses of Bergamo (first half of the century) was an important Greek scholar and grammarian, but also wrote a rhyming poem in praise of Bergamo. Also important is the anonymous *Gesta Friderici* on Frederick Barbarossa.

The Hildebert tradition of religious poetry continued with Petrus Pictor (*fl. ca.* 1100), whose many poems included a lone one on the Mass. A major poet in this tradition was Peter Riga from Rheims; his greatest work was the *Aurora,* a versified Bible. He also wrote a very popular poem on *Susanna* (incorporated in the *Aurora*) and a long collection of shorter poems known as the *Floridus aspectus* (which became entangled in anthologies with the short poems of Hildebert and Marbod). Matthew of Vendôme (*fl.* 1185) wrote, among other things, the *Tobias,* a verse treatment of the *Book of Tobit.* In 1194 Henry of Settimello wrote a long moralizing poem on Fortune.

Hymn writing received a new impetus not only from the varied melodies of the sequence but also from the newly developed form of the "regular Victorine Sequence" (or *Stabat mater* stanza), which takes its name from Adam of St. Victor (*ca.* 1110–1192), who himself wrote more than forty such hymns. This meter was very popular, especially for religious verse, throughout the rest of the Middle Ages. Its earliest examples are characterized by symbolism, particularly the "typology" of Christ and the Virgin—that is, the prefiguration of the New Testament by the Old.

Educational tools and handbooks included two dictionaries: Osbern of Gloucester's *Panormia* and the very widely distributed *Liber derivationum* (1190–1192) by the canonist Huguccio (*d.* 1210). Two versified (and thus easily memorable) Latin grammars were the *Graecismus* by Evrard of Béthune (*d.* 1212) and the *Doctrinale* by Alexandre de Villedieu (*ca.* 1170–1250). The quantities of syllables were illustrated by Serlo de Wilton's *De differentiis.* The art of writing poetry was treated in several works. Matthew of Vendôme, himself a major poet, wrote the *Ars versificatoria.* The Englishman Geoffrey of Vinsauf (*fl.* 1200) wrote the *Poetria nova* (dedicated to Pope Innocent III) and the *Documentum de modo de arte dictandi et versificandi.* In classical scholarship we may note the commentaries on Ovid and Lucan by Arnulf of Orléans (second half of the twelfth century).

This is not the place to write about the great scientific advances of the age—the emergence of Arabic science, the rediscovery of Aristotle, and the work of such notable writers as Hildegard of Bingen, Adelard of Bath, and Honorius Augustodunensis—but science and literature were not always far apart. Medical studies flourished at Salerno—and were satirized by Nigel of Canterbury. The *Regimen sanitatis Salerni,* attributed to Arnald of Villanova (*ca.* 1240–1311), was a digest of practical medical lore and epigrams; it remained popular for centuries (and was printed very early) and was expanded into the much longer *Flos medicinae.* An older interpretation of the phenomenal world was consolidated by the Neoplatonists of Chartres; their world view stimulated major literary "scientific mythology" in Bernard Silvester's *Cosmographia* (*ca.* 1143–1148), a *prosimetrum* in the style of Martianus Capella and Boethius. Bernard also wrote a commentary on Vergil's *Aeneid,* Books I–VI; other commentaries (probably including the rather well-known and important one on Martianus Capella in the Cambridge University Library); and various poems, including the *Mathematicus.*

The most important philosophical poet, whose works greatly influenced both Jean de Meun and Chaucer, was Alan of Lille (*b. ca.* 1116–*d.* 1202–1203). His hexameter epic *Anticlaudianus,* in nine books, provides a new myth for the nature of mankind; his prosimetrum *De planctu Naturae* ("The Pleynt of Kynde," as Chaucer calls it) is a complaint by the goddess Natura against unnatural sexual practices, but it also explores the whole nature and purpose of human love and sexuality. Alan also wrote theological works, a biblical concordance, hymns, and a treatise on preaching.

A philosopher-poet of a different kind was Peter Abelard (*ca.* 1079–*ca.* 1142), one of the most fascinating men of the Middle Ages; his ill-starred personal life is described in his *Historia calamitatum.* Most of his works are theological or philosophical (such as the *Sic et non*), but he also wrote hymns, a proverb collection for his son Astralabe, a series of dramatic *Planctus* (the individual laments) by biblical characters, and (by his own account) secular popular songs. He ended his days at Cluny, where the abbot, Peter the Venerable (*ca.* 1092–1156), was himself a noted writer.

The founder of the Cistercian order, Bernard of Clairvaux (1090–1153), left many deeply devotional hymns. Other French poets of the century include Guy de Bazoches (*ca.* 1146–1203), Peter of Poitiers (*d.* 1205), and Arnulf of Lisieux (*d.* 1184). We may also mention Abelard's pupil Hilary, who wrote, among other things, some religious plays.

For many modern readers, Medieval Latin is especially associated with satire. The satirical tradition flourished in the twelfth century in many forms; in prose we see it in many parodies and in the *De nugis curialium* by Walter Map. One of the butts of Map's satire, as of the *Speculum ecclesiae* by Gerald of Wales, was the Cistercian order. Satirical epic is seen in John of Hauville's rambling epic, the *Architrenius* (Arch-lamenter) of 1184, in nine books of hexameters; it drew heavily on classical sources, was frequently copied (particularly in anthologies), and was very influential (particularly on Walter of Wimborne). Medieval Latin satire is not usually personal or topical like Classical Latin satire (though imitations of Martial's epigrams are common) but general, aimed primarily at sin, especially avarice. A striking example is the *De contemptu mundi* by Bernard of Cluny, whose interminable *dactylici tripertiti* were very popular and often imitated. Almost equally popular was the *Parvus contemptus mundi* in leonine hexameters and the *Sacrilegis monachis* (variously ascribed in manuscripts to Gualo, Nicholas of Caen, Roger of Caen, and others). Other satirists who used the rhymed hexameter include Serlo of Bayeux (*ca.* 1050–1113/1122) and his namesake Serlo de Wilton.

The most amusing and accomplished English satire is the *Speculum stultorum* by Nigel of Canterbury (also known as N. Wireker and N. de Longo Campo) (*ca.* 1130–1200). An epic in elegiac couplets, it recounts the wanderings of the ass Burnellus in his search for a longer tail. In passing, it satirizes doctors, universities, merchants, and the whole range of religious orders; in the thirteenth century it was supplemented to include friars. Nigel also wrote a prose satire, *Tractatus contra curiales,* and many short poems. The beast fable was very popular as a vehicle both for satire and for moralizing; Alexander Neckam's *Novus Avianus* and *Novus Aesopus* have already been mentioned. Reynard the Fox's exploits are recounted in the epic *Ysengrimus* (*ca.* 1148) by Nivard of Ghent. A long series of fables (which were later used by John Lydgate and Robert Henryson) was written by Walter the Englishman, chaplain of Henry II. Satires and epigrams were also written by the historian Henry of Huntingdon (1080/1085–1155) and by the French poet Paganus Bolotinus.

Hugh (Primas) of Orléans (twelfth century) gained a reputation for his skillful and witty rhyming epigrams, usually satirical. The anonymous Archpoet of Cologne (*fl.* 1159–1165) wrote satires mainly in the new goliardic stanza, including the famous "Confessio Goliae" with its famous line "Meum est propositum in taberna mori." The names Primas, Archpoet, and Golias are used by medieval scribes to indicate the heroes of a kind of literary myth (like the sixteenth-century Pasquin); the word *goliardus* is sometimes used similarly, but there is no evidence for a class of wandering scholars composing satirical verse. The goliardic stanza was used sometimes for sacred verse; several poems on the martyred Becket are in this meter. The most gifted poet in the so-called goliardic tradition was Walter of Châtillon (*b.* ca. 1135). His most substantial work, the epic *Alexandreis*, has already been mentioned, but he is nowadays more famous for his lyrics, love poems, and particularly satires against the Roman curia. Many anonymous poems are in the goliardic meter, including the "Metamorphosis Goliae," which surveys all the famous Parisian philosophers, including Abelard. The "Apocalypsis Goliae," an extremely popular satire against the whole ecclesiastical hierarchy, is written in rhythmical asclepiads, a common meter for satire.

The new rhythmical meters put life into an ancient literary form, the poetic debate (well known from Vergil's *Eclogues*, the Alcuinian Spring-Winter conflict, and the school text *Ecloga Theoduli*). The popular *Phyllis and Flora* debates the merits of Clerk and Knight as lovers; similar is the *Council of Remiremont*, which (like many such poems) is set in a dream framework. Probably the most popular poem in the Middle Ages was the *Visio Philiberti*, a debate between Body and Soul at the moment of death. It is extant in more than 160 manuscripts and has many analogues, imitations, and translations. There are also verse debates between Winter and Summer, Wine and Water, Wine and Beer (all popular themes), Lily and Rose, and the various religious orders. Often these debates are clearly school exercises in rhetoric.

The *comoedia*, or verse drama, first appears in the twelfth century. Vitalis of Blois (*fl.* 1150) wrote the *Aulularia* and the *Geta* (based on Plautus' Amphitryon, but with satire on contemporary philosophy).

William of Blois (*fl.* 1170) wrote the *Alda*. Another example is the anonymous *Pamphilus, Gliscerium et Birria;* probably of English origin are the *Baucis et Thraso* and the *Babio*. Whether these *comoediae* were actually performed is the subject of much scholarly debate, but there is evidence (as in the fourteenth-century *Visio Thurkilli*) for open-air theater. Religious drama is seen in the Christmas and Easter plays preserved in the *Carmina burana* and in the *Ludus de Antichristo*.

Toward the end of the twelfth century we begin to see anthologies of Medieval Latin poems, including work by Hildebert, Petrus Riga, Marbod, and Petrus Pictor, but usually dominated by anonymous poems, many of which remain little noticed by modern scholars. These anthologies soon eclipsed the florilegia based on the ancient poets, which nevertheless continued to be produced into the thirteenth century.

The twelfth and thirteenth centuries—the High Middle Ages—are sometimes called the *aetas Ovidiana,* the age of Ovid. This appellation reflects first the immense popularity of his works as school texts, which resulted in many imitations, such as Baudri of Bourgueil's *Letters of Helen and Paris.* Themes from Ovid were often used by medieval poets—the *armorum judicium* (judgment of arms) between Ajax and Ulysses; Dido's lament on the departure of Aeneas; Pyramus and Thisbe—and the anthology of "rhetorical poems" in Glasgow MS Hunterian V. 8. 14 (thirteenth century) contains many Ovidian poems. The character of the *vetula*, the aged go-between, found first in Ovid's *Amores* and *Ars amatoria*, became a stock figure not only of Latin but also of vernacular medieval literature—La Vieille in the *Roman de la Rose,* Chaucer's Wife of Bath, Villon's Helmet-maker. Her activities form the plot of the comoedia *Pamphilus de amore*, and the curious poem *De vetula* (which is full of scientific information) is also based on this character. Surprisingly, Ovid's influence is also seen in scientific writers, who used the cosmology of the first book of the *Metamorphoses* and several tales of transformation. Echoes from Ovid's love poems are found not only in the learned love lyric, but also in antifeminist literature.

The concept of courtly love has been questioned in recent years, and with it the status of Andreas Capellanus' *De amore* (written 1174–1186), which has been called "a systematic code of courtly love." No one, however, doubts that from the twelfth century onward the literature of love increases greatly. The few love lyrics in the *Cambridge Songs* anticipate the large numbers in the *Carmina burana* and in the Bekynton, Arundel, Ripoli, and similar collections. The new sequence meters were especially suited to the love lyric, and genres such as the love-debate and pastourelle became common in both Latin and the vernacular languages. The nature of human sexuality is examined more seriously in Alan of Lille's *De planctu Naturae* (1160–1175). Antifeminism is part of the same tradition. Its major Medieval Latin monuments are Book I of Jerome's (fourth century) treatise *Adversus Jovinianum,* which incorporates a Latin translation (the sole extant text) from Theophrastus' *De nuptiis,* and Walter Map's *Dissuasio Valerii ad Rufinum* (which he incorporated into his *De nugis curialium*). Antifeminist literature makes frequent use of Ovid's *Ars amatoria* and *Remedium amoris.*

THIRTEENTH CENTURY

During the thirteenth century the cathedral schools gradually became more recognizably universities, with degrees, formal teaching and curricula, statutes and privileges. In England, although scholars still attended Paris, the rise of Oxford and Cambridge resulted in more home-grown writers. More aids for literary study and writing appeared. Two more dictionaries were compiled, the great *Catholicon* (1286) by Giovanni Balbi of Genoa (one of the first books to be printed by Gutenberg) and the *Dictionarius* by John of Garland (*ca.* 1195–1272). John of Garland also wrote a *Dictionarius metricus,* a *Compendium grammaticae* in 4,000 hexameters, works on the art of poetry, and religious poems. Other writers on rhetoric include Gervase of Melkley and Evrard the German, whose *Laborintus* has an account of many Medieval Latin verse forms. The art of letter writing *(ars dictaminis)* was analyzed by Thomas of Capua (*d.* 1243). Conrad of Hirsau's *Accessus ad auctores (Dialogus super auctores)* (*ca.* 1070–1150) gives an account of Latin writers from Vergil to Theodulus, and so laid the basis for literary histories such as Hugh of Trimberg's *Registrum multorum auctorum* (*ca.* 1280) and Henri d'Andeli's *Battle of the Seven Liberal Arts.* Many great monasteries began to catalog their library holdings; one of the most informative lists is the *Biblionomia* of Richard de Fournival (*d.* 1260).

John of Garland's *Integumenta Ovidii* is one of the first major interpretations of the *Metamorphoses* and an early landmark in the genre of mythography—the interpretation and rationalization of myths. Mythography has its roots in Greek Alexandrian scholarship. Besides John of Garland, other notable medieval exponents include what are misleadingly called (from the Vatican manuscript in which the treatises are preserved) the "three Vatican mythographers." "Mythographus tertius," the most interesting of the three (identified in the Middle Ages with Alexander Neckam), is now known to be Alberic of London, who also wrote a collection of miracles of the Virgin.

The interests, themes, and forms of the twelfth century continued. This was the great age of the poetic anthology, such as the Codex Buranus (containing the *Carmina burana*); the Florence Antiphonary; the Bekynton, Arundel, and Ripoli collections; the "Later Cambridge Songs"; and many others. These collections are our principal sources for the Medieval Latin lyric. More *comoediae* appeared, such as the *Pamphilus de Amore.* Among the satirists we must mention Philip, chancellor of Paris (*d.* 1236), who is often associated with Walter of Châtillon and the so-called goliardic poets. Antifeminist literature was amplified by the very popular anti-matrimonial poem *De coniuge non ducenda* (in asclepiadic quatrains); this work in turn was used by Matthew of Boulogne in his *Lamentationes Matheoluli* (1290–1291), more than 5,500 lines of rhyming hexameters advising against marriage.

The single most important factor in the literature of this century is the rise of the mendicant orders, particularly the Franciscans and Dominicans. The latter produced perhaps the two greatest minds of the Middle Ages, Albertus Magnus and Thomas Aquinas, but it is to the Franciscans that devotional poetry owed its new impetus. The emphasis on the human pathos of Christ's Passion and the Virgin's sorrows goes back to the mystical writings of the twelfth century (especially to Cistercian writings) and was thoroughly exploited by Franciscan poets. In England, for example, Walter of Wimborne's (*fl.* 1260) *Marie carmina* retells the life of Christ, mainly from the viewpoint of the Virgin; Walter's main source for his Marian imagery was the compilation *De laudibus beatae Virginis Mariae* (written 1239–1245) by the Dominican Richard of St. Laurent. Walter also wrote many satirical poems. Another English poet, John of Howden (identified by some with a holy person who died in 1275), was influenced by the same movement; he wrote the *Philomena* (in both Latin and French), an elaborate poem on the life of Christ, and several other long religious poems, many to the Virgin. Another Franciscan, John Peckham (Pecham), archbishop of Canterbury (1279–1292), wrote another poem called *Philomena,* using the nightingale as an allegory for the soul. Peckham also wrote a verse debate between Religion and the World, in addition to his theological works. The *Dies irae* is attributed to another Franciscan, Thomas of Celano. The principal Franciscan poet outside England was St. Bonaventure (*ca.* 1217–1274), the leading Franciscan theologian of the century. The friars unwittingly gave rise to a great deal of satire in the thirteenth and fourteenth centuries; they were intensely unpopular with the secular clergy and the regular monks. (The proliferation of all nonmonastic orders except Dominicans, Franciscans, Carmelites, and Augustinians was halted by the Second Council of Lyons in 1274.) The Franciscans were especially important in Oxford; Roger Bacon was a member of the community.

Other major poetry of the century includes Albert of Stade's *Troilus* on the Trojan War; Albert (*d.* 1265) also wrote a world chronicle. The Sicilian Guido delle Colonne wrote a long and influential prose history of the Trojan War. Adam de la Bassée (*d.* 1286) wrote the *Ludus super Anticlaudianum,* a "poetical fantasy" based on Alan of Lille. The Danish historian Saxo Grammaticus (*ca.* 1150–1220) composed a *Gesta Danorum,* in which apparently ancient Germanic songs are translated into complex Latin lyric meters. Henry of Avranches (*d. ca.* 1262), a court poet of Henry III of England, wrote several verse saints' lives and many poems on a variety of subjects. He was pitted in a debate—an extravagantly rhymed "flyting" in leonine hexameters—against the English poet Michael Blaunpayn (the Potter) of Cornwall. The fable genre is well exemplified by the *Asinarius* and *Rapularius,* of German origin. Of the Italian poets we may mention Bellino Bissolo, whose *Speculum vitae* is a collection of short stories in elegiacs; he also wrote a *Liber legum moralium* and *De regimine vitae et sanitatis.*

Among prose writers of literary significance we must mention Jacques de Vitry (1180–1240), whose *Historia* is stocked with exempla and interesting anecdotes. Caesarius of Heisterbach (*ca.* 1180–1240) compiled a collection of marvels in his *Dialogus miraculorum.* Jacobus de Voragine (*ca.* 1228–1298) compiled the *Legenda aurea* (a collection mainly of lives of saints) from earlier sources. Popular science was conveniently summarized by Bartholomaeus Anglicus (*fl.* 1230–1250) in his *De proprietatibus rerum;* technological writing was graced (for the first time) by an elegant Latin style in Theophilus' *De diversis artibus.* Prose chroniclers abound. For English history one of the most interesting is Matthew Paris (*d.* 1259).

FOURTEENTH AND FIFTEENTH CENTURIES

Historians of Medieval Latin literature tend to run out of interest after the end of the twelfth or, at best, the thirteenth century. Consequently, there are few "maps" of the later period, and many texts remain unprinted and their authors unknown, even to specialists. In some respects, this neglect reflects a genuine decline in literary activity in Latin. The spread of literacy among the laity produced a much larger reading public, but one that read the vernacular languages rather than Latin. Creative writers naturally sought the widest possible audience, and therefore turned to their own native tongues. For some time Latin remained the language of scholarship, philosophy, and theology, but as the language of poetry and entertainment it eventually disappeared, except as a scholar's pastime. Nevertheless, Latin remained the dominant literary language much longer than is generally realized.

In France, the Dominican Petrus Berchorius, or Pierre Bersuire (*ca.* 1290–1362), in addition to translating Livy into French, wrote a massive *Reductorium morale,* of which Book XV is a moralization of the *Metamorphoses;* the prologue to Book XV is a treatise on the pagan gods. The Latin literary works, mainly poems, of Dreux (Drogo) of Haut-Villers occupy three manuscript volumes but remain unprinted.

In Italy, Petrarch (1304–1374) wrote a great deal of Latin verse, including an unfinished epic, the *Africa.* Most of his prose works are in Latin. Boccaccio (1313–1375) also wrote as much in Latin as in Italian. His *Olympia* is a possible source of the Middle English poem *Pearl,* and his *De claris mulieribus* and *De casibus virorum illustrium* were very influential on Chaucer and on Lydgate (who translated them). The last two books of his *De genealogia deorum gentilium* (a treatise on mythography) deal with poetry and the defense of poetry. Even Dante wrote much Latin prose, including the *De monarchia.* With these writers, however, we are almost in the Renaissance, as we certainly are with humanists such as Leonardo Bruni of Arezzo (who translated Italian works into Latin) and Aeneas Silvius Piccolomini (later Pope Pius II), though their themes are often medieval.

In England in this late period, poems in Latin on contemporary political and military events are common. In 1312 the English Carmelite friar Robert Baston was captured by the Scots and forced to write a poem on the Battle of Bannockburn. The other poems attributed to him are not his. The death of Edward II's hated favorite, Piers Gaveston, produced a spate of poems, and the military successes of Edward III stimulated poems against the French and the Scots. The controversies between the friars and the secular clergy, especially at Oxford, were the cause of much satirical verse. "John of Bridlington"'s *Prophecy* (written during the reign of Edward III) is only one of many political prophecy poems, though it is the most elaborate and was published with a commentary by John Erghom. John Gower's *Vox Clamantis* is an elaborate political allegory; after the Peasants' Revolt of 1381 he wrote a new first book in the form of a beast fable. In the fifteenth century Thomas Elmham and various anonymous authors celebrated the victories of Henry V in both prose and verse. There are two English religious poets of note: the Franciscan Richard Ledrede, who wrote a series of hymns (some adapted from Walter of Wimborne's *Marie carmina*), many set to popular tunes; and the mystic Yorkshire poet Richard Rolle, famous for his *Incendium amoris* and many Latin and English poems.

The collection of allegorized tales known as the *Gesta Romanorum* was compiled in the early fourteenth century. Knowledge of classical literature prospered in a group of fourteenth-century English friars, including Thomas Waleys and John Ridewall. Ridewall's *Fulgentius metaforalis* is another piece of mythography. John of Tynemouth compiled a collection of the lives of English saints. In the *Philobiblon*, Richard de Bury (1287–1345) extolled the value of books. Another English man of letters was Nicholas Trivet (*b. ca.* 1260–*d.* after 1334); he wrote not only chronicles and biblical exegesis but also commentaries on classical authors such as Livy, Juvenal, and Seneca. John of Bromyard's *Summa praedicantium* (1348) is an alphabetically organized encyclopedia of material for preaching and includes many stories. The *Visio Thurkilli* by Richard of Coggeshall recounts a peasant's vision of hell. In the fifteenth century Thomas Walsingham wrote not only a chronicle of his abbey, St. Albans, and a treatise on music, but also several literary studies, including the *Prohemia poetarum* (lives of poets), the *Dites ditatus* (an expansion of Dictys Cretensis' account of the Trojan War), and the *Arcana deorum* (a commentary on the *Metamorphoses*, based on earlier mythographers). John Wethamstede, abbot of St. Albans

(1420–1440, 1451–1465), wrote several literary works, including the *Granarium*, a classical encyclopedia, and the *Palearium poetarum*, a collection of classical proverbs and sayings.

Anthologies, of both old and contemporary poems, proliferated in all countries of Europe, and some of the best texts of earlier authors (such as Walter of Châtillon) are found in fifteenth-century copies. The *Summa recreatorum*, a Bohemian collection of "therapeutic" texts, includes two books of poems and stories. Bohemia was the center of religious disaffection; the leader of the reformers was John Hus (who also wrote some Latin hymns), and the Hussites received support from English Wycliffites. Bohemia and eastern Europe produced many satires and parodies during this period; also, many of the Bohemian anthologies of earlier goliardic satire show textual affinities with English collections of similar material. The neglected anthologies of the fifteenth century undoubtedly contain the works of many unknown Latin poets, whom only further research will unearth.

MEDIEVAL LATIN IN RECENT TIMES

Latin, as a universal language, continued to be a tool for philosophical, theological, scientific, scholarly, and even literary purposes. In 1635 Chaucer's *Troilus* was translated into Latin to make it more accessible to readers. Purely Medieval Latin, however, is deemed to end with the Middle Ages, and is replaced by Neo-Latin (that is, Renaissance Latin). Rhyme and rhythm disappeared from Latin verse in favor of classical quantitative meters (which had, of course, continued to be written throughout the Middle Ages). Under the influence of scholars such as Erasmus, the medieval arts curriculum was replaced by one based on the pagan classical authors, especially those of the Golden Age of Augustan Rome. The standards of Latinity—for style, grammar, and vocabulary—became those of the Roman Republic and early Empire. Consequently, schools and universities stressed the ancient classics, and Medieval Latin did not become a university subject until relatively recently; it thus attracted little original research.

The study of documents, however, required a knowledge of the language; the first dictionary of Medieval Latin (by Du Cange) was begun in the seventeenth century. Texts—of medieval theology, philosophy, chronicles, saints' lives—were edited by scholars in the appropriate disciplines; purely literary texts, however, generally took a back place behind the ancient authors. (One exception was anticlerical satire, which was revived in the sixteenth century by Protestant polemicists such as John Bale and Flacius Illyricus.) Medieval Latin authors were, until recently, generally treated fairly by literary histories, whether those of religious orders (by John Tritheim, Luke Wadding, Jacques Quétif, Jacobus Echard, and others) or those of nations (the *Histoire littéraire de la France*, and works of John Bale, John Pits, Thomas Tanner, and Thomas Wright). Such histories, however, rarely provided more than the barest bibliographical information; genuine literary study and the careful editing of Medieval Latin literary texts have been rare and slow.

Interest revived in the nineteenth century, especially in Germany, where the great *Monumenta Germaniae historica* series stimulated editors and scholars to work on Medieval Latin literature for its own sake. In the twentieth century Scandinavian countries, especially Sweden, have done much. In the English-speaking world Medieval Latin has been ancillary to the studies of the medieval vernacular languages, particularly English. This development has been beneficial to the literary criticism of Medieval Latin, but has often unfortunately resulted in a divorce between classicists and medievalists, to the detriment of both. There are signs, however, that interest is increasing in Medieval Latin literature in its own right.

BIBLIOGRAPHY

Erich Auerbach, *Literary Language and Its Public in Late Latin Antiquity and in the Middle Ages*, Ralph Manheim, trans. (1965); Robert R. Bolgar, *The Classical Heritage and Its Beneficiaries* (1954); Richard A. Browne, ed., *British Latin Selections A.D. 500–1400* (1954); Ernst R. Curtius, *European Literature and the Latin Middle Ages*, Willard R. Trask, trans. (1953); Charles H. Haskins, *The Renaissance of the Twelfth Century* (1933); Karl Langosch, *Lateinisches Mittelalter* (1963); Martin R. P. McGuire and Hermigild Dressler, *Introduction to Mediaeval Latin Studies*, 2nd ed. (1977); Max Manitius, *Geschichte der lateinischen Literatur des Mittelalters*, 3 vols. (1911–1931); Frederic J. E. Raby, *A History of Christian-Latin Poetry from the Beginnings to the Close of the Middle Ages*, 2nd ed. (1953), and *A History of Secular Latin Poetry in the Middle Ages*, 2 vols., 2nd ed. (1957); Beryl Smalley, *English Friars and Antiquity in the Early Fourteenth Century* (1960); Karl Strecker, *Introduction to Medieval Latin*, Robert B. Palmer, trans. (1957).

A. G. RIGG

[See also **Acrostics–Wordplay; Anthologies; Carolingian Latin Poetry; Carolinginas; Classical Literary Studies;**

Drama; Encyclopedias and Dictionaries; Goliards; Hisperic Latin; Ovid in the Middle Ages; Parody, Latin; Troy Story; Vergil in the Middle Ages; and individual authors.]

LATIN METER. The meters of Medieval Latin poetry can be described essentially under two headings: nonrhyming, according to Classical practice, and rhyming, either metrical or rhythmical, a purely medieval phenomenon. Examples of Medieval Latin verse are here taken mainly either from the *Oxford Book of Medieval Latin Verse*, cited by number and line, or from the thirteenth-century *Laborintus* by Evrard (Eberhard) the German of Bremen, edited by Edmond Faral.

NONRHYMING METRICAL VERSE

Dactylic. The main dactylic meters of Classical Latin poetry, combinations of the dactyl (- ‿ ‿) and spondee (- -), were the hexameter (as in Vergil's *Aeneid*) and the elegiac couplet, which consists of a hexameter plus a pentameter (as in Ovid's *Amores*). These two verse forms continued throughout the Middle Ages and remained the most popular meters, the hexameter especially for epic poems (such as Josephus Iscanus' [Joseph of Exeter's] *Bellum Troianum*), and the elegiac couplet for lighter verse and satire (such as Nigel of Canterbury's *Speculum stultorum*). Such verse depended on the length or quantity of the syllable (not its stress). Classical rules for syllable length are generally observed in Medieval Latin poetry, but some writers clearly had difficulty with natural length, which is known only by memory, not by any deductive rules: Serlo de Wilton's *De differentiis* (twelfth century) was designed partly to inculcate a knowledge of the true length of vowels, distinguishing, for example, between *fides* and *fides*. A fairly common departure from Classical practice is the lengthening of short vowels at the caesura (see *Oxford Book*, no. 188/13). Classical rules of elision are generally observed where appropriate, but many poets avoided elision and hiatus altogether.

Iambic, trochaic, and lyric. The iambic dimeter, iambic dimeter catalectic, and trochaic septenarius (trochaic tetrameter catalectic) survived principally in hymns. Lyric meters, such as sapphics, alcaics, and pherecratics, were known not only through the treatises of metrical theoreticians (such as Bede) and texts of Horace's *Odes* (which were relatively rare, compared to the *Satires* and *Epistles*), but also through the *metra* contained in Martianus Capella's *De nuptiis Mercurii et Philologiae* and Boethius' *Consolation of Philosophy*. They were, however, rarely imitated, though sapphics and alcaics were written in the Carolingian period, notably by Gottschalk of Orbais. For Alan of Lille's sapphic ode, see *Oxford Book*, no. 241; for Sigebert of Gembloux's alcaics, see *Oxford Book*, no. 148. One writer who made frequent use of such relatively rare meters was Saxo Grammaticus (thirteenth century): in his *Gesta Danorum* he used lyric meters to translate Old Norse songs. Generally, however, the lyric meters of Medieval Latin poetry were rhythmical.

THE INTRODUCTION OF RHYME

Classical poets avoided assonance or "consonance," except for special effects, but even in Vergil there are examples of "rhymes" within his hexameters. It is in the hymns that we first see fairly regular rhymes, particularly in Sedulius (fifth century), though these are usually vocalic only (that is, on the vowels, not the consonants) and are, to modern ears, very inexact. The origins of rhyme remain obscure, but the most likely source is rhetorical prose, in which final "consonance" was often used as an ornament: the chants of the liturgy also lent themselves to devices to emphasize parallelism and echoes. Rhyme is found in some pre-Carolingian writers, but the poets of the Carolingian court circle seem to have preferred to imitate Classical metrical verse. Not until the eleventh century do we see regular disyllabic rhymes as a structural device; from then on, rhyme is common both in dactylic quantitative verse and in the new rhythmical poems, and disappears only after the Renaissance. Rhymes are particularly valuable for determining the pronunciation of Medieval Latin.

RHYMING DACTYLIC VERSE

Rhymes in dactylic verse can be divided into those that depend on the caesura and those that depend on the metrical foot. Caesura rhymes will be considered first. In the quantitative hexameter there is a regular break, or caesura, in each line, either after the first syllable of the third foot (the strong caesura), for instance in Ovid, *Metamorphoses* I, 1:

In nova fert animus ‖ mutatas dicere formas

or after the second syllable of a dactylic third foot (the weak caesura), for instance in Vergil, *Aeneid* I, 87:

insequitur | clamorque ‖ virum | stridorque rudentum

(in which case there are reinforcing caesuras in the second and fourth feet). The pentameter consists of two first halves of a hexameter, separated by a caesura, for instance in Ovid, *Amores* I, 1, 6:

Pieridum vates ‖ non tua turba sumus

From these caesuras—the strong hexameter caesura, the reinforcing caesuras in lines with weak caesura, and the pentameter caesura—arise the main possibilities of internal rhyme.

(1) The simplest form is Leonine rhyme, between the syllables before the strong caesura and at the end of the line, for instance in Marbod (*Oxford Book*, no. 153/1):

moribus esse feris   prohibet me gratia veris

The term "Leonine" and the noun *Leonitas* become common in the early twelfth century; they appear to derive from the use of the rhymed prose cursus in documents of Pope Leo I. Analogous rhyme schemes are *unisoni* couplets, *collateralles*, and *cruciferi*.

(2) *Unisoni* (single-sound) couplets can be found in Primas (*Oxford Book*, no. 176a):

pontificum spuma,   faex cleri, sordida struma,
qui dedit in bruma   mihi mantellum sine pluma

and in an anonymous elegiac couplet, *Oxford Book*, no. 137/1–2:

Pergama flere volo   fato Danais data solo
solo capta dolo   capta redacta solo

(3) *Collaterales*, also known as *ventrini* (internal), in which the words at the caesuras rhyme together, are in, for instance, Petrus Pictor (*Oxford Book*, no. 149/1–2):

Flandria dulce solum   super omnes terra beata
tangis laude polum   duce magno glorificata

and similarly, in an elegiac couplet, *Laborintus*, 718–719:

si tibi nota seges   est morum gratus haberis
si virtutis eges   despiciendus eris

(4) In *cruciferi* (crossed), also known as *serpentini* (serpentine), there is a cross-rhyme between the caesura of the first line with the end of the second, and vice versa (verse cited by Norberg, p. 68):

angelico verbo   castus tuus intumet alvus
ut fieret salvus   homo tentus ab hoste superbo

and in an elegiac couplet, *Laborintus*, 732–733:

est Domini donum   puri devotio cordis
contemptus sordis   initiale bonum

(5) All the above schemes depend on the strong caesura; the weak caesura, with its reinforcing caesuras in the second and fourth feet, breaks the line into three parts, thus making possible *trinini salientes* (jumping threesomes), for instance, in Marbod (*Oxford Book*, no. 150/1–2):

> stella maris   quae sola paris   sine coniuge prolem
> iustitiae   clarum specie   super omnia solem

(Note the rhyme *iustitiae:specie,* which is slightly obscured by the classicized spelling; in medieval orthography it would appear *justicie:specie.*)

(6) Other types of caesura rhyme are found in the *Laborintus:*

> virgo beata salusque parata   benigna precanti
> dona rogata   dabis cumulata   tibi famulanti
> (777–778)

> cum sentis   mentis sit pax   mala fare reatus
> ad matrem   patrem   matris fuge flere paratus
> (784–785)

> tradideris miseris sceleris   purgamina servis
> tutus erit   poterit   reperit   qui te pia quaerit
> (796–797)

> felices illae   sunt linguae   dicere mille
> (798)

> quae poterunt tibi laudes   caeli culmine gaudes
> (799)

> grata   parata   veni quaerenti   certa   reperta
> dia Maria   Dei genetrix pia   digna   benigna
> (800–801)

These hexameter and couplet rhyme schemes are often found in combination, especially those involving the strong caesura. By far the most common form, however, is the simple Leonine line, which is often the sole meter throughout a long poem.

(7) Other dactylic rhyme schemes involve the metrical foot, and consequently the lines are constructed in such a way as to avoid having a traditional caesura altogether. The most common are *dactylici tripertiti* (three-part dactyls), which rhyme in couplets finally, and internally after the second and fourth feet (see Bernard of Cluny, *Oxford Book*, no. 160/1–2):

> Hora novissima   tempora pessima   sunt vigilemus
> ecce minaciter   imminet arbiter   ille supremus

These lines are from Bernard of Cluny's *De contemptu mundi,* a very popular poem. To the modern reader, at least, there is considerable monotony in three whole books of these dactyls; there were, however, several imitators of the meter.

(8) Other examples of noncaesura (metrical foot) rhyme schemes are given in the *Laborintus:*

> fac   pia regia   flagito clamito   stirpe puella
> hostica caelica   spernere cernere   splendida stella
> (788–789)

or, using the spondee, in various combinations,

> spes miseroroum   duxque piorum   florida vitis
> fons bonitatis   lex pietatis   sis mihi mitis
> cellula mellis   fundis ororem   virgo serena
> nescia fellis   cui dat honorem   nostra camena
> optima rerum   lux mulierum   dirige clerum
> hanc homo cura   flectere pura   non prece dura
> (790–795)

(9) In addition to these internal rhymes, both caesural and noncaesural, *caudati* (tailed lines) are also very common: these lines rhyme in the final syllables only. They are most often found in combination with other types of rhymed hexameter; sometimes they are in quatrains, as in these from Reginald of Canterbury's *Vita Sancti Malchi* (extract, *Oxford Book*, no. 145/1–4), which contains series of almost every kind of rhyming hexameter:

> angele qui meus es custos pietate superna
> me tibi commissum serva tueare guberna
> terge meam mentem vitiis et labe veterna
> assiduusque comes mihi sis vitaeque lucerna

Elegiac couplets are also sometimes rhymed finally, as in *Laborintus,* 713–714:

> non lignis flamma nec   rebus cor satiari
> praecupidum poterit   in ratione pari

RHYTHMICAL VERSE

Rhythmical verse depends not on the length of a syllable, as does metrical verse, but on its accent. In the prose reading of a word, the stress falls on the penultimate syllable if the penultimate is long (*amábat*), but on the antepenultimate if the penultimate is short (*amavéritis*). The regular combination of stressed and unstressed syllables, usually in rising (iambic ˘ ¯) or falling (trochaic ¯ ˘) pairs, produced an enormous range of new verse types in the later Middle Ages. Rhythmical lines are described by the number of syllables in the line, together with the notation *p* or *pp*: *p* indicates a line (or half-line) with paroxytonic stress—that is, a line in which the stress at the end of the line falls on the penultimate syllable; *pp* indicates a line with proparoxytonic stress, in which the final stress falls on the antepenultimate syllable. Thus, the line

> Apparebit repentína   dies magna Dómini

is described as $8p + 7pp$. Elision is rare in rhythmical verse, and vowels $+ m$ are not elided. Hiatus is quite acceptable.

Fifteen-syllable lines. Most rhythmical meters, apart from the Goliardic line and the sequence meters, can be interpreted as developments from equivalent quantitative metrical meters. We may begin with one that gave rise to several rhythmical lines and combinations, the trochaic septenarius (also known as the trochaic tetrameter catalectic); quantitatively, this line consisted of four trochaic metra ($- \smile - \smile$) with the penultimate syllable of the final metron suppressed, for instance, Venantius Fortunatus (*Oxford Book,* no. 54/1):

> Pāngĕ līnguă / glōrĭōsī / prōĕlĭūm cēr / tāmĭnĭs

A prose, accentual reading of the same line results in a fifteen-syllable line divided into $8p + 7pp$; see *Oxford Book,* no. 13/1:

> Apparebit repentína   dies magna Dómini

This, in turn, may be divided into two separate lines, of eight and seven syllables, respectively; the following stanza, by Philip the Chancellor (*Oxford Book,* no. 251/1–6), can be described as 3 ($8p$, $7pp$) rhyming *a b a b a b*:

> Pange lingua Magdalénae
> lacrimas et gáudium
> sonent voces laude plénae
> de concentu córdium
> ut concordent philoménae
> turturis suspírium

Repetition of the eight-syllable line produced the very popular stanza, rhyming *a a b c c b,* known either as the Victorine Sequence, from its major author, Adam of St. Victor (*ca.* 1110–*ca.* 1180), or as the *Stabat mater dolorosa* stanza, after one of its most famous examples (*Oxford Book,* no. 285/1–6):

> Stabat mater dolorósa
> iuxta crucem lacrimósa
> dum pendebat fílius
> cuius animam geméntem
> contristantem et doléntem
> pertransivit gládius

Variations on the pattern of 2 ($8p$) 1 ($7pp$) 2 ($8p$) 1 ($7pp$) *a a b c c b* are achieved by splitting the eight-syllable line into two halves, producing a half-stanza, thus: $4p4p$ $4p4p$ $7pp$; for instance, *Oxford Book,* no. 147/4–6:

> dulce melos   tangat caelos
> dulce lignum   dulci dignum
> credimus melodia,

or by increasing the number of eight-syllable lines, to three and then to four, as in the same poem, lines 68–72:

> Assistentes crucis laudi
> consecrator crucis audi
> atque servos tuae crucis
> post hanc vitam serae lucis
> transfer ad palatia

This meter became one of the most popular in the later Middle Ages for devotional hymns.

Eight-syllable lines. (1) 8 *pp.* The quantitative iambic dimeter consisted of two iambic metra ($\smile - \smile -$), as in St. Ambrose's *Hymn at Cockcrow* (*Oxford Book,* no. 9/1–2):

> Āetērnĕ rērūm cōndĭtōr
> nōctēm dĭēmquĕ quī rĕgīs

The rhythmical reading of this line produced $8pp$, as in Marbod, *Oxford Book,* no. 152/1–4:

> Omnes immundi currite
> fons patet indulgentiae
> nullus desperet veniam
> qui servat paenitentiam

(2) $8p$. This line could have arisen from a rhythmical reading of the trochaic dimeter ($- \smile - \smile / - \smile - \smile$), but the latter is so rare that the rhythmical line is best explained as arising from the first half of a rhythmical trochaic septenarius. Marbod formed quatrains of it, as in *Oxford Book,* no. 151/1–4:

> Cum recordor quanta cúra
> sum sectatus peritúra
> et quam dura sub censúra
> mors exercet sua iúra

Seven-syllable lines. (1) $7p$. The quantitative iambic dimeter catalectic consisted of two iambic metra, with the penultimate syllable suppressed, as in Prudentius' *Hymn Before Sleep* (*Oxford Book,* no. 17/1–2):

> Ădēs pătēr sŭprēmē
> quēm nēmŏ vīdĭt ūnquām

The rhythmical reading of this line produces $7p$, as in John of Howden, *Oxford Book,* no. 271/1–2:

> Maria laus divína
> virginea regína

(2) *7pp*. This could have arisen from the quantitative trochaic dimeter catalectic, as in Horace, *Odes* II, 18, 39:

pāupĕrēm lăbōrĭbŭs

This line, however, is never independent in classical verse. The rhythmical line, like that of *8p*, is best explained as the second half of a rhythmical trochaic septenarius. With an *a b a b* rhyme scheme it appears in Walter of Châtillon, *Oxford Book,* no. 193/1–4:

Importuna Véneri
redit brumae glácies
redit equo céleri
Jovis intempéries

Twelve-syllable lines. The quantitative asclepiad has as its nucleus the choriamb (‑ ᴗ ᴗ ‑); the popular Lesser Asclepiad has two choriambs, as in the first line of Horace's first *Ode:*

Maēcēnās ătăvīs ēdĭtĕ rēgĭbŭs

The rhythmical reading of this line produced a twelve-syllable line split into two halves, *6pp* + *6pp*, as in *Oxford Book,* no. 101/1–2:

O Roma nóbilis orbis et dómina
cunctarum úrbium excellentissima

Quatrains of this line, rhyming *a a a a,* were very popular for satirical verse such as the famous *Apocalypse of Golias* (extract in *Oxford Book,* no. 203/1–4):

A tauro torrida lampade Cynthii
fundente iacula ferventis radii
umbrosas nemoris latebras adii
explorans gratiam lenis Favonii

Other rhythmical combinations. There is no space here, nor is there any need, to list all the possible rhythmical verse lines, whether based on quantitative lines or not, or the combinations of such lines into rhyming stanzas; rhythmical imitations of sapphics, alcaics, adonics, and other meters are occasionally found, and for many lines of fixed syllable length one can find a corresponding quantitative line. Once the basic rhythmical pattern of iambics and trochaics had been accepted, there was no limit to the invention of new rhythms or new rhyme patterns. One particular new rhythm and stanza became very popular, that known as the Goliardic line and stanza, consisting of *7pp* + *6p*, usually in quatrains rhyming *a a a a.* This stanza is used for some devo-

tional verse, but is usually employed in satirical poems, or, in the case of the famous *Archpoet's Confession* (*Oxford Book,* no. 183/45–48), personal verse:

Meum est propósitum in taberna móri
ut sint vina próxima morientis óri
Tunc cantabunt laétius angelorum chóri
Sit Deus propítius huic potatóri

Walter of Châtillon and some of his followers wrote the Goliardic stanza *cum auctoritate*—that is, with the final line of each stanza from a classical poet, usually in dactylic meter as in Walter of Châtillon's poem (*Oxford Book,* no. 198/1–4) in which the last line is from Juvenal's first satire:

Missus sum in vineam circa horam nonam
suam quisque nititur vendere personam
ergo quia cursitant omnes ad coronam
semper ego auditor tantum nunquamne reponam

THE SEQUENCE

This analysis has so far concentrated on meters that (apart from the Goliardic line) could have had antecedents in Classical Latin quantitative verse; music has been ignored. Music, however, may have had much to do with the development of certain rhythmical forms, as it certainly did with the sequence. The liturgy contained many nonmetrical verses, such as the Psalms; the pattern of verse followed by response naturally produced a tendency to alternation, and it is in this alternation that we see the development of the sequence. Between the reading of the Epistle and the Gospel, melodies developed extending the final *-a* of the *Alleluia.* In time, these melodies were fitted with words, to be sung by the choir. Tunes acquired their own names, and words were written to fit the music: examples of tune names can be seen in the secular poems among the Cambridge Songs, which are designated the "Modus Liebinc," "Modus Ottinc," etc. (that is, to be sung to the Lieb tune, the Otto tune, and so forth). This practice is seen again 300 years later in the *Red Book of Ossory,* where sacred songs by Richard Ledrede are headed with the opening words of the secular songs, to the tunes of which the sacred hymns were to be sung.

The words attached to the melodies were known as a *sequentia* or *prosa.* Sequences of French origin first demonstrated their origin in the *Alleluia* by ending every line with *-a,* but German sequences differed: the German sequence is associated with Notker Balbulus. The choir would sing the first verse together, and from then on each half of the choir would alternate stanzas, concluding on a shared stanza. It is this alternation that determines the sequence. With the introduction of rhyme, reinforced by the alternation between two halves of the choir, elaborate rhyme schemes developed. The Victorine sequence can be described in terms of either its musical origin (the alternating stanzas) or its metrical form, 2(8p) 1(7pp) 2(8p) 1(7pp) *a a b c c b.* The sequence is primarily a religious form, but was soon extended into secular use: many of the *Carmina burana* are love lyrics in sequence form.

BIBLIOGRAPHY

Edmond Faral, ed., *Les arts poétiques du XIIᵉ et XIIIᵉ siècle* (1924); Paul Klopsch, *Einführung in die mittellateinische Verslehre* (1972); Dag Norberg, *Introduction à l'étude de la versification latine mediévale* (1958); Frederick J. E. Raby, ed., *Oxford Book of Medieval Latin Verse,* 2nd ed. (1959).

A. G. RIGG

[See also **Anthologies; Classical Literary Studies; Cursus; Hymns, Latin; Poetry, Liturgical; Sequence;** and individual authors.]

LATIN STATES IN GREECE. After the French and Venetian crusaders captured Constantinople in 1204, making it the capital of a short-lived Latin empire, they established lordships for themselves throughout Greece and the Aegean islands, an area they called Romania. Matteo Orsini of Apulia had already taken the Ionian islands of Cephalonia (Kefallinía) and Zante (Zákinthos). The Byzantine Empire lay in fragments, and its nobles held on to what they could.

In October 1204 the crusaders agreed to the Partition of Romania, a wholesale division of Byzantine territory. The Latin emperor received one quarter, while the remaining three quarters were divided evenly between the Venetians and the other crusaders.

Boniface of Montferrat, the new king of Thessalonica (Thessaloniki), then marched south to take possession of the allotted lands and to distribute them as fiefs to his companions. The Byzantine lord of Nauplia, Leo Sgouros, took his stand at the pass of Thermopylae, but one look at the Frankish cavalry sent him racing back to Acrocorinth. The town of Bodonitsa (modern Mendenitsa), commanding the pass, was granted to Guido Pallavicini. Ancient Am-

phissa was bestowed on Thomas of Autremencourt (de Stromoncourt), who built the castle of Salona above it. Otho de la Roche from Burgundy was recognized as lord of Athens, and by 1211 held Thebes as well. The coastal island called Negroponte (ancient Euboea) was taken by James of Avesnes, who was soon replaced by Ravano dalle Carceri of Verona. Boniface forced the isthmus of Corinth, left a detachment to besiege Leo Sgouros at Corinth, and went on with the main body of his troops to lay siege to Nauplia.

Meanwhile, Geoffroi de Villehardouin, nephew of the chronicler, had gone to the Holy Land and was on his way to rejoin the crusaders on the Bosporus when rough weather forced his ship to put in at Modon (Methone). He assisted a local magnate in taking some nearby land, and then went to join Boniface before Nauplia. There he found an old friend, William of Champlitte, and apparently convinced him that it would be easy to conquer the rich land of the Peloponnese, commonly known as the Morea. With 100 knights and 400 mounted sergeants they set out early in 1205. In the northwest they took Patras, Andravida, and Pondikos. Bypassing Arcadia, they occupied the land to the south, and beat off a large Greek army led by Michael Doukas of Epiros. Local nobles (*archontes*) acknowledged Latin sovereignty, were confirmed in their property and customs, and were readily assimilated into the feudal system taking shape in the Morea. On 19 November 1205, William of Champlitte was recognized as the ruler of the Morea, with the title "prince of Achaea," by Pope Innocent III, and the land was divided into fiefs.

Venice, deeply involved in the enterprise from the beginning, was not to be left without its rewards. The partition of the empire gave the republic more land that it could occupy. In 1206 it sent out a fleet which took Corfu, then Modon and Coron (Korone) in the southwest Morea, sailing thence to begin a long struggle for control of Crete. On Negroponte the Venetian bailli acquired more and more influence until that island became the Signoria's center of power in the Levant. But the Venetian government did not have the resources to take over the Aegean islands, and left this to private citizens.

Venetians had long lived in the East, and with the Latin conquest of 1204 they came close to setting up an autonomous state there. In 1205 the Venetian governor in Constantinople, Marino Zeno, entitled himself "podesta and despot of the empire of Romania and lord of a quarter and a half of the same

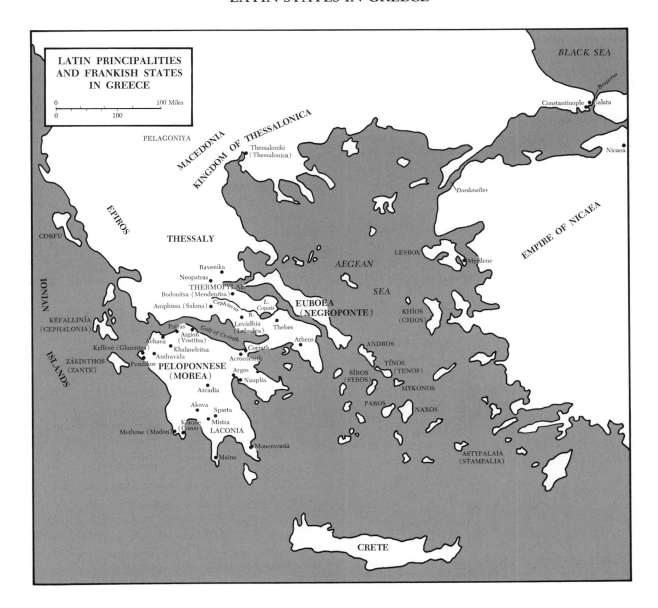

LATIN PRINCIPALITIES AND FRANKISH STATES IN GREECE

0   100 Miles
0   100

empire." Within a decade, however, the *comune* had made it clear that there could be no more talk of a "second Venice," and the title was taken over by the doge at home.

In 1207 a wealthy Venetian, Marco Sanudo, equipped a fleet at his own expense, and with several compatriots took possession of the Aegean islands. He kept Naxos, Paros, and Syros (Síros) for himself, assumed the title of duke of the Archipelago (*Egeopelagus,* from Greek *Aighaion pelagos,* the Aegean Sea), and was recognized as a vassal of the Latin emperor in Constantinople. Among his own vassals were his cousin Marino Dandolo of Andros, the Ghisi family on Tenos (Tínos) and Mykonos, and the Querini on Astypalaia (Stampalia).

Venice thus evolved a twofold structure in its eastern empire. There were the direct possessions, tightly under the control of the central government, administered by baillis, consuls, rectors, castellans, or on Crete dukes, who were appointed by the *comune* usually for two-year terms with clearly limited powers. Then there were the feudal lordships in the Aegean, whose rulers were vassals of the Latin emperor (this title continued even after the Byzantine reconquest of Constantinople in 1261). But these feudal lords were also citizens of Venice and were never allowed to forget it, for their domains came ever more under the rule of the central government. In 1395 the pilgrim Nicola de Martoni observed that there were many lords throughout the Aegean sub-

377

ject to the duke of the Archipelago, but that "all of them are under the rule of Venice."

By early 1209, William of Champlitte had died, and Geoffroi de Villehardouin assumed power in the Morea. In May, at a parliament held in Ravenika, he was confirmed by the Latin emperor Henry. In June he formed an alliance with Venice, recognizing its suzerainty and granting it extensive commercial privileges. Joining forces with Otho de la Roche of Athens, he seized the strongly fortified Acrocorinth, then Argos, and, in 1210–1211, Nauplia; he imposed his rule over Arcadia, Laconia, and Sparta. This enabled him to grant fiefs to the increasing number of young knights who came, mostly from France, to settle in the Morea. A conflict with the Roman church over the secularization of ecclesiastical property was settled by negotiation in 1223.

The despot of Epiros, Theodore, captured Thessalonica from the Latins in 1224 and soon had all of Macedonia and Thessaly in his power. A few years later Geoffroi de Villehardouin died, leaving the Morea to his son Geoffroi. Marco Sanudo died about the same time, and Otho de la Roche retired to Burgundy, leaving his lands to his nephew Guy. Although Guy's domain was known as the duchy of Athens, its center was actually Thebes with its flourishing silk industry.

Geoffroi II, prince of Achaea and lord of the Morea, lived in almost legendary splendor with an entourage of eighty knights with golden spurs. Young nobles came from France to learn knighthood and to seek fame and fortune. Geoffroi was generally regarded as kind and just, concerned with the welfare of the common people. He was succeeded in 1246 by his brother William II. Both were capable rulers and well liked by the Greeks; their reigns marked an unparalleled period of peace and prosperity. Their courts were renowned throughout the West for magnificent tournaments and displays of knightly gallantry. William further secured possession of the Morea by taking Monemvasia and erecting the powerful fortresses of Mistra and Maina. He was connected by marriage with the French royal family and joined King Louis IX for the Egyptian part of his crusade in 1249–1250.

Society in the Morea was highly structured according to the feudal pattern, with several high barons, peers of the prince, at the top. Holding fiefs from them were knights, sergeants, and local archontes (gentils hommes grecs), who had been the landed proprietors under Byzantine rule and whose lives were probably not much changed under the Latins. Even less changed was the lot of the peasants, the old paroikoi. The Chronicle of Morea provides abundant information about the feudal organization of the principality, and the Assizes of Romania delineate its law code. Although Andravida served as the administrative capital, the prince often resided in Kalamata or elsewhere; the chief port was Glarentsa (Kyllēnē), on the west coast.

There seems to have been a high degree of cultural exchange. The Latins came to speak Greek, and French chansons were translated into Greek. Both Latins and Greeks took part in the government. Marriages between the two seem to have been common, with the children generally becoming Orthodox. The sons of illegitimate unions, gasmouloi, eventually played an important role in the Byzantine reconquest.

While the diocesan framework of the church was retained, almost all the Greek bishops were replaced by Latin ones. The metropolitan sees were Thebes, Athens, Corinth, and, most important, Patras. The Latin church in Greece was a church without roots, but a prelacy or canonry there could provide an ambitious cleric with revenue and the beginnings of an ecclesiastical career. Some Latin monasteries were established, while older Greek ones remained and even expanded. Despite occasional restrictions, the Greek priests continued to minister to their people.

In 1255 a disputed feudal succession in Negroponte pitted William II against Venice, with the other Frankish lords lining up on either side. Bitter warfare ensued until William won a clear victory in 1258. But more serious threats were taking shape. William had formed an alliance with Despot Michael of Epiros, who hoped to take territory from the Byzantine emperor in Nicaea. But there Michael VIII Palaiologos had usurped power and, early in 1259, sent a strong army under his brother John to Macedonia. In the summer the forces met in battle on the plain of Pelagoniya in Macedonia. Michael of Epiros deserted his Frankish allies, and his son John went over to the enemy. The Latins were surrounded and defeated, and William and many of his knights were taken prisoner.

The Byzantine army then marched through Thessaly and plundered Thebes. Michael Palaiologos insisted that William surrender the Morea, but he refused. The Byzantines recaptured Constantinople on 25 July 1261; William gave in and ceded the important strongholds of Mistra, Monemvasia, and Maina. Toward the end of the year this action was ratified by the parliament of Achaea, composed mostly of Frankish ladies whose husbands were in Byzantine dungeons. William and his knights were then set free, but the coming of Byzantine rule to Mistra meant that the principality of Achaea would never really be at peace again.

The peace agreed to in 1261 quickly collapsed, and warfare between Latins and Greeks continued sporadically. Seeking to strengthen his much-weakened position, William turned to Charles of Anjou, who had become master of Sicily. On 24 May 1267, before Pope Clement IV in Viterbo, William ceded his lands to Charles, with William retaining his lands and his rights for the period of his life. The two further agreed that William's daughter Isabel would marry one of Charles's sons, who would succeed to Achaea on William's death.

On 1 May 1278, William II died in Kalamata, and since Isabel's husband, Philip, had died the previous year, Achaea passed to Philip's father, Charles of Anjou, who governed it through baillis. He died in 1285 and was succeeded by his oldest son, Charles II. On 16 September 1289, Philip's widow, Isabel, married Florent of Hainault, and Charles granted Achaea to her.

Florent proved himself a brave knight and a wise ruler, whose reign was generally prosperous. There was some fighting with the Byzantines, and a long conflict over feudal rights in the duchy of Athens, ruled by Helena, regent for her son Guy de la Roche, and her second husband, Hugh de Brienne. In 1296 the conflict was settled in Florent's favor, but he fell ill and died, probably on 23 January 1297, leaving Isabel with a three-year-old daughter, Mahaut. While the little girl was betrothed to the young duke of Athens, in 1301 Isabel married Philip, nephew of the count of Savoy, who was invested as prince.

While brave, Philip was autocratic and provoked some clashes with the Moreote barons. His feudal obligations to the Angevins of Naples involved him in some desultory warfare in Epiros. In the spring of 1304 he convened a parliament in Corinth which turned into three weeks of jousting and festivities. But Philip had not performed the required homage and was reluctant to continue fighting for the Angevins in Epiros. As a result, on 5 June 1306, King Charles declared him deposed, although Isabel kept protesting until her death in 1311.

The principality then reverted to Philip of Taranto, son of Charles II, who made a show of military force in Greece, although his army soon fell apart in Epiros. He returned to Italy and named the young duke of Athens, Guy II, who had married Isabel's

daughter Mahaut, as his bailli for Achaea. But Guy died on 5 October 1308. The duchy of Athens was then awarded to his cousin Walter de Brienne.

In the meantime, a band of mercenaries, the Catalan Grand Company, led by a former Templar, Roger de Flor, which had been fighting against the Angevins in Sicily, entered Byzantine service and was employed against the Turks in Asia Minor. But Roger was murdered by the Byzantines, and the company ravaged Thrace and Macedonia. In 1310 they were hired by Walter de Brienne and aided him in subduing Thessaly. The duke then refused to give the Catalans the land they expected as well as their back pay. To get rid of them he assembled a huge army, including 700 knights, which met the much smaller Catalan force on 15 March 1311 on the banks of the Cephissus River and Lake Copais. The French chivalry charged recklessly into the swampy ground and was slaughtered. Almost all the knights were killed, including de Brienne. The Catalan company took over Thebes and Athens and the French duchy of Athens ended. The Customs of Barcelona were adopted as the law code, and the title of duke was given to the royal family of Sicily and later of Aragon, who administered the duchy by a vicar-general.

The popes at Avignon excommunicated the Catalans at regular intervals but with little effect. Venice was generally able to deal with the situation by diplomatic means. Walter de Brienne, whose father had lost the duchy, made several unsuccessful efforts to regain it. Under the leadership of Alfonso Fadrique, son of King Frederick of Sicily, vicar-general from 1317 to 1330, the Catalan duchy prospered. In 1318, Don Alfonso captured Neopatras to the north, and a second duchy was formed. The Catalans mixed more and more with the native Greeks and, despite wars and uprisings, continued to prosper. But civil strife broke out in the 1360's and 1370's, and external foes drew near: the Navarrese "White Company" and the Acciaiuoli from Corinth.

As for the Morea, in 1313 it once again reverted to a Villehardouin. In that year Mahaut, daughter of Isabel and widow of Guy II of Athens, received the Morea from Philip of Taranto and married Louis of Burgundy as part of larger dynastic arrangements involving the houses of France, Naples, and Burgundy.

In the summer of 1315 the infante Ferdinand, son of King James I of Majorca, claimed the Morea and landed near Glarentsa. Louis gathered a large army, including Byzantine troops. On 5 July 1316, Ferdinand was defeated and killed. But Louis died suddenly a month later, leaving Mahaut a widow again. In January 1322, after some years of uncertainty, the principality was given to John of Gravina, youngest brother of King Robert of Naples; Mahaut died in captivity a few years later.

The instability and weakness of Frankish rule in the Morea were in marked contrast to the increasing strength of the Byzantines operating from their base at Mistra in the southern Peloponnese. By 1322 the Byzantines had reduced the Franks to the coastal regions in the north and west. The most prosperous of the remaining Frankish lands was the ecclesiastical barony of Patras with its busy port and fertile hinterland, ruled by its archbishop. Practically independent, it was on good terms with the papacy and Venice. Not far away were the flourishing baronies of Vostitsa (Aigion) and Khalandrítsa, both of which were sold by their French lords, the first to the Florentine Nerio Acciaiuoli and the second to the Genoese Martin Zaccaria.

In 1325 a costly expedition led by John of Gravina against the Byzantines and the Orsini family in Epiros failed completely, and John contented himself with appointing baillis to govern the Morea. In 1332 he sold his rights to Robert, son of his brother Philip of Taranto and Catherine of Valois.

Catherine, as regent for Robert, led a large, well-equipped expedition to the Morea in 1338. She was accompanied by her three sons and her close adviser Nicholas Acciaiuoli, a Florentine who had risen rapidly in Naples and had already acquired some fiefs in Greece. They remained in the Morea for two and a half years, trying to enforce feudal obedience and strengthen the defenses of the principality.

By this time, however, it was clear that the Morea needed a resident ruler. The barons began negotiations to give it to John Kantakouzenos, then Byzantine grand domestic, or to King James II of Majorca. These efforts came to nothing, and the situation in the Morea, except for Patras, continued to deteriorate.

Although the Venetian government was deeply involved in the affairs of Greece, the Genoese government was not. There were Genoese colonies on the Black Sea and the important one of Galata across the Golden Horn from Constantinople. Other territories on the Asiatic coast and on Chios were governed by merchant companies such as the Maona. In 1354 the Genoese privateer Francesco Gattilusio helped John V Palaiologos recover his capital and, as a reward, was given the emperor's sister and the island of Mytilene (Lesbos). There he established a

lordship which remained in his family until taken by the Turks in 1462. Mytilene became a naval and commercial power and played an important role in the transmission of classical learning to the Italian humanists.

While Venice had diplomatic and commercial establishments in Constantinople and elsewhere, its territories were concentrated in lower (bassa) Romania, the most important being the islands of Crete and Negroponte. It exercised a more indirect control over the duchy of the Archipelago and other islands held by Venetian nobles. In the Morea its key possessions were Modon and Coron, "the two eyes of the comune." Toward the end of the fourteenth century it acquired the area around Argos and Nauplia, and also Corfu, which it held until its own demise in 1797.

Venetian colonial policy focused on keeping the trade routes to the east open; for this end naval bases were required, not large tracts of land. In 1381 the chancellor, Raffain Caresini, wrote that "the proper task of Venice is to cultivate the sea and to pay less heed to the land." Not following this policy on Crete caused great trouble and expense.

Venice relied on a highly centralized system in which everything affecting its colonies was debated in the senate, and inspectors (provisores) were sent out at regular intervals. The republic treated the church well and in return received the support of Rome. Venetian clerics, staunchly loyal, were named to influential positions in the Latin church in Greece.

The duchy of the Archipelago, ruled by the Sanudo family from its castle on Naxos, flourished for a century or so before pirate raids began taking their toll. To obtain assistance the dukes had to submit to stricter Venetian control. A good example was the second marriage of Fiorenza Sanudo, daughter and heiress of Duke John I. When he died in 1361 a spirited diplomatic struggle was waged by Venice to keep her from marrying a non-Venetian; it ended with her being kidnapped, conveyed to Crete, and forced to marry the republic's choice, Niccolò Sanudo "Spezzabanda."

Fiorenza was succeeded in 1371 by her son by her first marriage, Niccolò dalle Carceri, who was so disliked that he was assassinated in 1383. A new dynasty was then founded by Francesco Crispo. The duchy, though, lived in constant dread of Turkish pirates and suffered greatly from their raids.

The Ghisi family on Tenos and Mykonos died out in 1390, and Venice took over directly. Pietro Zeno, a great statesman and lord of Andros, died in 1427, and the Sommaripa family succeeded. The Querini of Stampalia even extended their dominions. Most of the nobles, however, were dependent on the limited assistance that Venice could provide.

William II, proclaimed duke of the Archipelago in 1453, the year in which Constantinople fell to the Ottomans, was compelled to pay them tribute the following year. The fortunes of the islands then varied according to whether war or peace reigned between Venice and the Turks. The Crispis survived in their duchy only with difficulty and were finally removed by the sultan in 1566.

Although in steady decline from the 1360's, the principality of Achaea still attracted claimants. Despite a challenge by Hugh de Lusignan, Philip II of Taranto was recognized as prince in 1370; he was, however, more interested in Neapolitan affairs. After his death in 1373, his widow, Joanna, was acknowledged as princess. In 1376 she leased the principality to the Hospitalers for five years, but they found it too costly and returned it to her in 1381. She was soon imprisoned by Charles of Durazzo, who had been invested as king of Naples by Pope Urban VI. James of Les Baux next claimed the principality and was recognized by the Navarrese mercenaries there. But he died in 1383, and the Navarrese, led by Peter Bordo de St. Superan, became the real rulers of Achaea.

In 1387, Urban VI cited feudal law to claim the principality of Achaea for the Holy See and appointed Archbishop Paolo Foscari of Patras as his regent. Foscari apparently did not take it seriously and left the Navarrese in charge. Backed by Avignon, Amadeo of Savoy put forth a tenuous claim and for five years (1386–1391) engaged in convoluted diplomatic negotiations with all parties, but nothing came of it all.

Meanwhile the Byzantine despot in Mistra, Theodore Palaiologos, seized Argos, which Venice had purchased from Marie of Enghien. The Venetians enlisted the aid of the Navarrese against him and his father-in-law, Nerio Acciaiuoli. Nerio had been lord of Corinth since at least 1372, and in 1388 took possession of the acropolis at Athens. The Navarrese captured him in September 1389, and in May of the following year he was freed after, among other things, agreeing to obtain the surrender of Argos. But it was not until 1394 that the despot handed it over. In February 1395 the Navarrese joined forces with the Turks to take Akova from the Byzantines. In June, however, the Navarrese were themselves defeated, and St. Superan was held captive until Venice paid his ransom six months later.

Nerio Acciaiuoli died on 25 September 1394, leaving Corinth to his daughter Francesca, wife of Count Carlo Tocco of Cephalonia. Theodore regarded Corinth as his and used force to make good his claim. In 1397 a large Turkish army ravaged the Morea, taking and sacking Argos in June and besieging Acrocorinth. In desperation the despot sold Corinth, and then the entire despotate, to the Hospitalers, but soon bought it back.

Nerio Acciaiuoli willed Athens to the church of St. Mary (the Parthenon) under the protection of Venice. His illegitimate son Antonio had been given Levádhia (Lebadea) and Thebes, and in 1402 he also took Athens from the Venetians. After a long and generally peaceful reign, Antonio was succeeded in 1435 by a young cousin, Nerio II. By the time Nerio died in 1451, Athens was tributary to the Turks, and on 4 June 1456 was finally taken by them, with Thebes suffering the same fate four years later.

St. Superan died in November 1402, leaving the principality of Achaea under the regency of his widow, Maria, sister of Centurione Zaccaria, baron of Arcadia, one of the most powerful nobles in the shrinking realm. In April 1404 he paid the king of Naples to invest him with the principality. His brother Stephen became archbishop of Patras and had to contend with fiscal problems and Turkish raids.

Emperor Manuel II Palaiologos spent a year (1415–1416) combatting rebellious nobles and strengthening the authority of his son Theodore II in the Morea. His oldest son, John, inflicted several defeats upon the Zaccaria brothers in 1417–1418. In 1423 a huge Turkish army devastated the peninsula, but that did not bring Greeks and Latins together. In June 1424, Theodore II captured Centurione, and, since Stephen had died in January, the power of the Zaccaria family was finished. In 1427–1428, Carlo Tocco was forced to surrender the last of his lands in the Morea. In 1430, Constantine Palaiologos captured Patras. The previous year his brother Thomas compelled Centurione to give him most of his possessions and his daughter in marriage. On Centurione's death in 1432, Thomas took the rest of the land, and the principality of Achaea came to an end.

With these events, the whole of the Morea, except the Venetian strongholds, was under Byzantine rule. By 1460, however, it had all been taken by the Turks.

BIBLIOGRAPHY

Antoine Bon, *La Morée franque: Recherches historiques, topographiques, et archéologiques sur la princi-*

pauté d'Achaïe (1205–1430), 2 vols. (1969); George Dennis, *Byzantium and the Franks, 1350–1420* (1982); Giorgio Fedalto, *La chiesa latina in Oriente*, 3 vols. (1973–1978); David Jacoby, *Société et démographie à Byzance et en Romanie latine* (1975), and *Recherches sur la Méditerranée orientale du XIIᵉ au XVᵉ siècle* (1979); Raymond J. Loenertz, *Byzantina et Franco-Graeca*, 2 vols. (1970–1975); Jean Longnon, "The Frankish States in Greece, 1204–1311," in Kenneth Setton, ed., *A History of the Crusades*, II, *The Later Crusades, 1189–1311* (1969), 235–276, and III, *The Fourteenth and Fifteenth Centuries* (1975), 104–339, for chapters by Anthony Luttrell, Kenneth Setton, and Peter Topping; Harold Lurier, *Crusaders as Conquerors: The Chronicle of Morea* (1964); Kenneth Setton, "The Latins in Greece and the Aegean from the Fourth Crusade to the End of the Middle Ages," in *Cambridge Medieval History*, 2nd ed., IV, pt. 1 (1966), 388–429, 908–938, *Catalan Domination of Athens 1311–1388* (1948, rev. repr. 1975); Freddy Thiriet, *La Romanie vénitienne au moyen âge* (1959; 1975); Peter Topping, ed. and trans., *Feudal Institutions as Revealed in the Assizes of Romania, the Law Code of Frankish Greece* (1949), with trans. of the *Assizes of Romania*, and *Studies on Latin Greece, 1205–1715* (1977); Denis Zakythinos, *Le despotat grec de Morée*, 2 vols. (1932–1953; rev. ed. by C. Maltezou, 1975).

GEORGE T. DENNIS

[See also **Boniface of Montferrat; Byzantine Empire; Catalan Company; Crete; Crusades and Crusader States; Epiros, Despotate of; Latin Empire of Constantinople; Venice; Villehardouin, Geoffroi de.**]

LATINI, BRUNETTO (*ca.* 1220–1294), Florentine notary, magistrate, politician, and author. His fame rests mainly on the central role assigned to him in canto xv of the *Inferno*, on the basis of which a "master-pupil" relationship has been generally assumed between Latini and Dante. Although he is traditionally considered a minor figure in the history of Italian literature, there is evidence to suggest that Latini had a significant influence on late-thirteenth-century Florentine political and cultural life, as stated by the historian Giovanni Villani, some fifty years after Latini's death:

> He was a great philosopher and an excellent teacher of rhetoric, both in speaking and in writing . . . and he was secretary of our commune. He was a worldly man, but we have mentioned him, because he was the initiator and master in refining the Florentines, in making them perceive the importance of good speech, and in teaching them how to guide and sustain our republic according to the art of politics.

Villani's statement stresses the didactic function of Latini's life and works, extending to the whole city what for Dante had been expressed in a more personal and subjective way: "For in my memory is fixed, and now saddens my heart, the dear, kind, paternal image of you, when in the world hour by hour you taught me how man makes himself eternal" (*Inferno*, xv, 82–85).

Latini's involvement in the political life of Florence coincided with the most turbulent portion of the city's history. He belonged to the Guelph faction, and came to prominence in the period immediately preceding the tragic battle of Montaperti (4 September 1260), in which the opposing Ghibelline forces, led by Farinata degli Uberti and supported by King Manfred of Sicily, inflicted a disastrous defeat on the Florentine Guelphs. Since war appeared to be imminent, Latini was sent on a mission to Spain to seek an alliance with Alfonso X the Wise of Castile. News of the defeat at Montaperti reached him on the return journey, probably near Montpellier, as Latini himself relates in the *Tesoretto*. He remained in France for the next six years. There he practiced law, enjoying the protection and patronage of a rich Florentine Guelph who is praised in the three major works written during the exile: *Tesoretto, Trésor,* and *Rettorica*. Latini returned to Florence after the defeat of the Ghibellines at the battle of Benevento (28 February 1266), in which King Manfred was killed. His importance in the political life of the city is evident from the numerous and important positions he held thereafter.

In Dante's works there are other references to, and echoes of, Latini. The first, and most explicit, occurs in *De vulgari eloquentia* (I, xiii, 1), where Latini is relegated, with other Tuscan poets, to the category of "municipal" poets (as opposed to Dante's, Cino da Pistoia's, and Guido Cavalcanti's "new style") for their obscurity and for their "plebeian" language. A further, though less explicit, reference to Latini is found in *Convivio* (I, xi), where Dante condemns to "perpetual infamy . . . the evil men of Italy, who commend another people's vernacular and scorn their own" and alludes to the *Trésor*, written in French.

Despite Dante's apparently terse rejection of his mentor, modern scholars have provided evidence for a complex, and at times subtle, series of references to Latini's works in Dante. The opening canto of the *Inferno*, for example, is clearly reminiscent of the *Tesoretto*. Opening with an image of the grandeur of Florence, and with references to the mission to

Spain, the anguish at the news of the defeat of Montaperti, and of the exile from Florence, the *Tesoretto* (1265 or 1266) is an allegorical, didactic poem of close to 3,000 rhyming couplets. Though it is rooted in a specific personal and political reality, the historical and autobiographical elements soon give way to a series of encounters with allegorical figures: Natura; the Empress Virtue, attended by the cardinal and other virtues; and the God of Love.

Traditionally considered an artistic failure, the *Tesoretto,* upon closer examination, reveals a creative treatment of sources (Boethius' *Consolation of Philosophy,* Alan of Lille's *Planctus naturae,* and the *Ovide moralisé,* to name the most important ones) by which the experience of the protagonist, uprooted from his city and caught up in the chaos of history, is reintegrated into a higher order of existence. This reintegration is not to be interpreted in the context of Christian grace, since it evolves within unmistakable naturalistic parameters, drawing its inspiration from the Platonic cosmological and philosophical tradition of the school of Chartres (William of Conches, Bernard Silvester).

Li livres dou trésor (*ca.* 1265) is a more extensive, three-book prose work in the medieval encyclopedic tradition. The first book provides the reader with an extensive compilation of philosophical, doctrinal, historical, and scientific topics. The principal sources are the Bible, Isidore of Seville, and Orosius. The second book deals mainly with matters of ethics, based on Aristotle's *Nicomachean Ethics,* and with practical economics, William of Conches' *Moralium dogma philosophorum* being its principal source. The third and most important book concerns rhetoric and politics, two subjects that for Latini are inseparable and represent the noblest pursuit of the civic-minded citizen: "the highest science and the noblest profession ... because it teaches us to rule ... a people and a commune in times of peace and war, according to reason and justice" (*Trésor,* I, iv, 5).

For this concept Latini relied on his translation of the first part of Cicero's *De inventione.* The latter also formed the substance of the *Rettorica,* the last main work written in exile, which can be defined as a manual for the orator-politician. Latini's adaptation of Cicero as the model for a prehumanistic view of existence can be traced in all his works. The *Favolello* (after 1282), which usually accompanies manuscript and printed editions of the *Tesoretto,* is based on Cicero's *De amicitia.* He also translated into Italian three speeches by Cicero: *Pro Ligario,*

Pro Marcello, and *Pro rege Deiotaro.* This revival of Cicero, of great significance for the proper understanding of Latini's rhetorical-political ideas, can be seen as the beginning of what would become a cornerstone of late-fourteenth- and early-fifteenth-century Florentine civic humanism.

The encounter between Latini and Dante in *Inferno* xv, although more specifically pertinent to Dante studies, presents an interesting series of problems that affect our perception of Latini, his life and works, and their impact on the subsequent generations and on Dante himself. The debate continues, for example, on the meaning of the sin against nature (sodomy) for which Latini is condemned. André Pézard has impressively argued that it is to be interpreted allegorically, as Dante's way of condemning Latini for having written the *Trésor* in French, thus violating the sacredness of his natural language. The thesis has not been generally accepted by Dante scholars. Another problem concerns the exact nature of Latini's teachings to Dante. Were they literary or philosophical? How can the affectionate and respectful words of the pilgrim in the *Divine Comedy* be reconciled with such a doctrinally repulsive sin?

The most important and most recent contributions have focused on the differences between the old and the young poet on matters of grace and salvation, which have required a closer reading of Latini's works. This, in turn, has resulted in a long-due reevaluation. What remains unquestioned in the canto is Latini's representiveness as the embodiment of civic-minded duty who could be used to fulminate against the Florentine people for their corruption and for the outrage of Dante's exile, and who could aptly be used to prophesy his greatness.

BIBLIOGRAPHY

Editions. Il Tesoretto, in Gianfranco Contini, ed., *Poeti del duecento,* II (1960), 169–277; *La Rettorica,* and *Pro Ligario,* in Cesare Segre, ed., *Volgarizzamenti del due e trecento* (1969); *Li Livres dou trésor,* Francis J. Carmody, ed. (1948).

Studies. Charles T. Davis, "Education in Dante's Florence," in *Speculum,* **40** (1965), and "Brunetto Latini and Dante," in *Studi medievali,* ser. 3, 8 (1967); Hans Robert Jauss, "Brunetto Latini als allegorischer Dichter," in *Festschrift für Paul Böckmann* (1964), 47–92; Fausto Montanari, "Brunetto Latini," in *Cultura e scuola,* **13–14** (1965); André Pézard, *Dante sous la pluie de feu* (1950).

ELIO COSTA

[See also **Dante; Florence; Guelphs and Ghibellines; Italian Literature: Allegorical and Didactic.**]

LAUDA, or more precisely *lauda spirituale* (spiritual praise), was the most important form of popular religious song in medieval Italy. *Laude* were characterized by nonliturgical texts (usually in the vernacular) and simple musical and formal structures. Texts dealt with familiar religious subjects drawn from the Christian narrative, the most common being the Nativity, Passion, and Resurrection of Christ, and traditional Marian themes.

Lauda texts often made reference to the saints, chief among them St. Francis of Assisi. St. Francis himself is associated with the early history of the *lauda*. His "Canticle of the Sun" opens with the words *Altissimu, omnipotente bon Signore / tue so le laude, la gloria et l'onore* (Good Lord, most high and omnipotent, yours are the praise, the glory, and the honor), and is preserved in at least one source with staves for music. Throughout the Middle Ages, the connection between the *lauda* and the Franciscan friars was strong. The most accomplished *lauda* poet, Jacopone da Todi (1230–1306), was a Franciscan. Performers and composers of *laude* were most often, however, members of lay confraternities. The earliest documented confraternities of *laudesi* (singers of *laude*) appear in the early thirteenth century. By the latter half of the century, some cities in northern Italy boasted as many as forty such institutions. The singing of *laude* was often part of the public religious fervor of such penitential organizations as the *disciplinati* or *flagellanti*. *Laudesi* were most prevalent during times of war and pestilence. Tuscany witnessed an increased interest in the performance of *laude* after the plagues of the mid thirteenth and fourteenth centuries.

The musical history of the medieval *lauda* is somewhat amorphous, owing to the lack of notated musical sources. Only two large collections of monophonic *laude* survive (at Cortona and Florence). The melodies of the *laude* are in general quite simple, although several are set in the more melismatic style associated with the troubadours and trouvères. The form of the *lauda* was that of a refrain *(ripresa)* sung in alternation with a variable number of verses. As with most medieval monophonic repertoires, the rhythmic interpretation of the *laude* remains an open issue. No aspect of the notation of these songs reveals whether they were meant to be performed in free or isochronous rhythm, or according to the principles of the rhythmic modes of contemporary polyphony.

The fourteenth century witnessed a number of developments in *lauda* style, many of which may have originated among the very active confraternities of Florence. These developments included the use of Latin texts and the composition of polyphonic musical settings, usually for two voices. On the basis of the contemporary statutes of religious companies, it appears that such songs were often incorporated into popular offices based on the model of the (somewhat lengthier) liturgical prayer hours. Confraternities often employed professional singers to perform the polyphonic *laude* in these "marginal liturgies," as they have been termed.

Polyphonic *laude* for two or three voices were composed throughout the fifteenth century. Although the newly composed polyphonic *laude* were generally set in a simple syllabic style, some were contrafacta of more elaborate secular art songs *(travestimenti spirituali)*. By the end of the fifteenth century, polyphonic *laude* were serving a new function as musical interludes in the religious dramas *(rappresentazioni sacre)*, popular in Florence through the middle of the sixteenth century.

BIBLIOGRAPHY

Cyrilla Barr, "Lauda Singing and the Tradition of the Disciplinati Mandato," in *L'ars nova italiana del trecento*, IV (1978); Frank A. D'Accone, "Le compagnie dei laudesi in Firenze durante l'ars nova," in *L'ars nova italiana del trecento*, II (1969); Fernando Liuzzi, *La lauda e i primordi della melodia italiana* (1935); John Stevens and William F. Prizer, "Lauda spirituale," in *The New Grove Dictionary of Music and Musicians*, X (1980), 538–543.

MICHAEL P. LONG

[See also **Italian Literature: Drama; Italian Literature: Religious Poetry; Jacopone da Todi.**]

LAUDES (praises), a specific kind of textual formula, or acclamation, to be corporately shouted or sung in praise or glorification of a person or object or in ratification of an act. Acclamations of various kinds were widely used in ancient Greece and Rome and particularly in Byzantium, where they served primarily to express public recognition and approval of important dignitaries and to ratify legislative or judicial decisions and imperial elections. They played much the same role in early ecclesiastical councils of the Christian church, with the election of a bishop often being confirmed by the Christian community through the acclamation "Axios!" (Worthy!).

Acclamations occur in all traditional Christian liturgies. Elaborate litany-like acclamations for honoring public dignitaries evolved during the sixth to the tenth centuries. In Byzantium these included the *polychronia* or *polychronismata,* which wished a long life and prosperity to the emperor, and the *euphemiai,* which were addressed to high ecclesiastics. Such melodies, many of which were performed by two choirs, survive only from the end of the empire, although they may well be much older than the sources that preserve them.

The oldest example of a similar set of acclamations from the Latin West is known as the *Laudes regiae.* The text of these *Laudes* is first found in a Frankish manuscript copied about 796–800, but the music makes its appearance only in early-tenth-century sources. These Carolingian acclamations, probably patterned after contemporary Byzantine salutations, seem to have originally been intended as a panegyric for Charlemagne; even so, they were soon adopted for honoring other important secular dignitaries as well as bishops and popes.

Variant forms of the *Laudes regiae* evolved during the Middle Ages, but all shared in common the following elements: (1) a threefold glorification of Christ, "Christus vincit, Christus regnat, Christus imperat" (Christ conquers, Christ rules, Christ commands), which was sung at least three times to open the *Laudes* and served as a refrain or response sung by all, either in whole or in part, at various points within the acclamations and sometimes at the end; (2) acclamations for the person or persons being acclaimed, each of which was introduced by the petition "Exaudi, Christe" (Hear, O Christ) and was followed by invocations of a number of saints, each coupled with the petition "Tu illum adjuva" (Help him) in an effort to secure the saints' intercessions on behalf of those being acclaimed; (3) a section consisting of several acclamations proclaiming the attributes of Christ; and (4) a series of doxologies addressed to Christ. Sometimes congratulatory wishes addressed to those being acclaimed were appended to the final statement of "Christus vincit"; often found among these was the ancient Roman imperial formula for wishing the emperor a long life: "multos annos."

The music to which the *Laudes* were sung was simple because all present were expected to participate. Rarely did a syllable of text receive more than two notes and most received only one. Also, the range was limited, and in most melodies (which closely resembled one another) it did not exceed a

sixth. It was these same features that, throughout the centuries, kept alive the tradition of singing *Laudes* on certain liturgical occasions and led to the publication in the 1920's of a somewhat modified version of the ancient *Laudes regiae* for use in connection with the newly instituted feast of Christ the King (1925).

BIBLIOGRAPHY

Chants divers pour les saluts du très saint sacrement, 3rd ed. (1924), 251, 252, contains two modern versions of *Laudes.* The second is largely based both textually and musically on the ancient Frankish *Laudes,* whereas the first is a highly distorted work that should be ignored; Ernst H. Kantorowicz, *Laudes regiae: A Study in Medieval Ruler Worship and Liturgical Acclamations* (1946), a comprehensive treatment of the *Laudes regiae* with an appendix by Manfred Bukofzer in which the musical aspects of these are thoroughly explored; Egon Wellesz, *A History of Byzantine Music and Hymnography* (1949; rev. 1961), an excellent study of Byzantine music that treats of the *polychronia* in some detail.

ROBERT J. SNOW

[See also **Acclamations.**]

LAURENTIUS HISPANUS (*d.* 1248), professor of canon law at Bologna and bishop of Orense (1218–1248). He studied at Bologna, possibly heard Azo lecture on Roman law, and most likely taught there from about 1200 to 1214. Huguccio of Pisa greatly influenced his work. After leaving Bologna, he became *Magister scholarum* of Orense in 1214 and was elected bishop in November 1218. A contemporary Spanish historian, Lucas de Túy, who knew Laurentius while he was bishop, called him a "regula iuris"—a rule of law.

Laurentius wrote glosses on Gratian's *Decretum* and the first three *Compilationes antiquae.* His siglum (l.; lau.; laur. his.) appears in the margins of many manuscripts and in the commentaries of later canonists, especially Johannes Teutonicus, Tancred, and Bernardus Parmensis. Until recently, it was thought that he never wrote a complete apparatus to the *Decretum,* or, if he did, that it had not been preserved. But Alfons Stickler has argued that a widely disseminated and influential commentary on the *Decretum,* the *Glossa Palatina* (fourteen manuscripts are known), was Laurentius'. Without a doubt, the *Glossa Palatina* contains much Laurentian material.

Nevertheless it is not certain that the entire work may be attributed to him. Laurentius may also have produced an independent set of glosses to Gratian's tract on penance (*De penitentia*).

The canonists systematically collected and glossed new papal decrees after about 1190, and Laurentius turned his attention to this material. Although the manuscripts of the first three *Compilationes antiquae* contain many glosses atrributed to him, scholars have not located complete commentaries on *Compilationes prima* and *secunda*. These glosses were probably never part of a formal apparatus but taken from his lectures in the classroom. After much debate over which manuscripts preserved Laurentius' commentary to *Compilatio tertia*, Knut W. Nörr established that this work exists in two manuscripts (Karlsruhe, Landesbibliothek, MS Aug. XL and Admont, Stiftsbibliothek, MS 55). Unfortunately, it remains unedited.

Laurentius' thought is marked by intellectual vigor and creativity. Even though the number of his works is small, he influenced canonists for the next century. Johannes Teutonicus incorporated many of his glosses into his Ordinary Gloss to the *Decretum*. In the early fourteenth century, the scriptoria in Bologna attached Laurentius' name to many of the glosses in Johannes' Apparatus that they considered to be his. At the end of the thirteenth century, the most important glossator of his time, Guido de Baysio, wrote a supplementary commentary to Gratian, the *Rosarium*, in which he cited Laurentius frequently. Modern historians have found his thought touching issues of constitutional law particularly interesting.

BIBLIOGRAPHY

None of Laurentius' works have been printed. Antonio García García, *Laurentius Hispanus: Datos biográficos y estudio crítico de sus obras* (1956), Knut Wolfgang Nörr, "Der Apparat des Laurentius zur Compilatio tertia," in *Traditio,* **17** (1961), and Alfons M. Stickler, "Il decretista Laurentius Hispanus," in *Studia Gratiana,* 9 (1966), discuss the manuscript traditions of his works. Stickler also examines his thought touching a number of issues, in particular the relationship of church and state. Laurentius' importance for constitutional thought is discussed in Kenneth Pennington, *Pope and Bishops: The Papal Monarchy in the Twelfth and Thirteenth Centuries* (1984), chap. 1.

KENNETH PENNINGTON

[See also **Glossators; Gratian; Law, Canon.**]

LAURENTIUS OF MONTE CASSINO (early eleventh century), bishop of that city and author of the *Passio sancti Venceslai,* an account in Latin prose of the sufferings of the Bohemian martyr Wenceslas. It contains numerous references to classical Latin authors and occasionally introduces verse. Laurentius follows the common format for such a work—youth, praise of holiness, prophecies—but succeeds, nevertheless, in conveying real feeling for his subject.

BIBLIOGRAPHY

Opera: Laurentius monachus casinensis Archiepiscopus Amalfitanus, Francis Newton, ed. (1973). See also Beda F. Dudik, ed., *Iter Romanum,* I (1855), 304–318; Max Manitius, *Geschichte der lateinischen Literatur des Mittelalters,* II (1923), 304–306.

W. T. H. JACKSON

[See also **Hagiography.**]

LAURENTIUS SAGA, one of the so-called bishops' sagas, is an Icelandic life of Laurentius Kálfsson (1267–1331), bishop of Hólar, Iceland, during 1324–1331; it was written about 1350 by the priest Einar Hafliðason (1370–1393). It is chiefly preserved in two vellum manuscripts, both probably from the sixteenth century. The last pages of the saga have been lost in both manuscripts.

The saga is considered a valuable source for the history of Iceland and the Icelandic church. It tells the story of a young and poor Icelander who becomes a priest and acquires considerable knowledge of canon law. He is educated as a church lawyer in Nidaros (Trondheim), capital of the Norwegian-Icelandic archdiocese, and some of the troubles he encounters in later life develop out of a disagreement over legal and political matters between the archbishops of Nidaros and large portions of the Icelandic clergy in the period after 1264, when the Icelanders had accepted the king of Norway as their ruler. There was from time to time a good deal of friction between the two countries in secular as well as ecclesiastical matters. Another matter of importance was the dispute in Iceland between laymen who wanted to control property donated to the churches and the church officials who fought to establish the right of the church.

Laurentius' struggles with adversity are reported

in some detail. He is imprisoned in Nidaros; becomes an adversary of his benefactor, Jörundr, bishop of Hólar from 1267 to 1313; and one of his Norwegian antagonists becomes bishop of Hólar (Auðunn rauði, 1313–1322), yet Laurentius becomes bishop at the recommendation of Auðunn. There is a distinct patriotic touch to the story and a certain hagiographic delight in its happy ending. The bishop's son Árni Laurentiusson wrote *Dunstanus saga.*

Einar Hafliðason, author of the saga, was much interested in history and is generally believed to have composed *Lögmannsannáll,* an important annalistic compilation. He was educated at Hólar, belonged to this diocese throughout his career, and was close to Laurentius in the bishop's last years.

BIBLIOGRAPHY

Editions. Jón Sigurðsson and Guðbrandur Vigfússon, eds., *Biskupa sögur,* I (1858); Guðni Jónsson, ed., *Byskupa sögur,* III (1948); Einar Hafliðason, *Laurentius saga biskups,* Árni Björnsson, ed. (1969). A translation is Einar Haflidason, *The Life of Laurence Bishop of Hólar in Iceland,* Oliver Elton, trans. (1890).

Studies. Peter G. Foote, "Bischofssaga," in *Reallexikon der germanischen Altertumskunde,* III (1978); Jørgen Højgaard Jørgensen, *Bispesagaer—Laurentius saga* (1978); Magnús Már Lárusson, "Laurentius saga," in *Kulturhistorisk leksikon for nordisk middelalder,* X (1965).

HANS BEKKER-NIELSEN

[See also **Bishops' Sagas; Dunstanus Saga; Iceland.**]

LAUSAVÍSA (pl., *lausavísur*), a single or "loose" Old Norse skaldic stanza. Many hundreds of these eight-line strophes have come down to us. Some were almost certainly composed as independent units; others are probably fragments of longer poems. The styles, genres, and contents of the stanzas are various. *Dróttkvætt* is the dominant meter, but there are *lausavísur* in *munnvorp, hrynhent, runhent, tøglag, kviðuháttr,* and *fornyrðislag.* Love, blame, praise, travel, nature, pictorial, and memorial poetry are all found as single stanzas. The poet may be a king, a farmer, a ghost, or a berserk; he may lament a fallen lord, describe seaweed burning on the beach, or sneer over a boiled sausage.

Almost all *lausavísur* have been preserved in prose narratives from the thirteenth century or later. Sometimes a saga author cites a stanza as a historical footnote to corroborate what his prose says; at other times, he quotes a stanza as the impromptu utterance of a character in his saga. Each of these stanzas normally has an accompanying prose link that adapts the verse to the specific needs of the narrative. It is probably safest to take the details supplied by the saga author regarding the narrative context of a *lausavísa* as nothing more than one medieval author's imaginative reconstruction of how such a stanza came to be uttered.

Most *lausavísur* are attributed to professional skalds. Some of the finest are preserved under the names of Egill Skallagrímsson, Kormákr Ogmundarson, Eyvindr Finnsson skáldaspillir, and Gísli Súrsson. The authenticity of many of the *lausavísur* quoted in thirteenth-century sagas and attributed to skalds who lived two or three centuries earlier is sometimes suspect. Although there is perhaps no reason why early poems—even those composed for informal occasions—could not have been remembered over several centuries, there is also no reason why a man telling or writing a saga in the twelfth or thirteenth centuries could not have attributed a stanza of his own devising (or of someone else's) to his tenth-century hero. We cannot yet distinguish confidently between "genuine" and "spurious" *lausavísur.*

BIBLIOGRAPHY

Peter G. Foote, "Beginnings and Endings: Some Notes on the Study of Scaldic Poetry," in Régis Boyer, ed., *Les vikings et leur civilisation* (1976); Russell G. Poole, "Skaldic Poetry in the Sagas: The Origins, Authorship, Genre, and Style of Some Saga *Lausavísur*" (diss., Toronto, 1975); Klaus von See, "Skaldenstrophe und Sagaprosa," in *Mediaeval Scandinavia,* 10 (1977); Jan de Vries, *Altnordische Literaturgeschichte,* I, 2nd rev. ed. (1964), 167–171, 190–201.

ROBERTA FRANK

[See also **Drottkvætt; Egill Skallagrímsson; Eyvindr Finnsson Skáldaspillir; Gísla Saga Súrssonar; Skaldic Poetry.**]

LAUSIAC HISTORY. See **Palladios.**

LAVRA (Laura), a cluster of cells or caves occupied by hermit monks in the monastic organizations of the eastern Mediterranean. Often loosely organized and lacking architectural distinction, the *lavra* had a common center with a church and sometimes a refectory, kitchen, and guesthouse. This special type of monasticism was originated in the early fourth century by St. Hilarion in Palestine, where it became extremely popular. In contrast to the cenobitical system, where members of the congregation lived together, occupants of a *lavra* gathered only for worship and meals on Saturdays and Sundays.

BIBLIOGRAPHY:

Derwas J. Chitty, *The Desert a City* (1966); Richard Krautheimer, *Early Christian and Byzantine Architecture,* 3rd ed. (1979); Henri Leclercq, *Dictionnaire d'archéologie chrétienne et de liturgie,* VIII, pt. 2 (1929), 1,961–1,988.

ROBERT OUSTERHOUT

[See also **Monasticism, Byzantine; Monasticism, Origins.**]

LAW, ARMENIAN. We know virtually nothing about the administration of law in ancient Armenia prior to the rule of the Arsacid dynasty (64–428). Our knowledge about the Arsacid period is also very limited and dependent on what the sources from the mid fifth century say about the different types of legislation of the kings of Armenia. The lack of documents makes it very difficult to reconstruct the legal system in ancient Armenia. The earliest legal documents that exist in Armenian are translations of the canons of the councils of Nicaea, Antioch, Gangra, Laodicea, and Neocaesarea, which were put into circulation in Armenia in the 430's. The canons of the Armenian council of Šahapivan (444) were added later. These canons, as well as the later canons of the Armenian church, and the Scriptures served as major literary sources for upholding the feudal social structure of medieval Armenia. During the fifth and sixth centuries, the Persian court occasionally tried to introduce Iranian law and traditions but always met strong resistance and was forced to abandon such designs. The emperor Justinian, however, succeeded in enforcing a number of strict measures in Byzantine Armenia and replaced the ancient Armenian tribal and feudal traditions with Roman law.

According to some modern scholars, medieval Armenian society could not have functioned without civil law. Therefore, they argue, Armenian jurists translated and adapted the Syro-Roman code of laws, a compilation of the late fifth or early sixth century, originally composed in Greek, that is now extant only in Armenian, Syriac, and Arabic versions. It is assumed that the Armenian translation,

rendered from a lost Syriac version, was made at an early date and used in Armenia throughout the Middle Ages. This view, however, is not supported by the testimonies of the jurist Mχitᶜar Goš and his contemporary Nersēs, bishop of Lambron, who clearly state that until their time the Armenians had no codification of any kind of civil law. If the Syro-Roman code had been in wide circulation in Armenia, neither Nersēs nor Mχitᶜar would have been ignorant of its existence.

During the late Sasanian, Byzantine, and early Arab periods of domination, the unwritten feudal laws and canon law prevailed in Armenia. Under the later period of Arab domination, during the eighth and ninth centuries, the legal status of the Armenians was that of the dhimmis. It is very doubtful that under such circumstances they could have put into practice any kind of civil law. We have no specific idea about the legal system in the Bagratid kingdom (884–1045). The scanty documentation concerning solemn oaths requiring the presence of high-ranking church dignitaries and the excommunication of princes and kings indicates that the country was still under unwritten feudal and canon law.

The earliest legal work other than the canons is a penitential consisting of ninety-seven articles composed in the first half of the twelfth century by the priest Dawitᶜ of Ganjak, son of Alawik. These articles are intended for parish priests and concern such themes as contamination caused by impure animals (such as mice), murder, stealing, usury, bribery, and perjury. This work served as a source for the *Codex* of Mχitᶜar Goš, which is the major collection of laws in Armenian. Mχitᶜar was also from Ganjak; he was born about 1140 and educated in eastern Armenia, where he attained the rank of *vardapet* (doctor). He continued his studies in the monasteries of Cilicia and attained the rank of *vardapet* for the second time. After his return to eastern Armenia he spent his entire life teaching and writing. The *Codex,* which was completed in 1184, is Mχitᶜar's major work. It was composed at the request of Katᶜołikos Stepᶜanos of Albania on the eve of the rise of the Zakᶜarid feudal family in northeastern Armenia. Later, Mχitᶜar produced a revised, second edition of his work, rearranging the chapters to separate the ecclesiastical laws from the civil laws. He also tried to simplify and clarify the text. A third, abbreviated edition appeared a few decades after his death in 1213. All three editions have survived and have been published.

The first edition consists of a prologue where the

author presents the purpose of his work and presents his views about the office and jurisdiction of a judge and about the types of cases that should be taken to court. He also talks about the number of witnesses and their function and about the oath. Among his sources he mentions customary law of the pagans and the Muslims, which he considers acceptable, the canons of the church, the Scriptures, and legal interpretations drawn from scriptural texts. The second part of the codex consists of 251 chapters or articles. There is no apparent logical sequence to the arrangement of the articles, but there are occasional clusters of articles with similar themes. About half of the articles deal with ecclesiastical matters and ecclesiasts with various legal problems. The *Codex* is particularly rich with laws that deal with marital problems and family matters. It also has sections on criminal law, inheritance, the legal status of minors in criminal cases, and feudal relations. The *Codex* prohibits masters from killing their slaves and recognizes the rights of non-Christians.

Although never accepted as an official code in any Armenian kingdom or principality, Mχit^car's work served as the major legal reference book for Armenians throughout the world, and was still in use in the nineteenth century. In 1519 the Armenians of Poland translated it into Latin for local use. Soon thereafter it was translated into Kipchak Turkish for the benefit of the Armenians living in the Crimea. In the early part of the eighteenth century it was translated into Georgian and incorporated into the code of King Wakhtang VI, which was put to official use in Georgia.

Soon after Mχit^car Goš had produced his codex in eastern Armenia, the Armenians in the west and especially in Cilicia, having realized the need for civil law, appealed to the *kat^cołikos* Grigor Tłay to provide a code of laws. According to a colophon written by Bishop Nersēs of Lambron, the *kat^cołikos* commissioned him to translate a legal work from Syriac, since there were no codifications of civil laws in the archives of the patriarchate. In 1193 Nersēs completed the translation of a Syriac work that is, according to some scholars, the Syro-Roman code of laws. The same bishop also translated a number of Byzantine legal texts. In the mid thirteenth century the *sparapet* (commander-in-chief) Smbat (1208–1275), the brother of King Het^cum I of Cilicia, translated the Assizes of Antioch, a work whose original is now lost. None of these, however, were sufficient for the legal needs of the people of the Armenian kingdom of Cilicia. Consequently, Smbat

composed a new work in 1265 that was, according to his own testimony, an adaptation of an older work—presumably the codex of Mχit^car Goš.

Modern scholars have shown the close relationship between the works of Smbat and Mχit^car. Smbat omitted all the biblical and canonical references and presented the material in the Middle Armenian dialect of Cilicia. His arrangement of the articles is also different; he has a tendency to group together, occasionally under a heading, the articles that deal with similar or the same topics. Smbat's codex was the official lawbook of the Cilician kingdom. However, it never attained the popularity and prestige of Mχit^car's work and fell out of use after the fall of the Armenian kingdom of Cilicia.

According to Armenian law, the ruling classes and the ecclesiastical hierarchy alone enjoyed the full protection of the law. Peasants and serfs had limited rights, whereas slaves had none. The law protected everyone's life. Criminal law differentiated between premeditated and meditated crime and accidental behavior. The court consisted of a judge and two associate magistrates or consultants. There were different kinds of courts: royal, ecclesiastical, and lower. Different punishments were clearly designated in the codes according to the severity of the crimes. A person above the age of fifteen was considered an adult. Those between the ages of ten and fifteen were at an intermediary stage and therefore were not tried as adults, and received lighter punishment. Children also could be tried and punished for criminal action, but the punishments were relatively light.

BIBLIOGRAPHY

Sources. Asorakan datastanagirk^c [Syrian Code of Laws], Arsen Łltčean, ed. (1917); Carl [Karl] G. Bruns and Eduard Sachau, eds., *Syrisch-römisches Rechtsbuch aus dem fünften Jahrhundert* (1880); *Kanonagirk^c Hayoc^c* [Armenian Book of Canons], Vazgen A. Hakobyan, ed., 2 vols. (1964–1971); Mkhithar Gosh [Mχit^car Goš], *Datastanagirk^c Hayoc^c*, V. Bastameanc^c, ed. (1880), and *Girk^c datastani*, Xosrov T^corssyan, ed. (1975); *Penitential of David of Ganjak,* C. J. F. Dowsett, ed. and trans. (1961); Sparapet Smbat, *Armenisches Rechtsbuch, I, Sempadscher Kodex aus dem 13. Jahrhundert,* Josef Kraft, ed. (1905), *Assises d'Antioche,* Ghevont M. Alishan [Łewond M. Ališan], ed. (1876), and *Sudebnik* (Armenian with Russian trans. and commentary by A. G. Galstian, and with French summary) (1958).

Studies. S. H. Hovhannissian, *Amusna-ĕntanekan iravunk^cĕ vał avatakan Hayastanum IV–IX dd.* (1976), and "'Asorkan' kam 'Asorahṙomeakan' koč^cvac datastanagirkᶜi ałerse hay iravunkᶜi het [The Connection of the Judicial Code, Called 'Syrian' or 'Syro-Roman,' with Armenian Law]," in *Patmabanasirakan Handes,* 2 (1970), 159–178; X. Samuēlean, *Hin hay iravunkᶜi patmutᶜyunĕ* [History of Old Armenian Law], with Russian summary (1939), and *Mxitᶜar Goši datastanagirkᶜn u hin Hayocᶜ kᶜałakᶜacᶜiakan irawunkᶜĕ* (1911); Aram Ter-Łewondyan, "Hay žołovrdi iravakan vičakĕ xalifayutᶜyan tirapetutᶜyan nerkᶜo," in *Lraber Hasarakakan Gitutᶜyunneri,* 4 (1975); A. T. Tᶜovmasyan, *Hin ew mijnadaryan hay kᶜreakan iravunkᶜ,* 2 vols. (1962–1977).

KRIKOR H. MAKSOUDIAN

[See also **Mxitᶜar Goš; Nerses Lambronacᶜi; Smbat Sparapet.**]

LAW, BYZANTINE. The codification of Roman law, accomplished under Justinian I (527–565) and known as *Corpus iuris civilis,* is the basis of the further development of Byzantine legislation. It is also the last major legal work published in Latin, except for most of the *Novellae,* but its more important parts were soon translated into Greek, and were accompanied by detailed commentaries, also in Greek. The gradual Hellenization of the empire that was already perceptible under Justinian prevailed under his successors and resulted in a new legal system written only in Greek and aimed at serving and uniting the mainly Greek-speaking populations of the middle Byzantine period. The values of Christianity as well as the Hellenistic traditions of the East, already taken into consideration by the sixth-century legislators, had an ever-increasing impact on the development of Byzantine law.

SEVENTH TO NINTH CENTURIES

During the seventh and eighth centuries, and even later, the Justinianic legislation was enriched by important commentaries that clarified and updated the traditional Roman law, which remained unchanged because it was considered an everlasting framework for the regulation of constantly changing human relations. However, despite all its high qualities, the *Corpus iuris civilis* presented major problems for everyday use because of its vast scope. Therefore, beyond the ad hoc legislation of individual emperors—about which little is known because of the scarcity of evidence—there were during this period deliberate and coordinated efforts to compose legal studies that served as shorter, more handy legal codifications for use by judges and lawyers in everyday practice.

One of the most important of these legal handbooks, the *Eclogue,* issued by the Isaurian emperors Leo III and Constantine V in 726 (or 741 according to Burgmann), introduced considerable modifications to Justinianic law on the basis of Hellenistic and Christian traditions. Further elaborations of this law code resulted in the composition of private legal handbooks, such as the *Ecloga privata* and the *Ecloga privata aucta.*

Around the same period (end of the seventh and beginning of the eighth centuries) the Farmer's Law *(leges rusticae, nomos georgikos)* seems to have been issued. It is not clear whether this code, which was in fact a practical handbook, was the private work of a provincial official or a work officially sanctioned by imperial decree. In either case it is undoubtedly a very important source for the history of the Byzantine countryside. It provides much information about the free landholders, who were organized in village communities, owned land privately or collectively, and assumed collective fiscal obligations toward the state.

Another code of law with a very specific and practical character was the Rhodian Sea Law *(lex rhodia de jactu, nomos rodion nautikos),* which was probably composed sometime between the sixth and the eighth centuries. It is a collection of ordinances concerning such matters of shipping and naval trade as the distribution of the profits and regulations concerning security on ships and the sharing of responsibility in cases of theft or damage to the cargo or the ship. Although influenced by the principles of the *Corpus iuris civilis,* the Rhodian Sea Law was mainly based on local customs.

In the area of administrative law there is the work of George of Cyprus with its description of the Byzantine provinces and the *Taktikon Uspenski,* which contains the hierarchical enumeration of the state officials (*ca.* 842–843).

NINTH TO TWELFTH CENTURIES

A major effort for the renewal of the legal codifications occurred in the ninth and tenth centuries. It was inspired by Emperor Basil I the Macedonian (867–886), who, although poorly educated—or possibly for that reason—realized that the legal system had become extremely complicated because the large number of laws issued by successive emperors had superseded the existing codifications. The most recent codification had been the Isaurian *Eclogue,* strongly resented for being issued by iconoclast emperors. Basil I launched a major project that he named Purification of the Old Laws (*Anakatharsis palaion nomon*). All existing legislation was reexamined, and laws that were recognized to have lost their de jure or de facto validity were retrieved from circulation and collected in a special book, which has not survived. During Basil's reign two short, well-organized legal codes were published: the *Procheiros nomos* appeared between 870 and 879, and the *Epanagoge* between 879 and 886. Both were easy to consult, served the practical purposes that the emperor had set forth, and were inspired by the Justinianic legislation and subsequent law codes (including the abhorred *Eclogue*) as well as by local customs. However, neither of them was the major, systematically renewed codification that Basil had desired.

His son and successor, Leo VI (886–912), continued along the same lines. Before 900 Leo had issued a collection of 113 *novellae*, which dealt primarily with the requirements of the *Anakatharsis*. He was mainly concerned with abolishing legislation that had fallen into disuse, such as the legislative powers of the Senate, the self-government of the cities, and the operation of the ordinary consulate, as well as with giving the force of law to certain customs, such as making mandatory the blessing of any marriage by the church. Toward the end of Leo's reign the vast project conceived by Basil I was brought to completion; the Basilics, a vast codification of all Byzantine law, was published to replace the Justinianic *Corpus,* and soon thereafter it was accompanied by rich commentaries.

During this period of purification and codification of the law several treatises of an administrative character were composed: the *Military Tactics (Taktika)* and the *Military Laws*, attributed to Leo VI; the treatise of Philotheos, written in 899 and establishing the order of precedence of the court dignitaries and officials; and the *Notitia episcopatuum*, issued by Leo VI probably in 904 and establishing the order of precedence of the clergy. More important was the *Book of the Eparch (To eparchikon biblion)*, a collection of rules issued in 911 by Leo VI concerning the regulation of trade and industry in Constantinople, and the protection of the guilds (*systemata*) of the notaries; goldsmiths; bankers; merchants of silk, linen, perfumes, and soap; grocers; butchers; fishermen; bakers; and saddlemakers. For all arts and crafts the prefect of the city (*eparchos*) and his assessor (*symponos*) had authority to control the quantity and the quality of the goods sold to the pub-

lic as well as their prices. The *Book of the Eparch,* in spite of its regulatory character, reflects in a most interesting and precise way the stipulations of commercial law in the middle Byzantine period.

During the reign of Leo VI, the empire was shaken by the Tetragamy quarrel, a bitter schism inside the church caused by the emperor's fourth marriage. From about 920 on, a new principle of law emerged, making questions of family law more and more dependent upon ecclesiastical rather than imperial legislation.

From the tenth century there are a considerable number of writings concerning administrative law, such as the *taktikon Benesevic* (934/944) and the *taktikon* of the Escorial (971/975). Above all, there are the impressive works of Emperor Constantine VII Porphyrogenitos: *On the Themes (De thematibus),* in which he describes the provinces of the empire; *On the Administration of the Empire (De administrando imperio),* a treatise addressed to his son Romanos and providing him with detailed information and advice concerning the foreign relations of Byzantium; and *On the Ceremonies (De ceremoniis aulae byzantinae),* a vast compilation of court ritual. There are also two handbooks concerning the taxation of land, one preserved in a manuscript of the Marciana Library and one recently discovered in the library of the Greek monastery of Zaborda. Scholars date the composition of both these texts sometime between the tenth and the twelfth centuries.

From the tenth century on, there are a large number of legal handbooks whose main purpose was to rearrange the legal material in a way that would facilitate consultation. In spite of their more or less private character, these handbooks seem to have enjoyed a certain prestige and to have had a wide circulation. They include the *Ecloga ad Prochiron mutata,* the *Prochiron legum,* the *Prochiron Vaticanum,* the *Epanagoge aucta* (issued under Leo VI), the *Epanagoge cum Prochiro composita,* the *Epitome legum* (issued ca. 920/921), the *Epitome ad Prochiron mutata,* the *Epitome Laurentiana* (ca. 945), the *Ecloga privata aucta,* and, above all, the *Synopsis major* of the Basilics (mid tenth century), summarizing the contents of the Basilics and giving on each subject the necessary references to the original lengthy text. This practical handbook, which had gone through more than a dozen revised editions by the thirteenth century, was enriched by appendixes in which the important new legislation was recorded.

This new legislation of the tenth century was primarily concerned with the protection of the free peasantry from the rapacity of the big landowners. A series of imperial *novellae,* starting with those of Romanos I Lekapenos (920–944) and continuing with those of Constantine VII Porphyrogenitos (945–959), Romanos II (959–963), Nikephoros II Phokas (963–969), and Basil II (976–1025), had as their main objective the erection of legal obstacles to the increase of large landholdings at the expense of small landholders, more specifically, of the soldier-peasants, who constituted the backbone of the Byzantine army. The motivation of this legislation was fiscal rather than social, and thus it did not have lasting results. Nonetheless, the basis of this legislation, which was the revived right of preemption, remained valid until the end of the empire.

The legislative activity of the eleventh century was not particularly impressive. Yet there was a very interesting work, the *Peira* of Eustathius Rhomaios, divided into seventy-five titles. This work contains summaries of judicial rulings rendered by Eustathius and other judges of the supreme court of Constantinople from the last years of the tenth century through the first four decades of the eleventh. Classified according to subject, the material is especially important because it shows how the written law was applied and the extent to which local customs influenced the imperial tribunal.

Until the eleventh century law was taught only inside the corporation of the notaries. A major change in this practice occurred under Constantine IX Monomachos (1042–1055). At the beginning of his reign, he created a law school (*didaskaleion ton nomon*) housed, with its specialized library, in the vast complex of the monastery of Mangana in Constantinople and headed by a high state official called the guardian of law (*nomophylax*). The first person to occupy this position was John Xiphilinos, who later became patriarch (1064–1075).

In spite of this new and prestigious school, Byzantine legal studies never surpassed the high levels they had attained in the ninth and tenth centuries. There are two works of some interest from the late eleventh century: the *Synopsis ton nomon* of Michael Psellos, a 1,400-verse poem, addressed to Psellos' student, the future emperor Michael VII Doukas (1071–1078), that contains a summary of the legislation; and the *Ponema nomikon* of the judge Michael Attaleiates, which does not contain any substantial innovations in spite of the fact that it focuses particuarly on penal law.

TWELFTH TO FIFTEENTH CENTURIES

The last centuries of Byzantium are relatively poor in legal literature. Lay jurists lost importance in comparison with the ecclesiastical ones, such as the archbishop of Ochrid, Demetrios Chomatianos, and the metropolitan of Naupaktos, John Apokaukos, whose rulings were a prime source for legal procedures at the beginning of the thirteenth century. From the thirteenth century there is also a new compilation, the *Synopsis minor* of the Basilics, based on the *Synopsis major* and on the *Ponema nomikon* of Michael Attaleiates. Another compilation, the *Procheiron auctum,* appeared around 1300. However, the only really important work of the period was the *Hexabiblos,* published in 1345 by the Thessalonian judge Constantine Harmenopoulos. This code, completely updated, and carefully and methodically organized, remained the major legal handbook not only for the last century of Byzantium but also for the later centuries of the Turkish domination in the Balkans.

As for administrative law, there are several lists of precedence from the thirteenth to the fifteenth centuries and one major work, a detailed treatise on the court offices composed in the mid-fourteenth century by an unknown author called the Pseudo-Kodinos.

It should be stressed, finally, that throughout its history Byzantine law strongly influenced the legislation of the neighboring Orthodox countries, especially those of the Slavs, who translated several Byzantine codes of law and applied them in their own states.

BIBLIOGRAPHY

Most Byzantine legal texts are in Panagiotes I. Zepos and Ioannes D. Zepos, eds., *Jus Graecoromanum,* 8 vols. (1931), and in the series *Fontes minores* published since 1976 by Dieter V. Simon. For other editions and translations of individual texts, see Walter Ashburner, *The Rhodian Sea-law* (1909, repr. 1976), "The Farmers Law," in *Journal of Hellenic Studies,* 30 (1910), and "The Byzantine Mutiny Act," in *Journal of Hellenic Studies,* 46 (1926); L. Burgmann, ed., *Ecloga: Das Gesetzbuch Leons III. und Konstantinos V.* (1983); Jean Darrouzès, ed., *Notitiae episcopatuum Ecclesiae constantonopolitinae* (1981); Gustav E. Heimbach, ed., *Kōnstantinos Harmenopoulos: Manuale legum sive Hexabiblos* (1851, new ed. by Konstantinos G. Pitsakes entitled *Procheiron nomon he Hexabiblos,* 1971), partially translated by Edwin H. Freshfield, *A Manual of Byzantine Law, Compiled in the Fourteenth Century by George Harmenopoulos* (1930); Jules Nicole, ed. and trans., *Le livre du préfet; ou l'édit de l'empereur Léon le Sage sur les corporations de Constantinople* (1893, repr. with intro. by Ivan Dujčev 1970); Pierre Noailles and Alphonse Dain, eds., *Les novelles de Léon VI, le Sage* (1944); Nicholas Oikonomides, ed., *Les listes de présénce byzantines des IXe et Xe siècles* (1972); Nicolas G. Svoronos, *Recherches sur la tradition juridique à Byzance: La Synopsis major des Basiliques et ses appendices* (1964); Jean Verpreaux, ed., *Pseudo-Kodinos, Traité des offices*, rev. ed. (1976).

The best summary of Byzantine law is P. E. Pieler, "Byzantinische Rechtsliteratur," in Herbert Hunger, ed., *Die hochsprachliche profane Literatur der Byzantiner*, II (1978). For a short but dated description in English, see H. J. Scheltema, "Byzantine Law," in *Cambridge Medieval History*, 2nd ed., IV, pt. 2 (1967). For the influence of Byzantine law on neighboring countries, see Alexandre V. Soloviev, "L'influence du droit byzantin sur les pays orthodoxes," in *Proceedings of the X Congresso Internazionale di Scienze Sociale, Roma 4–11 Settembre 1955* (1955).

NICHOLAS OIKONOMIDES

[See also **Attaleiates, Michael; Basil I of Macedonia; Basil II "Killer of Bulgars"; Basilics; Byzantine Empire: History; Caesaropapism; Constantine VII Porphyrogenitos; Constantine IX Monomachos; Constantinople; Corpus Iuris Civilis; Doukas; Eclogue; Epanagoge; Eparch, Book of the; George of Cyprus; Harmenopoulos, Constantine; Isaurians; John Xiphilinos; Justinian I; Leo VI the Wise, Emperor; Nikephoros II Phokas; Procheiros Nomos; Psellos, Michael; Pseudo-Kodinos; Romanos I Lekapenos; Romanos II.**]

LAW, CANON: ARMENIAN. The ecclesiastical rules of the Armenian church derive from (1) the pronouncements of the first three ecumenical councils and the local councils of the early church, (2) the councils of the Armenian church, (3) the decrees and writings of certain early church fathers, (4) the decrees and writings of certain Armenian church fathers, and (5) the Scriptures. The Armenian Book of Canons (*Kanonagirk^c Hayoc^c*) constitutes the main corpus of ecclesiastical laws in the Armenian language and has survived in several medieval and late-medieval editions, of which there are more than 200 extant manuscripts.

The *Kanonagirk^c Hayoc^c* was first compiled in the early eighth century by Kat^cołikos Yovhannēs Ōjnec^ci (717–728). The source of this information is a colophon that was written by Yovhannēs himself and is thought to have been originally attached to the end of the thirty-two canons that appear under

his name. Yovhannēs' corpus consists of the following twenty-four groups: "the canons of the Apostles," which were translated from Syriac; the canons of Clemens, also translated from Syriac; "the canons of the fathers who followed the Apostles," presumed to be of Armenian origin; the canons of Nicaea and Ancyra; the canons of Caesarea, which have no Greek original; the canons of Neocaesarea, Gangra, Antioch, and Laodicea; canons attributed to St. Gregory the Illuminator; the canons of Sardica, Constantinople, and Ephesus; the canons of Athanasius, which are attributed to Timotheus of Alexandria in the Greek canons; the canons of St. Basil of Caesarea, canons attributed to St. Sahak, bishop of Armenia (*ca.* 387–439); the canons of the Armenian council of Šahapivan (444), the canons of Bishop Sewantos, which are unknown in Greek and Syriac; the canons of Kat^cołikos Nersēs (548–557), Neršapuh, bishop of the Mamikoneans; the canons of Kat^cołikos Yovhannēs Mandakuni (484–490); the canons of Abraham, bishop of the Mamikoneans; the canons of Kat^cołikos Sahak III (677–703); and the canons of Kat^cołikos Yovhannēs Ōjnec^ci. Yovhannēs states in his colophon that the corpus was intended as a reference work and was to be kept in the Armenian patriarchate, which was in Dwin at that time. The collection itself obviously had no authority, but the individual canons did.

The *Kanonagirk^c* was supplemented over the years by additional canons. By the 990's sixteen new groups had been appended and seventeen more were added in 1098, thus raising the total number to fifty-seven. Further additions were made in the fourteenth, fifteenth, and seventeenth centuries. In these supplements are found the canons of the Armenian councils of Partaw (768), Dwin (645), and Karin (690's?), as well as several canons and canonical writings attributed to various apostles, Armenian church fathers, and Syrian and Greek church fathers and councils that are not authentic. Many of the individual canons in these groups are drawn from earlier canons; some of the sections are taken from medieval collections of homilies, letters, and other types of documents, and are presented here as canonical writings. For example, the letter of Makarios, bishop of Jerusalem, to Bishop Vrt^canēs of Armenia appears as chapter 39 in the corpus, and the "Second Nicaean Canons," which comprise chapter 34, have nothing to do with the second council of Nicaea, but are drawn from the canons of the first council of Nicaea and those of the local councils.

Even though the authority and the contents of the Armenian *Kanonagirk^c* were never officially promulgated by any council or synod, the corpus was and is still used. Until the emergence of the twelfth-century jurists, it was used for deciding ecclesiastical as well as civil cases.

BIBLIOGRAPHY

Kanonagirk^c Hayoc^c, Vazgen Hakobyan, ed., 2 vols. (1964–1971). The introduction and the copious notes in this work contain a thorough bibliography. See also Tiran Nersoyan, "A Brief Outline of the Armenian Liber Canonum and Its Status in Modern Times," in *Kanon: Jahrbuch der Gesellschaft für das Recht der Ostkirchen: I Acta Congressus 1971*, 76–86.

KRIKOR H. MAKSOUDIAN

[See also **Armenian Church; Armenian Literature; Armenian Saints.**]

LAW, CANON: BYZANTINE. The Byzantine church never produced an exhaustive and juridically consistent corpus of canon law, but it did recognize the permanent authority of a body of conciliar decrees and patristic opinions issued at various times and in various circumstances. On the other hand, the harmony that was supposed to exist between church and empire, as defined particularly by Emperor Justinian I (527–565), made it inevitable that imperial decrees came to be authoritative for the church as, reciprocally, the empire recognized that ecclesiastical canons had the force of law. In cases of conflict between ecclesiastical canons and state laws, the canons were to be preferred. This system meant that in practice many areas of church discipline, such as the system for electing bishops and rule of marriage, were covered by state legislation, while in turn the emperors were formally bound by ecclesiastical canons (for example, the church opposition to the fourth marriage of Emperor Leo VI).

SOURCES OF BYZANTINE CANON LAW

Decrees of ecumenical councils. These were the decrees of Nicaea I (325); Constaninople I (381); Ephesus (431); Chalcedon (451); the Quinisext Synod, also known as the Council in Trullo (692), which issued canons on behalf of Constantinople II (553) and Constantinople III (680); and Nicaea II (787).

Apostolic canons. These represent eighty-five disciplinary rules going back to the first half of the fourth century. Originating in Syria, they were given formal canonical authority by the Council in Trullo.

Canons of local councils. These were the canons of Ancyra (314), Neocaesarea (314–325), Antioch (341), Sardica (343), Gangra and Laodicea (both in the fourth century), and Constantinople (394). There were also the canons of Carthage (418), which included decrees of several councils of the North African episcopate held from the third to the fifth centuries, as well as the later canons of Constantinople (859–861), also known as the "First-Second" Council, and Constantinople (879–880), sometimes referred to as the "Eighth Ecumenical."

Canons of the Fathers. These were a collection of patristic excerpts that were given formal canonical authority by the various councils. They included texts by Dionysius of Alexandria (*d.* 265), Gregory of Neocaesarea (*d.* 270), Peter of Alexandria (*d.* 311), Athanasius of Alexandria (*d.* 373), Basil of Caesarea (*d.* 379), Gregory of Nyssa (*d. ca.* 394), Gregory of Nazianzus (*d.* 389/390), Amphilochius of Iconium (*d.* 395), Timothy of Alexandria (*d.* 355), Theophilus of Alexandria (*d.* 412), Cyril of Alexandria (*d.* 444), and Gennadius of Constantinople (*d.* 471). Later Byzantine collections added a few more texts to this original list.

Imperial legislation on ecclesiastical affairs. First and foremost was the *Corpus iuris civilis* of Justinian I, followed by the *Novellae* issued by him and succeeding emperors. Many texts concerning the church are contained in the imperial legislation found in the *Ecloga* (731–741) and particularly in the legislation of the Macedonians: the *Procheiros* (or *Procheiron) nomos* (870–878), the *Basilics* (867–912), and the *Epanagoge* (perhaps written by Photios *ca.* 880–886).

Nomokanons. These were systematized collections of imperial laws *(nomoi)* and ecclesiastical rules *(kanones)* arranged according to topic. The most important were the *Nomokanon in L Titles,* which goes back to the patriarch John III Scholasticus (565–577) and the *Nomokanon in XIV Titles,* issued by Patriarch Photios in 883. The latter served as the basis for the major Slavic canonical collection, known as *Kormchaya kniga,* edited by St. Sava of Serbia (thirteenth century) and subsequently accepted in all Slavic lands.

Authoritative commentaries. Commentaries on canonical legislation listed above appeared particularly in the twelfth century. The commentary of John Zonaras attempted, somewhat artificially, to classify canons according to their relative importance and authority. Alexis Aristenos emphasized their historical context. Theodore Balsamon, titular patriarch of Antioch during the reign of Manuel I Komnenos (1143–1180), produced a major commentary on the entire *Nomokanon in XIV Titles* that attempted to coordinate the ecclesiastical legislation of the previous centuries and the civil legislation contained in the *Corpus iuris civilis* and the Basilics.

Patriarchal and synodal decrees. The permanent synod *(synodos endēmousa)* at Constantinople regularly issued decrees on canonical and doctrinal issues. Since the archives of the patriarchate were almost totally destroyed by successive invaders, only a small part of the decrees have been preserved in their original text. In the last two centuries of the empire, as the power of the emperors diminished, the patriarchs—without even pretending to powers comparable with those of the popes—assumed a wider role and greater competence in the affairs of society far beyond the shrinking borders of the Byzantine Empire. This new role was expressed in the concept "universal leadership" *(kēdemonia pantōn)* used in patriarchal decrees of that period (1261–1453).

The entire body of canonical texts was, in the understanding of the Byzantines, entrusted to the stewardship *(oikonomia)* of the bishops, with local provincial synods as well as the permanent synod at Constantinople *(synodos endēmousa)* acting as courts of appeals, or as supreme tribunals. The principle of *oikonomia* implied a certain discretion given to the bishops in applying sanctions against repentant sinners. Politically minded patriarchs tended to expand the concept of *oikonomia,* more especially when imperial and political interests were involved, whereas the monks stood for a stricter interpretation of church rules. On several occasions controversies, and even schisms, occurred over the issue of the use of *oikonomia* (for example, the "moechian" schism in the early ninth century, on the occasion of the adulterous marriage of Emperor Constantine VI, and the "Tetragamy" of Leo VI in the tenth century). However, everyone agreed on the principle that one could practice *oikonomia* only, in the words of Eulogius of Alexandria, "whenever orthodox doctrine remained unharmed."

BIBLIOGRAPHY

A complete collection of texts is in G. A. Rhalli and M. Potli, *Syntagma tōn theiōn kai ierōn kanonōn,* 6 vols. (1852–1859). For a catalog of these texts in French, see Venance Grumel, ed., *Les régestes des actes du patriarcat de Constantinople,* I, *Les actes des patriarches,* 6 fascs. (1932–

1979). See also Hans-Georg Beck, *Kirche und theologische Literatur im byzantinischen Reich* (1959), 27–120; John Meyendorff, *Byzantine Theology,* (1974, 2d ed. 1979), 79–90; Ivan Žužek, *Kormchaya kniga: Studies on the Chief Code of the Russian Canon Law* (1964).

JOHN MEYENDORFF

[See also Basilics; Byzantine Church; Byzantine Empire: History; Corpus Iuris Civilis; Councils (Ecumenical); Councils, Byzantine; Eclogue; Epanagoge; Justinian I; Leo VI the Wise, Emperor; Liturgy, Byzantine Church; Nomokanon; Photios; Procheiros Nomos; Russian Orthodox Church; Zonaras, John.]

LAW, CANON: TO GRATIAN. Canon law is so called because it is a law that has been measured according to an ecclesiastical canon or rule and has been approved in some fashion by the general consensus of the faithful, by an individual either public or private, or by a group or groups of authorities. Among the numerous overlapping systems of law operative in the early Middle Ages, few touched as many facets of life as canon law. Not only were the lives of clerics regulated by this law, but in a myriad of ways laymen, both Christian and non-Christian, were touched by its provisions. If one surveys even briefly the rubrics of canon-law collections from the fifth to the twelfth century, one is quickly impressed with the enormous range of subjects covered. There are canons on clerics, monks, and laymen, the sacraments and their liturgical administration, moral and ethical norms, the economic systems by which clerics and laymen lived, and so forth. Rather than surveying the development of legal provisions for each of these subjects prior to Gratian, this article will concentrate on the development of the sources or *fontes* in which these provisions on various subjects can be found.

In the study of canon law one of the most basic distinctions is between the material sources *(fontes materiales)* and the formal sources *(fontes formales).* The material sources are the basic, original, or the "legislative" sources, such as those of councils, popes, the Bible, and the like, while the formal sources are the intermediate sources by which the law was transmitted, the canonical collections.

FONTES MATERIALES

From her very beginnings the church, which grew out of an Old Testament and Jewish tradition heavy with a sophisticated system of law, had its own institutions and inchoate legal systems. Some scholars have claimed that the early church was a largely spiritual entity that was directed by charismatic figures without a legal structure. And while it cannot be denied that there were these charismatics whose teaching cut through existing legal structures, there were also undoubtedly a system or systems of institutions and "legal" customs operative from the first years of the church. Many of these—ceremonial law, prayers, fasts, and the like—clearly come from the Old Testament and were either observed in actuality or cited as archetypes for Christian use. There were also the fundamental moral precepts, such as the Ten Commandments. But beyond these the primitive church developed its own system of norms or regulations. Among these were the directives given by Christ and the apostles as recorded in the various books of the New Testament. Especially important were the sayings of Jesus and the letters of the apostles and others of the apostolic age that dealt with disciplinary and doctrinal matters. Further, deliberative or quasilegislative or judicial bodies, such as the Council of Jerusalem reported in Acts, dealt with a number of disputed matters. And finally, there appears to have been a developing body of customary law or tradition reported by New Testament authors.

As the church prospered, these sources of primitive church law continued not only as norms in themselves but also as models for further development and refinement. Hence, the Old Testament laws were either refined and interpreted in Christian fashion or rejected as inapplicable to the New Covenant. The sayings of Jesus were canonized in the Gospels, and the epistles and writings of the apostles were gathered together and given canonical status. The decisions of the apostles were further augmented by writings of their successors, not only the official leaders of the churches, such as bishops and presbyters, but also by others, and in some instances these came to be included in the canon of Christian scripture as well. Further, assemblies continued to be held to decide on wider questions, and among the first of these after the apostolic Council of Jerusalem were those in Asia Minor called to deal with the important issue of the date of Easter, the so-called Quartodeciman controversy. And, finally, the sense of tradition or custom was refined so that authenticity could be assigned to certain decisions with an appeal to the tradition or proper sense of interpretation inherent in the church.

By the late patristic period additional sources had taken on normative status. Among these were: the theological works of such important authors as Jerome, Augustine, and others; Roman law, which was now binding for Christians in an empire where their religion had been accepted and made the official religion; liturgical material used in the rites and rituals of the Christian cult; monastic codes followed by increasing numbers of Christians who lived their regulated lives outside of or within society at large; and apocryphal material that attempted to present systems which anonymous writers thought represented the positions of the apostles and the saintly worthies of the church. But most important among the developing sources of canon law were the decisions of the councils and bishops.

The decisions of the councils went under a variety of names: dogmata and anathemas for doctinal matters; and *canones, constitutiones, statuta, decreta, edicta,* and *sanctiones* for disciplinary matters. These decisions were enacted at councils or synods held at a variety of levels: ecumenical councils, whose decrees came to be accepted by the entire church; councils for only a part of the empire *(pars imperii),* such as that of Arles in the West in 314; provincial and regional councils; and local synods.

Pontifical decisions, now usually called decrees or decretals, were essentially the decisions of pontiffs or bishops, including the bishop of Rome, or the pope, given either in response to a question or *de novo* (anew). Although in classical Roman law there were fairly clear terminological distinctions among *decretum, mandatum, interdictum* and the like, pontifical decisions went under a variety of terms in the patristic and medieval church including *decretum, sententia, monitum, responsum, regula, praeceptum, epistula, littera, scriptum,* and *litterae decretales.*

FONTES FORMALES

As these material sources of canon law multiplied, they were gathered into collections, which then became the intermediaries through which the original sources came to be known. In studying these *fontes formales* several basic notions must always be kept in mind.

First, there is the question of how authoritative each collection in its present form might be. This depends on whether it was a private collection made not by a legislator or other official but by an individual or individuals for private use, or whether it was an official collection, approved or authorized by a "legislative" authority.

Second, the principle of organization of a collection must be determined, because the significance of canons or decrees in a particular historical circumstance often turns on this question. Among the various principles of organization of the collections there were four major ones: a historical arrangement, sometimes called chronological, in which the canons or decrees were ordered according to some historical sequence without regard for the subjects covered; a systematic or topical arrangement in which individual canons or decrees were specifically selected and ordered according to topic; a *Quellenblock* arrangement in which blocks or series of canons and decrees taken from earlier sources were ordered according to some principle; and a farraginous arrangement in which no consistent system is now obvious.

Third, in many collections there exist multiple layers of sources. Rarely in early medieval collections did the compiler return to the *fontes materiales*. Rather, he depended heavily on other *fontes formales* that reflected in varying degrees the original enactments.

Fourth, in making their collections, compilers were selective. They might include or omit complete enactments of councils or ecclesiastical officials; and even if a larger text were included, the compiler might omit certain portions of the text he felt were unnecessary or counter to the law as he perceived it.

And, finally, just as compilers altered the meaning of larger texts through selectivity, so they could alter individual texts and their attributions either by mistake, with an intent to deceive, or to justify what the compiler thought "should have been."

PRIMITIVE COLLECTIONS

Long before the Middle Ages the church had begun to collect and codify her law, and some of this eventually found its way either indirectly or directly into several medieval collections.

The earliest collections are called pseudoapostolic because they went under the names of the apostles. The law in these collections may in part reflect the tradition of apostolic teaching, but they were all written after apostolic times. Moreover, with one exception, all of these pseudoapostolic collections were written in the East and played little role in the development of Western canon law, even though some were translated into Latin and survive in a limited number of Latin manuscripts.

The earliest of these pseudoapostolic collections is the *Doctrina duodecim apostolorum,* or *Didache,*

written in the late first or early second century. Although it was known in the patristic period and was even translated into several languages, it was lost until the late nineteenth century. It is a rather short collection with its provisions divided into three sections: moral precepts couched in terms of the "Children of Light and Darkness"; liturgical prescriptions, especially baptism; and regulations about the structure and hierarchy of the church.

A century after the appearance of the *Didache,* it was incorporated in the East into a larger work known as the *Didascalia apostolorum,* which dealt with the church hierarchy, the care of the poor and orphans, Jews, fasting, and liturgical questions. Almost contemporary with the *Didascalia* was the *Apostolic Tradition* attributed to Hippolytus of Rome. Although it seems to be the oldest Western collection, it was written in Greek and played a larger role in the East than in the West. Its first section deals especially with ordination and the second with the administration of sacraments; hence this collection has been extremely important in liturgical studies.

These pseudoapostolic collections from the first through the third centuries exercised considerable influence on later primitive collections written in Greek, Syriac, Coptic, Arabic, and Bohairic from the fourth through the sixth centuries. Among these are the *Canones Hippolyti, Constitutiones per Hippolytum, Canones ecclesiastici sanctorum apostolorum,* and *Testamentum domini nostri Jesu Christi.* But of special importance because parts of it would enter Western medieval canon law is the collection entitled the *Constitutiones apostolicae.* This collection in eight books consists of an amplified *Didascalia,* the *Didache,* an amplified *Apostolic Tradition,* and the addition of eighty-five apostolic canons. These were later extracted from the collection, and although they were rejected in the famous *Decretum Gelasianum* as apocryphal, fifty of them were used in the influential Western collection of Dionysius Exiguus and hence entered the whole tradition of Western canon law.

PRIMITIVE COLLECTIONS IN THE WEST

Even as these pseudoapostolic collections were being drawn up, the church at large continued to legislate, laying down her law in the form of conciliar canons and pontifical decrees. Moreover, as the church grew and expanded, its internal organization developed. Certain episcopal sees rose in importance, and cities, regions, provinces, and other geographical divisions were established and recognized. With this development in structural organization came an increase in the legal norms under which the church operated.

Part of the development in the structural organization of the church was the establishment of archives and *scrinia* in imitation of civil practice. In these archives copies and registers of the most important disciplinary decrees of councils and bishops, both local and foreign, were maintained. In the process of organizing these and publicizing the decisions, small collections of canons were made. Certainly such collections existed in the East; hence they probably also existed in the West as well.

At first these collections seem to have been both private and local or regional. Although the exact origin of each is sometimes unknown or is controverted, scholars generally group these primitive collections by geographical region.

African collections. The African collections are some of the earliest in the West. Not only were local or regional decisions included in the collections, but also texts of oriental councils, some of which had been attended by African bishops who presumably brought back texts. Of these later texts the best known is probably the *Versio Caeciliani,* named after Caecilianus, who had attended the first Council of Nicaea (325), but likely compiled at the beginning of the fifth century. Slightly later during the Apiarian controversy, the African church, to support its position against Rome, asked for and got from the Eastern church translated decisions of various Eastern councils.

Besides these oriental decisions, the African church also kept collections of its own councils' decisions. For example, the Third Council of Carthage (397) included in its own canons the *Breviarium Hipponense,* or summary of earlier canons. Similarly at the seventeenth Council of Carthage (419) a summary of previous conciliar decisions was given. Called the *Codex canonum ecclesiae Africanae* by Justel, these were known in the West through the later work of Dionysius Exiguus.

Spanish collections. Spain was also represented at the Eastern councils by such figures as Osius of Córdoba, one of the most significant fathers at the First Council of Nicaea, and it appears that the Spanish church knew early of the collections of the Eastern conciliar canons. These were in the *Collectio Isidoriana,* or *Hispana,* so called because they would later appear in the *Collectio hispana* of the seventh century, but they were actually compiled in Africa. Also, papal decrees were very early sent to Spanish sees,

and a collection of these would later come to play a role in Spanish conciliar decisions and the *Collectio hispana.* Clearly the Spanish church had begun to collect its own decisions, and these were later reflected in the *Collectio Novariensis* and *Epitome hispanica.*

These collections of ancient canons were known also to the *ecclesia lusitana,* or Portuguese church, because antique canons were read at the first Council of Braga (*ca.* 561). Slightly later a systematic collection of eighty-four capitula, especially from the Greek and Hispanic councils, which went under the name of St. Martin of Braga, was approved at the Third Council of Braga (572).

Gallican collections. The early church in Gaul had collections of the canons of oriental councils (in the *Versio gallica* and *gallo-hispana* and several others), Hispanic collections, and decrees of popes, especially those sent to Gallican bishops. But the two most important primitive Gallican collections were the *Statuta ecclesiae antiqua* and the *Collectio Arelatensis.*

The *Statuta* was compiled after 470 (perhaps *ca.* 475) probably by Gennadius, presbyter of Marseilles, but was attributed through the Middle Ages to the Fourth Council of Carthage (398) or the Council of Valence (374). It is in reality a *Weihebuchlein* or small book for ordinations that contains a creed, a large number of disciplinary canons, and finally rubrics for the Gallican rite of clerical ordination, which were widely diffused and used in the Roman rite of ordination down to 1972.

The *Collectio Arelatensis,* or *Concilium Arelatense II,* was not a group of canons of a council held in Arles, the prime see of Gaul, but a collection of some fifty-six canons drawn up sometime between 442 and 506 and deriving from the first Council of Nicaea and various Gallican councils.

Italian collections. Before the fifth century the churches in Italy displayed only a modest amount of canonistic activity, but it is known that by the fifth century and the Apiarian controversy the Roman church had a collection, called the *Versio antiqua romana,* with the canons of Nicaea and Sardica. Also by the early fifth century a paraphrase of the Nicene canons had been made by Rufinus of Aquileia. Between 419 and 451 the Roman church, like the African church, had translations of Eastern conciliar canons in the *Versio Isidoriana* in its three forms of *antiqua* (compiled in Africa), *vulgata,* and *gallica.* Also, after 451 the Roman church had a collection of Eastern canons, known as the *Versio*

Prisca or *Itala*. This collection differed in some ways from the *Versio Isidoriana*, particularly with the addition of the canons of the Council of Chalcedon (451).

Papal decrees were also being collected by the fifth century. The earliest of these collections is what scholars call the *Canones urbicani*, perhaps compiled in Gaul during the pontificate of Pope Sixtus III (432–440), followed shortly thereafter by the *Epistolae decretales*, compiled in Italy and perhaps in Rome, to which Pope Leo I alluded.

COLLECTIONS OF THE "GELASIAN RENAISSANCE"

At the very end of the fifth century and early in the sixth a thoroughgoing revision and systematization of canon law was carried out in the Western church. Although Pope Gelasius I (492–496) is usually connected with the revisions, his own role seems to have been fairly modest, and the intense canonistic activity continued into several later pontificates. Hence, the term "Gelasian Renaissance" is somewhat of a misnomer.

Major collections. The most famous and influential collection compiled during the "Gelasian Renaissance" was the work of the Scythian monk Dionysius, who styled himself Exiguus. He came to Rome just after the death of Pope Gelasius I (492–496) and, besides compiling canonistic revisions, worked for harmony between the Eastern and Western churches and on a reform of the calendar that began the method of dating the Christian era still in use. He died after 525, probably toward the middle of the sixth century.

In his canonistic revisions Dionysius seems to have had at least four aims: to collect universal laws; to pass over pseudoapostolic law, dogma, history, and other material that had been worked into prior collections; to collect the best texts possible and to translate accurately the Greek canons; and to put some order into the confusion of materials collected in the past by arranging his work according to source and in a chronological order.

Dionysius was responsible for collections of both conciliar canons and papal decrees. These seem to have been done separately and were then joined into a codex, or *corpus canonum*, that today goes under the name *Collectio Dionysiana*. The compilation of canons went through three redactions. The first, compiled probably about 497–500 and now found in only two manuscripts and a fragment, contained a dedication to a bishop Petronius, a list of rubrics, fifty of the apostolic canons, the canons of many of

the Eastern councils, including the ecumenical councils of Nicaea, Constantinople, and Chalcedon, and canons attributed to the Council of Carthage of 419. The second redaction, compiled at the beginning of the sixth century, was dedicated to Bishop Stephen of Salona and contained the other material of the first recension, but slightly rearranged, renumbered, and in some cases augmented. The third redaction is now lost except for its preface, found in only one manuscript. In this preface the work is dedicated to Pope Hormisdas (514–523), who ordered its compilation; and Dionysius says that he is now omitting the apostolic canons and several other canons because they are not universally recognized.

In two of the manuscripts of the second redaction of the *Dionysiana* there is a series of thirty-eight papal decrees from the period 384–498 that Dionysius compiled probably during the latter part of the pontificate of Pope Symmachus (498–514). Dedicated to Julian, cardinal presbyter of S. Anastasia in Rome, these include *praecepta* (precepts) from Pope Siricius (384–398) down to Pope Anastasius II (496–498). According to some scholars Dionysius would have had access to the papal archives for copies of these papal decretals.

Although the third recension of the *Dionysiana* seems to have been commissioned by a pope, the collection remained basically a private one. Nevertheless, it had great prestige in Rome and was cited as the *Dionysiana* as early as the pontificate of John II (533–535). Moreover, as will be seen, it was quickly augmented and diffused in large numbers of manuscripts throughout Europe in the early Middle Ages.

Minor collections. Among the minor collections compiled during this period, two (the *Collectio Frisingensis*, named after one codex, from Freising, of the two manuscripts in which it is found, and the *Collectio Teatina*, named after the manuscript from Theate or Chieti in which it is found) were private and not very influential. Three other collections, however, often designated as minor have been shown by Hubert Mordek to have enjoyed far more popularity in the early Middle Ages than has previously been thought.

The first of these, the *Collectio Quesnelliana*, named after its first editor, Quesnel (*d.* 1719), is now found in more than ten manuscripts and fragments. Although some scholars argue that it was compiled in Gaul, most agree that it was Roman, but not the official Roman collection. Its compiler tried to collect antique and universal laws, but he also worked into it some doctrinal material and Roman law.

The *Collectio Sanblasiana,* named after the only manuscript, from Sankt Blasien (in southwest Germany), in which it was originally found, is now known to exist in seven manuscripts and a fragment. Compiled probably under Pope Hormisdas, the collection contained a mixture of conciliar canons, papal decrees, and the Symmachian forgeries.

Resembling the *Collectio Sanblasiana* because it too contains the Symmachian forgeries is the *Collectio Vaticana,* once found only in Vat. Lat. 1342, but now known to exist either in whole or in part in six manuscripts.

REGIONAL AND NATIONAL COLLECTIONS
FROM DIONYSIUS TO THE CAROLINGIAN PERIOD

The consolidation of antique canon law in the *Dionysiana* occurred at the time of the breakup of the Roman Empire and the ascendency of the peoples who either had migrated into the confines of the empire or had assumed the governance of territories formerly controlled by Rome. And just as the secular law in these regions became "national" or "tribal," so canon law took on a regional or "national" character. Hence, scholars usually survey the development of canon law after the time of Dionysius according to region.

North Africa. After the Vandal invasions of the 430's, the creation and collecting of canon law in the North African church virtually ceased. But between the ascendency of the Vandals and the Muslims, there was a slight revival during the Justinianic period. During this time two systematic collections were compiled, one of which would have an extraordinary distribution in Europe during the early Middle Ages.

The first of these collections is the *Breviatio canonum* of the Carthaginian deacon Fulgentius Ferrandus, who compiled this work for Bishop Boniface about 546/547. The collection of 232 capitula on a variety of topics did not contain the full text of canons but rather rubrics with summaries of the canons of oriental and African councils.

Much more important, however, was the *Concordia canonum Cresconii,* said to have been compiled by an African bishop to supplement the work of Fulgentius. Compiled sometime in the sixth or seventh century, the collection is extraordinary for its time because its texts, based largely on the *Collectio Dionysiana,* are arranged in a systematic fashion with rubrics. Because of its convenience, the *Concordia* had a very wide distribution. Raymund

Kottje and Mordek have shown that the manuscript diffusion was heaviest in northern Italy, which may corroborate the disputed theory that the collection was compiled in Italy, perhaps by Dionysius himself. In any event, during the reforms of Charlemagne, when an augmented version of the *Collectio Dionysiana* called the *Collectio Dionysio-Hadriana* had been made quasi-official, the *Concordia* continued to be reproduced more heavily in northern Italy than the *Dionysiana.* Moreover, the *Concordia* was recast in various forms, including a Gallican recension, an excerpted form, and an abbreviation.

Italy. As might be expected, the *Collectio Dionysiana* and its systematized version in the *Concordia Cresconii* continued to be popular in Italy. But the collection itself was altered in a variety of ways. Additional material was included in the *Dionysiana Bobiensis,* so called from a manuscript from Bobbio (south of Pavia); the *Dionysiana adaucta,* compiled in Rome; and the *Collectio Dionysio-Hadriana,* sent by Pope Hadrian I (772–795) to Charlemagne in 774. There were abbreviations as well, such as the *Breviarium ad inquirendum sententias infra* and the *Epitome Hadriani.*

Beyond these collections based heavily on the *Collectio Dionysiana* were other Italian collections containing the more recent decrees of popes, theological materials, apocryphal material, and the like. These are broadly divided into three classes: (1) Collections with conciliar material, usually found in only one manuscript and apparently not especially influential (for example, the *Collectio Theodosii diaconi, Collectio Wirceburgensis,* and the many manuscripts with purely dogmatic conciliar material, such as *Verona BC LVIII* or *LIX*); (2) Mixed collections such as the *Collectio Colbertina* with its combination of the *Collectio Sanblasiana,* the *Quesnelliana,* and decretal texts; (3) Decretal collections, such as the *Collectio Avellana* of the mid sixth century with its papal letters of 368–553, unknown in other sources, or the *Collectio Mutinensis,* generally believed to have been compiled shortly after 600 with its brief notices of letters from popes drawn from the *Liber pontificalis,* Symmachian forgeries, and letters of popes up to Gregory I (590–604).

Spain. From Roman times through the Visigothic era, canonistic activity in both legislation and collecting was intense. After the Visigothic kings had renounced Arianism and become Catholic, there was a long series of councils, especially in Toledo, and the canons of these were combined with the collections of oriental and Gallican canons, papal decrees, and other materials to form extremely influential collections of canon law.

The *Collectio Novariensis,* named after a codex from Novara in northern Italy in which it was originally found, was compiled between the mid and late sixth century and contained canons from Eastern, African, Italian, and Spanish sources. Strangely, it is represented not in manuscripts from Spain but almost exclusively in codices from northern Italy, where Spanish emigrés fled during the Muslim invasion. It is now known to exist in full or fragmentary form in at least ten manuscripts, and while it played some role in the formation of Spanish canon law, its wider role came at the end of the ninth century when it was used by the northern Italian compiler of the *Collectio Anselmo dedicata.*

The *Epitome hispanica,* a small collection compiled about 598–600 probably in Tarragona, contains brief summaries of historically arranged canons from oriental, African, Gallican, and Spanish councils together with pontifical decrees, to which has been added an epitome of the Pseudo-Hieronymian tract on the ecclesiastical orders now entitled *De septem ordinibus ecclesiae.* Like the *Collectio Novariensis,* the *Epitome hispanica* is found not in Spanish manuscripts but in its full form in northern and central Italian manuscripts.

The *Collectio hispana chronologica* was clearly the most important early Spanish collection and was considered even into the twelfth century the authentic collection of Spanish ecclesiastical law. Moreover, long beyond the time of Gratian it was repeatedly copied, with as many as forty manuscripts dating from the sixteenth to the nineteenth century. Of the nearly two dozen extant early manuscripts and fragments of the collection, fifteen of them, mostly written in Spain, are nearly complete and are being used for the new edition of the collection.

For centuries a debate has raged over the authorship of the *Hispana,* with many Spaniards opting for Isidore of Seville on the basis of similarities of the prologue of the collection and the *Origines.* Nonetheless, most scholars deny this, holding that Isidore may have used in his *Origines* earlier definitions of the councils.

The collection itself is a very extensive one. The first section contains conciliar texts arranged geographically, then chronologically. The Greek councils from Nicaea to Chalcedon derive from the ancient *Versio hispana.* The African councils from I Carthage (251) to Mileve derive from a source like that which influenced the Council of Tours (567).

The Gallican councils from Arles (314) to Orléans (511) probably came from a collection known in 516 in Tarragona. And the Spanish councils are from a collection made shortly after 589 to which later ones were added. Following the conciliar canons come papal decretals from Damasus I (366–384) to Gregory I, arranged in historical order. The sources for these are quite diverse, but preeminent were the *Collectio Dionysiana* and a collection like that used by the compiler of the *Epitome hispanica.*

Because of the intense conciliar activity of the Spanish church, canons were added to the *Collectio hispana* for almost seventy years, and hence there are a number of recensions in several different forms. The first recension, the *Isidoriana,* was compiled in the time of Isidore between 633 and 635. The second recension, the *Juliana,* probably has nothing to do with Julian of Toledo but was compiled during his time shortly after 681. It is found in a Toledan form in Spanish manuscripts and a Gallican form in manuscripts largely from France. The final recension, the *Vulgata* depending on the *Isidoriana,* was completed about 694–702 and is in two forms, a common form in manuscripts largely from the interior of Spain and a Catalan form in manuscripts from Catalonia.

From the *Hispana chronologica* several re-elaborations of a systematic type were quickly made. Between 656 and 675, *excerpta* consisting of résumés of the canons were compiled and attached to the Spanish manuscripts of the *Hispana chronologica.* From these there developed a systematic collection, the *Collectio hispana systematica,* found in Latin manuscripts from the south of France and in Arabic manuscripts in Spain and Portugal. Also compiled from the *excerpta* were *tabulae* of a systematic nature, perhaps originating in Catalonia in the tenth century, according to Antonio García y García.

By the eighth century the *Hispana* was well known north of the Pyrenees and came to influence many collections of the Carolingian period and afterward.

Gallican collections. Until the recent monumental work of Mordek, it had generally been thought that most of the collections compiled in Gallican territories before the Carolingian period were very minor ones, usually contained in one manuscript and written for local churches. But multiple manuscripts are now known for many of these collections, and their influence is known to have been felt well into the eleventh century throughout Europe.

The earliest collections seem to have originated in

southern France and were clustered around Arles. Most of them are historically arranged or mixed with papal and conciliar canons, especially those emanating from Gallican provincial and regional councils. Because originally each collection was known from a single manuscript, they sometimes go under the names of those codices: the *Collectio Albigensis, Burgundiana, Lugdunensis,* and so forth. These collections have often been plundered for the *fontes materiales* they contain by editors of texts, but they have not really been edited or studied extensively by modern scholars as canonical collections.

As was the case with these historically arranged Gallican collections, so it was formerly thought that the Gallican systematic collections played little role in the development of early medieval canon law. But now it is known that a variety of these collections exercised great influence in early medieval canonistic activity.

The most important of these collections is one formerly called the *Collectio Andegavensis II* but now rechristened by Mordek as the *Collectio vetus gallica.* This collection is now known to exist in thirteen full manuscripts (only one of which is related to another), two fragments of full manuscripts, two large *excerpta,* numerous smaller *excerpta,* and dozens of later collections that include selections from it.

The author of the *Vetus gallica,* clearly a reforming cleric desirous of compiling an easy-to-use systematic collection of authentic texts, had among his major concerns the regular assembly of synods, the ordination, deposition, and duties of clerics, the rights of the metropolitan, the administration of the sacraments, and ecclesiastical properties. He depended almost exclusively upon conciliar canons to compile his collection. In later redactions more papal and patristic texts were added. Since one of the author's special themes was the protection of metropolitan rights and some of his canonical sources appear to have come from Lyons, probably from the archives there, the author must have worked in Burgundy, almost certainly in Lyons itself. As for the date, the *terminus ante quem* for the original compilation must have been 585, the date of the Burgundian II Council of Mâcon, whose canons are in the collection; and the *terminus a quo* must have been 626/627, the date of the Council of Clichy, which used the collection. Given these *termini,* the well-known correspondent of Gregory I, Etherius of Lyons, appears as the most likely ecclesiastical au-

thority responsible for the compilation of the *Vetus gallica.* And from the date of compilation, it appears that there was important canonistic activity in Gaul between 585 and 670 and that Lyons quickly replaced Arles as the center of this activity after the latter's decline in the mid sixth century. From Lyons the *Vetus gallica* traveled northward, where after its use at Clichy, presided over by Treticus of Lyons, it was augmented in another redaction in the circle of Leger of Autun. When this saintly bishop was exiled to Luxeuil, the *Vetus gallica* may have gone with him, and then to Corbie with the founding monks from Luxeuil. At Corbie, in whose distinctive pre-Carolingian *a-b* script the earliest extant manuscript of the collection was written, more additions were made, resulting in the *Generalredaktion* of the second quarter of the eighth century.

The major Gallican systematic collection deriving from the *Vetus gallica* is the *Collectio Herovalliana,* named for the owner of the single manuscript from which it was originally edited. It is now known that there exist eight manuscripts and several *excerpta* of the collection, and it is clear that its influence was extensive in later canonical collections and even liturgical books down to the twelfth century. Basically, the *Herovalliana* follows the contents of the *Vetus gallica,* but it omits and adds material.

The *Vetus gallica* was also a source for one of the most interesting systematic collections of the eighth century, the *Collectio Sangermanensis,* so called because it was originally studied from a manuscript from the Parisian abbey of St. Germain. The collection is now known to exist in a full form or in extensive extracts in four manuscripts, and isolated fragments are present in many more. Its systematic organization is much more like that of later collections than earlier systematic collections, and many of the texts are cast in the form of a dialogue between master and disciple. Besides the *Vetus gallica,* its sources are the Insular *Collectio canonum hibernensis,* conciliar and papal canons, the works of the Fathers, and liturgical material.

Insular collections. Insular Christians of Ireland, England, Scotland, and Wales began to make ecclesiastical laws and compile collections of canons very shortly after the conversion of these lands. The legislation came in several forms, as did the collections. The earliest of the legislation has generally been included in the collections of penitentials, but there were synods also that laid down canonical regulations. The *Hispana* and *Dionysiana* seem to have come early to Ireland, and these together with other material were used to make one of the earliest formal collections of canon law for the Irish church.

One of the earliest of the Insular collections is a fairly minor one, if it can indeed be called a canonical collection at all, the *Liber ex lege Moysi.* It was compiled in Ireland about 700 and, unlike the continental collections, contains exclusively moral and legal precepts drawn from the Pentateuch. This collection seems to have enjoyed some popularity in Brittany and Frankish territories, but its main importance is that is shows clearly the influence of the Old Testament on the Celtic church.

Much more important than the *Liber,* however, was the *Collectio canonum hibernensis,* compiled in Ireland about 700. It is in two major recensions, each with numerous manuscripts, several subrecensions, and at least five abridgments. Further, miscellaneous canons from it are scattered throughout canonical collections, theological and liturgical florilegia, and even biblical commentaries reaching well into the twelfth century. Its canons are arranged in a systematic fashion under titles on a variety of disciplinary, social, and spiritual topics. Each title is followed by a group of canons. These may be correctly or incorrectly attributed to the proper source, and they may be extensively reworked, abridged, or even expanded. In fact, in the prologue to the collection the compiler openly says he intends to do precisely this.

The collection is extraordinary in that, together with the expected canonical material, its nearly 1,600 canons (at least in the *A* recension) contain some 646 texts from the patristic fathers, 304 from the Old Testament, and 144 from the New Testament. Among the fathers cited are, surprisingly, such Eastern fathers as Gregory of Nazianzus, John Chrysostom, and Basil of Caesarea.

The influence of the *Collectio hibernensis* on continental canonical collections of the early Middle Ages was not perhaps as great as that of the *Dionysiana* and *Hispana,* but it would eventually come to enjoy an unexpected popularity in collections in central and southern Italy from the tenth to the twelfth centuries.

CANON-LAW COLLECTIONS
OF THE CAROLINGIAN ERA

In matters ecclesiastical the Carolingian era was characterized by attempts at reform and unification. The aim of the former was to curb what was seen to be the anarchy characterizing the Merovingian church, and the aim of the latter was to counteract the particularism of the Merovingian church.

Attempts at ecclesiastical reform actually antedated Charlemagne himself and go back to 742, when there began a series of reform councils. By the early ninth century the number of these councils had increased dramatically so that in a single year as many as three major councils could be held in various parts of the empire. Together with this conciliar activity there was also an outpouring of capitularies, both secular and episcopal, whose aim was reform of the church. At the same time, in the penitential discipline there was a reform of the older types of penitential books with the introduction of a new style that attempted to use largely antique and universally recognized canons.

In the attempts at ecclesiastical reform and unification, collections of canon law played a major role, and it is generally held that Charlemagne ordered a return to antique, universal, and genuine ecclesiastical law by suppressing the older collections and introducing what he believed was a "pure" collection of Roman canon law in the form of the *Collectio Dionysio-Hadriana.* To some extent this is true, but it is now known that the popularity of many of these older collections reached a zenith precisely in the Carolingian era. Mordek has shown, for example, that most of the manuscripts of the *Vetus gallica* were copied during this period, one even in the court of Charlemagne. Kottje has shown that in northern Italy the *Concordia Cresconii* was the preferred collection. And the *Collectio hibernensis* clearly continued to be a popular collection in western and northern France, if one can judge by the number of late-eighth- and ninth-century manuscripts from these areas.

Nonetheless, it is true that there was an attempt to introduce the best of antique canon law in the form of the *Collectio Dionysiana.* Pope Hadrian I sent to Charlemagne a copy of what he thought was this collection, the already mentioned *Collectio Dionysio-Hadriana.* In reality it was not a pure copy but one that was heavily augmented. Among the additions were subscriptions of conciliar participants after the lists of conciliar canons, creeds, papal decrees, and a series of letters of Pope Gregory II (715–731). This version of the collection clearly was a recommended form of the *mos romanus* being urged upon the Carolingian church. And as a result, scores of exemplars were made throughout Europe. By 1870 Friedrich Maassen had found some seventy of these manuscripts, and to this Mordek has added another twenty-four, many of which go back to the late eighth and ninth centuries. Moreover, there are multiple examples of *excerpta* and fragments.

Augmented as it was, the *Dionysio-Hadriana* lacked a great deal of older material that could be of value in ecclesiastical reform, and this was provided by forms of the *Collectio hispana* brought into Frankish territories both by visitors to Spain and by Spanish emigrés and the Visigothic population in the Spanish March and southern France. One of these forms was the *Collectio hispana gallicana* and the other was the *Collectio hispana systematica*, still found in two Carolingian-script codices from Lyons filled with corrections and marginalia in Visigothic script. These two forms of the *Collectio hispana* would quickly work their influence on two collections compiled in the Carolingian period, the systematic *Collectio Dacheriana* and chronological *Collectio hispana gallica Augustodunensis*. (Although it is often said that the *Hispana* was combined in the Carolingian period with the *Dionysio-Hadriana* to form the *Collectio Hispana-Hadriana*, Mordek has suggested that the combination may have come in the period of the so-called Gregorian reform in the later eleventh century.)

The *Collectio Dacheriana*, named after its seventeenth-century editor Jean Luc d'Achéry, is, unlike the *Collectio Dionysio-Hadriana* and *Collectio hispana chronologica*, a systematic collection. Because it is based heavily on the *Collectio hispana systematica*, and many of the earliest manuscripts are from Lyons and the vicinity, it is believed that Bishop Agobard of Lyons may have been its author. In its arrangement of texts the *Collectio hispana systematica* was clearly used, but a variety of sources, including the *Dionysio-Hadriana*, provided texts.

Besides a preface, which is sometimes separable in the manuscripts, the *Dacheriana* contains three books on penance, matrimony, and the ecclesiastical hierarchy. This collection, as a systematic one, became extremely popular, and beyond the twenty-two manuscripts known to Maassen, Mordek has found some thirty additional ones. Moreover, Kottje has shown that in southern and western France the *Dacheriana* seems to have been preferred even to the quasi-official *Dionysio-Hadriana*. So popular was the collection that it went through at least three recensions, even to being altered in the mid ninth century with the substitution of texts from the Pseudo-Isidorian forgeries discussed below.

Beyond the *Dacheriana*, a host of smaller, more local collections were compiled in response to calls for reform. For example, in Salzburg in the first quarter of the ninth century there was compiled a liturgicocanonical collection in two books, called the *Collectio duorum librorum* and still found in four manuscripts or fragments, whose aim seems to have been to supplement the *Dionysio-Hadriana* with didactic liturgical texts and Gallican canons. And in the vicinity of Cambrai, a farraginous collection, known as the *Collection of Laon* and still found in two manuscripts, was compiled using texts from the *Dionysio-Hadriana, Vetus gallica, and Hibernensis,* and liturgical didactic and formulaic texts.

SPURIOUS COLLECTIONS
OF THE CAROLINGIAN PERIOD

The ecclesiastical reforms undertaken by Pepin, Charlemagne, and Louis the Pious had been of great benefit to the church. Her hierarchical ordering had been regularized; the lives and education of clerics had been improved; large parts of the empire had been Christianized; and some of the best and most genuine texts of antique canon law had been reinstated.

In order to effect these reforms, however, secular rulers had had to involve themselves in the control of the church. This they had done directly and indirectly through the appointment of archbishop-metropolitans. But by the second quarter of the ninth century this interference had created tension among the bishops.

There was also another remnant of ecclesiastical government left over from patristic antiquity that created tension among the bishops by undercutting their authority. This was the continued existence of chor bishops, who were often created irregularly by single bishops and who wandered about without fixed sees.

It was in this climate of both reform and tension that there was composed what Emil Seckel called "the most audacious and vastest forgery of ecclesiastical legal sources ever undertaken and by which the world has been deluded for centuries." These forgeries were the product of a highly organized, skilled, and clever atelier working in the archdiocese of Rheims probably in the employ of Hincmar of Laon, who was locked in a bitter feud with his uncle Hincmar, archbishop of Rheims. According to the traditional account, the forgeries were issued in four parts, but over the past dozen years it has been shown that the forgeries were continuously being modified and issued in different forms. Moreover, it is clear that not all of the products of the forgers' atelier have yet come to light and have been published. Finally, it is not at all certain what texts properly belonged to the forgeries, given the fluidity of the textual tradition. In any event there are four major collections known to have been issued by the forgers.

Collectio hispana gallica Augustodunensis. This collection is named after an Autun manuscript (now Vat. Lat. 1341), which Bernhard Bischoff says was written in the Corbie scriptorium in the late ninth century. Other exemplars are now known to exist, however. The collection is usually said to have been the first collection the forgers completed about 847, but it is clear that it was influenced by what were formerly thought to have been the later forgeries. The collection is a revised version of the *Collectio hispana gallica,* but many of its canons have been altered and apocryphal sections added to deal with such issues as legal procedures against bishops, matrimony, and chor bishops.

Capitula Angilramni. Some seventy-one capitularies are attributed to Angilramnus of Metz (768–791) and said to have been sent to him by Pope Hadrian I or made as a gift for Hadrian. This short collection is especially concerned with matters touching the rights of clerics vis-à-vis seculars, such as the *privilegium fori* and accusations. Not only were the *Hispana Augustodunensis* and *Dionysio-Hadriana* used as sources, but also several patristic works and the *Breviarium Alarici.*

Capitularia Benedicti Levitae. This purports to be a continuation of the ninth-century *Capitularia* by Ansegis and in the manuscripts often follows that work as books 5 to 7. The author calls himself a deacon from Mainz, but clearly he worked in the atelier of the forgers. The *Capitularia* is a falsified attempt to gain support for the forgers' cause, especially regarding lay incursions and chor bishops, by citing secular sources and showing their agreement with ecclesiastical decrees and the works of the fathers. Among its many sources, not only are the Frankish capitularies used, but also Roman law, tribal law, the *Dionysio-Hadriana,* the *Vetus gallica,* the *Hibernensis,* the penitentials, the Bible, and the patristic fathers.

Pseudo-Isidorian Decretals. This is the largest section of the forgers' work and in the manuscripts is attributed to Isidorus Mercator or Peccator, although it has nothing to do with Isidore of Seville. It is a magnificently forged set of papal decretals

reaching back to the primitive age of the church and based on at least 10,000 textual fragments woven together.

The first section is largely made up of forged decretals from Pope Clement I (88–97) to Pope Melchiades (Miltiades, 311–314) in chronological order together with a number of genuine pieces. Then follow a number of forged pieces, including the earlier Donation of Constantine, and canons of fifty-four councils and synods in the form of the *Hispana Augustodunensis.* Finally, there are both genuine and spurious conciliar canons and papal decretals from Pope Sylvester I (314–335) to Pope Gregory II (715–731).

Among the multiple aims of the collections were the independence of clergy from lay control; the inhibition of judicial actions by laity against clergy; the diminution of the power of the metropolitans by making appeals to Rome available to lower clergy; and the suppression of chor bishops by equating their order with that of simple presbyters.

By 852 the forged decretals were being used in the dispute between Hincmar of Rheims and his suffragans, and they quickly became immensely popular. The success of the decretals is seen in the large numbers of manuscripts made almost immediately and their several recensions: A-1, A-2, B, A/B, and C. Moreover, the decretals were used almost immediately to revise canons in such collections as the *Dacheriana* and to compile new collections. In fact, from the mid ninth century to the time of Gratian there was hardly a major canonical collection that was not in some way influenced by the decretals.

Even from their origins the forgeries were held in suspicion by many churchmen. Hincmar of Rheims, for example, knew that they were forged, although he used them when they supported his position. And in the eleventh century Bernold of Constance, the Norman Anonymous, and Pope Urban II were aware of the forgery. The modern attack on their authenticity began in the fifteenth century with Lorenzo Valla's examination of the Donation of Constantine and during the Reformation when the veracity of the forgeries was disputed. Definitive proof of the forgery, however, came only in the seventeenth century with the work of the Reformed scholar David Blondel.

COLLECTIONS FROM THE MID NINTH CENTURY
TO THE MILLENNIUM
The earliest collections to follow Pseudo-Isidore were largely those based directly on it. Among these

are the *Collection of Berlin DSB Phill. 1764*, the *Pittaciolus* of Hincmar of Laon, and a group of collections in single manuscripts, including Troyes BM 1406 and Paris BN 2449. But certainly the most important is the *Collectio canonum* attributed to Remedius of Chur. This collection, made up almost entirely of extracts from Pseudo-Isidore and widely diffused in manuscripts, clearly postdated Remedius of Chur (*ca.* 790–806). The early manuscript diffusion seems to indicate a southern German origin of about 870, but there is also evidence for its diffusion in northern France. The canons from Pseudo-Isidore have sometimes been altered, and the topics dealt with are much the same as those in Pseudo-Isidore.

Not long after the Pseudo-Remedian collection was compiled, a more systematic collection based on Pseudo-Isidore appeared in northern Italy, the *Collectio Anselmo dedicata*. This collection was directed to bishop Anselm II of Milan (882–896) by a cleric who calls himself the smallest sheep of Anselm's flock. Some scholars argue that he was a cleric in Milan itself, others Vercelli, Ravenna, or Bobbio. In any event, the collection seems to have enjoyed almost as much popularity north of the Alps as in Italy because, of the nine major medieval manuscripts or fragments, four were written north of the Alps.

The collection, according to its dedication, is a systematic one in twelve books corresponding to the twelve apostles. The books deal with the Roman church and the higher ecclesiastical dignitaries, bishops, councils, presbyters and deacons, lower clerics, religious and widows, the laity, virtues, liturgy and sacraments, heretics, Jews, and pagans. Each book is divided into three sections corresponding to the *fontes* used: canon law texts from various sources, fragments from Gregory I, and Roman law from the *Lex romana canonice compta*. The sources used are, among others, the papal decretals from Pseudo-Isidore, manuscripts of which had reached northern Italy by the third quarter of the ninth century, conciliar canons from the *Dionysio-Hadriana*, and the Spanish *Collectio Novariensis*.

Beyond the *Collectio Anselmo dedicata*, there were several minor collections appearing in northern Italy, including those in Milan Bibl. Amb. A 46 inf., G 58 inf., and Verona BC LXIII. Three collections of the tenth century from the south, now in eleventh-century codices, should be singled out because they draw on somewhat unlikely material, the Irish. The first of these is the *Collection of Rome Bibl. Vallicelliana Tom.XVIII*. The manuscript itself,

written in part in Beneventan script, contains not only a long recension of the Irish *Collectio hibernensis*, but also an extensive and influential collection based on the *Collectio hibernensis*, penitentials, *Dionysio-Hadriana*, Pseudo-Isidore, and even the *Epitome Juliani*. Also written in Beneventan script is the *Collection in Nine Books of Vat. Lat. 1349*. This large collection of some 1,300 capitula is fairly well organized, but the extracts are grouped according to the sources from which they were drawn, including the *Concordia Cresconii*, the *Collectio hibernensis*, the Fathers, and a source something like that in the *Collection of Vallicelliana Tom.XVIII*. The compiler seems to favor the Byzantines, many of whom could be found in southern Italy, and uses many canons attributed to Basil of Caesarea. The third collection, that of Vatican S. Pietro H 58, was compiled in Rome itself and borrowed much from the *Collectio hibernensis* and a source resembling the *Collection of Vallicelliana Tom.XVIII* or the nearly contemporary *Collection in Five Books*. But it also contains Halitgar's ninth-century new-style penitential, and liturgical *ordines* and expositions have been scattered throughout.

As was the case in Italy in the late ninth and tenth centuries, so in Germany a host of minor systematic collections was compiled, and most survive in only one or a few manuscripts, such as the collections of Munich Clm 3851 and 3853 or Cologne DB 124. But one collection compiled in the early tenth century did have a wide distribution and provided the basis for many later collections. This was the *Libri duo de synodalibus causis et disciplinis ecclesiasticis* of Regino, abbot of Prüm (840–915). Compiled about 906 at Trier on the urging of Archbishop Ratbod and dedicated to Hatto of Mainz, the collection was made to help effect a decision made at the Council of Tribur (895) that bishops should make periodic diocesan visitations in which the lives and religious practices of clerics and laymen would be examined and that synods be held where witnesses would testify regarding crimes, scandals, and the like. And to aid bishops in this task Regino compiled his handbook with appropriate canons and lists of questions to ask in visitation. The collection is broken into two books, the first on clergy and the second on the laity, to which three appendices were later added. Each book begins with a series of simply put questions, and this is followed by the canons on which the bishop could make his judgements. In these canons Regino did not simply present the ancient texts, but he often modified them the better to suit his reforming purposes. Moreover, to give certain canons more authenticity he would change the inscriptions and occasionally give his own comment. As sources Regino used the *Dionysio-Hadriana,* the *Hispana,* the *Dacheriana,* Pseudo-Isidore, and various penitentials.

In France after the spectacular canonistic output represented by the Pseudo-Isidorian forgeries, original and important canonistic activity remained fairly dormant for the next two centuries. There were, to be sure, a number of *excerpta* of the Pseudo-Isidorian forgeries and a number of minor collections in single manuscripts, such as that in Montpellier BEM 137. There is only one collection that stands out, however, the *Collectio* of Abbo (*ca.* 945–1004), monk at Fleury, schoolmaster at Ramsey Abbey, and finally abbot of Fleury. Soon after becoming abbot he began to compile a short collection of canons in fifty-two capitula whose aim was to protect the rights and immunities of Fleury. Hence, his compilation is one of those collections recently styled by Theo Kölzer as monastic collections of canon law. To defend the monastic enterprise Abbo insisted on immunity from episcopal and lay domination, despite the fact that the collection is dedicated to Hugh Capet and his son Robert. To do this Abbo had to stress the power of the papacy in the assurance of this immunity, and one would have expected him to have supported himself with the Pseudo-Isidorian forgeries, which are clearly reflected in his other works. Strangely, however, he seems to have been hesitant about this suspect material, and hence he used other sources from diverse papal decrees, conciliar canons, capitula, and the works of the Fathers. Abbo's innovation was in his acknowledgment that there were canons of the past that disagreed with one another because of differences in place, time, and circumstances of enactment. Thus, he argued that occasionally laws must be changed because of some necessity or utility.

COLLECTIONS OF THE FIRST HALF

OF THE ELEVENTH CENTURY

Long before the so-called Gregorian reform took place in the second half of the eleventh century, ecclesiastical reform had been introduced into the church. It began in the first and second quarters of the eleventh century north of the Alps with the appointment of some very capable bishops by the late Ottonian and early Salian emperors, and to accompany this reform several collections of canon law were compiled. While these collections did not stress the role of the papacy in the administration of the church as would later reforming collections, they did aim at far-reaching renewal and regularization of ecclesiastical life.

Certainly the most important of these collections was the *Decretum* compiled by Burchard, the bishop of Worms (1000–1025). Along with Ivo's later *Panormia,* the *Decretum* was one of the two most popular early medieval collections used throughout the entire Middle Ages. Even apart from book XIX, which had an enormous diffusion of its own, manuscripts of Burchard's *Decretum* blanket European libraries. When Otto Mayer completed his great study on Burchard by 1935, he had drawn attention to seventy-four manuscripts. In the more recent work of Mordek, Kottje, Gérard Fransen, and Horst Fuhrmann scores more have been reported. There seem to have been several reasons for its popularity. First, it was an extensive (but not overly extensive), practical, and conservative handbook. Second, it contained a synodical *ordo* and sermon which could be used in the holding of synods, and thus it would have been a natural book to copy and frequently consult in cathedral libraries. In fact, on the first folio of one northern Italian codex of the *Decretum* there is a diagram and description of how the archbishop of Milan and his suffragans were to arrange themselves in a circle during synods.

The *Decretum,* which was compiled between 1008 and 1012, was not the work of Burchard alone, according to later sources. Brunicho, the *praepositus* of the Worms cathedral, had asked for the composition of the book and, together with Bishop Walter of Speyer, was later described as one of Burchard's collaborators. But the major collaborator seems to have been a certain Olbert, who was eventually to become the abbot of Gembloux.

The *Decretum* is made up of 1,785 capitula spread over twenty books. It begins with books on the Roman church, clergy, ecclesiastical goods, sacraments, and various crimes, then works its way down to book XVIII on visitations of the sick. Then follow two books that were so popular that they were eventually separated and circulated independently. Book XIX, entitled *Corrector sive Medicus,* is a very practical guide for hearing confession. It is really an extraordinary penitential that goes into great detail regarding various sins. Book XX, called the *Speculator,* is a handbook of dogmatic theology with sections on heaven, hell, judgment, providence, and other matters of eschatology.

The sources from which Burchard drew his canons were multiple, but especially important were Re-

LAW, CANON: TO GRATIAN

gino and the *Anselmo dedicata*. Also used were the *Dionysio-Hadriana*, Pseudo-Isidore in the "Cluny" recension, episcopal capitula, the *Collectio hibernensis*, the church fathers, and Roman and tribal law.

In using these sources Burchard took great liberties with them in order to make his collection as practical and authentic as possible. Hence, he very often altered the inscriptions of canons to lend them more authority, especially when they were suspect penitentials. Moreover, in the texts of the canons themselves Burchard often altered older forms by rearranging them to fit his era, by adding material that he thought necessary, and by suppressing material he felt was inappropriate. In a sense his working methods were not totally unlike those of the Pseudo-Isidorian atelier.

The overall picture given by the *Decretum* is a canonical collection written by a practical reformer in the *via media*. Burchard welcomes secular help in his reform attempts, but as a bishop he insists on his own rights. He recognizes the pope but does not overplay his power. He encourages monastic and religious life but insists on his own prerogatives over them. He is against simony, and although he defends the sanctity of marriage, he acknowledges that there are some cases in which divorce is justifiable for the innocent party.

Beyond its obvious influence reflected in scores of manuscripts still extant in European libraries, the *Decretum* was heavily used in at least forty later collections. Even in the first half of the eleventh century it had begun to be used as a source in its own right in the *Collection in Twelve Books*. This collection, compiled in southern Germany sometime between 1020 and 1050, has come down to us in at least two forms in some six manuscripts. The arrangement of the collection is very much along the lines of Burchard, but the texts are borrowed not only from Burchard but also from the *Anselmo dedicata*, some of whose manuscripts come from southern Germany.

As the *Decretum* of Burchard was being compiled north of the Alps, there was also intense canonistic activity in Italy also. This came in the form of the *Collection in Five Books*, styled by Carlo Guido Mor as the *vade mecum* of Italian clerics and monks in the eleventh century. Although its influence was great, the collection itself is now found in only three large manuscripts, all written in central and southern Italy and all reflecting southern Italian influence. Its 1,288 titles, most of them containing multiple canons, are arranged in five books dealing with the sacred orders and ecclesiastical hierarchy, clerical

and monastic obligations, the sacraments and liturgy, penance and virtues, and matrimony and chastity. Among the sources used are the *Collectio hibernensis*, a compilation like the *Collection in Nine Books of Vat. Lat. 1349*, Pseudo-Isidore, the *Dacheriana*, the *Concordia Cresconii*, several penitentials, Roman law, and even several laws attributed to Henry II.

The general impression given by the collection is that of a great canon law code *cum* theological and liturgical compendium, especially for use in monastic circles. It is much more conservative than Burchard's *Decretum* and not so intensely directed at reform.

As will be seen, the influence of the *Collection in Five Books* was very substantial from the middle of the eleventh century, but it must be noted here that very quickly after its compilation and first extant manuscript from Monte Cassino dated to about 1025, it was combined with Burchard's *Decretum* or a Burchard-like source that was in Italy. In a hitherto unreported collection, now in an early or mid-eleventh-century codex whose provenance is Viterbo but which is presently in Toledo BC 22–32, extracts from the *Collection in Five Books*, especially from the penitential sections, are combined with Burchardian material in a convenient *vade mecum*.

COLLECTIONS FROM THE MID ELEVENTH CENTURY TO GRATIAN

Italian collections. Even as the reform of the church sponsored by the papacy from the middle of the eleventh century was under way, canonical collections of a traditional type continued to be compiled, especially in Italy. Most of these were either extracts from the *Collection in Five Books* or were mixtures containing the *Collection in Five Books*, other Italian sources, and Burchard's *Decretum*, which by this time was heavily represented in Italian manuscripts. Most of these collections are found in single manuscripts, and in 1916 Paul Fournier examined a series of them, including ones in Naples BN XII.A.28; Florence BML 4.4, Ricc. 300; Monte Cassino 216; Vat. Lat. 4977 and 8487; and Rome Vallicelliana F 54, F 92, F 2, E 62, and B 32. Beyond these collections and manuscripts studied by Fournier, there exist extracts from the *Collection in Five Books* in the following hitherto unreported manuscripts: Rome Bibl. Vallicelliana Tom.XXI, B 63, R 32, Bibl. Angelica 1447, Vat. Lat. 3830, 4317, and 7818; Madrid BN 373; El Escorial Z III 19; and New York, Hisp. Soc. Amer. 380/819.

Of particular interest among these manuscripts are the Farfa *Multiloquiorum in Seven Books* and the *Collectio Angelica*. The *Multiloquiorum in Seven Books* (*ca.* 1090–1099, probably originating at the imperial abbey of Farfa and now in Vat. Lat. 4317), is heavily dependent on a source like the *Collection in Five Books,* a lost codex of which was at Farfa. But it is filled with theological and liturgical pieces, especially on the Eucharist, reflecting perhaps the new concerns on the subjects being raised in the second half of the eleventh century by such figures as Berengar of Tours and the liturgicocanonical scholar Bernold of Constance. The *Collectio Angelica,* now found in the manuscript Rome Bibl. Angelica 1447, is a collection in at least thirteen books, the first and most of the second of which are lost. In this collection blocks of material have been borrowed from the *Collection in Five Books* and arranged according to a new order. There are, however, a few other sources introduced, such as Roman law from the *Lex romana canonice compta.*

A third and most interesting collection of the second half of the eleventh century is the *Collectio canonum regesto Farfensi inserta,* recently edited by Kölzer. This Farfese monastic collection by Gregory of Catino consists of five books deriving primarily from Burchard's *Decretum,* the *Collection of Five Books,* and Pseudo-Isidore. Bound as it is together with charters and other documents in Vat. Lat. 8487, it is particularly concerned with protecting ecclesiastical and monastic goods and immunities.

From the numbers of these collections of a traditional kind compiled from the middle of the eleventh century into the twelfth, it is clear that this type continued to play an important role in the ecclesiastical discipline and life of the Italian church. But a new type of collection had begun to be sponsored by the reforming papacy, one that emphasized papal prerogatives and jurisdiction and that depended not on the traditional collections of the immediate past but on what was called the *traditio canonica,* the decretals of popes, authentic canons, and the texts of such primitive fathers as Cyprian, Ambrose, Augustine, Leo I, and Gregory I. To this end there seems to have begun a search through the papal archives and patristic dossiers to find canons to create such collections. It is known that Hildebrand, the future Gregory VII, asked the canonist Peter Damian to collect in a single volume texts related to the apostolic see. And in one collection of about 1090, now found in a single Italian manuscript in London and hence called the *Collectio Britannica,* there is just

such a collection of papal decrees from Gelasius I down to Urban II, to which has been added material from the Justinianic laws. Also, it is clear that such collections as the *Dionysio-Hadriana* and Pseudo-Isidorian Decretals were carefully combed for canons in support of the reforming popes, and the result was the compilation of several remarkable Italian collections.

One of these, the *Capitulare,* or *Defloratio canonum* of Atto, cardinal of S. Marco in Rome, is a minor one. Compiled perhaps in the 1070's and found in only one manuscript, this small collection is chronologically arranged and uses texts from a Pseudo-Isidorian source close to that used by Atto's contemporary Cardinal Deusdedit, extracts from papal letters, and extracts from the *Dionysio-Hadriana.* The canons chosen and the interpolations occasionally made in them clearly reflect a concern for papal prerogatives, but because of its small size and the existence of other more important collections, the influence of Atto's collection was slight.

Far more successful was the *Diversorum patrum sententie,* or the *Collection in Seventy-four Titles.* It is unclear who the author of this collection was, but it may have been compiled in Italy by 1067 and was certainly in use during the pontificate of Gregory VII (1073–1085). The vast majority of its canons come from Pseudo-Isidore, but whether they come from it directly or through an intermediate source, such as the *Collection in Four Books,* as John Gilchrist has suggested, is unclear. In any event the decrees from Pseudo-Isidore at times were modified when necessary. The 315 canons of the collection are fairly systematically arranged under seventy-four titles. According to many scholars the first and predominant theme dealt with is papal primacy, but Fuhrmann has argued that the sections dealing with the papacy are just as heavily concerned with criminal and other legal procedures affecting the clergy and laity. Moreover, there are many canons dealing with other matters, such as the prerequisites for entrance into clerical life, simony, translation of bishops, ordination, monastic liberty, and liturgical practice. Manuscripts of the collection were rather widely distributed in Italy, southern Germany, France, and Belgium, and the collection went through three or perhaps four recensions. But, more important, it heavily influenced subsequent collections.

Chief among these collections in Italy was the *Collectio canonum* compiled about 1083 by Anselm of Lucca (*d.* 1086). This is a systematically arranged collection that is still found in fifteen manuscripts and that went through at least four major recensions: *A, B, C,* and *Bb.* Although it depended heavily on the *Seventy-four Titles,* it goes beyond this collection in its completeness and in the number of additional sources used. For the heavy papal and procedural sections, the *Seventy-four Titles* and Pseudo-Isidore were clearly preferred (700 out of 1,200 canons). But when it came to matrimonial and penitential concerns, the traditional canon law books were turned to, and hence Burchard's *Decretum* was included in the reform collections.

Almost contemporary with Anselm's collection is another *Collectio canonum* compiled about 1087 by Cardinal Deusdedit. This collection is divided into four large books concerning the privileges of the Roman see, Roman clerics, ecclesiastical goods, and the liberties and immunities of the church. Like Anselm, Deusdedit drew on the *Seventy-four Titles,* other older collections, and patristic sources. But he also made extensive use of material more recently found in the search to support the papal cause: texts from Cyprian, the liturgical *Ordines romani,* the *Liber pontificalis,* and even Roman law texts from the *Authenticum.*

Of these Italian collections of the second half of the eleventh century that were especially concerned with papal prerogatives, only one, the *Collectio canonum* of Anselm of Lucca, seems to have been used by Gratian in his *Concordia discordantium canonum,* or *Decretum,* and that in a mixed form. But two similar collections compiled in Italy in the first quarter of the twelfth century did play a much larger role in Gratian.

The first of these was the *Polycarpus* by Cardinal Gregory of San Chrisogono in Rome. This collection, which was compiled during the pontificate of Pope Paschal II (1099–1118) and still exists in eleven manuscripts, together with manuscripts of a French recension, was widely diffused in Spain and perhaps even Germany. It is divided into eight books, each subdivided into titles, and its order and sources follow Anselm of Lucca in emphasizing papal prerogatives and procedural matters. Nonetheless, among the many additional sources Gregory used were texts from Burchard's *Decretum* and Roman law. Although it is not absolutely certain that Gratian later depended directly on the *Polycarpus* itself for texts, it is most likely that he at least used derivatives from it.

Very near in time to Gratian's *Decretum* (ca. 1125–1140) was the *Collection in Three Books,* compiled in central Italy between 1112 and 1123. Still ex-

tant in three manuscripts, the three books deal with the pope, clergy, and faithful and are subdivided into titles, each with its summary, after which there follow a number of texts. The major sources are the Italian reforming collections with their stores of papal decrees. Unlike the *Polycarpus* but like Gratian later, there is little use of Burchard's *Decretum.* To what extent Gratian used the *Collection in Three Books* directly is yet to be ascertained, but in a number of instances readings of the canons used by Gratian are those found in the *Three Books.*

A final major Italian collection written during the so-called Gregorian reform, actually during the pontificate of Urban II (1088–1099), was the *Liber de vita christiana* by Bonizo of Sutri. Although Bonizo was one of the more rigorous proponents of the reforming positions espoused by the Gregorian party, his collection is not so much concerned with papal prerogatives as with the Christian life. It begins with baptism and ends with penance, and of some 780 canons only eighty-nine are drawn from Pseudo-Isidore, and that probably through other collections. Rather, large parts of Burchard or Burchardian derivatives were used. Most interesting are Bonizo's *dicta* and his alteration of canons to suit his own rubrics or personal preferences.

Beyond these major Italian collections from the mid eleventh century to Gratian that in varying degrees represent the reforms of this period, there were a host of minor collections found in one or a few manuscripts, among which are the *Collection in Two Books,* the related *Collection of Assisi BC 227,* the *Collection in Five Books of Vat. Lat. 1348, Collection of Lord Ashburnham, Collection of Santa Maria Novella, Collection of Palermo, Collectio Gaddiana, Collection in Seven Books, Collection in Nine Books, Collection of Vat. Lat. 3829, Collection of Turin BN E.V.44,* and the *Collection of Vat. Lat. 1361* with its combination of Anselm of Lucca and the northern *Panormia* of Ivo of Chartres.

Transalpine collections. One of the earliest manifestations of papal support for reforming efforts north of the Alps came in the celebrated episode of 1049 at Rheims with Leo IX's attack on simonical clerics. Hence, it is interesting that the first of the reforming collections in France should be a *Collection of Rheims* and reflect this same concern. This compilation, recently brought to light and studied by Linda Fowler-Magerl, is found in five manuscripts and a fragment and worked its influence on at least three southern French, Catalan, and Italian collections of the late eleventh century and early twelfth century. This collection is an excellent example of a compilation arranged according to the *Quellenblock* principle. One of the blocks of materials is especially interesting because it came from a reforming circle in Tuscany and together with the other blocks clearly reflects material and manuscripts available at Rheims in the 1060's. The major concerns of the collection illustrate the situation there shortly after 1059, that is, a concern to protect the privileges of Rheims, to put down simony, and to promote a learned clergy.

Not long after this collection of Rheims was compiled, manuscripts of larger Italian reforming collections, such as the *Collection in Seventy-four Titles* and Anselm's *Collectio canonum*, began to make their way northward, and these were combined with existing northern collections such as Burchard's *Decretum* to form yet another generation of reforming collections.

Among these is a group that has been called the "Poitevin Collections," not because they all necessarily came from Poitou but because they contain texts compiled there, such as the canons of the Synod of Poitiers of 1078, or they reflect the situation in the area that is portrayed in such texts as the confessions of Berengar on the Eucharist. Among these collections are the *Collection in Thirteen Books*, whose manuscript came from Poitou; the *Collectio Tarraconensis*, now known in five manuscripts; the *Collection of Bordeaux*, existing in two manuscripts in different forms; the *Collection in Seventeen Books*, of whose four manuscripts two reflect canonistic activity in Poitiers and two reflect canonistic activity in Worms; and the Turin *Collection in Seven Books*.

Far more important than this early group of Poitevin collections were those by Ivo of Chartres (*ca.* 1040–1115). Not only was one of Ivo's collections, the *Panormia*, diffused in scores of manuscripts, but his work was also drawn upon later by Gratian. The largest of his collections was the *Decretum* with 3,760 canons divided into seventeen books. Because of its size it does not appear to have been very popular and is found now in only nine manuscripts or fragments, although its first modern editors used two others now lost. Like several other collections of the reforming period, the *Decretum* is as much a theological compendium as it is a canonical collection; hence it begins with faith, baptism, confirmation, the Eucharist, and the like, and then moves into canonistic material. Among the many sources Ivo used to compile this vast collection were especially Burchard

(about 1,600 canons) and Pseudo-Isidore (at least 248 canons), although some of these may have come from intermediate compilations.

A second collection attributed to Ivo, one which was widely diffused in Europe and clearly influenced Gratian's *Decretum*, was the *Tripartita*. This important collection, now being edited for the first time, is traditionally divided into *Collections A and B*. The first of these is in two parts: the first contains in chronological order some 655 papal decrees of popes through Urban II; the second contains conciliar canons and patristic texts. *Collection B*, containing 861 texts drawn from Ivo's *Decretum* under twenty-nine titles, has generally been considered to have been the work of Ivo, but recently Peter Landau has cast doubt on this with his finding that the texts from the *Decretum* came not from the French recension of the text but from a later recension known in England.

By far the most popular of Ivo's collections was the *Panormia*, a compact, convenient, and well-arranged collection in eight books. Many manuscripts of this collection begin with a prologue discussing the sources of the collection and the distinction between precepts and counsels. The arrangement of the *Panormia* is much like that of the *Decretum*, beginning with faith, baptism, confirmation, and the like, but the number of canons from the *Decretum* has been reduced to some 920. Further, about 120 canons have been added from such sources as the *Collection in Seventy-four Titles*, perhaps through the intermediary of the *Collection in Four Books*.

Scattered throughout European libraries are not only full texts but multiple *excerpta* of these canonical collections of Ivo. Beyond this influence, however, Ivo's work was incorporated into a number of independent collections before the time of Gratian. Several of these, such as the *Collection of Ste. Geneviève*, are found in single manuscripts and are fairly minor. But there are several others which enjoyed a wider circulation. In northern France and more especially in the area of Therouanne, several collections incorporating material from Ivo were compiled in the early twelfth century. The *Collectio Sangermanensis*, not to be confused with the earlier collection of the same name, is represented in two manuscripts. The *Collection in Ten Parts*, compiled about 1023 and based heavily on Ivo's *Panormia*, can be found in six manuscripts or fragments. And from this collection an abridgment or *Summa*, now found in four manuscripts, was compiled by Haimo, archdeacon and then bishop of Châlons. In Châlons-sur-

Marne itself two collections based on Ivo were compiled, one in eighteen books and the other in thirteen.

Ivo's influence was present also in what may have been a major *vade mecum* for twelfth-century Spanish and southern French clerics, the *Collectio Caesaraugustana,* named for Zarragosa, near which an early manuscript was found. Appearing in two recensions in a number of manuscripts, including ones from Salamanca and Barcelona, this collection draws heavily on the *Decretum* of Ivo and is also another good example of a collection where blocks of material have been used in its compilation.

At the time Gratian was completing his *Decretum,* drawing on many of these reforming collections, both transalpine and Italian, England under Archbishop Theobald of Canterbury (1139–1161) was finally receiving systematic collections, such as those of Burchard and Ivo, from the Continent. Before that time the official collection in England had been the *Collectio Lanfranci,* created by the prior of Bec, who became archbishop of Canterbury (1070–1089). Widely diffused in manuscripts in England, Lanfranc's collection was an abbreviated version of the Pseudo-Isidorian Decretals, in a form like Vat. Ottob. 93, together with the *Capitula Angilramni* and Greek conciliar canons according to a version of the *Dionysio-Hadriana.* This official English collection is a striking example of the vitality of ninth-century canon-law collections in the twelfth century, just prior to the transformation of ecclesiastical law throughout Europe by the *Decretum* of Gratian.

BIBLIOGRAPHY

Bibliography. Bulletin of the Institute of Research and Study in Medieval Canon Law, in *Traditio,* **11** (1955) to **26** (1970), and thereafter *Bulletin of Medieval Canon Law,* n.s.

Editions. Editions of collections are cited in many of the books and articles listed below, but a convenient, although at times untrustworthy, list of editions can be found in M. Fornasari, *Initia canonum a primaevis collectionibus usque ad Decretum Gratiani, I, A–G,* in *Monumenta Italiae ecclesiastica, Subsidia* 1 (1972) XXXIII–LI.

Works dealing with collections throughout the early Middle Ages. Pietro and Girolamo Ballerini, *De antiquis collectionibus et collectoribus canonum* (1757), in *Patrologia latina,* LVI (1855), 11–354; Paul Fournier and Gabriel Le Bras, *Histoire des collections canoniques en Occident depuis les fausses décrétales jusqu'au Décret de Gratien,* 2 vols. (1931–1932; repr. 1972); Gérard Fransen, *Les collections canoniques,* in Léopold Genicot, ed., *Typologie des sources du moyen âge occidental,* fasc. 10 (1973); Antonio

García y García, *Historia del derecho canónico, I, El primer milenio* (1967); Peter Landau, "Neue Forschungen zu vorgratianischen Kanonessammlungen und den Quellen des gratianischen Dekrets," in Dieter Simon and Walter Wilhelm, eds., *Ius Commune: Veröffentlichungen des Max-Planck-Instituts für Europäische Rechtsgeschichte Frankfurt am Main,* XI (1984), 1–29; Hubert Mordek, "Kirchenrecht und Reform im Frankenreich: Die Collectio vetus gallica, die älteste systematische Kanonessammlung des fränkischen Gallien, Studien und Edition," in *Beiträge zur Geschichte und Quellenkunde des Mittelalters,* 1 (1975); Roger E. Reynolds, "Basil and the Early Medieval Latin Canonical Collections," in Paul J. Fedwick, ed., *Basil of Caesarea* (1981), 513–532, "The 'Isidorian' *Epistula ad Leudefredum:* An Early Medieval Epitome of the Clerical Duties," in *Mediaeval Studies,* **41** (1979), "The Ordinals of Christ from Their Origins to the Twelfth Century," in *Beiträge zur Geschichte und Quellenkunde des Mittelalters,* 7 (1978), and "The Pseudo-Hieronymian *De septem ordinibus ecclesiae:* Notes on Its Origins, Abridgments, and Use in Early Medieval Canonical Collections," in *Revue Bénédictine,* **80** (1970); Alphons M. Stickler, *Historia iuris canonici latini, I, Historia fontium* (1950); Alphons van Hove, *Prolegomena ad Codicem iuris canonici,* 2nd ed. (1945).

Pre-Carolingian collections. Gonzalo Martínez Díaz, *La colección canónica Hispana, I, Estudio* (1966); Friedrich Maassen, *Geschichte der Quellen und der Literatur des canonischen Rechts im Abendlande,* I (1870, repr. 1956); Hubert Mordek, "Il diritto canonico fra tardo antico e alto medioevo: La 'svolta dionisiana' nella canonistica," in *La cultura in Italia fra tardo antico e alto medioevo: Atti del convegno tenuto a Roma. Consiglio nazionale delle ricerche, dal 12 al 16 Novembre 1979* (1981), 149–164; Roger E. Reynolds, "Excerpta from the *Collectio hibernensis* in Three Vatican manuscripts," in *Bulletin of Medieval Canon Law,* n.s. 5 (1975).

Carolingian collections. Horst Fuhrmann, "Einfluss und Verbreitung der pseudoisidorischen Fälschungen von ihrem Auftauchen bis in die neuere Zeit," in *Schriften der Monumenta Germaniae historica,* **24** (1–3) (1972–1974); Herwig John, ed., *Collectio canonum Remedio Curiensi episcopo perperam ascripta,* in *Monumenta iuris canonici,* ser. B: *Corpus collectionum,* II (1976); Raymund Kottje, "Die Bussbücher Halitgars von Cambrai und des Hrabanus Maurus," in *Beiträge zur Geschichte und Quellenkunde des Mittelalters,* 8 (1980), and "Einheit und Vielfalt des kirchlichen Lebens in der Karolingerzeit," in *Zeitschrift für Kirchengeschichte,* **76** (1965); Roger E. Reynolds, "Canon Law Collections in Early Ninth-century Salzburg," in Stephan Kuttner and Kenneth Pennington, eds., *Proceedings of the Fifth International Congress of Medieval Canon Law: Salamanca, 21–25 September 1976,* in *Monumenta iuris canonici,* ser. C, subs. 6 (1980), 15–34, and "Unity and Diversity in Carolingian Canon Law Collections: The Case of the *Collectio hibernensis* and Its Derivatives," in Uta-Renate Blumenthal, ed., *Carolingian Es-*

says: Andrew W. Mellon Lectures in Early Christian Studies (1983), 99–135.

Collections from the tenth century to the Gregorian reform. Paul Fournier, "Un groupe de recueils canoniques italiens des Xᵉ et XIᵉ siècles," in *Mémoires de l'Académie des inscriptions et belles-lettres*, 40 (1916); Theo Kölzer, ed., *Collectio canonum Regesto Farfensi inserta*, in *Monumenta iuris canonici*, ser. B, *Corpus collectionum*, V (1982); Roger E. Reynolds, "Odilo and the *Treuga Dei* in Southern Italy: A Beneventan Manuscript Fragment," in *Mediaeval Studies*, 46 (1984), and "A South Italian Ordination Allocution," *ibid.*, 47 (1985).

Collections of the Gregorian Reform. John T. Gilchrist, *The Collection in Seventy-four Titles: A Canon Law Manual of the Gregorian Reform* (1980), *Diversorum patrum sententie: Sive Collectio in LXXIV titulos digesta*, in *Monumenta iuris canonici*, ser. B, *Corpus collectionum*, I (1973), and "The Relationship Between the Collection in Four Books and the Collection in Seventy-four Titles," in *Bulletin of Medieval Canon Law*, n.s. 12 (1982).

Collections of the late seventh and early twelfth centuries. Linda Fowler-Magerl, "Vier französische und spanische vorgrat i anische Kanonessammlungen," in *Aspekte europäischer Rechtsgeschichte*; *Festgabe für Helmut Coing zum 70. Geburtstag* (1982), 123–146; Peter Landau, "Das Dekret des Ivo von Chartres," in *Zeitschrift der Savigny-Stiftung für Rechtsgeschichte, Kan. Abt.*, 70 (1984); Roger E. Reynolds, "The Turin Collection in Seven Books: A Poitevin Canonical Collection," in *Traditio*, 25 (1969).

ROGER E. REYNOLDS

[See also **Abbo of Fleury; Anselm II of Lucca; Apostolic Constitutions; Burchard of Worms; Capitulary; Carolingians and the Carolingian Empire; Charlemagne; Church, Early; Church, Latin; Clergy; Councils (Ecumenical); Councils, Western; Decretals, False; Decretum; Deusdedit, Cardinal; Dionysius Exiguus; Donation of Constantine; Hincmar of Rheims; Isidore of Seville, St.; Lanfranc of Bec; Martinus Braga; Merovingians; Papacy, Origins and Development of; Regino of Prüm; Rufinus of Aquileia; Urban II, Pope.**]

LAW, CANON: AFTER GRATIAN

GRATIAN AND HIS SUCCESSORS

The Bolognese monk Gratian published his *Concordia discordantium canonum* around 1140. In its original form the *Concordia* consisted of a great collection of the canons organized in a series of treatises on the main subjects of church law, such as the nature and types of law, the structure and function of the church hierarchy, and marriage. Gratian treated his subjects by using the method developed by Peter Abelard for theological discourse. He stated a proposition or asked a question, set out canons supporting different positions on the matter, and reconciled conflicts in a dictum that served also to enunciate a doctrine.

In the first part of the book, Gratian covered subjects in a relatively orderly procession from general to specific topics, although he digressed often. The treatise on the nature of law develops in this way: it begins with a general definition of law, explains that law is either divine or human, then defines the types of divine and human law.

The second part of the work consists of thirty-six hypothetical cases (*causae*) of the type a professor might use in class. The treatise on marriage is made up of ten cases (*causae 27–36*). There are also cases on legal procedure, the legal status and condition of monks, and the use of force by ecclesiastical authorities.

The *Concordia* was revolutionary. The Master, as Gratian was later called, had gathered more canonical material than any of his predecessors and had gone beyond them in a decisive way by organizing it into a comprehensive and coherent statement of church law. By applying to the canons the rational techniques of the theological school of Peter Abelard, he had created a new canonical jurisprudence.

Gratian intended his book to serve as the basis for the teaching of canon law, whatever ulterior political or social purposes he might have had. But the work was not entirely suited for classroom use. The professors of law who first used it restructured it to fit their needs. They divided the first part into 101 distinctions, and they added texts left out by Gratian. The most important of the additions were contained in two long treatises: a treatise on penitence, which was inserted into the third question of *causa* 33, and a long section appended to *causa* 36. This was the treatise on the sacraments (*De consecratione*), which the Schoolmen considered to be the third part of the work. Both of these treatises were subdivided into distinctions. In addition, nearly all the selections from Justinian's *Corpus iuris civilis* were inserted after the *Concordia* left the atelier of Master Gratian. Whether the Master himself participated in making all these changes is not known.

While making the *Concordia* into the basic textbook for the study of the new canonical jurisprudence, the teachers gave it a new name, the *Decretum* or *Decreta*, a title that emphasized the book's function as the repository of the ancient law of the church. By the 1140's a school of canonists at Bologna had founded their work on the *Decretum* and had begun to produce glosses, lectures, questions, and other literary products of the classroom. The success of the course on the *Decretum* is indicated both by the number of its copies extant from the first decades of the school and by the abbreviations of the work that circulated in Europe. The shortened versions were reference works for church officials who heard cases. Although some older collections of canon law, such as those of Ivo of Chartres (completed in the 1090's), continued to be used in northern European churches to the end of the twelfth century, Gratian's book became overwhelmingly popular as those who had studied at Bologna won positions of influence in the hierarchy. By the 1170's the *Decretum* was being used virtually everywhere as the basis for teaching and as the basic reference work. It had become the basic manual of the Roman curia.

The new jurisprudence was attractive to litigants as well as to students. By 1150 Bernard of Clairvaux, the leading Cistercian abbot, complained that the papacy of Eugenius III (1145–1153) was preoccupied with lawsuits. In succeeding papal reigns the preoccupation grew steadily. The evidence of the growth of legal business is the increasing number of decretal letters produced by the papal curia. Decretal letters cannot be distinguished from other papal correspondence by form or by the procedure through which they were issued, but they had a distinctive role as sources of law. The papal chancery issued them as instructions to local judges delegated to hear cases appealed to the papal court, as responses to queries about legal doctrine received from episcopal courts, and as declaratory judgments about the rights of ecclesiastical persons or corporations. Even some papal privileges came to be regarded as decretals because they contained statements or illustrations of legal principles. What all these forms share is that they were included in collections used by lawyers and judges; they formed a corpus of new law.

The increasing use of decretals did not affect the priority of the *Decretum* in the schools or in the libraries of churches. Until the 1180's study of the canon law consisted in study of the *Decretum* only; this study would, it was presumed, prepare students to deal with the new law being created by the courts.

Those who lectured on the *Decretum*, called decretists by historians, produced a growing mass of commentary that was handed down from generation

to generation of teachers. Beginning in the early 1160's, legal scholars began to collect the body of commentary into large works, called apparatus. Like Gratian, the authors of these works not only collected and sifted the comments of their predecessors, but also provided new comments and connective passages that tied the material into a coherent whole. After 1188, the great Bolognese canonist Huguccio produced a massive apparatus on the *Decretum*. This work was the dominant one in the school—its main parts absorbed in the works of Huguccio's successors—until about 1216, when Johannes Teutonicus, also a teacher at Bologna, incorporated its most important parts into a new work. This work of Johannes became the standard apparatus on the *Decretum*, the *Glossa ordinaria*. It was revised somewhat by Bartholomew of Brescia in 1245.

The work of Huguccio brought to a close the most creative period of the work of the decretists. The shaping of his work into the *Glossa ordinaria*, though an advance, did not contribute a great deal that was totally new to the tradition of commentary on the *Decretum*. During the 1190's the canonists of Bologna turned their attention to the decretal law and began, effectively, the long period of creative work by the decretalists. During the first two decades of this movement many legal writers, such as Johannes Teutonicus himself, contributed to both the decretist and decretalist tradition, but the latter received more attention.

DECRETALS

The shaping of the corpus of decretals, which served as the basis for the work of the decretalists, began as a result of the choices and interests of the canon lawyers, particularly of the teachers. The professors inserted a very small number of decretals into the *Decretum*, among the older texts they added to the work. But by about 1160 the lawyers stopped enlarging the *Decretum* itself and began to make appendixes. The earliest of these consisted mostly of pre-Gratian texts, but increasingly these collections came to be dominated by decretals. By the mid 1170's the new material was no longer treated as an appendix to the *Decretum*, but as an independent collection of decretals, although many of the early decretal collections occur in manuscripts that also contain a copy of the *Decretum*.

The earliest post-Gratian collections of legal texts, almost completely made up of decretal letters, have the appearance of unorganized dossiers of papal letters. Scholars have called these collections "primitive" both because their compilers did not organize the material topically and because the letters are copied out in full. In fact, the canonists were still making collections of this sort in the 1190's, after "systematic" collections had become common. The primary characteristics of the systematic collections are the edited form of the texts and the distribution of texts and parts of texts among titles that treat the main doctrines and subjects of the law. Late primitive collections have titles, but their compilers did little editing of the texts, and the topical organization is not so strong as it is in the systematic collections.

The majority of decretals were issued as instructions to judges delegate. One or both litigants of a case would appeal to the papal curia for justice, and the pope would issue a letter appointing local prelates to hear the case and defining the law of the case. Such letters contained much material that legal scholars and lawyers considered unimportant, and in the 1180's the compilers of collections began to edit this matter out. The narrative of the case, the names of the parties and of the *res litigiosae,* and the procedural history of the case might be essential information for the prospective judges, but the lawyers were interested only in the newly defined law. This narrow interest is evident in the systematic collections. In some cases, scholars can trace the course of editing; in others, only the truncated version of a letter is known.

The first systematically organized collection was compiled in Bologna just before the Third Lateran Council (March 1179). It is known from a Parisian manuscript and therefore is called the Second Paris Collection *(Parisiensis secunda).* Scholars believe that its author was the famous Bolognese professor Bernard of Pavia and that he created it while preparing his treatise on canonical election, *Summa de electione.* His citations in the treatise make it clear that he used the collection.

The Third Lateran Council produced the most important body of canonical legislation since the publication of the *Decretum,* and its decrees became an important subject of study by lawyers. But the council was also a watershed in the history of the decretal law. The prelates who attended the meeting brought with them legal assistants and much legal business, and the interaction of these people at the meeting spread the idea of systematic decretal collections. In the early 1180's such collections were appended to copies of the conciliar legislation. If the Bolognese master Bernard provided the model for a systematic treatment of the decretal law, the northern lawyers, particularly those in the Anglo-Norman realm and in northern France, were apparently the first to create a course on that law. During the 1180's the northern schools were teaching decretal law as well as the basic course on the *Decretum.*

At Bologna it was Bernard of Pavia who organized a course on the decretal law in 1190 or 1191. He created for this course a new textbook of decretal law, the *Breviarium extravagantium* (later known as the *Compilatio prima*). This work was divided into five books and topically ordered, and it was enlarged in at least two revisions. But the flow of decretals from the curias of Celestine III (1191–1198) and Innocent III (1198–1216) was too great to be incorporated in Bernard's basic text. His successors, the Englishmen Gilbert and Alan, made new collections to supplement it. Gilbert's collection was completed about 1202 and revised once or twice afterward. Alan completed his work about 1206. It too was revised. The decreasing time between the making of new textbooks is an indication of the increasing activity of the papal court.

Pope Innocent III effected another watershed in the history of the canon law. Between 1140 and 1209 the lawyers, both teachers and practitioners, had shaped the decretal law by making the collections that contained it. A great many decretal letters never got into the collections and therefore never influenced the development of the law. Innocent acted to end this anarchic evolution of the law.

The occasion of his action was the appearance of a collection of his own decretals made by the lawyer Bernard of Compostela the Elder, an archdeacon of the Holy See. The pope disapproved of some of Bernard's choices and some of his editing, so he commissioned the papal notary Peter of Benevento to compile an approved collection. The new collection contained the decretals issued by Innocent's chancery between 1198 and 1208. Toward the end of 1209, the pope sent this collection to Bologna. He did not issue it as an act of legislation, but as a basic collection of his decretals authenticated with respect to both their texts and their intentions by the pope himself.

The new collection rendered the collections of Gilbert and Alan partially superfluous, since both contained early letters of Innocent now incorporated in the collection of Peter. Consequently John of Wales, a professor at Bologna, undertook to cull from the two earlier textbooks the material that remained unique to them. The result was a new collection of letters that predated Innocent. As a result, about 1210 the decretal course at Bologna had three textbooks: Bernard of Pavia's collection, John of Wales's collection, and Peter of Benevento's collection. All were organized in five books subdivided into titles, in the systematic order established by Bernard in the first volume.

Like its predecessor of 1179, the Fourth Lateran Council (1215) produced a large body of legislation contained in seventy-one decrees, and the canonists eagerly incorporated the new law into their corpus of material. Shortly after the council Johannes Teutonicus, who about the same time was completing the *Glossa ordinaria* on the *Decretum,* compiled a new decretal collection made up of the conciliar decrees and of letters of Innocent III issued since the publication of Peter's collection. In 1216 or 1217 Johannes completed his collection, which became the fourth textbook of the decretal course. Finally, Honorius III (1216–1227), Innocent's successor, commissioned the Bolognese professor Tancred to make a collection of his decretals. In 1226 this work became the fifth textbook of the course.

The decretal collections of Bologna, popular and influential as they were, did not define the decretal law throughout the church. In the north older collections continued in use, and the importance of Bernard's and his successors' collections was only grudgingly accepted. A manuscript from Rouen (now Paris, B.N. 3922A) shows how a northern lawyer incorporated the Bolognese texts of Bernard and Gilbert into his basic reference book. The Rouen lawyer noted the order of the new collections, copied the letters he did not have elsewhere, and entered cross-references. When he had finished, he could use his old book against someone who was relying on the Bolognese texts.

The state of affairs indicated by the example from Rouen, and by many other contemporary books, made litigation in church courts difficult and hindered the development of a coherent post-Gratian canon law. The basis of legal research and argument was indeterminate. In 1230 Pope Gregory IX (1227–1241), himself a lawyer, commissioned the famous Spanish lawyer Raymond of Peñafort, then serving in the papal curia, to compile a grand new collection, which the pope would promulgate as the official corpus of decretals. Raymond based his new work on the five textbooks of the Bolognese tradition, which became known as the *Compilationes antiquae.* He used the structure and order that had become standard since the first compilation by Bernard

of Pavia, but he edited the texts much more severely than his predecessors. In 1234 Gregory issued his decretals by sending them to Bologna. The new book, with its carefully edited texts, was to replace all previous collections—it alone defined the body of decretal law. The canonists, in recognizing the book as the second standard work after the *Decretum,* called it the *Liber extra.*

From the 1190's the canonists had devoted the main part of their energies to glossing the decretals, an activity animated by the addition of new collections every few years. Now the decretals of Gregory IX became the basis of new apparatuses of glosses, which incorporated much of the earlier commentary on the *Compilationes antiquae.* The tradition of apparatuses on the decretals led to Bernard of Parma's *Glossa ordinaria,* the first redaction of which was completed in 1241. Bernard himself revised it more than once—for a final time in 1263, three years before his death.

The compilation of a commentary recognized as standard naturally dampened the creativity of the community of canonists, but in the mid thirteenth century some of the greatest medieval lawyers were at work. In particular, Henry of Susa, the cardinal bishop of Ostia (hence called Hostiensis), and Sinibaldo Fieschi, who became Pope Innocent IV in 1243, are considered among the greatest legal minds of the Middle Ages. Moreover, the papacy continued to produce new decisions and to hold important councils. Innocent IV, for example, made much new law in his decretals and held a great council at Lyons in 1245. He and his successors issued collections of *novellae,* which they intended to be inserted into or appended to the *Liber extra* and which became the basis for new creative work by legal scholars.

The number of these new collections produced a certain amount of confusion, much like that which had existed before 1234, so in 1298 Pope Boniface VIII promulgated a new collection, organized on the same model as the decretals of Gregory IX. This work became the third standard text of canon law; the canonists, referring to the five books of the decretals, called it the *Liber sextus.* Most of the material in the new collection came from the chancery of Boniface, but it also incorporated important texts from the two councils of Lyons (1245, 1274) and from the courts of earlier popes, particularly Innocent IV.

The *Liber sextus* became the basis for a new spurt of creative activity in the schools. By 1301 the canonists had produced elaborate apparatuses on the

Sextus; the one by Johannes Andreae, a lay canonist, became the *Glossa ordinaria* on the book. Johannes produced a first redaction of this commentary about 1301, and enlarged it later.

In 1317 a further collection added to the renewed activity of the decretalists. Pope John XXII issued the *Constitutiones Clementis V (Constitutiones Clementinae),* which contained the decrees of the Council of Vienne (1311–1312) and decretals from the chancery of Clement. Again Johannes Andreae produced the *Glossa ordinaria* on the *Clementinae,* as these constitutions came to be known. This commentary was completed about 1322.

The *Clementinae* was the last official addition to the corpus of standard canon law books, but the papacy continued to produce new law, and canonists were bound to take note of it. During the late Middle Ages several of these collections were in circulation, but only two became accepted as unofficial parts of the *Corpus.* The first was a small collection of the decretals of John XXII compiled about 1325 by the canonist Zenzelinus de Cassanis. Zenzelinus also provided the collection, called the *Extravagantes Johannis papae XXII,* with an apparatus of glosses. In the fifteenth century another collection of *extravagantes* was compiled, containing seventy decretals; in 1503 the canonist Chappins added four decretals. It was organized according to the plan of the *Liber extra* and bears the title *Extravagantes communes.* These two private collections became generally recognized appendixes to the corpus after 1582, when Pope Gregory XIII had them printed along with the corrected, and henceforth official, Roman edition of the whole corpus.

This Roman edition brought to a close the final chapter in the history of the canon law of the Middle Ages. The papal commission that produced it grew out of the reforms instituted by the Council of Trent and was appointed by Pope Gregory XIII. It was in this period of reform that the books studied by law students and used in the courts came to be seen as a corpus, and the term *corpus iuris canonici* was first used officially in Gregory's letter giving approval to the edition produced by the *Correctores Romani.* But the publication of an approved edition did not make the *corpus* into the exclusive lawbook of the church. The work produced by the commission was merely the recognized basis of the law, the purified medieval tradition that would serve as the cornerstone of a canonical legal system that included new judicial decisions and conciliar legislation. This corpus based on the *Decretum* and the decretal collec-

tions was replaced in 1917, when Pope Benedict XV promulgated the *Codex iuris canonici.* The code took effect in 1918. It was revised by a commission established in 1963 by Pope John XXIII, and the revised code was promulgated by Pope John Paul II in 1982.

BIBLIOGRAPHY

The study of medieval canon law, particularly of the classical period (1140–1378), is now centered at the Institute of Medieval Canon Law at the University of California, Berkeley. The Institute publishes an annual *Bulletin,* which since 1956 has contained a bibliography of works on all aspects of scholarship on canon law, and it publishes a series of texts and studies, the *Monumenta iuris canonici.* The Institute also maintains a research library of microfilms of medieval manuscripts and of published materials. The annual bibliography, together with the literature cited in the following works, provides the best guide to scholarship on all aspects of medieval canon law.

The classic history of canon law is Alphons van Hove, *Prolegomena ad codicem iuris canonici* (1945). This work can be supplemented by Gabriel Le Bras, ed., *Histoire du droit et des institutions de l'église en occident,* VII, *L'age classique, 1140–1378* (1965); and Helmut Coing, ed., *Handbuch der Quellen und Literatur der neueren europäischen Privatrechtsgeschichte,* I, *Mittelalter (1100–1500)* (1973). There is no comprehensive history of canon law in English.

The history of canonistic literature for the period 1140–1234 is now based on Stephan G. Kuttner, *Repertorium der Kanonistik (1140–1234)* (1937), supplemented by his many later studies. The most important of these, some of them concerned with the thirteenth and fourteenth centuries, are collected in three volumes: *The History of Ideas and Doctrines of Canon Law in the Middle Ages* (1980), *Medieval Councils, Decretals, and Collections of Canon Law* (1980), and *Gratian and the Schools of Law, 1140–1234* (1983). Each of these volumes contains *retractationes* in which Kuttner corrects and brings the articles up to date.

There is no comprehensive history of canonical private law, but see Willibald M. Plöchl, *Geschichte des Kirchenrechts,* 4 vols. (1953–1969). Hans E. A. Feine provides a briefer summary in *Kirchliche Rechtsgeschichte,* I, *Die katholische Kirche* (1950, 5th rev. ed. 1972). An increasing amount of work on the influence of canon law on European legal systems is being done. See Hans Liermann, "Das kanonische Recht als Grundlage europäischen Rechtsdenkens," in *Zeitschrift für evangelisches Kirchenrecht,* 6 (1957–1958).

S<small>TANLEY</small> C<small>HODOROW</small>

[See also **Abelard, Peter; Bernard of Clairvaux, St.; Bologna, University of; Boniface VIII, Pope; Corpus Iuris Civilis; Councils, Western; Decretals; Decretum; Glossa-**

LAW, CIVIL—*CORPUS IURIS*, REVIVAL AND SPREAD.

As part of his effort to restore the grandeur of the Latin Roman Empire, the Byzantine emperor Justinian (r. 527–565) appointed a commission early in his reign to gather together the disparate sources of the law. In 533 Justinian promulgated the commission's chef d'oeuvre, the *Digest* or *Pandects,* a collection in fifty books of excerpts from the writings of the classical jurists dating from the late Roman Republic to the beginning of the third century A.D. It was arranged by topic, largely according to the traditional arrangement of the ancient Roman actions in the praetor's edict. The same year also saw the promulgation of the *Institutes (Institutiones),* an elementary textbook in four books. In 534 Justinian promulgated the commission's revised *Code (Codex Justinianus),* a collection in twelve books of imperial legislation and decisions in cases arranged by topic and chronologically by emperor, beginning in the second century up to and including Justinian. Justinian's legislative efforts did not stop here: the remaining thirty years of his reign saw numerous *Novels (Novellae,* or new laws), which were privately collected during his reign and the reigns of his successors.

These four works, the *Institutes,* the *Digest,* the *Code,* and the *Novels,* which the Latin West knew under the title of *Corpus iuris civilis* (Body of civil law), rank with the Bible in the list of the most important books in the history of Western civilization. Knowledge of the *Corpus iuris* as a whole, however, was virtually lost in the West from the beginning of the seventh century until the end of the eleventh. Around the end of the eleventh century, the *Digest* began to be studied again at Bologna. The succeeding centuries saw a revival and spread of knowledge of the entire *Corpus iuris* throughout Western Europe, although its influence varied from country to country and from time to time. Academic study of the *Corpus iuris* continued throughout the later Middle Ages, but in the fourteenth and fifteenth centuries the focus of study tended to shift to commentaries based on it, while the text itself receded into the background. Despite the importance of canon law as an object of academic study (it was an impor-

tant object of legal studies in most places, in some places the sole object), the *Corpus iuris* remained overall the most important book for academic legal studies throughout the period from the twelfth through the fifteenth centuries. The influence of the *Corpus iuris* radiated out from the academy into the fields of politics, ecclesiastical administration, and native customary law.

To say that knowledge of the *Corpus iuris* was virtually lost in the early Middle Ages is not to say that all knowledge of Roman law was lost. Prior to Justinian's time the rulers of some of the Germanic kingdoms in the West had promulgated compilations of Roman law for the Latin-speaking peoples in their domains. These were based on the Theodosian Code (*Codex Theodosianus,* published in 438), a predecessor of Justinian's *Code,* and on post-Classical practice books and abridgments of juristic writings. Perhaps the most important of these compilations was the *Breviary of Alaric* (the *Lex romana Visigothorum*), promulgated by the Visigothic king Alaric II in 506. Although the *Breviary* remained in effect as law for no more than a century and a half, it was a principal source of knowledge of Roman law in the West until the eleventh century. Clerical notaries, too, kept alive some Roman practices in the early Middle Ages, and many Roman legal principles can be found in ecclesiastical legislation and in the writings of churchmen of this period.

We are badly informed about the teaching of law generally, and particularly of Roman law, in the early Middle Ages. There is evidence, however, of some Roman law instruction at Ravenna, at least in the eleventh century; and the teachers of Lombard law, who concentrated around Pavia, made some use of Roman principles and ideas in expounding their material.

Portions of the *Corpus iuris* are known to have circulated in the early Middle Ages. Knowledge of the full text of Justinian's *Institutes* was never lost in Italy. There was a Latin epitome of the *Novels,* the *Epitome Juliani,* and beginning in the ninth century an epitome of the *Code* (about a quarter of the whole) began to be expanded as fuller texts became available. While the subject remains somewhat controversial, it would seem that prior to the end of the eleventh century the *Digest* as such was not known at all in the Latin West and the *Novels* and the *Code* were known in only imperfect and incomplete versions.

In the middle of the eleventh century a complete manuscript of the *Digest* was rediscovered, probably in the south of Italy. The manuscript, "beautiful as a star," seems to have been written in the late sixth century and is known from its present location in the Laurentian Library in Florence as the *Codex Florentinus* or *Litera Florentina*. The *Florentina* was copied, perhaps at Monte Cassino, and this copy was collated with another manuscript of the *Digest*, now lost. The collated copy, also lost, became the archetype of all Western manuscripts of the *Digest*. The *Florentina* itself went to Pisa, where it remained until the capture of Pisa by the Florentines in 1406.

Sometime in the late eleventh century a manuscript of the *Digest* was brought to Bologna. A century and a half later the glossator Odofredus (d. 1265) reports the traditional Bolognese account of what happened:

> Sir Irnerius was among us the lamplight of the law. For he was the first who taught the laws in this city. The first *studium* in this city was in arts; and when the *studium* at Rome was destroyed, law books were brought to the city of Ravenna and from Ravenna to this city. On account of this, the law books which were brought from the city of Ravenna to this city were studied in the arts curriculum. A certain Sir Pepo began on his own authority to read in the laws, although whatever there was of his science was of no repute. Sir Irnerius taught in this city in arts and began by himself to study in our books; and studying he began to want to teach in the laws. He was of very great repute, and he was the first illuminator of our science; hence we call him the lamplight of the law.

A number of points in this text require modification. The implication that there was a law school at Rome is almost certainly wrong, nor does the relationship between Ravenna and Bologna seem to have been quite as direct as the text makes it out to be. But the basic outlines given in the text seem to be true. The founders of the *studium* in law in Bologna were Pepo (active in the last quarter of the eleventh century) and Irnerius (Guarnerius, *ca.* 1055–*ca.* 1130). Pepo is the earlier and the more mysterious of the two figures. Perhaps he is to be identified with the late-eleventh-century schismatic bishop of Bologna named Peter. We know more about Irnerius. He is found in documents associated both with Matilda of Tuscany (1046–1115) and with the emperor Henry V (1086–1125), and is last mentioned as alive in a document of December 1125. All that survives of his academic work are brief introductions to the *Code* and the *Institutes,* some glosses, and a tradition that he was the instructor of the "four doctors," the next generation of Bolognese teachers of law. By the time of Irnerius' death, in addition to the *Digest,* the full Latin text of the first nine books of the *Code* had been recovered, and Irnerius and his followers used a much fuller Latin version of the *Novels,* known as the *Authenticum.*

Irnerius' students, the "four doctors"—Bulgarus de Bulgarinis (d. 1166?), Martinus Gosia (d. ca. 1160), [H]Ugo de Porta Ravennate (d. ca. 1166/1171), and Jacobus de Porta Ravennate (d. 1178)—were all present at the Diet of Roncaglia in 1158 and obtained privileges from the emperor Frederick I Barbarossa both for themselves and for their students at Bologna. This event, coupled with the close association of the doctors with the legal and political life of the city, seems to have ensured the survival of the teaching of civil law at Bologna. From the mid twelfth century, we can trace chains of masters and students into the fourteenth century and beyond. A third generation of students, which died out before the end of the twelfth century, includes such figures as Rogerius (d. ca. 1170), Vacarius (d. ca. 1198), Johannes Bassianus (d. ca. 1190), and Placentinus (d. 1192). A fourth generation, which died out in the first half of the thirteenth century, includes Pillius Medicinensis (d. ca. 1210), Hugolinus (d. ca. 1235), Roffredus (d. ca. 1243), and, perhaps the greatest of all, Azo (d. 1220). The efforts of these four generations of glossators were summarized in the mid thirteenth century by Azo's student Accursius (Francesco Accorso, d. 1263) in the great "ordinary gloss" (*Glossa ordinaria*) on the entire *Corpus iuris.*

The *Digest* is an extraordinarily difficult text. The extracts that Justinian's commissioners gathered together in the short space of three years clearly shows some powerful minds at work, but the authors of the extracts wrote from different points of view at different times about an ever-changing body of law. The commissioners were supposed to remove all contradictions in the texts to make them reflect the law of Justinian's time, but their efforts in this regard were by no means complete. Further, the classical Roman jurists had a tendency to assume as common knowledge the fundamentals of their discipline and to deal instead with the more complicated issues of special interest to their readers. This gap in fundamentals is only partially filled by Justinian's *Institutes.* The *Code* is also a difficult text. The greatest part of it postdates the period of the jurists, and many of the extracts, like those in the *Digest,* also assume the fundamentals of the topics with which they are dealing.

The first effort of the Roman law glossators, then,

was to uncover and explain what the texts meant. They read the texts aloud to their students, noting down, first between the lines, then in the margin of the text, the meaning of obscure terms, cross-references to other texts that seemed to deal with the same problem, and the principles on which the texts seemed to be based. Most of the known glosses of Irnerius are of this type.

The glossators next began to deal with some of the more fundamental problems of the *Digest.* The texts are not all consistent, and some method had to be found to reconcile them. The methods of reconciliation were standard ones in the dialectic of the day. Seeming contradictions were resolved largely on the basis of distinctions, either inherent in the texts themselves or brought to bear from the outside; historical explanations of the contradictions were rarely used. By and large the glossators preferred to make the texts appear to be a coherent whole.

The glossators did not always agree in their interpretation of the texts, and as time went on they cited the opinions of their predecessors, either without comment or before adding their own view. Ultimately, apparatus of glosses came to be published in the form of *lecturae* or *commentaria,* in some of which the original text is omitted, except for the key word on which the gloss is hung, and the glossatorial development alone is reported. Accursius' great "ordinary gloss" is an example of this kind of literature. Accursius selected from the divergent views of many glossators those that he believed belonged to the mainstream; he also wrote many of his own glosses. Accursius' apparatus, however, unlike that of certain others—for example, Azo's—came to be copied along with the full text of the *Corpus iuris.*

The gloss itself is the earliest form of juristic literature on the *Corpus iuris.* Relatively soon after the first glosses were written, however, other forms of literature appeared, mostly in connection with one or another aspect of the glossators' teaching function. After lecturing on the texts themselves, the master might lecture generally on the subject matter of the title of the *Digest* or *Code* in which the texts appeared. The relationship of this summa (comprehensive summary) to the text is looser, the master attempting in this case to "put it all together." The earliest summae deal with particular titles: Bulgarus, "On fraud" (D.4.3) and "On ignorance of law and fact" (D.22.6); and Martinus, "On the law of dowries" (D.23.3).

The next development is a more ambitious summa of the whole of the Roman law, loosely ar-

ranged according to the titles of the *Code.* This work, called the *Summa Trecensis* (from the location of the chief manuscript), was formerly thought to be by Irnerius, but it is now known to date from the middle of the twelfth century. It was probably composed by a pupil of Martinus, perhaps the youthful Rogerius, and it exhibits an interest in equity—in relaxing the strictures of the law to make it conform to moral principle—that is characteristic of the *gosiani,* the followers of Martinus. Rogerius is known to have composed a second summa, which he left unfinished. His pupil Placentinus finished it sometime in the 1170's and then went back and wrote his own summa on the titles that Rogerius had already treated. Both of these works show the same characteristics as the *Summa Trecensis.* The most influential summa on the titles of the *Code* is that by Azo (between 1208 and 1210), which marks a return to the mainstream of the Bolognese tradition.

The Bolognese law professor might test students' knowledge by posing questions while he was expounding the text. Particularly apt questions, with the professor's answer, were recorded either in the gloss or separately in collections of *Quaestiones legitimae.* A more elaborate form of question, usually involving a hypothetical set of facts, was reserved for a debate. From this second type of question there seem to have developed the various collections of "Disagreements of Masters" *(dissensiones dominorum).* In these questions, too, we can see the beginning of the practical element in the training of students, how they were taught to apply the law to facts, how they learned to marshal arguments on one side or another, even how they applied laws of the first six centuries to the twelfth century.

The medieval student also needed guides to aid his memory. Summaries of the texts of the *Corpus iuris* were published separately as *casus* or *commenta.* Telling arguments made in dispute were published separately in the form of *notabilia* or *brocardia.* Schemata of the various distinctions that appeared in the gloss or the questions were sometimes also published separately.

The intellectual origins of the glossators' methods are somewhat obscure. The tradition reported by Odofredus that Bolognese legal studies began in the arts curriculum suggests that the elements of the trivium played some role. Perhaps the most important element was dialectic, as part of the study of rhetoric. The first two generations of Bolognese masters began their work before French scholasticism had had much of an impact in Italy. The development of the scholastic method probably gave powerful support to the methods of the glossators, but the origins of their methods must be sought in developments that antedate Peter Abelard (*ca.* 1079–*ca.* 1142). In this regard the parallels between the glossatorial methods of the biblical scholars of a slightly earlier period and those of the first glossators of Roman law demand further study.

The glossators' teaching of Roman law proved powerfully attractive. Students flocked to Bologna; instruction in Roman law began to take place in cities other than Bologna, even in places outside Italy; and the canonists adopted the glossators' methods and some of their legal principles.

There seems to be some connection between the establishment of the legal *studium* at Bologna and the struggle between empire and papacy as it worked itself out in the investiture controversy. The association of both Pepo and Irnerius with Matilda of Tuscany suggests that they hoped the Roman law might provide some support for the papal position. On the other hand, the evidence also points to an imperial connection for both Pepo (if he was indeed the schismatic bishop of Bologna) and Irnerius and certainly to an imperial connection for the four doctors. Later lawyers and publicists used texts of Roman law to support secular power against that of the papacy. Philip IV the Fair (*r.* 1285–1314), for example, associated Roman lawyers with his court at the time of his struggles with Boniface VIII. Some have even seen the development of a canon law *studium* at Bologna in the early decades of the twelfth century as a kind of counter to the study of Roman law, an effort to give respectability to the papal side of the controversy.

If there is undeniable evidence that the struggle between empire and papacy was connected with the origin of both *studia* at Bologna, it is equally clear that much of what the early glossators accomplished—both in civil and canon law—had little to do with the the political controversies of their day. There is relatively little in the *Corpus iuris* that concerns public law. Principles of government were derived from the texts, and they were, as one might expect, imperial Roman and, to a certain extent, Byzantine principles. But the texts of the *Digest*, almost exclusively, and those of the *Code*, in large measure, concerned matters of private law. While the glossators of the Roman law certainly did not ignore those portions of the *Code* and *Novels* that deal with public law, their efforts began with the *Digest* and were quite evenly spread over the whole of the *Corpus*

iuris. This means they must have spent the bulk of their time on texts that deal with the great topics of Roman private law—persons, property, obligations, and actions. The greatest immediate effect of their activity on the practical level was in the area of procedure, and while we may see a program of political reform in the Romano-canonic procedure of the twelfth century, the procedure itself was not the subject of much political controversy in its day.

What little is known about the students who studied civil law at Bologna in the twelfth century and who did not become professors suggests that a great variety of careers were available to them. Some of them worked in the imperial chancery; others found positions in the administration of the cities; others in the courts of princes; still others, perhaps a growing number toward the end of the century, seem to have moved into canon law and into the church. The connection between what the professors were teaching and what many of their students ultimately did is tenuous. It would seem that the method that the professors of Roman law taught was of more practical utility than the content of the law itself. The method, in turn, could be used to support either side of the controversy between empire and papacy, or to resolve lesser disputes far removed from the great controversy.

The first and greatest impact of the revival of Roman law studies occurred at Bologna itself. Sometime in the 1120's or 1130's a monk named Gratian began to teach canon law at Bologna, employing the same methods that the glossators had been using with Roman law. Since he had no authoritative text handed down to him in the way that the *Corpus iuris* had been handed down to the glossators, he composed his own compilation of the previous canonic collections and interleaved the texts with his own commentary, calling the whole work the *Concordia discordantium canonum* (Concordance of discordant canons). (The text was later called the *Decreta* and later still the *Decretum;* ultimately it was to form the first and largest book of the *Corpus iuris canonici,* a conscious parallel to the *Corpus iuris civilis.*) Gratian's text was itself glossed and commented on, distinctions were made, questions were posed and debated, and summae written. Canon law teaching and writing quickly took on many of the characteristics of Roman law teaching and writing.

Although Gratian employed the methods of the glossators of the Roman law, there was relatively little in his *Concordance* borrowed directly from Roman law. His students, however, inserted a number of Roman texts in the *Concordance,* and the twelfth-century canonists made increasing use of ideas and rules belonging to Roman law, although they were also conscious of the fact that canon law differed from Roman. The two disciplines advanced along separate but parallel paths, and there was considerable interchange between them. Despite later efforts to prevent the study of Roman law by certain clerics and in certain universities, throughout the Middle Ages some knowledge of Roman law was a necessary part of the intellectual equipment of a good canonist.

The first and perhaps the most important practical effect of the revised studies of Roman and canon law was on the procedure of the church courts, especially the papal court in the mid twelfth century, a time of great expansion of appeals to the papacy. The first of the treatises on Romano-canonic procedure was written by Bulgarus, and although it is largely based on Roman law, it was written at the request of the chancellor of the Roman church. The papacy adopted and refined the Romano-canonic procedural system, and under the leadership of the papal court, church courts throughout the Western church did the same. Its influence was felt in many secular courts as well. Procedural literature proliferated throughout the twelfth and thirteenth centuries, written by men who had been trained either in Roman or in canon law or in both. The two most influential procedural works of this period, Tancred's *Ordo judiciarius,* composed early in the thirteenth century, and Durantis' (Guillaume Durand's) *Speculum iudiciale,* first published in the 1270's, were both written by canonists trained in Bologna. In both works the Roman and the canonic elements are inextricably intertwined.

The twelfth-century glossators did not teach only at Bologna. This does not mean that they established law faculties in other cities; by and large, those were a product of the thirteenth century, not of the twelfth. Instruction in Roman law, however, was taking place in a number of Italian cities by the end of the twelfth century, and a number of Bolognese glossators went even further afield. Placentinus, for example, taught and wrote at Mantua and at Montpellier, Phillius Medicinensis at Modena. Vacarius taught in England, probably at the cathedral school of Theobald, archbishop of Canterbury.

The spread of the teaching of Roman law in Italy in the thirteenth century is intimately connected with the foundation of new centers of study. Of the numerous centers, some acquired privileges that allowed them to become universities. The most important of these were Padua (founded by scholars who migrated from Bologna in 1222) and Naples (founded by Frederick II in 1224). The former came to rival Bologna as a center for legal studies; the latter was notable for the practical quality of the writings of its professors from its very beginnings. It is not until the end of the century, however, that the mainstream of Italian legal science turned its attention to the customs and statutes of the Italian cities.

Outside of Italy, there seems to have been a considerable amount of academic activity connected with Roman law in twelfth-century Provence. A number of short treatises based on Roman law and designed for the practical instruction of lawyers are probably of Provençal origin. The most famous are the *Petri exceptiones* and the *Tübingen Lawbook.* Certainly of Provençal origin is a summa on the *Code* in Provençal, known as *Lo Codi.* Whether we should associate the three earliest systematic *summae* based on the titles of Justinian's *Code* with Provence is more controversial. At least Placentinus' *Summa* seems to have been composed at Montpellier.

The later scholarly division of France into the land of written and the land of customary law (*pays de droit écrit* in the south, and *pays de droit coutumier* in the north) would have us believe that the southern third of France was given over entirely to Roman law. This is a considerable exaggeration, as recent research has shown. But the early revival of Roman law studies in the south of France, coupled with the tendency of southern French customary rules to parallel Roman rules, suggests both a greater continuity with the Roman tradition and a marked early influence of Roman law teaching.

Similar developments seem to have occurred in Spain. The seventh-century Visigothic Code (*Leges Visigothorum*) contains a number of elements derived from Roman law. Roman law teaching was revived in non-Arabic Spain by the early thirteenth century, and by the middle of the century the various redactions of the *Fuero real* (between 1252 and 1255) and the *Libro de las leyes* (a later redaction of which is known as *Las siete partidas*) show a native legal system imbued with Roman ideas.

In the north of France, the influence of Roman law was more indirect. Paris had a school of canon law but not of Roman law. There was, however, a Roman law faculty at the University of Orléans and another at that of Toulouse. Some thirteenth-century academic products of these universities have survived, suggesting that these institutions were lively intellectual centers. Beyond the university, the penetration of Roman ideas in the north of France was slow, but unmistakable. *Li livres de jostice et de plet* (written *ca.* 1260) is a curious mixture of Roman law and customary law from west-central France, probably produced by a student at Orléans in the middle of the thirteenth century. Philippe de Rémi, Sire de Beaumanoir's (*d.* 1296), great treatise on the law of the small customary jurisdiction of Clermont en Beauvaisis (*Coutumes de Beauvaisis*) shows a firm grasp of local detail that owes nothing to Roman law, qualified by an underlying structure that is decidedly Roman in its flavor.

The situation was somewhat different in England. Vacarius taught Roman law in England but seems to have left no pupils who themselves taught Roman law. During the thirteenth century, however, instruction in both Roman and canon law was given at Oxford. In that century learning in Roman law in England seems to have been quite widespread. Bracton's great treatise *On the Laws and Customs of England (De legibus et consuetudinibus Angliae)* is full of Roman law, so much so that in some parts we may doubt the accuracy of his description of English law. After the thirteenth century, however, the influence of Roman law seems to have died out so far as the central royal common law courts are concerned. It remained, of course, of considerable importance for the church courts, and, probably through the medium of the canon law, it had some influence on the development of at least the procedure of the High Court of Parliament and the King's Council. The end of the Middle Ages witnessed the development of two civil law courts, Admiralty and the court of the Constable and Marshal. Beyond this there is an unmistakable, but as yet ill-defined, influence of civilian ideas on the Chancellor's court, and a vaguer and quite controversial influence of civilian ideas on the general development of English jurisprudence.

Outside the imperial court and the church courts, there is relatively little evidence of a practical impact of Roman law in Germany and the Low Countries in the twelfth and thirteenth centuries. (Switzerland may have been something of an exception.) Instruction in Roman law began with the foundation of such universities as those of Prague, 1348/1349; Cologne, 1388; Louvain, 1425; and Basel, 1459/1460. During the fourteenth century, and more noticeably in the fifteenth century, ideas coming from Roman law began to penetrate the writing on the diverse customary laws of the Empire. There was also a growing popular literature on law, based largely on Roman and canon law, apparently designed to instruct local lawyers and officials who could not afford university training. The extraordinary development of writing about Roman law in the Empire which followed the formal reception of Roman law by the *Reichskammergericht* in 1495 had medieval antecedents, but the writing itself belongs more to the legal history of the early modern period than to that of the Middle Ages.

The first wave of Italian scholarly work on Roman law culminated in the great gloss of Accursius. After Accursius the direction changed. The text of the *Corpus iuris* with the Accursian gloss became the received text. It was taken for granted and commentary on it, together with monographic literature on particular topics, became the chief means by which each instructor advanced his own ideas. The fourteenth and fifteenth centuries also witnessed a proliferation of collections of *consilia,* the opinions of various great jurists on particular cases. The quantity of published *consilia,* particularly in the fifteenth century, suggests that the world of practice rather than the lecture hall had become the place where the important developments in law were taking place.

The period of the late thirteenth century through the fifteenth century is known as the time of the commentators. The phrase refers not only to the type of literature that the law professors produced in this period but also to the shift in emphasis from the explication of the text of the *Corpus iuris* to its adaption to the more practical concerns of the day. In this respect Odofredus is a transitional figure. He wrote commentaries in a style that foreshadowed the new fashion, but their content was little more than a prolix repetition of the work of the glossatorial period that had preceded him. Jacobus de Ravanis (Jacques de Révigny, *d.* 1296) and Petrus de Bellapertica (Pierre de Belleperche, *d.* 1308) in France and Cinus de Pistoia (Cino da Pistoia, 1270–1336) in Italy were considerably more innovative. The greatest of the commentators were Bartolus de Saxoferrato (Bartolo da Sassoferrato, 1314–1357) and Baldus (Baldo degli Ubaldi da Perugia, 1327–1400), master and student. The latter also wrote extensively on canon law.

All of these writers revealed in their commentaries an interest in system-building, and the systems they built are in many cases far from that of the Roman texts on which they are ostensibly commenting. They expanded on distinctions that the glossators had introduced into the law of property to take account of the realities of the postfeudal age; they began to discuss public law and the relationship between general and local law in a systematic way; and they described the marital property systems of the time, using the terminology, but not the rules, of the *Corpus iuris.* The commentators' mastery is impressive even today; their range is great, and their books voluminous. Bartolus, in particular, became something of a legend: "No one is a good jurist who is not a Bartolist" *(Nemo jurista nisi sit bartolista)* was the maxim.

The fifteenth century witnessed the continuation of the work of Bartolus and Baldus. Practical needs came more and more to the fore. Paulus de Castro (Paolo di Castro, *d.* after 1441) and Alexander Tartagnus (Alessandro Tartagni, *d.* 1477) were particularly notable for their *consilia,* the latter in both civil and canon law. Toward the end of the century there were early signs of the reaction that characterized at least some of the thinking in the next hundred years, and that a later age would call "humanist jurisprudence." Doubt was cast on much of what had been developed in the two previous centuries as humanist legal scholars attempted to return to the text of the *Corpus iuris* or even to the texts that lay behind it, shorn of the layers of commentary.

The humanist effort ultimately proved to be unsuccessful in the practical legal realm, however much humanist writings influenced political thought. When the Holy Roman Empire formally received Roman law in the sixteenth century, it did not receive the law of the classical jurists or even the law of Justinian, but rather the law of Bartolus. While the story of the reaction to the Bartolists belongs essentially to the early modern period, Bartolus himself was firmly embedded in the Middle Ages. He and the writers around him created a *ius commune,* a common law. Unlike the common law of England, this common law was not one that applied in every place. Rather, it was a combination of Roman and canon law that was taught in the universities. It was applied more fully in some countries, less fully in others, but it served in all of them, with the possible exception of England, as a common base that allowed those learned in the law to communicate with one another. The existence of this academic tradition had the potential, never fully realized, to iron out the differences in the customary

laws of the various regions. It was even specifically stated in some regions that if there was no customary rule, the *ius commune* would apply. In all of Europe, the *ius commune* shaped the habits of thought of the university-trained lawyer.

The *Corpus iuris* provided much of the material for political discourse in the later Middle Ages. This seems to have been almost as true of England as it was of the Continent, where more lawyers were trained in the *ius commune.* The political theory underlying the *Corpus iuris* is equivocal. While the emphasis is on the legislative power of the emperor—hence the usefulness of the *Corpus iuris* to those seeking to advance a position both absolutistic and secular—there is enough in it that survives from Republican Rome to provide support for those who would ground political power not in a grant of God made to the governor but in the grant of assent made by the governed. Further, there is much in the *Corpus iuris* to support a view of private law as a rational, autonomous system, not completely dependent on the will of the ruler.

If we separate the two contributions of scholarship based on the *Corpus iuris* to the later Middle Ages, the *ius commune* and the body of political ideas, we may find that the former is the more important. It has certainly had more staying power—there is more of the *ius commune* in the modern European codes than there is of ideas inspired by the *Corpus iuris* in modern political theory. It may even be that the *ius commune* was more important at the time. But that will not be known for certain until modern scholarship dealing with continental legal history penetrates beyond the academic writings about law to the records of the courts themselves. Only these records can reveal the effect of academic law on the law as it was actually applied.

BIBLIOGRAPHY

General. Helmut Coing, ed., *Handbuch der Quellen und Literatur der neueren europäischen Privatrechtsgeschichte,* I, *Mittelalter* (1973), a comprehensive bibliographic guide to the sources and literature; Robert Feenstra, "Droit romain au moyen âge (1100–1500)," in John Glissen, ed., *Introduction bibliographique a l'histoire du droit et à l'ethnologie juridique* (1979), fasc. B/10, is a more selective guide; Harold Dexter Hazeltine, "Roman and Canon Law in the Middle Ages," in *Cambridge Medieval History,* V (1926, repr. 1957); Friedrich Karl von Savigny, *Geschichte des römischen Rechts im Mittelalter,* 7 vols., 2nd ed. (1834–1851)—for a new edition of Savigny see *Jus romanum medii aevi* being published by Societé d'histoire des droits de l'antiquité (Milan, 1961–); Walter

Ullmann, *Law and Politics in the Middle Ages* (1975); Paul Vinogradoff, *Roman Law in Medieval Europe* 3rd ed. (1961, repr. with new foreword 1968); Franz Weiacker, *Privatrechtsgeschichte der Neuzeit*, 2nd ed. (1967). See also Francesco Calasso, *Medio evo del diritto, I, Le fonti* (1954).

Specific. On Justinian's codification, see Herbert F. Jolowicz and Barry Nicholas, *Historical Introduction to the Study of Roman Law*, 3rd ed. (1972), 478–498. On the beginnings of the *studium* at Bologna, see P. Fiorelli, "Clarum Bononiensium Lumen," in *Per Francesco Calasso* (1979); Hermann Kantorowicz and Beryl Smalley, "An English Theologian's View of Roman Law: Pepo, Irnerius, Ralph Niger," in *Mediaeval and Renaissance Studies*, **1** (1941–1943); Enrico Spagnesi, *Wernerius Bononiensis Judex* (1970). On "the four doctors," see Johannes Fried, *Die Entstehung des Juristenstandes in 12. Jahrhundert* (1973); Hermann Kantorowicz, *Studies in the Glossators of the Roman Law* (1938); H. Koeppler, "Frederick Barbarossa and the Schools of Bologna," in *English Historical Review*, **54** (1939). On questions and *dissensiones,* see Hermann Kantorowicz, "The Quaestiones Disputatae of the Glossators," in *Tijdschrift voor Rechtsgeschiedenis,* **16** (1939). On Gratian and the development of canon law, see Stephan Kuttner, *Repertorium der Kanonistik* (1937, repr. 1972); Gabriel Le Bras, Charles Lefebvre, and Jaqueline Rambaud, *L'âge classique (Histoire du droit et des institutions de l'église en Occident, 7* [1965]). On Roman law and canon law, see Paul Legendre, *La pénétration du droit romain dans le droit canonique classique de Gratien à Innocent IV* (1964). On Roman law in France and England, see André Gouron, "Les étapes de pénétration de droit romain au XIIᵉ siècle dans l'ancienne Septimanie," in *Annales du Midi*, **69** (1957); Eduard Maurits Meijers, *Études d'histoire du droit*, Robert Feenstra and H. F. W. D. Fischer, eds., III (1959); Henry G. Richardson, "The Oxford Law School Under John," in *Law Quarterly Review*, **57** (1941); Richard W. Southern, "Master Vacarius and the Beginning of an English Academic Tradition," in *Medieval Learning and Literature: Essays Presented to Richard William Hunt*, Jonathan J. G. Alexander and Margaret T. Gibson, eds. (1976). On legal humanism, see Domenico Maffei, *Gli inizi del umanesimo giuridico* (1972). On political ideas, see Myron P. Gilmore, *Argument from Roman Law in Political Thought, 1200–1600* (1941, repr. 1965); Gaines Post, *Studies in Medieval Legal Thought* (1964); Walter Ullmann, *The Medieval Idea of Law, as Represented by Lucas de Penna* (1946, repr. 1969). On the *ius commune*, see Ennio Cortese, *La norma giuridica*, 2 vols. (1962–1964).

CHARLES DONAHUE, JR.

[See also **Azo; Baldus; Bartolo da Sassoferrato; Beaumanoir, Philippe de; Bracton, Henry de; Bologna, University of; Bulgarus; Cino da Pistoia; Corpus Iuris Civilis; Decretals; Glossators; Hugo; Irnerius; Jacobus; Law, Canon: After Gratian; Law, Schools of; Martinus Gosia; Petri Exceptiones; Placentinus; Rogerius; Vacarius.**]

LAW CODES: 1000–1500. "To codify" laws means to reduce them to a code, to create a systematic collection of laws. A codification is quite different from a compilation, which is a collection of laws brought together in a volume. The legal force of the laws in a compilation dates to the time of their promulgation, and the act of compilation adds nothing to it. A codification is a collection of laws (some or all of which may predate the compilation) that is sanctioned by a ruler or governmental body at a particular time. The laws derive their force from the moment of the code's promulgation, and earlier versions of the laws are not valid. Sometimes, preceding laws excluded from a code are declared to be void. A ruler's prerogative to codify law presupposes his right to legislate new and to abrogate old laws.

Before the year 1000 in Western Europe, there were many compilations of laws. Customary law codes composed for the Germanic kingdoms contained the customary practices of the peoples for whom they were written and remained in force until the eleventh century. With the growing complexity of commercial and social life, the rediscovery of Roman law, and the establishment of law schools in Italy, these customary codes were no longer suitable instruments for regulating society. Modern ideas of codification have their origins in the codes of the twelfth and thirteenth centuries. The rediscovery of Justinian's *Corpus iuris civilis* in the late eleventh century provided a model for early codes. Justinian had outlined his purpose and methodology in the constitutions with which he promulgated his new lawbooks. His example shaped the theory and practice of codification throughout the Middle Ages. The law schools that taught Roman law were also important. They produced many of the private codes of the twelfth century, and even after monarchs began to exercise their legislative prerogatives, the compilation of codes was often delegated to the professors of the schools.

Justinian had ordered that a thousand years of Roman law be compressed into a single manageable code, which would supersede all earlier law. The codifications of the Middle Ages rarely claimed such completeness. In the eighteenth century, lawyers argued that a code should cover every possible legal situation, and several codes were fashioned in accord with this belief. The most famous was Frederick II the Great's Prussian *Landrecht* of 1794. Frederick's code was a failure, and modern codifications no longer place a high value on absolute comprehensiveness.

A "wave of codification" swept over Western Europe in the twelfth and thirteenth centuries, beginning with the *Constituta usus et legis* of the city of Pisa (1160) and ending with the *Liber sextus* of Pope Boniface VIII (1298). These early codifications had a number of common features. They were issued at the command of a ruler or government and often stipulated that the "community of the realm" had consented to them. The consent of subjects to laws and their approval of codifications became an important principle of the late Middle Ages. When monarchs issued these codes, they gave the following reasons: the confirmation of customary law, the expansion of older law by the addition of new, the replacement of older law by new, and the simplification of older law. In the prooemium of the *Liber Augustalis* (1231), Emperor Frederick II declared:

> We therefore desire that the present laws under our name should be in force only in the Kingdom of Sicily and order that these constitutions should be inviolably observed by all in the future. We abrogated the older laws and customs of Sicily contradicting these constitutions. We have commanded that earlier laws of the kings of Sicily and our own should be included in this collection, so that those which are not contained in this collection of our constitutions may have no force or authority either within or outside the law courts.

Three years later Pope Gregory IX promulgated the Decretals, a new code of canon law, under his name and expressed slightly different concerns:

> Diverse constitutions and decretal letters of our predecessors are dispersed in varied volumes. Some of these canons were repetitious, others contradictory, others produced confusion by their prolixity. . . . We therefore have provided, for the common utility and that of the students especially, that these be collected in a single volume.

Both of these collections were intended to supersede the older versions of the laws they contained and to have legal force in their present form from the moment of their promulgation. They were true codifications. They signaled the acceptance of new principles of kingship derived from Roman law: The prince had the duty to shape and correct the laws of his realm, and was the source and interpreter of all law.

PRIVATE COLLECTIONS OF LAW

The realization that the king could make and shape the legal system of his kingdom came slowly. The earliest codes of the eleventh century were private compilations or were products of the newly formed law schools; they were not, strictly speaking, codes. These compilations were important sources of law in Western Europe until the fourteenth century, and the evolution of public, official codes cannot be understood without reference to them.

Lombard law reigned in northern Italy and was based on legislation of the Lombard kings, dating back to the seventh and eighth centuries. These laws were arranged in chronological order by anonymous compilers in the first half of the eleventh century, in a work known as the *Liber Papiensis*. At the end of the century, the materials of the *Liber* were systematically ordered into three books and each book was further divided into titles treating various topics of law. A number of recensions exist of this new work—dubbed the *Lombarda*—which was used to teach Lombard law in the schools, especially at Pavia.

The oldest compilation of feudal law was also a product of Italy. The *Compilatio antiqua* was probably composed in Milan around 1150. It depended on the *Lombarda* and the legislation of the German emperors Conrad II (1037) and Lothair II/III (1136). Later recensions incorporated the legislation of Frederick I and Frederick II. These *Libri feudorum* were added to the *Corpus iuris civilis* and eventually, about 1250, were glossed by Accursius as part of his *Glossa ordinaria*.

In Germany and France customary law reigned until the fifteenth century. Eike von Repgowe of Anhalt, probably a lay judge (*Schöffen*) who had no public authority, translated his Latin treatise on German territorial and feudal law into Low German (*ca.* 1224–1227). The *Sachsenspiegel*, the title given to his translation, soon won widespread acceptance as a source of canon law. It was modified during the thirteenth century for other parts of Germany; the *Schwabenspiegel* used it as a model and adapted it for southern Germany (*ca.* 1275/1276). Because Germany never developed a strong central authority until the second half of the nineteenth century, these *Spiegel* were in effect until 1900 in parts of the country.

The first customary lawbooks in France, called *coutumiers,* were composed about 1200. The *Très ancien coutumier de Normandie* (1198–1218) and the *Grand coutumier de Normandie,* in its Latin redaction the *Summa de legibus* (*ca.* 1226–1258), were probably, like the *Spiegel*, written by judicial officers of the French local courts. The *Grand coutumier* was accepted as the "official" customary law of Normandy in the fourteenth century. Although the French kings issued statutes as early as the twelfth century, they did not promulgate codes of royal law during the Middle Ages. They did, however, issue official redactions of customary law in the fifteenth century. Charles VII in 1454 issued the *Ordonnance de Montil-les-Tours,* in which he ordered the customs of the land to be approved by the king in his great council and then promulgated as lawbooks. The result was a series of customary "codes": Burgundy (1458), Touraine (1462), Anjou (1463).

CANON LAW

The step from private collections to official codes is most clearly visible in canon law. There had never been an official code of law in the early church. A number of influential collections of canon law were produced during the early Middle Ages, but none achieved general recognition. The investiture controversy, the great contest between the empire and the papacy in the second half of the eleventh century, generated numerous private compilations of canon law, as churchmen perceived that many legal issues raised by the dispute needed definitive answers. The compilers exercised ingenuity and creativity. They no longer found the simple chronological ordering of decretals that appeared in early medieval collections useful, and soon divided their collections into books and titles, which greatly enhanced their comprehensibility and usability. Two collections compiled with the practical needs of the courts and students in mind, Burchard of Worms's *Decretum* (1008–1012) and Ivo of Chartres's *Panormia* (1094–1095), were the most influential lawbooks of this type. The investiture controversy further stimulated a renewed interest in and concern for law, spawning collections with a strong emphasis on papal legislative authority.

The systematic collections of the eleventh century prepared the way for the work of Gratian in the middle of the twelfth. While teaching canon law at Bologna (*ca.* 1130–1140), Gratian composed the *Concordia discordantium canonum* (later simply the *Decretum*), in which he reconciled conflicts found in legal texts. The *Decretum* quickly supplanted all earlier collections and became the standard introduction to canon law in the schools. Although the papacy never officially authenticated it, a legend grew

up in the early thirteenth century that a pope had approved it. This fictitious approval probably was needed to explain the primacy of place the *Decretum* held in the schools.

After the *Decretum* a new genre of collection appeared, the decretal collection. Small collections of papal letters and decisions (given the technical name of decretals) were added as appendixes or placed in the margins of *Decretum* manuscripts. Their purpose was to supplement Gratian. As the rate of papal legislative activity increased, particularly during and after the pontificate of Alexander III (1159–1181), these collections grew in size and sophistication. They became self-contained works. In 1190–1191 Bernard of Pavia put together a collection called the *Breviarium extravagantium,* later known as *Compilatio prima* (First compilation). He arranged it in five books, dividing each book according to titles. His classification—ecclesiastical offices (I), procedure (II), rules governing the clergy (III), marriage (IV), and criminal offenses (V)—became the pattern of almost all later collections. Other collections quickly followed, of which those of Gilbertus Anglicus (1203), Alanus Anglicus (1206), and Bernard of Compostela the Elder (1208) were the most important.

At this point, for the first time, the papacy became directly involved in the lawyers' work of codification. In 1209/1210 Pope Innocent III sent a collection of his decretals, compiled by Peter of Benevento, to the law school at Bologna with his official approval and assurance that all the decretals were authentic. This collection was called *Compilatio tertia* (Third compilation). In spite of Innocent's precedent, the next two major compilations were private. Nevertheless, John of Wales's *Compilatio secunda,* whose composition shortly postdates, but whose contents predate, *Compilatio tertia,* and Johannes Teutonicus' *Compilatio quarta* (1215–1216), another collection drawn exclusively from the decretals of Innocent III, were accepted by the schools. This phase of development ended in 1225, when Pope Honorius III ordered Tancred, an eminent teacher of law at Bologna, to compile a collection of his decretals. He sent the collection to Bologna with a bull of promulgation, *Novae causarum* (*ca.* 1226), in which he left no doubt that the papacy had taken the initiative in shaping its legal system. Honorius' collection was not, however, a comprehensive code, covering only legislation of his pontificate. It also, somewhat surprisingly, contained laws of Emperor Frederick II.

A few years later Honorius' successor, Pope Gregory IX (1227–1241), entrusted the compilation of a new and comprehensive collection of papal decretals to Raymond of Peñafort, a distinguished jurist who had become an important figure at the papal curia. Raymond drew his material from the decretal collections postdating Gratian. He radically altered the texts that he chose by eliminating large sections of narrative; by adding words and phrases; by rewriting sentences; and by reducing each text to its essential point of law. Consequently, the original intent of a decretal was often lost. The changes he made were not arbitrary but were influenced by the writings of previous canonists who had commented extensively on each decretal. Almost every emendation of substance that Raymond made can be traced to a doctrine found in the glosses of the canonists. He incorporated 195 new texts of Gregory IX into the collection, approximately one-third of them general, abstract statements of law. Many of them may have been drafted by Raymond, and they indicate a major shift toward legislation by statute. On 5 September 1234 Gregory sent Raymond's work, called the Decretals of Gregory IX or the Gregoriana, to the law schools and forbade that anyone presume to make another collection without papal permission. He prohibited the citation in the schools and courtroom of any pre-1234 decretal not in this collection. The Gregoriana has almost all the attributes of a modern code.

Pope Boniface VIII (1294–1303) and Pope John XXII (1316–1334) issued codes of canon law that were modeled on the Gregoriana. Boniface's *Liber sextus* (Sixth book [of decretals]), promulgated on 3 March 1298, collected conciliar and decretal legislation from 1234 to 1298. It was divided into five books on the same pattern as its predecessors. John's collection was called the *Clementines* or *Clementinae* because it contained the decretals of Pope Clement V (1305–1314) and the canons of the Council of Vienne (1311–1312). With these two collections, the official codification of canon law during the Middle Ages ceased for reasons that are still not understood. Nonetheless, these three codifications, together with Gratian's *Decretum,* became the *Corpus iuris canonici* and remained the official code of canon law until 1918.

CODIFICATION IN THE ITALIAN CITY-STATES AND THE EMPIRE

Many Italian city-states established communal forms of government during the late eleventh and early twelfth centuries. As self-governing states, they created rules regulating their constitutional structure and law courts. The first known codification, the *Constituta usus et legis* of Pisa, was a product of this environment. Promulgated on 31 December 1160 by the citizens of Pisa, the code had been compiled by a commission established in 1156. Just as the officials of the city-state held yearlong terms of office, so the members of the commission were replaced each year. Called *sapientes* (men learned in law), they drew the materials of the new code from Roman law, the *Lombarda,* and customary usages of Pisa. In the prologue to the *Constituta,* the compilers noted that judges had conducted their courts for Pisans and foreigners according to custom. Because judges differed in their knowledge and understanding of law, they rendered contrary judgments in similar cases:

> Whence the Pisans who desire to observe justice and equity almost more than all other citizens [*cives*] have ordered their customs which they hold on account of intercourse with different peoples written down and henceforth preserved for the knowledge of all who want to know them.

It is not known who the compilers were, but it can be assumed that they were probably jurists and judges who heard cases in Pisan courts.

The code was divided into two parts, one devoted to custom (*usus*) and the other to law (*lex*). This division corresponded to the jurisdiction of the three law courts in mid-twelfth-century Pisa. The court of custom (*curia usus*) was presided over by five judges, one of whom had to be learned in law (*iurisperitus*). The court of law (*curia legis*) had three judges, all of whom were learned. Finally, there was a court of appeals in which five judges sat, of whom two were learned. The *Constitutum legis* treated civil procedure, marriage, inheritance, and family law. The *Constitutum usus* also dealt with procedural matters, but treated predominantly law merchant, the law of the sea, and feudal law. The entire code was a full and comprehensive system of civil law. After 1160 the *Constituta* was constantly revised, augmented, and glossed. A thirteenth-century manuscript in Florence (Biblioteca Laurenziana, Acq. e Doni 62) contains rich layers of marginal glosses.

Precociously early and lacking immediate successors, the *Constituta* seems to have been the first official codification of the High Middle Ages. Its priority may be misleading, however, for it depends on the chance survival of earlier, out-of-date codes, which, since they no longer had any legal force, were often not preserved. The next earliest codes date to the thirteenth century. In this and the following century, almost all the major city-states of Italy issued codes: Vercelli (1241), Venice (1242), Reggio (1242), Bologna (1250), Viterbo (1251), Parma (1255), Vicenza (1264), Padua (1276), Perugia (1279), Pistoia (1296), Siena (1296), Modena (1306–1307), Lucca (1308), Brescia (1313), Milan (1330), Florence (1355), and Genoa (1363).

The Bolognese statutes of 1288 are typical of these urban codes. In 1287 a commission was formed to emend earlier statutes and arrange them in one volume. Two lawyers, four notaries, and four citizens comprised the commission. Their letter of appointment gives reasons for a new codification:

> Since it is certain and well known to all that statutes, decrees, provisions, reforms of the people as well as of the commune of Bologna are scattered in many volumes, because of their number and confusion, they cannot be held in many large books. Moreover, they contain so many similarities, contrarieties . . . that it is impossible for the memory of anyone to hold them all.

The commission examined 250 books of statutes, reforms, and provisions promulgated since 1250. The amount of material was daunting. Although much of it is now lost, an inventory of 1243 listed ten volumes of old statutes in the commune's archives. The resulting codification was divided into twelve books, beginning with constitutional law (books 1–3), procedure (books 4 and 6), regulation of notaries (book 7) and of the university (book 8), and ending with statutes governing guilds (book 12).

Intense legislative activity and codification were not limited to the city-states. Other corporate groups promulgated bodies of statutory law through which they ordered the activities of their members. The University of Bologna's earliest statutes date from the middle of the thirteenth century. A commission led by the prominent canonist Johannes Andreae completed the school's first code in 1317. Other universities followed Bologna's example. The guilds of the city-states also issued statutes, and there are numerous compilations of guild law from the thirteenth and fourteenth centuries. The same movement occurred in religious corporations. In 1228 the Dominicans promulgated a series of statutes at Paris that Raymond of Peñafort later revised (1238–1241). During the thirteenth century Franciscans, Cistercians, and other orders participated in this wave of legislation. Codification of legislation became an important means of structuring corporations, both large and small.

The most important codification of secular law in the thirteenth century—and the most modern in its form and substance—was the *Liber Augustalis* (also called the Constitutions of Melfi), issued by Emperor Frederick II for the Kingdom of Sicily in 1231. The *Liber Augustalis* is the first major royal codification of the High Middle Ages, and its longevity is remarkable—it remained in force in southern Italy until the early nineteenth century.

Frederick appointed a commission to work on the new law code in 1230; Jacobus, the archbishop of Capua, was probably a member and may have directed the project. The commission worked swiftly. Each province sent to Capua four representatives who declared local law, and the committee drew material from royal statutes of the Norman kings of Sicily and Frederick's legislation. Lombard, Roman, canon, feudal, and Byzantine law also left their imprint on the compilation to varying degrees. Jacobus had been trained at Bologna, and the codification bears the imprint of learned law.

The *Liber Augustalis* was divided into three books, which were subdivided into titles. Each title treated a different area of law. Book 1 dealt primarily with public order and royal institutions; book 2 with civil and criminal procedure; and book 3 with feudal and private law. The last also contained many statutes stipulating punishments for specific crimes, such as penalties for mothers who prostitute their daughters, for dispensers of love potions, and for tampering with coinage. Frederick enhanced the prerogatives of the crown through the *Liber Augustalis,* particularly at the expense of the feudal nobility and the cities. The emperor restricted their privileges and liberties to exercise justice and to elect their magistrates.

Shortly after promulgating the new code, Frederick introduced it into the curriculum of the university he had established at Naples in 1224. As a part of the law school's curriculum, it became part of the body of learned law. Marinus de Caramanico wrote the *Glossa ordinaria* to it between 1270 and 1280; and this gloss, along with that of Andrea d'Isernia, was printed several times from the fifteenth to the eighteenth century. The code remained in force until 1809 in Naples and until 1819 in the Kingdom of Sicily.

CODIFICATION IN SPAIN AND NORTHERN EUROPE

After the reconquest of the Iberian peninsula, the kingdoms of Valencia, Aragon, and Castile established codes of laws. James (Jaume) I the Conqueror

(1213–1276) drove the Muslims out of Valencia in 1238 and added the kingdom to the crown of Aragon. The following year he ordered that the customs of Valencia be written down. The resulting compilation, known as the *Fori Valentiae,* was revised in 1251, 1261, and 1271, but the texts of these thirteenth-century redactions have not been preserved. Between 1301 and 1341 Berenguer March added new legislation *(novellae)* to the collection, and during the fourteenth century it was translated into the vernacular.

In 1247 at Huesca, with the counsel and consent of the nobility, James promulgated the *Firi Aragonum,* also known as the Codex of Huesca. He ordered that this collections of laws be used in the courts to settle all cases. It was originally divided into eight books and later expanded to twelve. With the addition of new laws, it remained the law of Aragon until 1547, when the Codex was completely reorganized after the model of Justinian's *Code.*

During the reign of Alfonso X the Wise (1252–1284), the kingdom of Castile-León produced a series of lawbooks. The most important were the *Fuero real* (1252–1255) and the *Libro de las leyes* (1256–1258), which in later redactions was known as the *Siete partidas.* The *Fuero real* contained laws for cities, and the *Libro de las leyes* was a collection of territorial laws. It is not clear, however, what role Alfonso X and his successors played in creating these collections. There was considerable resistance to the *Fuero real* in the cities, which limited their implementation by the crown.

A number of northern European kingdoms produced no codes during the Middle Ages, even though the kings enacted a considerable body of legislation. In England and France royal statutes were registered. During the reign of Edward I, the statutes of the realm were placed in statute rolls, which became permanent records. A similar register was established for *ordonnances royales* at Paris during the fourteenth century. These registered statutes were far from being comprehensive codes, but represented an attempt to record all new legislation.

The history of codification during the Middle Ages reflects two important developments in law: the establishment of law schools after the rediscovery of Roman law and the ever-increasing juridical and legislative activity of European monarchs that gave great impetus to the "wave of codification" of the High and late Middle Ages. Most significantly, the Schoolmen worked on systematizing and organizing legal systems inside and outside of royal courts and communal councils, and very likely encouraged kings and towns to bring order to their law. In large part the work of these men, often anonymous but, even when known, laboring behind the facade of monarchical authority, accounts for the magnitude and the breadth of legislative activity, and the large number of official and private codifications in Western Europe from 1000 to 1500.

BIBLIOGRAPHY

General. The best survey of the history of codification in the Middle Ages, with a detailed bibliography of the sources and literature, is in Helmut Coing, ed., *Handbuch der Quellen und Literatur der neueren europäischen Privatrechtsgeschichte,* I, *Mittelalter (1100–1500): Die gelehrten Rechte und die Gesetzgebung* (1973). Two essays in this volume are of particular importance: Armin Wolf, "Die Gesetzgebung der entstehenden Territorialstaaten," and Knut Wolfgang Nörr, "Die Entwicklung des Corpus iuris canonici." Until recently it had been assumed that the medieval state had no theory of legislation. Fritz Kern, *Gottesgnadentum und Widerstandsrecht im früheren Mittelalter* (1914, 3rd ed. 1962), trans. with intro. by Stanley B. Chrimes as *Kingship and Law in the Middle Ages* (1939, repr. 1948, 1956), gave this thesis its most learned presentation. Sten Gagnér, *Studien zur Ideengeschichte der Gesetzgebung* (1960), and Gaines Post, *Studies in Medieval Legal Thought: Public Law and the State, 1100–1322* (1964), have established that medieval monarchs legislated and medieval lawyers produced sophisticated theories to support their legislative prerogatives. Armin Wolf, "Gesetzgebung und Kodifikationen," in *Die Renaissance der Wissenschaften im 12. Jahrhundert* (1981), sums up recent work. For the influence of Roman law on codification in Western Europe, see Alan Watson, *The Making of the Civil Law* (1981).

Private collections. Karl von Amira, *Germanisches Recht,* I, *Rechtsdenkmäler,* Karl August Eckhardt, ed., 4th ed. (1960); Gunter Gudian, "Coutumes," in Adalbert Erler and Ekkehard Kaufmann, eds., *Handwörterbuch zur deutschen Rechtsgeschichte,* I (1971); Paul Ourliac, "Législation, coutumes, et coutumiers au temps de Philippe Auguste," in Robert Henri Bautier, ed., *La France de Philippe Auguste: Le temps des mutations* (1982); Alan Watson, *Sources of Law, Legal Change, and Ambiguity* (1984), chap. 2.

Canon law. Leonard E. Boyle, "The *Compilatio quinta* and the Registers of Honorius III," in *Bulletin of Medieval Canon Law,* 8 (1978); Steven Horwitz, "Magistri and Magisterium: Saint Raymond of Penyafort and the Gregoriana," in *Escritos del Vedat,* 7 (1977); Stephan Kuttner, "Raymond of Peñafort as Editor: The 'Decretales' and 'Constitutiones' of Gregory IX," in *Bulletin of Medieval Canon Law,* 12 (1982); Kenneth Pennington, "The Making of a Decretal Collection: The Genesis of *Compatio* tertia," in Stephan Kuttner and Kenneth Pennington, eds., *Proceedings of the Fifth International Congress of Medieval Canon Law* (1980); Jane E. Sayers, *Papal Government and England During the Pontificate of Honorius III (1216–1227)* (1984).

On Italian city-states, see Peter Classen, *Studium und Gesellschaft im Mittelalter,* J. Fried, ed. (1983); Hermann Dilcher, *Die sizilische Gesetzgebung Kaiser Friedrichs II.* (1975); James M. Powell, ed., *The Liber Augustalis; or, Constitutions of Melfi* (1971).

Spain and northern Europe. A. Ferreirós, "Alfonso X el Sabio y su obra legislativa: Algunas reflexiones," in *Anuario de historia del derecho español,* **50** (1980); Arcadio García Sanz, "La sistemática de las compilaciones del derecho valenciano," in *Ligarzas,* **1** (1968); Rafael Gibert y Sánchez de la Vega, *Historia general del derecho español* (1968); Eelco Nicolaas van Kleffens, *Hispanic Law Until the End of the Middle Ages* (1968); Theodore F. T. Plucknett, *Legislation of Edward I* (1949, repr. 1962).

KENNETH PENNINGTON

[See also **Alfonso X of Castile, King; Aragon, Crown of; Bologna, University of; Boniface VIII, Pope; Burchard of Worms; Communes, Italian; Corpus Iuris Civilis; Custumals of Normandy; Decretals; Decretum; Eike von Repgowe; Frederick II; Gratian; Gregory IX, Pope; Innocent III, Pope; Ivo of Chartres, St.; Johannes Andreae; Johannes Teutonicus; John XXII, Pope; Kingship, Theories of; Law, Canon; Law, Schools of; Law, Spanish; Melfi, Constitutions of; Pisa; Raymond of Peñafort, St.; Sachsenspiegel; Schwabenspiegel; Siete Partidas; Tancred (Canonist).**]

LAW, DANISH. Laws in early Denmark developed from the interplay of freemen in their regional assemblies; a centralizing monarchy; a church gradually becoming institutionalized and more committed to supranational allegiances; and, later, a rising nobility. The inscription "That Harald . . . who made the Danes Christians" on the Jellinge stone (*ca.* 960) must reflect kingly lawgiving, and royal decree continued to be conspicuous in support of the church. An important instance was abolition of judicial ordeal (by hot iron) after its proscription by the Fourth Lateran Council in 1215. (Presence of this mode of proof provides a valuable terminus ante quem for individual laws and texts.) The king must also have had some supreme say in military affairs and generally the strength to ensure local acquiescence. There was no precise early conception of lèse majesté; only those who had sworn personal loyalty to the king could behave treasonably. It has been argued that a royal edict on the crime of lèse majesté was issued as

early as 1139/1140, but it may have been 100 years or more later. Certainly by the mid thirteenth century it was acknowledged that the king gave laws and the people accepted them, though the right of the people to propose law was also recognized. Nevertheless, our medieval texts contain different sets of laws for the three provincial amalgamations, Skåne, Zealand (or Sjælland), and Jutland, and there was no unified national code until Christian V's "Danish Law" of 1683.

Skåne laws (SkL) covered the (now Swedish) Halland, Skåne, Blekinge, and (still Danish) Bornholm, with Lund the center. They are known in a Danish form originating between 1202 and 1216 (though derived from twelfth-century sources) and a Latin "paraphrase" by Anders Sunesøn, archbishop of Lund from 1201 to 1223. Either the Latin was based on the extant Danish, or both followed the same source. Neither text can be regarded as an official code. The Danish text exists in many manuscripts, many with additions. The two oldest date from about 1300; one of them is the Codex runicus, AM 28 8vo.

Zealand (Sjælland) laws (SjL) covered that island and associated minor ones, with Ringsted the center. The extant texts are of a private, not official, character, even though the two main recensions go under the names of Waldemar (VSjL) and Eric (ESjL). The complex interrelations of the laws and law texts are well illustrated by SjL. VSjL is known in: (1) a text concerning inheritance and "unatonable" offenses, originating before 1216, that also influenced and was preserved among Skåne laws; (2) an "Older Redaction," from before 1250 (oldest manuscript fragment, *ca.* 1280–1290) and probably Jutlandic in origin, with additional sections on family, property, and tenancy law, much borrowed from SkL; and (3) a "Younger Redaction," also made before 1250 (oldest manuscript, *ca.* 1300), which is expanded with sections on slaves and theft. ESjL is based on the "Older Redaction" of VSjL but is twice the length, and its book three has many further correspondences with SkL. Its oldest manuscripts are from about 1300. There is also a fifteenth-century Low German translation.

Jutland laws (JL) covered that long peninsula from the Eider to the Skagerak, Fyn, Langeland, and lesser islands, with Viborg probably the original center. They are known in a lawbook promulgated by Waldemar II and ratified by a council of state shortly before his death in 1241. JL's prologue, often attributed to Bishop Gunnar of Viborg, is in the main a

Danish statement of canon-law precepts, and there is clear clerical influence on the laws themselves. A supplement, "Thord's articles," was compiled around 1300 and subsequently (in either 1326 or 1354) received royal confirmation as part of JL. It is assumed that JL was based on older, private law texts. The oldest manuscripts are from about 1300. A fourteenth-century Latin translation was itself rendered into Low German for use in Slesvig.

JL was organized in three books, but SkL and SjL were not originally so divided. A cursory analysis of JL (excluding "Thord's articles") will show the range of subjects included. Book one (fifty-seven sections) concerns family and inheritance law; land law, roads, and mills; book two (114 sections) concerns permanently appointed jurymen; homicide, maiming, rape, and fornication; boundary disputes; outlawry; atonement; breaking and entering; robbery; damage or death from chattels; damage to property; juries, especially in robbery cases; property in common; pledges; payments; warrantors; men under penalty; crop robbery; unlawful use of land; highway molestation; fines payable by stewards; bishop's juries; not observing holy days; and theft. Book three (sixty-eight sections) covers the military levy; atonement payments for homicide; bees; oaths taken for someone else; property relations between man and wife; misuse of land, crops, and animals; stray cattle; fences; drift and shipwreck; coining; arson; highway robbery; and fire damage in the countryside.

The form of the typical legal statement varies in early Scandinavian law texts. In Danish the "interrogative" conditional clause is very common (although less so than in Swedish), as, for example, in JL II.21, "Do men dispute about boundary marks, then the jurymen of the district are to establish them either with sticks or with stones. . . ." It is more frequent than the "if" type (usual in Norwegian and Icelandic, as in Latin and English), for example, JL II.36, "If someone drowns in another man's well . . . he [the owner] atones . . ." and the "whoever" type, for example, JL II.26, "Whoever knowingly houses an outlaw, let him atone. . . ." In JL the "interrogative" outnumbers the "if" type by about five to one.

Unlike the medieval law texts of the other Nordic countries the Danish contain no section on church law. It was largely left to the clerics. Two brief and virtually identical Danish texts called the Skåne Church Law (1171) and the Zealand Church Law (1170?) seem to contain only points where compromise between clerical and secular claims was urgent. The latter often appears as a pendant to VSjL.

The oldest Danish law for any kind of corporation is the Vederlov, cited in the Latin histories of Sven Aggesøn and Saxo about 1200, and known in Danish in a fifteenth-century manuscript. The relationship between the Danish and Latin versions is a matter of debate. It concerns the king's *hird,* his body of sworn retainers, and is attributed to Cnut the Great (*d.* 1035). Later (*ca.* 1400) a so-called "Gaardsret" (household law) was applied in the court and royal domains, and its use was also permitted on noble and monastic estates.

Many towns were established by royal charter in the eleventh, twelfth, and thirteenth centuries; as elsewhere, they developed their own regulations. The bylaws of Slesvig are the oldest known, probably from about 1200, certainly before 1241. They and others for Flensburg, Aabenraa, Haderslev, Ribe, Roskilde, and Copenhagen are (or were) in Latin, but some are also known in Danish redactions. The early Copenhagen bylaws were more episcopal than municipal in origin; there are extensive Danish regulations for the city from 1443. In Lund the maritime and commercial regulations known as the Birkeret were applied, known in a Danish text originating after 1216 but possibly before 1250 (oldest manuscript *ca.* 1400). It also held in Helsingborg and elsewhere in the SkL province. (The word *birk,* detached from the compound, became the general Danish name for a trade fair or other area with a jurisdiction separate from that of the local district.) Within the towns guilds operated with their own privileges and regulations. We have thirteenth-century texts for the guild of St. Cnut in Flensburg and Odense; they contain certain archaic elements of general interest to the legal historian.

Some maritime matters are mentioned in the provincial laws, and more extensive regulations having to do with shipping contracts and seafaring are in the early municipal laws. They chiefly reflect the general Nordic customs developed in the late Viking age and early medieval period, best known to us in the Swedish Bjarkörätt and the Norwegian Farmannalög. Later in the Middle Ages the misnamed Visby Sea Law (ultimately derived through various intermediaries from the *Jugements ou Rôles d'Oléron*) was used.

BIBLIOGRAPHY

Johannes Brøndum-Nielsen and Poul Johannes Jørgensen, eds., *Danmarks gamle Landskabslove,* 8 vols. (1933–1961); Ole Fenger, *Romerret in Norden* (1977); Åke Ernst Holmbäck and Elias Wessén, eds., *Svenska landskapslagar tolkade och förklarade för nutidens svenskar*, 4 vols. (1943); Poul Johannes Jørgensen, *Dansk Retshistorie* (1965); Erik Kroman, ed., *Danmarks gamle Købstadlovgivning*, 5 vols. (1951–1961); Erik Kroman and Stig Juul, eds., *Danmarks gamle Love paa Nutidsdansk*, 3 vols. (1945–1948); Thomas Riis, *Les institutions politiques centrales du Danemark 1100–1332* (1977); Carl Ivar Ståhle, *Syntaktiska och stilistiska studier i fornnordiskt lagsprak* (1958).

PETER G. FOOTE

[See also **Denmark; Law, Swedish; Saxo Grammaticus.**]

LAW, ENGLISH COMMON: TO 1272. Anyone who seeks the origins of the English common law must ultimately settle on the reign of Henry II (1154–1189), for it was his legislation that combined old practices with new needs and conditions to create the process and substance of a new law. Although much of his legislation initiated procedures to be used in the apprehension and punishment of criminals, his provisions for settling land disputes led to the growth of a large body of land law that has invariably been identified in modern times as the heart of the common law.

FEUDALISM AND ENGLISH LAW

Certain of the components of the common law existed before Henry II's reign, and at least three of these go back to the Norman conquest or even beyond, into the Anglo-Saxon period. One of these components was the royal writ, an efficient and effective instrument of communication whereby the English king could command judicial procedure to be applied to a given case and, in doing so, create what may be called royal justice. Another was the sworn inquest or jury system, in which neighbors gave information or evidence that was usually tantamount, in land cases, to judgment itself. A third component was the court system, and especially that part of it called the Curia Regis, or court of the king, which William I the Conqueror modeled on his ducal court in Normandy. But the most important institution that William brought to England was feudalism, which determined the nature of the king's court and of landholding and established both as the roots from which the tree of the common law would grow.

Feudalism transplanted from Normandy to England in 1066 meant that William the Conqueror gave vast estates or fiefs to his followers who had helped him in the conquest of England. These men were to hold such lands "in chief" of him as king. These followers or companions were thereby called tenants-in-chief or barons and held their estates from the king in return for many services, the most prominent of which was military service. These barons in turn gave many of their estates to their own followers, who, as their vassals, were obliged in turn to give them military service, which the barons used in partial fulfillment of their own service to the king. Vassals or knights to whom the tenants in chief gave fiefs were thought of as subinfeudated tenants, since they held their fiefs not directly from the king but from intermediate persons. The subinfeudated tenants often conferred some of their lands on other persons who, as their feudal tenants and vassals, owed them military service. This process of lords giving fiefs to vassals who then became lords of vassals below them often extended downward two, three, or more levels. The association of landholding with military service was the most prominent characteristic of feudalism.

Next in importance to military service, and almost equally prominent among the obligations of the feudal system, was the duty of each vassal to attend the court of his lord, usually held in connection with certain of the great feast days. The vassal was said to owe counsel (*consilium*) to his lord in such a court, but he also engaged in litigation there with his fellow vassals, mainly over landholding matters. Because of this obligation of suit to court, a large number of feudal courts—as many presumably as there were feudal lords—came into existence after 1066. The greatest of all feudal courts was the king's court (Curia Regis), to which his tenants in chief came to give him counsel and also to engage in litigation with one another, as plaintiff or as defendant.

ANGLO-SAXON LEGACY

While the Curia Regis and the feudal courts were the particular products of the Norman Conquest, the Norman kings of England inherited from the Anglo-Saxons a system of local courts that experienced varying fortunes under the new rulers. One of these, the manorial (domanial) court, was common to England and the Continent before 1066. Just as the Anglo-Saxon thane was usually a manorial lord, so was the new feudal lord after the Conquest when the manor became identifiable with the fief. If the Norman aristocrat held a fief, he had a largely unfree peasant population that worked his estate and sought justice in his manorial court, where regulations for accomplishing the agricultural routine were enforced and where peasants brought their suits against their fellows in such cases as trespass and debt.

The hundred court and the shire (county) court were two public courts also inherited from the Anglo-Saxon period. The better known of the two was the hundred court, which had appeared in the tenth century. With its monthly sessions, to which the entire free population came to receive and give justice, it treated the bulk of criminal and civil cases in the pre-Conquest period. The introduction of the feudal system doomed the hundred court to a diminishing role as a legal tribunal. On the one hand, many hundred courts came under the private control of feudal lords, since the fief often enveloped all or part of the hundred. This process created what has been called private, or "franchisal," justice, and in such cases the feudal lord tended to merge the hundred court with his manorial court. On the other hand, much of the legal business formerly transacted in the hundred court was transferred to other courts or done in other ways.

The shire court did not make its appearance until the late tenth century, and its functions and jurisdiction remained unclear both before and for some time after the Conquest. It met twice a year, in contrast to the monthly meeting of the hundred court, and while it was open to all freemen, it is probable that only the more important persons of the shire attended. Its presiding officer was the sheriff (shire reeve), who used it as the place to publicize royal proclamations. Although it was the highest local court and had both civil and criminal jurisdiction, it did not deal with as large a case load as did the hundred court.

William the Conqueror forbade bishops and archdeacons to hold ecclesiastical pleas in the hundred court, thereby separating church courts from lay courts in England for the first time. But he made no comment on the new or old functions of the shire court (after the Conquest, the county court), and it was left to his son Henry I, about 1110, to remind his subjects that the hundred and county courts were to meet as they had met before the Conquest with respect to place and time. Henry I made an important stipulation in ordering that any plea between his barons concerning the occupation or division of land would be held in his own court; that such pleas between vassals of the same lord would be tried in the lord's court; and that similar pleas between vassals of different lords would be held in the county court. In this way he assigned to the county courts a

specific new function. While little is known of the county court's operations and exact jurisdiction during the first century after the Conquest, that condition changed substantially with Henry II's great body of legislation.

Yet another local court was that of the borough. In the Anglo-Saxon period the borough had been originally a military and administrative center; gradually it developed into a place of trade. With the economic revival of Western Europe in the eleventh century, and with the patronage of the Norman kings, many of these boroughs became thriving centers of commerce. At first, the inhabitants of the boroughs were subject, like the rest of the free population, to the jurisdiction of the hundred and shire (county) courts. Gradually, certain of these urban centers—London being the most prominent—grew large and important enough for the kings to favor them with royal charters that enlarged the jurisdiction of the borough court. William the Conqueror's writ to the burgesses of London simply confirmed the liberties (whatever they were) that they had enjoyed under his predecessor, Edward the Confessor (*ca.* 1005–1066). Henry I in his charter of about 1130 not only gave the Londoners the right to elect their sheriff and to control their private and public business but also granted them their own court with elected judges and immunity from being impleaded in any case outside the city. At the same time, the city court (the hustings) was to try pleas of the crown, that is, those pleas arising from certain criminal acts.

Like the court system itself, the other two components in the origins of the common law, the writ and the inquest, cannot be seen as clearly as could be wished in the period before Henry II. In his reign a royal writ was a carefully worded order or mandate to an official or some person to accomplish or to comply with the message contained in the writ. These royal orders often concerned administrative matters, but they could also initiate a lawsuit or an action concerning a lawsuit, and therein lay their great importance for the origins and development of the common law.

It was once unclear whether William I brought this particular instrument with him from his duchy on the Continent, or whether he adapted to his own use an important device created and widely used by the Anglo-Saxon kings. There is no doubt now that the latter alternative is correct and that the English kings had used the royal writ as early as the tenth century. But while Anglo-Saxon kings clearly used the writ, it is not at all certain how often and in what ways they used it in the strictly legal sphere—that is, to affect legal process and justice.

There is the well-known case of Snodland Manor in Kent, which became in the late tenth century the subject of dispute between the bishop of Rochester and various members of a local noble family. Initially the gift of a wealthy widow to the bishop's church, the estate became subject to litigation when the woman's son regained possession of the title deeds and thereby of the land. After unsuccessful attempts to retrieve the deeds, the bishop brought the case before the king and a court made up largely of the king's ministers. This is important in showing that such a case fell under royal purview. Unfortunately, the process by which it came to the king's jurisdiction is unknown. At first the case was adjudicated through a compromise; then, several years later, the land was taken from the bishop by enemies. Time passed, and the bishop's successor brought the question before another king. On this occasion the king sent his writ, with a seal, to the archbishop of Canterbury, instructing him to assemble a large group of king's thanes to decide the suit after hearing each party's arguments. This time an effective settlement was achieved.

The important point is that an Anglo-Saxon king in this particular instance used a royal writ to turn a private complaint into a lawsuit, stipulating the persons to judge the case and, presumably, the time and place of the hearing. The evidence does not say how often Anglo-Saxon kings used royal writs in this manner, but it did occur on occasion, and the handling of this case resembles in several respects the manner in which William the Conqueror used royal writs for similar purposes.

In William's reign, the crucial difference was the system of feudalism, which made him profoundly interested in the legal condition and tenancy of land which owed him, first of all, the various feudal services that underpinned his rule. He therefore interfered quickly, frequently, and repeatedly if necessary, to see that land disputes between his barons were justly settled. Perhaps "interfered" is not the correct word, for he had the right (suit to court) and the obligation (as feudal overlord) to see that justice was done among his tenants in chief. That had not been the situation under his predecessors, the Anglo-Saxon kings.

William was quick to see the value of the Old English royal writ and to adapt it to judicial uses. He also, undoubtedly, used it more frequently than had

his predecessors, and the examples that have survived are almost certainly only a small fraction of the total number of incidents. An example of his use of the writ to initiate legal proceedings among his barons comes from about 1079 and was addressed to Lanfranc of Bec, archbishop of Canterbury (1070–1089), and Geoffrey, bishop of Coutances, whom he designated as presiding judge in this case:

> See to it that *sac* and *soc* [jurisdiction], between Bishop Wulfstan [of Worcester] and Walter, abbot of Evesham, are determined as they were on the day that, in the time of King Edward [the Confessor], geld [taxes] was last taken for the building of a fleet. And for holding the plea, be you, Geoffrey, presiding officer in my place; and be sure that Bishop Wulfstan fully has what is his right. Also see to it that the bishop justly has the houses in Worcester which he claims against the abbot, and that all those who hold lands of him are always prepared for my service and his.

The king's points of interest in this case are evident. He was concerned that the bishop and abbot settle their dispute in an orderly manner, and since both men were his tenants in chief and he their feudal overlord, he intended to provide the means for an orderly settlement. But it is also easy to see that he wished to settle the dispute so that they and their vassals, whom they had subinfeudated with lands (or fiefs), would always be prepared to render him the feudal services that they owed him. Just as he provided a tribunal for cases of this kind on numerous occasions, so did his sons, William II Rufus (1087–1100) and Henry I (1100–1135). The royal writ became the indispensable means of providing justice during the hundred years between the Conquest and the reign of Henry II.

ANGLO-NORMAN INQUEST AND THE JURY

Often in such cases, the king's justices, acting in his name, needed to have a legal question answered in an incontrovertible fashion, and for this they resorted to determination of the fact by men, usually neighbors, who knew the truth of the matter and who would testify or give such knowledge under oath. This institution, given the name of the Norman Inquest during the early part of its history, has also been called the jury of recognition, for its sole purpose in such cases was the recognition of a fact. The procedure was to ask a question, such as: which of two parties held a certain piece of land on a certain date?

The origin of the sworn inquest in English law has long remained a highly controversial question.

Supporters of one view staunchly argue that it was strictly a Norman importation from the Continent, where it has been traced to Carolingian kings and beyond them to the late Roman Empire. The opposing school maintains that the seed of the sworn inquest, whatever its particular form, can be seen in the Anglo-Saxon law code issued by King Ethelred II (r. 978–1016) at the close of the tenth century for the inhabitants of that part of England called the Danelaw. This code provided for a jury of twelve senior thanes who swore that they would not wrongly accuse an innocent man or conceal a guilty one. This wording makes it appear that such a jury made presentments or indictments in the criminal sphere rather than recognitions. While this is not what the early Norman Inquest did, the example has been used to support the argument that the idea of the jury was in England before the Conquest, perhaps as a contribution of the invading Danes who settled the northern part of the country in the ninth century.

Scholarly attention has focused upon a different kind of sworn testimony that occurred about 1053 in a land dispute between the abbots of Thorney and Ramsey. The dispute had gone on for some time until friends of both brought men of the neighborhood together to say under oath how the matter lay. This case and its resolution did not take place in a law court or on the orders of the king. Because it was done outside of court and between persons who were willing to accept a solution in that manner, it has been called a popular inquest rather than a royal inquest. Additional incidents of this kind of recognition occurred in the century after the Conquest, suggesting that such an institution was well rooted at the popular level.

Whatever the truth of the matter, both schools agree that the Anglo-Norman kings were the first to employ the jury of recognition as a royal instrument. A notable early instance of its use occurred in 1082, when the king sought to settle a land dispute between the abbot of Ely and various other persons. At a given time and place, by orders contained in the king's writ, several Englishmen who knew the facts of the case as they existed in 1066 (at the time of the Confessor's death) were asked to present these facts under oath. The presiding officers of this court were an archbishop, a bishop, and a lay baron, whom the king had appointed as royal justices to hear and determine the matter for him. Once more this was an example of the king providing justice for his vassals.

The most concentrated use of the sworn inquest by William I did not occur in law cases but in the gathering of vast amounts of information in 1086 for the famous Domesday Book, for which dozens of juries in every English county gave sworn recognition of facts about the landed estates, income, and population. This represented an administrative use of the inquest, and while Anglo-Norman kings would continue to use the jury in that way, they also continued to employ it occasionally in law cases, until Henry II expanded and multiplied its uses as he developed the common law.

While the origins and rise of the common law may well be attributed to the genius of Henry II, it is important to remember that the weakness and anarchy of the reign before his posed a great challenge to rebuild and reconstruct, and evoked his ability in law and statecraft in an unusual way. William the Conqueror and his two sons were strong kings; each kept and increased the power of the royal office. And while the first two had a certain reputation for cruelty, and all three exercised a relentless fiscal policy, they also showed a keen interest in the rendering of justice, viewing it as indispensable to the stability and order that in turn buttressed their claim to rule. Henry I, in particular, made great advances in creating more effective legal institutions and processes, but when he died without a surviving son, his sister's son, Stephen of Blois, made good his claim to succeed his uncle as king of England.

Stephen's reign (1135–1154) was a period of anarchy. His lack of strong will and resolution led him to give to powerful feudal lords who challenged him much of what they demanded, as a calculated concession to win their support. But the support of such men was never durable, and so the royal authority and the royal substance were diminished. At the same time, the daughter of Henry I, Matilda, with her husband, Geoffrey, count of Anjou, and their young son, the future Henry II, opposed Stephen's claim to rule, with the result that intermittent civil war took place in both England and Normandy. Stephen finally agreed in 1153 that upon his death Henry should become king, both death and accession occurring less than a year later.

HENRY II AND THE COMMON LAW

Henry II came to the throne convinced that the feudal system which his grandfather had controlled in a highly centralized fashion had suffered serious dislocation during Stephen's anarchy, and that royal as well as individual rights had suffered greatly in the process. He was consumed with the idea of reconstructing the feudal monarchy of Henry I and repeatedly referred in the early part of his reign to restoring things as they had been in his grandfather's time. He suspected that the church had encroached on royal rights, and his attempts to reestablish the "proper" relationship between church and monarch led to his first large body of legislation and also to the disastrous struggle with Thomas Becket. He knew that the royal demesne had been encroached upon by great lords in various ways and that the royal manors were seriously dilapidated. He also came gradually to realize that the prosecution of crime had been grievously neglected; this knowledge drove him to the most visible and impressive of his legal innovations.

But what was equally visible to Henry was the dispossession, or disseisin, of individual landholders within the feudal system. Great lords had in some cases become feudal tyrants, violating and abusing the regulations and customs that governed the relationship with their vassals. Landholding was not only the economic base of feudalism; it was also the major source of legal dispute among members of the feudal hierarchy. Even in time of peace, confusion easily arose over possession, or seisin, of land; and disseisin, or eviction, of persons from their lands had been a problem since the Conquest. The previously mentioned case of 1082, involving the abbey of Ely, concerned essentially the question of seisin.

Anglo-Norman custom permitted the dispossessed party, within a certain number of days and with his friends' help, to eject his disseisor and recover his seisin. This action was called self-help, and it was clearly not the best way to accomplish conflict resolution. The Anglo-Norman kings, including Stephen, tried to discourage self-help and intervened on numerous occasions with royal writs ordering individuals and sometimes sheriffs to reseise persons who complained of having been disseised.

Before Henry II these royal orders to reseise were usually of a peremptory nature; they have been called executive writs. Such a writ was a particular order addressed by the king to a particular circumstance and purchased by the plaintiff for a considerable price. It was not a remedy in formulaic style which anyone could obtain to apply to similar situations. No inquiry into the facts of the disseisin was contemplated in the writ. The disseisor was simply ordered to return the land to the plaintiff. While many wrongs could be made right in this manner, the reverse was also true. There were such things as just disseisins and unjust reseisins. A writ of Henry I, made about 1102, illustrates the content of such

writs: "Henry, king of England, to Roger the sheriff, greeting. I order you to reseise abbot Aldwin of the land which William son of Osmund holds unjustly. And afterwards if he claims something there, let the abbot do him right in his court." The language of this writ suggests, as it does in many similar writs of this period, that the disseisor made the disseisin unjustly. There is no mention of an investigation that may have determined this. The king, in effect, ordered William to abandon self-help and, if he had a just claim, seek orderly redress through litigation in his lord's (the abbot's) court.

Technically, in the feudal system, there was no ownership of land, only possession, or seisin—unless we say, with a certain fiction, that the king owned all the land. The concept of ownership or "right," however, persisted in the feudal age and served to limit the free disposition of land by the more powerful members of society.

Too much can be made of the confusions between seisin and right. After all, Roman law recognized that *possessio* and *proprietas* were two different things, as does twentieth-century law. It is certainly true, however, that conflicting claims of seisin and right made for some extraordinarily complex litigation. In disseisins, the disseisor was often acting on a claim of proprietary right. In addition, as lands were demised to succeeding tenants over generations, the question of proprietary right was complicated by issues of inheritance, and litigants came to speak not of having right but of having a better right to land.

This system had its troublesome aspects in time of peace and stability, but war, rebellion, a weak ruler, and usurpation by the strong against the weak compounded the grievances. These conditions characterized Stephen's reign, and this deterioration was foremost in Henry's mind as he addressed the problem after 1154.

The significance of Henry II's work as the father of the common law lies in what he accomplished in the fields of seisin and right, working largely through the returnable writ and the inquest or jury of recognition. By his use of the writ and the jury and by opening his own court either immediately or ultimately to those seeking remedy, he gave system and effectiveness to the adjudication of disputes over seisin and right.

Neither seisin nor right was a peculiarly English problem in the twelfth century; most of the feudal states of Western Europe had to deal with them in some measure. Furthermore, all these states could look to certain principles which provided theoretical support for the remedies that were created. In the case of the protection of seisin, the theoretical support came from certain precepts laid down in the Pseudo-Isidorian decretals of the ninth century. The influence of Pseudo-Isidore came into England after the Conquest and was strongly felt in the twelfth century, when Henry took up the question of seisin.

Pseudo-Isidore was compiled mainly to protect bishops from archbishops who claimed to have power to remove bishops from office. Pseudo-Isidore argued that only the pope (who was very distant and weak in the ninth century) had that power. The principle that protected the office of the bishop was stated in Latin as *spoliatus ante omnia restituendus* and was also expressed in Gratian's *Decretum* in the mid twelfth century. It meant that whatever had been taken away had to be restored to the party before anything else (such as litigation) could occur. Another principle, also from Pseudo-Isidore, maintained that no one should be made to plead in court while he was disseised *(nemo placitet dissaisitus)*. This points up the essentially conservative nature of the answer to the problem of seisin. In effect, a disseised tenant was to be repossessed of his land before he was made to plead in court about it.

Henry II ruled for twelve years before he took his decisive step in the matter of seisin. During these years he continued to order reseisin in the old manner by way of the executive writ used by the Anglo-Norman kings before him. It was probably in 1166 that he decided to deal with disseisins in a sharply different way. He devised a royal writ of common form, obtainable in chancery, and available to everyone who had cause and was willing to purchase it. The writ was addressed to the sheriff and informed him that because of the party's complaint of disseisin, he was to have the land in question viewed by twelve free and lawful men of the neighborhood. He was furthermore to summon these same twelve men to appear before the king or his justices on a certain day to state under oath whether the plaintiff had been, in fact, unjustly disseised of his free tenement. Reseisin followed if the answer was affirmative. The order or statute creating this remedy has not survived, but within a few years it was referred to as the "assize of novel disseisin." The word "assize" in twelfth-century England could refer to an assembly or council meeting or to the laws made by such a body. It could also refer to a specific legal action or remedy, as in this particular case. "Novel" means "recent" (as opposed to a disseisin occurring in the

distant past), and so the term may be translated as "the remedy (or action) on recent disseisin."

Because this remedy on disseisin was fundamental to the establishment of the common law, it is desirable to reproduce the entire writ as contained in the law tract called Glanville, written at the end of Henry's reign:

> The king to the sheriff, greeting. N. has complained to me that R. has unjustly and without judgment disseised him of his free tenement in such a vill after my last voyage to Normandy. I therefore command you that if N. will give you security to prosecute his claim, see that the tenement is reseised with the chattels which were taken in it, and have that tenement with its chattels remain in peace until the Sunday after Easter. And meanwhile have twelve free and lawful men of the neighborhood view that tenement, and have their names endorsed on this writ. And summon them by good summoners that they then be before me or my justices prepared to make the recognition. And put by gage and safe pledges the aforesaid R. or his bailiff if he himself cannot be found, that he then be there to hear that recognition. And have there the summoners and this writ and the names of the pledges. Witness etc.

The assize of novel disseisin was a special action for several important reasons. It used the returnable writ, which did not exist before Henry II. It was returnable because of the last sentence, which compelled the sheriff to answer for the entire process by returning the writ, properly endorsed, to the king's court so that it could become a matter of record. Nothing was left loose-ended, every step in the process was stipulated, and everything commanded in the writ had to be accomplished. The steps were: (1) accepting security from the plaintiff; (2) putting the tenement into peace, or restoring it with its chattels to its predisseisin status; (3) finding twelve lawful men to view the tenement; (4) seeing that they appeared before the king or his justices; (5) compelling the defendant to post bond and find sureties, to guarantee his court appearance; and finally (6) producing the summoners and the writ at the day and place assigned.

Henry II intended above all for the process to be speedy. The defendant could not delay the process in any way, as he could do in other common-law actions at this time. He could not essoin (excuse) himself, and the recognition proceeded whether he was present or not. Because it did not permit delays, process under this writ was called a summary action. At the same time, it did not ignore the defendant's right to be heard. He could plead, and usually did, before the jury gave its recognition. Whatever questions or objections he raised could be answered by the jurors, who knew the circumstances and history of the case. Lastly, the assize of novel disseisin was important because the writ with its many details was now made of "common form." Chancery clerks, working from a set formula, simply filled in names, places, and dates; they no longer crafted a particular writ made on an individual's petition with respect to particular conditions, as was done during the previous century.

The assize of novel disseisin, in working order by 1166, was not the first systematic use made of the jury of recognition by Henry II. Only two years before, in 1164, he and his council had produced the first large body of legislation of his reign that brought him into serious confrontation with the church. These laws were called the Constitutions of Clarendon and, in sixteen chapters, reduced to writing for the first time what the king thought were the customary rules governing the important areas of contact between ecclesiastical and royal authority. In the hundred years since the Conquest the identification of which lands were held by the church free of all worldly service and which lands were held of a lord in return for feudal service had sometimes become difficult and uncertain. Church land that owed no secular obligation was said to belong to free alms; land that owed feudal service was in lay fee. Conflict arose because a lord would claim that land was held of him in lay service while the church argued that it was free alms. Henry decided that in such disputes the question would be settled through the recognition of twelve lawful men of the neighborhood who stated under oath the true condition of the contested land. This process received the name of the assize *utrum*, the Latin word referring to the question "whether" the land belonged to free alms or to lay fee. Each time such a question arose, the plaintiff could obtain from the royal chancery a writ addressed to the sheriff, who would arrange for the assize to be taken. The purpose of the recognition was to determine jurisdiction of law cases that came out of such disputes. If the land was free alms, any dispute concerning it was to be tried in the church courts; if lay fee, unless both parties agreed to trial in the court of the same bishop or of the same feudal lord, the case would be tried in the king's court. The law strongly suggested that if the land were in lay fee further litigation might well concern the question of seisin or right.

While no known statute or ordinance lies behind the assize of novel disseisin, the opposite is true of

the second assize made by Henry II to protect seisin. Novel disseisin protected a landholder from unjust disseisin. But another kind of disseisin was at work in the twelfth century—another legacy of Stephen's chaotic reign. Upon the death of a feudal tenant, his lord was by custom bound to recognize the hereditary interest of the dead man's son by investing him with his late father's fief. For many reasons a lord would sometimes fail to do this. The king's interest in such a case was undoubtedly due to his desire to keep the feudal system stable and orderly, but he must also have seen the injustice of a disseised heir. In 1176, Henry and his council made a large body of legislation called the Assize of Northampton. Although its major concern was the prosecution of crime, one chapter addressed the problem of the deceased tenant, stipulating the various acts that should occur at such a moment for an orderly transition. The heir should remain in seisin and perform all services for the fief. If underage, he should be placed in wardship. The widow should have her dowry. But if the lord refused seisin to the heir, the latter could obtain a writ from the royal chancery that would cause a jury of recognition to state in the presence of royal justices whether the plaintiff's father was lawfully seised of the tenement on the day he died. This remedy quickly became known as the assize of mort d'ancestor. If the recognition was affirmative, the lord was compelled to deliver seisin to the heir. Although the language of the statute makes one think that the ancestor was always a father, in practice the ancestor could also be a mother, brother, or sister.

The third and last of Henry's remedies to protect seisin was called the assize of *darrein presentment* (last presentment). It concerned the right of a patron to appoint a new priest to a church whose previous priest had died. It was probably made about 1179, for in that year the Third Lateran Council decreed that bishops would name priests to churches after they had remained vacant for three months. Seeking to forestall such actions, Henry hastened the process by which vacant churches were filled. The right to present was an integral part of the feudal system, in which churches were supported by lands held by feudal lords, either lay or ecclesiastical. Just as there could be dispute about seisin and right in free tenements, so could two parties contest the presentation of new priests to vacant churches. The issue was not seisin of land but seisin of the right to present, and Henry's solution was to have the plaintiff obtain a writ to impanel a jury to recognize which party presented the last priest. That person would then have the right to present the next. While it did not work as successfully as the other two assizes, it did simplify greatly an otherwise often protracted and messy procedure and prevented the church from assuming jurisdiction in such matters.

These three assizes were known as possessory assizes, for they concerned seisin or possession rather than right or ownership. And while they brought order and justice into litigation over land, the question of proprietary right remained untouched. One could always, and sometimes did, move from a judgment on seisin to a suit on right. On occasion, the person who was reseised had less right than the defeated disseisor, and the latter might then begin a process on proprietary right. In such an action, he became the demandant in the new process, and the party in possession became the tenant. Nevertheless, custom and the law favored the tenant rather than the demandant.

Glanville made the well-known statement that by custom of the realm, "no one is held to answer in the court of his lord concerning any free tenement of his without a writ of the lord king or of his chief justice." This principle has usually been interpreted as referring to the requirement that a demandant could not implead a tenant in his lord's court without the king's writ; and that particular writ has commonly been identified as the writ of right, which gave the king a forcing position on a lord who might default in doing right to a demandant in his feudal court.

There were in fact two writs of right after Henry had completed his legal reforms. Process on right, like other legal actions in the feudal system, was considered to be in the jurisdiction of the lord's court of whom the demandant claimed to hold. If the demandant held "in chief" of the king, he obtained the writ praecipe, which ordered the sheriff to bring the matter immediately to the king's court. If the demandant claimed to hold of a mesne, or intermediate, lord, he was, from the beginning of Henry's reign, obliged to obtain a royal writ of right patent, which was addressed to the lord and which directed him to do right to the demandant. This writ, probably the earliest to be given common form by Henry II, was first prepared several years before the assize of novel disseisin. It was the writ referred to by Glanville when he stated that no one should answer for his tenement without the king's writ. But occasionally the tenant in the suit did not hold of the demandant's lord, and the case would then have to be

moved to the king's court. If the demandant knew this at the outset, he might use the praecipe and save time. If he conducted his case in the lord's court but came to the opinion that he would not obtain justice there, he could, by a complex process, have the case moved eventually to the king's court.

The demandant began his case in court by claiming a title or right by hereditary descent. This kind of action provides a good example of the connection between seisin and right. In effect, the demandant claimed right by virtue of an ancestor's seisin and specified by name the king in whose reign his ancestor had seisin. In this way, it appears, right descended from an older seisin. The demandant also had to state that his ancestor received the income from that land over a certain time. Then he carefully traced the descent of that right from his ancestor, step by step, to himself as descendant.

The tenant might reply, and often did, that he held the land as a grant from some third party, and this claim gave him the opportunity to vouch that third party to warranty. This was a well-known process in the common law, and it arose from the fact that the grantor usually warranted himself and his heirs to personal confirmation of the grant at a later date should the need arise. If the third party came and admitted his obligation to warrant, he then replaced the tenant in the process. That was the nature of warranty. If the warrantor then won the case, his tenant kept the land. If the warrantor lost, the demandant received the land and the warrantor had to compensate his tenant with other land.

If the tenant denied the seisin of the demandant's ancestor, and thereby the demandant's right, the issue then had to be settled by battle, a solution brought in by the Normans at the time of the Conquest. That is, trial by battle in process on right was compulsory up to Henry's time. He and his councillors felt at last that battle was too uncertain a method to settle such an important question and probably in 1179 devised a process called the grand assize, whereby the question of right would be settled by a jury of recognition. Glanville in explaining this system waxed eloquent on the civilized nature of the new solution as against the barbarity of the old system.

It was the tenant's privilege, not the demandant's, to choose this process. If the demandant did not wish to submit to the assize, he had to give some reason. A usual reason was that he and the tenant were related, in which case, if the tenant admitted the kinship, the case would be verbally pleaded until a resolution was achieved. If a tenant knew that he could not prove a greater right, he would almost certainly opt for battle, hoping to achieve by an uncertain method what he was sure not to gain by a jury. If he was equally certain that he could demonstrate the better right, he would be sure to choose the jury.

Process in the grand assize was more complex than in the possessory assizes. If the case was being sued in the court of the demandant's lord, a royal writ put the process "in peace." Another writ ordered the sheriff to send four knights from the neighborhood to Westminster, where they would elect twelve other knights, also of the neighborhood, who best knew the facts of the case and who would then declare on oath which party had the greater right in the disputed land. But this is to make the process appear simpler than it was. Unlike the possessory assizes, which limited or eliminated delays, the process on proprietary right permitted all delays normally given in other actions. Furthermore, the difficulty of getting the four knights to Westminster on the appointed day was foreseen to be great enough that further delays were provided for in the operation of the process, and finally it appears from Glanville's description that other complications could arise in bringing twelve knights together from the same neighborhood who knew the facts well enough to be willing to swear to them. Despite its great improvement over battle, the grand assize, while offering a humane and more legal solution, was a slow and cumbersome process. But these disadvantages did not prevent its success, for in one year alone during the reign of Richard I (1189–1199) at least 135 cases on proprietary right were settled by the grand assize. Glanville seems to have been correct when he said that the grand assize was a royal benefit given to the people by the goodness of the king and with the counsel of his magnates.

In developing the possessory assizes, the writ of right patent, the praecipe, and the grand assize, Henry II is said to have founded the common law. His innovations in the fields of seisin and right systematized process by means of the returnable writ and the jury of recognition. Formerly addressed to the circumstances of an individual, the writs became standardized. Chancery clerks working from set formulas produced writs for the assizes and for process in right without consulting the king on each petition or complaint. By being returnable, and by having a series of penalties for failure to proceed, the writs compelled litigation to commence and to proceed toward judgment. The jury of recognition gave de-

cisive movement toward the conclusion of a case, for the jurors' swearing to a particular fact determined the nature of the judgment. With this system, Henry regularized legal process for conflicts in landholding.

In addition, these new remedies were not available only to the tenants in chief, who had always had access to the king's court. Rather, all freemen (meaning first of all the entire subinfeudated class of military tenants) were invited to find their remedies in these particular cases by suing in the king's court rather than in the lord's court. It was a more certain and impartial justice. From this central fact of the king's court being opened to all freemen came the important idea that the king's law was the common law, coming from a single authoritative source and available to the entire free population.

It has been suggested that Henry's development of the common law was part of a deliberate royal program to reduce the feudal courts to impotence so that the king's personal rule would be unchallenged. This thesis, as eye-catching as it may be, does not accord with what we know. The king certainly intended to control the feudal system. To do this, he had to ensure order and stability throughout the structure. He did intend that justice in the feudal courts be effective and sure, especially in the area of landholding, and he expected the lords of feudal courts to be responsible in that way. His remedies were all directed to old grievances, to faults and flaws that had already appeared and that could only be corrected by his legislation. The lords, for their part, acquiesced and appeared willing to accept his solutions to questions they could not adequately resolve.

HENRY II AND CRIMINAL LAW

The work accomplished by Henry II in the area of criminal law was scarcely less significant than his contributions to the field of civil actions. While little is known of the prosecution of crime under the Anglo-Norman kings, the concept of pleas of the crown clearly emerged from that period. This title was applied to certain criminal acts which were defined as breaches of the king's peace. The prosecution of such pleas belonged to the king or to his justices and to no one else. The law book called *The Laws of Henry I,* compiled about 1115, named thirty-six offenses as pleas of the crown, the most prominent being treason, murder, robbery, rape, and counterfeiting. The Normans also brought in the institution of the appeal, in which an injured person, called the appellor, appealed the alleged criminal of the specific crime and of breaking the king's peace. The criminal process of appealing felons would continue through the thirteenth century as one way to prosecute crime. By 1166, however, Henry II realized that the prosecution of crime needed new effort.

Since the Conquest the king had given prosecution of crown pleas to various officials, at first to the sheriff of each county, then to local justiciars resident in the county and appointed by the king. Occasionally he would send a commission of justices to try his pleas in certain counties; Henry I took this idea and developed out of it the system of circuit or eyre justice. He had such commissions operating in 1116 and again in 1129 and 1130. But while he is considered the founder of the eyre system of traveling, or itinerant, justices, little is known of the system during his reign, and the practice disappeared during Stephen's anarchy. It was the eyre system of his grandfather, but with new machinery, that Henry II revived in 1166, when he issued the Assize of Clarendon.

This body of legislation contained twenty-two chapters of instructions that dealt in unprecedented detail with the indictment, apprehension, trial, and punishment of robbers, murderers, thieves, and the receivers of the same. For the indictment of criminals, Henry used the jury of presentment, which because of its procedure can be seen as the ancestor of the present-day grand jury. In every county twelve lawful men from each hundred and four from each vill were put on oath to say who was accused or suspected of being a robber, murderer, or thief. This jury was clearly different from the jury of recognition; it made presentments or accusations, and hence its name. Sheriffs were to apprehend the accused persons and have them before the itinerant justices when they came through the county. Compurgation and ordeal by cold water were the methods of proof. Even those who "made their law" and were cleared, if they were men of notorious reputation, were to leave the realm or be declared outlaws.

In addition to establishing the jury of presentment, the Assize of Clarendon revived the eyre as a continuing institution in English life. Henry dispatched two groups of justices to tour large sections of England in 1166, and in 1168 the eyre covered the entire kingdom. This new system was to continue as long as the king wished. In 1176 he issued new legislation under the name of the Assize of Northampton; its main purpose was to renew and clarify the

criminal jurisdiction set up ten years before. The evidence from the Pipe Rolls (annual statements of the king's expenses and revenues) shows that from the beginning, while the major purpose of the eyre was the prosecution of crime, the possessory assizes could also be heard, and other legal actions were soon included. This led to the idea of a general eyre for all pleas (ad omnia placita), which became great campaigns of circuit justice that would periodically cover the kingdom and entertain all pleas, civil and criminal. The general eyres created by Henry II were to continue to the end of the thirteenth century as one of the most prominent institutions for bringing royal justice to the English population.

A fitting tribute to Henry II's development of the common law appeared at the end of his reign in the book commonly called "Glanvill" (Glanville). A detailed treatment of the substance and process of the common law, it was the first book to be written on the subject. Whether Ranulf de Glanville, a justiciar of Henry II, or some other legal specialist of the period wrote it has never been determined. Its general title is, in translation, *Treatise on the Laws and Customs of England.* When compared to the *Laws of Henry I,* the only other published law book up to that time, Glanville's work is scientific, systematic, and modern, while the earlier work is a jumbled and archaic presentation of doubtful laws and legal principles. Among other things, the *Treatise* can be considered the earliest register of writs. It contains some seventy-five writs which were obtainable from the chancery and which initiated and continued process in a dozen fields of legal action. Around the writs, the author built extended explanations and treatments of the process and substance of the common law. Without the *Treatise* we would not know how much the common law had grown during Henry II's reign. It gives immeasurably more information than can be gleaned from the documentary materials of Henry II's legislation and the Pipe Rolls. No comparable law tract was produced by any other Western European state before this time. Glanville's book was an altogether suitable monument to the role of Henry II in the making of the English common law.

For all that Glanville accomplished in his book, he neglected to identify or describe the royal courts of justice that administered the law. His neglect may have been due to the embryonic state in the late 1180's of what fifty years later would be clearly visible central law courts. The king's court was, of course, the original and highest feudal court in England. And as the king delegated authority to justices to hear cases for him, he began imperceptibly to create different royal courts. Not only was his own court a traveling court, but he sometimes commissioned justices—his great ecclesiastical and lay barons at first—to hear and decide cases in distant places where he could not be present. Henry I appointed local justiciars who resided in the counties and heard all pleas belonging to the king. This extension of the king's judicial presence into the counties disappeared in the early years of Henry II, perhaps because the systematic eyres were a better means of taking the king's court to the countryside.

The justices who traveled with Henry II as he moved about his realm may be considered the nucleus of the court that came to be called the king's bench in the thirteenth century. The pleas they heard were *coram rege* (in the presence of the king), a partly fictitious expression since the king was not always present, nor did he need to be. This court became visible under John (1199–1216), then disappeared during Henry III's minority, finally reappearing in 1234.

Another royal court, resident at Westminster, began to develop in the last years of the twelfth century. It may have grown out of the Exchequer, the great financial office that already had almost a century of development behind it. It may also have grown out of the king's wish to have a group of justices in a central place for ease of access by litigants, especially during the long absences of Richard and John. Within the thirteenth century this court acquired the name of the common bench (later, the court of common pleas). There is no certain date for the origin of either of these two central courts, and in their early history they and the eyre courts heard the same types of cases, with the exception that the king's bench had a superior jurisdiction over the other two courts in matters of error, and that it also paid particular attention to cases that touched the king or his interests.

The justices for these three royal courts came at first from the great barons, but by the beginning of the thirteenth century they were drawn from the lesser tenants in chief and even from the lesser nobles and knightly families. Throughout the thirteenth century, both clerics and laymen served as judges of the two benches and of the eyre commissions. These men were considered to be a professional judiciary, with careers that sometimes extended over twenty years. In certain cases, the clerical judges used their service to the king as stepping stones to a bishopric.

COMMON LAW FROM HENRY II TO EDWARD I

The period from the death of Henry II in 1189 to the accession of Edward I in 1272 saw the steady growth of the common law. The reign of Henry III (1216–1272) covers most of the period, but Henry himself seems not to have played a central role in legal development. On the contrary, law and legal remedy in this period expanded through decisions and innovations of the judges themselves. New remedies were needed, but judges created these, with the compliance of the chancery, as the occasion arose. Proof of this expansion can be seen in the official record—the plea rolls—of both the king's bench and the common bench, and in the most important book written on medieval English law, the treatise by Henry de Bracton entitled, in translation, *On the Laws and Customs of England*. Since his and Glanville's titles are almost identical, the two books are usually referred to by the names of their supposed authors—for it has recently been discovered that Bracton, one of Henry III's justices, probably did not write all of the treatise that bears his name. While Bracton wrote on all of the topics found in Glanville, he also treated areas not covered by the latter, and one of the most notable areas was on entry.

The actions on entry probably represent the most important of many ways in which the common law changed and expanded in the thirteenth century. These writs to recover land attended to problems not addressed in the possessory assizes. The assize was only between disseisor and disseisee; it did not lie against the heir of the disseisor, nor could it be used by the heir of the disseisee.

Glanville did not mention entry, but he did have a writ of gage in which the plaintiff had demised land to the defendant as security for debt. Because the plaintiff was now ready to pay the debt, the defendant no longer had right to the land and was obligated to restore it. In effect, the land had been granted for a term that had passed (*ad terminum qui praeteriit*), and this remedy pointed the way to the writs of entry which began to appear just after 1200.

The writ of entry alleged that the tenant had entry in the land only by a defective title or grant. The demandant could claim that the tenant had no entry except through *X (per)* to whom (*cui*) *Y* had granted it, and that this *Y* had disseised the demandant's ancestor. This writ was called "entry in the *per* and *cui*." The demandant had to specify the steps or degrees from the original defect to the present tenant, and a jury usually determined the issue. While the writ of entry lay between the questions of seisin and right, it tried to exclude the question of right. Finally, the Statute of Marlborough of 1267 permitted the demandant to skip the enumeration of steps and simply claim that the tenant had entered after *(post)* the disseisin, thereby creating the writ of entry in the *post*. Through the writs of entry, the king completed his jurisdictional control over all litigation concerning freehold land.

Beyond the writs of entry there were other fields of legal action that prospered in the thirteenth century. Glanville devoted an entire chapter to the action of debt, but he could not have dreamed of its future prominence. The action of detinue was akin to debt in that it had the nature of something withheld. The same was true of the action on account, arising from the failure of a bailiff or person of comparable office to render account of money and goods for which he was responsible. Still another action, which appeared in the early years of the century and continued to develop, was that of trespass.

These newer remedies, like the older ones, were sued under the system of the returnable writ. When Bracton expressed his strong opinion (about 1250) that for every wrong or injury there ought to be a remedy, he knew, but said little or nothing, about wrongs and injuries which had for many years been brought without writ to the two central courts as well as to the eyre courts. It is important to realize that throughout the thirteenth century, while returnable writs continued to be the lifeblood of the common law, freemen could bring suit to the king's courts without writ, by the process of plaint (querela), or what is often called procedure without writ.

Not only were older actions expanded and new ones created in the thirteenth century, but statutory provisions began to alter and amend both old and new. The first statute to play this role was the Magna Carta. Some eighteen chapters of an original sixty-three concerned legal and judicial matters. Most of these, however, touched on procedure rather than on substance. Chapter thirty-four, for example, prohibited the issuance of the writ praecipe whereby any freeman *(liber homo)* might lose his court. The barons had insisted on the inclusion of this provision to prevent the king's summary interference in their own feudal courts on writs of right. The understanding of this provision has remained controversial, as has that of chapter thirty-nine, which said that no freeman would be arrested, imprisoned, disseised, outlawed, or exiled except by the lawful judgment of his peers. While this clause contained the seed of later due process, it did not, contrary to popular

opinion, guarantee or provide for trial by jury. Magna Carta also provided that common pleas would not follow the king but would be held in some fixed place. The clause was probably unnecessary, since a central court resident at Westminster had already become a tradition.

Henry III's reign was not noted for a large volume of legislation. Apart from the reissues of Magna Carta the only two effective bodies of law were the Statute of Merton in 1236 and the Statute of Marlborough in 1267. Magna Carta was a large general body of reforms, addressing the problems of the feudal system, of local and central administration, and of law. Merton and Marlborough were directed almost exclusively to adjusting, refining, and expanding the substance and procedure of the common law.

Among other adjustments of remedy, Merton struck at those who withheld a widow's dower after her husband's death and made her sue for it. Those who were convicted of such deforcement would thenceforth pay damages, that is, the full value of the dower from the day of the husband's death. On another front, disseisors who redisseised tenants after the assize had restored seisin were upon conviction to be imprisoned until they paid a fine or otherwise made peace with the king. These are examples of the ways in which Merton, a modest piece of legislation, amended and corrected flaws in legal remedies.

The Statute of Marlborough was Henry III's largest piece of lawmaking and was directly related to the upheaval caused by the period of the baronial rebellion, 1258–1267. That rebellion produced the baronial political program of 1258 known as the Provisions of Oxford and also, in the fall of 1259, the Provisions of Westminster, a program of legal reform dealing mainly with inadequacies in the common law. This legal program was never executed because of the baronial wars; but in 1267, when peace was reestablished, the Statute of Marlborough was published largely as a reenactment of the Westminster document. Of twenty-nine chapters in Marlborough, some twenty repeat legal reforms included in the earlier program. Notable among these was the provision for damages in the assize of mort d'ancestor, because the lord had compelled the heir, upon attaining his majority, to sue for his ancestor's holding. The Statute of Marlborough not only completed Henry III's involvement in the expansion of the common law, but it also pointed the way to Edward I, who would enact more legislation affecting the law than any king after him until modern times.

Although there was still need and room for

growth, the fundamental body of the common law had been established by the end of Henry III's reign. While his role as a lawmaker did not approach that of Henry II a century before, he was no less aware than his grandfather of the royal and divinely imposed duty to provide justice for his people. Bracton noted that "a king is created and chosen for this purpose that he might do justice to all." The coronation oath of English kings from the earliest times enshrined that obligation. The king's awareness of this duty intensified during the twelfth century, although more stress than is warranted has been placed on the king's desire to see his revenues grow by drawing into his hands a comprehensive administration of justice. That was at best a minor motive for the king's behavior. The feudal monarch in England saw the absolute need for law and stability and was convinced that only he could, and should, provide it. Not only did this belief derive from the view of the king as lawgiver, but in England after the Conquest it was peculiarly strengthened and made a reality by the needs and operations of a centralized feudal landholding system. As supreme feudal lord, the English king was bound to exercise effective control over those needs and operations, and this consideration loomed large in the origins and development of the English common law.

BIBLIOGRAPHY

The older and still standard historical studies of the early history of the common law are those of Frederick Pollock and Frederic W. Maitland, *The History of English Law Before the Time of Edward I,* 2nd ed., 2 vols. (1968); William S. Holdsworth, *A History of English Law,* I–III (many editions); and Theodore F. T. Plucknett, *A Concise History of the Common Law,* 5th ed. (1956). A recent general history of medieval English law is by Bryce D. Lyon, *A Constitutional and Legal History of Medieval England,* 2nd ed. (1980).

More technical and specialized studies are Doris M. Stenton, *English Justice Between the Norman Conquest and the Great Charter, 1066–1215* (1964); R. C. van Caenegem, *The Birth of the English Common Law* (1973); and Stroud F. C. Milsom, *Historical Foundations of the Common Law,* 2nd ed. (1981). The statutes of Henry II and related primary sources are translated in *English Historical Documents,* II, *1042–1189,* David C. Douglas and G. W. Greenaway, eds. (1953). Translations of the Magna Carta and the statutes of Merton and of Marlborough, with related primary sources, are in *English Historical Documents,* III, *1189–1327,* Harry Rothwell, ed. (1975). The standard edition and translation of Ranulf de Glanville is that by George D. G. Hall, ed. and trans., *The Treatise on the Laws and Customs of the Realm of England Com-*monly Called Glanvill (1965). For Henry de Bracton's treatise, see *Bracton on the Laws and Customs of England,* George E. Woodbine, ed., Samuel E. Thorne, trans., 4 vols. to date (1968–1977).

FRANKLIN J. PEGUES

[See also **Assize, English; Bracton, Henry de; Clarendon, Assize of; Clarendon, Constitutions of; Common Pleas, Court of; Curia, Lay; Danelaw; Domesday Book; England; Exchequer, Court of; Feudalism; Glanville, Ranulf de; Henry II of England; Inheritance; Jury; Justices Itinerant; Justices of Common Pleas; Justices of the Peace; Langton, Stephen; Magna Carta; Seisin, Disseisin; Statute; Tenure of Land.**]

LAW, ENGLISH COMMON: AFTER 1272. By the time that King Henry III died in 1272 and Edward I inherited the throne of England, the common law had developed a large momentum of growth. In the century just past, beginning in the reign of Henry II (1154–1189), the king's courts had defined themselves as a distinct system. They had asserted their jurisdiction over felonies and over most questions of the ownership of free lands and tenements (real property), while standing open for important cases of debt, contract, and trespass. Most important, they had shaped a single law for the kingdom; this was the English common law. The justices had come for the most part to be professional judges. In the court, professional counsel spoke for clients and a corps of professional attorneys formed around the court of Common Pleas to represent absent litigants. Resting upon these practitioners' appreciation of all that had been accomplished, and buoyed by their anticipation of future attainments, the law's momentum for growth continued throughout the later Middle Ages.

THE COURTS AND THE LEGAL PROFESSION

One expression of the law's momentum was the improvement in the organization of the king's courts. The system that had been built by 1272 provided that the royal judicature should appear locally, in the counties, in the persons of itinerant justices. These might be sent to hold an "eyre for all pleas," that is, to exercise comprehensive common-law jurisdiction, or they might have a limited commission, as justices "of assize" (for cases of novel disseisin and mort d'ancestor), of "gaol delivery" (to try felonies), or of "oyer and terminer" (to "hear and determine" particular cases). Many such commissions issued them, but each had to be given specially; they did not provide regularly recurring sessions.

At the center of the judicial system were several king's courts with continuous being and jursdictions over the whole realm. Since the 1230's these had been the court of Common Pleas, the Exchequer, the King's Bench, and the parliaments. Their principal work was to hear in the first instance lawsuits of special importance. Of these, the Exchequer heard the king's revenue cases and the King's Bench received other business in which the king had an interest. The Common Pleas took the ordinary suits between subject and subject. Under Edward I even the parliaments which capped the system were opened to first-instance work on behalf of the king or of petitioners. The Exchequer, King's Bench, and parliament also functioned as courts of appeal. They received knotty cases referred by itinerant justices and the Common Pleas, or, in the parliaments, from the Exchequer and the King's Bench themselves. More formally, upon the complaints of litigating parties, the King's Bench reviewed the judgments of itinerant justices and the Common Pleas, and the parliaments (in principle more than in practice) had a like jurisdiction "in error" over the King's Bench and the Exchequer.

The structure of the four central courts saw little change. It only happened that in the fourteenth and fifteenth centuries the parliaments proved less and less able to handle either formal proceedings in error or the discussion of difficult cases referred by the justices. They met less frequently than they had in the thirteenth century. Furthermore, they lost the mixed character that they had possessed in those earlier days when justices and administrators as well as magnates, knights, and burgesses came to make or seek decisions, and they took on instead an overwhelmingly political cast. They made a satisfactory legislature but not a good supreme court. Nothing was done, however, to provide a better court of error over the King's Bench and nothing effective to provide a similar court over the Exchequer. For the resolution of problems which they wished to refer, as distinct from proceedings in error, the justices of the central courts found a substitute for parliaments in the meetings they convened among themselves. All the justices of Common Pleas and King's Bench, and sometimes the judges ("barons") of the Exchequer and others, gathered in the Exchequer Chamber, and the decisions of the group so constituted were, naturally, highly authoritative. Under the parliaments and by their default, the Court of Exchequer emerged as a supreme court for referred cases.

Deeper changes came over the itinerant justices. Here the keystone of the old system was the eyre for all pleas, which brought into each county visited the whole authority of the king's court. Gradually during the middle and later years of the thirteenth century these eyres ceased to function. Commissions were issued less and less often, until they stopped almost entirely after 1294 and quite entirely after 1348. The eyre was unpopular. It took money out of the county and conducted a review of local government that was upsetting to the community. Edward I tried to counteract its unpopularity by directing the justices to redress all sorts of oppressions by the official and the powerful, but this served chiefly to offend the oppressors and to burden the justices with too much work.

For civil litigation at the common law, mainly concerned with free lands, the result was a rush to the Common Pleas. From about 1300 nearly all civil cases at common law had to go there, from far and near in the kingdom and among persons both great and small; there was no other resort. For business that could by no means be taken to the Common Pleas, the government contrived by the 1330's a sort of substitute for the eyres. Itinerant justices were sent to visit every county two or three times a year. They had no such comprehensive jurisdiction as belonged to the old justices in eyre, but held instead several of the limited commissions that were known to the law. They had the commission of assize, for actions of novel disseisin and mort d'ancestor, and this provided a handy name for them in all their powers: "justices of assize." They probably did more actual business under their other commission of gaol delivery, which empowered them to try felonies. Still more important was the commission of *nisi prius* in the Statute of Westminster II (1285). Under this the justices of assize acted as delegates of the Common Pleas, that is, they were directed to try a case "at *nisi prius*"—before the scheduled trial at Westminster. Most of the cases that flooded into that central court came to the point where they required trial by jury on one issue or another. Twelve jurors were needed from the county where the case arose. Since it was impossible to bring to the capital thousands of juries from near and far, the Common Pleas delegated the holding of trials to the justices of assize on their visit to the county whence the jurors were to be drawn. The justices would report the verdict so the Common Pleas could proceed.

Another plan, developed about the same time as the circuits of justices of assize, provided each county with several resident common-law justices called justices of the peace. When their functions were finally stabilized by the 1360's (beginning with the statute of January 1361), their powers were restricted to criminal law, but within this field were very full. They could investigate offenses, receive indictments, and try the accused.

These expedients did more than make up for the breakdown of the eyres. They provided a better structure of courts than the common law had known before. By the end of the fourteenth century they had rendered nearly obsolete the commission issued specially or upon application, with all the irregularities that it used to occasion. Justices of the peace became permanent fixtures in each county, and justices of assize visited regularly. The Common Pleas was effectively open to everyone, and the justices of assize handled without much delay the trials by jury required for cases there. England lived with this system for centuries, and much of it endures to the present day.

Organized in this way, the king's court experienced a vast growth in their jurisdiction at the expense of the courts of counties, hundreds, and franchises. This came about in part through the appointment of the justices of the peace. Their concern for the general peace and quiet of their counties brought before them many indictments for small trespasses—misdemeanors which before their time would have been handled in hundred courts or in the franchisal courts leet. A statute enacted in 1461 stated that such indictments should be turned over to the justices of the peace for trial. This addition to the work of the king's courts was in part specious. These small offenses had always been judged within the local community, and so they continued to be. The authority of the justices of the peace, however it may have borne the stamp of their commissions as royal justices, was from many points of view simply a fresh way of organizing the community for this purpose. In civil matters, on the other hand, there was an undoubtedly genuine flow of business away from local courts into the Common Pleas and King's Bench. Beginning in the reign of Edward I litigants more and more sought these central courts for their actions of replevin, debt, and trespass.

Replevin was an action brought by a tenant of lands whose lord had impounded his cattle (or other moveable property) without good cause. It could be brought only in the county court. But when an action of replevin came up in that court the lord would commonly contend that he had impounded the cat-

tle, as well he might, in order to enforce payment of customs and services due to him from the land. If the tenant replied, as he often did, that his land did not owe the customs and services which the lord claimed, it would thus appear that the case "touched free tenement." Anything that touched free tenement was a traditional concern of the king's courts. The county courts were not well equipped to handle it. In 1285 the Statute of Westminster II, therefore, allowed the lord who claimed customs and services in replevin to remove the action to the Common Pleas if he liked, and in the event the lords frequently did so.

The jurisdiction of local courts in actions for debt seems to have been curtailed by overzealous supervision from the king's courts. From the 1290's they allowed defendants in actions for debts of 40 shillings or more to remove the cases to the Common Pleas upon a bare allegation of bias in the sheriff or other presiding officer. The removal caused the plaintiff delay, disrupting the process of his suit. Plaintiffs almost unanimously judged that under these circumstances it was best to bring their actions in the Common Pleas to begin with.

It is less clear why actions for trespass also tended more and more to be brought in the king's courts. In their nature they were private suits for damages for miscellaneous offenses, and at first the king's courts were reluctant to hear them. The Statute of Gloucester of 1278 ruled that the Common Pleas and King's Bench would receive none where the alleged damages were less than 40 shillings. The plaintiff also had to allege a breach of the king's peace. But with some debasement of currency in the fourteenth century, 40 shillings came to represent less value than it had in 1278, while on the other hand the king's courts accepted cases where the breach of the king's peace was, to say the least, only constructive. Finally, in the 1360's, the king's courts abandoned altogether the requirement that it must be alleged. Plaintiffs availed themselves fully of the access to the king's courts which was thus granted them, and much of this business thereby flowed away from the local courts. After the 1360's, when breach of peace no longer needed to be charged, many cases of the sort that later generations would segregate as "trespass on the special case" came to the king's court. A plaintiff might sue his neighbor for damage that resulted from the neighbor's failure to keep in repair his share of a seawall. A lodger might sue his innkeeper if unknown thieves stole from the lodger's room. Patients might sue medical doctors for malpractice, and so forth, in unending variety. The category of trespass was also stretched to cover enforcement of unwritten contracts. The party who had suffered from a breach of such a contract could bring an action of trespass in the form assumpsit, charging that the defendant had undertaken to do something or assumed (assumpsit) a responsibility or obligation and then failed to fulfill his obligation. Especially with the influx of trespass cases, the jurisdiction of the king's courts changed in character on the civil side. No longer was it centered on property in free lands and tenements.

Improvement in organization and expansion in jurisdiction were matched by better definition of the legal professions. Two professions were distinguished, the attorneys and the serjeants-at-law. Attorneys represented absent clients, conducted the routine of lawsuits (seeing that orders went out to summon defendants, and the like), and gave elementary legal advice. Serjeants constituted a much higher profession as counsel who advised clients in doubtful or contentious matters and pleaded and argued cases in court.

For attorneys, regulation came from the several central courts. Each court admitted those who might practice before it, accepting the able and honest to the number needed to serve its public, excluding others, and exercising disciplinary power. We first hear of such a system in 1292, when the Common Pleas was ordered to institute it. A statute of 1402 directed it to be used by the King's Bench and Court of Exchequer as well. The regulation of serjeants-at-law took a different form. Every court needed attorneys, but the forensic skills of serjeants were especially associated with pleading civil cases between subject and subject. Such cases went to the Common Pleas; in the time of Edward I one normally became a serjeant by being accepted as such by that court. By the 1460's all serjeants were chosen by the chief justice of the Common Pleas in consultation with the other justices of the central courts and formally appointed by authority of letters patent. Thus precisely defined, their professional dignity served in turn to define that of the justices themselves, for in the 1300's it became the rule that those whom the crown appointed as justices must be found among the serjeants. The rule did not apply to justices of the peace or to the barons of the Exchequer, and in the other central courts it served only to shape a judicial professionalism which in the main had been established long before. But for itinerant justices it brought about an important change. In earlier times

the limited common-law commissions (assize, gaol delivery, oyer and terminer, and others) had often been given to laymen who thus became temporary amateur justices. In the fourteenth century and thereafter the new justices of assize who received the limited commissions, and who became almost the only persons to receive them, had to be serjeants. There appears to have been a large gain in competence and impartiality.

The serjeants had a monopoly of pleading in the Common Pleas, but men who were training to be serjeants, called "apprentices," could act as counsel in other capacities, working in the Exchequer and King's Bench, before justices of assize, and even in the Common Pleas for purposes other than pleading. The apprentices seem to have remained unregulated in the Middle Ages, but the foundations were being laid then for their future professional direction or control. On the edge of London, toward Westminster, there grew up four societies of apprentices, the Inns of Court: Lincoln's Inn (the records of which began in 1422), Gray's Inn, the Inner Temple, and the Middle Temple. In the fifteenth century, apprentices had to belong to one or another of these societies, for only fellows of the Inns were called to be serjeants. The Inns were hospices, fraternities, and above all schools for training in the skills of serjeants. Length of membership in the Inn and standing in the stages of its curriculum gave some measure of the qualificaitons of an apprentice. Later on, in the sixteenth century, the courts used such measures in a formal way to determine which apprentices (then called barristers) might be received to act before them.

THE RULES OF LAW

Better organization of the courts and the legal professions was accompanied by fuller specification of rules of law. By 1500 the common law had become a far richer body of doctrine than it was around 1250. In the time of Henry III the law was unclear about, for example, what constituted good title to franchise. Franchises were privileges belonging to subjects which allowed them to take a profit or exercise a power that in principle was the king's; they ranged from hunting preserves to judgment of capital crimes. Could subjects claim franchises by virtue of immemorial usage alone? No one knew. In 1290 the Statute of Quo Warranto resolved that immemorial usage was to be acceptable, and defined it as usage since 1189.

Only important men and women held franchises,

but hundreds of thousands of ordinary English people were tenants of free lands. In the mid thirteenth century there remained some doubt whether a free tenant could legally give or sell his holding without the approval of the lord of whom he held. Again in 1290, the statute *Quia emptores* determined that he could do so, provided that when he alienated in fee simple (giving the outright ownership) the new tenant must hold immediately of the lord.

From time to time an owner of land might find that property of his was being held against him by an adverse claimant. Where there was a dispute about title, the adversary might move in and take control either surreptitiously or by violence. Where property had been leased out, the lessee might for some reason refuse to give it up when, as the owner believed, the lease had expired. Where the owner's widowed mother held a piece of property for her life, she might abuse her rights by selling outright, in fee simple, to a stranger.

These and hundreds of other tangles could arise from misunderstandings or unscrupulous ambition, and medieval Englishmen, an assertive breed, often found themselves embroiled in them. It was important for owners to know how far the law allowed them to "enter," that is to go and seize control of their lands in face of an adverse possessor, and how far it required them to make good their own through the courts. In the thirteenth century the law had rules for this kind of action, but these rules were vague and imprecise. The principal doctrine was that the owner who wished to enter must do so without undue delay. There was nothing to tell for certain, in many cases, what would count as undue delay. In the fourteenth century the ambiguities were all resolved by decisions of the courts, which held that delay on the owner's part should not tell against him at all. It was too difficult to define. The owner might enter when he liked, early or late. But he must not use any force to effect his entry, and he lost the right of entry if there was a "descent cast," that is, if his adversary died in possession leaving an heir to succeed him. The descent cast would not, however, destroy the right of entry if the owner had "made continual claim." He "made claim" by going to the property, or as near as was safe, and publicly stating his right; the claim was "continual" if made within a year before the adversary died. There was far more in the rules, for we can do no more than illustrate them. A mature body of law was created, complicated but also firm and detailed.

Procedural law was also elaborated, especially for the practice of pleading. Pleading is the statement of his stand by a party to a lawsuit, and may be distinguished from argument—which is the attempt to show that the rules of law support one's position—and from evidence, the attempt to establish the truth of the facts on which one relies. Pleading may amount to nothing more than a statement of a charge or claim and the defendant's denial of it in reply. If we can judge from the records, it commonly came to nothing more than that in the earliest period of the common law, around 1200. Defendants always retained the right to plead in this briefest of all possible ways if they liked. To a claim for debt on a contract the reply might be, "I owe nothing"; to a charge of disseisin, "I did no wrong or disseisin"; to a charge of felony or trespass, "Not guilty."

But as the thirteenth century went on, defendants were increasingly allowed and encouraged to plead specially, that is, to define their stands more particularly. A defendant who flatly denied a charge might accompany the denial with an explanation meant to account for whatever plausibility the charge possessed, as though to say, for example, "I did not drive the plaintiff's cattle off the common as he charges; that area was my private land." He might admit some of the facts that his opponent alleged, restricting his denial to a few, perhaps to one point alone. He might admit everything the adversary said but add other facts that destroyed the merits of his case: "True, I disseised you, but you afterwards released your rights to me." Pleadings in this last form were bound to elicit a reply on the plaintiff's part, and there might be further answers and counteranswers. In that case it sometimes happened that the parties agreed on all the facts, each merely contending that under the circumstances the law if rightly understood was on his side.

The development of special pleading was well under way by 1272. Under Edward I skill in this business became the chief qualification of a serjeant. But as the art and science of special pleading was elaborated the need was felt for rules to govern it. The courts provided these. Thus, it was made clear that a plaintiff need not reply further to special statements of the defendant's which only served to explain a general denial; that any party who pleaded a release must have the deed in court at the time; that it could not suffice a defendant to dispute only certain kinds of details of a plaintiff's case, such as the date when he said an offense was committed. There was a great deal more.

Successes of this kind in the articulation of law

were made possible by a growing professional literature. In its infancy in the twelfth century the common law seems to have been extensively shaped by acts of legislation, but in those days the acts were forgotten when they had taken effect in the practice of the courts. In the thirteenth century this way of absorbing legislation was left behind; decisively so when a long series of important enactments was issued through the years 1267–1299. In those years official copies came to be kept on the Statute Rolls, and lawyers began to have made for them little books of the statutes. The tradition was established forevermore that legislation took the form of an authoritative text to be preserved in its very words.

Even more important than collections of statutes were the law reports. Since the twelfth century the king's courts had kept written records, but while these were good for many purposes they were difficult to use for professional study. From the 1270's a new type of writing, the reports, appeared to serve legal science. The authors were anonymous and their work unofficial. They wrote accounts of cases in court that seemed of special interest for lawyers, leaving routine aside and trying to catch the unusual maneuver, the fresh decision, and the unresolved doubt. They cast most of their work in dramatic form, purporting to reproduce the actual give-and-take among serjeants and justices, though what they give is in fact artful reconstruction. Most of the manuscript copies through which reports were disseminated were arranged chronologically, as "yearbooks," but "abridgments," digests of reports under topical heads, were also made. In the reign of Henry VII some yearbooks and an abridgement called Statham appeared in print. The law knew no strict doctrine that precedents must be followed, and the reports therefore could not be cited like statutes as authoritative texts. But in illustrating practice as they did they gave lawyers an abundant literature from which to draw exact learning.

THE CAPACITY OF REFORM

Where so much of importance was done, and so well done, to organize the courts, regulate the professions, and specify the law, the law might have become too sharply fixed to adapt itself to new conditions. In some ways it did. But on the whole it retained remarkably well the ability to meet changing times.

The superior legislative power of parliament was always recognized; parliamentary statutes could alter the law. For example, the law of the mid thirteenth century had known no imprisonment for debt. The Statute of Acton Burnell (1283) and the Statute of Merchants (1285) introduced it for merchants' debts which had been specially registered, and the Statute of Staples (1353) made some additional registries available. If debts so registered were not paid, the debtor would be imprisoned for his default. Then in 1352 another statute established that any creditor who sued and got a judgment in the king's courts could choose to have the debtor put in gaol until the claim was satisfied. Thus the law was changed in an unpleasant way, especially as no proceedings in bankruptcy were provided to relieve the insolvent debtor. However well or badly, the law did show the capacity for change. In this case it was refashioned to meet the needs of a society where moneylending was increasingly common.

A happier story lies in the history of benefit of clergy. The common law of felony was put into its final stated form, as far as concerns the Middle Ages, around 1250. It was an unintelligently harsh form. Death by hanging, with loss of all real and personal property to the felon's family, was (with minor exceptions) the penalty for every felony from larceny to organized murder and without regard to extenuating circumstances. Conviction was normally through trial by jury, and juries rendered the law more supple in practice by refusing, ordinarily, to convict for the less serious felonies (among which they evidently counted forcible rape) or for those, including homicide, that were committed under extenuating circumstances. Still, their exercise of flexible judgment was off the record and out of the lawbooks, so that in making the law less harsh they also made it less certain.

Benefit of clergy was the privilege of clerics ("clerks") not to be convicted or punished for felony in the king's courts but only in their own church courts. The church courts could give no sentences of death; in fact they seldom gave any sentences at all for felony but almost automatically acquitted the accused through their special form of trial called canonical purgation, in which the accused could "purge his innocence" by bringing with him to the canonical trial a number of men (compurgators) who would swear they believed he was telling the truth about his innocence. In the later fourteenth century the king's courts modified their common law of felony by allowing benefit of clergy to anyone who could read a bit of Latin. In the fifteenth century the spread of literacy therefore spread benefit of clergy, and if more was needed the courts gave it by recognizing as clergy anyone who could appear to read Psalm 51:1 (known as the "neck-verse") when it was pointed out in the book. Benefit of clergy thus became available to most accused felons. A guilty man who was entitled to the privilege did not get off wholly without trouble. He could be indicted, arrested, arraigned in the king's court, and turned over to the bishop to abide in his prison for some time before being allowed to make his canonical purgation, and all his property would be held by the sheriff all the while. But he paid therewith a far lighter penalty than death and total loss of property. Under Henry VII it was judged that the pendulum had swung a little too far toward mildness. A sensible correction was made by a statute of 1488 which enacted that benefit of clergy could be used only once. The man who was convicted of a second felony must pay the full common-law penalty.

The change in the law of felony that was brought about through benefit of clergy was effected for the most part by judicial decisions, not by statute. In the late Middle Ages judicial decisions also served to simplify radically the common law's procedures for litigation about free lands and tenements. Beginning in the 1160's King Henry II offered specially designed procedures in the king's courts for certain classes of cases. From that starting point, the king's courts for free lands and tenements grew over a period of time with the invention of more and more special procedures for particular kinds of dispute. The fashioning of the many diverse procedures was a crudely effective way of providing improved justice and creating, by 1272, a near monopoly of cases concerning free lands and tenements in the king's courts. Nevertheless, it meant when the development was complete that the king's courts had to deal with dozens of different procedures, the famous "forms of action." If a landowner's complaint was that he had been ejected he must have novel disseisin. If his father whose heir he was had been ejected he must have "entry sur disseisin." But if his father had died in possession and he had been kept as heir from entering the holding he needed mort d'ancestor. If his mother's land had been alienated by his step-father, the son as his mother's heir must bring "entry *cui in vita*." If it were, on the other hand, a question not of an owner suing for recovery of land but of a lord wishing to make good a right to his customs and services from land, the suit might according to circumstances be in replevin, *ne vexes*, "customs and services," *contra formam feoffamenti*, or *de secto subtracto*.

New forms of action continued to be invented as late as the 1280's, but then the process stopped. The forms had done their work so well that their particularities were rendered superfluous. To most people it now seemed that litigation about free lands and tenements belonged naturally to the king's courts. The forms bred their own artificial problems, however, in borderline cases where it was doubtful which form was right and in other cases where there were characteristics belonging to two different forms. To resolve these problems, lawyers and the courts, from the reign of Edward I, worked toward achieving a unified procedure. They did so by broadening the applicability of a few favored forms of action.

For litigation about customs and services, the courts singled out replevin. Traditionally, replevin had a serious limitation: through it the lord could recover his dues or the tenant successfully fend off the claim, but only on the basis of recent seisin. If the lord was entitled to customs and services that had not lately been acknowledged and rendered, or if conversely a tenant had for some time paid more than was due, replevin could not set the matter right. In a series of decisions in the early fourteenth century the courts removed this limitation. They substituted for it a rule that the tenant could plead whatever lawful matter he liked to disburden himself of the dues that the lord claimed, and that the lord must reply to it. Handled in this way, replevin resolved any and all disputes about customs and services.

In much the same way, where ownership of lands and tenements was in question the courts chose to broaden the assize of novel disseisin. In the old law the principal limitation of that form was that it would serve to recover land only for an owner who had been disseised by the defendant. An owner who had never been in occupation of the land but wished perhaps to claim a right of inheritance must betake himself to some other form. So must a litigant who had leased out his land and who, in the face of some difficulty or other, had to sue to reclaim it when the lease expired. Even someone who had been disseised might find that the assize could not help him if the perpetrator of the disseisin died and the property passed to his heir, for novel disseisin was good only against the disseisor.

The restrictions on novel disseisin were interpreted away in a long, slow process and by means of an ingenious series of decisions from the 1270's to the 1380's. The new and firmer definition of the owner's right of entry, already discussed above, was made during this same period as part of this work. The courts deliberately formed that definition in such a way as to give the true owner a right of entry in most cases where he might find his property being held against him. They proceeded to make it their doctrine that when a true owner lawfully entered upon his property he instantly acquired seisin of it in the eyes of the law, even without establishing actual control. Since the owner was seised in the eyes of the law, any adversary who from that moment held out against him committed a disseisin in the eyes of the law, and the owner could therefore recover by the assize of novel disseisin. In the hearing of the assize he would as a rule have to demonstrate that he was the true owner, for only if he were would his bare entry put him in legal seisin so that he could rightly complain of being disseised. When he showed that he was the true owner, the adversary could of course dispute it, and the parties would then go on to try the title to the property: any title that carried a right of entry. Thus novel disseisin became a general-purpose action for trying titles to free lands and tenements.

No sooner had this been accomplished (by the 1380's) than the assize of novel disseisin began to be replaced by the action of trespass. If an owner who made a bare entry upon his property could complain that his adversary, by holding on, had from that moment disseised him and so sue by novel disseisin, he could equally, and at his option, complain that the adversary had trespassed on his property and sue by an action of trespass. In the action of trespass the owner's title would be set forth and tried just as in novel disseisin. But actions of trespass could do even more than try titles to free lands and tenements. They could also try titles to leaseholds. Though in no sense unfree, leaseholds were for ancient reasons not counted among the "free tenements" and so lay outside the ambit of novel disseisin. And of course actions of trespass could also try the myriad matters quite outside the land law for which they were originally designed. By the end of the Middle Ages the action of trespass was the usual form of trying a vast range of matters from land titles to breach of contract. The common law was approaching a unified procedure for civil litigation.

The flexibility of the law appears again in the important development of entails of lands. In the thirteenth century landowners often wished to give property to favored relatives on terms that would assure keeping it in the family. When a child married, the father might give him lands "to have and to hold

to him and the heirs of his body." The intent was that the child must keep the land so that it would pass on eventually to his descendants. But around 1280 the courts insisted on interpreting a gift of land in this form, or in any like form, as yielding the donee an outright ownership in fee simple as soon as a child was born to him. The courts had technical reasons for this, but their interpretation frustrated the intentions of the donors. A tenant in fee simple was free to give the land away or sell it to anyone he liked.

In 1285 the statute *De donis conditionalibus* (part of the Statute of Westminster II) did away with the courts' unsuitable interpretation. It enacted that the donor's wishes must be respected and the property pass on to the heir of the donee's body. The apparent intent was to restrain alienation only for one generation, through the donee's lifetime. But the courts interpreted the statute so as to alter this rule drastically. The land should remain inalienable, they held, as long as there was any heir of the body of the donee. Since a donee might have descendants to the end of time, the land might remain forever inalienable.

Dynastically minded men of property appreciated the facility that was thus opened to them for entrenching their families permanently in their social positions as landowners. But the entail (as the arrangement was called) was a legal monstrosity and a danger to society. It meant rule by the dead hand of the past. A tenant of an entail was prevented from disposing of the land if he wished to do so, because of the decision to entail made by the original donor perhaps many generations before. It also tended to create a society of castes. The upper classes of England were made up of large landowners. Access to these circles was possible for new men rising from the lower classes if they could use their luck or talents to acquire lands. But when land was entailed it was taken out of the market. As new lands were put into entail from time to time, the supply of marketable land shrank and the entrance of successful new men into the highest classes became more difficult, perhaps nearly impossible. In developing the entail the law had taken a disastrously bad turn.

The statute *De donis conditionalibus* was not repealed, nor was the judicial interpretation of it repudiated. But the traditions of the law were rich and varied; discoveries could be made in them. By about 1475 lawyers had found the means to undo the law of entail. They discovered, or invented, the common recovery.

The basis of this device was an important body of doctrine long known to the law about warranties of land. If *A* owed to *B* a warranty for lands that *B* held, *A* must compensate *B* in the event that the lands were lost to a third party because of a defect in the title. When sued for the lands by the third party, *B* would "vouch *A* to warranty," which meant haling him into court to take over the defense of the case. If the case was finally lost, the judgment would provide that *A* must give *B* other lands out of his own holdings. They must be of equal value with those that *B* had lost, and *B* would hold them on the same terms as he had held the lands that he lost. In the commonest case warranties were due where lands had been given or sold: the grantor and his heirs would owe a warranty to the purchaser and his heirs and assigns. But anyone could undertake an obligation to warrant a tenant, either by giving him a sealed deed to acknowledge the obligation or by making his acknowledgment in the king's court, where it would be recorded.

In the late fifteenth century a tenant of entailed land who wanted to break the entail by giving or selling the land to a stranger would arrange for his would-be purchaser to sue him for the land as though he had some old claim to it. In court, the tenant would vouch a warrantor, who would appear and acknowledge an obligation to warrant. The warrantor would then deliberately lose the case; this could most easily be done by departing in contempt of court. By judgment in consequence, the purchaser would recover the property and the erstwhile tenant would recover land of equal value from the warrantor, which he would hold as an entail since that was how he held the land that he had lost. The entail as such was not destroyed at all but preserved in the land that was recovered by judgment against the warrantor. Therefore, no one who might in any future generation become entitled to the entail could claim the land that the purchaser acquired. In respect of that land, the entail had indeed been broken. The workability of the device depended upon the tenant's being able to find someone who would warrant and then throw away the case and let himself be subjected to the judgment for compensation. But some such person was always to be had. The judgment for compensation could be enforced only by taking lands and tenements of the warrantor's. Anyone could afford to act as warrantor who had no lands and tenements. The tenant would have a judgment for compensation, but no compensation in fact. It was enough that the compensation should exist in

the judgment, for it was by judgment that the purchaser had taken the entailed land. The common recovery was a tortuous device, but it worked. Through its mechanism entailed property became freely alienable.

The law again showed itself triumphantly able to adapt when it developed the "use of lands." In the fourteenth century the interest of the tenant of lands in fee simple became very much like an absolute ownership. It was protected by the king's courts, and the tenant could alienate as he liked. The right of the superior lord to customs and services was considered to be a distinct tenement of the lord's. Strictly regulated as it was, it seemed to limit the tenant's rights only in the same way as did the boundaries of his lands, externally as it were, leaving his ownership complete within its bounds. Although the common law itself furnished the basis for this sense of ownership, the law held several doctrines that nevertheless clashed painfully with it. There was the learning about the lord's right to "incidents." When a tenant in fee simple died and the holding descended to his heir, the heir had to pay the lord a substantial sum as "relief." If the heir was underage and the land was held by knight's service, then the heir would have to enter wardship to the lord, who would then take the income and sell the right to marry the heir. If there was no heir or if the tenant had committed a felony, the land would pass to the lord forever as his "escheat."

In addition to these incidents, there was an ancient rule that tenants might not bequeath their lands by last will and testament. In a world of free alienation it made no sense. Neither did it make sense that the law, which recognized free alienation, restricted to a very few kinds the different interests that the owner might give or sell. He could lease his lands for a fixed period; he could give them for someone's life; he could give them as an entail; or finally, he could give them in fee simple. But the "estates" that he could create were limited to these four.

All these doctrines seemed confining, vexatious, and even downright unjust. The time had become ripe for their removal. The required changes in law were effected with the rise of the use of land in the fifteenth century. The use was an arrangement in which a tenant of land held it for the enjoyment of another, and so entirely so that this beneficiary occupied and managed the land and collected its income by and for himself. The tenant was merely the nominal owner, the "feoffee to uses" (who received the feoffment but with the obligation to allow the use to another), while the beneficiary was "the one who uses," *cestui que use*. A use could be set up by express provision, as when property was given "to *A* to the use of *B*," or by tacit understanding, as for example when a tenant struck a bargain for the sale of his land but then abstained from conveying title to his purchaser. In this latter instance, he held to the purchaser's use by virtue of the bargain and sale.

The law refused to take notice of uses. It held that every tenant had by definition the beneficial use of his property, so that a gift "to *A* to the use of *B*" made sense only in respect of *A,* and the additional phrase concerning *B* was therefore disregarded. It held that interests in lands and tenements were created only by express statements and that tacit understandings could create none. Where a use was set up, *cestui que use* was therefore wholly free from the burdens and restraints that the law laid upon tenants of lands. Since the law ignored him, no "incidents" could ever come due under the law when he died or committed a felony. When he died he could bequeath the land by leaving instructions that the feoffee to uses was thenceforth to hold to the use of another whom he named.

In this way upon his death, or otherwise during his lifetime, he could transfer interests in any form he chose to others, without restriction to the four estates known to the law. He might, for example, instruct the feoffee to uses to hold to the use of *A* until *B* reached age twenty-five or married, but then to the use of *B*. The burdens and restraints of the law that *cestui que use* then escaped all rested of course upon the feoffee to uses, the tenant in the eyes of the law. But because his interest was only nominal, the burdens could always be evaded without inconvenience and the restraints mattered not at all. The incidents were evaded by arranging for several feoffees to uses, holding together as joint tenants. When one of them died (or committed a felony) his interest, according to an old rule of the common law, accrued to the survivors free of any incidents. Since the feoffees' bare legal interest carried no enjoyment of the property, there was no reason why they should wish to bequeath it, and no reason why they should wish, while they held, to hold in one estate rather than another. For technical reasons they always held in fee simple.

Since the law did not notice *cestui que use*, it could not protect his interest. In most circumstances he was none the worse for that. If legal rights in the property had to be vindicated or defended, *cestui que*

use could instruct the feoffees to uses to do what was necessary, paying their expenses. *Cestui que use* remained unprotected only in his relation to the feoffees themselves. If they betrayed his trust or if misunderstandings arose between him and them, he was legally helpless. But in the fifteenth century the chancellors of England lent their help when that happened. The chancellor, for these purposes, was not a justice and therefore was not bound by the doctrines of the law which determined that *cestui que use* must be ignored. Free to consider whatever facts there were, he could take notice of the relationship of trust between *cestui que use* and his feoffees. Taking notice of it, he was prepared to insist as a matter of conscience that it must be respected. If *cestui que use* had a complaint against his feoffees he could petition the chancellor for redress. His interest was therefore secure enough. Under these circumstances the use of land became increasingly popular, and landowners gained thereby a much freer hand with their property.

Petitions of grievance that came in to the chancellor in the fifteenth century usually had to do with uses of lands, but he received others as well. Men solicited his aid who were (so they alleged) too poor to be able to sue at law, and so did foreign merchants who had to leave England and could not abide the law's delays. Others whom the law left unprotected might, like *cestui que use*, seek their remedy with the chancellor. Tenants of unfree lands (now called "copyhold") were mere tenants-at-will in the eyes of the king's courts, which referred them to the protection of their manor courts alone. If the lord of a manor court arbitrarily overrode the custom of his manor, the copyhold tenant could in the fifteenth century petition the chancellor with good hope of finding relief. Victims of frauds sought the chancellor too, for the law of the king's courts, though it proscribed some particular fraudulent practices, gave no remedy for fraud as such. Petitions also came to the chancellor from men who had in one way or another fallen afoul of the growing rigor of the law. For example, when a plaintiff at law could base a claim on a written and sealed document, the courts in many cases held this in such high regard as evidence and so fully respected its content that substantial injustice might result. Thus a defendant who was sued for debt on the evidence of his sealed bond could not successfully plead that he had paid the debt unless he had a sealed acquittance to set against the sealed bond. If he had paid without getting such an acquittance he had no defense at law however well he might otherwise be able to prove the payment. Again, if a written and sealed agreement between parties provided a preset penalty for default by one of the parties, and if in the event the party did default, the courts would impose the penalty as it was stipulated without regard to whether it was reasonable or whether there were mitigating circumstances. In such cases where these rules of law could work hardship, a petition to the chancellor might win relief.

In these ways and others the chancellors both supplemented the law and modified its rigors, and in doing so developed a body of rules of their own outside the law. Men came to speak of the "equity" of the chancellor in contrast to the "common law" of the law courts. But the separateness of equity and common law existed only in that they were stated bodies of doctrine. The law that governed the lives and business of the people was a unity, namely the common law as supplemented and modified by equity. As the chancellor gave protection to the beneficiaries of uses and afforded his help to others, his work figured as another resource whereby the governing law adapted itself to the times.

WEAKNESSES AND STRENGTHS

The history of England in the late Middle Ages is strewn with evidences of the failures of the law. In a society where power had in some measure moved away from the king's government into the hands of the aristocracy, great men were too often able to manipulate the machinery of the law in their favor or obstruct it when it worked against them. The special commission to itinerant justices had often been one of their instruments, until these commissions ceased to be given in the fourteenth century. Thereafter, they may have availed themselves of appointments as justices of the peace. Certainly they sought weaknesses of the law in the sheriff and his staff (the executive agents of the courts) and in the jury, learning to control these people by fear or favor. More sinister than individual abuse was the strain of contempt for law that ran through society from top to bottom. From the fourteenth century the stories of Robin Hood and other gallant outlaws began to circulate. The rebellious commons of 1381 chose lawyers, among others, as special objects of their hatred. After the long, weary warfare of the late Middle Ages began in 1294, during the reign of Edward I, enormous numbers of pardons for felony, given to

recruit soldiers and to purchase political support, showed that the government itself thought the law a poor thing. In some respects the law deserved to be looked down upon. Imprisonment for debt, which developed in this time, was a cruel and unjust punishment. Condemned traitors were executed in a manner that became more grisly and obscene as this age went on, though these horrors may not have been at all unpopular in their time. Widespread resentment certainly was raised, and rightly so, by the Statute of Laborers of 1351. The terrible mortality of the Black Death in the years just before had brought a shortage of labor, and wages had accordingly risen. The statute required wages to be kept at their pre-plague levels. In the long run the legislation was unsuccessful, but it failed only after vigorous and sustained efforts were made to enforce it.

From such facts it would be easy to draw a picture of degeneration and disaster. But it would be wrong to do so; the common law in this period was not like that. The technical evolutions that we have followed show that on the whole the law must have been serving the nation justly and efficiently and thus must have been widely appreciated. Otherwise, we cannot understand the redesigning of the organization of the king's courts on a plan that remained in use for five centuries thereafter, or the flow of business into the king's courts from the local jurisdictions. The ongoing adaptation of the law to changing ideas during these centuries would have been beside the point if the nation had not been under the direction of its laws. Notwithstanding its many failures in particular, the law was in sound condition.

There was, indeed, something more than fundamental soundness. The ways in which the law was shaped savor of high generosity and a little of genius. Steady work was done as we have seen to make the doctrines of the law clearer, firmer, and more detailed. There was in this much care shown for particulars, but the whole enterprise was informed by something that transcended honest workmanship in detail; through it all there was a consistent thrust of policy. The articulation of the law on its procedural side, as in the elaborate rules of pleading, presently made it natural to speak of "due process of law" and to claim the enjoyment of due process as a right of the subject. The phrase "due process of law" crops up in the statutes of 1341 and 1354 and begins from those dates its long history.

Even more revealing is the rise in the late Middle Ages of a belief in the high antiquity of the common law. The *Mirror of Justices,* a strange essay on the law probably written between 1285 and 1290, perhaps intended partly as a joke, professes to accept a common law that has come down from the time of the Anglo-Saxons. In the 1460's Sir John Fortescue, serjeant-at-law and chancellor, wrote in high seriousness of a common law of England, older than the Roman law, descended unchanged in its main stock from the times of the ancient Britons. Lamentable as history, the belief nevertheless reflected an overwhelming sense of the importance of tradition and of continuity in the law. This powerfully felt need for continuity, and the talk of due process, point the way to an ideal pursued in all that was done to articulate the law, an ideal of government by laws and not by men. A belief of this kind in law was not at all new in English civilization. But it had never before been nearly so well served as it was in the late Middle Ages.

The service of this ideal might easily have deprived the legal system of the aiblity to adapt to changing conditions, imposing on the nation a canon of transcendent law above men's manipulation. Conversely, the need to adapt might have pressed itself upon the lawmakers as primary and in so doing might easily have been taken to demonstrate that the dream of a government of laws was merely foolish, as though laws could be anything other than a human artifact and wholly under the control of the men of each generation. But with a practical brilliance that must be rare in history the leaders of the English law found the means to keep their doctrines flexible enough without sacrificing any part of the ideal. Changes were brought about through discoveries within the fabric of the law, whose system was so full and whose literature so abundant that no man could know them completely and every man however learned might always find further matters to explore.

Where discovery was not relied on, statutes could be enacted to alter the law. From the fourteenth century statutes were always made in the parliaments. The law was every man's heritage, but every man was present in parliament through his representative and could there agree, in making a statute, to surrender something of his own for his own greater advantage or for the common good, just as an owner might by his voluntary act alienate land that was his heritage. Finally, where all else failed, law could change through the intervention of the chancellor. The common law might indeed be frustrated in its effects, but it would remain unchanged in itself, a

heritage for the nation, bearing untouched the rule of law.

BIBLIOGRAPHY

There is no general history of the law in the late Middle Ages alone, but the period is well covered in several works dealing with the whole course of English legal history. The most recent of these, and highly authoritative, is John Hamilton Baker, *An Introduction to English Legal History,* 2nd ed. (1979). Bibliographies appended to the several chapters of this work set forth the literature of the field. Baker has also written an account of the law as it stood in the early sixteenth century, around and just after the close of the Middle Ages, in his introduction to *The Reports of Sir John Spelman,* II (1978) (Selden Society, **94**), 23–396. Other histories of more general bearing which deal well with the late Middle Ages are: Alan Harding, *The Law Courts of Medieval England* (1973); Sir William Searle Holdsworth, *A History of English Law,* 7th ed., I–III (1956); Stroud F. C. Milsom, *Historical Foundations of the Common Law* (1969); Theodore F. T. Plucknett, *A Concise History of the Common Law,* 5th ed. (1956).

The history of parliament is presented in George O. Sayles, *The King's Parliament of England* (1974). For the general eyre and its ultimate breakdown, see Helen M. Cam, *Studies in the Hundred Rolls* (1974); and David Crook, *Records of the General Eyre* (Public Record Office Handbooks, no. 20, 1982). The foundation of the new circuits of justices of assize is traced by Ralph B. Pugh, *Imprisonment in Medieval England* (1968), and the growing powers of the justices of the peace by Bertha H. Putnam, "The Transformation of the Keepers of the Peace into the Justices of the Peace, 1327–1380," in *Transactions of the Royal Historical Society,* 4th ser., **12** (1929). Margaret Hastings, *The Court of Common Pleas in Fifteenth-century England* (1947), describes the operation of that central court in its medieval maturity. Transfer of business from local courts to the king's courts is explained by Robert C. Palmer, *The County Courts of Medieval England* (1982). For early business of the chancellor in equity, see Margaret E. Avery, "A History of the Equitable Jurisdiction of Chancery Before 1460," in *Bulletin of the Institute of Historical Research,* **42** (1969).

For legal professions, statutes, and reports, see George O. Sayles, ed., *Select Cases in the Court of King's Bench,* VII (1971) (Selden Society, **88**), xxviii–xli; Alfred W. B. Simpson, "The Early Constitution of the Inns of Court," in *Cambridge Law Journal,* **28** (1970); H. G. Richardson and George O. Sayles, "The Early Statutes," in *Law Quarterly Review,* **50** (1934); Theodore F. T. Plucknett, *Legislation of Edward I* (1949), and *Early English Legal Literature* (1958).

For criminal law, see John G. Bellamy, *The Law of Treason in England in the Later Middle Ages* (1970), and *Crime and Public Order in England in the Later Middle Ages* (1973); Leona C. Gabel, *Benefit of Clergy in England in the Later Middle Ages* (1969); Thomas A. Green, "The Jury and the English Law of Homicide, 1200–1600," in *Michigan Law Review*, **74** (1976).

For land law, franchises, and the forms of action, see John M. W. Bean, *The Decline of English Feudalism, 1215–1540* (1968); Richard H. Helmholz, "The Early Enforcement of Uses," in *Columbia Law Review*, **79** (1979); Charles M. Gray, *Copyhold, Equity, and the Common Law* (1963); Frederic W. Maitland, *The Forms of Action at Common Law*, A. H. Chaytor and W. J. Whittaker, eds. (1965); Alfred W. B. Simpson, *An Introduction to the History of the Land Law* (1961); Donald W. Sutherland, *Quo Warranto Proceedings in the Reign of Edward I, 1278–1294* (1963), and *The Assize of Novel Disseisin* (1973).

The law of debt and contract is studied in Alfred W. B. Simpson, *A History of the Common Law of Contract: The Rise of the Action of Assumpsit* (1975). For the law of bonds and preset penalties, see also the same author's "The Penal Bond with Conditional Defeasance," in *Law Quarterly Review*, **82** (1966).

Some of the tactics employed in abuse of the law appear in E. L. G. Stones, "The Folvilles of Ashby-Folville, Leicestershire, and Their Associates in Crime," in *Transactions of the Royal Historical Society*, 5th ser., **7** (1957); and Natalie Fryde, ed., "A Medieval Robber Baron: Sir John Molyns of Stoke Poges, Buckinghamshire," in *Medieval Legal Records (Edited in memory of C. A. F. Meekings)*, R. F. Hunnisett and J. B. Post, eds. (1978), 198–221. For the Statute of Laborers see Bertha H. Putnam, *The Enforcement of the Statutes of Labourers During the First Decade After the Black Death, 1349–1359* (1908).

The anonymous *Mirror of Justices* (to which the name of Andrew Horn or Horne has been attached as "compiler") is edited by William J. Whittaker with an introduction by Frederic W. Maitland (1895) (Selden Society, 7). Sir John Fortescue's most interesting writing is his *De laudibus legum Angliae*, Stanley B. Chrimes, ed. (1942).

DONALD W. SUTHERLAND

[See also **Assize, English; Common Pleas, Court of; England; Exchequer, Court of; Inheritance; Inns of Court; Jury; Justices Itinerant; Justices of Common Pleas; Justices of the Peace; Mirror of Justices; Nisi Prius; Parliament; Seisin, Disseisin; Sergeant; Statute; Tenure of Land; Trespass.**]

LAW, FRENCH: IN NORTH. As the Carolingian Empire and its successor, the separate West Frankish kingdom, collapsed, each region began to develop its own system of law. The process was speeded up by conquest, as in the case of the Viking conquest of Normandy, and by earlier racial and linguistic divergences, as in the Breton peninsula. In the end, there were separate codes of law for every major, and many minor, feudal principalities. To take two extremes, the great duchy of Normandy had, as might have been expected, its own highly developed and very sophisticated law code. Yet, one of the great treatises on northern French law was written for the tiny county of Beavaisis.

The multiplicity of law codes in the north should not obscure the fact that on many points of substantive law and procedure there was basic agreement. To take one essential point, many decisions were made by the "good men" of the neighborhood and not by the judge. This principle was put into rigid legal form by the development of the Norman jury, but in many other jurisdictions the "good men" had the deciding voice. For example, when there was an argument about substantive law (such as rights of inheritance) or procedure (what is a legal summons) a panel of respected members of the community was asked to declare what the practice in the past had been. This reliance on community opinion made the task of the presiding officer easier, but it also limited his power.

The courts were neighborhood courts; the "good men" of the village, the town, the lordship, or the county were supposed to attend. As might be expected, the older and wealthier men of the community were more apt to be present; they could afford the time and the loss of income that attendance involved.

Formal appellate courts developed very slowly during the thirteenth and later centuries. They were staffed by legal experts and were often too distant from the scene of the dispute to allow much direct neighborhood participation. On the other hand, they could send out requests to local officials to call together a group of neighbors to determine the facts in a case, or the controlling custom of the region.

A basic principle of northern French law was that no one should judge his own case. Thus the king had his lawsuits judged by the great men in his court—a body that by the thirteenth century developed into the Parlement of Paris. The duke of Normandy sent his cases to the Exchequer, the count of Champagne had his *Grands Jours,* and so on. The men who staffed these courts were at first not legal experts, but simply great lords. As time went on, however, the need for legal training and expertise became more apparent, and by the end of the thirteenth century the great law courts (the Parlement of Paris, the Exchequer of Normandy, the *Grands Jours* of Champagne) were composed largely, but not entirely, of men who had had long experience with legal problems.

The development of a class of professional lawyers was paralleled by the development of a group of law treatises written for the professionals. If precedents were to be followed, then it was well to know what the precedents were. Thus in Normandy there was an early (*ca.* 1200) version of the customs of Normandy, followed, after the conquest of the duchy by the king, by a large and well-arranged summary of Norman law (*ca.* 1254), a summary that dominated Norman jurisprudence until the final version of Norman customs was approved in 1583. For other regions there is the *Livres de jostice et de plet* (*ca.* 1260) and, most important, Beaumanoir's *Coutumes de Beauvaisis* (1283). The district of Beauvais was not very large, no larger than a small county in the United States, but Beaumanoir was a great scholar, and his discussion and explanation of the law of his county illustrate many problems in the history of the law of northern France. He also considered the question, increasingly important after 1300, of the degree to which the ruler could interpret, modify, and introduce new concepts into the law.

There had, of course, been innovations in both procedure and substantive law long before 1300. Growth in population had led to the clearing of land and the foundation of new villages. Growth in trade had increased the size and complicated the economic patterns of the towns. It had also led to the foundation of new urban settlements. Obviously men were not going to undertake the backbreaking work of clearing new land and building houses in a new town or a new suburb without some inducements. Thus charters, spelling out in some detail the rights, privileges, and duties of settlers in their new communities, had to be issued. These charters usually gave the settlers some rights of self-government, some assurances against arbitrary exactions, and quite specific rules about land tenure, the competence of and procedure in new courts that had to be set up, and definitions of the authority of the founder, or of his representatives, in the town or village. Older settlements naturally wanted similar rights, and thus town charters (often copied from an older and well-regarded charter) became common throughout the north. They were the basis for municipal law.

In rural areas, which included the majority of the population, the pressure for fixed and settled rules of

law came largely from landed proprietors, who were concerned with problems of inheritance and tenure. What were the rights of younger sons, of grandsons, of widows and daughters? When two men claimed the same land, or a profitable monopoly such as a mill, how could the question be settled without violence? Courts could arbitrate, encourage compromises, persuade a claimant with a weak case to drop his claim, but without fixed rules how could one prove that the case was weak?

In Normandy, where the duke was especially powerful (and even more so after his conquest of England), some basic rules were adopted to aid the courts in reaching decisions. An "inquest," that is, a jury, was called to answer simple questions—Who was the last in possession? Who was the nearest heir? and so forth. Fair enough, but the questions were not always so simple, for example, What is possession? What sort of rights can be possessed? So definitions and interpretations had to be made, and by the thirteenth century these were collected in semi-official form, in such works as the *Très ancien coutumier de Normandie* and, in the mid thirteenth century, the *Summa de legibus Normannie*. The latter work remained the official law code of Normandy during the rest of the Middle Ages.

Beaumanoir and the unknown author of the *Summa de legibus* wrote the most elegant and intelligent treatises in the law of a northern French province, but there were many other useful, more or less contemporary works on other districts: the *Conseil à un ami* (Vermandois) by Pierre de Fontaines (*ca.* 1258); the *Livres de jostice et de plet* (Orléans region), author unknown (*ca.* 1260); and the so-called *Établissements de St. Louis* (c. 1270), which does indeed begin with an ordinance of St. Louis, but goes on with material from an anonymous customal of Touraine-Anjou that was written around 1246, followed by an equally anonymous work on the customs of the Orléans region (mid thirteenth century). *Établissements* influenced the law of much of northern France—Touraine, Anjou, Orléanais, Artois, and, to a lesser degree, Brittany and Champagne.

Champagne had its own *Coutumier* (1253–1270, but based on an earlier work of 1250–1260), which also included a series of judgments of the court of the county. This practice of collecting judgments of a court to serve as precedents for future decisions was not confined to Champagne. It had begun in Normandy at least as early as 1207. Important decisions of the king's court at Paris were being preserved in the royal archives at least as early as 1200. By 1254 the decisions of this court, by then called the Parlement, were being regularly recorded.

There were many variations in the substance of the law as one went from province to province, variations especially in rules of inheritance. On the other hand, the basic procedure was very much the same in the whole area. A group of men of the region was called together and was asked questions about the case. What was the custom of the district in regard to rights attached to a landed estate (monopoly of milling, of markets, of fisheries, and so forth)? What rights did relatives of various degrees have when there was no direct heir? Who had the right to nominate the village priest—a lay patron, an abbot, or the bishop of the diocese?

The jury that gave a formal, unanimous, and decisive verdict on such matters was known only in Normandy. Elsewhere, however, if all the men questioned agreed on an answer, this was almost as binding. The problem of how to handle a divided set of answers was more difficult. One dissenter could be ignored, but was the opinion of a slim majority decisive? The safest procedure was to keep asking questions until the group agreed on one or more points, but this result could not always be achieved. If the presiding officer (one cannot yet call him a judge) was strong enough, or could gain enough support, he could make a decision based on the arguments he had heard, but such a decision was not always definitive. In case after case the issue was raised again, or the losing party simply refused to carry out the order of the court, resorting to violence if necessary.

These difficulties eventually led to the development of a system of appeals to a higher court, but "appeal" was a dangerous word. It meant a direct personal accusation that could be settled only by combat. Thus Beaumanoir advises suitors who see that the decision of a court is going against them to challenge immediately the first two or three men who are giving an unfavorable opinion; otherwise they will have to fight the entire panel.

The growth of the power of the king's court—the Parlement of Paris—eased this situation. The king's court in its judicial capacity heard very few cases before 1200; it was not nearly as active or as sophisticated in its procedure as the court of the duke of Normandy. From 1200 on, however, as royal power grew with the expansion of the royal domain, the king's court perfected its organization, its procedure, and its record keeping. By 1300 there was already a

collection of precedents, going back to 1254, known as the *Olim*. There was also a regular procedure by which a case was officially accepted, evidence collected by local inquests and discussed by a group of masters of the Parlement, and a final decision prepared.

This organization made it easy to deal with the problem of appeals. The addition of the Midi (southern France) to the royal domain meant that a region with a very different legal tradition (basically Roman) was now subject to the final authority of the Parlement. The south had been used to appeals, and appeals from decisions of southern courts went to Paris, though not in very great numbers. However, a tradition was established, and litigants from the north began to appeal to the Parlement.

The largest number of appeals came from Paris itself—naturally enough since the court of the provost of Paris heard many difficult and important cases and no long journey was necessary to appeal from him to the Parlement. By 1300 almost all northern disricts were sending appeals to Paris. Normandy was an exception, since its highest court, the Exchequer, was staffed by a delegation composed of members of the Parlement. On the other hand, appeals did run from the highest court in Champagne, even though it was also staffed by men from the Parlement. Appeals were useful in putting pressure on powerful and semi-independent lords, such as the king of England/duke of Aquitaine, and the count of Flanders. On the other hand, there were at first very few appeals from the duke of Burgundy, who was a kinsman and a loyal supporter of the king—at least until the duchy passed to a very ambitious branch of the royal family in the fourteenth century.

At first laws were "found, not made"—that is, the appropriate court, after careful investigation, defined the law applicable in a given case, and this served as a precedent. Most of the acts assembled for the earlier sections of the *Ordonnances* of the king of France were administrative decisions or decisions of the royal court that had general applicability. From the middle of the twelfth century on, however, there were acts that were purely legislative in character, dealing, for example, with the status of the Jews or the financing of a crusade. Beaumanoir (late thirteenth century) gave a general definition of lawmaking: it must be for the common welfare, for reasonable cause, and by the advice of many competent men. This last phrase could be interpreted in several ways; in the end it meant that the ordinance must be registered in the Parlement and that the Parlement could refuse, or at least delay, the registration of an ordinance that it thought was unreasonable. In actual practice, however, the advice came from the leading men of the king's council, and refusal of registration by the Parlement was rare.

Even after the making of ordinances became a regular and not very difficult procedure, relatively few changes were made in substantive law. Thus to define the way in which the right of bourgeoisie could be acquired and maintained (1287) did not introduce a new concept; it simply clarified an old class distinction. The difficult problem of amortization (limiting free transfer of lands, and rights associated with land, from laymen to the church) was the subject of two ordinances; again the problem was old, and definition of the rights of both parties was useful. An ordinance of 1287 ordering lords with the rights of justice to have only laymen as judges and "sergeants" (that is, policemen) did introduce a new element into the existing customs, but it did not change substantive law.

After 1300 almost every judicial district in the north of France had its official or semi-official statement of its customs. Some covered fairly wide areas, such as Normandy (though even in Normandy there were local variations). At the other extreme were collections of municipal customs, which dealt with very small areas; in fact the charter which gave a town its rights of justice did not necessarily include all the suburbs into which the town expanded.

One can recognize affinities, both in procedure and in substance, in all these compilations, but there are endless points of difference—for example, on such a fundamental problem as rules of inheritance. As a result, attempts to write manuals that summed up the law of the north were interesting failures. Jacques d'Ableiges, in the 1380's, compiled a work called the *Grant coutumier de France*. The title is correct if "France" is given its original meaning—the region centered on Paris that we now call the Île-de-France. A little later, about 1395, Jean Boutillier composed a very interesting work which he called the *Somme rural*. He covered a much wider area than his predecessor—Normandy, Artois, Tournai, and the northeast—but he did not try to reconcile differences among customs, he simply noted them.

In sum, the law of northern France was customary, not written, and local, not general. It had many common ideas, both in substance and in procedure. It also had very wide variations, even in such a common problem as inheritance. All agreed that the rightful heir should receive the property of a deceased relative, but who were the rightful heirs and what share should each receive? One need only to look at the map in Jean Yver's *Égalité entre héritiers* (1966) to see how great the differences were and how little uniformity there was even in small regions. In procedure, there was a considerable difference in the way in which testimony was to be received, running from the unanimous group verdict of a Norman jury to the questioning of individuals, one by one, by a judge, which was the common usage in most royal courts outside Normandy. Finally, while custom was the basis of law, custom could change, either through disuse or through the active intervention of a powerful ruler—for instance, in making it more difficult to convey land to the church.

Like most people, the inhabitants of northern France realized that the main purpose of law is not to do abstract justice but to stop a fight. Northern French law was not entirely successful in this effort, but it was acceptable enough so that legal solutions to quarrels prevented a large number of disputes from degenerating into feuds and private wars. Going to court was often expensive, and the decisions of the courts were not always acceptable to the loser, but private war was more expensive and the results might be even more disastrous to the loser.

BIBLIOGRAPHY

The basic books are all in French, but some understanding of the law of northern France may be found in John F. Benton, "Philip the Fair and the Jours of Troyes," in *Studies in Medieval and Renaissance History*, 6 (1969); Charles H. Haskins, *Norman Institutions* (1918); Joseph R. Strayer, *The Administration of Normandy Under St. Louis* (1932), "Normandy and Languedoc," in *Speculum*, 44 (1969), and *The Reign of Philip the Fair* (1980).

In French: Arthur Beugnot, *Les Olim* (1839–1848); Edgard Boutaric, *Actes du Parlement de Paris* (1863–1867); Émile Chénon, *Histoire générale du droit français* (1926–1929); Joseph Declareuil, *Histoire générale du droit français* (1925); Gustave Ducoudray, *Les origines du Parlement de Paris* (1902); Paul Guilhiermoz, *Enquêtes et procès* (1892); Charles Victor Langlois, *Textes relatifs à l'histoire du Parlement depuis les origines jusqu'en 1314* (1888).

JOSEPH R. STRAYER

[See also **Beaumanoir, Philippe de; Champagne, County of; Châtelet; Coutumes de Beauvaisis; Custumals of Normandy; Établissements de St. Louis; France; Inheritance; Inquest; Jury; Livres de Jostice et de Plet; Normans and Normandy; Parlement of Paris.**]

LAW, FRENCH: IN SOUTH. The southern, or occitan, part of what would become modern France developed a legal tradition in the Middle Ages that differed considerably from that of northern France. The north is described as the region of customary law (long uncodified) and the south as the region of written (that is, Roman) law. This facile distinction between the written law of the south and the customary law of the north, however, distorts reality, exaggerating differences for most of the medieval period. Occitan law was strongly based on custom. Its rules of procedure long resembled those of the north. Southern law also resembled the north in possessory actions and in many aspects of family law. One must thus be wary of overstating the differences in legal traditions between the two great linguistic regions of France.

The differences that did exist relate to the variant historical experiences of the north and the south. Roman civilization and law had a much greater impact in the south than in the north; under the fifth-century Germanic invasions, the south fell to the Goths, who were themselves more Romanized than the conquering Franks in the north; and later in the Middle Ages the south was far more influenced by Italian legal and political traditions than was the north.

THE EARLY MIDDLE AGES

In the fifth century, Roman law consisted of the legislative acts of later emperors, fragments of earlier legislation, and a mass of legal opinions and treatises that had accumulated over several centuries. In 438, Emperor Theodosius II had a codification of this material published. About 481, King Euric issued a separate code for his Visigothic subjects that showed strong Roman influence. In 506, using the *Theodosian Code* as a base but simplifying it to suit the needs of his less sophisticated regime, the Visigothic ruler Alaric II promulgated a *Lex romana Visigothorum*, also called the *Breviarium Alaricianum* or *Breviary of Alaric*, for his subjects of Roman origin. The *Breviary of Alaric* was to be the standard source of Roman law in the Latin West for the next six centuries.

The *Corpus Iuris civilis* of Justinian I, compiled at Constantinople in the early sixth century, became the authoritative compilation of Roman law for the part of the Roman Empire that remained under imperial control. It would not influence the West until the study of Roman law revived in the twelfth century. Lawyers and judges were then trained by legal academicians in the principles of Roman law set forth by Justinian. Also in the twelfth century, the canon law of the church, which had maintained some continuity from the days of imperial Rome, enjoyed an authoritative collection composed by Gratian as the *Decretum*, or *Concord of Discordant Canons*.

The Roman law of the *Breviarium* and the subsequent simplification that it underwent applied only to persons of Roman origin. The Goths and the Franks were subject to the laws and customs of their own people, sometimes codified under Roman influence, but different in origin and conception. When two parties to a case were subject to different laws, it was necessary to employ complex rules to determine which law to follow. By the end of the Carolingian period in the late ninth century, this regime of "personality of law" had given way to a system of "territoriality of law," as the regional and local customs of an increasingly sedentary society prevailed in the face of the progressive blurring of ethnic distinctions.

Differences between the law of the north and that of the south began to appear at this time. When regional custom supplanted personal law, the north with its heavier Germanic concentration drew more heavily on Frankish law. In the Midi, Frankish settlement was much lighter and the predominant ethnic groups—Goths and Gallo-Romans—lived under codes that bore the common imprint of pre-Justinianic Roman law. The laws of these two groups had, in fact, been combined in Visigothic Spain in the late seventh century. They had a major impact on occitan territorial custom.

Where the customs of northern and southern French law retained similarities in post-Carolingian Europe, these similarities seem to have been confined to two principal areas—judicial procedure and "family law" (that is, law relating to the extended family and its property). Otherwise, the disintegration of Carolingian political power followed different lines and produced different legal results in the two parts of what is now France.

In the north, courts lost their public character and became the private property rights of great lords. In the Midi, the fragmentation of political power in the hands of local lords came even earlier than in the north. Where a dozen great families wielded effective power around the year 900, more than 150 did so by 975, when much of the north of France was still being ruled effectively by counts. Yet in the south law and justice never lost their public character. While the stronger legal legacy of ancient Rome must have been a factor in preserving this conception of law, Ourliac has argued that the perceptions of the law that survived in the Midi were seen as a legacy of the Carolingian Empire. This phenomenon was more clearly marked in Languedoc than in Aquitaine. Besides the idea of public authority, the Midi also retained a conception of ownership of property that differed from the concept of seisin that accompanied the spread of feudal institutions in the north.

To confront the threat of disorder implicit in the fragmentation of political power, the Midi did not institute private personal ties or establish "feudal" relationships and private courts. To resolve disputes, the southern magnates used the techniques of arbitration and conciliation in ad hoc assemblies convened to administer the public law of the land. This type of assembly, called a *guirpitio,* was a meeting of the powerful men of a locality, who would attempt to arbitrate a dispute or hammer out a compromise. Once agreement was reached, the participants were committed to enforce the law with their considerable power.

These ad hoc assemblies did not always achieve peaceful solutions any more than did the feudal courts of the north, but in each case the respective parts of France turned to procedures consistent with their legal customs in order to deal with a serious problem. The *guirpitio* of southern France influenced a new type of ad hoc assembly that first appeared in the 980's to establish the Peace of God. The peace assemblies generally were convened by prelates, and, rather than trying to arbitrate a specific dispute, they were designed to commit the local strong men to a general policy of preserving the peace. Although spawned by the occitan tradition of ad hoc assemblies to arbitrate disputes, these peace assemblies were of a different order. In parts of the Midi, they gradually achieved institutional form, while in their original ad hoc form they soon penetrated other parts of Europe, unlike most other occitan legal traditions.

REVIVAL AND SPREAD OF ROMAN LAW

When the revived study of Justinian's law began to affect southern France after 1100, it was a development of great importance. Scholars have argued at length about this "reception" and "diffusion" of Roman law. There seems little doubt that the ultimate source of this learned law was northern and central Italy, which had maintained much more con-

tact with the Byzantine Empire and had become deeply embroiled in the Investiture Controversy during the second half of the eleventh century. This conflict stimulated papalists and imperialists to study the laws, both canon and civil. Law became the subject of debate, analysis, and systematic compilation. In the late eleventh century, there appeared in Provence a short manual of practical rules for administering Roman law, known as the *Petri exceptiones.* It was based on Justinian's compilation, not on the *Theodosian Code* and the *Breviary of Alaric.* The first vernacular treatise on Roman law, *Lo Codi,* was written in the Rhône region about 1160, perhaps at Valence or St. Gilles or Arles.

The geographic spread of Roman law in southern France took place between about 1130 and 1220. It seems to have involved three parallel developments—the use of certain terms and concepts from Justinian's *Corpus;* the spread of the institution of the notary, and the rise of the consulate as a form of municipal government. The three developments exhibited similar patterns of territorial expansion. After 1220 they became more firmly entrenched in regions already affected, rather than spreading to new geographical areas. Gouron has detected three phases of this expansion—one ending around 1150, another ending around 1195, and a third ending by 1220.

During the first phase, consulates, sometimes ephemeral, appeared at Avignon and Arles on the lower Rhône; and at Nîmes, Tarascon, Montpellier, St. Gilles, and as far west as Narbonne. An isolated consulate was noted at Nice in eastern Provence, perhaps a result of direct Italian influence, while elsewhere in the Midi the three developments mentioned above reflected more indirect Italian contact and radiated from centers on the Rhône.

In the second phase, consulates spread eastward from the Rhône to Marseilles and northward from the coast to Millau; but the main territorial expansion came in the third phase (1195–1220), when consulates penetrated into Gascony, northwestward into the Rouergue, Quercy, and Périgord, northward to Alès, the Albigeois, Dauphiné, and even to the Auvergne. In the first century of expansion, the major towns were affected, and expansion occurred most readily along the major waterways. Lesser places within these geographical areas acquired consulates later.

The institution of the notary spread in a manner that paralleled the consulates, and with the notariate we find oaths, contracts, and judicial procedures reflecting the influence of Justinian's *Corpus*. Terms from Roman law that had not been used since the sixth century began to be used again during the twelfth. Commercial and financial contracts, property acts, marriage contracts, and witnessed wills began to display Roman terminology. In the last decades of the twelfth century, Roman lawyers were found increasingly far up the Rhône. In Provence, where Roman law had penetrated both from the east and from the west, the two separate zones of penetration finally merged, and this region developed the most Romanized legal system of the south by the fourteenth century.

Throughout the Midi, the customary law became a written law influenced by Roman models, but the learned law did not overthrow legal custom. Roman law was accepted in specific areas where people saw it as a means of improving and perfecting customary procedures. Other areas of law saw little impact of Justinianic practice.

The increasing influence of notaries was fundamental to the spread of Roman legal models. In addition, the legal practitioners who operated municipal and seigneurial courts were increasingly men trained in the learned law, and they were ready to adopt it in cases where it facilitated effective judicial operations.

Legal learning, therefore, was an important part of the evolution of southern French law. It had not completely disappeared in the earlier Middle Ages but had largely been confined to abstracts and glosses of earlier compilations designed for those who had to administer canon law. When Justinian's *Corpus* first became an object of study in the West, legal scholarship centered in Italy, especially at Bologna, where most of the lawyers in southern France received their training in the period prior to the last third of the thirteenth century. (The earliest legal scholars, the glossators, had already been flourishing in Italy during the twelfth century.)

The first center of legal study in what is now southern France was in the Rhône Valley around Valence and Die. It was active by the second quarter of the twelfth century. It has now been demonstrated that no monastic school or center of learning in France possessed works on Justinian's law antedating this period. The most celebrated center for the study of Roman law in France was to be Montpellier, where the glossator Placentinus resided and studied in the 1160's. He may have been preceded there by another legal scholar, Rogerius, but there is no evidence that either man established any sort of

school. It is possible that the lawyers of southern France, having studied law in Italy, engaged in teaching when they returned to Languedoc. Placentinus was, in any case, an important legal scholar who contributed to the greater compatibility of Roman and canon law.

Finally, in the late 1260's, a century after Placentinus came to Montpellier, we have clear evidence of a studium in that town for the training of lawyers. By the end of the thirteenth century, there were several studia in southern France, as occitan lawyers trained in Italy began to come together and teach their countrymen. As the studium at Montpellier began to take shape in the 1260's, the documents reveal the names of *doctores legum* who served as teachers, jurists, and attorneys in and around the city in ever greater numbers.

From the first, Montpellier had strong ties with Bologna, where so many occitan lawyers had studied. Regulations were similar, as were the very origins of the two schools. Both had developed without papal sponsorship, without special privileges or concessions, and without any prior school of canon law. At length, in 1289, Pope Nicholas IV conferred a charter on the studium at Montpellier. At last the jurists were on the same footing as the medical doctors, whose statutes date from 1220, and it was not long before the law school became as significant as the medical school at the University of Montpellier. The proximity of the Avignon papacy gave further stimulation to legal study at Montpellier, and after 1320 the school began attracting students from other parts of Europe. A period of decline set in after 1380, as the city lost its political autonomy, and war, plague, and papal schism made their impact.

The establishment of the studium at Montpellier coincided with an important landmark in the history of legal study. The work of the glossators (the tradition to which Placentinus belonged) reached its culmination in the achievement of the Italian scholar Accursius, whose gloss has been considered the ultimate interpretation of Justinian's *Corpus* by a medieval scholar. With Accursius as the standard gloss, the pre-Accursian glosses became obsolete. Subsequent legal scholars are generally called the post-glossators. They moved beyond Accursius, adapting his interpretation of Justinian's law to the practical problems of late medieval government and jurisprudence. Unlike most pre-Accursian commentaries, their treatises were addressed to juridical practice. It was at this point in the later thirteenth century that Roman law began to have importance for governments. It was also in this period that the French royal government acquired control of most of Languedoc.

ROYAL INFLUENCES, REGIONAL CUSTOM

The expanding French royal domain in the thirteenth century absorbed territories which in some cases possessed more sophisticated institutions of government than the old royal lands. Languedoc and its judicial institutions are an example. The royal government tended to preserve such local institutions and adapt them to its own needs, but in Languedoc it did not immediately make use of local judicial models in the royal courts. The first royal acquisitions in Languedoc, in 1229, consisted of the coastal regions and district nearest the Rhône, where Justinian's law had made its first impact a century earlier. Seigneurial and municipal institutions of law and justice were rapidly adopting the procedures of Roman law by this time, but the new royal administration lagged behind, only gradually emulating the nonroyal institutions. At this time, southern French lawyers, many of them now trained in Languedoc, were advising both royal and nonroyal administrations in the region, but the crown adopted Roman legal forms only when royal subjects made their preference felt, either through petitions or by their avoidance of royal courts.

One such preference was for the separation of administrative and judicial offices. French field administration characteristically employed two or more tiers of officials who combined military, financial, and judicial responsibilities. In 1254, however, Louis IX acceded to the complaints of his subjects in Languedoc and ordered that seneschals consult with local judges and that *viguiers* (the second tier of officers) consult with *iurisperiti.* An early result of this order was the appointment of the *iudex maior,* or chief judge of the seneschal. He was always an important and experienced southern lawyer.

Occitan lawyers henceforth were prominent advisers of the royal officers who governed Languedoc. By the late thirteenth century, the law faculty at Montpellier had increased in size and influence to the point that its members began to hold important judgeships. The *iudex maior,* no longer just the seneschal's judge, became the chief judge of the district. About the same time (the late 1280's), the crown began to employ regular proctors to represent its interests in the royal courts of Languedoc.

As the legal institutions of the Midi continued to grow in sophistication, the nonroyal jurisdictions continued to lead the way. They began to separate original from appellate jurisdiction. By 1330 the royal courts emulated this step with the establishment of ordinary judges at the *viguerie* level. They had original jurisdiction in less important cases, and their appointment marked the full separation of judicial duties from the other functions of the *viguiers.* By 1350, the flowering of Roman law in Languedoc and the establishment of a judicial apparatus separate from the traditional royal administration had made southern French justice quite different from justice in the north. Not until nearly 1500 do we begin to find separate judicial institutions in the Languedoïl.

By the end of the thirteenth century, the king of France was making his own distinctively northern contributions to some aspects of southern judicial institutions. Among the most important court creations for contract law were the courts of voluntary jurisdiction without territorial limitation, such as the Cour du Petit Scel at Montpellier. In many other places in the Midi in the second half of the thirteenth century, courts carrying the title "sceaux aux contrats" and endowed with considerable independence of action were instituted by the king of France. These southern courts were an imitation of an earlier set of courts in northern lands of customary law, where, since the second half of the twelfth century, ecclesiastical courts had gained the competence to ratify contracts by the apposition of a seal and where one found specialized jurisdictions such as those of the wardens of the Champagne fairs and the Châtelet of Paris. In the south of France, the notarial act stood alone without the need for further authentication, but submission to a voluntary jurisdiction such as that of the Petit Scel, which had a reputation for the rapid execution of judgment in the case of abuse, provided an additional assurance to the acts carrying its seal.

The distinctive character of royal justice in the south developed through the adoption of local practices influenced by Roman law, not through the direct impact of schools of Roman law. In fact, legal developments in southern France flowed in three distinct, and often quite separate, currents: the academic law of the schools, the codified customs that drew selectively on Roman law without direct influence from the schools, and specific administrative acts and judicial decisions. The first and last of these currents could be entirely divorced in their operation. For instance, in the twelfth century, during the early expansion of the learned law, the surviving acts from the Rouergue reveal virtually no traces of Roman law when they were written in occitan, whereas those drafted in Latin, presumably by more learned scribes, do reflect the imprint of Roman law.

The fact that scribes or notaries had training in the learned law did not, however, mean that they regularly fostered its use at the expense of regional custom. Notaries might be more precise in rendering the procedural phrases, but contracts continued to reflect traditional practice, and cases were argued without significant appeals to the *Digest* or the writings of the glossators. The penetration of the learned law varied according to the type of case involved. Disputes over property, testamentary law, and marriage contracts continued to emphasize traditional custom, even though the spread of the notariate ensured that Roman terms and forms of procedure were much more widely used.

Throughout southern France during the twelfth and thirteenth centuries, towns had their customs put into written form. The customs of Montpellier, some dating to as early as 1196, were codified in expanded form in 1204 and went on to influence the customs of a number of other towns in lower Languedoc as they in turn were reduced to writing. In this sense the Midi did become a land of written law, and the drafting of these *coutumiers* was surely prompted by the diffusion of the learned law. More often than not, however, the attitude of the drafters of the *coutumiers* was not so much to incorporate the new learning as to prevent it from encroaching in certain areas and to specify when it could be applied. The statutes of Montpellier contain statements that invoke Roman law in the absence of *mores et consuetudines* (customs); Marseilles also included canon law as well as Roman law as a frame of further reference after the municipal statutes themselves. However, in specific cases, the drafters of municipal statutes were not averse to affirming principles that contradicted Roman law, either explicitly stating the variance or leaving it unstated.

CONTRACTS AND COMMERCIAL LAW

The development of a law of contracts was quite advanced in the south by the end of the twelfth century. Many legal terms with overtones of Roman law were in use by 1200, the result of the influence by lawyers, jurists, and notaries. Acts written by notaries, as public record keepers instituted by authorities with regalian rights, carried the force of proof in a court of law by the thirteenth century. Particularly significant in regard to contract law were the

formulas of renunciation of certain Roman law actions protective of the debtor in which the creditor might be constrained in his ability to see that the contract was honored in a court of justice. These renunciations of actions protected the freedom of southerners and particularly merchants to enter into contractual agreements. For instance, merchants regularly renounced the *exceptio non numeratae pecuniae,* which protected the defendant against the plaintiff's claim for restitution in the case where the former had issued a recognizance for debt before receiving all the funds. Renunciation of the *Senatusconsultum Velleianum,* which in Roman law forbade women's assumption of legal liability for others, gave women greater contractual freedom. While historians have disputed the significance of the multitude of renunciation formulas in notarial acts, Pryor has argued convincingly for their legitimate application in contract law.

The *lex mercatoria,* or commercial law, in the Midi evolved as a form of customary law which reflected the impact of the many legal traditions of the south. The contractual techniques of Provençal and Languedocian merchants from the major towns of Toulouse, Montpellier, and Marseilles in the High and late Middle Ages have been labeled as backward in comparison with those of Italian merchants. Yet, the contracts that appear in the notarial registers of Provence from the mid thirteenth century and from Montpellier from the late thirteenth century are relatively sophisticated business instruments, frequently derivative of earlier Italian prototypes but adapted to specific southern French needs. They run the gamut from techniques of partnership, such as the *commenda* or the *societas terrae,* to financial instruments such as the sea loan, the *mutuum* loan, and the contract of exchange. Some of these contracts, such as the *societas terrae,* have Roman roots, but Pryor has shown that some, like the *commenda,* were purely medieval in synthesis, having drawn on elements of Jewish, Islamic, Byzantine, and Roman traditions.

The Roman-law concept of purchase and sale, *emptio venditio,* was divided into two contracts by the medieval notaries: *emptio,* when the buyer as first party of the act promised the seller to pay for things received or anticipated, and *venditio,* when the seller as the first party acknowledged the receipt of payment for goods delivered or to be delivered. Many of the sales in the surviving southern French notarial registers were made on credit.

In the area of property law, Roman and Germanic

influence can be noted in some landholding arrangements. Throughout the Midi, the Roman term *emphyteusis* is a commonly found designation for the long-term lease with fixed dues. But closely associated with the term *emphyteusis,* indeed in apposition in many notarial acts, is that of *accapitum* or *accaptum,* which can be traced back to Carolingian legislation. It implies a long-term tenure in both feudal and nonfeudal contexts.

LAW AND THE FAMILY

Municipal statutes governed some of the areas of commercial and property law, while notarial tradition and actual practice molded others as need dictated. What was generally at issue when the municipal statutes deviated from Roman-law provisions was the whole range of law dealing with the extended family and its control over property. It was in this area of law that the two parts of France had retained the greatest similarity since Carolingian times. It was also in this area that occitan custom diverged most clearly from the law of Justinian.

By the same token, Tisset, Ourliac, and Hilaire speak of a Romanizing terminology shrouding the originality of legal practice. Terms like *dos, testamentum,* and *patria potestas* have symbolized the supposed differences between the lands of written law and those of oral custom, but a closer look at the documents suggests the deceptiveness of the Roman-law terminology in use in the Midi. By the middle of the fourteenth century the notaries, who preserved much Roman-law terminology in their jargon, were constructing new formulas to reflect the evolution of institutions away from early-thirteenth-century statutory forms as well as from Roman-law models.

The Roman law had provided for wills that allowed a person to dispose of his property freely; in the case of intestate succession, a person's property was to be divided equally among his heirs. These principles survived into the Middle Ages, but early in the Carolingian period the testament disappeared, and with it the right of free disposition. The lineage began to exercise rights over the property of its members, and in some regions custom provided that property return to the side of the family from which it had come.

The church, whose law kept alive Roman traditions, and which stood to profit from pious bequests, endeavored to preserve or revive the testamentary law and had partial success. The church alone appeared occasionally as a will-designated heir in the tenth and eleventh centuries. Pious bequests to churches often provoked violent reactions from relatives of the deceased. The peace assemblies of the eleventh century frequently had to deal with depredations against church property, and it has been shown that many of these incidents were perpetrated by people whose relatives had alienated family land to the church.

The revival of Roman law reinforced the pressure from the church to restore the will and the Roman right of free disposition. In the thirteenth century, this pressure was reinforced further by the growing wealth of the urban merchant class. For this class, property increasingly took the form of movables that constituted the capital of a family business. The right of free disposition became important, and the bourgeois exerted growing pressure to change the customs. Not only did they seek the right of free disposition, but they pursued another objective not provided for in Roman law—the exclusion of dowried daughters from the inheritance. Again, it was the desire to protect the family's movable capital that led them to pursue a policy that, in this case, had no basis in the learned law.

Noble families with wealth consisting mainly of real property had nothing to gain from the right of free disposition, which tended, at the outset, to enrich the church at the expense of the lineage. As the right of free disposition began to gain ground, lineages pursued a number of strategies to limit its effects on the family patrimony. One of these, the *laudatio parentum,* gave relatives the right of first refusal before a property could be sold. Later there appeared the *retrait lignager,* which could be invoked after a sale, with the relatives having the right to step in and substitute themselves for the buyer who had purchased the property.

The most serious threat to noble lineages, however, was the fragmentation of property among heirs. To preserve the status of the lineages, they came to prefer some sort of unigeniture, either established by will or guaranteed by law in the event of intestate succession. As the Roman will gradually regained ground at the expense of customary law, the lineage was concerned to avoid a division of the property in the case of default of the designated heir. As early as 1121, we find the device called substitution, specifying who would take the place of the designated heir and in what order. It was two centuries later before Roman lawyers reluctantly accepted this device, which was not contemplated in Justinian's law. Still, in Provence, Aubenas could find in the late

Middle Ages poor nobles working like peasants in their fields, the victims of partible inheritance, which had over time fragmented family holdings.

While the Roman law exerted one kind of pressure on the customs of medieval Languedoc, another pressure came from feudal law—in particular, that part of the customary law of the north which dealt with the succession to fiefs. The feudal system for a long time remained virtually unknown in the Midi, but two events brought feudal law into sharp contact with occitan custom. First, the marriage of Eleanor of Aquitaine to Henry Plantagenet in 1152 led to the introduction of Norman feudal custom into Aquitaine. Second, the triumph of northern French barons in the Albigensian Crusade led to the Statutes of Pamiers in 1212, which sought to introduce a feudal regime into Languedoc. In neither case did feudal law enjoy an unqualified triumph, but in both cases it encouraged noble lineages to adopt the measures used in northern France to prevent fragmentation of the patrimony. One result was the adoption of the "right of the eldest," a form of primogeniture that gave the bulk of the inheritance and a preponderant role in the affairs of the lineage to the eldest son. In addition, the military obligations attached to the fief worked in practice against female inheritance as well as against equal inheritance. The influence of feudal law thus reinforced the pressure on custom, already being exerted by the urban merchant class for the exclusion of dowried daughters.

In short, the inheritance law of southern France from the twelfth century onward involved the interplay of three forces—the regional traditions embodied in the newly drafted *coutumiers,* the revival and spread of Justinian's law, and the injection of feudal law from northern France. The economic interests of different classes determined the extent to which custom would stand firm against the outside influences or be modified to accommodate, selectively, the elements of Roman law or feudal law that served those interests.

The interplay between occitan custom and Roman law may also be seen in matrimonial law. Roman marriage contracts provided for a dowry *(dos)* from the parents of the woman and a gift *propter nuptias* from the husband. This matrimonial regime did not survive through the early Middle Ages. Pre-twelfth-century marriage contracts at Montpellier followed one of two different forms: (1) the *sponsalitium,* which consisted of a gift to the woman from the husband alone (essentially a Germanic custom), and (2) contracts in which the wife received a dowry from her own family but nothing from her husband. In the twelfth century Roman practice was rediscovered, and a third type of marriage contract developed, in which a dowry from the wife's family was combined with a gift from the husband derived from the *sponsalitium.*

After 1160, this third form of contract completely replaced the other two, but it still did not recreate the marriage law of the *Corpus.* The two gifts received by the bride were not integrated into a single contract or made rigorously equal. They remained independent, and each donor retained propriety over the property, which was brought together as a usufruct for the period of the marriage. At the dissolution of the marriage, the property was transmitted to the direct heirs of the marriage or, in the absence of such heirs, returned to the heirs of the respective spouses. In some occitan customs, both parts of the matrimonial property were administered by the husband. Elsewhere, the husband and wife might administer them jointly. In short, Roman law influenced marriage contracts where it was found useful, but customary law was only modified, not supplanted, by Roman practices.

Roman law also made only gradual inroads in another aspect of family law, that relating to the power of the father. The Roman regime of *patria potestas* subordinated the juridical personalities of children to a system of rigorous paternal authority from which only death or a formal emancipation could release them. By the eighteenth century, this system would be established in the Midi—in contrast to that of northern France, which gave children greater rights. In the Middle Ages, however, southern France had varied customs and did not yet follow the rigorous Roman practice. One custom of the thirteenth century did not hold a father responsible for debts contracted by a son. Another forbade the lending of money to a son in the power of his father. Another put the son totally in the power of his father, whose consent was required for all transactions.

To safeguard the unity of patrimonies, occitan custom widely practiced the community of family property. This practice gave extensive powers to the head of the family, but the power of the father over property coming into the family from the mother was often modified by the counterclaims of the wife's lineage. And in certain customs, communal family property could make the children virtual partners of the father, rather than compelling their strict subordination as in Roman law. The right of the eldest could actually reduce the power of the father by preventing him from alienating patrimonial land without his son's consent. Indeed, the consent by family members to sales of real property was a common feature of notarial contracts. A further elaboration on the community of family property is found in the Provencal *frayresque,* which was a formal contractual arrangement for the mutual sharing of all property among brothers. Once again, however, one finds that the spread of the notariate and the rise of Roman formulas had very mixed results in modifying custom. The community's perceptions of its needs always affected the degree to which the learned law was accepted in medieval practice.

CONCLUSION

The evolution of southern French law in the Middle Ages was subject to many legal influences while remaining responsive to family, business, and community pressures. The differences between northern and southern French law were not always sharply drawn in the medieval period. They would be accentuated by the sixteenth-century renaissance of Roman law in the Midi and by the concurrent drafting in written form of the evolved customary law in the north. A unification of the civil and criminal law systems in France would have to await the Napoleonic legislation of the early nineteenth century.

BIBLIOGRAPHY

Roger Aubenas, *Étude sur le notariat provençal au moyen âge et sous l'ancien régime* (1931); Jean-Baptiste Brissaud, *A History of French Private Law,* Rapelje Howell, trans. (1912); Mireille Castaing-Sicard, *Les contrats dans le très ancien droit toulousain, X^e–XIIIe siècle* (1959); Louis de Charrin, *Les testaments dans la région de Montpellier au moyen âge* (1961); André Gouron, "Les étapes de la pénétration du droit romain au XIIe siècle dans l'ancienne Septimanie," in *Annales du Midi,* 69 (1957), "Diffusion des consulats méridionaux et expansion du droit romain aux XIIe et XIIIe siècles," in *Bibliothèque de l'École des chartes,* 121 (1963), *Les juristes de l'école de Montpellier* (1970), and "The Training of Southern French Lawyers During the Thirteenth and Fourteenth Centuries," in *Studia Gratiana,* 15 (1972); André Gouron and Jean Hilaire, "Les 'sceaux' rigoureux du Midi de la France," in *Société d'histoire du droit et des institutions des anciens pays de droit écrit: Recueil de mémoires et travaux,* 4 (1958); Jean Hilaire, "Les régimes matrimoniaux aux XIe et XIIe siècle dans la région de Montpellier," in *Recueil,* 3 (1955), and *Le régime des biens entre époux dans la région de Montpellier du début du XIIIe siècle à la fin du XVIe siècle* (1957); Archibald R. Lewis, *The Development of Southern French and Catalan Society, 718–1050* (1965); *Mélanges Roger* Aubenas (1974); John H. Mundy, *Liberty and Political Power in Toulouse, 1050–1230* (1954); Paul Ourliac, *Études d'histoire du droit médiéval* (1979); Paul Ourliac and J. de Malafosse, *Droit romain et ancien droit,* 2 vols. (1957–1961); Jacques Poumarède, *Les successions dans le sud-ouest de la France au moyen âge* (1972); John H. Pryor, *Business Contracts of Medieval Provence: Selected Notulae from the Cartulary of Giraud Amalric of Marseilles, 1248* (1981); Jan Rogoziński, "Ordinary and Major Judges," in *Studia Gratiana,* 15 (1972), and *Power, Caste, and Law: Social Conflict in Fourteenth-century Montpellier* (1982); Joseph R. Strayer, *Les gens de justice de Languedoc sous Philippe le Bel* (1970); Pierre C. Timbal, *Droit romain et ancien droit français,* 2nd. ed. (1975); Pierre Tisset, "Placentin et son enseignement à Montpellier: Droit romain et coutume dans l'ancien pays de Septimanie," in *Recueil,* 2 (1951); Paul Vinogradoff, *Roman Law in Mediaeval Europe* (1909); Paul M. Viollet, *Histoire du droit civil français* (1905, repr. 1966).

KATHRYN L. REYERSON
JOHN BELL HENNEMAN

[See also **Aquitaine; Bologna, University of; Breviary of Alaric; Cathars; Châtelet; Codex Theodosianus; Commenda; Consuls, Consulate; Corpus Iuris Civilis; Decretists; Decretum; Fairs of Champagne; France; Glossators; Gratian; Investiture and Investiture Conflict; Languedoc; Lo Codi; Marseilles; Montpellier; Peace of God; Petri Exceptiones; Placentinus; Provence; Rogerius; Toulouse.**]

LAW, GERMAN: EARLY GERMANIC CODES.

The Germanic barbarians had no written codes of law before their entry into the Roman Empire. Their law was essentially customary, based on traditions passed down by word of mouth from previous generations. It was presumably kept in the memories of the elders of the community, who, when needed, came together "to speak the law." No one individual guarded this custom; and justice, if it was to be obtained, depended heavily on the initiative and support of the kindred, backed by the threat of the blood feud, rather than the state. The composition of the courts of the premigration Germans is not certain, but even if they were not popular courts, they nonetheless represented community rather than royal justice.

The barbarian migrations took place under the leadership of kings whose royal position had but recently developed. The shift from loosely organized Germanic confederations, whose leaders were primarily military leaders, to more closely knit groupings under the leadership of individuals who were political and judicial as well as military leaders was a development that had taken place largely as a result of contact with Rome. Once established, however, the royal power advanced rapidly and the Germanic kings were soon exercising the functions of Roman-style kings.

ROMAN LAW AND THE GERMANIC CODES

The barbarians' legal response to the challenge of Roman culture varied. Those nations that entered the empire early and settled in the more advanced southern sections encountered a large Roman population and a well-established Roman legal culture. As a result, the legislative activities of their kings reflected considerable influence by Roman law and legal practices, and they also reflected genuine concern to administer a well-recognized code of Roman law for the Roman part of the population. On the other hand, the law codes issued by the rulers of those Germanic peoples who settled in the more backward northern part of the Roman Empire reflected little if any influence by Roman law, and the rulers of these northern kingdoms were little concerned about providing a code of Roman law or judges learned in the Roman law for the remnants of the Roman population in their kingdoms.

There seems little point in trying to establish the theoretical basis of the legislative function of the barbarian kings. It is difficult to determine the extent to which the kings regarded themselves as the source of law versus the extent to which they were dependent on the support of their people, or at least on the elders or magnates of their people, for knowledge of the law. Most of the barbarian codes contain phrases indicating that the king had consulted with his faithful followers or the elders of the community, or acted with the consent of his people, but the phraseology is so formal and perfunctory that it would be unwise to conclude that Germanic law proceeded ultimately from the people. At least in his role as a codifier of his nation's laws, the Germanic king seems to have been following Roman precedent.

The oldest surviving barbarian laws are associated with the Visigoths, who were allowed to establish a federate kingdom in the southwestern part of Gaul (Aquitaine) about the year 418 and who expanded their territory into Spain later in the fifth century. After defeat by the Franks in 507, the Visigoths lost Aquitaine and thereafter controlled Spain and a strip of territory along the Mediterranean coast of Gaul east to the Rhone called Septimania.

The Visigothic kings faced the problems of ruling one of the most culturally advanced parts of the Western empire while at the same time controlling the relatively rude and basically illiterate Visigoths. So far as is known, the first efforts of the Visigothic kings to legislate date from about 458, during the reign of the Visigothic king Theodoric II. Theodoric's statement of law, known as the *Edictum Theodorici,* was until recent years ascribed to the Ostrogothic ruler Theodoric and dated in the early sixth century; however, the edict is now generally attributed to the earlier Visigothic ruler. It dealt primarily with the resolution of cases that had arisen between Goths and Romans. In general, the provisions of the edict were derived from Roman sources, especially from the Theodosian Code and the *sententiae* of Paul. But this Edict, whether of Visigothic or Ostrogothic origin, can hardly be described as a complete code of law. It seems to be a mere collection of cases haphazardly listed as they arose with little attempt to organize the material by subject matter.

The earliest surviving laws that can be regarded as constituting a true code are fragments of a code issued by the Visigothic king Euric (*ca.* 466–485) some time between 476 and 483. Euric's code was issued for the use of the Visigoths in their suits with each other and probably for cases that arose between Goths and Romans. Although most of this code has been lost, enough survives by incorporation as *antiquae* in later compilations to indicate strong Roman influence, especially in the use of written instruments, in recognition of the last will or testament, and in provision for credit and interest transactions. In addition, it may reflect some Christian influence in its emphasis on impediments to marriage between those within the prohibited degrees of relationship.

For the use of their Roman subjects, the early Visigothic kings sponsored the issuance of a special collection of Roman law less complex than the Theodosian Code, which had been compiled in 438 during the reign of the Eastern Roman emperor Theodosius II. The Visigothic code for Roman provincials was issued by Alaric II (485–507) about 506—it is known as the *Lex romana Visigothorum* or the Breviary of Alaric. The Breviary was compiled by a commission of jurists working under instructions from Alaric II, who may have been influenced by the need to conciliate his Catholic Gallo-Roman subjects as the threat of the Catholic Franks became an important factor to the Arian Visigoths. In any event, the Roman jurists who accomplished this task used many sections of the Theodosian Code (thus preserving the greater part of it) plus material from the *Sententiae* of the Roman jurist Paul and from a compendium of the Institutes of Gaius, as well as from some less important Roman law sources. The Breviary was thus a very respectable statement of Roman law in use at that time.

So far as Visigothic Spain was concerned, the Breviary remained in use among the Roman provincials only until the middle of the seventh century, when a new collection of Visigothic law issued by King Recceswinth in 654 offered a unified code for both Visigoths and Romans and prohibited the use of any code except this combined one. Thereafer the Breviary was not used in Visigothic Spain, but its influence did not end. It remained in use among the Gallo-Roman inhabitants of southwestern Gaul (Aquitaine) and of the Rhône Valley, both of which areas had come under Frankish rule in the early sixth century, and it was also known in northern Gaul as well as in northern Italy. It was one of the most important sources of Roman law in Western Europe prior to the revival of the Roman law of the *Corpus iuris civilis* in the eleventh and twelfth centuries.

The revised Visigothic code, which was corrected and expanded by royal enactment after its introduction, is commonly known as the *Leges Visigothorum* or the *Forum judicum*. This Visigothic lawbook remained in use in Spain even during the period of Moorish domination, and in the thirteenth century was incorporated in Castilian translation (*fuero juzgo*) in a code, the *Siete partidas,* issued by Alfonso X of Castile. Through the *Siete partidas* some elements of Visigothic law were eventually to find their way to Spanish America.

The Visigothic code is the most romanized of the early Germanic law codes. It reflects a conscious effort on the part of the Visigothic kings to rule a state with a unified system of law just as their decision to embrace Catholicism created a people bound together in a single church. That the church was Roman rather than Germanic is significant—so too the law became basically Roman. Although these developments imply a unified Visigothic society based upon an amalgam of Visigoth and Roman, with the latter predominating, it appears that the religious and legal facade of Romanism was established as much for propaganda purposes as for religious or political purposes. The Visigothic church, despite its formal connection with Rome, showed strongly independent tendencies throughout the Middle Ages. Likewise, the disappearance in the *Leges Visigothorum* of such typically Germanic legal concepts as

collective family responsibility, symbolized by the blood feud, and the absence of popular participation in the judicial or legislative process overstate the Roman influence on Visigothic law. Much of the content of the Visigothic code does indeed show Germanic influence, but the procedures outlined there are basically Roman, dependent as they are on a strong state where the king is the source of law, and the judicial system, backed by strong state control and operated by state magistrates, supersedes private or family justice.

The Burgundian people who settled in the Rhône Valley in southeastern Gaul seem to have been much fewer in number than the Visigoths. The Burgundians also established a federate kingdom in a very thoroughly romanized part of the empire, and the new Burgundian rulers also faced the problem of providing a stable rule for a population partly Germanic and partly Gallo-Roman, with the Gallo-Romans in the majority. As in the case of the Visigoths, this effort necessitated a reduction to writing of the old Burgundian customary law and a modification of that law to adjust it to the more settled circumstances of the new Burgundian life. At the same time, the Burgundian rulers attempted to guarantee that the Roman part of the population would continue to enjoy its rights and its own law. Accordingly, the Burgundian king Gundobad (474–516) and his son and successor Sigismund (516–523) issued codes for both the Burgundian and Roman populations. The Germanic code was issued in several parts between the years 483 and 532 and is known as the *Liber constitutionum* or the *Lex Gundobada*. The laws for the Roman population were probably issued about the year 517 and collectively are known as the *Lex romana Burgundionum*. The Burgundian rulers were clearly following Visigothic precedent in these affairs, and, as in the case of the Visigoths, the Burgundian rulers almost certainly employed Roman jurists in the preparation of their compilations.

The two Burgundian lawbooks had markedly different fates. The Burgundian kingdom was conquered by the Merovingian Franks in 534/535, but this conquest did not mean the end of Burgundian law. The Franks, even more than the other barbarians who entered the empire, retained their respect for the personal concept of law. Accordingly, for centuries after they were conquered by the Franks, Frankish subjects of Burgundian descent continued to claim the right to be judged by Burgundian law. So Burgundian customary law as modified by contact with Roman provincials and recorded in the fifth and sixth centuries remained alive for many years and eventually contributed significantly to the development of a distinctive form of medieval law in southern France. On the other hand, the use of the *Lex romana Burgundionum* was very brief. When the Franks conquered the Burgundian kingdom, the *Lex romana Burgundionum* was replaced by the more comprehensive Visigothic Breviary, which would be the chief source of Roman law in the Frankish empire.

The Ostrogoths moved into northern Italy at the close of the fifth century and, with the approval of the Eastern Roman emperor, established a kingdom nominally dependent on Constantinople. Ostrogothic rule in Italy did not bring a radical break with the past. Before he became king, the Ostrogoth Theodoric (sole ruler in Italy, 493–526) had lived at the Roman court in Constantinople for some years as hostage for the good behavior of his people and there he had acquired a great respect for Roman politics and culture. Consequently, the administration of the Ostrogothic kingdom was a conscious continuation of the former Roman administration. Even in the matter of personnel, many of the officials remained the same, for Theodoric even more than the Visigoths and Burgundians made extensive use of Romans in official positions—Boethius (*d. ca.* 524) and Cassiodorus being simply the best-known of them.

That several judicial edicts were issued by Theodoric is attested by a number of contemporaries, but no collection of these edicts has survived. Through references in that voluminous collection of the writings of Cassiodorus known as the *Variae* we know that Gothic counts heard suits between the Goths and that a Gothic count and a Roman acted together in hearing suits between Goths and Romans. Suits between Romans were heard by a Roman magistrate. We do not know the source of the law applied in any of these instances, although the Roman judges should have had access to the Theodosian Code as well as to such other Roman works as the *Sententiae* of Paul; possibly they also had the Visigothic Breviary after 507.

Whether recorded in writing or not, Ostrogothic law did not long survive in Italy. Shortly after Theodoric's death in 526, the Ostrogothic kingdom was invaded and eventually overthrown by the Eastern Roman armies of the emperor Justinian (552), and a few years later (568) the Italian peninsula was invaded by the Germanic Lombards. As a result of these developments, the Germanic content of medieval Italian law became Lombard rather than Ostrogothic.

As Ostrogothic law left no trace behind it, so also was the case with Vandal law. The Vandals had crossed the Rhine from Germany into Gaul about the year 406. They passed through Gaul into Spain, where they established themselves temporarily. Threatened by the Visigoths, the Vandals crossed the Straits of Gibraltar in 429 and about 435 forced Roman North Africa to accept them as rulers. They established a kingdom in which the Roman provincials were to a considerable extent expropriated. This action plus religious friction (Arianism versus Catholicism) meant that there was little progress toward amalgamation in Vandal Africa. In any event, information about the Vandals is not extensive, and if the Vandals codified their laws in written form, these laws have not survived. Most Vandal influence in Africa disappeared shortly after the kingdom was overthrown by the armies of the Eastern Roman emperor Justinian in 534.

The earliest written codification of Frankish law was accomplished during the reign of Clovis (481–511). At the beginning of Clovis' reign, the Franks occupied a relatively small territory in northeast Gaul where they had been established as federate allies of the empire since the mid fourth century. By the end of Clovis' reign, Frankish power had pushed westward to Brittany and southwestward to the Pyrenees, and in the east the Franks had pushed east of the lower and middle Rhine. Southeast Gaul (Burgundy) was added later by Clovis' sons (534). The Frankish state was thus a very extensive one. In addition to their own Salian Franks, the Frankish kings ruled such other Germanic peoples as the Ripuarian Franks, the Alamanni, and the Bavarians, as well as Gallo-Romans and such partially romanized Germans as the Visigoths from Aquitaine and the Burgundians from southeast Gaul. The legal complexity of the Frankish state was somewhat simplified by continued application of the traditional Frankish concept of personality of law—each ethnic group might claim its own law. However, if the customary Frankish law was to compete with the other legal systems, now written, Frankish judges needed a more reliable source of law than the memories of the elders of the community. Furthermore, the community was now so scattered as the result of expansion that consulting such persons was not always possible.

Presumably the laws of the Franks had existed in unwritten form before the time of Clovis, but to

Clovis almost surely belongs the oldest written version of the Salic (Salian) law (the sixty-five-title version) dating from the last years of the sixth century (probably 506–511). Unlike his Burgundian and Visigothic forerunners who issued separate Germanic and Roman codes, Clovis confined his "legislative" activities to the issuing of a single written code, primarily for the Salian Frankish part of the population. Legal life in the Salian part of the kingdom nonetheless involved both Frankish and Roman law. Both Franks and Gallo-Romans came under the provisions of Salic law in areas covered by that code, superseding Roman law in these matters. Where the Salic law offered no guidance, however, the conclusion seems inescapable that the vulgar Roman law was still followed by the Gallo-Romans. The specific sources of this Roman law in northern Gaul are not easy to trace, but it was there whether in the form of the Visigothic Breviary or some other compilation, and it increasingly influenced Frankish law.

Some of the success of the Merovingian Frankish rulers in their attempts to rule an expanding empire may be laid to their policy of recognizing non-Frankish law. Not only was Roman law in use by the Gallo-Romans and churchmen of the Frankish empire, Burgundian law by Burgundians, and Visigothic law by Visigoths, but the more purely Germanic peoples of the eastern frontier were allowed to retain their own "national" law as well. Since the laws of these last peoples were still unwritten, however, written codes for them were produced under Merovingian leadership. The *Lex Ribuaria* appeared in the early seventh century, as did the *Pactus legis Alamannorm* (another code, *Lex Alamannorum*, appeared a century later); and the earliest written version of the Bavarian law *(Lex Baiuvariorum)* may go back to the mid seventh century. These three "codes" (Ripuarian, Alamannian, and Bavarian) are alike, however, in that they were prepared under Frankish leadership and reflect significant Salian influence. Revisions of these codes as well as the preparation of codes for the Saxons *(Lex Saxonum)*, Frisians *(Lex Frisionum)*, Thuringians *(Lex Thuringorum)*, and Chamavian Franks *(Lex Francorum Chamavorum)* resulted from similar policies pursued by Charlemagne in the early ninth century.

To the Salian Frankish laws originally issued by Clovis, other capitularies were added later in the sixth century by Clovis' sons and grandsons. This early version of the law is usually known as *Pactus legis Salicae*. In the sixth and seventh centuries the Salic law underwent further modification as the Germanic Frankish law encountered the influence of Roman law and of Catholic Christianity. Not only was it modified by such influences, it was also modified through use. Early Frankish custom recorded in Latin, which frequently did not have an equivalent word or concept for the Frankish custom, caused problems for both the scribes (almost certainly Gallo-Romans or trained by Gallo-Romans) and judges. As knowledge of Classical Latin declined, the uncertainty of the scribes in transcribing the laws increased. Barbarisms crept in and were handed on to other scribes. To explain the Germanic phrases (some of which were undoubtedly still Germanic in form but others hardly more than garbled transcriptions), the so-called Malberg glosses were added and handed down in some of the manuscript traditions.

So the original issue of Clovis expanded (in some of the manuscripts) by the capitularies issued by Childebert I (*r.* 511–558), Chlotar I (*r.* 558–561), and Chilperic I (*r.* 561–584) existed in many versions, all more or less barbarized, by the late Merovingian period. The new Carolingian dynasty undertook reform. The first attempts at this were taken by Pepin the Short in 763–764, producing a lawbook in 100 titles (or 99 titles in some versions) of the entire corpus of Frankish law. This version was reissued in slightly revised form by Charlemagne (*Lex salica emendata),* probably in 798. The 100-title text meanwhile underwent further reform (802–803). The Malberg glosses (now virtually unintelligible) were eliminated, and minor changes were made in the order and content of the chapters. But basically the result was an updated version of Clovis' 65-title text in 70 titles: this version is known as *Lex salica karolina.*

Lex salica is not a very comprehensive code of law, inasmuch as its content is largely devoted to establishing monetary or other penalties for various criminal acts or to setting up rules of legal procedure. Such private-law concerns as marriage and the family, succession, gifts, and contracts—which play such a large role in the Visigothic, Burgundian, and Lombard codes—are almost entirely absent. Thus, the very nature of the Frankish legislation goes far to explain why there is less Roman influence on the Frankish code than on any other of the early Germanic codes except the Anglo-Saxon.

The law of *Lex salica* was never extended to all parts of the Frankish kingdom nor was it extended beyond Gaul as a result of Charlemagne's conquests.

It was the law of the northern half of Frankish Gaul, where the bulk of the Frankish settlements were concentrated; elsewhere it was invoked only as the personal law of individual Franks, and as a result had disappeared outside of northern France by the time of the revival of the Roman law of the *Corpus iuris civilis* in the eleventh and twelfth centuries. But in northern Gaul, the Frankish law was extremely tenacious. It held its own beside feudal custom when that developed, and it was strong enough to retain much of its content even after medieval French kings encouraged the study of the revived Roman law. Its continued use in modified form would account for the fact that at the outbreak of the French Revolution, northern France was still described as the land of customary (that is, Germanic) law *(pays du droit coutumier)* in contrast with southern France, the land of the written (Roman) law *(pays du droit écrit)*.

When the various Germanic peoples known as the Anglo-Saxons settled in Britain between the middle of the fifth and the middle of the sixth centuries, they encountered an area that had been part of the Roman Empire since the mid first century, but it was an area that had been unprotected by Roman legions since the late fourth or early fifth centuries. There had been a Celtic revival, and it was this sub-Roman kingdom that faced the Germanic invaders and held them at bay for a time. So the Germanic Anglo-Saxons encountered a Britain that had been cut off from its Roman contacts for some time and that had always been out on the fringes of Roman territory. As a result, Roman survivals were much weaker here than in any of the other Germanic kingdoms. Latin disappeared as the language of the people, and the Germanic Old English triumphed instead. Romanized Britons and Celtic Christianity retreated before the conquering Germans, and, as a result, a reconversion of England was necessary.

From the standpoint of law, these considerations would have certain practical consequences. There was no need to retain Roman-law courts or Roman law in Britain, and therefore Roman legal ideas (except those associated with the church) seems to have had little if any influence on Anglo-Saxon law; the Anglo-Saxon kings issued no laws for their Roman population, and no Roman lawbooks seem to have survived in England. Furthermore, in issuing laws for their Germanic population, the Anglo-Saxon rulers alone of the early Germanic kings employed their native Germanic tongue rather than Latin—after all,

they had no Roman personnel to employ in their administrations. As a result of these factors, the Anglo-Saxon codes are closer to pure Germanic custom than any of the other early Germanic legislation.

The first Anglo-Saxon laws were issued by Aethelbert of Kent shortly after the year 600. This legislative activity seems to have been associated with the arrival in Kent of the missionary Augustine, sent there by Pope Gregory I to convert the "angelic" Angles. Later Kentish laws were issued by Hlothere and Eadric (673–685) and by Wihtred a few years later. Laws for Wessex were issued by Ine (688–694) and by Alfred (871–900). Laws for a united Saxon kingdom were issued by Edward the Elder (900–925) and Aethelstan (925–939). The eleventh-century laws of Cnut and Edward the Confessor, although technically still Saxon, hardly belong to the period of the early Germanic kingdoms.

The Anglo-Saxon laws represented in the work of Aethelbert, Hlothere and Eadric, Wihtred, and Ine are extremely brief and for the most part set up what would be essentially new regulations for cases arising outside the bounds of the Anglo-Saxon customary law, new regulations required by the introduction of a new institution, Roman Catholic Christianity. From the beginning, ecclesiastical motivation ranked high in the written Anglo-Saxon laws, and this influence was to continue throughout the Anglo-Saxon period. It should also be noted that there was no separate body of church law and no separate church courts in Anglo-Saxon England. The Anglo-Saxon courts heard all cases, bishop and ealdorman presiding jointly.

It is only with the later Anglo-Saxon issues that one sees something more of the basic system, and these later laws were not reduced to writing until the time of Alfred, at the close of the ninth century. Alfred's laws seem to mark a new period in the history of English law; he and his successors went to great lengths to codify the law of their consolidated kingdom. It was this law, with later modifications, that was in use in England at the time of the Norman Conquest in 1066 and that would then combine with other elements (especially Norman-French feudal custom and some aspects of Roman civil law) to form the basis of the medieval English common law.

The Lombards were the last major Germanic people to invade the empire. They entered in the second half of the sixth century, invading an Italy torn by a long-drawn-out war between the Ostrogothic kingdom and the Byzantine Empire. The Byzantines had at last won the war and established a provincial administration in Italy, but before Byzantine rule could become well established, the Lombards invaded from the north and with relatively little difficulty overcame the weak Byzantine garrisons which had been left in the major towns. The Italo-Roman population seems to have stood aside passively and to have observed the successful entry of the Lombards—perhaps Lombard rule promised relief from heavy Byzantine taxation.

The experience of the Lombards was not radically different from the experience of the Visigoths and Burgundians in their attempts to rule a people more culturally advanced than themselves and to provide an administration that could protect the lives and property of both Germanic and Roman subjects. Much of the Roman provincial administration had been disturbed if not destroyed by the long Ostrogothic-Byzantine wars; but the Lombard kings undoubtedly had some Roman advisers, and the municipal civitas remained the basis for the Lombard local administration.

Although the Lombard judges were learned only in the Lombard law and the Lombard courts do not seem to have offered a means of settling disputes among the Roman part of the population, it is clear from the Lombard legislation that the Lombards recognized Roman law in Italy and that the Roman part of the population continued to settle its disputes and to regulate its legal transactions in accordance with it. It is not clear how this Roman law was administered, for unlike the situation in the Ostrogothic, Visigothic, and Burgundian kingdoms, the Lombard courts took no cognizance of Roman law.

The value of the Lombard legislation lies in the continuing legislative activity of the Lombard kings and the development of a fairly sophisticated legal reasoning, revealed in the successive issues of these laws. The earliest laws were issued by King Rothair in 643 in a law code known as Rothair's Edict (*Leges Rotharis*). Rothair's Edict is almost entirely Germanic custom modified only slightly by the experiences encountered by the Lombards in the process of migrating into and settling in Italy. It deserves the designation "code" more than almost any other of the Germanic issues inasmuch as it is a nearly complete statement of Lombard legal principles and is organized according to a number of general categories: offenses involving damages or violence, family law, and property law.

A brief supplement to Rothair's Edict was added by Grimwald in 668, and a long series of supple-

ments (153 laws) was issued by King Liutprand between 713 and 735. Finally, brief additions were made by Ratchis in 745 and 746 and by Aistulf in 750 and 755. All of the laws issued after Rothair's Edict added to and modified the original edict, and accordingly there was little sense of organization among them. In general, it would seem that the later Lombard kings were issuing laws inspired by specific cases that had arisen in their kingdoms. So these laws are clearly not Germanic custom but are instead new laws worked out to meet new conditions. Not surprisingly, much of this new legislation owes a great deal to the influence of Roman law, although it also owes much to the influence of the church (the originally Arian Lombards became Catholic in the seventh century).

After the conquest of the Lombards by the Franks in 774, Italy was administered as a separate kingdom by Charlemagne and his successors, and Lombard law, supplemented by a number of Carolingian capitularies, continued to be the law of the greater part of the population. This law could be consulted in the numerous manuscripts that circulated in Italy, but it was also taught in a law school that had been established at an uncertain date in the Lombard capital of Pavia. By the eleventh century it was the subject of increasingly sophisticated study and was endorsed by the ancients, who wished to keep pure the Lombard element in the law, in contrast to the modernists, who wished to expand Lombard law by the incorporation of elements from the Roman law. Before the rise of Bologna in the late eleventh and early twelfth centuries as the most prestigious place in which to study Roman law, the law school at Pavia was the best-known school of Roman law in Western Europe, and students who studied there would carry their knowledge of the Roman law to such distant places as Normandy and England.

Each of the early Germanic law codes is distinct, and there is a vast difference between the most Romanized of them, the Visigothic, and the most Germanic, the Anglo-Saxon. Nonetheless, all were composed under roughly similar circumstances and all enjoyed certain characteristics. They were the products of a new royal power, even when nominal acknowledgment is given to consulting the "elders" or "the people." Each reflected the fact that much of the responsibility for maintaining peace and order in the community had passed from the family to the state. Each envisaged a judicial system staffed by royal appointees who either conducted the proceedings alone or presided over a court that contained representatives of the community. They handled criminal offenses as injuries against an individual or property, and the judicial action to resolve the issue was essentially a suit for civil damages.

With the exception of the Visigothic code, all the early Germanic law codes reflect a society where the cooperation of the family was necessary in order to obtain justice, for the state as such merely provided the tribunal before which the parties essentially presented their cases for arbitration. Once the issue had been settled in court, the parties could no longer resort to the blood feud.

The early Germanic law codes thus constitute a fusion of primitive Germanic practice and sophisticated Roman reasoning. They offer a legal parallel to the racial and cultural fusion that was taking place in Western Europe in the first centuries following the fall of the Roman Empire.

KATHERINE FISCHER DREW

SPECIAL CHARACTERISTICS OF GERMANIC LAW

Kinship was basic to any primitive society; it was essential to social organization and interpersonal relationships. In fact, primitive society as such is inconceivable without the notion of kin. The concepts of lineage and its expression through marriage, the rearing of children, the defense of rights, and the burden of duties were all grounded in kinship and given substance by blood. The type of kinship manifested by the Germans were derived from the father and his male ancestors. Therefore, Germanic society was patriarchal. Kin also signified that the family was particularly important in Germanic society. It protected the individual in time of need, and most importantly, it protected him from the blood feud. Without relatives, an individual could not be protected from the vendetta and would himself fall victim to it.

At the time that the Germanic tribal laws were put into writing, Germanic society was undergoing changes, many of which were initiated and encouraged by the German kings. One of the most important of these changes replaced the blood feud with the payment of money. As a result of this change, any crime perpetrated by an individual would have a corresponding monetary value and supposedly would not be followed by more violence. Therefore, more serious crimes, such as murder, arson, or abduction, would be compensated with a higher payment than less serious crimes, such as assault and battery. The new custom of monetary payment was especially important for the consequent abatement of violence, which earlier was likely to follow the crime of murder. Under the new law, taking the life of another would be compensated with the victim's wergild, that is, the monetary value of a person's life, and the wergild would be payable to the victim's relatives.

Wergild was also closely connected to the idea of class, since Germanic society as evident in its tribal laws was characterized by a class system. Theoretically, classes were three in number: slave, freed, and free (although the second class given here, that of freedmen, was actually a subclass). Freedman were former slaves who had been liberated or manumitted, but a freedman never completely lost the stigma of having been a slave at one time. The greatest variety within a class occurred only among the free, and in this class there were numerous divisions: ordinary freemen, counts, dukes, and the king's personal bodyguard, as well as the king himself. Although social mobility was somewhat difficult in Germanic society, it was not impossible. A person could raise his status by marrying into a higher class, or he could lower his status by marrying into a lower class. He could also have his status lowered to that of slave because he could not pay the compensation demanded when he was found guilty of a crime.

The status of women in Germanic law is also noteworthy. Women were always placed under the protection or guardianship of some male, but this protection varied depending on whether the guardian was the father, husband, uncle, or brother. The church also offered protection to women when the latter were cloistered. The guardianship under which women were placed was called the *Mundium*, and it signified that a woman lacked legal rights, including the right to defend herself in a court of law. Therefore, women always needed some male relative to speak for them. Neither women nor slaves possessed full legal rights because they could not defend themselves with weapons.

Germanic law reveals how cases were brought before the courts and how crimes were compensated. The plaintiff brought his case before his local court (the *mallus* or placitum), over which a judge presided. The jurisdiction of this local judge could be supplemented, if necessary, by the authority of counts, dukes, and ultimately the king himself. When a case was brought before the local court (which originally was simply the tribal assembly), all freemen were expected to be present. After the plaintiff publicly stated his case, the defendant was summoned to court to answer the charge made against him, but it was the plaintiff's burden to prove his case. Apart from the presentation of evidence, the defendant substantiated his innocence by taking an oath, which was supported by a certain number of predetermined oathtakers who believed in his innocence and swore to that effect. This procedure of oathtaking is known as compurgation, and it signified the sanctity of the spoken word in an age when literacy was almost nonexistent. The oath itself was taken upon some sacred object or upon weapons. The more serious the charge, the greater was the number of required oathtakers. More oathtakers were also required from those defendants who came from a lower class than from those who came from a higher class. The evidence that the defendant presented in his defense was also supported by witnesses who swore to his truthfulness. Witnesses who testified falsely against a man, as well as plaintiffs who could not prove their case, were condemned to the punishment they would have inflicted upon the accused. If the accused refused to come to court, then he was found liable.

If the oath was unsatisfactory to the court or if the evidence conflicted widely, the judge would put the parties through a trial by ordeal, of which there were several different types. Sometimes the ordeal served as an alternative to compurgation. Various types of ordeal included the ordeal of hot iron, in which a hot object was carried in the bare hand for a specified distance, or the ordeal of boiling water, in which an object (usually a stone) would be grasped by hand from a vessel of boiling water. In both of these ordeals, the guilt or innocence of the person would be concluded from how quickly the wound healed. The most common type of ordeal was known as judicial combat, trial by battle, or wager of battle, and it resulted in an armed contest between experienced fighters who fought on behalf of the respective plaintiff and defendant. Judicial combat always took place in public and in the presence of the judge. The victor of all these ordeals was assumed to be innocent because victory presupposed the judgment of God and the triumph of truth in the conflict. Guilt and legal liability were associated with the losing party of the ordeal. Torture was also used to obtain confessions, supposedly confessions of guilt.

The ultimate authority for any lawsuit was the king, but because of his importance, he might be unreachable by the ordinary person. Nevertheless, the king could and did extend protection both to individuals, when he believed they were in need of it, and to the population at large. The type of protection extended to the latter evolved into what is called the king's peace, that is, the public peace. The breaking of the public peace was punished by the payment of a fee *(fredus)* to the public treasury. In most Germanic kingdoms, the recipient of the *fredus* was the king, with the exception of Alamannia and Bavaria, where dukes had sovereignty.

The roots of feudalism, which can be traced in various historical sources (notably formulae, cartularies, and capitularies), are also evident in Germanic law, particularly in the laws of the Franks and in those laws influenced by Frankish law. Although the laws supply us with little or no information about the feudal concepts of commendation and benefice, they do contain references illustrating the evolution of the retinue. It is known by way of Germanic law that the early Germanic institution of the comitatus, that is, the personal retinue or armed retainers of a chieftain, evolved into the *trustis* of the Merovingian and Carolingian kings. Because members of this personal bodyguard, called the *antrustiones,* fought for and rendered service to their king, they acquired a higher status with increased privileges and a triple wergild. These *antrustiones* later became the vassals of the Middle Ages.

THEODORE JOHN RIVERS

BIBLIOGRAPHY

For the most recent and reliable editions of the various codes, see the *Leges* volumes of the *Monumenta Germaniae historica* (1835–1969) and the volumes (with German translation) in the *Germanenrechte* series originally published by the Akademie für Deutsches Recht (1935–1940) and more recently by the Historisches Institut des Werralandes (1947–1962). English translations are: Frederick L. Attenborough, *The Laws of the Earliest English Kings* (1922); Katherine F. Drew, *The Burgundian Code* (1949 and 1972), and *The Lombard Laws* (1973); Theodore J. Rivers, *Laws of the Alamans and Bavarians* (1977); Agnes J. Robertson, *The Laws of the Kings of England from Edmund to Henry I* (1925); and Samuel P. Scott, *The Visigothic Code* (1910).

For material about the law codes, see *A General Survey of Events, Sources, Persons, and Movements in Continental Legal History* (1912); K. von Amira and K. A. Eckhardt, *Germanisches Recht,* I and II, 4th ed. (1960–1967); Heinrich Brunner, *Deutsche Rechtsgeschichte,* I, 2nd ed. (1906); Louis Halphen, *Les barbares des grandes invasions aux conquêtes turques du xie siècle* (1926); P. D. King, *Law and Society in the Visigothic Kingdom* (1972); E. A. Thompson, *The Goths in Spain* (1969); J. M. Wallace-Hadrill, *The Bar-*

barian West, 400–1000 (1952), and *The Long-haired Kings* (1962); and Wilhelm Wattenbach and Wilhelm Levison, *Deutschlands Geschichtsquellen im Mittelalter: Vorzeit und Karolinger,* II, *Die Rechtsquellen* (by Rudolf Buchner) (1953).

KATHERINE FISCHER DREW

[See also **Barbarians, Invasions of; Breviary of Alaric; Codex Theodosianaus; Corpus Iuris Civilis; Law, Canon; Law, English Common; Law, French; Law, Schools of; Lombards, Kingdom of; Merovingians; Oath; Ordeals; Siete Partidas; Vandals; Visigoths; Wergild.**]

LAW, GERMAN: POST-CAROLINGIAN. Along with updating their own Salic (Salian) Frankish code (*Lex salica*), the Carolingians had overseen revisions—or first written codifications where none existed previously—in the laws of the German tribes they conquered. In doing so, they preserved the separate legal traditions of the tribes, so that the breakup of the Carolingian Empire did not have a particularly great impact on German law.

In ninth-century Germany, local courts still decided disputes among free people, mainly over property damage and theft, acts of violence, and failure to keep promises. The most common local court, the people's court (*Ding* or *Thing*), traditionally met at regular intervals about three times a year and held its sessions by daylight under open skies. It convened at a familiar location, preferably on a small hill; sometimes court sites were shaded by old trees having sacred or magical associations. In the absence of much consciousness of a ruler's responsibility for trials— only in rare instances was royal or ducal power involved—nearly all proceedings took place at the request of a plaintiff. In fact, the saying prevailed: "Where there is no plaintiff, there is no judge." Plaintiff and defendant confronted each other, alternately speaking and presenting witnesses before a judge.

If the credibility of a defendant's spoken word was tarnished, he could sometimes be subjected to a form of trial by "God's judgment." This usually meant plunging his arms to the elbow in boiling water, carrying a piece of glowing-hot iron, or walking barefoot on glowing-hot plowshares. In some instances, he could ask for trial by combat to prove his innocence; if the defendant was a woman or too infirm for combat, a substitute would fight instead.

The Carolingians had introduced the term "count" (*comes, Graf*) for "judge," but until the later Middle Ages his function was the ancient Germanic one of umpire, keeping the rules while the adversaries contended before him. He did not decide cases himself in the popular courts but left this either to the public in attendance, or, particularly in Frankish areas and those influenced by the Franks, to a jury of seven or twelve men. These would, as the phrase went, "find a judgment," which the judge would then announce. Eventually, jurors replaced the free public in this role entirely. Jurors or "lay judges" (*Schöffen*) in the popular courts of medieval Germany were not chosen at random; rather, they were supposed to be wise and experienced men with a good recollection and understanding of the law. Because of this, English sources sometimes call them "assessors," and their courts "assessors' courts," to avoid confusing them with randomly chosen "jurors" who had no expertise in law. In areas influenced by the Franks, the duke or his deputy had a hand in their selection; otherwise they were chosen locally by the free citizens.

Even in the German towns, legal proceedings were first held on open stone porches at the town halls, perhaps in deference to the custom of holding court under open skies, although the porch gave way to the closed courtroom by the High Middle Ages. Towns and cities developed their own legal traditions, and, as written law codes played increasingly large parts in settling disputes, cities and towns developed their own, often by copying them from one another.

Most medieval Germans felt that a law was valid if it was familiar to and followed by citizens of a particular community. Only gradually did the principle make headway that a law was binding if it was written, and subject to some doubt if it was not written in a law code. Charlemagne had attempted to give written law a clear preference over unwritten customary law, but the idea of even contrasting the two was not widely entertained in Germany before the twelfth century.

In a thorough if slightly rambling way, the prologue to the Bavarian code (*Lex Baiuvariorum*) covers the main points in the typical pre-twelfth-century German view of law:

> A custom of long standing is considered as law. Law is a written enactment. Traditional usage is unwritten law or custom which has proven itself for ages. For law (*lex*) has its name from reading (*legendo*) since it is written. Traditional usage (*mos*), however, means a custom from olden times which has its strength from being followed for so long. Custom itself is a sort of

law sanctioned by usage so that it is accepted as law. Law should be everything established with good reason which furthers order and common well-being. It is called custom, however, because it is in common use.

Here no real difference is perceived between written law and that handed down by tradition. It is just that it is convenient to have the traditional law written down for reference.

The eighth and thirteenth centuries in Germany experienced waves of ethnic law-code writing. Charles Martel began the Carolingian attempt to refine Frankish laws, and to have those of the peoples subject to them recorded as well, with the writing of the Alamannian Code (Lex Alamannorum) around 717–719. The Bavarian Code (Lex Baiuvariorum) followed at a less certain date, but probably before 749. The Ripuarian Frankish Code (Lex Ribuaria) was written down probably in the early seventh century, retaining its differences from the Salian Frankish Code, the original version of which dates from the last years of Clovis' reign (507–511). After conquering the Saxons, Charlemagne had some of their laws codified as the Lex Saxonum in the first years of the ninth century.

The laws were written entirely in Latin. At least fragments of the laws of the Alamannians, Bavarians, and Ripuarian Franks had been written down before, but the Carolingians expanded them and cleaned up the crude Latin of the older parts. Einhard notes that the general improvement of law was on Charlemagne's mind, although it seems clear that its intertribal standardization was not, for he did not bring even Salian and Ripuarian Franks under one code. His aim was rather to fill in what was missing and get rid of inconsistencies within the codes. His own additions to the older codes were quite modest, and he did not succeed in supplying full written codes for all peoples under his empire. Even his collection of Saxon laws does not cover the material found in the four older codes.

A striking characteristic of these eighth-century codes is their relative avoidance of physical, let alone capital, punishment for free men and women. Nearly everything could still be settled by some sort of compensation to the injured person, or, in the case of homicides, to the next of kin. Here, as generally in medieval German law, the term "peace" is often stated as the law's aim. The main idea was the restoration of peaceful feelings in the tribe through adequate payments for wrongdoing, thus allowing things to go on as they had before the misdeed occurred. As long as injured parties were reasonably

content with financial settlement, the life and health of the offender could be preserved.

The treatment of serfs was, of course, something else. They were supposed to be given their day in court for most crimes, but they were not considered able to make serious monetary settlements and were much less immune than free people to torture under the law. Often we find their lords sharing responsibility for their misdeeds, much as free men are responsible for damage done by their livestock. The peculiarity of their legal position is illustrated by articles 42.1–2 of the Salic Code, which provide that if a serf is guilty of a theft which would cost a free man a fine of fifteen solidi, that serf shall be stretched over a bench and beaten with 120 blows; if he confesses before the beating begins, he is to pay only three solidi and his lord is to make compensation to the victim.

By the twelfth century, when canon law and imperial law were increasingly applied in the German lands, the initial hope was that they would both harmonize not only with each other but with the different tribal and city codes. Canon law meant the same thing in Germany as elsewhere, but imperial law meant something special. Imperial law came to mean Roman law, as contained in the great Theodosian and Justinian codes, explained by the comments or glosses of many scholars, and added to by the German emperor and the imperial diet. It was not always perceived, however, with these specifications; at first it was likely to mean simply the ordinance of a contemporary emperor. Furthermore, interest in the idea of a comprehensive imperial law as a sort of federal capstone to tribal and city laws can be documented well before the revival of learning allowed true Roman law to be taught and applied in Germany.

Dim perceptions of such an imperial law play a large part in the Book of Emperors (Der keiser und der kunige buoch; later called the Kaiserchronik), written anonymously in the mid twelfth century. The work is not so much a history as a compilation of good and bad rulers—stereotypes for popular consumption. It makes reverence for the imperial law a constant attribute of good ancient Roman and German emperors alike, inasmuch as they "call for" the lawbooks "to be brought forth" to help them fulfill their major role of judge. While good pagan emperors, such as Titus and Trajan, relied on it as they found it, Constantine and Sylvester added to it, thus making it a joint imperial-ecclesiastical effort. By the time of Charlemagne, it had fallen into disuse, and so with the help of an angel and in cooperation with Pope Leo, Charlemagne restored it:

And all the lords who ruled the lands swore to him that they would defend the Imperial Law as they would their lives, and that not even for the sake of wife or child would they shield injustice.

There is no particular Roman-German contrast in the details of the imperial law as it appears in the *Kaiserchronik.* For example, much attention is given to German customs regarding peasants. According to it, a peasant is to wear only black or gray clothes, and

he is to spend six days at the plow. On Sunday he is to go to church, carrying his animal goad openly in his hand. If a sword is found on a peasant, he is to be tied to the churchyard fence and flayed, hide and hair. If enemies threaten him, let him defend himself with a pitchfork.

Throughout, the *Kaiserchronik* articulates the twelfth-century German veneration of this partly imaginary imperial law, a law that was thought to help emperors gain strength enough to impose a meaningful peace in harmony with church interests, to oversee good order in feudal and manorial relations, and to stop strong men from taking justice into their own hands. It was only later that secular Roman law, the province of scholars, would be perceived as the foundation of imperial law, and Roman law would be placed in contrast with primitive and inconsistent elements of German law.

The manifestation of law closest to the popular ideal of twelfth-century Germany was probably the land-peace ordinance of Emperor Frederick I Barbarossa, issued in 1152. It prohibited private wars and feuds and offered help with the enforcement of local laws against large-scale violence. Nobles guilty of breaking the peace were to forfeit their fiefs to the emperor, who would bestow them on law-abiding counts. This example of imperial law was "Roman" law only in the sense that, like the old laws of the Roman Empire, it was issued by the imperial head of state.

The thirteenth-century wave of German lawbook writing was not merely a repetition of the earlier attempt to write down customs for the sake of consistency and convenience. Instead, writers of the new lawbooks seem to be striving to preserve certain laws from change, or alternately, to graft some new ideas onto folk law.

They were reacting to the partial replacement of native legal usage by canon law or items of Roman law imported by graduates of law schools in the universities of Italy or France. If a student studied law in the new universities, it was a study of the Latin laws of the church for a "doctorate of decretals" or of the civil code of the ancient Roman Empire for a "doctorate of laws."

Then, too, by the thirteenth century the whole concept of a tribe had broadened considerably. Up through the eleventh century, "tribe" meant roughly "ethnic group" in the sense of a people united by a distinct dialect of German, by traditions of a fairly independent ducal leadership, and by roots in a certain region of Germany (hence the persistent, if awkward, English translation "stem duchy" for the *Stammherzogtümer,* ethnic groups under dukes preserving older tribal identities). But then the concept of the "territorial principality" began to make inroads on ethnicity. Duke Henry the Lion, for example, tried to bring every bit of territory he could get into his jurisdiction without regard for the ethnicity of the indigenous populations.

The territorial principle clearly won out in the thirteenth century, when German dukes, while retaining the older stem-duchy titles, now ruled Saxony rather than "the Saxons" and Bavaria rather than "the Bavarians." As a matter of law, however, this development was less definitive. People kept claiming the validity of their old tribal laws, while admitting that they were subjects of dukes who ruled ethnically mixed territories. It is, therefore, no surprise that the struggle between empire and papacy, each seeking to use law in any available form, appears in thirteenth-century German lawbooks.

Independent of all these factors, thirteenth-century-German lawbooks reflect a growing sensitivity to legal rights as felt by the various classes. While the eighth-century codes had separated punishments involving free and unfree people clearly enough, the growth of a money economy created new divisions between wealthier elements and those free people barely able to stay out of debt. Sermons and popular poetry of the day reflected the strong feelings that the rich and powerful were trying to turn justice to their own interests; that the increasing complexity of law and the cost of legal proceedings were undermining the law's protection of the free poor of the towns; and that the landed nobility was attempting to assert new claims of manorial rights over their serfs.

Against this background of shifting concepts and sentiments, we have the *Sachsenspiegel* (Saxon mirror), written first in Latin and then in Low German between 1220 and 1235 by Eike von Repgowe, a Saxon knight who was both a jurist and a historian. It is a compilation of customary Saxon laws as the author knows them from his own experience. The idea, as Eike explains, is to let the Saxons have a good look at what they cannot otherwise see as a whole through their own eyes, "like a woman looking at her face in the mirror" (prologue). He divides his work into two main parts, the general laws of the land (*Landrecht*) and those governing feudal contracts (*Lehnrecht*).

A striking thing about the *Sachsenspiegel* is its mildness in comparison with both the ancient Roman law codes studied in medieval universities and the partial law code set down for the Saxons by Charlemagne, which decreed capital punishment with less hesitation than the older codes of the Franks, Allamanians, and Bavarians. As with these older codes, the *Sachsenspiegel* usually attempts to avoid extreme corporal punishment, although there is an imprint of the later Middle Ages in the gravity of offenses involving property and money. Stealing grain has become a capital offense (II, Art. 38. [39.]), rather than something a free man can compensate for with ninefold restitution, as in the old Bavarian code (Art. 9. §1). Counterfeiting is now much more serious: where a supplemental law from 818 or 819 to the Salian code demanded the loss of a hand for counterfeiting, the *Sachsenspiegel* demands the loss of a hand for mere possession of false coins and death for attempting to make purchases with them (Art. 27. [26.]).

The *Sachsenspiegel* still retains rather much of the old-style faith in oaths to procure innocence. A father not under a criminal charge himself can free his accused son (one time only, to be sure) by swearing by the saints that he is innocent (II, Art. 18. [17.] §2), and a lord can do the same thing once for his serf (II, Art. 20. [19.] §2). For some crimes, tests of innocence are stipulated for second offenders whose oaths would be doubted. These tests are the old ones of carrying glowing-hot iron or plunging the arms to the elbows in boiling water, still with the option of combat (I, Art. 39.). Possibly because of the growing influence of Roman-law procedures, it became necessary to point out that a judge cannot present accusations himself (III, 53. §2)—something that would have been taken for granted in older German law.

While Eike sets forth the rules of feudal tenure of land at great length, he regards with some suspicion the growth of independent feudal power under the hereditary principle and stresses that fiefs are meant to be held only for the lifetime of a man or woman (III, Art. 73.). Although he accepts the fact that some persons are unfree and must be treated as such, he portrays the whole institution of serfdom as if it were some sort of novelty which greedy men have imposed, in contrast with true law. He notes specific rights of serfs here and there; for example, if a serf loses his own horse in the service of his lord, his lord must give him another (III, Art. 6. §3). At the same time, he warns his readers not to look for an exhaustive list of serfs' rights, "for these are so numerous that no one could list them" (III, Art. 42. §2).

Opposing any Roman-style standardization of law, he stresses that each of the peoples of Germany has special laws from truly ancient days. Like popular historians a century earlier, he gives the main German tribes a continuous existence back into the time of the Roman Republic and portrays their conquest by Julius Caesar as having integrated them into the Roman Empire as separate peoples with separate rights, when the (legendary) ancient kings of the Saxons, Bavarians, Franks, and Swabians were made dukes in the nascent Roman Empire. Thus diversity of law among German tribes is sanctified both by the passage of centuries and by Roman approval.

Then there is the matter of primacy of the great law-giving figures, emperor and pope. Always interested in harmony, Eike presents the Doctrine of the Two Swords fairly evenhandedly:

> The Pope has been given the spiritual sword, the Emperor the secular one. . . . Any force which opposes the Pope beyond his power to subdue it with spiritual law should be brought under control by the Emperor with secular law. The spiritual power should also support efforts of worldly justice when it is needed. (I, Art. 1.)

In this connection, he mentions the symbolism of the emperor holding the pope's stirrup, but he interprets it as a sign of reciprocity in duties rather than accepting its rather obvious meaning of the emperor's being the pope's vassal.

Eike does not doubt the secular ruler's right to make laws, but he does stress the elective origins of monarchical power in Germany, which implies at least an indirect popular voice in current lawmaking. "The Germans," he states, "should choose their king according to law" (III, Art. 52. §1). In the selection of an emperor, he acknowledges the principle of the electoral college but maintains that the electors "should vote not just according to their own will but for the man all the princes choose" (III, Art. 57. §1).

In the 1260's an unknown author translated most of Eike's work into High German but introduced enough other elements to satisfy himself that he was producing a general German legal "mirror." He noted that he was infusing elements of law issued by kings and taught by "masters of law," which meant Roman jurists. Although this *Deutschenspiegel* does not contain much Roman jurisprudence, it is significant that the author thought that adding these foreign elements would both improve the *Sachsenspiegel* and make it into what we might call a national law code.

The influence of the *Deutschenspiegel* as such appears to have been slight, but around 1275 another anonymous author borrowed heavily from it and added materials from Roman and canon law to produce the *Schwabenspiegel*. With all these borrowings, he was obviously not writing a true "Swabian mirror," nor was he trying very hard to do so. The fact was that for traditional law to be taken seriously in a day of juristic education in Roman and canon law it had to be written down, but once it was written down it derived its authority more from the relative permanence which went with being recorded than from being remembered by members of an ethnic group as part of their heritage. As German historians of the Romantic period would later put it, the folk law lost its closeness to the people—and sacrificed its spontaneous springing from the legal life of the people—when it was written down and modified by commentaries and foreign addenda. The final result was no longer a tribal code but one more appropriate for an ethnically mixed territorial principality.

As with Eike, the author of the *Schwabenspiegel* inserts a version of the Doctrine of the Two Swords into his work; however, he clearly leans to the papal side. In his variation, God first gave the two swords to St. Peter, the first pope; subsequent popes bestow the secular sword in turn on emperors. There had been an equally partisan imperial version a century earlier: according to Rainald of Dassel, Frederick I's chancellor and archbishop of Cologne, both swords were entrusted to the emperor, who granted the use of one to the pope, but that view was not represented in the thirteenth-century lawbooks.

Regardless of their circumstances, medieval Germans all professed to honor the law above men. There were apparently no critics or opponents of the sentiment conveyed by the opening lines of the

anonymous, early-twelfth-century vernacular poem "Of the Law": "There is no man so sublime as the law truly is, as long as God is truly a just judge." Reverence for the law, however, was not necessarily extended to those who made a living by it. As in later times, a low regard for the scruples of at least some professional lawyers appears in the popular literature.

The use of Roman and canon law had increased the complexity of law in Germany to the point of making it advisable to hire professional lawyers (unknown to the older courts) educated at universities which taught the corresponding Latin codes, although Saxon or Swabian law might still be applicable in cases they presented. The popular reaction was predictable: a denunciation of those who used the law to make a good living for themselves and whose specious learning twisted the law in favor of their rich clients.

In the early fourteenth century, in his very lengthy, but popular, didactic poem, *Der Renner* ("The Runner," as it carries a message through the lands), Hugo von Trimberg, a schoolmaster near Bamberg, fervently praised love of the law, while inveighing against those who use it selfishly. He uses the term "jurist" as a German word for those who study Roman and/or canon law. If they live up to their name, he says, they are "upright people" who "stand by justice." True jurists are opposed, however, by those who derive their name from Judas, who sold his master for silver. Both types study lawbooks, which for Hugo means the Latin codes rather than the "mirrors":

> He who studies lawbooks for the sake of justice labors for the right reason, but the soul of him who studies them to satisfy greed will suffer great torment. . . . Lawbooks cannot be written so just, but what things can be found in them to increase earthly injustice.

The Theodosian and Justinian codes provided for more standard procedures and punishments than the diverse German laws, but they were also harsher. The later Roman emperors had been less motivated by a desire to let the defender absolve himself with financial penalties and regain his "peace" in the community than by a felt need to set deterrent examples of punishment. Then, too, the role of the state was different. German law, which had seen the governing powers in a very limited role, left legal controversy largely to the individuals concerned. Medieval Germans agreed that it was evil for individuals to exact revenge without going before a judge, and when injured individuals or their survivors were satisfied by a judgment the law had done its work. The Roman-law view was that law worked through the state and justice was done when the judgment reflected the law as applied by the appointed authorities.

While Roman law was undoubtedly more sophisticated, it was also more bizarre at times and was quite capable of making executions in medieval Germany more grisly than before for the most abstract of reasons. The punishment for parricide in the Roman Republic (sewing the offender in a sack with an adder and dropping the sack in the Tiber) had been embellished under the Roman Empire by the addition of other animals to drown with the criminal. The closest analogy in medieval German law—and not a very close one at that—was the (rare) punishment of thieves by hanging them by their feet on a gallows between dogs suspended by their hind feet. Modern anthropological research has traced that grim custom back to the pre-Christian practice of offering criminals to Wotan as sacrifices and sacrificing dogs at the same time, although it is not clear whether this was to offer Wotan a gift of his favorite animal or to stress the criminality of the victim as having the worst canine characteristics.

At any rate, it was under the influence of Roman law (a fourteenth-century commentator on the *Sachsenspiegel* at the court of the elector of Brandenburg cites the *leges* as authority) that the recommended punishment for parricide became drowning in a sack in which the culprit was sewn up with rocks, an adder, a dog, a monkey, and a rooster. The commentator explains the symbolism thus: the blindness of the dog during his first nine days symbolizes the blindness to human decency of the offender who killed a parent; the crowing rooster signifies his unbridled presumption and arrogance; the adder signifies family murder (the female bites off the head of the male after he impregnates her, while the young kill their mother in birth by biting their way out; finally, the monkey is a false image of man, just as this sort of criminal is a human-looking creature devoid of a human heart. If this recommended sentence was seldom carried out, the infrequency is more traceable to the high cost of monkeys in medieval Germany than to any humane sophistication in Roman law as taught at the time.

The later Middle Ages in Germany, as elsewhere in Europe, were times of severe and recurring threats. The disastrous effects of plagues in the cities, increasingly severe outbursts of the fear of witch-

craft, and the destructiveness of late-feudal warfare all tended to cheapen human existence. Disappointed expectations multiplied individual crimes, while class-based violence aimed at overthrowing or maintaining patrician control of city halls became a recurring phenomenon. Gallows and wheel by this time were permanently mounted outside the city gates among the "raven stones," where birds could pick the bones of hapless offenders.

With far more independence than their counterparts in western Europe—in fact, with little imperial direction beyond charters issued to them—mayors and councils of the German cities were determined to make the law work within their corporate limits. Their aim was, of course, to allow citizens to pursue their occupations without fear of violence and fraud and to punish offenders in a sufficiently deterring way to assure this. Apart from guaranteeing law and order, they sought to promote trade and make sure that business obligations were met.

This independence of the German cities made their lawbooks more significant than those of municipalities in France and England, and the more serviceable of the German city codes were copied by others. The Magdeburg code, in particular, served as a model for countless cities in Germany, Poland (including Warsaw), and others eastward to the Dnieper. As German colonization in eastern Europe developed, the laws of the older cities were adapted for the new settlements, and a system arose whereby cases could be appealed to the higher courts or to cities from which the "daughter city's" laws had been borrowed. Magdeburg law was probably favored in this connection because it allowed greater freedom to nonpatrician elements than did most other "laws." Some of the colonists in the east had even insisted on having Magdeburg law promised as the law of the settlement before they would undertake founding a new town. As early as the twelfth century, Magdeburg law had guaranteed that leaders of specified guilds should be chosen only by their own members. Through the appeals system, the Magdeburg superior court became the most influential in central and eastern Europe. In northern Germany, the laws of the maritime cities—particularly Lübeck, the dominant city in the Hanseatic League—went beyond municipal concerns to produce an early code of international commercial law.

Popular resentment against those learned in Roman law continued through the end of the Middle Ages. Between 1300 and 1500 many folk sayings coupled *Juristen* (lawyers) with *böse Christen* (evil

Christians) in rhymes. But the advance of Roman law could not be stopped. While the clergy preferred canon law in cases of conflict, the study of canon and Roman law increasingly went together, with aspiring students obtaining doctorates "in both kinds of law." Then, too, periods beset by the threat of anarchy make central authority look desirable. Both the emperors and those dukes ruling territorial principalities attempted to increase their control over their region, the former with very limited success, the latter with more. Regardless of their degree of success, however, they had every reason to stress the validity of Roman law, which not only confirmed the power of the ruler with few or no limitations, but also implied the importance of a permanent state apparatus under the rulers to provide law enforcement. Following this development would take us into military history, for it led to the justification of standing armies. There was no real difference for medieval German jurists between an armed force for defense against external enemies and one for keeping the ruler's peace internally.

In the legal system through the time of the *Book of Emperors* and even that of the *Sachsenspiegel*, the ruler was regarded as the chief judge. By the end of the Middle Ages, he was still recognized as the highest secular judge, but his role of enforcer had become more important. Where the older German law had been ideal for settling disputes among individuals in a community, revived Roman law was more suited to backing territorial pacification efforts.

BIBLIOGRAPHY

Sources. Der keiser und der kunige buoch oder die sogenannte Kaiserchronik, Hans F. Massmann, ed., 3 vols. (1849–1854); *Deutsche Kaiserchronik*, Edward Schröder, ed., in *Monumenta Germaniae historica: Deutsche Chroniken*, I (1892, repr. 1964); "Vom Rechte," in Albert Waag, ed., *Kleinere Deutsche Gedichte des 11. und 12. Jahrhunderts* (1890), 66–81; Karl A. Eckhardt, ed., *Die Gesetze des Karolingerreiches*, 3 vols. (1934); *Monumenta Germaniae historica: Legum*, 5 vols. (1835–1889).

Eike von Repgowe, *Sachsenspiegel*, Carl R. Sachsse, ed. and trans. (*Landrecht* part only; nearly exhaustive index) (1848), and *Sachsenspiegel*, Karl A. Eckhardt, ed., *Monumenta Germaniae historica* (both *Landrecht* and *Lehnrecht* parts) (1933). An edition of both parts is in preparation as vol. XXX of *Ausgewählte Quellen zur deutschen Geschichte des Mittelalters*.

Studies. Geoffrey Barraclough, ed. and trans., *Mediaeval Germany, 911–1250: Essays by German Historians*, I, *Introduction* (1938), 75–137; Otto H. Becker, *Kaisertum, deutsche Königswahl und Legitimitätsprinzip in der Auffassung der späteren Staufer und ihres Umkreises* (1975); Georg von Below, *Die Ursachen der Rezeption des römischen Rechts in Deutschland* (1905); Hermann Conrad, *Deutsche Rechtsgeschichte, ein Lehrbuch*, I, *Frühzeit und Mittelalter* (1954); Georg Dahm, "On the Reception of Roman and Italian Law in Germany," in Gerald Strauss, ed., *Pre-Reformation Germany* (1972); Otto Freiherr von Dungern, "Constitutional Reorganization and Reform Under the Hohenstaufen," in Barraclough, *Mediaeval Germany*, II; Wolfgang Kunkel, "The Reception of Roman Law in Germany: An Interpretation," in Strauss, *Pre-Reformation Germany*; Prince Hubertus zu Loewenstein, *The Germans in History* (1945), 91–96; Heinrich Mitteis, "Feudalism and the German Constitution," in Barraclough, *Mediaeval Germany*, II; R. J. Schoeck, "Recent Scholarship in the History of Law," in *Renaissance Quarterly*, 20 (1967); Claudius von Schwerin, rev. ed. of Hans Thieme, *Grundzüge der deutschen Rechtsgeschichte*, 4th ed. (1950); Indrikis Sterns, "Crime and Punishment Among the Teutonic Knights," in *Speculum*, 57 (1982).

Bibliographical. Hans Planitz and Thea Buyken, *Bibliographie zur deutschen Rechtsgeschichte*, 2 vols. (1950).

HENRY A. MYERS

[See also **Carolingians and Carolingian Empire; Codex Theodosianus; Eike von Repgowe; Germany; Hugo von Trimberg; Kaiserchronik; Rainald of Dassel; Sachsenspiegel; Schwabenspiegel; Two Swords, Doctrine of.**]

LAW, IRISH, often called brehon law (from Old Irish *brithem* [a judge]), was the customary law of Ireland at least from the time of the earliest surviving records. It yielded much ground to English feudal law after the Anglo-Norman invasion of the twelfth century and was finally abolished by statute and replaced by English law in the early seventeenth century.

From the beginning of legal documentation (fifth to sixth centuries), this customary law was preserved, expounded, and elaborated in different law schools by a tightly knit professional caste of poet-jurists, the lineal descendants of the druids described by the Greco-Roman writers. The teaching of the schools was entirely oral: law was transmitted in the form of gnomic maxims and verse (*roscada*) composed in meters that indicate the flowering of a long tradition. Ireland escaped romanization, but Latin learning came peacefully with Christianity in the fifth century—if not earlier. As a result, the secular learning of the law schools came to be written down from the late sixth century. The lawyers—who only slowly and reluctantly separated themselves from the poets *(filid)*—clung to an archaic and hieratic concept of social order not only because of their natural conservatism but perhaps also because society changed so quickly in the sixth and seventh centuries that they no longer had any empathy with it. Honored preservers of the *mos maiorum,* they were reluctant to change all the more because the growing concentration of power in the hands of the kings encroached steadily on their preserve. Indeed, the law tracts, with their stress on private justice, do not at all reflect the real powers of the seventh-century kings. The earliest verse tracts *(fénechas)* represent, as D. A. Binchy says, the first penetration of writing into the Irish law schools. Linguistically these tracts are very old, legally they are profoundly archaic. Their language *(bélre Féne)* is obscure, allusive, highly technical, and deliberately intended to exclude the uninitiated.

For all their conservatism the lawyers were soon heavily influenced by Christianity. In the course of the seventh century, probably under the influence of written canon law, the legal schools worked up extensive prose tracts that paraphrased and elaborated the older materials in verse. These tracts, in form, vocabulary, and frequently in content, are influenced (sometimes heavily) by the teachings and canons of the churches. The impression one gets from them is that the churches were deeply concerned with law and had a large part in molding it. This is very much the case with the texts emanating from the *Nemed* law schools of the south. These lay particular stress on the dignity and legal standing of the ecclesiastical scholar *(saí litre)* and on the high status of bishops and abbots; one tract goes so far as to cite matter from the Old Testament as precedent. Another early tract *(Córus Béscnai),* which belongs to the northern *Senchas Már,* is such a mixture of secular and ecclesiastical law that it can only have been redacted in a church establishment.

Influence also flowed in the other direction, and the *Collectio canonum hibernensis,* the materials of which date from the seventh century, is profoundly influenced by the rules and institutions of secular law. This influence can be traced to the early seventh, perhaps the sixth century, in regard to suretyship in particular. The rules of a synod of perhaps the same date concerning the wounding of a bishop and the compensation due him faithfully echo the institutions described in the archaic secular tract *Bretha Déin Chécht;* it is clear that these institutions were obsolete by the end of the seventh century. The

presence of legal terms and concepts of purely secular origin (in Latin translation or adaptation) in the earliest canon law and increasingly in the later strongly suggests that the two legal streams flowed together and that churchmen practiced as secular and canon lawyers—a state of affairs for which there is solid evidence in the contemporary annals from the ninth to the twelfth centuries. The manuscript transmission of the law and much of its practice was the work of clerics until the dramatic organizational changes that took place in the church in the twelfth century. During the so-called "twelfth-century reform" law was apparently again separated from the church and secular law schools developed; they subsequently flourished until the defeat and collapse of Gaelic Ireland in the sixteenth and early seventeenth centuries.

The late seventh and early eighth centuries were periods of collection, compilation, and editing. From this time dates the *Senchas Már* (The great tradition), a compilation that won increasing authority in the schools and very largely displaced rival collections. As one would expect, the teachings of the schools differed, and there were regional and local variations. There was no central political authority to make law or enforce uniformity. In fact, Irish law is for the most part jurist-made law, though there is evidence for the enactment of laws by local kings and their magnates (lay and clerical) as early as the last quarter of the seventh century. The lawyers were conscious antiquarians: nothing old was discarded, little that was new consciously admitted. From the period of compilation they confined themselves to copying and commenting upon what by now had become a sacred and immutable text—while practice diverged sharply, and their own understanding of it grew dimmer and dimmer. The vast apparatus of gloss and commentary accumulated over the later centuries is therefore of limited value. The institutions and rules of the texts were conservative if not obsolete when they were first written. By the end of the seventh century, the social structures and political framework differed greatly from those in the texts, and it would appear that the legal rules and remedies described in them were equally obsolete. The later collections of commentaries provide little that is reliable on the subsequent development of Irish law from the ninth to the sixteenth centuries.

The law tracts then are most valuable for the very early period. Here there are extensive materials on procedure, suretyship, real securities, private distraint, status, contract, clientship, compensation for injuries and sick-maintenance, land law and trespass, marriage law, inheritance, legal relations of church and secular society, penalties and mulcts, and a wide range of other topics. In addition, the texts contain a great deal of information on broader aspects of life: kingship; the nature and relationships of petty kingdoms (túatha); kinship, wergild, and kindred liability; the grades of society and of the professions (especially of the poet-jurists); the functions of nobles and commoners; the nature of the rural economy; and many other matters. Though there are considerable linguistic, technical, and historical difficulties of interpretation, the records of Irish law are invaluable for the comparative study of early European sociolegal institutions because they provide detailed descriptions of rules and remedies that survive only vestigially in the early laws of other societies. They are the principal source for the earliest social and legal institutions of Ireland. In addition, they throw a great deal of light on the early functioning of Christianity in a nonromanized society and on the emergence of early canon law.

BIBLIOGRAPHY

Editions. William N. Hancock, Thaddeus O'Mahoney, Alexander G. Richey, and Robert Atkinson, eds., *The Ancient Laws of Ireland,* 6 vols. (1865–1901), is unsatisfactory on most counts; the translation is very inaccurate and the text unreliable. Daniel A. Binchy, *Corpus iuris hibernici,* 6 vols. (1978), is a scrupulous diplomatic edition of the entire early text (including later commentaries and glosses), but without translation or index.

Studies. Ludwig Bieler, *The Irish Penitentials* (1963); Daniel A. Binchy, "Ancient Irish Law," in *Irish Jurist,* **1** (1977), and "Irish History and Irish Law," in *Studia hibernica,* **15** (1975), **16** (1976); Kathleen Hughes, *Early Christian Ireland: Introduction to the Sources* (1972); John (Eoin) Mac Neill, *Celtic Ireland* (1921, repr. 1981), and "Prolegomena to a Study of the Ancient Laws of Ireland," in *Irish Jurist,* **2** (1967); Maurice Sheehy, "Influences of Ancient Irish Law on the Collectio canonum hibernensis," in International Congress of Medieval Canon Law, 3rd, Strasbourg, 1968, *Proceedings,* Stephan Kuttner, ed. (1971).

DONNCHADH Ó CORRÁIN

[See also **Ireland; Irish Society; Law, Welsh.**]

LAW, ISLAMIC (*shariᶜa,* system of moral and legal precepts, the "path" ordained by God), is an aspect of religion, although defined separately from theology because it comprehends the practical issues that

touch upon everyday life. The term *fiqh* means "understanding" of the divine law, expressed in the rules of positive law formulated by the jurists as a result of their pious scholarly activity.

Islamic law had its beginnings in the developed urban societies of Iraq and Syria as well as in Medina, the home of the Prophet. It evolved with a character and methodology of its own that made it different in the most essential ways from the confessional systems that preceded it. From the earliest period there were Muslims who aspired to an ideal society based on the new faith, and who went so far as to wish to transform all social behavior to conform to the ideal set up by religion. Thus even the secular structures that had preceded Islam were rejected as diluting the ideal.

Furthermore, although Islam took on the egalitarian aspects of Judaism, the Muslims did not regard their community as the only divinely guided community, but as one among others that had received the blessings of a revelation. It was natural, then, that they follow the pattern established by the other confessional communities, that of a distinct group with its own law for its own members. When Islam came to rule vast areas, the opportunity was created to bring the divine guidance in its uncorrupted form to all peoples. Thus the concept of universality was introduced.

There was also the emphasis of the Koran on direct human responsibility before God, without church or priests to mediate in ritual worship. Except under certain conditions, even group responsibility was not stressed. The consequences of this were important. Because all Muslims were on an equal footing before God, the law could envision no hereditary class structure. Nor could there be territorial distinctions with respect to the law. Rights and duties are not laid down by a state within national boundaries but are determined by God alone, and so these rights and duties are everywhere the same.

These important tendencies came into being during the formative period of Islamic law and help to explain its nature. The idealistic effort to make all social behavior conform to religious norms accounts for the vast scope of the law. A man's dealings with his fellows are seen in terms of his duties toward God. Thus, in effect, the law takes in the whole field of human conduct. It deals not only with subject matter that in the West would be enforced in the courts—contracts and obligations, civil wrongs, criminal law—but also with all the religious obligations, such as prayer and fasting, with regulating family life, and, tentatively, with the law of war and public law. Even social behavior is viewed as appropriate subject matter for Islamic law.

Another aspect of this idealistic approach is the distinct ethical bias of Islamic law. Moral and ethical standards are rarely separated from strictly legal rules. Contract law, for example, is closely bound up with ideas of fair play, honesty, and mutual help among businessmen. For instance, taking interest or engaging in any other form of unjustified enrichment is strictly prohibited because the basic norm is a moral and ethical one, incorporated into strictly legal thinking. The jurists' works contain many discussions in which such concepts as intention are dealt with from a religious and moral perspective, and actions are ranked on a scale according to their status in the eyes of God.

Furthermore, the notion of a universal Muslim community meant that Islamic law would be personal, applying to the individual Muslim wherever he might live, in contrast with systems in which law is territorial and effective within political boundaries. On the other hand, Islamic law is not applicable to non-Muslims living in Muslim countries. It provides protected status for these communities, to the extent that they are governed by their own religious law, or occasionally European law. This feature helped preserve the independence of the *sharī͏ᶜa* against the increasing absolutism of temporal rulers, and at the same time maintained the unity and common identity of Muslims all over the world.

Finally, the most important feature of Islamic law is its sacred character. It is given by God in the precepts of the Koran and in the traditions reflecting the personal decisions and model behavior of the Prophet. Hence, classical doctrine holds that the law is not subject to change. It is the task of the jurists to discover God's will from this raw material, using strictly defined techniques. Thus, even though it is sacred law, Islamic law is not irrational, because it was shaped by rational methods of interpretation.

The legal doctrine of the *sharī͏ᶜa* is embodied and expressed not in the Koran alone, nor in any single comprehensive legal text or code, but in the vast corpus of discussions and commentaries of the jurists, who began to set down their work toward the end of the eighth century. Furthermore, because normative and right behavior is already defined by God, there could be no case law, nor precedents in court decisions. The courts are there not to rule on new situations, but to apply the law as it is known from the writings of the jurists.

The practical working-out of the system took many generations, and it was not until the first half of the ninth century that its full development, reflecting thoroughly Islamic norms, was achieved. There was no institution to provide everyday guidance; but there was the ideal example, as some believed, of the early community at Medina, whose members shared the aim of a godly life. In particular, there was the example of Muḥammad himself. It was gradually assumed that he and his close companions lived according to a social code that, if not divinely ordained, was at least in accord with a deep awareness of the commands of God. Could not their behavior be a guide for all men? Even if they were no longer living, it must be possible to collect information, inherited from contemporaries, about their views and behavior. Thus it was that eyewitness accounts, reporting details about Muḥammad and his community at Medina, gradually grew, presumably transmitted from one generation to the next. These short narratives, introduced by the names of the transmitters, or guarantors of their authenticity, are called traditions (*aḥādith;* sing., *ḥadīth*). They reflect the *sunna,* the practice of the Prophet and his companions.

The picture of this small and culturally homogeneous society, as it was reconstructed many generations after its existence, was an idealized one. It was, in fact, an interpretation in terms of the religious attitudes of later times. What is crucial is the process by which the religious scholars living in the great urban centers of the late Umayyad and Abbasid periods arrived at this formulation. Modern scholarship maintains that the development of Islamic law was closely linked to the social, political, and economic conditions of the early Abbasid period, and that positive law was the product of much creative human reasoning, not to mention the influences of other legal systems and the customary law of the areas in which it was formulated.

For some time, law and the administration of justice were generally restricted to the framework of Arabian customary law and the administrative rules created by the Umayyad caliphs. The Koran itself gives relatively little guidance on legal topics, and more frequently its style is to exhort the community, to offer moral injunctions and not legally enforceable ones. Most Muslims took for granted certain other norms, but these were convictions only and not formal rules. In the new urban environment of the military towns and other places where Muslims had settled, disputes were adjudicated by qadis, legal assistants appointed by the provincial governors. These men gave judgment in specific cases, according to their own discretion or individual reasoning. They based their decisions on what had been custom, on their understanding of the Koran, on the administrative regulations, and on their common sense. The result was that in these early times, positive law differed according to the geographical center and had considerable diversity in detail.

About the beginning of the second Muslim century, these and other men interested in problems that affected Muslims increasingly became specialists. Meeting together in informal scholarly circles in Basra and Al-Kufa, Mecca and Medina and Damascus, they now became concerned with applying religious norms to the whole field of law. They began examining acts and institutions in the light of general Koranic teaching, and evaluating the locally determined legal rules accordingly.

At the same time, there emerged two important features that dominated the development of Islamic law throughout the century. The first was the result of the gradual growth of agreement on legal doctrine in each urban center or "school," the *ijmā^c* (consensus, or average opinion of the majority of the center's scholars). The second was the belief among the scholars of each center that the local doctrine had continuity with the past, that it represented the well-established precedent *(sunna)* and the normative, ideal doctrine—when in fact it represented actual local custom and judicial decisions with an overlay of Koranic values. In this belief, they invoked the authority of earlier generations of scholars to provide a stronger foundation for their legal thought and to lend authenticity to the continuity of transmission. After a series of backward steps, it was inevitable that the ultimate authority of the Prophet himself should be claimed. Thus local tradition became transformed into the ideal tradition of the early community at Medina, and the practice of each local school was now called the *sunna* of the Prophet.

Concurrently, groups in opposition to the local schools arose to claim that it was not enough to derive rules of law from the general teaching of Muhammad or the example of his companions. These "Traditionists" rejected the systematic reasoning of the schools and insisted on *ahādīth* alone as the basis for legal decisions. In this way the activities of circulating, collecting, and preserving traditions came about. A small core of genuine traditions may have existed, but these were submerged in the flood of fictitious ones, some reflecting local customary law, some foreign law, some private interests. At first, the early legal scholars tried to reduce their effect by interpretation, but in general they tended to accept traditions insofar as these agreed with their own doctrines. In the course of time, traditions became more detailed and the attached chains of authorities transmitting the texts were made fuller and more consistent. Many traditions expressed opposing or disparate views, reflecting those of rival groups or of different geographical locations. Eventually the knowledge embodied in these traditions—which not only were legal but in fact were comprehensive in their subject matter—came to be considered by devout Muslims as the highest kind of knowledge. Vast numbers of people traveled far and wide to seek them out, to hear them personally from individuals who had preserved them in their memories. Many felt that seeking traditions was the most pious activity. No less important, the wide and intensive pursuit of this knowledge encouraged a new kind of cultural and religious homogeneity among Muslims.

A new science arose whose object was the collection, sifting, and authenticating of traditions, as well as the establishment of a generally accepted corpus. The traditions may fall short of historical accuracy in reporting the actual decisions of the Prophet, but in a rough way they preserve and represent the body of opinion of the religious scholars of the period, for what was not acceptable to their own system of values was rejected.

After approximately the year 770, individual scholars began to record their opinions and technical analyses of the legal subject matter. Sometimes these were based on traditions, sometimes on their own discretionary reasoning. Some scholars attracted influential personal disciples who carried on and elaborated their views. Four names represent the four schools of law surviving today within the Sunni world: Mālik ibn Anas of Medina (*d.* 795); Abū Ḥanīfa of Al-Kufa (*d.* 767); Shāfi^cī (*d.* 820), who lived in several centers; and Aḥmad ibn Ḥanbal of Baghdad (*d.* 855). Schools now became associated with the name of an individual, as they are today, rather than with a locality.

Until Shāfi^cī became active, Islamic law was pervaded by diversity of doctrine and rivalry among the local schools, each of which claimed to have the true code of conduct. Moreover, those who supported the use of reason were in uneasy compromise with those who insisted on the precedents of the Prophet. It was Muḥammad ibn Idrīs al-Shāfiᶜī who imposed unity by formulating a coherent and brilliant legal theory.

The basis of Shāfiᶜī's jurisprudence was the identification of the sunna not with the local practice, nor even with the practice of the early community at Medina, but with Muḥammad's acts only, as expressed in the traditions. Because the Koran commands Muslims to obey God and his Prophet, Muḥammad's legal decisions, he asserted, are divinely inspired. Earlier, Muḥammad had always been a human interpreter; Mālik, for example, could reject a tradition in favor of local usage. But Shāfiᶜī now made Muḥammad's decisions the source of the divine will. Furthermore, according to Shāfiᶜī it is the traditions that reveal how to interpret the Koran, not the other way around, giving them overriding importance in the scheme of legal sources.

The principle of the consensus of the local scholars was transformed by Shāfiᶜī into the agreement of all the faithful, thus emptying it of practical importance. His purpose, as part of his effort to eliminate diversity in the law, was to deny the consensus of a particular locality. But shortly after his time the old idea was revived—that if the majority of scholars were agreed on a point of law or conscience, it was considered binding on the whole community. This has remained the keystone of classical theory, and in Sunni Islam it is the final infallible authority.

Shāfiᶜī's insistence on strict systematic reasoning, and his repudiation of its more arbitrary forms, completed his theory of jurisprudence. New decisions were now to be made by drawing analogies to rules already established by the Koran and *sunna*. This method of analogical (in logic, syllogistic) reasoning, called *qiyās*, is governed by complex and rigidly defined rules, and was meant to reduce differences to a minimum. In fact, however, discretionary reasoning was subtly reintroduced by most schools alongside *qiyās* under such concepts as equity, juristic preference, and the public interest, in the continuing attempt to respond creatively to social needs.

Shāfiᶜī established balance and uniformity, and with some modifications his ideas governed jurisprudence. Positive law continued to be elaborated within each school. It was recorded in the handbooks and commentaries on the works of the masters, and in the works of many subdisciplines within Islamic law; these became the core of higher studies

everywhere. Diversity of views continued to prevail, not only among schools but also among individuals within each school. A Muslim follows the doctrine of one school in all its details. This is normally the one that is dominant where he lives, because for a variety of historical reasons, the courts in different parts of the Muslim world gradually came to apply the positive law of one particular school. Thus, broadly speaking, Ḥanafī law became established in the Middle East, central Asia, and the Indian subcontinent; Shāfiᶜī law in east Africa, southern Arabia, and throughout Indonesia, Malaysia, and the rest of southeast Asia; and Maliki law in northern, western, and central Africa, and in Islamic Spain. While the tradition-bound Hanbali school did not have adherents in widespread geographical areas, it exerted an intellectual influence on important thinkers and is today officially recognized in Saudi Arabia.

Islam does not insist on absolute uniformity in the law. Since man cannot always know the will of God in the elaboration of the basic precepts, legal thinking is necessarily based on what is most probable, rather than on what is certain. Thus, the differences among schools on a given point of law or conscience are judged to be alternative interpretations of what is not explicit in God's commands. By consensus, then, the Sunni schools recognize one another's doctrines as equally valid.

If divine revelation is the fixed and constant element in Islamic law, then the reasoning of the jurists, their approach to law, has been historically the variable and fluctuating element. Creative solutions continued to be pursued as scholars debated issues. Thus the solid structure of the law that was built up in early Abbasid times, governing the whole field of ethics, ritual, and private and public behavior, formed the most important institution in Islamic society, guaranteeing the unity of Islam everywhere.

BIBLIOGRAPHY

Robert Brunschvig, "Logic and Law in Classical Islam," in G. E. von Grünebaum, ed., *Logic in Classical Islamic Culture* (1970); N. J. Coulson, *A History of Islamic Law* (1964); Ignaz Goldziher, *The Zahiris: Their Doctrine and Their History*, Wolfgang Behn, trans. and ed. (1971), and *Introduction to Islamic Theology and Law*, Andras Hamori and Ruth Hamori, trans. and eds. (1981), with intro. and additional notes by Bernard Lewis; George Hourani, "The Basis of Authority of Consensus in Sunnite Islam," in *Studia islamica*, **21** (1964); Herbert J. Liebesny, *The Law of the Near and Middle East: Readings, Cases, Materials* (1975), 129–209, selections from recent legislation; Joseph Schacht, *The Origins of Muhammadan Juris-*

prudence (1950, rev. and enl. 1967), and *Introduction to Islamic Law* (1964); Bernard Weiss, "Interpretation in Islamic Law: The Theory of *ijtihad*," in *American Journal of Comparative Law,* **26** (1978).

JEANETTE A. WAKIN

[See also **Abū Ḥanīfa; Family, Islamic; Fasting, Islamic; Ḥadīth; Ḥanbal, Aḥmad ibn Muḥammad ibn; Islam, Religion; Koran; Mālik ibn Anas; Qadi; Shāfiᶜī, al-; Sunna; Warfare, Islamic.**]

LAW, JEWISH. The term "Jewish law," in its widest sense, is synonymous with the Hebrew *Halakhah* and embraces all the normative rules of Judaism, both those connected with man's relationship to God (which nowadays are usually called "religious norms" in the sense of *fas* or *ius divinum*) and those governing a man's relations with his fellow men or with society ("legal norms," in the sense of *jus* or *ius humanum*). The term "Halakhah" is used in contradistinction to "Haggadah," which is part of Judaism treating morals, ethics, and philosophy and which serves as an ideological and philosophical background for the Halakhah.

In the sources of the Halakhah there is no separate term for the legal norms (the "judgments" [*mishpatim*] of Exodus 21:1 refer to all sections of the Halakhah, as is evident from the continuation in chapters 21 and 22). This is because all the norms of Judaism, whether "religious" or "legal," stem from one source—the written Torah (that is, the Pentateuch) and the oral law (that is, the totality of Jewish tradition). Throughout all sections of the Halakhah the same creative methodology, canons of interpretation, logic, and terminology are applied. Similarly, many principles are applied identically in both the "religious" and "legal" parts of the system. For example, the same laws of agency apply to matters of Temple consecration, tithes, and ritual slaughter, as well as to matters of marriage, divorce, and modes of acquisition. The very principal-agent relationship is derived in the Talmud from scriptural verses treating the Paschal lamb and tithes; and the first time it is mentioned in the Mishnah concerns the precentor representing the congregation at prayer. Frequently, "religious" rules are based on "legal" norms, and occasionally they supplement them. For example, a rabbinical enactment adopted in the town of Usha in the second century provided that a man must support his children until the age of six. The courts, however, coerced parents to support older children on the basis of a principle in the laws of charity that a person can be compelled to give charity if he can afford to and if there is a pauper who needs it. The fact that all parts of the Halakhah stem from a common source also influenced the question of the relationship between law and morality; although Jewish law recognizes a substantive distinction between legal norms, which are accompanied by sanctions, and moral norms, which cannot be enforced, both types of laws shared a special, reciprocal relationship. Occasionally the legal system itself—as well as the courts in their rulings—refers to moral norms as such, and sometimes over time a moral norm is transformed into a legal norm that can be enforced with sanctions.

At the beginning of the twentieth century, the term *mishpat ivri* (Hebrew law) came to refer to that part of the Halakhah usually included in contemporary legal systems. The new name was coined in order to delineate the parameters of scientific legal research as well as those of that section of the Halakhah that would be necessary for application in the Jewish state. The name *mishpat ivri* continues to be used in both of those contexts; in this article, the terms "*mishpat ivri*" and "Jewish law" are used interchangeably.

Notwithstanding the general unity of the Halakhah, a clear distinction is made between matters involving money (*mamona*) and prohibitions regarding ritual law (*issura*). Although this differentiation is not identical to that between "legal" rules and "religious" rules, it did have a decisive influence on the special development of the part of the Halakhah included in *mishpat ivri*. The distinction first appeared in the first century, in the days of Bet Hillel and Bet Shammai, the two great schools of jurisprudence, and over the centuries it became firmly entrenched. For example, in matters involving money the parties have freedom of stipulation even if their stipulation contradicts a rule of Torah, because it is assumed that from the outset the Torah did not establish its civil norms as *ius cogens* but rather as dependent on the will of the parties to the transaction, *ius dispositivum*, except if the stipulation causes injury to a person's freedom or the public welfare. Similarly a contract entered into for a lawful purpose is recognized and enforced by the court even if a transgression was committed in drawing it up, for example, if it was written on the Sabbath, contrary to the rule *ex turpi causa non oritur actio* (a cause of action does not arise from a base claim). Also, different decisional rules are applied to ritual matters and legal matters and no analogy may be made from one to the other.

THE BASIC NORM
AND THE SOURCES OF JEWISH LAW

In Jewish law, as in other systems, the term "sources of law" has three connotations: literary sources, historical sources, and legal sources.

The literary sources. These serve as an authoritative and recognized repository of Jewish law, and are recognized as such by Jewish law. The Pentateuch is the source of the authority delegated throughout the system. It also constitutes the primary authoritative source—both chronologically and in importance—from which the system can be known. The literary source that follows the Pentateuch is comprised of the books of the prophets and the Hagiographa. A significant portion of what we know about Jewish law in that period is derived from contemporary legal and general literature. Later literary sources of Jewish law include the Aramaic translations of Scripture, the halakhic midrashim, and the Mishnah, which was redacted in Palestine at the end of the second century and constitutes the *corpus iuris* of Jewish law after the Pentateuch. The sages of the mishnaic period, known as tannaim (sing., tanna), also authored the Tosephta, the *baraitot* in both Talmuds and *Megillat Taᶜanit*. These sources were followed by the Jerusalem Talmud, redacted in Palestine at the end of the fourth century, and the Babylonian Talmud, redacted in Babylonia a century later. The sages of both Talmuds are called amoraim (sing., amora). The Babylonian Talmud was given its final redaction and sealed by scholars known as savoraim (sing., savora), who were active until the end of the sixth century (or, according to some scholars, until the middle of the seventh century).

The historical sources. These sources supply the economic, social, and moral background that led to the creation of legal norms. It is exceedingly difficult to identify a clear, unequivocal historical cause for a legal norm, and most suggestions in this area must be classified as speculation.

The legal sources. These are the ways and means by which Jewish law itself gives force to a legal norm. In Jewish law there are six such sources: (1) tradition (cabala), the authoritative transmission that began with Moses, who received it from God (Mishnah *Avot* 1:1). This source, by definition, is not given to development or change; (2) interpretation (midrash), exegesis of the Pentateuch and of laws that de-

veloped in the various periods—from which new laws emerge. In time, interpretation of documents and communal enactments was added; (3) enactments and decrees (*takkanot* and *gezerot*) are the legislation of authorized halakhic bodies or of authorized communal bodies; (4) custom and usage (*minhag*); (5) case and precedent (*maᶜaseh*), principles drawn from the decisions in a specific case or from the behavior of an authority; (6) legal logic (*sevarah*), the human logic of the halakhists, such as the principle that the onus of proof lies on the claimant. The last five sources are recognized by Jewish law as legitimate ways to solve new problems and to change previously existing norms in the light of social, economic, and moral developments. In this manner Jewish law simultaneously regulates life and is influenced by it, while showing its constant concern for the continued creativity of the Halakhah and bearing the great responsibility for the preservation of its spirit. This mission is the sole preserve of the halakhic authorities of every generation (see Deuteronomy 17:9–12 and *Sifrei* on those verses) in accordance with the doctrine that "the court of Jephthah is as authoritative as the court of the prophet Samuel" (the Babylonian Talmud, *Rosh Ha-Shanah* 25b)—although the latter was far more erudite, learned, and pious than the former. Superhuman power, such as prophecy or "voices from heaven" (*bat kol*), has no authority in halakhic decision or creativity.

Thus, regarding the sources and the basic norm, or *grundnorm*, of Jewish law, everything in the Pentateuch is of binding force. This norm is evident in the substance of the Pentateuch and is the immutable constitution of Jewish law. It is the valid source of authority for the whole system; it delegates, in the form of the legal sources of Jewish law, the valid methods for its development and creativity. The source of the binding authority of this basic norm itself is beyond the scope of jurisprudence; it belongs to the realm of faith. The basic dogma of Judaism is that the Torah's authority flows from God, who gave it, and that it represents his will. In the passage from Deuteronomy referred to above and in additional passages of the Torah, the sages of the Halakhah discovered the methods (that is, the legal sources) by which to ensure the ongoing vitality of Jewish law.

THE POST-TALMUDIC PERIOD

The nature of talmudic law as opposed to post-talmudic law. Jewish literature has a history of more than three millennia, which is divided into two general periods: the period through the conclusion of the Talmud and the period after it. However, as far as the continued development of the Halakhah is concerned, this periodization is of no great significance. Jewish law not only continued to develop after the Talmud, but in many areas of creativity became even more intense both quantitatively and in the literary methods of creativity. The talmudic period is special for the authenticity that Judaism attributes to talmudic Halakhah—the interpretation of the oral law—and the conclusions to be drawn from it. "All Jewry agreed to it," wrote Maimonides in the introduction to his *Mishneh Torah*. The Pentateuch remains the constitution of the Halakhah, but the Mishnah, the two Talmuds, and the other halakhic literature of the period are the direct source for the study of the law and its application. Talmudic law has maintained this special status even after the composition—over some fifteen centuries—of a wide and ramified literature that, from the point of view of scope, arrangement, and convenience of use, is superior to talmudic literature. The special status of talmudic literature affords great possibilities of maneuver for deciding the law in the post-talmudic period. If a judge, in examining each case in the light of talmudic law, can find a basis for his conclusion by using the accepted talmudic methodology, then his decision is legitimate. This is true even if it contradicts other post-talmudic authorities, since those do not have the force of binding precedent (according to Asher ben Jehiel, *ca.* 1250–1327). Similarly, it was the talmudic sages who established the forms of halakhic logic, expression, legal sources, and methodology that defined the guidelines for the ongoing creativity and development of Jewish law.

The gaonic period. The period after the conclusion of the Talmud is divided into two main subperiods. The first of them is the period of the geonim (sing., gaon), which extended from the seventh century to the middle of the eleventh century. The appellation "gaon" was the official title of the heads of the academies (*yeshivot;* sing., *yeshiva*) in the towns of Sura and Pumbedita in Babylonia. During most of the gaonic period, the Babylonian academies wielded spiritual hegemony over all world Jewry and most Jewish communities accepted their important decisions in the various branches of *mishpat ivri* as binding. The Babylonian geonim established the Babylonian Talmud as the authoritative source of Halakhah for all Jews. One can already discern at that time the beginnings of the tripartite division in

post-talmudic halakhic literature: commentaries and novellae, codes, and responsa, a division that still exists.

Because of internal Jewish developments as well as changing external conditions, the connections between the Babylonian geonim and the Jews of North Africa and Spain became progressively weaker. From the middle of the eleventh century the phenomenon of one center holding spiritual sway over the Jewish Diaspora—as had also been the case earlier when Palestine was that center—came to an end, and the individual Jewish centers began to turn to their own leadership or occasionally to that of a neighboring center. This fragmentation greatly influenced the subsequent development of Jewish law and led to the new phenomenon of a multiplicity of local customs and laws, which differed from center to center and even from community to community within one region. The gaonic period also marks an important development in the adoption of enactments by the geonim and their academies in various branches of *mishpat ivri.*

The rabbinic period: commentaries and novellae, codes, and responsa. Following the period of the geonim is the rabbinic period, which is usually divided into three subperiods: that of the early scholars, that of the later scholars, and, in modern times, the period of the abrogation of Jewish judicial autonomy. The period of the early scholars, or "first ones;" (*rishonim,* sing., *rishon*), extending from the middle of the eleventh century until the sixteenth century, saw the creation of the classic works in all three genres of post-talmudic halakhic literature: commentaries and novellae, codes, and responsa.

The commentaries explain talmudic texts in order to facilitate their study and understanding. The commentary par excellence on the Babylonian Talmud is that of Solomon ben Isaac (known as Rashi), who lived in northern France and Germany in the eleventh century. The novellae literature compares associated and cognate passages of the Talmud and the commentaries and attempts to resolve contradictions between them, thus yielding new commentaries and halakhic principles. The prime example in this genre is the work of the tosafists, who were active mainly in Germany and France during the twelfth and thirteenth centuries. In the genre of commentary and novella in this period, the talmudists of Spain and southern France were noteworthy as well.

Most of the great codes of Jewish law were compiled in this period, which was also witness to deep and incisive discussions as to the role of codification in Jewish law and the appropriate methodology to be adopted. Some of the codes are arranged according to the order of the tractates of the Talmud and present a condensed discussion of the talmudic passage under consideration followed by the authors' legal decision. Examples include *Sefer ha-Halakhot* of Isaac Alfasi (eleventh century) of North Africa and Spain and *Piskei ha-Rosh* of Asher ben Jehiel of Germany and Spain. In this manner the connection between the codes and the talmudic sources was maintained. Other codes were arranged thematically according to legal subjects. These include *Mishneh Torah* of Maimonides (Spain and Egypt, twelfth century); *Sefer ha-Turim* of Jacob ben Asher (Germany and Spain, fourteenth century); *Shulḥan Arukh* of Joseph Caro (Spain, Turkey, Palestine, sixteenth century).

From the point of view of codification per se, Maimonides' *Mishneh Torah* is the greatest and most important creation. It is the only code that embraces the totality of the Halakhah, including even laws that were no longer applicable in the author's time and that were not treated in the other codes, such as the laws relating to sacrifices and the Temple and the laws of ritual purity and impurity. Maimonides was the first to collect all the laws scattered throughout talmudic and gaonic literature and classify them under headings and subheadings. The code is written in a pure Hebrew style, unadulterated with Aramaic—unlike the rest of halakhic literature. Maimonides' most audacious innovation was to present only the opinion with which he agreed (excluding the many others), recording it anonymously and without indicating its talmudic source. He justified his method by claiming that he intended to introduce uniformity into the Halakhah and prevent the proliferation of different opinions and approaches. Nevertheless, it aroused fierce opposition from contemporary and subsequent halakhists. His critics charged that his method threatened Jewish law by severing it from its talmudic sources. Furthermore, they opined that it hampered the judge, since it was specifically the multiplicity of opinions that afforded great latitude in decision making—the judge could return to the talmudic sources to find a basis for the decision which the specific case before him required.

The most extreme of Maimonides' critics was his older contemporary Abraham ben David of Posquières in southern France, who composed critiques on *Mishneh Torah* in which he attacked its approach and frequently disagreed with its specific halakhic conclusions. The latter's view came to be accepted, and thus the Halakhah preserved one of its unique and important characteristics—pluralism of opinion and approach, which allowed wide maneuverability within the framework of the Halakhah. Maimonides' monumental code, which had intended to unify Jewish law, instead engendered hundreds of commentaries, both pro and con, a phenomenon that again led to a great proliferation of different opinions and approaches.

In order to preserve the special nature of Jewish law, Joseph Caro first composed a commentary, *Bet Yosef*, on Jacob ben Asher's *Sefer ha-Turim*. In it he cites all the opinions on every subject and names their authors and their sources. It was only after he had written this, his main work, that he composed *Shulḥan Arukh*, a digest of his decisions. Moses Isserles of Poland (sixteenth century) followed the same path, first composing a major commentary, *Darkhei Moshe* on *Sefer ha-Turim*, and only afterward writing his glosses on *Shulḥan Arukh*. Caro's *Shulḥan Arukh*, with Isserles' glosses, still stands as the definitive binding code of Halakhah and a summary of talmudic law through the sixteenth century. In the course of subsequent generations, hundreds of commentaries were written on *Shulḥan Arukh* which explain its text, indicate the talmudic sources on which it draws, support or oppose its decisions, and supplement it with material composed after it was written. Thus was preserved the continuity with the Talmud.

The responsa literature (*sheʾelot u-teshuvot*) contains the decisions and conclusions written by halakhic authorities in answer to questions that were addressed to them in writing. This literature constitutes the case law of *mishpat ivri*. Reponsa became a separate genre of halakhic literature in the eighth century and are still being written today. (It is estimated that some 300,000 responsa exist.) Disputes between individuals were usually brought before their local court; if the judge of that court had difficulty reaching a decision he forwarded the question to one of the recognized halakhists of the region. Cases involving matters of principle, as well as litigation between an individual and the community or between two communities, were usually referred to such an authority in the first instance.

The responsa literature constitutes the main material of Jewish law in the post-talmudic period. Its study reveals how Jewish law developed as well as its great creativity in all its areas and branches. To some degree the responsa can be likened to the *responsa prudentium* of Roman law and, as far as their authority and creative power is concerned, even more so to the *fatwā* of Muslim law. The responsa literature also reveals the essential nature of Jewish law. The main creativity of *mishpat ivri* lies in decisions rendered in real cases and not in the establishment of abstract principles. This afforded the halakhists great maneuverability and flexibility; they could draw an analogy from, or make a distinction between, previous decisions and the case before them and thus arrive at an appropriate verdict. In this aspect, Jewish law is very much like the Anglo-Saxon system; both are made up in large part of "judge-made" law. In the English system the decisions are collected in the *Law Reports;* in Jewish law after the Talmud, in the various collections of responsa. Through the fifteenth century the activity flourished in Spain, Germany, France, and North Africa, and afterward—with the decline of the Spanish center—in many other centers, not only in North Africa but also in Italy, the Balkan countries, Turkey, Egypt, Palestine, Poland, and Lithuania.

Great creative activity continued in the period under discussion in all areas of Jewish law by way of enactments *(takkanot)*, which were adopted in various ways: (1) by various halakhic authorities such as Rabbenu Gershom (the "Light of the Exile") in Germany at the end of the tenth century, Meir of Rothenberg and Perez of Corbeil in Germany and France respectively in the thirteenth century, Jacob Weil and Israel Bruna in Germany in the fifteenth century, and various halakhists in other centers; (2) at conventions attended by the outstanding rabbis of a particular center, such as the convention in Troyes in the twelfth century which was attended by Samuel ben Meir and his brother Rabbenu Tam, two of the greatest tosafists, and the conventions convened at the beginning of the thirteenth century. The legislation adopted by the latter is known as "The Enactments of Shum." ("Shum" is an acronym for the three towns represented, Speyer, Worms, and Mainz.) Other rabbinical conventions were held in various locations in Italy, Spain, and North Africa; and (3) by way of communal enactments adopted by the lay communal leaders, usually with the participation of the halakhic authorities or with their blessing.

The period following that of the early scholars, known as that of the later scholars *(aharonim)*, lasted until the onset of Emancipation and the cessation of Jewish judicial autonomy at the end of the eighteenth century. The tripartite creativity in ha-

lakhic literature continued during this period, and the responsa literature reached its peak as far as quantity is concerned. The main collections of communal enactments that have survived date from this period.

In addition to the literary sources described above, others were created in the post-talmudic period. Among these should be listed: collections of deeds, which include the formulations in use in various fields of the law; introductions to the Talmud and the Halakhah (the first was the tenth-century epistle of Sherira Gaon); encyclopedias (such as *Pahad Yizhak* by Isaac Lamproti of Italy, in the eighteenth century); biographies of great halakhists; bibliographies of halakhic works; and lexicons and dictionaries such as *Arukh* by Nathan ben Jehiel of Rome, in the late eleventh century (supplemented in the nineteenth century by Alexander Kohut's *He-Arukh ha-Shalem*). However, as has been shown, the Talmud always remained the central source, and the entire subsequent halakhic literature was created with reference to it and as a continuation of it.

THE PRACTICAL APPLICATION OF JEWISH LAW

The great growth of Jewish legal literature in the post-talmudic period was not the result of abstract and theoretical study, but came about because until the end of the eighteenth century Jewish law was a living and relevant system according to which Jewish communities throughout the world regulated their affairs. For most of the long history of Jewish law, the Jewish people did not enjoy political sovereignty; they lived outside their homeland, the land of Israel, scattered throughout the world without a unified center. Nevertheless, the Jews enjoyed judicial autonomy, and, indeed, the main creations and developments of Jewish law—the Babylonian Talmud and the post-talmudic literature—occurred in exile. This phenomenon is explained by internal and external factors.

The internal explanation for the ongoing creativity of Jewish law lies in its national-religious character. Its source is revelation, and just as the Jew is obliged to observe the "religious" commandments, so too is he obliged in the Torah itself to keep the "legal" commandments that apply to all other areas of human intercourse. *Mishpat ivri* was also the national law of the Jewish people and its entire development is the creation of that people, as opposed to canon law or Moslem law, each of which was created by believers of various nations. The Jewish people continued to exist in exile as a nation and not as a religious sect or denomination; thus it uninterruptedly needed its national heritage to express itself in all areas of life.

The Bible mandated the establishment and operation of a judicial system by a direct, positive commandment (Exod. 18:21–27; Deut. 16:18). Throughout the dispersion, the Diaspora, from the Babylonian exile to the period of Emancipation, the court (bet din) was the cornerstone of Jewish autonomy. Rabbis and communal leaders imposed strict internal discipline to prevent Jews from resorting to non-Jewish courts; great efforts were made to persuade the general authorities to grant the Jewish communities privileges that would ensure their judicial autonomy and the right to enforce the decisions of the Jewish courts by coercion. Such jurisdiction covered most areas of civil law (ownership, obligations, torts, personal status, and succession) and areas of public administrative law connected with the regulation of local government, such as elections, taxes and their collection, and the relationship between the individual and the community. In many places judicial autonomy even included criminal law, although its scope and methods of execution varied with the time and place. In certain centers, the Jewish courts were empowered to impose capital punishment, particularly on informers.

This judicial activity is amply attested in the responsa literature up to the sixteenth century. Approximately 60 percent of that literature treats civil, administrative, and criminal law; some 20 percent is devoted to family law and only another 20 percent to religious law (such as prayer, festivals, and dietary laws). In the seventeenth and eighteenth centuries the proportion of the responsa on religious matters increased somewhat; and in the nineteenth century, with the abrogation of judicial autonomy, a drastic change occurred—from then on the overwhelming majority of the responsa dealt with religious matters and family law.

The usual methods of enforcing the courts' decisions were expropriation of property, fines, and physical punishment; some communities maintained their own prisons. At times the Jewish community had to apply to the non-Jewish authorities for help in executing court decisions and imposing penalties, particularly with regard to capital punishment. The proclamation of a ban (ḥerem) on the recalcitrant was an accepted form of coercion and was perhaps one of the most effective. It was needed because the Jewish community lacked political sovereignty and, therefore, the usual means of enforcement. The na-

ture of the ban and its severity varied from place to place and according to the crime and the degree of coercion required. To a greater or lesser degree the banned person was excluded from the religious and civil life of the community, a punishment considered to be so grievous that many halakhic authorities refrained from imposing it except in the most serious cases.

The prohibition against a Jew resorting to a non-Jewish court is a prime manifestation of the religious-national character of Jewish law. The prohibition originated soon after the destruction of the Temple and applied even if the foreign tribunal's law was identical to Jewish law. To transgress this prohibition was to be likened to "one who has blasphemed and cursed [God] and raised his hand against the Torah of Moses" (Maimonides, Yad, Laws of Sanhedrin 26:7). Notwithstanding the freedom of stipulation afforded in civil matters, most halakhic authorities believe that the prohibition applies even if the parties to the litigation agree otherwise and, similarly, that the principle "the law of the land is law" (dina de-malkhuta dina) does not apply with regard to this matter. Bowing to necessity, Paltoi Gaon in the ninth century allowed that the Jewish court could permit recourse to an alien court if the defendant was a violent and powerful man who could not be coerced into appearing before a Jewish court. At times recourse to non-Jewish courts was also permitted in matters of special interest to the general authorities—cases involving real property, taxes, coinage, and other such issues. On the whole, however, the prohibition was observed meticulously, an obedience encouraged by severe sanctions.

Arbitration and lay tribunals. The halakhic authorities strove to preserve Jewish judicial institutions of arbitration and lay tribunals, even if their rulings were only tenuously based on Jewish law—again, to prevent recourse to non-Jewish tribunals. In Jewish law arbitration is known from the second half of the second century, when the autonomy of Jewish courts was temporarily curtailed. Rather than sanction recourse to non-Jewish courts, the sages referred litigants to arbitration courts, on which even "cattle herdsman," who judged according to their own understanding of the matter, could sit. The arbitration tribunal was composed of three arbitrators, similar to the bet din, on which at least three judges sat, and not, as was usually practiced in Roman law, of a single arbitrator. The institution of lay tribunals may have begun before the destruction of the Second Temple in 70; some scholars believe it started after the Bar Kokhba rebellion of 132. Such a tribunal, too, was composed of three persons; at least one of them was required to be "somewhat learned," and the others had to have the capacity to understand a matter when it was explained to them. The tribunal was authorized to coerce the parties to appear before it and had jurisdiction in all areas of civil law, but not in criminal law. With a view to preventing recourse to non-Jewish courts, the requirement that at least one member be "somewhat learned" was dispensed with in special circumstances as long as the magistrates were "good men who fear God and despise ill-gotten gain and who are possessed of sound sense." In special circumstances such lay tribunals were given jurisdiction even in criminal cases (*Resp. Rashba*, vol. 2, no. 290). Lay tribunals functioned in most Jewish centers alongside the regular courts, which heard most cases. The lay tribunals judged according to communal enactments, commercial custom, assessment, and their innate sense of equity and justice. In some matters they even made use of foreign laws on occasion, and they frequently turned to the halakhic scholars for advice and opinion. The field of taxation was usually within their jurisdiction, and occasionally an a priori division of jurisdiction between them and the regular courts was made. The halakhic authorities were well aware of the dangers of judging solely according to a sense of justice and assessment, particularly since the weaker segments of society were not represented on such tribunals, and they frequently warned their communities against the negative manifestations.

The external factors bearing on the growth of Jewish legal literature in the post-talmudic period are rooted in the attitude of the general authorities to Jewish judicial autonomy, which must be understood in the light of legal and political theory current until the eighteenth century. Legal systems dealt with individuals according to their personal and group affiliations, and the state recognized the jurisdiction of the legal systems of the various ethnic, social, and religious groups living within its borders. During the Middle Ages, the states were corporate in nature. As they were composed of diverse autonomous estates or bodies, such as the aristocracy, burghers, and guilds, the situation allowed for the existence of an autonomous Jewish "estate" as well. In giving the Jews autonomy, the secular authorities were moved by various motives, including a degree of tolerance toward other religions (under Muslim rule), reasons of theology, and, mainly, financial considerations. The general authorities and the estates

saw it as their duty and privilege to impose heavy taxes on the Jews as payment for the right to live among them. Usually, for reasons of convenience, the taxes were imposed on the community as a whole and not on its individual members. This state of affairs necessitated an autonomous Jewish community whose leaders could then be held responsible for collection of the taxes. The scholar Yeḥezkel Kaufmann wrote: "It was judicial autonomy which caused the Jewish people in exile to be truly a state within a state. . . . Jewish autonomy was, in essence, judicial autonomy" (*Golah ve-Nekhar* 1:518, 2:312).

CREATIVITY AND CHANGE

The processes of creativity and development in Jewish law are reflected differently in the different legal branches. In some of the areas, such as family law and succession, criminal law, procedural law, and the law of evidence, the process did not substantially affect the actual framework or content, notwithstanding the far-reaching novelties that had been introduced. Of such novelties it is sufficient to mention the enactments of Rabbenu Gershom prohibiting polygamy and divorce against the wife's will and the Spanish (fourteenth century) and North African (fifteenth century) enactments granting rights of inheritance to unmarried daughters equal to those of sons, and permitting testimony from relatives or interested parties if, in the view of the court, they were truthful, and circumstantial evidence even in criminal hearings, as well as self-incrimination, given willingly and corroborated.

Certain areas of Jewish law changed more substantively with regard to both classification and content, for example, the laws of obligation. Jewish law unequivocally and in principle forbids seizure of an obligor's person in order to collect an obligation. Instead, the obligee is given, at the moment the obligation is created, an automatic lien on all the property of the obligor. As a result many of the laws of acquisition, such as the rule that a nonexistent article or one outside the domain or control of the vendor cannot be sold, were also applied to obligations. Over time, substantive changes were gradually instituted: obligation could be established whether or not the obligor had possessions and even if the possessions were not yet in existence, thus transforming the obligation into a personal obligation, with the existence of possessions of secondary importance.

In the post-talmudic period far-reaching and substantive changes were introduced into the laws governing modes of acquisition and the establishment of obligation by way of the legal source, custom. In Jewish law custom serves as the decisive factor when there is a disagreement as to the law and custom follows one of the opinions. It also supplements the law when a problem arises for which the existing law offers no solution. In civil law, custom can even override existing law (contra legem), since the parties to a transaction have freedom of stipulation; and if the entire community follows a specific custom, it is assumed that the parties entered into the transaction on that basis, even against the law. In early Jewish law, modes of acquisition were very formal—the purchaser had to perform the physical act of lifting the item being purchased or pulling it into his domain—which became very cumbersome as commerce developed and became more sophisticated. The Talmud had already ruled that if it was commercial practice to effect a transfer of goods by way of a specific act—such as the purchaser putting his seal on the barrels of wine he was buying—that act was sufficient and there was no need to use one of the more formal modes, although according to strict law the goods remained the property of the vendor. In the post-talmudic period, Jewish law applied this principle widely, such that any act for effecting a transfer of goods or establishing an obligation that conformed to current commercial practice—such as a handshake, payment of a deposit, or the transfer of keys—was considered valid. From the thirteenth century on, even a verbal agreement alone was considered sufficient, if such was accepted commercial practice.

Other manifestations of change are evident in public administrative law, in which all the central features are post-talmudic. In ancient times Jews related to an individual ruler, such as the king and later the patriarch in Palestine and the exilarch in Babylonia. Beginning in the tenth century, when no one center any longer enjoyed spiritual hegemony over the whole Jewish Diaspora, the power and independence of the communities increased. The government of a community, or a federation of communities, was now vested in a collective body that was either appointed or elected. The new conditions created many legal problems that talmudic law had not addressed, such as whether the majority could force the minority to abide by its decisions, and questions concerning the relationship of members of a community to its institutions, the composition of the institutions, franchise, appointments and legislation by the community, the management of the communal institutions, and tax assessment and col-

lection. As a result, an entirely new and comprehensive branch of Jewish administrative law came into being. The community, or its representatives, was given the authority to adopt—by a majority vote—enactments in all areas of civil, criminal, and public law (but not religious law); those enactments were binding on all members of that community, even if the enactments, in one matter or the other, contradicted the established provisions of Jewish law. In ancient Jewish law, such extra-halakhic legislative authority had been given to the king. Many halakhists compared the status of the community to that of the court, which is authorized to adopt enactments that change the existing law if the circumstances warrant it. However, under no circumstances could the enactments diverge from standards of proper public order or from the principles of justice and equity of Jewish law. It was for this reason that Solomon ben Abraham Adret invalidated a communal enactment that did away with the position of internal comptroller of community institutions. Similarly, the principle was established that the majority could not, by its decision, negate the basic rights of the minority, since it may not act "in the way of robbers." Thus an enactment which provided that a pauper must pay taxes was overturned at Mainz (thirteenth century), as was one which provided that a wealthy man must pay property tax in his own community on realty held in another community where he also paid taxes, because double taxation is like robbery. Many complete and partial collections of communal enactments have survived the centuries, and the texts of hundreds of enactments have been preserved in the responsa literature, where they are cited in the discussions of the questions posed.

Another example of a new branch in the Jewish legal system is conflict of laws. Although Jewish law applies to all Jews, and, in theory, it is of no halakhic relevance if a contract drawn up in one country is to be executed in another, the reality of geographic dispersion created problems of conflict of laws arising from the proliferation of local enactments and customs and the need to decide among them. The principle that "the law of the land is law" also contributed to this problem.

FACTORS LIMITING THE DEVELOPMENT
OF JEWISH LAW

The fact that from the tenth century on the Jewish people lacked a central spiritual authority whose rulings were binding on all led to some contraction in the development of Jewish law, from the point of view of territoriality and content. From then on the enactments of halakhic authorities were directed only at the Jews of their own regional center; the rabbis did not have the authority to obligate Jews of other centers. The local nature of Jewish legislation was further intensified because a significant part of it, from the tenth century on, was legislated by the community and its leadership by means of communal enactments. By definition, such legislation was limited to the community or group of communities by whom and for whom it had been adopted. The outstanding example of this "territoriality" is Rabbenu Gershom's enactment forbidding polygamy, which reflected the economic and social conditions prevalent in Germany at the end of the tenth century and which was influenced by the general law in those countries which prohibited polygamy. This enactment introduced crucial changes into Jewish family law and was not accepted by large and important oriental Jewish communities until very recently. Many other substantive enactments and decisions met the same fate. This "territoriality" also applied to various decisions on matters of principle which were handed down in Jewish law. Nevertheless, local legislation and local decisions did become an integral part of the Jewish legal system.

Another fundamental change that occurred after the gaonic period and intensified over time was the tendency to refrain from utilizing the legal source of legislation in matters concerning the validity of marriages and divorces that, according to existing Halakhah, were valid. There had always been great legislative activity in this field during all the periods up to and including the gaonic period. Enactments had been adopted that canceled or annulled marriages in certain circumstances, such as improper behavior on the part of the husband, or in order to prevent the wife from becoming "a chained wife" (*agunah*, that is, one whose husband has deserted her, leaving her still married and thus unable to remarry). After the gaonic period—and particularly from the twelfth century on—outstanding halakhic authorities ruled that they no longer had the authority to annul valid marriages. Later most halakhists adopted the attitude that although theoretically it was valid to annul the marriage of one who transgresses, in practice such enactments should not be adopted. Thus, legislation with regard to the validity of marriage and divorce progressively diminished until to all intents and purposes it ceased entirely.

This contraction in legislation was also due mainly to the new historical conditions after the

gaonic era. The fact that legislation had become local raised the very real fear of a proliferation of conflicting enactments that could undermine legal uniformity in the delicate area of family law. While forbearance from legislating in this area of law prevented this undesirable consequence, it also created problems.

CLASSIFICATION OF LEGAL BRANCHES

Jewish law rests on its own set of fundamental principles, as does any other legal system. Sometimes these are unique to Jewish law and reflect its weltanschauung (on questions such as personal freedom and rights, the nature of legal and moral obligations, ownership and the attitude toward it, the nature of justice, and modes of proof), and sometimes they resemble principles in other systems. In view of this, great caution must be exercised against the automatic projection of systems of classification—which are by no means the same in all non-Jewish systems—onto Jewish law. Consideration must also be given to the unique Hebrew terminology. The fact that the detailed classification of Jewish law only started with Maimonides' code (and was used in some of the subsequent codes) adds to the general difficulty of creating categories; and it is still not possible to view any classification as final and definitive.

THE RELATIONSHIP BETWEEN JEWISH LAW AND FOREIGN LAW

There are two aspects to this subject. The first is the degree to which there is a relationship of reciprocity and influence between Jewish law and alien law such that they absorb legal rules from one another. The second aspect involves the recognition by one system of the validity of provisions of another, but without absorbing them. Since the seventeenth century, the problem of mutual influence has been a favorite subject of scholars. Their research is, however, usually tainted by apologetics for one or the other legal system. It is also hampered by the objective difficulty of proving influence, since it is entirely possible that similar circumstances and conditions led Jewish and gentile jurists independently to similar conclusions. However, generally speaking, it can be said that Jewish law was influenced by the law of its surroundings and vice versa. The halakhic authorities were acquainted with non-Jewish law, praised it when its procedure was superior, and occasionally even recommended the adoption of foreign usages. When a foreign principle was taken over, it was "digested" and adapted to the principles and aims of Jewish law, and if it did not fit it was ejected.

The recognition of non-Jewish law by Jewish law is reflected in the legal principle "the law of the land is law," which was first formulated by the amora Samuel in Babylonia in the third century. Various rationales were suggested for this principle in the post-talmudic period, the main one being rooted in the political theory that an agreement exists between the citizens and the ruler according to which the former accept upon themselves the laws of the latter in return for the protection he affords them. Since Jewish law recognizes freedom of stipulation in civil matters even if the stipulation is against Jewish law, such acceptance is valid. Other halakhic jurists explained the principle on the basis of the ancient notion of the "Noahide Laws"—that certain fundamental laws are common to all nations, and Jewish law can, therefore, recognize their validity. However, the principle holds in civil matters only and not in religious or ritual matters. Recognition of alien law could very well have been detrimental to the development of Jewish law since that depended on its ongoing practical application. This was why most halakhists in the post-talmudic period restricted the principle to specific subjects in the field of the relationship between the general government and the community; according to them it did not apply to private, criminal, or internal administrative law, otherwise "all Jewish laws will be abrogated" (*Bet ha-Behirah, Bava Kamma* 113b). Even those halakhists who rejected this limitation were not consistent in their stand, and others found different methods by which to limit the application of the principle.

The great and uninterrupted creativity which continued in the various areas of Jewish law in the post-talmudic period proves that the application of "the law of the land is law" remained marginal and did not damage the operation of the Jewish legal system in practice. Furthermore, by discerning utilization of the principle, the halakhists transformed it into a factor that worked for the preservation of the Jewish legal system, since a limited acceptance of some foreign laws made it possible for the Jewish community to adapt itself as far as was necessary to its non-Jewish surroundings.

Even in the limited areas in which the principle "the law of the land is law" was applied, Jewish law would not recognize the validity of a foreign law if it did not concord with the basic Jewish principles of equity and justice. Therefore, the halakhists ruled that a law promulgated by the king is valid only if it applies to all the citizens of the kingdom without discrimination—otherwise "it is robbery" (Maimonides, *Yad*, Laws of Robbery and Lost Property 5:14). Similarly, the imposition of a fine on the whole community because of the crimes of individuals is "absolute robbery," since Jewish law does not allow collective punishment (*Resp. Rivash ha-Hadashot*, no. 9). This critical attitude led to a state of affairs in which the validity of foreign laws was not only recognized by the Halakhah from time to time, but even absorbed into it.

SUMMARY

The post-talmudic period in Jewish law, from the sixth century to the eighteenth—which more or less corresponds to the Middle Ages in general history—was one of enormous creativity and development, notwithstanding the occasional aberration. This was because for the whole of that period the Jewish people throughout the Diaspora enjoyed judicial autonomy and Jewish law continued to develop uninterruptedly as a functioning system. This is evident from an examination of the Halakhah's response to changing social and economic conditions and the resulting problems, for which the existing law did not provide explicit solutions or for which the accepted solutions were inadequate. Jewish authorities imposed severe internal discipline on their members in order to preserve *mishpat ivri*. Indeed, where recourse to Jewish law declined, its development and creativity also declined. But so long as spiritual creativity depended on practical life, the system developed organically and retained its vitality. This was due to the fact that for the whole of that period the Jewish people throughout the Diaspora enjoyed judicial autonomy and imposed severe internal discipline on its members in order to preserve *mishpat ivri* and live according to its provisions, which were viewed as the practical manifestation of its heritage.

BIBLIOGRAPHY

Salo W. Baron, *The Jewish Community: Its History and Structure to the American Revolution* (1948); Haim Hillel Ben-Sasson, *A History of the Jewish People: The Middle Ages* (1976); Boaz Cohen, *Jewish and Roman Law* (1966); Menachem Elon, *Freedom of the Debtor's Person in Jewish Law* (in Hebrew) (1964), *Jewish Law: History, Sources, and Principles* (in Hebrew), 2nd ed. (1978), idem, ed., *The Principles of Jewish Law* (1975), and *Digest of the Responsa Literature of Spain and North Africa* (Hebrew with English intro.) (1981–); Louis Finkelstein, *Jewish Self-government in the Middle Ages*, rev. ed. (1964); Asher Gulak, *The Fundamentals of Jewish Law* (in Hebrew)

(1922, repr. 1966/1967); Isaac Herzog, *The Main Institutions of Jewish Law* (1936, 2nd ed. 1965–1967); Nathan Isaacs, "Influence of Judaism on Western Law," in Edwyn R. Bevan and C. J. Singer, compilers, *Legacy of Israel* (1927); Kopel Kahana Kagan, *Three Great Systems of Jurisprudence* (1955); Jacob J. Rabinowitz, *Jewish Law: Its Influence on the Development of Legal Institutions* (1956); Moshe Silberg, *Talmudic Law and the Modern State* (1973).

MENACHEM ELON

[See also **Abraham ben David of Posquières; Dietary Laws, Jewish; Exegesis, Jewish; Family and Family Law, Jewish; Gaonic Period; Jacob ben Meir (Rabbenu Tam); Jewish Communal Self-government; Karaites; Maimonides, Moses; Nahmanides, Moses; Rashi (Rabbi Solomon ben Isaac); Responsum Literature, Jewish; Saadiah Gaon; Talmud, Exegesis and Study of.**]

LAW, JEWRY, the corpus of legal and judicial measures evolved by Christian authorities in order to govern relations between Christians and Jews. It was one of the responses given by Christian Europe to the "Jewish problem," the existence of Jewry within a society that defined itself on religious grounds as an organic and uniform *Ecclesia*.

The permanent tensions generated by this contradiction forced the authorities repeatedly to redefine their Jewish policies and take action in the legal-judicial sphere. Jewry law reflects this activity in its local and temporal manifestations. It is highly varied, owing to the different circumstances that affected specific acts, and to the extent of ideological commitment that motivated the authorities in specific cases. It is also highly uniform in essentials, a demonstration of the general character of both the problem that generated it and the legal-judicial solutions adopted. Jewry law affected the evolution of Jewish society in all areas open to contact with Christians. Its impact on Jewish law can be appreciated by the very wide and varied application of the principle "the law of the state is law."

Students of Jewry law usually distinguish between three main types: Roman Jewry law, canon law, and secular law. Each type has its specific machinery of legislation and law enforcement, a more or less coherent body of laws and regulations, and a reasonably clear delimitation of scope and validity. Yet they were never exclusive. They evolved under reciprocal influence and were mutually dependent in that each provided complementary action to the others and needed theirs in return. All three will be found,

in various combinations and variations, and elaborated in subtypes, in any medieval Jewry law.

Roman Jewry law was created in the late Roman empire (fourth to sixth centuries), through legislation and codification. It survived the disintegration of the empire in the West and retained its force thanks to continued legislation and codification in the Germanic kingdoms (Alaric II, Theodoric), the reception of Byzantine texts, and the study and application of Roman law to certain populations (such as the Gallo-Romans) and groups (such as clerics and Jews). Its body of law was preserved in the *Codex Theodosianus* and its epitomes, the *Codex Justinianus* and Justinian's *Novellae* with their translations, epitomes, and commentaries, and the *Breviarium Alarici*.

The gradual weakening of Roman law in the still Romanized provinces and its virtual extinction in the completely Germanized provinces (in Gaul south and north of the Loire, respectively) had corresponding effects on Roman Jewry law. It gradually disappeared as the valid law for Jews qua Roman citizens, although some of its elements were adopted by the other types of Jewry law. Its revival followed the renaissance of the twelfth century, when it reappeared as an authoritative learned law. The "reception" of Roman law in northern Europe since the late Middle Ages reestablished there Roman Jewry law in the university and in the courtroom, but its growing influence is evident in the south as well (for instance in Marquardus de Susannis' *De Judaeis*).

The canon-law type of Jewry law was created by ecclesiastical authorities acting as ideological, legislative, and judicial arbiters in religious and spiritual matters. They form two corresponding hierarchies, one of conciliar legislation and the other of legislation, judicial decisions, and policy statements made by ecclesiastical functionaries. Both hierarchies influenced the creation of Jewry law on all levels, from the synodal to the ecumenical council, from the bishop with his administration to the pope in his curia. The elaboration of canon law as a learned law added a third source of law creation, the canonists, and resulted in securing the universality and uniformity of this type of Jewry law to a considerable extent. The corpus of its literary sources comprises mainly conciliar legislation received in the canonical collections (such as the *Quesnelliana* and the *Hispana*), official publications of conciliar *Acta*, papal decretals (the texts preserved in Gregory I's *Register*), and above all the *Corpus iuris canonici*. The extensive literature produced by the canonists on this subject can be found in monographs and in works of general scope.

Until the High Middle Ages this type was directed not at the Jews, but at Christians coming into contact with Jews. As the Jews were not considered to be members of the church, they were not bound by its laws. From the thirteenth century on, the canon-law type of Jewry law was radically expanded; henceforth it dealt directly with Jews, whenever they were implicated with converts and relapsed converts suspected of heresy and blasphemy, or accused of anti-Christian activity. This expansion was accompanied by the penetration of ecclesiastical law enforcement agencies (such as the Inquisition) into spheres traditionally avoided (such as economic activity, and ritual), or reserved to the secular authorities (such as trials of Jews).

Secular Jewry law was created by secular authorities. It consists of numerous subtypes, reflecting the political and legal divisions of European society, from the universal empire to the national monarchies, the territorial princedoms, and the municipal enclaves. Its subtypes were conditioned by the political systems in which they originated; the more comprehensive, the better delineated, and the better enforced were evolved by political systems that achieved unified and effective control over their subjects.

Carolingian Jewry law still consisted of a loose and varying complex of subjective rights, granted to individuals in charters of protection, but the existence of a *magister Iudeorum* in the court suggests that the Jewish grantees were recognized as a special group, distinct from other protected individuals. Grants of special rights to individuals and groups persisted till the late Middle Ages and remained an important element in any secular Jewry law, but attempts to deduce the status of the Jews as a distinct religious group from an objective legal order were made from the late eleventh century on.

The idea that the Jews stand in direct, unmediated relation with the imperial chamber (Worms privilege, about 1090) was later defined as the "chamber serfdom" of all Jews (by Frederick II in 1236, probably under the influence of canon law). At the same time the state assumed responsibility for the safety of all Jews when they were included in land-peace proclamations, alongside other "defenseless" groups, such as clerics, merchants, and women (for the first time in Mainz, 1103). Both principles were to exert a great influence on the evolution of any secular Jewry law.

The German state utilized the principle of "chamber serfdom" in its fiscal and protective policies toward the Jews, but its inability to evolve an effective administration largely nullified the practical implications of this principle. Even the theoretical right to make grants of Jews (as regalia) to feudatories and cities, though consistent with the principle of serfdom, left the inefficient chamber very little opportunity to apply it in practice. This principle determined other secular Jewry-law systems as well, for instance in England (enunciated *ca.* 1135), Aragon (1176), and France (end of the twelfth century), but its application varied from one state to another.

English Jewry law was the most comprehensive and effective. From the beginning of the thirteenth century the crown controlled all the activities of Jews it had an interest in, using for this purpose a body of law (enacted law and a complex of precedents and decisions), and an efficient administration (the Exchequer and Justices of the Jews). The French Jewry law distributed the ownership of Jews between the crown and the magnates (definitive regulations in 1223–1230), but in practice this Jewry law was largely dominated by the crown, thanks to the expansion of the royal domain and to the power exercised by the royal administration outside the boundaries of this domain. It underwent a radical change in the fourteenth century following the expulsion of Jews in 1306 and their temporary readmission to the kingdom. Henceforth they depended entirely on the favor of the king and the magnates; the objective status of serfdom was replaced by the subjective rights of foreigners tolerated at the discretion of the ruler. The Iberian Jewry-law systems exhibit most of the elements typical of the other monarchies, but differ in that they allowed the Jewish communal authorities *(aljama)* an important role in the government of the Jews, which amounted to a virtual autonomy in certain areas, and permitted Jews to occupy senior positions in government and to influence, consequently, the evolution of Jewry law and its practical application.

Political disunity, for example in Germany and Italy, was accompanied by legal diversity, and Jewry law in these regions became a complex mosaic of imperial and royal legislation, customary territorial law, and locally valid enactments of magnates and municipal authorities. Municipal Jewry-law systems functioned in towns that enjoyed autonomy and had a sizable Jewish population, but the more comprehensive and the more authentically urban types were evolved in the framework of the typical town law.

Some of them spread far and wide, such as Magdeburg town law, which spread to Eastern Europe during the thirteenth to sixteenth centuries. Municipal Jewry law is known chiefly from charters of protection (*Judenschutzbriefe*) granted by territorial princes and urban authorities, from lawbooks (such as the *Wiener Stadtrechtsbuch* and Johannes Purgoldt's *Rechtsbuch*), and from collections of court decisions (such as Magdeburg's *Schöffensprüche* and the *Brünner Schöffenbuch*). This was one of the more important types of secular Jewry law, due to the predominantly urban character of medieval Jewry.

The scope of Jewry law consists of the following categories:

Protection of Jewry. Roman Jewry law protected Jewry on the ground of the Roman citizenship of the individual Jews and of the recognized status of Jewry as a lawful national religion. The canon-law type based its protection on the theological principle that the survival of Jewry is a vital element in God's "economy of salvation." It was embodied in the official bull of protection (*Sicut Iudaeis*), issued many times since Calixtus II, and in numerous interventions by popes and prelates occasioned by particular persecutions (crusades, ritual-murder charges, the Black Death).

Secular Jewry law combined these principles in its rationale for protection, which proved to be the ultimate guarantee of survival of any Jewry. This category included protection of life, limb, and property, defense against forced conversion, toleration and protection of recognized religious activities and establishments (ritual, holidays, synagogues, and cemeteries). The commitment of Jewry law to this category was progressively eroded from the fifteenth century on, and when secular authorities abandoned it and acted against it, the existence of Jewry was terminated (for instance in England, France, Spain).

Segregation and degradation. This category derives from predominantly religious sources, and exists already in the earliest versions of the Roman Jewry law and canon-law types of Jewry law. Initially devised to prevent proselytism and apostasy (a function it never lost), it was also employed to reinforce the missionary pressure exerted on the Jews. With time it also served other causes, specific to Christian society and only marginally conditioned by the actual activities of the Jews.

Segregation and degradation in the religious sphere were the aims of Jewry-law regulations dealing with proselytism, appearance in public during Christian holidays, commerce in Christian liturgical vessels, right of asylum in church for Jews and their property, legal capacity in trials concerning clerics, payment of tithe, participation in religious debates, commerce in commodities prohibited to Jews by halakhic law (such as meat and wine under certain circumstances).

Segregation and degradation in the social sphere were the aims of Jewry-law regulations dealing with appointments to government offices and functions, ownership and possession of non-Jewish slaves, employment of Christian servants, wet nurses, and midwives, legal capacity in trials involving Christians, mixed marriages and sexual relations with Christians, restricted living quarters, distinguishing garments and badges, restrictions and prohibitions on certain economic and professional activities, and exclusion from feudal relationship. This category becomes progressively harsher from the thirteenth century onward, and expands to new areas during the late Middle Ages.

Active missionary policy. This category derives, generally, from the canon-law type; the other types usually followed its lead, although its aims and means frequently contrasted with those of the protection category. In its earlier phases it consisted of regulations dealing with the different aspects of conversion of Jews (questions of legal age, consent, and good faith, economic aspects, contact with former coreligionists and with Christians, family ties with Jewish relatives). From the thirteenth century on this category expanded, and it dealt—usually under the heading of the fight against blasphemous and heretical activities—with matters traditionally regarded as specifically Jewish and hence outside Jewry-law jurisdiction, such as control of Talmudic studies and literature, destruction of condemned literature, control and "purification" of Jewish ritual, defense of Jewish "orthodoxy" against "heresy," forced public religious debates, forced attendence at sermons. Some elements of this category assume—and complement—a prior use of illegal force, though without according it formal legitimation.

Profitable regulation. This category depends on the previous categories for its ideological guidance, but its bulk consists of pragmatic answers to practical problems involved in the pursuit of Jewry law goals. Secular authorities played the leading role in this respect, and this category reflects their prime concern, that is, how to obtain maximum profits by operating an efficient government machinery. This goal did not always accord with those enunciated in the previous two categories, but it had the important support of the state behind it. All questions related to the role of the Jew in the general judicial system (such as problems of judicial status, procedure, conflict of laws and of courts) had to be dealt with. The evolution of the special Jewry oath, which permitted the use of a non-Christian formula, was of prime importance in a system that built much of its law of evidence around the religious oath. The category further deals with the whole domain of the economic activities of the Jews, mainly their financial and credit transactions; this domain, a state monopoly, was tightly controlled and protected as well as thoroughly exploited. It encouraged and sometimes directly undertook the creation of communal authorities capable of fulfilling various administrative duties more efficiently than the ordinary state machinery, fiscal as well as judicial. From the late twelfth century on, these purely operational aims became increasingly subservient to the ideological aims of the two earlier categories, with the dispositions typical to this category being redesigned accordingly. The offensive and degrading character became much more pronounced, and usury legislation was sharpened in order to achieve total expropriation. At the same time, unbridled appropriation of Jewry resources diminished its economic value to such a degree that economic advantages were no longer expected from the traditional methods of exploitation. Here again, a Jewry-law category aimed at the profitable regulation of Jewry was replaced by the militant policies of segregation, degradation, and missionary pressure.

BIBLIOGRAPHY

General studies include Guido Kisch, "Research in Medieval Legal History of the Jews," in *Proceedings of the American Academy for Jewish Research*, 6 (1934–1935), repr. in Robert Chazan, ed., *Medieval Jewish Life* (1976), 97–144; Kenneth Stow, *Catholic Thought and Papal Jewry Policy, 1555–1593* (1977).

Studies of Roman Jewry Law include Petrus Browe, "Die Judengesetzgebung Justinians," in *Analecta Gregoriana*, 8 (1935); Jean Juster, *Les Juifs dans l'empire romain*; 2 vols. (1914); A. Linder, *Roman Imperial Legislation on the Jews* (1983), and *The Jews in Roman Legislation* (1986); A. M. Rabello, "A Tribute to Jean Juster," in *Israel Law Review*, 9 (1976).

Studies of the relationship of canon law and Jewry law include Solomon Grayzel, *The Church and the Jews in the Thirteenth Century*, rev. ed. (1966); W. Holtzman, "Zur päpstlichen Gesetzgebung über die Juden im 12. Jahrhundert," in *Festschrift Guido Kisch* (1955), 217–235; A. Linder, "Christlich-Jüdische Konfrontation im kirchlichen Frühmittelalter," in K. Schäferdiek, ed., *Die Kirche des früheren Mittelalters* (1978), 397–441; Shlomo Simonsohn, "Prolegomena to a History of the Relations Between the Papacy and the Jews in the Middle Ages," in *Sefer Zikkaron le-Yitzhak F. Baer* (1980), 66–93.

Studies of secular Jewry law include Yitzhak F. Baer, *A History of the Jews in Christian Spain*, Louis Schoffman, trans., 2 vols. (1961–1965); Robert Chazan, *Medieval Jewry in Northern France* (1973); Vittore Colorni, *Legge ebraica e leggi locali: Ricerche sull'ambito d'applicazione del diritto ebraico in Italia dall'epoca romana al secolo XIX* (1945); A. C. Cramer, "The Origins and Functions of the Jewish Exchequer," in *Speculum*, 16 (1941); Jean Juster, "La condition légale des Juifs sous les rois Visigoths," in *Études d'histoire juridique offertes à P. F. Girard* (1912), 275–335; Guido Kisch, "Magdeburg Jury Court Decisions as Sources of Jewry-Law," in *Historia judaica*, 5 (1943), *Jewry-Law in Medieval Germany: Laws and Court Decisions Concerning Jews* (1949), and *The Jews in Medieval Germany: A Study of Their Legal and Social Status* (1949, 2nd ed., 1970); Gavin I. Langmuir, " 'Judei nostri' and the Beginning of Capetian Legislation," in *Traditio*, 16 (1960), and "The Jews and the Archives of Angevin England: Reflections on Medieval Anti-Semitism," in *Traditio*, 19 (1963); E. Patlagean, "Contribution juridique à l'histoire des Juifs dans la Méditerranée médiévale: Les formules grecques de serment," in *Revue des études juives*, 124 (1965), 137–156; Henry G. Richardson, *The English Jewry Under Angevin Kings* (1960); V. Zimmermann, *Die Entwicklung des Judeneides: Untersuchungen und Texte zur rechtlichen und sozialen Stellung der Juden im Mittelalter* (1973).

AMNON LINDER

[See also **Jewish Communal Self-Government; Jews.**]

LAW, PROCEDURE OF, 1000–1500. The history of legal procedure in Western Europe can be described as the evolution of irrational systems of proof into rational systems. As with every sweeping generalization, one may object to each term. The older, unilateral ordeals (primarily oaths, water, and hot iron) held sway over judicial procedure until the twelfth century. They have been termed "irrational" because they did not depend on oral and written testimony nor on a body of legal theory and principles, but on God's intervention into human affairs. Men did not judge other men; they simply "read" God's will as revealed through the ritual of the ordeal. In Italy these judgments of God were called "paribiles," that is, "open and manifest judgments." We now understand, however, that the ordeals were not so irrational as they appear at first glance. They followed strict rules, involved the community in each case, and often provided the community an opportunity to seek a compromise between the two parties. Further, the procedure developed to replace the ordeals during the twelfth and thirteenth centuries, upon which modern legal procedure grew, is not so rational as we might wish. It too sometimes seemed to put a greater value on formal rules than on truth and reason. Nevertheless, during the twelfth and thirteenth centuries, the courts of Western Europe replaced the ordeal inherited from the Germanic tribes with a procedure resting on oral and written evidence. Judges evaluated the evidence presented to the court and rendered judgments according to it. This change marks an important point in the transformation of Western European society into one in which reason, not the supernatural, provided a resolution of conflicts in human affairs.

Reason did not win a swift victory. Although Pope Innocent III (1198–1216) promulgated a canon (no. 18) at the Fourth Lateran Council (1215) forbidding clerics to participate in ordeals, his legislation did not mark the first nor the last step in eliminating the old modes of proof. The courts in Western Europe had already begun to use alternative procedures during the previous century; on the other hand, the ordeal lasted long after 1215 in many parts of Europe. In England, for example, the defendant's right to offer trial by battle was not abolished until 1819. But the judgments of God did eventually disappear. Two developments were particularly important for initiating this change: the revival of Roman jurisprudence in the late eleventh century and the centralization of governmental authority during the twelfth century.

PROCEDURE IN ROMAN LAW

By the end of the imperial period, the ancient Romans had created a system of procedure with intricate and sophisticated rules. This system of proof, called the *cognitio extraordinaria,* is the original model after which most of the procedure in modern civil law jurisdictions (France, Germany, Italy) is fashioned. Roman procedure required oral and written testimony with stringent rules of evidence and emphasized the authority of the judge to oversee the proceedings, interrogate witnesses, and render decisions. The *cognitio extraordinaria* and Roman law gradually disappeared in the West after the collapse of Roman authority in the western provinces of the empire. The Germanic ordeal replaced it as a system

of proof. All the elements of Roman procedure can be found in Justinian's great codification, *Corpus iuris civilis,* but Roman lawyers did not unduly concern themselves with questions of procedure and did not produce a large literature treating procedural questions. Consequently, when Justinian's *Corpus* was rediscovered and taught in the late eleventh century, medieval lawyers had to reconstruct the workings of the *cognitio extraordinaria* from widely scattered texts and rules in the *Digest* and *Code.* In the first half of the twelfth century they began to write tracts based on Roman procedure and created, for the first time, procedural law as a branch of jurisprudence. One of the first of these tracts was written by one of the Four Doctors of Roman law in the twelfth century, Bulgarus, in the form of a letter to Haimeric, the chancellor of the papal curia (1123–1141). Bulgarus defined for Haimeric the most important elements of Roman procedure—the judge, advocates, plaintiff, defendant, witness, and appeal—describing the function of each in the judicial process. He wrote in simple terms that a layman could understand. More than a dozen of these tracts have survived from the twelfth century, and their content became increasingly technical. These tracts provide striking evidence of intense theoretical and practical interest in Roman procedure. As a result, Roman rules slowly began to be recognized in the procedure of Western European courtrooms during the second half of the twelfth century.

CENTRALIZATION OF GOVERNMENTAL AUTHORITY

Simultaneously with the revival of Roman law, kings, princes, and city-states consciously extended the judicial authority of central organs of government during the twelfth century. This movement was more marked in England and Italy than elsewhere, but was almost everywhere discernible. Nowhere, however, is the process through which Roman law influenced court procedure more visible than within the church. Ecclesiastical courts had employed the ordeal as a mode of proof, but it had never been totally accepted. As early as the ninth century, Pope Nicholas I (867) prohibited judicial duels and Pope Stephen V, between 886 and 889, condemned the ordeals of hot iron and water. These decrees were known in the eleventh century from their inclusion in canonical collections, and Gratian, when he composed his *Decretum* (*ca.* 1140), placed them in a long section on procedure (*Causa* 2) where he discussed ordeals (C. 2, *q.* 5, *cc.* 20 and 22). He also included other authorities that permitted certain ordeals and seems to have accepted them as modes of proof under certain circumstances or was, at least, hesitant to condemn them. However, by the end of the century, Huguccio of Pisa (d. 1210)—the most distinguished canonist of the period—vigorously opposed the use of the ordeal in ecclesiastical courts.

Although some canonists may have been willing to consider the ordeal as a mode of proof during the twelfth century, in practice the ecclesiastical courts had rejected the old proofs almost entirely. The centralization of papal legislative and judicial power introduced far-reaching changes in how ecclesiastical justice functioned. The *Dictatus papae* of Pope Gregory VII (1075) stipulated that "no one shall dare to condemn one who appeals to the apostolic chair" (no. 20). Appeal from a decision of the ordeal—the judgment of God—was impossible. The inexorable logic of the pope's dictum demanded that the old systems of proof not be used. The papal court became the court of last resort, and ecclesiastical procedure had to adapt to a system of proof that was based on evidence. In response to requests from litigants throughout Christendom, the papal court delegated cases to judges with instructions to investigate and settle disputes, or to send them for final judgment to Rome. These events did not pass unnoticed. During the pontificate of Pope Eugenius III (1145–1153), St. Bernard of Clairvaux lamented that the laws of Justinian, not of the Lord, resounded in the papal palace.

Twelfth-century papal decretals illustrate these developments. They established rules for papal judges-delegate and regulated the testimony of witnesses, often in accordance with Roman law. Bulgarus' instructions on Roman legal procedure to the papal chancellor, Haimeric, would have been superfluous by the end of the century. Ecclesiastical procedure had become thoroughly "Romanized." Indeed, from the twelfth century on, it is through canon law that Roman procedure exercised its influence on secular procedure.

Around 1216 Tancred of Bologna composed an *Ordo iudiciarius* in which he described ecclesiastical judicial procedure in great detail. He divided his treatise into four parts: the first discussed the persons who participated in court cases (judges, lawyers, plaintiffs, and defendants), the second instructed these persons in their various roles, the third set out the rules governing procedure in the courtroom, the fourth defined judicial judgments, their execution, and appeals. Tancred's *Ordo* was enormously pop-

ular and influential. It was translated into French and German and remained the standard work on procedure in canon law until it was replaced by the magisterial and exhaustive *Speculum iudiciale* of Guillaume Durand. His *Speculum* was encyclopedic in its coverage. He wrote the first recension between 1271 and 1276 and a second between 1289 and 1291. Like Tancred he divided the work in four parts. The first two parts followed Tancred's *Ordo* and covered the same topics, while the third treated criminal procedure and the fourth listed formulas used in judicial documents. It is not an exaggeration to say that Durand's *Speculum* became the standard work on procedure for the next three centuries. Textbooks observe that "Romano-canonical procedure"—with its emphasis on the investigative authority of the judge, often referred to as "inquisitorial" procedure—is the foundation of modern civil law procedure. Durand's *Speculum* is the best introduction we have to the mature development of that procedure.

PROCEDURE IN SECULAR COURTS

Kings legislated, codified law, established royal courts, and sent royal judges into the countryside (itinerant justices or justices in eyre) during the twelfth and thirteenth centuries. The centralization of royal jurisdiction and the quickening pace of royal judicial and legislative activity occurred at markedly different tempos in various kingdoms. In the Norman kingdoms of Sicily and England, royal authority was strong by the mid twelfth century. The French monarchy developed more slowly, while German political institutions fell into complete disarray after the death of Emperor Frederick II in 1250. In Italy, after the waning of imperial authority, the city-states developed independent, nonfeudal political institutions with corresponding legal institutions. However, none of the secular states adopted Roman forms and rules as thoroughly as the church had during the Middle Ages. And England, in particular, evolved its own distinctive procedure.

Several general trends can be noted. As the law schools produced large numbers of trained lawyers, these men found employment in the chancelleries of Western Europe. Often they were appointed royal judges, and these "learned" judges gradually replaced their unlearned predecessors. By the end of the Middle Ages, the doctrine arose that the prince who was not learned in the law should not judge in court. Beginning in the twelfth century, written evidence and documents were given greater authority. Perhaps most importantly, the defendant no longer bore the burden of proof in a trial, but the plaintiff was required to establish the justice of his case ("onus probandi incumbit ei qui dicit": the burden of proof falls on him who brings the action).

The growth of cities also had an effect on attitudes toward older systems of proof. Townsmen seem to have viewed the ordeals and trial by combat with repugnance. In southern Italy Troia (1127) and Bari (1131) obtained privileges that freed them from being subjected to the ordeal as a mode of proof. Cologne's inhabitants were granted the same rights in 1179. Although the ordeal had almost universally disappeared from northern Italian cities by the end of the twelfth century, there is evidence that it was still used in the countryside (Friuli in 1234, Benevento in 1230, and Apricale in 1267). In many parts of Europe, particularly in Central and Eastern Europe, the ordeal did not fall into desuetude until the end of the thirteenth or in the fourteenth century.

Legislation abolishing ordeals was common in the thirteenth century. The Emperor Frederick II declared in his Constitutions of Melfi (1231) that only simple people believed in ordeals since they were contrary to "true legal learning" and the "nature of things." He forbade that they be imposed on his subjects in all the courts of his realm. Only the crimes of treason, secret murder (committed by unknown persons or persons who are shielded by the local community), and death by poison were subject to trial by combat. Frederick made this exception because he thought these murderers should be subjected to combat as a terrifying example to others, not because the procedure was just (Book 2, titles 31–33). His Constitutions reveal a well-developed system of proof, relying on written evidence presented to a judge, and modeled in large part after the procedure of Roman and canon law. Other secular rulers followed Frederick's lead. King Louis IX of France abolished trial by battle with a royal ordonnance in 1258.

By the end of the Middle Ages, the courts of most European states had adopted the "Romano-canonical procedure" of the ecclesiastical courts. England, however, was a notable exception. During the reign of King Henry II the jury became a common feature of English procedure. The jury was not unique to England in the twelfth century, but was found in northern France, the Low Countries, parts of Germany, and Sweden. It consisted of a group of men, free and lawful, ranging in number from seven to over fifty, who testified before a court about a partic-

ular crime. They were selected from the locality, and their original purpose was to present evidence as the voice of the people (vox populi) or the verdict of the country. They swore an oath—they were "jurati"—to tell or "find" the facts. This was a jury of accusation, and the royal assizes used it to bring criminals to justice. The jury and the ordeal worked together. The Assize of Clarendon (1166) decreed that juries of twelve men should present evidence of wrongdoing to the courts. Those who were indicted had to prove their innocence through an ordeal.

At the same time new forms of actions were introduced, called writs (breves). Each writ governed a distinct procedure and was intended as a remedy for a specific complaint. By the beginning of the thirteenth century these writs had become so numerous that they were compiled in a Register of Writs. The doctrine soon arose that litigants could only have access to the courts after they had obtained the proper writ. The earliest writs often stipulate that a sheriff should convene a jury to give evidence about the complaint. The combination of these two institutions, juries and writs, became the main features of procedure in English law by 1200.

Van Caenegem has argued that two factors account for England's deviation from the Romano-canonical model adopted by the rest of Europe. First, English royal government developed precociously during the twelfth century. English kings, particularly Henry II, were able to create a national legal system using royal writs and royal courts to administer justice throughout England. Second, royal authority matured in the second half of the twelfth century, before English ecclesiastical courts had fully assimilated Romano-canonical procedure. If royal institutions had evolved more slowly, or if ecclesiastical courts had matured more quickly, perhaps England would have adopted the system of proof similar to most other European countries. Van Caenegem's thesis is persuasive, but difficult to prove. Other historians have pointed to other factors that might account for English developments. Whatever the case, when English courts were forced to abandon ordeals in criminal trials after the Fourth Lateran Council, they could turn to the jury as a well established institution. Gradually, the jury became a body that heard evidence as well as presented it. However, the "inscrutable" or impartial jury was not a product of the Middle Ages, but of the early modern period. For a long time, jurors were expected to know the facts of a case as well as hear testimony and render a judgment. The jury became a fundamental part of English procedure during the thirteenth century, and England, unlike other countries where the jury existed, never gave it up for the Romano-canonical inquest.

BIBLIOGRAPHY

There have been several recent attempts to explain the change in modes of proof during the twelfth century: Peter Brown, "Society and the Supernatural: A Medieval Change," in *Daedalus,* **104** (1975); Paul R. Hyams, "Trial by Ordeal: The Key to Proof in Early Common Law," in Morris S. Arnold *et al.,* eds., *On the Laws and Customs of England: Essays in Honor of Samuel E. Thorne* (1981); Charles M. Radding, "Superstition to Science: Nature, Fortune, and the Passing of the Medieval Ordeal," in *American Historical Review,* **84** (1979). John W. Baldwin has examined the legal and theological opposition to the ordeals in "The Intellectual Preparation for the Canon of 1215 Against Ordeals," in *Speculum,* **36** (1961). The best short description of Romano-canonical procedure is C. Lefebvre, "Procedure," in *Dictionnaire de droit canonique,* VII (1959), 281–296. Knut Wolfgang Nörr discusses the influence of Roman law on procedure in "Die Literatur zum gemeinen Zivilprozess," in Helmut Coing, ed., *Handbuch der Quellen und Literatur der Neueren Europäischen Privatrechtsgeschichte,* I, *Mittelalter* (1973), 383–397, with a comprehensive bibliography. R. C. van Caenegem wrote a brilliant essay of synthesis, "La preuve dans le droit du moyen âge occidental: Rapport de synthèse," in *Société Jean Bodin pour l'histoire comparative des institutions, La preuve,* II (1965), 691–753. He has also explored the developments in English law, with a continental viewpoint, in *The Birth of the English Common Law* (1973). For the history of procedure in the various nation-states the older general histories of law still contain much useful information: Adhémar Esmein, *Histoire de la procédure criminelle en France et spécialement de la procédure inquisitoire depuis le XIIIe siècle jusqu'à nos jours* (1882); Theodore F. T. Plucknett, *A Concise History of the Common Law,* 5th ed. (1956); Giuseppe Salvioli, *Storia del diritto italiano,* III, pt. 2, *Storia della procedura civile e criminale,* 9th rev. ed. (1930).

KENNETH PENNINGTON

[See also **Clarendon, Assize of; Corpus Iuris Civilis; Dictatus Papae; Durand, Guillaume; Jury; Melfi, Constitutions of; Ordeals; Tancred.**]

LAW, RUSSIAN (MUSCOVITE), 1300–1500.

The centuries during which the principality of Muscovy extended its hegemony over most of northeast Russia witnessed an extraordinary growth in law and legal institutions. Not only did the main pre-Mus-

covite codes continue to be copied, but new law was created in many of the areas that came under Muscovy's domination by the early sixteenth century. Finally, Muscovy itself produced major codes that attempted to unify judicial practice throughout the principality.

SOURCES OF THE LAW

The bulk of the extant legal texts of early Muscovy survive in complex clerical collections that came to be known as the *Kormchaya kniga* (Pilot's book). Borrowing most of its contents from Byzantine nomocanons, the *Kormchaya kniga* consisted of the canons of the ecumenical and local church councils, canons of notables in the church, and numerous secular Byzantine codes like the *Eclogue* and *Procheiros nomos.* Along with miscellaneous Byzantine texts, the *Kormchaya* also preserved the basic text of medieval Russian law—the *Russkaya pravda* (Russian truth).

The *Russkaya pravda* is generally believed to have originated at some point in the eleventh century; subsequently it was revised and supplemented, perhaps in the twelfth century. In this form the *Pravda* survives in two fundamental redactions—Short and Expanded. The Short *Pravda* bears several indications that it was used in Russia in the eleventh century during the reigns of Yaroslav the Wise (grand prince of Kiev during the period 1019–1054) and his sons, but it is extant only in two fifteenth-century copies of chronicles and in a number of much later copies.

The Expanded *Pravda,* on the other hand, is extant in nearly 100 copies, the oldest of which is included in the oldest *Kormchaya kniga* (1282) of the so-called Russian redaction. Likewise, most of the other medieval copies—the majority of them date from the fifteenth century—are known to us by their inclusion in copies of the *Kormchaya.* The Expanded redaction of the *Russkaya pravda* is approximately three times longer than its shorter counterpart and contains much detail on matters of substantive and procedural law untouched in the Short *Pravda.* That the Expanded *Pravda* springs from the twelfth century seems certain because it mentions Vladimir Vsevolodich Monomakh, who was grand prince of Kiev from 1113 to 1125.

The repeated copying of the *Pravda* in the fourteenth, fifteenth, and even sixteenth century introduced some minor changes in the law, but on balance the medieval scribes seem to have regarded the *Pravda* as a continuing source of law. One significant revision was carried out perhaps as early as the end of the fifteenth or early sixteenth century. As a result of severe condensation, the copyists in Muscovy produced the so-called Abbreviated *Pravda,* a text that harmonizes rather well with Muscovy's own legislation.

While the *Russkaya pravda* enjoyed distribution throughout all the territories of medieval Russia, several local centers also produced codifications of their own law. The medieval town of Novgorod had its own statutes, which in time were joined in a Judicial Charter. Only a fragment of the Charter survives, and it comes from a single copy of late origin (*ca.* 1471). But the harmony of its contents with some of the *Russkaya pravda*'s regulations and the clues provided by the Charter's text suggest that the Charter probably was used in Novgorod at least by the end of the fourteenth century. Pskov, too, left a Judicial Charter; it is extant in a single complete copy of late provenance (late sixteenth to early seventeenth century), and in addition, its last twelve articles survive in a separate manuscript. Since Pskov was really part of Novgorod's administrative system for much of the late medieval period, it seems likely that many of the regulations extant in the Pskov Charter had parallels in Novgorod's law.

Legal texts from Smolensk confirm that the norms of *Russkaya pravda* continued to have weight in the west Russian territories at least through the thirteenth century. Smolensk, like Novgorod and Pskov, came into contact with European traders, and Smolensk law itself was preserved in Latin copies from the city of Riga and the trading island of Gotland.

The establishment of a new legal order was the work of the Muscovite princes Ivan III (1462–1505) and Ivan IV (1547–1584). Several regulations governing territories within Muscovy appeared in the course of the fifteenth century, but no Muscovite code antedates the *Sudebnik* of 1497. It too is preserved in a single copy, which has been dated to a time very close to 1500. Essentially a schedule of fees for the prince's judicial administration and a description of various judicial documents, the 1497 *Sudebnik* contains relatively little substantive law. This has encouraged speculation that the *Russkaya pravda* and other customary norms continued to have the force of law in the overwhelmingly agrarian society of early Muscovy, especially since it was precisely at the time of the promulgation of the *Sudebnik* that the copying of *Pravda* reached record dimensions.

With the publication of the 1550 *Sudebnik,* Muscovite law had solidified and procedure as well as substantive law was rewritten to accommodate the needs of the state, now successfully centralized. Not until the seventeenth-century Muscovite sovereigns undertook major revisions did the law undergo any alteration in principle.

Church law too experienced significant growth in the late medieval period. The first of the Russian redactions of the *Kormchaya kniga* dates from the late thirteenth century, and the collection underwent several revisions in the succeeding three centuries. In addition, several legal texts for churchmen appeared in the fourteenth century. The *Merilo pravednoe* (Just measure) seems to have been composed for the Metropolitan's own court. This bulky composition—each of the five extant copies numbers several hundred folios—consisted of two parts. The first section contained exhortatory texts addressed to judges to ensure that justice would indeed prevail. The second section includes several legal texts, including the Expanded *Russkaya pravda,* church statutes, extracts from the *Procheiros nomos* and Mosaic law, several novels of the Byzantine emperor Alexios I Komnenos, and numerous other texts.

One of the codes included in the *Merilo pravednoe* was the *Zakon sudnyi liudem* (Court law for the people), a revision of the eighth-century *Eclogue* adjusted to meet the needs of Slavic society. The *Zakon* is preserved in two fundamental redactions—Short and Expanded. All of the copies of both redactions are extant only in medieval Russian manuscripts. It is certain that the Expanded redaction originated somewhere in Russia, perhaps in Novgorod in the thirteenth century, but the Short redaction almost certainly was compiled outside the Russian lands. There are several viewpoints associated with different national groups, but the lexicon of the Short redaction seems to indicate that this code was compiled for the West Slavs sometime around the turn of the ninth century.

Both redactions contain regulations addressed to questions of testimony and delicts associated especially with agriculture. The harsh sanctions of the *Eclogue*'s seventeenth title (normally several kinds of mutilation), from which much of the *Zakon sudnyi* was borrowed, are replaced in the Slavic reworking with clerical penances. The Expanded redaction maintains this distinction but further adjusts the code's regulations to conform to medieval Russian practice.

Another church text of the fourteenth century was the first in early Muscovy to prescribe afflictive sanctions. The *Pravosudie mitropoliche* (Metropolitan's justice) represents a kind of amalgam of local precedent and severe sanctions. It prescribes penalties like decapitation for homicide and makes provision for documents of litigation; it is perhaps the first of Russia's texts to include consideration of transcripts.

Church guarantees also flourished in the early Muscovite period. Churchmen, like many private landlords, enjoyed varying degrees of judicial immunity into the sixteenth century. Special guarantees for clerical immunity from secular prosecution were built into a series of compacts that bear the names of well-known medieval princes. Vladimir's Statute, ascribed to the tenth-century prince Vladimir Sviatoslavich (980–1015), who forcibly converted his subjects to Orthodoxy, included guarantees that no cleric would be subject to any secular court, and that certain offenses—principally offenses against marriage and morality—would be judged exclusively by churchmen. Yaroslav's Statute, ascribed to Vladimir's son, Yaroslav the Wise, who is also mentioned in the *Russkaya pravda,* listed specific cases over which clerical courts held jurisdiction and prescribed penances and fines to be paid into the church's treasuries. Both documents survive only in late copies. The oldest copy of Vladimir's Statute belongs to the fourteenth century and the oldest copy of Yaroslav's Statute is fifteenth-century, so that critics have long maintained that neither statute originated with the prince whose name it bears. What is indisputable is that in the fourteenth and fifteenth centuries these texts enjoyed wide currency among both clergy and laity. Extant Muscovite documents demonstrate that early in the fifteenth century and again in the sixteenth century, Muscovy's secular rulers reaffirmed the right of the church to immunity from secular jurisdiction for its own personnel and the exclusive right to adjudicate crimes of morality.

PROCEDURE

Presumably, therefore, two separate court systems were in action in the early centuries of Muscovy's history. Neither secular nor clerical courts, however, have left satisfactory records of actual trials with which one might reconstruct court practice. The codes must serve instead.

The *Russkaya pravda* nowhere describes a trial as such. Rather, like the so-called barbarian codes of the European West, the *Pravda* describes a process of private prosecution. Homicides were liable to revenge, at least until sometime in the eleventh cen-

tury, when composition (a compensation payment of money) was prescribed. Discovery of theft initiated a public announcement to that effect, whereupon the possessor of the stolen property was expected to return the goods in question within three days. If he himself was not the thief, then he was to assist in a series of regressing interrogations until the thief was discovered. Catching the thief in the act allowed the victim to settle the matter on the spot, and everyone in the community was obliged to assist in the hot pursuit of thieves. Failure to join the posse invited charges of complicity, and the law broadened responsibility for repayment to include those who would not take part in the chase. Assault cases fell under similar regulations. Initially talion ruled, but the *Pravda* came to detail a series of financial remedies for almost any conceivable offense.

None of this involved any third party. Only the victim and offender (together with their kin) were expected to take any part in litigation. Neither redaction of the *Pravda* even mentions a judge, and no regulations governing court appearances or procedure are included. Even pleas of innocence are absent, since the *Pravda* left all these matters to the community's own judgment.

The inattention of the *Pravda* to matters of trial and procedure contrasts strongly with the content of later legal codes. The Novgorod Judicial Charter begins with a call to judges to execute their task without regard for the social or financial station of litigants. The code continues by outlining courts of the Novgorod archbishop, the mayor, the prince's assistants, and the town official charged with presiding over commercial suits *(tysiatskii).* Novgorod's courts required various forms of documents in order to further prosecution, and unruly partisans were specifically banned.

Procedure also demanded several ceremonial acts that, the Charter's compilers hoped, would guarantee the integrity of the outcome of the suit. All litigants were expected to kiss the cross as a proof of their honesty. Evidence was of three kinds: documentary, testimonial, and results of ordeal. Novgorod law expressed special preference for documentary evidence, and guaranteed that any suitor who provided appropriate documentary proof when his opposite did not would win the case. To that end each judicial decision was written up, affixed with an authenticating seal, and handed over to the winning suitor to use as proof of his claim in any subsequent litigation. Witnesses were also heard in court, but they seem not to have testified to questions of fact.

Rather they were witnesses of reputation, as their name *(poslukh)* indicates. At any rate, the Novgorod Charter relates few specifics governing testimony except to rule out testimony from foreigners and slaves.

Evidently some form of ordeal was practiced even in early Russian society. Although the *Russkaya pravda* makes no specific provision for its use, the iron ordeal is recalled in one article of the Expanded *Pravda,* in which the code lists fees paid to officials who administered the ordeal. Novgorod law, at least as it survives, does not mention the iron ordeal or any of its parallels. Consequently, the ordeal seems to have been relegated to a subsidiary function in Novgorod law, where documentary evidence and, to a lesser extent, testimony provided the main proofs.

The Pskov Judicial Charter also begins with an enumeration of Pskov's courts and calls upon judges to render decisions without consideration of friendship or vengeance. As in Novgorod, clerical courts operated side by side with courts of the town mayor and the prince's assistants, and the Pskov Charter makes special mention of the judges' duty to consult the law in coming to their decisions.

Again procedure was governed primarily by documentary evidence. Winning litigants received official records of their victory, and a copy of the trial record was deposited in the town archives. Consequently unofficial documents, presumably those without authenticating seals and for which no copy existed in the town archives of the Holy Trinity Cathedral, were not recognized in court. Introducing them brought the litigant no satisfaction and merely obliged the court to offer the plaintiff his choice of ordeals—kissing the cross, taking the oath, or engaging in the duel. Wager of law decided the matter.

Witnesses too played a part in Pskov, but again their role seems to have been limited to questions of the litigant's repute. Land suits, for example, could be decided by the squatter asking his neighbors to come to court in his behalf to attest to his veracity in claiming long-time tenancy. The Charter does not quite ask them the facts of the case, and indeed other provisions make clear that witnesses had no role in deciding questions of fact. Complaints of assault could include reference to witnesses, but the judge only asked where the victim spent the night. It remained for the victim himself to describe the conditions of the attack, and declare before whom he had announced his complaint. Finally witnesses were summoned to determine if in fact the victim had, as he said, announced his assault to them. Witnesses were expected to parrot the complainant's charge exactly, but they were never asked the circumstances of the assault. Even if the witness exactly matched the litigant's charge, nothing was proved. It remained for the victim and the accused to do battle or engage in some other form of ordeal.

Use of ordeals to determine the outcome of litigation in Pskov was evidently well established. The duel was prescribed in more than a dozen cases, and the deciding oath and the risk of kissing the cross were assigned even more frequently. The popularity of ordeals in the law very likely was due to the inexperience of Pskov's citizens in dealing with written guarantees. Simple theft cases continued to be resolved as before, by means of the bald announcement of one's loss and the expectation of the prompt return of the stolen property. Failing that, the accused had to produce the person from whom he had acquired the stolen goods. Should memory fail him, he was allowed to purge himself with a simple oath, on the assumption that he already enjoyed a good reputation in Pskov.

In short, the law of both Pskov and Novgorod continued many of the procedural forms known to the *Russkaya pravda.* New were the specific provision for trials, and the confidence in written guarantees. Muscovy's elaboration of these principles was to result in a significant change in the law. Primarily, the law codes of 1497 and 1550 extended the range within which documentary evidence was accepted. As in Pskov and Novgorod, court records were admissible, but Muscovy also took cognizance of other forms of documentation unknown to previous justices. The surviving spate of court records from land litigation that took place late in the fifteenth and early in the sixteenth century demonstrates that witnesses could introduce various documents to support their claims. Immunity charters, cadastral records, gift documents, testaments, and other written instruments were often introduced as proof of ownership. Not infrequently the judges recorded their preference for documentary evidence and noted its role in deciding the case.

Nevertheless, testimony too played a significant role in a society that was still overwhelmingly illiterate. Again Muscovy's law introduced a significant advance in detailing what kind of testimony was acceptable: witnesses *(svideteli)* were obliged to relate only that which they had seen. The 1497 code, which introduced this prescription into trial testimony, did not produce immediate changes in the traditional character of testimony, if one is to judge from the extant cases. But plainly the significance of demanding eyewitness testimony was clear to Muscovy's jurists, because the succeeding code, the 1550 *Sudebnik,* reproduced the demand for eyewitness testimony and ridiculed hearsay evidence.

It is difficult to determine precisely the source of Muscovy's changed view of testimony, but it now seems likely that churchmen were influential in effecting the new requirements. Not only did documents like the *Merilo pravednoe* detail rigorous examination of witnesses, but several texts extant in copies from the fifteenth and sixteenth centuries reproduce Byzantine legislation on testimony. Most important is a work entitled "On Witnesses," which is included in at least two sixteenth-century miscellanies. It was extracted from the *Procheiros nomos* and edited for local consumption, but it stands out by virtue of both its contrast with early Muscovite practice and its similarity with the demands of the new Muscovite codes.

Nevertheless, ordeals continued to have an important place in Muscovite procedure. The codes detail all the fees payable in the event of a duel, and while some modern commentators doubt the application of the wager of law, Baron Sigismund von Herberstein (who visited Muscovy early in the sixteenth century) provides a complete description of a duel he seems to have witnessed. Other forms of ordeal also continued in practice. Surviving case records indicate that litigants were expected to agree to submit their case to decision by kissing the cross (a form of oath), casting of lots, or judicial duel. It may be, as some transcripts suggest, that all these forms of the law's wage were simply formulaic, routine parts of litigation without which the litigant had no hope of a successful outcome. On the other hand, it is clear that irrational modes of proof were declining in number, and with the rise of detailed regulations governing testimony the fate of ordeals was sealed.

CRIMINAL LAW

Criminal law too underwent dramatic change in the interval between the composition of the *Russkaya pravda* and the publication of the 1497 *Sudebnik.* In early medieval Russian law, there was no distinction between criminal and civil law. All offenses were simple torts, and appropriate restitution was specified. The *Russkaya pravda* itself documents the earliest history of talion (retaliatory) justice. Both the Short and Expanded redactions of the *Pravda* begin with a provision that sanctioned revenge for homicide. The law imposed limits upon those eligible to

avenge the homicide, and it may be that identification of specific kin who might press for revenge represents the very first step in restricting talion. Nevertheless, only in cases where there was no one to seek vengeance was composition for homicide acceptable.

Sometime late in the eleventh century revenge was removed from the list of acceptable legal satisfactions, and composition replaced it. Homicides henceforth were to be compensated according to a prescribed schedule in which the prince's servitors were protected by a bloodwite (a fine to the ruler) as well as a wergild (compensation to the family). Homicides of ordinary free men called for payment of the wergild, which in reduced size also applied to women, slaves, and various categories of dependents. Other offenses also were subject to composition. Assault, slander, and all categories of theft each had a fixed rate of restitution by which the victim was to be compensated.

Consequently, the *Russkaya pravda* provides little evidence of any distinction between civil and criminal law. All offenses were conceptualized as simple torts, and detailed schedules of compensation provided a framework within which all disputes could be settled. Only the barest glimpse of afflictive sanctions is visible in the *Pravda.* In one article in the Expanded *Russkaya pravda* there is a single provision which seems to indicate that in the event of a homicide that had no provocation, the offender and his family could be subjected to physical punishment. Parallel readings in the various copies of the redaction indicate that the medieval copyists did not very well understand the code's provisions in this matter, so it may be doubted that any of the medieval princes had occasion to apply the sanction. More credible is the hint in the *Russkaya pravda* that in addition to the wergild payable in cases of homicide the prince came to expect the bloodwite as well. Certainly the prince extracted payment in the event of the homicide of any of his servitors, but precisely how the bloodwite was generalized to the larger population is not clear. All that is certain is that already sometime in the eleventh century there was an official of the prince's administration charged with collecting the bloodwite, and in time the princes succeeded in extending application of the homicide sanction beyond the narrow confines of the princely circles.

Finally, the Expanded *Russkaya pravda* unmistakably initiated the practice of punishing various offenses by financial sanction. Indeed, often the compensation figure remained identical to its parallel in the Short *Pravda*, but it prescribed a fine (payable to the state or the judge) instead of composition (payable to the victim or the family). In this way officials of the prince's judiciary gradually succeeded in converting the law into an instrument of centralized social control.

The criminal law of the Novgorod and Pskov Judicial Charters gives some sign of moving still further away from notions of tort. Pskov law clearly stipulated execution for a series of crimes—horse theft, arson, recidivist theft, and so on—but only called for the collection of the bloodwite in cases of homicide. It may be that the customary composition payments were also at work here, but the code's compilers simply omitted mention of the obvious. Certainly much of the Pskov Judicial Charter recalls the composition schedules of the *Russkaya pravda*. Theft of various forms of livestock, for example, brought the victim composition just as it did in the *Pravda*. The Novgorod Charter provides less information on criminal law, probably because only a fragment of the Charter survives. Nevertheless, from what remains it is clear that in Novgorod too the courts were increasingly inclined to separate criminal infractions from civil loss. Land litigation, for example, could lead to heavy financial fines for the losing party convicted of forcible seizure of property.

Muscovite law brings to fruition the long drive toward isolating criminal law from civil law. Undoubtedly the legal precedents of Pskov and Novgorod were in the minds of the compilers of the 1497 *Sudebnik* when they examined questions of criminal offense. Repetition of theft would lead to execution, just as homicides, church thieves, arsonists, traitors, and all "notorious" criminals were dispatched immediately for execution. False accusation too was to be punished by execution, but inasmuch as the *Sudebnik* authorized torture to extract confessions from the accused, one may question the utility of the code's suspicion of slanderous accusation.

Whether any executions ever took place is unknown, since no records of criminal litigation survive. Certainly the updating of Muscovite law that took place in 1550 built upon the provisions included in the 1497 code, so that at least the formal conception of criminal law in early Muscovy remained fixed. Compensation continued to be active, however, although in slightly different circumstances. Muscovite victims might well earn damages for injury done to their honor in the event of false

accusation. But only in this one area did the 1550 code introduce any substantial additions to the corpus of criminal law.

CIVIL LAW

While the gradual differentiation of criminal law from the rest of the law did indeed take place in medieval Russia, the growth of a body of civil law was irregular. The Short *Pravda* contains no regulations whatsoever that might qualify as civil law, and the Expanded *Pravda* offers only slightly more attention to this part of the law. The *Pravda* introduced an important concept in limiting liability for disaster beyond the control of the contracting party, and the provision was repeated in close rewording in the 1497 *Sudebnik*. Litigation over loans, storage contracts, and acceptable levels of usury are the subject of several provisions enacted probably sometime in the twelfth century, but as noted above, in principle civil law remained indistinguishable from criminal.

The Expanded redaction of the *Russkaya pravda* also devoted considerable space to inheritance law. The regulations govern not so much inheritance as they do rights of survivorship, inasmuch as they pay no attention to the instruments of inheritance, and examine instead forms of natural succession. Escheat, widow's bench, ultimogeniture, and complications caused by succession when two or more marriages are involved all find consideration. Also of relevance to the development of civil law in medieval Russia is the *Pravda*'s large codex on slavery. The statute defines the various types of slavery, conditions of enslavement, and a slave's legal responsibility. Both the inheritance and slavery sections probably continued to have legal weight in the fifteenth and early sixteenth centuries in Muscovy, inasmuch as no significant corrections were introduced into Muscovite law on these matters. Quite the contrary, it was precisely in this interval that Muscovite copyists were reproducing the Expanded *Pravda* in record quantities, and as scholars of Muscovite slavery have noted, these copyists did update the *Pravda*'s slavery law, but their work indicates only minimal changes in the law.

Since both Novgorod and Pskov were very much involved in medieval trade, it seems reasonable to assume that civil law was significant in both towns. In fact, the surviving part of the Novgorod Charter gives no evidence of an interest in commercial law. Slavery, inheritance, debt resolution, and all other matters treated in the *Pravda* do not surface in the Novgorod code. Pskov, however, which borrowed much of its political organization and judicial content from its mother-city, Novgorod, does produce a few statutes on these themes. Storage contracts and procedures governing loans are spelled out in considerable detail, specifying acceptable limits for evidence of default of contractual obligations. The Pskov Charter also defines the relations between hired artisan and his employer, between agricultural tenant and landlord, and between apprentice and master. Succession too occupies a significant place in the Pskov code, and reproduces some of the fundamental provisions of the *Pravda*. Pskov also recognized the widow's bench, although ultimogeniture seems not to have been practiced in Pskov. The code is not specific on this point but does make the elder brother responsible for the deceased father's debts, although repayment evidently was made from lands inherited jointly by the sons.

Muscovite law paid attention only to those matters already well developed in the civil law of both Novgorod and Pskov. Land litigation was at the heart of the civil law provisions of the *Sudebnik*, but Muscovy's regulations clearly stemmed from procedures already worked out in the northwestern city-republics. After repeating the *Pravda*'s defense of merchants ruined by matters beyond their control, and after defining in brief the forms and means of enslavement and manumission, the *Sudebnik* devotes a single article each to relations between hired labor and employer, interstate succession, and rights of peasants to move (in reality, this represented a constriction of peasant rights and the foundation of serfdom). The *Sudebnik* also examined details of land litigation. The code determined where fences were acceptable, allowed protection of boundary markers, and described the means and limits of litigation over land.

In other respects, however, Muscovite jurists made no noticeable attempt to enlarge the corpus of civil law bequeathed them by the *Russkaya pravda* or the Novgorod and Pskov Judicial Charters. Even the 1550 *Sudebnik* only amplified upon the relatively terse statements of civil law contained in the 1497 code.

SUMMARY

Medieval Russian law underwent significant, though uneven, growth. Criminal law, virtually indistinguishable from civil law in the earliest codes, came to constitute a separate jurisdiction in which an entirely distinct notion of penalty emerged well before 1500. Procedure too underwent dramatic

change. Muscovy's fully staffed courts—judges, secretaries, seal-keepers, bailiffs and clerks—contrast vividly with the informal adjudication described in the *Russkaya pravda*, according to which the citizen himself prosecuted his case. Indeed, even vengeance justice seems to have passed from the realm of legal remedy only sometime late in the eleventh century. Testimony, at first primarily simple reputation and attestation testimony, gradually came to be eyewitness testimony directed to questions of fact. Written proofs, unmentioned in the *Russkaya pravda*, came to constitute the final and deciding evidence in Muscovy's litigation over land.

Consequently, while it is not possible to identify early Muscovite law with modern legal notions, some fundamental steps toward rationalizing the law had already been taken by 1500.

BIBLIOGRAPHY

General bibliographies on Russian law that treat Muscovite law include William E. Butler, *Russian and Soviet Law* (1976); Marc Szeftel, "Russia (Before 1917)," in John Gilissen, ed., *Bibliographical Introduction to Legal History and Ethnology*, D/9 (1966).

Translations into English are: George Vernadsky, *Medieval Russian Laws* (1947, repr. 1965), which includes the *Russkaya pravda* and the Pskov and Novgorod Judicial Charters; Horace W. Dewey, *Muscovite Judicial Texts, 1488–1556* (1966), which includes both Muscovite *Sudebniki, idem* and Ann M. Kleimola, trans., *Russian Private Law in the XIV–XVII Centuries* (1973), and *Zakon Sudnyj Ljudem (Court Law for the People)* (1977).

See also Daniel H. Kaiser, *The Growth of the Law in Medieval Russia* (1980), summarized in "Modernization in Old Russian Law," in *Russian History*, 6 (1979); Ann M. Kleimola, *Justice in Medieval Russia: Muscovite Judgment Charters (Pravye Gramoty) of the Fifteenth and Sixteenth Centuries* (1975).

DANIEL H. KAISER

[See also **Eclogue; Ivan III of Muscovy; Muscovy, Rise of; Nomocanon; Novgorod; Ordeals; Procheiros Nomos.**]

LAW, SCHOOLS OF. Law was perhaps the most influential intellectual force in the development of universities throughout Europe in the Middle Ages. After beginning in Bologna, law schools were established in other Italian cities, southern France, Spain, Germany, and England. The professionalized legal education fashioned in these schools, moreover, shaped the subsequent legal evolution of Europe.

Only England's indigenous common law withstood the influence of the *ius commune* of the medieval schools.

Most medieval law schools adopted a variant of the university organization found in Bologna, but they also had in common a mode of instruction that set them apart from earlier forms of legal education. Schools treated law as a theoretical science. It was not taught by observing the actions of legal practitioners or studying particular cases (as it was in the English inns of court). It was taught by professional teachers who expounded on rules of law contained in authoritative texts and compilations: the *Corpus iuris canonici,* assembled during the Middle Ages, and the *Corpus iuris civilis,* compiled at the order of the Byzantine emperor Justinian I in the sixth century (consisting of the *Codex* of imperial laws, subsequent legislation known as *Novellae,* an introductory legal textbook called the *Institutes,* and a large collection of jurisprudential writings called the *Digest*).

BOLOGNA AND THE
DEVELOPMENT OF LEGAL EDUCATION

In a strict sense there were no law schools prior to the establishment of the university in Bologna. Instruction in law before the twelfth century was largely practical in nature, designed to equip a small class of lay judges and notaries for the tasks of drafting legal documents and conducting cases. In formal terms, because it involved the use of words, law was bound up with study of the trivium and the *ars dictaminis,* which provided the rudiments of judicial rhetoric. In substantive and procedural terms, law figured as a branch of ethics.

Because Roman law continued to be the personal law of many people in Italy, it was still studied in Pavia, Ravenna, and Rome following the Lombard conquest of Italy. Here too, however, the emphasis was largely practical. Legal knowledge took the form of epitomes, compendiums of applicable rules extracted from Roman legal texts, mainly the *Codex* and the *Novallae* (an example being the *Epitome codicis* of the eighth century). Otherwise, entire parts of the Justinianian *Corpus* were ignored or forgotten, such as the last three books of the *Codex* and most of the *Digest.*

From perhaps the mid eleventh century there was renewed interest in the Roman law. Works such as the *Brachylogus iuris civilis* assembled bits of several texts *(Codex, Digest, Institutes)* in a topical or institutional arrangement. The relationship between different passages and statements of law was becoming a concern. But it was only in Bologna that the elements of the *Corpus iuris civilis* were reassembled in their entirety and considered for the first time as a whole (and called a corpus).

The recovery of the *Corpus,* especially of the *Digest,* was probably the accomplishment of Irnerius *(d. ca.* 1130), who began lecturing on it in Bologna early in the twelfth century, supposedly at the suggestion of Countess Matilda of Tuscany. The *Digest* was recovered in three parts: D.1 to D.24.2, called the *Digestum vetus;* then D.39 through D.50, the *Digestum novum;* and finally the missing middle segment, dubbed the *Infortiatum.* Irnerius may have also lectured on and glossed the *Institutes,* which again came into prominence as a textbook. The *Institutes* presented an image of the law focused upon interrelated legal rules. The *Digest* contained rules and concepts applied in general or hypothetical situations *(casus)*—a very professorial law. With these textual tools law could be seen as a separate object of study and a coherent system of rules. This perception was aided by the fact that the Roman texts presented the law as timeless and universally valid, and with little attention to procedural issues (an area of the law greatly at variance with existing practices). The long-ignored last three books of the *Codex,* the *Tres libri,* and the *Authenticum,* a collection containing the *Novellae,* also surfaced in Bologna.

Irnerius and his successors employed a characteristic method of textual exegesis, explaining difficult passages and resolving contradictions. The same exegetical and dialectical method was employed by the monk Gratian, who composed a systematic textbook of canon law. His *Concordantia discordantium canonum* (written around 1140 and better known as the *Decretum*) related a variety of canonical sources by means of logical *distinctiones.* This unofficial but successful textbook also drew heavily on the language of Roman law and combined features of the *Institutes* and the *Digest.* As a result of Gratian's work, canon law was separated from theology, and study of Roman law became an essential prerequisite for canonistic studies.

Civil and canon law were considered to be universally valid. Thus they had an "international" character as a common law *(ius commune)* of Christendom and the empire. Impetus for the study of this law came from two sources: the investiture controversy between the two universal powers, the papacy and the empire, and the communal movement in Italian cities, of which Bologna was a part. Legal ideas fed into the polemical and legal battles between popes and emperors, on the one hand, while they began to articulate elements of the legal order of the communes and their relations to the rest of the world, on the other.

The prestige of the *ius commune* and of the teachers in Bologna attracted students from all over Italy and the rest of Europe. The large contingent of foreign students in Bologna not only accentuated the international character of the law but also proved a decisive factor in the institutional development of the university there. As foreigners, students did not have the protection of the statutes of the commune of Bologna, especially the lay students of civil law, who could not claim clerical status and immunities. Emperor Frederick I, desirous of furthering education in "imperial" laws, afforded these students some initial protection by means of the decree *Habita* (1158). From this basis students were able to establish their independence from the commune and their control over their teachers through the formation of *universitates* of foreign (cismontane and ultramontane) students.

Instruction in Bologna was privately arranged; doctors of law were highly dependent on student fees, and thus vulnerable to organized pressure. The *universitates* regulated the fees and even imposed fines on teachers who failed to cover their texts completely and competently in their lectures. Students also faced problems with the town of Bologna and reacted with the threat to migrate elsewhere to study—a threat with serious economic consequences. Brief migrations to Vicenza in 1204 and Arezzo in 1215 preceded an almost total exodus in 1217–1220, when students refused to give Bolognese officials an oath not to migrate. A compromise was eventually arranged through Pope Honorius III, but town–gown problems continued to surface and student migrations occasionally occurred thereafter, most notably in 1321.

LATER LAW SCHOOLS:

THE EXPANSION OF LEGAL EDUCATION

Migrations of students and teachers from Bologna contributed to the establishment of law schools elsewhere in Europe. Not all of these new schools were permanent, and some flourished only after a history of desultory revivals and extinctions. One of the most important daughters of Bologna was Padua. The glossator Martinus Gosia may have taught there before 1169, but a true *studium generale* existed only from the time of the great migra-

to Padua in 1222. During the rule of Ezzolino da Romano (1237–1260), the school in Padua was at a low ebb, but its fortunes revived after 1260 and it became one of the leading universities of Europe.

Other schools grew up around individual teachers. Vacarius journeyed to Oxford and initiated the study of civil and, especially, canon law there. Legal studies began in Montpellier with the arrival of Placentinus around 1166, although the school did not flourish until 1289. The law school at Orléans resulted from yet another type of migration. In 1219 Honorius III forbade the teaching of civil law in Paris. The civil-law faculty shifted to Orléans, where it provided the necessary scientific background for canon-law studies, which continued, with papal encouragement, in Paris.

Finally, other law schools owed their existence in the thirteenth century to deliberate efforts and patronage by emperor, pope, or prince. The first such was at Naples, founded by Frederick II in 1224. Professional legal education there was designed to produce graduates to fill the emperor's needs in the legal and administrative affairs of his southern Italian kingdom. Civil-law norms figured in Frederick's compilation of laws and customs for his kingdom, the *Liber Augustalis*. Likewise, the school of Salamanca in Spain (originally founded before 1227/ 1228) was revived by Alfonso X the Wise, whose *Siete partidas* established the need for trained jurists. Papal patronage led to the foundation of a university at Toulouse in 1229 (mainly for theology but also offering legal instruction) and to a school of civil and canon law at the papal court in 1244/1245.

Throughout the thirteenth century, however, Bologna remained preeminent. As other schools struggled, Bologna produced a steady stream of graduates who found ready employment, especially in the church, where law aided in the consolidation of ecclesiastical order. Only toward the end of the century did other universities flourish, mainly with princely and communal support. Even in Bologna the commune began to salary professors and take a more active interest in the university. The use of foreign jurists in cities (such as the Italian podesta) and the utility of "universal" law in handling competing rights and claims increased the demand for trained jurists.

In southern France *studia* at Toulouse, Cahors, Avignon, and Montpellier flourished, and *causidici* were trained locally rather than at Bologna. In Italy, Piacenza, Siena, Florence, and Pavia established universities and sought to attract renowned teachers and flocks of students. Unquestionably one of the most successful universities was that of Perugia, founded in 1308, which attracted the teachers Jacobus de Belviso, Johannes Andreae, and Bartolo da Sassoferrato. In all these universities teachers of law held higher status and received higher salaries.

Legal education came later to Germany and the Holy Roman empire. German students, mainly in canon law, generally went to Italy or southern France. The first German universities followed the Parisian model, offering only canon law. Only on the eve of the reception of Roman law in Germany did universities such as Tübingen (1476/1477) arise, with the express mission to teach civil law, and did existing universities, such as Prague (founded 1347/1348), Vienna (founded 1365), and Heidelberg (founded 1385), gather a faculty in civil law. In other northern European universities, colleges were endowed for the study of law, in contrast with the thirteenth-century colleges that fostered mainly the arts and theology.

TEACHING METHODS AND CURRICULA

The expansion of legal education owed a great deal to social, economic, and political developments. Princes, cities, and individuals, as well as the church, had need of law and legal expertise. But the expansion of legal education must also be attributed to the concepts, methods, and curricula of the schools. In a world of overlapping jurisdictions (ecclesiastical, feudal, communal) of diverse legal origins (customary, Germanic, civil, canonical), teaching of the *ius commune* provided a form of legal expertise adaptable to various circumstances.

Courses of study and degree requirements followed general patterns everywhere. At Bologna a student acquired the status of bachelor after a fixed course of "ordinary" instruction lasting four or five years in canon law and five or six in civil. Thereafter he attended "extraordinary" lectures and participated in public repetitions and disputations. A sequence of examinations (after about seven or eight years in canon law, eight in civil, ten for a doctorate in the two laws [*in utroque iure*]) completed a prospective lawyer's education. A student was examined privately by his chosen mentor, who then presented him for examination before a board of *doctores*. If he passed, he was officially licensed to teach (*licentiatus*). Then, if he could sustain the costs, the student proceeded with the ceremonial doctoral examination conducted publicly in the cathedral.

Basic legal instruction took the form of lectures, which consisted of reading part of an authoritative legal text, summarizing the points of law, and analyzing any difficulties. Lectures were given in the morning by the teaching masters. They provided detailed exposition of the chief texts and magisterial rulings on related problems. Extraordinary lectures occurred in the afternoon; they covered the chief texts or less important ones, and could be given by bachelors. Lectures were supplemented by repetitions (recapitulations, required of advanced students) and by disputations. In the latter, *quaestiones disputatae* (rather than texts) were debated pro and con. Advanced students and teachers had the opportunity to hone their dialectical skills in disputations and to consider various problems and fact situations.

The *quaestio disputata* is one example of the use of dialectical reasoning in law schools. The harmonizing of contradictory passages or points of law was embedded in legal education from the time of Irnerius. However, the use of dialectic changed between the glossators and the commentators. The first interlinear glosses and later marginal ones extracted key phrases and related them to other passages. This process was geared not to reconstructing fact situations or to delineating specific legal problems, but to reforming the texts into a normative unit through subdivisions (*distinctiones*) under a common concept. In this manner textual contradictions were resolved in accord with the conviction that the *Corpus* was a normative unit. The glosses, as a scientific production, became fixed as a professional apparatus, the "ordinary gloss." This was assembled by Accursius (*d. ca.* 1263) for civil law; similar glosses were constructed for canon law. Thereafter texts almost always appeared with the marginal ordinary gloss.

The commentators paid attention to the marginal apparatus almost to the exclusion of the text. They treated law as a system not necessarily confined to the texts, thus fashioning a more active interpretive role for themselves. The first major commentator was Cino da Pistoia (*d.* 1336/1337). His achievement was distinguishing the *casus* of a text from the unresolved *quaestio* of the law, the definition and resolution of which required not only the text and glosses but also statutes and other sources of legal reasoning. His work was extended greatly by the two most famous and authoritative commentators, Bartolo da Sassoferrato (*d.* 1357) and Baldus (or Baldo) degli Ubaldi (*d.* 1400). By their efforts a variety of norms and normative sources, even Aristotelian philosophy with Baldus, became linked dialectically into a system.

The commentators had a larger body of texts to confront. Canon law underwent considerable expansion. Following Gratian's *Decretum* attempts were made to gather papal decretal letters. Gregory IX finally promulgated an official compilation in five books, the *Liber extra vagantium* (1234). Boniface VIII added a collection (the "sixth" book, *Liber sextus*) in 1298; and in the fourteenth century the *Clementinae, Extravagantes,* and *Extravagantes communes* completed the corpus of canon law. In contrast, the *Corpus iuris civilis* was much more fixed, but additions were made following the model of the *Novellae.* Thus the feudal law, *Liber feudorum,* compiled in the 1150's and reedited in the 1220's, was included as the tenth collation of the *Authenticum.* Lombard law, still studied at Pavia in the eleventh century, did not acquire the same status. However, renewed studies of Lombard law did produce an apparatus of glosses assembled by Carolus de Tocco (*ca.* 1200).

These texts held different statuses within the curriculum. The most important texts were treated in ordinary lectures: *Codex, Digestum vetus, Decretum,* and *Liber extra vagantium.* The *Digestum novum, Infortiatum, Liber sextus,* and *Clementinae* were generally treated as *extraordinaria.* Other texts were treated only occasionally, although Bologna eventually provided for salaried lecturers in *extraordinaria* to assure regular treatment of the *Institutes, Tres libri, Authenticum,* and *Liber feudorum.*

THE SIGNIFICANCE OF MEDIEVAL LAW SCHOOLS

In a society of competing rights, privileges, and jurisdictions, there was endless opportunity for employment of the dialectical and disputational expertise of the law graduate. The articulation of juristic and political principles by these men played a powerful role in shaping governments and ideologies. Even humanism, often antithetical to legal notions and arguments, owed its origins in part to law. Above all, laws schools and their graduates shaped the law, and therein lay their most pervasive influence.

Professionalized legal studies served to distinguish the *doctor legum* from the judge. While schools developed law as a science, lawmakers and judges were left to chart a course in unexplored realms of law. In their doing so, the dialectical skill of deducing subordinate principles from general ones proved useful, and it enabled commentators to influence legal practice once again by incorporating statutory law within their purview. The work of the commenta-

tors and their immediate predecessors, the "post-glossators," went hand in hand with the expansion of universities in the late Middle Ages.

The more prestigious and technically precise *ius commune* served as a basis for coordinating statutes and customs, conceived as *ius proprium* (local law). The overarching *ius commune* was the framework within which the limited *iura propria* were seen to work. Civil and canon law were treated as enclosing all particular laws on the level of theory and procedure, a treatment aided by the development of notarial and procedural formularies.

Relating statutes to *ius commune* in the course of actual litigations took two forms. On the one hand, jurists occasionally became involved in the editing and compiling of statutes, intruding their concepts and terminology in the process. On the other hand, and more regularly, they became involved in the interpretation and application of law in a consultative role, through *consilia* (legal opinions). In the fourteenth and fifteenth centuries there was a major shift from exegesis of the juristic sources to application of the law by use of *consilia.* Jurists composed opinions for the guidance of judges, litigants, and others on doubtful points of law that arose in judicial and legislative practice. The greatest jurists wrote numerous *consilia,* which were prized and collected. The demonstrated relevance of academic jurisprudence to legal practice was a stimulus to the spread of legal education. The reception of Roman law in Germany was a reception not so much of particular norms as of scientific jurisprudence and (written) procedure. Far from representing a supposed decadence of legal scholarship or its mortgaging to powerful interests, *consilia* were the instrument of a rationalization and extension of the law of the schools into society.

BIBLIOGRAPHY

On the organization of law schools and universities, see Giorgio Cencetti, *"Studium fuit Bononie,"* in *Studi medievali,* 3rd ser., 7 (1966); Alan B. Cobban, *The Medieval Universities: Their Development and Organization* (1975); André Gouron, "The Training of Southern French Lawyers During the Thirteenth and Fourteenth Centuries," in *Studia Gratiana,* 15 (1972); Charles Homer Haskins, *The Rise of Universities* (1957); J. K. Hyde, "Commune, University, and Society in Early Medieval Bologna," in John W. Baldwin and Richard A. Goldthwaite, eds., *Universities in Politics* (1972); Hastings Rashdall, *The Universities of Europe in the Middle Ages,* new ed., F. M. Powicke and A. B. Emden, eds., 3 vols. (1936); Helene Wieruszowski, *The Medieval University* (1966).

On civil and canon law, see Lauro Martines, *Lawyers*

and Statecraft in Renaissance Florence (1968); Walter Ullmann, *Law and Politics in the Middle Ages* (1975); Alan
Watson, *The Making of the Civil Law* (1981).

THOMAS KUEHN

[See also **Baldus; Bartolo da Sassoferrato; Bologna, Uni-
versity of; Corpus Iuris Civilis; Dictamen; Frederick II;
Gloss; Glossators; Gratian; Irnerius; Johannes Andreae;
Law, Canon; Martinus Gosia; Naples; Placentinus;
Ravenna; Siete Partidas; Trivium; Universities.**]

LAW, SCOTS. The history of Scots law in the Middle Ages conforms to a recognizable pattern of
Western European legal development, by which a
distinct system of law—in the case of Scotland, a national system coextensive with the Kingdom of Scotland—gradually emerges, as the civil law, the canon
law, and the feudal law react with royal ordinances
against a background of customary law. Scots law,
however, diverges from the European norm in two
important respects: first, the customary law base was,
to some extent at least, Celtic rather than Germanic,
and second, although Scottish political development
was not interrupted by a Norman conquest, the influence on Scotland of the Norman and early Plantagenet kings of England, and of the nascent English
common law, was very great.

In the Dark Ages documentation is sparse in the
extreme, and legal history is largely a matter of inference. The non-Indo-European strain among the
Picts is reflected in matrilineal succession in the
royal line. The law of the Britons of Strathclyde
would be cognate with the early Welsh laws. In
Lothian and the Merse, the northern tip of the kingdom of Northumbria, Anglo-Saxon law codes applied. The ancient Irish law tracts, already in writing
in the eighth century, hold the key to the law of the
Scots, whose dynasty, hailing originally from Ireland, gradually extended its rule over Picts, Britons,
and Angles alike.

By the middle of the eleventh century the medieval kingdom of Scotland had taken shape; by the
middle of the twelfth century feudalization was proceeding rapidly. To a great extent England provided
the model. Glanville's *De legibus et consuetudinibus
regni Angliae* was influential in Scotland and forms
the basis of the most important treatise on medieval
Scots law, *Regiam majestatem,* which probably
dates from the early fourteenth century. Both in the
substance of the law, particularly in land law and
succession, and also in procedure, there are strong

parallels between Scotland and England. Thus procedure by brieve (writ) and by inquest was borrowed
from England; Scotland too had its brieve of right,
brieve of novel dissasine (anglicé disseisin), and
brieve of mortancestry (anglicé mort d'ancestor). In
Scotland, as in England, royal administration was
con ducted by justiciars, sheriffs and bailies, a chancellor, and a chancery.

Yet there were also many points of difference. In
England a strong monarch was early able to eliminate or control baronial franchises. In Scotland
courts of barony and courts of regality continued to
function and to multiply throughout the medieval
period. In England a separate legal profession
emerged in the thirteenth century. In Scotland this
was not to happen until the fifteenth or sixteenth
century. Also, even during the period of greatest
English influence, in the twelfth and thirteenth centuries, the English model had not been uncritically
adopted, but had been altered to meet Scottish needs.
G. W. S. Barrow's apt comment that the office of justiciar, borrowed from England, soon "took on the
protective colouring of a thoroughly native species"
applies equally to many other importations. Thus
Scots law, so heavily influenced by the common law
in its infancy, took its own course, especially after
the Wars of Independence, and remained open to
civil- and canon-law influences.

The older customary law was never abolished but
merged insensibly into the new. Daniel A. Binchy
has suggested that in Ireland the Celtic obligation of
clienthood *(celsine)* may have been the precursor of
the feudal relationship. This is likely to have been
the case in Scotland also. Certainly the Celtic *mor-
maer* became the feudal earl *(comes),* and, in some
cases, the Celtic *toiseach* became a thane and later
a baron. The Celtic *britheamh* (judge) appears in
twelfth-century legislation as the Latin *judex* and
long survived the introduction of justiciar and sheriff. The Celtic exaction of *cain* (royal tribute) outlasted the Middle Ages. Nor was the Anglo-Saxon
inheritance rejected: the jingle "cum sacca et socca
et toll et theme et infangthief" is repeated in many
grants of baronial jurisdiction, and hamesucken
(Anglo-Saxon: *hamsocn*) remains a crime in the law
of Scotland to this day. Actions of assythment
(compensation) for slaughter, of customary origin,
whether Celtic or Anglo-Saxon, remained a commonplace until the seventeenth century.

In 1426 it was enacted that "the kingis liegis of
the realme leif [live] and be governyt undir the
kingis lawis and statutis of this realme alanerly

[alone] and undir na particular lawis na speciale privalegis na be na lawis of uthir cuntreis nor realmis." However, the ideal of one system of law under one monarch was not to be fully realized until the downfall, at the end of the fifteenth century, of the MacDonald lords of the isles, who had established a powerful principality in the west highlands and islands that threatened the stability of the kingdom. Under the MacDonald lords, who had close ties with Ireland, Celtic law enjoyed a new lease on life. Also in the fifteenth century, the northern isles of Orkney and Shetland, which had belonged to Norway, were effectively incorporated into the Scottish kingdom, although traces of udal law affecting land ownership were to survive until the twentieth century.

No specialized central civil court existed in Scotland until the end of the medieval period. In the fourteenth and fifteenth centuries Parliament was the supreme court of law; and when Parliament could not be called, there was no ordinary court superior to that of the justiciar and the chamberlain, although the king's council might in some cases provide a remedy. During the fifteenth century various expedients were tried to cope with the flood of legal business to Parliament and council. When a central civil court, the Court of Session, finally emerged and was established as the College of Justice in 1532, it combined the ordinary jurisdiction of the feudal courts with the extraordinary jurisdiction of the council, thus ensuring that in Scotland there would be no divide between law and equity. As originally constituted, the court's composition was as much ecclesiastical as lay, thus ensuring that the civil and the canon law, including the Romano-canonical procedure, would continue to influence the law of Scotland.

BIBLIOGRAPHY

There is no standard work on the history of Scots law; however, the following general works may be consulted: William Croft Dickinson, *Scotland from the Earliest Times to 1603*, 3rd ed., rev. and ed. by Archibald A. M. Duncan (1977); Alexander A. M. Duncan, *Scotland: The Making of the Kingdom* (1975); Cosmo N. Innes, *Lectures on Scotch Legal Antiquities* (1872); Hector McKechnie, ed., *An Introductory Survey of the Sources and Literature of Scots Law* (1936); Ranald Nicholson, *Scotland: The Later Middle Ages* (1974); George C. H. Paton, ed., *An Introduction to Scottish Legal History* (1958).

More specialized works include John W. M. Bannerman, "The Lordship of the Isles," in Jennifer M. Brown, ed., *Scottish Society in the Fifteenth Century* (1977), and "The Lordship of the Isles: Historical Background," in

K. A. Steer and John M. Bannerman, *Late Medieval Monumental Sculpture in the West Highlands* (1977); G. W. S. Barrow, "The Scottish *Judex* in the Twelfth and Thirteenth Centuries," in *Scottish Historical Review*, **45** (1966), and, as "The Judex," in his *The Kingdom of the Scots* (1973), and "The Scottish Justiciar in the Twelfth and Thirteenth Centuries," in *Juridical Review* (Edinburgh), n.s. **16** (1971), and, as "The Justiciar," in his *The Kingdom of the Scots* (1973); T. M. Cooper, *Select Scottish Cases of the Thirteenth Century* (1944), and introduction to *Regiam majestatem* (1947); William Croft Dickinson, introduction to *Sheriff Court Book of Fife, 1515–1522* (1928), introduction to *Court Book of the Barony of Carnwath, 1523–1542* (1937), and "The Administration of Justice in Medieval Scotland," in *Aberdeen University Review*, **34** (1952); Archibald A. M. Duncan, "Regiam Majestatem: A Reconsideration," in *Juridical Review* (Edinburgh), n.s. **6** (1961).

Robert K. Hannay, *College of Justice* (1933); A. Harding, "Medieval Brieves of Protection," in *Juridical Review* (Edinburgh), n.s. **11** (1966); Hector McKechnie, *Judicial Process upon Brieves, 1219–1532* (1956); Arthur R. G. M'Millan, *Evolution of the Scottish Judiciary* (1941); James J. Robertson, "The Development of the Law," in Jennifer M. Brown, ed., *Scottish Society in the Fifteenth Century* (1977); Thomas Broun Smith, *Short Commentary on the Law of Scotland* (1962), chap. 1; Peter Stein, "Roman Law in Scotland," in *Ius Romanum medii aevi*, part V, 13b (1968), and "Source of the Romano-canonical Part of *Regiam Majestatem*," in *Scottish Historical Review*, **48** (1969); David M. Walker, *Scottish Legal System*, 5th ed. (1981), chap. 4; J. M. Webster and Archibald A. M. Duncan, Introduction to *Regality of Dunfermline Court Book, 1531–1538* (1953).

DAVID H. SELLAR

[See also **Chancery; Glanville, Ranulf de; Justiciar; Scotland: History; Sheriff.**]

LAW, SPANISH. For two centuries, the history of Spanish law has been a battlefield of conflicting ideologies. Diversity of political views has led to contradictory interpretations that remain unresolved in the late twentieth century. By attempting to provide a short summary of the development of Spanish law, this study avoids the more elaborate political and scholarly controversies and seeks instead to keep close to the common body of knowledge that has been agreed upon by most scholars.

Spanish law does not necessarily mean the legal system of medieval Spain. Throughout the Middle Ages, the Iberian peninsula had great diversity in its political, legal, and cultural institutions. There was in fact no Spain as a legal entity until long after the dawn of the modern age. Here, the emphasis will be upon the development of law and legal mechanisms in the kingdom of Asturias and Castile—that is, the area that became ascendant within Spain and imposed, with some minor exceptions, its law and institutions on the rest of the Spanish kingdoms.

The Iberian peninsula came under Roman influence early, and over the course of time it became one of the most romanized areas of the empire. However, the extent of romanization varied from area to area within the peninsula. Iberia received a large influx of colonists from Italy, and these colonists brought with them their legal prerogatives and institutions. Urban centers generally hewed to the institutional and legal patterns created by Rome, and areas easily accessible to Roman influence, such as the eastern coast and the south, were more receptive to the spread of Roman legal institutions than the mountainous areas of the north (Asturias, the Cantabrian Mountians, and the Basque region) that were never really conquered by the Romans.

Spanish legal historians have paid a great deal of attention to the early indigenous customs. The have discussed their survival after the establishment of Roman rule in Spain, and they have detected their influence in later legal systems. To support these findings, scholars point to the Roman practice of respecting local traditions and also to the overwhelmingly urban nature of Roman colonization. They then infer that, in the rural world and in remote areas, the Celtic-Iberian customary law remained in existence with, as one scholar puts it, "persistent vitality." One must add the caution, however, that we know very little about these original customs, and that attempts to recreate them have been largely futile. Although it is possible that their influence was widespread, the importance that some scholars attach to them seems unwarranted and possibly motivated less by evidence than by a patriotic desire to discover indigenous national legal origins. In fact, recent legal historians point to the survival of these customs, if at all, only as isolated and disjointed concepts.

García Gallo dates the juridical romanization of Spain to the years between 74 A.D., when Vespasian granted Latin rights to the inhabitants of the peninsula, and 250 A.D. Roman commercial and municipal law, edicts of Roman magistrates, imperial constitutions, and the work of noted Roman jurists served as the sources for the development of law in Roman Spain, as they did elsewhere in the empire. The influence of Ulpian, Paul, Gaius, Papinian, and others can

be seen in the numerous references to their works found in legal decisions and textbooks in late Roman Spain. Roman legal, cultural, social, and institutional achievements survived the disasters of the third century and were transmitted, if often in modified form, into the barbarian period.

By the early fifth century, the Iberian peninsula had ceased to be a part of the empire. The short rule of the Vandals was quickly followed by the Visigothic invasion in the late fifth century. The Visigoths came to Spain as *foederati*—theoretically representatives of imperial authority. Always a small minority among the Hispano-Romans, they were received—as Orosius reports in a few pages dealing with the fall of Spain—with open arms by the inhabitants of the peninsula. Rather efficient warriors, the half-romanized Visigoths brought back some semblance of order to Hispania. Their occupation of Spain was a slow and never completed process, however, and many areas, especially in the north and northwest, escaped their rule.

As everywhere, at least in the early period of barbarian Europe, the conquered peoples of Spain continued to live under the legal system of Rome while the Germanic conquerors followed their own tribal customs. Although there were fundamental differences between the Roman and Germanic concepts of law, the two systems did tend to grow together over time, as legal practice among the Hispano-Romans was progressively barbarized, and as Germanic customs, in this case Visigothic tribal laws, were modified by contact with the more sophisticated Roman legal system.

This movement toward a unified legal system seems to have been encouraged by the Visigothic kings, who stood to gain from the adoption of Roman political concepts. The Visigothic kings did in fact substantially increase their powers, and in particular they managed to limit the number and power of those electing the king to an extent unknown in early Germanic tradition. This is not to say that in Visigothic Spain the kings fully enjoyed the prerogatives of post-Diocletian emperors. Rather, the Germanic tradition of elective kingship remained a troublesome element of Visigothic political life, and in the kingdoms of Asturias, León, and Castile later on.

There is evidence that this royal policy in favor of legal unification started early. Some of the legislation of Theodoric I (418–451) and Theodoric II (453–466) appears to have been designed to apply to both Hispano-Romans and Visigoths. Further evidence comes from the first surviving law code, which dates from the reign of Euric (466–484). Euric's Code, written sometime around 475, though some scholars disclaim any certainty in this dating, brought together elements of Roman law (mainly borrowed from the *Codex Theodosianus,* which was published at Constantinople in 438), Germanic customs, and some of the canons of the Arian church (the predominant confession among the Visigoths). Written in Latin, probably by jurists trained in the Roman law, at Euric's court in Toulouse in southern Gaul, this legal collection was intended to serve as a code for all the king's subjects.

Euric's son, Alaric II (484–507), was forced after his defeat by the Franks to consolidate his position south of the Pyrenees. Moved perhaps by these political considerations, he ordered the edition of a collection of post-classical Roman law (the *Codex Theodosianus,* later imperial edicts, and the writings of Roman jurists). Alaric's *Breviarium* or *Lex romana Visigothorum,* as the end product of these labors was called, did not include any Germanic elements and was an attempt, according to van Kleffens, "to bring up to date and to codify Roman law." Although there has been a long debate as to for whom this law was promulgated, either Hispano-Romans or Visigoths or both, the *Breviarium* had little impact on Visigothic Spain. Its importance lies elsewhere, in its influence on Frankish law. More important for the Visigothic legal tradition was the reestablishment and correction of Euric's Code carried on under Leovigild (568–586). Most scholars maintain that Leovigild's legislation was aimed only at the Visigoths, but others, Galo Sánchez among them, have disagreed. Leovigild's reforms did expand the Roman legal elements of Euric's Code. In addition, Leovigild married a Catholic and was sympathetic in his policies toward Catholics. In general, his reign tended to diminish the differences between Visigoths and Hispano-Romans. Leovigild's successor, Recared I (586–601), converted to Catholicism, bringing an end to the distinctions between Hispano-Romans and Visigoths.

Recared's conversion made a dual legal custom unnecessary, if indeed such a system was still in force, which is not at all certain considering the progress already made toward a unified legal system. Recared also introduced further modifications into Leovigild's revisions of the Code of Euric through laws clearly influenced by Roman legal precedents.

In the seventh century the legal work of four Visigothic kings, with the active participation of the church, through the famous councils of Toledo (the Eighth and Twelfth), led to the compilation of a highly romanized code, the *Liber iudiciorum* or *Lex barbara visigothorum* (not to be confused with the earlier *Lex romana visigothorum,* or Breviary of Alaric). Began probably under Chindaswinth (642–652), with work continuing under his son Recceswinth (653–672), the *Liber iudiciorum* became the sole guide for the administration of justice in Visigothic Spain. All previous legislation ceased to have binding force in the king's court. The sources for the *Liber* were Leovigild's Code, Justinian's law codification (one must remember the Byzantine presence in southeastern Spain after 535), other assorted Roman legal texts, and St. Isidore's *Etymologies.* In the 680's King Erwig (680–687) and his succesor, Egica (687–701), ordered their jurists, with the help of the church, to prepare a second edition of the *Liber iudiciorum.*

The *Liber* consisted of twelve books. It included discussions of the law and the legislator, judicial organization and procedure, civil and criminal law, and a variety of other topics such as treatment of heretics, Jews, and the sick. This material, as scholars have noted, was put together without much respect for logical order. Van Kleffens notes the harshness and cruelty of its provisions, but he also praises the law's "well-developed sense of justice."

The *Liber iudiciorum* was undoubtedly the greatest legacy of Visigothic Spain. It far outlived the barbarian kings, influencing later Spanish legal systems and the law of Spanish colonies around the world. Its influence at the time, however, should not be overstated. Although in theory the *Liber iudiciorum* applied throughout Visigothic Spain, its enforcement was severely restricted by the limitations on the political power of the Visigothic kings. Large areas of the peninsula were outside their control. Moreover, as Thomas F. Glick has shown in his book *Islamic and Christian Spain in the Early Middle Ages* (1979), the Visigoths presided over the demise of Roman urban society and the progressive ruralization of Spain. In the north and in the countryside local customs, of which we know next to nothing, may well have been the only law.

The coming of Islam in 711 brought Visigothic rule in Spain to a swift end. The Arabs and Berbers established their rule in the peninsula without great difficulty, and by the tenth century the Córdoba caliphate reached its political and cultural apex.

There is considerable scholarly debate as to the influence that Muslim law, mostly religious in nature, may have had on the Christian kingdoms of Spain. Certainly in areas such as Valencia and Andalusia, Muslim institutional arrangements were part of the very fabric of life. How did they affect the legal system? The issue has not yet been satisfactorily resolved.

In this connection, it is important to note that the Hispano-Romans and Visigoths who came under Muslim rule and retained their religion continued to be judged by the *Liber iudiciorum*. In this manner, these people, who came to be called Mozarabs, preserved the legal accomplishments of the seventh century. In the tenth century Mozarabs fleeing Muslim rule carried the *Liber* with them to the north.

Prior to the early tenth century, the legal systems of the small and divided Christian kingdoms in the north reflected the fragmentation and particularism of the country. Visigothic law had little or no impact in Asturias, the mountain areas of the Bay of Biscay, and far-off Galicia, because Visigothic power had never been strong in these isolated, impoverished, and thinly populated areas. In Asturias, however, under Alfonso II (791–842), there was an attempt to revive the Visigothic administrative and court structure, and the *Liber iudiciorum* was introduced into the kingdom. Yet it was not until the late ninth and early tenth centuries, during the reign of Alfonso III (866–910), that the *Liber iudiciorum* found any significant acceptance in Asturias-León. Even then, the tenuous hold which the Asturian-Leonese kings of the tenth century had upon the realm weakened the enforcement of a unified territorial law. This was most evident in the development of localized customs in places such as Galicia (with its strong Celtic background) and above all Castile.

Many of the peculiarities of regional and local customs resulted from diversity in the patterns of landholding, from variations in the relationship between the nobility and the rest of the population, and from differences in the repopulation efforts. For example, in Galicia the rapid seignorialization of the land led to the emergence of customs quite different from those in the open frontier of Castile, where free peasants often cultivated their lands with few or no obligations. The repopulation of León, sponsored to a large degree by the crown, also contrasts with that of the frontier in Castile, which was undertaken by freeholders or directed by the counts and monasteries.

In any case, Castile developed its own peculiar institutions and legal instruments, of which the most important was the *fuero*. The *fueros* (charters of privilege or exemption) and also the *cartas de población* (charters to promote repopulation) reflected long-unwritten customs. They were granted by the Castilian counts and, later on, the Castilian and Leonese kings to new towns, to special groups (such as foreigners, the nobility, the merchant class), to whole regions, and eventually to the entire realm.

There were two different types of *fueros*, brief (*breve*) and extensive (*extensivo*). An example of the first is the *fuero* of León (1017 or 1020), which included territorial and local (city of León) customs, laws, and privileges. An example of the second type of *fuero* is the elaborate *fuero* of Cuenca (late twelfth century) with its numerous "family" of other *fueros* derived from it.

In Old Castile and the Basque region one also finds the so-called *fuero*, or *juicio, de albedrío*. When, in the tenth century, Castile rejected the *Liber iudiciorum* (according to the legends by public burning of the *Liber* in Burgos) as it had rejected Asturian and Leonese political rule, its counts forbade the use of the old Visigothic code or appeals to the authority of the Asturian-Leonese kings. Instead, the judges were to examine and decide in each instance according to the merits of the case and by using their own judgment (by *albedrío*). These legal decisions (*fazañas* or *faciendas*) were recorded and had binding force for any future cases of similar nature.

One must add to the above the impact of Frankish law and feudal practices, which, although they made a strong imprint only in Catalonia, did nevertheless have some influence in the development of law in the western kingdoms. Particularly important in this respect were the numerous French and other trans-Pyrenean merchants (known in Spain as *Francos*) who settled in the cities along the road to Santiago de Compostela and influenced the commercial legislation of the Castilian kings. Such then were the conditions at the beginning of the thirteenth century.

When Ferdinand III (1217–1252) effected the permanent union of Castile and León, one of his main tasks was to provide the realm with a unified system of law. Much as been made of the reception of Roman law in Spain and of the impact that the recovery of Justinian's *Corpus* and the work of the Bolognese jurists had on the political and legal development of Castile. This emphasis underestimates the direction that the political and legal centralization had already taken in Castile and elsewhere in western Europe. Roman law or not, political conditions pointed to the emergence of a unified legal system in Castile.

It must be admitted, however, that the reception of Roman law from the twelfth century on was of great significance. As Galo Sánchez and García Gallo have shown, the acceptance of the *Corpus iuris civilis* was not a dramatic and immediate event. Rather, the way for its reception was paved by the previous study of other romanizing legal works. Among them one should mention the *Decretum, Panormia,* and *Tripartita* of Ivo of Chartres, the *Petri exceptiones legum Romanorum* (extracts of Justinian's Code), and *Lo Codi,* written in Provençal and translated into Catalan, Castilian, and other languages. Moreover, from the mid twelfth century on, many Castilians traveled to Bologna, Montpellier, and other centers for the study of law, bringing back with them their newly acquired knowledge. In Castile itself the universities of Palencia, founded in the early thirteenth century, and later on Salamanca served as training centers for lawyers versed in Roman law. As in other parts of Europe, many of these lawyers soon became judges and officials of the crown. The stage was therefore set for the legal work of Ferdinand III, his son Alfonso X (1252–1284), and their successors.

Ferdinand III's military victories (the conquest of Córdoba in 1236 and Seville in 1248) brought most of Andalusia under his rule. To the newly conquered cities he granted as their local *fuero* or municipal charter the *Liber iudiciorum.* This Visigothic code had been translated into Castilian and now with the name of *Fuero juzgo* became the local charter of many towns in the south. This practice of granting the same *fuero* to different cities while preserving the fiction of granting it individually to each urban center was continued, with some variations, by the succeeding four kings. Ferdinand III also ordered the composition of the *Setenario,* a legal work which was only completed under Ferdinand III's son, Alfonso X. Following in the footsteps of his father, Alfonso X had his jurists embark on an ambitious legal program. The first task was to complete the *Setenario.* Unfortunately, we do not have an extant complete version of this work, which was really more of a religious and speculative work than a law code.

The first important legal work to be finished by Alfonso X's jurists was the *Fuero real* or *Fuero de las leyes.* According to García Gallo it was written between 1252 and 1255 and granted to many cities from 1255 on. In the prologue, the *Fuero real* was described as the work of the king, his court, and his lawyers, and its stated aim was to provide *fueros* for places that did not have them. However, it was also given to places that already had *fueros.* In essence, it replaced the *Fuero juzgo* in the royal campaign to provide uniformity of law throughout the kingdom. Consisting of simple rules of law arranged in an unsystematic manner, it was divided into four *libros* (books) dealing with religious and political matters, procedure, and civil and criminal law. Its extensive treatment of contracts, debts, sureties, and other commercial subjects made the *Fuero real* well suited for its role as the law of urban centers. Sources for the *Fuero real* were the *Fuero juzgo,* Roman law, and unidentified local customs, one of which, Galo Sánchez affirms, was the *fuero* of Soria.

Two important historiographical questions are how widely the *Fuero real* was applied and what sort of resistance it met from supporters of the old *fueros* and customs. The view has been that after 1272 (when the nobility rebelled against Alfonso X) the king, already in serious political and economic difficulties, bowed to aristocratic pressure and allowed a return to the old customs. Although there were a few instances in which this was true, my own research shows that this was not the case in the main cities of Castile and that the *Fuero real* remained in force long after 1272.

Although there are serious questions about its dating (some historians placing its composition in the court of Sancho IV), traditionally legal historians have emphasized as Alfonso X's most important legislation the code known in the later thirteenth century and thereafter as the *Siete partidas.* The *Siete partidas* was clearly intended as a uniform law code for the whole kingdom, even though the first redaction, known as the *Libro del fuero* (probably written between 1256 and 1260) was described as a guide for royal judges in cases that did not come under the jurisdiction of or were not covered by the local *fueros.* (According to García Gallo this is the version known as the *Espéculo,* which closely resembles the first portion of the code's second redaction. There is not, however, unanimity on the dating of the *Espéculo,* or indeed of its being a first version of the code later known as the *Siete partidas.*) Further revisions and redactions of the *Siete partidas* throughout the next hundred years emphasized the theoretical aspects of the work, making it more a book of reference than the code of law which it was originally intended to be. The political complications faced by the Castilian kings throughout most of the hundred years after the mid thirteenth century prevented the full implementation of the *Partidas*. Nevertheless, its strong romanizing elements and its thoroughness as a law treatise made the *Partidas*, and above all the third redaction, dating from the late thirteenth century, an undisputed set of references and a widely used source for the decisions of Castilian jurists and legislators.

The last years of Alfonso X's reign were a period of turmoil, and little was accomplished. One should note, however, the increased activity of the Castilian Cortes. Representatives of the clergy, the nobility, and especially the merchants came together in the Cortes, which played an enhanced role after the 1250's. Petitions from the Cortes to the crown on a wide range of economic, social, and political issues, when accepted by the king, had the force of law and were widely publicized throughout the realm.

In addition, municipal and royal officials often asked the king for clarification of legal points of the *Fuero real* or for guidance on matters not covered by the law. Royal answers to these inquiries also had the force of law. The *Leyes del estilo*, a private collection from around 1310, illustrates this type of royal clarification of the *Fuero real*.

There were also a number of private and anonymous redactions of Castilian territorial law. Two collections stand out. One is the *Libro de los fueros de Castilla*, a collection of customs from the area of Burgos written in the second half of the thirteenth century and containing royal privileges, *fazañas*, and local customs. The other collection is the *Fuero viejo de Castilla* or *Fuero de los fijosdalgo*, which is from the same period as the *Libro de los fueros de Castilla* and bears some similarity to it.

The next important phase in the development of Castilian law came in the reign of Alfonso XI (1312–1350). A capable and forceful king, Alfonso XI exercised increased control over the aristocracy but still moved cautiously in the area of legal innovations. Significant legislative work and judicial streamlining were carried out at the Cortes of Burgos in 1328 and at the Cortes of Segovia in 1347. In 1348, the Cortes meeting at Alcalá de Henares produced the very important *Ordenamiento de Alcalá de Henares*, which confirmed previous laws; set up new rules on matters of procedure, wills, contracts, and royal dealings with the nobility; and above all, established the order of precedence of the law then in force in Castile and León. This is the same order of precedence that, allowing for later additions, was

more or less maintained in Castile until the nineteenth century.

In this order of precedence, the *Ordenamiento* ranked as the most important legal source, having undisputed authority throughout the realm. It was followed by the municipal *fueros*, by now mostly the *Fuero real*. These *fueros* could be modified or set aside by the king. Finally, legal matters outside of the jurisdiction of either the *Ordenamiento* or the *fueros* were to be judged by the *Siete partidas*. This was the first time this code received anything like the general enactment that was originally intended. A new redaction of the *Siete partidas* was prepared at this time.

The death of Alfonso XI in 1350 marked the beginning of a troubled period that lasted, with a few short periods of peace, until the reign of Ferdinand and Isabella. Except for the administrative and judicial reforms of Juan I (1379–1390), little was done until 1480, when Ferdinand and Isabella ordered a collection of those Castilian laws not included in the *Ordenamiento de Alcalá de Henares*. The task was assigned to Alonso Díaz de Montalvo, a trained lawyer who after five years of work presented Ferdinand and Isabella with the finished version of the *Libro de las leyes u ordenanzas reales de Castilla*, also known as the *Ordenamiento de Montalvo*. This same lawyer also took an active role in the other great collection of this time, the *Leyes de Toro* (1505), an attempt by the jurists as Ferdinand and Isabella's court to bring into concordance the contradictory aspects of previous legislation.

From the reign of Ferdinand and Isabella, the legal structure of Castile remained basically unchanged until the nineteenth century; and over the centuries it was slowly imposed on the rest of Spain. In particular, the work of centralization carried out by the Bourbon kings in the eighteenth century swept away many of the traditional liberties and privileges of the different regions of Spain.

BIBLIOGRAPHY

General. Luis García de Valdeavellano, *Curso de historia de las instituciones españolas*, 3rd ed. (1973); Alfonso García Gallo, *Curso de historia del derecho español*, 2 vols., 5th ed. (1950), and *Manual de historia del derecho español*, 2 vols., 3rd ed. (1967); Eduardo de Hinojosa y Naveros, *Historia general del derecho español* (1887); Ernesto Mayer, *Historia de las instituciones sociales y políticas de España y Portugal durante los siglos V a XIV*, 2 vols. (1925–1926); Galo Sánchez, *Curso de historia del derecho*, 9th ed. (1960); E. N. van Kleffens, *Hispanic Law Until the End of the Middle Ages* (1968).

Roman Spain. A. García y Bellido, "Las colonias romanas de Hispania," in *Anuario de historia del derecho español,* **29** (1959); Theodor Mommsen, "Die Stadtrechte der latinischen Gemeinden Salpensa und Malaca in der Provinz Baetica," in his *Gesammelte Schriften,* I (1905); Álvaro d'Ors, "Estudios sobre la 'Constitutio Antoniniana,'" in *Anuario de historia del derecho español,* **15** (1944) and **17** (1946); Marcelo Vigil, "Romanización y permanencia de estructuras sociales indígenas en la España septentrional," in *Boletín de la Real Academia de la Historia,* **152** (1963).

Visigothic Spain. Teodoro Andrés Marcos, *Discurso leido . . . : Constitución, trasmisión y ejercicio de la monarquia hispano-visigoda en los Concilios Toledanos* (1928); Alfonso García Gallo, "Nacionalidad y territorialidad del derecho en la época visigoda," *Anuario de historia del derecho español,* **13** (1936–1941); Álvaro d'Ors, "La territorialidad del derecho de los visigodos," in *Estudios visigóticos,* I (1956); Claudio Sánchez-Albornoz, "Pervivencia y crisis de la tradición jurídica romana en la España goda," in his *Estudios sobre las instituciones medievales españolas* (1965); Manuel Torres, "El estado visigótico," in *Anuario de historia del derecho español,* **3** (1926).

Christian Spain. Joaquín Cerdá Ruiz-Funes, *Consideraciones sobre el hombre y sus derechos en las Partidas de Alfonso el Sabio* (1963); Ignacio de la Concha, "Consecuencias jurídicas, sociales y económicas de la reconquista y repoblación," in *La reconquista española y la repoblación del país* (1951); Gifford Davis, "The Incipient Sentiment of Nationality in Mediaeval Castile: The *Patrimonio Real,*" in *Speculum,* **12** (1937); Luis García de Valdeavellano, "Las 'Partidas' y los orígenes medievales del Juicio de residencia," in *Boletín de la Real Academia de la Historia,* **153** (1963); Rafael Gibert, "El derecho municipal de León y Castilla," *Anuario de historia del derecho español,* **31** (1961); Juan Martínez de la Vega y Zegri, *Derecho militar de la edad media: España* (1912); Gaines Post, "Roman Law and Early Representation in Spain and Italy, 1150–1250, in his *Studies in Medieval Legal Thought* (1964); Evelyn S. Procter, "The Castilian Chancery During the Reign of Alfonso X," in *Oxford Essays in Medieval History Presented to H. E. Salter* (1934), and *Curia and Cortes in León and Castile, 1072–1295* (1980); Percy Ernst Schramm, "Das Kastilische Königtum und Kaisertum während der Reconquista (11. Jahrhundert bis 1252)," in *Festschrift für Gerhard Ritter* (1949).

TEOFILO F. RUIZ

[See also **Alfonso X; Aragon; Asturias-León; Barbarians, Invasions of; Barcelona; Basques; Catalonia; Codex Theodosianus; Corpus Iuris Civilis; Ivo of Chartres, St.; Lo Codi; Navarre, Kingdom of; Petri Exceptiones; Seville; Spain, Christian-Muslim Relations; Spain, Muslim Kingdoms of; Valencia; Visigoths.**]

LAW, SWEDISH. Swedish sources make several references to *laghsagha,* or "law-saying"—that is, the recitation of orally preserved laws at assemblies by elected "lawmen." A fourteenth-century text gives a list, first compiled around 1250, of nineteen lawmen of Västergötland. The earliest names on the list date from the pre-Christian times of the early eleventh century. From comments in the list, it appears that lawmen were not mere repositories of law but legislators and justices as well.

Äldre Västgötalagen, or "the older law of Västergötland," says that the lawman should be a "yeoman's son"—that is, a representative of resident landowners and householders, and not a nobleman or a king's officer. In the early thirteenth century, however, the lawman in Västergötland was Eskil Magnusson. Eskil, who died around 1227, was a magnate from Östergötland. His family was of such prominence that his brother Birger, who died in 1266, was the highest officer of the state (*jarl*) and father of the kings Valdemar and Magnus I Ladulås. Another brother, Karl, was bishop of Linköping. Eskil's nephew Magnus Bengtsson was lawman in Östergötland around 1250; and Magnus' son Bengt held the same office from 1269 to 1294.

Snorri Sturluson knew Eskil Magnusson personally, and he probably based his account of the Swedish legal system on Eskil. Snorri wrote his account, which is perhaps somewhat idealized, around 1225 as a part of his *Óláfs saga helga* (it is in chapter 60 in the "separate" saga, and chapter 77 in *Heimskringla*).

The extant Swedish law texts are variously interrelated, but interest centers on their connections with *Upplandslagen,* "the law of Uppland," the region which from pre-Christian times had been the national religious center and seat of the monarchy. *Upplandslagen* was produced by a commission consisting of lawmen, judges, yeomen, noblemen, and the cleric Anders And, a Paris *magister* and dean of Uppsala. The code brought about the amalgamation of the three separate jurisdictions that had previously existed in Uppland. It received royal assent in 1296.

Other provincial laws may depend in varying degrees on the 1296 *Upplandslagen,* but they may also reveal earlier Uppland influence. A short text called *Hednalagen,* or "the heathen law," is probably a fragment of early Uppland law. It discusses dueling procedure in case of verbal injury.

It should be noted that canon law exerted an influence on Swedish law from early times. Swedish bishoprics were organized between 1025 and 1125, and Uppsala got metropolitan status in 1164.

The Götaland laws are *Äldre Västgötalagen, Yngre Västgötalagen* ("the younger law of Västergötland"), and *Östgötalagen* ("the law of Östergötland"). The *Äldre Västgötalagen* appears to have been codified in the time of Eskil Magnusson. It exists in two manuscripts in the Kungl. Biblioteket in Stockholm. Holm. B 193 is a fragment of two leaves from around 1250. Holm. B 59 dates from 1280–1290. *Yngre Västgötalagen* is a recension made about 1300. It is found in Holm. B 58, in a manuscript dating from soon after 1345. *Östgötalagen* probably dates from around 1290. It exists in Holm. B 50, which dates from around 1350; in Holm. B 197, a manuscript from around 1600; and in a 1607 edition printed from a lost manuscript.

The laws of the central and northern provinces are *Upplandslagen, Södermannalagen* ("the law of Södermanland"), *Västmannalagen* ("the law of Västmanland"), and *Hälsingelagen* ("the law of Hälsingland"). The *Upplandslagen* exists in Uppsala Universitetsbiblioteket B 12, which dates from 1300–1350; in four other fourteenth-century manuscripts; and in a 1607 edition. The *Södermannalag* goes back to a pre-1296 original. It exists in Holm. B 53, dating from around 1325, and in a manuscript from around 1340 that is in the Kongelige Bibliotek in Copenhagen (Ny. kgl. Saml. 2237 4°). The *Västmannalag* shows both pre-1296 and post-1296 Uppland influence, but it also has much independent material. It exists in Holm. B 56 and B 57, both from 1300–1350, and Holm. B 55, from 1350–1400. The text in Holm. B 54, from around 1350, is customarily distinguished as *Dalalagen*, or "the law of Dalecarlia"; but more probably it represents an early version of the *Västmannalagen*, and there never was a law of Dalecarlia as such. *Hälsingelagen* did not originate until around 1320. It exists in Uppsala Universitetsbiblioteket B 49 and in a 1609 edition from a lost superior manuscript.

The laws for the island of Gotland—the *Gutalagen*—were probably written as an official code around 1220. They show some connections with Norwegian law that may go back to the early eleventh century. The *Gutalagen* is in Holm. B 64, which dates from around 1350. It is also in AM 54 4°, from 1587. There are also German and Danish translations of independent value. The German translation is in Holm. B 65, from 1401, and the Danish translation is in AM 55 4°, which dates from around 1550.

Birka, the famous trading island in Lake Mälaren that flourished between 800 and 1000, gave its name to municipal and maritime laws used throughout early Scandinavia (WN *Bjarkeyjarréttr;* Swedish *Bjärköarätt*). The only complete Swedish text is a set of regulations first made for Stockholm sometime after 1250. This text exists in Holm. B 58, which dates from around 1345.

Bjarköarätt was a source for King Magnus II Eriksson's *Stadslag*, a "town law" for Stockholm dating from around 1350. It was also a source for this king's *Landslag* and for bylaws from Visby, Schleswig, Lübeck, and elsewhere. The *Stadslag* is in Holm. B 170, from 1387, and in five other fourteenth-century manuscripts. The *Visby Stadslag* is in Holm. B 63, which dates from around 1350. It was issued in German in the 1340's, but much of it depends on ancient customs developed among Gotland traders from the eleventh century onward.

Differences in procedure, penalties, social composition, and ecclesiastical and secular administration can be observed from province to province. A centralizing influence was legislation concerning *epsørisbrot,* offenses regarded as a reproach to the king, who, as long as they were unpunished, had failed to keep the oaths he swore on his election. Public order and legal organization became more and more a royal interest. The culmination was King Magnus Eriksson's *Landslag,* a "national law" based on the *Upplandslagen,* the *Västmannalagen,* the *Östgötalagen,* and royal edicts. The *Landslag* was produced around 1345, and it exists in AM 51 4°, dating from around 1350, and in some twenty-five other fourteenth-century manuscripts. A revision was issued by King Kristoffer in 1442. The *Landslag* was not immediately introduced everywhere (it did not reach Västergötland and Värmland until after 1389, for example), nor was it comprehensive enough to supersede the old provincial laws entirely.

Cursory citation of the headings in *Äldre Västgötalagen,* the oldest of the recorded laws, and in *Upplandslagen,* the best-organized of them, may give a representative idea of the contents. *Äldre Västgötalagen* fills some sixty-four pages in Schlyter's edition. It was divided into sections (*bolkær* or *balker*) dealing with church affairs, homicide, wounding, accidental injuries, beatings, unatonable offenses, inheritance, land, mills, theft, misuse of another's property, damage to another's property, strolling players (this is a kind of legislator's joke), and a miscellaneous section beginning with articles on the king, the bishop, and the lawman. *Upplandslagen* fills some 270 pages in Schlyter's edition. It has sections on church affairs, the king, inheritance, personal injuries (including theft), land, commerce, community affairs, and procedure. Each section is divided into articles.

The "interrogative" conditional statement is a marked characteristic of Swedish legal style. Some of the texts, or parts of them, are further distinguished by crisp narrative illustration of the rule stated, aphoristic utterance, parallel and triplet structure, climax, and assonance and alliteration. Such features are rare in other Norse legislation (though they may occur in formulas and set speeches to do with procedure). In the Swedish texts these devices are usually regarded as evidence of the old oral style, which used them for mnemonic as well as expressive reasons. It seems plausible to think that the first literate law framers would adopt a style that had popular appeal (laws continued to be "said" long after they were first written) and that orally preserved law provided their nearest model. This view has recently been challenged in favor of a theory which sees the stylistic devices rather as literary embellishment; in particular it has been shown that cultivation of alliterative formulas expands with the written law. Probably there is truth on both sides.

BIBLIOGRAPHY

Sources. The texts are available in H. S. Collin and C. J. Schlyter, *Samling af Sweriges gamla lagar (Corpus iuris Sueo-Gotorum antiqui)*, 13 vols. (1827–1877). Facsimile editions of the principal law manuscripts are in *Corpus codicum Suecicorum medii aevi*, 20 vols. (1943–1967). Five introductions in these volumes by Elias Wessén are reprinted in revised form and with an additional chapter on *Hälsingelagen* in vol. I of his *Svensk medeltid* (1968).

Studies. A useful encyclopedia is the *Kulturhistorisk leksikon for nordisk middelalder*, 22 vols. (1956–1978); see in particular "Bjärköarätt," "Dalalagen," "Gutalagen," "Hälsingelagen," "Södermannalagen," "Upplandslagen," "Visby stadslag," "Västgötalagarna," "Västmannalagen," and "Östgötalagen." Other studies include Harald Ehrhardt, *Der Stabreim in altnordischen Rechtstexten* (1977); Peter Foote, "Oral and Literary Tradition in Early Scandinavian Law," in H. Bekker-Nielsen, *et al.*, eds., *Oral Tradition, Literary Tradition* (1977); Gösta Hasselberg, *Studier rörande Visby Stadslag och dess källor* (1953); Åke Holmback and Elias Wessén, *Svenska landskapslagar*, 5 vols. (1933–1946), *Magnus Erikssons Landslag* (1962), and *Magnus Erikssons Stadslag* (1966); Ivar Lindquist, *Väst-*
götalagens litterära bilagor* (1941); Alvar Nelson, "Envig och ära," in *Saga och sed* (1944); Dieter Strauch, *Das Ostgötenrecht* (1971); Carl Ivar Ståhle, "Medeltidens profana litteratur: Lagarna," in E. N. Tigerstedt, ed., *Ny illustrerad svensk litteraturhistoria*, I (1955), 39–52, and *Syntaktiska och stilistiska studier i fornnordiskt lagspråk* (1958); Elias Wessén, *Svenskt lagspråk* (1965); Per-Axel Wiktorsson, *Avskrifter och skrivare: Stukdier i fornsvenska lagtexter* (1981).

PETER G. FOOTE

[See also **Birka; Óláfs Saga Helga; Scandinavia, Political and Legal Organization; Snorri Sturluson; Sweden.**]

LAW, WELSH. Although English law had been making territorial inroads ever since the first contacts with the Anglo-Saxons, some native Welsh law continued to be administered up to the sixteenth century.

Reliable written materials before the twelfth century have to do mainly with land law. There are land charters and similar documents from about the eighth century on, and there is evidence on land settlement in the border areas in the Domesday Book, as well as in later extents and surveys. But the main source is the Welsh lawbooks.

Some eighty manuscripts of the laws survive, half of them from the medieval period. Six are in Latin; the remainder, in Welsh. The oldest surviving manuscript dates from the late twelfth century.

The first printed edition was published as *Leges Wallicae* (1730). The most comprehensive edition to date appeared in 1841, and is still of great value. It makes use of a large number of manuscripts; the practice among more recent scholars has been to edit a single manuscript, if necessary filled out from others closely related to it. Some individual manuscripts have been edited in Welsh; others, in English. Several English translations of collections have been made. Most editors and translators provide introductions to the subject, and there are a number of separate studies, collections of articles, bibliographies, and a glossary. Further, there is a subcommittee of the Board of Celtic Studies, at the University of Wales, Cardiff, devoted to the Welsh laws that organizes colloquiums from time to time.

All texts of the laws cover substantially the same ground, but no two are exactly alike. They are divided by scholars into three main codes, named after lawyers mentioned in the texts: the books of Cyfnerth, Blegywryd, and Iorwerth. Some copies lack whole sections, others add a body of miscellaneous rules for the use of practical lawyers. A complete text together with its associated "case law" would, at the expense of some repetition, approach 50,000 words in length.

For anyone who knows Middle Welsh or Medieval Latin, the lawbooks are easy to read, with the exception of a few technical terms. Yet there are great difficulties in interpretation. Most problems are those common to other early law texts, such as the practice of giving minor details while omitting the basic rule, and the introduction of excessive schematism and logicalization. (The horse is a one-legged animal, because the person who breaks its leg must pay the worth of the whole horse.)

More important, there are many contradictions between one text and another, and even within each text. Most copies open with a preamble claiming that the laws were codified at the behest of King Hywel Dda (Howel the Good, who ruled over the greater part of Wales from 942 to ca. 950), and the consensus among scholars is that this account is basically true. But of course there must have been considerable evolution during the succeeding centuries. The scribes and redactors, however, undertook only partial revision at each stage. The result is that a thirteenth-century text will contain several chronological layers of law.

One popular line of research is to seek to determine what remains in the texts of the law and custom pertaining to the tenth century, or earlier. Techniques include comparison with legal matter in early Welsh tales and the drawing of parallels with other early law tracts, particularly those of Ireland, in which a more primitive stage of law is rather more consistently recorded.

The law texts are divided into two sections: the laws of the king's court and the laws of the territorial unit (gwlad). This latter section comprises a number of tractates, each dealing with a particular aspect of law. Among them are the following: laws relating to women; surety, oath, and contract; bail and protection; laws pertaining to military and other obligations; land suits and laws relating to land; laws concerning children; homicide, theft, and arson; the worth of wild and tame creatures, and of other property; joint plowing; and cattle trespass.

The picture given in the first type of tractate is of a great hall presided over by a powerful king, evidently meant to represent the ruler of one of the three provinces, if not of the whole of Wales. He is accompanied by twenty-four officials, each with his own rights and obligations. The gwlad mentioned in the remaining tractates, however, is not necessarily the territory of such a king. Rather, it is represented as being made up of one or more cantreds (cantred being the anglicized form of the Welsh cantref, of which there were about forty-eight to fifty in medieval Wales).

It is now generally accepted that the list of court officials and their functions in the first tractate was borrowed, evidently for effect. But somewhere within these twenty or thirty pages there must be some genuine native material pertaining to the establishments of Welsh kings, down to the king of a single tribal area. However, it is well buried, and it is only with much sifting of evidence, both internal and external, that the investigator can begin to unearth it.

It is otherwise with the law of the gwlad. Here the state layer, whether native or foreign in origin, is thin and patchy, and of doubtful applicability outside the particular gwlad. The great bulk, continually updated though it will have been, is still recognizably tribal law. All freeman may serve together as judges, while half their number are required as oath helpers in certain cases of compurgation. And order is ensured not by the sudden decree from above but by the quiet application of rules that have been formulated over the years.

After the Edwardian conquest of 1282, some cantreds became part of the private domains of the English king; others were converted into lordships and conferred upon the king's nominees. Meanwhile, native legal custom appears to have continued largely unchanged, except in those cases in which public order was threatened (for example, homicide in native law could result in a violent feud between two kins; under the new regime the state took over the prosecution of such cases). After 1536, however, changes occurred rapidly as a result of the Act of Union passed that year, in which was stated that "the laws, ordinances, and statutes of the realm of England . . . and none other . . . shall be had, used, practised, and executed . . . in the dominion of Wales."

BIBLIOGRAPHY

Thomas Peter Ellis, *Welsh Tribal Law and Custom in the Middle Ages* (1926); Hywel D. Emanuel, ed., *The Latin Texts of the Welsh Laws* (1967); Dafydd Jenkins, ed., *Celtic Law Papers* (1973), *idem.* and Morfydd E. Owen, eds., *The Welsh Law of Women* (1980); Timothy Lewis, *A Glossary of Medieval Welsh Law* (1913); Aneurin Owen, ed., *An-*

cient Laws and Institutes of Wales, 2 vols. (1841); Melville Richards, trans., *The Laws of Hywel Dda* (The book of Blegywryd) (1954); A. W. Wade-Evans, ed. and trans., *Welsh Medieval Law* (1909, repr. 1979).

DONALD GWYON HOWELLS

[See also **Homicide; Oath; Trespass; Wales: History.**]

LAXDŒLA SAGA, a thirteenth-century Icelandic feud saga, recounts the history of eight generations of Ketill flatnefr's (flatnose's) descendants. Ketill fled Norway and settled in Scotland around 990. Some twenty-five years after that, his daughter Unnr left the British Isles for Iceland, where, with the aid of her brothers, she established herself as matriarch of the Breiðafjǫrðr region. The main action of the saga takes place in the seventh generation, around the time of the conversion to Christianity, and concerns Guðrún Ósvífrsdóttir, Kjartan Ólafsson, and Bolli-Þorleiksson, whose relationship bears a strong and deliberate resemblance to the fatal love triangle Brynhild-Sigurd-Gunnarr of heroic tradition. Like Brynhild, Guðrún is cheated of the man she loves and retaliates by plotting his death with her husband. Her husband, Bolli, is himself slain in an act of retribution that is avenged in the following generation by Guðrún's son. It is clear from *Landnámabók* (Book of settlements, twelfth century) that *Laxdœla saga* rests on actual events, but it is equally clear that its grasp of historical fact and chronology is weak. Conspicuously lacking in *Laxdœla saga* is the sort of original skaldic verse that normally serves in saga narrative as a source of historical detail.

In its subscription to the heroic ethos and in its focus on bloody retribution, *Laxdœla saga* is a typical feud saga. Less typical, however, is its extended attention to niceties of dress and behavior, a feature that is taken to indicate the author's familiarity with continental romance. Emphatically atypical is the amount of space and interest devoted to women and marital matters. The early chapters are dominated by the commanding person of Unnr, and even the main action, the feud itself, is clearly structured around the marital career of Guðrún; her death concludes the saga. Guðrún's story, punctuated though it is by community matters, may be counted as one of the first secular women's biographies in European medieval literature; certainly it stands alone in early Scandinavian tradition. Several of the "female" details of *Laxdœla saga* carry over into the later *Njáls*

saga. They are seen in quite a different light, however, and one suspects that the author of the latter wished to provide a counterbalance to the former.

In the form in which it is preserved, *Laxdœla saga* dates from the middle of the thirteenth century; one manuscript fragment survives from around that time. Some of the manuscripts suffix *Bolla þáttr,* a short narrative relating the later career of Guðrún's son. Although *Laxdœla saga* is anonymous, it has been variously ascribed to Ólafr Þorðarson hvítaskáld, Sturla Þórðarson, Snorri Sturluson, and an unidentified woman.

BIBLIOGRAPHY

A. Margaret Arent, trans. and ed., *Laxdœla Saga* (1964); Ursula Dronke, "Narrative Insight in *Laxdœla* Saga," in Mary Salu and Robert T. Farrell, eds., *J. R. R. Tolkien, Scholar and Storyteller: Essays in Memoriam* (1979); Rolf Heller, *Die Laxdœla Saga: Die literarische Schöpfung eines Isländers des 13. Jahrhunderts* (1976); Helga Kress, "Meget samstavet må det tykkes deg: Om kvinneopprör og genretvang i Sagaen om Laksdölene," in *Historisk Tidsskrift (Norsk)* (1980); A. Margaret Arent Madelung, *The Laxdœla Saga: Its Structural Patterns* (1972); Magnus Magnusson and Hermann Pálsson, trans., *Laxdæla Saga* (1969); Njörður P. Njarðvík, "Laxdœla saga—en tidskritik?" in *Arkiv för nordisk filologi,* 86 (1971).

CAROL J. CLOVER

[See also **Brynhild; Family Sagas, Icelandic; Landnámabók; Njáls Saga.**]

LAY. See Lai/Lay.

LAYAMON. See Brut, The.

LAYAS, LAYAZZO. See Āyās.

LAZAR HREBELJANOVIĆ (*ca.* 1329–1389), a Serbian nobleman at Stefan Dušan's court, with holdings between the West Morava and Ibar rivers, rose to prominence after King Vukašin's death in the Battle of the Marica River (1371). Lazar soon acquired a rich mine, Novo Brdo. Participant in a victorious coalition against the nobleman Nikola Altomanović, Lazar obtained in 1373 Altomanović's Serbian lands, including the mining town Rudnik. Becoming a

Hungarian vassal during or shortly after the Altomanović war, Lazar met little Hungarian opposition to his expansion north toward the Danube, which he reached in about 1379, when, by defeating the Rastislalići, he obtained Braničevo. By the mid 1370's Lazar, bearing the title prince (knez), had a sizable principality in the Pomoravlje, to the north of the earlier Serbian centers, with Kruševac as his capital. The most powerful of Serbian princes, his strength resulted from possession of the richest silver mines and from the region's increased population. The latter was a consequence of Serbian migrations northward away from Turkish pressure.

Closely associated with the church, Lazar in 1375 restored communion with the patriarchate of Constantinople—which had excommunicated the Serbian church in 1351. Lazar built many churches (including the monastery of Ravanica), granted the church land, and did much to spread Christianity in these northern lands, where, except for certain towns on the Danube, little evidence of earlier Christian penetration exists. The church sponsored his pretensions to revive under himself a greater Serbian state, and about 1378 crowned him "Lord of the Serbs and the Danube, Stefan [the Nemanjići's royal name] Prince Lazar, Autocrat of All Serbs." Though called tsar in epics, Lazar's title always remained prince. By 1386–1389 two major lords living beyond his borders, Vuk Branković and Djuradj (George) II Balšić (both of whom were his sons-in-law), recognized his suzerainty. Because Lazar resisted accepting Ottoman suzerainty, the Turks under Sultan Murad I invaded Serbia. Lazar headed a coalition which met the Turks at the Battle of Kosovo in June 1389. Both he and Sultan Murad I died there, and Lazar's heirs had to accept Ottoman suzerainty. The Serbian church canonized Lazar in the 1390's. The battle (and Lazar's death) became a subject for Serbian epics.

BIBLIOGRAPHY

O Knezu Lazaru (papers from Kruševac Symposium on Knez Lazar, Beograd) (1975).

JOHN V. A. FINE, JR.

[See also **Byzantine History; Marica River; Murad I; Serbia.**]

ŁAZAR PᶜARPECᶜI (Lazar of Pᶜarp, *fl. ca.* 500), an Armenian historian from the village of Pᶜarp at the foot of Mt. Aragats, author of a *History of Armenia* dedicated to his patron, Vahan Mamikonean, marzpan (governor) of the country from 485 to 505.

The work falls into three distinct sections. Part one reviews the work of two earlier Armenian historians, Agatᶜangełos and Pᶜawstos Buzand, and takes up the history of Armenia from the division of that country into Iranian and Roman spheres of influence in 387. It also discusses the invention of the Armenian alphabet by Maštocᶜ and the beginnings of Armenian literature; but surprisingly, Łazar does not mention Koriwn, Maštocᶜ's pupil and biographer. Łazar then describes the final collapse of the Arsacid monarchy (428) and the efforts of the Iranian shah to impose Syrian patriarchs on the Armenian church. A vision of St. Sahak I (*d.* 438), patriarch of Armenia at the time, was later inserted in this section. Also found in a Greek translation, it foretells the return of the Arsacid line and the restoration of the patriarchate to the line of St. Gregory the Illuminator in 350 years' time. Part one ends with the deaths of Maštocᶜ and Sahak.

The second part discusses the revolt of the Armenians against Iran in 450–451 led by Vardan Mamikonean (the uncle of Łazar's patron) and the fate of the Armenian prisoners in Iran. These events are described in more detail and somewhat differently by the historian Ełišē in *History of Vardon and the Armenian War*.

The third and longest part is devoted to the exploits of Vahan Mamikonean during the reign of Shah Pērōz (459–484), culminating in a second armed rebellion which ended with the recognition of Vahan as marzpan. This part of Łazar's work is particularly valuable, as he is the only contemporary Armenian source for this period.

The *History* proper is followed by a letter addressed to Vahan in which Łazar defends himself from the slander of various monks. After a brief sketch of his early years, he exculpates himself from the charges of (unspecified) heresy and emphasizes his superior learning. The style of the *Letter* is quite different from that of the *History,* and its genuineness may be doubted.

The printed text of the *History* (based on manuscripts which date from the seventeenth century or later) contains many medieval forms. Recently, some fragments of the *History* dating from the tenth and eleventh centuries have been discovered which indicate that the printed editions do not represent the original text very closely. Although the variants so far discovered are more of style than of historical substance, the problem of the differing recensions of this *History* has not yet been resolved. It remains, however, a most valuable source for the history of Persian Armenia in the fifth century, despite the author's extreme bias in favor of the Mamikonean family.

BIBLIOGRAPHY

The *History* of Łazar was first published in 1793 in Venice. The only critical edition is that of Galowst Ter-Mkrtch^cean and Step^can Malkhasiants^c, eds., *Łazaray P^carpets^cwoy Patmut^ciwn Hayots^c* (1904). The only full translation into a Western language is in Victor Langlois, ed., *Collection des historiens anciens et modernes de l'Arménie*, II (1869), 259–368. For a translation, with commentary, from the critical text of Book III, 60–85, see C. Sanspeur, "L'Arménie au temps de Peroz," in *Revue des études arméniennes*, n.s. **11** (1975–1976). For the early fragments see C. Sanspeur, "Le fragment de l'histoire de Lazare de P^carpi, retrouvé dans le Ms. 1 de Jérusalem," in *Revue des études arméniennes*, n.s. **10** (1973–1974); and C. J. F. Dowsett, "The Newly Discovered Fragment of Lazar of P^carp's History," in *Le muséon*, **89** (1976). For the vision of Sahak see Gerard Garitte, "La vision de S. Sahak en grec," in *Le muséon*, **71** (1958).

R. W. THOMSON

[See also **Agat^cangełos; Armenia: History of; Armenian Literature; Armenian Saints; Ełišē; Historiography, Armenian; P^cawstos Buzand; Vardan Mamikonean, St.**]

LAZARUS, RAISING OF. Lazarus is an abbreviated form of the Hebrew name Eleazar (God has helped). The New Testament mentions two persons named Lazarus, most notably the brother of Mary and Martha, whom Jesus raises from the dead in John 11:1–44. According to Eastern tradition, Lazarus and his two sisters were placed in a leaky boat and set adrift by Jews. The boat landed in Cyprus, where Lazarus is said to have become bishop of Citium (Kittim). His relics, discovered in the late ninth century, were later transported to Constantinople. The Eastern church celebrated his feast on the Saturday before Palm Sunday, the Western church on 17 December.

Depictions of the raising of Lazarus in medieval art include a scene in Giotto's *Life of Christ* (Scrovegni Chapel, Padua, ca. 1301–1306), a mosaic in S. Apollinare Nuovo in Ravenna, a miniature in the *Gospels of Emperor Otto III*, 983–1002 (Munich, Bayerische Staatsbibliothek), and a wall painting in Sant'Angelo in Formis (1072–1100).

BIBLIOGRAPHY

Charles R. Dodwell, *Painting in Europe, 800 to 1200* (1971); George W. Ferguson, *Signs and Symbols in Christian Art* (1954).

JENNIFER E. JONES

LAZICA. See **Georgia: Geography.**

LE LOUP, JEAN. See **Loup, Jean.**

LEAGUE, a measure of length for land and sea distances in the British Isles, generally of 15,840 feet (4.827 kilometers) or 3 miles of 5,280 feet each. However, various other lengths were used during the Middle Ages: 7,500 feet (about 2.29 kilometers) or 1.5 miles of 5,000 feet each; 7,680 feet (about 2.34 kilometers) or 12 linear farthingdales of 40 perches each, the perch containing 16 feet; 7,920 feet (about 2.41 kilometers) or 12 furlongs of 40 perches each, the perch containing 16.5 feet; 8,910 feet (about 2.72 kilometers) or 13.5 furlongs of 40 perches each, the perch containing 16.5 feet; 9,375 feet (about 2.86 kilometers) or 15 furlongs of 125 paces each, the pace containing 5 feet; and 10,000 feet (about 3.05 kilometers) or 16 furlongs of 125 paces each, the pace containing 5 feet. In medieval manuscripts the league appears under such variant spellings as leuce, leuga, leuca, leuk, lewa, lewge, leghe, lywe, lege, leuge, leeke, leuke, lewke, lieke, leege, legge, and lig.

RONALD EDWARD ZUPKO

[See also **Weights and Measures, Western European.**]

LEATHER AND LEATHERWORKING. Leather was produced by three methods, tanning, dressing, and tawing, with little variation in technique until the late nineteenth century. Heavy hides and some calfskins were tanned with a vegetable tanning agent, usually oak bark. The tanning process consisted of three stages. First, the hide was prepared to receive the tannage by removing the epidermis or outer layer with the hair and the adipose tissue or underlayer. All particles of flesh had to be removed.

This was done by soaking the hide in a lime solution and then scraping both sides with a knife. The lime also helped to separate the fibers of the hide, which allowed better penetration of the tanning solution. A further treatment was applied when a particularly soft leather was wanted. This was either bating or puering—immersion in either a cold infusion of pigeon or hen dung or a warm infusion of dog dung. Judging the correct length of time for liming, bating, and puering was a skilled matter.

The second stage was the tanning itself, which brought about a chemical change in the hide and made it imputrescible. Tannin is a natural substance found in many vegetable materials, but in western Europe oak bark was the principal source of tannin until sumac was introduced from the Near East in the fifteenth century. Hides were soaked in infusions of oak bark for periods varying from six months to two years, depending on the quality of the hide and the strength of the infusions. The hides were moved through a series of infusions of increasing strength, with the tanner judging when to make the moves. The third stage, the work of the currier, was the finishing. The oils that had been removed from the hide by the other processes were replaced in order to make it supple and water-resistant. The hide was then shaved to the required thickness.

Other types of skin were dressed, rather than tanned, either with train oil (from whale blubber) or with alum and salt. Oil-dressed leather, commonly referred to as chamois after the breed of goat whose skin was widely prepared in this way, was treated by soaking the prepared skins in troughs of train oil and repeatedly beating them to encourage the penetration of the oil. The final step was to expose the skins to the air so that oxidation of the oils would take place, causing the skins to become imputrescible.

Alum-dressed leather was produced by craftsmen called whittawyers, or white tawyers. The process of tawing involved immersion in a liquor containing alum and common salt. The leather produced was stiff and white; the stiffness was remedied by staking, pulling the damped leather in all directions over a blunt-edged blade, and by working fats into the fibers. Cordovan was a fine alum-dressed leather associated from the eighth century with the city of Córdoba in Spain. Similar leather was produced in Britain and called cordwain; those who made and used it were called cordwainers, a term which later came to mean simply a shoemaker.

The production of leather requires certain raw materials; their availability must to some extent have governed the location of major leather-producing centers. A supply of hides could be obtained in any town where there was a cattle market. Oak bark was supplied from forests; the monks of Tintern Abbey were buying bark from Wentwood at twopence a load in the thirteenth century. Walsall was well supplied with hides from local cattle, oak bark from Cannock Chase or the Forest of Arden, lime from local pits for loosening the hair, and a good water supply. Bedford had eleven tanneries in 1297, and the borough records for medieval Leicester list a number of producers of leather and workers in leather before 1300. It is to be expected that other towns had their tanneries and associated trades, but the evidence for this is often little more than a few street names on old maps.

Leather was an important material, and its users belonged to many trades. Glovers, saddlers, pursers, pouchmakers, girdlers, bottlemakers, and shoemakers all worked with leather, and each trade formed organizations to protect its members. Their spheres of influence varied enormously, with some London guilds controlling the trade throughout the country. One such was the Worshipful Company of Saddlers, whose recorded history begins with an agreement with the church of St. Martin le Grand at the end of the twelfth century. Theirs was one of the most powerful groups in London by the fourteenth century, and their power to search all saddlers' premises for defective goods was not restricted to London until 1558.

Outside London, provincial boroughs were acquiring their own guilds. Cardiff, for example, had a guild of cordwainers and glovers set up in 1324 that prevented outsiders from starting businesses within seven miles of the town. This protection of local craftsmen from too much competition was one side of a coin, the other side of which was quality control. A petition of 1372 to the mayor and aldermen of London stated that it was forbidden for a pouchmaker to try to pass off sheep leather scraped on the back as roe leather (the penalty was the burning of the offending articles) and requested that this prohibition be extended to calf leather made to look like roe leather. There were many such rules, which were enforced by men of each trade who were entrusted with the authority to search out defective work.

BIBLIOGRAPHY

Clare E. Allin, *The Medieval Leather Industry in Leicester* (1981); Philip R. Green, *A History of the Walsall*

Leather Trades (1977); Kenneth S. Laurie, *The History of the Guild of Saddlers*, 3rd rev. ed. (1963); Edward Mayer, *The Curriers and the City of London* (1968); George Unwin, *The Gilds and Companies of London*, 4th ed. (1963); James F. Wadmore, *Some Account of the Worshipful Company of Skinners of London* (1902); John W. Waterer, *Leather in Life, Art, and Industry* (1946), *Leather and Craftsmanship* (1950), *Leather Craftsmanship* (1968), and *Spanish Leather* (1971).

VICTORIA GABBITAS

[See also **Guilds of Artists.**]

LEBANON. The name denotes the Lebanon mountain range along the Syrian coast and, by extension, the territory of the present-day republic of Lebanon, extending from the crest of the Anti-Lebanon and Mount Hermon to the Phoenician littoral. As in other parts of Syria, the rural areas in this territory were arabized between the third and sixth centuries of the Christian era; the coastal cities, however, became arabized only after the Islamic conquest (634–641). Under Byzantine rule, the population of these cities was Aramaic in native speech and culture but included hellenized and colonial Greek elements.

As part of Muslim Syria, the modern Lebanese territory was divided between the *ajnād* (provinces; sing., *jund*) of Jordan and Damascus, the dividing line being the lower course of the Litani River. Under the crusaders, the coastal areas south of Nahr al-Khalb (the Lycus, or Dog, River) fell within the Kingdom of Jerusalem; those to the north formed part of the county of Tripoli; the inland areas remained under the Muslim rulers of Damascus. Later, under the Mamluks, the Lebanese territory was divided between the *mamālik* (provinces; sing., *mamlaka*) of Safad, Damascus, and Tripoli, remaining so until the Ottoman conquest of Syria in 1516.

The Islamic conquest of the seventh century was followed by a rapid spread of Islam in all the Lebanese regions except the parts of the Lebanon range north of Nahr al-Khalb. Starting with the ninth century, as the rift between the orthodox, or Sunni, Muslims and the heterodox Shiite sects (Imāmīs, Ismailis, and Nuṣayrīs) began to deepen, only Beirut and Sidon (and perhaps Tripoli) remained bastions of Sunnism; elsewhere, Shiites of various kinds predominated. While Syria was under the rule of the Ismaili Fatimid caliphs of Egypt, Ismaili peasants and tribesmen in the southern Leba-

non and Wādī al-Taym (the valley of the upper Jordan) became converts to a new Ismaili sect, that of the Druzes, which held that the Fatimid caliph al-Ḥākim bi-Amr Allāh (996–1021) was the living manifestation of the unity of God. After the Fatimids left Syria, the Druzes of the Lebanon cooperated politically and militarily with the Sunni regimes that succeeded one another in Damascus, while the older Shiite communities did not and were therefore persecuted.

Meanwhile, the northern Lebanon remained a predominantly Christian enclave, inhabited mainly by Maronites. This community originated in the valley of the Orontes and the adjacent hills of the Lebanon and the Anti-Lebanon, where the local Christian peasants and tribesmen were led by the monks of Dayr Mārūn (a rural monastic foundation established in the fifth century), apparently in opposition to the urban and hellenized church of Antioch. The followers of the orthodox patriarch of Antioch were called Melchites. In 680, when the Sixth Ecumenical Council at Constantinople condemned the Monothelite doctrine (officially established as orthodoxy in 638) as heresy, the Maronites parted company with the Melchites, remained Monothelite, and began to elect their own patriarchs. From the start, these patriarchs established themselves in the northern Lebanon. As enemies of Byzantium, the Maronites later joined forces with the crusaders, and under their influence abandoned the Monothelite doctrine and entered into union with Rome by stages, beginning around 1180. One Maronite patriarch attended the Fourth Lateran Council (1215), and another got himself into serious trouble with the Mamluk authorities in Tripoli by sending a representative to attend the Council of Florence (1439) on his behalf. Despite some episodes of persecution (including the burning of one Maronite patriarch at the stake in Tripoli in 1367), the Maronites fared well under the Mamluks and were allowed a considerable measure of autonomy under their *muqaddamūn* (village or district chiefs, sing., *maqaddam*), who acted as fiscal agents for the Mamluk governors of Tripoli.

Economically, the various Lebanese regions went into stagnation between the seventh and the ninth centuries, as a result of the recession of the maritime commerce in the Mediterranean at the time. The seaports lost their former affluence and dwindled into villages. By the tenth century, however, the revival of the Mediterranean commerce brought a return of prosperity to these seaports and, before long, also to the hinterland. This prosperity reached its peak under crusader rule, when Genoese and Pisan merchant colonies were established in the Syrian seaports, including those of the Phoenician coast (Tripoli, Jubayl, Beirut, Sidon, and Tyre). When the Mamluks finally drove the crusaders out of coastal Syria (1289–1291), the Genoese and Pisan colonists left. The Mamluks, however, favored Venice, which rapidly inherited the commercial privileges formerly enjoyed by Genoa and Pisa in the Syrian seaports. From 1291 until 1516, Beirut in particular flourished on a reexport trade in Eastern spices, with Venice as the unrivaled European customer. The position of Beirut with regard to the spice trade at the time came second only to that of Alexandria, in Egypt.

Profiting from their association with the spice trade, the Druze emirs (or chiefs) of the house of Buḥtur, who were entrusted by the Mamluks with military duties in Beirut, gained a considerable local influence, and also an ascendancy over other chiefs in the southern Lebanon. The quasi-hereditary tenure of their mountain *iqṭāᶜ* (fiscal fiefs) was recognized by the Mamluks after 1313; later, after 1390, their *iqṭāᶜ* became in fact, though not in theory, a private domain. Nevertheless, the Buḥturs never became the founders of an autonomous principality, and their fortunes went into rapid decline after the Ottoman conquest.

Among the Lebanese communities, the Maronites and the Druzes, beginning with the twelfth century, were the only ones whose historical individuality stands out, partly because their organization and leadership were strictly local, with no external attachments, and partly because they inhabited mountain areas close to the coast. Other communities of rural or tribal Sunnis and Shiites had their chiefs at the time; historically, however, those do not appear to have been of much consequence.

BIBLIOGRAPHY

M. Gaudefroy-Demombynes, *La Syrie à l'époque des Mamelouks, d'après les auteurs arabes* (1923); Philip K. Hitti, *Lebanon in History*, 3rd ed. (1967); Henri Lammens, *La Syrie: Précis historique* (1921); Muḥammad ᶜAlī Makkī, *Lubnān, 635–1516* (1977); Kamal S. Salibi, *Maronite Historians of Mediaeval Lebanon* (1959) and *Syria Under Islam* (1977).

KAMAL S. SALIBI

[See also **Crusades and Crusader States; Druzes; Fatimids; Ḥakim bi-Amr Allâh, al-; Islam, Conquests of; Mamluk Dynasty; Maronite Church; Melchites; Monothelitism; Ottomans; Sects, Islamic; Syria.**]

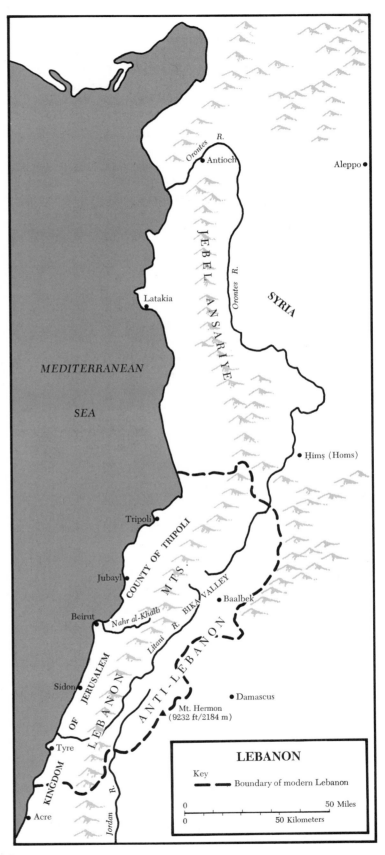

LECTIONARY, a book containing readings for liturgical services, especially, but not exclusively, for the Mass and Divine Office. Lectionaries for the Mass contained readings drawn largely from the Scriptures. This material could be read through continuously or arranged in centonized and harmonized fashion. The major types of Mass lectionaries were complete Bibles or parts of Bibles with marginal notations indicating the pericope (selection from Scripture) to be read; Bibles or parts of Bibles such as evangeliaries (books of Gospels) with *capitularia* or tables of incipits and explicits indicating where the pericopes for reading were to be found for each liturgical feast; and books of pericopes such as evangelistaries arranged according to a liturgical cycle.

Lectionaries for the Divine Office contained readings from the Bible, writings of the Fathers, accounts of the lives and sufferings of the saints, and homilies. Because lectionaries were used in the night Office they could be called *nocturales* or *matutinales,* and because of their size they could be separated into those for winter or summer use. The lections or readings themselves could be gathered into separate sections within the lectionaries according to the temporale (a liturgical cycle arranged according to feasts of the ecclesiastical year) or sanctorale (a liturgical cycle arranged according to the feasts of saints), or they might be mingled. Monastic and secular lectionaries were arranged differently because the Divine Office celebrated in monastic and nonmonastic settings differed, but both might be enriched with materials from the Divine Office such as responses, antiphons, *capitula* (short readings), collects, and hymns.

BIBLIOGRAPHY

V. Fiala and W. Irtenkauf, "Versuch einer liturgischen Nomenklatur," in *Zur katalogisierung mittelalterlicher und neuerer Handschriften (Zeitschrift für Bibliothekswesen und Bibliographie, Sonderheft)* (1963).

ROGER E. REYNOLDS

[See also **Alcuin of York; Breviary; Canonical Hours; Divine Office; Evangeliary; Mass; Pericopes.**]

LEFÈVRE, RAOUL (*fl.* 1460–1467), priest and author. He was probably not chaplain to Philip the Good as is usually asserted in older literature, but was a professional author-scribe who collaborated with the miniaturist Loyset Liédet (*d. ca.* 1479) in

Hesdin. Lefèvre composed *L'histoire de Jason* around 1460 and *Le recueil des histoires de Troie* shortly before 1467. Both works remained popular in the Netherlands for the rest of the century. They also became popular in England through the translations of William Caxton.

BIBLIOGRAPHY

Raoul Lefèvre, *L'histoire de Jason*, Gert Pinkernell, ed. (1971).

ANNE HAGOPIAN VAN BUREN

[See also **Liédet, Loyset.**]

LEGATE, PAPAL. From early times the papacy had its representatives outside Italy. Until the eleventh century the most important of these were the apocrisiars, semipermanent diplomatic agents at the imperial court of Constantinople, and the apostolic vicars, who exercised quasi-papal spiritual jurisdiction over areas of the church. There were also legates acting on specific tasks or who, in the capacity of *legatus ad gentes* (legate to the nations), undertook missionary activity (the supreme example of this last is probably St. Boniface). From the eleventh century, and specifically as a result of the policies of the popes of the Gregorian reform period, the use of legates changed. They became the chief agents in the construction of a centralized papal monarchy over the church.

Contemporaries and later historians have often confused the roles of legates and nuncios, but there was a crucial difference that was strictly maintained in the papal commissions. The legate, unlike the nuncio, was capable of independent activity to fulfill his commission, which was less a series of precise instructions than a power of attorney to achieve an end. Papal legates were not completely free agents, however; there remained a right of appeal to the pope against their actions.

By the end of the thirteenth century canon law distinguished between three distinct types of papal legate. The least important were the *legati nati* (legates by birth), prelates like the archbishops of Canterbury, Salzburg, and Arles, who held the title of legate ex officio in areas subject to their metropolitan spiritual jurisdiction. Possibly the title derived from the earlier apostolic vicariates, but by 1300 it was largely honorific. It did, however, blur the nature of their powers, making it uncertain whether such prelates were acting locally with independent authority or by virtue of a papal delegation. The other grades of legate were more important and more active, being individually commissioned by the popes. Here the essential difference was one of standing: the *legatus missus* was not a member of the college of cardinals; the *legatus a latere* was. In addition to these three legal categories, which had developed only slowly, a fourth made a fleeting appearance in the twelfth century. At the time some secular princes claimed the powers of papal legates within their realms to restrict papal activity and increase their own control over the church. Only in Sicily were these claims upheld, based as they were on the commission originally granted by Pope Urban II to Count Roger I in 1098, which survived to produce the privilege known as the *Monarchia sicula*.

The powers of papal legates were extensive, supplanting all local ecclesiastical authorities. These powers concentrated considerable authority in the hands of the legates. Each legate was in many respects a local pope. The ceremonial and administrative activities of legates, particularly legates *a latere*, emphasized this status as papal doppelgänger. Because of the powers enjoyed by legates, kings and princes were chary of admitting them to their domains for fear that serious difficulties of protocol might arise.

Until the fourteenth century, legates were the chief agents for implementing papal political and spiritual objectives in the localities. The scope of legatine activity varied enormously, depending on individual commissions. Several legates were closely involved in secular politics. In England, Henry of Blois, bishop of Winchester, exploited his legatine powers between 1139 and 1143 to influence the succession struggle between King Stephen (his brother) and Empress Matilda. Later, between 1216 and 1221, the legates Gualo and Pandulf (*d.* 1226) were influential in the last days of King John and the minority of Henry III.

From the start of the crusading movement, papal legates were intimately involved in the leadership and direction of such activity, as the pope's representatives. Adhemar of Monteil, bishop of Le Puy (*d.* 1098), was appointed legate for the First Crusade at the Council of Clermont in 1095, even before the expedition had been organized. Such activity continued later, both in crusades to the Holy Land and in those which took place within Europe during the thirteenth and fourteenth centuries (especially against the Albigensians of southern France, and in Italy).

The rulers of the Papal States in Italy occasionally enjoyed legatine powers, as did Cardinal Albornoz in the 1350's. Legates were also often engaged in investigating and reforming local churches. John of Abbeville in Spain in the 1220's and Nicholas of Cusa in Germany in the 1450's both attempted reform but failed; but Otto and Ottobono were more successful in thirteenth-century England.

The position of papal legates was, of course, not static. In the fourteenth and fifteenth centuries the *legatus missus* virtually disappeared for reasons not yet properly elucidated. That role was taken over by the papal nuncios, whose powers correspondingly increased. The status of the legate *a latere* also changed in the fifteenth century with the nature of the cardinalate. The ending of the requirement that the cardinals reside at Rome meant they could stay in their localities, some being given the title and powers of legates *a latere*, which they then exploited for their own purposes. By the sixteenth century the normal diplomatic activities of papal legates had virtually disappeared, having been taken over by the papal nuncios.

BIBLIOGRAPHY

The historical writing on papal legates is immense; the most important recent statement is in Richard A. Schmutz, "Medieval Papal Representatives: Legates, Nuncios, and Judges-Delegate," in *Studia Gratiana*, **15** (1972).

Other sources include: J. Deer, "Der Anspruch der Herrscher des 12. Jahrhunderts auf die apostolische Legation," in *Archivum historiae pontificiae*, **2** (1964); Robert C. Figueira, "The Classification of Medieval Papal Legates in the *Liber extra*," in *Archivum historiae pontificiae*, **21** (1983); Clifford I. Kyer, "*Legatus* and *Nuntius* as Used to Denote Papal Envoys, 1245–1378," in *Mediaeval Studies*, **40** (1978); George L. Lesage, "La titulature des envoyés pontificaux sous Pie II (1458–1464)," in *Mélanges d'archéologie et d'histoire*, **58** (1941–1946); Gino Paro, *The Right of Papal Legation* (1947); Kenneth Pennington, "Johannes Teutonicus and Papal Legates," in *Archivum historiae pontificiae*, **21** (1983); Jane E. Sayers, *Papal Judges Delegate in the Province of Canterbury, 1198–1254* (1971); Franz Wasner, "Fifteenth-century Texts on the Ceremonial of the Papal 'Legatus a Latere,'" in *Traditio*, **14** (1958).

R. N. SWANSON

[See also **Church, Latin: Organization; Curia, Papal; Nuncio, Papal; Papacy, Origins and Development of.**]

LEGENDA AUREA. See **Golden Legend.**

LEGENDARY SAGAS. See **Fornaldarsögur.**

LEINSTER, an early province of eastern Ireland. Early Christian Leinster, which embraced the basins of the Liffey, Barrow, and Slaney rivers, was a compact geographical area and, to a degree, a land of defense. From the earliest historical period the Laigin or Leinstermen were under attack on their northern frontier from the Uí Néill, to whom they had lost the plain of Meath (Mide) immediately before the historical period. The belt of bogland in the counties of Offaly and Kildare was to remain the border of their province.

The early Leinster dynastic poems—and other equally early sources—reflect a Leinster in close contact with the Roman world. It is very likely that there were Laigin settlers on the west coast of Roman Britain, and it has been claimed that the Laigin were ethnically different from the rest of the population of Ireland. These same dynastic poems reflect a Leinster ruled by a number of early dynasties—Uí Enechglais, Uí Bairrche, Uí Garrchon (Dál Messin Corb), and Uí Máil—who were later reduced to the status of subject peoples and whose kingship of the province was not admitted by the historians of the later dominant dynasties, Uí Dúnlainge (ruled until *ca.* 1037) and Uí Chennselaig (ruled 1042–1171). Of the subject peoples of the province the most important without doubt were the Uí Failge, who appear to have suffered heavily at the hands of the Uí Néill but maintained themselves as powerful territorial lords in northwestern Leinster throughout the early Christian period. Among the other subject peoples were the disunited and splintered Fothairt (Fotharta), who claimed Brigit, the patroness of Leinster, as one of their own and who left their name on the baronies of Forth in Carlow and Wexford, and the Loígis, who formed a compact local kingdom in western Leinster and who were traditionally regarded as the defenders of the border.

The Uí Dúnlainge, who were to dominate Leinster until the eleventh century, came into prominence in the early seventh century, immediately before the onset of the great plagues, and firmly linked their fortunes to those of the great monastery of Kildare. Indeed, in the ninth century the association of the royal family with the rule of the monastery was so close that Kildare may be regarded as the dynastic capital. Their principal rivals were the Uí Chennselaig, their kinsmen in the genealogical schema, who apparently tried to seize the plain of Kildare—the center of Uí Dúnlainge power—in the first half of the seventh century. They were defeated and moved into south Leinster, where they carved out a place for themselves in close association with the great monastery of Ferns. They suffered another crushing defeat in 738, which left the Uí Dúnlainge securely in power until the eleventh century.

Uí Néill aggression was so successful in the late eighth and early ninth centuries that they were nominating kings of Leinster; one of their kings is called *satrapa Lagenarum,* which probably means that he was provincial governor under the Uí Néill. By then there were three mature and rival segments within the dynasty, and Uí Dúnlainge were reduced to being rulers of their dynastic homeland, as Uí Chennselaig were of theirs in the south.

The shaky hegemony of the Uí Dúnlainge finally collapsed in a series of fierce struggles in the early eleventh century. Diarmait mac Máel na mBó, king of Uí Chennselaig, seized the kingship of Leinster in 1042. His descendants held it until the Norman invasion and the dissolution of the kingship of Leinster on the death of Diarmait Mac Murchada (Dermot Mac Murrough) in 1171. From 1042 until his death in 1072, Diarmait mac Máel na mBó made Leinster a power to be reckoned with in Irish politics, and for much of that period he was the most powerful king in Ireland. His immediate successors, however, failed to maintain that position; it was left to his great-grandson, Diarmait Mac Murchada, to attempt to restore the power of Leinster. To this ambition he devoted a long, stormy and—even by twelfth-century standards—ruthless career that ended in his expulsion in 1166 and his introduction of Anglo-Norman adventurers in an attempt to regain his kingdom. After his death in 1171, the greater part of his kingdom passed into the hands of Anglo-Norman lords.

BIBLIOGRAPHY

Francis J. Byrne, *Irish Kings and High-Kings* (1973); Gearóid MacNiocaill, *Ireland Before the Vikings* (1972); Donnchadh Ó Corráin, *Ireland Before the Normans* (1972); Alfred P. Smyth, "The Húi Néill and the Leinstermen in the Annals of Ulster," in *Études celtiques,* **14** (1974), and "Húi Failgi Relations with the Húi Néill in the Century After the Loss of the Plain of Mide," *ibid.,* **14** (1975). On the archaic Leinster poetry, see James Carney, "Three Old Irish Accentual Poems," in *Ériu,* **22** (1971); Myles Dillon, "The Consecration of Irish Kings," in *Celtica,* **10** (1973); Kuno Meyer, "Über die älteste irische Dichtung," in *Abhandlungen der K. Preussischen Akade-*

mie der Wissenschaften (1913), no. 6; M. A. O'Brien, ed., *Corpus genealogiarum Hiberniae* (1962, repr. 1976), 1–9, 334. For the later political history, see Francis X. Martin, *No Hero in the House: Diarmait Mac Murchada and the Coming of the Normans to Ireland* (1977); Donnchadh Ó Corráin, "Irish Regnal Succession: A Reappraisal," in *Studia hibernica*, **11** (1971), "The Career of Diarmait mac Máel na mBó," in *Journal of the Old Wexford Society*, **3** (1970–1971) and **4** (1972–1973), "The Uí Chennselaig Kingship of Leinster, 1072–1126," *ibid.*, **5** (1974–1975) and **6** (1975–1976), and "The Education of Diarmait Mac Murchada," in *Ériu*, **28** (1977); Brian Ó Cuív, "Diarmaid na nGall," in *Éigse*, **16**, pt. 2 (1975).

DONNCHADH Ó CORRÁIN

[See also **Brigit, St.; Ireland; Uí Néill.**]

LEIÐARVÍSAN (Pointing the way) is an anonymous Icelandic poem dating from the second half of the twelfth century. Composed in forty-five *dróttkvætt* stanzas, the poem is in symmetrical *drápa* form: prologue *(upphaf)*, twelve stanzas; refrain section *(stefjubálkr)*, twenty-one stanzas, divided between two refrains (stanzas 13, 17, 21, and 25, 29, 33); and conclusion *(slæmr)*, twelve stanzas. The subject is the observance of Sunday. The poet begins the prologue with a prayer for poetic inspiration and expresses his eagerness to recite the poem, asking for attention as he sings of Sunday. He briefly sketches the legend of the Sunday Epistle, first attested in sixth-century Spain but thereafter widely disseminated. A letter from heaven, written in gold, is found in Jerusalem on a Sunday; in it the Lord commands (here in unornamented, direct discourse) the observation of his day and promises punishment to those who violate it or refuse to pay their tithe.

The central refrain section recounts events of salvation history that are supposed to have taken place on Sunday: six from the Old Testament (creation of angels, establishment of peace between heaven and earth, landing of Noah's Ark, crossing of the Red Sea, giving of the Ten Commandments, water from the rock) and six miracles of Christ (changing water to wine at Cana, loaves and fishes, another miraculous feeding, entry into Jerusalem, the Resurrection, gift of the Holy Ghost). Between these two series of miraculous events—each of which is divided by a refrain into sets of three—are three transitional stanzas concerning events preceding Christ's ministry: the Annunciation, the Nativity, and Christ's baptism. The conclusion is concerned with the Last

Judgment (also to take place on Sunday) and with admonitions to observe Sunday and to pray for mercy. In stanza 43 the poet credits Rúnolfr, "an excellent priest," with substantial assistance in setting the poem's foundation *(grundvǫllr)* and develops this metaphor further by calling the poem a "strong building" *(ramligt hús)*. In the penultimate stanza the poem is named "Pointing the Way."

It will be obvious that the number three is central to the structure: threefold division into numbers divisible by three (twelve, twenty-one, twelve), subdivision of the *stefjubálkr* into units of three, termination of the refrain in stanza 33, and the appeal to the members of the Trinity in stanza 3 to establish the poem's form.

Early scholars speculated concerning the poet's lack of experience (because of certain metrical weaknesses), the dedication of a church as the possible occasion for the poem (based largely on literal reading of the poet's "strong building" metaphor), and the identification of Rúnolfr from among at least four possibilities, including Rúnolfr Ketilsson (*d.* 1186), to whom is attributed a verse on the completion of the new church (which he calls "strong hall") at Skálaholt in 1154. None of these speculations can be substantiated, but the poem can be generally dated by its relation to other twelfth-century *drápur.*

BIBLIOGRAPHY

Sources. Editions include Finnur Jónsson, ed., *Den norsk-islandske skjaldedigtning* (1908–1915), A I, 618–626 (diplomatic), and B I, 622–633 (normalized); Ernst A. Kock, ed., *Den norsk-isländska skaldediktningen,* I (1946), 302–308; Hugo Rydberg, *Die geistlichen Drápur und Dróttkvættfragmente des Cod. AM 757 4to* (1907), 4–11 (diplomatic). A translation is Wolfgang Lange, trans., *Christliche Skaldendichtung* (1958), 38–45.

Studies. Reidar Astås, "Om Leiðarvísan: En Studie i norrøn Kristendomsforståelse," in *Edda*, **70** (1970); Jakob Benediktsson, *"Leiðarvísan,"* in *Kulturhistorisk leksikon for nordisk middelalder,* X (1965); Finnur Jónsson, *Den oldnorske og oldislandske litteraturs historie,* 2nd ed. (1920–1924), II, 118–119; Wolfgang Lange, *Studien zur christlichen Dichtung der Nordgermanen 1000–1200* (1958), 150–157; Fredrik Paasche, *Kristendom og kvad* (1914), 98–108; Vemund Skard, "Harmsól, Plácítusdrápa og Leiðarvísan," in *Arkiv för nordisk filologi,* 68 (1953); Edward O. G. Turville-Petre, *Origins of Icelandic Literature* (1953), 159–160; Jan de Vries, *Altnordische Literaturgeschichte,* 2nd ed., II (1967), 59–61.

GEORGE S. TATE

[See also **Skaldic Poetry.**]

LEJRE CHRONICLE (*Chronicon Lethrense*), a Danish chronicle, the subject of which is legendary history (Danish: *oldhistorie*). In medieval histories, legends about national origins and early kings form a necessary prologue to any account of documented facts, and Danish historiography is no exception to this rule. Sven Aggesøn and Saxo dedicate sizable portions of their works to *oldhistorie*. The Lejre Chronicle is probably the earliest Danish specimen of the genre. The passionate hatred of Germany expressed by its anonymous author makes it likely that it was written around 1170, when Frederick I Barbarossa (*r.* 1152–1190) was trying to force Waldemar I (1157–1182) to recognize him as his overlord. The traditional title of the chronicle does not imply that its author worked at Lejre (Leire); it is more probable that he was a priest in nearby Roskilde, but the Danish kings whose legends he tells all reigned, according to popular tradition, from the early royal seat of Lejre and are buried there.

The chronicle begins with a short description of the Danish territory, then goes on to relate the reign of Dan, son of Ypper, who helped the Jutes fight off the forces of Augustus Caesar and incorporated Jutland, Funen, and Skåne into Denmark. Significantly, the Roman invasion is said to have taken place along the border with Germany. There follows an account of the reign of Ro and the foundation of Roskilde (etymologized as "Ro's source"). Next comes the story of King Halfdan, his brother Helgi the pirate, and the latter's siring of Hrólf kraki. During Hrólf's infancy, Denmark is conquered by the Swedes, who place a dog as king over the Danes in order to humiliate them. The animal, bitten to death in a fight with other dogs, is succeeded on the throne by Snyo, a shepherd who had the courage to announce the dog's death to the king of Sweden. Snyo later is eaten alive by lice. The stories of the dog king and the lice-ridden king (*hundekongen* and *lusekongen*) are well known in folk tradition. In saying that the Danes "always remember the name" of Snyo, the author is perhaps making an insulting pun on the name of Erik II Emune (the memorable), comparing him to the verminous shepherd. The chronicle ends with a brief account of Hrólf kraki and of his slaying by his sister Sculd and her husband Hiarwart, who is here made a German. The final chapter concerns Harald hildetand and the battle of Bravalla.

The Lejre Chronicle has been preserved as part of the annals of Lund, and was perhaps mutilated (shortened and in part rewritten) so that it could be incorporated into that work. It is preserved in the oldest manuscripts of the annals: AM 843 4° and AM 841 4° (where it follows a world chronicle compiled from Isidore of Seville and Bede), both manuscripts in the Arnamagnaean collection, and the Erfurt codex 23 8°, leaves 184–221. A Swedish translation was incorporated into the *Prosaiska Krönikan* after 1452.

BIBLIOGRAPHY

Chronicon Lethrense, Martin Clarentius Gertz, ed., in *Scriptores minores historiae Danicae medii aevii*, I (1917), 34–53. Also Bjarni Guðnason, *Um Skjöldungasögu* (1963), 167–175; Ellen Jørgensen, *Historieforskning og historieskrivning i Danmark indtil aar 1800* (1931), 27–28; Jørgen Olrik, "Sagnkrøniken i Lundeårbogen," in *Historisk tidskrift*, 7th ser., II (1899–1900), in Danish.

JOAQUÍN MARTÍNEZ-PIZARRO

[See also **Denmark; Hrólfs Saga Kraka.**]

LE LOUP, JEAN. See **Loup, Jean.**

LENSES AND EYEGLASSES. An elaborate mythology has grown up around the medieval use of lenses and the invention of eyeglasses. It is certain that burning glasses were available in antiquity; they are referred to in literary sources, such as Aristophanes' *Clouds,* and ancient double-convex glasses and crystals that seem likely to have served that purpose have been discovered. It has been hypothesized, and it does indeed seem likely, that the magnifying properties of such glasses were recognized, and that they were utilized as magnifiers in such crafts as gem cutting. To what extent the use of burning glasses and magnifiers persisted into the early Middle Ages cannot be judged from the available evidence, but it would be surprising if the practice disappeared totally.

By the thirteenth century it was a commonplace that the refraction of light could be employed to produce magnification of distant objects. Robert Grosseteste (*d.* 1253) wrote in *De iride* that the third part of perspective, which treats refracted light,

> if perfectly understood, shows us how to make very distant objects appear close, how to make nearby objects appear very small, and how to make a small object placed at a distance appear as large as we wish, so that it would be possible to read minute letters from incredible distances or count sand, seeds, blades of grass, or any minute objects.

As for the cause of these wonders, Grosseteste merely refers in general to the principles of refraction and the fact that the size of a visible object is judged from the angle between the visual rays that perceive its extreme points:

> The way in which these astonishing things occur is made manifest as follows. The visual ray penetrating through several transparent substances of diverse natures is refracted at their junctions, and its parts, in the different transparent media existing at those junctions, are joined at an angle. . . . We add the following principles, which the optical theorist appropriates from the natural philosopher, namely that the size, position, and order of the visible object are determined from the size of the angle and the position and order of the rays under which the object is seen and that it is not great distance that makes an object invisible, except accidentally, but rather the smallness of the angle under which it is observed. From these principles, it is perfectly evident by geometrical reasoning how an object of known distance, size, and position will appear with respect to location, size, and position.

Nothing in these passages points to knowledge of lenses. The object of Grosseteste's admiration is not the magnifying lens but the rules of refraction, through the application of which one should (in principle) be able to perform marvels of magnification.

Roger Bacon (*d. ca.* 1292) made similar remarks in the second half of the century. But Bacon went further, referring explicitly to the magnifying lens:

> But if a man should look at letters and other minute things by means of crystal or glass or some other transparent substance placed above the letters, and this substance is less than a hemisphere and has its convexity toward the eye, and the eye is situated in air, he will see the letters far better, and they will appear larger to him. For according to the truth of the fifth rule [given above], all conditions are right for magnification, since the angle under which the thing is seen is larger, and the image is larger and closer. . . . And therefore this instrument is useful to the elderly and those with weak eyes. (*Opus maius*, John Henry Bridges, ed. [1900], II, 157)

It is clear from this passage that magnifying lenses were used for reading and examining small objects by the second half of the thirteenth century.

It should not be supposed, however, that medieval scholars worked out anything approaching an adequate geometrical theory of lenses. The principles of refraction were perfectly understood, but their application was almost always restricted to a single refracting interface. For example, the "fifth rule" to which Bacon referred in the passage quoted above was concerned with refraction at a single spherical interface; in applying this rule to a plano-convex magnifying lens, he ignored refraction at the plane surface (perhaps because that surface was conceived to be in direct contact with the observed object). There were very few exceptions to this practice of limiting attention to a single refraction. One such exception was in the theory of the rainbow, where Theodoric of Freiberg considered the twofold refraction of light in individual raindrops. More significant was the analysis of the burning sphere and burning hemisphere. A number of thirteenth-century writers (Grosseteste, Bacon, and John Peckham, for example) argued that a spherical crystal or a spherical globe of water would bring solar rays to a focus. Bacon went further, applying the same idea to a hemispherical crystal or a spherical vessel half full of water. This is as far as the theoretical analysis of lenses went during the Middle Ages; it was concerned only with the convergence of solar rays to produce combustion, and it would not have assisted anybody in grinding spectacle lenses or magnifiers of the proper shape.

It might be inquired whether a more complete theory of lenses could be found in attempts to trace radiation through the crystalline lens of the eye. Medieval scholars certainly recognized the lenticular shape of this organ and applied ray geometry to it. However, according to the visual theory of the perspectivists (the only medieval scholars with a serious interest in ray geometry), the radiation efficacious in producing sight is that which falls perpendicularly on the crystalline lens; this radiation enters the crystalline lens without refraction and maintains its rectilinear course until it is refracted at the rear surface of the lens. All other radiation is ignored: once again the medieval scholar restricts his attention to a single refracting interface.

It is clearly a short step from magnifying lenses to eyeglasses. But if a distinction is nevertheless made between these two instruments, the scanty evidence indicates that the latter was invented late in the thirteenth century. The earliest known reference to eyeglasses is in the rules of the guild of Venetian crystal workers for 1300: "Nobody in the said guild of crystal workers shall dare to buy, or cause to be bought, or sell, or cause to be sold, any work in colorless glass which counterfeits crystal; for example, buttons, handles, disks for small barrels and for the eyes. . . . " If this reference seems slightly ambiguous, the matter is made perfectly clear in a rule promulgated a year later, which laid down the procedure to be followed by anybody "wishing to make eyeglasses for reading (vitreos ab oculis ad legendum)." References to eyeglasses became quite common thereafter, such terms as ocularii vitri and unum par ochialium being employed. The earliest known depiction of eyeglasses is in a portrait of Hugh of St. Cher, painted in 1352.

Two documents bear on the question of the identity of the inventor and the date of his invention. The first is a sermon given by Giordano of Pisa in 1306, which contains the following remark: "It is not twenty years since there was found the art of making eyeglasses which make for good vision, one of the best arts and most necessary that the world has. . . . I have seen the man who first invented and created it, and I have talked to him." On the basis of this passage, it has been argued that eyeglasses were probably invented about 1286 or shortly thereafter. Giordano's account is confirmed in a general way by an entry in the Ancient Chronicle of the Dominican Monastery of St. Catherine at Pisa (Giordano's own monastery), written after 1313. This entry asserts that one of the monks, Alessandro Spina, who died in 1313, saw a pair of eyeglasses invented (the inventor refused to share the secret) and successfully reproduced them. What can be concluded from this evidence is simply that eyeglasses were probably invented late in the thirteenth century. From Giordano's failure to describe their invention as a monastic achievement, it can be inferred that the inventor was probably a craftsman; from the localities of the early references to eyeglasses, he was likely a Pisan or a Venetian.

If all of the references thus far encountered are to positive or converging lenses (thicker in the center than at the edges), as historians have universally supposed, when did negative or diverging lenses (thicker at the edges than in the middle) first appear? (Positive lenses correct for presbyopia; negative lenses, for myopia.) The earliest unambiguous reference to negative lenses is in a letter sent from Ardouino da Baesse in Ferrara to Piero di Cosimo de' Medici in Florence, dated 25 August 1451, noting that of four pairs of spectacles recently received, three were for "distant vision." Another letter, sent by Duke Francesco Sforza of Milan to Nicodemo Tranchedini da Pontremoli, his ambassador to Florence, in 1462, requested three dozen pairs of glasses: "one dozen of those apt and suitable for distant vision, that is for the young; another [dozen] that are suitable for near vision, that is for the elderly; and the third [dozen]

for normal vision." It is apparent that by this time eyeglasses were highly fashionable at the Milanese court, even for those whose vision was normal. No theoretical analysis of negative lenses appeared until the next century.

There has been much useless debate over the question of why no theoretical analysis of spectacle lenses appeared until almost 300 years after their invention. The best-known answer is that of the physicist-historian Vasco Ronchi, who has argued that theoretical scientists were prejudiced against lenses and therefore entered into a conspiracy of silence. Without resorting to such an implausible account, however, the absence of theoretical analysis of spectacle lenses can be explained as follows.

First, by the time eyeglasses were invented, the creative period in medieval mathematical optics was over. After John Peckham, who probably completed his Perspectiva communis by 1279, it is very hard to find a significant writer in the mathematical tradition until the middle of the sixteenth century. In short, nobody was writing the sort of treatise in which a mathematical analysis of spectacle lenses might reasonably be expected to appear.

Second, no writer in the mathematical tradition (before, during, or after its creative period) was in the business of solving practical problems. The writer of optical treatises was not an applied scientist, but a natural philosopher. His goal was factual knowledge and theoretical understanding, and as far as refraction was concerned, there was nothing to be gained from a consideration of lenses. Medieval students of optics had quite a thorough and impressive understanding of the principles of refraction at a single interface, and although these principles could easily have been extended to thin lenses, such an extension would not have taught them anything about the principles that they did not already know.

Third, not only did a theoretical analysis of lenses have nothing to offer the natural philosopher, but it promised the spectacle maker no benefits. The latter would not have been helped by a knowledge of the path of radiation through a lens, but only by rules that would assist in correcting for myopia and presbyopia. Such an analysis, had it been attempted, is unlikely to have succeeded until after Johannes Kepler had developed his theory of the retinal image in the seventeenth century. Fitting a myope or presbyope with proper spectacles was a problem best solved by trial and error, and that is precisely how the spectacle maker solved it—not only during the Middle Ages, when he had no alternative, but as late as the twentieth century, when the theoretical avenue was open to him.

BIBLIOGRAPHY

See H. C. Beck, "Early Magnifying Glasses," in *Antiquaries Journal*, 8 (1928); Alistair C. Crombie, *Robert Grosseteste and the Origins of Experimental Science, 1100–1700* (1953, 3rd ed. 1971); Edward Grant, ed., *A Source Book in Medieval Science* (1974); Vincent Ilardi, "Eyeglasses and Concave Lenses in Fifteenth-century Florence and Milan: New Documents," in *Renaissance Quarterly*, 29 (1976); David C. Lindberg and Nicholas H. Steneck, "The Sense of Vision and the Origins of Modern Science," in Allen G. Debus, ed., *Science, Medicine, and Society in the Renaissance: Essays to Honor Walter Pagel*, I (1972); Edward Rosen, "The Invention of Eyeglasses," in *Journal of the History of Medicine and Allied Sciences*, 11 (1956).

DAVID C. LINDBERG

[See also **Bacon, Roger; Glass, Western European; Grosseteste, Robert; Optics, Western European; Peckham, John.**]

LENT (from OE *lencten*, perhaps related to the "lengthening" of spring days) is the period of preparation for the Christian festival of Easter. Although the medieval church inherited the basic outlines of Lent from earlier centuries, there was considerable evolution and local variety in the nature of this preparation and in the computation of the traditional forty days. Earlier, Lent was both a period of catechism for converts preparing to be baptized on Easter, and a time of prayer and fasting by all Christians, following Jesus' scriptural journey to Jerusalem. Medieval Lent lost the catechetical dimension and became primarily a time of penitent fasting. This change was completed in Byzantium in the ninth century by the liturgical reform of the Studite monks, and somewhat earlier in the West.

Varying customs of fasting compounded the problem of calculating the biblical forty days of preparation. In Byzantium, Lent ended when "Lazarus" Saturday and Palm Sunday ushered in Holy Week. Although there was no fasting on Saturdays and Sundays, they too were days of preparation included in the forty; thus five weeks of seven days, plus five days, put the beginning of Byzantine Lent on a Monday. The Roman tradition emphasized fasting and penitence almost exclusively (it omitted the joyful word "Alleluia") and thus counted only fast days, including Saturdays and Holy Week, in the forty; thus six weeks of six fast days, plus four days added after Gregory I the Great but before the ninth-

century Gelasian Sacramentary, put the beginning of the Western Lent on a Wednesday, later called Ash Wednesday for the penitential symbol placed on the foreheads of worshipers (first mentioned in the twelfth century).

The extent and severity of the actual fasting also varied, but the general exclusion of meat yielded "carnival" or "meat removal" (Mardi Gras, or Shrove Tuesday) just before Lent.

BIBLIOGRAPHY

See *The Lenten Triodion*, Mother Mary and Kallistos Ware, trans. (1984).

PAUL ROREM

[See also **Easter; Fasting, Christian; Penance and Penitentials.**]

LEO I, POPE (*ca.* 400–461), the most decisive and energetic pope of the fifth century, known to history as Leo the Great. Said to be of Tuscan origin, he first appears in records as deacon in Rome under Celestine I; he was an influential adviser to this pope and to his successor, Sixtus III. Absent on a mission to Gaul when Sixtus died, Leo was summoned to return, acclaimed as his successor, and ordained bishop on 29 September 440.

As pope, Leo worked tirelessly to uphold the status of his see and to promote a rule of law and moderation throughout the universal church. Firmly convinced of the right of the Roman see to universal primacy, he believed that, in the person of the pope, Peter continues to exercise his role of "confirming the brethren." He was just but unyielding in enforcing ecclesiastical discipline when matters of doctrine or principle were at stake. His reliance upon conciliar decrees and the decisions of his predecessors as expressions of policy was influential in the development of canon law.

While recognizing the emperor's authority in temporal matters, Leo vigorously resisted any attempt by the civil power to control the church. In the face of the Western Empire's collapse, Leo stepped into the vacuum to defend the citizens. He went out to meet Attila near Mantua in 452 and persuaded him to withdraw. Again, in 455, he met with Genseric (Gaiseric) the Vandal outside the walls of Rome to plead for the city.

Leo was equally assertive in dealing with the Eastern churches. When the abbot Eutyches (*d. ca.* 454) began teaching his Monophysite Christology in 446,

Leo kept fully informed through correspondence, especially with Patriarch Flavian of Constantinople. To him he addressed the famous letter known as the *Tome of Leo* (449), defining the theological issue in clear terms. A council that Emperor Theodosius II (401–450) convened at Ephesus in 449, however, rehabilitated Eutyches, deposed Flavian, spurned Leo's letter, and insulted his legates. The pope denounced this synod as a *latrocinium* (robber council) and annulled its decrees. Supported by the new emperor, Marcian (*d.* 457), Leo directed the new council, which convened at Chalcedon in 451. His legates presided, and the council reversed the decisions of 449 and adopted the teaching of the *Tome*, acclaiming, "Peter has spoken through Leo." Leo ratified the decrees of Chalcedon but firmly rejected its famous canon 28, which conferred primacy in the East upon Constantinople.

Leo's extant writings include about 120 authentic letters and 97 sermons. The letters, doubtless edited by curial stylists, are valuable sources for the events of the times. The sermons are finely crafted compositions, probably edited for publication after delivery. Originally preached during the liturgy, they reveal Leo as devoted pastor, instructing his flock and urging them to fidelity. While not an original theologian, he had a profound grasp of the Christian mystery and a gift for communicating it. His writing displays the clarity and logic of the Roman mind and the noble sobriety of a refined Latin style.

BIBLIOGRAPHY

Sources. Leo's letters are in *Patrologia latina*, LIV, (1846), 581–1218; his sermons in *Corpus Christianorum, series latina*, CXXXVIII–CXXXVIIIA (1973). English translations of selected letters and sermons are in *Nicene and Post-Nicene Fathers*, XII (1894, repr. 1979).

Studies. C. Bartnik, "L'interpretation théologique de la crise de l'empire romain par Léon le Grand," in *Revue d'histoire ecclésiastique*, 63 (1968); Aloys Grillmeier and Heinrich Bacht, *Das Konzil von Chalkedon*, 3 vols. (1951–1954); Germain Hudon, *La perfection chrétienne d'après les sermons de saint Léon* (1959); Trevor G. Jalland, *The Life and Times of St. Leo the Great* (1941); Hubert Jedin and John Dolan, eds., *History of the Church*, II (1980); Marie-Bernard de Soos, *Le mystère liturgique d'après saint Léon le Grand* (1958, repr. 1972); Peter Stockmeier, *Leo I. des Grossen Beurteilung der kaiserlichen Religionspolitik* (1959).

CLAUDE J. PEIFER, O.S.B.

[See also **Councils (Ecumenical); Eutyches; Monophysitism; Theodosius II the Calligrapher.**]

LEO III, POPE (*d.* 816). A curial official unconnected with the Roman nobility, Leo moved quickly after his consecration as pope (27 December 795) to secure in Charlemagne the protector he needed for maintaining order in the papal territories and for emancipating the papacy from Byzantine control. This delicate relationship between pope and king reached a climax on Christmas Day 800, when Leo crowned Charlemagne in St. Peter's as emperor of the Romans. The precise political motives behind this action are still being debated, but the coronation long remained in the European mind as a potent image of the central position the pope held in Western medieval polity.

Leo's reign was clouded at its beginning and end by factional violence and by accusations about his own conduct. Seriously wounded by enemies at Rome in 799, he escaped to Charlemagne at Paderborn. Ultimately he cleared himself of the charges against him only by swearing a public declaration of innocence (the exact nature and content of which remain controversial) in the presence of Charlemagne on 23 December 800.

Not himself a theologian, Leo supported the Carolingian opposition to adoptionism at a Roman synod in 798 or 799. But in the dispute between Eastern and Western Christians (especially Charlemagne) over the *Filioque*, which the Franks called on Leo to resolve in 810, he established the mediating papal policy that lasted for the next two centuries: acceptance of Western Trinitarian theology as orthodox coupled with a firm refusal to add the term *Filioque* to the Nicene Creed over Byzantine objections.

Leo's name entered the Roman Martyrology only in 1673. His status as saint appears to depend heavily on accounts that treat as miraculous the recovery from the wounds he received in 799. Leo's extraordinary benefactions toward the churches of Rome are recorded at length in the *Liber pontificalis* and formed an important part of his later reputation.

BIBLIOGRAPHY

Horace K. Mann, *The Lives of the Popes in the Early Middle Ages*, 2nd ed., II (1925), is the fullest account in English summarizing the primary sources. For the political background and controverted historical questions see Walter Ullmann, *The Growth of Papal Government in the Middle Ages*, 3rd ed. (1970); Robert Folz, *The Coronation of Charlemagne, 25 December 800*, J. E. Anderson, trans. (1974); Luitpold Wallach, *Diplomatic Studies in Latin and Greek Documents from the Carolingian Age* (1977). For the *Filioque* dispute see Richard Haugh, *Photius and the*

Carolingians: The Trinitarian Controversy (1975). For information about archaeological remains of Leo's reign see Gerhard B. Ladner, *Die Papstbildnisse des Altertum und des Mittelalters* (1941).

ROBERT BARRINGER

[See also **Adoptionism; Charlemagne; Filioque; Kingship, Rituals of: Coronation; Papacy, Origins and Development of; Rome; Trinitarian Doctrine**.]

LEO IX, POPE (1002–1054). Born Bruno of Egisheim of noble parents in Egisheim, Alsace, he studied with Adalbert of Bremen (*ca.* 1000–1072) at Toul, where he became a canon in 1017. Although a deacon, Bruno in 1026 commanded an army of Emperor Conrad II in suppressing a revolt in Lombardy. The following year he was elected bishop of Toul. During his episcopate Bruno introduced reforms, inspired by Cluny and Lorraine, into monasteries within his see: Moyenmoutier, Remiremont, St. Aper, and St. Dié. When Pope Damasus II died in 1048, Emperor Henry III secured the election of Bruno as pope at Worms.

During his procession from Worms to Rome Bruno, dressed as a pilgrim, was accompanied by the archbishop of Trèves, the bishops of Metz and Verdun, Abbot Hugh of Cluny, and Hildebrand. In Rome Leo IX gathered around him a group of reform-minded advisers mostly from Lorraine: Archdeacon Frederick of Liège (or Lorraine), Hugh of Remiremont, Abbot Humbert of Moyenmoutier (soon bishop of Silva Candida), Udo of Toul, and Archbishop Halinard of Lyons. These gave the papacy new vigor and wider authority within the church. Out of this nucleus evolved the college of cardinals.

Leo summoned a synod in Rome, which outlawed simony and nicolaitism, and imposed regular living upon the secular clergy. Dubbed "the Apostolic Pilgrim," Leo spent most of his reign traveling in Italy, Germany, and France, holding synods that denounced simony, clerical marriage, church appointments made without election by clergy and people, violence against churches, military service by the clergy, mistreatment of the poor, illegal withdrawal of monastic vows, improper possession of churches by laymen, and collection of fees for burials and administration of the sacraments. An indirect result of the increased flow of papal privileges was the development of the papal chancery. The pope's visibility enhanced papal prestige and encouraged other reformers. In Rome about 1050 appeared the canonical collection in seventy-four titles, which utilized previous decretals to uphold the pontiff's legal prerogatives. The pope also arbitrated disputes among secular princes.

Leo's assault on simony influenced sacramental theology. Although he agreed with Humbert's view that simoniac bishops could not confer valid orders, the more moderate opinions of Peter Damian prevailed. In 1050, at the synods of Vercelli and Rome, Leo intervened against Berengar's denial of eucharistic transubstantiation.

Leo attempted to ally with Henry III and the Byzantine emperor Constantine IX Monomachos (*r.* 1042–1055) to expel the Normans from southern Italy. He led an army south but was defeated at Civitate in June 1053 and taken prisoner. Peter Damian (*d.* 1072) condemned his military venture as unseemly for a pope.

Angered by the papal attack in south Italy, Patriarch Michael Keroularios closed the Latin churches in Constantinople, ostensibly because they used unleavened bread. In response, the Roman curia sent an embassy to Constantinople headed by Cardinal Humbert. But the papal legates anathematized Keroularios and declared various Greek doctines and usages heretical. The Eastern Schism occurred in July 1054, following Leo's death on 19 April.

The program of the later Gregorian reform is evident in Leo IX's aggressive pontificate. Under him the papacy emerged as an independent, universal institution that provided spiritual and ecclesiastical direction for much of the clergy of Europe. Leo IX was canonized in 1087.

BIBLIOGRAPHY

Sources. Acta sanctorum, Apr. 2, 648–665; *Analecta Bollandiana,* **25** (1906), 258–297; *Patrologia latina,* CXLIII (1853), 457–798.

Studies. Augustin Fliche, *La réforme grégorienne,* I (1924); Hartmut Hoffmann, "Von Cluny zum Investiturstreit," in *Archiv für Kulturgeschichte,* **45** (1963); Eugène Martin, *Saint Léon IX* (1904); D. M. Nicol, "Byzantium and the Papacy in the Eleventh Century," in *Journal of Ecclesiastical History,* **13** (1962); Lucien Sittler and Paul Stinzi, *Saint Léon IX, le pape alsacien* (1950); H. Tritz, "Die Hagiographischen Quellen zur Geschichte Papst Leos IX," in *Studi Gregoriana,* **4** (1952).

THOMAS RENNA

[See also **Adalbert of Bremen; Berengar of Tours; Cardinals, College of; Constantine IX Monomachos; Decretals;**

Henry III of Germany; Holy Roman Empire; Investiture and Investiture Conflict; Law, Canon: To Gratian; Nicolaitans; Papacy, Origins and Development of; Schism, Great; Simony.]

LEO I, EMPEROR (*r.* 457–474), apparently the first Byzantine emperor to have a coronation, his predecessors having used the older Roman method of acclamation. Leo, however, was crowned by the patriarch of Constantinople. A military tribune born in Thrace, he came to the throne with help from the Goths, but he soon replaced them with the Isaurians, marking the end of Germanic influence in the empire. In 466 his elder daughter, Ariadne, married the Isaurian chieftain Tarasicdissa, who later became emperor under the name Zeno. Under Leo I the Byzantines launched a large and unsuccessful naval expedition against the Vandals in Africa.

BIBLIOGRAPHY

George Ostrogorsky, *History of the Byzantine State*, Joan Hussey, trans. (1957, rev. ed. 1969), 61–62.

LINDA C. ROSE

[See also **Byzantine Empire: History.**]

LEO III, EMPEROR (*ca.* 680–741). Leo seized the throne in a military coup (717) provoked by the threat of an imminent Muslim attack on Constantinople. Like four of the six preceding emperors who reigned between 695 and 717, he had no claim to rule other than a successful army career. But, in contrast with the accomplishments of their brief reigns, Leo undertook a spirited defense of the empire and a steady improvement in administrative efficiency that constituted a turning point in Byzantine history.

Leo's long reign was marked by a strengthening of imperial control over coinage, taxation (especially in the rebellious provinces of Sicily and southern Italy), the judiciary (with the legal handbook *Ekloga*, issued in 740 primarily to assist provincial justices), and the church. He is best known, however, for the introduction of iconoclasm (the destruction of icons), which became the official policy of the Eastern church in 730. Leo initiated this attempt to reduce the prominence of visual aids in worship after considerable discussion about the dangers of idola-

try. Although the patriarch and several devout iconophiles were punished and sent into exile for their opposition, this reform was generally accepted by the court, the episcopate, and Leo's supporters in the army. A decade of iconoclast rule culminating in the victory over the Arabs at Akroinon (740) forged the peculiar combination of religious and military success that characterized the government of Leo's son, Constantine V.

Because of the polemical nature of iconoclasm and its final condemnation in 843, nearly all its official acts and related imperial documents have been destroyed. Conversely, its iconophile opponents have been given retrospective prominence by later historians equally hostile to Leo. Recent research has sifted the prejudices to reveal more of his background and the circumstances in which he established a new ruling dynasty. His family came from Germanikeia (Maraş, or Marᶜaš) in northern Syria, and he was baptized Konon. In an official resettlement of population they were moved from the southeast to the northwest frontier when he was still young. After joining the army he adopted the name Leo, was promoted by Justinian II, and finally became *strategos* (military governor) of the Anatolikon province (*thema*). In 717, as Constantinople was threatened by a Muslim blockade, he displaced the ineffectual Theodosios III. The triumphant defeat of this twelve-month siege established Leo's reputation as a master of military strategy and diplomacy. It was probably more significant for medieval Christendom than the Battle of Poitiers (732).

Leo was clearly aware of the danger of Muslim domination posed by the caliphate of Damascus and determined to revitalize imperial defense. In addition to military and naval reforms, he made sure that his son would succeed him, thus restoring the traditional Byzantine pattern of family rule. His new imperial dynasty—Leo III, Constantine V, Leo IV, Constantine VI—held power for eighty years and is most conveniently identified as Syrian. Although the epithet Isaurian has frequently been employed, there is no firm evidence that Leo's family originated in Isauria. There is, however, a certain confusion in the sources, a confusion exaggerated by later writers responsible for alterations designed to brand Leo as a heretic. These also aimed to exonerate Patriarch Germanos, who resigned in 730, from any connivance in the early stages of iconoclasm. They therefore minimized the support Leo received and ignored the widespread concern about the power of images, both Christian and pagan, that is reflected in a collection of stories made in the early eighth century (*Parastaseis syntomoi chronikai*).

Leo III certainly contributed to the schism with Rome and the eventual loss of Byzantine Italy, but his rule ensured the survival of Byzantium under fierce Muslim pressure and made possible its expansion and growing prosperity later in the eighth century.

BIBLIOGRAPHY

Averil Cameron and Judith Herrin, eds., *Constantinople in the Early Eighth Century: The Parastaseis Syntomoi Chronikai* (1984), with introduction, translation, and commentary; Patricia Crone, "Islam, Judeo-Christianity, and Byzantine Iconoclasm," in *Jerusalem Studies in Arabic and Islam*, II (1980); Gilbert Dagron, *Constantinople imaginaire* (1985); *Ecloga*, L. Burgmann, ed. (1983); Stephen Gero, *Byzantine Iconoclasm During the Reign of Leo III* (1973); Judith Herrin, "The Context of Iconoclast Reform," in Anthony Bryer and Judith Herrin, eds., *Iconoclasm* (1977); George Ostrogorsky, "Les débuts de la querelle des images," in *Mélanges Charles Diehl*, I (1930); Dieter Stein, *Der Beginn des byzantinischen Bilderstreites und seine Entwicklung bis in die 40*er *Jahre des 8. Jahrhunderts* (1980).

JUDITH HERRIN

[See also **Byzantine Empire: History; Constantine V; Germanos I; Iconoclasm, Christian; Islam, Conquests of.**]

LEO V THE ARMENIAN, EMPEROR, Byzantine emperor (813–820), was responsible for the revival of iconoclasm by the Council of 815, which held essentially the same ideas as that of 754. Formerly *strategos* of the Anatolikon theme, Leo wished to restore the military power of the empire and successfully defended Constantinople against two sieges by the Bulgarian khan Krum. He rebuilt some of the cities in Macedonia and Thrace, and constructed stronger walls around the capital. Leo was murdered in front of the high altar at Hagia Sophia by followers of Michael the Amorian, who then became Emperor Michael II (820–829).

BIBLIOGRAPHY

George Ostrogorsky, *History of the Byzantine State*, Joan Hussey, trans. (1957, rev. ed. 1969), 200–203.

LINDA C. ROSE

[See also **Byzantine Empire: History; Iconoclasm, Christian; Krum.**]

LEO VI THE WISE, EMPEROR (866–12 May 912), Byzantine emperor. Leo studied under Photios and earned the epithet "the Wise" by his writings, chiefly orations and poems. At the death of Basil I in 886, Leo became senior emperor, with his younger brother Alexander as a very subordinate coemperor. Almost at once he replaced Photios as patriarch of Constantinople with his own brother Stephen. During the first part of his reign, Leo's chief adviser was Stylianos Zaützes, with whom he completed the legislative work of Basil I by publishing the massive Basilics, a systematically organized collection of laws based on the *Code* of Justinian I that, especially because it was in Greek, became the definitive Byzantine lawbook. Leo updated the Basilics with a group of novellae.

Leo faced severe challenges at home and abroad. In 894 war broke out with Czar Symeon of Bulgaria, who defeated the Byzantines at Bulgarophygon in 896 and won a favorable peace. Zaützes died in 899, and his family conspired against Leo in 900. Although Byzantine forces defeated an Arab army near Adana in 900, Arab naval forces sacked Demetrias in 901, took Taormina in 902, and, worst of all, sacked Thessaloniki in 904. The Arabs, however, were defeated in the Aegean in 905. In 905–906 the rebel Andronikos Doukas rose, with Arab backing. In 911–912 a Byzantine expedition against Arab-held Crete ended in failure.

In the meantime, Leo had been widowed three times without producing a male heir. In 905 a son, the future Constantine VII Porphyrogenitos, was born to his mistress, Zoë Karbonopsina. Leo married her in 906, in violation of a canon that forbade fourth marriages. In 907 Leo replaced Patriarch Nikolaos I Mystikos, who would not tolerate the marriage, with St. Euthymios. Though Leo procured a dispensation for his marriage from Pope Sergius III, the "tetragamy" caused a continuing schism in the Byzantine church. Leo's main achievement was to survive the crises of his reign without lasting damage to the empire.

BIBLIOGRAPHY

Romilly J. H. Jenkins, "The Chronological Accuracy of the 'Logothete' for the Years A.D. 867–913," in *Dumbarton Oaks Papers*, 19 (1965), with many notes on the chronology of Leo's reign; Patricia Karlin-Hayter, *Vita Euthymii* (1970), text and trans. of a fundamental source for the reign, with a commentary and complete bibliography; George Ostrogorsky, *History of the Byzantine State*, Joan M. Hussey, trans., rev. ed. (1969), 241–260.

WARREN T. TREADGOLD

LEO I/II OF ARMENIA

[See also **Basilics; Byzantine Empire; History; Corpus Iuris Civilis; Islam, Conquests of; Law, Canon: Byzantine; Nikolaos I Mystikos; Photios.**]

LEO I/II OF ARMENIA (*d.* 2 May 1219), first king of Cilician Armenia, was the youngest son of Stepᶜanos and the brother of the Rubenid baron Ruben III. Leo received the title Baron Leo II upon his brother's retirement to a monastery in 1187. Leo became head of the Rubenid line at a time when Cilicia was becoming an important factor in the struggles of the Crusader states of Antioch, Tyre, and Tripoli against Saladin; sensing this growing importance, Leo lost little time in requesting recognition as king of Cilicia from both the pope and Emperor Frederick I Barbarossa. Barbarossa's death in 1190 postponed Leo's coronation at Tarsus by the German imperial chancellor, Conrad, archbishop of Mainz. There is some dispute among historians over the exact date of this event, since some Armenian and Western sources give the year as 1198 and others 1199.

Leo is often referred to after his coronation as King Leo I, rather than Leo II. His letter of thanks indicates that his crown was given in the name of both the emperor and the pope, an act for which he formally recognized the primacy of the Roman see. His struggle over the succession of Antioch, however, soon resulted in tensions between Cilicia and Rome. Some Armenian chronicles and colophons state that Leo received a crown, probably honorific, from the Byzantine emperor Alexios III Angelos as well.

Leo's struggles with the principality of Antioch, to whose suzerainty he was subject, characterize the greater part of his reign. The conflict dated back to 1191, when Leo recaptured the Templar fortress of Baghrās from Saladin but refused to return it to the Templars. His forceful control of the fortress, which was located on the border between Antioch and Cilicia, posed a direct threat to Bohemond III, the ruler of Antioch. Further intensifying the situation were Leo's capture of Bohemond in 1193 and his unsuccessful attempt to annex Antioch to Cilicia. Leo later tried to place Raymond Ruben, the son of his niece and heiress presumptive, Alice, and of Bohemond's eldest son and heir, Raymond, on the throne of Antioch following Bohemond's death in 1201. These designs, however, opposed by both Raymond's younger brother and the Templars, who still demanded the return of Baghrās, failed.

Despite this diplomatic and territorial loss, the twenty-year reign of Leo I/II marked the height of Cilician power. He extended the boundaries of the kingdom; conquered the strategic Hetᶜumid fortress of Lambron, a longtime goal of the Rubenids; and attempted a reconciliation between the two rival houses by naming Hetᶜum, lord of Lambron, as his chief ambassador to the West. He made important marriage alliances with the emperor of Nicaea, and with the Lusignans of Cyprus and Jerusalem; he also enjoyed the support of the Teutonic Knights and the Hospitalers, to whom he granted sizable territories.

As regards the economic life of the kingdom, Leo made Cilicia's ports more accessible to Western merchants as early as 1201, when a trade agreement granting commercial privileges to the Genoese was signed; another with Venice soon followed. As a result, the ports of Koṛikos and, especially, Ayas (Lajazzo) began to prosper during this period as major entrepôts of the eastern Mediterranean.

The tone at Leo's court was decidedly influenced by his Frankish neighbors, and his reign marked the beginning of a latinization of Cilician culture. Latin titles such as "constable," "count," and "chamberlain" replaced their Armenian counterparts, and the nature of the feudal offices was altered accordingly. The traditional independence of the Armenian nobles from their king was transformed into a more European feudal dependence upon the sovereign. Most important, the medieval law code of Mχitᶜar Goš was gradually replaced by that of the Frankish Assizes of Antioch. Leo had named his grandnephew, Raymond Ruben, as heir but later decided in favor of his daughter, Zabel (Isabel), who succeeded to the throne upon Leo's death.

BIBLIOGRAPHY

Ghevond Alishan, *Léon le magnifique, premier roi de Sissouan ou de l'Arméno-Cilicie* (1888); Claude Cahen, *La Syrie du nord à l'époque des croisades et la principauté franque d'Antioche* (1940); Édouard Dulaurier, "Étude sur l'organisation politique, religieuse, et administrative du royaume de la Petite-Arménie," in *Journal asiatique,* 5th ser., **17** (1861) and **18** (1861); Smbat Lambronacᶜi (high constable of Armenia), *Chronicle* (1856, repr. 1956), in Armenian, and *La Chronique attribuée au connétable Smbat,* Gérard Dédéyan, ed. (1980).

ANI P. ATAMIAN

[See also **Cilician Kingdom; Cilician-Roman Church Union; Crusades and Crusader States; Hetᶜumids; Law, Armenian; Mχitᶜar Goš; Rubenids.**]

LEO V/VI OF ARMENIA (1342–29 November 1393), last king of Cilician Armenia. Probably the illegitimate son of Soldane and Jean de Lusignan, Leo was called to the throne during the regency following the death of Constantine IV/VI and was crowned at Sīs with his wife, Margaret of Soissons, on 14 September 1374. He fled Sīs during the Mamluk siege and was held prisoner in Cairo, but was released in 1382 through the intercession of the kings of Aragon and Castile. His family having died in prison, Leo spent his last years in Europe, seeking aid for the defense of Cilicia. Froissart's *Chronicle* relates that Leo at one time acted as a mediator between France and England during the Hundred Years War. He died at Paris and was buried in the Church of St. Denis.

BIBLIOGRAPHY

Ghevond Alishan, *Sissouan; ou, L'Arméno-Cilicie* (1899); K. J. Basmadjian, *Léon VI de Lusignan* (1908); Jean Dardel (chaplain to Leo V/VI), "Chronique d'Arménie," in *Recueil des historiens des croisades: Documents arméniens*, II (1906); Jehan Froissart, *Oeuvres de Froissart—Chroniques*, Baron Joseph Kervyn de Lettenhove, ed., XII (1871).

ANI P. ATAMIAN

[See also **Cilician Kingdom**.]

LEO OF OSTIA or Leo Marsicanus (*ca.* 1046–22 May 1115), archivist of the monastery of Monte Cassino, was born into the family of the counts of Marsi. He became a monk at Monte Cassino about 1060 and was elevated to cardinal bishop of Ostia sometime between about 1102 and 1107. A scribe, an illuminator, and librarian of Monte Cassino, he was also author (between about 1087 and 1105) of the early chapters of the *Chronicon monasterii Casinensis*, the most important literary source for the history of the abbey.

BIBLIOGRAPHY

Sources. Editions of the *Chronicle* include *Chronica monasterii Casinensis*, in W. Wattenbach, ed., *Monumenta Germaniae historica: Scriptores*, VII (1846), 551–841; *Die Chronik von Montecassino*, in Hartmut Hoffmann, ed., *Monumenta Germaniae historica: Scriptores*, XXXIV (1980).

Studies. Herbert A. Bloch, "Monte Cassino, Byzantium, and the West in the Earlier Middle Ages," in *Dumbarton Oaks Papers*, 3 (1946), and *Monte Cassino in the Middle Ages* (1981); Harmut Hoffman, "Der Kalendar des Leo Marsicanus," in *Deutsches Archiv für Erforschung des Mittelalters*, 21 (1965), "Die älteren Abtslisten von Montecassino," in *Quellen und Forschungen aus italienischen Archiven und Bibliotheken*, 47 (1967), and "Studien zur Chronik von Montecassino," in *Deutsches Archiv für Erforschung des Mittelalters*, 29 (1973); Wilhelm Smidt, "Die vermeintliche und die wirkliche Urgestalt der Chronik Leos von Montecassino," in *Quellen und Forschungen aus italienischen Archiven und Bibliotheken*, 28 (1938).

ROBERT P. BERGMAN

[See also **Monte Cassino**.]

LEO THE MATHEMATICIAN (*ca.* 790–after 869), a leading Byzantine intellectual of the ninth century. A cousin of John VII Morocharzianus the Grammarian (patriarch 837–843), he was regarded as one of the greatest minds of his age. Equally versed in mathematics, medicine, and philosophy, he became the head of the university at the Magnaura Palace that had been set up by Bardas Caesar. Leo's fame was so widespread that the caliph al-Maʾmūn (813–833) invited him to Baghdad, but the emperor Theophilos (829–842) did not want to lose this luminary and gave him a salary and a teaching position in one of the churches of Constantinople. Legend has it that the caliph then wrote to Theophilos offering him "eternal peace and 2,000 pounds of gold" if he would send Leo to Baghdad just for a short visit, probably *ca.* 831. Leo was later elected archbishop of Thessaloniki but was deposed for his iconoclastic views.

BIBLIOGRAPHY

Aleksandr A. Vasiliev, *History of the Byzantine Empire, 324–1453* (published in Russian 1917, 2nd rev. Eng. ed. 1952, repr. 1970); Paul Lemerle, *Le premier humanisme byzantin* (1971), 148–176.

LINDA C. ROSE

[See also **Bardas Caesar; Byzantine Empire: History; Constantinople; Iconoclasm, Christian; Maʾmūn, al-**]

LEONARDO DI SER GIOVANNI (*fl.* third quarter of the fourteenth century), Florentine goldsmith and follower of Orcagna. Leonardo collaborated with Francesco di Niccolò on the altar of S. Jacopo, Pistoia Cathedral, 1361–1364 and 1367–1371. He worked with Betto di Geri on the silver altar depicting scenes from the life of St. John the Baptist for S. Giovanni, Florence (now in the Museo dell'Opera), 1366–1377.

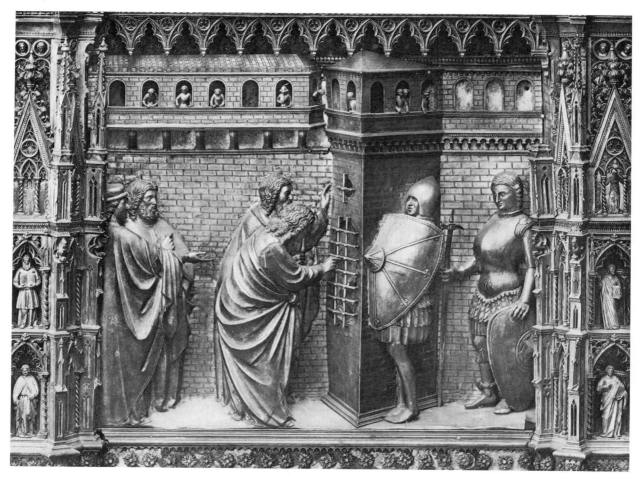

St. John the Baptist in prison. Silver altar relief by Leonardo di Ser Giovanni for S. Giovanni, Florence, *ca.* 1367. SCALA/ART RESOURCE

BIBLIOGRAPHY

Pèleo Bacci, *Gli orafi fiorentini e il 2° riordinamento dell'altare d'argento di S. Jacopo,* 2nd ed. (1906); Hugh Honour, *Goldsmiths and Silversmiths* (1971); Filippo Rossi, *Italian Jeweled Arts,* Elizabeth Mann Borghese, trans. (1957).

BRUCIA WITTHOFT

[See also **Metalsmiths, Gold and Silver; Orcagna.**]

LEONINUS (Leonius, Léonin) (*ca.* 1135–1201), French poet and composer of organum, credited with the creation of the *Magnus liber,* a collection of two-part settings of graduals, alleluias, and responsories for important feasts of the church year at the Cathedral of Notre Dame in Paris. Documentary evidence indicates that Magister Leonius, later called Leoninus, was a canon at the collegiate church of St. Benoît on the Left Bank and was later associated with St. Victor. His association with the Cathedral of Notre Dame, where he became a canon by the 1180's, extended from at least 1159 to 1201.

Leoninus was a highly educated cleric, well known for his Latin poetry (there are several sources for his verse setting of the first eight books of the Old Testament). Our only source for a knowledge of the musical achievements of Leoninus is the treatise of an anonymous English monk (known as Anonymous IV to music historians). Writing between 1172 and 1180, after a term of study in Paris, the unknown writer described something of the recent history of music in Paris:

> Note that Magister Leoninus, according to what is said, was the best composer [or singer?] of organa, who made the great book [*magnus liber*] or organa from the Gradual and Antiphoner in order to augment the divine

service. And it was in use up to the time of the great Perotinus, who abbreviated it and made many more and better *clausulae* or *puncta*, because he was the best composer [or singer?] of discant, and better than Leoninus was. But this may not be said for the refinement of [Perotinus'] organa etc.

After enumerating some of Perotinus' works, Anonymous IV added: "The book or books of Magister Perotinus [have been] in use ... in the choir of the great church of the Blessed Virgin in Paris ... up to the present day." Since some of Perotinus' work is datable to 1198, it seems reasonable that Leoninus' musical activity began about 1160 (construction of the new cathedral began in 1163; the altar was dedicated in 1182).

According to Anonymous IV, Leoninus' greatest achievement was the creation of the *Magnus liber*. This, with the additions of Perotinus, is the first group of polyphonic pieces that gained a very wide circulation and was copied even into the beginning of the fourteenth century. It is difficult to measure fully Leoninus' achievement because the three surviving complete copies of the *Magnus liber* postdate Leoninus' work by a half century and more. As Anonymous IV states, Leoninus' work was soon subject to revision and modernization by Perotinus. Thus, the original characteristics of Leoninus' style cannot be isolated. Attempts have been made to reconstruct the original corpus of the *Magnus liber,* but these are not fully convincing.

Leoninus used two styles to set the solo parts of responsorial chants; the chorus parts continued to be sung monophonically by the full choir. For predominantly syllabic sections of a chant, a highly ornate, rhythmically free melismatic upper voice *(duplum)* was set over sustained notes of the chant (tenor). This style was called *organum purum.* The original rhythmic nature of the *organum purum* is a matter of controversy, since the notation was subject to reworking and modernization by later copyists. For melismatic parts of the chant, the setting was note-against-note; that is, the notes of the tenor move almost as fast as the *duplum* in what is called discant style. Both the melismatic and the discant styles of polyphony were cultivated before Leoninus in the St. Martial style of organum, but in Leoninus' discant sections, the voices were precisely measured according to the principles of the rhythmic modes. (What role Leoninus may have had in the formulation of the rhythmic modes is unknown; his poetry, in quantitative Latin verse, does not provide an immediate analogy to the system of musical rhythm.)

As Anonymous IV attests, it was the discant style that captured composers' imaginations. The further development of organum lay in the direction of "more and better *clausulae.*" The clausulae, which are substitute discant sections, were inserted into the old *organa pura,* and further sections of *organum purum* were recomposed in discant style, thus "abbreviating" the *Magnus liber* and rendering the shape of Leoninus' original unrecognizable.

BIBLIOGRAPHY

The identification of the composer Léonin with the poet Leoninus has only recently been made. See Craig Wright, "Leoninus, Poet and Musician," in *Journal of the American Musicological Society,* **39** (1986). A complete edition of the *Magnus liber* according to one of the three surviving sources is in William G. Waite, *The Rhythm of Twelfth-century Polyphony: Its Theory and Practice* (1954). This book must be used with caution. The sections of *organum purum,* fully rhythmized according to principles of the rhythmic modes, do not reflect twelfth-century practice but rather the practice of the late thirteenth and early fourteenth centuries. The same must be said of all other readily available examples of organa from the *Magnus liber:* Archibald T. Davison and Willi Apel, eds., *Historical Anthology of Music,* rev. ed., I (1949), 24 (item 28c) and 27–30 (item 29); Richard H. Hoppin, ed., *Anthology of Medieval Music* (1978), 50–56; W. Thomas Marrocco and Nicholas Sandon, eds., *The Oxford Anthology of Music: Medieval Music* (1977), 90–95.

LAWRENCE M. EARP

[See also **Anonymous IV; Ars Antiqua; Magnus Liber Organi; Notre Dame School; Organum; Perotinus.**]

LEPROSY. In the High and later Middle Ages, the leper was legally and religiously cut off from the rest of society. He was seen as morally unclean. Special hospitals served to segregate lepers. Fear of the disease, religious impulses, and social attitudes combined to create this situation. In order to better understand the medieval leper, it is necessary to consider his disease, its diagnosis, and the legal and religious machinery set in motion by that diagnosis. Once declared a leper, a person had a limited set of alternatives of which life in a leper hospital is the best known.

THE DISEASE

Leprosy, also known as Hansen's disease, is a bacterial infection caused by *Mycobacterium leprae,* which has the longest generation time of any known microorganism and a latency period in human beings of up to several years. Its mode of transmission is still not understood, though it is probably passed both via the respiratory route and via contact. The former is thought to be more important.

Its manifestations are protean but grouped about two poles. The expression of the disease in humans depends on host immunity rather than type of organism. There is only one known pathogen, with no variation in virulence. The patient's immune response determines the course. Tuberculoid leprosy represents a hypersensitivity response and is usually self-limited. Lepromatous leprosy results from a specific immune deficiency (of the cell-mediated or T-cell-dependent type) in the face of *M. leprae*. It is the latter form that leads to the severe deformity and disfigurement generally associated with the disease. Lepromatous leprosy has a very long course.

The disease was well described during the Middle Ages, and the best descriptions, such as those of Theodoric of Cervia (1205–1298), Gilbertus Anglicus (Gilbert of England, *fl.* 1245), and Guy de Chauliac (*ca.* 1300–1368), leave no doubt that leprosy is in fact the disease in question. Although Charles Creighton and more recently Bonser have argued against any reliable diagnosis of leprosy in the Middle Ages, examinations of skeletal remains have permitted the diagnosis in about 80 percent of cases reported by Moller-Christensen, Anderson, and Schmitz-Cliever. This figure is amazingly high since no osseous changes occur in many cases.

MEDIEVAL ATTITUDES TOWARD LEPROSY

Leprosy was held to imply moral uncleanness. This view was already well entrenched in Carolingian times, when it was expressed by Hrabanus Maurus, among others. Partly, this view derived from Old Testament injunctions applying to leprosy, but it must also be attributed to the nature of the disease itself, which, when untreated, is horrifying and repulsive.

Another possible explanation of the considerable written comment and legislation regarding leprosy is that, contrary to much historical opinion, the disease may have been more prone to assume its worst form among members of the upper classes. Lepromatous leprosy is more likely, other factors being equal, to occur in well-fed persons. The organism requires cholesterol as a growth factor, specifically macrophage cholesterol, which represents part of the body's rapidly exchangeable pool. The meat-rich diet of the upper classes favored lepromatous, rather than tuberculoid, leprosy.

It is worthwhile to recall the many literary motifs involving noble and occasionally royal lepers. Various cases of actual legal decisions involving disputed or malicious diagnoses of leprosy involve persons of the upper classes. It is worth considering the possibility that much of the perceived burden of the disease fell on the rich, and that this helped to make the disease a matter of great concern and the object of many pious benefactions.

The disease is generally felt to have peaked in prominence in the High medieval period and to have declined in the fourteenth and fifteenth centuries. This decline has often been attributed to plague, but the hypothesis is now untenable. In the first place, as has been summarized by Richards, the evidence clearly points to a steep decline before 1348. Second, leprosy appears to confer immunity to plague. Indeed, lepromatous lepers have exaggerated antibody responses to several bacteria. The notion that leprosy was on the rise in the eleventh through the thirteenth centuries is based largely on the increasing numbers of leper houses. As we shall see when we consider these hospitals, this assumption is also very weak.

DIAGNOSIS AND ITS CONSEQUENCES

A diagnosis of leprosy in the Middle Ages was in some ways more a legal and religious decision than a medical one, for it set upon the leper the weight of a whole apparatus of sanctions. Lepers were legally excluded from ordinary society. Already in 757 Pepin the Short accepted leprosy as grounds for divorce, though almost simultaneously Pope Stephen II denied this, as did Alexander III in 1180. The Third Lateran Council of 1179 stated that lepers should not mix with others, nor share church or cemetery with the healthy. This was also civil law in England by 1220. In 1346, Edward III reaffirmed these principles, though stating for one of the first times that fear of contagion partly prompted these measures.

In most of France, lepers in the High and late medieval periods were denied all or most rights of ownership. A vassal found to be a leper might forfeit his property to his lord, a rule that could lead to tremendous injustice. Despite papal pronouncements to the contrary, leprosy continued in some localities to be cause for divorce.

Diagnosis of leprosy was not undertaken lightly.

In general a body of knowledgeable men made the decision, but unfortunately most of the time the diagnosticians were not trained physicians but local notables. Guy de Chauliac enunciated the principle that isolation should depend on the certainty of diagnosis and that doubtful cases should be observed at home. Considering the almost phenomenal diagnostic accuracy apparent from skeletal remains, this principle was probably observed.

Once diagnosed, the leper was supposed to be cut off from society. In most of Western Europe there was an actual religious rite of seclusion of lepers. In this rather elaborate ceremony, the priest threw dirt on the leper's feet (ritually burying him), saying, "Be you dead to the world, but alive again to God." The leper was prohibited from, among other things, entering a church or market, washing or drinking directly from a well or stream, going about without leper's garb, touching merchandise directly, having sexual relations with anyone but his spouse, and touching children. Sometimes lepers were obliged to ring bells to announce their approach and to step aside to let others pass.

Such harsh rules were, of course, largely unenforceable. The wealthy could, at worst, seclude themselves at home, if unable to avoid the diagnosis altogether. A leper could lead a wandering life also. Thus we ought not to imagine that the leper's lot was so bleak as the law intended it to be.

HOSPITALS

One of the means of seclusion of the leper was entry into a leprosy hospital. These hospitals had a highly religious character, and the lepers led an almost monastic life. Leprosariums were primarily a phenomenon of the twelfth and thirteenth centuries and must be viewed within the context of that period.

In the first place, the term "hospital" should not be taken in its modern sense. Most hospitals represented pious benefactions of individuals or families. To the extent that they looked after the sick at all (some merely provided lodging for the poor, widows, orphans, or other disadvantaged groups), hospitals fed and clothed them and provided for their spiritual well-being. Therapy was neither a major intent nor a practical reality.

Moreover, the hospital was a source of benefit to its staff as well as its patrons. Much medieval care for the sick was viewed as a boon to the physician or other person looking after the patient. This atti-tude is perfectly expressed in the Rule of St. Benedict, which states, "Above all tend the sick . . . for Christ said, 'I was sick and you visited me.'" The intent to help the sick reflected back upon the actor to his spiritual benefit. We need only consider the idealized image of the leprosarial monk who kissed the leper's sores and slept in his bed to realize the extent to which the sick were seen to offer an opportunity for spiritual advancement.

The hospital founder or patron derived his spiritual benefit at a safer distance and realized some practical gains as well. Many patrons of leprosaria and other hospitals stipulated that they be allowed to live in the establishment in their old age. Others requested that the establishment conduct their funeral or say masses in their behalf.

Turning to the hospitals themselves, the most striking feature is their number and the relatively short interval over which they were founded. The total number of leprosariums in France around 1300 has been estimated at 2,000. At the same time there were around 200 in Britain. In the year 1000, Spain had 2 leper houses; in 1500 there were 91. Most of these hospitals were founded in the twelfth and especially the thirteenth centuries. Toulouse, with a population in 1250 of about 25,000, had 7 leprosariums, all founded between 1150 and 1250, according to Mundy. In Germany, there were a few leprosaria before 1000, but rapid increase took place in the thirteenth century. In the Low Countries major foundations took place in Ghent in 1146, in Brussels in 1150, in Namour and Tournai in 1153, and in Louvain in 1217. In England there are not known to have been any leper hospitals before the Conquest.

One way to explain this sudden spate of foundations is to posit, as some authors have, that the disease itself was dramatically on the rise. This is very risky. There is no real way to estimate the incidence or prevalence of leprosy. Richards estimates that there were probably never more than 2,000 leprosarial inmates in Britain at one time. Contreras Dueñas estimates that late medieval Spain had 8,000 hospitalized lepers and 60,000 total. These estimates are to be viewed as extremely tentative, and there is no way even to estimate the prevalence of leprosy *before* the period of hospital foundations.

The foundation of the leprosaria is evidence instead of a variety of social processes and attitudes. Charitable work in general and medicine in particular ceased in the High Middle Ages to be primarily a monastic function. New institutions of many sorts arose: other hospitals, religious confraternities, even guilds. Leprosaria should be seen in the light of this increasing corporatization and social reorganization rather than as a response to an increasingly problematic disease.

Though some leper houses were converted dwellings, many were designed and built expressly for the purpose they served. Often there was an attached chapel for religious services. If space allowed, a cemetery or crypt was also included, since lepers were usually denied ordinary cemeteries. Generally leprosaria lay on the periphery of a city, near the gates or in the suburbs. If the city expanded, the leper house might be obliged to move further away.

Life in a leper hospital had a monastic flavor and lepers who refused to obey the rules could be ejected. A uniform of sorts, often russet in color and with a hood, mimicked a monk's robes. If husband and wife resided in the same hospital they were obliged to remain continent. A leper might be expected to bring some household utensils with him, but most goods were held in common, again on a monastic model.

Other persons than lepers might reside in leprosariums. These establishments also provided for the elderly, usually for a fee or donation. Of course, some leprosariums tried to charge even lepers an admission fee, sometimes quite high.

Most of the support of leprosariums came from gifts. This voluntary support could, of course, dry up. Provisioning could be a severe problem, as could firewood for the winter. Some cities, such as fifteenth-century Venice, required notaries to remind anyone making a will that he could leave money to the Lazaretto. This unsubtle technique had dubious results but the need for it is telling. As the sporadic nature of leprosarial financing became more of a problem, governments, whether communal or royal, tended to assume responsibility for leprosariums and other hospitals. This trend was begun but left incomplete at the end of the Middle Ages.

BIBLIOGRAPHY

J. G. Anderson, "Studies in the Medieval Diagnosis of Leprosy in Denmark" (M.D. thesis, Copenhagen, 1969); Wilfrid Bonser, *The Medical Background of Anglo-Saxon England* (1963); Saul N. Brody, *The Disease of the Soul: Leprosy in Medieval Literature* (1974); Félix Contreras Dueñas and Ramón Miquel y Suárez Inclán, *Historia de la lepra en España* (1973); Stephen R. Ell, "Plague and Leprosy: Medieval Accounts in the Light of Modern Medical Research," in *Fifteenth Century Studies*, 5 (1982); V. Moller-Christensen, *Bone Changes in Leprosy* (1961); John

H. Mundy, "Charity and Social Work in Toulouse, 1100–1250," in *Traditio*, 22 (1966); Peter Richards, *The Medieval Leper and His Northern Heirs* (1977); Egon Schmitz-Cliever, "Zur Osteoarchaeologie der mittelalterlichen Lepra," in *Medizinhistorisches Journal*, 6 (1971), and "Das mittelalterliche Leprosarium Melaten bei Aachen in der Diozece Luttich (1230–1550)," in *Clio medica*, 7 (1972).

STEPHEN R. ELL

[See also **Hospitals and Poor Relief; Medicine, History of.**]

LÉRIDA FERRER THE ELDER. See **Ferrer I (the Elder), Jaime.**

LESSER ARMENIA. See **Armenia: Geography; Cilician Kingdom.**

LETALD OF MICY (active late tenth century), a monk at the Benedictine abbey of St. Mesmin-de-Micy near Orléans, and author of polished hagiography and poetry. His humor shines in an epic about a man swallowed by a whale. He probably died in exile, judging from the way Abbo of Fleury denounces him as a monastic rebel.

BIBLIOGRAPHY

Jean-Paul Bonnes, "Un lettré du Xᵉ siècle: Introduction au poème de Létald," *Revue mabillon*, 33 (1943), 23–47; Cora E. Lutz, "Letaldus: A Wit of the Tenth Century," in *Viator*, 1 (1970); Jan Ziolkowski, "Folklore and Learned Lore in Letaldus's Whale Poem," in *Viator*, 15 (1984). Letald's biographers have heretofore overlooked his authorship of a *Life and Miracles of Martin of Vertou*, demonstrated by Bruno Krusch in *addenda* appended to *Monumenta Germaniae historica: Scriptores rerum Merovingicorum*, IV (1902), 771–774.

JOHN HOWE

LETTER OF TANSAR (Tòsar). Document written by a Zoroastrian high priest under Ardešīr I (*ca.* 224–240) to Gušnasp, king of Ṭabaristān, a mountainous region in northern Iran south of the Caspian Sea. It is a reply to Gušnasp's letter, not preserved, protesting Ardešīr's usurpation of power from the Arsacids and the suppression of local sovereignty, and refusing fealty to the new king. Gušnasp evidently accused Ardešīr of having taken away and extinguished fires from fire temples.

The text of the *Letter* survives in the thirteenth-century translation into New Persian from Arabic, preserved in the *History of Ṭabaristān* of Ibn-i Isfandiyār; there are also citations of it in earlier Arabic works. Ibn al-Muqaffaᶜ (*d. ca.* 756) translated into Arabic a Pahlavi version of the *Letter*, which reflects editorial embellishments of the time of Xusrō I Anōšarwān. Tōsar is mentioned in the *Dēnkard* (D. M. Madan, ed. [1911], 412–415) as the priest to whom Ardešīr granted full authority in religious matters, and who also began the compilation of the Avesta. The name Tōsar is read unambiguously in a Sasanian inscription (see P. Gignoux in *Travaux de l'Institut d'études iraniennes*, **9**, p. 46 and n. 24), but in the Zoroastrian Book Pahlavi the name appears in two variants, *tnsr* and *twsr*. The writing of both *n* and *w* with a simple downward stroke accounts for the misreading Tansar.

Gušnasp's accusation that Ardešīr quenched sacred fires and Tansar's retort that these had not been sanctified by central authority reflects the Sasanian policy, actively pursued by Kartīr as well, of reforming and sometimes suppressing Zoroastrian temple cults in provinces outside Pārs. Tansar's apologia for Sasanian rule is couched entirely in the terms of Zoroastrian piety: Ardešīr is praised for bringing order, prosperity, and cultivation to a country that had suffered demonic misrule and chaos. Ardešīr's "pure intelligence" is the *āsn xrad* (innate wisdom) praised in the Pahlavi books as the source of religion and creation. Other features of the *Letter* have been compared to Sasanian *andarz* (wisdom) literature.

BIBLIOGRAPHY

Persian text is *Tansar's epistle to ʾGoshnaspl...*, Mojtaba Minovi, ed. (1932). English is *The Letter of Tansar*, Mary Boyce, trans. (1968). See also Edward W. West, *Pahlavi Texts*, V (1897), with a translation of books VII and V of Dēnkard, where Tansar is spelled Tanvasar; Robert C. Zaehner, *Zūrvan: A Zoroastrian Dilemma* (1955, repr. 1972), 8–10, 35–36, 44.

JAMES R. RUSSELL

[See also **Ardešīr I; Avesta; Dēnkard; Kartir; Muqaffaᶜ, ᶜAbd Allāh ibn al-; Xusrō I Anōšarwān; Zoroastrianism.**]

LETTER WRITING. See Dictamen.

LETTERS, BOOK OF. See Girk Tᶜłtᶜocᶜ.

LEVI BEN GERSHOM (Gerson) (1288–1344), also known as Gersonides, was born and spent all of his career in the French Provence. Relatively little is known about his life. Of greater importance, however, were his various and many writings, all written in Hebrew. Levi was a mathematician, astronomer, biblical exegete, commentator on Averroës' commentaries of Aristotle, and finally a philosopher in his own right. In mathematics he commented upon the works of Euclid and attempted to prove the notorious "parallel postulate" as well as some of the other axioms of Euclid's geometry. He wrote a treatise on trigonometry that was translated into Latin under the title *De sinibus, chordis, et arcubus,* and had some influence upon Western mathematicians such as Regiomontanus.

His research in astronomy was of even greater importance. In addition to his invention of an astronomical instrument for measuring the angular distances of the heavenly bodies (Jacob's staff), he was a meticulous observer of the astral and planetary positions and recorded these facts in very accurate tables. He was especially interested in planetary theory and in lunar eclipses, and one of the lunar craters is named after him. He wrote a long astronomical work, parts of which were translated into Latin and enjoyed some reputation even in the time of Kepler, who sought out these chapters. In his own day he was consulted on astronomical matters by several important Provençal clerics and was commissioned to write some short essays on specific astronomical problems. These survive in Latin translation.

Levi's biblical exegesis, widely known among Jews, was eventually incorporated into the standard printed rabbinic Bibles in spite of its very obvious philosophical character and sometimes "unorthodox" opinions. His supercommentaries upon Averroës (Ibn Rushd) are also marked for their independence; he often criticizes Averroës' interpretations of Aristotle and frequently injects his own views on the subject into his explanations.

Levi's most important philosophical work, *The Wars of the Lord (Sefer Milḥamot Adonai),* written over a twelve-year period, 1317–1329, treats virtually all the important and most controversial topics in medieval philosophy, especially those that were most debated in the Arabic-Hebrew philosophical literature. Levi was most influenced by Aristotle, Maimonides, and Averroës. In addition to philosophical material, *The Wars of the Lord* contains many astronomical and scientific discussions, such as an interesting treatment of the problem of free fall.

Among Levi's more significant philosophical views developed in *The Wars of the Lord* is his detailed defense of the Platonic cosmology, according to which the universe was created out of formless eternal matter and will continue to exist forever. He vigorously rejected, therefore, both the traditional theological view of creation ex nihilo as well as the Aristotelian-Averroist philosophical thesis of the eternity of the universe. He also denied the traditional view that God has knowledge of particular events, including future human actions, and argued that God's cognition consists only of general facts, or laws. This claim forces him to redefine the notion of divine omniscience: God knows everything that is *knowable;* but knowledge of particular future contingent events is *unknowable to anybody.*

Levi was not completely radical in the philosophical positions he adopted. Against the Averroist doctrine that in immortality the individual loses all self-identity, he defended the traditional theological thesis that the individual would retain his personal identity. This doctrine is also consistent with his rejection of the Aristotelian-Averroist claim that divine providence extends to the human species only, not to individuals. On this issue he sided with the more traditional view of Maimonides that the individual, by virtue of his moral and intellectual achievements, merits divine solicitude.

Levi's philosophical views stimulated considerable interest among the later Hebrew philosophical writers, although most of them found him too radical for their taste. By contrast, Spinoza, the destroyer of the medieval world, considered him too conservative and carried some of his results to their logical and extreme conclusions, such as the denial of creation in any form.

BIBLIOGRAPHY

A complete English translation of Levi's major work is Levi ben Gershom, *The Wars of the Lord,* Seymour Feldman, trans. (1984–). See also Seymour Feldman, "Gersonides' Proofs for the Creation of the Universe," in *Proceedings of the American Academy for Jewish Research,* 35 (1967), "Platonic Themes in Gersonides' Cosmology," in *Salo Wittmayer Baron Jubilee Volume,* I (1974), and "Gersonides on the Possibility of Conjunction with the Agent Intellect," in *Association for Jewish Studies Review,* 3 (1978); Bernard R. Goldstein, *The Astronomical Tables of Levi ben Gerson* (1974); Menachem M. Kellner, "Gerson-

ides, Providence and the Rabbinic Tradition," in *Journal of the American Academy of Religion,* 42 (1974); Charles Touati, *La pensée philosophique et théologique de Gersonide* (1973), an excellent comprehensive study.

SEYMOUR FELDMAN

[See also **Aristotle in the Middle Ages; Plato in the Middle Ages; Rushd, Ibn.**]

LEWES. See **Song of Lewes.**

ŁEWOND (eighth century), the author of a historical work in Armenian on the Arab period of domination in Armenia (640–ca. 788). In the majority of the manuscripts of this work the author is referred to as "the great *vardapet* [doctor] of the Armenians." The tenth-century historian Step^c anos Asołik Taronec^c i, however, who is the first to mention him and use his work, knows him as Łewond erēc^c (presbyter).

The medieval sources are absolutely silent about Łewond's biography. Since the *History* ends with the description of Kat^c ołikos Step^c anos' accession to the patriarchal throne, an event that took place in 788, scholars have assumed that Łewond lived in the eighth century. The evidence in the *History* suggests that the author favors the Bagratid family and its political orientation. In the colophon at the end of the book it is stated that Łewond composed his treatise at the request of Šapuh Bagratuni. The latter is thought to be the son of Smbat Bagratuni, the *sparapet* (commander-in-chief) of Armenia who was killed in battle against the Arabs in 775.

In the title of the earliest manuscript of the *History,* which is from the thirteenth century, the work is described as a treatise "about the appearance of Muḥammad and his successors, as to how or in what they ruled the world, and especially our Armenian nation." The *History,* however, in its present state, begins with the death of Muḥammad in 632 and ends abruptly without a final statement. This has led modern scholars to think that the beginning and final sections of the work are missing. Moreover, one-fifth of the extant text, which consists of the correspondence between the Byzantine emperor Leo III and the caliph ^c Umar II (chapters 13–15), is considered to be an interpolation, since there are differences between Łewond's language and style and those of the correspondence.

The information in the *History* appears to be authentic and reliable. The author occasionally refers to oral accounts of eyewitnesses, and seems to be a contemporary of the events that transpired in the second half of the eighth century. Łewond is one of the earliest historians who considered the adversity that befell the Armenian people a punishment from God for all the sins committed by Christians. His outlook on life is narrow and his knowledge of matters outside of Armenia is very limited. Nevertheless, Łewond's *History* is an important source for Armenian history and also valuable for Arabists, since it is earlier than the works of major Arab historians.

BIBLIOGRAPHY

Edition in Armenian is *Patmut'iwn Łewondeay meci vardapeti Hayoc*ᶜ, K. Ezeancᶜ, ed. (1887). Translations include Léonce Ghévond, *Histoire des guerres et des conquêtes des Arabes en Arménie*, Garabed V. Chahnazarian, trans. (1856); *History of Lewond, the Eminent Vardapet of the Armenians*, Zaven Arzoumanian, trans. and ed. (1982), with extensive bibliography; and a translation into modern Armenian by Aram Ter-Ghewondyan, *Levond, Patmut*ᶜ*yun* (1982). See also Joseph Laurent, *L'Arménie entre Byzance et l'Islam depuis la conquête arabe jusqu' en 886* (1919, new ed. 1980); Aram Ter-Lewondyan [Ghewondyan], *The Arab Emirates in Bagratid Armenia*, Nina G. Garsoïan, trans. (1976).

KRIKOR H. MAKSOUDIAN

[See also **Armenia; Stepᶜanos Asolik Taronecᶜi.**]

LEYS D'AMORS. The codification of rules governing the writing of poetry was written for the Subragaya companhia del Gai Saber of Toulouse by Guilhem Molinier in a number of different versions between 1330 and 1355. In addition to an exposition of grammar, versification, rhyme, figures, and genres, there are dissertations dealing with ethical matters such as the virtues, the nature of God, and love.

BIBLIOGRAPHY

Joseph Anglade, ed., *Las flors del gay saber*, I (1926), and *Las Leys d'Amors, manuscrit de l'Académie des Jeux Floraux*, 4 vols (1919–1920); Robert Lafont, "Les *Leys d'Amors* et la mutation de la conscience occitane," in *Revue des langues romanes*, 77 (1966–1967), 13–59; John H. Marshall, "Observations on the Sources of the Treatment of Rhetoric in the *Leys d'Amors*," in *Modern Language Review*, 64 (1969), 39–52.

ROBERT TAYLOR

[See also **Provençal Literature.**]

LIBER USUALIS, a book originally published by the monks at Solesme in 1896 under the title *Paroissien romain*. It is an anthology of chants for the Mass and Divine Office, most of which appear in the more comprehensive *Graduale* (1908) and *Antiphonale sacrosanctae romanae ecclesiae* (1912), both publications of Solesme. The *Liber* contains those chants, both proper and common, needed for regular dominical services and includes chants for those saints commonly venerated in the Catholic Church. It should be used with caution as a source for plainsong since it draws its repertory from many varied sources dating from the Middle Ages and later.

BIBLIOGRAPHY

A useful introduction to the contents of the *Liber usualis* is contained in Appendix A of Richard H. Hoppin, *Medieval Music* (1978), 527–529. For an account of the activities at Solesme down to 1913, see Dom Pierre Combe, *Histoire de la restauration du chant grégorien d'après des documents inédits* (1969).

JAMES GRIER

[See also **Gregorian Chant.**]

LIBERGIER, HUGUES (*d.* 1263), architect, began the abbey church of St. Nicaise, Rheims, in 1231 and directed construction of the nave, facade, and two towers until his death. The facade of the abbey church, with its continuous screen of seven gables, pierced towers, and west window composed of a rose atop two traceried lights, was one of the most innovative works of the second quarter of the thirteenth century. The extreme sophistication of Libergier's style, achieved through unexpected disalignments and decorative richness, heralds directions taken by later Gothic architects. Libergier was buried in St. Nicaise, and his elaborate tombstone is preserved in the north transept of Rheims Cathedral.

BIBLIOGRAPHY

Carl F. Barnes, Jr., "Libergier, Hugues," in *Macmillan Encyclopedia of Architects*, III (1982); Maryse Bideault and Claudine Lautier, "Saint-Nicaise de Reims: Chronologie et nouvelles remarques sur l'architecture," in *Bulletin monumental*, 135 (1977); Robert Branner, *Saint Louis and the Court Style in Gothic Architecture* (1965), 23–24, 30–31; Henri Deneux, "L'ancienne église Saint-Nicaise de Reims," in *Bulletin monumental*, 85 (1926); Paul Frankl, *Gothic Architecture*, Dieter Pevsner, trans., Nikolaus Pevs-

Hugues Libergier (d. 1263) portrayed holding a church on his tomb slab, now in Rheims Cathedral. PHOTO: WIM SWAAN

ner, ed. (1962), 94–96, 110–112; Charles Givelet, *L'église et l'abbaye de Saint-Nicaise de Reims* (1897); Erwin Panofsky, *Gothic Architecture and Scholasticism* (1957), 26, 73–74.

MICHAEL T. DAVIS

[See also **Gothic Architecture; Rheims Cathedral.**]

LIBERTY AND LIBERTIES. Liberty is freedom (*franchise* in medieval French). It meant in the Middle Ages what it usually meant in the nineteenth century and what it often means today: an absence of restraint or claim or coercion by another person. "Liberty is the natural power of every man to do as he wishes," according to the *Institutes of Justinian.* In a ceremony for the emancipation of a serf, his former master showed him an open door and an open road.

From such an understanding of liberty it would follow that no one could be wholly free, since no one could live entirely without constraint by others. "Perfect liberty is not to be had in this mortal life," as William of Ockham observed in the fourteenth century. Nevertheless, those medieval people who were not slaves or serfs were commonly able to feel that somehow they were decisively free men and women. Often they simply relativized the idea of liberty, considering themselves free because the claims that they had to meet were lighter than those which fell upon others. The serf was burdened with "servile customs" due to his lord; notably lesser services that some of his neighbors might owe the lord could figure therefore as "free customs" rendered by free men.

But the sense of freedom was also maintained, for those who had it, by the feeling that liberty was not detracted from by any commitment that one made voluntarily as an individual, not even if it were a life-long commitment that would surely be enforced upon him. Contracts had to be kept; so did marriage, monastic, and other vows. Men and women determined their affairs and their very lives when they made such commitments, but in the medieval view they remained nonetheless free for that. Then too, any reasonable security in freedom depended for everyone upon belonging to a group—kingdom, town, affinity of a lord—whose members agreed to defend the freedom of each. Membership always entailed obligations, at least to respect fellow members and to contribute to the defense of all. The obligations might be burdensome, and they could be enforced with heavy penalties. Yet if the individual joined of his free will, either expressly or implicitly, the duties and penalties were not thought to prejudice liberty. On the contrary, membership in the group, as being the effective guarantee of liberty, seemed to be liberty itself. To belong to the community of a city was to have "the freedom of the city," and in later centuries "franchise" consequently took for a time the sense of the right of the citizen to vote, as a member of the group. And since medieval society was marked by a very large number of small groups of this kind and by endless diversity of the laws with which they regulated themselves, the distinctive laws of his own group easily seemed to the free man to be his very liberty. In 1073 the Saxons told King Henry that they would obey him "if he would govern justly, lawfully, in the established ways. . . . If not, they would wage war against him . . . for their liberty." It would render free men unfree after all if their laws were changed, if laws were made for them without their consent; among free men, "what concerns all must be approved by all," according to Justinian's *Corpus iuris civilis* (C 5, 59, 5, 2).

Christians were under the rule of the church. This could be stringent, as it was in exacting tithes and punishing sins and heresy. Yet the sense had to be convincingly maintained that Christians were characteristically free. Here the theory of voluntary commitment was pressed into some service: in receiving baptism, it was held, the individual joined the church and so came freely under its law. But since nearly all medieval Christians had been baptized as infants, the free consent to baptism was almost always a fiction and would hardly have supported a sense of liberty without the aid of another theory that was effective on both religious and secular sides of medieval culture. "Liberty is the natural power of every man to do as he wishes," but, as Plato had demonstrated and St. Augustine taught, every man wishes for the good. The good is justice, truth, and communion with God. The unjust man, the liar, the damned, only seek the good where it cannot be found. To seek thus in vain can never be to do as one wishes, but must be the failure of one's desires; sin, error, and perdition are not liberty. If the law of the church then constrains men toward the good, it furthers their freedom thereby. So in secular government it could also be argued, against the consensual theory, that "laws and customs may be changed for the better even without consent," in the words of Bracton.

As meaning absence of claim or restraint, "liberty" also denoted what we call an "exemption" or a "right" in the sense of an immunity, as a right not to testify against oneself. Thus medieval people often spoke of "liberties" in the plural. The liberties of a church or lordship were exemptions that it enjoyed from public burdens and outside interference. Fundamentally exemptions or immunities, many such liberties nevertheless carried immediate corollaries of an affirmative sort. If a king gave to an owner of lands by the seaside liberty from the royal claim to wrecked ships washed up on the shore, the owner was thereby entitled to take such wrecks for himself. When a community or its lord was conceded some liberty from outside interference in the collection of revenues or enforcement of justice, the power was thereby given to collect the revenues and the duty to enforce that kind of justice. The medieval administrative landscape was thickly sown with liberties, or "franchises," which figured thus as entitlements, powers, and duties: "wreck of the sea," "pleas and plaints," "free prison," and others in varied profusion. In some cases, such as the franchise of holding a market or collecting a toll, this sense of affirmative authorization was easily primary, and that is the sense in which "franchise" has survived in use to the present day. Meanwhile, in yet a further extension of sense, "liberty" was also used in the Middle Ages to denote the territory to which certain franchises applied, the district of a privileged lord or church or town.

BIBLIOGRAPHY

Marc L. B. Bloch, *Feudal Society,* L. A. Manyon, trans. (1961), esp. 255–274; Helen M. Cam, *Liberties and Communities in Medieval England* (1944, repr. 1963); Alexander J. Carlyle, *Political Liberty: A History of the Conception in the Middle Ages and Modern Times* (1963); Alan Harding, "Political Liberty in the Middle Ages," in *Speculum,* 55 (1980); Arthur S. McGrade, *The Political Thought of William of Ockham* (1974), esp. 78–172; Gaines Post, *Studies in Medieval Legal Thought: Public Law and the State, 1100–1322* (1964); Richard W. Southern, *The Making of the Middle Ages* (1953), esp. 98–117; Gerd Tellenbach, *Church, State, and Christian Society at the Time of the Investiture Contest,* R. F. Bennett, trans. (1940), esp. 1–25; Walter Ullmann, *The Individual and Society in the Middle Ages* (1966).

DONALD W. SUTHERLAND

[See also **Commune; Feudalism; Law, English Common; Law, French; Ockham, William of; Serf, Serfdom: Western European.**]

LIBRARIES

LIBRARY HISTORIOGRAPHY

Although the idea of libraries was inherited from the ancients, libraries as institutions and theoretical models developed significantly during the Middle Ages. Library management and methodology changed, libraries expanded collections and their scope, specializations evolved, and the number of libraries multiplied extraordinarily. This proliferation of repositories and book stock, plus the formation of liberal policies, created more access to information resources in the West on a remarkably different scale than in the ancient world. Libraries became integrated into formal and informal education, and were instrumental in the growth of literacy and information exchange.

Usage. Different terms were used regionally and in time to denote a library until *libraria* became commonplace for libraries that lent books, while *biblioteca* came to mean, although not exclusively, a nonlending research depository. The latter, derived from the Greek *bibliotheke* (bookcase, book chest), dominated medieval usage as popularized by St. Jerome for the books of the Bible *(Biblia)*. Its meaning was expanded in early Christian circles to describe where the Bible was kept. In Old English, as in Aelfric's reference to Jerome's Vulgate, *bibliothece* meant also a collection of books to be read together. *Libraria* in Latin and *libraire* in Romance meant instead a licensed distributor, so that a "librarian" was a dealer rather than a curator, custodian, or keeper of the books as meant by the Carolingian terms *bibliothecarius, custos librorum,* or, in Hrabanus Maurus, *clavipotens frater* for the librarian at Fulda who had authority over the keys that locked up the books.

Libraria was derived from *liber,* which meant, as in Chaucer's translation of Boethius (ca. 1374), either a single compilation or a collection of books. Monks sometimes used simply *domus* as "home" for books. Conversely, the specific type of storage or container, whether an arc or chest *(arca, archiva),* stack attached to a desk *(scrinium),* or book press and dresser *(armarium),* could designate a medieval library. This general idea combined with that of the compartment, originally the ambry used for eucharistic reservation, grew into a book room, and finally by the twelfth century into a building called a "library," as through the centuries increased lending blurred original distinctions between places for bookkeeping or accounting *(archiva),* for book manufacture *(scriptoria),* for distribution *(libraria),* and for the safekeeping of books *(biblioteca).* Justus Lipsius in his library history, *De bibliotecis* (1607), recognized three meanings for *biblioteca:* (1) books themselves, (2) a bookcase, and (3) the place where encased books were kept. "Bibliothecary" and "bibliothecarian" were used widely in English through the mid eighteenth century, when they gave way to "library" and "librarian."

Library history. The library had been largely ancillary to other foci in historical scholarship, but much early work was synthesized by James Westfall Thompson in the masterful and comprehensive, but premature and not wholly accurate, *The Medieval Library* (1939). Thompson's Victorian typology is still common, as is the treatment of all historical evolution as progress toward modern types: from monastic to cathedral chapter libraries, from cathedral school to university and academic libraries, from private to public libraries, from subscription to free libraries, and from royal to national libraries. Most medieval libraries, however, defy such rigid classification and fall more realistically under the modern rubric of "special" library. Nor is the clearcut distinction between archives and libraries, so dear to classicists and well defined by Neil Ker's criteria, always appropriate. Library history has benefited from the enlargement of paleography to codicology in recent years; the fusion of literary and textual interest with art historians' emphasis on the decorated book as artifact and symbol; the rhetorician's investigation of the interplay between writing and speaking, orality and literacy, and patterns of artistry and thought; and attention to the library as an architectural development. Quantification in historical method, typified by Carla Bozzolo and Ezio Ornato's *Pour une histoire du livre manuscrit au moyen âge* (1980), adds new dimensions to older text-based work.

ANCIENT HERITAGE

There is little direct continuity between ancient and medieval libraries, except in allusions to monarchical and temple repositories of Babylonia and Egypt. The archtype for all myth relating to libraries from ancient times is the Alexandrian library, which flourished from the third to the first century B.C. For the medieval learned man, this library—with its 700,000 rolls and its directors portrayed as scholarlibrarians par excellence—represented an ideal to be emulated. Other library sites, like Ephesus, Smyrna, Edessa, and Timgad, never caught the medieval imagination as much, and yet without them the early Christian corpus would not have been possible.

In Roman culture archives were as plentiful as literary libraries, and there was little to distinguish between them. Private Roman libraries of notables like Cicero and Pliny, or that of Lucullus, used by Cato and described by Plutarch, were known in the Middle Ages. The library built by Asinius Pollio (d. 4

A.D.) from the spoils of Dalmatian wars was known from Pliny and later was described by Isidore of Seville and John of Salisbury. There was also a Roman imperial library tradition, modeled after Alexandria, which shifted to the Byzantine East when Constantine the Great moved the capital and imperial patronage.

With the growing influence of Christianity and demise of classical civic religion, Roman libraries were left unsupported. They failed as much from neglect as from wanton destruction. The famous epitaph of Ammianus Marcellinus in 378 that all "libraries, like tombs, were closed forever," must be understood in context as a diatribe from his *Res gestae*. But although the libraries as Roman institutions did not survive, the idea of the library continued.

EARLY CHRISTIAN LIBRARIES

Religious motivation has dominated library development in the West. The initial impetus was the need to codify an oral tradition for transport to foreign lands; books were bolstered by letters and rudimentary archives. The New Testament records the early formation of letter collections kept with the few books of Christian communities in various cities (2 Tim. 4:13; Luke 1:1; Acts 23:25–30). The foundations of the earliest Christian libraries lay in the largely unknown assemblage of the Bible in the East. The Bible became a focal point, drawing to its domicile the *Didache* (a short early Christian collection of oral sayings about morals and church customs), apologetic literature, scriptural commentaries and exegetical literature, and patristic writings. The first libraries may have been stored and carried in travel chests. By the fourth century scrolls had been replaced by more durable and transportable codices. Their primary purpose was archival, to preserve Scripture in standardized form; their secondary role was catechetical.

Early library sites tended to be ecclesiastical centers, episcopal and metropolitan sees, including Jerusalem, Antioch, Ephesus, Caesarea, and Alexandria, where the earliest systematic Christian theology was recorded. Christian reading rooms, perhaps from the days of Roman persecutions, were "secret" libraries *(secretum)*, in the archival and private sense. Catechumens were taught orally by catechists, who relied increasingly on library materials in the hands of the evolving priestly class in Christian communities. Epigraphic evidence suggests that

early Western sites may have been private villa libraries, since the Christians had no immediate access to official libraries.

St. Jerome's travels indicate that christianized Roman libraries were available to him at Rome and even on the frontier at Trier; other Western sites included Carthage, Milan, and Lyons. St. Augustine's reliance on a nuclear grammar-school library and his augmentation of Christian writings at Hippo Regius indicate the merger of the late classical and early Christian libraries and preservation of classics along with the new Christian works. His famous decision in *De doctrina christiana* that Christians could take from pagan learning those works compatible with Christianity, as though these non-Christian scholars unjustly possessed the truth, provided a justification for Christian libraries to retain the classics. However, the priority of the Christian scriptorium was dissemination of Scripture and development of a new synthesis, a Christian culture. As Roman government waned, the resources to support classical libraries diminished. Neglect, new priorities, and sporadic Christian persecution of secular centers of pagan learning spawned a replacement of the older, larger libraries with smaller but more numerous Christian ones.

The transition in Rome from classical to Christian libraries was perhaps typical. The earliest known library of the Roman church was founded in the 380's by St. Jerome's contemporary, Pope Damasus I, in the church of S. Lorenzo. The papal collection held both classical works and the elementary Christian corpus of the Bible, commentaries, and select writings of the Greek apologists. Its scope was narrowed before the pontificate of Gregory I (590–604) and during his purge of astrology, but there was a sufficient supply of books to send a nuclear collection to England with Augustine of Canterbury in 597. Thereafter the papal library was not well supported until a revival under Zacharias (741–752), who separated the library from the archives.

In contrast to such metropolitan sites, monastic communities built communal libraries in remote areas. The earliest "desert father" eremitic tradition did little to promote libraries, but anchoritic forms provided a corporate organization capable of sustaining a library. Pachomius (*ca.* 290–346) at Tabennisi in Egypt provided for book storage in window-like recesses *(fenestra)* in the walls of his monastery and called for an inventory check each evening to assure the return of his community's precious few books to their domicile. Similar monastic libraries have been identified ar Athribis in Upper Egypt, St. Epiphanius at Thebes, and the Nitrian communities in the deserts of Libya.

In the West early monastic library sites included Arles, Tours, and Lérins. Scribal tradition, however, was not as strong in the Latin West. John Cassian's foundation (ca. 414) of two monasteries near Marseilles and the writings of Caesarius of Arles witness only limited copying and, by inference, small libraries.

EARLY MEDIEVAL LIBRARY DEVELOPMENT

While Boethius (ca. 480–524/526) epitomizes the continuity of Latin letters via the late Roman civil service into the early Germanic regimes, the promotion of scribal endeavors so essential for Western library development is associated with two monastic leaders. St. Benedict of Nursia (ca. 480–543), in compiling his Rule, set the standard for regularized reading in choir, in cells for meditation, in the refectory, where food for the mind accompanied physical nourishment, and in the infirmary, in keeping with Egyptian ideas of books as medicine. Books were housed in all four locations in Benedictine monasteries. Books were used liturgically and symbolically, for reading aloud and silent meditation, and for perpetuating a mnemonic tradition. One book as both a penance and privilege was selected each Lent for a monk to read throughout the coming year. This was an intensive education program and a means of disseminating a text orally throughout large communities.

The most unequivocal advocacy of monastic scribal practice and library development is found in the *Institutiones divinarum et saecularium litterarum* of Cassiodorus (d. ca. 583), who prescribed translating, transcription, and copying manuscripts as the most meritorious of monastic labors. His monastery at Vivarium (ca. 551–562) seems to have had a more centralized library closely associated with the scriptorium, perhaps because of its direct continuity with the old Roman villa library.

In certain areas, especially Spain, the monastic and episcopal traditions blended in the organization of a monastic community as a support to a see, and in the institution of the monk-bishop. In such cases the copying and reading emphasis in monastic circles would have been merged with the more activist, legal, practical, and educational interests of the episcopacy. Contact, both overland and by sea, between

libraries was intermittent, and pockets of learning often became isolated. Greek and Hebrew survived in such pockets, as at the monastic and episcopal center at Dumio near Braga in Portugal, as well as at distant Armagh in Ireland, where St. Patrick represents the archtype of the wandering monk, bishop, and missionary. Houses at Clonard, Clonmacnoise, and Bangor are linked to Iona, and to the scriptoria housed at Durrow, Kells, and Derry in the mid sixth century, just before contact between Rome and southern England was revived by the Roman missionaries.

St. Isidore of Seville (ca. 560–636), known as an encyclopedist, is as important for his explicit remarks on the care of books and as representative of the blended interests of the monk-bishop. Early library sites, which cannot be distinguished as monastic or episcopal because they were both, can be identified at Arles, Vienne, Bordeaux, Riez, Rheims, Clermont, Auxerre, and Lyons. Over 220 monasteries existed in Merovingian Gaul, but fewer than 300 manuscripts dating between 400 and 750 have survived from the earliest Romano-Gallic scriptoria. This does not mean that libraries did not exist, but that the political stability required to sustain large, permanent libraries was not achieved.

The Carolingian reliance on written texts and legal codification in preference to earlier customs and oral traditions, and conscious preservation programs, altered the nature of libraries. Continuities are more readily identifiable in the Mediterranean areas such as Visigothic Spain and Ostrogothic Italy, where imperial patronage sustained Latin and Greek libraries respectively at Verona and Ravenna. At places like Tours little is known about library functions and scribal production, except that an author like Defensor (ca. 700) was still able to find there a usable collection. There had to be something to revive in order to have a Carolingian revival of book learning.

CONTEXTUAL DEVELOPMENTS

Byzantine libraries. Continuity between late Roman libraries and medieval developments is easier to identify in the Greek East than in the Latin West, although the takeover of Christian areas in Armenia and Syria by Islamic factions was almost as disruptive as the barbarian invasions of the West. Late Roman government as represented in the Theodosian Code (438) provided for the tax support of copyists and librarians. Both Diocletian and Constantine, at Nicomedia and Constantinople respectively, patronized imperial libraries. The palace library at the capital was enlarged by Theodosius II (*d.* 450), and his successor Zeno rebuilt parts destroyed by fire in his early reign. It flourished under Justinian (527–565) and supported the great legal codification associated with his reign. This library, like the Alexandrian one, encompassed most of the functions associated with today's universities. Collection development suffered under the iconoclasts, especially Leo III (717–741), parallel to the stagnation of library development in the West.

Both East and West experienced revivals of book learning at the same time, and hence revitalization of libraries. Because of church and state union in the East, ecclesiastical and imperial library patronage and developments seem closely entwined. Patriarch Photios' *Myrobiblion,* a classified digest of some 280 works and bibliophilic treatise, was a set sometimes thought of as a *biblioteca* in itself. Reference collections seem to have constituted libraries in themselves, or at least the intensely used portion of a larger, less accessible backup collection. It became typical to separate public and private or secret parts of a library, and to treat materials separately by primary language, Greek or Latin.

All libraries in Constantinople suffered losses in the 1204 sacking of the city by the crusaders. Emperor Michael VIII Palaiologos after 1261 attempted to repair the damages and losses, but book production diminished.

Islamic libraries. Islam, like Judaism and Christianity, was book oriented. When Muslims inherited or conquered metropolitan areas that had late antique libraries, these were islamized in ways similar to the Christianization of pagan libraries in the West. Religious works were replaced and old priorities were displaced, but scribal technology was not abandoned nor were libraries neglected. In addition to the ancient inheritance of the richest libraries in the East, Islam developed its own tradition of academic and mosque libraries as counterparts to Christian school and church libraries. Umayyad patronage fostered library growth at Damascus, while Abbasid rule favored Baghdad, which had thirty-six known libraries. Under al-Maʾmūn the Great (813–833), the Abbasid "House of Learning" or "of Wisdom," as the caliphal library was called, reached its apogee. Agents of al-Ḥakim in 1004 conducted several expeditions to augment its collections. Following the Alexandrian model and as a counterpart to the Byzantine imperial library, it included a museum, laboratories, archives, and the library proper, as one complex.

Smaller libraries in provincial cities continued to flourish, as at Tripoli and Gaza. Crusaders in 1109 exaggerated book counts for some of these libraries, upward to 3 million books by their bewildered estimation. At Cairo the Fatimid collections grew to a more realistic 1.1 million volumes from a nascent library begun by al-ᶜAzīz (975–996). It was partially destroyed in the Fatimid takeover but was rebuilt, only to suffer from Sunnite purges after 1175. Nevertheless, these library centers grew to much larger collections than anything realized in the West, developed well-supported and sophisticated scribal enterprises to build book stock in addition to forced consolidation of smaller collections from conquered peoples, and are seen as major conduits for the passage of Greek learning to the West to replace what was lost in the early Middle Ages.

The crusades displaced book collections, but voluntary trade did so as well. Norman ports in Sicily served as conduits, especially Naples and Salerno. In Spain scholars and books crossed the frontier between the Ibero-Christian kingdoms and the caliphate of Córdoba, or later, the *taifas* kingdoms. Andalusia possessed over seventy libraries, many connected with mosques. The caliphal library at Córdoba was the largest, boasting a realistic volume count of 400,000 in the accounts of al-Ḥākim II (961–976). Access was provided by a forty-four-volume catalog maintained with the collection by over 500 employees at its peak under ᶜAbd-al-Raḥmān III (912–961). Seville, Toledo, Málaga, and Granada also had large holdings accumulated to sustain Islamic culture far away from its homeland.

Christian scholars, such as John of Gorce in 953, journeyed south to use these libraries, despite obstacles created by the sporadic reactivation of the Reconquest. Such contacts were important for the Ottonian revival of learning in Germany. Gerard of Cremona, Adelard of Bath, Gerbert of Aurillac (later Pope Sylvester II), and others studied Greek sources available south of the Pyrenees that had not survived in their libraries. The Christian centuries-long Reconquest assuredly destroyed libraries, but the occupation was slow enough and the indigenous population strong enough to accommodate considerable assimilation and cross-cultural transmission of texts and oral learning.

Judaic libraries. Spain was also a bridge between

Latin Christendom and Jewish learning. From their ancestral homeland Jews inherited the temple library tradition. Jerusalem's temple complex, as described by the Maccabees (2 Macc. 2:13) before the Roman destruction of this cultural center, from the time of Nehemiah (fifth century B.C.) contained a library proper with an archive (Esther 6:1) and a treasury. Jewish communities under Christian and Muslim regimes supported their libraries to preserve their own cultural identity. One of the most famous medieval caches was the Cairo genizah in the eleventh century, but auction lists such as that for the sale of Abraham ben Samuel he-Ḥasid's collection (in twelfth-century Speyer) attest the development of considerable private libraries by wealthy Jewish merchant families. Books were transportable assets. Talmud Torah schools flourished in concentrations of Jewish settlement, especially in Italy at Rome, Ferrara, Reggio Emilia, Pisa, Leghorn, and Verona. Some Jewish libraries were confiscated by Christian rulers to enhance their collections, as in the case of Judah Leon Mosconi's library at Majorca, which was supposed to be auctioned in 1377 but was seized by the king of Aragon. Menahem ben Aaron's collection in fifteenth-century Volterra went to the Vatican. Some Jewish scholars, like Judah ibn Tibbon (d. 1170), built libraries of their own translations from Hebrew and Arabic into Latin, which were important vehicles across language barriers and between cultures.

MEDIEVAL DEVELOPMENTS

Rapid library development in the medieval West is associated with two major revivals of learning or "renaissances"—in the Carolingian era and during the twelfth century—and then with the advent of printing in the late Middle Ages and the Renaissance.

Carolingian revival. The first period of growth was characterized by political consolidation of the Franks and Charlemagne's patronage of a major palace school at Aachen, and in ecclesiastical counterparts during the reform of monastic schools associated with major episcopal sees. The result was a new educational system, cultural preservation, and a concentration on writing form and technology (script clarification, punctuation, vocabulary control, and orthographic standardization), which were the prerequisites for the technical improvement of libraries. The revival created a new elite in ecclesiastical and civil service, the *literati*, who perceived literacy as the ability to communicate in the new standardized Latin as a medieval lingua franca. Such standardization was perhaps necessary because of the language divergence that had occurred in Romance, and the convergence of scholars from three directions at once: (1) from Italy, where the papacy and various northern scholarly centers had continuity from late antique Roman schools and libraries; (2) from Spain, where Romano-Visigothic Christians, *Hispani*, fled the Islamic conquest of 711–714; and (3) from England's monastic centers, which were in contact with numerous continental houses founded after 590 by St. Columbanus and his followers. A combined monastic and episcopal reform, and spread of the mission church by St. Boniface (d. 754), gave birth to centers at Mainz, Salzburg, Fulda, Eichstätt, and Würzburg, among others. All developed writing schools, unique scripts, and libraries that are renowned for their preservation of the classics.

Alcuin of York (*ca.* 730–804) was instrumental in many of these reforms, carrying with him training inherited from the Irish and Insular reforms a century before, to develop the palace school at Aachen, and then do the same for the monastic site and episcopal see at Tours. The Carolingian libraries at these centers were not voluminous by today's standards: St. Gall held 400 volumes in 841 and Bobbio 650 volumes in the early 1100's. It took a corporation nearly one century to accumulate 400 codices to be added to the permanent collection.

The decreasing cost of book production and a streamlining of the technique almost to an assembly-line process, especially with the piecemeal system after 1150 and the tendency to subcontract or to farm out artwork, allowed for larger libraries to be assembled by institutions and smaller ones to be owned privately. Books were still valuable commodities; before 1200 the value of large liturgical books and Bibles without ornate bindings could still equal an annual knight's fee, and around 1300, after quasi-industrialization of previous artisan production, a book for an English student would have cost as much as his annual room and board.

Episcopal collections formed the nuclei for cathedral school libraries, and the religious orders all began to sponsor organized library development. Cluny, founded in 909, developed its library more rapidly than older houses unsupported by a congregation system; by the 1110's it held 570 volumes in its main library. The Carthusians (founded 1084) and Cistercians (1098) both had in their governance provisions for libraries and rules for required reading. The libraries of individual houses may not have been large, but these orders, combined with the diocesan and archdiocesan structure of the secular church, proliferated libraries and formed information-sharing networks throughout Europe.

Twelfth-century expansion. The growth of book stock, extension and intensification of the book trade, and manufacture of smaller, transportable, and individualized books characterize the twelfth-century revival. Whereas older libraries grew out of monastic operations, new foundations supported libraries that were accessible to a broader public. The friars rather than the monks are associated with this second acceleration of library development; the new libraries tended to be urban-based rather than rural, and they were often related to the new universities.

Cathedral libraries, of the bishop, his chapter, or both, supported episcopal schools, which in turn spawned universities. York, Durham, and Canterbury are perhaps the most famous cathedral libraries in England; Notre Dame in Paris, Orléans, and Rouen are representative of France; Bamberg and Hildesheim were known in Germany; and Toledo dominated Spain. The *pecia* system was introduced before 1180 at Paris, Oxford, and Cambridge to supply less expensive books to students, and libraries began to separate their collections into major and minor libraries. The latter collected duplicates and nonexemplar copies to be used more freely by faculty and ultimately to be lent to students. The trauma of witnessing a private library being made available to students in anticipation of its supporting a cathedral school is captured in the *Philobiblon* by Richard de Bury, the bishop of Durham (1333–1345). At Paris the university, organized in the 1170's and recognized by a charter in 1200, relied on the libraries of Notre Dame, St. Victor, and Ste. Geneviève, until the benefaction of Robert de Sorbonne provided a central academic library for its purpose. By 1338 the Sorbonne held 1,700 volumes. Oxford's library owes its collection growth to a series of gifts from Humphrey, duke of Gloucester (the largest bequest was in 1439), after a century with very modest library resources.

Nuclear royal libraries were founded at various palaces, but it would be wrong to regard these as miniature national libraries. Rather, they were private institutions, treated as royal patrimony and under property or inheritance law. The papal library at the Lateran Palace operated similarly, but was neglected after 855 and was last mentioned by Honorius III (*d.* 1227). The Avignon Library, separate from the Vatican, was built largely after Boniface VIII's post-1303 revival of canonical studies. The Vatican Library, perceived today as heir to centuries of continuous development, was really artificially re-created in the mid fifteenth century by Nicolas V's librarian, Tortelli, as a Renaissance institution of 1,200 volumes, and under Sixtus IV (1471–1484), when it doubled in size.

Municipalities like Antwerp had small libraries associated with their archives, but secular institutions tended not to develop libraries except through gifts of private collections. Private collecting became increasingly common among the nobility in the late Middle Ages, and library development became increasingly less dependent on the church and more reliant on a diversified patronage.

Printing. The impact of printing on medieval library development was pervasive, although, rather than revolutionary, change was evolutionary, an extension beyond previous developments. The major changes were in how books were acquired; the scriptorium moved away from the library and merged with the chancery and archives, since noisy, mass-production printing shops could not be accommodated in library environments. Previous in-house production became external and contractual, and this had repercussions as well for binding and finishing work. Text blocks were acquired in wrappers and were finished for libraries in separate shops. Thus the medieval centralization of book copying and use in the library was reversed; technical services became less concerned with content and more interested in the business of book production. Such tendencies forced greater standardization in the texts themselves as well as in physical production, bibliographic control, and cataloging. The geometric explosion of collection size pressured libraries to move from cloisters to larger quarters in separate buildings such as tower vaults, but library architecture adhered to old church-based models largely because stack weight still had to be borne by wall structures and column supports. Manuscripts and custom-printed works were relegated to "special collections," and archives were also separated as distinctions between primary, secondary, and tertiary sources became clearer. Thus late medieval and early modern libraries with their enlarged collections also became more specialized, more departmentalized, and increasingly reliant on printed works despite eloquent protests by defenders of the old scribal culture that hand-scripted works should remain the bulwark of permanent library collections.

INFORMATION SERVICE

Reference. Apart from the small lending libraries and the backup research collection, a third, special collection became identifiable after the twelfth century: a tertiary literature providing access to the primary sources and secondary commentaries—hence, reference. Most of the tools associated with modern reference service were invented and refined in the Middle Ages. The encyclopedic tradition was strong, from Isidore of Seville to Vincent of Beauvais, and from Carolingian times onward lexical enterprises became more common, especially in the standardization of Latin and attempted revival of Greek. The tenth-century *Lexikon* of Suidas was important for the latter. Merging the two with alphabetization created regularized access in encyclopedic dictionaries. Alphabetization was very important for subsequent library approaches to file control. Histories in series, as chronicles, stressed chronology as the second major ordering principle.

Abstracting abounded as a means to extract essentials from a wide variety of circulating literature. Florilegia served as summaries and master plots, and digests such as the Patriarch Photios' *Myrobiblion*, were equally popular forms of condensation. This type of synoptic work is epitomized in John Balbus' *Catholicon* (1286), a manuscript book having a widespread audience ready for a still larger printing market. Such compilations needed improved access within volumes, which prompted the creation of tables of contents by librarians (an explicit responsibility for the librarian at Tegernsee) in imitation of canon tables for control of rotating Gospel readings. Alphabetical indexing depended on orthographic standardization and easier foliation by using Arabic rather than Roman numerals. Indexing methodology seems to have been a northern twelfth-century Cistercian development. Annotated bibliographies blended with digests, and were made accessible by tertiary treatments, early illustrated by Muḥammad Al-Nadīm's *Index of the Sciences* (987) and imitated thereafter.

By the thirteenth century the construction of tertiary reference works to order the ancient inheritance and produce a medieval synthesis began to be a regular occupation of librarians and junior schol-

ars, to such an extent that original creative writing seems to have been neglected at times. Since such tools were intensely used, they were often not circulated even within a library, but were chained to work stations as *libri catenati,* along with valuable exemplars.

Access and circulation. In monastic circles the precentor or cantor, or his subordinate, the succentor, often served as librarian, stationed at his carrel or reading cell in command over the library. He reported directly to the abbot. In Benedictine houses these protolibrarians selected books for the Lenten reading cycle, controlled circulation by a registry system, and took inventory each evening. They often kept watch over materials unacceptable for common reading, and as censors they prohibited "curious" (versus "necessary") reading in these according to St. Bernard's criteria and following Isidore's dictum against consuming heretical works because it was better to be ignorant than mentally or spiritually poisoned. Hugh of St. Victor in his *Didiscalicon* thought all texts deserved to be preserved and read for research needs, but was ambivalent about how accessible questionable books should be to nonfaculty readers.

To facilitate selection, the Franciscans and Dominicans in Paris displayed quarterly all new exemplars in order to gauge interest and estimate how many copies needed to be made. Sermons, like booktalks, highlighted their contents and provided summaries as a prologue to selection for a library. Subsequently access could be restricted depending on the librarian's placement of volumes in an appropriate armarium as *libri vagantes* or traveling books in the *parva biblioteca,* which might be lent externally (literally an extramural loan outside the walls of the precinct), in the *libraria communis* for in-house use, in closed reference, or among the *libri prohibitorum.*

Seniority often determined who got a desired book when demand required sequential circulation. Check-out procedures were controlled by the registration; in 1212 at Rouen borrowers had to swear that they would not personally lend books without going through the librarian. It was common to require surety to a book loan, a voucher sufficient to cover its replacement; that alone discouraged interinstitutional lending. Book lending, however, was declared by the Council of Paris in 1212 to be an act of mercy, and anathemas previously invoked against illicit borrowers and lenders were revoked.

The spirit of the Fourth Lateran Council in 1215 promoted increased borrowing and copying, especially of books seen as weapons in the fight against the Albigensians. Records of friars' libraries dating to 1233 show increased extramural lending and the growth of the *biblioteca publica.* As the rules for using the Sorbonne library indicate, "public" meant not what it means today, but a defined clientele. The Sorbonne limited use outside the library to one day. In some cases borrowing privileges were contractual and created miniature networks for interlibrary loan. Confraternities, congregations of religious orders, and circuits within ecclesiastical provinces served as networks. Copy-circles were active, as in the ninth century, when books and scribes traveled along well-defined circuits between Fulda, Würzburg, and Holzkirchen. Rome lent to archiepiscopal sees like Canterbury and Paris, while metropolitan-sponsored institutions lent regionally to diocesan-based institutions, and mother abbeys lent to dependencies. In the case of Nicholas of Clairvaux, the enterprising secretary of St. Bernard, books were lent only to borrowers who returned the original with a fair copy, which the librarian used to build the circulating collection and to save the exemplar for the research collection. By the twelfth century librarians were experimenting with union catalogs to coordinate collection development and to identify locations to secure an interlibrary loan.

SYSTEMS AND OPERATIONS

Inventory control. Early libraries, like archives, used inventories to control their permanent holdings. These were like shelflists, often listing Bibles first, then glosses, fathers of the church with St. Augustine at the head, philosophy, law, and grammar, and sometimes medicine at the end. The earliest "catalogs" such as that at Fulda (*ca.* 744–749) are nothing more than such short-title lists. Since titles themselves were not standard, the *tituli* were often inferred, or the incipit would be used. They originated on flyleafs in cartularies or in the premier book in a case, and sometimes appeared with relic lists and other property-control devices such as inventories.

Bibliographic control. Most extant catalogs are fourteenth- and fifteenth-century sequels to earlier inventories. They are incomplete and often list books in clusters by uninformative titles such as *liber diversorum,* or multitract and composite volumes by

name of the first treatise only. There were obvious precedents for improved ordering of books into a rational collection, both in the talmudic approach to controlling the sequence of books in the Bible and in the Christian approach to a "canon," whether in Scripture, liturgy, or law.

Librarians were charged with imposing control over collections often well after works were acquired. Contents notes after short titles appear in the twelfth-century catalog of Titchfield Abbey. Misattributions were common, and the form of the main entry (author or title, seldom corporate entry) in cataloging was uncontrolled. Data as complete as that recorded in the Dover catalog of 1389 were uncommon: author or attribution, short title, copy derivation, volume contents, and pagination.

The purposeful instability of friars and laxity of rules for monastic stability promoted the formulation of union catalogs. Savigny tried to implement one for its congregation, the colleges at Paris cooperated to list their holdings together, and the registers of the English friars were used similarly. Perhaps the most sophisticated attempt at sharing catalog data was the English Augustinian effort of John Boston of Bury in the early fifteenth century.

Classification. Medieval men tended to favor an epistemological subject approach to classification, and only slowly after the advent of the "new learning" and revival of Aristotelianism did the identity of individual works for easy retrieval really matter. Greek notions about man, function, and behavior dominated the approach.

The earliest subject approach to cataloging appears in the Le Puy cathedral library during the eleventh century, remotely like earlier subject classification in the preceding century at Cairo. Hugh of St. Victor in the 1120's advocated a synoptical approach to the arts, dividing them into the theoretical, practical, and mechanical as subdivisions of the traditional liberal arts. Between 1150 and 1200, with debate about Aristotle's *Organon,* the juxtapositioning of faith and reason, and new distinctions between rhetoric, dialectic, logic, theology, and philosophy, there were attempts to refine older discipline-based classes. A pervasive classification mentality spread throughout Europe, exemplified by Gratian's *Decretum* (1140) and Peter Lombard's *Sentences* (*ca.* 1150). But book catalogs were slow to change. Sorbonne cataloging rules and synodal decrees at Canterbury in the thirteenth century indicate that books were divided practically by faculties using them most, that is, into classes for theology, law, medicine, and philosophy.

COLLECTION DEVELOPMENT

Collection management. Libraries as physical entities frequently cannot be located in early medieval edifices. Books were often stored in cloister alcoves close to chapter rooms and the church, but also in the sacristy and treasury, choir, refectory, infirmary, and individual cells. There was a tendency from Carolingian times until the twelfth century to consolidate holdings and the authority of the librarian, but thereafter developments favored dispersal again, as in the establishment of departmental libraries for medieval universities.

As books were removed from central control, it became necessary to legislate proper handling. Peter Damian specified that books should be used with gloves to avoid thumbing and oil transfer with excessive use, and that books were to be stored away from smoke, heat, and exposure to intense light. In keeping with such efforts at conservation, the twelfth-century catalog of Lanthony in England noted the condition of bindings and wrappers, perhaps because physical condition was a consideration in permitting use. At St. Victor's in Paris the librarian was supposed to inspect the collection three times a year and make necessary repairs.

Deliberate misuse of a book or destruction without cause were always regarded as sinful; medieval anathemas against book theft are notorious. Canons against abuse date from the Council of Torillo in 692 almost continuously through the Middle Ages. Safekeeping under lock and key was the most common solution for conservation problems. Then as now, preservation and accessibility were polarizing attitudes. Resorting to chained books was an attempt at compromise.

Contents. Apart from the idea of "canonical" works in assemblage of the Bible, there seems not to have been any sense of a "core" collection for medieval libraries. Prescribed lists for acquisitions seem uncommon; practicality and opportunity directed acquisitions. The following general categories and representative authors dominated most collections: Bibles and commentaries; psalters and liturgical texts; fathers of the church, especially Augustine, Ambrose, Jerome, and Gregory the Great, and less so the Eastern fathers, who were represented mainly by Basil, Gregory of Nazianzus, and John Chrysostom; reference tools and digests, like Peter Lombard's

Sentences; monastic custumals and the Rule of St. Benedict; and transitional works, like Boethius' *Consolation of Philosophy,* Cassiodorus' *Institutiones,* and Isidore's *Sentences.* Popular works achieving wide distribution were by Petrus Alfonsi (*Disciplina clericalis*), Hugh of St. Victor (*Didiscalicon*), and Bernard of Clairvaux (*Sermons* and the spurious *Meditations*). Academic staples included Thomas Aquinas (*Summa theologica*), Robert Grosseteste, and old and new logic (Aristotle and Porphyry). Later authors most widely disseminated were Ockham and Duns Scotus. Law included the *Corpus iuris civilis* and *Canonici,* Gratian's *Decretum,* and Gregory IX's *Decretals;* and classics such as Vergil and Ovid, Terence, Cicero, Seneca, and grammarians like Donatus and Priscian. Carolingian authors fell out of favor by the twelfth century, but earlier authors such as Julian of Toledo, Eusebius of Caesarea, and Martinus Braga were revived. It is this happenstance, uncontrolled approach to collection development that ensured by sheer chance the survival of so many authors and works.

Acquisitions and growth. Despite numerous efforts to estimate the size of medieval libraries, few methods seem reliable. Statistical counts are at the mercy of unstandardized catalogs with mixed levels of entry, nonuniform methods of counting, variant vocabularies, incomplete catalogs and sporadic survivals, and exaggeration in secondary narrative accounts. Extant library catalogs seem to account only for the permanent collections in the libraries per se, which were perhaps intensively used, but were not the most extensively used books in the institution. Little is known about circulating collections or use from registries. Libraries have been better book keepers than accountants of their own records or compilers of their own history. Nor do modern inventories of medieval books allow any telling reconstruction; about 4,200 manuscript codices attest libraries in over 500 English monasteries before their suppression in the sixteenth century, but the losses are incalculable; estimates have ranged as high as 300,000.

More is known about the diversity of methods used to acquire books. "Opening day" collections were not uncommon, when mother abbeys sent nuclear libraries to their foundations. Starting collections were often supplemented by gifts of duplicates from judicious weeding of larger collections. The most famous long-distance acquisition program was perhaps that of Benedict Biscop, who made five trips to Rome in the seventh century for books to be used at Wearmouth and Jarrow, where they influenced Bede and later scholars. Libraries relied on their own scriptoria to copy books routed on circuits, imitating the encyclical model; or by abstracting. Inscription evidence from 1248 points to round-robin solicitation letters, especially to replace libraries lost in disasters. Other means included forfeiture of books left on deposit and the copying of books left as pledges for loans. There were donations by patrons and exchanges in medieval diplomacy; the gift book was then as now a memorial. As the book trade grew, books became more accessible at bookfairs such as those held at Paris, Oxford, and London, where unlicensed bookdealers appeared in 1170.

Rapid growth, however, came only with the amalgamation of other libraries, often made possible by royal patronage. The library Charles I (1220–1285) built at Naples was captured by the French and carried northward in 1485. Charles V (1338–1380) generously supported his librarian, Gilles Mallet, to build the royal collection at the Louvre to nearly a thousand volumes. Although it suffered losses from raids during the Hundred Years War by the duke of Bedford, it was rebuilt in 1461 by Louis XI, who added to it the ducal libraries of Berry and Burgundy. The composite library was moved to Blois about 1500 by Louis XII, but it was returned to Paris in 1595 and served as the manuscript core of the Bibliothèque Nationale.

Funding. Patronage and gifts have received the most attention in book-centered studies because the great medieval codices known for their art value were special commissions and presentations. Collections and collectors are less well known than many of these rare manuscripts. In addition to royal patronage, the founders of libraries were often seen as the fathers of universities; Robert de Sorbonne's gift of his library after 1257 to the college was noteworthy as well for his endowment for their upkeep. By 1289, the collection had expanded to over 1,000 titles. Bishops, of course, had similarly endowed episcopal and chapter libraries. Bequests through wills, such as John of Salisbury's gift to Chartres in 1180, were not uncommon. Bibliophiles like Richard de Fournival, chancellor of Amiens, were civic benefactors, as were many late medieval and Renaissance officials such as Coluccio Salutati and Nicolò Niccoli of Florence. Petrarch, Boccaccio, Janus Lascaris, Pico della Mirandola, Johann Reuchlin, Duke Federico of Urbino, Cosimo and Lorenzo de Medici

and their librarian Vespasiano da Bisticci, Nicholas of Cusa as well as Cardinal Bessarion, who brought so many Greek manuscripts from Byzantium to Venice, were all private collectors who held high office or belonged to privileged elites and who assembled core collections of now famous libraries.

Less well known are mechanisms of support for the institution and daily operations of libraries. The abbot of Fleury in 1146 began to tax his abbey's dependencies to support a central library. Abbatial account books through the fourteenth century indicate reserves set aside for library maintenance. Budgets for scriptoria tended to decrease as acquisitions budgets increased for purchasing on the open market. Universities profited from licensing authority over *librari* or book agents, but as control of the book market was lost, statutes tried to protect libraries from price gouging by dealers.

The various estimates of the cost of books all suggest the tremendous expense in building a library. Labor and materials for a Bible commission could equal 1,500 or more hours and vellum from a dozen animals; while Peter Lombard's *Sentences* would have cost only half an average Bible, Vincent of Beauvais's 1244 version of his encyclopedia would have been three times as much. When costs are considered, it is amazing how many books there were in medieval libraries, and, although modest in size, how many libraries were built.

LIBRARY FACILITIES

Furnishings. Libraries require large capital investment in space and furnishings. Isidore of Seville's references to Pollio's archtypical Roman library caused many medieval founders to imitate a classical model by using colored tile and glass and placing in libraries' entrance halls marble busts, columns, and statuary as adornments "in the Roman style." The ideal dictated how large institutional libraries should look once they outgrew their old cloister settings: that image has influenced library architecture to the present day.

Most medieval libraries, however, were modestly outfitted. The standard stack was a book cupboard or press, in which codices were first stored flat, as depicted in the famous eighth-century *Codex Amiatinus*. Press capacity with fewer shelves was increased with the conversion to upright storage. These armaria were designed for permanent housing, replacing old damp stone niches in the walls themselves. When times were threatening, as in the

MEDIEVAL LIBRARY DEVELOPMENT

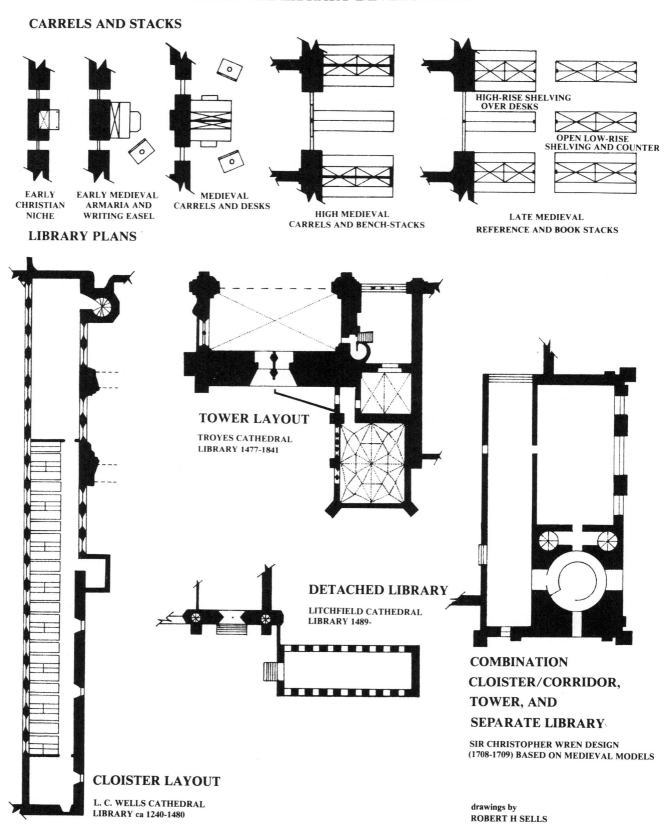

CARRELS AND STACKS

EARLY CHRISTIAN NICHE

EARLY MEDIEVAL ARMARIA AND WRITING EASEL

MEDIEVAL CARRELS AND DESKS

HIGH MEDIEVAL CARRELS AND BENCH-STACKS

HIGH-RISE SHELVING OVER DESKS

OPEN LOW-RISE SHELVING AND COUNTER

LATE MEDIEVAL REFERENCE AND BOOK STACKS

LIBRARY PLANS

TOWER LAYOUT

TROYES CATHEDRAL LIBRARY 1477-1841

DETACHED LIBRARY

LITCHFIELD CATHEDRAL LIBRARY 1489-

CLOISTER LAYOUT

L. C. WELLS CATHEDRAL LIBRARY ca 1240-1480

COMBINATION CLOISTER/CORRIDOR, TOWER, AND SEPARATE LIBRARY

SIR CHRISTOPHER WREN DESIGN (1708-1709) BASED ON MEDIEVAL MODELS

drawings by
ROBERT H SELLS

568

mid ninth century, portable book chests reappeared, as pictured at Tours in miniatures dating from the 840's. Books were also shipped and stored in barrels.

The physical placement of libraries in larger complexes changed over the years and varied by institution and region. In monastery plans after the Aniane reforms in the early ninth century, north annexes to the church were used for libraries, corresponding to the use of the south annex for the sacristy and treasury as in the case of Cluny. In two-story structures the lower level was the scriptorium and the upper level was a library. The elevation provided natural restrictions on access, increased security, and a measure of preservation against dampness. When libraries were erected as separate buildings the preferences to elevate the reading room above a lower entry, to use upper window bays for light, and to banish the business of production and trade to the basement were retained.

The influence of monastic design was enduring. Armaria, or ambries, were at first placed along walls between columns in Romanesque structures, so that a light source was nearby but also because the weight had to be supported by the walls themselves. Gothic structures spread support away from the walls to inner rows of columns, so that armaria could be turned sideways to form book-lined cells between arches with the windows in full view. Lecterns had been in use, as were pulpits for public reading. Their design was transferred to long desks with slanted shelves on them, to fit into now elongated carrels or miniature cells. Some cells could be private, as for the librarian, while others were for multiple use and benches were added to seat several readers at a time. These desk units could face each other in the middle of an alcove, or face the armarium shelving, leaving a single center aisle. In the latter case more books could be accessible from a single seated position, and longer chains pulled through brackets could ensure security and yet provide access to several books from a single seat. The desk-shelf combinations held eighteen to twenty volumes each, far more than the enclosed armarium of the early Middle Ages. One to three shelves could be stacked on top of a desk to form a rack or *classis*. The Sorbonne in 1330 had twenty-eight desk arrangements in its main library.

When universities after 1300 began to experiment with open stacks and reference collections on free-standing stacks within a large reading room, the library was arranged like pews in an early modern church. Stacks simply moved inward away from the walls to rows and aisles ordered from front to back,

Scribe pricking his manuscript and producing an exemplar. Note writing desk, reading lectern, armarium, and clasped books. 15th-century woodcut. ILLUSTRATION PROVIDED BY AUTHOR

with the librarian's pulpit up front in a commanding position from where public reading might also be delivered. In basilican layouts, the librarian's station was centered in a cruciform, with stacks radiating outward in four directions, each with its own light source. Private collections like memorials in churches remained in the cell-like alcoves along the outer walls, while public collections moved into the central area, where they could be used with better overhead light and under observation of the librarian as overseer in his elevated pulpit. Whereas bench-desk units were used in the cells, open stacks on the floor were usually standing desks (*lectrinum, stallum, bancus, analogium, subsellium*, etc.). Reference librarians "worked the floor" or were assigned "floor duty," as modern usage echoes long-standing customs.

LIBRARIANSHIP

Evolution of the office of librarian is unclear, except that it was intimately tied to communal property control and the idea of a *custos librorum* just as there were custodians for other church treasures. As indicated by the Rule of St. Augustine, the librarian was in charge of several functions that later became more specialized: he "charged out" books, but also managed scribal operations for collection development. Some maintain that this was a high office, since it often reported directly to the superior. In late antiquity the Roman *procurator bibliothecarius* was a magistrate, and in early grammar schools librarianship was entry to becoming a headmaster. The Theodosian Code of 438 suggests that this office was a viable career ladder for those of ignoble status. This is evidenced in monastic communities, where the librarianship, regardless of actual name, was a prelude to the abbacy. Sometimes the office is called *armarius,* a synonym for the library itself used as a reminder of how closely interwoven were the character of the librarian and the books he controlled. The earliest abbatial institution of the office is *ca.* 835 at Bobbio, as indicated in a brief of Abbot Wala. At St. Gall in 874, as a document of Charles the Bold indicates, the abbot was the librarian and retained both office titles. The Roman librarian Anastasius (*ca.* 815–879) kept the honorary title of *bibliothecarius* as a surname.

The authority of librarianship could be invested in other offices. Isidore of Seville's Rule charged the sacristan with book keeping. More commonly it became associated with the precentor or cantor, then the succentor or subcantor, as the office became more specialized and simultaneously removed from central authority, when the office itself took on a restricted, particular authority. Lesser officers in reporting lines included the *librarius,* who, like dealers later, took charge of circulation; the *antiquarius,* who cared for less used, older materials, including recopying; and the *vilicus* or clerical support person. *Armarius* later could refer simply to the registrar rather than to the chief librarian.

BIBLIOGRAPHY

General surveys include Karl Christ, *The Handbook of Medieval Library History,* Theophil M. Otto, trans. (1984); Alfred Hessel, *A History of Libraries,* Reuben Peiss, trans. (1950); Sidney L. Jackson, *Libraries and Librarianship in the West* (1974); Elmer D. Johnson and Michael H. Harris, *History of Libraries in the Western World,* 3rd rev. ed. (1976); James Westfall Thompson, *The Medieval Library* (1939, rev. ed. 1957).

For further reference see *Encyclopedia of Library and Information Science,* 35 vols. (1968–1983); and bibliographies in *Codicologica* (1976–), *Gazette du livre médiéval* (1982–), *Scriptorium* (1946–).

Studies. James S. Beddie, *Libraries in the Twelfth Century: Their Catalogs and Contents* (1929), and "The Ancient Classics in Medieval Libraries," in *Speculum,* 5 (1930); Bernhard Bischoff, *Die süddeutschen Schreibschulen und Bibliotheken in der Karolingerzeit,* 2nd ed. (1960),

and "Die Hofbibliothek Karls des Grossen," in *Karl der Grosse, Lebenswerk und Nachleben,* II (1965); Arthur Brall, ed., *Von der Kosterbibliothek zur Landesbibliothek* (1978); Colloque international sur la paléographie grecque et byzantine, Paris, 1974, *La paléographie grecque et byzantine,* Jean Glénisson, Jacques Bompaire, and Jean Irigoin, eds. (1977); Lloyd W. Daly, *Contributions to a History of Alphabetization in Antiquity and the Middle Ages* (1967); Elizabeth L. Eisenstein, "Some Conjectures About the Impact of Printing on Western Society and Thought," in *Journal of Modern History,* **40** (1968), and *The Printing Revolution in Early Modern Europe* (1983); Lucien P. V. Febvre and Henri-Jean Martin, *The Coming of the Book: The Impact of Printing, 1450–1800,* David Gerard, trans. (1976); G. B. Flahiff, "The Censorship of Books in the Twelfth Century," in *Mediaeval Studies,* 4 (1942); H. W. Garrod, "The Library Regulations of a Medieval College," in *The Library,* 4th ser., 8 (1928); Rudolf Hirsch, *Printing, Selling, and Reading, 1450–1550* (1967); Kenneth W. Humphreys, *The Book Provisions of the Medieval Friars, 1215–1400* (1964), and "Medieval Views of the Role of a Librarian," in *Liber amicorum Herman Liebaers* (1984); Jean Irigoin, "Centres de copie et bibliothèques," in *Byzantine Books and Bookmen* (A Colloquium at Dumbarton Oaks, 1971) (1975); Neil R. Ker, *Medieval Libraries of Great Britain: A List of Surviving Books,* 2nd ed. (1964); Pearl Kibre, "The Intellectual Interests Reflected in Libraries of the Fourteenth and Fifteenth Centuries," in *Journal of the History of Ideas,* 7 (1946); Paul O. Kristeller, *Latin Manuscript Books Before 1600: A List of Printed Catalogues and Unpublished Inventories of Extant Collections* (1960); Max L. W. Laistner, *Thought and Letters in Western Europe, A. D. 500–900* (1931, new ed. 1957); Jack D. A. Ogilvy, *Books Known to the English, 597–1066* (1967); James F. O'Gorman, *The Architecture of the Monastic Library in Italy, 1300–1600* (1972); Graham Pollard, "The *Pecia* System in the Medieval Universities," in *Medieval Scribes, Manuscripts, and Libraries* (1978); Leighton D. Reynolds and Nigel G. Wilson, *Scribes and Scholars: A Guide to the Transmission of Greek and Latin Literature* (1968); Pierre Riché, *Education and Culture in the Barbarian West, Sixth Through Eighth Centuries,* John J. Contreni, trans. (1976); Richard Rouse, "The Early Library of the Sorbonne," in *Scriptorium,* **21** (1968); Herman J. de Vleeschauwer, *Libraria magna et libraria parva dans la bibliothèque universitaire de XIIIᵉ siècle* (1956); Nigel G. Wilson, "The Libraries of the Byzantine World," in *Greek, Roman, and Byzantine Studies,* 8 (1967); Francis Wormald and Cyril E. Wright, eds., *The English Library Before 1700* (1958).

LAWRENCE J. MCCRANK

[See also **Alphabetization, History of; Archives; Canon Table; Codex; Codicology; Manuscript Books, Production of; Monasticism, Origins;** and individual persons, works, and places.]

LIBRO DE BUEN AMOR. See **Ruiz, Juan.**

LIED VOM HÜRNEN SEYFRID, DAS, a poem of 179 stanzas in the so-called "Hildebrandston." It is extant in twelve prints from the sixteenth and seventeenth centuries. Neither story nor style has much to recommend it, but the text has attracted a good deal of attention because it was long thought to shed light on the medieval form of the German Siegfried legend. Briefly, the story tells how Seyfrid, son of King Sigmund of Niderland, is banished from court because of his unruliness. He takes service with a village smith, but his behavior is so wanton that the smith seeks relief by sending him to a dragon's lair. He destroys a whole brood of dragons, bathes in their molten hides (thus becoming "hürnen," that is, "horny" or hardened), then does service with King Gybich for eight years to win the hand of his daughter Krimhilt. One day Krimhilt is abducted by a flying dragon and imprisoned on a cliff. Seyfrid sets out and, with the aid of the dwarf Eugel, succeeds in liberating her after killing the giant Kuperan and the dragon. He carries off a treasure but sinks it in the Rhine because he realizes that his days are numbered. At Gybich's court his marriage to Krimhilt is celebrated with great splendor, but the poet foresees that envy will set in and that his brother-in-law Hagen will murder Seyfrid at a cold spring in the Odenwald. The reader is referred to "Sewfrides hochzeyt" for an account of his eight years of marriage.

It has frequently been speculated that *Das Lied vom hürnen Seyfrid* reflects old versions of the Siegfried legend not preserved elsewhere, but the story can be adequately explained from known sources. Seyfrid's service with a smith and first dragon slaying derive from the so-called "Brünhildenlied," a lost twelfth-century poem underlying the first part of the *Nibelungenlied* and the equivalent section of *Þiðreks saga.* The remainder of the story was fashioned, with some elaboration of the giant and dragon lore, from a unique redaction of the *Nibelungenlied.* This redaction is lost except for a table of contents known as the "Darmstädter Aventiurenverzeichnis." Adventures six through nine of the lost redaction told the story of Krimhilt's abduction and release. A few details in *Das Lied vom hürnen Seyfrid,* for example the name of Krimhilt's father, Gybich, are taken from the heroic tale *Rosengarten A.* The form of the story is thus late and eclectic and of limited use in restoring anterior versions. The most immediate historical value lies in the confirmation of certain details pertaining to Siegfried's youth as they are told in *Þiðreks saga.*

The composition of *Das Lied vom hürnen Seyfrid* is crude. The poet fails to combine his sources smoothly, and the narrative seam resulting from the fusing of the "Brünhildenlied" with the *Nibelungenlied* is palpable.

BIBLIOGRAPHY

Sources. Wolfgang Golther, ed., *Das Lied vom hürnen Seyfrid nach der Druckredaktion des 16. Jahrhunderts. Mit einem Anhange: Das Volksbuch vom gehörnten Siegfried nach der ältesten Ausgabe (1726), Neudrucke deutscher Litteraturwerke des XVI. und XVII. Jahrhunderts,* LXXXI–LXXXII (1889, 2nd ed. 1911); Kenneth Charles King, ed., *Das Lied vom hürnen Seyfrid: Critical Edition with Introduction and Notes* (1958).

Studies. Elisabeth Bernhöft, *Das Lied vom Hörnenen Sigfrid* (1910); Helmut de Boor, "Die Bearbeitung m des Nibelungenliedes (Darmstädter Aventiurenverzeichnis)," in *Beiträge zur Geschichte der deutschen Sprache und Literatur* (Tübingen), **81** (1959); John L. Flood, "Neue Funde zur Überlieferung des Hürnen Seyfrid," in *Zeitschrift für deutsche Philologie,* **87** (1968); Hendrik Willem Jan Kroes, *Untersuchungen über das Lied vom Hürnen Seyfrid: Mit Berücksichtigung der verwandten Überlieferung* (1924); Willy Krogmann, "Der Hürnen Sewfrid," in *Die deutsche Literatur des Mittelalters: Verfasserlexikon,* IV (1953); Gerhard Philipp, *Metrum, Reim und Strophe im "Lied vom Hürnen Seyfrid"* (1975).

THEODORE M. ANDERSSON

[See also **Brynhild; Nibelungenlied; Rosengarten; Sigurd; Þiðreks Saga.**]

LIÉDET, LOYSET (*fl. ca.* 1448–1479), commercial illuminator active in Hesdin and Bruges. He was paid in 1460 for illuminating Jean Mansel's translation of Livy, now in the Paris Arsenal; in 1468 for volume III of the *Chroniques de Hainaut* (Brussels, Bibliothèque Royale); and in 1472 for the *Histoire de Charles Martel* (in the same library). His contrasted palette and hard style, in the manner of Dirk Bouts, is found in many manuscripts made for the Burgundian court.

BIBLIOGRAPHY

L. M. J. Delaissé, *La siècle d'or de la miniature flamande (Collection de l'histoire de la miniature,* III) (1959); Joseph van den Gheyn, *Histoire de Charles Martel* (1910);

Miniature by Loyset Liédet from *Histoire de Charles Martel,* 1472. FROM FRIEDRICH WINKLER, DIE FLÄMISCHE BUCHMALEREI DES XV. UND XVI. JAHRHUNDERTS (1925)

Friedrich Winkler, *Die flämische Buchmalerei des XV. und XVI. Jahrhunderts* (1925).

ANNE HAGOPIAN VAN BUREN

[See also **Flemish Painting; Gothic Art: Painting and Manuscript Illumination.**]

LIERNE, a subsidiary vaulting rib that connects the major ribs to form an intricate weblike pattern. Unlike the tierceron or main diagonal ribs, the lierne does not originate at the springing points of the vault but starts at intermediary locations. It appeared first in England about 1300.

BIBLIOGRAPHY
Jean Bony, *The English Decorated Style: Gothic Architecture Transformed 1250–1350* (1979), 46–48; Robert Willis, "On the Construction of the Vaults of the Middle Ages," in *Transactions of the Royal Institute of British Architects,* **1** (1842).

STEPHEN GARDNER

[See also **Gothic Architecture; Vault.**]

LIÉVIN VAN LATHEM. See **Lathem, Liévin van.**

LIFE OF MARY, MASTER OF THE (*fl. ca.* 1460–1480), anonymous Cologne painter, named for a series of eight panels of the Life of the Virgin (now in Munich and London) from the Cologne church of St. Ursula. Tall, thin figures, stiff yet meticulously rendered, recall the Netherlandish masters Dirk Bouts and Rogier van der Weyden, as does much of the other German art of this period (for example, the work of Caspar Isenmann and Hans Pleydenworff).

BIBLIOGRAPHY
Herbst des Mittelalters (1970), 36–37; *Late Gothic Art from Cologne* (1977), 46–55; Heribert Reiners, *Die Kölner Malerschule* (1925), 124–145; Hans M. Schmidt, *Der Meister des Marienlebens und sein Kreis: Studie zur spätgotischen Malerei in Köln* (1978); Alfred Stange, *Deutsche Malerei der Gotik,* V (1952), 25–37.

LARRY SILVER

[See also **Isenmann, Caspar; Pleydenworff, Hans;** and illustration, p. 574.]

Lierne vaulting by William Vertue from St. George's Chapel, Windsor, 1506–1511. PHOTO: WIM SWAAN

LIGATURE, in musical square notation, a symbol representing a series of two or more pitches to be sung to a single syllable, joined graphically. Beginning in the late twelfth century, Notre Dame polyphony indicated regular metrical rhythms ("rhythmic modes") by patterns of two- and three-note ligatures. By the time of Franco of Cologne (*fl.* 1250–1280), however, the shape of the ligature rather than the context conveyed the rhythmic meaning. Only relatively long notes could be written in a ligature. The proliferation of shorter rhythmic values, together with the introduction of printing,

The Annunciation. Panel by the Master of the Life of Mary, from Church of St. Ursula, Cologne, before 1480. MÜNCHEN, ALTE PINAKOTHEK

in the fifteenth and sixteenth centuries resulted in the gradual replacement of ligatures with single-note symbols.

BIBLIOGRAPHY

Willi Apel, *The Notation of Polyphonic Music, 900–1600* (1942, 5th rev. ed. 1961), is the standard work in English for all questions of polyphonic notation. For further reading see the list of theorists and bibliography in David Hiley, "Notation III.2," and Margaret Bent, "Notation III. 3," in *New Grove Dictionary of Music and Musicians* (1980).

DIANE L. DROSTE

[See also **Franco of Cologne; Music in Medieval Society; Musical Notation, Western.**]

LIGHTING DEVICES of the Middle Ages were based on the use of torches, oil lamps, and candles. Outside the church, lamps and lanterns formed an indispensable part of the domestic equipment, especially in the case of writers, while banquets and funerals as well as imperial triumphs provided opportunities for a lavish display of lights. In Byzantium, the most elaborate lighting devices were reserved for the church, where their supply and maintenance sometimes absorbed as much as one-third of the church revenues.

BYZANTINE LIGHTING DEVICES

Spouted lamps of the early Christian period were part of the Greco-Roman heritage. They were commonly made of clay or of bronze, with the clay lamps somewhat different in form and decoration from the

Griffin lamp in cast bronze, 4th–5th century. RICHMOND, VIRGINIA MUSEUM OF FINE ARTS (66.10)

bronze. Both kinds consisted of a bulbous oil chamber and a spout with the wick hole.

Clay lamps were mold-made in specialized, local factories and represent the most numerous group. They were mainly intended for daily use, although some of them appear to have been employed as cult objects and funerary offerings. Their decoration relies largely on Roman models, with proper Christian iconography first appearing in the fifth century. The manufacture of clay lamps appears to have declined in Byzantium during the early Middle Ages.

Bronze lamps were single- or multinozzled and were employed as standing, hanging, or swinging lamps by the more affluent. Some of the most elaborate examples of bronze lamps, for instance sandaled foot lamps, griffin and dove lamps, or lamps in the shape of a boat, reflect popular Roman models. All these fell out of use by the end of the seventh century, however, with the exception of dove lamps, which were associated with a new, properly Christian symbolic content.

Lampstands in the early Christian period appear to have been intended mostly for private use. They consist of a base, usually on three supports, and a shaft carrying the drip pan with the pricket. Supports in the form of dolphins and lions or lion feet and animal hoofs are quite common. Elaborate stands sometimes display figural shafts. Far more common are baluster-shaped shafts or shafts in the form of a Corinthian or other column. A small group of collapsible stands appears to have been made especially for travel.

Pricket candlesticks (manoualia) are currently recorded in church inventories from the eleventh century onward. Most of the extant examples are found in pairs that stood before the bema royal doors, at the two sides of the holy altar, or before votive icons or funerary monuments. Animal supports, especially lions, are common. In some cases, the shaft is baluster-shaped or consists of two superimposed knotted colonettes.

Float-wick lamps were lit by oil floating on water, with a bronze, *S*-shaped strip hung from the rim of the lamp acting as a wick holder. They were usually made of glass, though a few examples of rock crystal or semiprecious stone are also to be seen. Conical or bowl-shaped and stemmed glass lamps were produced in great quantity for the early Christian *polycandela*. Larger, bowl-shaped glass lamps were fitted into openwork metal containers *(kaniskia)* or into especially made metal mounts that transformed them into suspension lamps.

Candlestick from the Great Lavra, Mount Athos, 10th century.
PHOTO: P. VOCOTOPOULOS

Polycandela appear to have been a Byzantine invention widely employed in churches. An early type is that of a crown with detachable dolphin brackets carrying glass lamps. Far more popular, however, were the disk-shaped *polycandela* of bronze or silver

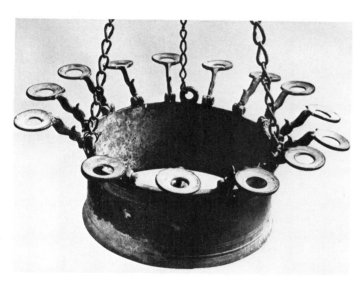

Float-wick glass lamp, 11th century. VENICE, S. MARCO, TESORO

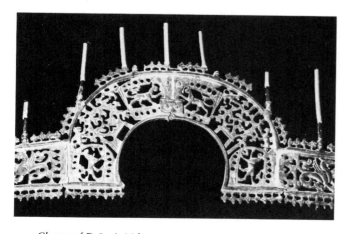

Polycandelon with dolphin brackets, 5th century. MÉTSOVO, GREECE, AVEROFF COLLECTION

Choros of Dečani, 14th century. PHOTO SUPPLIED BY AUTHOR

and gold, pierced with circular holes into which conical or stemmed glass lamps were inserted. The Kumluca treasure in the Dumbarton Oaks Collection includes three sixth-century types of silver *polycandela*: disk- or cross-shaped and in the form of a rectangular tray.

Choroi were lighting devices especially designed to fit domed churches and consist of a polygonal frame, carved in timber or cast in bronze, which was suspended from the dome cornice by means of openwork strips. This frame carried single lights or *polycandela* and candles. The *choroi*, which are first recorded in twelfth-century monastic typica, recall the Romanesque Jerusalem chandeliers.

ISLAMIC LIGHTING DEVICES

Spouted lamps of the early Islamic period resemble contemporary Byzantine examples. However, they developed distinctly Islamic forms around 800 and remained in use long after the decline of Byzantine spouted lamps.

Clay spouted lamps that have been excavated in Egypt appear to date roughly between 800 and 1500. The earliest are mold-made and oval-shaped with a stub handle. Eventually they become wheel-made, with a spheroidal or cylindrical body, loop handle, long spout, and wide neck with flaring sides. Islamic clay lamps for the most part display a tinted tin or lead glaze.

Bronze lamps include an important group of elaborate lamps with earlier Coptic antecedents: the animal-shaped lamps in which the animal forms become increasingly stylized. Plain Islamic lamps have a prismatic spout that appears to be separately cast and soldered to the bulbous body. A distinct, late group, which is usually attributed to twelfth-century Iran, consists of elaborate lamps with a flat upper part, tall faceted foot, and ovoid handle decorated with animal finials or bosses.

Lampstands of the early Islamic period recall Byzantine baluster stands. However, the base is transformed into a domical or polygonal shape, the drip pan with the pricket is usually replaced by a wide disk, and two prismatic knobs often mark the two ends of the shaft, with a plain or ribbed column between them. A more elaborate type of stand, developed in twelfth-century Iran, has a base analyzed into six almond-shaped depressions. Such stands are often decorated with engraved floral patterns and inscriptions.

Socket candlesticks (sham^cdān) have the characteristic form of a truncated cone, the socket often echoing the shape of the body. The latter can be faceted, with straight or concave flanks. These candlesticks were hammered or hollow-cast in brass and decorated with dedicatory inscriptions and benedictions which were inlaid with silver, copper, gold, and niello. The form is thought to have originated in the late twelfth century, but the majority of the surviving examples date from the thirteenth and the fourteenth centuries.

Glass float-wick lamps of the early Islamic period adopt the established Byzantine forms, especially that of stemmed bowl-shaped lamps or footed conical beakers, as well as that of the handled glass lamps on a flaring foot, which by the thirteenth century developed into the oversize glass mosque lamps. These are made of colorless bubbly glass and decorated with multicolored enamel and gilding. Their elaborate inscription bands include the Koranic *Āyāt-al-Nūr* (verse of light, 24:35), dedicatory inscriptions, and medallions enclosing blazons and floral motifs, which often provide useful dating indications.

Openwork lamps (misbāh) display a form very similar to that of glass mosque lamps, namely the same bulbous body, flaring neck, and suspension rings fitted to their body by means of shield-shaped attachments. Such lamps were equipped with float-wick glass containers and appear to have been primarily intended for use in mosques all over the Islamic world.

Polycandela were essentially Byzantine lighting devices that were adopted by Muslims all along the North African coast, especially in Egypt, as well as in Syria and Mesopotamia, but only rarely in Iran. Here again, stemmed bowl lamps of glass and conical goblets are fitted into an openwork metal disk that is usually cast in bronze and occasionally inlaid with copper and silver.

Lanterns (pyramidal chandeliers [tannūr]) are thirteenth-century Seljuk devices. The lantern from Konya is box-shaped, with a pyramidal roof and hinged doors for the insertion of lamps or candles. The general form of this lantern goes back to late Roman lamphouses. Mamluk examples of the fourteenth and fifteenth centuries are bigger and become increasingly more elaborate, with domical or pyramidal shades.

Many-tiered chandeliers (thurayyā) are a further development of such pyramidal lanterns. They are octagonal, dodecagonal (sixteen-sided), prismatic, or conical in shape. Their walls are completely perforated and carry multiple glass containers arranged in tiers.

Hanging lamp from the Alhambra, Granada, 1305. EDISTUDIO, BARCELONA

LIGHTING DEVICES IN THE LATIN WEST

The first lighting devices of Western Europe that are clearly differentiated from those of Byzantium appear roughly around 1000. The rapid advance of German metalwork in the course of the eleventh and twelfth centuries contributed to the creation of new monumental and distinctly Western lighting devices, such as the Jerusalem chandeliers and the seven-branched candlesticks intended for ecclesiastical use.

Jerusalem chandelier from Gross-Komburg, Stiftskirche, *ca.* 1130. PHOTO: H. WENTZEL

These reveal the mastering of the lost-wax casting technique for the production of works of unprecedented scale.

Jerusalem chandeliers (radleuchter) were the most ambitious lighting devices of the German workshops. That of Hildesheim (*ca.* 1055–1065) consists of a circular band, almost 7 meters wide, carrying seventy-two candleholders with towerlike lanterns spaced around it; the lamp was thought to evoke the walls of Heavenly Jerusalem. Other important examples include the *radleuchter*s of Stiftskirche at Grosskomburg (1102–1139) and the Barbarossa *leuchter* of Aachen (1165–1170).

Seven-branched candlesticks seem to have been popular in Western European churches between 1000 and 1200. The earliest example, in Essen Minster, was commissioned by the abbess Matilda (974–1011). It is cast in lost-wax bronze and is 2.5 meters (8.2 feet) high. The square base stands on claw-supports with cast personifications of the four winds at the four corners. The stem and branches are all interrupted by cast openwork knops. Each of the seven branches ends in an openwork capital carrying the drip pan. Other important examples include the twelfth-century candlestick of Brunswick and the Milan candlestick of the thirteenth century, which is 6 meters (19.7 feet) high.

Candlesticks. Some candlesticks were intended for use on the altar. The most elaborate example is that of Gloucester, which was commissioned by Abbot Peter of the Benedictine Abbey of St. Peter at Gloucester around 1110. It is cast in three sections in the lost-wax method and displays intricate animated scrollwork and combat scenes of men and beasts, as well as the four symbols of the Evangelists. It has repeatedly been noted that this candlestick shares a number of features with earlier candlesticks produced in Hildesheim. German workshops also produced numerous smaller candlesticks for ecclesiastical use. These often display three-dimensional grotesque forms, such as dragons, and are embellished with rock crystal knops or enamel. From the thirteenth century, Italian workshops, especially in Venice, produced elaborate altar candlesticks of silver and rock crystal, which were clearly inspired by Byzantine models.

Paschal candlesticks, carved in marble and mostly dating from the twelfth and thirteenth centuries, represent an Italian peculiarity and are closely connected to the celebration of the Easter eve. They have the form of a column, and were intended to carry candles that are 2 to 3 meters tall.

Crusies are humble lamps for domestic use and are in many ways similar to the classical spouted lamps. The crusies were already in use in Roman times and remained so long after the fifteenth century. The lamp consists of a pear-shaped or oval pan that is attached at the back to a flat upright band with a hook-and-spike suspension device. Crusies are made of brass, tin, and iron, and may have more than one spout. Oil-burning crusies were not unknown in twelfth-century Greece, and in medieval Western Europe they usually burned either fish oil or tallow.

BIBLIOGRAPHY

Byzantine lighting devices. Daniel Alcouffe, *et al., The Treasury of San Marco in Venice* (1984), nos. 2, 24; Donald M. Bailey, "Pottery Lamps," in Donald Strong and David Brown, eds., *Roman Crafts* (1976), 93–103; Laskarina Bouras, "Two Byzantine Candelabra from the Metamorphosis Monastery of the Meteora," in *Byzantina,* 5 (1973), and "Byzantine Lighting Devices," in *Jahrbuch der Österreichischen Byzantinistik,* 32 (1982); S. A. Boyd, "The Sion Treasure: Status Report," in *Fifth Annual Byzantine Studies Conference* (abstracts of papers) (1979); Oscar T. Broneer, *Isthmia,* III (1977); Grace M. Crowfoot and D. B. Harden, "Early Byzantine and Later Glass Lamps," in *The Journal of Egyptian Archaeology,* 17 (1931); D. R. Dendy, *The Use of Lights in Christian Worship* (1959); V. H. Elbern, "Leuchterträger für byzantinische Soldaten," in *Aachener Kunstblätter,* 50 (1982); Walter B. Emery and L. P. Kirwan, *The Royal Tombs of Ballana and Qustul* (1938); Robert J. Forbes, *Studies in Ancient Technology,* VI (1958), 119ff.; Fritz Fremersdorf, *Antikes, Islamisches und Mittelalterliches Glas* (1975), nos. 875, 877; G. Galavaris, "Some Aspects of Symbolic Use of Lights in the Eastern Church: Candles, Lamps, and Ostrich Eggs," in *Byzantine and Modern Greek Studies,* 4 (1978); Hans R. Hahnloser, ed., *Il Tesoro e il Museo* (1971), 149, 150; John W. Hayes, *Ancient Lamps in the Royal Ontario Museum,* I (1980), and *Greek, Roman, and Related Metalware in the Royal Ontario Museum* (1984), nos. 214, 215; Jacqueline Lafontaine-Dosogne, ed., *Splendeur de Byzance* (1982), nos. Br. 3–5, 20; Judith Perlzweig, *Lamps of the Roman Period* (1961); F. W. Robins, *The Story of the Lamp* (1939, repr. 1970); Marvin C. Ross, "A Tenth Century Byzantine Glass Lamp," in *Archaeology,* 10 (1957), and *Catalogue of the Byzantine and Early Mediaeval Antiquities in the*

Dumbarton Oaks Collection, I (1962), nos. 15, 29, 32–44; D. Todorovic, "Le grand polycandilion de Markov Manastir," in *Zograph,* 9 (1978); Frederick O. Waagé, *Antioch on the Orontes III: The Lamps* (1941).

Islamic lighting devices. Esin Atil, "Two Īl-Hānid Candlesticks at the University of Michigan," in *Kunst des Orients,* 8 (1972), and *Renaissance of Islam: Art of the Mamluks* (1981), 57–58, 120–122, 134–137; Eva Baer, *Metalwork in Medieval Islamic Art* (1983), 10–39, 41, 43; Fritz Fremersdorf, *Antikes, Islamisches und Mittelalterliches Glas* (1975), 96ff.; Dalu Jones and George Mitchell, eds., *The Arts of Islam* (1976), 168, 169, 172, 196; W. B. Kubiak, "Medieval Ceramic Oil Lamps from Fustat," in *Ars orientalis,* 8 (1970); Jean Lacam, "Étude et classement des lampes a huile musulmanes," in *Cahiers de Byrsa,* 3 (1953); Carl J. Lamm, *Mittelalterliche Glaser und Steinschnittarbeiten aus dem nahen Osten,* 2 vols. (1930); Assadullah S. Melikian-Chirvani, *Islamic Metalwork from the Iranian World* (1982), 56–60, 87–89, 100–104; R. H. Pinder-Wilson and George T. Scanlon, "Glass Finds from Fustat: 1964–1971," in *Journal of Glass Studies,* 15 (1973); D. S. Rice, "The Seasons and the Labors of the Months in Islamic Art," in *Ars orientalis,* 1 (1954), and "Studies in Islamic Metal Work V," in *Bulletin of the School of Oriental and African Studies,* 17 (1955); Topkapi Palace Museum, *The Anatolian Civilisations III* (1983).

Lighting devices in the Latin West. Daniel Alcouffe et al., *The Treasury of San Marco in Venice* (1984), 274ff.; P. Bloch, "Siebenarmige Leuchter in christlichen Kirchen," in *Wallraf-Richartz Jahrbuch,* 23 (1961); Joseph Braun, *Das christliche Altargerät in seinem Sein und in seiner Entwicklung* (1932); D. R. Dendy, *The Use of Lights in Christian Worship* (1959); Otto von Falke and Erich Meyer, *Romanische Leuchter und Gefässe: Giessgefässe der Gotik* (1935); Hans U. Haedeke, *Metalwork,* Vivienne Menkes, trans. (1970); A. Harris, "A Romanesque Candlestick in London," in *Journal of the British Archaeological Association,* 27 (1964); Hayward Gallery, *English Romanesque Art: 1066–1200* (1984), 249; K. Jahrmuth, *Lichter Leuchter in Abendland* (1967); Peter Lasko, *Ars sacra 800–1200* (1972), 171, 178; A. MacGregor, ed. *Tradescant's Rarities* (1983), 268ff.; Charles C. Oman, *The Gloucester Candlestick* (1958); I. A. Richmond, "Stukeley's Lamp," in *The Antiquaries Journal,* 30 (1950); Frederick W. Robins, *The Story of the Lamp* (1939); Heinrich Strauss, "The History and Form of the Seven-branched Candlestick of the Hasmonean Kings," in *Journal of the Warburg and Courtauld Institutes,* 22 (1959); H. Torp, "Monumentum Resurectionis: Studio sulla forma e sul significato del candelabro per il cero pasquale in Santa Maria della Pieta di Cori," in *Acta ad archaelogiam et artium historiam pertinentia,* 1 (1962).

LASKARINA BOURAS

[See also **Glass, Western European; Metalsmiths; Metalworkers; Polycandelon.**]

LÍKNARBRAUT (Way of mercy), a late-thirteenth-century Icelandic poem, is a devotional *drápa* in *dróttkvætt* meter celebrating Christ's passion and the virtues of the cross. In the prologue (*upphaf*, stanzas 1–12), the poet prays for poetic inspiration ("sprinkle my mind's land with precious heavenly seed"), acknowledges sins of the tongue (he is "young"), appeals to "brothers and sisters" for supportive prayers, and explores the commingling of joy and sorrow that his subject evokes in him. Stanza 12 concerns the nativity, and in the next stanza the poet offers Christ a "high refrain" as a gift as he begins the central refrain section (*stefjabálkr*, stanzas 13–29). This four-line refrain extolling the power of the cross recurs in every fourth strophe (13, 17, 21, 25, 29) as the poet depicts the passion, harrowing, resurrection, and the appearance of the cross at the Last Judgment. Stanzas 30–45, which, though lacking refrain, seem to function as the equivalent of the second refrain subsection (*stefjamél*) typical of Christian *drápur*, constitute an *adoratio crucis* and draw heavily on that portion of Good Friday liturgy. The poet alludes to "creeping to the cross," quotes the recurrent phrase "popule meus" (*mín þióð*) from the Reproaches, and borrows details from the passion hymns of Venantius Fortunatus (*ca.* 530–*ca.* 601). Several stanzas of this section are devoted to exegetical figures of the cross (balance, ladder, key, ship, bridge, and shield). Stanzas 46–52 contain the elements usually associated with the *slœmr* (conclusion): The poet confesses his unworthiness, requests a blessing as reward, and names the poem in the penultimate stanza (as is done in his models *Harmsól* and *Leiðarvísan*). If stanzas 30–45 are weighed as a second *stefjamél* rather than as part of the *slœmr,* the poem's structure both is more symmetrical—12/33(17 + 16)/7 (like most Christian *drápur,* for instance, *Harmsól* 20/25/20, *Leiðarvísan* 12/21/12)—and is based on symbolic numbers. The high frequency of *ár* (year) supports de Vries' suggestion that the total number of stanzas (fifty-two) represents the weeks of the year.

The poem gives evidence of the range of the anonymous poet's learning: earlier skaldic poetry, Icelandic homilies (one of which he follows closely in stanzas 38–41), and Latin exegetical literature, such as a passage by Honorius Augustodunensis (1075/1080–*ca.* 1156) from which he draws the image of the cross as a ladder whose poles represent "twofold love." The poet is probably a cleric (possibly a monk), and the poem's close connection to Good Friday liturgy suggests the possibility of its having functioned, like Einarr Skúlason's *Geisli,* as a verse sermon.

The dating of the poem is based on its borrowing from *Harmsól* and *Leiðarvísan* (late twelfth century) and its influence on *Lilja* and on Árni Jónsson's *Guðmundardrápa* (mid fourteenth century), on formal elements suggesting transition (for example, reduction of kenning frequency and occasional extension of lines), on linguistic features such as full rhyme of historical *æ/æ* in *brœðr/kvæði,* and on its iconographic and emotional concord with contemplative Franciscan passion poetry of the late thirteenth and fourteenth centuries.

BIBLIOGRAPHY

Sources. Finnur Jónsson, ed., *Den norsk-isländske skjaldedigtning,* II (1915), A 150–159 (diplomatic ed.), B II 160–174 (normalized ed.). Ernst A. Kock, ed., *Den norsk-isländska skaldediktningen,* II (1949), 85–91; George S. Tate, *"Líknarbraut:* A Skaldic *Drápa* on the Cross" (diss., Cornell, 1974, diplomatic and normalized eds. with trans. and commentary).

Studies. Anne Holtsmark, *"Líknarbraut,"* in *Kulturhistorisk leksikon for nordisk middelalder,* X (1965); Finnur Jónsson, *Den oldnorske og oldislandske litteraturs historie,* II, 2nd ed. (1923), 120–121; Fredrik Paasche, *Kristendom og kvad* (1914), 126–134; George S. Tate, "Good Friday Liturgy and the Structure of *Líknarbraut,*" in *Scandinavian Studies,* 50 (1978), and "The Cross as Ladder: *Geisli* 15–16 and *Líknarbraut* 34," in *Mediaeval Scandinavia,* 11 (1978–1979); Jan de Vries, *Altnordische Literaturgeschichte* II, 2nd ed. (1967), 76–79.

GEORGE S. TATE

[See also **Dróttkvæt; Einarr Skúlason; Eysteinn Ásgrímsson; Gamli Kanóki; Honorius Augustodunensis; Iceland; Skaldic Poetry; Venantius Fortunatus.**]

LILJA. See **Eysteinn Ásgrímsson.**

LILLE, today a large industrial city of northeastern France in the *département du Nord,* was in the French-speaking area of the county of Flanders during most of the Middle Ages. Lille, a French word, comes from the ancient word *isla,* the vulgar form of the Latin *insula* (meaning island), which came into usage in the twelfth century. Not until the thirteenth century did the vernacular word *Lille* prevail. Prior to the tenth century the region around Lille had been occupied first by the Romans and then by the Franks. With the disintegration of the Frankish Carolingian state in the ninth century this region became part of the county of Flanders and Lille became the center of one of the castellanies of Flanders.

Late in the tenth century, after the departure of marauding bands of Normans, some merchants and artisans settled on the left bank of the Deûle River. This area, referred to as a *forum,* became the site of a market and the nucleus of the town that arose in the eleventh and twelfth centuries just to the south of the castle built late in the tenth century to protect the mercantile community. The growth of Lille resembled that of such Flemish towns as Bruges, Ghent, and neighboring Ypres and Tournai. Referred to in a document of 1066 (a charter to the canons of St. Pierre de Lille) as a town of merchants, Lille became known during the next century for its wool industry. The chronicler Guillaume le Breton stated that the fine quality of the wool cloth brought riches to the Lille merchants, who sold it at the fairs of Champagne and also became affiliated with the Hansa of London. The trading quarter expanded rapidly in the twelfth century and then remained stable in the thirteenth and fourteenth centuries. When the English export of wool dwindled in the fourteenth century, the economic slump that befell the wool industry was partially neutralized by the fabrication of lighter and finer cloths.

Lille obtained elementary social, economic, and legal privileges not by armed revolt, as did many nearby towns such as Cambrai, but by peaceful negotiation with the Flemish counts during the eleventh century. Like the other leading Flemish towns, it also acquired the right of self-government during the civil war following the assassination of Count Charles the Good in 1127. Located along the French border, it was the scene of much warfare between the French kings and Flemish counts during the thirteenth and fourteenth centuries. To punish Count Ferrand for his alliance with King John of England, King Philip Augustus of France occupied and burned Lille in 1213. Philip the Fair of France besieged Lille three times in three years and took it in 1297. Recaptured by the Flemish in 1302, it fell again to the French in 1304 and remained under royal authority until 1369, when it reverted to Flemish rule. Between 1384 and 1477, when the Burgundian dukes ruled Flanders and most of the Low Country states, Lille experienced a revival as an important administrative center with a population of between 5,000 and 6,000 inhabitants. Here the dukes located their Chambre du Conseil, a council of professional administrators and judges who wielded supreme control over the finances and justice not only of Flanders but of the other Low Country states under Burgundian rule. Ravaged by later wars between the Habsburgs and Bourbons and sharply altered by nineteenth-century industrialization, Lille preserves today few monuments from its medieval past.

BIBLIOGRAPHY

The foremost authority on Lille is Alexandre de Saint-Léger, whose numerous studies include *Histoire de Lille des origines à 1789* (1942), with select bibliography. For further information see Max Bruchet, *Bibliographie des travaux publiés sur l'histoire de Lille antérieure à 1789* (1926). The social and economic history of medieval Lille receives some attention in Jean Lestocquoy, *Les villes de Flandre et d'Italie sous le gouvernement des patriciens (XIe–XVe siècles)* (1952). The best account of Lille as an administrative center under the Burgundian dukes is Henri Pirenne, *Histoire de Belgique,* 3rd rev. ed. (1922), II, 343–415. See also Robert Marquant, *La vie économique à Lille sous Philippe le Bon* (1940); Pierre Pierrard, *Histoire de Lille* (1982).

BRYCE LYON

[See also **Flanders and the Low Countries; Textiles; Trade, European; Wool.**]

LIMBOURG BROTHERS. Pol, Herman, and Jean (*ca.* 1386–1416), nephews of Jean Malouel, were from Nijmegen in Guelders and became the principal manuscript illuminators for Jean, duke of Berry. As youths they went to Paris to serve their apprenticeships under a goldsmith, but had to leave because of an outbreak of the plague. Imprisoned in Brussels in 1399 on their way home, they were ransomed by the duke of Burgundy, Philip the Bold. They served him from 1400 to 1404, illuminating a Bible for him, now lost. The three brothers may have been in the service of Jean of Berry by 1405. They enjoyed a particularly amicable relationship with the duke, often exchanging lavish gifts. All three appear to have died in an epidemic in 1416.

Pol executed some paintings for the duke's Château de Bicêtre in 1408, but these were destroyed in 1411. The brothers painted some miniatures for the *Très belles heures de Notre Dame* (Paris, Bibliothèque nationale, MS nouv. acq. lat. 3093), a miniature for the *Petites heures* (Paris, Bibliothèque nationale, MS lat. 18014), and some scenes in grisaille

The month of June, with Palais de la Cité and Ste. Chapelle, Paris, in background. Miniature by the Limbourg Brothers from the *Très riches heures*, ca. 1416. CHANTILLY, MUSÉE CONDÉ; PHOTO: LOUIS LANIEPCE, PARIS

for a *Bible moralisée* (Paris, Bibliothèque nationale, MS fr. 166). Their most famous works are the miniatures in the *Belles heures* (New York, The Cloisters), perhaps finished by 1408–1409, and the *Très riches heures* (Chantilly, Musée Condé), painted between 1413 and 1416. The latter remained unfinished at their death.

Their miniatures, particularly in the *Très riches heures*, are representative of the height of the International Gothic style in France. The Limbourgs combined courtly elegance, sumptuous coloration, and a mixture of fanciful and remarkably naturalistic landscape settings. They used Italian and classical sources for their motifs and iconography, and created innovative, expanded cycles of narrative miniatures unprecedented in previous books of hours.

BIBLIOGRAPHY

Jean Longnon and Raymond Cazelles, *The Très Riches Heures of Jean, Duke of Berry* (1969); Millard Meiss, *French Painting in the Time of Jean de Berry: The Limbourgs and Their Contemporaries*, 2 vols. (1974); Millard Meiss and Elizabeth H. Beatson, *The Belles Heures of Jean, Duke of Berry* (1974).

ROBERT G. CALKINS

[See also **Book of Hours; Gothic Art, Painting and Manuscript Illumination; Gothic, International Style; Jean, Duke of Berry.**]

LIMITANEI were the frontier troops of the late Roman (later the Byzantine) Empire. Established by the reforms of Diocletian and Constantine, they were natives of the areas in which they were stationed on permanent assignment. Commanded by military dukes, the Limitanei were expected to absorb the first shock of an invasion and delay it, thus giving the better-armed *comitatenses* time to gather and present a more effective resistance. Eventually they were given land in exchange for their service—a form of payment which gave them an additional stake in the defense of their territory. These *limitanei* may have evolved into the *stratiotai*, who later formed the basis of the theme system.

BIBLIOGRAPHY

George Ostrogorsky, *History of the Byzantine State*, Joan Hussey, trans. (1957, rev. 1969).

LINDA C. ROSE

[See also **Byzantine Empire: History; Constantine I, the Great; Stratiotai; Themes; Warfare, Byzantine.**]

LINCOLN, RITE OF. Evidence of the pre-Reformation liturgical rite of the cathedral and diocese of Lincoln is scarce. No indisputable service books are extant, and only two manuscript witnesses of the Divine Office have been identified. The Lincoln rite, with the exception of a few local modifications, was similar to the Sarum rite. The most prominent differences are the selections for the readings of the epistles and gospels.

Evidence of the customs of the cathedral church is far more abundant than that of the Divine Office. The *Vetusissimum registrum*, which is contained in a fourteenth-century compilation called the *Liber niger*, records the customs of the cathedral church. Also included in the *Liber niger* are an account of the history of Lincoln as well as other charters and writs. William Alnwick, Bishop of Lincoln (1436–

1449), compiled the *Novum registrum ecclesiae Lincolniensis* to take the place of the earlier customs recorded in the *Vetusissimum registrum*. Alnwick contributed to present knowledge of the history of the Lincoln rite by identifying Remigius de Fécamp, bishop of Lincoln (1072–1094), as the man responsible for introducing the rites of the church of Rouen to Lincoln.

BIBLIOGRAPHY

Henry Bradshaw and Christopher Wordsworth, eds., *Statutes of Lincoln Cathedral,* 3 vols. (1892–1897); William G. Henderson, ed., *Missale ad usum insignis Ecclesiae eboracensis* (1874), II, 343–348; Archdale A. King, *Liturgies of the Religious Orders* (1955), 397–408, and *Liturgies of the Past* (1959), 276–374.

CLEO LELAND BOYD

[See also **Liturgy, Treatises on; Sarum Rite.**]

LINDISFARNE GOSPELS, a richly illustrated Hiberno-Saxon Gospelbook produced at Lindisfarne about 700, now at London, British Library, Cotton MS Nero D.IV. A colophon (fol. 259r.) names the monastery, the scribe (Eadfrith, bishop of Lindisfarne from 698 to 721), the men responsible for the binding and the ornamental cover (Aethelwald and Billfrith), and the author of the colophon (Aldred), who also provided Anglo-Saxon glosses to the Latin text. Although the colophon was added centuries later (*ca.* 970), it is believed to be accurate. Aldred was a prior of Lindisfarne and presumably conversant with the monastery's history; also, an invented colophon would probably have attributed the Gospelbook to the most famous bishop of Lindisfarne, St. Cuthbert (*ca.* 635–687). The Lindisfarne Gospels is usually dated about 696–698, on the assumptions that the elaborate decoration (thirty-three pages of illustrations plus enlarged initials throughout the manuscript done in forty-five different tones of color) was done without significant interruption and must have taken at least two years to produce; and that Eadfrith was both the scribe and the illuminator and would not have had time to devote himself to the manuscript after he became bishop in 698. The Lindisfarne Gospels is also closely related to the reliquary of St. Cuthbert and is associated with the translation of the saint's relics in 698.

The Lindisfarne Gospels generally follows the format of the Book of Durrow but is more richly

St. Matthew. From Lindisfarne Gospels, *ca.* 696–698. LONDON, BRITISH LIBRARY COTTON NERO D. IV, f. 25ᵛ (cat. 9)

decorated and incorporates other sources. A greater variety of colors is used in Lindisfarne (although the bright yellow of Durrow is rare), and the ornamental vocabulary is richer, including elements such as unframed interlace bands that were not found in the earlier Gospelbook. However, most of Lindisfarne's decorative motifs were anticipated in metalwork, for example, in the Sutton Hoo treasure (*ca.* 625–650). Decorated initials in the Lindisfarne Gospels, unlike those of the Book of Durrow, are rectangular, resembling those of most later deluxe Insular manuscripts. The initials are sometimes expanded to fill an entire page; Lindisfarne contains the earliest known full-page elaboration of the *chi-rho* initials at the beginning of Matthew's Gospel. The decoration of the Lindisfarne Gospels is more uniform in scale and quality than that of the Book of Durrow; the pricks and rulings that governed the layout of the ornament are still discernible. Influences foreign to the Book of Durrow are also found in Lindisfarne. Italian sources have been suggested for the text and liturgical apparatus of Lindisfarne. The substitution of a sixteen-page sequence of arcaded canon tables for the twelve pages of rectangular tables in Durrow has also been connected with Italian models; and Mediterranean influence has been seen in the replacement of the full-page evangelist symbols by portraits of the evangelists accompanied by their symbols.

The evangelists' portraits are largely consistent in location and type: each follows the Gospel preface on the verso of the folio preceding the decorative frontispieces to the Gospel. The portraits all carry two inscriptions, one identifying the symbol in Latin (for example, *Imago hominis* for Matthew), the other identifying the evangelist in Greek transliterated into Latin characters *(O Agios Mattheus)*. The portraits were all done by the same hand, use the same setting and same type of garments, and include the same type of full-length evangelist symbol (sometimes partially obscured by the evangelist's nimbus), with wings and a halo, holding a book or scroll. The portrait of Matthew presents a second figure, probably Moses, peering out from behind a curtain, apparently inspiring the evangelist. The portraits contain little Insular ornament and suggest the availability of new sources in Northumbria. A variety of influences on the Lindisfarne evangelist portraits has been traced. The portrait of Matthew is based on the same model used for the seated figure of Ezra in another Northumbrian manuscript, the *Codex Amiatinus* of about 716; it seems likely that both derive from an Italian exemplar (the *Codex grandior* or the *Novem Codices*) written by Cassiodorus (ca. 490–ca. 583) and sent to Northumbria during the last quarter of the seventh century. The bilingual inscriptions, the not quite frontal position of three of the seated evangelists, and the figure (ultimately derived from an inspiring muse) that accompanies Matthew suggest Greek influence, and the style of the figures has been connected with a group of ivory panels—the so-called St. Mark Grado chair ivories—probably produced in Byzantium in the seventh century. The evangelists' symbols are without precedent, but are related to those on the reliquary of St. Cuthbert, those surrounding the miniature of the Majestas Domini in the *Codex Amiatinus,* and the sixth-century mosaic examples at S. Vitale in Ravenna. The Lindisfarne symbols may adapt Italian types current in late-seventh- and early-eighth-century Northumbria. The Mediterranean models and classicizing style of the Lindisfarne portraits are also evident in the *Codex Amiatinus* and the Ruthwell cross and may reflect the impact of illustrated manuscripts

brought from Rome by Benedict Biscop in the last quarter of the seventh century or gifts from Rome presumably brought by Theodore of Tarsus, a Greek emissary of the pope, when he came to Lindisfarne in 678 to consecrate the new church.

BIBLIOGRAPHY
Jonathan James G. Alexander, *Insular Manuscripts Sixth to Ninth Century* (1978); Thomas Downing *et al.,* eds., *Evangeliorum Quattuor: Codex Lindisfarnensis* (1956–1960), facsimile edition and commentary; Françoise Henry, "The Lindisfarne Gospels," in *Antiquity,* **37** (1963); Carl Nordenfalk, "Eastern Style Elements in the Book of Lindisfarne," in *Acta archaeologica,* **13** (1942), and *Celtic and Anglo-Saxon Painting: Book Illumination in the British Isles, 600–800* (1977).

LESLIE BRUBAKER

[See also **Canon Table; Carpet Page; Celtic Art; Evangelist Symbols; Gospelbook; Initials, Decorated and Historiated; Manuscript Illumination; Sutton Hoo;** and frontispiece, this volume.]

LINEN. Linens were the first textiles to be manufactured from a vegetable fiber and were already in evidence about 7000 B.C. In Europe they remained the most important textiles woven from such fibers until cotton manufacturing came to predominate in the Industrial Revolution. The source of that fiber is the domesticated flax plant *Linum usitatissimum* (most useful), a herbaceous annual of the family Linaceae, derived from one variety of wild flax *Linum angustifolium* (which probably provided the fibers for the very earliest linens). The former is also the source of commercial linseed oil, extracted from the flowering plant's seed bolls. Though domesticated flax may have originated in the mountainous regions of China and India, from where it spread westward, ancient Egypt was evidently the first to cultivate flax specifically for linen textiles, whereas the ancient Greeks grew it only for the linseed oil. The diffusion of both flax cultivation and linen manufacturing throughout Europe were very slow processes that commenced in the pre-Roman (perhaps, Phoenician) era and were completed only in the Middle Ages. Up to the early fourteenth century, Egypt and Syria continued to be regarded as the sources of the very finest flax and linen.

Of all the natural textile fibers, linen is the strongest, but also the most difficult and laborious to prepare for spinning. The bast fibers themselves (related to hemp), almost pure cellulose, lie between the outer bark of the stalk and the woody inner core and are bound together by gummy resins. The flax plant grows best in well-drained, fertile alluvial soils with a temperate climate; it is harvested when the stalk reaches about a meter in height, but before the plant has fully ripened, to prevent lignification, that is, the conversion of the bast fibers to woody tissue. Harvesting was effected by pulling the plants out by the roots rather than by reaping, since cutting injured the fibers and reduced the amount that could be extracted. The flax stalks were then loosely bound into bundles called beets and placed in stocks for desiccation in the sun in order to commence the rippling process: the removal of the leaves, flowers, and globular seed bolls. When it was not done by hand, a long comb fitted with big, well-spaced iron teeth was used. In the next and most crucial process, retting, the flax stalks were submerged with weights in a bath of warm water, ideally heated to 27° C (80° F), for one to three weeks, to undergo bacteriological fermentation, by which micro-organisms dissolved the resinous bonds of the bast fibers and, along with the water-softening effects, began the separation of the fibers from the outer bark and inner core.

The fully retted stalks were then dried once more in the sun to be subjected to flax breaking. Until the later Middle Ages, this process meant pounding the stalks with a wooden mallet against a flat stone or on a wooden block with raised diagonal surface strips in order to break the stalks into smaller pieces and to further the separation of fibers from bark and core. Then, in the late thirteenth or early fourteenth century, a much more efficient, mechanical flax breaker was invented, possibly in Holland. It consisted essentially of three wooden planks standing on edge in parallel to one another: two outer planks fixed to a wooden base and a third plank or blade pivoted between them by a bolt (or axle) at one end and fitted with a handle at the other end. The artisan placed the flax stalks across the two outer fixed planks and then brought the blade down forcibly to break up and crush the stalks against the wooden base, rotating the stalks with the left hand while operating the blade with the right. The broken stalks were then subjected to scutching: the pieces were bent over the edge of a thick wooden board or block and beaten with a flat blade of wood or metal to remove the larger remnants of bark and woody core. The final, complete separation of the linen fibers from all foreign materials was achieved by a form of combing called hackling, which also served to disen-

tangle the linen fibers, forcing them to lie parallel to each other. The hackle itself had two forms. The earlier one closely resembled the age-old iron combs of the worsted and woolen industries (with finer teeth, set more closely together, than those of the flax-rippling comb). The other, later instrument was akin to the later medieval wool cards: a wooden hackling board, about 45 cm by 15 cm (17.7 in x 5.9 in), containing numerous protruding iron spikes arranged in several rows of graduated height, through which the fibers were repeatedly drawn. The long linen fibers, drawn out and fully separated by such combing, were known as line fibers; they were taken directly as rovings, wound in coils, to be attached to the spinner's distaff or wheel. The short, broken, tangled fibers that wound themselves around the hackle's teeth were called tow fibers; they were generally reserved for such coarse uses as cordage.

The ensuing processes of spinning and weaving were virtually identical to those of the woolen and worsted industries. Linen fibers are best spun moistened and counterclockwise (S-spun), since they naturally rotate to the left. In ancient Egypt and in other eastern Roman provinces, linen was so S-spun; but in the West it was generally Z-spun (clockwise), as was wool. Linen yarns, of both the East and the West, were almost always woven in a simple plain or tabby weave, that is, with each weft passing over and under a single warp; indeed, this weave was commonly known as "linen weave."

Linen cloth, when taken down from the loom, is fully manufactured (not requiring the fulling, tentering, napping, and shearing of woolens); but its natural gray-brown color necessitates extensive bleaching. In medieval Europe, linens to be bleached were first scoured and boiled in a bath containing lye extracted from wood ashes (which also removed any remaining resinous impurities) and were then spread out on wooden posts in the open air and exposed to sunlight for eight to sixteen weeks, according to the thickness of the fabric. Finally, the linen cloth was polished to a very smooth and hard finish by a linen rubber: a large, heavy, flattened glass or marble ball, vigorously rubbed over the surface of the cloth.

Among the properties that accounted for the widespread popularity of linens in the ancient, medieval, and early modern worlds are their great tensile strength and durability (particularly important for sailcloth), their very smooth and lustrous handle (in the finer grades), and their very bright whiteness when bleached (associated with purity and cleanliness). Linens are also highly absorbent, but dry quickly and free of lint. They are very easily laundered and provide very cool apparel, by conducting heat away from the body. Their chief disadvantages were (and are) that they wrinkle easily and were difficult to dye, because the fibers were not receptive to most medieval dyestuffs.

Medieval and early modern Europe manufactured a wide variety of linens (and fustians, having a linen warp and a cotton weft): very coarse and heavy canvases, sailcloths, tarpaulins, carpet backings, cordage, bagging, fishnets; medium-grade fabrics in curtains, upholstery, towelings, bed and table linens, embroidery foundations, and numerous forms of apparel; and extremely fine-grade, costly cambrics, lace, handkerchiefs, sheet curtains, veils, and delicate apparel. In terms of apparel, the wardrobe accounts of Henry VI for 1438/1439 indicate that the prices of linens per yard ranged from 20 percent (Brabant) to 142 percent (Rheims) of the average price of English woolen broadcloths. Linen manufacturing was widespread in medieval Europe, but the chief producers for international trade were located in northeastern France (the best at Rheims), the Rhineland, and the Low Countries.

BIBLIOGRAPHY

Fred Bradbury, *Flax Culture and Preparation* (1920); Walter Endrei, *L'évolution des techniques du filage et du tissage du moyen âge à la révolution industrielle* (1968); Robert J. Forbes, *Studies in Ancient Technology*, III, 2nd rev. ed. (1964); Agnes Geijer, *A History of Textile Art* (1979); R. Patterson, "Spinning and Weaving," in Charles Singer *et al.*, eds., *A History of Technology*, II (1956); M. L. Ryder, "The Origin of Spinning," in *Textile History*, 1 (1968–1970); J. P. Wild, *Textile Manufacture in the Northern Roman Provinces* (1970).

JOHN H. MUNRO

[See also **Flax; Hemp; Textile Technology; Textiles.**]

LIPARIT IV ORBĒLEAN (*fl.* eleventh century to 1060) was a prominent general and political figure in Caucasia. The Orbēlean family, a branch of which moved from Armenia to Georgia in the second half of the ninth century, was at times the most valuable support of the Georgian kings and their most dangerous rival. At a time when the Byzantine emperor Basil II (976–1025) was coercing the weakened Armenian and Georgian princes to cede their ancestral lands to the empire (early 1020's), Liparit, as duke of the district of Tᶜrialetᶜi and later as commander-in-chief of the armies, appeared as the defender of Georgia's boy king Bagrat IV (1027–1072). Liparit's prowess as a general was demonstrated in 1034 when, together with other Georgian and Armenian nobles, he defeated a Shaddadid army in Arrān. In 1038 Liparit was on the verge of capturing the Georgian city of Tiflis (Tbilisi), which had been a Muslim stronghold for centuries. But fearing his growing power, the Georgian nobles thwarted the plan. As a result of this betrayal, Liparit began actively cooperating with foreign powers (the Byzantines, and later the Seljuks) for vengeance on the Caucasian lords. In 1039 King Bagrat's rebellious half-brother Dmitri entered Georgia with Byzantine troops. Liparit supported him and enjoyed numerous successes against the king. Following Dmitri's death in 1042, Liparit became the agent of Byzantine expansionist policies in Caucasia.

During the Seljuk campaigns in western historical Armenia in 1048, Liparit (who had been fighting on the Byzantine side) was captured. Sent as a prisoner to Isfahan, he quickly earned the trust and respect of Alp Arslan. The following year he was sent at the head of a Seljuk army to ravage the Georgian district of Javaχetᶜi. In the absence of King Bagrat, who had fled to Byzantium, Liparit ruled Georgia (1050–1053) and even installed Bagrat's son as king. After Bagrat's return, Liparit warred against him. Eventually in 1060 he was betrayed by his followers and sent to King Bagrat, who forced him into a monastery.

BIBLIOGRAPHY

Sources. Aristakēs Lastivertcᶜi, *Patmutᶜiwn Aristakisi Lastivertcᶜwoy*, K. N. Yuzbašyan, ed. (1963), chap. 13, pp. 80–82; *Kᶜartᶜlis Cᶜχovreba*, in Marie Felicité Brosset, *Histoire de la Georgie depuis l'antiquité jusqu'au XIXᵉ siècle, Iᵉ partie* (1856), 311–323; Matthew of Edessa, *Patmutᶜiwn Mattᶜēosi Urhayecᶜwoy* (1869), chap. 54, pp. 122, 125–128; Vardan Arewelcᶜi, *Hawakᶜumn Patmutᶜean Vardanay Vardapeti lusabeneal* (1862), chap. 55, pp. 98, 99.

Studies. William E. Allen, *A History of the Georgian People* (1932, repr. 1971), 88–90; Vladimir Minorsky, *Studies in Caucasian History* (1953), 56–57; Cyril Toumanoff, "Armenia and Georgia," in J. M. Hussey, ed., *The Cambridge Medieval History*, IV.1 (1966), 621–622, and "The Mamikonids and the Liparitids," in *Armeniaca* (1969), 125–126, 128–129.

ROBERT BEDROSIAN

[See also **Basil II; Caucasia; Georgia: Political History.**]

LIPPO MEMMI (*fl.* 1317–1357), Sienese painter and assistant and brother-in-law to Simone Martini. His principal works include a signed *Madonna and Child Enthroned* in the Altenburg, Lindenau Museum; the signed *Madonna del Popolo* in S. Maria dei Servi, Siena, and the copy after Simone Martini's *Maestà* fresco in the Palazzo del Popolo, S. Gimignano, signed and dated 1317. He is also the author of the SS. Ansanus and Margaret that form wings to Simone's 1333 *Annunciation*, now in the Uffizi, Florence.

BIBLIOGRAPHY
Bernard Berenson, *Italian Pictures of the Renaissance: Central Italian and North Italian Schools*, I, II (1968); Antonio Caleca, "Tre polittici di Lippo Memmi: Un'ipotesi sul Barna e la bottega di Simone e di Lippo," in *Critica d'arte*, **41** (1976); Enzo Carli, "Ancora dei Memmi a San Gimignano," in *Paragone*, **14** (1963); Luigi Coletti, *I primitivi: I senesi e i giotteschi* (1946).

ADELHEID M. GEALT

[See also **Gothic Art: Painting; Maestà; Siena; Simone Martini; Trecento Art.**]

Madonna del Popolo. Lippo Memmi, mid 14th century. Siena, S. Maria dei Servi. ART RESOURCE

LIPSANOTHECA, a small casket for holding relics. Such reliquaries, made of a variety of materials, are preserved from the fourth century on. The term is rarely used except as applied (perhaps incorrectly) to the famous ivory *lipsanotheca* of Brescia, which dates from the third quarter of the fourth century.

BIBLIOGRAPHY
Richard Delbrück, *Probleme der Lipsanothek in Brescia* (1952).

LESLIE BRUBAKER

[See also **Early Christian Art; Reliquary.**]

LITANIES, GREATER AND LESSER (*litaniae maiores et minores*), also called rogations, were processions with supplicatory prayers. The Greater Litany, so called by at least the time of Pope Gregory I (590–604), was held on 25 April. It originally had no connection with the feast of St. Mark, by whose name the procession was often called. Rather, the Greater Litany derived from a pagan procession, Robigalia, that was held on that day. In Rome this pagan procession followed a northerly course up the Via Flaminia to a grove beyond the Milvian Bridge, where a sheep and a rust-colored dog were sacrificed to the god Robigus to ward off rust blight from the newly sown cereals. According to the twelfth-century liturgical commentator John Beleth, it was under Pope Liberius (352–366) that the celebration was christianized. By the early Middle Ages in Rome, the procession began at the *collecta* church of S. Lorenzo in Lucina near the Via Lata and continued north on the Via Flaminia with a station at the church of S. Valentino near the Milvian Bridge. Rather than continuing northward to the grove of sacrifice, the Christian procession crossed the Tiber and turned south toward the Vatican, where the Christian sacrifice was offered at the stational basilica of St. Peter. In the procession the pope, his court, and the people chanted supplications to God and litanies to the saints for a successful spring planting. The festive nature of the procession eventually took on penitential overtones, and the starting point or *collecta* was changed to the Lateran. The Greater Litany practiced in Rome spread to other churches throughout Europe as the Roman liturgy was widely accepted.

The origin of the Lesser Litany, generally celebrated on the Monday, Tuesday, and Wednesday preceding Ascension Thursday, was early attributed to Bishop Mamertus of Vienne (*ca.* 470), who as a result of an earthquake and other natural disasters ordered a three-day fast together with a penitential procession to various stational churches in the city. Historically, the Lesser Litany also probably had roots in the antique *ambervale,* or rural springtime rogation procession. By the time of Caesarius of Arles (*ca.* 470–542) the custom was said to have been celebrated by the church throughout the world. Certainly, during the seventh and eighth centuries the Lesser Litany was adopted by churches north of the Alps, and in Rome it was introduced by Pope Leo III (795–816). The exact days of celebration could, however, vary from church to church. In Spain, for example, a council of Gerona in 517 ordered that the rogations were to be celebrated on the last three days of Pentecost week. And in Milan the Lesser Litany was celebrated on the first three days of the week following Ascension Sunday, although there was vigorous objection to this because according to the teaching of St. Ambrose these days were still in the festive season of Easter, when fasting was not to take place.

The Lesser Litany might take place in cities or the countryside and include nobility, clerics, and common folk processing from church to church, sometimes barefoot, vested in hairshirts, and covered with ashes. Litanies of the saints, psalms, and other chants were intoned during the procession, and special lessons, collects, and antiphons were used during the Mass and Divine Office on the days of the litany.

BIBLIOGRAPHY

Mario Righetti, *Manuale di storia liturgica,* II, 2nd ed. (1955), 225–232.

ROGER E. REYNOLDS

[See also **Litany; Processions.**]

LITANY

LITANY applies, in the broadest sense, to almost any prayer with a highly repetitive form, particularly if it includes lists of divine titles or saints' names, whether Christian or not. In a narrower sense, it refers to a particular group of texts chanted at certain points in the medieval Christian liturgy.

ETYMOLOGY

In Homer, the verb *linaneuō* meant "entreat" or "implore" (*Iliad* 9.581; *Odyssey* 7.145). This word and the noun *litaneia* occur rarely in the Septuagint but not at all in the New Testament. In a first-century B.C. papyrus (Tebtunis Papyri 284.9), the noun is used of a pagan prayer. Early Christian writers tended to use this, and the related noun *litē,* in the sense of public and corporate rather than private and individual prayer—particularly, prayer for the general welfare or forgiveness of sins. Such prayers were often occasioned by earthquakes, plagues, and other calamities, and soon came to be associated with public processions. As a result, the various forms of the word shifted their meaning, so that in documents of the fifth and sixth centuries, such as an epistle of the Council of Ephesus of 431 and a report on the Council of Tyre of 518, they seem to connote the procession itself. In the Greek Orthodox Church the primary meaning of the word remains "procession."

As early as the year 396, the Latin form *litania* was in use, for it occurs in an imperial decree of that year, preserved in the Theodosian Code and later in the Justinianic Code. In medieval Latin it was frequently spelled *letania,* and developed some meanings not found in Greek. Because processions came to be commemorated on certain fixed days of the calendar, as in the seventh-century Greek *Chronicon Paschale,* the Latin word frequently was used to designate the procession days customary in the West, particularly the rogations celebrated on 25 April and the weekdays before Ascension. In a separate development, the word was also applied to the repetitious prayers that were chanted during these processions, when a deacon or cantors would intone the various petitions to be prayed for or the names of various saints, and the people would respond with a fixed refrain such as "Kyrie eleison" (Lord have mercy) or "ora pro nobis" (pray for us).

Although this meaning is rare and atypical in Greek, it became the most important one in Latin. Thus it is from this final sense that our modern word "litany" derives its meaning.

DERIVATION

Many writers have attempted to derive the medieval Christian litanies from one or another of the repetitious prayer forms proper to ancient Jewish and pagan worship. Though such lineage is not impossible, specific relationships are at best difficult to demonstrate. Such prayers are common to most world religions, past and present; no explanation for their use in medieval Christianity is required. Nevertheless, parallels have been noted with such phenomena as the pagan use of the divine title Kyrie, as well as the *hoshanot* processions of the Jewish Feast of Tabernacles. The presence of repetitious prayers and hymns in early Christian literature and papyri is also noteworthy, though these too are not necessarily related to the medieval processional chants.

THE GREEK LITURGIES

In the Greek Byzantine rite there are five main types of texts that, according to Western terminology, would be called litanies: (1) the synapte, (2) the aitesis, (3) the ektene, (4) the dismissal litanies, and (5) the prayers of the *litē*. Each of these is led by the deacon, and can therefore also be called *diakonika*, though the word is most often applied to the synapte.

The synapte (from the Greek *synaptē*, "joined together") is known in several different forms, of which the most important is the "great synapte." This is begun by the deacon with the words "In peace let us beseech the Lord"; the people respond "Kyrie eleison" throughout. Because the first three petitions deal with peace, the great synapte is also called the *eirēnika*. On certain occasions, for example in the Office for the Dead and at the great blessing of the waters on Epiphany, special petitions may be inserted into the text.

The great synapte may once have been a processional chant, for it originally stood before the Trisagion at the beginning of the Greek Mass (but after the Trisagion, in the Armenian Mass). The *Tupikon tēs Megalēs Ekklēsias* or Typikon of the Great Church (Hagia Sofia in Constantinople) still mandated the use of the synapte before the procession on Easter Monday. In the later Byzantine Mass, however, three antiphons were sung before the Trisagion, with the entrance procession accompanying the third of them. The great synapte was then moved to precede the first antiphon.

Preceding each of the other two antiphons was a highly abridged version called the "little synapte," beginning "Again and again in peace let us beseech the Lord." The great and little synaptai also bracket the variable psalmody of the morning and evening offices.

Texts related to the great synapte stand in place of the prayer of the faithful in the Byzantine Mass, the Greek liturgies of St. James and St. Mark, and the Apostolic Constitutions. A fragment of another such text survives in a sixth-century Egyptian papyrus.

The aitesis (request) has no fixed beginning but always includes a petition "for an angel of peace, a faithful guide and guardian of our souls and bodies." The response to most petitions is "Grant, O Lord," but the first few petitions may be answered by "Kyrie eleison." It occurs already in the Apostolic Constitutions as the last of a series of dismissal litanies for the morning and evening offices. In the Typikon of the Great Church it always appears as a supplement to the synapte, while in the later (that is, monastic) Byzantine Office it acts as a supplement to the ektene. In the Byzantine Mass it is said after the great entrance and again before the Lord's Prayer, where it was formerly used in the West Syrian Mass as well. A form of it occurs in the Armenian Mass at the prayer of the faithful, and it is among the Syriac *karozwata* (proclamations) of the Nestorian and Chaldean Mass and Divine Office.

The ektene (fervent supplication) begins "Let us all say with our whole soul, and with our whole mind let us say: Kyrie eleison." The Kyrie is repeated three times in response to each petition. In the Typikon of the Great Church it is called the Great Ektene or the Great Kyrie eleison, and is normally sung at stopping places during the processions. It is used after the Gospel or the prokeimenon in the Office, after the Gospel in the Byzantine Mass, and before the Gospel in the Greek liturgy of St. James. Its use at processions and its insistent repetitions of the Kyrie render the ektene perhaps the most representative or typical genre of litany.

Already the dismissal litanies of the Apostolic Constitutions began with the deacon's monition "Let us all pray fervently," and it was the ethos of the ektene that was most readily grasped in the foreign nations to which the Greek litanies were exported. Thus in the Slavonic rite all litanies are called *ektēniya*, even the synapte and aitesis. Most Latin litanies of the preces type also betray the influence of the Greek ektene.

An abridged form of the ektene, beginning "Have mercy, O Lord, according to thy great mercy, O Lord, hear and have mercy," occurs at several places in the Byzantine Office. Its few petitions are almost exclusively for the emperor and the bishops, and it is similar to the habitual prayers recited by the bishop himself during processions. A similar ektene for the dead is sometimes recited after the great ektene in the Byzantine Mass; a form of it is already quoted in a sixth-century life of St. Eutychius.

The dismissal litany for the catechumens was said on those occasions when the unbaptized catechumens were dismissed, primarily before the great entrance at Mass and at the Liturgy of the Presanctified. In the latter place it is sometimes followed by another dismissal litany for the *photizomenoi*, those awaiting baptism at the very next Easter. In each case, the deacon begins by instructing those being prayed for to pray silently and then asks the already baptized to respond to the litany. They respond with the Kyrie eleison once after each petition.

Fully developed dismissal litanies already occur in the Apostolic Constitutions, which directs their use at every morning and evening Office as well as at Mass. This source includes two other dismissal litanies: for those undergoing canonical penances, and for those who are possessed by demons. At the dismissal of the catechumens, the Constitutions direct that the deacon should mention the name of each individual, after which the people should shout "Kyrie eleison," especially the children. This identical practice was also reported in fourth-century Jerusalem by Egeria.

The litē is a procession that sometimes takes place near the end of Vespers, after the ektene and aitesis. The litany of the *litē* is chanted when the procession pauses in the vestibule of the church. The deacon begins with "O God, save your people and bless your inheritance" (Psalms 28:9) and continues with long lists of prayers for the welfare of the Christian people, calling on many saints by name. Each group of petitions is answered by "Kyrie eleison," repeated three, eight, twelve, forty, or fifty times, depending on the source one consults; a threefold repetition is mentioned in the fifteenth-century commentary of Symeon of Thessaloniki.

Incessant repetitions of the Kyrie eleison have a long history. A sixth-century description of the monastic office of Mount Sinai mentions twelve or thirty or three hundred repetitions; the Coptic Office has forty-one near the end of each hour. Particularly striking is the rite followed at Constantinople on the feast of the Exaltation of the Cross (September 14), at which the people shouted "Kyrie eleison" one hundred, then eighty, then sixty times as the patriarch repeatedly held up a relic of the True Cross.

ADDITIONAL EASTERN RITES

Some of the other Eastern rites use or formerly used litanies which, though similar in form to the Greek litanies, are almost completely different in content. Thus the Maronite Mass had litanies at the blessing of the incense before the Trisagion that opens the Mass, after the Gospel, before the kiss of peace, and before the Lord's Prayer. The Armenian Office has litanies of a type known as *charoz*—the word may be related to the Syriac *karozutha* (proclamation).

Two types of Ethiopian litany are the *liton* and the *mehellā*. Each anaphora has its own *liton*. Among the many nonliturgical private litanies is the *mehellā* called *sebhata fequr* (praise of the beloved) by Emperor Zarᶜa Yaᶜqob (1434–1468). Litanic private prayers are characteristic of the Western church, however. Not only is there a considerable literature of devotional litanies in Latin, Celtic, and other languages, but the earliest extant sources of some liturgical litanies are personal prayer books for private use.

THE KYRIE IN THE WEST

It is possible that the Kyrie eleison was prayed in Latin at a very early date. The fourth-century hymn *Miserere Domine, miserere Christe* by Gaius Marius Victorinus (*d.* after 363) probably reflects an awareness not only of the Kyrie but also of the Christe eleison, a form that was never used in the East. In the same century Egeria, describing the dismissal litanies in Jerusalem, reported that "the many children are always responding 'Kyrie eleison,' as we say 'Miserere Domine.'" An anti-Arian tract of uncertain date seems to indicate that the Greeks, the Latins, and the Goths each said the Kyrie in their own language.

The first certainly datable evidence of the Kyrie in the West is canon number 3 of the Council of Vaison in Gaul, which met on 5 November 529. This canon reads: "Because both at Rome and in all the provinces of Italy and the Orient, the sweet and extremely wholesome custom has been introduced of saying 'Kyrie eleison' repeatedly with great sorrow and remorse, it has pleased us also that, God willing, this holy custom might be introduced in all our churches at the morning and evening Office and at

Masses." At about the same time, the Rule of St. Benedict directed that "supplicatio litaniae, id est Kyrie eleison," be said in the Office.

The statement of the Council of Vaison that the Kyrie should be said "repeatedly with great sorrow and remorse" recalls the fervor of the Greek ektene, and indeed, the Council probably had in mind Latin litanies similar in structure to the Greek ones, for that is the type that was then being used "at Rome and in all the provinces of Italy and the Orient." Such Latin litanies are known as preces or *deprecationes*.

The preces used in Rome was introduced by Pope Gelasius (*r.* 492–496) and is therefore known as the Deprecatio Gelasii. Its opening phrase recalls the Greek ektene, "Let us all say: Lord hear and have mercy." But this is followed by an invocation to the Trinity, a peculiarity found in some other Western litanies but never in the East. The content of the petitions differs somewhat from the usual petitions of Eastern litanies, but it closely follows the content of the *orationes solemnes*, a series of nonlitanic prayers said after the Gospel in the Roman Mass, which the Deprecatio Gelasii evidently replaced. The first fourteen petitions of the Deprecatio were answered with a single Kyrie eleison, the next four with the words "Grant, Lord, grant [*praesta*]." This and the petition for "an angel of peace" unquestionably recall the Greek aitesis. The final petition of the Deprecatio is answered by the Latin "Domine miserere." It is believed that the Deprecatio was later moved to the beginning of the Roman Mass, where it became an ancestor of the ninefold Kyrie.

The Council of Vaison stated that the Kyrie eleison was being said also "in all the provinces of Italy." The most important litanies after the Deprecatio Gelasii are two that were said at Milan during Lent, immediately after the entrance chant of the Ambrosian Mass. The first of these, the *Divinae pacis,* used on the first Sunday in Lent (the second Sunday by modern reckoning), recalls the Greek ektene with its opening line: "Favored with divine peace and forgiveness, entreating with our whole heart and with our whole mind we pray you: Lord have mercy." After each petition, the response is "Domine miserere" in Latin. The end of this litany echoes even more clearly the opening of the Greek ektene, with the words "Let us all say: Lord have mercy," followed by three repetitions of the Kyrie eleison in Greek.

The other Ambrosian litany, used on the second Sunday of Lent (the third in modern books), opens like the Greek ektene with "Let us all say: Kyrie eleison." A single Kyrie is used as the response to each petition, but there are three at the very end. (In the sixteenth century, the Sundays of Lent were renumbered, so that the litanies were moved back a week earlier.)

The Ambrosian litanies also occur in a couple of manuscripts from elsewhere in Italy. Some litanies related to the *Dicamus omnes* are found at Pistoia and in the Celtic Stowe Missal. The Celtic litany, called the *Deprecatio sancti Martini pro populo*, also shows the influence of the synapte and aitesis, in that the first petition asks "for the peace from above," and the last three end with "Grant, Lord, grant."

The most extensive body of preces-type litanies is found in the Mozarabic rite, where they were used at Lenten Masses, throughout the Office on penitential days, and in the burial service. These preces show the least dependence on Greek models and the most creative originality: many of them are metrical, some are abecedarian or acrostic, some even make use of rhyme. A wide variety of responses were used, such as "Et miserere" and "Quia peccavimus tibi." Nevertheless, there are some that seem related to the Greek ektene.

During Lent, the Mozarabic preces were sung at Mass between the psallendo and the New Testament readings; the arrangement is perhaps analogous to that of the Greek Liturgy of St. James and the Stowe Missal, wherein the litanies come between the psalmody and the Gospel. On Good Friday, the rite for the veneration of the Cross recalls the Eastern rite for the exaltation of the Cross, with its hundreds of repetitions of the Kyrie. The Mozarabic service calls for hundreds of repetitions of the word "Indulgentia," the response to the preces said on that day.

Because one Mozarabic manuscript preserves the burial service written in a decipherable notation, melodies survive for those preces that are included. A few Mozarabic preces occur also in the Bobbio Missal and in notated French manuscripts of Gregorian chant, indicating that they must have been used in the Gallican rite as well. Other Gallican preces in the same sources have no Mozarabic counterparts.

The most enigmatic preces of all was sung in many dioceses and some religious orders at the Tenebrae service of Holy Week. It had both the responses "Kyrie eleison" and "Domine miserere," and verses referring to the passion of Christ, often beginning "Qui passurus advenisti propter nos." The breviary of the Roman curia had the gradual *Christus factus est* sung as an antiphon in this position, and therefore in some uses—such as the Breviary of York and the Dominican Breviary—both pieces are intertwined, with successive lines from each sung in alternation.

Some metrical compositions of Carolingian hymnographers resemble litanic preces. The most famous is *Humili prece et sincera* by Hartmann of St. Gall.

THE LITANY OF THE SAINTS

The most important type of litany in the Western church has not been the preces, but rather the litany of saints, in which long lists of saints' names were intoned by the leader, with the people responding "pray for us" *(ora pro nobis)* after each name.

Following the list of saints' names, there was often a second list of calamities from which the petitioners sought deliverance, with the response "Deliver us, Lord" *(Libera nos Domine)*.

Although Eastern antecedents of the litany of saints can be seen in several obscure Greek litanies, an antecedent is most clearly discerned at the end of the synapte, in the tendency to multiply saints' names after the commemoration of the Blessed Virgin. In some of the earliest manuscripts (books of individual devotion rather than the corporate liturgy), the Western litany is given in Greek rather than Latin.

The litany of saints was a processional litany, associated particularly with the Rogation days. The Greater or Roman Rogation took place on 25 April, which coincidentally was also the Feast of St. Mark. The origin of this rogation is traditionally ascribed to Pope Gregory the Great, who, according to the historian Gregory of Tours, on the occasion of a plague in 590 commanded the clergy and laity to assemble in the seven districts of Rome to hold processions, "crying 'Kyrie eleison' through the streets of the city." Despite the claims of many medieval writers, however, the processions of 590 did not take place on 25 April.

Some writers have supposed that the 25 April celebration was intended to supplant the pagan Robigalia—an agricultural festival that celebrated the pagan god Robigus, and involved processions and the sacrifice of a dog—that traditionally took place the same day.

The Lesser, or Gallican, Rogations were celebrated on the three weekdays preceding Ascension Thursday (the following week in the Ambrosian rite). A sermon of Avitus, bishop of Vienne (d. 518), attributes the origin of these rogations to his predecessor, Mamertus. But a canon preserved in the collection of Regino states that all the Gallican bishops assembled at Vienne instituted the practice to counteract an attack by wolves. It has also been speculated that these rogations were meant to supplant the pagan Ambarvalia—an agricultural festival connected with the worship of Dea Dia (a deity perhaps related to Ceres).

Besides the Rogation days, processions with the litany took place on many other occasions: before Mass at the Easter Vigil, on fixed days during Lent and other penitential seasons, before the stational Masses when bishop and people would assemble at one church and go in procession to another one where the Mass would be celebrated, and in time of drought, earthquake, famine, or other calamity. Before the litany, one or more processional antiphons would be sung, with texts usually expressing the people's sorrow for their sins.

The actual text of the litany of saints varied enormously from one locality to another, depending on the selection and number of saints' names and the other material at the beginning and end. St. Angilbert's Ordo for St. Riquier *(ca.* 800) mentions four different types of litany text: "laetaniam generalem," "Gallicam," "Italicam," and "Romanam." In other sources, the type called "Letania gallica" usually begins by addressing the persons of the Trinity in turn, "Pater de caelis Deus, miserere nobis . . . ," continuing with a list of saints, and with the response "ora pro nobis" after each name. At the end is a list of petitions resembling those of the preces. The "Letania italica" usually begins with "Agnus Dei qui tollis peccata mundi, miserere nobis," and/or "Exaudi Deus voces nostras." The response to the saints' names tends to be "intercede pro nobis," a form also used in the Ambrosian litanies of saints. At the end is a list of petitions for the pope, the emperor, the bishop, and other rulers. The characteristics of Angilbert's "laetania generalis" and "romana" remain as yet unidentified.

As early as the late eighth century, Ordo Romanus 24 directed that the litany during the Easter Vigil be said seven times, then five, then three. Many later sources preserve three distinct litanies for this purpose, entitled "letania septena," "quina," and "terna."

A text form of particular interest is represented by the litany that begins the Mass in the Stowe Missal. Other litanies of this kind, with "Christe audi nos" at the beginning and "Agnus Dei . . ." at the end, are found in both Latin and Greek in several Celtic and Anglo-Saxon liturgical manuscripts. Expanded texts, with the processional antiphon *Peccavimus Domine peccavimus,* are also extant.

Some forms of the litany of saints had special functions. The *commendatio animae,* recited over a dying person, tended to begin with the Kyrie eleison, "Christe audi nos," and "Salvator mundi, adjuva eum," with a particular emphasis on Old Testament saints. Similar litanies were used in the East for the same purpose, as far back as the Apostolic Constitutions.

Another special form of the litany, the *laudes regiae,* included many petitions for the emperor, the king, the pope, and other rulers and bishops. These petitions probably owe something to the acclamations sung for the Byzantine emperor, described in the tenth-century *De caerimoniis* of Emperor Constantine VII Porphyrogenitos. The *laudes regiae* often began with "Christus vincit, Christus regnat, Christus imperat" (Christ conquers, Christ reigns, Christ commands), and the response to each saint's name was frequently "Tu illum adiuva" (you help him). *Laudes* were sung at ceremonies in which the bishop or king took part, particularly at pontifical Mass, where they were joined to the Kyrie. At Beauvais, they were evidently joined to the "Ite missa est."

From the twelfth century, litanies began to be addressed exclusively to the Virgin Mary, with the saints' names replaced by Marian titles such as "Virgo virginum" (virgin of virgins), "Mater purissima" (purest mother), and "Regina angelorum" (queen of angels). The most famous such Marian litany is the so-called *Litaniae Lauretanae* (Litany of Loreto), named for the Italian village where a venerated house was reputed to have been the Virgin's own, miraculously transported from Palestine by angels.

The litanies of the Virgin exemplify a larger phenomenon, in which every major part of the medieval liturgy received a Marian parody, including the Mass and the Divine Office. By the sixteenth century, similar litanies had developed for other objects of medieval devotion, such as the Holy Eucharist.

THE KYRIE AS SUBSTITUTE

Simple repetitions of "Kyrie eleison" occur at several places in the medieval liturgy, and they appear at least sometimes to be abbreviations of complete litanies. This is thought to be the case with the ninefold Kyrie at the start of the Roman Mass; in a famous letter, Pope Gregory I wrote that "in daily Masses we omit the other things that are customarily said," apparently the petitions of a litany. Some have speculated that the "things that are customarily said" might be the rest of the Deprecatio Gelasii—but no surviving text of the Deprecatio includes the phrase "Christe eleison" of the middle part of the ninefold Kyrie. As Gregory himself pointed out, the Greek litanies do not use "Christe eleison" either.

The form of the ninefold Kyrie, with three repetitions of "Kyrie eleison," three of "Christe eleison," and three again of "Kyrie," is first documented in the late-eighth-century Ordo Romanus 4. In the earlier Ordo Romanus 1, the number of repetitions could still be varied by a signal from the pope. The Gallican Mass also began with a Kyrie eleison; according to the mystical commmentary of Pseudo-Germanus, it was sung by three boys.

Multiple repetitions of the Kyrie eleison are especially characteristic of the Ambrosian rite: a triple Kyrie is sung after the psalmody of each hour of the Office, after the Magnificat at Vespers, after the Gloria in excelsis at Mass, and often after the exchange "Dominus vobiscum / et cum spiritu tuo." A twelvefold Kyrie is sung at the end of Vespers during Holy Week, and various other multiple repetitions occur at other places. Similar practices are laid down in an appendix to the monastic rule of Aurelian of Auxerre.

The previously cited practice reported by Egeria and the Apostolic Constitutions, according to which the Kyrie was sung by children, persisted in some cases well into the Middle Ages. The twelfth-century Roman pontifical directed that, at a procession during the blessing of a church, the women and children were to sing "Kyrie eleison" while the clergy sang the responsory "Erit mihi dominus." Nor is this the only case in which the Kyrie seems to have served as a popular substitute for a chant sung by the clergy. Honorius in his *Gemma animae* wrote that the people responded to the bishop's sermon with Kyrie eleison, but the clergy with the Credo. More than a century later, the *Rationale divinorum officiorum* of Durandus reported that this practice was still followed in some places.

This use of the Kyrie, apparently as a substitute for a chant not known to the people, may lie behind the usage of Kyrie eleison refrains in vernacular hymns and secular songs. Such refrains are known as early as the early-tenth-century *Petruslied,* and in such popular later hymns as *Crist ist erstanden.* German secular songs with these refrains are known as *Leisen* (apparently from "eleison"); a similar song in French is called a *kyriolé*. A Kyrie refrain is also found in one of the oldest surviving songs in English, the twelfth-century *Crist and sainte Marie* of St. Godric of Finchal.

BIBLIOGRAPHY

General. Anton Baumstark, *Comparative Liturgy,* Bernard Botte, rev., Frank L. Cross, trans. (1958), 71–80; Edmund Bishop, *Liturgica historica* (1918, repr. 1962), 116–164, 314–332; Fernand Cabrol and Henry Leclercq, eds., *Reliquiae liturgicae vetustissimae,* II (1913), 122–129, 138–142, 147–148, 188–201; Balthasar Fischer, "Litanies," in *Dictionnaire de spiritualité ascétique et mystique,* IX (1976); Michel Huglo *et al.*, "Litany," in *New Grove Dictionary of Music and Musicians,* XI (1980); Bruno Stäblein, "Litanei," in *Die Musik in Geschichte und Gegenwart,* VIII (1960; John Wilkinson, ed. and trans., *Egeria's Travels to the Holy Land,* rev. ed. (1981), 57, 124, 255.

Eastern texts. Frank E. Brightman, ed., *Liturgies, Eastern and Western, I, Eastern Liturgies* (1896, repr. 1965); Oswald H. E. Burmester, *The Egyptian or Coptic Church* (1967), 96–107; Franz X. von Funk, *Didascalia et constitutiones apostolorum,* 2 vols. (1905), 478–493, 545–549, 551–552; Pierre-Edmond Gemayel, *Avant-messe maronite* (1965), 13, 286–288; François Halkin, "Une litanie des saints dans un office grec pour un mourant," in *Corona gratiarum: Miscellanea patristica, historica, et liturgica Eligio Dekkers O.S.B.,* II (1975), 51–59; Isabel F. Hapgood, ed. and trans., *Service Book of the Holy Orthodox-Catholic Apostolic Church,* 4th ed (1965); Sarhad Y. Hermiz Jammo, *La structure de la messe chaldéenne du debut jusqu'à l'anaphore* (1979), 125–136, 139–150; Heinrich Husmann, ed., *Die Melodien des chaldäischen Breviers Commune nach der Traditionen Vorderasiens und der Malabarküste* (1967); Augusta Longo, "Il testo integrale della 'Narrazione degli abati Giovanni e Sofronio,' attraverso le hermeniai di Nicone," in *Rivista di studi bizantini e neoellenici,* n.s. **2–3** (1965–1966), esp. 251–252; Juan Matéos, ed., *Le Typicon de la Grande Église* (1962–1963), I, 28–31, II, 202–203, 296–297, and *La célébration de la parole dans la liturgie byzantine* (1971), 27–33, 115–118, 148–173; Frans van de Paverd, *Zur Geschichte der Messliturgie in Antiocheia und Konstantinopel gegen Ende des vierten Jahrhunderts: Analyse der Quellen bei Johannes Chrysostomos* (1970), 138–221, 445–464; Alphones Raes, *Introductio in liturgiam orientalem* (1947, repr. 1962), 189, 193–194; Anselm Strittmatter, "Notes on the Byzantine Synapte," in *Traditio,* **10** (1954); Robert F. Taft, *The Great Entrance* (1975), 311–349.

Western texts. Analecta hymnica medii aevi, **50** (1907), 146–147, 176–178, 183–184, 208, 237–238, 246–247, 253–255; Michel Andrieu, *Les ordines romani du haut moyen âge* (1951), II, 84, 159, III, 296; Terence Bailey, *The Processions of Sarum and the Western Church* (1971); Bernard

Capelle, "Le Kyrie de la messe et le pape Gelase," in his *Travaux liturgiques,* II (1962); Paul de Clerck, *La prière universelle dans les liturgies latines anciennes: Témoignages patristiques et textes liturgiques* (1977); Maurice Coens, "Anciennes litanies des saints," in his *Recueil d'études bollandiennes* (1963), 129–322; Helmut Hucke, "Die Neumierung des althochdeutschen Petruslied," in *Organicae voces: Festschrift Joseph Smits van Waesberghe* (1963); Michel Huglo, "Les 'preces' des graduels aquitains empruntées à la liturgie hispanique," in *Hispania sacra,* 8 (1955); Josef Jungmann, "Marius Victorinus in der karolingischen Gebetsliteratur und im römischen Dreifaltigkeitsoffizium," in *Kyriakon: Festschrift Johannes Quasten,* Patrick Granfield and Josef A. Jungmann, eds., II (1970), 691–697; Ernst H. Kantorowicz, *Laudes regiae: A Study in Liturgical Acclamations and Mediaeval Ruler Worship* (1946); Art. B. Kuypers, ed., *The Prayer Book of Aedeluald the Bishop, Commonly Called the Book of Cerne* (1902); Gérard G. Meersseman, *Der Hymnos Akathistos im Abendland,* II (1960), 214–256; Wilhelm Meyer, *Die Preces der mozarabischen Liturgie* (1914); Jean-Baptiste Molin, "Les manuscripts de la 'Deprecatio Gelasii': Usage privé des psaumes et dévotion aux litanies," in *Ephemerides liturgicae,* 90 (1976); Bernhard Opfermann, "Litania italica: Ein Beitrag zur Litaneigeschichte," *ibid.,* **72** (1958); Pierre Salmon, *Analecta liturgica* (1974); 123–194; Hermann Schmidt, ed., *Hebdomada sancta,* I (1956), 294, II (1957), 861–866; J. B. Trend, "The First English Songs," in *Music and Letters,* 9 (1928), esp. 120–123; Geoffrey G. Willis, *Essays in Early Roman Liturgy* (1964), 1–48; André Wilmart, *Precum libelli quattuor aevi karolini* (1940).

PETER JEFFERY

[See also **Apostolic Constitutions; Kyrie; Liturgy, Byzantine Church; Processions.**]

LITERACY, BYZANTINE. In the modern world, literacy implies the ability to read and understand printed books, periodicals, and documents as well as to write. In the medieval world, in which books were rare and expensive and in which the language of literature was usually distinct from that of everyday conversation, a man might be able to read and write more or less easily without ever acquiring or seeking to acquire the familiarity with books which literacy entails today. In seeking an understanding of medieval literacy generally and Byzantine literacy specifically, it is helpful to distinguish clearly between functional literacy and high-grade literacy.

Literacy in Eastern and Western Europe. In the West, with the possible exception of Italy, literacy—which demanded a knowledge of Latin—was until the later Middle Ages largely confined to the clergy, who were not merely an occupational group, but an order in society with a special legal and social status. The functions of the clergy called for high-grade literacy. Financial administration, for example, was largely a clerical monopoly. A ruler might be illiterate, but his chancellor would be a literate clergyman. The transmission of literacy was also in the hands of clerics. If a man did not read Latin, he usually did not read at all.

In the Byzantine world, however, neither functional literacy nor high-grade literacy was a clerical preserve. Offices requiring literacy were open to laymen, and the teaching of reading and writing was often the work of laymen. The language in which books were written was a form of Greek and could be at least partially understood without special study. Literacy was more evenly spread horizontally, and probably also vertically, than in Western Europe. It is symptomatic that only two Byzantine emperors are said to have been illiterate, while at least ten were themselves authors of works that still survive.

The acquisition of literacy. Throughout the Byzantine period the rich often employed private tutors to teach the rudiments of reading and writing to their sons and, occasionally, to their daughters as well. But most literate Byzantines got their elementary education at school. A school was not a continuing institution. All it implied was a teacher and a room. The teacher usually depended for his livelihood on fees paid by his pupils, though in some cities the ancient institution of the public teacher may have survived in the early Byzantine period or been revived later. Further education in the understanding and use of literary Greek, based on the study of ancient Greek poetry or sometimes of the psalms, was given by the *grammatikos*. The third stage was the study and practice of rhetoric under the *rhetor*. The same teacher sometimes combined both functions. Years of study were required to acquire the command of literary Greek necessary for a career in the higher bureaucracy of state and church. But a much shorter period of study could enable a student to read and appreciate literary texts.

Distribution of schools. Elementary teachers were to be found in most cities and sometimes even in villages throughout most of the Byzantine period. Their economic and social position was probably precarious, and they sometimes combined teaching with the drawing up of legal documents and with letter writing for the illiterate. Those who wished to pursue their education beyond the elementary stage

had to go to one of the great cities of the empire, and most often to Constantinople. Many men of distinction received an elementary education in their native city and then proceeded to the capital to study grammar and rhetoric. For example, Constantine (Cyril), the apostle of the Slavs (826/827–869), who learned to read and write in Thessaloniki, found he could not fully understand the church fathers and went to Constantinople, where he learned grammar and read the whole of Homer in three months. Other examples are: Athanasios (920–1002), founder of the monastery of Great Lavra on Mount Athos, who went to school in his native Trebizond, then was sent by a rich patron to the capital for his secondary education; and the Patriarch Gregory of Cyprus (1241–*ca.* 1290), who learned to read and write in Latin at a Frankish school in Cyprus, then traveled to Ephesus and made his way on foot to Constantinople to seek training in grammar and rhetoric. For every youth who attended school in his hometown and then went on to study in the capital there must have been many who remained at home, able to read and write but not at ease in the language of literature nor accustomed to reading books. That it was no uncommon thing for a boy to go to school is shown by the inclusion in the *Euchologion* (the prayer book of the Greek Orthodox Church) of prayers for the first day at school and for the improvement of slow learners. The mention of a barefoot schoolboy in a twelfth-century poem suggests that attendance at school was not restricted to the well-to-do. The cities of Syria and Palestine, which were taken over by the Muslims with little fighting or disturbance of the social order, seem to have preserved the ancient tradition of publicly maintained teachers of grammar and rhetoric after it had been abandoned in provincial cities remaining under Byzantine rule. Several Byzantine men of letters of the eighth and ninth centuries acquired their higher education in Damascus or Jerusalem.

Evidence of documents. From the tenth century onward many Byzantine documents survive, mainly belonging to monastic archives and concerned with landed property. The study of these throws some light on the distribution of functional literacy in society. In general, clergymen, state functionaries, and monks signed their names, while most other parties made a cross. Monks who signed their names must in most cases have learned to read and write as children. It is not easy for an adult to learn his letters, and in the Byzantine world it was looked on as something of a miracle. Some monks attended a monastic school for boys hoping to adopt the religious life, but the majority attended a lay school with other boys before choosing to become monks. Among laymen who signed their names, urban tradesmen were more prominent than peasants. But there was clearly much individual variation even within the same family. Very few women signed, and those who did evidently belonged to the richest families, who could employ private tutors.

Of those who did sign their names, some used the flowing and confident hand of the habitual writer, others wrote an awkward and clumsy hand with an untidy mixture of majuscule and minuscule forms, others again could only draw capital letters painfully and helplessly. The first two groups were functionally literate, the third probably not. We do not know how Byzantine schoolmasters taught writing. It is likely, however, that they began with the invariable majuscule forms and only later introduced their pupils to the variable forms and ligatures of the minuscule hand. Those whose education was broken off early might be familiar only with the capital letters used in inscriptions in churches and elsewhere, and be unable to read the minuscule hand in which books were written.

Evidence of legal texts. Justinian observes (Novel 73) that in villages it was hard to find persons who could write or witness documents, thus underlining the difference between town and country in the matter of literacy. The *Ecloga,* a simplified manual of law for judges issued by Leo III in 726 and addressed in particular to "those living outside our God-guarded city," provides some evidence on literacy in the provinces in the so-called "dark age" of the Byzantine Empire. It treats written wills as normal. They could be signed or crossed in the presence of seven witnesses. An oral will also had to be declared before seven witnesses. The presumption is that the witnesses could at least write their names. Written contracts of betrothal and marriage were also regarded as normal, though not obligatory for the poor. A *transactio* (a compromised settlement of a dispute) had to be in writing and signed by three witnesses, though Justinianic law had permitted oral *transactiones.* Records of judicial proceedings in Byzantine courts regularly mention the production of documents, nearly always signed. The authenticity of signatures was sometimes challenged. All this evidence suggests that at least functional literacy was not uncommon in the provinces, though probably largely confined to the property-owning classes in country towns.

Ownership of books. Before the invention of printing, and especially before the widespread use of paper in the thirteenth century, books were extremely costly in comparison with most other commodities. There is a presumption that if a man owned a book he read it, and there is much evidence of the lending of books among friends. Thus, ownership of books by persons for whom literacy was not a professional necessity is prima facie evidence that they were not merely functionally literate but were able to read literary texts with ease. The copying or writing of books by such persons is even more compelling evidence of their literacy. Colophons and marginal notes in manuscripts bear witness to both ownership and copying of books by senior military officers from the tenth century onward. Two such officers, in the thirteenth and fifteenth centuries respectively, boast of their extensive private libraries. These military men are unlikely to have had a thorough literary education. Kekaumenos, an eleventh-century general who owned, read, and wrote books, states expressly that he had not had such an education. Many laymen holding nonmilitary offices owned books. Eustathios Boilas, a former government official living in retirement on his estates in Armenia in the eleventh century, possessed a library of about eighty books. A few upper-class women also owned and copied books, and several ladies of the imperial family were either authors, like Anna Komnena, or patrons of literature, like her niece by marriage, the sebastocratorissa Eirene. It would appear that high-grade literacy was widespread among the upper classes; presumably even the less literate members of this group knew enough to keep their accounts or write a private letter.

General conclusions. Rather than a clear-cut distinction between the literate and the illiterate, the Byzantine world shows a gradation from those fully at home in the manipulation of the literary language, through those who could read it but not write it with confidence or who could on occasion read books but could not fully comprehend the literary language, to those who could only laboriously trace out the letters of their name. Beyond these lay the mass of the wholly illiterate, who formed the majority of the Byzantine, as of any medieval, society. Within this graduated scale urban dwellers scored higher than countrymen, males much higher than females, the vast majority of whom were totally illiterate. The number of those persons in the top section of the scale was always very small, and probably at its smallest in the seventh to ninth centuries. It was largely confined to Constantinople, and in the later Byzantine period also to Thessaloniki, though in most cities the bishop and his immediate entourage would form a nucleus of high-grade literacy and a source of patronage for ambitious and talented youths. Numbers in the lower sections of the scale were until the fourteenth or fifteenth century higher than in most Western societies, and more widely spread. The concept of a scale of literacy explains the adaptations into more popular language of some classicizing literacy texts, such as the histories of Anna Komnena and Niketas Choniates. It also provides the background against which the rise of literature in vernacular Greek from the thirteenth century can be most readily understood. Literacy served as a vehicle of social mobility. For some it opened avenues to power and wealth. But little stigma attached to illiteracy, though it was a bar to certain careers.

In medieval terms highly literate, the Byzantines were not pedantic. Bookmen might fuss about orthography; yet the grossest misspellings were tolerated on the seals of high officials and on the numerous inscriptions in churches, an indication that many members of a congregation probably could not read. Surprisingly, many signatories of documents could not spell their own names.

Literacy, even of the most elementary kind, was always acquired through the study of texts in literary Greek, usually Homer or the psalms. Teaching in or from the vernacular tongue was unknown. This conservative tradition must have limited the scope of literacy.

Literacy in other languages. While Greek was the majority language and the language of state and church, many Byzantines, especially before the Arab conquests of the seventh century, spoke another language as their mother tongue. Some of these languages, such as Syriac, Coptic, Latin, Armenian, Georgian, and Old Slavonic, were themselves vehicles of literature. The Syriac community, whether or not it formed part of the Byzantine state, had a high level of literacy. Many Byzantine Armenians were literate in Armenian. On Mount Athos and elsewhere there were monasteries in which the liturgy and the life of the community were conducted in a language other than Greek. The Jewish community in the Byzantine Empire was literate in Hebrew and occasionally wrote vernacular Greek in Hebrew characters. Literacy in more than one language was not rare, and there were occasional men of letters who wrote in more than one language.

BIBLIOGRAPHY

Robert Browning, "Literacy in the Byzantine World," in *Byzantine and Modern Greek Studies,* **4** (1978); Paul E. Lemerle, *Le premier humanisme byzantin* (1971); Ann Moffatt, "Schooling in the Iconoclast Centuries," in Anthony Bryer and Judith Herrin, eds., *Iconoclasm* (1977); Évelyne Patlagean, "Discours écrit, discours parlé: Niveaux de culture à Byzance aux VIIIe–XIe siècles," in *Annales: Économies, Sociétés, Civilisations,* **34** (1979), 264–278; N. G. Wilson, "Books and Readers in Byzantium," in *Byzantine Books and Bookmen* (1975).

ROBERT BROWNING

[See also **Anna Komnena; Athos, Mount; Byzantine Church; Byzantine Empire: History; Byzantine Literature; Clergy, Byzantine; Colophon; Constantinople; Cyril and Methodios, Sts.; Family, Byzantine; Greek Language, Byzantine; Historiography, Byzantine; Kekaumenos; Law, Byzantine; Law, Canon: Byzantine; Niketas Choniates; Rhetoric: Byzantine; Universities, Byzantine.**]

LITERACY, WESTERN EUROPEAN. The origins of medieval literacy are to be found in Roman antiquity. The Romans provided the letter forms, the scripts, the modes of book production, the techniques of education, and the language that medieval men used to give graphic representation to their thoughts. Yet, while the Middle Ages owed much to the Roman literate world, the era was nevertheless different in many significant aspects. In Rome in the late Republic and Empire, literacy, the ability to read with comprehension and to write, was widely diffused within the confines of the upper classes. The election slogans scrawled on the walls of Pompeii and the vignettes of daily life in the comedies of Plautus and Terence suggest a society where considerable numbers could read and write. Roman schools produced grammatical texts that made Latin literature available to those of moderate intellectual abilities who had the leisure to attend public grammar schools. A major impetus to the spread of literacy among Roman patricians was the use of the alphabet borrowed from the Greeks. In contrast to Egypt, Mesopotamia, and China, where writing was dependent on thousands of pictographs, Roman writing was phonetic and based on the mastery of twenty-one phonemes. This distinction undoubtedly increased the percentage of the population who had the necessary skills for reading and to a lesser extent those for writing. Roman grammarians taught their pupils to read by starting with the letters of the alphabet, proceeding to syllables and the construction of words, and finally to sentences. With only minor exceptions, Roman writing until the fall of the empire continued to be an accurate representation of the sounds of spoken Latin.

The close bond between spoken and written language profoundly influenced the character of literacy in the Roman world. Reading was customarily an oral exercise and frequently a group activity. Men of letters read their own works to their friends in seances in private homes. In Roman libraries readers read aloud, and even in private study the educated Roman was encouraged to murmur as an aid to memory. The Roman manner of writing on scrolls, without word separation, punctuation, and distinction between upper- and lower-case letters, both reflected and encouraged the oral character of literacy. Roman composition was also an oral activity; the author murmured to himself as he wrote or, more commonly, dictated his works to a recording scribe. Even book publishing was done orally with a dictator reading the exemplar to a group of scribes gathered in a scriptorium.

Christianity originated among Jews with their own literary traditions. The Roman Christians, however, with the exception of their preference for parchment over papyrus and their use of certain abbreviations modeled on those employed in Hebrew, owed relatively little to their Jewish antecedents. The Western Fathers spoke and wrote Latin and, on the whole, practiced the reading and study habits of the pagans, consummating a marriage between the church and *latinitas* that was to mold the culture of the medieval West. However, the interest of Christians both in proselytization and in Scripture, even in Roman times, gave a peculiar orientation to Christian literacy as opposed to that of other Romans. While the codex (collected and bound leaves of manuscript) was apparently a pagan novelty and not a Christian invention, the Christians adopted it widely at an earlier date than did contemporary pagan society. The codex allowed early Christians, who were often persecuted, to have portable copies of the Gospels, and the format provided the possibility of numbered leaves, establishing convenient points of access. Christians, also taking the Gospels as a model, popularized the division of books into chapters and adopted the principle of writing Scripture in lines of sense, *per cola et commata,* a method of punctuation that facilitated reading for those who read poorly and aided any reader seeking a particular place in the biblical text.

The fall of Rome and the closing of grammar schools in Italy and southern France in the sixth century left Latin letters solely in the hands of Christians. In certain respects little changed. The old Roman aristocracy who filled the high offices of the church continued to use Roman methods of education in the privacy of their own homes to instruct their children in literature. Cassiodorus at Vivarium and Pope Gregory the Great were scions of the patrician class, and their command of written language was equal to that of any literate Roman in the late empire. The Christian Fathers, to be sure, preferred the Bible as recast in metrical verse to Vergil, and Lactantius to Cicero, but until the beginning of the seventh century they shared a common ideal of style and eloquence that their Roman forebears would not have found offensive. The succeeding waves of barbarian invasions in conjunction with the decline of secular education inevitably altered the relationship between the custodians of Latin letters and the unlettered people by whom they were surrounded. By the beginnning of the seventh century, the Roman literary tradition was becoming encapsulated within the class of monks and priests as lay literacy first declined and then, at least north of the Alps, entirely disappeared. In Roman times, Latin literacy had been the province of an elite comprised of many professions who had shared a common language with an illiterate majority. When an educated Roman read aloud, illiterate members of the lower classes understood his words even if they could not appreciate the art with which he turned phrases and constructed sentences. In the eighth century in northern Europe and even in Italy, the language of the church was quite clearly a language apart from that of the common people. Ironically, the church, which had adopted Latin to spread the Gospels because it was the vulgate of the empire, now found that the same language was unintelligible to the laity who attended Mass. Latin literacy thus became a part of the mystery of the church that set priests and monks apart from other men and enhanced the perception of clerics as possessors of divine powers. The terms *laicus* and *illitteratus* became synonymous in a world in which priests and monks alone were presumed to be literate.

The bilingual culture of the Middle Ages was central to the new reading and study habits that came to characterize medieval society. In the medieval cloister, pedagogical techniques began to change in response to the growing gap between Latin, the language of literacy, and the vernacular. In Ireland and

England, to compensate for the fact that Latin was not the native tongue, scribes introduced word separation to aid the reader. To substitute for the lack of naturally learned Latin, clerical authors composed artificial dialogues as a means of instilling correct grammar and building vocabulary. The medieval student needed word lists to aid in the artificial learning of unfamiliar terms. To meet this need, the Latin glossary, a new genre of book, emerged. The earliest of these works were systematically classified by subject or arranged by first-letter alphabetical order. As word separation and the idea of the word as a visible unit were more widely accepted, rigorous alphabetical forms of organizing glossaries evolved. In 1053, Papias completed the *Elementarium doctrinae erudimentum*, a dictionary arranged alphabetically through the fourth letter of individual words, and in 1272 Guillelmus Brito composed a fully alphabetized dictionary with over 2,500 entries, known as *Summa* or *Expositiones difficiliorum verborum de Biblia*. By the end of the Middle Ages, these dictionaries became the companions to the grammar texts inherited from antiquity as the basic books for primary education.

The demise of Latin as the vernacular tongue was a contributing factor as well in the declining use of writing as a tool of government administration and commerce. In Rome, written documents had been used extensively to conduct affairs of state and commerce, and Roman scribes had evolved a cursive script especially for this purpose. The new barbarian peoples forsook pen, papyrus, and parchment and relied on custom and vernacular oral tradition to conduct their affairs. Whereas in the Roman Empire the corpus of administrative documents written in cursive far exceeded the number of books in libraries, the reverse was true in Europe from the sixth to the tenth centuries. At no period in Western history was the book more exclusively the mode of written communication than in the High Middle Ages. In the monasteries of Monte Cassino, St. Gall, Corbie, Tours, and St. Denis, only the most important transactions were recorded in writing in the form of parchment charters. The writing of casual memoranda on slips and in notebooks, which had existed in antiquity, disappeared, and the cursive script employed for them evolved into the cumbersome and difficult-to-read book scripts. These scripts were in turn replaced in the ninth century by the Caroline *textualis* (or Caroline minuscule), modeled on the half-uncial book script of Roman antiquity. From the sixth century to the twelfth century, marginal notes in codices were usually written in the same formal script as the text. The virtual nonexistence of an informal mode of writing reflected a monastic world that placed greater emphasis on the copying of already extant works than on the composition of new ones. Throughout the early medieval period, to copy a book was an act of devotion, and as a consequence the choice of texts copied became increasingly restricted. Thus, many classical works were lost or survived in only a single early medieval codex, while thousands of Bibles and patristic texts were produced. Medieval monks, in contrast to the ancient Romans, developed a highly intensive pattern of reading. The elite early medieval literate class, consisting of less than 2 percent of the general population, copied and read the same works over and over again and learned many of these aurally by heart. When monks composed new texts, they were able to construct them by memory out of strings of phrases borrowed from the Bible and church fathers. Apart from the use of vocabularies, reference reading had little place in the literacy of the early medieval world.

Consciously, the tiny literate class of the early Middle Ages was primarily concerned with the conservation of Christian texts, and innovations in the presentation of the written text went unmentioned by contemporary scribes. Of these, the introduction of word separation was the most significant. This practice, which began in Insular texts of the seventh century, did not achieve general acceptance across Europe until the second half of the eleventh century. Although it may not have been the intent of those who introduced it, word separation allowed for swift silent reading. The Romans had read syllabically to sound out words. The placing of spaces between words permitted each word to become a unique visible image immediately recognizable by the brain; the initial result was that the reader no longer had to mumble as he read. Exemplars written in blocks of letters or with full word separation permitted the scribe to retain an image of a given fragment of text and, therefore, to copy it silently. Christians in Roman times had professed the ideal of silent monastic labor, but they had not applied it to reading and writing. In the ninth century, the first regulations requiring silence in the monastic scriptorium appeared, and in the twelfth century, the silent work of monastic scribes was explicitly described. Word separation also had its impact on pedagogy, for the old method of reading from the letter to the syllable to the word was supplemented by one in which the pupil recognized words as *distinctiones* of letters. The uniform acceptance of word separation in manuscripts throughout Europe in the twelfth century indicated an increased rate of reading and nurtured the fermentation of ideas that was to explode in the scholastic age.

In the second half of the twelfth century, the most profound paleographic change of the medieval period took place: the introduction of Gothic textual and cursive scripts. These modifications in writing were closely related to the greatly increased production of books and documents. Gothic textual script, because of its angularity and use of abbreviations, was swifter to write than Caroline script. Gothic cursive, which emerged in England at the end of the twelfth century and on the Continent in the thirteenth century, enhanced productivity even further by permitting the scribe to write flowingly without lifting pen from parchment.

By mid thirteenth century, Gothic cursive was serving a function analogous to that of the cursive writing of antiquity; notaries used it for public and private documents, and authors used it for annotating existing books or for drafting new ones. The evolution of Gothic scripts reflected a world in which a new emphasis was placed on original literary compositions, because university instruction and increasingly complex affairs of state and commerce required written documentation. The shift in manuscript production from monasteries and cathedral schools to universities was indicative of an expanded literacy. The student population of universities, estimated to have numbered in the thousands, was far greater than had existed at the monasteries and cathedral schools. Universities of such size were needed to train the clerics employed in growing numbers both by the church and by the emerging monarchies.

It is difficult to estimate the percentage of increase of Latin literacy in the thirteenth, fourteenth, and fifteenth centuries. There can be no doubt that written documents touched the lives of many; by the end of the thirteenth century even some English peasants possessed documents to vouch for the tenure of their land. The emergence of mercantile archives and books confirms that some merchants, particularly in Italy, could read. In fourteenth-century Italy, grammar schools were supported by communal governments, and in northern Europe in the fourteenth and fifteenth centuries, the sons of merchants began to attend the parish grammar schools that had been first

established in the sixth century to recruit clerics. Beyond the bold assertion that literacy increased quantitatively, one can only repeat the observations of close contemporaries such as Ludovico Guicciardini, who in the mid sixteenth century supposed that over half of the merchants in the Netherlands were literate, and Sir Thomas More, who in 1520 observed that 60 percent of Englishmen could read. These estimates are very late, and they also include vernacular literacy, making them even more problematical.

If it is difficult to discuss with precision the quantity of Latin literacy in Western Europe, much can be said about the evolving quality of literacy. University-trained scholars read far more extensively than had the monks and clerics before 1200. The new additions to medieval books were far more complex in structure and content than were earlier works. No longer was it possible to retain through aural memorization a single common literary corpus. Newly prepared manuscripts of the Bible and patristic authors and newly authored works were divided into chapters and subdivided into *distinctiones* to encourage reference consultation. Alphabetical and analytical tables facilitated access to lengthy works for readers in search of information on a specific subject, but who, because of the phenomenal growth in knowledge, could no longer read all pertinent works in their entirety. In the classroom, students were required to bring the text from which the professor lectured in order to follow visually the subtleties of his arguments, which had become too complex and numerous to be understood only aurally. The new uses to which the book was put, in turn, engendered new techniques of book production, such as the *pecia* system, in which authenticated unbound copies were circulated in quires, thereby allowing for the production of greater numbers of more standardized texts. Libraries also changed by establishing chained reference collections allowing readers permanent access to the most frequently cited works. In these new libraries, where scholars now came to read and study, silence was mandatory. A new genre of reference book, the classified library catalog with alphabetical author indices, made readily available a vast amount of written information.

The principles of reference organization of books that evolved in the milieu of the university were applied by university-trained clerics to the organization of documents. In the twelfth, thirteenth, and fourteenth centuries in the papal chancellery and in the chancelleries of France and England, clerics began to construct alphabetical indices for the registers containing the various statutes, mandates, and official communications. The well-organized archives of the end of the Middle Ages facilitated the transactions of affairs of state and aided chroniclers and other men of letters to cite specific historical documents or even to refer to them as being written on specific folios in specific registers. At the universities and in administration, the structured format for organizing information reduced redundancy and fostered precise expression of thought.

In the late Middle Ages, the corpus of written Latin literature expanded greatly, although the continuation of Latin as the primary written language still limited the growth of a literate public. Given the inadequate institutions for elementary education, Latin was simply too difficult for most laymen to master. The more frequent appearance of the signatures of noblemen on charters merely signified a basic mastery of the alphabet and should not be mistaken for an ability to read with comprehension. Certainly, many noblemen could sound out the Psalter phonetically, but it is dubious if any but a handful could comprehend Latin treatises such as Egidius Colonna's *De regimine principum,* dedicated to the young Philip the Fair. Significantly, no copy of this or similar texts survives with reading notes attributable to the hand of a king or great prince.

At the end of the Middle Ages, the need for a simpler language suitable for laymen was met by the vernacular, and particularly French, the international language of the lay aristocracy. In the early thirteenth century, the Italian Brunetto Latini chose French to compose his *Trésor,* the first vernacular encyclopedia. German and Flemish noblemen in the fourteenth and fifteenth centuries regularly read in French, and in England, until the time of Edward IV, French remained the principal language of letters for the royal court. In contrast to Latin, French could be learned not only from books but by sending children to France to serve in noble households, where the language could be acquired easily. In the thirteenth century, written French was still a phonetic transcription of speech without standard orthography. The limited vernacular literature was intended for the ear and not the eye, and French romances and poetry were often oral compositions set down on parchment and intended to be read aloud. In mid fourteenth century, university scholars began to devise canons for a standard orthography for French. Unlike Latin, written French could not be read from

the letter to the syllable to the word without a prior knowledge of silent and aspirate letters and syllables. Modern studies of the psychology of reading indicate that these silent letters, while making pronunciation problematical, assisted the silent reader, who found unpronounced letters helpful in speedy visual recognition of words.

In the second half of the fourteenth century, the practice of reading French texts silently spread. Charles V established the first royal library in the Louvre with furnishings and arrangements of books modeled on those of contemporary university libraries. The king also sponsored the translation of numerous Latin treatises for reference consultation. Nicole Oresme prepared glossed French versions of Aristotle's *Ethics* and *Politics* accompanied by carefully designed alphabetical tables of contents. The custom of having substantial French libraries numbering hundreds of volumes spread to the courts of the Low Countries, Brittany, Provence, and England. As lay aristocratic readership grew in the fifteenth century, the script used for copying French texts changed from Gothic textualis to batarde, a new hybrid script that laymen with university training found easier to read. While French remained the premier vernacular language of Western Europe until 1500, other vernacular tongues, notably Italian, English, and Dutch, experienced a similar evolution toward more standardized orthography and more legible scripts.

With the acceptance of the vernacular for the written word, the remaining barrier to widespread literacy in Western Europe was the scarcity of books. Despite the increasing number of used books inherited by each generation, the institution of the *pecia* system in the thirteenth century, and the wide use of cursive script and paper as a substitute for parchment in the fifteenth century, manuscript books continued to be expensive items scarcely affordable by small grammar schools and members of the mercantile and artisan classes. The great cost in book production was that of labor, for it took a skilled scribe two and a half months to copy a codex of 200 leaves. The invention of the printing press radically reduced within three generations the labor required to produce a single volume, thereby making truly inexpensive texts possible. The aggregate corpus of books in Western Europe expanded at a rate far greater than the increase in population. The pervasive presence of the printed word marked the end of the constraints of medieval literacy and ushered in a new age in which reading matter was readily available at every level of education.

BIBLIOGRAPHY

Carlo M. Cipolla, *Literacy and Development in the West* (1969); M. T. Clanchy, *From Memory to Written Record: England, 1066–1307* (1979); Lloyd W. Daly, *Contributions to a History of Alphabetization in Antiquity and the Middle Ages* (1967); Nicolas Orme, *English Schools in the Middle Ages* (1973); Malcolm B. Parkes, "The Influence of the Concepts of *Ordinatio* and *Compilatio* on the Development of the Book," in *Medieval Learning and Literature: Essays Presented to Richard W. Hunt* (1976), and "The Literacy of the Laity," in David Daiches and Anthony Thorlby, *Literature and Western Civilization,* II (1974), 555–577; Pierre Riché, *Les écoles et l'enseignement dans l'Occident chrétien de la fin du Ve siècle au milieu du XIe siècle* [*Écoles et enseignement dans le haut moyen âge*] (1979); Richard H. Rouse and Mary A. Rouse, *Preachers, Florilegia, and Sermons: Studies on the Manipulus florum of Thomas of Ireland* (1979); Paul Saenger, "Silent Reading: Its Impact on Later Medieval Script and Society," in *Viator,* 13 (1982).

PAUL SAENGER

[See also **Alphabetization, History of; Cassiodorus, Senator; Grammar; Latin Language, Libraries; Manuscripts and Books; Oresme, Nicole; Paleography; Schools; Scriptorium.**]

LITERATURE. See national literatures and individual entries.

LITHUANIA. The name Lithuania has acquired two meanings. In a narrow sense, it refers to the land along the southeastern shores of the Baltic Sea inhabited by ethnic Lithuanians. In a wider sense, it denotes a historical political entity that encompassed not only modern Lithuania but most of today's Belorussia as well.

A land with few natural resources, no metals, sulphur, or coal, Lithuania lay far away from the centers of European civilization. While such a location delayed Lithuania's inclusion in the European cultural world by several centuries, it also allowed the Lithuanians to maintain their independence and distinctiveness. Their state was the last pagan political entity in Europe.

THE BALTS

Ethnic Lithuanians are an Indo-European people whose language belongs to the Baltic group. The only other living language in this group is Latvian. Old Prussian became extinct around 1700; Curonian, Semigallian, and Selian disappeared between 1400 and 1600.

On the basis of archaeological evidence and hydronymy, it is evident that at the beginning of the first millennium A.D., Baltic tribes inhabited a large area stretching from the Pripet Marshes to the Northern Dvina River, between the Baltic Sea and the Oka River. By 500, the Eastern Balts, inhabiting the area of the Oka, the upper Volga, the Northern Dvina, and the Dnieper rivers, were pushed out by expanding East Slavs. During the seventh and eighth centuries, the Middle Balts were likewise pushed out of their homes in what today is Belorussia.

The earliest known references to the Balts mention the westernmost tribes, the Old Prussians, who lived in the area later designated East Prussia. In his *De Germania* (A.D. 98), Tacitus refers to *Aestii (gentes aestiorum),* a people who collect amber and who are more energetic cultivators of crops and fruits than the Germanic people whom they resemble in appearance and customs. It is unclear whether he is concerned with all Balts, the Old Prussians, or merely the amber-collecting Old Prussians settled along the Baltic coast. The *Aestii* reappear in the writings of Jordanes (*ca.* 550), the letters of Cassiodorus (sixth century), Einhard's *Vita Caroli Magni* (*ca.* 830–833), and the writings of King Alfred's voyager Wulfstan (*ca.* 880–890). Archbishop Adam of Bremen provides a graphic description (*ca.* 1075):

> The Sembi or Prussians are a most humane people. They go out to help those who are in peril at sea or who are attacked by pirates. Gold and silver they hold in very slight esteem.... Many praiseworthy things could be said about these peoples with respect to their morals, if only they had the faith of Christ, whose missionaries they cruelly persecute. At their hands Adalbert, the illustrious bishop of the Bohemians, was crowned with martyrdom. Although they share everything else with our people, they prohibit only, to this very day indeed, access to their groves and springs, which, they aver, are polluted by the entry of Christians. They take the meat of their draught animals for food and use their milk and blood as drink so freely that they are said to become intoxicated. These men are blue of color [meaning either blue-eyed or tattooed blue], ruddy of face, and long-haired. Living, moreover, in inaccessible swamps, they will not endure a master among them.

Although the composite picture obtained from such descriptions is one of Old Prussian society, it is logical to assume that their less accessible kinsmen,

LITHUANIA IN THE
FIFTEENTH CENTURY

- - - Boundary of Lithuania
      1377–1434
✸ Battles
≈ Marshes

0 _____ 400 Miles
0 _____ 400 Kilometers

the Lithuanians, did not differ greatly. Agriculture provided the mainstay of the economy. Sometime between the ninth and twelfth centuries, the earlier two-field system seems to have been replaced by a three-field system. In a number of settlements, other crop grains began to predominate over wheat and barley. During the tenth century, a currency began to supplement barter. Fingerlike silver bars with one flattened side weighing from 100 to 200 grams are characteristic finds in graves from the period. They continued in use until the fifteenth century.

THE ORIGINS OF THE LITHUANIAN STATE

Of the Baltic peoples, the Lithuanians were least affected by foreign incursions. Nevertheless, rudiments of political organization, doubtlessly stimulated by defense needs, began to appear during the second half of the first millennium. Fortified hills or castles are known from the period 500–800. Wulfstan mentions many "towns," each with its own "king." Almost all excavated earthworks dating

from the tenth to the thirteenth centuries show considerable enlargement. The largest and most powerful castles became military and administrative centers of tribal districts, and their "kings" tended to extend their rule over adjoining districts. Chronic petty warfare among the rulers made stable government practically impossible. The system could be maintained only as long as neighbors lived under similar systems.

The first extant mention of the name Lithuania occurs in the Annals of Quedlinberg in the account of the martyrdom of Bishop Bruno of Querfurt (1009), who had been sent by King Bolesław the Brave of Poland to convert the Prussians. Along with eighteen companions, he met his end "in confinio Rusciae et Lituae." The name Lithuania is in this instance rendered in its Slavic form, which suggests that it must have had currency among the Slavs at an earlier date.

Written evidence of the Lithuanian relationship with the East Slav world dates from the tenth cen-

603

tury. In 983, Great Prince Vladimir of Kiev claimed to have subjugated the Baltic Yotvingians (Iatviagi), a tribe occupying the southeastern portion of present-day Lithuania and the northeastern corner of modern Poland. It proved a temporary victory, as his successor Yaroslav the Wise was unable in 1038 to reimpose domination. The chronicle is silent about Yaroslav's 1040 campaign into Lithuania; most likely, it was not successful. A century later, during the winter of 1131–1132, Great Prince Mstislav attacked Lithuania but could do little more than ravage the land and take prisoners. His rearguard was destroyed.

The decline of Kiev was followed by Lithuanian incursions into the East Slav lands. At times, some Slav princes made alliances with Lithuanians in the petty civil wars that had become endemic in the Kiev realm. Polotsk, a populous and rich land, was the first target of Lithuanian expansion. By 1187, Lithuanians dominated the West Dvina River, the lifeline of the trading community, and threatened the city of Polotsk itself. Prince Iziaslav Vasilkovich, referred to in *The Lay of the Host of Igor,* perished in the struggle against them. By the end of the century, Lithuanian raids into Novgorod and Pskov were also noted. These wide-ranging raids into the decaying Kiev state laid the groundwork for subsequent Lithuanian expansion into the area.

During the late twelfth century, German expansion posed a new threat from the west for the Baltic peoples. The Semigallians and the Latvians were its first victims. In 1186, a German outpost was established at the mouth of the Daugava (Western Dvina) River. In 1201 the city of Riga was founded, and the following year the Order of Sword-Bearing (Livonian) Knights was established. Slowly, their control was extended over present-day Latvia and Estonia. The German expansion from Livonia soon affected the Lithuanians as well. They managed to offer effective resistance, however.

A more serious threat to the Lithuanians came with the appearance in 1233 of the Teutonic Knights in East Prussia. This military order, founded in 1190 in Palestine to fight the Saracens, was invited by Conrad of Mazovia to subjugate his neighbors, the pagan Prussians. The task took over a half century. But even before it had been completed, the knights began to threaten Lithuania as well.

Raiding activity coupled with the appearance of the German threat laid the groundwork for the emergence of a Lithuanian political entity. During the period from 1201 to 1236, at least forty Lithu-

anian raiding expeditions are known (twenty-two on Germans in Latvia, fourteen into East Slav lands, and four into Poland). The scope of the ventures implies that these must have been more than actions by one or more local lords. Known agreements seem to indicate rudiments of a political organization during the first quarter of the thirteenth century. In 1219, for instance, a group of twenty-one Lithuanian princes tendered a peace offer to Galicia-Volhynia. The account in the Chronicle of Galicia-Volhynia (1201–1292) of the signing seems to denote a strict hierarchical structure among the Lithuanian chieftains, though it remains unclear exactly how close the confederation was. Strong elements of hierarchical military organization are also attested to in the funerals of leaders and their retinues.

The tribal confederation of Lithuanians appears to have been led by a group of senior rulers (*kunigai*), and political power at this stage seems to have been concentrated in the hands of a few interrelated families. By the late 1230's, two principal centers of power are known. One was in Samogitia, the western part of Lithuania, where the standing of Prince Vykintas had been enhanced by the crushing defeat which he inflicted on the Livonian Order at Šiauliai (Saule) in 1236. One in ten knights returned from that campaign, and the Livonian Order, in order to survive, subordinated itself in 1237 to the Teutonic Order of East Prussia. The second was in the Kernavė area, not far from Vilnius, where, from 1238, Mindaugas (Mindovg) emerged as undisputed ruler. The formation of the Lithuanian state is closely connected with his rise.

Although it is unclear how Vykintas lost out, there is no doubt that Mindaugas' road to power was tortuous and bloody. In 1249–1250, he was faced with a formidable coalition, including the Livonian Order, the Yotvingians, Galicia, and southern Samogitia. His success in extricating himself from this predicament attests to his capability as a politician. He split the alliance ranged against him by promising the Livonian Knights a district, Samogitia, which he did not control and which the knights were in no position to take. Furthermore, he underwent a formal conversion to Latin Christianity. Pope Innocent IV sanctioned his coronation during the summer of 1253. A year later, the coalition fell apart. In 1260, on the occasion of a massive incursion by the Teutonic Knights into Samogitia, Mindaugas apostatized. The core element of the Lithuanian state, which he had in a sense founded, remained pagan for over another century.

The incursion of the Mongols into Eastern Europe (1237–1240) radically altered the political configuration of the area and offered opportunities for eastward Lithuanian expansion. Control over the East Slav trading principalities added to the resources of Lithuanian rulers struggling against the Teutonic Knights. Although Lithuania itself suffered one Mongol raid (1258–1259), it remained an independent center of power attractive to the neighboring East Slav principalities for its ability to offer protection against Tatar raids. The process of absorption of such principalities into the Lithuanian state was apparently a peaceful one. There are no records of great campaigns. While Lithuanian princes became rulers of such principalities, local customs and laws retained force. Frequently, the Lithuanian overlords themselves became Orthodox Christians and were slavicized. Some Lithuanians of prominent backgrounds even figured in East Slav areas that never came under Lithuanian control. Vaišvilkas, the third son of Mindaugas, for instance, became an Orthodox monk. Later, as elected prince of Pskov, he led two attacks (1266 and 1267) against his former country.

The expansion of Lithuania into the East Slav world altered the character of the Lithuanian state. In addition to its pagan Lithuanian core area, the entity also included East Slav principalities with a different tradition of political and cultural existence. The East Slav lands provided military resources to the state. Their trading cities formed part of a longstanding mercantile network. They possessed organized administrations with defined obligations and ranks that were adopted by the Lithuanian princes in the core area. Their written language, Chancery Slavic, became the language of state administration.

It can be surmised that continuing bloody internal politics which attended the emergence of Mindaugas likewise accompanied his demise. For reasons that remain unclear, a coalition of opponents murdered him in 1263 together with two of his sons. Civil war and a period of uncertainty followed, and it is difficult to ascertain from extant sources who ruled what when. The Samogitian leader Treniota, who had figured in the anti-Mindaugas coalition, was himself killed by followers of the slain ruler. The name Traidenis is associated with a particularly heavy defeat inflicted on the Teutonic Knights in 1279. His death in 1281 or 1282 coincided with an intensification of the German push after the completion of the conquest of Prussia in 1283. Samogitia, forming a land bridge between Livonia and Prussia,

was particularly threatened. Between 1300 and 1315, some twenty campaigns by the knights into Lithuania are known. The renewed German push may have contributed to a political settlement within Lithuania. After 1295/1296 Vytenis emerged as supreme ruler and managed to introduce a lasting concentration of power. The other pretending families were no longer able to provide alternate candidates, and he maintained his position until his death in 1315.

THE APOGEE OF THE PAGAN STATE

The brother and successor of Vytenis, Gediminas (Gedimin, Gedymin) (1315–1341), made Lithuania into a regional power. As had been the case with his predecessors, his rule proved one of almost constant warfare with the Teutonic Knights. His immediate predecessor had already successfully utilized differences between the knights and the city of Riga, which had an interest in the pursuit of trade with Lithuanian-controlled areas. Gediminas pursued this policy further. His alliance with Riga was used to channel letters, six of which have survived, to Pope John XXII and other Western European leaders. These formed an attempt to break the papal interdict on trade by Christians with Lithuania, especially in iron, arms, salt, and horses. They provide a glimpse into the political mood then prevalent at the Lithuanian court. An element of tolerance and pragmatism emerges. Gediminas pointed out that the knights' policy of destruction was preventing the baptism of Lithuania. He invited foreign craftsmen to settle in the country and offered them his protection, pointing to the foreigners, including Christian clergymen, already active in Lithuania. The hopes for Gediminas' imminent baptism into the Latin Christian fold proved deceptive. Most likely, Gediminas realized that his gains from such a move would be limited because the efforts of the Teutonic Knights to impose their control would not end. His alternate attempt to form closer ties with the Western world by marrying his daughter Aldona to Casimir, son of the Polish king Władysław Lokietka, also proved abortive.

During the reign of Gediminas, the pattern of Lithuanian competition with Muscovy for the widest possible political influence in the East Slav world emerged. Novgorod, Pskov, and Tver were not part of the Lithuanian realm. Nevertheless, they began to use Lithuanian support against the inroads of Ivan Kalita of Muscovy. The attempt by Gediminas to establish a separate Orthodox metropolitanate for

Lithuania underscores his policy of seeking to separate East Slav lands under Lithuanian rule from the jurisdiction of a hostile church leadership in Moscow. The effort proved abortive, since the Lithuanian see existed only until 1330.

Gediminas died in the winter of 1341–1342. His realm was divided among seven sons. The youngest, Jaunutis (Iavnut), received Vilnius and the title of Great Prince. His reign, however, proved ephemeral. Sometime during the winter of 1344–1345 he was deposed by two of his older brothers, Algirdas (Olgerd) and Kęstutis (Keistut, Kenstut), who effectively divided the realm between themselves. As the older of the two, Algirdas assumed the title of Great Prince. He received Vilnius and the Orthodox portions of the state and concentrated on eastern affairs. Algirdas emerged as one of the greatest politicians of medieval Eastern Europe. His reign was marked by a spectacular Lithuanian expansion in the east. Smolensk was annexed in 1356, Bryansk around 1358, and Kiev around 1362. The victory against the Tatars at Blue Waters (Sinie Vody) in 1363 extended Lithuania to the Black Sea.

The rivalry with Moscow continued. Algirdas' wife was a sister of the Great Prince of Tver, another rival of Moscow, who in 1368 fled to Lithuania after a Muscovite attack. Algirdas besieged Moscow twice, in 1368 and 1370. Two years later, however, both sides avoided a battle that could have proved decisive. Like his father, Algirdas attempted to secure a separate Orthodox church administration for Lithuania and succeeded, but only temporarily, in establishing a separate metropolitan for his realm.

Establishing his capital at Trakai (Troki) near Vilnius, Kęstutis assumed leadership of the pagan core area of Lithuania and spent his reign struggling against the increasingly severe incursions by the Teutonic Knights. The new threat began in 1337 when Emperor Louis IV (d. 1347) "granted" Lithuania to the order. In 1343, the order signed a peace with Poland; Livonia settled its differences with Denmark. All efforts could be concentrated on Lithuania. During the period from 1345 to 1382, ninety-six campaigns are known to have been launched. The brunt of the attacks fell on Samogitia and the fortresses along the Nemunas (Niemen) River. In 1362 the key fortress at Kaunas, defended by Kęstutis' son Vaidotas, fell after most of the garrison had been wiped out by hunger. The knights' attacks began to penetrate the region of the twin capitals of Trakai and Vilnius. Their intensity increased mark-

edly during the 1370's as the order, realizing its inability to subjugate Lithuania in a single campaign, adopted a policy of laying waste the land and also making arrangements with malcontent Lithuanian princes. Lithuanians also counterattacked in the knights' territory. Kęstutis besieged Riga in 1345. In 1370 Königsberg was attacked from two sides.

THE ACCEPTANCE OF LATIN CHRISTIANITY

After his death in 1377, Algirdas was succeeded by his eldest son, Jogaila (Iagailo, Jagieło). Policy differences between the young man and his uncle led to internal strife which rendered the diarchy unworkable. Kęstutis, the last representative of pagan Lithuania, sought to continue the two-front struggle, resistance against the Knights and expansion in Russia. Jogaila favored concessions to the knights in order to gain a free hand in Russia. Moscow's position was strengthened after its victory against the Tatars at Kulikovo (1380). Kęstutis moved to unseat Jogaila in 1380. Two years later he was in turn dethroned by his nephew, and murdered. Vytautas (Vitovt, Witold), the eldest son of Kęstutis and his heir, was imprisoned. One of Jogaila's younger brothers, Skirgaila (Skirgaillo, Skirgieło), was installed as Jogaila's formal co-ruler.

Having secured power, Jogaila proceeded to implement his policy. Concluding a truce with the order, Jogaila ceded part of Samogitia and agreed to become a Christian. He suffered a setback when his cousin Vytautas, dressed as a servant girl, escaped imprisonment and made his way to the knights. Using him as a convenient tool, they broke the truce with Jogaila and installed Vytautas as their vassal. The succeeding campaign inflicted heavy losses on Lithuania. Vytautas deserted the order, made peace with Jogaila, and was installed in his patrimony.

Jogaila now began to seek outside allies. He considered accepting Orthodox Christianity and an alliance with Moscow. Sofia, the daughter of Prince Dimitrii Donskoi, was offered to him in marriage. But such an arrangement would have had little effect on his main problem, the knights, and he refused the Muscovite insistence that he become a "younger brother," that is, vassal, of Dimitrii. Instead, Jogaila pursued the possibility of an alliance with Poland. The outcome was a grand Polish embassy at Krėva (Krewo), where an agreement for a close relationship was concluded in August 1385. Jogaila would marry Jadwiga, heiress of Poland, and become king of that state. Together with his relatives, he agreed to accept Latin Christianity and to baptize all of pagan Lithuania. Other clauses in the agreement covered freeing all Polish captives in Lithuania, a common struggle to regain lands lost by both sides to others, and compensation to Wilhelm von Habsburg, to whom Jadwiga had been promised. The new Polish-Lithuanian relationship was defined in the agreement by the laconic term *applicare,* which has received a variety of definitions and interpretations. In practice it is evident that Lithuania continued to exist as a separate state in which the Poles were considered allies though foreigners.

The formal acceptance by Lithuania of Latin Christianity took place in 1387, a year after Jogaila's assumption of the Polish throne as Władysław, his Christian baptismal name. The Latin church was introduced into Lithuania through the establishment at Vilnius of a diocese which, through extensive grants from the Great Prince, became one of the largest landholders of the realm. The cultural latinization of the state that followed the baptism had the effect of making the Orthodox population of the state second-class citizens, which gave Moscow an added advantage in its struggle with Lithuania. The acceptance of Latin Christianity by the Lithuanians, however, deprived the Teutonic Knights of moral justifications for crusades. The order was forced to seek other pretexts for intervention. Such pretexts were not hard to come by. Vytautas, dissatisfied with his fate, went over to them for a second time after an unsuccessful attempt at seizing Vilnius. The campaign that followed demonstrated that Jogaila could not be king of Poland and, at the same time, maintain control over Lithuania. By 1392, the greater part of the realm was in the hands of Vytautas, though he was unable to win a decisive victory. He again broke with the order. A negotiated settlement with Jogaila gave him the title of Great Prince and de facto if not de jure independence.

THE REIGN OF VYTAUTAS THE GREAT

The long reign of Vytautas (1392–1430) was the pinnacle of Lithuanian power. The threat from the Teutonic Knights was eliminated, and the Lithuanian position in Russia maintained. Warfare with the order resumed soon after Vytautas' accession. Between 1392 and 1394, six attacks into Lithuania were launched, which penetrated deeper than any previous campaigns. The order's inability to subjugate Lithuania, however, led in 1398 to a compromise peace according to which Vytautas recognized its possession of Samogitia.

Settlement in the west allowed Vytautas to devote attention to the southeast. Here, however, his attempt to intervene in a civil war among the Tatars resulted in a major setback at the Battle of Vorskla (1399), during which three-fourths of his army perished. The defeat forced Vytautas formally to reiterate his vassalage to Jogaila. After his death, Lithuania passed to Jogaila and to the Polish crown. Lithuanian ties with Poland were subsequently again reaffirmed at Horodlo (1413). On this occasion, the principal points of the Kreva agreement were maintained. It was furthermore agreed that each partner would have veto power over the selection of the other partner's ruler. Offices in Lithuania and noble titulary were patterned after Polish models; forty-seven Lithuanian families adopted Polish coats-of-arms.

In 1409, an uprising in Samogitia against the order provided Vytautas with an opportunity for intervention. A conflict between the order and Poland had also simultaneously broken out. On 15 July 1410, the joint Polish-Lithuanian army inflicted a crushing defeat on the Teutonic Knights at Grunwald (Tannenberg) from which the order never fully recovered. The Peace of Toruń (Thorn) returned Samogitia to Lithuania and imposed an indemnity on the knights. Three years later, the region, which had by then undergone formal baptism, was organized into a diocese. Samogitia was ceded in perpetuity to Lithuania by the order according to the terms of the Peace of Melno (1422) following an uneventful war—the last beween Lithuania and the knights. The resulting border between Lithuania and Prussia remained unchanged until the twentieth century.

While the success of Vytautas in the west was phenomenal, his Russian policy remained inconclusive. Control over Smolensk was successfully reasserted in 1404, but an attempt to take Pskov foundered. As had been the case with his predecessors, his attempts to establish an Orthodox metropolitanate proved abortive. A modest success in Russia came during the last years of his life when in 1426 his daughter Sofia, widow of Vasilii I, came to Smolensk with her son Vasilii II to place themselves under Vytautas' protection.

Circumstances thwarted the formal recognition of Vytautas' position through a coronation. Holy

Roman Emperor Sigismund (*d.* 1437) had proposed such a step in 1429. Polish opposition, however, held up delivery of the royal regalia. Vytautas died uncrowned in 1430. Some years after his death, the Polish historian Długosz characterized Vytautas:

> To our day opinions among people are maintained that no contemporary prince could equal Witold in excellence of thought and diligence in affairs ... and it is a fact that the greatness of Lithuania originated under him and ended with his death.

A decade of civil war preceded a stabilization of political succession. After 1501, when Alexander of Lithuania was elected to the Polish throne, the Great Prince of Lithuania was always likewise king of Poland. A closer political union between the two states was achieved at Lublin in 1569, an arrangement that lasted until the partitions of the Polish-Lithuanian commonwealth at the end of the eighteenth century.

SOCIETY AND STATE ORGANIZATION

In the absence of primary sources on the structure of society, information has had to be gleaned from a variety of German, East Slav, and Polish chronicles, some letters of Lithuanian rulers, and customary practices included in the sixteenth-century codification of law.

It is clear that constant warfare shaped the character of medieval Lithuanian society. Forests and water provided natural obstacles that made Lithuania in effect impregnable during rainy times. Fortresses with standing garrisons were erected at strategic sites, particularly along the Nemunas (Neman) River. At the end of the thirteenth century, some twenty castles in Samogitia alone figured in German accounts. The fighting force was predominantly a militia composed of all able-bodied men of a particular district. As swords were expensive, spears were the principal weapons. The special role of cavalry is attested to in burials, written sources, and folklore.

The military burden affected all classes. It prevented the nobility from developing into an independent social class owing its position to the control of particular lands. The land and the peasants who worked it were under the control of the Great Prince. The practice of sending nobles to East Slav lands for temporary upkeep *(kormleniia)* enabled some among them to acquire wealth. Latifundia, however, were absent from the core area of Lithuania. Most nobles, prior to the fifteenth century, had few or no serfs. Up to the thirteenth century, most peasants were free and fulfilled obligations to the

state in the form of payment in kind or military service. Serfs fell into two categories: the *kaimynai,* or those who had been settled on noble lands as war captives; and the *veldamai,* who owed obligations for the use of particular lands, which they had rented as free individuals.

Lithuania had few cities. By the thirteenth century, some urban development appeared around castles. Only three, however, were of any significance: Vilnius, Trakai, and Kaunas. The principal commercial ties were with Riga; merchants from that city constantly operated in Vilnius. After the union with Poland, the trade routes with Lublin and Krakow acquired particular significance. Lithuania provided a cheap source of some goods demanded in Western Europe, particularly furs and wax, which came in large quantities as tribute to the Great Prince and were exported. The West sold in return arms, iron, salt, cloth, and various luxury items not produced locally.

During the fourteenth century, the state consisted of districts, each of which was based on a city and ruled by a governor responsible for administrative, judicial, and military affairs. The districts were divided into counties, each of which generally had a castle of the Great Prince serving as a seat of administration, and were headed by a *tijunas.* The first mention of these counties dates from 1389, when Jogaila ordered them to provide for priests of the parishes then being founded. Counties varied in size and their boundaries were not clearly defined. The local units centered around the *pristavy,* or collectors of tribute for the Great Prince. It should be remembered that Lithuania was a very heterogeneous state. The East Slav lands were largely ruled according to their customary forms. In the ethnic Lithuanian regions, the core area of Aukštaičiai was run by rather strong central control. Administration was considerably looser in Samogitia.

State organization was based on the concept that all lands were the patrimony of the Great Prince, who could divide his realm among his sons. Primogeniture was evidently not the principal criterion for succession of power. The exact nature of the ruler's power was not clearly defined. Mindaugas was referred to in the Hypatian chronicle as "autocrat" and in the Volhynian Chronicle as Great Prince. Gediminas called himself "King or Prince of the Lithuanians," "King of Lithuania and Russia," or "King of Lithuania and Russia and Ruler and Prince of the Samogitians." Although it would seem that as owner of the land, the Great Prince would be an autocrat, it is evident that in practice he would have had difficulty in making important decisions without the concurrence of important nobles. A system of consensus apparently was operative. The Chronicle of Peter Dusburg mentions a gathering of notables in 1306, though this could have been a one-time occasion. In 1324, twenty notables were present when Gediminas negotiated with papal envoys. A 1338 trade treaty with Livonia refers only to Gediminas' children as "kings"; all others are nobles. During the reign of Vytautas, the establishment of a noble council formally excluded autocracy as a form of government. The principle of election of the Great Prince, paralleling royal elections in Poland, appeared later during the fifteenth century.

RELIGION

Lithuania formally became Christian in 1387. The new creed, however, took a long time to permeate the villages, where the old religion lingered. The customs, mythology, and folk art symbolism of the Lithuanians, as well as of the Latvians, possess only a recent Christian stratum. Folklore provides considerable insight into basic elements of the natural animism forming the basis of Baltic religious beliefs. Accounts of several chroniclers provide some additional details, albeit for the most part about rites and practices unintelligible to foreigners. The Baltic pantheon consisted essentially of natural phenomena, the sky, the sun, the moon, the stars, and thunder. Anthropomorphic images of the gods represented by those elements were not strongly developed, with the exception of *Dievas* (the sky) and *Perkūnas* (Thunder). *Žemyna* (the earth) was the great life-giving force from which came humans, animals, and plants. All manifestations of the earth's fecundity were protected, especially particular groves and streams. Fire, sacred and eternal, was venerated. Sacred fires were tended and guarded by priests.

There was belief in an afterlife. While bodies were burned, souls or *vėlės* went to live on a sandy hill. Collective graves testify to obligatory death for surviving husband, wives, or children upon the death of a member of the family. It was evidently felt that all would live together in the hereafter. Western chroniclers expressed surprise at the readiness of Lithuanians to commit suicide in adverse circumstances. The most noteworthy incident occurred in 1336 during the siege of the castle at Pilėnai by the knights. When hope of successful resistance ended, the Lithuanians threw their possessions into a fire, killed their wives and children, and asked their chieftain Margiris to decapitate them. An old woman axed one hundred volunteers before splitting her own head as the invaders approached. Wigand of Marburg, who described the scene in his rhymed chronicle (1393–1394), commented, "However, it is not amazing, since they did that according to their religion and they regarded death as much easier." The pagan religion remained loosely organized, and its priesthood was not hierarchically centralized. This may have contributed to its survival long after the formal Christianization of the state.

BIBLIOGRAPHY

Oswald P. Backus, *Motives for West Russian Nobles in Deserting Lithuania for Moscow, 1377–1514* (1957); Marija Gimbutas, *The Balts* (1963); Zenonas Ivinskis, *Geschichte des Bauernstandes in Litauen von den ältesten Zeiten bis zum Anfang des 16. Jahrhunderts* (1933, repr. 1965), and *Lietuvos istorija: Iki Vytauto Didžiojo mirties* (1978); Lietuvos TSR Mokslų akademija, Istorijos institutas, *Lietuvos TSR istorija,* I, K. Jablonskis, J. Jurginis, Juozas Žiugžda, eds. (1957), and *Gedimino laiškai* (1966); Henryk Łowmiański, *Witold wielki książę litewski* (1930); Matvei K. Lyubavskii, *Ocherk istorii litovsko-russkogo gosudarstva do Lyublinskoi Unii vklyuchitelno* (1910); Jerzy Ochmański, *Historia Litwy* (1967, 2nd ed. 1982); Vladimir T. Pashuto, *Obrazovanie Litovskogo gosudarstva* (1959); Josef Pfitzner, *Grossfürst Witold von Litauen als Staatsman* (1930); Adolfas Šapoka, ed., *Lietuvos istorija* (1936); Juozapas Stakauskas, *Lietuva ir vakarų Europa XII-me amžiuje* (1934).

ROMUALD J. MISIUNAS

[See also **Baltic Countries; Balts; Chivalry, Orders of; Jagiełło Dynasty; Poland.**]

LITURGICAL BOOKS. See individual entries.

LITURGICAL DRAMA. See **Drama, Liturgical.**

LITURGICAL FURNISHINGS. See **Furniture, Liturgical.**

LITURGICAL POETRY. See **Poetry, Liturgical.**

LITURGY, BYZANTINE CHURCH. The liturgical forms and traditions developed in Hagia Sophia, also known as the "Great Church," built at the order of Emperor Justinian I and inaugurated in 537, exercised a decisive influence on the development of the liturgy throughout the Christian East in the Middle Ages. Although Hagia Sophia served as the cathedral of the "ecumenical" patriarch, who exercised primacy in the Orthodox world after the schism between East and West, there is no direct evidence in the East of any deliberate or administrative effort to impose its liturgical practices as the only acceptable ones. However, the prestige of the imperial capital as a political, religious, and intellectual center, and of the "Great Church" itself, was sufficient to assure its overwhelming influence throughout the Middle East and, later, in the Eastern European countries evangelized by the Byzantine church.

HISTORY

At the time when Constantinople acquired its dominant position, strong local liturgical traditions had already been established, particularly in Syria, Palestine, Egypt, and the Latin West. The new pattern created in the imperial capital incorporated many of these existing forms. At its beginnings the liturgy of the church of Constantinople was, therefore, eclectic. Inevitably it preserved a nucleus of the pre-Constantinian liturgy, which included, in particular, the sacramental rite of baptism and the major structure of the eucharistic canon.

Throughout the medieval period the baptismal rite in Byzantium retained the essential elements it had acquired in the second and third centuries. Performed through triple full immersion, in the name of the Holy Trinity, it represented the mystery of the death and resurrection of Christ in which the new Christian was participating. It was immediately followed by anointment with "holy chrism" *(myron)*, which corresponds to the Western confirmation. This "chrismation" was normally performed by a priest, although the chrism had to be blessed by a bishop. Since baptism and confirmation were bestowed simultaneously, newly baptized children were immediately admitted to eucharistic communion.

While the baptismal rite preserved its relatively primitive forms, in the eucharistic liturgy, which involved the participation of numerous clergy, of big crowds of people, and (at Hagia Sophia) of the imperial court, ceremonial embellishments and symbolic accretions were much more numerous. The central part of the mystery, the eucharistic liturgy, however, largely preserved the wording and the character of a third- or fourth-century Christian Eucharist. The short liturgy, traditionally attributed to St. John Chrysostom (*d.* 407), but probably of early medieval origin, gradually became the most usual eucharistic form in the Byzantine church, and has remained so in the Orthodox church since that time. However, on ten specific festal occasions a much longer and elaborate eucharistic liturgy, edited most probably by St. Basil the Great of Caesarea (*d.* 379), who was using an existing tradition of early Christian origin, was also in use. A third liturgy, attributed to St. James, "brother of the Lord," remained in local usage, particularly in Jerusalem.

In the Byzantine tradition the eucharistic liturgy has always been a very solemn and festal celebration. Except in monasteries it was celebrated only on Sundays and feast days. No practice of low or private Masses ever developed. During Lent, except on Saturdays and Sundays, the celebration of the Eucharist was forbidden by the Council in Trullo (692); it was replaced by a vesperal rite of Communion with reserved sacrament, known as the Liturgy of the Presanctified, traditionally attributed to Pope Gregory I (590–604).

In the Eucharist the Byzantines used ordinary leavened bread and, beginning in the eleventh century, strongly criticized the Latin and Armenian practice of using unleavened bread (azymes). They referred to the literal meaning of the New Testament accounts of the Last Supper, where the word *artos* (leavened bread) is used. Another point of contention with the Latins was the consecratory invocation of the Holy Spirit upon bread and wine (epiclesis). In the Byzantine and other Eastern eucharistic liturgies, the epiclesis follows the words of institution ("This is my body...," "This is my blood...") and crowns the consecratory prayer, whereas in the medieval Roman rite it is absent. Thus, in the Latin church the words of institution alone were considered as the consecratory formula. Controversies on the moment of consecration occurred often at encounters between Latin and Greeks in the late medieval period. While giving a very realistic interpretation to the eucharistic mystery, the Byzantines used such terms as *metabolē* (change) and *metastoicheiōsis* (transelementation) to designate it. The term "transubstantiation" *(metousiōsis)* appears only in the writings, under obvious Latin influence, of George (later Gennadios) Scholarios (fifteenth century).

In Byzantine theology there was neither a clear distinction between sacraments and sacramentals, nor a formal and definitive number of sacraments. Thus, St. Theodore of Studios (759–826) speaks of six sacraments: baptism, Eucharist, chrismation (confirmation), orders, monastic tonsure, and burial, whereas other authors include marriage, anointing of the sick, penance, the blessing of water on Epiphany day.

The overall liturgical ordo of the Byzantine church was shaped, on the one hand, by what has been called the "cathedral" rite—that is, the practice of large city churches—and, on the other hand, by the monasteries. Thus the manuscript Patmos 266 preserves the ordo followed in Hagia Sophia in 802–806. In general, the cathedral ordo gave little time to scriptural readings and psalmody, but encouraged hymnography and developed the "dramatic" character of the liturgical ceremonial. Clearly designed for large audiences, it encouraged devices to attract the attention of mass congregations. Under the influence of the *Ecclesiastical Hierarchy* of Pseudo Dionysius (late fifth or early sixth century), inspired by Neoplatonism, the liturgy was frequently conceived as a symbolic reflection on earth of unchangeable divine realities. Some of the symbolism implied by this approach was arbitrary—for instance, the conception of the eucharistic liturgy as a detailed reenactment of the earthly life of Jesus.

Concurrently with the liturgical development taking place in city churches, the monastic communities practiced a system of worship divided into autonomous units and distributed throughout the day and night: vespers, compline (*apodeipnon*), midnight prayer (*mesonyktikon*), matins (*orthros*), and the canonical hours (first, third, sixth, and ninth). Ideally, monks prayed without ceasing: at the Constantinopolitan monastery of the "Non-Sleepers," the chanting of the Divine Office never stopped, with monks taking shifts in the choir. Monastic worship, as distinct from the cathedral rite, originally was based almost exclusively on psalmody and Scripture readings. Having first showed reluctance to use hymnography, the monks, especially beginning in the ninth century (Theodore of Studios), adopted it on a large scale, and enriched it with texts of ascetical inspiration. Nevertheless, in the tenth century the ordo at Hagia Sophia and that at the monastery of Studios in Constantinople were still clearly distinct.

A full integration of the secular and the monastic liturgies seems to have occurred first not in the capital but at Jerusalem, perhaps in the eleventh century.

At the end of the Latin occupation of Constantinople (1204–1261), the typicon (or ordo) at the monastery of St. Sabas near Jerusalem was gradually adopted throughout the Byzantine Orthodox world. This adoption was promoted by patriarchs belonging to the hesychast monastic revival of the fourteenth century, particularly Philotheos Kokkinos (1353–1354, 1364–1376). The new liturgical synthesis included much of the hymnography originally destined for the cathedral rite, but it was now elaborately combined—in each liturgical unit, and in each of the daily, weekly, and yearly cycles—with the monastic ordo, accepting monastic spirituality as the general liturgical pattern.

In practice this meant greater detachment from the world and a strongly eschatological understanding of the liturgy. The magnitude and length of the services required by the typicon often implied the total impossibility of observing it completely outside of a monastery. The severe penitential discipline attached to the reception of sacraments revealed the church as signpost of the kingdom to come, irreducible to the present age. It is in this form that the Byzantine liturgy contributed much to the preservation of the Christian faith during the dark age of Muslim rule in the Balkans and the Middle East.

THE LITURGICAL CYCLES

The Christian liturgical year has traditionally been composed of cycles—daily, weekly, and yearly—that were largely borrowed from the Jewish tradition and established connections between human life and the mysteries of the Christian faith. In Byzantium all these cycles remained centered upon the resurrection of Christ, which since the first days of Christianity had been celebrated on the day after the Jewish Sabbath—that is, Sunday, the focus of the weekly cycle—and on Easter, the Christian Passover (Greek: *Pascha*). After some debate the date of Easter was fixed by the First Council of Nicaea (325) on the Sunday following the full moon after the vernal equinox. In the late Middle Ages some problems arose in connection with that date because the Julian calendar gradually fell behind the astronomical date of the vernal equinox.

The centrality of the Resurrection in the liturgy reflects a paschal understanding of the Christian faith, as a "passing over" from death to life, from the "old Adam" to the "new Adam." This passage occurs because Christ himself passed from death to life—the liturgy is commemorating this event, which happened in the past—and also because each mortal person freely appropriates this divine gift, joining the New Israel on the way to the promised land, following the Messiah. This human aspect of the paschal mystery always remains incomplete, because human ascetical efforts are always imperfect, but it is always based on a vision of the victory already won by Christ and an anticipation of the kingdom that is to come both as triumph and as judgment.

In each of its individual units and its cycles, the Byzantine liturgy used not only theological concepts to formulate the mystery but also the means that in a sense were more adequate to the purpose: poetry, music, pictures, and colors. Also, each day and night, and each changing season, served as occasions for—and as pointers at—the passage involving God and man, life and death, and joy and sorrow.

The daily cycle was structured around an unchangeable pattern made up of scriptural texts, primarily the Psalter. Monastic in character and style, this basic structure was embellished with hymnography that changed according to the days and seasons. The service of vespers, which began the liturgical day, was composed of Old Testament texts evoking the "old creation," still in need of salvation (Psalm 104) and the helplessness of "fallen" humanity (Psalms 140, 141, 129, 116). However, it also included an ancient hymn exalting light *(Phōs hilaron)* and ended with the Canticle of Simeon (Luke 2:29–32), proclaiming the coming of the messianic age. Matins also alternated the themes of necessary repentance and hope. Celebrated before daybreak, it was a solemn meeting of darkness with sunlight, used as symbol of the coming of Christ. Also based on Psalms, matins included other pieces of Old Testament poetry, such as the paschal canticles of Moses (Exod. 15:1–18; Deut. 32:1–43) and of the Three Youths in Babylon (Dan. 3:26–56, 67–88), culminating in the magnificat (Luke 1:46–55), the *benedictus* (Luke 1:68–79), the Psalms of lauds (148, 149, 150), and, at daybreak, the doxology.

The feast of Easter was preceded by Holy Week and six weeks of Lent. The hymns proper to this period were contained in a special liturgical book, the triodion, which was compiled primarily at the monastery of Studios in Constantinople. Easter was followed by fifty days of celebration, the proper hymnography being found in the *Pentekostarion,* which covered the entire period between Easter and Pentecost. After Pentecost, a cycle of eight weeks repeated itself until the beginning of Lent the following year. The hymns of each week used a particular musical

mode *(echos).* This explains the title of the book, the *Oktoechos* (Book of the eight modes). It is traditionally associated with St. John of Damascus (eighth century).

Thus, every day of the year was marked by liturgical characteristics or forms connected with the central celebration of Easter. However, in addition to and in combination with these forms, there were proper offices for each day of the calendar year, that is, feasts celebrating events in the life of Christ and the Virgin Mary, the commemoration of individual saints or of other events of Christian significance. Like the Western sanctorale, this layer of liturgical materials was of later origin. It reflected historical interest in past events and in individual personalities, as well as local piety directed at the veneration of saints and their relics. The entire body of hymns of this yearly cycle was included in the *Menaion* (Book of months). The content of the *Menaion* changed throughout the centuries, as new saints were canonized. The quality of the hymnography in the *Menaion* was varied. The hymns for the major feasts of Christ—Christmas, Epiphany, Transfiguration—and of the Virgin were written by the great hymnographers of the eighth and ninth centuries, incorporating also some of the kontakia of Romanos. A significant difference from the Latin sanctorale was that Old Testament figures—kings, prophets, and others—were commemorated side by side with Christian saints. Obviously, in the consciousness of Byzantine orthodoxy, the just men and women of pre-Christian Judaism, who met Christ at his descent to Hades, were alive in the communion of the church. The numerous feasts commemorating John the Baptist, the last prophet to announce the coming of the Messiah—his conception, his birth, his beheading—are expressions of the same theology. The cycle of John the Baptist served as a model for the later cycle of feasts celebrating the Virgin Mary—the Annunciation, the Nativity, the Dormition—which acquired a great popularity with the ever growing veneration of the Mother of God *(Theotokos).*

HYMNOGRAPHY

A few of the hymns used in the Byzantine liturgy were inherited from the first Christian centuries, but new hymnography began to be introduced on a large scale in the cathedral rite, as it developed in Constantinople in the sixth and seventh centuries. Its origin is primarily associated with Syria, where St. Ephraem (306–373) was known as a great religious poet, although it is improbable that any of his poetry was used in the liturgy in his time. Under Emperor Anastasios I (491–518) another Syrian, Romanos, known as the Melode (Greek: *Melōdos,* sweet-singer), came to Constantinople and became the real founder of Byzantine medieval hymnography. Born at Emesa possibly of Jewish parentage, he composed kontakia (metrical homilies) that were to be recited or chanted by a cantor and accompanied by a simple refrain sung by the entire congregation. The form of the kontakia was ideally suited for corporate worship of large assemblies, like the ones at Hagia Sophia and other large churches built in the age of Justinian. Written in a relatively simple Greek, using as themes the major events of biblical history, and relying on imagery and drama, the kontakia were both poetic and didactic in character. Eighty-five authentic kontakia by Romanos are preserved, and parts of them have been integrated into liturgical books used in the following centuries. In its integrity the kontakion form has been preserved in the *Akathistos Hymn,* of which Romanos may also have been the author. Praising the Virgin Mary as protectress of Christians, and particularly of the city of Constantinople, it is one of the most famous examples of Byzantine liturgical hymnography.

The length of the kontakia of Romanos made it impossible to integrate them into the existing framework of the daily cycle, based on the text of the Psalter and adapted to the monastic liturgy. By the seventh and eighth centuries the monks had abandoned their opposition to hymnography, and had begun to interpolate into the psalmody of biblical texts short poetic pieces called troparia or *stikhera.* It is this compromise between the monastic and the cathedral rites, with numerous later enrichments, that eventually provided the final form of Byzantine liturgical cycles. The form known as the *kanōn* replaced the kontakion and became the central part of matins. It was composed of the biblical poetry, with special short hymns known as *heirmoi* establishing a connection between the biblical text and the event celebrated by the hymns, and whose rhythm and melody set the pattern for short troparia interspersed between the biblical verses. Among the most famous authors of *kanōnes* in the eighth and ninth centuries were Andrew of Crete (d. 740), who composed the famous penitential *Great Canon;* John of Damascus; Kosmas of Maïuma; Theodore of Studios; Joseph the Hymnographer; and others.

The volume of Byzantine medieval hymnography is immense and very diverse in character and style. Together with hagiographical legends and poetic ex-

aggerations, it contains remarkable expressions of the Christian faith, as well as doctrinal formulations *(dogmatika)* that the authors clearly distinguish from mere poetry. For centuries, when Eastern Christians under Muslim rule were deprived of schools and preaching, the liturgical texts—together with iconography—were the source of religious knowledge. They played the same role among non-Greek Orthodox Christians. The entire body of the Byzantine liturgical books was translated into Georgian (sixth century), Arabic, Slavic (ninth century), and, more recently, many other languages. Much of it was adopted, in Syriac, by the Syrian Jacobites, as well as Armenians and Copts in their own languages.

BIBLIOGRAPHY

Frank Edward Brightman, *Liturgies Eastern and Western* (1896, repr. 1965); Aleksei Dmitrievsky, *Opisanie liturgicheskikh rukopisei,* 2 vols. (1895–1901); *The Festal Menaion,* Mother Mary and Archimandrite Kallistos Ware, trans. (1969); Alphonse Raes, *Introductio in liturgiam orientalem* (1947); Alexander Schmemann, *Introduction to Liturgical Theology* (1966); R. Taft, *The Great Entrance,* 2nd ed. (1978), with bibliography of the Byzantine eucharistic rite; *The Lenten Triodion* (1978); N. D. Uspensky, *Vsenoshchnoe bdenie* (1978), containing a complete history of the daily cycle.

JOHN MEYENDORFF

[See also **Akathistos; Azymes; Basil the Great of Caesarea, St.; Baptism; Byzantine Church; Canonical Hours; Confirmation; Death and Burial, in Europe; Epiphany, Feast of; George Scholarios; Hagia Sophia (Constantinople); Hymns, Byzantine; John Chrysostom, St.; John of Damascus, St.; Kanōn; Kontakion; Mass; Philotheos Kokkinos, Patriarch; Romanos Melodos; Sticheron; Theodore of Studios; Troparion.**]

LITURGY, CELTIC. There is no liturgy comparable to Roman, Gallican, Ambrosian, or Mozarabic liturgy that can be termed Celtic—that is, there are scarcely any distinctive liturgical features common to the whole area that was inhabited by Celts. It was not until the late seventeenth century that the term "Celts" was used in liturgical matters. The earlier records spoke of usage common to the *Scoti,* which term, at least until the end of the twelfth century, basically denoted the Irish. Moreover, the differences in levels of information on liturgical particularities of the Irish church (which term can include Irish clerics abroad) and of churches in other Celtic regions is immense. Even though Irish records have suffered from destruction to a particularly high degree, they are the only ones from "Celtic" lands that contain actual liturgical texts. (The *Book of Deer,* sometimes described as the only one to contain liturgical texts proper to the old Scottish church, is a Scottish manuscript with contents of the Irish type.)

The date of Easter, the form of tonsure, and particulars at baptism, at the consecration of bishops, and in the arrangement of the Mass have often been regarded as distinctive features of the Celtic church. The acceptance of the Roman computation of Easter by the Synod of Whitby (663) is considered the end of the Celtic church in England. Special links between Wales and Ireland are referred to in Irish hagiography. The continuance of some distinctive features in Brittany up to the ninth century, and in Scotland up to the eleventh century, is testified to indirectly and summarily rather than directly and specifically. In Ireland the eighth constitution of the Synod of Cashel (1172)—"The divine office shall be henceforth celebrated in every part of Ireland according to the form and usages of the Church of England"—marked the end of a development that had started with the reform movement (Gilbert of Limerick, *De statu ecclesiae,* 1106; Synod of Rathbraesail, 1111). Since 1881 the list of liturgical texts of the old Irish church has been steadily increased, but the only major text has remained the Stowe Missal. Apart from it, the only sacramentary texts preserved in Ireland are the fragments contained in the Book of Armagh, the Book of Dimma, and the Book of Mulling. Fragments of sacramentaries associated with Ireland and written in the eighth and ninth centuries, however, have been preserved in libraries in England (Cambridge, London), France (Colmar, Paris), Germany (Karlsruhe, Munich), Switzerland (St. Gall, Zurich), and Italy (Milan, Piacenza). How much these texts were used by the Irish on the Continent is not certain. The deplorable state and the dispersion of these texts over a wide area have been an obstacle to their comprehensive study.

The points in which contents and wording of those sacramentaries differ from those of churches in other areas would hardly justify their description as records of a different liturgy. They are considered to be records of the old Irish church, first of all, on account of their script. Moreover, some of them contain Gaelic words, glosses, or names of Irish saints not known or scarcely known outside Ireland, or show particularities in spelling or terminology of Hiberno-Latin. Their contents are predominantly Communia, notably of all the saints, of the Holy Trinity, and of the Blessed Virgin, and votive Masses for the sick, for captives, for penitents, and for the dead. There are also prayers for blessing the sick and for the consecration of virgins and of widows. The comparatively large number of texts relating to the sick and to women is remarkable.

It is a distinctive feature of the old Irish liturgy that antiphonaries can be singled out as a separate type of liturgical literature. The Bangor Antiphonary (*ca.* 680–691) is the only one that has been preserved (almost) in its entirety (Milan, Ambrosian Library) and, like other liturgical texts stemming from Ireland, was once preserved at Bobbio; part of a version of it is also in Turin. Fragments of other antiphonaries are in Oxford, Paris, and Karlsruhe. These texts are representative of the monastic character of the old Irish church. Irish saints are claimed to have been the authors of some of them. Ireland has been the country where the plea made by Hilary of Poitiers for *hymnorum carmina* (liturgical or devotional) has been answered most intensely.

A large number of fragments of Psalters and evangeliaries (and commentaries on them) show the eminent position that the Bible occupied in the spiritual life of Irish monasticism. The notes of the Cathach of St. Columba (second half of the sixth century) clearly indicate its liturgical purpose. A feature common to Psalters associated with Ireland is that the *cantica* are arranged in groups after each section of fifty psalms. Some of the evangeliaries are famous for their rich ornamentation, notably the Book of Durrow, the Book of Mulling, and the Book of Kells. The tract on the Mass in the Stowe Missal (recorded again in the late-fourteenth-century *Leabhar Breac* [Speckled book]), the versified tract on the canonical hours, the tract on the consecration of a church, and the tract on liturgical colors (in *Leabhar Breac*)—all in Gaelic—and many Latin texts containing Gaelic words or glosses offering explanations of their spiritual or liturgical contents, show that extensive use was made of the vernacular in liturgiological teaching.

Ireland was the first country in the Western world to develop an ecclesiastical terminology and literature in the vernacular. In the liturgy there are not only loanwords such as *oiffriund* (*offerendum,* for "Mass"), *sacart* (*sacerdos*), and *cailech* (*calix*), but also entirely original words such as *tocbál* (elevation), *fobdod* (submersion), and *combuig* (confraction). Unfortunately, adequate knowledge of both the liturgical history and the old Irish language has rarely been combined in one scholar. This combination would be particularly desirable in view of the fact that in the old Irish church the border between liturgical and devotional literature was much broader than in other parts of the church. The existence of a large paraliturgical literature in the vernacular shows that the language of religious life was Gaelic. Apart from the collections of Latin prayers in the Book of Nunnaminster, the Book of Cerne, the Royal Library Prayer Book, and the *Liber Hymnorum* (this in Latin and Gaelic), there are the litanies—all in Gaelic—of the saints, of those with biblical, dogmatic, and moral themes, and of the *féliri,* that is, metric versions in Gaelic of anniversaristic lists of saints.

The term "martyrology" is hardly applicable in the context of the old Irish church because it had practically no martyrs of its own. For the same reason the term "relic" has a different connotation, denoting objects used or garments worn by a saint rather than bodily remains and having no liturgical significance. The close connection of this literature with the liturgy is significantly expressed by the epilogue to *Félire Oengusso,* written about 800 at Tallaght (as was the Stowe Missal). It is the largest work of its kind (consisting of one quatrain for each day of the year), its recitation being the equivalent (*arrae;* Latin: *arraeum*) of seven Masses, of the 150 Psalms (the recitation of which was one of the practices of Irish monasticism), of an *aurtach* (here probably meaning a feast liturgically celebrated, as distinguished from a mere commemoration, *féil*), of a "giving of *coibsen*" ("confession"; the Irish are credited with having introduced private confession), of three triduums, of a Communion, or of a canticle of psalms.

The lack of uniformity not only over the Celtic area, but even within the Irish church, resulted mainly from the monastic rather than the diocesan structure; there were no urban centers in pre-Norman Ireland. Most churches bore the name of a person credited with having founded or built them; the recording of a name in the *Félire* amounted simply to describing the person as *noibh,* a Gaelic word equivalent to *sanctus* in the broad original sense (Acts 26:18), certainly not implying liturgical veneration. The absence of diocesan structure was due to, or resulted in, the bishop's being a member of the monastic hierarchy rather than the head of a region. The abbot had no liturgical authority beyond his monastery and the land belonging to it.

To the names extracted from the *Martyrologium Hieronymianum* the Martyrology of Tallaght

added, in separate paragraphs (thus perhaps indicating the difference in status), as many Irish names, mostly of persons of whom nothing else is known except possibly their traditional association with a place. Thus, the Martyrology of Tallaght appears to be an attempt to collect local commemorations; the selection of names made from it by *Félire Oengusso* was dictated by reasons of versification—certainly not of liturgical relevance. In the sacramentary texts of the old Irish church there are few traces of a temporale, notably in the Stowe Missal: the Nativity, the calends (1 January), the stars (6 January), Easter, the Ascension, and Pentecost. The prayer at the end of the Gospel of St. Matthew in the Book of Armagh is not a collect proper to a feast of this apostle but a private devotion to him. In view of the extensive knowledge of, and private devotion to, the saints of Ireland and of other areas, the absence of a sanctorale is the most significant feature common to the liturgical texts associated with Ireland. Whether in this case Ireland preserved an ancient tradition proper to the city of Rome or whether it can be ascribed to connections with the Eastern church (as is obvious, for instance, in the confraction rite) is a question that probably can never be answered with certainty. In any case, the absence of a sanctorale is one of the aspects of the conservatism characteristic of the old Irish church (a prayer in the Stowe Missal speaks of "the pious emperors," a relic of the time when two emperors were commemorated in the Latin Mass).

It was due to Irish influence that the date of the feast of All Saints was assigned to November 1, which in the pre-Christian Irish calendar was the feast of the dead, marking the end of harvest time and the beginning (with *Imbolc,* St. Brigit's day [1 February], marking the middle, and *Bealtaine* [1 May], the end) of the second half of the year. In contrast with the earlier Roman commemoration of all the martyrs (who were too numerous to be named individually), this commemoration corresponds to the Irish votive Masses commemorating (in clear connection with the Eastern church) all the choirs of saints, patriarchs, prophets (Ireland played a prominent part in promoting Christian devotion to Old Testament saints), apostles, martyrs, confessors, virgins, anchorites, monks, bishops, and abbots in a natural rather than a historical order of time, the main difference being that the former is cyclical, while the latter is linear (thus inevitably containing the idea of increasing distance of the event).

It has been suggested that the absence of a sanctorale was due to an abbreviation of the sacramentary to make it more easily portable for missionaries. While the idea of *peregrinatio pro Christo* was widespread in the Old Irish church, only a small number of clerics actually put it into practice. Although texts for private devotion may have been less subject to destruction than liturgical ones, the proportion of texts classed as paraliturgical is nevertheless surprisingly high. Hymns, litanies, *féliri,* and collections of prayers are rarely written in the first-person plural; they express a high standard of private devotion separate from, though in keeping with, the liturgy. This may have occurred because the Irish monastic structure contained a large number of anchorites and other persons living—and possibly doing pastoral work—in loose contact with monastic organizations.

BIBLIOGRAPHY

Edmund Bishop, *Liturgica historica* (1918, repr. 1962), 137–165; Klaus Gamber, *Codices liturgici latini antiquiores,* I (1968), 130–152; John Hennig, "Ireland's Contribution to the Devotion to Old Testament Saints," in *Irish Ecclesiastical Record,* **104** (1965), "Old Ireland and Her Liturgy," in R. McNally, ed., *Old Ireland* (1965), "The Sources of the Martyrological Tradition of Non-Irish Saints in Medieval Ireland," in *Sacris erudiri,* **21** (1973), and "Ireland's Place in the History of the Function of the Martyrology," in *Ephemerides liturgicae,* **93** (1979); James F. Kenney, *The Sources for the Early History of Ireland,* I, *Ecclesiastical* (1929, rev. and enl. 1980), 687–718; Archdale Arthur King, *Liturgies of the Past* (1959), 186–275; John T. McNeill, *The Celtic Churches* (1974); Frederic E. Warren, *The Liturgy and Ritual of the Celtic Church* (1881).

JOHN HENNIG

[See also **All Saints' Day; Antiphonal; Brigit, St.; Celtic Church; Colors, Liturgical; Columba, St.; Durrow, Book of; Evangeliary; Kells, Book of; Martyrology, Irish; Sacramentary.**]

LITURGY, ISLAMIC. Islamic worship centers around the prayer ritual called the salat (*ṣalāt*), which has daily, weekly, annual, and occasional forms. Our oldest and most valuable historical source on the salat is the Koran, which provides a contemporary record of its origin and early development during the lifetime of the prophet Muḥammad (*d.* 632). Other primary sources on Islamic liturgy include the hadith collections, various theological and legal treatises, and many popular worship manuals. The most highly respected hadith collections, by al-Bukhārī (*d.* 870) and Muslim (*d.* 875), are now available in English translations, as is the popular compendium called *Mishkāt al-maṣābiḥ,* completed in 1337. One of the most influential and informative treatises on Islamic liturgy is the section on worship (salat) in the *Iḥyāʾ ʿulūm al-dīn* by the famous theologian al-Ghazālī (*d.* 1111). Many popular manuals on Islamic worship are discussed in Padwick's *Muslim Devotions,* and some entire treatises are translated in Jeffery's *A Reader on Islam.*

Proper observance of the daily salats, the Friday service, and other Islamic rituals is regarded as an obligatory (*fard*) religious duty for all Muslim men. The essential elements of these rituals came to be prescribed by Islamic law and customary practice during the early centuries of Islam, and they have remained basically the same down to the present.

The mosque. The preferred place for performing most forms of Islamic liturgy is the mosque. The first mosque was the courtyard of Muḥammad's residence in Medina, which later became the Mosque of the Prophet, Islam's second-holiest place. After Muḥammad's death this mosque became the model for others built in towns and cities throughout the Islamic world. In older, conquered cities, such as Damascus and Cairo, churches and synagogues were sometimes converted into mosques, often with very little architectural alteration. The architectural features that became characteristic of the mosque are (1) the tower or minaret, from which the call to prayer is given, (2) the niche (mihrab), which indicates the qibla or direction of Mecca, (3) the pulpit (minbar), a staircase with an enclosure at the top from which the Friday sermon is delivered, and (4) a fountain or other source of water for ablutions. The most important mosque officials are the leader (imam) of the salat and the preacher (khaṭīb), who delivers the Friday sermon. In smaller mosques one person often fills both of these roles. The muezzin (*muʾadhdhin,* "caller"), who issues the call to prayer, and the Koran reciter (*qāriʾ*) also have prominent roles in Islamic liturgy in the mosque.

The daily salats. The salat had its origin in the early years of Muḥammad's ministry; but, according to the Koran, until sometime after he and his followers moved to Medina in 622 daily performance of this ritual seems to have been required only of the Prophet, and it was performed only twice each day, at sunrise and sunset (suras 11:114, 17:78–79, 50:39–40, and 76:25–26, which also mention the night vigil that was later shortened and made voluntary by the

Medinan verse, 73:20). Then in Medina performance of the salat came to be required of all Muslims, and a third observance (called "the middle salat" in sura 2:238) was added, possibly influenced by the fact that the Jews performed their prayer (the *tefilla*) three times a day. For the first year or so in Medina the Muslims also followed the Jewish practice of facing toward Jerusalem during the performance of their prayer. Then at the time of the so-called "break with the Jews" the direction of prayer was changed from Jerusalem to Mecca, and the Meccan *qibla* has been an essential feature of the salat ever since. Within a century of the prophet's death the number of required daily salats was increased to five, probably by combining previously voluntary ones, customarily performed by Muḥammad, with the obligatory ones. These five, and the times when they may be performed, are (1) the morning salat, from dawn to sunrise, (2) the noon salat, from just after noon until midafternoon, (3) the afternoon salat, from midafternoon until sunset, (4) the sunset salat, from sunset until dusk, and (5) the evening salat, anytime after dark. There are also voluntary salats in the morning and at night, and there are additional, supererogatory liturgical cycles before and after the required ones of each salat.

The exact performance of the salat varies among the different legal schools or rites, but there is uniformity of practice regarding thirteen "essentials" (*arkān*)—six actions or positions, six utterances or recitations, and the requirement that these twelve must proceed in the prescribed order. The variations involve numerous customary (sunna) elements that are recommended but not required. The description that follows is based largely on the explanation given by al-Ghazālī. The beginning of the period for performing each prescribed daily salat is announced by a public call to prayer (the *adhān*) given by the muezzin. The worshipers must be in a state of ritual purity, accomplished by performing either the minor ablution (*wuḍūᶜ*) for minor impurities, or the major one called (*ghusl*) for major ones. The salat itself, following the order of prescribed positions and utterances, begins with the worshipers in (1) the standing position (*qiyām*), facing Mecca. In a congregational salat a second call to prayer (the *iqāma*) is recited, followed by the statement, "Worship has begun." Then comes (2) the statement of intention (*nīya*), indicating which prayer is about to be performed, followed by (3) a *takbīra*, the statement, "God is most great" (*Allāhu akbar*). Remaining standing the worshipers then begin the first liturgical cycle (*rakᶜa*) with (4) the recitation (*qīrāᵓa*) of the first sura and one other portion of the Koran. Next comes (5) the bowing (*rukūᶜ*), bending the upper part of the body to a horizontal position with the hands on the knees, while saying "Glory be to God" or a longer statement of praise that varies among the different rites. The worshipers then assume (6) the upright position (*iᶜtidāl*) with the hands raised to the sides of the face, while saying "May God hear him who praises Him" or a longer formula. Then follows (7) the first prostration (*sujūd*), with the toes, knees, palms, and forehead all touching the floor or ground, while saying "Praise be to Thee, my Lord, the Most High." This is followed by (8) the half-sitting, half-kneeling position (*julūs*) in which another *Allāhu akbar* is recited. Then there is a second prostration, which completes the first cycle of the salat. The second follows immediately as the worshipers stand and recite the opening sura of the Koran again and then proceed through the same sequence of essentials. The morning salat has two required cycles, the sunset one has three, and the others each have four. After the second prostration of the last cycle, the salat then concludes with the final four essential elements. The worshipers assume (9) the sitting position (*quᶜūd*) and recite (10) the confession of faith (*tashahāda*), "There is no god but God; Muḥammad is the Messenger of God," (11) a blessing on the prophet and his family, and (12) the *salām*, "Peace be upon you," pronounced once with the head turned to the right and once to the left. In the salat, which culminates in the twofold prostration before God, faithful Muslims perform daily a ritual that symbolizes the essence of Islam, submission (*islām*) before God.

The Friday service. Since the time of Muḥammad Muslims throughout the world have congregated in their local mosques at noon on Fridays for a worship service called the "assembly" (*jumᶜa*). Friday, called in Arabic "the day of assembly" (*yawm al-jumᶜa*), is the closest Islamic parallel to the Jewish Sabbath and the Christian Sunday or Lord's Day; but it was not instituted as a day of rest for Muslims, and it has remained essentially different from the Jewish and Christian counterparts. Friday was chosen as the day for the weekly Islamic service because it was the market day in Medina, already called "the day of assembly," when everyone came into Medina to shop. The Koran admonishes the people to cease their commerce for the Friday noon service and then permits them to resume their business activities (sura 62:9–10).

According to Islamic law and custom the Friday service is held only in the main mosque of each town and in the larger mosques of the cities, those designated as a "central mosque" (masjid jāmiᶜ). The essentials of the Friday service are a sermon (khuṭba), traditionally presented in two parts, and, following that, a salat of two cycles called "the Salat of the Assembly" (ṣalāt al-jumᶜa). It is considered sunna (customary and meritorious, but not obligatory) to perform a major ablution before the Friday service, to wear one's best clothes or newly washed ones, and to perform a sunna salat of two cycles before the service begins. Wearing perfume, arriving early, reciting certain verses from the Koran, and uttering blessings for the Prophet are also recommended.

In the larger mosques the jumᶜa traditionally proceeds as follows. On arriving at the mosque the worshipers remove their shoes at the door and assemble in the main hall or in the courtyard, arranging themselves in straight rows facing Mecca, just as for any other congregational salat. Those who arrive early perform a sunna salat of two cycles and then sit quietly. In some mosques a Koran reciter chants a sura of the Koran until the time of the sermon, when the call to prayer is recited. The preacher or the imam then climbs the stairs of the pulpit and delivers the first part of the sermon, which should include a recitation from the Koran, a statement of praise to God, a prayer for blessings on the prophet, and an exhortation to the worshipers. Then he says, "Pray to God" and sits down. After some private prayers, ending with "Amen, amen," the preacher arises and delivers the second part of the sermon. Although it is supposed to include the same four elements as the first part, it has a different character, being essentially a eulogy asking for blessings on the Prophet and the current rulers. Then the preacher descends the pulpit, the muezzin chants the second call to prayer (the iqāma), and the imam leads the worshipers in the Salat of the Assembly. The service officially ends when the imam departs, but some worshipers usually remain for additional prayers and meditation.

Annual and occasional services. The most prominent annual Islamic liturgical rites are those observed during the months of Ramadan and Dhul-Hijja. Ramadan, the month of fasting, was in medieval times a time of many special religious observances. The mosques were illuminated with extra candles, and their floors were covered with luxuriant Ramadan carpets. The evening salat was followed by a service called the Salat of the Pauses (tarāwīḥ),

consisting of twenty cycles with long pauses after every four. Also, Koran reciters often performed in the mosques during the thirty nights of Ramadan, reciting one-thirtieth of the Koran each night.

Ramadan ends with the "feast of the breaking of the fast" (ᶜīd al-fiṭr), sometimes called "the minor feast." On the tenth of Dhul-Hijja, the month of the great pilgrimage to Mecca, pilgrims and other Muslims throughout the world celebrate the other great annual feast, the "feast of the sacrifice" (ᶜīd al-aḍḥā), also called "the major feast." Both feasts are marked by a special service called the Salat of the Feasts, consisting of two cycles followed by a sermon in two parts. It differs from other salats in having no call to prayer (adhān) or second call (iqāma), and in having several more takbīras.

A similar ritual called the Salat of the Eclipse (ṣalāt al-khusūf) has traditionally been performed during an eclipse of the sun or moon. Said to have been instituted by Muhammad, it is mentioned frequently in the hadith collections and legal treatises. Another ritual that goes back to Muḥammad is the Salat for Rain (ṣalāt al-istisqāᵓ), performed preferably in the morning in a field outside the town or city. It consists of two cycles followed by a sermon in two parts, during which the worshipers turn around their cloaks or outer garments in an ancient sympathetic rite intended to produce a change in the weather. The "Funeral Salat" (salāt al-jināza), sometimes called the "Salat for the Dead," has, instead of the cycles of most salats, four parts, each beginning with a takbīra: a recitation of the first sura of the Koran, a eulogy on the Prophet, a prayer for the deceased, and a prayer for those taking part in the service. Like other salats it ends with the twofold salam, "Peace be upon you."

BIBLIOGRAPHY

Muḥammad ibn Ismāᶜīl al-Bukhārī, *The Translation and the Meanings of the Ṣaḥīḥ al-Bukhārī: Arabic-English*, Muḥammad Muḥsin Khan, trans., 3rd rev. ed. (1976), I–III; Edwin E. Calverley, *Worship in Islam: Being a Translation, with Commentary and Introduction, of al-Ghazzālī's Book of the Iḥyāᵓ on the Worship*, 2nd ed. (1957); Solomon D. Goitein, "The Origin and Nature of the Muslim Friday Worship," in *Muslim World*, **49** (1959); Arthur Jeffery, ed. and trans., *A Reader on Islam* (1962), 463–486, 521–549; Muslim ibn al-Ḥajjāj al-Qushayrī, *Ṣaḥīḥ Muslim*, ᶜAbd al-Ḥamīd Ṣiddīqī, trans. (1971–1975), I–IV; Constance E. Padwick, *Muslim Devotions* (1961); Muḥammad ibn ᶜAbd-Allāh al-Khaṭīb al-Tibrīzī, *Mishkāt al-masābīḥ*, James Robson, trans. and ed. (1960–1965), I–II; Gustave E. Von Grunebaum, *Muhammadan Festivals* (1951);

W. Montgomery Watt and Alford T. Welch, *Der Islam*, I (1980), 262–299, 318–322.

ALFORD T. WELCH

[See also **Bukhāri, al-**; **Ghazāli, al-**; **Ḥadith**; **Imam**; **Islam, Religion**; **Koran**; **Mecca**; **Medina**; **Mosque**; **Muezzin**; **Muḥammad**; **Preaching and Sermons, Islamic**; **Qibla**.]

LITURGY, JEWISH. Liturgy consists of prescribed orders of prayer and ritual. Jewish liturgy provides a framework for popular, ongoing participation in the religious experience of Judaism. The deity is worshiped as a being who, although wholly different in nature from creation, is continually concerned with its proper functioning and with the well-being of his creations. In need, men approach him in prayer; enjoying his sustaining gift, they gratefully praise him. Liturgical formulas express declarations of faith in, or gratitude for, God's generous benevolence, his wise laws, and his righteous judgments. The Jewish worshiper feels justification, on the basis of his faith, in approaching his God with complaints.

There is a strong communal aspect to Jewish worship; God desires and delights in the daily service of the congregations of his people. Jewish liturgy developed set forms over the ages in the fulfillment of this end. At the same time, Jewish worshipers needed means for the communication of unique personal expression. In addition, in order to maintain their enthusiasm in the daily service of their Lord, many felt that they needed the aesthetic and intellectual stimulation that could be provided by alternating (if not by composing new) liturgies.

Both the need for constancy and the desire for change are reflected in the Jewish liturgy of the Middle Ages. The fixed order is largely a development of the berakhah (pl., berakhot, blessing, benediction) style adopted by the early mishnaic rabbis. The importance of this form can be seen in the fact that the major tractate in the Mishnah dealing with liturgy is called *Berakhot*. Paradoxically, the very multiplicity of occasions for which berakhot were formulated provided the potential for much variety. One scholar, Natronai bar Hilai, a ninth-century gaon of Sura in Babylonia, claimed to have enumerated over one hundred benedictions to be recited in a day. The major opportunities for liturgical variety, however, were provided by the ongoing composition of poetic hymns and elegies called piyyutim (sing., piyyut, from the Greek: *poiētēs*, poet). Each of these liturgical types will be described in turn.

Berakhot derive their name from the fact that the introductory formula of each benediction begins with the word *barukh* (blessed, praised): *barukh atah, adonai elohenu, melekh ha-olam* (Blessed be You, Lord our God, King of the universe). There is an exception if the benediction is a member of a series. Then, only the first will open with the formula, whereas all subsequent ones will begin directly with the subject of the benediction, as in the second and subsequent benedictions of the grace after meals or the *Amidah* prayer. When the statement of the subject runs to two or more clauses, a short concluding eulogy, also beginning with *barukh*, will recapitulate the invocation and the subject of the benediction. Heinemann (1977) describes this and other traditional Jewish liturgical forms in terms of their origins, style, and methods of composition.

Benedictions may be categorized as benedictions of praise and thanksgiving, benedictions upon the fulfillment of a ritual requirement, and those included in the fixed order of daily services. An appropriate benediction of praise or thanksgiving must be recited upon taking nourishment, enjoying other benefits of creation, admiring prodigies of nature, or visiting locations of Jewish religiohistorical significance. Many ritual observances, such as lighting Sabbath candles, donning phylacteries, slaughtering animals, or circumcising a male infant on the eighth day of life, are preceded by a benediction formula whose introduction has been augmented by the addition of the following clause: *asher kiddshanu be-mitzvotav ve-tzivanu* . . . (who has sanctified us by his commandments [in general] and [in particular] commanded us [concerning . . . or, to . . .]). They are called *birkhot mitzvah*, blessings upon ritually prescribed acts.

Standard liturgical services were offered three times daily: morning (Shaḥarit), afternoon (Minḥah), and evening (Maʿariv, Arvit). An additional service (Musaf) was offered before concluding the morning worship on the Sabbath, new moon, and festivals. Persons unable to join a communal service could recite their prayers in private, although Judaism ascribed special sanctity and importance to the ongoing maintenance of public services. To this end, it transferred the aura that had surrounded the Temple cult to the service of the synagogue following the destruction of the Second Temple in 70.

A petitionary prayer is recited, standing in silent devotion, at each one of those services. It is known as *ha-tefillah* (the prayer), the *Amidah* ([prayer recited while] standing), or the *Shemoneh Esreh* ("eighteen," after the original number of benedictions comprising the weekday *Amidah*). The *Amidah* has a complex structure. A set of three eulogistic benedictions introduces the core section of petition, which is followed by another set of three benedictions. The introduction and conclusion vary little from one occasion to the next, but the petitionary core does. One weekdays it contains twelve (according to Babylonian usage, thirteen) short petitionary benedictions, whereas the Sabbath and festival *Amidah* has one composite core benediction (and the New Year's *Musaf* has three long core benedictions).

Although its purpose is petitionary, the *Amidah* is communal and nationalistic by design. To express his personal needs, each worshiper concluded with a private petition. In addition to this, at weekday services, petitionary lectionaries and prayer texts (*tahanunim, tehinhot,* or *devarim*) followed the *Amidah*, especially in the morning and the afternoon. On the new moon and other festivals, Psalms 113–118, collectively called the *Hallel,* were recited instead.

On each Sabbath, festival, or fast day a section of the Torah would then be read, followed by a selection from the Prophets (the *haftarah,* "concluding" scriptural reading). In addition, a small section from the following Sabbath's Torah portion is read three times during the week. The Sabbath readings follow the order of the Torah so that the entire Five Books of Moses is completed each year (according to Palestinian usage, every three years).

Besides the *Amidah,* the other major component of the fixed order of daily prayer is *keriat Shema u-virkhoteha* (the recitation of the *Shema,* with its attendant benedictions). The *Shema* derives its name from the first word of this group of three passages from the Torah (Deut. 6:4–9, 11:13–21; Num. 15:37–41). They declare the unity of God (the central article of Jewish faith), mandate the allegiance of his people to him and to the study and observance of his precepts, describe the blessings of loyalty together with the penalties of disloyalty, and conclude by stating the purpose of Israel's election—to become a holy people in order to preserve its special relationship with God. Because the *Shema* had to be recited twice daily, at morning and at night, it was formulated as part of a liturgical complex for *Shaharit* and *Arvit.*

This complex precedes the *Amidah.* It consists of two benedictions, the *Shema* passages, and another, concluding benediction that serves as a bridge to the *Amidah* (in *Arvit* there would be one or two additional benedictions, depending upon the rite). The opening benediction provides a universal context for this service, celebrating the orderly daily renewal of creation as manifested in the renewal of light or in the orderly passage of time and the seasons. The second benediction acknowledges the Lord for the revelation of his Torah and the election of Israel. This context implies a correlation between the orderly functioning of nature and the orderly functioning of human society. The benediction following the *Shema* has two components. Beginning with the formula "true and certain," it consists in the worshipers' declaration of their faith in the *Shema* passages just recited. The theme of the redemption from Egypt alluded to at the end of the *Shema* is thereupon developed, which prepares for the concluding eulogy, "who has redeemed Israel." The stage is now set for the worshipers to approach their Lord with their petitions, and the *Amidah* follows.

Allusion has been made to the two original rites in use in the Middle Ages, the Palestinian and the Babylonian. Both derived from the same early traditions (the *Shema* complex and the *Amidah* were both known to the Mishnah, *ca.* 200), which then developed variously in their Palestinian and Babylonian milieus. Nonetheless, there were some differences in formulation or in specific liturgical practices, texts, and versions. Furthermore, in the areas of worship that were not fixed, the differences were greater. Local or personal idiosyncrasies may account for some of the variations perceived between these two major rites. Lawrence Hoffman has documented the efforts of the Babylonian geonim in the eighth to eleventh centuries to standardize Jewish liturgical practice throughout the known Jewish world. The tension between the toleration of divergent practice and the need to purify the liturgy of sectarian or stylistic errors (or merely competing norms) was resolved in various ways throughout the period. The first two known prayer books, that of Amram Gaon (*d. ca.* 875) and that of Saadiah Gaon (882–942), are very different in structure, approach, and even wording of their prayer texts.

The Palestinian rite was not well known until the discovery of the Cairo genizah (a storeroom for discarding sacred writings) in the late nineteenth century. The texts preserved there in both complete and fragmentary form revolutionized scholars' understanding of the fixed, standard liturgies and of piyyut. Genizah evidence shows that the Palestinian rite was used in Egypt at least until the twelfth century. The Palestinian rite influenced Italy and, via Italy, other parts of Europe—north through Germany, northern France, and England, and east to

Greece and Romania. Nonetheless, as Babylonian gaonic authority gained prominence throughout the Diaspora in the ninth and tenth centuries and, later, as the Babylonian Talmud itself was adopted and taught in Europe, all communities responded by standardizing their rites to accord with their interpretation of Babylonian rulings. In Spain, the Babylonian rite had been the original, direct influence. Not only had Natronai Gaon's list of one hundred benedictions been written for a Spanish community, but Amram Gaon's prayer book was compiled in response to a request from the developing Jewish community in Spain.

The Palestinian and Babylonian traditions diverged the most in regard to the poetic alternatives to the standard prayers, the piyyutim. These compositions constitute the major creative medieval contribution to Jewish liturgy. Piyyut may be used in a specific sense to refer to hymnal, lyrical synagogue poetry in contradistinction to penitential (selihot) and elegiac compositions (kinot). It is also used in a more inclusive sense as a term for all of the religious poetry of the age period under discussion here. There are three major schools of piyyut: the Eastern, or Oriental, school and the roughly contemporaneous Italo-Ashkenazic (including Germany and other areas settled by Ashkenazic Jewish migration) and Spanish (Sephardic) schools.

Byzantine Palestine was the birthplace of piyyut. In the Eastern stage, piyyut had three major periods, which may be designated preclassical (fourth and fifth centuries), classical (sixth through eighth centuries), and, finally, late Eastern (ninth through eleventh centuries), when it declined and shifted to Babylonia, Italy, and North Africa. The monumental achievement and seminal influence of Palestinian piyyut could be appreciated only in the light of the fragments, poems, and even payyetanim (liturgical poets) discovered among the Cairo Genizah documents. Understanding this phenomenon has been a major task of twentieth-century liturgical scholarship.

Preclassical piyyut was being written while the standard prayer traditions were still being formed. Thus, among the poetic compositions embedded in the standard liturgy can be found piyyutim from this period. Stylistically they are characterized by their alphabetical acrostic structure, their loose rhythm of two major beats per versicle, which latter are usually arranged in lines of four (or two) versicles, thereby allowing for a structure deriving from the traditions rooted in biblical poetry based upon parallel pairs of

units of expression, and their heavy dependence upon biblical Hebrew vocabulary and forms.

A number of major accomplishments are rooted in the preclassical period. The major genres of payyetanic composition were largely established then, as was the custom that cantors (hazzanim, sing.: hazzan) would recite such compositions in place of the standard forms of prayer recited by their congregants. (Some of the precentors were also the payyetanim.) By going beyond the themes of prayer to treat of a Sabbath's scriptural readings or themes connected with a festival or fast, the payyetanim enriched their poetry and ensured variety. They further enhanced their compositions by drawing upon the rabbinic literature then being formed. Yose ben Yose, the first payyetan known by name, flourished toward the end of the preclassical period (probably fifth or sixth century). He used a technique of ending each line in a poem with the same word (word rhyme) and played on its variations of connotation and meaning. This technique paved the way for the development of rhyme in poetry; it also made possible a new way of structuring the poetic line that was based upon the poet's own inspiration in forming his expression and manipulating his syntax, rather than upon the demands of parallelism.

The shift to the classical period can be seen in the greater utilization of rabbinic sources, the increasing structural complexity of genres of composition, the insertion of the poet's name, in addition to the alphabet, into his acrostic sequences, and the use of rhyme. The payyetanim were evidently the first poets anywhere to use rhyme consistently in their compositions, whence it spread to Syriac (Christian) poetry and to Christian poetry written in the various European languages. Compressed expression, dense syntax, and enigmatic, allusive language render much of this poetry extremely difficult, for which it has been both harshly criticized and highly praised over the centuries. A "neoclassical" shift from their largely literary rabbinic Hebrew back to biblical norms, beginning in the late Eastern period, also made the classical payyetanim difficult to understand (for example, Abraham ibn Ezra). The major classical payyetanim are Yannai, Simeon ben Megas, Eleazar ben Kallir (or Killir), Haduta ben Abraham, Joshua ha-Kohen, and Joseph ben Nisan from Shaveh Kiryatayim. Eleazar ben Kallir, in particular, is associated with the difficult style, which is often described as "Kallirian."

As the classical period closed, payyetanic generic forms had grown too long, and various standard liturgies were fixed. Worshipers in the late Eastern period expected the cantor to repeat the text of the standard liturgy and to interpolate piyyutim as supplementary embellishment rather than as an alternative liturgy. Old, complex compositions were used selectively, whereas new compositions were less epic in proportion and style. Payyetanim were active in North Africa, Babylonia, and Italy, as well as in Palestine. The major center of innovation shifted to Babylonia, where Saadiah Gaon, having undertaken a revaluation of Hebrew philology, initiated a return to biblical principles as he understood them, thereby anticipating the approach of the great Spanish poets. His student, Dunash ben Labrat (d. ca. 990), caused a revolution in Hebrew prosody with his introduction of quantitative meter, in imitation of Arabic style. Dunash settled in Córdoba, where his innovation took hold and spread during the following two centuries.

The major period of liturgical creativity (1020–1150) came during the Islamic Golden Age in Spain. The language of Hebrew poetry was refined and perfected with an emphasis on *tsahat* (biblical) purism, in the same way that Islamic poetry was imitating and innovating according to the model of the classical language of the Koran. The new learning in the sciences and philosophy came to replace rabbinic literature as a source of material for poetic discourse. The personal religious concerns of the individual man also became a popular subject of this poetry. Though they are most widely known for their secular poetry, many of the major poets of the Spanish period excelled in religious poetry as well. They are among the finest poets who ever created in Hebrew: Joseph ibn Abitur, Solomon ibn Gabirol, Isaac ibn Ghayyat, Moses ibn Ezra, Judah Halevi, and Abraham ibn Ezra.

Gifted payyetanim, who were flourishing in Byzantine southern Italy as early as the mid ninth century, evidence the influence of classical Palestinian (Eastern) style. Important names surviving are those of Silano, Shefatiah, and his son, Amittai. Solomon ben Judah ha-Bavli (tenth century) in northern Italy reinvigorated his style with a Kallirian intricacy of structure and language, setting the tone for subsequent payyetanim. In addition to the difficult style, recourse to rabbinic sources and modes of thought characterized Italian piyyut, through which it came to dominate that of central Europe. This came about as Italian payyetanim (notably members of the Kalonymus family) moved to Germany in the tenth century, when Germany and France were just becoming

centers of learning, among whose scholars were to be numbered many payyetanim. In fact, these people drew heavily upon the rabbinic literature of the Babylonian Talmud and the late midrashim as well as the early Palestinian materials. Piyyut also spread from Italy to Greece and the Balkans. Although some Spanish influence came through Provence in the twelfth century, the Italo-Ashkenazic style of piyyut retained its Kallirian, rabbinic flavor. Major Ashkenazic figures were Moses ben Kalonymus, Meshullam ben Kalonymus, Simeon ben Isaac, and Gershom ben Judah Me'or ha-Golah in the tenth century; and Ephraim ben Isaac of Regensburg and Ephraim ben Jacob of Bonn in the twelfth century.

Paytanic creativity began to decline in the thirteenth century; by the fourteenth and fifteenth centuries most areas tended to accept certain cycles (*mahzorim,* sing.: *mahzor,* whence comes the Ashkenazic term for the festival prayer book) of piyyutim as traditional. Innovation had long been limited to some extent as the compositions of gifted predecessors came to be fixed in the cycles of local or regional rites. Nevertheless, piyyutim continued to be written on into the twentieth century, even if not in the major paytanic genres. Moreover, even with the fixing of rites, cantors retained the authority to select from among a number of alternatives collected in the manuscript copies of their liturgies (an editorial policy reflected in early printed editions of many rites, as well). Generally, cantors were the only ones in their congregations to possess copies of the piyyut cycles. Moreover, in some areas, they had to recite their selections by heart, thus increasing their monopoly over the selection. Copies of the smaller, more widely used, standard liturgies (*siddurim,* sing.: *siddur*) were much more common.

The basic rites of the Middle Ages, with the incorporation of piyyut, resolve themselves along the stylistic lines described above. From the earlier Palestinian traditions arose the Romanian (Byzantine, Greek, Balkan) and the Roman (Italian, with regional variations) rites. Out of the latter, came the rites of northern France (and England) and Ashkenaz (Germany). The Ashkenazic rite subdivided into a western (Rhine) and an eastern branch (Austrian or Bohemian, later Polish, reflecting the direction in which it spread). Called the "Palestinian group" because its standard fixed prayers were originally Palestinian, the preceding rites have all been modified to accord with Babylonian usage. The other major group of rites is called "Babylonian," because its standard prayers derived directly from the Babylonian geonim and their talmudic traditions. This latter group also shares traditions of piyyut created under the influence of Islamic styles. It may be subarranged as Sephardic, or Spanish, rites (with North African, Catalonian, and Aragonese branches), the very similar Provençal rite, and the Yemenite rite.

BIBLIOGRAPHY

For texts of the various liturgical rites see Ismar Elbogen, *Ha-Tefillah be-Yisrael be-Hispathuto ha-Historit* (1972), an updated translation of *Der jüdische Gottesdienst in seiner geschlichtlichen Entwicklung* (1913). A few rites exist only in manuscript, and only two of the others have been systematically translated into English—the Ashkenazic and the Sephardic.

Ashkenazic rite, daily and holiday. Philip Birnbaum, trans. and ed., *Daily Prayer Book* (1949 and reprints), and *High Holyday Prayer Book* (1960 and reprints); Abraham Rosenfeld, trans., *The Authorised Selichot for the Whole Year* (1956 and reprints), and *The Authorised Kinot for the Ninth of Av* (1965 and reprints); Isidore Singer, trans. and Joseph H. Hertz, ed., *The Authorized Daily Prayer Book* (1944 and reprints). Useful Hebrew commentaries are Isaac Seligman Baer, *Seder ᶜAvodat Yisrael* (1868 and reprints); A. L. Gordon and Enoch Zondel ben Joseph, *Siddur Otsar ha-Tefillot* (1914 or 1915 and reprints); Bernhard S. Jacobson, *Netiv Binah* (1964–1973), which is translated under the titles *Meditations in the Siddur* (1978), *The Weekday Siddur* (1978), and *The Sabbath Service* (1981).

Piyyut. The most comprehensive editions of Ashkenazic piyyut, with valuable introductions to the history of the liturgy, its texts and rites, are Ernst D. Goldschmidt, *Seder ha-Selihot* (1965), *Seder ha-Kinot le-Tishᶜah be-Av* (1968), *Mahzor le-Yamim ha-Noraᵓim* (1970), and, posthumously completed by Jonah Frankel, *Mahzor Sukot, Shemini ᶜAtseret, ve-Simhat Torah* (1981).

Because of its difficult language, piyyut has not often been translated. A comprehensive selection is found in T. Carmi, ed. and trans., *The Penguin Book of Hebrew Verse* (1981), 14–34, 51–55, 201–492, 583. Ezra Fleischer's comprehensive introduction, *Hebrew Liturgical Poetry in the Middle Ages* (in Hebrew) (1975), and his study, *The Yozer, Its Emergence and Development* (in Hebrew) (1984), are definitive. Indispensable in piyyut research is the listing of sources for the poems with an author index in Israel Davidson, *Thesaurus of Mediaeval Hebrew Poetry* (in Hebrew), 4 vols. (1924–1933, repr. with supplement through 1938, 1970). This is further supplemented by Jefim Schirman, "Studies in Hebrew Poetry," in *Kiryat sefer,* **26** (1950). In addition the Israel Academy of Sciences and Humanities has established the Mifᶜal le-Heker ha-Shirah veha-Piyyut ba-Genizah, Jerusalem, which continues the work on manuscript sources of the Institute for the Research of Medieval Hebrew Poetry, formerly of Berlin and Jerusalem. The Mifᶜal, directed by Ezra Fleischer, has an elaborate indexing system for poems in manuscript.

For introductory works, see Abraham Z. Idelsohn, *Jewish Liturgy and Its Development* (*ca.* 1932, repr. *ca.* 1967); Abraham E. Millgram, *Jewish Worship* (1971); Raphael Posner et al., eds., *Jewish Liturgy: Prayer and Synagogue Service Through the Ages* (1975); Shalom Spiegel, "On Medieval Hebrew Poetry," in Louis Finkelstein, ed., *The Jews: Their History, Culture, and Religion,* I, 3rd ed. (1960). Comprehensive modern studies of the fixed liturgy include Joseph Heinemann, *Prayer in the Talmud: Forms and Patterns,* Richard S. Sarason, trans. (1977), and Lawrence A. Hoffman, *The Canonization of the Synagogue Service* (1979). Review essays on research (mainly on the standard liturgy) include Jakob J. Petuchowski, ed., *Contributions to the Scientific Study of Jewish Liturgy* (1970), introduction. Most important is Richard S. Sarason, "On the Use of Method in the Modern Study of Jewish Liturgy," in William S. Green, ed., *Approaches to Ancient Judaism* (1978). For a review of piyyut scholarship, see Jefim Schirman, "Introduction," in Davidson, *Thesaurus,* I.

JAY ROVNER

[See also **Abraham ben Meïr ibn Ezra; Ashkenaz; Cairo Genizah; Gershom ben Judah; Hebrew Poetry; Judah Halevi; Judaism; Kalonymus Family; Saadiah Gaon; Sephardim; Solomon ben Judah ibn Gabirol.**]

LITURGY, STATIONAL, was the practice whereby according to an established cycle the bishop of a city celebrated Mass or other liturgical services at different churches on important days. The term "stational," coming from the Latin *statio,* referred in the early Christian period to an assembly at a designated place on a designated day. Most probably the term had a liturgical meaning as early as the second century. The practice certainly existed early in the Eastern churches. In the West the paradigm for stational liturgy was Rome. During the very early period of the Roman church the people and clergy met to celebrate Mass with their bishop or the pope, who represented the unity of the worshiping community. But as the Christian community grew and more buildings became necessary, individual presbyters began to celebrate Mass locally throughout the city, even as the bishop celebrated it in his basilica. These local celebrations took place in halls or private houses called *tituli,* after the name or title of the donor who had provided them for worship. The *tituli* were in a sense the parish churches of the city. In these local celebrations a symbol of unity with the bishop's Mass was provided in the *fermentum* or piece of leavened bread consecrated by the bishop and sent to the local *titulus,* to be mixed with the consecrated species there. But on major celebrations certain churches throughout the city came to be designated as stations where the clergy and people of the city or their representatives could gather for Mass in union with the pope himself. The practice itself had probably developed by the third century, and by the fourth century the churches in which the pope said Mass on these designated days were called stations. Following ancient pagan practice there could on occasion be a procession, or *litania,* to the stational church, during which litanies were chanted, and the procession would begin at a *collecta,* or the church where the people had collected.

The growth of the list designating days with their stational churches and *collectae* was slow and somewhat haphazard from the fourth century until the time of Pope Gregory I (*d.* 604), who seems to have been responsible for fixing most of the cycle. In general, the course of development appears to have been that on Sundays and the most important days the stational liturgy was celebrated in the large basilicas of Rome to accommodate the crowds; on important weekdays, such as those in Lent, the stations were at the smaller *tituli;* and on the feasts of martyrs and saints the stations were held in cemetery chapels or in the church dedicated to the saint. After the cycle of days and churches for stational liturgy had been fixed in the time of Gregory I there were a few additions made, such as the inclusion at the time of Pope Gregory II (715–731) of stational liturgies for the previously aliturgical Thursdays in Lent, or the creation in 1006 of St. Trypho as the stational church for the first Saturday of Lent.

Shortly after the time of Gregory I the designations of the stational churches and *collectae* came to be added to the rubrics for the liturgical texts in sacramentaries, lectionaries, homiliaria, ordines, and the like. And as manuscripts of these texts were spread, so the existence of the Roman stational liturgy came to be known throughout Europe, even in locations where no stational liturgy was practiced. In several cities, however, there was a local stational liturgy, which in some instances was as old as that in Rome. Among the cities with stational liturgies were Ravenna, Vercelli, Tours, Metz, Paris, Strasbourg, Liège, Mainz, and Cologne. In Rome itself the practice of stational liturgies was discontinued when the popes moved to Avignon in the early thirteenth century, although the designation of the sta-

tional churches with their days was continued in liturgical books down to the twentieth century. A modified Lenten stational liturgy was revived in Rome during the first half of the twentieth century, largely under the aegis of the *Collegium cultorum martyrum.* And in a tradition begun by Pope Paul VI the pope opens the Lenten season in a procession with litanies from the modern *collecta* of S. Anselmo to the ancient stational basilica of Sta. Sabina, where ashes are imposed and Mass is celebrated. Throughout the remainder of Lent the list of churches where daily Masses are celebrated is remarkably like that established in late patristic antiquity and the early Middle Ages.

BIBLIOGRAPHY

Geoffrey G. Willis, *Further Essays in Early Roman Liturgy* (1968), 1–87.

ROGER E. REYNOLDS

[See also **Lent; Processions.**]

LITURGY, TREATISES ON. During the Middle Ages, scores of treatises, commentaries, and *expositiones* on the liturgy were written and widely circulated. Almost all liturgical acts were explained in one or more of these treatises, sometimes alone or sometimes in combination with others. However, the vast majority of expositions dealt with the following topics: the Mass; the Divine Office; baptism and confirmation; liturgical ministers or orders and vestments; dedication of churches; sickness, death, and burial; and the liturgical year, or kalendar.

In their explanations of the liturgy, medieval commentators examined their subjects with a variety of approaches. The explanation might simply be a description of the way a cultual act was performed, that is, a rubrical approach. Beyond this approach there might be an account of the origins of the activity, that is, a historical approach. Related to this was an etymological approach, an explanation of the liturgical act on the basis of the origin of the term or terms used to describe it. Finally, there were theological and moral approaches. In the former the theological significance of the rites was explained according to allegorical, anagogical, spiritual, mystical, and tropological meanings. The latter approach had as its aim the improvement of religious life by appeals to liturgical precedents. In medieval treatises on liturgy these various approaches could be used either singly or in combination.

Because medieval liturgical rites followed certain ordines and were repetitive, the explanations were usually bound by these regular patterns. For example, a commentator explaining the Mass usually followed the order of the rite itself beginning at some fixed point, such as the introit or the *Dominus vobiscum* before the canon. Bound by the patterns of the liturgical rites, the medieval liturgical commentators usually felt obliged to follow to some extent previous commentaries on a particular rite. Occasionally, a brilliant commentator, such as Amalarius of Metz (d. *ca.* 850), Bernold of Constance (d. 1100), or Ivo of Chartres (d. 1115), would innovate; but the vast majority of commentaries are largely repetitive, amassing layer upon layer of previous commentary on various cultic acts. Hence, in using any medieval treatise on the liturgy, the reader must always be aware of the multiple layers of earlier sources that were used. Among these sources were: Scripture and scriptural commentaries; texts of the Fathers; canon law and monastic rules; sermons, admonitions, and allocutions; and the liturgical formulae themselves—rubrical, exhortational, and prayers.

As for the contexts in which medieval liturgical treatises appear, the most usual case finds a commentary combined with others of its kind. There was a tendency in such cases to compile vast florilegia of liturgical explanations. Sometimes these florilegia would deal with a single liturgical rite, such as the Mass, or sometimes with a variety of rites, such as baptism, the Mass, and ordination. But liturgical commentaries could be joined to other types of material. In canon-law manuscripts, for example, liturgical commentaries could be used to introduce or conclude a group of legal norms concerning a particular liturgical subject, such as the Eucharist or sacred orders. Further, in manuscripts containing the formulaic texts for the liturgy, such as sacramentaries, ordines, and the like, the commentaries could be intruded, perhaps to function as didactic or inspirational pieces to be read before or after the performance of the liturgical rite. Liturgical commentaries might also be juxtaposed to more strictly theological tracts or inserted into sentence collections to initiate, illustrate, or explain more profound points made there. Finally, liturgical expositions could be combined with sermonic material to be presented catechetically, as exhortations, or in homilies.

From the very beginnings of the church there were writers who described in varying degrees of completeness her cultual activity. Like the many books of the Old Testament, the New Testament books refer to various liturgical rites, such as baptism, the Eucharist, and ordination. Not only were the rites described, but they were often interpreted. The biblical books themselves are filled with liturgical texts, such as prayers, acclamations, benedictions, and doxologies. Also, directives were given for different sacred rites, such as postures to be assumed, the duties of ministers, and the reading of Scriptures.

PATRISTIC TREATISES

After New Testament times, the Fathers of the late first and second centuries often referred to liturgical matters, especially baptism and the Eucharist. The *Didache* gives directions for the Eucharist; Clement I (*ca.* 92–101) speaks of a liturgical celebration; and the epistles of Ignatius and Barnabas, the *Shepherd of Hermas,* and the *Epistle to Diognetus* all mention elements of sacred ritual. The Apologists of the second century continued this tradition with Justin Martyr (d. *ca.* 165) giving a brief description of the Eucharist, but without text, and Irenaeus of Lyons (d. *ca.* 202) furnishing valuable material regarding baptism, the creed, Eucharist, and the priesthood.

By the third century, commentaries in Latin on aspects of Christian worship began to appear, and the language in these works played an important role in fixing liturgical usage in the Western church. Chief among these Latin commentators were the North African Tertullian (d. *ca.* 225) and Cyprian (d. 258), who described baptism, the manner of prayer, penance, fasting, and the consecration of virgins. Contemporary with these influential Latin commentators were several who wrote in Greek. Clement of Alexandria (d. *ca.* 215) alluded in his writings to liturgical practice, and Origen (d. *ca.* 254) wrote at length on baptism, the creed, Eucharist, orders, anointing the sick, and the liturgical year. Perhaps more important, however, was the *Apostolic Tradition,* generally attributed to Hippolytus of Rome (d. *ca.* 236), which dealt with baptism, ordination, and the consecration of oils, and even contained a text for the Eucharist.

The *Apostolic Tradition* became the basis for a further group of pseudoapostolic writings that provided additional comment on liturgical materials. Among these were the *Apostolic Constitutions,* the *Testamentum domini nostri Jesu Christ,* and the *Canones Hippolyti* (dating from *ca.* 500). The material in these compilations, which in reality were canon-law collections, was augmented in the fourth century with the catechetical lectures in Greek by Cyril of Jerusalem (*d.* 386), explaining baptism and the Eucharist, and the letters of the Cappadocian fathers, who frequently alluded to liturgical rites.

In the Western church from the fourth century on, there was a plethora of miscellaneous comment on the liturgy. Throughout their writings such Fathers as Jerome and Augustine dealt with aspects of the liturgy; the epistles of Pope Leo I (440–461) are a treasure trove on the rite celebrated at Rome; and monastic writings of such figures as John Cassian (*d. ca.* 435) and Benedict of Nursia (*d. ca.* 550) are of capital importance for explanations of the Divine Office. Two figures in the West devoted entire or nearly entire treatises to very different types of liturgical commentary. Ambrose of Milan, in his *De sacramentis* and *De mysteriis*—both often copied in medieval manuscripts—described the ritual and meaning of baptism, confirmation, and the Eucharist. Etheria (also Aetheria or Egeria), a Spanish pilgrim to the Holy Land at the end of the fourth century, gives in her *Itinerarium* an extraordinary account of the liturgy of Palestine for some of the most important feasts of the Christian year.

PRE-CAROLINGIAN TREATISES

With the gradual evolution and elaboration of liturgical rites, commentators began to describe their meaning with symbolic and mystical approaches. Particularly important in the East was a Pseudo-Dionysius of the end of the fifth century, whose *De ecclesiastica hierarchia* dealt with baptism, confirmation, the Eucharist, orders, and funeral rites. His work eventually became known in the West and played a significant role there in sacramental theology.

In very late patristic antiquity and the beginning of the early Middle Ages in the West, scholars from Spain were in the vanguard of liturgical scholarship and commentary. Isidore of Seville (*d.* 636) was by far the most important of these figures, and two of his works had an enormous influence on liturgical commentary throughout the Middle Ages. The first of these, the *De ecclesiasticis officiis* or *De origine officiorum,* written between 598 and 615 and dedicated to Fulgentius, bishop of Ecija, was divided into two books with chapters, although it was perhaps Braulio, bishop of Saragossa (*d. ca.* 651), who made these divisions. The first book (*ca.* 45 chapters) deals with the Office and its components, the kalendar, and the Mass; the second (*ca.* 26 chapters) deals with the liturgical ministers, religious men and women, and baptism. It is often stated that Isidore's treat-

ment reflects the liturgical practice in the Old Spanish or Mozarabic rite, but there has also been an argument that he was simply stating personal preference. The sources used in the *De ecclesiasticis officiis* are extensive. For the first book the major sources were the works of Hilary of Poitiers (*d.* 367), Nicetas of Remesiana (*d. ca.* 414), Augustine, Gregory I, Cassian, and various canon-law prescriptions; and for the second book two of the major sources were the canonistic *Statuta ecclesiae antiqua* (*ca.* 475) and the Pseudo-Hieronymian *De septem ordinibus ecclesiae.* The *De ecclesiasticis officiis* had an extraordinarily large circulation in medieval manuscripts, and excerpts from it were used in the influential *Institutio canonicorum* of 816/817, which itself also had wide manuscript diffusion. Beyond this, extracts from the *De ecclesiasticis officiis* are found in some form in virtually every major liturgical commentary of the Middle Ages.

Not long after he had completed the *De ecclesiasticis officiis,* Isidore put the final touches to his version of the *Etymologiae* or *Origines,* a vast encyclopedia in twenty books of all religious and secular knowledge treated from an etymological perspective. Two of the books (6 and 7) deal with liturgical topics, such as the Christian year, the Mass, the Office, baptism, penance, and clerical orders and ordination. The sources again are numerous and, as might be expected, are often the same as those in the *De ecclesiasticis officiis.* Besides the dominant etymological approach to his topics, Isidore also used historical and allegorial explanations. The *Origines,* especially the first books including those on liturgy, had an extraordinarily prolific manuscript tradition of over a thousand manuscripts. Moreover, extracts from the liturgical section are often found in manuscripts and in other texts, such as Beatus of Liébana's celebrated commentary on the Apocalypse. As was the case with the *De ecclesiasticis officiis,* there is hardly a liturgical treatise in the Middle Ages that does not use Isidore's *Origines* in some way.

Sometime during the seventh or eighth century in Spain a treatise on the liturgical duties of clerics was composed and attributed to Isidore. The tract, in the form of a letter to Bishop Leudefredus of Córdoba, lists the various clerical grades and their cultual duties. The letter had an extremely wide circulation in the Middle Ages, particularly in canon-law collections and ordination admonitions.

The liturgical work of Isidore quickly passed to Ireland, where it was used and combined with the imaginative liturgical commentary of Irish scholars.

Among these Irish works are those on the Mass, such as the *Indaltoir fiugor indingrimme* in the early-ninth-century *Stowe Missal*; on the Office, such as the *Ratio decursus qui fuerunt eius auctores*; and on orders, such as the *De officiis septem graduum* and Ordinals of Christ. Of these last tracts, the former lists the ecclesiastical orders together with their liturgical obligations and the latter, the orders with some event or saying in Christ's life that sanctions the liturgical duty of the officer. These Irish tracts on orders enjoyed extensive circulation on the Continent inasmuch as they were transmitted through such compilations as the canonical *Collectio hibernensis*. In many of the early Irish liturgical treatises there is a particular fascination for etymology and numerical meaning.

The early influence of Isidore in territories where the Gallican rite was practiced is also found in the celebrated *Expositio brevis antiquae liturgiae gallicanae*, attributed to Germanus (Germain), bishop of Paris (*d.* 576), but written after his time. In this exposition of the distinctive Gallican liturgy, not only are the parts of the Mass explained but also aspects of the Office.

CAROLINGIAN TREATISES

With the ecclesiastical reforms of Charlemagne in the late eighth and early ninth centuries there came a flood of liturgical commentaries. This was largely in response to a series of directives, both secular and ecclesiastical, requiring clerics to know and understand liturgical texts and rituals, especially those of the Roman rite, which was at that time being promoted. Particularly important among these liturgical rites were baptism and the Mass, the former because large numbers of adult pagans were being baptized as a result of Charlemagne's conquests, the latter because it was the one continuously repeated rite that publicly signified membership in a renewed Christian society.

Susan Keefe has shown that over sixty treatises on baptism, many in multiple manuscript exemplars, were compiled in the Carolingian period. Many of these tracts were the result of a letter in 812 by Charlemagne asking how his archbishops and their suffragans "teach and instruct the priests of God and the people commissioned to [them] on the sacrament of baptism." In response to this inquiry dozens of brief descriptions of baptismal practice were written, and from these other tracts were compiled. Although most of the tracts are anonymous, several are attributed to such ecclesiastical luminaries as Alcuin of

York (*d.* 804), Theodulf of Orleans (*d.* 821), Leidrad, archbishop of Lyons (*d.* 817), Magnus of Sens, Jesse, bishop of Amiens, Maxentius of Aquileia, and Hildebald, bishop of Cologne (*d.* 819). Much of the material in these tracts is based on biblical and patristic sources and etymological analysis, but they are of extraordinary interest because they illustrate the diversity of baptismal practice and interpretation in the Carolingian empire.

The requirement that clerics be able to understand and explain the Mass also resulted in several early commentaries written about 800. Among these are the *Dominus vobiscum, Primum in ordine, Quotiens contra se*, and a section of the *Missa pro multis causis*. Of particular interest is the *Dominus vobiscum*, because the text commented on is the Roman Mass canon, which at the time was widely circulated with the Gregorian Sacramentary as the quasi-official Mass book of the Carolingians. The *Dominus vobiscum* is usually attributed to Amalarius of Metz (*d. ca.* 850), but its earliest-dated manuscript was written about 813, and in a Salzburg manuscript of about 825 the tract is attributed to Alcuin. Like the baptismal treatises, the *Dominus vobiscum* is based heavily on patristic sources, reaching back even to the Venerable Bede, and its interpretive approaches are descriptive, etymological, typological, and at

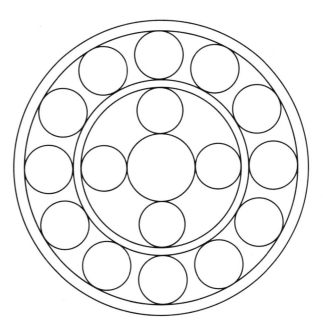

Distribution of eucharistic hosts, representing (from outside) the angelic chorus, the four Evangelists, and the Son of God. After diagram in the *Revelation to Eldefonsus* (845). VATICAN, VAT. LAT. 1341, FOL. 188ʳ

times historical. Of the forty-six manuscript exemplars thus far discovered, fifteen are from the ninth century. During the eleventh and twelfth centuries the tract again enjoyed a degree of popularity, because it was incorporated into both liturgical florilegia and collections of canon law, especially in central and southern Italy.

Closely related to the baptismal tracts, some of which were in dialogue and interrogatory form, were several early texts cast in this same erotematic style. Among these are the *Disputatio puerorum* attributed to Alcuin, which deals with the liturgical ministers and the Mass, and the *loca episcopi ad sacerdotes* and *loca monachorum,* in which priests and monks are asked questions on, and furnished with answers to, a wide variety of liturgical topics. As *ioca* or jokes, these tracts often contain an element of whimsy. Similarly whimsical is another Carolingian tract of a slightly later date on the making of eucharistic hosts and their distribution on the altar. This tract, a revelation made to bishop Eldefonsus of Spain on the seventh day of the tenth month of 845, is in at least three manuscripts, several of them canonistic, and together with the numerological fantasies regarding the Eucharistic hosts, there are illustrative diagrams in the manuscripts (overleaf).

Much more celebrated than any of these early Carolingian liturgical treatises are those by three major liturgiologists of the ninth century, Amalarius of Metz, Hrabanus Maurus, archbishop of Mainz (*d.* 856), and Walafrid Strabo (*d.* 849). Of these three, Amalarius was clearly the greatest and most influential, despite the condemnations of his work and the scorn heaped on his allegorizing methods by his contemporaries (as well as by twentieth-century critics). Among the factors that made Amalarius one of the greatest early medieval liturgiologists were his training under Alcuin, his study and prestigious position under Louis the Pious, his trips to Rome and Constantinople, where he carefully observed liturgical practices, and his active searching out and reforming of liturgical texts. Amalarius' major commentaries on the liturgy are generally divided according to those on the Mass and Office and his *magnum opus,* the *Liber officialis.* Among his works on the Mass are the *Canonis missae interpretatio* and *Missae expositionis geminus codex.* Also belonging either to Amalarius or influenced by his work are the *Eclogae de ordine romano, Introitus missae quare,* and the major portion of the *Missa pro multis causis.* After he had compiled his own antiphonary, Amalarius wrote an exposition on the Office called the *Liber de ordine antiphonarii,* in which he commented on the formulas found in his sources.

Amalarius' greatest work, the *Liber officialis,* found in over sixty manuscripts, went through three editions. In the first of these, from the early 820's, there were three books. The first dealt with the kalendar, the second with the ember days, orders, ordination, and vestments, and the third with the Mass. He wrote a fourth book on the Office in 829; it is found in the manuscripts of the *Liber officialis* either as an addition to the first edition of books 1–3 or worked into the second edition of about 826/827 and third edition of about 831/832. As sources for the work, Amalarius used both Roman and Gallican liturgical books together with patristic authorities from Cyprian to Bede. Influenced by the latter, he used at least four types of interpretation—historical, allegorical, tropological, and anagogical—although he is most celebrated (and condemned) for his allegorical explanations of the liturgy. In any event, Amalarius did not slavishly follow the Fathers but was extremely original, even claiming immediate inspiration of God.

The influence of Amalarius on medieval and even modern liturgiology has been incalculable. Besides numerous manuscripts and excerpta of his works, Amalarius' tracts were modified and reissued by such figures as William of Malmesbury (*d. ca.* 1143) and the author of the *Liber quare.* The number of later liturgical expositions that use Amalarius' texts or ideas is enormous.

Much more traditional and derivative in his liturgical commentaries was Amalarius' contemporary Hrabanus Maurus, who wrote the *De clericorum institutione* and the *Liber de sacris ordinibus.* The former, compiled at the request of the monks at Fulda, is in three books and deals with the liturgical ministers and vestments, baptism, the Mass, the Office, fasting, penance, and the kalendar. The latter, dedicated to Thiotmar, deals especially with baptism and the Mass. In his work Hrabanus borrows from Scripture extensively; of the Fathers used, Isidore with his *De ecclesiasticis officiis* and *Origines* stands out.

Hrabanus' student, Walafrid Strabo, wrote the *Liber de exordiis et incrementis quarundam in observationibus ecclesiasticis rerum* between 840 and 842 during his temporary deposition from the abbacy of Reichenau. The work, divided into thirty-two chapters dealing with ecclesiastical buildings and furniture, prayer, the Mass, baptism, and ecclesiastical ministers, is always cited as a prime example of a ninth-century liturgical tract using a historical approach. Walafrid deals with the origins of various liturgical practices and is keenly aware of the differences in rites as practiced in Rome and in Frankish territories.

Resembling the historical approach taken by Walafrid was one taken by Agobard, bishop of Lyons (d. 840), in his *Liber de correctione antiphonarii* and *Contra libros IV Amalarii*, and by Florus of Lyons (d. ca. 860) in his *Liber de divina psalmodia* and *De actione missae*. Both of these Lyonese clerics attacked Amalarius for his allegory and theories going beyond the Fathers. In turn they interpreted the liturgy along literal and historical lines, making extensive use of the works of the Fathers.

The tract of Florus on the Mass was to demonstrate its influence slightly later in the celebrated Mass commentary of Remigius of Auxerre (d. ca. 908), the *Expositio missae*. Using Florus' work together with an *Expositio missae* found in a mid-ninth-century manuscript from the Loire area (Troyes BM 804) and an *expositio* entitled *Missa, ut beatus Isidorus dicit*, Remigius put together an explanation combining both allegorical and historical approaches.

TENTH- AND EARLY-ELEVENTH-CENTURY
TREATISES

Remigius' tract, in turn, found its way into the only tenth-century commentary on the liturgy of any significance, the *Liber de divinis officiis*, incorrectly attributed to Alcuin. The anonymous compiler of this tract, who perhaps worked in southern France, took material from Isidore's *De ecclesiasticis officiis*, Amalarius' *Liber officialis*, the baptismal *expositio Primo paganus*, *Ordo romanus XXXIV* on ordinations, expositions on the paternoster, and the works of Helperic of Auxerre and Remigius of Auxerre, and arranged them in several chapters on the kalendar, orders, tonsure, ordination of a bishop, vestments, the Mass, sickness, death, funerals, and the mind's day. Because of the variety of his sources, many types of liturgical interpretation are used: etymological, literal, typological, and spiritual. Although it is generally thought that the tract played little role in later liturgical commentaries, it is now known that it exists in whole or part in at least thirty-nine manuscripts.

Another Mass commentary, probably written in the tenth century and almost totally ignored by modern scholars, is found in at least fifteen manuscripts of the eleventh and twelfth centuries from southern

and central Italy. Entitled in many manuscripts *Ordo quod sacerdos debet sacrificare*, the tract grew out of an early Carolingian canon attributed to Pope Damasus and St. Jerome on the hour of the Mass and then developed into a commentary on the trinitarian significance of aspects of the Mass. For example, even the priest or presbyter before the altar represents the Trinity, because in his name there are three "persons": "pres," representing the Father; "by," representing the Son; and "ter," representing the Holy Spirit. This tract, found in at least seven recensions, came to play an important role in early-eleventh-century canon-law collections from southern Italy as an introduction to canons on the Mass.

Just as this Mass commentary was being incorporated into the collections, a Mass commentary of a very different type was being composed by Berno, abbot of Reichenau (d. 1048). In the first two chapters of his *Libellus de quibusdam rebus ad missae officium pertinentibus*, Berno took a much more historical approach to the Mass. The first chapter largely repeats material found in the *Liber pontificalis*; and the second is a historical explanation of why the presbyter should sing the Gloria not only on Easter but every Sunday. In the remaining five chapters on the kalendar and feasts, however, Amalarian spiritual interpretation is much more in evidence.

TREATISES FROM THE MID ELEVENTH
TO THE LATE TWELFTH CENTURY

Liturgical commentary, which had been at a fairly low ebb from the end of the ninth to the middle of the eleventh century, experienced a revival just at the time the church at large was undergoing reforms promoted especially by the papacy, and hence it is no surprise to find that many of the ecclesiastical figures most prominent in that reform were also the authors of treatises on the liturgy.

In Italy, the canonist Bonizo of Sutri (d. ca. 1095) wrote a short tract entitled *Libellus de sacramentis*, which discusses baptism, the Eucharist, salt, and holy oils. The approach taken is like Berno's, that is, liturgical development is traced back historically through papal practice to the New Testament.

A not dissimilar papal emphasis is also found in the finest liturgical commentary since Amalarius' work, the *Micrologus de ecclesiasticis observationibus* of Bernold of Constance (d. 1100). This commentary, dealing with the Mass, ember days, and kalendar, had as its objective the Romanization of the liturgy. Bernold made repeated reference to the Roman tradition and attempted to prune liturgical practices that had grown up outside of Rome during the tenth and eleventh centuries, such as the multiplication of prayers in the Mass. Although Bernold knew and used allegorical interpretation, his approach was a more descriptive, practical, and historical one, and hence the *Micrologus* is generally included among commentaries of a literal type. The influence of the *Micrologus* was very substantial. At least forty-five manuscript exemplars still exist; and in one area, Hungary, the bishops in synod are said to have established the *Micrologus* as the norm for the performance of the Roman rite.

Just as Bernold was compiling his *Micrologus,* a commentary of an old Amalarian type, the *Liber quare,* was enjoying a wide circulation throughout Europe. The commentary, cast in dialogue form and explaining the kalendar, the Office, orders, and vestments, resembles the old catechetical commentaries, but it is shot through with material borrowed from Amalarius. There is a possibility that this tract came from the school of Anselm of Laon because many of the fifty-six extant manuscripts are in French, but the question of authorship and date of composition is still open.

Also dependent on Amalarius is a group of late-eleventh-century commentaries composed in what might be called a Norman school. The first of these was the *De officiis ecclesiasticis* written by John of Avranches (*d.* 1079) and dedicated to Archbishop Maurilius of Rouen. The tract, dealing with the clerical state, canonical hours, Mass, and kalendar, is marked by two things. First, it displays a precise knowledge of the rites and texts in Normandy and a thorough knowledge of contemporary liturgical books and actual celebration of the liturgy. Second, the tract shows a thorough assimilation of the ideas and methods of Amalarius' *Liber officialis,* although John could modify its ideas and imagery to fit different situations. Unlike Bernold's work and the *Liber quare,* John's *De officiis ecclesiasticis* seems to have enjoyed little circulation, and it is now found in only three manuscripts in differing recensions. But Ronald Zawilla has recently discovered that John's work was revised and abbreviated in a work called the *Quia quattuor elementis,* and this abbreviation can be found in at least ten manuscripts scattered throughout European libraries. From this tract a derivative commentary was made, probably in southern Germany, and incorrectly attributed to the liturgist and canonist Ivo of Chartres (*d.* 1115).

Copies and excerpta of pre-twelfth-century liturgical treatises continued to be made after 1100, but a new generation of commentators began to produce a flood of treatises using not only the older approaches but also newer ones influenced by the developing scholastic method. Further, although the traditional liturgical rites and the kalendar continued to receive comment, there was a tendency to concentrate on the Eucharist, which, since the Berengarian controversy, had become the object of intense theological speculation and popular devotion.

One of the more interesting of the twelfth-century commentaries is the largely descriptive *Ordo et caeremoniae ecclesiae Ambrosianae Mediolanensis* of Beroldus of Milan. In this treatise the local rite of Milan is described, including the ceremonies, clergy, Office, Mass, and kalendar.

Of the twelfth-century commentaries that follow a more literal approach, three stand out. There is first the *Expositio in canonem missae* of Odo of Cambrai (*d.* 1113), in which the various prayers of the canon are discussed with clarification of words and some theological speculation. Then there is the *De differentia quattuor temporum* by Sigebert of Gembloux (*d.* 1112), in which the ember days are explained and justified with frequent references to papal practice and directives. But far more important was the later work of the Parisian master John Beleth (*d.* 1182), the *Summa de ecclesiasticis officiis (ca.* 1160), still extant in over 180 manuscripts. The tract, dealing with the kalendar, ministers, Office, and Mass, explains the liturgy largely through etymological derivations, historical analysis, and the opinions of earlier authors, both the *antiqui,* such as Augustine, Bede, and Amalarius, and the *moderni,* such as Rupert of Deutz (*d.* 1129), Honorius "of Autun" (Honorius Augustodunensis), and Gratian.

Although these more practical and literal commentaries have received the lion's share of praise from modern liturgiologists, it was the allegorical and spiritual commentaries that seem to have been more popular in the twelfth century and beyond. Among the earliest of these are the sermons attributed to Ivo of Chartres. The liturgical subjects treated in them are baptism, orders and ordination, vestments, dedication of churches, the Mass, and the kalendar. Throughout these sermons Ivo used the allegorical methods of his predecessors and was heavily dependent on their works as sources. But particularly striking is his use of the Old Testament, not simply as an analogy to later Christian worship, but as presenting a conformity (*convenientia*) to various parts of liturgical rites. The influence of Ivo's sermons was enormous. For example, *Sermo II* on orders is found in at least sixty manuscripts, and portions of it entered dozens of later liturgical commentaries and even the *Sententiae* of Peter Lombard (*d.* 1160), the standard text that all students in theology used and commented on throughout the high and later Middle Ages.

Reflecting Ivo's work is the *De sacrificio missae,* attributed to Alger of Liège because of the text's proximity to an authentically Algerian work in Paris (BN 812). The author divides the Mass into two parts and emphasizes the role of Christ the high priest between the Mosaic and sacramental priesthood.

Also emphasizing events in Christ's life as the rationale for the various canonical hours is the short *De divinis officiis* of Cardinal Drogo of Ostia (*d.* 1138). Similarly in the *Tractatus de sacramentis ecclesiae mysteriis atque ecclesiasticis ritibus* of Bruno of Segni (*d.* 1123) the dedication of churches, baptism and confirmation, and vestments are related to sayings and events in Christ's life.

The conservative Benedictine theologian Rupert of Deutz was the author of the *De divinis officiis* (1111), a treatise in twelve books on the Office, vestments, the Mass, and the kalendar. Clearly in the tradition of Amalarius, Rupert went beyond him in two respects. First, he introduced a greater number of biblical images into his commentary; and second, his elaborations on such subjects as the Eucharist display new theological insights of the eleventh and early twelfth centuries.

Attributed to Hildebert of Le Mans (*d.* 1133) are two liturgical commentaries, the *Versus de mysterio missae* and *Liber de expositione missae,* only the first of which is genuinely his. In the *Versus,* a novel versified Mass commentary is based on the work of Amalarius and Ivo. This work was used as a basis for lectures and further commentaries throughout the twelfth century. The *Liber* is a much less original work and depends heavily on Isidore, the Carolingian *Missa pro multis causis,* Amalarius, Paschasius Radbertus (*d. ca.* 860), and the contemporary Honorius Augustodunensis.

Honorius, one of the most enigmatic authors who wrote in the first half of the twelfth century, may have been from England or southern Germany (Augsburg?), but not Autun. He composed at least two major commentaries on aspects of the liturgy, the *Gemma animae* and *Sacramentarium.* Of particular importance is the *Gemma,* found in at least thirty manuscripts, which deals with the Mass, ecclesiastical buildings, vestments, orders, the Office, the kalendar, and scriptural passages used in the liturgy. Honorius is heavily dependent on Amalarius but goes beyond him in multiplying symbolic interpretations. Moreover, he is especially careful to draw parallels between liturgical actions and events in the life of Christ.

In Norman England William of Malmesbury composed for his friend Robert (perhaps the bishop of Bath, *d.* 1166) an abbreviation of Amalarius on the Mass, orders, and vestments . Although Amalarius' organizational scheme and allegorizing methods are used, William was much more interested in the historical background of the liturgy and often used his own reading of the *Liber pontificalis* to supply details. Further, he was not afraid to modify Amalarius' allegorical explanations and to improve on them with his own mastery of numerological meanings. Finally, William seems to have used liturgical sources beyond those of Amalarius, and there are clear echoes of the Norman John of Avranches and the *Quia quattuor elementis,* the manuscripts of which were in England during William's time.

Attributed to Hugh of St. Victor (*d. ca.* 1141) are two treatises dealing with liturgy, the *De sacramentis* and *Speculum ecclesiae,* the latter actually composed between 1160 and 1165 in Hugonian style long after Hugh's death. The *De sacramentis,* Hugh's masterpiece found in whole or part in over 230 manuscripts, is divided into two books, the second of which deals with orders and vestments, dedication of churches, baptism and confirmation, the Mass, marriage, confession and penance, unction and death. Because the treatise as a whole is on the sacraments, sacramental theology reflecting new trends of the late eleventh and early twelfth centuries is dominant, but liturgical commentary has been worked into the theological discussions. For sources Hugh drew heavily on the Fathers and such *moderni* as Ivo of Chartres, Anselm of Laon, William of Champeaux (*d.* 1122), and even Abelard, but large parts of the work are clearly original.

The Pseudo-Hugonian *Speculum ecclesiae* consists of nine chapters dealing with the mystical and allegorical meaning of the church, Office, kalendar, orders, vestments, Mass, and Scriptures. The author of the treatise drew heavily from the works of Amalarius, Ivo, and Hildebert; and the incipient scholastic theological synthesis of the authentically Hugonian *De sacramentis* is clearly present also.

The short treatise in ten chapters on the Mass, entitled the *Libellus de canone mystici libaminis* and sometimes assigned to John of Cornwall (Johannes Cornubiensis), has again recently been attributed by

Mary Schaefer to Richard the Premonstratensian. This tract is especially interesting for its use of Old Testament typology to interpret the Mass liturgy and for its extensive number symbolism, the descendant of the numerological explanations of the early Irish commentators.

Sometime between 1162 and 1167 Isaac of Stella (d. ca. 1169) addressed an *Epistula de officio missae* to the nearby bishop of Poitiers on the canon of the Mass. This letter, found in some twenty-two manuscripts in three recensions, likens the three oblations of the canon—that of the bread and wine, of the body and blood of Christ, and of the heavenly offering of Christ as the eternal high priest—to the sacrifices on the three altars of the Jerusalem temple. Although the letter is reminiscent of Ivo's sermon on the Mass in its comparison of Old and New Testament practice, it is clearly original in many respects.

In the *Tractatus de sacramentis altaris*, likely written by Stephen of Autun (d. 1189) in the last quarter of the twelfth century, doctrinal questions regarding the Eucharist are mixed with a variety of liturgical topics, including orders, vestments, and the Mass. The sources used are largely Odo of Cambrai, Ivo, and Hildebert through the *Speculum ecclesiae* of Pseudo-Hugh of St. Victor. Added to these topics is a short summary of the historical development of the parts of the Mass, especially as introduced by various popes.

Robert Paululus of Amiens (d. ca. 1184) wrote the *De caeremoniis, sacramentis, officiis et observationibus* at the request of a friend and in his preface says that his work is an attempt to offer an abbreviation of liturgical explanations he had found in diverse books. In the treatise, divided into three books dealing with the dedication of churches, baptism and confirmation, penance, anointing of the sick, marriage, ordination, vestments, the Mass, the Office, and the kalendar, the principal sources are Rupert of Deutz and Isaac of Stella. But traces of a host of others can be found, including Jerome, Hilary, Augustine, Gregory I, Isidore, Bede, Hincmar, Ivo, Hildebert, Honorius, and Gratian.

One of the longest and most influential liturgical commentaries of the twelfth century, the *Mitrale seu de officiis ecclesiasticis summa*, was written in the last decade of the century by Sicard of Cremona (d. 1215). It is a veritable summa of information on the liturgy and was used extensively a century later by Guillaume Durand (d. 1296) in his enormously popular *Rationale divinorum officiorum*. The *Mitrale* consists of nine books on ecclesiastical buildings and furnishings, orders and vestments, the Mass, and the kalendar. Sicard's work was largely derivative, depending on Amalarius, Rupert, Honorius, and John Beleth, and to a lesser extent on Ivo and Isaac. Particularly striking throughout are the allegorical interpretations of the liturgy as related to events in Christ's life.

HIGH AND LATER MEDIEVAL TREATISES

Between 1195 and 1197 the future Pope Innocent III, Lothario dei Segni (d. 1216), wrote what was to become an immensely popular Mass commentary, the *De missarum mysteriis*. The treatise, found in over 200 manuscripts and divided into six books, actually begins with a commentary on orders and vestments. Among the principal sources are the Carolingian commentaries of Amalarius, Florus of Lyons, and Remigius of Auxerre together with such *moderni* as Rupert of Deutz. The work seeks to show how the persons, actions, words, and objects used in the mysteries of the Mass reflect events in Christ's life. For this reason the bulk of the treatise is devoted to illustrating these parallels.

The thirteenth-century writings of many scholastic theologians are filled with references to liturgical practice. One of the reasons, of course, is that the twelfth-century *Sententiae* of Peter Lombard, upon which they comment and expand in their summae, contains liturgical commentary. But there were several thirteenth-century masters who wrote more specifically on the liturgy, among them, the Dominican Hugh of St. Cher (d. 1263) in his *Expositio missae*; Gilbert of Tournai (d. ca. 1170) with his *Tractatus de officio episcopi et caeremoniis ecclesiae*; and a tract *De sacrificio missae* often attributed to Albertus Magnus.

But the most important and influential of all thirteenth-century treatises on the liturgy was the *Rationale divinorum officiorum* by Guillaume Durand, bishop of Mende, the distinguished liturgiologist and canonist—often called the *Speculator* in the Middle Ages from his legal work, the *Speculum iudiciale*. It seems that before he became the bishop of Mende in 1285, Durand had compiled his influential *Pontificale romanum*, and when he assumed the bishopric he wrote the *Rationale* as a liturgical encyclopedia for the education of diocesan clerics.

Durand's magnum opus is divided into eight books on (1) the altar, church, images, and churchyard; (2) orders and ordination; (3) vestments; (4) the Mass; (5) the Office; (6) the *Proprium temporis*; (7) the *Proprium sanctorum*; and (8) the kalendar. The sources used are extremely diverse, running the gamut from scriptural citations to Carolingian commentaries through eleventh- and twelfth-century expositions. Innocent III's *De mysteriis* is particularly well represented: of its 176 chapters, 152 are used by Durand. Given the plethora of sources underlying the *Rationale*, it is not surprising to find a variety of interpretations used.

Beyond the thirteenth century the influence of Durand was overwhelming. His *Rationale*, both in full and in part, can be found in hundreds of manuscripts, and in 1459 it was one of the first printed books. By the turn of the fifteenth century the *Rationale* had gone through at least thirty-one editions, and in the sixteenth century, thirty-nine more. Nonetheless, a number of later medieval authors continued to produce liturgical commentaries. Among the most significant of these were: Radulphus de Rivo (d. 1403), whose *De canonum observantia liber* and *Tractatus de psalterio observando* championed the old Roman liturgy; Denis the Carthusian (d. 1471), who wrote an *Expositio missae*; and Gabriel Biel (d. 1495), who compiled a great literal and mystical exposition of the Mass in eighty-nine *lectiones*.

BIBLIOGRAPHY

General works. Adolph Franz, *Die Messe im deutschen Mittelalter: Beiträge zur Geschichte der Liturgie und des religiösen Volkslebens* (1902); Pierre-Marie Gy, "*Expositiones missae*," in *Bulletin du Comité des études [de la] compagnie de St. Sulpice*, 22 (1958); Angelus A. Häussling, "Messe," in *Dictionnaire de spiritualité*, X (1979); Douglas L. Mosey, "Allegorical Liturgical Interpretation in the West from 800 A.D. to 1200 A.D." (diss., Toronto, 1985); Roger E. Reynolds, "The Ordinals of Christ from Their Origins to the Twelfth Century," in *Beiträge zur Geschichte und Quellenkunde des Mittelalters*, 7 (1978); Cyrille Vogel, *Introduction aux sources de l'histoire du culte chrétien au moyen âge* (1975); André Wilmart, "Expositio missae," in *Dictionnaire d'archéologie chrétienne et de liturgie*, V, 1 (1923).

Pre-Carolingian treatises. Roger E. Reynolds, "The Pseudo-Hieronymian *De septem ordinibus ecclesiae*: Notes on Its Origins, Abridgments, and Use in Early Medieval Canonical Collections," in *Revue bénédictine*, 80 (1970), "The Isidorian *Epistula ad Leudefredum*: An Early Medieval Epitome of the Clerical Duties," in *Mediaeval Studies*, 41 (1979), "The *De officiis vii graduum*: Its Origins and Early Medieval Development," *ibid.*, 34 (1972).

Carolingian treatises. Jean-Paul Bouhot, "Les sources de l'*Expositio missae* de Remi d'Auxerre," in *Revue des études augustiniennes*, 26 (1980); Susan A. Keefe, "Baptismal Instruction in the Carolingian Period: The Manuscript Evidence" (diss., Toronto, 1981), and "Carolingian Baptismal Expositions: A Handlist of Tracts and Manuscripts," in Uta-Renate Blumenthal, ed., *Carolingian Essays* (1983); Roger E. Reynolds, "Unity and Diversity in Carolingian Canon Law Collections: The Case of the *Collectio Hibernensis* and Its Derivatives," *ibid.*; Raphael Schulte, "Die Messe als Opfer der Kirche," in *Liturgiewissenschaftliche Quellen und Forschungen*, 35 (1959).

Tenth- and early-eleventh-century treatises. Roger E. Reynolds, "Marginalia on a Tenth-century Text on the Ecclesiastical Officers," in Kenneth Pennington and Robert Somerville, eds., *Law, Church, and Society: Essays in Honor of Stephan Kuttner* (1977), and "An Early Medieval Mass Fantasy: The Correspondence of Pope Damasus on a Nicene Canon," in Peter A. Linehan, ed., *Proceedings of the Seventh International Congress of Medieval Canon Law, Cambridge, 23–27 July 1984.*

Treatises from the mid eleventh to the late twelfth century. Richard W. Pfaff, "The *Abbreviatio Amalarii* of William of Malmesbury," in *Recherches de théologie ancienne et médiévale*, 47 and 48 (1980 and 1981); Roger E. Reynolds, "Ivonian *Opuscula* on the Ecclesiastical Officers," in *Studia Gratiana, Mélanges Gérard Fransen* II, 20 (1976), "Liturgical Scholarship at the Time of the Investiture Controversy: Past Research and Future Opportunities," in *Harvard Theological Review*, 71 (1978), "Patristic Presbyterianism in the Early Medieval Theology of Sacred Orders," in *Mediaeval Studies*, 45 (1983), and "At Sixes and Sevens—and Eights and Nines: The Sacred Mathematics of Sacred Orders in the Early Middle Ages," in *Speculum*, 54 (1979); Ronald J. Zawilla, "The *Sententia Ivonis Carnotensis Episcopi de Divinis Officiis*: Text and Study" (diss., Toronto, 1982); Mary Schaefer, "Twelfth-century Latin Commentaries of the Mass" (diss., Notre Dame, 1983).

High and later medieval treatises. David Wright, "A Medieval Commentary on the Mass: Particulae 2–3 and 5–6 of the *De missarum mysteriis* (ca. 1195) of Cardinal Lothar of Segni (Pope Innocent III)" (diss., Notre Dame, 1977).

ROGER E. REYNOLDS

[See also **Agobard; Amalarius of Metz; Apostolic Constitutions; Baptism; Benedict of Nursia, St.; Cassian, John; Celtic Church; Divine Office; Durand, Guillaume; Ecclesiology; Florus of Lyons; Germanus of Paris, St.; Honorius Augustodunensis; Hrabanus Maurus; Hugh of St. Victor; Isidore of Seville, St.; Itinerarium Egeriae; Ivo of Chartres; Law, Canon; Mass; Milanese Rite; Mozarabic Rite; Remigius of Auxerre; Rupert of Deutz; Walafrid Strabo; William of Malmesbury.**]

LITURGY, WESTERN EUROPEAN. See individual entries.

LIUDOLFINGIANS. See Saxon Dynasty.

LIUTHARD (*fl.* ninth century), a scribe and possibly illuminator, signed three manuscripts produced at the court of Charles the Bald about 870: a Psalter (Paris, Bibliothèque Nationale, Lat. 1152) and two books of Gospels (Munich, Bayerische Staatsbibliothek, Clm. 14000, and Darmstadt, Landesbibliothek, MS 746). The Gospelbook now in Munich, known as the *Codex Aureus aus St. Emmeram in Regensburg,* was signed by Liuthard and his brother Beringar. An important group of Carolingian ivory carvings is named for Liuthard.

BIBLIOGRAPHY

Jean Hubert, J. Porcher, and W. F. Volbach, *The Carolingian Renaissance* (1970); Wilhelm R. W. Koehler and Florentine Mütherich, *Die karolingischen Miniaturen,* V, *Die Hofschhule Karls des Kahlen* (1982); Percy E. Schramm and Florentine Mütherich, *Denkmale der deutschen Könige und Kaiser* (1962), 131, 134; Amy Vandersall, "The Relationship of Sculptors and Painters in the Court School of Charles the Bald," in *Gesta,* **15** (1976).

AMY VANDERSALL

[See also **Carolingians and the Carolingian Empire.**]

LIUTPRAND OF CREMONA (*b. ca.* 920–*d.* 972), bishop, was born in Pavia. He grew up in the court of Hugh of Arles, king of Italy, in whose service both his father and his stepfather had worked. The family appears to have had some influence: Liutprand's father and stepfather were sent to Constantinople as ambassadors of Hugh, on missions which they executed successfully. Liutprand's first trip to that city in 949 was undertaken in the name of Berengar of Ivrea, who, having disposed of Hugh, wanted "to know with what affection he was regarded" by the Byzantines. Soon thereafter Liutprand entered the service of Emperor Otto I the Great of Germany, to whom he remained faithful until his death. He accompanied Otto I on his second invasion of Italy (961/962) and became bishop of Cremona (installed by the emperor). He visited Constantinople again; his most famous embassies were in 968 and 971, when he had the delicate task of restoring friendly relations between Otto I and the Byzantines by arranging a marriage between a Byzantine princess and the future Otto II. Having failed the first time, Liutprand succeeded in 971.

Liutprand wrote two historical works, the *Liber de rebus gestis Ottonis magni imperatoris* and the *Antapodosis.* His most famous work, however, is probably the *Relatio de legatione Constantinopolitana,* written after his failure in 968. The *Antapodosis* is a catalog of marvels: he was overwhelmed by the grandeur of Constantinople, the palaces, and the emperor. The *Legatio* presents a different picture; the Byzantines are presented as weak, luxurious, effeminate, and perfidious. Even the city of Constantinople, which he saw during the reign of Nikephoros II Phokas, seemed to him to be in decline. He ridiculed the trappings of the Byzantine imperial office as he had previously extolled them, and he described the emperor as a short, fat, dark, ugly man. Underlying the bias, however, were significant issues. The conflict between the Byzantines and the Western emperors for Italy is omnipresent, as is an interesting attitude on the part of Westerners. Liutprand considers the Byzantines to be Greeks and not Romans. He also defends the "young" faith of the Saxon church, "among people whose faith is seconded by works." The writings of Liutprand of Cremona are among the clearest early indications of the growing split between Eastern and Western Europe and of the myths that widened the split.

BIBLIOGRAPHY

Frederic A. Wright, *The Works of Liutprand of Cremona* (1930).

ANGELIKI LAIOU

[See also **Constantinople; Nikephoros II Phokas; Otto I the Great, Emperor.**]

LIVERE DE REIS DE BRITTANIE ET LE LIVERE DE REIS DE ENGLETERRE, a composite Anglo-Norman history, dating originally from the late thirteenth century. The kings of Britain from the arrival of the legendary Brutus down to the reign of the historical Edward I are treated in *Le livere des reis de Britannie,* and a longer history of the English kings from the time of Ethelbert, king of Kent (sixth century), to 1274 is given in *Le livere des reis de Engletere.* The two surviving manuscripts containing both parts also have continuations. In Cambridge, Trinity College, MS R. 14. 7, the "Wroxham Continuation" goes as far as 1306, and in an unnumbered Vatican MS the "Sempringham Continuation" takes the history to 1326.

BIBLIOGRAPHY

Rerum Britannicarum medii aevi scriptores, XLII, John Glover, ed. (1865).

BRIAN S. MERRILEES

[See also **Chronicles; Historiography.**]

LIVRE. The principal unit of weight throughout France. During the late eighth century the "livre esterlin" was fixed at 5,760 grains (367.1 grams) and consisted of 20 sous or 12 onces or 240 deniers or 480 oboles. This livre was the first state standard, and it was retained until the middle of the fourteenth century, when the government of King John II the Good (1350–1364) authorized the employment of a new, heavier livre called the "livre poids de marc" or the "livre de Paris." Totaling 9,216 grains (489.506 grams), it was subdivided in two different ways: for valuable goods such as gold and silver it consisted of 2 marcs or 16 onces or 128 gros or 384 deniers or 221,184 primes, while for cheaper commodities it was 2 demi-livres or 4 quarterons or 8 demi-quarterons or 16 onces or 32 demi-onces. The apothecaries used this livre also but subdivided it into 128 drachmes or 384 scrupules, while physicians employed a medical livre of 5,760 grains (367.1 grams) which had 12 onces of 480 grains or 96 drachmes or 288 scrupules or 576 oboles. The "livre marchande" of 15 onces (459 grams) was reserved solely for silk weighings. Locally, however, there were numerous other livres utilized, the vast majority of them dating from the period of the thirteenth and fourteenth centuries. Most of them were identified under the names poids de table, poids de balance, grosse, poids de ville, poids de marchandises et denrées, poids de crochet, poids de vicomté, pour les laines, poids de fourneau, and others.

BIBLIOGRAPHY

Ronald E. Zupko, *French Weights and Measures Before the Revolution* (1978), with extensive bibliography.

RONALD EDWARD ZUPKO

[See also **Weights and Measures, Western European.**]

LIVRE DE SEYNTZ MEDICINES, LE, a moralistic and confessional work written in Anglo-Norman French prose in 1354 by Henry, first duke of Lancaster. Filled throughout with prayers and striking comparisons, the book begins with an elaborate allegory wherein the bodily senses are likened to seven wounds fostering the Seven Deadly Sins. The second portion of the work sets forth an allegory of the holy medicines needed to cure the wounds.

BIBLIOGRAPHY

Émile J. Arnould, ed., *Le livre de seyntz medicines* (1940). See also Robert W. Ackerman, "The Traditional Background of Henry of Lancaster's *Livre,*" in *L'esprit créateur,* 2 (1962); and Émile J. Arnould, *Étude sur le Livre des saintes médecines du duc Henri de Lancastre* (1948).

ELLEN T. WEHNER

[See also **Anglo-Norman Literature; Seven Deadly Sins.**]

LIVRES DE JOSTICE ET DE PLET, LI, an anonymous French legal compilation from the third quarter of the thirteenth century, was produced in the region of Orléans. It is a striking example of the way in which northern French legal practitioners sought at that time to assimilate their newly acquired knowledge of Roman law, and to organize and reshape the custom of local and royal courts along more learned lines.

The work is known through only one manuscript, which is not the original. It does not appear to have had a wide diffusion. It begins with the text of Louis IX's "reform ordinance" of 1254, and follows it with the regulation of procedure in the court of the provost of Paris that also appears as the opening chapters of the *Établissements de Saint Louis.* (The relationship between *Li livres* and the *Établissements* is not clear. The regulation may not have been part of the original compilation but may have been added sometime between its first composition and the one surviving manuscript. The compilers of these two Orléanais works may likewise have copied the Parisian ordinance from the same source.) There then follow twenty books modeled directly on the ordering of Justinian's *Digest.* A large proportion of the compilation consists of translations, more or less accurate, from the *Digest* and from the Decretals of Pope Gregory IX. In addition, the author adapted many texts of both Roman and canon law by putting the words of Roman or papal authors into the mouths of "King Louis," "Queen Blanche," and a variety of royal officials active in the Orléans region in the 1250's and 1260's. In the course of this adaptation he turned praetors into baillis, senators into lords, and *theatra* into monasteries, and often altered or misconstrued the sense of the original texts.

Customary law of the Orléans region constitutes the smallest portion of the text. The sources of this material have never been traced, and may be lost. The compiler took this material from at least three different manuscripts, however, for on several occasions he copied the same text three times in slightly different forms. He was acquainted with the activities of the Parlement of Paris and cited a number of decisions that can be identified in the records of that court between 1255 and 1259.

It is hard to know how seriously the author took his work. It may have been nothing more than a school exercise, or it may have been an attempt to incorporate into the case law of royal courts the norms of Roman and canon law by giving them false pedigrees. Whichever it may be, the author's methods suggest the importance of authoritative decisions as a source of law in late-thirteenth-century France. If the norms of learned law were to be adapted to thirteenth-century secular practice, it could be only by giving them the cover of contemporary local rulings.

BIBLIOGRAPHY

An edition is *Li livres de jostice et de plet*, Louis Nicolas Rapetti, ed. (1850). Studies include Eduard M. Meijers, *Études d'histoire du droit*, III (1959), 56–58; H. Stein, "Conjectures sur l'auteur du 'Livre de jostice et de Plet,'" in *Nouvelle revue historique de droit français et étranger*, 40 (1917).

Fredric L. Cheyette

[See also **Corpus Iuris Civilis**; **Établissements de St. Louis**; **Law, French: In North**.]

LJÓSVETNINGA SAGA. This relatively little-known family saga recounts a feud, spread over two generations, between the leading families of two districts in northern Iceland. Guðmundr the Powerful (resident at Mǫðruvellir [Madderfield]) and the sons of Þorgeirr the Chieftain (resident at Ljósavatn [Lake of Lights], hence the title of the saga) come into conflict over the faulty payment of a debt. The dispute results in three killings but is eventually settled.

The second phase of the conflict centers on the slandering of Guðmundr. A comparison of husbands between Guðmundr's wife and the wife of Þórir Hel-

gason brings to light a rumor that Guðmundr is homosexual, a rumor spread by Þórir and Þorgeirr the Chieftain's son Þorkell hákr. Through an ingenious sequence of legal maneuvers and long-range strategy Guðmundr succeeds in exiling Þórir and killing Þorkell. After Guðmundr's death his son Eyjólfr and Þorgeirr's grandson Þorvarðr agree to keep the peace, but a new conflict arises over a paternity case. The hostilities culminate in a full-scale battle in which Eyjólfr's brother Koðrán falls. Ensuing litigation results in the outlawing of his killer and the exile of three other Ljósvetningar. The saga concludes with an account of their various fates and Eyjólfr's further revenge against Þorvarðr's brother Þórarinn.

Ljósvetninga saga is extant in two redactions, a short version *A* and a fuller version *C* (containing three additional loosely connected episodes from the life of Guðmundr). Virtually all the literature on the saga is devoted to this philological problem. No final solution has been reached, but it seems most likely that redaction *C* is closer to the original and that *A* is an abbreviation. There are no obvious criteria for dating the composition of the saga, but it is now generally considered to belong to the second half of the thirteenth century.

The artistry of the saga is mixed. Easily the most successful section is the account of Guðmundr's vengeance against the rumormongers. The maneuvering behind the scenes, the guessing game on both sides, the thrusting and parrying, and the building and last-minute deflection of the reader's expectations, all this is managed as expertly as in any saga. The attack on Þorkell hákr is vividly described and is in the best scenic tradition. Elsewhere, especially in the second part of the saga, the narrative is overloaded and difficult to follow. Perhaps the most notable feature of the saga is the unsavory standard of conduct. Deceit is the rule, even between the brothers Guðmundr and Einarr. Guðmundr shrinks back in the final encounter with Þorkell hákr, relying on an advantage of twenty to one, and Þorkell's dying witticism tends to make the charge of homosexuality stick. If we had no other saga to judge by, our view of life in medieval Iceland would be anything but heroic.

BIBLIOGRAPHY

Sources. Björn Sigfússon, ed., *Ljósvetninga saga með Þáttum; Reykdæla saga ok Víga-Skútu* (1940); Gudbrand Vigfusson and F. York Powell, trans., "The Story of the Men of Lightwater," in *Origines islandicae*, II (1905), 355–427.

Studies. Adolfine Erichsen, *Untersuchungen zur Liós-vetninga Saga* (1919); Björn Sigfússon, *Um Ljósvetninga sögu,* with English summary (1937); Barði Guðmundsson, *Ljósvetninga saga og Saurbæingar* (1953); Hallvard Magerøy, "Sertekstproblemet i Ljósvetninga saga," in *Avhandlinger utgitt av Det Norske Videnskaps-Akademi i Oslo,* II, no. 2 (1956), 3–99; Theodore M. Andersson, *The Problem of Icelandic Saga Origins: A Historical Survey* (1964), 150–165; Cecilia Borggreve, "Der Handlungsaufbau in den zwei Versionen der Ljósvetninga saga," in *Arkiv för nordisk filologi,* 85 (1970), 238–246.

THEODORE M. ANDERSSON

[See also **Family Sagas, Icelandic; Iceland.**]

LLULL, RAMON. See **Lull, Ramon.**

LLYWELYN AP GRUFFYDD (d. 1282), the last prince of an independent Wales, succeeded to the lordship of the principality of Gwynedd jointly with his brother Owain on the death of Dafydd ap Llywelyn in 1246. Their joint succession permitted some real opposition to Henry III's armies, and although the terms of the 1247 Treaty of Woodstock were harsh, they allowed the brothers to retain control of much of Gwynedd. Of the two, Llywelyn was clearly the more able leader; and when they fell out in 1255, Owain was defeated and imprisoned.

Over the following twelve years, Llywelyn added extensively to the lands he controlled—in 1256 he invaded Meirionydd; in 1257, Powys. A truce with the English king was made in 1258, and in the same year Llywelyn accepted the homage of the Welsh princes (with one exception), from that time calling himself Princeps Wallie. Hostilities with England were renewed in 1262 when Henry, acting on a rumor of Llywelyn's death, claimed his lands for the crown. Llywelyn supported Simon de Montfort the Younger in his battles with Henry, and in 1265 received Simon's promise to recognize him as prince of Wales in the king's name. This promise was fulfilled in the Treaty of Montgomery in 1267, the climax of Llywelyn's career. The treaty created a principality of Wales ruled by Llywelyn and his successors and stabilized its relationship to the English crown.

Llywelyn's real troubles began with the death of Henry III and the accession of Edward I in 1272, and the following four years saw continually worsening relations with the crown. Llywelyn did not attend Edward's coronation, and several subsequent attempts to arrange a meeting where he might do homage failed. In 1275 Llywelyn was married by proxy to Simon de Montfort's daughter Eleanor, but she was captured on the way to Wales and imprisoned in Windsor Castle.

Gruffydd ap Gwenwynwyn, prince of Powys, had accepted Llywelyn's overlordship in 1263, but in 1274 was accused of complicity in a plot on Llywelyn's life. After being forced to give up his son as hostage, relinquish some of his lands, and beg forgiveness before Llywelyn on his knees, Gruffydd was granted asylum in England. In September 1275 Llywelyn complained to Pope Gregory X that the terms of the Treaty of Montgomery were not being observed.

In 1276 Edward opened war on Wales. The tactics that Llywelyn had used earlier against an England divided by the baronial wars appear not to have been successful against the united England of Edward. The Peace of Conway (1277) left Llywelyn with only the Gywnedd lands he had begun with in 1246, and at Christmas 1277 he finally did homage to Edward in London.

The apparent reconciliation was strengthened when Llywelyn formally married Eleanor de Montfort at Worcester Cathedral in 1278, in a ceremony attended by Edward, but over the next few years the relationship worsened through a series of territorial disputes. Shortly before Easter 1282, Llywelyn's brother Dafydd captured the English-held castle of Hawarden, and revolt spread through Wales with great speed. The rebellion took Edward by surprise, but he assembled an army and moved on Wales from both the northeast and the southwest. By autumn he had control of the south and west, and turned his attention to the north.

On 11 December 1282 the royal army met Llywelyn's forces at Irfon Bridge near Builth. Llywelyn became separated from his army for reasons that are now unclear; in attempting to return to it, he met an English scouting party and died at the hands of Stephen de Frankton, who realized only later whom he had killed. Llywelyn's head was exhibited at the Tower of London. His wife had died in childbirth, and his daughter was placed in the nunnery of Sempringham in Lincolnshire, where she remained all her life. Llywelyn's brother Dafydd continued the revolt but was betrayed and was executed at Shrewsbury on 2 October 1283.

Many of the details of Llywelyn's death will probably never be known. The *Brut y Tywysogion* suggests that he was betrayed, but this is unsupported by any other sources. What does seem clear, though, is that although Llywelyn styled himself prince of Wales, he never established a complete supremacy over the Welsh, and that even at the time of the Treaty of Montgomery his position as overlord was built on a shaky foundation. His death was lamented throughout Wales, and two fine elegies survive. One is an extraordinary poem of great power, apocalyptic in its imagery, by Gruffydd ap yr Ynad Goch; the other, a more traditional elegy by Bleddyn Fardd. A series of political poems on Llywelyn was written by Llygad Gwr (*ca.* 1273). A statue of Llywelyn stands in the Cardiff City Hall.

BIBLIOGRAPHY

J. E. Caerwyn Williams, *The Poets of the Welsh Princes* (1978), 34–35; A. D. Carr, *Llywelyn ap Gruffydd* (1982); John Edward Lloyd, *A History of Wales from the Earliest Times to the Edwardian Conquest*, 3rd ed., II (1939, repr. 1967), 716–764; John Edward Morris, *The Welsh Wars of Edward I* (1901, repr. 1967); John Morris-Jones and T. H. Parry-Williams, eds., *Llawysgrif Hendregadredd* (1933), 66–67, 214–219; D. Stephenson, *The Last Princes of Wales* (1980).

DAVID N. KLAUSNER

[See also **Conway, Peace of; Edward I of England; Henry III of England; Simon de Montfort the Younger; Wales: History.**]

LO CODI, a systematic handbook of Roman law, written in Provençal about 1150 and based on the *Codex* of Justinian. As a vernacular treatise, it is strong evidence for the early diffusion of Justinianic law among legal practitioners in southern France, and indeed beyond, as it was translated into Old French and Castilian. Ricardus Pisanus also translated it into Latin. The Provençal text was probably written somewhere in the Rhône Valley, possibly at Arles or St. Gilles.

BIBLIOGRAPHY

Robert Caillemer, "Le Codi et le droit provençal au XIIᵉ siècle," in *Annales du Midi*, **18** (1906); Felix Derrer, *Lo Codi: Eine Summa codicis in provenzalischer Sprache aus dem XII. Jahrhundert: Die provenzalische Fassung der Handschrift A (Sorbonne 632): Vorarbeiten zu einer kritischen Textausgabe* (1974); Hermann Fitting and Hermann Suchier, *Lo Codi: Eine Summa codicis in provenzalischer Sprache aus der mitte des XII. Jahrhunderts*, I, *Lo Codi in der lateinischen Übersetzung des Ricardus Pisanus* (1906).

WILLIAM K. WEST

[See also **Law, French: In South; Petri Exceptiones.**]

LOCHNER, STEPHAN (*b.* 1400/1410, *fl.* 1442–1451), probably born in Meersburg (on the Bodensee), was the most important fifteenth-century painter of Cologne. Like most Cologne painters, he never signed a work. His most important commission was a fifteen-foot-wide triptych, the *Adoration of the Magi Altarpiece* (*ca.* 1442), which includes St. Ursula and St. Gereon, patron saints of Cologne, in the wing panels. Originally painted for the chapel of the city hall, it is now in Cologne Cathedral. Another important altarpiece, formerly in the Cologne parish church of St. Lawrence, depicts the *Last Judgment* in its center panel (now in the Wallraf-Richartz-Museum, Cologne) and the martyrdom of the apostles on its wings (now in the Städelsches Kunstinstitut, Frankfurt). Lochner's *Presentation in the Temple* (Hessisches Landesmuseum, Darmstadt) is dated 1447. Stephan Lochner is also credited with a number of small devotional panels, such as the *Madonna in a Rose Garden* (Wallraf-Richartz-Museum, Cologne) and *Madonna with a Violet* (Erzbischöfliches Diözesan-Museum, Cologne). In these latter panels, as in most of his work, the artist emphasized rich color and decorative gold in combination with meticulous natural description, derived from his presumed study in the Low Countries.

BIBLIOGRAPHY

Otto Förster, *Die Kölnische Malerei von Meister Wilhelm bis Stephan Lochner* (1923), and *Stefan Lochner, ein Maler zu Köln* (1952); *Late Gothic Art from Cologne*, exhibition catalog (1977), 42–45; Heribert Reiners, *Die Kölner Malerschule* (1925); Alfred Stange, *Deutsche Malerei der Gotik*, III (1938), 94–118; Hubert Schrade, *Stephan Lochner* (1923).

LARRY SILVER

[See also **Altarpiece; Cologne; Gothic Art: Painting and Manuscript Illumination; Panel Painting.**]

Adoration of the Magi Altarpiece. Stephan Lochner, *ca.* 1442, Cologne Cathedral. PHOTO: WIM SWAAN

LOCK, ADAM (Lok) (*d.* 1229), English master mason. He was responsible for the construction of Wells Cathedral in Somerset from about 1214 (or earlier), when work resumed after the interdict, until his death. He certainly worked elsewhere, most likely at Bristol Cathedral.

BIBLIOGRAPHY

John Bilson, "Notes on the Earlier Architectural History of Wells Cathedral," in *Archaeological Journal*, **85** (1928), 65–67; L. S. Colchester and John H. Harvey, "Wells Cathedral," in *Archaeological Journal*, **131** (1974), 203–204; John Harvey, *English Mediaeval Architects: A Biographical Dictionary Down to 1550* (1954), 170; J. Armitage Robinson, "Documentary Evidence Relating to the Building of the Cathedral Church of Wells," in *Archaeological Journal*, **85** (1928), 11.

STEPHEN GARDNER

[See also **Chapter House; Gothic Architecture; Masons and Builders.**]

LOCULUS, a burial slot hewn into a catacomb wall. Many loculi from the third and fourth centuries are preserved in Rome. They are normally narrow rectangular niches arranged in long galleries with as many as six carved vertically up the wall. Loculi were closed with stone slabs, tiles, or mortar; the closure was inscribed and/or decorated to identify the body within.

LESLIE BRUBAKER

[See also **Catacombs.**]

639

LOCUS SANCTUS (literally, holy site or place) refers to a location hallowed by sacred history. Connected with important events of the Old and New Testaments—such as Moses' encounter with the burning bush near Mt. Sinai, the Nativity at Bethlehem, or the Crucifixion at Jerusalem, or with the life or tomb of a saint, *loca sancta* provided a significant stimulus to the elaboration and dissemination of Christian imagery. The monumental decorative programs of these shrines, which often included topographically specific elements, were translated into a myriad of small-scale objects, such as painted panels, manuscripts, ampullae, ivories, bread stamps, and other pilgrim souvenirs. Architecturally, *loca sancta* inspired the development of complex and innovative plans that frequently employed ambulatories and multiple subsidiary chapels. These structures were able to accommodate the holy site or shrine and to provide adequate space for the circulation of pilgrims as well as regular liturgical services.

BIBLIOGRAPHY

Dmitrii V. Ainalov, *The Hellenistic Origins of Byzantine Art,* Elizabeth Sobolevitch and Serge Sobolevitch, trans., Cyril Mango, ed. (1961); André Grabar, *Martyrium: Recherches sur le culte des reliques et l'art chrétien antique,* 2 vols. (1943–1946, repr. 1972), and *Les ampoules de Terre Sainte* (1958); Kurt Weitzmann, "*Loca Sancta* and the Representational Arts of Palestine," in *Dumbarton Oaks Papers,* **28** (1974); Kurt Weitzmann *et al., Age of Spirituality: Late Antique and Early Christian Art* (1979), 564–591, 640–643.

MICHAEL T. DAVIS

[See also **Early Christian Art; Early Christian and Byzantine Architecture; Pilgrimages, Western European; Pilgrim's Guide.**]

LOGIC. See **Dialectic.**

LOGIC, ISLAMIC. Islamic logic was not an indigenous development but reflected the assimilation and elaboration of Greek logic. Syriac-speaking Christians had transplanted the Hellenistic learning of Alexandria to the Persian empire, and it was there that the Arabs, by right of conquest, as it were, took possession of Greek learning in the ninth century—logic included. The textual basis of Islamic logic was the *Organon* of Aristotle and the logical opuscules of Galen (which the Arabs possessed in toto). Logic rode into Islam on the coattails of medicine and owed much to Galen's contention that the competent physician must be trained in logic. The rapidity and thoroughness of this appropriation was phenomenal. Early in the tenth century, Baghdad was effectively the only center of logical studies in Islam; around 920 virtually no Islamic logician was to be found outside its precincts. But the second half of the century saw a swift diffusion of logical studies throughout the Arabic-speaking domain. By 1000, Greek logic was not only arabized but also well en route to being islamized—in its personnel, its geographical distribution, and its influence.

The canon of logic as seen by medieval Islam, following Syriac precedent, organized the subject into nine branches: "introduction," categories, hermeneutics, analytics, apodictics, topics, sophistics, rhetoric, and poetics. The *Isagoge* of Porphyry furnished the canonical text of the first; the remainder were based on the corresponding Aristotelian treatises. The order from apodictics to poetics was seen as one of declining probative rigor.

Islamic logic developed in three phases. The first, spanning the ninth century, was the period of translation and assimilation of the Greek logical texts. The next phase, extending roughly from 900 to 1300, was a period of relatively independent discussions and expositions of logical issues. The final phase, after about 1250, was the time of schoolmasters rather than thinkers, with the commentary on earlier texts as the sole mode of writing.

Al-Fārābī (870–950) was the first important Islamic logician. He was particularly active as a commentator on Aristotle, and was dubbed the "second teacher"—that is, the successor to Aristotle, the first teacher. His commentaries cover the whole of the *Organon* (as well as many other Greek philosophical and scientific works). His principal contribution lay in his effectiveness in making the issues and problems of Greek logic available within a setting of Arabic language and Islamic culture.

Ibn Sīnā (980–1037), known as Avicenna to the medieval Schoolmen, was the son of a high public official in Persia. An encyclopedic writer in many fields, he wrote treatises on virtually every branch of logic. His originality and critical independence of tradition are manifest throughout. In the interest of a full and comprehensive treatment of logical issues, Ibn Sīnā did not hesitate to fill gaps left in the discussions of his predecessors or to make corrections in their work. He was interested not in commentary but in systematization, and did not balk at innovation when the adequate treatment of a problem called for a new approach. The theory of temporal modalities described below was apparently in large measure his creation.

Ibn Rushd (1126–1198), also known as Averroës, was the greatest Arabic philosopher of Spain, where logical studies flourished throughout the eleventh and twelfth centuries. He produced (inter alia) a monumental set of commentaries covering virtually all of Aristotle's works (St. Thomas referred to him as "the Commentator"). A rigid Aristotelian, Averroës sought, and in creditable measure was able, to get back to the conceptions of the master himself. His work represents the high-water mark—and the conclusion—of Arabic commentaries on Aristotle.

The main creative innovation of Islamic logic was the theory of temporal modalities that sprang up in the tradition of Ibn Sīnā on the basis of precursor ideas in Stoic logic. The modal propositions at issue have such forms as "All S are sometimes P" or "Some S are always P." This paves the way for such syllogistic inferences as

> All M are sometimes P.
> Some M are always S.
> . . .
> Some S are sometimes P.

On this basis a very sophisticated theory of modal distinctions was generated, and a highly complex apparatus of modal syllogistic was developed that made possible the detailed analysis of temporal relationships.

After the time of Ibn Sīnā, logical treatises of Greek origin were worked over by only a handful of Spanish-Muslim logicians, of whom Ibn Rushd was effectively the last. Henceforward, logical studies were to be based exclusively upon indigenous Arabic treatises (themselves of course ultimately based on Greek logic). Increasingly, logic was studied from encyclopedias and manuals, rather than from works of research exploring a vital domain of inquiry. Although at first sight this seems like a step in the direction of originality, in fact any basis for original work and independent inquiry was soon eroded away.

Texts have survived from the pens of some 150 Islamic logical writers during the seven centuries from 800 to 1500, representing a fairly stable series of roughly six identifiable logicians per human generation of thirty years. As a feature of cultural history, Islamic logic was clearly something of an epi-

phenomenon. Moreover, while the great majority of Islamic logical texts were written in Arabic (the Latin of the medieval Mediterranean world), the great majority of the logicians were Persians.

The place of logic in Islamic thought was hotly contested. The important theologian al-Ghazālī (1058–1111) exempted logic from his general critique of the views of the "philosophers," and it ultimately gained a place in the training program for theologians of various sects. Nevertheless, some theologians strongly opposed logic, the most influential being the Hanbalite Ibn Taimiyyah (1263–1328). In practical effect these opponents won the day. Though logic continued to be taught after the thirteenth century, it was effectively dead in Islam as a branch of inquiry. In this final stage the Aristotelian texts were virtually abandoned, and the study of logic addressed itself to commentaries or sterile handbooks and epitomes. Logic was preserved by continuing generations as a kind of museum piece, some acquaintance with which was viewed as desirable for theological students and philologists.

BIBLIOGRAPHY

Studies. Nicholas Rescher, *Studies in the History of Arabic Logic* (1963), and *The Development of Arabic Logic* (1964), a general account with full bibliography. The theory of temporal modalities is described in "The Theory of Modal Syllogistic in Medieval Arabic Philosophy," in his *Studies in Modality* (1974).

NICHOLAS RESCHER

[See also **Aristotle in the Middle Ages; Fārābī, al-; Ghazālī, al-; Philosophy and Theology, Islamic; Rushd, Ibn; Sīnā, Ibn.**]

LOGOS (Greek: the word) is a term for the second person of the Trinity, Christ, who is the Word of God. The identification of Christ and Logos is first used in the prologue to the Gospel of John, where the Logos is described as God from the eternity, the Word that became incarnate in the man Jesus of Nazareth. In John 8:31,43, Christ is synonymous with a single Logos or message, which conveys truth and eternal life. To the evangelist, the message or Logos of Christ is inseparable from his person: Christ is both the preexistent word of God and the physical affirmation of it.

There are few adequate formulas for representing God the Son as Logos in medieval iconography. Logos is unincarnate, except when represented as

Jesus Christ during the period of Incarnation. References to Logos can be found in the mosaics at Capua Vetere and on the Triumphal Arch in Sta. Maria Maggiore, Rome. In both, an empty throne represents God the Father and the book resting on the seat the Son or Logos. Visions of Christ in the Second Coming can also be considered as depictions of the Logos (see apse mosaics of Hosios David in Thessaloniki and S. Vitale, Ravenna).

BIBLIOGRAPHY

Otto Demus, *Byzantine Mosaic Decorations* (1948); Charles Harold Dodd, *The Bible and the Greeks* (1935), and *The Interpretations of the Fourth Gospel* (1953), 263–285; André Grabar, *Martyrium: Recherches sur le culte des reliques et l'art chrétien antique* (1943), and *Christian Iconography: A Study of Its Origins* (1968).

JENNIFER E. JONES

LOGOTHETE, a high Byzantine state official charged mainly with financial responsibilities. The office first appeared in the fifth century, and from the eighth century on, logothetes headed several departments of the central administration. The more important among them were the following: the logothete of the genikon *(tou genikos)*, concerned with taxation, appeared in the seventh century, lost his prerogatives in the eleventh, but was still attested as an honorific title in the fourteenth; the logothete of the stratiotikon *(tou stratiotikos)*, concerned with recruiting and financing the armed forces, appeared in the seventh century, disappeared after 1088, and reappeared as an honorific title in the fourteenth century; the logothete of the oxys (dromos) or logothete par excellence, concerned with financing and maintaining the road network and the imperial mail service, and the reception of foreign ambassadors, appeared in 759/760 and was purely a honorific title in the fourteenth century; the logothete of the agelai *(praepositus gregum)*, who provided the palace and army with horses and mules, appeared in the ninth century but was only an honorific title in the fourteenth century; the logothete of the *sekreta,* an office created by Alexios I in 1081 for coordination of the central administrative services, by the end of the twelfth century was called the grand *(megas)* logothete and, by the fourteenth century, was in charge of foreign correspondence.

BIBLIOGRAPHY

Rodolphe Guilland, "Les logothètes," in *Revue des études byzantines,* **29** (1971); Nicolas Oikonomides, *Les listes de préséance byzantines des IXe et Xe siècles* (1972), 311, 313, 314, 338, and "L'évolution de l'organisation administrative de l'empire byzantin au XIe siècle (1081–1118)," in *Travaux et mémoires,* **6** (1976).

NICOLAS OIKONOMIDES

[See also **Byzantine Empire: Bureaucracy.**]

LOHENGRIN is a Middle High German narrative of 7,670 verses written in a ten-line tripartite strophic form known as "Clingors schwarzer Ton" and transmitted in three manuscripts and two fragments. (The otherwise unknown author is a Bavarian, possibly with connections to Augsburg, who reveals his name, Nouhusius [Neuhäuser] or Nouhuwius [Neuhuber], in an acrostic in stanzas 763–765.) A series of allusions to contemporary political institutions and situations during the reign of Rudolf of Habsburg narrows the probable period of composition to between 1283 and 1288/1289.

The work begins with a frame (stanzas 1–25, 27–28, and 30 are borrowed from the riddle contest in the *Wartburgkrieg*), in which Clingsor poses various riddles to Wolfram von Eschenbach before asking about an unnamed knight whose story Wolfram then proceeds to narrate (stanzas 31ff.). Elsam of Brabant, whom Friedrich of Telramunt has unjustly accused of having broken a vow to marry him, prays for a champion to defend her. Her prayer is heard in the Grail castle, where Parzival dispatches his son Lohengrin to Antwerp in a boat drawn by a swan. Lohengrin defeats Telramunt in judicial combat before the emperor Henry and then must marry Elsam, making her promise never to ask his name and lineage lest he be compelled to leave her. The hero demonstrates exemplary ability fighting for Henry against Hungarian invaders and Saracens. After his return from the emperor's coronation in Rome, Elsam cannot refrain from asking the forbidden question, whereupon Lohengrin sadly takes leave of her and their two sons before the assembled nobility and departs in the boat drawn by the swan. The work concludes with a survey of the Ottonian dynasty through Henry II.

Lohengrin presents an unusual conglomerate of historical and Arthurian narrative in which the fictional hero becomes a historical figure localized in a contemporary thirteenth-century political setting. The *Sächsische Weltchronik* served as principal source for the historical passages; further details appear to derive from the *Buch der Könige* and the *Schwabenspiegel*. The chronicle material is carefully selected to project a favorable imperial image, a concern that is also noticeable in the fictional portrait of Henry II's Italian campaign and crusade. The combination of a glorified historical ruler and the wealth of contemporary detail suggest that *Lohengrin* was written to support the policies of Rudolf of Habsburg. Similar use of the legend for purposes of dynastic self-mythologization was made by many noble families.

The sources of the Lohengrin legend—versions exist in nearly every European language and extend into the nineteenth century—are extensive and still incompletely investigated. The principal French narrative, the *Chevalier au Cygne,* exists in a number of redactions. Early German versions are the conclusion of Wolfram von Eschenbach's *Parzival,* Albrecht von Scharfenberg's *Jüngerer Titurel,* and the *Schwanritter* of Konrad von Würzburg. *Lohengrin* provided the material for *Lorengel* (or shared its source), a late-fifteenth-century version by Ulrich Füetrer, and the opera by Richard Wagner, first performed in 1850.

BIBLIOGRAPHY
Thomas Cramer, *Lohengrin: Edition und Untersuchungen* (1971), contains the text of the poem and a full discussion in German of all the critical issues of its composition.

ARTHUR GROOS

[See also **Arthurian Literature; German Literature; Habsburg Dynasty; Konrad von Würzburg; Schwabenspiegel; Wartburgkrieg; Wolfram von Eschenbach.**]

LOKASENNA. The anonymous Eddic poem *Lokasenna* is the best-known example of blame literature in the north. In it the god Loki bullies his way into the god Ægir's court (from which he has previously been expelled for breaking the peace) to castigate the assembled gods and goddesses with his "wound words" and "slanderous staves." He begins by accusing Bragi of cowardice. When Iðunn objects, Loki turns on her, charging her with promiscuity. Gefjon's protest meets with the same response. To

Odin's intervention on behalf of Gefjon, Loki replies by claiming that the war god has decided battles unfairly. Odin answers with a rhetorical concession ("It may be that I allowed the weaker man to win") followed by the counterclaim that Loki spent eight years as a woman, milking cows and bearing children. Loki responds with a similar charge of effeminacy against Odin. The poem goes on in this fashion until all thirteen gods and goddesses, as well as Freyr's servants Byggvir and Beyla, have been exposed. The taunts in the earlier part of the poem refer to instances of sexual deviance or misbehavior; those in the latter part concern Ragnarǫk and the frailty of the gods' defensive efforts. The last and longest exchange, reminiscent in many respects of *Hárbarðsljóð,* is with Thor, who enters the scene at the eleventh hour brandishing his hammer. Loki dances verbal circles around the mentally inept thunder god, but bows finally to the latter's threat of brute force: "To the gods, and to the sons of the gods, I have said what was on my mind; only before you will I retreat, for I know you fight to kill." He departs with a curse on the host and guests.

The rude treatment of the gods and goddesses in *Lokasenna* has prompted the view that the poem is an expression of Christian antipathy toward the earlier religion. It should be recalled, however, that Loki brings up very little that is new; the divine misdeeds he enumerates are known from other sources—including sources not otherwise regarded as especially antagonistic to the old religious order. In general it would seem that the tales of moral shame are too many and too tightly woven into the Norse mythological fabric to be considered Christian addenda. What distinguishes *Lokasenna* is not the uncomplimentary content of the insults, nor even their patronizing tone, but their concentration in a form which is nothing more than a display case for witty invective.

It has been argued (by Schröder and others) that the symposium format derives from Greek tradition, possibly via an undocumented medieval version of Lucian's satire on the gods. If so, the *Lokasenna* poet has done a splendid job of grafting a foreign idea onto a native form, for the poem is one of the most elaborately realized flytings (exchange of abuse or ridicule) in Germanic literature. To the flyting tradition belong the banquet setting, focus on a threshold (Ægir's peace sanctuary), confrontation between an alien and insiders, stylized nature of the speeches, and use of tag line with proper name ("Þegi þú,

Týr!"), as well as the themes and phrasing of the boasts and insults themselves. Even the uncommon symposium format has its counterparts, albeit in late and possibly dependent forms (*Bandamanna saga, Ǫlkofra þáttr,* and *Njáls saga*).

Lokasenna is preserved in Codex Regius 2365, 4° (now in the Arnamagnaean Manuscript Institute, Reykjavik). Recent opinion holds that the poem proper dates from the twelfth century and that the prose prologue and epilogue are later additions. The numerous allusions to other Eddic and skaldic poetry, as well as certain of the phrasings, have led to speculation that the author was a skald.

BIBLIOGRAPHY

Sources. Gustav Neckel and Hans Kuhn, eds., *Edda: Die Lieder des Codex Regius nebst verwandten Denkmälern,* I, 3rd ed. (1962), 96–110; Henry Adams Bellows, trans., *The Poetic Edda* (1923, repr. 1957); Lee M. Hollander, trans., *The Poetic Edda* (1928, 2nd ed. 1977).

Studies. Magnus Olsen, *Edda- og skaldekvad,* II, Lokasenna (1960); Maria Elena Ruggerini, *Le invettive di Loki* (1979); Franz Rolf Schröder, "Das Symposion der Lokasenna," in *Arkiv för nordisk filologi,* 67 (1952); A. G. van Hamel, "The Prose-frame of Lokasenna," in *Neophilologus,* 14 (1929).

CAROL J. CLOVER

[See also **Bandamanna Saga; Eddic Poetry; Freyr; Gefjon; Hárbarðsljóð; Loki; Njáls Saga; Norse Flyting; Odin; Ragnarǫk; Skaldic Poetry; Snorri Sturluson; Thor.**]

LOKI. In Scandinavian mythology, Loki is an enigmatic figure numbered among the gods, according to *Snorra Edda,* although by descent he is half god, half giant. According to one text (*Lokasenna*) he is blood-brother to Odin, head of the gods. There is no evidence that Loki was ever worshiped, but he plays a major role in the mythology. Loki accompanies Thor on his visits to Útgarða-Loki and Þrymr; after the giant Geirrøðr has captured and starved him, Loki is freed when he promises to bring back Thor without his weapons; Loki betrays Iðunn and her apples of youth to the giants; he fathers the monsters Fenrir, Hel, and the Midgard serpent; he procures the cursed gold of the dwarf Andvari, a major motif in heroic legend; he is responsible for the building of Asgard, the stronghold of the gods; he acquires various treasures for the gods, from dwarfs and once,

curiously, from Freyja; he reviles all the gods at a banquet; and he arranges Baldr's death and makes it impossible for Baldr to return to the world of the living. For this he is punished by being bound to a rock under a bowl dripping poison; here he will remain until Ragnarǫk, when he will break his fetters and join the forces of chaos, or evil, in the last battle.

From this short catalogue it is apparent that Loki's actions sometimes benefit the gods, sometimes harm them. For example, he is the father of Thor's greatest enemy, the Midgard serpent, but he also provides Thor with the hammer Mjollnir, the weapon Thor uses against the Midgard serpent and the evil race of giants. Often, however, the benefits Loki provides to the gods result directly from one of his acts that threatens their interests, and these acts, in turn, reveal no ideological basis; in the absence of other compelling circumstances, Loki thinks only of and for himself. This has led some scholars to consider Loki in light of the trickster figures so common in many world mythologies. Incapable of forethought, a trickster acts only for the moment. His actions are sometimes harmful, sometimes beneficial, occasionally self-destructive. He is greedy, boastful, deceitful, and lewd—and therefore a useful narrative mechanism, to whom a whole cycle of tales may accrue.

Explanation of Loki as a trickster figure has been adequate for some scholars, particularly those who approach the problem from the perspective of folklore. These have included de Vries, whose argument is most persuasive, and Celander and Rooth, who have associated Loki with the spider. Those with a more philological orientation, however, have tended to seize on other aspects of Loki's mysterious personality. Association with fire goes back at least to Grimm, and Gras regarded Loki as a water demon. Olrik drew attention to similar tales among Baltic peoples and farther east in the Caucasus and suggested that a loan had been transmitted to Scandinavia via the Goths. Ström, on the other hand, emphasized the similarities between Loki and Odin and concluded that Loki was a hypostasis of Odin. Similarities with Ossetic lore (Ossets are Aryan people of the central Caucasus), and a possible Indo-European origin, have been investigated by Dumézil.

As the wealth of these studies indicates, the problem of Loki is still far from solution. All that is certain is that he shares aspects of the trickster figure and in the symbolic world of the mythology ultimately aligns himself with evil, killing Baldr and leading the forces of chaos at Ragnarǫk.

BIBLIOGRAPHY

Studies include Hilding Celander, *Lokes mytiska ursprung* (1911); Georges Dumézil, *Loki* (1948), and *Gods of the Ancient Northmen*, Einar Haugen, ed. (1973); Elizabeth Johanna Gras, "De Noordse Loki-mythen in hun onderling verband" (diss., Utrecht, 1931); Jacob L. K. Grimm, *Teutonic Mythology*, James S. Stallybrass, trans., I (1880, repr. 1966); Axel Olrik, "Loke i nyere folkeoverlevering," in *Danske studier* (1908–1909), "Myterne om Loke," in *Festskrift til H. F. Feilberg* (1911), "Efterslæt til Loke-myterne," in *Danske studier* (1912), and *Ragnarök: Die Sagen vom Weltuntergang* (1922), esp. chap. 5; Anna Birgitta Rooth, *Loki in Scandinavian Mythology* (1961); Folke Ström, *Loki: Ein mythologisches Problem* (1956); Jan de Vries, *The Problem of Loki* (1933). A survey emphasizing the studies of de Vries, Rooth, and Ström is Anne Holtsmark, "Loki: En omstridt skikkelse i nordisk mytologi," in *Maal og Minne* (1962).

JOHN LINDOW

[See also **Odin; Ragnarǫk; Thor.**]

LOLLARDS. The word "lollard" or "loller" appears to derive from Middle Dutch *lollen*, "to mumble," and was evidently known at the end of the fourteenth century as a name for a religious eccentric or vagabond, usually loosely attached to the church; William Langland in *Piers Plowman*, for example, applies it to Will, his narrator. Langland's use is odd, especially in the *C* text, since the word had, by the presumed date of the composition of this version, come to have a more specific meaning as one who held opinions derived from, or similar to, those of John Wyclif (*ca.* 1335–1384). The first official use of the term in this latter sense was in Bishop Henry Wakefield of Worcester's register under 1387, but in 1382 Henry Crumpe was accused by the chancellor of the University of Oxford of a disturbance of the peace "because he called the heretics Lollards." Attempts to suggest that John Ball, the leader of the Peasants' Revolt, should be regarded as a Lollard, and hence that Lollards in the more specific sense of that word existed before the condemnation of Wyclif and independent of him, must be considered misguided: they depend upon the evidence of a few chroniclers, writing with hindsight, who wished to link together all dissidents and who erroneously presented Ball as a disciple of Wyclif.

It seems clear that Wyclif's followers understood the appellation "Lollard" at first as a serious insult, a name used only by their enemies. Later they accepted the name, finding antecedent Lollers or Lollards in the apostles and in Christ, "lolling on the cross," as they put it. Other names seem to have been preferred by them: "true men" was probably the most widespread and long lasting. In Latin writings the term frequently used by their opponents was *Wycliffistae*. Some have held that this term should be restricted to Wyclif's early university followers, but it is plain that opponents, such as Thomas Netter of Walden, did not observe this distinction but used the term indiscriminately for all sympathizers with Wyclif's views, whether or not they had had direct contact with Wyclif and his writings. Both terms, *Wycliffistae* and *Lollardi/Lollards/Lollers,* are applied in the fifteenth century also to adherents of John Hus in Bohemia, usually by their opponents as indication of their ultimate origin.

Much doubt was expressed by historians in the 1950's and 1960's about the links between Wyclif and the Lollards; it was argued that Lollardy was essentially an outcome of economic and social forces, lacking any coherent program or intellectual framework, becoming increasingly a collection of idiosyncratic individuals without organization and power, and that Wyclif neither initiated nor desired to initiate any popular movement. More recently opinion on both scores has reverted to older views. Wider sources of evidence have revealed that the early Lollard movement had considerable learning and connections with political power, and that even the later groups of Lollards were by no means isolated or without intellectual stimulus. Further scrutiny of references in Wyclif's own writings indicate an interest in, and awareness of, the spread of correct views by "poor priests," a term later applied to Lollard evangelists. There is some clear independent evidence for the dissemination of Wyclif's views during his lifetime outside the university: in 1382 two of his closest Oxford disciples, Nicholas Hereford and John Aston, and two others had been teaching in the villages and towns of north Hampshire in such a fashion that a mandate against them was issued by Bishop Wykeham of Winchester. In Leicester by the same date a group of artisans was known as adherents and as copiers of Wycliffite literature. The stream of official injunctions against Wyclif and his followers had begun by 1384, the year of Wyclif's death.

The role of Oxford in the early years of the Lollard movement has been increasingly appreciated as having been vital. Though Philip Repingdon reverted to orthodoxy in October 1382, and doubtless other less celebrated Oxford disciples likewise took heed of the warning signals from William Courtenay (archbishop of Canterbury, 1381–1396) and the ecclesiastical hierarchy, it is plain that work in support of Wycliffite views continued in Oxford. Hereford maintained his position until 1389, though not in Oxford. But there are a number of well-attested Oxford disciples, such as William James and Robert Lechlade of Merton, Thomas Turk of Exeter, and William Taylor and Peter Payne of St. Edmund Hall, all of whom are recurrently mentioned as Wycliffites, many of them well into the fifteenth century. That Thomas Arundel (archbishop of Canterbury, 1396–1397, and 1399–1414) in his 1407 Constitutions felt impelled to infringe the closely guarded autonomy of the university to such an extent as to require monthly enquiry by wardens of halls into their undergraduates' opinions on matter of theology makes it plain that Wycliffism was still a potent force in Oxford. Bonfires of Wyclif's books were still possible in the city up to 1410, yet as late as 1454 Oriel College paid out sums for the purchase of three manuscripts containing Wyclif's writings in Latin. Equally, though it is in most cases impossible to assign an authorial name to the works, there are a number of early Lollard texts whose compilation must depend upon access to extensive libraries, the sort of library only to be found in larger monastic houses, a location closed to the Lollards because of their inherited opposition to all forms of "private religion," or in one of the universities. Texts of this kind include the Latin commentary on the Apocalypse, known from its opening words as the *Opus arduum,* which was written between Christmas 1389 and Easter 1390, declaredly in prison, but, from its copious and extensive quotations from patristic, canonistic, and scholastic authorities, the author evidently had access to many books. Also the vast *Floretum,* compiled between 1384 and 1396, a florilegium (collection) of quotations on alphabetically arranged subjects, including many quotations from Wyclif and having a plainly Wycliffite slant, heavily indebted to the academic compilation tradition and drawing on a very large number of sources. In English and falling into this same category are the *Glossed Gospels:* these divide each chapter of the four gospels into sections, giving first the Early Version Wycliffite translation, followed by an extensive commentary, drawing in part on such established works as the *Catena aurea,* but in many cases going back to the original sources from which these collections had been compiled. There are at least three versions of the *Glossed Gospels,* each of which seems to have had recourse to further books. These are the cases where an academic background is most readily demonstrable.

The early years of the Lollards are the least well documented, largely because the established church, unaccustomed in England to dealing with heresy, was often slow or erratic in moving against the new challenge. The episcopal registers provide some material, if hostile and formulaic, reducing complex views and groupings to a simple list of errors sufficient for a condemnation; some of these registers have been lost. It is also clear that heresy was often recorded in a less permanent form than the registers, and this has been destroyed. Secular records preserve some material in the patent and close rolls and in the largely unprinted and unindexed documents housed in the Public Record Office (London). Equally hostile are the chroniclers, many of them monastic and many writing with some degree of hindsight. There are also a number of extensive texts composed to refute Wyclif and his followers, from William Woodford or William Rymington in Wyclif's own lifetime to Reginald Pecock in the 1450's; although these need careful handling to yield valid historical evidence, they have been unduly neglected. Equally difficult to handle are the texts written by the Lollards themselves, but they are the only sources for the defense. Most are undated, many are undatable, almost all are anonymous, yet they allow a coherent assessment to be made of the views of the sect.

The first stage of the history of the movement runs from Wyclif's lifetime to 1401, when the statute *De heretico comburendo* first introduced into England the death penalty for heresy. The statute represented the decisive victory of the established church over the would-be reformers. The bishops had succeeded fitfully in engaging the secular authorities in their pursuit of the Lollards from the 1380's, but this represented a formalization of the united opposition. The early chroniclers, Henry Knighton and Thomas Walsingham, suggest that at the beginning of this period there was a group of knights favorable to the Lollard cause. From a careful scrutiny of documentary details, the modern scholar K. B. McFarlane argues that the chroniclers were essentially right; M. Wilks has developed this idea to suggest that these Lollard knights had considerable power at the court of Richard II as a national party in opposition to the internationalism of the church. Some of the knights certainly acted with apparently unchallenged brazenness in support of individual Lollard preachers, and were themselves undoubted sympathizers. The backing of such men would certainly explain the money and organization that the early Lollards demonstrably had for the composition and dissemination of their prolific texts. Equally, by the 1390's episcopal registers demonstrate that there were large and well-established groups of Lollards in many areas: evidence is good for the area between the Wiltshire downs and the Chilterns, for Bristol, Herefordshire, Leicester and its neighborhood, Northampton, and London. Many of these areas continued to produce Lollards, even though the social class from which they came shows a shift: while in this first stage adherents to Wycliffite opinions can be found in all classes from the gentry to laborers, and among the clergy, by the 1420's Lollardy had become more limited to the lower classes, with a few eccentric clerical supporters.

The next stage might be defined as that from 1401 to the Oldcastle revolt and its aftermath in 1413–1415. In the years after 1401 a number of major trials were held, and some Lollards were burned at the stake. The ecclesiastical authorities also moved further to eradicate the movement: most notable were Archbishop Arundel's Constitutions, drafted in 1407 and finally issued in 1409. The opening sections of the legislation were not overtly directed against the Lollards, but by tightening the rules concerning licenses to teach and to preach they made the work of the "poor preachers" much more difficult. Section 6 reiterated earlier bans on the ownership or reading of works by Wyclif; other sections forbade the discussion of tendentious matters of doctrine even in the universities and required the monthly investigation of undergraduate views on theological matters. Section 7 forbade the ownership of vernacular translations of Scripture, unless prior permission had been obtained from the bishop and unless the translation dated from before Wyclif. Since the prohibition extended beyond complete translations to any works that cited Scripture, this was a far-reaching provision. It went far beyond the position of undoubtedly orthodox men as recently as 1401.

Opposition to the Lollard movement was confirmed in all its worst suspicions by the events of the Oldcastle rebellion. Sir John Oldcastle was first detected of heresy in 1410, by which time he was evidently a leader of the Lollards but also, by virtue of his second marriage, a man of substance and, because of his eminent military service, in favor with the future Henry V. In 1413 some of his books were scru-

tinized, and Oldcastle was asked to reject the heresies they contained; the new king, Henry V, failed to persuade Oldcastle to submit. In September Oldcastle was brought to trial; his Lollardy was revealed as extreme, and he refused to recant. During the respite before execution, Oldcastle escaped from the Tower and went into hiding. Agents quickly endeavored to organize a rising for 9–10 January 1414, centered on London but involving Lollards from many areas. Intelligence reached the authorities beforehand, and the rebels were intercepted as they arrived in London and were easily defeated. Oldcastle evaded capture for some time and was not finally brought to trial and executed till December 1417. Extensive inquiries about his followers ensued immediately in 1414; some were executed and many more fined and forced to recant their heresy.

As a significant political force Lollardy never recovered from the Oldcastle rebellion. It seems that Lollards were involved in an attempted rising in 1431, whose main centers were Berkshire and Wiltshire but with minor troubles in London and the Midlands. The program for this revolt included disendowment of monasteries and friaries, and the removal of the wealth of some eminent lay lords; the leaders seem mostly to have been artisans, though a few minor gentry may have been implicated. But even though after 1415 Lollardy was under constant attack, it is plain that many groups survived and even flourished throughout the fifteenth century and up to the point where Wycliffism merged with Lutheranism. The bishops' registers reveal recurrent trials. A particularly full picture of a Lollard community can be reconstructed from the court book of Bishop William Alnwick of Norwich covering the years 1428 to 1431; this shows the groups of Lollards in a number of Norfolk and Suffolk villages, the ways in which the groups were built up and in which they communicated with each other, their contact with an equally flourishing group around Tenterden in Kent, and their beliefs. Almost equally full pictures can be found in the years 1511–1512 both in the Coventry area from the court book of Bishop Geoffrey Blythe and in the Tenterden area from the register of William Warham, archbishop of Canterbury (1503–1532). The persistence of beliefs and of methods of proselytization is noteworthy. In many areas of the south and the south Midlands the sixteenth-century reformers were able to gain ready support from people already sympathetic to their views about the Roman church and its sacraments, and about the importance of vernacular scripture; in some cases investigations during the 1530's are indeterminately of Lollards or of Lutherans. Several Lollard texts were copied and printed, mainly abroad, by the reformers during Henry VIII's reign.

In view of the long period during which Lollardy flourished and the wide diversity of education and class of its adherents, it is not surprising that it should be impossible to list the tenets always and unvaryingly held by the Lollards. With the exception of a few idiosyncratic opinions, in some cases probably erroneously associated with Lollardy by its opponents, most of the ideas are traceable in germ, if not in detail, to Wyclif himself. It seems, however, that in many cases other contemporary attitudes colored, slanted, and were caught up in this stream. The bishops plainly regarded the most characteristic view of the heretics as the denial of transubstantiation in the Eucharist, and a consequent disregard for the sacrament. Equally regularly found in Lollard trials is a condemnation of the worship of images and of the practice of pilgrimage. The first is directly attributable to Wyclif; the second and third are in line with his dislike for the outward trappings of institutionalized religion, but were not topics on which he wrote extensively. After 1407 ownership or knowledge of, or favor for, vernacular scriptures was also often cited as evidence of heresy (though it is clear that many owners of such scriptures were completely orthodox). These are the attitudes on which the bishops apparently found it easiest to convict. Some trials and many writings, both by opponents and by the Lollards themselves, reveal that the Lollards continued and developed Wyclif's opposition to "private religion" (that is, to all forms of religious life that separate the individual from the community), to the papacy, to all the temporal wealth and power of the church, and to the church's claim to the prerogatives of absolution and of excommunication. Many Lollards went further than Wyclif in claiming the "priesthood of all believers." Priests, they held, should devote themselves to preaching, should possess only what was sufficient for their immediate needs, and, if necessary, should labor with their hands for their food. Most held puritanical views about the sacraments, some even denying the need for baptism or for ecclesiastical ceremony at marriage. A number held pacifist views, and a few anticipated the Taborites in urging community of property.

The most celebrated English text with which the Lollards are connected is the first complete vernacular rendering of the Bible. Two versions of this are usually distinguished: the Early Version, an awkward rendering of the Latin following closely the syntax, word order, and vocabulary of its model; and the Later Version, a revision of this into idiomatic English. Over 250 manuscripts of these versions survive, despite ecclesiastical suppression and the losses due to time. While a recent attempt to argue for a version predating Lollardy seems misguided, older attributions of the Early Version to Wyclif, completed by Nicholas Hereford, and of the Later Version to John Purvey, are not to be trusted; both versions are the products of extensive group effort. Apart from the texts mentioned earlier there are a number of other English and Latin works of Lollard authorship. A large cycle of sermons survives, together with many other groups of sermons, tracts, and individual texts. Some were widely publicized, such as the Twelve Conclusions of the Lollards, posted on the doors of Westminster Hall and of St. Paul's Cathedral in 1395, or the Lollard Disendowment Bill, a broadside that appears to have been known over a long period and which some chroniclers allege was introduced into Parliament in 1407 or 1410. Most of the texts appear to have been written before about 1431, though circulation continued for another hundred years. Considerable care must be taken in identifying vernacular writings as Lollard, and early critics certainly ascribed to Wyclif and his followers many anonymous works of orthodox origins. The fact that the Lollards took up many ideas, particularly of an anticlerical cast, which were in circulation before Wyclif makes it hard always to be certain of the background of a text.

BIBLIOGRAPHY

Sources. Ernest W. Talbert and S. Harrison Thomson, "Wyclyf and His Followers," in *A Manual of the Writings in Middle English, 1050–1500,* II, J. Burke Severs, ed. (1970), 360–380, 521–533, for basic bibliography. The two versions of the Bible translation were printed (not always from the best manuscripts) in *The Holy Bible . . . Made from the Latin Vulgate by John Wycliffe and His Followers,* Josiah Forshall and Frederic Madden, eds. (1850). For the Old Testament in the Early Version translation, there is a more recent edition: Conrad Lindberg, ed., *MS. Bodley 959: Genesis-Baruch 3.20 in the Earlier Version of the Wycliffite Bible,* in *Stockholm Studies in English,* 6 (1959), 8 (1961), 10 (1963), 13 (1965), 20 (1969), and *The Earlier Version of the Wycliffite Bible* (Baruch 3.20 to end of Old Testament from MS. Christ Church 145), in *Stockholm Studies in English,* 29 (1973). Other recent editions are: Anne Hudson, ed., *Selections from English Wycliffite Writings* (1978); Christina von Nolcken, *The Middle English Trans-*

lation of the 'Rosarium Theologie' (1979); V. J. S. Scattergood, *The Two Ways*, in *The Works of Sir John Clanvowe* (1975).

Studies. Sven L. Fristedt, "The Wycliffe Bible," in *Stockholm Studies in English,* **4** (1953), **21** (1969), **28** (1973); H. Hargreaves, "The Wycliffite Versions," in *Cambridge History of the Bible,* II, G. W. H. Lampe, ed. (1969), and "Popularising Biblical Scholarship: The Role of the Wycliffite *Glossed Gospels,*" in *The Bible and Medieval Culture,* W. Lourdaux and D. Verhelst, eds. (1979).

History. Margaret Aston, *Lollards and Reformers: Images and Literacy in Late Medieval Religion* (1984); Henry L. Cannon, "The Poor Priests: A Study in the Rise of English Lollardry," in *Annual Report of the American Historical Association for 1899,* I (1900); James Crompton, "Fasciculi Zizaniorum," in *Journal of Ecclesiastical History,* **12** (1961), and "Leicestershire Lollards," in *Transactions of the Leicestershire Archaeological and Historical Society,* **44** (1968–1969); A. G. Dickens, *Lollards and Protestants in the Diocese of York 1509–1558* (1959); R. B. Dobson, *The Peasants' Revolt of 1381* (1970); A. Gwynn, *The English Austin Friars in the Time of Wyclif* (1940); Anne Hudson, *Lollards and Their Books* (1985); Malcolm D. Lambert, *Medieval Heresy: Popular Movements From Bogomil to Hus* (1977), 217–271; G. Leff, *Heresy in the Later Middle Ages,* II (1967), 559–605; K. B. McFarlane, *John Wycliffe and the Beginnings of English Nonconformity* (1952), and *Lancastrian Kings and Lollard Knights* (1972), 139–232; H. G. Richardson, "Heresy and the Lay Power Under Richard II," in *English Historical Review,* **51** (1936); Norman P. Tanner, *Heresy Trials in the Diocese of Norwich, 1428–31* (Camden Society, 4th ser., **20** [1977]); J. A. F. Thomson, *The Later Lollards, 1414–1520* (1965); M. Wilks, "*Reformatio regni:* Wyclif and Hus as Leaders of Religious Protest Movements," in *Studies in Church History,* **9** (1972), and "Royal Priesthood: The Origins of Lollardy," in *The Church in a Changing Society* (1978); H. B. Workman, *John Wyclif,* 2 vols. (1926).

ANNE HUDSON

[See also **Bible; England (1216–1485); Heresies, Western European; Heresy; Hus, John; Oxford University; Wyclif, John.**]

LOMBARD ARCH. See Arch.

LOMBARD ART presents in microcosm both the problems and the achievements of early medieval art in the West. When the Lombards entered Italy in 568 their artistic tradition was centered on small objects of personal adornment such as pins and buckles made of metal, and often decorated with inlaid gems. The objects were executed with great skill, but the complex decorative patterns and motifs generally did not include any human forms whatsoever, much less complex scenic representations or religious subjects. Suddenly the Lombards found themselves occupying a territory in Italy still displaying many large-scale works of classical and early Christian painting and sculpture, while the great cities of Rome and Ravenna long maintained a living tradition of monumental art. Contact with the Byzantine Empire in the East provided other sources of inspiration for Lombard artists and their patrons. By the end of the Lombard kingdom in the second half of the eighth century, a series of works of monumental sculpture and painting had been produced revealing something of the interplay of these diverse traditions and at the same time representing a new departure with its own character.

It is difficult to define Lombard art with precision. Much has been lost, and the fragmentary works that remain are often extremely difficult to interpret or even to date with any certainty. It is also likely that many works were executed for Lombard patrons by artists of other nationalities. The important series of paintings in Rome during the seventh and eighth centuries cannot be considered as part of the Lombard tradition, as Rome was always free from and generally opposed to Lombard rule, although Lombards were certainly influential. On the other hand important works, especially wall paintings, continued to be produced for the Lombard dukes of Benevento well into the ninth century, and in many areas of Italy works in a "Lombard" style were made as late as the tenth century—but these will not be considered here.

Even after entering Italy, Lombard metalworkers continued to employ northern techniques and northern animal styles brought with them from their Germanic homeland. By the early seventh century an increasing impact of Mediterranean motifs and techniques is apparent, as might be expected from the new location of the Lombards at the center of the Mediterranean world and its trade routes. Indeed, one of the most important questions concerning early Lombard metalwork, which is often of superb quality and distinct originality, is its likely role at this period in transmitting Mediterranean ideas to other Germanic tribes such as the Franks, and even the Anglo-Saxons, and particularly with reference to the so-called Style II animal ornament. Perhaps the

Lombard helmet plaque. Val di Nievole, early 7th century, now in Florence, Bargello. SCALA/ART RESOURCE

best-known class of Lombard works in metal are the gold-leaf crosses commonly buried with the dead, a clear example of continuing pagan habits even after the conversion to Christianity, and a type of work that seems to have spread from Lombard Italy to the north. From the early seventh century dates the famous helmet plaque from Val di Nievole (Florence, Bargello), with an enthroned monarch flanked by guards and Victories while receiving tribute. This rare figural scene in a highly abstract style entirely depends in its iconography upon traditional Roman imperial art.

Lombard decorative sculpture survives in very large quantities, but only relatively few pieces at such major centers as Brescia, Pavia, and especially at Cividale, present complex figural compositions. Since the bulk of this material dates only from the eighth century, it is difficult to trace a clear connection between Lombard sculpture and the preceding metalwork tradition. The impact of earlier Italian works still visible in situ was clearly felt by Lombard sculptors, and the influence of contemporary art in the Byzantine Empire was also an important and perhaps a dominant factor. Certainly a number of scholars have sought to explain the general similarities of Lombard sculpture to works from Spain and France by postulating a common use of Eastern models, although this theory remains inconclusive. Interlace

and even occasionally animal decoration continue in many sculptural pieces, although large works with royal or ducal patronage tend to employ Mediterranean styles of vegetal rinceaux and related patterns. Cividale del Friuli preserved the largest group of Lombard figural sculptures, especially the grand baptismal ciborium of Calixtus with its ornate capitals, arches, and closure slab (before 762), and the so-called Ratchis altar (ca. 737), with reliefs of the Visitation and Adoration of the Magi on the narrow ends and on the front a large *Majestas Domini*, Christ in a mandorla borne by angels. Most controversial are the decorative panels and the life-size stucco figures at S. Maria in Valle in Cividale, now generally accepted as works from the end of the eighth or early ninth century, although possibly executed by foreign artists rather than by Lombard craftsmen.

Lombard painting poses the most perplexing difficulties. A series of important surviving fresco cycles at Lombard sites in the north of Italy such as Cividale, Brescia, and especially at Castelseprio present exceptionally sophisticated works, while from the south San Vincenzo al Volturno and Benevento preserve paintings of high quality. Yet the southern works clearly date from the mid-ninth century, and the northern examples, more difficult to date, are scarcely earlier than about 800. The situation is sim-

650

Majestas Domini from the Ratchis altar, *ca.* 737, now at Cividale, Museo Cristiano. SCALA/ART RESOURCE

ilar with respect to manuscript illumination. The grand author portraits of the Egino Gospels (Berlin, Staatsbibliothek) are only the most splendid of a series of works datable about 800 and after. Yet for neither fresco nor manuscript painting is it possible to trace a strong continuous tradition back into the eighth century or earlier, and other evidence that seems to reflect lost Italian works of the period is inconclusive. Thus the critical question whether these paintings should be seen as truly Lombard art and as an essential background for Carolingian court art, or instead as derivative versions of new artistic traditions created outside of Italy, remains unresolved.

BIBLIOGRAPHY

Nils Åberg, *The Occident and the Orient in the Art of the Seventh Century*, II, *Lombard Italy* (1945); Hans Belting, "Probleme der Kunstgeschichte Italiens im Frühmittelalter," in *Frühmittelalterliche Studies*, 1 (1967), and *Studien zur Beneventanischen Malerei* (1968); Gian Piero Bognetti, ed., *Santa Maria de Castelseprio* (1948); Aleandra Cosmi De Fanti, *Il Battistero di Callisto a Cividale* (1972); Otto von Hessen and Adriano Peroni, "Die Langobarden in Pannonien und in Italien," in Helmut Roth, ed., *Kunst der Völker-wanderungszeit* (1979), 164–179; Wolfgang Hübener, ed., *Die Goldblattkreuze des frühen Mittelalters* (1975); Felix Kayser, *Kreuz und Rune: Langobardisch-romanische Kunst in Italien* (1965); Rudolf Kutzli, *I Longobardi e la Lombardia* (1978); Hans Peter L'Orange and Hjalmar Torp, *Il Tempietto Longobardo di Cividale* (1977); Wilfried Menghin, *Die Langobarden* (1985); Helmut Roth, *Die Ornamentik der Langobarden in Italien: Eine Untersuchung zur Stilentwicklung anhand der Grabfunde* (1973); Meyer Schapiro, review of Kurt Weitzmann, *The Fresco Cycle of S. Maria di Castelseprio* (1951), in *Art Bulletin*, 34 (1952); Joachim Werner, *Die langobardischen Fibeln aus Italien* (1950); David H. Wright, "The Canon Tables of the Codex Beneventanus and Related Decoration," in *Dumbarton Oaks Papers*, 33 (1979).

LAWRENCE NEES

[See also **Animal Style; Barbarians, Invasions of; Pre-Romanesque Art.**]

LOMBARD BANDS, in northern and central Italy and neighboring areas, the striping or banding of wall surfaces in courses of varying color, with alternating stripes either of red brick and white stone or of two colors of stone, usually marble. The term "Lombard" was once used to mean essentially Italian Romanesque. Banded walls are as common in Tuscany (Pisa, Siena) as in the Lombard plain of northern Italy (Verona). Islamic influence has been suggested (mosque in Córdoba).

BIBLIOGRAPHY

Arthur Kingsley Porter, *Lombard Architecture* (1916); Angiola M. Romanini, *L'architettura gotica in Lombardia* (1964); George E. Street, *Brick and Marble in the Middle Ages* (1855); John White, *Art and Architecture in Italy 1250 to 1400* (1966).

GREGORY WHITTINGTON

[See also **Gothic Architecture; Lombard Art; Romanesque Architecture.**]

LOMBARD LEAGUE. This term denotes a series of alliances formed by most of the cities of Lombardy in the twelfth and thirteenth centuries to resist the efforts of the Holy Roman emperors Frederick I Barbarossa and Frederick II to establish effective imperial authority over that region. The membership of the leagues varied with circumstances, but the most consistent members were Milan (usually the leader), Brescia, Piacenza, Bologna, Faenza, Mantua, and Lodi.

By the mid twelfth century, sworn communes controlled most of the cities of northern and central Italy and were exercising royal rights *(regalia)* within their districts. At the imperial diet held in Roncaglia in November 1158, Frederick I sought to turn de jure imperial authority over Lombardy into true sovereignty by reclaiming the *regalia,* asserting control of the elected communal consuls, and by appointing a new magistrate, a podesta, in the cities to govern in the name of the emperor.

Frederick then withdrew concessions granted to Milan, the most hostile anti-imperial city in Lombardy, and reduced the area under Milanese domination. Milan refused to accept a podesta and, with its allies Brescia, Piacenza, and Crema, joined Pope Adrian IV to oppose the emperor. Frederick defeated and destroyed Milan (March 1162) and was able to appoint podestas in most of the Lombard cities. Even the emperor's supporters, however, found the rule of the podestas to be oppressive.

The struggle for Italy was complicated by the divided papal election of 1159, with Frederick supporting antipope Victor IV against Alexander III, who encouraged the emperor's enemies. In 1164, Venice helped organize Treviso, Vicenza, Padua, and Verona into the anti-imperial Veronese League, while Alexander III fomented trouble for Frederick in Lombardy. Imperial officials were attacked in several cities, and the rebellion spread to many traditionally imperial cities. Cremona, Mantua, and Bergamo joined with Brescia to form the League of Pontida (in April 1167), which rebuilt Milan. Soon Piacenza, Parma, Ferrara, and Lodi were added to the Pontidan league.

The destruction of the emperor's army by pestilence (summer 1167) and Frederick's flight from Italy encouraged his opponents. On 1 December 1167 the First Lombard League (known as the *Societas Lombardiae*) was formed by the union of the Veronese League and the League of Pontida, as well as Venice, Milan, Bologna, and Modena. During the emperor's almost seven-year absence from Italy, the Lombard League grew to include some thirty-six cities of the Piedmont, Lombardy, Emilia, Romagna, and the Veronese Mark. The league members swore to support a common army financed by members' contributions and to maintain internal unity. Each member chose a rector to serve on an executive board that directed the league's affairs.

The league then constructed (1168) the new fortress of Alessandria, named for its papal supporter, to guard western Lombardy. Frederick returned to Italy (September 1174), but his siege of Alessandria failed and peace negotiations at Montebello (April 1175) foundered when the league insisted on an end to the papal schism as well. On 29 May 1176 the league soundly defeated Frederick I near Legnano, which convinced him to come to terms with Alexander III.

In the Peace of Venice (1 August 1177), Frederick gave recognition to Alexander III as rightful pope and made a six-year truce with the league. At the expiration of the truce, the league and the emperor concluded the Peace of Constance (25 June 1183). The league's seventeen remaining members formally recognized the emperor's sovereignty, while he abandoned the rights he had claimed at the diet of Roncaglia, which effectively left the cities with most of their communal autonomy undisturbed.

At Constance the league also gained the right to be renewed, and it revived frequently in the next quarter century when its leading cities perceived a threat to the concessions granted at Constance. Eleven cities renewed the league in 1195 to oppose

Emperor Henry VI; eight cities did so in 1198 to support Otto of Brunswick as the emperor Otto IV (d. 1218) against Philip of Swabia (d. 1208); six members joined to oppose Philip's imperial coronation in 1208 and then backed Otto IV against Frederick II. Milan and her allies were thenceforth ready to resist any attempt by Frederick II to exercise his authority in Lombardy.

Thus when Frederick summoned an imperial diet to Cremona in 1226, seventeen cities formed the Second Lombard League, which was an aggressive coalition bound by an offensive and defensive alliance. Pope Honorius III arranged a peace (1227), but he was succeeded in that same year by Gregory IX, an implacable opponent of imperial domination of Italy. At Frederick II's return from his crusade (1229), the league was renewed, but a peace was soon made at San Germano (July 1229). When the emperor called for a diet at Ravenna in 1231, however, the league again revived, although little of consequence occurred before another peace was arranged.

In 1234 the Lombards allied with the emperor's rebellious son Henry, but by May 1235 Frederick II was victorious. He declared war on the Lombards, which caused the league to be renewed by eleven cities. Frederick nearly destroyed the league's army at Cortenuova (27 November 1237), but his harsh peace terms forced Milan to resist, and the league rallied and went on the offensive. In 1239 it was actively joined by Gregory IX. Desultory warfare was the rule in the 1240's, with Gregory's successor Innocent IV leading the emperor's opponents. Not even the league's defeat of Frederick II at Vittoria in 1248, however, seriously threatened his general control of Lombardy.

The death of Frederick II (13 December 1250) crippled the imperial cause. Frederick's son Conrad IV attempted to continue his father's policies, while a league of eight Lombard cities (1251) was prepared to resist. There was little conflict, and the league ended with Conrad's death (1254). An attempt to revive the Lombard League to oppose Emperor Henry VII, who entered Italy in 1310, failed because of the internal divisions in the cities of Lombardy.

BIBLIOGRAPHY

Marshall W. Baldwin, *Alexander III and the Twelfth Century* (1968), 79–80, 137–153; Ugo Balzani, "Frederick Barbarossa and the Lombard League," in *Cambridge Medieval History*, V (1926); William M. Bowsky, *Henry VII in Italy* (1960); William F. Butler, *The Lombard Communes* (1906, repr. 1969); Gina Fasoli, "Federico Barbarossa e le città lombarde" and "Le lega lombarda—ante-

cedenti, formazione, struttura," in her *Scritti di storia medievale* (1968), and "Federico II e le lega lombarda: Linee di ricerca," in *Annali dell'Istituto storico italo-germanico in Trento*, 2 (1976); Edouard Jordan, *Les origines de la domination angevine in Italie* (1909, repr. in 2 vols. 1960), and *L'Allemagne et l'Italie aux XIIᵉ et XIIIᵉ siècles* (1939); Peter Munz, *Frederick Barbarossa* (1969); Marcel Pacaut, "Aux origines du Guelfisme: Les doctrines de la ligue lombarde (1167–1183)," in *Revue historique*, 230 (1963); *Popolo e stato in Italia nell'età di Federico Barbarossa* (1970), 209–220, 247–261; Michelangelo Schipa, "Italy and Sicily Under Frederick II," in *Cambridge Medieval History*, VI (1929); Giovanni Battista Testa, *History of the War of Frederick I Against the Communes of Italy*, rev. ed. (1877); Giovanni Treccani degli Alfieri, ed., *Dalle lotte contro il Barbarossa al primo signore (1152–1310)*, vol. IV of *Storia di Milano*, 17 vols. (1953–1966); Thomas G. Van Cleve, *The Emperor Frederick II of Hohenstaufen* (1972).

STEVEN C. FANNING

[See also **Frederick I Barbarossa; Frederick II of the Holy Roman Empire; Gregory IX, Pope; Guelphs and Ghibellines; Holy Roman Empire; Milan; Podestà**.]

LOMBARD, PETER. See Peter Lombard.

LOMBARDS. The term "lombard" in the thirteenth, fourteenth, and fifteenth centuries was an epithet applied in northern Europe to Italian pawnbrokers and petty moneylenders. Lombard and its twin *cahorsin* were virtually synonomous with usurer.

The first lombards were apparently merchants from the Piedmontese towns of Asti and Chieri who had settled in Savoy and France for the purpose of engaging in moneylending. The earliest firm date for the appearance of lombards in France is 1226. From about 1240 until the mid thirteenth century, lombard bankers from the Lombard and Tuscan towns of Italy settled in most of the population centers in an area that included the Dauphiné, Savoy, the Comté, Burgundy, Champagne, Lorraine, the Rhineland, Brabant, Flanders, Artois, the Île de France, and part of Normandy. Despite intermittent suppressions by public authorities, the lombards continued their activities in these regions through the later Middle Ages until they gave way in the sixteenth and seventeenth centuries to the *monts-de-piété*, or official pawnshops run by the church or public authorities.

The lombards plied their trade under licenses granted them for a fee by municipal authorities and territorial lords. Such grants conveyed a monopoly to lend money at interest against pledges of personal property. The businesses of the lombards were customarily organized through partnerships, frequently involving members of the same family. Profit and loss were assigned pro rata according to the capital or labor placed in the venture. Generally lombards worked with their own capital, although they occasionally accepted deposits or borrowed from third parties. Lombards worked out of houses large enough to quarter the resident partner or partners, hired assistants, and the goods taken in pawn.

The lombards' customers were drawn from all walks of life, including feudal princes and municipal authorities borrowing on behalf of their cities, but as might be expected the majority came from the poorer classes. These pawnbrokers accepted a wide variety of articles as pledges, but household utensils and clothing were the most common. The percentages of the value of pawns that the lombards could lend varied. For example, a partnership agreement drawn up at Troyes in 1260 by six financiers from the Tuscan town of Lucca (to regulate the operation of a pawnshop in the nearby locale of Poigney in the lordship of one Guido de Labersotto) explicitly stated that the resident partners could lend as much as 80 percent of the value of items of silver and gold and 75 percent of the value of other articles. The lombards of Sluis were allowed to lend up to 60 percent of the value of silverware. Lombards came in touch with trade when they sold their unredeemed pledges after a holding period of as much as a year or a year and a half.

In the thirteenth century interest charges allowed to the Lombards are not specifically mentioned in the surviving licenses. In the fourteenth and fifteenth centuries, however, grants openly allowed interest charges in the neighborhood of two pence a week per pound, which is an annual charge of 43.33 percent. In view of their extraordinary expenses in the form of license fees and fines, coupled with the constant risk of suppression and confiscation of their goods, it is difficult to judge whether the lombards' interest charges were extortionate. It is clear, however, that there was a strong and continuous market in medieval Europe for their services.

BIBLIOGRAPHY

Georges Bigwood, *Le régime juridique et économique du commerce de l'argent dans la Belgique du moyen âge* (1921–1922); Raymond A. De Roover, *Money, Banking, and Credit in Mediaeval Bruges* (1948); Kurt Grunwald, "Lombards, Cahorsins, and Jews," in *The Journal of European Economic History*, **4** (1975); Anna Maria Patrone, *Le casane astigiane in Savoia* (1959).

THOMAS W. BLOMQUIST

[See also **Banking, European; Banking, Jewish, in Europe; Fairs of Champagne; Mints and Money, Western European; Usury.**]

LOMBARDS, KINGDOM OF, usually refers to the period of the Lombard domination of northern and central Italy from 568 to 774. The Lombards (an evolved form of their own name, Langobards, "Long Beards") were a Germanic people who were living around the lower Elbe by the late first century B.C. Whether they were ethnically East Germanic or West Germanic is a matter of debate. In the mid second century A.D., they were raiding the Roman Empire along its Danubian frontier. The next three centuries of Lombard history are poorly known, but their legends of this period were included in the principal narrative source of the Lombards, the *Historia Langobardorum* of Paul the Deacon, himself a Lombard writing at the end of the eighth century. During this time, the Lombards either acquired or assumed the reputation of a small but fierce tribe.

By the end of the fifth century, the Lombards were in lower Austria, where they defeated the Heruli (*ca.* 508) and then moved into Pannonia under their king Waccho (*ca.* 510–540). Waccho formed marriage alliances with Merovingian kings, and concluded a treaty of alliance with Emperor Justinian I. Under King Audoin (546–*ca.* 565), the Lombards expanded into Noricum and served as Roman auxiliaries in Justinian's Persian wars and in the last phase of his war against the Ostrogoths in Italy. Audoin married the grand-niece of Theodoric the Great, which may have given the Lombards notions of succeeding the Ostrogoths in Italy.

King Alboin (*ca.* 565–572), Audoin's son, was to make the most important decisions of Lombard history at a time of great changes in the political world of the mid sixth century. Justinian died in 565, which may have signaled an end of the Lombard alliance with Byzantium, and the nomadic Avars arrived in the regions to the northeast. Alboin first allied with the Avars to crush the neighboring Gepids (567), and then he cast his eyes on Italy, not yet recovered from the devastation of the twenty-year-

KINGDOM OF THE LOMBARDS

Key ===== Roman roads

0   100 Miles
0   100 Kilometers

long Gothic wars. It was also racked by a recent onset of plague and divided religiously over the papacy's acceptance of the "Three Chapters." Recent veterans of Italian campaigning, the Lombards were not unaware of the weakened and divided state of Italy at a time when they were under Avar pressure but no longer allies of Constantinople. Thus in the spring of 568, Alboin led the Lombards and the mélange of other peoples associated with them into the supine and unprepared province.

Within a year the Lombards had captured the major cities north of the Po, with the exception of Pavia, which withstood the Lombard siege for three years. The Lombards crossed the Apennines and moved into western Emilia and north and central Tuscany. Perhaps even Rome was menaced. During this period, Lombard bands also took the southern territories of Spoleto and Benevento. Pavia fell into the hands of the invaders in 572, but Alboin was murdered in that same year. He was succeeded by Cleph (572–574), who reigned only briefly before he, too, was assassinated.

The dispersion of the Lombards, relatively few in number, during the invasion and early conquest had significantly decentralized them. This danger was exacerbated when their leading men chose no successor to Cleph, but instead the dukes, said to be thirty-five in number, ruled their own regions independently. They were unable to act in concert, however, and there were ill-fated raids into Frankish Gaul while a Frankish-Byzantine alliance led to attacks against the disunited Lombards.

The dukes found it necessary to restore the monarchy, choosing Cleph's son Authari as king (584–590). The king was given half of the ducal lands to provide a permanent domain as a material foundation for royal power. Authari withstood combined Frankish-Byzantine assaults, and allied with Bavaria by marrying Theodelinda, the Catholic daughter of its duke. When Authari died (September 590), Theodelinda selected Duke Agilulf of Turin to succeed Authari both as her husband and as king of the Lombards (590–616). Agilulf, a strong and active king, reestablished royal authority over the northern dukes and made peace with the Avars, who were threatening his northern border. He also resumed the conquest of Italy. By 605 the hinterland of Venetia had been seized, as well as the entire Po valley and eastern Emilia. The territory of Rome was assaulted by Agilulf and by the dukes of Spoleto and Benevento until Pope Gregory I was able to negotiate a piece with the Lombards.

During the reign of Agilulf, the Lombard and imperial frontiers of Italy began to stabilize. Imperial Italy was limited to the coastal regions of Venetia and Liguria, Ravenna and its district (the Exarchate), the Pentapolis (centered on Rimini and Ancona), the region around Rome and a string of strongholds along the Via Flaminia forming a corridor connecting Rome with the Pentapolis and Exarchate, and the Neapolitan region as well as the southern provinces of Apulia and Calabria. Italy was now divided politically, not to be reunited until 1870.

The Lombards were mainly pagan when they invaded Italy, but there were also Catholics and Arians among them. Pope Gregory I concentrated his efforts on trying to win the support of Theodelinda in influencing the northern Italian bishops to accept the papal position on the "Three Chapters." But in this he failed. Orthodox Christianity was growing among the Lombards, and this movement was accelerated by the arrival in northern Italy of the Irish monk Columbanus and his followers around 612. He was welcomed by Agilulf and Theodelinda and was given land at Bobbio for his monastery. Arioald (626–636) and Rothari (636–652) are the only indisputably Arian kings of the Lombards, but religious peace continued in the kingdom. Rothari conducted the last major attacks on imperial territory in the seventh century, conquering the Ligurian coastline in 643 and seizing the Venetian hinterland.

Rothari is best known for his issuance of the Edict, the first codification of Lombard laws (643). The code was written in Latin and was influenced by Roman vulgar law (especially concerning property law). But the Edict is essentially Germanic, and deals with such characteristic practices and institutions as the bloodfeud, wergilds, compensation tariffs, compurgation, and *mundium* (rights of guardianship and power held by men over women).

With the Edict and additions to it by subsequent kings, documentary sources, archaeological and onomastic evidence, and traditional narrative sources, a picture of the kingdom and society of the Lombards emerges. The relatively small numbers of Lombards were settled most densely in the Po valley (in the region that came to be called *Langobardia,* or Lombardy) and in the northeastern duchies of Friuli and Istria. Groups of related families (*farae*) were placed in strategic positions near cities as well as in fortified sites in the countryside. A military organization was maintained among the Lombards in the *arimannia* (similar to hundreds of the Franks and Anglo-Saxons), with the soldiers (*arimanni,* or *exercitales*) having a military obligation based on the equipment that their resources provided. Lombard traditions implied that at the time of Authari the Lombards were supported by receiving one third of the revenues of the land of great Italian landowners, but it is possible that the latter only had to relinquish their bondsmen to the Lombards. The law codes indicated that Lombard society was divided into the main classes of *gasindi* (royal councillors), *adelingi* (nobles), the *arimanni, aldiones* (half-free peasants tied to the land they worked by an obligation to a lord), and freedmen and slaves.

The kings' royal authority was supported by financial resources from their patrimony. Increasingly in the seventh century the royal court became centered at Pavia, and a bureaucracy developed. The duchies of Friuli and Istria were relatively free of royal supervision due to their character as frontier marches, and the two southern duchies of Spoleto and Benevento were geographically separated from the rest of the Lombard *regnum* by the Flaminian corridor. Thus their dukes normally functioned without regular intervention by the kings. The other dukes, in charge of a region similar to the Roman civitas, were under more effective royal supervision and commanded the military force of their duchies. The kings came to appoint gastaldi to administer the royal domain in the kingdom, and in time the gastaldi's authority grew to include military and judicial powers. Thus they served as royal officials rivaling the older, personal authority of the dukes and at times were even given ducal powers. Judges were royal appointees administering the royal law codes, and the kings also made use of notaries to perform some judicial functions.

The later seventh century was a time of civil wars and internal disorders within the kingdom. King Aripert I (653–661) is chiefly known for the claim that Arianism was exterminated during his reign. There were some Arian bishops among the Lombards, but the small number of Lombard Arians declined steadily, and they are not heard of past the seventh century. King Grimoald (662–671) was an active leader who routed a Frankish invasion of Italy, repelled a Byzantine army led personally by Emperor Constans II (663), and removed Avars from the duchy of Friuli. King Cunicpert (680–700) survived a major rebellion by Duke Alachis of Trent, and his victory over the rebels caused the northern bishops who had remained in opposition to the "Three Chapters" to accept the papal position, thus ending the long schism.

Liutprand (712–744) raised the Lombard kingdom to the height of its power. His early years were spent consolidating his hold on the kingdom, but he inaugurated a new series of conquests when the Iconoclastic Controversy sparked the virtual secession of the papacy and imperial Italy from Byzantium. He invaded the Exarchate and Pentapolis, and for a time he held the capital of Ravenna. He also seized some towns in the Roman duchy, and he dominated the two southern Lombard duchies.

The resurgence of an aggressive Lombard kingdom alarmed the papacy, which was bereft of any imperial support. Gregory III tried to form an alliance against the Lombards with the Frankish leader Charles Martel, but Liutprand and Charles were themselves close allies, and Charles ignored the papal blandishments. At Liutprand's death most of central and northern Italy, with the exception of the duchy of Rome, was in Lombard hands. In 749 King Aistulf (749–756) renewed the attack on the residue of imperial Italy, and in 751 he took Ravenna. He then moved aggressively against Rome. Pope Zacharias was successful in gaining the Frankish alliance that had eluded his predecessors. He supported Pepin III's seizure of the royal title from the Merovingian dynasty, and Pepin in his turn twice invaded Italy (755 and 756), easily defeating Aistulf each time. He turned over to the papacy the imperial lands that Aistulf had seized.

Duke Desiderius of Tuscany succeeded Aistulf (757–774), and at first he enjoyed good relations with the papacy as well as a marriage alliance with the Franks. But by 771 his relations with the Franks had broken down completely, and he was attacking the Exarchate (claimed by the papacy), and towns of the Pentapolis and Roman duchy. Pepin's son Charles responded promptly by invading Italy (773), defeating the Lombards and capturing Pavia (774). He then deposed Desiderius and brought an end to the independent Lombard kingdom by assuming for himself the title King of the Lombards.

Charles succeeded in bringing Spoleto under his authority (788), but Benevento remained outside of Carolingian Italy, and developed into the principalities of Benevento, Salerno, and Capua, which were conquered by the Normans in the eleventh century. The rest of Lombard Italy was incorporated into the Carolingian empire, although it was usually one of the semiautonomous subkingdoms, with its own king and administration under Frankish officials.

BIBLIOGRAPHY

Sources. Paulus Diaconus, *History of the Lombards,* William Dudley Foulke, trans. (1907, 1974); *The Lombard Laws,* Katherine Fischer Drew, trans. (1973).

Studies. Convegno internazionale sul tema: La civiltà dei longobardi in Europa, 1971, *Atti* (1974); Steven C. Fanning, "Lombard Arianism Reconsidered," in *Speculum,* 56 (1981), and "A Review of Lombard Prosopography," in *Medieval Prosopography,* 2.1 (1981); Gina Fasoli, *I Longobardi in Italia* (1965); Walter Goffart, *Barbarians and Romans, A.D. 418–584, the Techniques of Accommodation* (1980); Jan T. Hallenbeck, *Pavia and Rome: The Lombard Monarchy and the Papacy in the Eighth Century* (1982); Ludwig M. Hartmann, "Italy Under the Lombards," in *Cambridge Medieval History,* II (1913, repr.

1964); Thomas Hodgkin, *Italy and Her Invaders,* V–VI (1895); Lucien Musset, *The Germanic Invasions, the Making of Europe, A.D. 400–600,* Edward and Columba James, trans. (1975), 85–95; John M. Wallace-Hadrill, *The Barbarian West, A.D. 400–1000,* 2nd rev. ed. (1962).

STEVEN C. FANNING

[See also **Arianism; Barbarians, Invasions of; Columbanus, St.; Gregory I the Great, Pope; Italy, Byzantine Areas of; Law, German; Pepin (and the Donation of Pepin).**]

LONDON. When the Roman armies drew back to their mother city in 410, they left in Londinium a substantial town whose outstanding features were to determine the topography of the medieval city. These features included wooden wharves along the riverfront, two bathhouses, a forum and basilica at Cornhill surrounded by very extensive stone buildings, a Mithraic temple east of the stream later called Walbrook, monumental arches, and, most important, a stone wall of three miles in length that incorporated the earlier Cripplegate fort in its northwestern angle. This wall, which ran also along the riverfront and thus completely encircled the city, was breached at six points by gates. It encompassed not only the built-up town but also open fields.

EARLY LONDON

The years between the departure of the Romans and the conversion of their pagan successors to Christianity in the early seventh century are the darkest in London's history. The demoralized Britons and the conquering Saxons appear to have squatted in the once flourishing city. The telltale accumulation of dark earth over and around the earlier Roman structures suggests that the city was largely depopulated and abandoned. The potteries closed, the skills of the builder faded, and the circulation of money ceased entirely. Nevertheless, the Saxons had no reason to destroy the stone buildings left behind by the Romans, even if they lacked the skill to use them, and some vestiges of an urban consciousness may have remained. When the Christian missionaries arrived from Rome in 597, Bishop Mellitus was despatched to convert the people of the tribal kingdom of Essex, using London as his base. The Northumbrian historian Bede, writing in the early eighth century, described London as "an emporium for many nations who come to it by land and sea."

There is, however, so little archaeological evidence to support this description that historians have been inclined to believe that Bede was writing not of the contemporary town but of what he knew of its impressive Roman past.

Even if London was not such a great emporium, yet it must have been more than simply another occasional royal residence. The Roman buildings ensured it some preeminence. In the wake of Christianity came literacy and the earliest Anglo-Saxon law codes. In the last quarter of the seventh century Kentish kings in their codes refer to a royal base in London where tolls and dues may have been collected, and Kentishmen were buying and selling goods and property in the city. Other kings whose law codes do not survive may have done likewise. During the seventh century the small kingdom of Essex together with London seems to have fallen increasingly under the sway of the expansionist Midland kingdom of Mercia. By the 660's Wulfhere, king of Mercia, was free to sell the bishopric of London to his chosen candidates, and this would suggest Mercian control of the town. Certainly the landlocked kingdom of Mercia needed a port for continental trade, and the charter evidence indicates that by the eighth century it was the Mercian kings who were controlling and taxing that trade. The Mercian king Ethelbald (716–757) granted to certain religious houses the privilege of bringing a specified number of ships toll-free into the port of London. The wording of these grants suggests a thriving port with wharves crammed with goods and patrolled by an army of customs officials. Moreover, although the earliest English silver pennies were minted at Canterbury or Rochester, by the 790's both gold and silver coins were being produced in London for the great Mercian king Offa (757–796). During this period English coins seem to have been produced for international trade; they maintained the same weight standard as the Frankish coinage.

The written evidence suggests that London was an important trading port in the eighth and ninth centuries and yet archaeologists have been unable to find evidence of either pottery or structures within the city walls which can be dated to these years. Where, then, was Saxon London? There is now considerable archaeological evidence to suggest that the invading Saxons may originally have settled, not within the walls of the old Roman city, but on the Strand shore lying to the west of the Fleet River. Here an extramural settlement seems to have grown up where sailors beached their ships, merchants bought and sold goods, and tolls were collected for the Mercian kings.

In the ninth century the Vikings fell upon England with increasing regularity. Whereas the northern and eastern kingdoms of England were totally destroyed, further south the men of Kent and Wessex joined together in mutual self-defense. Mercia stood at the heart of the Viking/Saxon struggle. By 851 the eastern half of the Mercian kingdom had fallen to the Vikings, and twenty years later London was occupied by a Danish army. Meanwhile Alfred had become king of Wessex (871–899) and after early setbacks successfully organized English resistance to the Viking conquest. In spite of the significance of Alfred's dramatic defeat of the Danes in 878 after his sojourn on the Isle of Athelney in Somerset, his triumph in recapturing London from the Danes in 886 was probably a more significant achievement. Alfred drew attention to this by having coins minted in London that bore his name and portrait on the obverse and the old Roman monogram for London on the reverse. In a treaty that he drew up with Guthrum, the Danish leader, not long after the reconquest of London, Alfred tacitly acknowledged that these raiders had come to stay and that London stood on the frontier between English and Danish England.

King Alfred was fully conscious of the importance of London, and he took steps to secure it since potentially it was the most substantial of all the boroughs with which he could defend English England from the Danes. The King encouraged men to settle within the old Roman walls and granted land to bishops and *ealdormen* ("elders" or "aldermen"— those who exercised authority under the king) who could defend it, and in return they were allowed to collect the tolls and dues that by custom belonged to the king. Hence the military and economic roles of London were interdependent. The old Roman fort at Cripplegate became the headquarters or palace of Alfred's deputy in the city, the Mercian *ealdorman* Ethelred, who was married to Alfred's daughter Ethelflaed. The Cripplegate area became known as Aldermanbury, the borough (from *burh*, fortified place) of the *ealdorman*. The remains of substantial wooden buildings dating from the late ninth century have been found. There is, however, little suggestion that they were crowded together since there were as yet no constraints on space. Pottery finds within the walls are much more numerous, although Londoners seem neither to have made their own pots nor to have imported them from abroad (as in Saxon South-

ampton), but to have used pots made by potters in the London region. Alfred's coins, which bore the Roman monogram for London, declared not only that the city had been retaken from the Danes, but also that the Saxon community was now to be found within the walls of the old Roman city.

In the years between Alfred's reconquest of London and the Norman invasion of 1066, the evidence for the growth and urbanization of London is unambiguous. A sequence of Saxon houses excavated near the Thames at Billingsgate reveals that between the late ninth and mid eleventh centuries the buildings became larger as well as increasingly sophisticated in construction. The city continued to flourish as a royal mint, and in the reign of King Athelstan (925–939) more moneyers worked in London than in either Canterbury or Winchester. The evidence of surviving coins suggests that London in the reign of King Ethelred (979–1016) was producing twice the volume of silver coinage of all the other English mints put together. The importance of London as a port is demonstrated by the list of tolls payable on ships and merchandise coming into the port during Ethelred's reign. Among those expected to pay the tolls were merchants from Rouen and several Flemish towns, as well as the central European subjects of the Holy Roman Emperor. Archaeologists have found the remnants of substantial wooden quays, beyond the old Roman ones, built out into the river on reclaimed land; they were large enough to support buildings. It is not surprising, therefore, that the Danish king Cnut (1016–1035) was able in 1018 to raise a massive tribute of £10,500 from London alone.

There is evidence from this period not only of substantial building and foreign trade but also of communal activity. As early as the reign of King Athelstan the bishops and reeves (in Anglo-Saxon times high officers of the royal administration) of the London district banded together to maintain the peace, pursue wrongdoers, support each other in adversity, and compensate victims of crime. Although only two of London's hundred or so medieval parish churches can be traced back with certainty to a period before King Alfred, a dozen or more can be shown, either by archaeological evidence or by their dedications, to have been established in the tenth or early eleventh century. Sculptors of considerable skill and sophistication fashioned the early-eleventh-century carved cross, fragments of which can still be seen in the crypt of All Hallows, Barking, near the Tower of London. The brief Viking occupation of

London is perhaps commemorated in the Norse word Husting borne by the city's oldest court, and the strength of the Norse influence upon the city is also reflected in six churches dedicated to Olaf II Haraldsson, the saintly eleventh-century king of Norway.

The maintenance of bridges must be the work of communities. It is unlikely that the Roman wooden bridge in London survived the Dark Ages, and we do not know when it was rebuilt. But there was certainly a bridge spanning the Thames again by the reign of King Edgar (959–975), and the wooden bridge played a prominent part in the battles between the English and the Danes in the early eleventh century. It was also of considerable significance for the future development of London that Edward the Confessor (1042–1066) decided to rebuild the Benedictine abbey church on the island of Thorney in the Thames, to the west of London. This great monastic church (later known as Westminster Abbey) was modeled on the church at Jumièges in Normandy; it came to serve not only as a royal mausoleum and palace but also as one of the centers of the king's peripatetic government. That Edward chose to build his royal monastery not at Winchester, the seat of Alfred and Athelstan, but rather near London is a tangible indication that the kings of Wessex had been transformed into kings of England. London, in close proximity to the royal monastery at Westminster, had become the focal point of all England east of Offa's Dyke and south of Hadrian's Wall.

THE NORMAN-ANGEVIN PERIOD

The conquest of Anglo-Viking England in 1066 by a frenchified band of Norsemen coincided with, but did not cause, a period of great economic expansion in England and throughout most of western Europe. Duke William did not, in fact, win England at the Battle of Hastings in October 1066, but two months later, when the men of London decided to submit to the Normans. It was the submission of the Londoners and of the remaining English nobles who had been organizing resistance behind the city walls that made possible William's coronation in the abbey church at Westminster on Christmas day 1066.

The importance of London was acknowledged in William's charter addressed to the bishop, portreeve (chief officer of a town), and citizens of London, both French and English. Their laws and customs were to be preserved, as in King Edward's day, and every child was to be his father's heir. It is hard to know

how heavily the Norman yoke fell upon London. The city remained predominantly English; few Norman names or saints found their way into the dedications of city churches. The king built a palace fortress in the southeast corner of the city (the White Tower), and Norman lords like Ralph de Baynard and Gilbert de Montfichet were allowed to construct private castles in the west. Domesday Book (1086), so rich in detail about the shires of England, does not include London. There are signs, however, that London may have prospered while the other parts of England languished under the relentless pressure of Norman rule. The rapid proliferation of parish churches bears witness to the expansion of London's population, which may have reached 20,000 by 1100. Archaeologists have demonstrated that the extension of the wharves along the Thames continued at a rapid pace. The preeminence of London as the main minting center of the realm became ever more marked. We know of merchants trading in London from Rouen, the German Rhineland towns, and northern Italy. Traders from Cologne had established their own base near Dowgate, on the waterfront (later known as the Steelyard), by the end of twelfth century. There are signs of a flourishing trade with Spain at this period, and William Fitzstephen, who wrote at the end of the twelfth century, described—with some literary license—the Arabian gold, Chinese silks, Russian furs, Egyptian gems, and French wines that were imported into London. The bulk of the city's export trade probably consisted of wool, which was largely handled by Flemish merchants.

The Normans were accustomed to building in stone and began to leave their characteristic imprint upon the city. Between 1066 and 1200 large new stone buildings transformed the face of London in much the same way as the building of skyscrapers has done since 1945. The nave and choir of the Saxon cathedral of St. Paul was completely rebuilt, and all around the city walls great monastic churches were constructed. No fewer than seven new houses belonging to the fashionable order of Augustinian (Austin) canons were founded in the city or its suburbs between 1106 and 1197. Many of these were dedicated to the service of man as well as of God, and hospitals for the care of the sick and aged were attached to the priories, as at St. Bartholomew's in Smithfield and St. Thomas's in Southwark. Three leper hospitals were also founded in the twelfth century, and the two great crusading orders of the Knights Templars and Knights Hospitalers established their English headquarters in London. Only the crossing and choir of the great priory church of St. Bartholomew (founded 1123) and the Templars' characteristic round church (consecrated 1185) survive to recall this rash of stone buildings that spread across the face of London. Not all new buildings were constructed on the scale of St. Paul's or the Tower of London. Modest stone undercrofts of the twelfth century have been discovered, which show that merchants were beginning to abandon the timber structures of Saxon London for more substantial stone buildings in which they could store their wares and house their families.

Perhaps the most striking of all the great Norman buildings of this period was Peter of Colechurch's new stone bridge, begun in the 1170's and completed thirty years later. Like all medieval bridges its construction was a work of piety, and several guilds were founded to forward the work. In the center of the bridge a chapel, dedicated to London's most famous saint, Thomas à Becket (d. 1170), was built so that travelers might pray and make offerings for the maintenance of the bridge. In spite of the problems of bridging a tidal river, Peter built well, and his bridge survived intact until it was demolished in the nineteenth century. It was maintained throughout its existence by the income derived from its own Bridge House Estates, the landed endowment provided by Londoners throughout the medieval period. The bridge was a remarkable memorial to the competence of the twelfth-century masons who transformed the face of London.

From the twelfth century—characterized as London's age of stone—until the fifteenth century all substantial and important buildings in London were of stone. Some (like William Rufus' great hall at Westminster of 1097–1099, intended as the beginning of a new palace) were of imported Caen stone; others (like the Temple church) used Purbeck marble from Dorset; but most used ordinary ragstone quarried in Kent. Stone was expensive, difficult to transport, and hard to work; the sheer volume of stone building in twelfth-century London thus bears witness to the city's wealth.

In this age of stone Londoners began to press for definition of their corporate rights and customs as the increasingly efficient royal bureaucracy began to intrude upon their lives. The charter of William I had promised the citizens that no man should do them wrong; but what if it were the king who wronged them? In the reign of Henry I (1100–1135) the citizens secured the right to choose their own sheriffs who should be responsible for the city's "farm" or annual tax (settled at £300 per year) at the royal Exchequer. The citizens were also allowed to run their own judicial courts, and were exempted from payment of various tolls levied for the transit of persons or goods throughout the realm. In the civil war between Stephen and Matilda (1135–1154) Londoners lost this precarious independence, and Henry II (1154–1189) was careful not to restore it. But he was tactful in selecting men of the great London dynasties of Bucointe, Cornhill, or Haverhill to serve as sheriffs. At Henry's death royal control of London relaxed, and in the struggle between Richard I the Lionhearted and his brother John Londoners were able to wring from John in his brother's absence the right to hold a sworn commune, that is, to stand together as a corporate body, and to elect their own leader or mayor, and so secure by communal action what none of them could have gained individually. This "union" of leading Londoners was viewed with suspicion by English monarchs. Richard of Devizes, a twelfth-century chronicler, called the London union "not a commune but a conspiracy." When John (1199–1216) himself became king, his early charters to the Londoners did not formally recognize their right to act as a commune, although he did allow them to elect their own sheriffs.

By the end of the twelfth century the English kings had contrived, in theory if not in fact, to resist the demands of the Londoners to govern themselves as an independent community within the body politic. But King John's loss of his Norman lands in 1204 forced him to financial expedients that alienated both the Londoners and the magnates of the realm and drove them into common opposition. In 1206 John asserted the royal right to tallage the city, that is, to collect a tax without seeking the consent that was essential for a feudal aid. It may be that the commune of London formed the precedent for the sworn community of barons who led the struggle against the king. Robert Fitzwalter, one of the baronial leaders, was the lord of Baynard's Castle in the city. John sensed his danger and made a bid to secure the support of the citizens. On 9 May 1215 he granted to the "barons of our city of London" the right to elect their own "faithful, discreet, and fit" mayor to govern them on the king's behalf. But John's concession came too late. The citizens threw in their lot with the baronage and thereby secured the inclusion of their own clauses in Magna Carta. London was to pay aid (by implication, therefore, not tallage, although this remained a matter of bitter controversy throughout the thirteenth century), the Thames and Medway were to be kept free for navigation (not impeded by fish weirs), the standard weights and measures of the realm were to be those in use in London, and merchants were to be protected throughout the realm. The new mayor of London, William Hardel, was a member of the committee of twenty-five men appointed to see that the provisions of Magna Carta were carried out. Only when John had demonstrated to the barons' satisfaction that he intended to fulfill his obligations would the Tower and the city be handed back to his control. In July 1215 Robert Fitzwalter wrote to William d'Albini, "You well know what great benefit it is to you and to all of us to keep the city of London which is our refuge." In the civil war that followed the sealing of Magna Carta, London supported the king's opponents; but at John's death the citizens made peace with the loyal supporters of the young King Henry III. In return the charters of the city were confirmed, and in 1221 the phrase "mayor and commune of London" first appeared in royal records.

DEVELOPMENT OF THE COMMUNE

The thirteenth century was important in the history of London because, in the great struggles between citizens and monarchs, the privileges of the city were defined and secured. It is also the first century in which we have substantial records of civic government. Until the thirteenth century the evidence for London's history is tangential: chance references in chronicles, monastic cartularies, and royal administrative documents, supplemented only by archaeological evidence. Now, however, the commune began to keep its own records. The earliest surviving roll of deeds and wills registered in the city's Husting court dates from 1252, although it is clear that such records were being kept from at least the second quarter of the thirteenth century. The pleadings before the mayor in his court are preserved in rolls beginning in 1272, and the city's own precedent books, known as Letter Books, also begin in the reign of Edward I (1272–1307). We know that by the end of the century the sheriffs also kept rolls of the pleadings in their courts, that the wardens of London Bridge kept accounts, and that the city's own chamberlain kept not only accounts of civic expenditure but also registers of the men admitted to the freedom of the city (none of these records survive).

These records bear witness to the emergence of civic government and bureaucracy. From the reign of John there survives a collection of London customs that reveals, already at that early date, a measure of municipal adminstrative unity. Wards were the basis of this civic administration. Taxes were collected there and then brought to the central Guildhall, where justice was administered in the city's own courts according to civic custom and where records were stored. Citizens were capable of taking communal action, for example to prevent the risk of fire. By the end of the century, a civil service had come into being to assist the mayor and sheriffs in their tasks. A financial officer known as the chamberlain, a common clerk who acted as a superior secretary, and a common serjeant and recorder between them provided the necessary legal expertise to cope with the rising tide of English common law. All these men received salaries (the recorder, who was the most highly paid, received £10 per year) and were served by households of serjeants, valets, and clerks. At the local level citizens met together to elect their aldermen, admit men to the freedom, and choose scavengers and other minor officers to clean the streets and maintain the peace.

This growth in administrative coherence took place against a background of constant and wide-ranging conflicts between Henry III (1216–1272) and the citizens of London. At the root of the conflict was money; citizens struggled to resist Henry's demands for tallage and to prevent his intervention in their internal faction fights. The inability of Londoners to act together in the common interest enabled Henry to hold his own and to develop and patronize Westminster at the expense of London. In the conflict between Henry and the baronial leader Simon de Montfort, earl of Leicester, Londoners largely supported Simon, and a contingent of them rode out to help him achieve his great victory over the royal forces at Lewes in 1264.

Such overt support was misguided, for Montfort was killed at Evesham in the next year, and the treachery of the Londoners was punished with a swingeing fine of 20,000 marks. In this way citizens atoned in 1266 for the "great crimes and misdemeanors" that they had committed against their sovereign, his brother (Richard, earl of Cornwall), his wife (Eleanor of Provence), and his son (the future Edward I). But the right to elect their own mayor and sheriffs was not restored for another four years. Edward I (1272–1307) finally decided to bring London to heel, for civic turbulence and violence were becoming endemic as the "middling classes" struggled to push their way into civic government and oust the few great dynastic families of the early years of the commune. For thirteen years (1285–1298) Edward confiscated the Londoners' right of self-government and appointed instead his own warden, who presided over city courts and held the citizens down with a rod of iron. By the time the liberties were restored new men were ready and willing to take over civic government. The oligarchic stability of the early thirteenth century, when the great intermarried families might produce long-serving mayors like Richard Renger (1222–1227) or Andrew Bukerel (1231–1237), was broken forever by the twin forces of population explosion from below and royal intransigence from above.

LATER MEDIEVAL LONDON

In spite of Londoners' participation in the civil wars of the thirteenth century (in contrast to their marked detachment 200 years later) the city continued to grow and flourish. New wharves were built along the waterfront, the vacant spaces within the city were filling up with houses, and there is striking evidence that along the city's main street, Cheapside, and in the central part of the city, space was at a premium. Properties were subdivided, and street frontages were lined with numerous tiny shops selling a wide range of goods. London merchants continued to export wool to Flanders in exchange for cloth, and cloth and corn to Gascony in return for wine. In the early years of the fourteenth century some 15,000 sacks of wool and 25,000–50,000 sheepskins (in all, the produce of nearly 300,000 sheep) were exported through London each year and 6,000–8,000 tuns of Gascon wine were imported. The richest of London's merchant princes were vintners like the Hardels, and all of them sold goods to the royal household. It was this crucial commercial link that made quarreling with the crown such a dangerous business. For this reason, too, Montfort's support came less from the old patrician merchants and more from the new classes of artisans and victuallers such as fishmongers, weavers, and cutlers.

The increasing importance of London as a commercial and financial center and of Westminster as the administrative and legal heart of the kingdom led great men of the realm to acquire town houses near these twin centers of power. Already by 1200 the archbishop of Canterbury was established at Lambeth, and at least three other bishops had London inns, as did a clutch of wealthy abbots. By 1300 the archbishop of York, twelve more bishops, and fifteen abbots or priors had set up their inns in London. By now the western suburbs, along the Strand

and Holborn, were characterized by these magnificent palaces with their impressive gateways, great halls, pleasant gardens, and orchards. Within the city itself, the arrival of the friars led to the building of vast preaching churches. The Friars Minor (Franciscan), or Greyfriars, were established at Newgate (1224), the Dominicans first at Holborn (by 1224) and then in the southwest corner of the city on a site which later adopted their name, Blackfriars (1290's), and the Augustinian Friars near Bishopsgate (1253). The White Friars (or Carmelites) were established at about the same time in Fleet Street, the only friary to lie outside the city walls, and the Crutched (or Crossed) Friars arrived last and settled (*ca.* 1298) on a site just north of the Tower. These newcomers invigorated London life with their skilled preaching, their link with the nascent universities of Oxford and Cambridge, their great libraries, and their habit of public intellectual debate. The friars were called to work closely among the urban communities whom they served. Although this exposed them to criticism from some Londoners (note Geoffrey Chaucer's unflattering portrait of a friar in his *Canterbury Tales*), and to rivalry with the city's parish priests, yet their continuing popularity is attested by the frequency with which Londoners remembered them in their wills.

The history of London in the fourteenth century is characterized by a twin struggle: the continuing internal conflict between the artisan or craft mysteries on the one hand and the great merchant guilds on the other, and the external struggle, less intense but still active, against the power of the crown. The development of national parliamentary taxation levied upon goods and chattels removed some of the bitterness which had marked the earlier disputes between London and the crown.

In 1319 Edward II (1397–1327) granted the Londoners a charter that gave the guilds the right to control entries to the freedom of the city. To be a freeman, or citizen, of London entitled a man to certain important privileges: only a freeman might open a shop in the city, or sell goods by retail. Those who were not "free" had to work as journeymen (or day laborers) or else set up their shops outside the city's jurisdiction, for example, in Southwark south of the river. This shift from ward control (dominated by the alderman and the leading merchants of the neighborhood) to guild control is seen again in the changes in the manner of election to the Common Council. In the fourteenth century this body of about 150 men was achieving some definition of its role and procedures and, like the Commons in Parliament, was gradually securing control over finance, although its position was still subordinate, in most matters, to the omnicompetent court of aldermen. In the early 1350's, and again between 1376 and 1384, the electoral constituencies for the Common Council were the guilds and not the wards. Hence pinners, cobblers, and other craftsmen were secured representation on the Common Council; numerically, these craftsmen outnumbered the representatives of the merchant guilds, such as mercers or drapers.

In 1376 at the meeting of Parliament nicknamed "the Good" local London resentment against a group of wealthy and self-interested aldermen coincided with national indignation at the household corruption and mismanagement that characterized the declining years of Edward III (1327–1377). Three London aldermen were impeached and convicted of various corrupt practices and financial peculations. Their enemies in the city, who had probably helped to fuel the fire against them in Parliament, ensured that their dominance in city government was also undermined. After the dissolution of Parliament, a special meeting of the Court of Aldermen was held reinforced by the presence of representatives of forty-one different city guilds. The three men (two of whom had each served for thirty years) were expelled from their aldermanries, and new men were elected. The radicals, having thus got rid of some of the conservative faction, and led by a draper, John of Northampton, swept on to restore the craft-based system of election to Common Council, to revise all the city's ordinances, and to secure the annual election of aldermen. The resulting system of government was both more democratic and more turbulent. Mob violence became endemic in London, and gangs took to the streets to support their patrons for election as mayors or aldermen. It was the prevalence of this kind of urban "bastard feudalism" that allowed the men from the Home Counties during the Peasants' Rebellion in 1381 to secure entry to a divided and ill-governed city. The Londoners had, of course, suffered like the rest of the country from the novel poll taxes of 1377, 1379, and 1380. On the last occasion the tax of twelve pence per head had raised over £1,000 in the city. The forces of conservatism gradually eroded the radical innovations. In 1384 the election of common councilmen was restored to the wards, and in 1386 the book of revised civic ordinances was burned in public. In 1394 the annual elections of aldermen were abolished, and thereafter they normally held office for life. By degrees a measure of stability was achieved in civic government. In the fifteenth century the aldermen were conscious of the need to govern the city in the interests of all rather than of a narrow oligarchy of wealthy merchants.

The turbulence of London in the later fourteenth century must be understood in the context of considerable demographic and economic change. The Black Death of 1348–1349 probably reduced the population of London by as much as a third. The dramatically accelerated rate of will-enrollment in the city suggests that the death rate was eighteen times higher than normal in these years. Although the fabric of civic government survived, the devastating drop in population dislocated the social structure. The level of real wages rose. Industrial laborers (journeymen), like their agricultural counterparts, were conscious of their greater earning power and resentful of a political structure that excluded them—because they were not citizens—from an effective role in civic government. In London these journeymen tried to form their own guilds whereby they could press for higher wages and better working conditions. There is evidence from the years 1350 to 1400 of such "conspiracies" of journeymen in London among shearmen, weavers, saddlers, skinners, spurriers, cordwainers, and tailors.

At the other end of the social scale, the greater London merchants were also particularly prosperous during these years. The Italian bankers had been largely bankrupted by Edward III in the 1340's, and their exodus had opened the way for the rise of native English capitalist enterprise. At first it was the da la Pole merchants of Hull who were preeminent in royal finance, but by the 1360's men like the vintners Henry Picard and Richard Lyons, the mercers Simon and Adam Fraunceys, and the grocer John Pyel were to be found providing loans for the crown. During these years, also, English merchants for the first time seriously threatened the commercial monopoly of the Hanse League in the Baltic. Other merchants, like the goldsmith Adam Bamme or the mercer Richard Whittington, grew rich from the profits on sales of goods to the royal household or the King's Wardrobe (the name for the king's chief purchasing office and supply depot). In this period of intense social mobility throughout England, the opportunities offered by London beckoned very strongly. Competition was sharp in the city and provoked sharp violence in its turn.

The social upheavals aggravated the need for lawyers and attorneys, ready to proffer, and profit by, their expertise. The rapid acceleration of the land market and the desire to avoid the forfeiture and disintegration of landed estates help to explain the remarkable growth of the legal profession in the fourteenth century. That expansion culminated in the establishment of four inns of court and ten inns of chancery, all in the western suburbs of the city among the ecclesiastical town houses in Holborn and the Strand. This new legal professionalism threatened both manorial and civic custom, and it is not surprising that much of the peasant and urban savagery during the revolt of 1381 was directed toward lawyers, their servants, and their records.

Throughout the Middle Ages and beyond, London was unable to maintain its population level without continuous infusions of new blood from the surrounding countryside. These newcomers who came in search of prosperity also needed security and formed hundreds of small neighborhood guilds or fraternities in the later part of the fourteenth century. The guilds served as mutual friendly societies and as communal chantries in which members contributed towards the wages of a priest who would pray for the souls of living or dead members of the guild. In return for a small quarterly subscription ranging from two pence to six shillings and eight pence, which the brothers and sisters of the guild paid out of their earnings, the members secured help in times of trouble or sickness, a decent, well-attended funeral, continuing prayers for the soul after death, and conviviality and companionship in life. The popularity and proliferation of such guilds, particularly in London, led to some suspicion about their purposes. Although some overtly religious guilds may have been founded with subversive aims in mind, the majority simply reflected a desperate search for security in a time of great social and geographic mobility.

The greater prosperity of the Londoners found expression not only in the formation of these parish guilds (many of which were closely associated with a parish church and contributed to its rebuilding or refurbishment) but also in the foundation of small hospitals and colleges of priests. Although there had always been some Londoners who were wealthy enough to found religious houses in the city, the majority of London's great monastic houses had been established by "outsiders," members of the nobility or of the royal family. In the fourteenth century this pattern began to change. Londoners themselves became increasingly responsible for religious and charitable provision in the city. Money was bequeathed

so that secular and chantry priests might be grouped together in colleges attached to a parish church. In this way the priests were encouraged to live a communal and orderly life. Sir John de Pulteney established a college at his parish church of St. Lawrence in 1334, and Richard Whittington set up a similar college of priests attached to his parish church of St. Michael Paternoster in 1424. There were several others. Some of them had a more obviously educational purpose, and the college of priests attached to the Guildhall chapel had a library. The other characteristic fifteenth-century charitable enterprise was the almshouse, groups of dwellings established for the aged and infirm. These differed in two important respects from the earlier hospitals (although they were often called hospitals) in that they provided a measure of privacy and independence for their inmates and they were not administered by the church but, frequently, by the newly incorporated city companies. Richard Whittington's almshouses, founded in 1424 for thirteen poor men and women and administered by the Mercers' Company, were to serve as the model for various other company almshouses, such as those of the Companies of Shearmen, Drapers, Vintners, and Merchant Taylors.

The achievements of the fifteenth-century rulers of London are less dramatic than those of their predecessors. With a few exceptions, the annual elections of mayors and sheriffs were conducted peacefully; the court of twenty-five aldermen met frequently and labored to administer justice, keep the peace, and provide for the supply of wholesome and reasonably priced food for the citizens. By and large they served faithfully and their wills testify to their consciousness of the charitable obligations incumbent upon wealthy and successful men. Under their aegis a great new guildhall, chapel, and library were built in the years between 1411 and 1455, and the city's supply of fresh water, brought from the Tyburn in lead pipes from Paddington, was completely renewed at a cost of some £5,000. The money for this enterprise was raised by a combination of private charity and civic taxation.

The great merchants of London maintained their preeminent situation. London's share of the cloth exported from England rose from 45 percent in 1410 to 77 percent in 1530. The overseas trading company of Merchant Adventurers was dominated by a group of London mercers (including the printer William Caxton) who maintained a permanent base in Bruges. Some successful merchants, like the grocer John Crosby, invested their wealth in building magnificent London houses. Crosby's great house was constructed not only in stone but also in the newly fashionable brick, and it was considered sufficiently fine to serve as a temporary home for the future Richard III.

The steady prosperity of London is displayed less by Crosby's private palace than by the rash of new company halls that appeared all over the fifteenth-century city. Whereas in 1400 only half a dozen companies had halls, by 1538 a further forty had acquired such meeting places. The halls ranged from the magnificent Grocers' Hall in Conyhope Lane (near Poultry) to the Tylers' modest house on Broad Street. These halls express artisan as well as mercantile prosperity. So too the forest of fifteenth-century spires and towers added to earlier churches testifies to the helping hands of a wide range of parishioners. Wealth was more evenly distributed among Londoners, and this narrowing of the gap between rich and poor was reflected in the increase in the proportion of the adult male inhabitants of London who achieved the status of citizen. Whereas one in four adult males was a citizen in the early fourteenth century, the proportion may have risen to three in four by the end of the fifteenth century. This shift may have contributed to the greater political stability of the period, in spite of the fact that wealthier citizens began to separate themselves into an elite—the livery—within their companies.

By the end of the thirteenth century the king had acknowledged that the great barons or tenants-in-chief could not be assumed to speak for the whole community of the realm, and so knights from the shires and burgesses from the towns were also summoned to Parliament. Londoners, like other townsmen, increasingly perceived their own interests as being distinct from those of the magnates and country gentry. When pressed to support Richard II in November 1387 in his struggles with the "Lords Appellant," the mayor of London replied that the citizens of London could not help the king, since they were "in the main craftsmen and merchants with no great military experience and it was not permissable for them to devote themselves to warfare except in the city's defence." The mayor wished, it is true, to remain neutral, but William Hardel would not have answered the king in those terms in 1215. Merchants and craftsmen were now a distinct class within the national body politic. Whereas the brass on the tomb chest of a country knight displayed him in full armor, a London merchant wore the dress earlier reserved for the clergy, a long garment tied at the waist

with a pouch belt and surmounted with a hood or cloak. The merchants had beome men of peace, and as far as possible, they stood apart from the Wars of the Roses (1455–1485). When it was not possible to maintain this detached stance, their involvement, as in 1460–1461, when they supported the House of York against King Henry VI, tended to be financial rather than military.

From the end of the fifteenth century the population of England appears to have begun to rise once more. There are signs that the suburbs of Southwark and Westminster were expanding rapidly, although the pressure on the center of the city may not have come until the late sixteenth century. The royal takeover of the religious houses in London in the 1530's followed in 1548 by the sales of the lands of the dissolved chantries had a dramatic effect upon the topography of the city. The religious precincts with their houses and gardens were swept away; the old and patched Roman walls fell into disuse and decay; and the city became, ultimately, much more densely populated (50,000 in 1520, rising to 200,000 by the end of the century) and less sanitary. Poverty became a more obvious and extensive problem. Many Londoners who lived, as John Stow did, through the upheavals of the sixteenth century, must have shared his nostalgia for a lost medieval golden age, when the civic spirit of community had not fully given way to the anonymous commercialism of the Tudor age.

BIBLIOGRAPHY

Timothy Baker, *Medieval London* (1970); Caroline M. Barron, *The Medieval Guildhall of London* (1974), and "London and the Crown, 1451–61," in J. Roger L. Highfield and Robin Jeffs, eds., *The Crown and Local Communities in England and France in the Fifteenth Century* (1981); Martin Biddle, "London on the Strand," in *Popular Archaeology*, 6 (1984); Ruth Bird, *The Turbulent London of Richard II* (1949); Joanna Bird, Hugh Chapman, and John Clark, eds., *Collectanea Londiniensia: Studies in London Archaeology and History Presented to Ralph Merrifield* (1978); Christopher N. Brooke and Gillian Keir, *London 800–1216* (1975); Charles Gross, *A Bibliography of British Municipal History* (1897, 2nd ed. 1966), 286–329; Edgar B. Groves, ed., *A Bibliography of English History to 1485* (1975), 712–718; A. J. Hollaender and William Kellaway, eds., *Studies in London History* (1969); M. D. Lobel, ed., *Atlas of Historic Towns*, III, *Medieval London* (1986); Derek Keene and Vanessa Harding, *A Survey of Documentary Sources for Property Holding in London Before the Great Fire* (1985); Ralph Merrifield, *The Roman City of London* (1965); John Morris, *Londinium: London in the Roman Empire* (1982); Alec R. Myers, *London in the Age of Chaucer* (1972); William Page, ed., *Victoria History of London*, I (1909); Nikolaus Pevsner, *London, I, The Cities of London and Westminister*, 3rd rev. ed. (1973); Royal Commission on Historical Monuments of England, *An Inventory of the Historical Monuments in London*, 5 vols. (1924–1930); John Schofield and Tony Dyson, *Archaeology of the City of London* (1980); John Schofield, *The Building of London from the Conquest to the Great Fire* (1984); Sylvia Thrupp, *The Merchant Class of Medieval London* (1948); George Unwin, *The Gilds and Companies of London* (1908, 4th ed. 1964); Gwyn A. Williams, *Medieval London: From Commune to Capital* (1963).

CAROLINE M. BARRON

[See also **Aldermen; Chivalry, Orders of; Class Structure, Western; Commune; Chroniques de Londres; England; Guilds and Métiers; Hanseatic League; Hospitals and Poor Relief, Western European; Liberty and Liberties; Magna Carta; Markets, European; Mayor; Mendicant Orders; Parliament; Peasants' Rebellion; Reeve; Sheriff; Taxation, English; Trade, European; Urbanism, Western European; Wine Trade; Wool.**]

LONDRES, CHRONIQUES DE. See **Chroniques de Londres.**

LOPES, FERNÃO (*fl. ca.* 1380–ca. 1459), Portuguese historian. A professional civil servant, and possibly the greatest chronicler of medieval Europe, he wrote the official account of Portuguese history, covering the period from 1357 to 1433. He based his work on earlier narratives now lost and on the documentation of the royal archive, of which he was curator (1418–1454).

BIBLIOGRAPHY

Fernão Lopes, *Crónica de D. Pedro I*, Damião Peres, ed. (1932), *Crónica de D. Fernando*, 2 vols. (1933–1935), and *Crónica de D. João I*, 2 vols. (1945–1949). Also: Aubrey F. G. Bell, *Fernam Lopez* (1921); Peter Edward Russell, *As fontes de Fernão Lopes* (1941); Antonio José Saraiva, *Fernão Lopes* (1952).

DEREK W. LOMAX

[See also **Chronicles; Historiography, Western European; Portugal.**]

LÓPEZ DE AYALA, PERO (1332–1407), one of the most important figures in the political life of Castile during the second half of the fourteenth century. In addition to his minor positions, Ayala represented the kings of Castile in the courts of Portugal, Aragon, Paris, and Avignon; he was a member of the regency council during the minority of Henry III, and high chancellor of the realm. His literary activity was equally outstanding. As poet, historian, and translator, Ayala was the leading man of letters in the Castile of his time.

His poetic work is the *Rimado de Palacio*, a lengthy poem of some 2,150 stanzas, most of which are composed in *cuaderna vía* (four lines per stanza, each containing fourteen or sixteen syllables, with a single consonant rhyme). In the first part, some 700 stanzas, the *Rimado* is a moral treatise, in which are set forth the Ten Commandments, the Seven Deadly Sins, the works of mercy, and the five senses. There follows a description of the various states in life, beginning with the religious state, continuing with the secular states (kings, knights, advisers and counselors to the king, merchants, lawyers), and ending with an exposition of the cardinal virtues (justice, temperance, fortitude, and prudence). After a prayer in which the poet asks God to free him from worldly dangers and temptations, he speaks of the dangers encountered in life at court and of the right use of riches and power. This first section ends with the identification of nine points that manifest the power of the king (such as his selection of ambassadors, his messages, the coinage of his kingdom), and an explanation of the perilous life of the king's favorites.

The second part of the poem, approximately 200 stanzas of various meters, is a collection of poems of heterogeneous character, some addressed to the Virgin and others concerned with the Great Schism of the Roman church. The third part, again in *cuaderna vía*, is a metrical translation of the *Moralia in Job* of St. Gregory the Great. Ayala had previously translated and annotated the Gregorian masterpiece, and the final 1,250 stanzas of the *Rimado* are a versification of many passages of this work.

Ayala's poem is preserved in two manuscripts, one of which seems to contain the original redaction, while the other appears to be a revised version. A reliable critical edition of the *Rimado* is not yet available, although several editions have been recently published.

As a historian, Ayala wrote the chronicles of the kings Pedro I, Henry II, John I, and Henry III (the last remains incomplete). Despite some doubts about Ayala's objectivity in describing the reign of Pedro I, his mastery as a narrator is unquestionable, and the

Chronicles represent a great advance in Castilian historiography.

Finally, Ayala translated into Castilian classical and medieval Latin works of Livy, Boethius, St. Gregory the Great, St. Isidore of Seville, and Boccaccio. He also composed a *Libro de la caça de las aves,* and an anthology of the *Moralia* entitled *Flores de los "Morales de Job."*

BIBLIOGRAPHY

Sources. Jacques Joset, ed., *Libro rimado del Palaçio,* 2 vols. (1978); Michel García, ed., *Libro de poemas o Rimado de Palacio,* 2 vols. (1978); Cayetano Rosell y López, ed., *Crónicas de los reyes de Castilla,* I, II (see chronicles of John and Henry III) (1875, 1877); Francesco Branciforti, ed., *Las Flores de los "Morales de Job"* (1963); José Gutiérrez de la Vega, ed., *Libro de la caza de las aves* (1879).

Studies. Francesco Branciforti, "Regesto delle opere di Pero López de Ayala," in *Saggi e ricerche in memoria di Ettore Li Gotti,* 6 (1962), 289–317; José Luis Coy, "Las *Flores de los Morales sobre Job,* de Pero López de Ayala, y las notas de los MSS. 10136–38 de la Biblioteca Nacional de Madrid," in *Revista de Estudios Hispánicos,* 9 (1975), 403–23, and " 'Busco por que lea algunt libro notado': De las notas de los *Morales* al texto del *Rimado de Palacio,"* in *Romance Philology,* 30 (1976–1977); Franco Meregalli, *La vida política del Canciller Ayala* (1955); Luis Suárez Fernández, *El Canciller Pedro López de Ayala y su tiempo (1332–1407)* (1962).

JOSÉ LUIS COY

[See also **Castile; Cuaderna Vía; Spanish Literature.**]

LORE OF PLACES. See Dindshenchas.

LORENZETTI, AMBROGIO (*fl. ca.* 1317–1348), Sienese painter, brother of Pietro Lorenzetti. Ambrogio was the most daring and perhaps the most sympathetic and inventive member of the early Sienese school, which included Duccio di Buoninsegna, Simone Martini, and Pietro Lorenzetti.

Ambrogio's career is sketched out with relatively few documents and signed or dated works. In 1321 his name appears on some Florentine mercantile records; 1327 is the date generally given to his matriculation in the Florentine painters' guild, the *Arte dei Meidici e Speziali.* In 1332 he signed and dated the altarpiece for the Florentine Church of S. Procolo that survives in fragments reassembled in the Uffizi, Florence. Ambrogio and his brother Pietro signed the now-destroyed *Marriage of the Virgin* fresco for the hospital of S. Maria della Scala, Siena, in 1335. In 1338 and 1339 documents record Ambrogio's work on the allegorical frescoes depicting Good and Bad Government for the Palazzo Pubblico, Siena. In 1342 he signed and dated his *Presentation of the Virgin* panel intended for the Sienese Duomo, but now in the Uffizi. In 1344 he signed and dated his *Annunciation,* now in the Siena Pinacoteca.

Ambrogio's career, development, and oeuvre are to a great extent matters of speculation. There are, however, a number of important paintings whose qualities are such that they are generally accepted by most scholars as his paintings.

Ambrogio's earliest dated work is the 1319 *Madonna and Child* painted for the church of Sant'Angelo a Vico l'Abate, near Florence, and now in the Museo Arcivescovile, Florence. This bold, monumental work reveals that Ambrogio's style was already well developed. Ambrogio's Madonna exhibits a palpable fleshiness and her child a charming and lifelike animation never before so convincingly rendered in paint. The massive, monumental composition shows Ambrogio's understanding of contemporary Florentine developments and an affinity for the compositions of Giotto. His roots and training, however, lie in Siena with the art of Duccio, in whose shop he may have worked.

In Ambrogio's *Madonna del Latte,* now in the Palazzo Arcivescovile, Siena, the artist translated the subject into something unique. The interlocking structure underscores the act of nursing, through which mother and child are so deeply bonded.

Ambrogio's last and perhaps most endearing interpretation of the madonna and child is the *Rapolano Madonna,* in the Siena Pinacoteca. In this fragment of a dismembered polyptych, Ambrogio once more completely reinvented the images of the Virgin holding her child. Here the underlying structure is merged with the figures themselves. The *Rapolano Madonna* is Ambrogio's most natural and tender image of the Virgin and child.

Most likely the earliest surviving example of Ambrogio's narrative art can be found in the four panels depicting the life of St. Nicholas (generally dated in the early 1330's) now in the Uffizi. Lively, animated, full of anecdotal detail, these small panels demonstrate the scope of his narrative understanding and his sophisticated conception of fictive space. Ambrogio's best-known large-scale narrative painting is his fresco mural cycle depicting the Effects of Good and Bad Government painted for the Palazzo Pubblico in

Detail from *The Effects of Good Government.* Ambrogio Lorenzetti, 1338/1339, Palazzo Pubblico, Siena.
PHOTO: HANS HINZ, BASEL

Siena between 1338 and 1339, the earliest surviving large-scale landscape panoramas in Western art. *The Effects of Good Government* is appropriately the best preserved. Here, in a carefully crafted, tightly organized mural, Ambrogio moves the viewer easily and effortlessly through the rich fabric of city and country life.

Less well known but perhaps even more remarkable is his late-period fresco depicting the *Annunciation to the Virgin* in the Chapel of S. Galgano at Monte Siepi. Although covered with later alterations that reflect a more conservative taste, the sinopia (preliminary drawing) points out Ambrogio's daring and original interpretation of a traditional theme. The Virgin, instead of reacting with the usual obedient calm, is shown slumped on the floor, reacting to the apparition with shock and fear.

In addition to the narratives and images of the Madonna and Child, Ambrogio's originality is evi-

dent in a series of *Maestàs,* which further demonstrate his fertile imagination in re-creating, so to speak, a subject each time he painted it. The *Maestà*—so called because the Madonna is shown in majesty surrounded by a throng of worshipers including saints, donors, and angels—was particularly important to Siena and her territories because the Virgin was the patron saint of the city. The *Maestàs,* in successive order, are at Palazzo Preco Massa Marittima, the Pinacoteca and Church of S. Agostino in Siena, and the Chapel of S. Galgano at Monte Siepi.

Natural observation, exaggerations, the real, and the unreal were all grist for Ambrogio's mill. His object was to bring the viewer closer to the subject of his devotion. Never had a painter developed a greater arsenal of ideas to achieve that goal, and never were religious subjects treated with greater imagination or invention. Ambrogio's contributions

669

and gifts cannot be overestimated, nor can his influence on succeeding generations of painters.

BIBLIOGRAPHY

Eve Borsook, *Ambrogio Lorenzetti* (1966); Enzo Carli, *Ambrogio Lorenzetti* (1954), and *Pietro e Ambrogio Lorenzetti* (1971); Bruce Cole, *Sienese Painting from Its Origins to the Fifteenth Century* (1980); Ernst von Meyenburg, *Ambrogio Lorenzetti* (1903); George Rowley, *Ambrogio Lorenzetti*, 2 vols. (1958); Giulia Sinibaldi, *I Lorenzetti* (1933).

ADELHEID M. GEALT

[See also **Duccio di Buoninsegna; Fresco Painting; Giotto di Bondone; Gothic Art: Painting; Maestà; Siena; Simone Martini; Trecento Art.**]

LORENZETTI, PIETRO (*fl. ca.* 1315–1348), Sienese painter and brother of Ambrogio Lorenzetti. A pupil of Duccio who was influenced by Giotto, Pietro stands out among Sienese painters for his interest in Florentine painting.

His earliest dated work, the polyptych *Virgin and Saints* of 1320 painted for Guido Tarlati (Arezzo, Pieve di S. Maria), already reveals a mature style. His monumental figures are filled with emotional intensity and animation. Pietro's interest in juxtaposing numerous elements to strike a single, overpowering note in his images is already apparent in this work.

The enthroned *Madonna and Child,* in the Museo Diocesano, Cortona, and the half-length *Madonna and Child* in Castiglione d'Orcia are undated but most likely early works, based on their similarity to the Arezzo polyptych.

In 1329 Pietro was commissioned to paint a large altarpiece for the Church of S. Maria del Carmine, Siena (the Carmelite altarpiece), which survives in fragments in the Siena Pinacoteca. Here he realized his full potential as an artist, carefully and subtly manipulating the image to create the desired effect, which is both human and monumental. A half-length *Madonna and Child* in Monticchiello (recently restored) demonstrates a similar direct emotional tenor as the Carmelite altarpiece. From the same period, roughly the late 1320's and early 1330's, comes the magnificent *Crucifixion* in the Museo Diocesano, Cortona. Sometime later, Pietro must have executed the now partially ruined *Madonna and Child with Angels,* in the Uffizi, Florence.

Pietro's last known panel painting is his *Birth of the Virgin,* executed between 1335 and 1342 for the Siena Duomo and now in the Museo dell'Opera del Duomo. Here his interest in fusing formal and narrative considerations results in an image that originally and brilliantly tests the limits of the divided altarpiece by using the frame to create fictive architecture and space which exist in one continuum behind it.

Much of Pietro's activity as a fresco painter has been lost or damaged. In 1335 he and Ambrogio signed a now lost fresco depicting the *Marriage of the Virgin* for the hospital of S. Maria della Scala in Siena. A few years earlier, he probably executed his now damaged fresco of the *Crucifixion* for the Church of S. Francesco, Siena. Among his greatest surviving works are his frescoes depicting the Life of Christ in the lower church of S. Francesco of Assisi. Great problems of chronology and attributions for the smaller narrative images in the vaults still confound scholars.

Pietro's *Crucifixion, Deposition,* and *Entombment* are undoubtedly his most profound images. The epic *Crucifixion* is contrasted with the isolated, sparing images of the *Deposition* and *Entombment.* Here Pietro concentrated the action and minimized detail to reach a level of emotional intensity unequaled in Trecento art. If Pietro's career can be

Virgin and Child. Fresco by Pietro Lorenzetti, from his Life of Christ cycle at S. Francesco of Assisi. PHOTO: WIM SWAAN

characterized by an attempt to express the most essential qualities of an image, then his *Deposition* and *Entombment* are the highest achievements of that goal.

Like Duccio, Ambrogio Lorenzetti, and Simone Martini, Pietro Lorenzetti's originality stretched the limits of painting and anticipated many of the developments of the Renaissance.

BIBLIOGRAPHY

Enzo Carli, *Pietro Lorenzetti* (1956) and *Pietro e Ambrogio Lorenzetti* (1971); Emilio Cecchi, *Pietro Lorenzetti* (1930); Bruce Cole, *Sienese Painting from Its Origins to the Fifteenth Century,* (1980); Ernest Theodore DeWald, *Pietro Lorenzetti* (1930); Giulia Sinibaldi, *I Lorenzetti* (1933).

ADELHEID M. GEALT

[See also **Assisi, San Francesco; Duccio di Buoninsegna; Fresco Painting; Gothic Art: Painting; Siena; Simone Martini; Trecento Art.**]

LORENZO DI NICCOLÒ DI MARTINO (*fl.* 1393–1412), a Florentine painter, pupil and collaborator of Niccolò di Pietro Gerini and later Spinello Aretino. No frescoes and only thirteen panel paintings attributed to Lorenzo di Niccolò survive today. His earliest dated painting is the signed *S. Bartholomew* in the Collegiata of S. Gimignano. His greatest surviving work is the *Coronation of the Virgin,* signed and dated 1402, formerly the high altar for S. Marco in Florence, and today in S. Domenico in Cortona. A conservative artist, Lorenzo di Niccolò responded to the style of Gerini and later Lorenzo Monaco. His work strove for generalized, idealized forms, devoid of any stylistic or emotional excess, and it found favor in Florence and her outlying regions, Arcetri, Terenzano, and Prato.

BIBLIOGRAPHY

Bruce Cole, "A New Work by the Young Lorenzo di Niccolò," in *Art Quarterly,* **33** (1970); Everett Fahy, "On Lorenzo di Niccolò" in *Apollo,* **108** (1978); Richard Fremantle, *Florentine Gothic Painters* (1975), 391–402.

ADELHEID M. GEALT

[See also **Fresco Painting; Niccolò di Pietro Gerini; Spinello Aretino.**]

LORENZO MONACO (*ca.* 1370/1371—*ca.* 1424), Florentine painter, perhaps trained by Niccolò di

Pietro Gerini. Lorenzo is known to have been a Camaldolese monk by 1391. His early works, *The Agony in the Garden,* and *The Man of Sorrows* (both in Florence, Accademia) point to the influence of Gerini and Nardo di Cione. They are, however, artistically far beyond Gerini in their imagination and inventiveness. Monaco is sometimes credited with the development of the cutout crucifix, which replaced the more conventional type in the early quattrocento. An example is his *Crucifix* in Monte San Savino, Sta. Maria delle Vertighe. Later works included his triptych of *Madonna and Child with Saints,* 1410 (Florence, Accademia), *Coronation of the Virgin,* 1413 (Florence, Uffizi), and *Adoration of the Magi,* 1422 (also Uffizi). Monaco's last known works are his fresco cycle depicting the Life of the Virgin and his altarpiece depicting the Annunciation in the Bartolini Salimbeni Chapel of Sta. Trinità, which are dated in the early 1420's. The creator of a splendidly decorative, highly refined style, which emphasized line, color, elegance, and unearthly beauty, Lorenzo created images to marvel at, adore, and venerate. His art, which had many followers, represents a popular alternative to the heroic styles of Donatello and Masaccio.

Crucifix. Panel painting by Lorenzo Monaco, *ca.* 1415. Monte San Savino, Sta. Maria delle Vertighe. © INDIANA UNIVERSITY PRESS 1980

BIBLIOGRAPHY

Luciano Bellosi, *Lorenzo Monaco* (1965); Bruce Cole, *Masaccio and the Art of Early Florence* (1980); Marvin J. Eisenberg, "A Crucifix and a Man of Sorrows by Lorenzo Monaco," in *Art Quarterly,* **18** (1955), and *Lorenzo Monaco* (1986); Frederico Zeri, "Investigations into the Early Period of Lorenzo Monaco," in *Burlington Magazine,* **106** (1964) and **107** (1965).

ADELHEID M. GEALT

[See also **Donatello; Florence; Fresco Painting; Masaccio, Tommaso Cassai; Nardo di Cione; Niccolò di Pietro Gerini; Renaissances and Revivals in Medieval Art.**]

LORENZO VENEZIANO (*fl.* 1356–1379), Venetian painter and student of Paolo Veneziano. Signed and dated works include the *Coronation of the Virgin* altarpiece, dated 1368 (Milan, Brera); the *Madonna and Child Enthroned* dated 1361 (Padua, Pinacoteca); and his elaborate altarpiece of thirteen sections, dated 1357 (Venice, Accademia), which includes scenes of the *Annunciation* and various figures of saints. Considered less gifted than his master, Lorenzo perpetuated many of Paolo's ideas and passed them on to succeeding generations.

BIBLIOGRAPHY

Bernard Berenson, *Italian Pictures of the Renaissance: The Venetian School,* 2 vols. (1957); Michelangelo Muraro, *Paolo da Venezia* (1970).

ADELHEID M. GEALT

[See also **Paolo Veneziano; Trecento Art.**]

LŌṘI (also known as Lōṙi-Joraget and Tašir-Joraget). The medieval kingdom of Lōṙi was located in Gugarkᶜ, the northernmost province of Armenia, bordering on Georgia. The district of Lōṙi was originally part of the Bagratid kingdom of Armenia and frequently served the early Bagratid kings as a safe haven from the attacks of the Arabs and the Byzantines. In the 960's, the Bagratid king Ašot III the Merciful appointed his youngest son Gurgēn as governor of this region and subsequently allowed him to use the royal title and insignia. Gurgēn's royal status was also recognized by his elder brother Smbat II, who shared the royal throne with his father. Gurgēn himself probably ruled as a vassal king. Lōṙi emerged as an independent kingdom during the reign of Gurgēn's son and successor, Dawitᶜ (David)

Anhoḷin (996–1048/1049). The latter extended the borders of his realm in the north and east at the expense of Georgia and the Shaddadids of Ganjak. His attempt to sever ties with the Bagratids of Ani failed, and in 1001 he was forced to submit to King Gagik I, who had entered Lōṙi and occupied a number of fortresses. Subsequent efforts by Dawitᶜ to seize the lands of the Armenian kings also failed. Dawitᶜ was more successful in his diplomatic relations. A political marriage ultimately brought Kakhetᶜia under his influence. In 1040 he succeeded in warding off the threat posed by Abul-Aswār, the Shaddadid emir of Dwin. This success proved to be crucial for the survival of his kingdom until the beginning of the twelfth century.

Dawitᶜ was succeeded by his son Kiwrikē I, after whom the kingdom is occasionally called Kiwrikean. Kiwrikē ruled in peace until about 1090. The Seljuk raids of the mid eleventh century had no effect on the kingdom. In 1064, Kiwrikē willingly accepted the suzerainty of Alp Arslan, the Seljuk sultan. Subsequently, and much against his wishes, Kiwrikē also gave his daughter in marriage to the sultan.

The kingdom of Lōṙi, secure from external interference, flourished and prospered during the long reigns of Dawitᶜ and Kiwrikē. The presence of mineral deposits and the rich soil of the realm helped to create a sound economy, which was also enhanced by the transit trade on the caravan route that ran through the region. The present-day ruins of churches, monasteries, bridges, and fortresses in the area bear testimony to the former prosperity of the kingdom. Among the latter are the remains of the fortified city of Lōṙē, which was the capital of Lōṙi. After the fall of Ani to the Seljuks in 1064, Lōṙi also became renowned for its cultural centers at the monasteries of Haḷbat and Sanahin, where the medieval learning of Armenia was preserved from extinction.

King Kiwrikē's early years marked the apex of the prosperity of the kingdom. He was probably the only Bagratid king to have issued currency bearing his name. During his later years the kingdom began to wane. However, in 1088/1089 the king paid a visit to the Seljuk sultan Makikshāh and succeeded in securing the eastern borders of his realm from the onslaught of the emirs of Ganjak. Around 1110–1113 his weak successors lost the kingdom to the unruly Seljuks of the region. Kiwrikē's descendants continued to rule as princes in the fortresses of Tawuš and Macnaberd; at Nor Berd they survived until the fourteenth century.

BIBLIOGRAPHY

Léwond Movsêsian, "Histoire des rois Kurikian de Loři," Frédéric Macler, trans., in *Revue des études arméniennes*, 7 (1927); Rafayel I. Mat͑ewosyan, *Tašir-Joraget* (1982).

Krikor H. Maksoudian

[See also **Ani in Širak; Armenia, Geography; Armenia, History of; Armenian Muslim Emirates; Ašot III; Bagratids; Dwin; Gagik I; Georgia: Political History; Hałbat; Sanahin.**]

LOTE, STEPHEN (fl. 1381—1417/1418), English craftsman and architect. With Henry Yevele he worked at St. Paul's and Canterbury and helped design a royal tomb at Westminster. Although he seems mostly to have collaborated with others, he did succeed Yevele to become on his own the king's master mason at Westminster and the Tower of London.

BIBLIOGRAPHY

John H. Harvey. *English Medieval Architects: A Biographical Dictionary Down to 1550* (1954), and *Gothic England: A Survey of National Culture 1300–1550*, 2nd rev. ed. (1948); Arthur Oswald, "Canterbury Cathedral: The Nave and Its Designer," in *Burlington Magazine*, 75 (1939).

Stephen Gardner

[See also **Architect, Status of; Architecture, Liturgical Aspects; Canterbury Cathedral; Masons and Builders; Westminster Abbey; Yevele, Henry.**]

LOUIS, ST. See Louis IX of France.

LOUIS VI OF FRANCE (Louis the Fat) (1081–1 August 1137), king of France from 1108 to 1137. The son of Philip I and Berthe of Holland, he was raised and educated at the abbey of St. Denis to the north of Paris. In 1097 Philip repudiated Berthe and married Bertrada, the countess of Anjou. The latter attempted to displace Louis in the royal succession in favor of her own sons, first by direct assassination and then, it was rumored, by poisoning, to which contemporary chroniclers attributed Louis' unusual pallor. Nevertheless, Louis was knighted in 1098 and shortly thereafter was associated in the kingship

with his father. He acceded to the throne in 1108. In 1115 he married Adelaide of Savoy, with whom he had seven children, six of them sons.

Given to corpulence (he became so fat that at the age of forty-six he could no longer mount a horse unaided), Louis was an energetic, if unprepossessing, ruler. Contemporaries praised his sweetness of character and affability and considered him "simple in nature," but he proved adequate to the tasks facing the monarchy. Louis was the first Capetian king to confront directly the problem of the disintegration of royal authority. His reign marks the moment when Capetian kings initiated their long attempt to recover royal power in order to extend their authority throughout the realm of France.

Louis' special contribution to this policy was his conviction that if the Capetians were to achieve mastery as kings of France, they must first secure their own domain, those lands which they governed directly and which provided the territorial basis of the monarchy. Centered principally around Paris and Orléans in the region known as the Île-de-France, the royal domain in the twelfth century was riddled with the castles of turbulent feudal lords who used their strongholds as bases from which to plunder the countryside. So powerless was the king to prevent their violence that he could not even travel safely from Paris to Orléans. For almost thirty years Louis waged unremitting war against the lords of the Île-de-France, attacking the castles along the roads to Paris: that of Hugh de Puiset to the west, which he took and burned three times before subduing it; that of the Montlhéri to the south, which commanded the roads to Orléans and Melun; and to the north, that of Thomas de Marle, who murdered and plundered with impunity until Louis imprisoned him in 1130. These and other lords were pacified, their castles destroyed or taken away from them, and peace was at last established in the domain.

Louis was not, however, equally successful in dealing with the great barons whose counties ringed the royal domain. These included the great fiefs of Blois-Champagne to the east and south, Flanders to the north, and Normandy to the west, whose duke was also the king of England. When two wars against Henry I of England ended in disaster for the French king, Louis was forced to resort to harassing the English king by supporting the claims of William Clito, son of Robert, duke of Normandy, to the duchy. After Henry won Normandy at the battle of Tinchebray (1106), Louis used William Clito to interfere in the affairs of Flanders, whose count,

Charles the Good, was assassinated in 1127. Louis imposed Clito as his candidate for count, but the following year Clito's oppressive rule sparked a rebellion in which the Flemish towns and nobles elected their own count, Thierry of Alsace. William Clito's death prevented Louis from taking further action, but he was able to require Thierry to do homage to him for the fief of Flanders. Similarly, Thibaut of Blois, count of Champagne, remained largely hostile to Louis throughout the reign. But in 1124, when the German emperor Henry V allied with Henry I and threatened to invade France, Thibaut joined the royal forces.

Seeking extrafeudal sources of support, Louis encouraged the growth of towns, granting charters of privileges to communes in the royal domain and neighboring lands. He also maintained good relations with the clergy and protected ecclesiastical property from the attacks of petty lords. Although not an ardent supporter of ecclesiastical reform, Louis refrained from the blatant sale of church offices practiced by his father. Yet he generally manipulated ecclesiastical elections in favor of candidates loyal to the monarchy.

Having mastered the royal domain, the other great problem the king faced was to gain mastery over his own government. On his accession in 1108, the great offices of the crown—the seneschal, constable, butler, chamberlain, and chancellor—threatened to escape royal control by becoming hereditary. Filled for the most part by the same castellan families that Louis was in the process of subduing, these offices had become the virtual property of three families: Rochefort, Garlande, and La Tour of Senlis. The Garlandes monopolized three of the five offices, with Stephen of Garlande occupying the chancellorship and seneschalsy at the same time. For three years Louis waged war to dispel Stephen from his court, finally removing him from office in 1127. After Stephen's departure, Louis initiated a policy of leaving offices vacant, a practice continued by his successors. Stephen's prominent role as counselor, but not his offices, was transferred to Abbot Suger of St. Denis.

Below the level of the great offices, Louis recruited the new, lesser nobility of the Île-de-France to fill his councils and do the real work of government. Drawn from the class of knights of the towns and castles, these men owed their wealth and position solely to the king and formed the core of a growing body of royal familiars loyal to the king.

Secure in his domain and master of his govern-

ment, Louis enhanced the monarchy's prestige by negotiating a marriage between his son Louis VII and Eleanor, heiress to the powerful duchy of Aquitaine. Louis died in 1137, a few days after his son set forth for Aquitaine to celebrate the marriage.

BIBLIOGRAPHY

The best contemporary source is the biography by Suger, *Vita Ludovici Grossi regis*, in Henri Waquet, ed. and trans., *Vie de Louis VI le Gros* (1964). Standard monographs include Achille Luchaire, *Louis VI le Gros: Annales de sa vie et de son règne* (1890, repr. 1964), and *Les premiers Capétiens (987–1137)*, in Ernest Lavisse, ed., *Histoire de France*, II, pt. 2 (1901), as well as Augustin Fliche, *Le règne de Philippe Ier roi de France* (1912), for Louis's early activity. New work on the social composition of Louis's government is found in Éric Bournazel, *Le gouvernement capétien au XIIe siècle: 1108–1180* (1975). For the growth in royal authority see Jean-François Lemarignier, "Autour de la royauté française du IXe au XIIIe siècle," in *Bibliothèque de l'École des chartes*, 113 (1955); Louis Halphen, "La place de la royauté dans le système féodal," in *À travers l'histoire du moyen âge* (1950), 266–274.

GABRIELLE M. SPIEGEL

[See also **Capetian Family Origins; Commune; Eleanor of Aquitaine; Feudalism; Flanders and the Low Countries; France; Henry I of England; Kingship, Theories of: Western European; Knights and Knight Service; Nobility and Nobles; Normans and Normandy; St. Denis, Abbey Church; Suger of St. Denis; Urbanism, Western European.**]

LOUIS IX OF FRANCE (St. Louis) (25 April 1214– 25 August 1270) became king of France in 1226 at the age of twelve. He succeeded his father, Louis VIII, who had died in the south of France during a decisive expedition against the Albigensian heretics. The regent authorized by Louis VIII's testament was the new king's mother, Blanche of Castile. Baronial opposition to her rule—the rule not only of a woman but of a foreigner as well—culminated in a short-lived, unsuccessful uprising.

Military confrontations, stimulated in the north by baronial resentment of the growing coercive power of the Capetian monarchy and in the south by hatred of the northern conquerors, continued during the first twenty years of Louis IX's reign. They were aggravated by the English, particularly by the unwillingness of their king, Henry III, to accept as permanent his father's loss of Normandy and other patrimonial territories to the Capetians. Louis frustrated all the efforts of Henry and the French baronage to subvert his rule, and his successes confirmed an emerging pattern of authoritarian rulership in France.

In 1234 Louis married Margaret of Provence, by whom he had eleven children. The queen had a vigorous and independent temperament and especially resented the influence of her mother-in-law over the king in both political and personal matters. The resulting tensions that developed between Louis and his wife tended to deepen with age.

The tie between Louis and his mother, so much resented by Margaret, was undoubtedly strong. They were both deeply religious. The most famous expression of his piety was the Sainte Chapelle of Paris, which was constructed at his command in order to accommodate the relics of the Passion—crown of thorns, true cross, and other artifacts—that he had purchased from his cousin, Emperor Baldwin II of Constantinople. Completely unlike his mother, however, Louis found the perfect vehicle for his piety in the holy war. He departed for the East for the first time in 1248 after more than three years of preparations, including the construction of the port of Aigues-Mortes and the reform of key parts of his administration with the help of special *enquêteurs* who collected complaints against local officials. He was absent from France from mid 1248 to mid 1254, during which time his mother (until her own death in November 1252) again acted as regent.

After a few early successes on crusade (including the capture of Damietta), the king's army was routed at Al-Mansūra (1250) and he himself was captured. One month later he effected his release by surrendering Damietta to the Muslims. (It was his troops, not himself as is usually alleged, who were ransomed for money.) The king then spent the next four years in Palestine improving the defenses of the Christian principalities. He returned to France only after it became clear that further absence would be seriously detrimental to the kingdom.

In penitential recollection of his failure as a crusader, the returned king became what many of his contemporaries considered a model prince: he reintroduced the *enquêteurs* as a permanent element of government; he overhauled provincial officialdom, concentrating on the bailiffs and the seneschals; he investigated and reformed municipal (communal) administration as well as administration in Paris; he undertook a not altogether unsuccessful program providing incentives for the voluntary conversion of the Jews; and he became remarkably considerate of the poor, widows, orphans, and the sick, founding and endowing a score of hospitals and providing care and alms for lepers. He was, in short, a serious, hard-working prince, and one constantly on the move because of his interest in provincial government.

Louis' policies and religious devotions did not lack critics. His deep affection for the friars (expressed in his adoption of a mendicant-style tunic in personal dress, endowments of mendicant convents, and employment of friars as *enquêteurs*) was viewed with vehement opprobrium by secular clerks, such as Guillaume de St. Amour of the University of Paris. His preference for severe penalties (branding of the nose and lips) for blasphemers excited the opposition of his friend Pope Clement IV. His desire to wear a hairshirt was reproved by his own confessor. And his constraints on the judicial duel, private war, tournaments, feudal coinage, and feudal arbitrariness in the administration of justice (as in the case of Enguerrand de Coucy) inspired much spirited but peaceful opposition.

In foreign affairs with other Christian powers, Louis arbitrated a dozen or more disputes, including the quarrel between the English king and his barons. His judgment in that dispute has survived in the Mise of Amiens of 1264 and is an important personal statement of his authoritarian and paternalistic view of kingship. Arbitration, however, constituted only one dimension of the king's reputation as a peacemaker. By the treaty of Corbeil (1258), he successfully lessened tension with Aragon by renouncing Capetian claims in Spain. In return, James I of Aragon renounced his territorial claims in Languedoc (with the exception of Montpellier). Louis also induced Henry III formally to accept the loss to the Capetians of Normandy and other Angevin lands (not including Aquitaine and its marches) by the Treaty of Paris in 1259.

In his relations with the church Louis was judicious. Accepting the spiritual supremacy of the papacy, he was nonetheless unyielding before many political pretensions of the popes and of churchmen in general. This is clear from his opposition to using royal coercion to enforce submission of excommunicates. He supported the Inquisition, but kept close watch over its activities. In the contest of empire and papacy, he would not recognize Innocent IV's deposition of Frederick II and only after much hesitation permitted his brother Charles of Anjou to go to war against the Hohenstaufen on behalf of Rome.

The king has been credited, at different stages in the historiography, with the first real "legislation" in French history, with the effective creation of the Parlement of Paris, with introducing a fundamental moral element into the style of royal leadership in France, and with the making of the first French state. All of these propositions can be defended with much weighty evidence, but they are complex and still quite controversial issues.

Louis IX again took the cross in 1267. Already in poor health, he departed France in 1270 after three years of careful preparations. He died of natural causes soon after the first landings and skirmishes in Tunisia. He was succeeded by his son, Philip III, during whose reign the first efforts were made for his canonization. These efforts were brought to fruition during the reign of his grandson, Philip IV, in 1297. The feast of St. Louis Confessor is celebrated on 25 August.

BIBLIOGRAPHY

The standard biography is Louis Sébastien Le Nain de Tillemont, *Vie de saint Louis*, 6 vols., J. de Gaulle, ed. (1849), which was written in the seventeenth century. The most comprehensive biography is Henri Wallon, *Saint Louis et son temps*, 2 vols. (1875). A recent treatment of the king's rule, with an up-to-date bibliography, is William C. Jordan, *Louis IX and the Challenge of the Crusade* (1979). The narrative source from which all studies draw the most valuable information on Louis IX's reign is Jean de Joinville's recollection of the king written from 1305 to 1309, *Histoire de Saint Louis*, J. Natalis de Wailly, ed. (1872).

WILLIAM CHESTER JORDAN

[See also **Angevins: France, England, Sicily; Blanche of Castile; Crusade, Concept of; Crusades and Crusader States; Feudalism; France; Friars; Henry III of England; Kingship, Theories of: Knights and Knight Service; Nobility and Nobles; Paris, University of; Parlement of Paris; Ste. Chapelle, Paris; Warfare, Western European.**]

LOUIS XI OF FRANCE (1423–1483), king of France from 1461 to 1483, has become a famous character in literature, thanks to the colorful accounts of contemporary chroniclers and foreign ambassadors. Exploiting these narrative sources, novelists and popular historians have created an image of the king that obscures our lack of a serious study of the voluminous unpublished administrative records of the reign.

The elder, and for a long time the only, son of Charles VII, Louis was born at a time when the French monarchy was struggling for survival in the Hundred Years War. French fortunes had greatly improved by 1440, when Louis joined an unsuccessful princely rebellion against his father. Charles never really trusted him thereafter, and Louis retired in 1447 to his appanage of Dauphiné, where he pursued an independent policy until 1456, when he was forced into exile in the Netherlands. The estrangement from his father seems to have been prolonged and aggravated by the intrigues of members of their respective entourages. When Louis became king, he pointedly reversed many policies of Charles VII and dismissed many of his father's trusted advisers. These actions helped to provoke a new rebellion, misnamed the War of the Public Weal (1464–1465).

Louis extricated himself from this predicament by making concessions in separate agreements with key princes in the coalition. His ineffectual younger brother, Charles (1446–1472), remained a useful figurehead for his opponents until the birth of Louis' son in 1470. The king's main enemies were Charles the Bold (also called "the Rash"), duke of Burgundy, and Francis II, duke of Brittany, both of whom enlisted support from the ancient enemy, England. Louis found allies in the Bourbon branch of the royal house, marrying his able daughter Anne to Pierre de Beaujeu, the brother and heir of John II of Bourbon. The king's deformed younger daughter, Jeanne, who was incapable of bearing children, was married to the duke of Orléans, perhaps in the hope that this house would become extinct.

The reign of Louis XI is best remembered for the liquidation of a number of large princely appanages that appeared to threaten the integrity of the monarchy, but the king's legendary cleverness seems to have been less important in achieving this result than his good luck. The demise of the house of Anjou in 1481 brought Provence, Anjou, and Maine into royal hands. The dukes of Bourbon, Burgundy, and Brittany all lacked sons. Charles of Burgundy aroused the fear and hatred of the imperial cities of Switzerland and the upper Rhine. They inflicted three great defeats on Charles, who perished in the last of them (January 1477). Louis, having already bought off the invading English (1475) and negotiated a concordat with the papacy (1472), eventually managed to seize a good part of the Burgundian lands.

Having inherited a sound fiscal structure and a well-financed army from his father, Louis benefited from the French economic recovery and sharply increased taxation. He was able to pursue an effective, albeit expensive, diplomacy, but he came to be feared and hated by his subjects, who welcomed his death in August 1483.

BIBLIOGRAPHY

Although much has been written on Louis XI, little of it is of historical value. A useful corrective to traditional accounts is that of Karl Bittmann, *Ludwig XI. und Karl der Kühne: Die Memoiren des Philippe des Commynes als historische Quelle* (1964–). Richard Vaughan, *Charles the Bold* (1973), deliberately, and perhaps excessively, underplays the role of Louis XI but offers many important insights and a lengthy recent bibliography. A good scholarly introduction to the reign of Louis XI, but rather difficult to use, is Peter S. Lewis, *Later Medieval France: The Polity* (1968). The latest and probably the best of a disappointing group of popular histories is that of Paul M. Kendall, *Louis XI* (1971).

JOHN BELL HENNEMAN

[See also **Brittany; Burgundy; Charles VII of France, King; Comines (Commynes), Philippe de; France.**]

LOUP, JEAN (**Jean Le Loup**) (fl. early thirteenth century). According to the destroyed labyrinth inscription, Jean Loup directed construction at Rheims Cathedral for sixteen years. Several scholars have hypothesized that he was the first architect and designer of the cathedral, although it appears more plausible that he supervised the second major campaign of work (*ca.* 1220–1230). During his tenure Jean may have erected the north transept portals ("encommencea les portaux," according to one labyrinth transcription) and worked on the upper stories of the chevet and transept, where he redesigned the triforium along the lines of Chartres Cathedral.

BIBLIOGRAPHY

Jean Loup has been designated as the first architect of Rheims Cathedral by the following scholars: Elie Lambert, "Le labyrinthe de la cathédrale de Reims: Nouvel essai d'interpretation," in *Gazette des beaux arts*, 6th ser., **54** (1958); Erwin Panofsky, "Über die Reihenfolge der vier Meister von Reims," in *Jahrbuch für Kunstwissenschaft* (1927); Paul Savy, "Les étapes de la construction de la cathédrale de Reims du XIIIᵉ siècle," in *Travaux de l'Académie nationale de Reims*, **154** (1956). The following studies of Rheims Cathedral and its architects have placed Jean's activity later in the sequence of construction campaigns: Marcel Aubert, "Les architectes de la cathédrale de Reims," in *Bulletin monumental*, **114** (1956); Carl Barnes, Jr., "Jean d'Orbais," in *Macmillan Encyclopedia of Architects*, II (1982); Robert Branner, "The Labyrinth of Reims Cathedral," in *Journal of the Society of Architectural Historians*, **21** (1962); Francis Salet, "Le premier colloque international de la Société française d'archéologie: Chronologie de la cathédrale [de Reims]," in *Bulletin monumental*, **125** (1967), with annotated bibliography, 391–394.

MICHAEL T. DAVIS

[See also **Bernard of Soissons; Jean d'Orbais; Rheims Cathedral.**]

LUCA DI TOMMÈ (*fl. ca.* 1356–1389), Sienese painter. Possibly a pupil of Lippo Vanni, he was influenced by the Lorenzetti and was an occasional collaborator with Niccolò di Ser Sozzo Tegliacci. His principal works include a *Crucifixion* (Montepulicano, Museo Civico), an *Assumption of the Virgin* (New Haven, Yale University Art Gallery), a *Crucifixion*, signed and dated 1366 (Pisa, Museo di S. Matteo), and a polyptych of *Madonna and Child with Saints*, signed and dated 1370 (Rieti, Museo Civico). He collaborated with Niccolò di Ser Sozzo Tegliacci. Luca developed a naturalistic, volumetric style, full of animation and realism; it is still underestimated for its contribution to the development of early Renaissance painting.

BIBLIOGRAPHY

Bruce Cole, *Sienese Painting from Its Origins to the Fifteenth Century* (1980); Sherwood A. Fehm, Jr., *The Collaboration of Niccolò Tegliacci and Luca di Tommè* (1973); Gordon Moran and Sonia Fineschi, "Niccolò di Ser Sozzo—Tegliacci or di Stefano?" in *Paragone*, **27** (1976).

ADELHEID M. GEALT

[See also **Italy, Fourteenth and Fifteenth Centuries; Lorenzetti, Ambrogio and Pietro; Polyptych; Renaissances and Revivals in Medieval Art; Siena; Tegliacci, Niccolò di Ser Sozzo; Trecento Art.**]

LUCIDARIOS. See **Elucidarium and Spanish Lucidario.**

LUDUS DE ANTICHRISTO, an eschatological mystery play in Latin verse. It is preserved in a manuscript from the monastery of Tegernsee that dates from between 1178 and 1184 and is now in Munich, Bayerische Staatsbibliothek, Clm 19411. The text in the manuscript is only a copy. The orig-

Assumption of the Virgin. Panel painting by Luca di Tommè, late 14th century. YALE UNIVERSITY ART GALLERY, JAMES JACKSON JARVES COLLECTION

inal must have been composed after 1099, when the kingdom of Jerusalem was founded, since it figures in the play. Other than that, the text provides no conclusive evidence for a date of origin more precise than between 1099 and 1178/1184.

The play, in two parallel parts of striking symmetry, describes the events preceding the end of the world. In part one, the last emperor of the Holy Roman Empire and king of Germany establishes his supremacy over the Christian kingdoms (France, Greece, Jerusalem), repels an attack on Jerusalem by the pagan king of Babylon, and finally resigns his imperial power in the Temple at Jerusalem to the "King of Kings" and "Only Emperor."

In part two, Antichrist, claiming to be the king of kings, moves in the reverse order, from east to west, and subjugates the Christian world to his rule, including, after initial resistance, the German king and former emperor. Even the king of Babylon is forced into submission. The Jews, after having been converted to Christianity by the prophets Enoch and Elijah, are the only ones who turn against Antichrist and, consequently, die as martyrs. At the height of his power, Antichrist is suddenly struck down and everybody returns into the church's lap.

The author of the play uses traditional elements of Christian eschatology—the legend of the last emperor and the legend of Antichrist—for which he did not need any particular literary sources. In a highly original manner he integrates his material into a consistent philosophy of history. The play does not give the usual fanciful biography of a depraved individual of Jewish origin; instead its Antichrist strikes a delicate balance between corporate historical force and individualized political agent. Antichrist, the offspring of heresy and hypocrisy, is conceived within the church. He gains access to power by a deceptive claim to reform the church. The emperor's renunciation of his hegemony over the church is suspected of having paved the way for Antichrist. In accordance with the tradition, Antichrist uses indoctrination, force, bribery, and miracles as his political means.

The *Ludus de Antichristo* is not connected with the literary Antichrist tradition as it is known to us. Adso's *Libellus de Antichristo* from the middle of the tenth century does not qualify as a source since it diverges significantly from the play, and the later Antichrist plays are totally different. The author of the play frequently quotes and parodies passages from the liturgy.

It is ironic that in various times of nationalistic excitement in Germany—after 1870 and after 1933—the play was heralded as a monument of German patriotism, even though it portrays the German king as a dupe of Antichrist, and presents the synagogue in the role of the martyr.

The play is a work of strong theatrical power that shows a subtle understanding of politics and great independence of thought.

BIBLIOGRAPHY

Editions and translations. Rolf Engelsing, ed. and trans., *Ludus de Antichristo: Das Spiel vom Antichrist*

(1968); Friedrich Wilhelm, ed., *Der Ludus de Antichristo,* 3rd ed. (1932).

Studies. Klaus Aichele, "The Glorification of Antichrist in the Concluding Scenes of the Medieval 'Ludus de Antichristo,'" in *Modern Language Notes,* **91** (1976); Gerhard Günther, ed., *Der Antichrist: Der staufische Ludus de Antichristo* (1970); William T. H. Jackson, "Time and Space in the 'Ludus de Antichristo,'" in *The Germanic Review,* **54** (1979); Georg Jenschke, *Untersuchungen zur Stoffgeschichte: Form und Funktion mittelalterlicher Antichristspiele* (1971); Helmut Plechl, "Die Tegernseer Handschrift Clm 19411: Beschreibung und Inhalt," in *Deutsches Archiv für Erforschung des Mittelalters,* **18** (1962); Paul Steigleder, *Das Spiel vom Antichrist: Eine Geistesgeschichtliche Untersuchung* (1938); Karl Young, *The Drama of the Medieval Church,* 2nd ed., II (1962, repr. 1967), 369–396.

KLAUS AICHELE

[See also **Antichrist; Anti-Semitism; Crusades and Crusader States; Drama, Liturgical; Drama, Western European; Holy Roman Empire; Jews in Europe: After 900; Mystery Plays.**]

LUDWIGSLIED. A manuscript now in the public library of Valenciennes and formerly belonging to the monastery of St. Amand-les-Eaux nearby contains the Old French *Séquence de Ste. Eulalie,* followed, in the same hand, by a poem in German which celebrates the life of King Louis III of France (879–882), culminating in his victory over the Northmen at Saucourt on 3 August 881. It is reasonable to suppose that both poems were composed in a bilingual area where the Frankish aristocracy still spoke Frankish. The German of the *Ludwigslied* is a slightly archaic variety of Rhine-Frankish with some Low German features. The poem was recorded after Louis' death (5 August 882), but composed during his lifetime.

The poet has a theodicean view of history. The Viking invasion is sent by God to test the young king and to remind the Franks of their sins. (The contemporary archbishop of Rheims, Hincmar, saw the invasion as a divine punishment, and repentance as a precondition of victory.) Louis proves equal to the test, taking his orders directly from God, and many Franks repent.

The king is depicted as an ideal feudal ruler, serving God diligently and being rewarded for it. He goes to the aid of his oppressed people, rallying them to God's cause and promising rewards to those who survive as well as to the kin of those who fall in bat-

tle. Before the battle he leads them in a hymn, and during the battle he fights more bravely than any. The poem ends, after praise to God and thanks to the saints for Louis' victory, with praise for the king's unfailing help in need and with a prayer that God in his mercy may save him.

There are near-contemporary Latin poems which have been compared with the *Ludwigslied;* perhaps it is a vernacular representative of a Latin genre. Alternatively it may be the only German representative of the *Preislied,* a song in praise of a living ruler, a genre attested in Norse literature. More persuasively it has been thought to belong to a Carolingian tradition of Christian heroic poetry which gives us the chansons de geste, in which the king defends the faith and his people against the heathen. The *Ludwigslied* would thus be the earliest example of the genre, and the only one known in German.

BIBLIOGRAPHY

John Knight Bostock, *A Handbook on Old High German Literature,* 2nd ed. (1976), 235–248.

DAVID R. MCLINTOCK

[See also **Carolingians and Carolingian Empire; Chansons de Geste; Old High German Literature.**]

LÜBECK is associated inextricably with the memory of doughty seamen and merchants who opened the Baltic Sea to European trade and who, organized into the Hanseatic League, made the northern seas a German preserve through much of the medieval and early modern era. Lübeck, as the most important city of the league, helped to form that unique Hanseatic culture which still colors northern German life and politics.

The origins of the city lay in the Viking era, when trading centers sprang up at convenient locations on the rivers and islands of the north. Old Lübeck, a Slavic settlement several miles below the modern city on the Trave River, served as a transit point for German and Danish goods, which had to be carried overland to and from the Elbe River valley. Northern products such as fish, furs, and wax were exchanged for the finished wares of the Holy Roman Empire. That small settlement flourished on the unsubstantial trade of the period, but its growth was limited by the general availability of surplus products, the dangers of travel, the slow development of suitable mercantile vessels, and the cultural backwardness of all the peoples of the region. These obstacles were being overcome, thanks to the economic growth of twelfth-century Germany, but Old Lübeck never had the opportunity to profit from this growth; it was destroyed in the dynastic wars in 1138. The Wendish inhabitants who supported the international merchant settlement left the country when Wagria became part of Holstein in 1140.

In 1143 Count Adolf II of Holstein founded Lübeck anew on an island in the Trave River that was more defensible than the old site. The town was later considered impregnable (an important consideration when the citizens challenged counts and kings for control of trade and taxes), but not in 1147. In June of that year Niklot of Mecklenburg sailed up the Trave, found the inhabitants too drunk to fight, and destroyed the city and harbor; only the castle survived—and the settlement's furious women, who, according to legend, chased away the Wends with axes and skillets. Count Adolf built a strong fort on Lake Dassow northeast of Lübeck to prevent a recurrence of the disaster.

The early settlement was more promise than profit for Count Adolf, and he lost the promise early to the most ambitious of the northern dukes, Henry the Lion of Saxony (1129–1195), who had closed the market and destroyed the salt mines at Oldesloe after the Lübeck competition had ruined his profits from Lüneburg salt. Henry took Lübeck from its original lord after an annihilating fire in 1157 and refounded the city in 1158 with the intent of making it the mercantile center of the north. The new market and harbor were united, to make for greater ease in commerce. Understanding the needs of merchants, he gave the community the help that was needed for rapid commercial expansion. While scant evidence provides the merest glimpse of his policy, it is sufficient to project an outline of his plans: in the 1160's, at the time he reorganized the church in northern Germany, he moved the bishop of Oldenburg (Stargard) to Lübeck; he also removed taxes and tolls from local trade and even intervened in distant Gotland on behalf of his merchants; he obtained fishing rights in Schonen (Scandia) on the southern coast of modern Sweden, then part of the Danish kingdom; and his military prowess reduced the fear of robbery and of war. Such actions made Lübeck the center of religious, political, and economic life in the region.

Henry the Lion's activities were decisive in the history of the town. Soon Lübeck fishermen were bringing in large catches of herring and other Baltic fish that formed an enduring basis for civic prosperity; and the merchants were penetrating as far east

as Livonia (now in Latvia and Estonia) in search of trade. Henry's rule came to an end in 1181, when Emperor Frederick I Barbarossa came to the aid of rebel Saxon lords and destroyed Henry's power by confiscating lands and distributing them among the minor princes. After forcing the citizens to surrender, Frederick kept Lübeck for himself; later, in 1188, he granted the city a new charter.

Unfortunately, the promises of a distant emperor were of less use than the energetic support of a local duke. The merchants continued to extend their trade, penetrating even to Novgorod by 1199, but when they were faced with competition from Denmark, no effective aid was available from the emperor. In 1201, after the Holy Roman Empire was deeply involved in civil war, the Danish monarch, Waldemar II (1170–1241), made himself master of the southern shores of the Baltic. Lübeck became part of his domain.

Lübeck flourished under Danish rule. Waldemar opened new areas to commerce. His 1218 crusade to Estonia even resulted in the establishment of a new city at Reval that used Lübeck law as the basis for its government; and eventually more than 100 cities along the Baltic governed themselves by Lübeck law and submitted disputes to the Lübeck city council for resolution. Despite the advantages of belonging to the widely extended Danish state, ultimately the Lübeckers tired of royal overlordship. The opportunity to rebel came in 1223, when Waldemar was kidnapped by the count of Schwerin. Once Waldemar's allies were beaten at Mölln in 1225, the citizens committed themselves. In July 1227 the Lübeckers stood in the ranks of the allied army that faced the ransomed king at Bornhöved and routed his forces from the field. The far-distant emperor, now Frederick II, gave the citizens a new charter in 1226; from that date Lübeck was a "free city" in every respect.

The ensuing years were ones of intense struggle. On the seas the citizens had to protect their fishermen and merchants, and on land they had to contend with robbers and robber barons. Alone they could not have coped. In union with other cities they found the resources to defeat or coerce their enemies; when other means failed, they bought off the neighboring princes by hiring their services.

It was particularly vital to guarantee the overland trade to Hamburg and Lüneburg. The one city provided goods for exchange, the other produced salt, which was essential for preserving fish. The roads belonged to the counts of Holstein, who hoped to reorganize their lands, then regain control of Lübeck. The counts were too weak to attack prematurely, but they made no secret of their ambitions. Consequently, Lübeck had to be constantly on guard. To protect themselves against interference on the roads, in 1241 Lübeck, Hamburg, and Soest entered into a defensive pact. In 1247 the Lübeckers obtained Travemünde (at the outlet of the Trave on the Baltic) from the counts of Holstein as part of a bargain by which the counts were installed as protectors (Schirmvögte). The citizens, however, carefully kept the counts from exercising any of the governmental duties normally associated with such office, though they paid the counts well for their military and political aid. In 1256 Lübeck began talks with the Wendish cities of Wismar, Rostock, Stralsund, and Griefswald, and by 1299 these cities had formed a league with Lübeck as the acknowledged leader. Such combinations made it easier to fight pirates and obtain commercial privileges. By 1291 Lübeck had treaties with the rulers of Braunschweig (Brunswick), Mecklenburg, Pomerania, and Holstein. By the end of the century the city supplanted Visby on Gotland as the center of the international merchant community, and decisions of that community were ratified using the Lübeck seal. Soon negotiations with Cologne, Dortmund, Soest, Hamburg, and Bremen resulted in the formation of the Hanseatic League. After that Lübeck merchants had access to the English, Flemish, and Norwegian markets.

One aspect of this outward movement was the close cooperation with the crusading Teutonic Knights in Livonia and Prussia. Lübeck citizens were vital to the founding of Elbing in 1237, Königsberg in 1255, and Memel (modern Klaipeda) in 1252.

As the city grew, it became a tempting target for robber barons. Some were a comparatively minor nuisance, armed men who lived from tolls and ambushes along the roads. Normally, by traveling in a large company, perhaps escorted by hired knights, merchants avoided encountering them. Sometimes, as in 1350, expeditions were necessary to burn their lairs and reduce their numbers. Many of the highwaymen entered local legend as fearsome beasts beyond law and morality. To guard against them, the citizens built walls and strong gates along the island, and then extended their fortifications far into the countryside. Long walls and thorn hedges marked the boundaries of the city, sheltering farms and gardens from sudden assault and keeping cattle from straying.

The importance of the Lübeck bishops was considerable. In the beginning they sought to become the dominant figure in city politics, and for that reason the city council watched them carefully. Fortunately, the bishops soon understood how little power they had. They possessed little land directly, perhaps fewer than 500 plots (mansi) scattered throughout Holstein, and although they had the right to collect the tithe, they could not enforce it. In 1262 they abandoned that tax to the counts of Holstein in return for their service as vassals. Thus developed a feudal relationship, with a bishop holding both spiritual and secular overlordship of vassals who held all the power and responsibility in the region. As the counts raised taxes from episcopal lands, the bishops protested in vain; this common mistrust of the Holstein counts helped foster feelings of mutual understanding between the Lübeckers and their bishops. After the accession of Bishop Hinrich von Bocholt (1317), a long period of cooperation began; at last in 1430 the emperor Sigismund appointed the Lübeck mayors and councilmen executors to protect the church's privileges.

The wooden houses that characterized early urban construction went up in flames in 1276. That prompted the city council to order that all future houses be built of stone or brick. The rebuilt city began to take on the form it held until World War II, with the brick structures of the artisans and guildsmen lining the curving streets that led to the central market at St. Mary's (St. Marien), the civic church. The north-south streets led to the castle, the mill, and the harbor—as their names (Burgstrasse, Mühlenstrasse, Sandstrasse) indicate; the names of the crossing streets witnessed to the principal occupations. The episcopal residence and the cathedral were isolated at the south end of the island. A customary feature of the high gabled buildings was the use of the ground floor for business, the middle floor for living, and the attic for storage.

The German merchants, having established a monopoly for themselves in the North and Baltic seas, had to fight to keep it. For Lübeck the great enemy was Denmark, for the king controlled the Sound (the strait between Denmark and Sweden) and could interdict shipping between the North Sea and the Baltic. In 1307 the Lübeckers were forced to put themselves under the protection of King Eric VI Menved; they escaped Danish control only because the kingdom fell into disorder to Eric's death in 1319. Two decades later Waldemar IV of Denmark (r. 1340–1375) sought to win control of the seaways and make himself master of the north. The full extent of his ambition and the danger he represented were not known until 1361, when he conquered and utterly destroyed Visby. War was inevitable. The first Hanseatic effort was directed at Helsingborg. Mayor Johann Wittenborg led twenty-seven of the heavy sailing vessels called cogs *(Koggen)*, filled with 3,000 troops, to besiege the king in his castle; to make the assault, the mayor unfortunately set too many men on land; the king sallied out, captured twelve ships filled with supplies and weapons, and put the remaining troops in such a desperate position that they had to surrender. Wittenborg paid for his mistake with his head; a stone in the Lübeck market notes the place of execution. A peace treaty was signed in 1365, but it lasted only two years; Lübeck wanted revenge as much as it wanted its trading privileges restored.

The Hanseatic cities prepared a fleet as soon as they found an ally in Albrecht von Mecklenburg, who had been elected king of Sweden in 1364 by rebels opposed to Waldemar's tyranny. The conflict that began in 1367 was a critical moment that determined the course of politics and the economy for centuries to come. Lübeck was the acknowledged leader of the seventy-odd cities of the Hanseatic League, lending its seal and flag to the organization. The league laid taxes on all commerce to pay for the fleet and army, and attacked Denmark by land and sea.

The Lübeck mayor, Brun Warendorp, led out seventeen cogs to Copenhagen, taking the city in May 1367, then joining the land forces to capture most of the province of Schonen (Scandia, on the southern coast of Sweden); meanwhile, Holstein forces overran the Jutland peninsula. Ultimately, in 1369, the allies converged on Helsingborg and forced the castle to surrender. Warendorp did not live to see the victory, having died in the final weeks of the war; his body was buried in St. Mary's. The Hanseatic League dictated peace in 1370 at Stralsund, punishing the Danes and then frustrating the territorial hopes of their allies; Hanseatic permission became a necessary precondition before a Danish king could mount the throne. German merchants and fishermen were thenceforth the masters of the north, and as time passed everyone else came to work for them. Wealth poured into Lübeck. New churches, new houses, and a new city hall *(Rathaus)* flaunted these riches while the otherwise tight-fisted merchant leaders sought out new ways to avoid taxes, evade expensive wars, and increase profits.

The city expressed its pride in churches. The cathedral, begun in 1173, was a large Romanesque basilica with an elegant entryway called the Paradise; later Gothic additions made it resemble the cathedral at Braunschweig. St. Mary's, begun in 1251, was the first large brick Gothic hall church; colorfully painted and magnificently outfitted with stained glass, it was the model for a large number of churches in the Baltic region. Built at the same time were St. Jacob's, St. Peter's, and St. Aegidius', whose Gothic towers marked the skyline and helped make the city profile among the most memorable in Germany.

The city hall evolved from three thirteenth-century houses along the market. A common brick wall united them and provided the basis for subsesquent enlargement; by the end of the fourteenth century the building reached to St. Mary's and was one of the largest civic centers of that era; ultimately it was crowned by a Renaissance facade and impressive decorative towers.

The hospital of the Holy Ghost (Heiligengeist) dates from the 1280's (the association was founded in 1263) and was still being used during the twentieth century for its original purpose: the housing and care of the elderly. The interior hall, 8 meters by 8 meters (26 feet by 26 feet), was decorated with carvings and paintings, among which were several scenes from the legend of St. Elizabeth.

There were numerous cloisters—the Cistercian Johanneskloster (1247), the Dominicans, the Franciscans; the five refuges for the poor (the Beginen Koventen) were founded between 1260 and 1300. Two schools existed by 1262, one in the cathedral and one at St. Jacob's.

Fourteenth-century Lübeck left few records from which population figures can be reckoned, but those that survive indicate that an average of about 330 to 340 property owners lived in the town, with each owner possessing his property fifteen years, on average, before the coming of the plague and ten years afterward. The population of 15,000 to 18,000 souls was dominated by a comparative handful of men. The city was the second largest in Germany (after Cologne) and grew to 25,000 by 1502. Despite the small numbers of the patricians, the upper class was not closed; at least nine mayors were immigrants; new families rose or came in to replace those that disappeared due to natural or financial causes. The Lübeck patrician class was a fluid one. Life expectancy was short: from forty-six to fifty-one years for men, varying widely for women, but not shorter than for men. Men married between the ages of twenty-five and thirty; women between fifteen and eighteen years; widows frequently remarried; many persons of both sexes never married.

The plague carried away about a quarter of the population in 1350, and about a seventh in 1367; the figures are less complete than one would wish, but they are at least not complicated by political events that make the effects of the 1350 plague impossible to calculate. The 1350 plague came from Visby, not from the interior of Germany, a fact that itself testifies to the importance of the maritime trade in the east.

Immediately after the plague subsided, the citizens built the beautiful brick Gothic St. Catherine's Church on the site of the Franciscan monastery, rewarding in that way the efforts and prayers of the monks during the catastrophe. In 1356 the General Assembly of the Franciscan order was held inside the new cloister church. A later outbreak of plague, in 1451, prompted the painting of a 30-meter- (98-foot-) long *Dance of Death* in St. Mary's by the famed native son Bernt Notke.

International trade came to supplant fishing as the prime source of income. The merchants imported furs, wood, pitch, tar, wax, honey, and flax from the east, and exchanged them for cloth, tools, weapons, and luxury items. Fish they obtained from Scandinavia, grain from Livonia and Prussia; metal tools manufactured in Lübeck were traded for northern copper and iron; salt remained a staple of the trade, and large warehouses were built to store it.

The city was governed by four mayors (*Bürgermeisters*) and a council (*Rat*) elected by the burghers. The three meetings of the assembly of all citizens held each year discussed some matters but did not pass laws. Since laborers and artisans were excluded from the polls, and middle-class men had too little time to serve on committees, political power fell into the hands of the patricians on the council, which made the laws. The council hired professionals to perform the tiresome tasks—a chancellor (*cancellarius*), town clerks (*notarius* or *Stadtschreiber*), and a chaplain (*sacerdos*) headed the administration; they hired the remaining employees of the state such as toll collecters and gate watchers. The courts were staffed by professional officers and judges. Until 1347 the court and the police were overseen by an advocate (*Vogt*) appointed by the council; afterward lesser crimes and disputes were heard by the judges

(*Niedergericht*) and appeals heard by the entire council (*Obergericht*). The basic code was simple: each citizen had the right to buy and sell, even to give away, his possessions as he wished; all citizens were to attend the sessions of the assembly or pay a fine; only three matters could be decided in this meeting—inheritances, property sales, and civic needs. There was a provision forbidding anyone to give property to the church, lest it be lost to the tax rolls; and each citizen was to join the militia and assist with civil defense, though no one was required to serve outside the walls. Also, there were the usual lists of crimes and punishments, of duties and regulations, many of a commercial nature.

The pride Lübeckers had in their self-governance was raised to the level of a proverb after the ten-day visit by Emperor Charles IV in October 1375. The city was at its height of power, having forced the peace of Stralsund on all the neighboring kingdoms, and Charles was in need of money. It was an impressive occasion, marked by pageantry, dances, and tournaments. During the public reception, the emperor addressed the councilmen as "lords" ("Ihr Herren unserer Stadt"), and when the eldest of the four mayors demurred, Charles continued, "But you are lords! The oldest registers of the emperors show that Lübeck is one of five free cities that are to be permitted to enter the imperial council when its representatives are present; those five cities are Rome, Venice, Pisa, Florence, and Lübeck." It was flattery, not fact, but the citizens loved it.

There were weaknesses in the social structure that resulted from the maldistribution of wealth. The city's "lords" should have taken heed of lower-class rebellions that had occurred in several Hanseatic cities, but they did not. In 1380 trouble began in Lübeck. The renderers (*Knochenhauer*) met in St. Catherine's to demand increased political rights for all guilds; the merchants reacted swiftly and overawed the troublemakers. In 1384 the renderers (those who cut up dead animals) organized again, this time with plans of armed violence. At the last moment the government was alerted. The council called out the militia, arrested and tried the ringleaders, then executed eleven of them and exiled nineteen. The patriciate could not hold onto exclusive power, however, and as they allowed a fuller participation in government, they found themselves outvoted; in a desperate move, many patricians left the city in 1408, hoping to cause the collapse of the democratic regime. Their plan failed—a new election was held and the victorious guildsmen declared the exiles' property forfeit. Only intervention by the Hanseatic League in 1412 caused the guildsmen to moderate their program; in 1416 the exiles returned, festively received back into the city.

The digging of the Stecknitz Canal was completed in 1398 after eight years of work, opening the way to cheaper transportation of bulk products from the interior. The route was almost completely within Lübeck territory, thanks to the 1370 purchase of Mölln, Bergedorf, and several smaller territories from the ruler of Saxe-Lauenburg; the remaining sections were brought into the project after weary negotiations with the neighboring lords, who made difficulties even over the previously acquired properties; ultimately, knights were hired to govern and protect the Mölln district.

Simultaneously Lübeckers were fighting the notorious pirate band of the *Vitalienbrüder*, who had grown powerful during the wars of succession in Scandinavia. The first necessity was to end the wars, which the Lübeckers did by the Kalmar Union in 1397, making Margaret of Denmark queen of a united Scandinavia; the second was to drive away the pirates from their base on Gotland, a feat accomplished by the Teutonic Knights in 1398; and lastly, to chase down the surviving robbers, which a Hanseatic fleet accomplished in 1401.

A major crisis over tolls raised on ships sailing through the Sound began in 1426; eight years of war ended unsatisfactorily—only Lübeck, Hamburg, Rostock, Stralsund, Lüneburg, and Wismar obtained free passage, while all other Hanseatic cities had to pay the king's toll. The Dutch, dissatisfied with this, took steps against Denmark and the Hanseatic merchants that led to war; the resulting Hanseatic victory guaranteed German domination of trade for generations. Repeatedly in this century Lübeck intervened in Danish politics, seeking to maintain stability in a kingdom rent by rebellion and secession; as a result of the king's financial troubles Lübeck came to possess Kiel from 1469 to 1496 and Fehmarn from 1437 to 1491.

The troubles on the eastern Baltic coast were a similar source of difficulties. The war in Prussia (1454–1466) hurt commerce badly, as did the civil wars in Livonia; worst of all was the conquest of Novgorod by Ivan III of Moscow in 1478, which disrupted trade until 1514. Mayor Hinrich Castorp, mayor from 1472 to 1488 and acknowledged leader of the Hanseatic League, was fully occupied with the conduct of diplomacy. His careful handling of the difficulties with England led to the signing of the Peace of Utrecht (1474), which restored Hanseatic privileges in that kingdom.

The disorders of the period were coupled with the introduction of gunpowder. This prompted the city fathers to rebuild the walls and towers in a more extensive system of fortifications. The famous Holstentor gate, built between 1469 and 1478, was part of this.

Lübeck prospered in the difficult years of the early 1500's, but the days of the Hanseatic League were numbered. The Reformation divided the league members along religious lines, and newly powerful rulers ended the independence of many proud cities. While herring began to disappear from the Baltic, Dutch fishermen discovered new fishing grounds on the North Sea banks. As revenues declined, Lübeck faced a long-term financial crisis. The last diet of the Hanseatic League was held in Lübeck in 1669. The Thirty Years War ruined most of the member cities; only a handful, like Lübeck, survived with independence intact. Napoleon finally ended the era of self-governance, though subsequently a form of face-saving self-rule was devised that has lasted to the present day. Lübeck today is a state in the Federal Republic of Germany and is known as "*freie und Hansastadt Lübeck*" (free and Hanseatic town Lübeck).

BIBLIOGRAPHY

Sources. Die Chroniken der niedersächsischen Städte, 5 vols. (1884–1914); *Urkundenbuch der Stadt Lübeck*, 11 vols. (1843–1905).

Studies. Philippe Dollinger, *The German Hansa* (1970); A. B. Enns, *Lübeck: A Guide to the Architecture and Art Treasures of the Hanseatic Town* (1974); Max Hoffmann, *Geschichte der freien und Hansastadt Lübeck* (1889); Conrad Neckels, *Lübeck, Königin der Hanse* (1964); *Veröffentlichungen zur Geschichte der Hansestadt Lübeck* (1912–1969, 1974–); *Zeitschrift des Verein für Lübeckische Geschichte und Altertumskunde* (1885–).

WILLIAM URBAN

[See also **Baltic Countries; Chivalry, Orders of; Denmark; German Towns; Germany; Germany: Imperial Knights; Hanseatic League; Notke, Bernt; Trade, European; Wends.**]

LUIS DALMAÚ. See Dalmaú, Luis.

LUITPRAND OF CREMONA. See **Liutprand of Cremona.**

LUKAS NOTARAS (*d. ca.* 1453/1454), a rich and influential member of the nobility and the last Byzantine *megadux* (megaduke). He was also grand admiral of the fleet and the senior minister to the emperor Constantine XI Palaiologos (*r.* 1448–1453). He was an opponent of union with Rome and was one of the most energetic defenders of Constantinople during the last siege of the city by the Ottomans. It was Lukas who allegedly said that he would prefer the turban of the Turk to the tiara of the Pope.

After the fall of Constantinople, Lukas was released from captivity by the Ottoman sultan, who had thought of making him the governor of Constantinople. But when Lukas refused to send his young son to the sultan for his pleasure, both he and his son were executed.

BIBLIOGRAPHY

Michael Ducas, *Historia byzantina*, in *Corpus scriptorum historiae byzantinae* (1834); Steven Runciman, *The Fall of Constantinople, 1453* (1965).

LINDA C. ROSE

[See also **Byzantine Empire: History; Constantine XI Palaiologos.**]

LULL, RAMON (Ramón Llull, Raymond Lully the Blessed) (*ca.* 1232–1316). The date of Lull's birth, probably in the Ciutat de Mallorques (today Palma de Mallorca), can be calculated from the date of his conversion at the age of thirty to a religious life (*ca.* 1263). Lull was the son of rich parents who had taken part in the expedition in 1229 led by James I of Aragon, which conquered Majorca from the Muslims. He was brought up as a noble, married (before September 1257), and became the seneschal of James I's second surviving son, Prince James, who was destined to be the first ruler of an independent kingdom of Majorca.

Among the Christian thinkers of the thirteenth century who display interest in Islam, Lull is, according to Urvoy, "absolutely alone in adopting the mode of religious (as distinct from intellectual) thought of his interlocutors, the dialectic of the *kalām*," and in attaching "the greatest importance to Muslim attitudes, types of prayer, bodily postures, customs." This fact and the way, also pointed out by Urvoy, that Lull's poetry evolves from the troubadour interests of his youth into "a religious transformation of courtly love in the sense not of his Western contemporaries but of his immediate Muslim predecessors," notably the thirteenth-century Spanish Muslim al-Shushtārī (*d. ca.* 1212), are very significant. Lull's autobiography, *Vida coaetanea*, written in Paris in 1311, begins with his conversion (*ca.* 1263), immediately followed by an unexplained decision to dedicate himself to the conversion of Muslims. The facts stressed by Urvoy indicate that this apparently sudden conversion and the study of Arabic that followed originated in Lull's preexistent sympathy with the conquered Muslims who survived in Majorca.

Inspired by the example of St. Francis, Lull sold most of his possessions and undertook pilgrimages. He then spent nine years in Majorca (*ca.* 1265–1274) studying Arabic with a Moorish slave he had bought. He also studied Latin grammar and Christian philosophy and theology, either at the Cistercian monastery of La Real or, more probably, with the Franciscans or Dominicans.

During this period Lull wrote a *Compendium of the Logic of al-Ghazāli* and the very long *Book of Contemplation*, both either originally written in Arabic or based on Arabic models but extant only in Lull's own Catalan or in later Latin versions. About 1274 Lull received what he always regarded as a divine illumination on Mount Randa in Majorca. From this he derived the form in which he wrote his first *Art*, only extant in Latin (*Ars compendiosa inveniendi veritatem*). About 1275 Lull was summoned to Montpellier by Prince James; his books were examined and approved by a Franciscan theologian, and he was authorized to teach in public. The prince (who became James II of Majorca in 1276) then founded at Lull's request a monastery at Miramar in Majorca, where thirteen Franciscans could study Arabic and be prepared for missions to Islam. The foundation was approved by Pope John XXI on 17 October 1276.

For the years 1277–1287 there are no documents on Lull and the *Vita* is silent. He must then have composed many of the works based on his first *Art* and also his first major apologetic work, the *Book of the Gentile and the Three Wise Men*, and the *Book of the Order of Chivalry*. (This chronology follows the new arguments produced by Bonner, based on a close analysis of the use of Divine Attributes and figures in the different cycles of the *Art*.) The second major cycle begins with the *Ars demonstrativa* and can be dated 1283–1289. The third cycle (1289–1304) begins with the restructuring of the *Art* in the *Ars inventiva* and includes the *Tabula generalis* and *The Tree of Science*. The fourth cycle (1304–1316) includes the versions of the *Art* best known to posterity, the *Ars brevis* and the *Ars generalis ultima*. From 1290 most of Lull's works are dated by month, year, and place of composition.

From 1287 onward Lull undertook a series of journeys to the papal curia and to royal courts to ask aid for his missionary plans, for church reform, and (from 1292) for the crusades. Since James II of Majorca was excluded from the Balearics from 1285 to 1298, Lull's main hopes (apart from the papacy) were placed in Philip IV of France and James II of Aragon. Lull was in Paris in 1287–1289, 1297–1299, 1309–1311, and probably also in 1306. He dedicated many works, especially on the crusades and against the Averroists, to Philip IV and received in return commendatory letters in 1310. In 1299 Lull secured permission from James II of Aragon to preach in the synagogues and mosques of his realm. In 1305 he presented James with his most important work on the crusade, the *Liber de fine*, and later received financial aid from him; he remained in touch with the king throughout his life. In 1312–1313 he dedicated several works on missions to James's brother, Frederick III of Sicily.

Lull visited the papal curia in 1287, in 1291–1292, and in 1294–1296, and presented petitions to popes Nicholas IV, Celestine V, and Boniface VIII. In 1305 and 1309 he visited Clement V and was present in 1311–1312 at the Council of Vienne. It was there that he secured his main practical achievement, the creation (by canon 11) of chairs of Hebrew, Arabic, and "Chaldean" in five university centers.

Lull also undertook several missions to North Africa, to Tunis in 1293, to Bougie (in present-day Algeria) in 1307, and again to Tunis in 1314–1315. In 1301–1302 he traveled to Cyprus and Asia Minor, hoping to meet the Tatar Khan Ghāzān, then thought to be advancing on Jerusalem. The traditional account of Lull's martyrdom in Bougie in 1315 is contradicted by the existence of works by him dated in Tunis in December of that year. He probably died a natural death (he was about 84) in Majorca early the next year.

Lull hesitated between the Dominicans and Fran-

ciscans: the Dominicans had missionary colleges on which he modeled his monastery at Miramar, and he almost joined the order in 1293, but the greater interest shown by the Franciscans, especially the Spirituals, in his *Art* prevented this. A fourteenth-century tradition states that he became a Franciscan tertiary. Lull was buried in S. Francisco, Palma. His feast is celebrated in the Franciscan order on 3 July. From the sixteenth century, at least, he has been regarded as a saint in Majorca and Catalonia, but repeated attempts to canonize him have failed. In 1858 Pius IX confirmed his beatification.

LULL'S WORKS

Lull taught at the universities of Paris, Montpellier, and Naples. He attracted disciples especially at Paris. Of more than 290 works he wrote some 250 survive, about 190 only in Latin; many of his works are still unpublished. Almost all of Lull's important works were written first in Catalan; the Latin versions are less reliable.

Lull's main aim, the reunification of all mankind in Christ to be brought about by the reunion of the Eastern and Western churches, and the conversion of Muslims, Jews, and pagans (especially the Tatars), inspired all his writings. He contributed to the creation of Catalan as a literary language, using it not only for poetry, novels, and mystical works but also for discussions of theological, philosophical, and scientific themes. He was the first Western Christian to use a vernacular language for such subjects and thus stands apart from medieval scholasticism. Although his mystical works are often placed within the Franciscan tradition, Lull himself indicated that his masterpiece, the *Book of the Lover and the Beloved*, was modeled on the mysticism of Muslim sufis. *Blanquerna* (probably 1283–1285, though retouched later) and *Fèlix* (*ca.* 1288) are the earliest philosophical-social novels of Europe. The plan in *Blanquerna* for a society of nations presided over by the pope is less striking than the critique of contemporary institutions in both books.

Lull's life was a continual battle with Islam, not only in Spain and North Africa but also in Paris against the Averroists. Concern for the unitary nature of truth explains the biased version Lull presented of Averroism; he could not tolerate any basic opposition between philosophy and theology.

For Lull God, in so far as he can be known to man, consists of a series of Divine Attributes or "Dignities," which constitute the absolute principles of the *Art*. They are both the highest degrees of being and universal principles evident to all men. They are the instruments of all created perfection. In the later versions of the *Art* (from 1289) the Dignities are nine: Goodness, Greatness, Eternity, Power, Wisdom, Will (or Love), Virtue, Truth, and Glory. The *Art* works not by demonstration but by the metaphysical reduction of all creation to the Dignities, and in the comparison of particular beings in the light of the corresponding nine relative principles: Difference, Concordance, Beginning, Middle, End, Equality, Contrariety, Majority, and Minority (the last three only predicable of created things). For Lull the Dignities and first six relative principles have an intrinsic function in the life of God and help to illuminate the doctrine of the Trinity while their extrinsic function (and that of the last three relative principles) lies behind the Creation and Incarnation.

In Lull's *Art* these principles are combined in circular and other figures where letters are substituted for names (for example, *B* = Goodness and Difference), and are manipulated by algebraic logic. Since both Muslims and Jews (especially cabalists) conceded a major place in their theology to the Divine Attributes, the use of them as the basis of the *Art* could make possible dialogue between Christians, Muslims, and Jews. Algebraic logic and figures were a way to surmount linguistic difficulties. Urvoy suggests that Lull drew on earlier Arabic works containing "divinatory tables."

Minor treatises applied the method of the general *Art* to particular sciences. *The Tree of Science* (1296) attempted the classification of all knowledge in an enormous encyclopedia under a unitary plan.

Lull's philosophy, as distinct from the combinatory methods of the *Art*, was Neoplatonic realism influenced by the general Augustinian tradition but not, demonstrably, by specific later Christian thinkers. Lull knew some works of the Muslim al-Ghazālī (1058–1111) and the general approach of Muslim theologians, the *mutakallimūn*, who tried to provide a rational apologetic for dogma. Lull's "rationalism" and emphasis on action sprang from the polemical inspiration of his ideas. His stress on the active character of the Dignities was closer to the Muslim than the Christian view. His theory of correlative principles, developed from the 1280's, was an attempt to answer Muslim objections to the Trinity. According to Pring-Mill, each Dignity "unfolds into a triad of interconnected principles": agent, patient, and the action itself. This unfolding, seen as an image of the relations within the Trinity itself, impresses an "ineradicably Trinitarian structure" on creation.

Lull stated that he borrowed his correlative terminology from the Arabs. Against the scholastic theology of Islam, Lull argued that the Muslim who began with a belief in God's unity and in the Divine Attributes must logically end by becoming a Christian.

BIBLIOGRAPHY

Editions and translations. In Catalan: *Obres esencials,* 2 vols. (1957–1960); *Doctrine pueril,* Gret Schib, ed. (1972). In Latin: *Raimundi Lulli opera latina,* Friedrich Stegmüller, ed. (1959–). In English: *Selected Works,* Anthony Bonner, ed. and trans., 2 vols. (1985). For older editions and translations see the bibliographies in *Obres esencials,* II; Rudolf Brummer, *Bibliographia Lulliana: Ramon-Llull-Schrifttum 1870–1973* (1976); Manuel C. Díaz y Díaz, *Index scriptorum latinorum medii aevi hispanorum,* II (1959), 348–384.

Studies. Miguel Cruz Hernández, *El pensamiento de Ramon Llull* (1977); Jordi Gayà, *La teoria luliana de los correlativos: Historia de su formación conceptual* (1979); J. N. Hillgarth, *Ramon Lull and Lullism in Fourteenth-century France* (1971); Armand Llinarès, *Raymond Lulle, philosophe de l'action* (1963); Edgar Allison Peers, *Ramon Lull: A Biography* (1929); Erhard W. Platzeck, *Raimund Lull: Sein Leben, seine Werke, die Grundlage seines Denkens (Prinzipienlehre),* 2 vols. (1962–1964); Robert D. Pring-Mill, "The Trinitarian World Picture of Ramon Lull," in *Romanistisches Jahrbuch,* 7 (1955–1956); Juan Tusquet, *Ramón Lull, pedagogo de la cristianidad* (1954); D. Urvoy, *Penser l'Islam: Les présupposés islamiques de l'"Art" de Lull* (1980). See also the journal *Estudios Lulianos* (1957–).

J. N. HILLGARTH

[See also **Catalan Literature; Ghazālī, al-; Mysticism, European; Neoplatonism.**]

LUPOLD OF BEBENBURG (BAMBERG) (*d.* 1363) wrote his principal work, the *Tractatus de iuribus regni et imperii romani,* about 1340. Lupold studied law at Bologna, was attached to the cathedral at Würzburg from 1325 to 1352, and became bishop of Bamburg in 1353.

Lupold became involved in the great dispute between the papacy and the emperor Louis IV of Bavaria (*d.* 1347). Compared to the quarrels of the Hohenstaufen period, this was shadow boxing, since the pope was in Avignon and Louis never had any real power in Italy. In fact, even in Germany Louis faced opposition. Nevertheless, there was a long dispute as to whether Louis could exercise the powers of emperor without papal approval and coronation, which Pope John XXII (1316–1334) withheld. Louis tried to solve the problem by marching on Rome and crowning himself there, but this did not end the opposition. Finally the German electors, in the declaration of Rense (1338), affirmed that the man whom they chose had all the powers of an emperor, even if not crowned by the pope.

Lupold's *Tractatus* supported this position. Every people, he said, has the right to choose its own king when there is a vacancy; the people of the empire have given this right to the electors. Thus the man chosen by the electors has all the rights and powers of an emperor. Coronation by the pope may add prestige and fully confirm the right to the title, but it adds no real power.

Lupold was a realist and rejected many old legends. The "transfer of the Empire" from the Greeks to Charlemagne was a myth; Charlemagne was emperor because he and his ancestors ruled most of western Europe. The German kings had become emperors because they had taken over most of Charlemagne's lands. France and England perhaps should be in the Empire, but Lupold admitted they were not. What was important to Lupold was that Germany remain strong and united. As he said, he wrote his treatise "out of fervent zeal for Germany, my fatherland." It would be too much to say he envisaged a Europe composed of independent national states, but he was approaching this idea.

Lupold strongly supported the principle of majority rule in the choice of a king by the electors. Germany had suffered from disputed elections in which a minority of the electors had refused to accept—and rebelled against—the man chosen by the majority. The electors, said Lupold, form a corporation, and as in any corporation they must accept the decision of the majority.

BIBLIOGRAPHY

Ewart Lewis, *Medieval Political Ideas*, 2 vols. (1954), I, 310–312, II, 456–463; Charles H. McIlwain, *The Growth of Political Thought in the West* (1932), 288–292; Michael Wilks, *The Problem of Sovereignty in the Later Middle Ages* (1963), 187–197, 246–247.

JOSEPH R. STRAYER

[See also **Bavaria; Holy Roman Empire; Political Theory, Western European.**]

LUPUS OF FERRIÈRES (Lupus Servatus) (*ca.* 805–*ca.* 862), a leading scholar of the ninth century. Born into a family of political and ecclesiastical aristocrats, he became a monk at the monastery of Ferrières near Senones (Sens) sometime in the 820's. He spent eight years at the monastery of Fulda, Germany, where he studied under the direction of Hrabanus Maurus, a leading Carolingian master. In 841, five years after his return to Ferrières, Lupus became abbot of his monastery. He played an active role in the Frankish church as well as in the complex and risky world of Carolingian politics.

Lupus was one of the important scholars who took part in the Carolingian revival of education and culture. Despite his administrative and political duties, he exchanged letters with other scholars on theological and grammatical points, engaged in intellectual debate, taught students, sought out manuscripts of important authors, copied manuscripts, corrected and edited texts, and wrote two saints' lives and other treatises. The collection of Lupus' correspondence, gathered together by Heiric of Auxerre, his best-known disciple, as a model book for his own pupils, is an important source for monastic administration and Carolingian politics as well as for Lupus' own activities and interests.

Many of the manuscripts whose texts Lupus copied or corrected still survive. Together with his letters and notes that Heiric published from his teaching, they show a keen interest in the Latin language and in the literature of Rome, especially the work of Cicero. The purity of his own Latin and his fondness for classical authors have led modern writers to describe Lupus as a humanist. He was also deeply interested in Christian literature. His thoughts on the purpose of learning reflect the general Carolingian hope that learning should lead one to religious salvation.

BIBLIOGRAPHY

For a list of Lupus' works, see Franz Brunhölzl, *Geschichte der lateinischen Literatur des Mittelalters*, I (1975). Studies include Charles H. Beeson, *Lupus of Ferrières as Scribe and Text Critic: A Study of His Autograph Copy of Cicero's "De oratore"* (1930); Robert J. Gariépy, *Lupus of Ferrières and the Classics* (1967), "Lupus of Ferrières: Carolingian Scribe and Text Critic," in *Mediaeval Studies*, **30** (1968), and "Lupus of Ferrières' Knowledge of Classical Latin Literature," in Guy Cambier, ed., *Hommages à André Boutemy* (1976); Riccardo Quadri, *I collectanea di Eirico di Auxerre* (1966); Emmanuel von Severus,

Lupus von Ferrières: Gestalt und Werk eines Vermittlers antiken Geistesgutes an das Mittelalter im 9. Jahrhundert (1940).

JOHN J. CONTRENI

[See also **Carolingians and Carolingian Empire; Church, Latin; Classical Literary Studies; Clergy; Fulda; Hrabanus Maurus; Latin Language.**]

LUSIGNANS, French dynastic family that had its origins in tenth-century Poitou, and that later succeeded to the kingdoms of Jerusalem, Cyprus, and Cilicia. The French branch died out with Guy of Lusignan in 1308, after which date the family lands, including the principality of Angoulême, were sold to the French crown.

The Levantine branches trace their origins to Hugh VIII, "the Brown," lord of Lusignan, who went as a pilgrim to the Holy Land in 1164 and was taken prisoner by Nūr al-Dīn (d. 1174), the Zangid atabeg of Aleppo and Damascus. Hugh's son Aimery became constable of the kingdom of Jerusalem about 1180. Another son, Guy (d. 1194), married Sibyl, the widowed heiress of the kingdom, thus becoming an heir presumptive to the throne after the death of Sibyl's son Baldwin V in 1186. Guy failed in his struggle for the crown, however. In 1192, he bought the island of Cyprus from the Templars, thus laying the foundations for the Frankish domination of that island. He was succeeded in 1194 by his brother Aimery, who requested and, in 1197, received a royal crown from Emperor Henry VI of Germany. In that same year Aimery became king of Jerusalem through his marriage to the widowed Queen Isabel. Beginning with Hugh III of Cyprus in 1268, all the kings of Cyprus held the title "King of Jerusalem" as well. The Lusignans introduced the feudal system and other Western medieval institutions to Cyprus, seeking to maintain strong control over their vassals on the island. Nevertheless, they lost possession of Famagusta—the chief center of trade and commerce—to the Genoese in 1376, until that area was recovered by James II in 1464.

In 1342, another Guy of Lusignan succeeded to the throne of Cilician Armenia. The Lusignans of Cilicia reigned during a period of intense anti-Latin sentiment, particularly regarding union between the Roman and Armenian churches. This climate had as one of its consequences the assassination of King Guy (Constantine II) by the anti-Latin faction in

Lusignan Rulers of Cyprus

Guy of Lusignan (1192–1194)	Hugh IV (1324–1359)
Aimery of Lusignan (1195–1205)	Peter I (1359–1369)
Hugh I (1205–1218)	Peter II (1369–1382)
Henry I (1218–1253)	James I (1382–1398)
Hugh II (1253–1267)	Janus (1398–1432)
Hugh III (1267–1284)	John II (1432–1458)
John I (1284–1285)	Charlotte (1458–1460)
Henry II (1285–1324)	James II (1460–1473)
(Usurpation of Aimery, prince of Tyre, 1306–1310)	James III (1473–1474; regency of Caterina Cornaro)
	Caterina Cornaro (1474–1489)

1344. The last king of Cilicia, Leo V/VI of Armenia, was taken prisoner by the Mamluks upon the fall of the kingdom in 1375 and died in Paris in 1393. Thereafter, the title "King of Armenia" fell to the kings of Cyprus, and possession of that island was given to Venice in 1489 by Caterina Cornaro, a Venetian, and the kingdom's last ruler.

BIBLIOGRAPHY

Ghevont Alishan, *Sissouan; ou, L'Arméno-Cilicie* (1899); Sir George Hill, *A History of Cyprus,* 4 vols. (1940–1952); Louis de Mas-Latrie, ed., *Chronique de Chypre* (1891); Louis de Mas-Latrie, *Histoire de l'île de Chypre sous le règne des princes de la maison de Lusignan,* 3 vols. (1852–1861).

ANI P. ATAMIAN

[See also **Assizes of Jerusalem; Cilician Kingdom; Cilician-Roman Church Union; Crusades and Crusader States;- Cyprus, Kingdom of; Guy of Lusignan; Leo V/VI of Armenia.**]

LUSTERWARE. The earliest evidence for the use of a luster technique comes from excavations at Al-Fusṭāṭ (Old Cairo), where glass (but not pottery) shards were found dating from 773 and 779/780. In the early twentieth century, German archaeologists discovered large quantities of luster pottery at Samarra, the Iraqi court residence of the Abbasid caliphs that was founded in 836. This has led to the speculation that Mesopotamian craftsmen, who seem to be the first to have adapted luster to clay, borrowed the technique from Egyptian glassmakers. In early experiments with luster it was applied as an overall covering for dishes with relief molding, evidently to simulate the appearance of bronze, brass, or gold.

Another novel venture applied contrasting luster tones (ruby, vermilion, gold, brown, and green) against a creamy white ground. The technique required mixing silver sulfide, silver and/or copper oxides, plus red or yellow ochre (containing ferric oxide acting as a flux) in a vinegar suspension. This solution was then laid in a very thin film over white tin-glazed earthenware, which was refired at a slightly lower temperature in a reducing kiln (one poor in oxygen). When the fire required extra oxygen it bonded with the coloring oxides, leaving the pigment in a metallic state that produced an iridescent surface sheen. Polychrome luster and total luster coverage were superseded by designs in less expensive and less complex monochrome luster-painted ceramics, which the Abbasids exported as luxury items to such distant lands as India, Samarkand, and Spain.

After Egypt gained political independence from Baghdad, a fine series of native lusterwares was developed there in the tenth century, probably under the influence of immigrant or imported Mesopotamian potters. Originally Fatimid style and inconography were heavily dependent upon Samarra prototypes; but a distinctive Egyptian luster evolved that frequently used bold figural images (often realistically conceived in a Hellenistic tradition), a new group of animal types, and a characteristically flo-

riated Kufic writing. During the last quarter of the twelfth century Syria and Iran began to manufacture luster ceramics almost simultaneously. The secrets of luster production were probably transmitted by Egyptian craftsmen seeking new patrons after the collapse of the Fatimid dynasty in 1171.

Like later Fatimid pieces, early Persian lusterware uses large motifs in white against a lustered background relieved by tiny white spirals. This monumental style was gradually replaced by a miniature style. Closely allied to book painting, it frequently repeated elements on a small scale. Garments, plants, and abstract designs with complex and crowded ornamental patterns were juxtaposed, leaving few plain white areas (usually faces and halos). The negative forces of Mongol destruction curtailed, but never totally stopped, luster production in Iran; however, the rise of the Nasrids in Spain (ca. 1232) created a need for a distinctive Andalusian lusterware. The Spanish artisans drew upon Eastern and North African sources and combined them with Gothic designs. Their ware was exported from the port of Majorca, which lent its name to majolica, a European pottery that derived from the technical achievement of Islamic lusterware.

BIBLIOGRAPHY

E. Kühnel, "Die ᶜabbāsidischen Lüsterfayencen," in *Ars islamica,* **1** (1934); Arthur Lane, *Early Islamic Pottery: Mesopotamia, Egypt, and Persia* (1947), 13–16, 20–24, 37–40; David Talbot Rice, *Islamic Art* (1965), 40–42, 80–81; Henri Terrasse, *L'art hispano-mauresque dès origines au XIII*ᵉ *siècle* (1932).

MARINA D. WHITMAN

[See also **Abbasid Art and Architecture; Ceramics, Islamic; Glass, Islamic; Kashi; Majolica.**]

LUZARCHES, ROBERT OF. See **Robert of Luzarches.**

LUZZI, MONDINO DEI. See **Mondino dei Luzzi.**

LYDGATE, JOHN (*ca.* 1370–1449), English poet, was born in the village of Lydgate, in Suffolk, six miles from Bury St. Edmunds and its great Benedictine abbey. He took his name from his village when

Fatimid lusterware plate. Egypt, 12th century. COURTESY OF THE FREER GALLERY OF ART, SMITHSONIAN INSTITUTION, WASHINGTON, D.C. (41.12)

he entered the abbey, as was the regular practice with monks even where there was a family surname. Lydgate entered the monastery at an early age and received his education there as a novice. In 1389, having passed through minor orders, he was ordained subdeacon, and in 1397 he was ordained priest. Some time after this, and certainly between 1406 and 1408, he spent a period of time as a student at Gloucester College, the Benedictine house for students at Oxford, although he was probably not registered for a degree. During his time there he made the acquaintance of Thomas Chaucer, the poet's son, who lived at nearby Ewelme, and perhaps even of the Prince of Wales, the future Henry V, who wrote to the abbot and chapter of Bury recommending that Lydgate be allowed to continue his studies.

Henry was subsequently one of Lydgate's most important patrons, being directly responsible for the commissioning of the *Troy Book* in 1412, and associated, perhaps more indirectly, with the *Life of Our Lady.* Henry, in conjunction with his friend Edmund Lacy, dean of the Royal Chapel at Windsor, may also have been instrumental in encouraging Lydgate to develop an elaborate and ornate style in the composition of quasi-liturgical pieces in the vernacular. This at any rate is the conclusion suggested by the rubrics to three such pieces (*Benedic anima mea domino, Eight Verses of St. Bernard,* and *Gloriosa dicta sunt de te*) offered by John Shirley (1366–1456), copyist, bookdealer and general literary factotum, whose manuscripts are an important source for copies of Lydgate's minor poems and gossip about his life and career. Shirley was associated with the "Chaucer circle" and an agent perhaps in the network of contacts that the aspiring poet was building up. Lydgate wrote a charming poem, *At the Departyng of Thomas Chaucyer on Ambassade into France* (variously dated between 1414 and 1420), which shows his familiarity with the household, and it was through Thomas' daughter Alice that he got to know Thomas Montacute, earl of Salisbury (Alice's second husband), who commissioned the translation of Deguileville's *Pilgrimage of the Life of Man* in 1426, and William de la Pole, earl of Suffolk (Alice's third husband), who took an interest in Lydgate in the 1430's and 1440's. For Alice herself Lydgate wrote his exposition of *The Virtues of the Mass.*

By 1420, Lydgate's reputation was firmly established, and he was in regular demand for commissioned pieces of various kinds. Before the death of Henry V he wrote his laudatory poem *On Gloucester's Approaching Marriage* to Jacqueline of Hainault in 1422, and during this time too he was much concerned in the promotion of the policy of peace with France, following the Treaty of Troyes in 1420. He adverted to this theme, probably under the influence of his patrons but certainly also by temperamental inclination, in the Epilogue to the *Troy Book,* in the fine short poem *In Praise of Peace,* and above all in *The Siege of Thebes,* where he developed the classical story as a sober admonition against unwise government, wars of aggression, and internecine feuds. After Henry's death, Lydgate showed his attachment to the widowed Catherine in the envoy addressed to her that he appended to a Valentine poem in praise of the Virgin, *A Valentine to Her That Excelleth All,* and in the mutability poem *That Now Is Hay Sometime Was Grass,* which Shirley tells us Lydgate wrote at the commandment of Queen Catherine "as she walked by the meadows that were late mown in the month of July." Lydgate was at the command of other noble ladies too. For Margaret, daughter of the earl of Warwick and later countess of Shrewsbury, he wrote around 1425 a weighty version of the story of *Guy of Warwick* in honor of her father's family. For Warwick's third wife, Isabella, daughter of Lord Despenser, he wrote a celebration of *The Fifteen Joys of Our Lady;* for Anne, countess of Stafford, a poem in praise of her sainted namesake, the *Invocation to St. Anne;* and for Anne's daughter, also called Ann, widow of Edmund Mortimer, earl of March, the *Legend of St. Margaret.* There must have been many more commissions of a less pious and more ephemeral kind, of which we can now obtain only stray glimpses in Shirley's gossipy headings. Shirley tells us, for instance, that *The Temple of Glass* was made "a la request d'un amoureux" and that the *Ballade of Her That Hath All the Virtues* was written by Lydgate "at the request of a squyer that served in loves court." Shirley may not always be reliable, but he probably reconstructs the general circumstances of composition accurately enough.

During this period, Lydgate spent much time away from his abbey, at least until he returned there to settle permanently in 1434. He was often in London, where he stayed at the abbot's town house, "Buries Markes" (where Shirley tells us he wrote his *Gaude virgo mater Christi* as he lay in his bed at night), and often with the court on its various peregrinations, as to Windsor and Eltham. The grant of a lease of land in 1423 is a clear mark of preferment, and his appointment as prior of the small house of Hatfield Broadoak in Essex in the same year was probably to help him with his expenses as much as anything. In 1426 Lydgate was in France in the retinue of the earl of Warwick, at whose instigation he did a translation of Laurence Calot's propagandist poem on *The Title and Pedigree of Henry VI,* establishing Henry's claim to the throne of France. He also did at this time his version of the French *Danse Macabre* (Dance of Death) inscribed on the cloister walls of the Church of the Holy Innocents in Paris, a poem that he later revised at the request of John Carpenter, town clerk of London, in 1430 for the cloister walls of Pardon churchyard near St. Paul's. The major commission of the French years was the translation of Deguileville's *Pilgrimage of the Life of Man,* a long allegorical poem, which he did at the request of Thomas Montacute, earl of Salisbury. Lydgate must have been overwhelmed with work at this time, and the translation of the *Pilgrimage* (over 26,000 lines) is so bad that one suspects that Lydgate subcontracted the commission to a feebler hack, reserving only the Prologue to himself.

In 1429 Lydgate was back in England for the coronation of Henry VI, now nearly eight years old. In his capacity of poet-propagandist for the Lancastrian dynasty, he provided a number of poems for the occasion and celebrated above all the union of the two crowns of England and France in the young king. There is the *Roundell* to be sung "ayens his coronacioun," and the verses to accompany the "soteltes" at the coronation banquet. There is also the *Ballade to Henry VI on His Coronation* and the *Prayer for King, Queen, and People.* These are sonorous pieces which demonstrate Lydgate's competence in the unenviable role of poet laureate. Like a good public speaker, he was always able to say something appropriate to the occasion, something which would sound impressive, never offend, and at worst would only send the audience to sleep. Lydgate was active again when Henry VI returned in 1432 from his coronation in Paris, this time in organizing, in collaboration with John Carpenter, a great ceremonial entry for the king into London, the streets of which were decorated at fixed stations with elaborate allegorical tableaux appropriate to the occasion. Lydgate left some verses on this *Triumphal Entry* which have the character, and literary interest, of a souvenir program.

Throughout this period of his career Lydgate was also writing "mummings" for the entertainment of the court at Christmas and at civic occasions in London. There are Christmas mummings for the royal court at Eltham in 1424, at Windsor in 1429, and at Hertford in 1430, and for the Mercers and Goldsmiths and other civic dignitaries in the intervening years, including one for a kind of civic picnic at Bishopswood. Mummings are an ancestor of the masque and consist of animated tableaux with the voice of the narrator (perhaps Lydgate himself) speaking a commentary, and sometimes with genuine dramatic impersonation. They are usually allegorical and mythological and, being by Lydgate, hortatory to some degree. But the unexpected triumph of the group was the *Mumming at Hertford,* a lowlife burlesque of shrewish wives and henpecked husbands with a quite vigorous comic realism. Lydgate shows here his remarkable versatility and reminds us that his vocation as a monk seems to have inhibited not at all his activities in the secular sphere, except in certain obvious ways, and that his actual experience of court and city life was probably not much narrower than Chaucer's. The mention of the civic mummings reminds us also that the range of Lydgate's commissions was not confined to the court and aristocracy. He did a satirical piece on henpecked husbands and their wives, *Bycorne and Chychevache,* to accompany some painted hangings in the hall of "a werthy citeseyn of London" and to act as a kind of explanatory text. The poem *On the Sudden Fall of Princes in Our Days* was probably intended to accompany a similar display. The exact mode of "publication" of the *Legend of St. George* is not clear, but it was certainly written for the Guild of Armourers for presentation at their annual feast of St. George, their patron saint.

In 1431 Lydgate, at the height of his fame, received his grandest commission, a request for a translation of Boccaccio's *De casibus illustrium virorum* (Concerning the fall of famous men) from Humphrey, duke of Gloucester (*d.* 1447), virtual ruler of England during Henry's minority and the greatest patron of letters of the fifteenth century in England. The task was an awesome one, since Boccaccio's work is almost a dictionary of universal biography, an encyclopedia of ill fortune, and was made more formidable by the fact that Lydgate worked from the extensively amplified version in French by Laurent de Premierfait. All this, coupled with Lydgate's own habits of encyclopedic amplification and the specific request from Humphrey to add moralizing envoys to each story of disaster, meant that Lydgate did not finish the work until 1438, by which time he had returned to the cloister, an old man, and Humphrey was in political decline. Humphrey took a keen interest in the work during its early stages and offered advice and the benefit of his contacts with Italian humanism. But the development of Humphrey's political career and of his humanistic ambitions left the old monk far behind, and Lydgate carried on dispiritedly, complaining from time to time of the lack of encouragement and money from his patron. An interesting product of their association is a *Letter to Gloucester* in which Lydgate, still hopeful of support, makes some witty play on words concerning the sickness of his purse. *The Fall of Princes* is Lydgate's longest poem (36,365 lines) and should be his *magnum opus*, but it is not. It is a vast, sprawling biographical encyclopedia, shot through with passages of lugubrious grandeur, but with no organizing principle other than that the great men and women of the past, whatever their merits, always come to a sticky end. The moralizing, though endless, is factitious, and the attitude toward Fortune and destiny eclectic and contradictory.

Other tasks were not wanting during this period. Henry VI came with his court to Bury at Christmas 1433 and stayed till Easter, an exceptional mark of favor. It was a great event in the history of the abbey, and the abbot, William Curteys, asked Lydgate to do a new version of the *Life of St. Edmund* to commemorate the visit. Though massively amplified, this is one of Lydgate's most successful attempts at narrative, and he was clearly capable of rising to the occasion. But in 1439, when Abbot Whethamstede of St. Alban's asked him to do a *Life of St. Alban* on the same grand scale, he was not inspired, and the result is turgid. Other works which can be dated to this period reveal a continuing interest in affairs of state. *The Debate of the Horse, Goose, and Sheep,* written about 1437, is an allegorical debate on matters of war, trade, and foreign policy, while the prose *Serpent of Division,* an unusually ambitious work for its time, is a treatise against civil war which uses the wars between Caesar and Pompey as its model.

By now Lydgate was an old man, and he seems to have written little in the last years of his life. He was brought out of retirement to provide verses for the street pageants at *Queen Margaret's Entry into London* in 1445, and he seems to have been occupied spasmodically with a translation of the *Secreta secretorum,* a long treatise of political and moral instruction. It was left unfinished at his death and completed by Benedict Burgh, one of his admiring disciples.

Most of Lydgate's verse is occasional in origin, or written to specific commissions, and it is no diminution of its intrinsic merit to speak of it in relation to the circumstances of his life. His voice is nearly always that of the public orator or professional rhetorician, and in all his vast output (about 140,000 lines of verse) there is no hint of the man himself, of the pressure of experience, or of the need from within to write. Even a poem like the *Testament,* written as a personal act of penitence and confession of faith, is exemplary in character and generally hortatory in tone, and the "autobiographical" data it uses are the commonplaces of penitential literature. In this Lydgate is entirely representative of his age and should be recognized as such. In almost every respect, in fact, Lydgate's chief interest and value is in his representativeness. In him, on a massive scale and without the intrusion of poetic individuality, we can trace the characteristic habits of mind, processes of thought, preoccupations, and poetic ambitions of the late medieval poet, and provide ourselves with a vantage point from which we can better understand the exceptional poet like Chaucer or Langland.

Lydgate, as a typical medieval poet, conceives of poetry as essentially sententious and rhetorical, as a form of discourse in which moral truths are pressed home through an ornate and impressive eloquence. The characteristic procedure is amplification, as can be seen in Lydgate's most successful major poem, the *Troy Book.* Here, in his 30,117-line translation of the Italian jurist and moralist Guido delle Colonne's Latin prose *Historia destructionis Troiae* (ca. 1276, itself a reworking of Benoît de Sainte-Maure's French prose *Roman de Troie*), the interest is not in narrative, character, or tragic design, but in history as a repository of moral truth. Lydgate's moralizing is so persistent, and the story so intractable to simple moralization, that the effects are often indiscriminate and self-contradictory, but his talents are well matched to the later part of the story. Here at last, as Troy's heroes decline and the city falls into the shadows, Lydgate can give full expression to his Christian sense of the inevitable ruin that time and fortune make of human grandeur, and to the contemplation of the inexorability of fate, the transitoriness of worldly bliss, and the mutability of Fortune. The procedures of rhetorical amplification, especially apostrophe and *excalamatio*, here find their fittest subject matter, and the poem has eloquent moments. On the other hand, the poem is very long, and there is much in it that shows Lydgate at his most prolix. Prolixity is Lydgate's besetting sin, especially in the way he multiplies illustrations, examples, images, and analogies for commonplace moral assertions. A certain narrative situation, such as duplicity in the behavior of a character, triggers off a flood of associations, and the narrative does not move forward until the flood has subsided. Prolixity, as seen here, is the product not of simple incompetence but of high rhetorical ambition operating in conjunction with a rigid and mechanical mind.

The rigidity of Lydgate's poetic technique is what makes it difficult to give him more than grudging respect as a poet or to quote him for more than a few lines without a sense of betrayal. Chaucer gave Lydgate his poetic language, his meters, his precedent for practice in nearly all the genres of poetry, and Lydgate responded admirably by trying to improve on his master's performance. The *Troy Book,* for instance, is a much more ambitious work, from any point of view but the truly poetic, than *Troilus and Criseyde.* The *Siege of Thebes* similarly surpasses the Knight's Tale, the *Fall of Princes,* the Monk's Tale; the *Temple of Glass* and the *Complaint of the Black Knight,* Chaucer's dream poems. But in Lydgate ambition outruns performance. In his handling of Chaucer's pentameter, for instance, whether in couplet or in stanza, he tries to imitate Chaucer's subtle variation of rhythmical stress against metrical pattern, but his method of doing so is to schematize Chaucerian variants into rigid patterns, so that fluency, variety, and balance are lost. He thinks only of the structure of the line, never of the flow of the lines into the verse paragraph. Likewise, in his handling of sentence structure, Lydgate had a model in Chaucer for the blending of complex sentences into the flow of the lines. But Chaucer's skill is unique, and the effect of imitation in Lydgate is often a choked mass of verbiage, with long involved sentences pursuing their tortured course to no particular conclusion, with extensive use of loosely related participial constructions.

Some of these defects are less noticeable when Lydgate's ambitions are lulled, as for instance when he is not writing for a specific aristocratic commission. *The Siege of Thebes* is successful on a smaller scale than the *Troy Book,* partly for this reason, partly also because Lydgate has absorbed the story of his original, a version of the French prose *Roman de Edipus,* into a coherent pattern of political and moral interpretation. The style is simpler, more sober, and less inflated. There is also the added interest of a "Canterbury Prologue," in which Lydgate imagines himself riding to Canterbury and meeting with Chaucer's pilgrims. *Thebes* is the story he tells at their request. There is some attempt in this Prologue to emulate Chaucer's comic realism and

humor, and though Lydgate's wit is somewhat elephantine, the attempt is not completely ineffectual, and it is interesting that Lydgate should have made it. He was clearly not without a sense of humor, albeit a heavy one, as in the *Mumming at Hertford* and in a couple of sharply observed low-style satirical pieces, *Against Millers and Bakers* and the *Ballade of Jak Hare.* There is also more than a touch of humor in Lydgate's elaboration of Guido's antifeminist comments in the *Troy Book.* The mask of innocence, as Lydgate rebukes Guido while at the same time presenting in full and even elaborating on his sour asides, is well-maintained. But Lydgate adds some arguments of his own in "defense" of women: If, for instance, women are fickle by nature, how can men blame them?

In some of the courtly pieces dealing with matters of love, Lydgate manages to strike a balance between his ambition to write in a lofty style and his need to write sense. Chaucer is important as an ally here, since he provides a number of conventional structures of thought and expression in which Lydgate's verbosity can be constrained. *The Complaint of the Black Knight* is the finest of these poems. Modeled on *The Book of the Duchess,* it consists almost entirely of a conventionally elaborate garden setting and a long complaint of unrequited love by the knight. Lydgate brings nothing of allegorical subtlety to the former or of psychological subtlety to the latter, but his handling of the formal rhetoric of the two poetic themes is highly professional. The same can be said of *The Flower of Courtesy,* a tour de force in its description of the lover's lady, in which there is hardly a word of specification. *The Temple of Glass* is a more ambitious poem, a dream vision with an enclosed narrative; but the claims that have been made for the poem's originality are exaggerated, and it is chiefly memorable, again, for the formal rhetoric of its set speeches. The narrative is principally a thread on which these exercises in eulogy, description, and love-complaint can be hung. Nevertheless, the *Temple of Glass* is the longest poem by Lydgate for which there is no known source. *Reason and Sensuality,* by contrast, is a free translation of the first part of a French allegorical poem, *Les échecs amoureux* (Love's game of chess). The moral theme is handled with unusual lightness of touch, and there is scope for more of Lydgate's sly ironies at the expense of women. This is the only long poem by Lydgate, apart from the *Pilgrimage of the Life of Man,* in the short octosyllabic couplet.

There are a number of shorter poems in which

Lydgate deals with matters of love, such as the *Ballade of Her That Hath All the Virtues* and *A Gentlewoman's Lament,* which are graceful exercises in a conventional idiom. Those with a touch of bitterness against the fickleness of women, such as *The Servant of Cupid Forsaken* and *Beware of Doubleness,* are more sharply written.

Throughout his life Lydgate turned out moralistic verse of the most varied kind. There are versions of the fables of Aesop, the neatly told fable of *The Churl and the Bird* in the low style, and the prolifically amplified *Fabula duorum mercatorum* in the high style. There is a whole series of didactic poems with proverbial refrains with titles like *A Song of Just Measure* and *The World Is Variable,* in which Lydgate is able to indulge his fondness for gnomic sententiousness as well as for crippling syntax and the vapid amplification of the obvious. Even here, though, he can surprise the reader with an unlooked-for felicity, in *As a Midsummer Rose,* where a conventional meditation on mutability is suddenly elevated in the contemplation of the rose that does not wither, the rose of martyrdom in Christ.

Lydgate also turned his hand to informational and instructional pieces of every kind: a versified portrait gallery of the *Kings of England,* a *Pageant of Knowledge,* a *Dietary* or series of instructions to preserve health (actually Lydgate's most "popular" poem, in the sense that it is the one that occurs in most manuscripts), a verse treatise on household etiquette called *Stans puer ad mensam,* a *Treatise for Laundresses,* and much else. These have nothing to do with Lydgate's interest as a poet, but rather with his role as a provider for the voracious fifteenth-century appetite for edification and instruction.

Lydgate's religious poetry should, if we consider his vocation, be the summit of his achievement. It is not, with the exception of one poem, but it is very considerable in bulk. There are instructional pieces designed for specific purposes, such as the *Exposition of the Pater Noster* and the exposition of *The Virtues of the Mass.* There are a number of short verse prayers to particular saints, again probably done to order. There are a series of paraphrases of the hymns and psalms of the Church, such as *Vexilla regis prodeunt,* the *Te Deum,* and *Letabundus,* in which Lydgate develops in its most unlovely form the aureate style to which he was always inclined. Strictly speaking, aureation is not merely richness of diction but the deliberate transfer of Latinate vocabulary into English. In some of these poems, especially the *Te Deum,* the ostentation of the transfer is

so marked that the dividing line between the two languages begins to be obscured.

Lydgate wrote comparatively few poems of devotion to Christ, though there are some conventional poems on the Passion, including those such as *The Dolerous Pyte of Crystes Passioun* and *On the Image of Pity,* which reveal clearly the practical purpose for which they were designed, as meditative accompaniments to devotional pictures. There are many more poems addressed to the Virgin. None of them expresses any very intimate or vivid spirit of devotion, and the most characteristic of them are in a lofty vein of adulation, as to a remote queen rather than to a loving and weeping mother. The most elaborate of these pieces are the aureate version of the Marian antiphon *Ave Regina Celorum,* the prayer *To Mary Queen of Heaven,* and the *Ballade at the Reverence of Our Lady,* which is based on lines from the *Anticlaudianus* of Alan of Lille—a rare example of Lydgate stepping outside the relatively narrow circle of his reading.

Finally, there are a large number of saints' lives, some of which have already been mentioned in connection with the circumstances under which they were commissioned. Most of them demonstrate Lydgate's characteristic tendency to turn narrative into a series of occasions for rhetorical amplification, none more so than the profusely ornamented *Legend of St. Austin at Compton* and the *Legend of Dan Joos.* The *Life of Our Lady* is the great triumph of this kind, less a "life" than an enormously prolonged Marian hymn, a loosely strung series of meditations and rhapsodies on the major liturgical feasts dedicated to the Virgin. There are some unexpected touches of personal devotion, but the best writing is in the more formal passages, where Lydgate offers a richly evocative exploitation of traditional imagery. The *Life of Our Lady* is one of the best religious poems of the fifteenth century. It demonstrates that what Lydgate can do well he can sometimes do triumphantly. Its success is a characteristic success.

It is difficult to arrive at a measured estimate of Lydgate's importance as a poet. Lavishly praised in his own day, sometimes even compared favorably with Chaucer, still influential in the sixteenth century (as seen in *The Mirror for Magistrates,* which is much indebted to *The Fall of Princes*), he fell subsequently into neglect and disfavor. He is perhaps now most famous for the sardonic witticisms he has inspired from generations of literary critics who have much better things to do with their time than actually read his voluminous writings. Of recent years he has come in for more sympathetic and sober assessment, though it is unlikely that any case will ever successfully be made for him as a great poet in his own right or as an intellectual figure of any stature. He is, for instance, no humanist and no precursor of the Renaissance.

The importance of John Lydgate, as has been suggested above, is primarily as a representative of the medieval poet working in the characteristic mold of medieval literary tradition. In this role, whatever the intrinsic merits of his poetry, he has an undeniable significance for us. In another way, too, he can be assigned a vitally important historical role. It was Lydgate who used, smoothed, and wore to usefulness the literary language he inherited from Chaucer, who consolidated by patient labor the bridgehead that Chaucer had won by his genius. The road back to Chaucer would be much more difficult if Lydgate had not worn it smooth for us.

BIBLIOGRAPHY

Editions. Most of Lydgate's poems have been edited for the Early English Text Society *(EETS)*. The major texts are as follows (o.s., Original Series; e.s., Extra Series): Guillaume de Deguileville, *Pilgrimage of the Life of Man* (Lydgate's trans.), F. J. Furnivall and Katherine B. Locock, eds., *EETS,* e.s. **77, 83, 92** (1899–1904); John Lydgate, *The Dance of Death,* Florence Warren and Beatrice White, eds., *EETS,* o.s. **181** (1931); *Fall of Princes,* Henry Bergen, ed., *EETS,* e.s. **121-124** (1918–1919); *Life of Our Lady,* Joseph Lauritis *et al.,* eds. (1961); *Minor Poems,* Henry N. MacCracken, ed., *EETS,* e.s. **107,** o.s. **192** (1910, 1934); *Reason and Sensuality,* Ernst Sieper, ed., *EETS,* e.s. **84, 89** (1901–1903); *St. Albon and Amphabel,* C. Horstmann, ed., in *Festschrift der Realschule zu Berlin* (1882) (a more recent ed. is that of J. E. van der Westhuizen [1974]); *St. Edmund and Fremund,* C. Horstmann, ed., in *Altenglische Legenden* (1881); *Secrees of Old Philisoffres,* Robert Steele, ed., *EETS,* e.s. **66** (1894); *The Siege of Thebes,* Axel Erdmann and E. Ekwall, eds., *EETS,* e.s. **108, 125** (1911–1920); *The Temple of Glass,* J. Schick, ed., *EETS,* e.s. **60** (1891); *Troy Book,* Henry Bergen, ed., *EETS,* e.s. **97, 103, 106, 126** (1906–1920); *Two Nightingale Poems,* Otto Glauning, ed., *EETS,* e.s. **80** (1900). A useful bibliography of Lydgate's works is Alain Renoir and C. David Benson, "John Lydgate," in *A Manual of Writings in Middle English, 1050–1500,* Albert E. Hartung, ed. (1980).

Selections. Eleanor P. Hammond, ed., *English Verse Between Chaucer and Surrey* (1927); John Norton-Smith, ed., *John Lydgate: Poems* (1966).

Studies. R. W. Ayers, "Medieval History, Moral Purpose, and the Structure of Lydgate's *Siege of Thebes,*" in *PMLA,* **72** (1958); C. David Benson, *The History of Troy in Middle English Literature* (1980); Lois Ebin, "Lydgate's Views on Poetry," in *Annuale mediaevale,* **18** (1977), and *John Lydgate* (1985); Anthony S. G. Edwards, "The Influence of Lydgate's *Fall of Princes* c. 1440–1559: A Survey," in *Mediaeval Studies,* **39** (1977); Douglas Gray, *Themes and Images in the Medieval Religious Lyric* (1972); Richard F. Green, *Poets and Princepleasers: Literature and the English Court in the Late Middle Ages* (1980); Eleanor P. Hammond, "Poet and Patron in the *Fall of Princes,*" in *Anglia,* **38** (1920), and "Lydgate and Coluccio Salutati," in *Modern Philology,* **25** (1927); Isabel Hyde, "Lydgate's 'Halff Chongyd Latyne': An Illustration," in *Modern Language Notes,* **70** (1955); John Norton-Smith, "Lydgate's Changes in the Temple of Glas," in *Medium aevum,* **27** (1958), and "Lydgate's Metaphors," in *English Studies,* **42** (1961); Derek Pearsall, *John Lydgate* (1970), and *Old English and Middle English Poetry;* (1977), vol. I of the *Routledge History of English Poetry;* Alain Renoir, "The Binding Knot: Three Uses of One Image in Lydgate's Poetry," in *Neophilologus,* **41** (1957), "Attitudes Towards Women in Lydgate's Siege of Thebes," in *English Studies,* **42** (1961), and *The Poetry of John Lydgate* (1967); Walter F. Schirmer, *John Lydgate: A Study in the Culture of the XVth Century,* Ann E. Keep, trans. (1961); Anthony C. Spearing, *Medieval Dream-Poetry* (1976); Rosemary Woolf, *The English Religious Lyric in the Middle Ages* (1968).

DEREK PEARSALL

[See also **Alan of Lille; Boccaccio, Giovanni; Chaucer, Geoffrey; Henry V, Henry VI of England; Middle English Literature; Troy Story; Tudor, Owen.**]

LYDUS (Ioannes Laurentii Lydus) (490–*ca.* 565), Greek cultural historian and antiquarian in Constantinople from 511. He held a variety of administrative posts, including *exceptor* (scribe) of the prefecture, *chartularius* (archivist) of several bureaus, and *cornicularius* (adjutant) of the prefecture. For Justinian he wrote a panegyric and a history of the Persian War, for which services the emperor rewarded Lydus with an appointment at the University of Constantinople.

Lydus wrote three major works, which have been transmitted only in a damaged manuscript discovered in 1784. They are replete with citations from Greek and Latin writers, and reflect the new Justinianic spirit of Romano-Byzantine cultural continuity. *De mensibus* (On months) treats of the history of the various annual festivals, calendars from the earliest Italian reckonings, and the origins of the days and months. *De ostentis* (On omens from the sky) deals with the origin and progress of the arts of divination and augury. The *De magistratibus rei publicae romanae* (On officials of the Roman state) presents in detail and historical sequence the institutions, rights, and fate of the Roman magistracies from the time of Aeneas down to the reign of Justinian, the material being set forth in such a way as to show the continuity between the older Roman institutions and those of Justinian's time. The praetorian prefecture, its origin from the cavalry commander and its great power, its subsequent decline, and its staff are discussed at length. Particularly valuable are the numerous philological, historical, and encyclopedic digressions, and the abundant citations and explanations of Latin words and terms.

BIBLIOGRAPHY

Anastasius C. Bandy, ed. and trans., *Ioannes Lydus On Powers; or, The Magistracies of the Roman State* (1983); Thomas F. Carney, *Bureaucracy in Traditional Society: Romano-Byzantine Bureaucracies Viewed from Within* (1971).

ANASTASIUS C. BANDY

[See also **Byzantine Empire: Bureaucracy; Calendars and Reckoning of Time; Justinian I.**]

LYONESE RITE. The former diocese of Lyons, shaped as it was by a millennium of political and religious history, was one of the largest in the French kingdom during the Middle Ages. According to the rules of precedence, it was the first of all French dioceses, founded in the second century at the time of the bishops Pothinus and Irenaeus. The archbishop had—and still has—the title *primat des Gaules* (primate of all Gaul). In this diocese there developed a liturgy peculiar to the diocese and called the Lyonese rite.

The liturgical reform undertaken by Pepin the Short and completed by Charlemagne at the end of the eighth century imposed on all the dioceses of the Carolingian Empire the Roman books, brought directly from the Eternal City, and first of all the famous Gregorian Sacramentary, which was the personal missal of Pope Adrian I. From these basic texts a whole body of formulas and ceremonies, worked out locally, were gathered together, so that as early as the twelfth century they made up an impressive *corpus liturgicum*, representing the liturgical customs peculiar to the diocese of Lyons. It is clear that the Lyonese rite resulted from the acclimatization to Lyons of the Roman liturgical books, around which new adaptations developed locally.

The Lyonese liturgical genius worked out peculiar formularies and ceremonies for various occasions such as Candlemas, Ash Wednesday, Palm Sunday, Maundy Thursday, Good Friday, Holy Saturday, Major Litany (on the feast of St. Mark), other Rogation days, and the Vigil of Pentecost. In the same way, the sanctoral cycle was enriched with many feasts of local saints.

The two liturgical and popular events that crowned all these celebrations were, on the one hand, the ceremonies of Holy Week and, on the other hand, the imposing folk festival and religious feast of St. Pothinus, the first bishop of the diocese, who died a martyr in 177 along with forty-seven companions. This event, called the *fête des merveilles* (feast of wonders), was celebrated on 2 June with extraordinary pomp.

Few manuscripts of the period before the sixteenth century have survived. Still extant are four antiphonaries, thirteen breviaries, three kalendars, three graduals, three lectionaries with benediction formulas, a book of intonations, eleven books of hours, a manual, three martyrologies, thirty missals, two books of particular offices and masses, three ordinaries, six pontificals, five psalm books, and one ritual. These represent only about 3 percent of all the manuscript liturgical books that were being used in the diocese of Lyons when printing began.

BIBLIOGRAPHY

Robert Amiet, *Inventaire général des livres liturgiques du diocèse de Lyon* (1980); Dom Denys Buenner, *L'ancienne liturgie romaine: Le rit lyonnais* (1934).

ROBERT AMIET

[See also **Agobard; Amalarius of Metz; Carolingians and the Carolingian Empire; Carthusian Rite; Councils, Western (869–1179); Ecclesiology; Liturgy, Treatises on.**]

LYONS, a major city of the Rhône Valley in ancient, medieval, and modern times, is at the confluence of the Rhône and Saône rivers. Valleys connecting Lyons with the Loire to the west give it access to the Atlantic, while to the east Alpine passes lead to Italy. Lyons, therefore, has always been fitted geographically to be an emporium of converging trade routes in a vital region of Europe.

Its first inhabitants were the Segusians, a Celtic people. Julius Caesar marched through on his campaigns in Gaul, and in 43 B.C. the Romans placed a colony on a hill west of the Saône. The Roman commander Munatius Plancus called the colony Copia Claudia Augusta Lugdunum (Lugdunum meaning Hill of Lug, apparently a reference to a Celtic divinity). The area became medieval Fourvière, a corruption of Forum Vetus. The Roman colony extended to Condate in the foothills of Croix-Rousse across the Saône and to the peninsula and islands between the rivers.

Augustus made Lyons the capital of Gaul in 16 B.C. It developed into a splendid Roman city with a forum, theater, amphitheater, odeon, altar to Rome and Augustus, and temple to Cybele, aqueducts, and a road system. There was so much Roman art and architecture in Lyons that today it is one of the most productive archaeological sites in Europe.

Christianity arrived in the second century, survived the persecution under Marcus Aurelius, and provided continuity of social life when Lyons declined in the third century. The troops of Aurelian sacked the city in 273, a disaster from which it did not recover until many centuries later.

During the barbarian invasions Lyons fell to the Burgundians in the fifth century and to the Franks in the sixth. Little is known of the Merovingian period, and even the revival under the Carolingians was mainly ecclesiastical. When Bishop Leidrad sent a report to Charlemagne in 810, there were flourishing churches and monasteries but no urban institutions worth mentioning.

By the treaty of Verdun (843), Lyons, as part of Provence, fell within the "middle realm" of Lothar between France and the empire. Thirty years of disorder ended when Boso of Provence founded the second Burgundian kingdom in 879. The last of this royal line, Rudolf III, bequeathed his lands to Conrad II (r. 1024–1039) in 1032, and Lyons was incorporated into the Holy Roman Empire.

In 1157 Frederick I Barbarossa granted Lyons self-government under Archbishop Héraclius de Montboissier, who ranked as a prince of the Holy Roman Empire. A division of lands in 1173, ending a power struggle in the area, gave Lyons control of the Lyonnais extending west of the Saône to Forez and north to Beaujolais.

Romanesque art and architecture flourished in the eleventh century in Lyons. The Roman ruins at Fourvière and elsewhere were pillaged for stones and columns to be used in the cathedral of St. John and the church of St. Martin-d'Ainay, which, with its solid structure, squared-off lines, and rounded arches, remains an excellent example of the style.

Lyons's strategic position made it a point of de-

parture during the crusades. In 1096 an army of the First Crusade passed through the city. Those of the Third Crusade arrived in 1190, and St. Louis chose the same route in 1248 and 1270. The Lyonnais were stirred by the spiritual enthusiasm of the crusades and provided recruits for the Christian invasion of the Holy Land, where two of their bishops died.

Heresy shook Lyons in the 1170's when the Poor Men of Lyons, a visionary sect led by one Waldes (Peter Waldo or Pierre Valdès), appeared. Waldes was a rich merchant who gave away his wealth and wandered with his followers preaching poverty for all true Christians and the simplicity of apostolic times for the clergy. A contemporary of St. Francis of Assisi, Waldes was at first accepted by the church. Its attitude changed after Waldes began condemning such central Catholic beliefs as the efficacy of the sacraments and prayers for the dead. Banned by the pope, Waldes and his Poor Men (later called Waldensians) were driven from Lyons in 1184 by order of Archbishop Jean Bellesmains.

The rise of a bourgeoisie in Lyons produced a conflict with the archbishops and the canons of the cathedral. The archbishops held both religious and political authority. The canons were feudal lords controlling much of the land and its tenants. On the other side, urban leaders resented the constraints placed on them by the clergy. Wealthy merchants wanted greater freedom to make money and buy land.

The center of unrest was the Church of St. Nizier in the commercial quarter on the peninsula between the rivers. Laymen held mass meetings at St. Nizier and called for reforms. In 1193 the powerful Archbishop Renaud de Forez, needing loans, was forced to acknowledge basic rights in the city, especially those regarding markets and trade. In 1269 a rebellion forced the canons to flee the city, and a peace arranged by Louis IX (d. 1270) granted Lyons a commune to have a voice in running urban affairs.

Despite the political violence against the clergy, Lyons remained staunchly Catholic. Pope Innocent IV (d. 1254) selected it for the Council of Lyons that in 1245 condemned Emperor Frederick II for his defiance of the papacy. Innocent remained there until 1251, six years that gave increased legitimacy to the ecclesiastical and civil institutions of Lyons.

In 1274 the Second Council of Lyons, under Pope Gregory X (d. 1276), failed to end the schism of the Greek church. Gregory also failed to prevent further violence in Lyons. For nearly twenty years there were sporadic conflicts in which the archbishops, the canons, and the citizens strove against one another for localized power and land entitlements.

Almost from his accession to the throne of France in 1285, Philip IV the Fair (d. 1314) plotted to seize the Lyonnais from the empire. The decadence of the empire gave him his chance. Siding with the citizens against the clergy, he established in Lyons by 1293 an official with the title *gardiator* to exercise secular control. The quarrel between Philip and Pope Boniface VIII (1294–1303) occurred partly because of the king's increased control—and the diminution of ecclesiastical authority—over Lyons.

The clergy of Lyons found a way to curry favor with the king following the French defeat by the Flemish at Courtrai in 1302. Needing the financial means to rebuild his army, Philip imposed the most important tax of his reign in 1304, and the clergy of Lyons promptly raised the money grant he asked of them. Coming at a low ebb of his fortunes, the gesture made Philip more willing to look favorably on ecclesiastical rights in the city.

Philip visited Lyons in 1305 for the coronation of Pope Clement V (d. 1314), a Frenchman and former bishop of Lyons, at which time he received an enthusiastic welcome from the inhabitants led by the archbishop and the canons. Pleased by this, the king recognized the archbishop of Lyons as his vassal in 1307 and once more placed the city under ecclesiastical control.

Feeling betrayed, the citizens protested. They received assistance from a strange ally, the archbishop himself. Pierre de Savoy, who assumed the office in 1308, made a bid for the archiepiscopal sovereignty of his predecessors by refusing to take the oath of fidelity to the king of France. The archbishop gathered a military force large enough to capture the castle of St. Just, the strongpoint from which the king's officials watched over his rights.

Opposed by both the citizens and the clergy, Philip sent an army to occupy Lyons, where a royal governor was installed. In 1312 Lyons and all of the Lyonnais became part of a new sénéchaussée, and thus permanently French.

A royal charter of 1320 restored the commune and popular assemblies. Twelve consuls were elected each year by the *maîtres de métiers* (heads of the craft guilds), an indication of the importance of businessmen, traders, and bankers in Lyons.

The Black Death interrupted ordinary life in 1348. It killed many of the people, terrified the survivors, and produced near anarchy in the city and the countryside. Another disaster came with the French defeat at Poitiers in 1356, which loosed marauding English bands upon the Lyonnais.

These were dismal interludes in fourteenth-century progress as Lyons became increasingly self-reliant and prosperous. Paris allowed the people to raise royal taxes for themselves. An opulent aristocracy arose. Lyons had some 30,000 inhabitants in 1400.

The Burgundian war (1417–1435), a localized version of the Hundred Years War, created another crisis. Since Lyons sided with France, it was threatened by France's enemy, Burgundy. The Burgundians invaded the Lyonnais during the 1430's, overrunning Belleville, Trévous, Vimy, and Thoissey, but Lyons remained secure behind its fortifications. As the Hundred Years War moved toward a French victory after the epic of Joan of Arc, King Charles VII visited Lyons in 1434. He found it, like France, recovering from the devastation.

The treaty of Arras, ending the Burgundian war in 1435, brought more stringent royal authority to Lyons. The *gabelle* (salt tax) of 1436 caused rioting that was put down by the king's troops. A royal letter of 1447 declared the king's pleasure to be sufficient explanation of laws imposed on Lyons. The commune and popular assemblies were suppressed, and consuls and *maîtres des métiers* lost most of their political authority.

At the same time, Charles VII restored the Lyons fair that had lapsed during the 1420's in the havoc of war. The charter provided for the fair to be held each spring, summer, and autumn. The rules guaranteed liberty of commerce, exemption from taxes, lending at interest, simplified justice, and safe-conducts for foreign merchants. One of the first to take advantage of the Lyons fair was the great merchant and banker Jacques Coeur (d. 1456), who maintained a factor in the market until his financial collapse in 1451.

The fair made Lyons an indispensable stop for nearly everyone involved in international commerce. The Lyonnais sold an array of goods, from gloves and rope to lead and wine. They bought Flemish tapestries, German copper, Venetian glass, Spanish silk, and Portuguese dried fish. There was no Lyonnaise silk at the Lyons fair in the fifteenth century because this industry had not yet developed.

Lyons profited from the accession of Louis XI in 1461. The Lyonnais had supported Louis as dauphin in his public quarrels with his father, the king. Louis now favored them, especially after the magnificent reception they gave him in 1476. He revived their urban institutions, including the commune and the assemblies, richly endowed Notre-Dame de Fourvière, and welcomed the representatives of Lyons when they came to Paris with petitions.

The fair became more flamboyant. Merchants crowded into Lyons from all over Europe. The city was so strong a commercial center that even the Medici of Florence installed a branch of their bank near St. Nizier.

The fair's most lasting contribution to European culture was its book trade. Printers from Germany introduced the art of printing with movable type in 1473. This new industry quickly blossomed among the Lyonnais. Before Paris, Lyons published printed books in French. The use of woodcut illustrations became a high art. Jean (Johannis) Trechsel, issuing his edition of Terence in 1493, produced one of the finest of incunabula.

For all its éclat, the Lyons fair lapsed for five years during the 1480's. Charles VIII, succeeding Louis XI in 1483, listened to the mercantilists at court who held that the kingdom's gold was leaking away through Lyons, a frontier city frequented by foreigners. The king closed the fair in 1484. Then, convinced by experience and Lyonnaise pleas, he restored it in its semiannual form in 1489. The news was announced in Lyons to the ringing of church bells. Festive processions marched through the streets.

Charles VIII passed through Lyons in 1494 en route for Italy. At the end of the Middle Ages Lyons stood poised at the dawn of its own golden age, the early sixteenth century.

BIBLIOGRAPHY

Sources. Georges Guigue, ed., *Cartulaire des fiefs de l'église de Lyon, 1173–1521* (1893); Claude-Francois Ménestrier, *Histoire civile ou consulaire de la ville de Lyon* (1696); Jean-Baptiste Monfalcon, *Histoire de la ville de Lyon,* 2 vols. (1847).

Studies. Amable Audin, *Lyon, miroir de Rome dans les Gaules* (1965, repr. 1979); Pierre Bonnassieux, *De la réunion de Lyon à la France: Étude historique d'après les documents originaux* (1874); Marc Brésard, *Les foires de Lyon aux XVᵉ et XVIᵉ siècles* (1914); Louis Caillet, *Étude sur les relations de la Commune de Lyon avec Charles VII et Louis XI (1417–1483)* (1909); Jean Déniau, *La commune de Lyon et la guerre bourguignonne, 1417–1435* (1934); Marguerite Gonon, *La vie quotidienne en Lyonnais d'après les testaments, XIVᵉ–XVᵉ siècles* (1968); Arthur Kleinclausz, ed., *Histoire de Lyon,* I, *Des origines à 1595* (1939); Joseph R. Strayer, *The Reign of Philip the Fair* (1980); James B. Wadsworth, *Lyons, 1473–1503: The Beginnings of Cosmopolitanism* (1962); Pierre Wuilleumier, *Lyon, métropole des Gaules* (1953).

Vincent Buranelli

[See also **Black Death; Boniface VIII, Pope; Burgundians; Burgundy; Charlemagne; Charles VII of France, King; Clement V, Pope; Commune; Councils, Western; Crusades and Crusader States; Fairs; France; Frederick I Barbarossa; Frederick II of the Holy Roman Empire; Holy Roman Empire; Hundred Years War; Innocent IV, Pope; Louis IX of France; Louis XI of France; Medici; Merovingians; Philip IV the Fair; Poitiers, Battle of; Printing, Origins of; Prints and Printmaking; Provence; Romanesque Architecture; Romanesque Art; Trade, European; Urbanism, Western Europe; Waldensians; Waldes.**]

LYONS, COUNCILS OF. See Councils, Western.

LYRIC. See entries under individual languages.

MAᶜARRĪ, ABŪ ’L-ᶜALĀᵓ AḤMAD AL- (973–1057), son of ᶜAbdallah, son of Sulaymān al-Tanūkhī, was accorded the appellation "the poet of philosophers and the philosopher of poets." He was also known as the "twice-bound captive," a reference to his blindness and seclusion. Or as he later mused:

> Methinks, I am thrice imprisoned—ask not me
> Of news that need no telling—
> By loss of sight, confinement to my house,
> And this vile body for my spirit's dwelling.
> (Reynold A. Nicholson, trans.)

Abū ’l-ᶜAlāᵓ (a patronymic of distinction) was born into a cultivated family in Maᶜarrat al-Nuᶜmān, a Syrian town south of Aleppo. His grandfather was a judge, and his father was a poet of some note. He was scarcely four years of age when an attack of smallpox scarred his face and gradually rendered him totally blind. Al-Maᶜarrī, the last major medieval Arab poet, had a powerful intellect, vivid and reflective insights, and a prodigious memory made fabulous by fictitious accounts of its extraordinary nature.

His life can be divided into three periods. The formative years carried him to Aleppo, Antioch, and Tripoli in pursuit of diversified learning; this period was followed by an interval of semiretirement in Maᶜarrah. The second period saw his inopportune trip to Baghdad from 1007 to 1009, a venture that nevertheless represents a turning point in the life and intellectual development of Abū 'l-ᶜAlāᵓ. The third period was his active seclusion in Maᶜarrah, from his return from Baghdad until his death.

Al-Maᶜarrī commenced his poetic career as an encomiast, though, he asserted, not to win favors but, rather, to refine his poetic skills. His early *dīwān*, *Saqt al-Zand* (The spark of the flint)—on which there are eight commentaries, the oldest being one by al-Maᶜarrī himself entitled *Ḍawᵓ al-Saqt* (The flame of the spark)—consists of panegyrics, elegies, and occasional pieces. Arab critics laud this collection as the most efficient and grandiloquent expression of al-Maᶜarrī's poetic genius. The style is reminiscent of that of al-Mutanabbī—individualistic and unconventional, at once affected and lapidary, allusive though lucid, infelicitous yet charming. Select poems representative of Abū 'l-ᶜAlūᵓ's elegant and incisive utterances on the human tragedy are still memorized by Arab students:

> What boots it, in my creed, that Man should moan
> In Sorrow's Night, or sing in Pleasure's Dawn?
> In vain the doves all coo on yonder branch—
> In vain one sings or sobs: behold! he's gone.
> (Ameen F. Rihani, trans.)

> Tread lightly, for a thousand hearts unseen
> Might now be beating in this misty green;
> Here are the herbs that once were pretty cheeks,
> Here the remains of those that once have been.
> (Ameen F. Rihani, trans.)

His sojourn in Baghdad was vastly enriching, though turbulent and humiliating. His distinction as a masterful poet and an erudite savant had already preceded him to Baghdad, and he was cordially admitted to its circle of litterateurs, theologians, poets, and philosophers. He was soon imbued with wondrous, enriching religious and philosophical ideas. His fervent defense of his great mentor, al-Mutanabbī, and the callous envy that his extraordinary learning had generated, however, subjected him to various indignities that prompted his decision to depart. (He cited his mother's illness and his diminished resources as the basic reasons for his return to Maᶜarrah.) The death of his mother shattered his psyche, and soon after his arrival he adopted a vegetarian diet and other ascetic practices and went into a self-imposed seclusion until his death. This "earthly prison" could not, however, confine his boundless fame. Consequently, students and would-be scholars flocked to Maᶜarrah to benefit from his immense scholarship, wisdom, and philosophy, and so he spent his time actively teaching and writing. He dictated to his numerous amanuenses and votaries scores of epistles on virtually every known and possible discipline. To this period belong his most important extant works: a vast collection of poetry, *Luzūm Mā Lā Yalzam* or *al-Luzūmiyyāt* (The necessity of what is unnecessary), *Risālat al-Ghufrān* (The epistle of forgiveness), *The Letters of Abū 'l-ᶜAlāᵓ*, and *al-Fuṣūl wa 'l-Ghāyāt* (Chapters and purposes).

The significance of *al-Luzūmiyyāt* is attributable to its structural and thematic singularity. The cumbersome complex artifice of "necessitating" the same consonant preceding the rhyme vowel establishes word harmony but renders the poem artificial, pedantic, and at times monotonous. Yet one readily recognizes, as Nicholson asseverated, "the aptness of his diction, the force and opulence of his imagery, the surprising turns of his fancy, and the charm of a style unmistakably his own, whose melancholy dirgelike cadences blend with sharper notes of wit, satire and epigram." In *al-Luzūmiyyāt*, considered by Western scholars as his greatest poetic work, al-Maᶜarrī is at once a moralist, a philosopher and, as Von Kremer declared, a poet many centuries ahead of his time. His bold skepticism, moral philosophy, rationalism, irreverence for formal religion, haunting pessimism and fatalism, lyrical meditations on the human condition, and feverish disdain for human follies, hypocrisy, and injustice are vigorously and brilliantly exhibited in the quatrains, fragments, and long odes of the *Luzūmiyyāt*. Al-Maᶜarrī celebrated the supremacy of the mind (the only guide to truth) and considered religion its refractory offspring. Religion, he maintained, is the result of education and habit, a "fable invented by the ancients":

> They all err—Moslem, Christian, Jew, and Magian;
> Two make humanity's universal sect:
> One man intelligent without religion,
> And one religious without intellect.
> (Reynold A. Nicholson, trans.)

Life was his paramount theme and the human tragedy the incessant subject of his meditations:

> We laugh, but inept is our laughter;
> We should weep and weep sore,
> Who are shattered like glass, and therefore
> Re-moulded no more!
> (Reynold A. Nicholson, trans.)

Risālat al-Ghufrān (The epistle of forgiveness), the most illustrious of his prose works, is a *divina commedia*, as Nicholson described it, "an audacious parody of Muḥammedan ideas concerning the Afterworld." The scene is heaven, where the principal characters are the "forgiven" heathen poets (hence the title). They conduct imaginary dialogues with Ibn al-Qāriḥ, to whom the epistle is addressed, engage in literary disputes, and earnestly recite and explain their own poetry. It also abounds in "philological pedantry" and treats a miscellany of other disciplines.

The Letters of Abū ʾl-ᶜAlāᴼ, composed in ornate rhymed prose chiefly after his return from Baghdad, were collected by al-Maᶜarrī himself with a complementary handbook that has been lost. They are replete with proverbs, allusions, idioms, and literary conceits and display extravagant verbosity, pedantry, and erudition seldom encountered in medieval epistolography.

Al-Fuṣūl wa ʾl-Ghāyāt (Chapters and purposes), admittedly composed by al-Maᶜarrī to "celebrate the glory of God and to admonish," is considered by many as a parody of the Koran. For both this work and *al-Luzūmiyyāt*, al-Maᶜarrī was accused of heresy and subjected to ridicule and opprobrium.

This original, liberal thinker and critic had no coherent system of philosophy because he was essentially a poet—undisciplined, unbound by convention, and free of dogmatic prejudice. Perhaps in defense of his nihilism as the only cure for mankind, he desired to have the following verse inscribed on his grave:

> This wrong was by my father done
> To me, but ne'er by me to one.
> (Reynold A. Nicholson, trans.)

National celebrations commemorating al-Maᶜarrī's millennium were held in Damascus in 1944. Distinguished poets and scholars participated and their presentations were published in a book by the Arab Academy in Damascus the following year. There is an immense library on Abū ʾl-ᶜAlāᴼ. A thesis published in Arabic in Damascus (1978) lists in chronological order 722 sources for the study of the poet. It also lists the names of 101 works (mostly short epistles) attributed to Abū ʾl-ᶜAlāᴼ, the majority of which have not been preserved.

BIBLIOGRAPHY

Critical editions of al-Maᶜarrī's extant works are available in Arabic. English and French translations and studies include the following works: Henri Laoust, *La vie et la philosophie d'Abou-l-ᶜAlāᴼ al-Maᶜarrī* (1944); Abu ʾl-ᶜAlāᴼ-al-Maᶜarrī, *The Dīwān of Abu ʾl-ᶜAlāᴼ*, Henry Baerlein, trans. (1908); *Risalat al-Ghufrān: A Divine Comedy*, George Brackenbury, trans. (1943); *The Letters of Abu ʾl-ᶜAlāᴼ*, David S. Margoliouth, ed. and trans. (1898), and *The Quatrains of Abū ʾl-ᶜAlāᴼ*, Ameen F. Rihani, trans. (1904); Reynold A. Nicholson, "*The Risalatu l-Ghufrān*," in *Journal of the Royal Asiatic Society* (1900, 1902), *A Literary History of the Arabs* (1907, repr. 1969), 313–324, and *Studies in Islamic Poetry* (1921), 43–289; Georges Salmon, *Le poète aveugle* (1904).

MANSOUR J. AJAMI

[See also **Arabic Poetry; Mutanabbi, al-; Philosophy and Theology, Islamic.**]

MA FIN EST MON COMMENCEMENT, Guillaume de Machaut's enigmatic fourteenth-century rondeau in which the text provides the canon or instruction for interpreting the music. Two musical parts are notated, one being half as long as the other; only the longer one has the rondeau text underlaid to the music. The text appears upside down beginning at the end of the music.

The octasyllabic poem is as follows:

> Ma fin est mon commencement
> et mon commencement ma fin
> et teneure vraiement.
>
> Ma fin est mon commencement
> mes tiers chans trois fois seulement
> se retrograde et einsi fin.
>
> Ma fin est mon commencement
> et mon commencement ma fin.

Since "my end is my beginning," the cantus part (or principal melody), which normally carries the text, must start with the end of the musical line, reading all the notes backward. The text copied upside down accommodates this reading. Machaut thus provides an excellent example of cancrizans composition. The second line of the poem suggests that the beginning of the cantus part may also serve as the end of a second part derived by reading the cantus in the usual way. No text is provided for this forward reading of the music. Thus, the one musical line is composed such that it sounds well when played both forward and backward simultaneously. The third and fourth lines of the poem simply confirm what has been stated: "and this holds truly, my end is my beginning."

The fifth and sixth lines of the text refer to the other portion of music provided. This tenor part without text (erroneously designated *contratenor*, that is, complementary to the tenor, in some of the manuscript sources) is only half long enough to fit with the cantus. The poem suggests, however, that "my third song [or part] three times only reverses itself and thus ends." By performing the tenor in normal fashion and then reading all the notes backward, the music of this line fits with the complete cantus. Here again the instruction of the first two lines of the poem applies: the end of the tenor is also its beginning.

The cantus part is divided into two equal actions, *a* and *b*; the corresponding sections of the tenor are *a* (forward reading) and *b* (retrograde reading of *a*). These portions of music are performed with the eight lines of the poem as follows: *a b a a a b a b*. A complete performance of the rondeau involves, therefore, three retrograde versions of the tenor (*b*). This is the meaning of the phrase in the fifth line: "my third song three times only reverses itself."

The intellectual sophistry present in this rondeau by Machaut was not an isolated phenomenon. Clever canons or instructions were added to numerous compositions written by musicians during the last quarter of the fourteenth century.

BIBLIOGRAPHY

Guillaume de Machaut, manuscripts, Paris, Bibliothèque Nationale, f. fr. 1584 (folio 479v–480), 1585 (folio 309), 9221 (folio 136), 22546 (folio 153); Gustave Reese, *Music in the Middle Ages* (1940), 350–352; Leo Schrade, *Polyphonic Music of the Fourteenth Century*, III (1956), 156–157; Johannes Wolf, *Geschichte der Mensural-Notation von 1250–1460*, II (1904), 40 (facsimile of the original notation).

GORDON K. GREENE

[See also **Ars Nova; Chansonnier; Machaut, Guillaume de; Rondeau.**]

MABINOGI. The term *mabinogi* refers to a collection of eleven tales existing in two medieval Welsh manuscripts known as *The White Book of Rhydderch (Llyfr Gwyn Rhydderch)* (ca. 1300) and *The Red Book of Hergest (Llyfr Coch Hergest)* (ca. 1400). The term *mabinogion,* as if a plural of *mabinogi,* was once in vogue; it appears by mistake at the end of the tale of "Pwyll" in both the *White Book* and the *Red Book* and was adopted by Lady Charlotte

Guest as the general name for these tales in her popular nineteenth-century edition. However, scholars are now reluctant to perpetuate the medieval scribe's error, and the correct form *mabinogi* is the accepted current usage.

The meaning of the word is not entirely clear. The Welsh word *mab* means "son, boy," and it was long believed the *mabinogi* meant a tale either about or for a youth. A fourteenth-century Welsh version of a gospel about the boyhood of Jesus is entitled *Mabinogi Jesu,* where *mabinogi* is a translation of the Latin *infantia.* Eric Hamp has suggested that the term originally meant a collection of material relating to the British-Celtic god Maponos (divine youth).

The tales traditionally subsumed under this title are the so-called "four branches of the *Mabinogi*" ("Pwyll, Prince of Dyfed," "Branwen Daughter of Llŷr," "Manawydan Son of Llŷr," and "Math Son of Mathonwy"), the four native tales ("Culhwch and Olwen," "The Tale of Lludd and Lleuelys [or Llefelys]," "The Dream of Rhonabwy," and "The Dream of Maxen Wledig"), and the three Arthurian tales ("Owain; or, The Lady of the Fountain," "Peredur Son of Efrog," and "Geraint Son of Erbin").

It is generally agreed that the four branches, which constitute the *Mabinogi* proper, are the work of a single redactor/author, who wove together traditional ancient Celtic narrative materials that had been passed on orally, perhaps for some centuries. While this is certainly a defensible position, it is much more apparent to the casual reader that whoever wrote these tales down in the form we have them was working with materials of considerable diversity. The first branch deals with the adventures of a little-known legendary prince, Pwyll, his sojourn and rule in the otherworld, his marriage to Rhiannon, and their subsequent adventures, including the birth, loss, and restoration of their son Pryderi. The second branch deals with the family of Llŷr (Lear), a Celtic divinity known in Irish as Ler, the sea god. The prinicpals are Branwen and her brother Bendigeidfran (Bran the Blessed), who is depicted as a giant able to wade across the Irish sea. Branwen is given in marriage to an Irish king and is subsequently humiliated by him and his people. Much of the tale tells of Bendigeidfran's invasion of Ireland and his attempt to liberate his sister. The third branch treats of the further adventures of Rhiannon, her new husband Manawydan son of Llŷr, and her son Pryderi. The fourth, apparently more complex and less cohesive than the other three branches, has as its principals the family of Dôn, a goddess whose wider Celtic connections are reflected in the Irish Danu (the mythical Túatha Dé Danann are the tribes of the goddess Danu) and in continental river names such as the Danube (German: *Donau*). Thus, in spite of their stylistic unity, the four branches draw upon diverse traditions concerning a variety of mythical and legendary characters and events.

The geographical settings of the tales have an air of reality about them. The first branch is set in Dyfed in southwest Wales, the second at Harlech in north Wales and in Ireland, the third in Dyfed again and, briefly, in England, and the fourth mostly in Gwynedd (north Wales). There are few clues that identify the historical setting. A bishop and a priest appear in the third branch, and the characters swear by (presumably) the Christian God in each of the branches, but the tales can scarcely be called Christian. There are no references to known events, and the material culture depicted in the tales is vague and eclectic. The four branches thus share a timelessness that emphasizes their traditional nature.

Because of the relative paucity of prose narrative from medieval Wales (at least as compared with that from medieval Ireland), there is little within the Welsh literary tradition to elucidate the events of the four branches (a notable exception being the Welsh triads); the *Mabinogi* has, therefore, generated much scholarly discussion. Perhaps the most celebrated among the early commentators on the tales was Matthew Arnold. In a famous passage, he comments that the author of the tales is "pillaging an antiquity of which he does not fully possess the secret." By this, Arnold meant that in the four branches the detritus of countless generations of inherited tradition had come together, but that by the time when it was written down the material had lost its original cohesion. As Arnold says, the author "builds, but what he builds is full of materials of which he knows not the history, or knows by a glimmering tradition merely."

It remained for W. J. Gruffydd to make a serious attempt to come to grips with the diffuse strands of tradition in the *Mabinogi*. Gruffydd looked at the comparable narrative tradition of medieval Ireland and saw that cycles of tales existed there that told of the conception and birth of a hero, his youthful exploits, his search for a bride and marriage, and his death. The *Mabinogi*, he hypothesized, must originally have constituted some similar cycle, and since the only character that appeared in each of the four branches was Pryderi, he supposed that the four branches originally contained a life cycle of Pryderi. Though it is true that Pryderi is born and married in the first branch, that the second and third contain references to his various deeds (though they are hardly heroic), and that he meets death in the fourth branch, many scholars now generally concede that Gruffydd's theories went too far, beholden as they were to the excesses of the historic-geographic approach. Gruffydd sought to show how the narrative had become confused over the years, and he attempted to reconstruct the tales in an effort to reveal their original shapes. Proinsias MacCana built on Gruffydd's work in seeking to show the indebtedness of the second branch to Irish narrative, an attempt that also has not met with universal acceptance. The studies of the four branches during the twentieth century took the tales at face value and focused on analyzing themes or structures inherent in them.

It is, of course, impossible to ignore the fact that the four branches are indeed built on the foundations of inherited Celtic mythological matter. With few exceptions, the principal characters—Rhiannon, Branwen, Bendigeidfran, Manawydan, Lleu Llaw Gyffes, the family of Dôn—derive from Celtic antiquity, and many of the episodes are shaped by that antiquity. Rhiannon is at times a thinly veiled reflection of the widely worshiped Celtic horse goddess Epona. This may be seen in the fact that Rhiannon first appears in the story of "Pwyll" astride a magical horse that cannot be overtaken. Though her child seems to be born under normal circumstances in the kingdom of Dyfed, he in fact makes his first appearance in a stable, and his precocious growth as a child is explicitly linked to his expertise with horses. Rhiannon is twice punished in the four branches. In "Pwyll" she is forced to stand beside a horse block and offer to carry visitors to the court on her back; in "Manawydan" she is forced to wear an ass's collar about her neck. Thus is her equine nature—in both its regal and beast-of-burden aspects—emphasized.

While these mythological facts cannot be denied or ignored, the redactor/author does not exploit them; they are merely there as part of the traditional baggage. Although we know nothing of the author of this version of the tales or of his audience, it seems clear that their interests lay not in the myth of Epona but in the human entanglements of Rhiannon and her milieu. When we first meet her, she has come from her own land to avoid an unwanted suitor. She proclaims her love for Pwyll, virtually proposing to him, and urges him to set an early date for their marriage. At the wedding feast, before their marriage has been consummated, Pwyll inadvertently and unwittingly concedes Rhiannon to another man. She upbraids him for his stupidity and then explains to him how he will win her back. Eventually the two are reunited and successfully wed; a child is born to them, but he mysteriously disappears almost immediately. Rhiannon is charged with destroying the child and, after consulting with her counselors, agrees to accept punishment for that, even though she has been wrongfully accused. From her first appearance, Rhiannon is depicted as strong-willed, assertive, in control of the world about her. Others are weak and passive or conniving and malicious, whereas she is a paragon of maternal and familial virtues. The contrast between her behavior and that of those with whom she comes in contact provides much of the drama in the first and third branches. And the tension between its mythological underpinnings and the rational and natural progress of the narrative accounts for the occasional inconsistency and illogicality of the tale.

There is additional evidence that, although each of the branches contains its own kernel of inherited tradition and myth, each is primarily concerned with the characters and their relationships to one another as the story unfolds. In the second branch, Branwen, who is passive and softhearted, provides a neat contrast to Rhiannon. In the fourth branch, Gwydion is a powerful magician like his uncle Math, yet he pines for his own nephew and searches painstakingly for him: Blodeuedd is made of flowers; but she is human enough to fall in love at first sight with Gronw the hunter and thus to betray her husband Lleu.

The four native tales vary considerably in style and content from one to the other. "Culhwch and Olwen" is a long tale that differs stylistically from the four branches. It tells of a curse by Culhwch's stepmother that he shall never have a wife until he wins Olwen, daughter of the giant Ysbaddaden. The youth sets out for the court of Arthur, his first cousin, and, with his assistance, finds Olwen and asks her father for her hand. The Giant imposes a series of seemingly impossible tasks that Culhwch must accomplish before he can marry Olwen. Again with Arthur's help these are accomplished, the giant is slain, and Culhwch wins Olwen. Thus the tale belongs to a folk narrative tradition of the "giant's daughter" type. It also contains other motifs familiar to students of the folktale everywhere, including "love for an unseen maiden," "the jealous stepmother," "the impossible tasks," "the oldest ani-

mals," and "the helper animals." But despite those familiar motifs, the story is deeply rooted in Celtic tradition. It has themes and a structure in common with medieval Irish "wooing" stories, and it deals in part with traditions about the swine god, so well attested among the Celts. Its two catalogs (the long list of names of Arthur's retinue and the list of tasks set by the giant Ysbaddaden) unlock a vast horde of early Welsh tradition about which we would otherwise know nothing. Much of the narrative is occupied by the enumeration of the forty or so tasks set by the giant and the subsequent accomplishment of them. That an oral tradition underlies the tale is evident in part from the formulaic nature of the recitation of the tasks and from the fact that only a small portion of them are accomplished—and those in a different order and under revised conditions. Perhaps most important of all, the tale is the earliest prose account of the exploits of King Arthur, his companions, and his court. Indeed, the centerpiece of the tale is Arthur's fight with the king-turned-boar, Twrch Trwyth. The Arthur depicted here is hardly the feudal lord of medieval romance; his exploits include fights with witches and giants, and his retinue includes many men with supernatural talents.

"The Tale of Lludd and Lleuelys" is a short piece, containing traditions about the defense of Britain from three great plagues. The first was the advent of a people called the Coraniaid, whose knowledge was so great that anything spoken on the island—however softly—was heard by them. The second was a great scream that went up annually over the island and sapped the land and all of its inhabitants of their vitality. The third plague was that food and drink of however vast a quantity lasted but a single night in the king's court. These plagues occur during the reign of Lludd, who seeks the help of his brother Lleuelys in overcoming them. Brief though it is, the tale has an interesting analogue in an early Irish tale, "The Second Battle of Mag Tuired." Taken together, they offer corroborating evidence for a traditional tripartite dilemma, inherited from Indo-European antiquity.

"The Dream of Maxen Wledig" is based on a pseudohistorical account of the military commander of Britain, Magnus Maximus (fourth century). In a dream, Maxen (Maximus) sees a beautiful maiden; with the help of his messengers, he eventually finds this girl of his dreams, Elen, and marries her. "The Dream of Rhonabwy" is also cast as a dream vision. It is a curious tale, clearly a literary composition, and almost surrealistic at times. Though it deals with the legendary characters Arthur and Owain, its style is flamboyant, and, as a colophon reminds us, it cannot be known without a book.

The three Arthurian romances pose problems still unsolved by scholars. There is a clear connection between those three tales and the three romances of Chrétien de Troyes, *Yvain*, *Perceval*, and *Erec*, but exactly what the nature of that connection is and what the channels of transmission were between the two cultures may never be known.

BIBLIOGRAPHY

Matthew Arnold, *The Study of Celtic Literature* (1891, repr. 1970); Patrick K. Ford, trans. and ed., *The Mabinogi and Other Medieval Welsh Tales* (1977); and "Prolegomena to a Reading of the *Mabinogi*: 'Pwyll' and 'Manawydan,'" in *Studia celtica*, **16–17** (1981–1982); William J. Gruffydd, *Math vab Mathonwy* (1928), and *Rhiannon* (1953); Lady Charlotte Guest, trans., *The Mabinogion* (1838–1849); Eric P. Hamp, "Mabinogi," in *Transactions of the Honourable Society of Cymmrodorion*, (1974–1975); Thomas Jones and Gwyn Jones, trans., *The Mabinogion*, rev. ed. (1974); Proinsias MacCana, *Branwen Daughter of Llŷr* (1958), and *The Mabinogi* (1977); Alwyn Rees and Brinley Rees, *Celtic Heritage* (1961); Brynley F. Roberts, "Tales and Romances," in Alfred H. Jarman and Gwilym Rees Hughes, eds., *A Guide to Welsh Literature*, I (1976), 203–243; Ifor Williams, *Pedeir Keinc y Mabinogi*, 2nd ed. (1951).

PATRICK K. FORD

[See also **Arthurian Literature; Irish Literature; Mythology, Celtic; Welsh Literature.**]